A Garland Series

THE
ENGLISH BOOK
TRADE
1660-1853

156 Titles relating to the early history of

English Publishing, Bookselling,

the Struggle for Copyright

and the Freedom of the Press

Reprinted in photo-facsimile in 42 volumes

edited, with bibliographical notes,
by
Stephen Parks
Curator, Osborn Collection
Beinecke Library, Yale University

Biographical and Literary Anecdotes
of William Bowyer
1782

John Nichols

———————

with Two Memoirs of
John Nichols

Garland Publishing, Inc., New York & London

1974

Library of Congress Cataloging in Publication Data

Nichols, John, 1745-1826.
  Biographical and literary anecdotes of William
Bowyer.

  (The English book trade, 1660-1853)
  Reprint of Biographical and literary anecdotes of
William Bowyer, printer, F.S.A., and of many of his
learned friends, by J. Nichols, printed in 1782 by
and for the author, London; of Brief memoirs of John
Nichols, printed in 1804 by Nichols and Son, London; and
of Memoir of John Nichols, Esq., F.S.A., by A. Chalmers,
from the Gentleman's magazine for December 1826.
  1. Bowyer, William, 1699-1777. 2. Nichols, John,
1745-1826. 3. Printing--History--Great Britain.
I. Brief memoirs of John Nichols. 1974. II. Title.
III. Series.
Z232.B79N498 1974   686.2'092'2   74-16185
ISBN 0-8240-0971-1

Contents

Preface

A. Brit. Mus. 132.c.4. Many later writers have based their accounts of the 18th century book trade upon this important source. Nichols printed an early sketch of this work in 1778 and then prepared this expanded version.

B,C. *Brief Memoirs* was printed in only twelve copies. The copy reproduced belonged to Isaac Reed and is now in the Osborn Collection in the Yale University Library. Alexander Chalmers memorialized Nichols in the *Gentleman's Magazine* in December, 1826. The copy reproduced is from a separate printing, in the collection of Stephen Parks. A memoir of John Bowyer Nichols appeared in the *Gentleman's Magazine* for December, 1863; and a memoir of John Gongh Nichols was privately printed in 1874.

April, 1974   S.R.P.

H ΚΑΙΝΗ
ΔΙΑΘΗΚΗ

ORIGIN OF PRINTING
OPERÂ GUL. B.
MANU PUERI MEI
I. N.

GULIELMUS BOWYER,
ARCHITECTUS VERBORUM, Æt. LXXVIII.

Jacobus Basire ad vivum del. et sculp.

BIOGRAPHICAL AND LITERARY

ANECDOTES

OF

WILLIAM BOWYER, Printer, F.S.A.

AND OF

MANY OF HIS LEARNED FRIENDS.

CONTAINING

AN INCIDENTAL VIEW OF THE PROGRESS AND ADVANCEMENT

OF LITERATURE IN THIS KINGDOM

FROM THE BEGINNING OF THE PRESENT CENTURY

TO THE END OF THE YEAR MDCCLXXVII.

By JOHN NICHOLS,

HIS APPRENTICE, PARTNER, AND SUCCESSOR.

" To preferve the memory of thofe who have been in any way ferviceable to mankind, hath been
" always looked upon as difcharging a debt which we owe to our benefactors ;" and " it is but
" reafonable that they who contribute fo much to the immortality of others, fhould have fome
" fhare in it themfelves."   OLDISWORTH.

LONDON:

PRINTED BY AND FOR THE AUTHOR.

MDCCLXXXII.

TO THE PRESIDENTS,

VICE PRESIDENTS, AND FELLOWS,

OF THE

ROYAL AND ANTIQUARIAN SOCIETIES OF LONDON;

THESE ANECDOTES OF MR. BOWYER,

A PRINTER OF UNCOMMON EMINENCE,

WHOSE TALENTS WERE LONG AND LAUDABLY

EXERTED IN THEIR SERVICE,

ARE WITH TRUE RESPECT AND GRATITUDE INSCRIBED

BY THEIR MOST DUTIFUL SERVANT,

J. NICHOLS.

PREFACE.

THOUGH it would be improper to begin with an ill-timed excuse for the manner in which this work has been executed, it is neceffary to obferve, that the volume has been more than four years in the prefs *; and during that period many new and unexpected informations have fwelled it to the prefent fize, and far beyond what was originally intended.

" To adjuft the minute events of literary hiftory is te-" dious and troublefome; it requires indeed no great " force of underftanding, but often depends upon en-" quiries which there is no opportunity of making †." The refearches which have produced thefe Anecdotes have abundantly verified this remark. Though I have applied to the moft authentic fources, and in general have been favoured with the moft liberal communications, fome fub-fequent difcoveries has often rendered it neceffary to

* In 1778 a few copies of a flight fketch of this volume were printed in 8vo, and given to the intimate friends of Mr. *Bowyer.*
† Dr. *Johnfon*, in the Life of *Dryden.*

compile

compile a second article, sometimes a third or fourth, concerning the same writer. In such cases, it becomes neceffary to request the reader's indulgence, and to refer him to the Index. There are other inftances, where, after every poffible enquiry, it has hardly been practicable to collect a fingle circumftance of private perfons, though of eminence in letters, except the date of their death. " The in-" cidents which give excellence to biography are of a vo-" latile and evanefcent kind, fuch as foon efcape the me-" mory, and are rarely tranfmitted by tradition * ;" and " Lives can only be written from perfonal knowledge, " which is growing every day lefs, and in a fhort time " is loft for ever. What is known, can feldom be im-" mediately told; and when it might be told, it is no " longer known †."

I had once an intention to give an alphabetical lift of all the friends who have kindly affifted me with information: but they are now fo numerous, that to name them would certainly be confidered as oftentation; and to fome of them (to Sir *John Pringle*, Dr. *Richardfon*, Dr. *Fothergill*, and Mr. *Coftard)* thofe thanks would come too late, which to the furviving contributors are neverthelefs very cordially paid.

---

* Rambler, N° 60.   † Dr. *Johnfon*, in the Life of *Addifon*.

The

The life of a private tradefman, however diftinguifhed as a fcholar, cannot be expected to " abound in adventure * ;" and in fact the Anecdotes of Mr. *Bowyer* are few, when compared to the many that are introduced of his learned friends. But the principal figure of the piece ftands every where foremoft on the canvafs; and the other perfons of whom anecdotes are occafionally introduced were connected with him by the ties of friendfhip or of bufinefs.

Some anachronifms have unavoidably arifen, from the work's having been fo long paffing through the prefs : but thefe are obvious, and will readily be pardoned; as will alfo the variety of ftyle which may be difcerned throughout this performance. It was fometimes almoft impoffible to change the expreffions in which my intelligence was received; nor was it always neceffary. The volume may perhaps be not lefs amufing (I am fure it is more authentic) by being illuftrated with the notes of my friendly correfpondents, and very frequently by the genuine fentiments of the writers of whom memoirs are here exhibited.

Convinced that I am " walking upon afhes under which " the fire is not extinguifhed †," I have endeavoured

---

* *Goldfmith*, Life of *Parnell*.

† ——— " incedens per ignes " Suppofitos cineri dolofo." HOR. Carm. II. i. 7.

to guard againft every fpecies of mifreprefentation.   That errors may have intruded, is highly probable—but what work of fuch a nature was ever perfect?—I flatter my-felf that many of my friends, in various parts of this kingdom, will teftify, that neither trouble nor expence has been fpared in my enquiries; and in the Appendix I have chofen rather to appear triflingly minute, than to fuffer articles to remain which it was in my power to correct or improve.

The whole is now chearfully fubmitted to the publick; with an affurance, that whatever hints may lead to the improvement of a future edition will be moft thankfully received, and properly regarded.

June 11, 1782.

ANECDOTES

ANECDOTES

OF

WILLIAM BOWYER, Printer.

WILLIAM BOWYER, confeſſedly the moſt learned printer of the age he lived in, was born in *London*, on the 17th day of *December*, 1699; and may almoſt be ſaid to have been initiated in the art of printing from his infancy.

His father (whoſe name was alſo *William* ∗) was in the foremoſt rank of his profeſſion; his mother, *Dorothy*, was the daughter of *Ichabod Dawks*, who had been employed as a journeyman, from the year 1652 till 1657, in compoſing the celebrated *Polyglott* Bible of Biſhop *Walton* †.

The daughter of Mr. *Dawks* was born in 1664, and firſt married to Mr. *Benjamin Allport*, of *St. Botolph's, Biſhopſgate,* bookſeller, by whom ſhe had one ſon *Benjamin* (who was born after his father's death, and died before he was a year old) and one daughter ‡. She afterwards became the wife of Mr. *Bowyer*; who opened a printing-office ‖ in *Little-Britain*

∗ Son of *John Bowyer*, citizen and grocer, and *Mary* the daughter of *William King,* citizen and vintner (ſee the pedigree in p. 485.) He was born in 1663, and was admitted a freeman of *London*, *Oct.* 7, 1686.

† See the Origin of Printing, p. 133 & ſeqq. See alſo in this volume, pp. 453. 493.

‡ *Mary*, afterwards Mrs. *Bettenham*. See p. 13; where, in the firſt note, l. 2, ſhould be read " Mrs. *Bowyer's* daughter by a former huſband."

‖ His earlieſt book had this title, " A Defence of the Vindication of King *Charles* the " Martyr; juſtifying his Majeſty's title to ΕΙΚΩΝ ΒΑΣΙΛΙΚΗ, in Anſwer to a late Pam " phlet, intituled, *Amyntor*: by the Author of the Vindication. *London*, printed by " *W. Bowyer* at *The White-Horſe* in *Little-Britain*; and ſold by moſt Bookſellers in *Lon* " *don* and *Weſtminſter*, 1699," 4to. Of this book and its author, ſee hereafter, p. 631.

B   in

in 1699 (the year in which his fon was born) and foon after removed into *Dogwell-Court* *, *White-Fryars*, where he foon met with the patronage and encouragement he' fo well deferved.

After having for thirteen years purfued bufinefs with unremitted induftry and unfullied reputation, he was in one night reduced to abfolute want, by a calamitous fire, *Jan.* 30, 1712-13, which totally deftroyed his printing-office, and many confiderable works at that time in his warehoufe and under his prefs. Amongft other valuable articles which perifhed by this fatal accident, was a confiderable number of Sir *Robert Atkyns's* " Hiftory of *Glouces-* " *terfhire*;" a few copies of which work were fnatched from the flames, of which they ftill retain indelible marks. The whole damage to Mr. *Bowyer* and his neighbours, as afcertained upon oath, amounted to 5146*l*. 18*s*. To the honour of *Englifh* humanity, let it be known, that, by the contributions of his friends, and thofe of his own fraternity in particular, Mr. *Bowyer* received towards his lofs the fum of 2539*l*. 15*s*. 2*d*.; of which 1377*l*. 9*s*. 4*d*. arofe from his proportion of a public brief, the original return to which is now in the poffeffion of his only furviving grandfon.

The liberality of almoft every individual in the whole body of printers and bookfellers was fpeedily experienced on this melancholy occafion : amongft thefe, Mr. *Bowyer* always held himfelf particularly under obligations to Mr. *Timothy Goodwin* †, who was the firft promoter of the fubfcription ; and to Mr. *Richard Sare* ‡, as a liberal contributor.

The

---

* The houfe which he converted into a printing-office had been formerly *The George Tavern*, in which fome of the fcenes in " The 'Squire of *Alfatia*" are laid.

† Bookfeller in *Fleet-Street*.

‡ Bookfeller in *Holbourn*. His knowledge of books and men, the candour and ingenuity of his temper, the obliging manner of his behaviour, and the grateful acknowledgements of any favours and benefits received, effectually recommended him to the friendfhip of many perfons eminent both in ftation and learning ; particularly of Archbifhop *Wake*,

The good, the pious Mr. *Nelson** found here an ample field for the exercife of his munificence and friendfhip. He had

Wake, who had a great affection and efteem for him. His fortune, originally very moderate, was given to him by his father (a clergyman), with a declaration, " that he " might depend upon that little wearing like iron, fince there was not one difhoneft " penny in it." As this faying made great impreffion on him, the experience which verified it made confiderably greater. His integrity in trade was remarkable. He never fuffered himfelf, by any temptation of profit, to be concerned in publifhing books obnoxious to the cenfures of church or ftate, or any way prejudicial to religion or good-manners. He always expreffed great compaffion for perfons under any fort of diftrefs, and acted proportionably for their confolation and fupport. The Society for relieving poor widows and orphans of the clergy had moft happy experience of his prudent zeal and indefatigable diligence at a very critical juncture. In the latter years of his life he was afflicted with decays of bodily ftrength, and a fometimes much infeebled mind. He was buried at *Pancras*, *Feb.* 11, 1723. See his Funeral Sermon by Dean *Stanhope*.

* This worthy layman was born *June* 22, 1656; educated at *St. Paul's* fchool; and removed thence to *Trinity College, Cambridge*. He contracted an early acquaintance with Archbifhop *Tillotfon*, which ended but with the life of the latter, who expired in Mr. *Nelson's* arms. From principle, he long adhered to the communion of the deprived bifhops; but, on the death of Bifhop *Lloyd*, in 1709, returned to that of the church of *England*. He died *Jan.* 16, 1714-15; and left his whole eftate to pious and charitable ufes, particularly to charity-fchools. He publifhed many valuable and pious works; his " Practice of true Devotion," 1698; his " Companion for the Feftivals and " Fafts," 1703; his " Great Duty of frequenting the Chriftian Sacrifice," 1706; and his little tract " on Confirmation," in particular, deferve, and have received, the higheft commendations. He wrote " An account of Mr. *Kittlewell's* Life and " Writings," 1695; publifhed the *Englifh** works of his tutor the learned and pious Bifhop *Bull* in folio, 1713; and wrote his Life†. Mr. *Nelson* married *Theophila* ‡, fecond daughter of *George* earl of *Berkeley*, and widow of Sir *Kingfmill Lucy*, bart.; on the death of whofe fon Sir *Berkeley Lucy*, Mr. *Nelson's* library was fold by auction 1759, together with that of Sir *Berkeley*, forming united a moft extraordinary affemblage of devotion and infidelity. The reader will not, I believe, be difpleafed to fee fpecimens of his epiftolary correfpondence, now firft printed from the originals in *The Britifh Mufeum*. They are characteriftic of the benevolent writer:

I. To Mr. PRIOR.

" Dear Sir,   *Cranford, July* 20, 1706.
I have been fo agreeably entertained in my retirement at this place with the beauties of your charming Mufe, that mere fenfe of gratitude for the pleafure I have en-

* The Bifhop's *Latin* works were publifhed by Dr. *Grabe*, who added to them many learned annotations and an excellent preface, 1703, folio; they were reprinted in 1721 by Mr. *Bowyer*, who fuftained a lofs of almoft two hundred pounds by the impreffion.

† The Life (which, with a confiderable part of the Bifhop's Works, was confumed by the fire at Mr. *Bowyer's*) was reprinted in 8vo, and prefixed to four volumes of the Bifhop's Sermons, 1713, and 1716. A tranflation of *Bull's* Works on the Trinity was publifhed in 2 vols. 8vo, 1730, by *Francis Holland*, M A. chaplain to Lord *Weymouth*, and rector of *Sutton* in *Wilts*, who died in *July* 1731.

‡ This lady, who was old when Mr. *Nelson* married her, died in 1705; and by her deceafe enabled him to add confiderably to the charitable purpofes for which his fortune was always deftined. A letter from Mr. *Nelson*, with a monumental infcription in *Latin* by Dr. *Swift* on *Charles* earl of *Berkeley* her brother, afterwards placed in *Berkeley* church in the county of *Gloucefter*, is in the Dean's Works, vol. X. 4to. p. 45.

                                          joyed

had a peculiar regard for Mr. *Bowyer* (who had regularly ushered his valuable publications into the world); and, in the

joyed conſtrains me to pay my acknowledgements to the maſterly hand that adminiſtered it. And indeed, I muſt own, the banquet is ſo elegantly prepared, that at the ſame time that it raiſes my admiration, it gratifies and ſatisfies my appetite to the full; and yet I can return to it with freſh guſto: for *decies repetita placebit.*

Our age is moſt certainly happy in this, that, when our countrymen fight with ſo much bravery, we have a conſummate Poet, that ſecures their hardy deeds from oblivion, and places their battles in eternal light. You obſerve a decency throughout your whole Ode *, which is the effect of your true good ſenſe, that when with a liberal hand you beſtow your incenſe upon our great General, it ſtill riſes in thicker clouds towards Her who made his arms her choice. I could wiſh our Pulpit Orators underſtood the ſame decorum; and then all their particular praiſes would have had a relation to their main ſubject. Without the bias of friendſhip, I may venture to ſay you have improved thoſe hints you have borrowed from *Horace*; and, were I as well acquainted with *Spenſer* †, I believe I ſhould have reaſon to make the ſame judgement in reference to your ſtyle. I am ſure, whatever his is, your imagination is warm, and your expreſſions noble and majeſtic; and yet they never carry you out of ſight; but you are always pleaſed to be intelligible. I have but one query to make, which I doubt not but that you can reſolve; which is, that though the *Dane* deſerves the epithet *cruel* ‡ which you beſtow upon him, yet whether it was not neceſſary to have ſoftened it, for the ſake of that prince that is ſo nearly related to the ſubject of your poem. Pardon this criticiſm; for I am rather inclined to think it wrong, than to tax you with the leaſt imperfection. It is poſſible you may think this whole letter very impertinent, becauſe it comes from a perſon ſo little capable in judging of theſe matters, and in deſcribing countries where he has never travelled. But my mind was full; and I found it neceſſary to give it vent. Beſides, I thought it friendly to acquaint you how much I ſhare in your glorious ſucceſs, and that the ſhort journey you have made to *Parnaſſus* turns ſo much to your ſolid reputation. I ſhall conclude this trouble, when I have aſſured you that I have no ways deſigned to reproach you for not making me a preſent of your noble Ode. I live in too much obſcurity to be remembered by a perſon ſo thronged with acquaintance of the beſt ſort as you are; and yet I am willing to flatter myſelf with a ſhare in your friendſhip; and, if I can give no other reaſon, I can always alledge that value and reſpect with which I am, dear Sir,

Your moſt faithful, humble ſervant,   ROB. NELSON.

P. S. I had almoſt forgot to do juſtice to thoſe admirable materials you have provided for erecting a column ‖ to perpetuate the Queen's glory to future generations; and yet it ſtruck me with particular pleaſure, from that knowledge I have of thoſe monuments that have been raiſed to the two Emperors you mention. It is a great misfortune that we have no eminent Sculptor than can execute what you have ſo maſterly deſigned. Such a work would make *London* exceed *Rome* in a monumental pillar, as much as it does already outdo her in trade and commerce. But we will glory that it ſtands fixt in your verſes; where lateſt times may read *Anna's* immortal fame. I deſire to know whether the Queen has made you any preſent, to ſhew her ſenſe of your exquiſite performance. I wiſh it, for her ſake as well as your's."

---

* An Ode, humbly inſcribed to the Queen, on the glorious ſucceſs of her Majeſty's arms, 1706.
† Mr. *Prior*, in the Preface to this Ode, calls *Horace* and *Spenſer* "his two great examples."
‡ This epithet remains unaltered.   ‖ In the ſix concluding ſtanzas.

II.

the period of his diftrefs, not only gave largely himfelf, but exerted his endeavours fuccefsfully in foliciting the affluent and

great ;

II. To Mr. HARLEY.

" S I R,   *Aug.* 11, 1710.

I beg leave to take this way of congratulating that juftice which is at length done to your merit *, and of expreffing my fatisfaction in the conqueft you have gained over your enemies, who were earneftly bent upon your deftruction : ' their tongues imagined wickednefs, and with lies they cut like a fharp razor.' I cannot but think it happy for a nation, when perfons in great ftations encourage learning and the liberal fciences ; and that has been always fo much your character, that the rifing generation will chearfully apply themfelves to their ftudies, now they know there are patrons that are difpofed to diftinguifh their talents ; and it will be a comfort to thofe that do not expect favours, fecurely to depend upon their having juftice. I am, with great refpect, Sir, your moft obedient and moft humble fervant,   ROB. NELSON."

III. To the Earl of OXFORD.

" My Lord,   *June* 26, 1712.

It is very fit that every thing that is publifhed of Dr. *Grabe*'s fhould be laid before your Lordfhip, becaufe you were pleafed, in a very diftinguifhing manner, both in his life † and at his death, to fhew yourfelf to be his patron. The learned prefatory dif-

---

* He was appointed commiffioner of the treafury and chancellor of the exchequer, *Aug.* 10, 1710.

† Through the recommendation of Mr. *Harley*, Dr. *Grabe* received from the Queen a purfe of fixty guineas towards the printing of his Septuagint. A penfion of a hundred pounds a year, which had been fettled on him by King *William*, was alfo continued to him by Queen *Anne*. Yet we find this learned and pious Divine, in 1711, addreffing the Lord Treafurer in terms which demonftrate that he was then finking under the complicated load of penury and ill health :

" My Lord,   *St. Paul's Church-yard, Aug.* 22, 1711.

I find my conftitution, by the continual labours which I have undergone thefe fourteen years, fo much weakened, and my health fo much impaired, that within thefe four months I have had three fits of illnefs ; of the laft of which I am not yet fully recovered. Now thefe as well as other accidents have caufed to me more than ordinary expences this laft year, and made me, receiving nothing of her Majefty's penfion in twelve months, run into debts amounting to fourfcore and odd pounds. Of thefe I have paid indeed laft week a part out of the laft *Michaelmas* quarter's penfion, which a friend received for me at *Whitehall* ; but fince I owe ftill about threefcore pounds (which debt makes me under thofe frequent monitions of mortality very uneafy, and afhamed to fee fome of my creditors). And fince the phyfician thinks it abfolutely neceffary for the recovery of my health, that I fhould go without any delay to the *Tunbridge Wells*, which journey will occafion ftill more expences ; I humbly beg your Lordfhip, that you would be pleafed to order the payment of the three laft quarters, in all feventy-five pounds, now to be made to me, either by Mr. *Godfrey* at Mr. *Compton's* office, where I receive my penfion, or at the *Exchequer* ; which afterwards, when the penfion-money is paid into the faid office, may deduct this fum advanced unto me, and may pay then to Mr. *Godfrey* and his clerk their dues. I hope after two or three days to go abroad to the other part of the town, and will make then bold to wait either upon your Lordfhip for an anfwer to this very humble requeft, or upon my Lord *Harley* ; of whom befides I intend to hear, what day he will be pleafed, together with my Lord *Duplin*, to take a view of the *Alexandrian* manufcript, which I have copied out entirely fome time ago, but cannot give the remainder to the prefs for reafons which I will not trouble your Lordfhip with at prefent. I recommend your Lordfhip to the grace of Almighty God ; heartily wifhing, that as he has delivered and exalted you to the higheft degree of honour, fo he may fatisfy you with a long life, and at laft fhew you his falvation. I remain, with the moft profound refpect, my Lord,

Your Lordfhip's moft humble fervant,
JOHN ERNEST GRABE."

This letter is now firft printed from Harl. MSS. N° 7524. Dr. *Grabe* died *Nov.* 13, 1711 ; and was honoured by the earl of *Oxford* with a handfome monument in *Weftminfter Abbey*.

Dr. *Grabe*'s " Collatio Codicis Cottoniani Genefeos cum Editione Romana," which lay long unnoticed in the archives of the *Bodleian* Library, had ample juftice done to it in 1778, by the attention and accuracy of Dr. *Henry Owen*.

courfe

great; amongſt theſe, it would be unpardonable not to mention the earl of *Thanet*, lord viſcount *Weymouth*, and

courſe of Dean *Hickes* * gives him a title humbly to beg your Lordſhip's acceptance of the whole performance †. The catalogue of the Mſſ. which Dr. *Grabe* hath left behind him I preſume to offer to your Lordſhip, as what will enlarge your opinion of his extenſive learning and capacity, and at the ſame time afford your Lordſhip ſome agreeable entertainment. I have returned to Dr. *Bentley* the books which Dr. *Grabe* had borrowed from the Queen's Library; which I think myſelf obliged to acquaint your Lordſhip with, becauſe I underſtand you had the trouble of an application upon that ſubject. I ſhall not venture to take any ſtep towards printing the remaining part of the Septuagint ‡, till I have received your Lordſhip's directions in that matter. I am, with all imaginable reſpect, my Lord, your Lordſhip's moſt obedient and moſt humble ſervant, ROB. NELSON."

IV. To the ſame.

" My Lord, *April* 7, 1714.

I beg leave to acquaint your Lordſhip, that I believe greater expedition might be given to the plates § concerning the Charity Children, if the perſon (Mr. *Vertue)* who does them ſhould receive fifty pounds at preſent; which I gave him reaſon to expect. I am, with great reſpect, my Lord, your Lordſhip's moſt obedient and moſt humble ſervant, ROB. NELSON."

V. To the ſame.

" My Lord, *June* 18, 1714.

I am required by my worthy neighbour the Dean to return his moſt humble thanks to your Lordſhip, for the royal bounty you have procured for Mrs. *Elſtob* ‖: ſhe wants only that, to ſet the preſs to work; and therefore ſhe humbly begs that your Lordſhip would be pleaſed to diſpatch that affair. I crave leave, at the ſame time, to remind your Lordſhip of the Queen's encouragement for carrying on the plates of the machine erected for the Charity Children in *The Strand*, which are in great forwardneſs. I am, with the greateſt zeal and reſpect, my Lord, your Lordſhip's moſt obedient and moſt humble ſervant, ROB. NELSON."

VI. To the ſame.

" My Lord, *Oct.* 4, 1714.

I have endeavoured ſeveral times to pay my duty to your Lordſhip, ſince you have retired from public affairs; but never had the happineſs of meeting with your Lord-ſhip. I am obliged to acquaint you, that Mr. *Bird* has made a conſiderable progreſs in Dr. *Grabe's* monument; and that part of my agreement with him was, that he ſhould receive fifty pounds this *Michaelmas*; which he has put me in mind of. I hope to bring the whole expence under what your Lordſhip was willing to beſtow. Pray God protect your Lordſhip from the aſſaults of your enemies, and keep you ſafe againſt all their attempts! I am, with great reſpect, my Lord, your Lordſhip's moſt obedient and moſt humble ſervant, ROB. NELSON."

* Mr. *Nelſon* left Dean *Hickes* an annuity of 20*l.*; and Dr. *Grabe* bequeathed all his MSS. to him for life, and after his deceaſe to Dr. *Smallridge.*

† This was, " Some Inſtances of the Defects and Omiſſions in Mr *Whiſton's* Collection of Teſti- " monies from the Scriptures and the Fathers, againſt the true Deity of the Son and the Holy Ghoſt, " &c. 1712;" to which Dr. *Hickes* prefixed an account of the Life and Writings of Dr. *Grabe.*

‡ The *firſt* volume was publiſhed in 1707; the *ſecond* and *fourth* in 1709; the *third* not till 1720.

§ Theſe two plates, drawn and engraved by *George Vertue* for Sir *Richard Hoare,* then Lord Mayor, were preſented by his grandſon *Henry Hoare,* of *Stourhead,* eſq. to the Society of Antiquaries, who firſt publiſhed them in 1774.

‖ An account of this learned lady will be given, p. 10.

lord

lord *Guilford*. The University of *Cambridge* and the Dean and Chapter of *Canterbury* do honour to the lift of benefactors.

Mr. *Bowyer* received on this occasion from Dean *Stanhope*** one of the moft excellent and affecting letters that fo melancholy an event could be fuppofed to have fuggefted. It was written in hafte, and evidently came from the heart :

* Dr. *George Stanhope* was a native of *Hertifhorn*, in *Derbyfhire*. His father, the rev. Mr. *Thomas Stanhope*, was rector of that place, vicar of *St. Margaret's* church in *Leicefter*, and chaplain to the earls of *Chefterfield* and *Clare*. His mother's name was *Adleftry*, of a good family in the fame county. He was fent to fchool, firft at *Uppingham* in *Rutland*, then at *Leicefter*; afterwards removed to *Eaton*, and thence chofen to *King's College* in *Cambridge*, in the place of *W. Cleaver*. He took the degree of B. A. in 1681; M. A. 1685; was elected one of the fyndics for the Univerfity of *Cambridge*, in the bufinefs of *Alban Francis*, 1687; minifter of *Quoi* near *Cambridge*; vice-proctor 1688; was that year preferred to the rectory of *Tring* in *Hertfordfhire*, which after fome time he quitted. He was in 1689 prefented to the vicarage of *Lewifham* in *Kent* by lord *Dartmouth*, to whom he had been chaplain, and tutor to his fon. He was alfo appointed chaplain to King *William* and Queen *Mary*, and continued to enjoy that honour under Queen *Anne*. He commenced D. D. *July* 5, 1697, performing all the offices required to that degree publicly, and with great applaufe. He was made vicar of *Deptford* in 1703; fucceeded Dr. *Hooper* as dean of *Canterbury* the fame year; and was thrice chofen prolocutor of the lower houfe of convocation. His uncommon diligence and induftry, affifted by his excellent parts, enriched him with a large ftock of polite, folid, and moft ufeful learning. His difcourfes from the pulpit were equally pleafing and profitable ; a beautiful intermixture of the cleareft reafoning with the pureft diction, attended with all the graces of a juft elocution. The good chriftian, the folid divine, and the fine gentleman, in him were happily united. His converfation was polite and delicate, grave without precifenefs, facetious without levity. His piety was real and rational, his charity great and univerfal, fruitful in acts of mercy, and in all good works. He died *March* 13, 1728, aged 68 years; and was buried in the chancel of the church at *Lewifham*.

Dr. *Felton* fays, " The late Dean of *Canterbury* is excellent in the whole. His " thoughts and reafoning bright and folid. His ftyle is juft, both for the purity of " language, and for ftrength and beauty of expreffion ; but the periods are formed in " fo peculiar an order of the words, that it was an obfervation, nobody could pro- " nounce them with the fame grace and advantage as himfelf."

We cannot but lament that we are not furnifhed with fufficient materials to do juftice to the memory of this worthy man. Many of the above dates are now firft publifhed from Mr. *Baker's* MS. " Hiftory of *King's College*," Harl. MSS. Nº 7038. His writings, which are an ineftimable treafure of piety and devotion, are, " A Paraphrafe and Comment " upon the Epiftles and Gofpels," 4 vols. 1705, 8vo. " Sermons at *Boyle's* Lectures," 1706, 4to. " Fifteen Sermons," 1700, 8vo. " Twelve Sermons on feveral occafions," 1727, 8vo. " St. *Auguftine's* Meditations," 1720, 8vo. " *Thomas a Kempis*," 1696, 8vo. " *Epictetus*," 1700, 8vo. " *Parfon's* Chriftian Directory," 1716, 8vo. " *Rochefocault's* Maxims," 1706, 8vo. " A Funeral Sermon on Mr. *Richard Sare*, Bookfeller, 1724," two editions, 4to.

"Good!

" Good Mr. BOWYER,

It is with very great concern, that I heard of the fad difafter befallen you. You and your family have been in great part the fubject not only of my waking, but even of my fleeping thoughts, from the moment the ill news reached me. You are a perfon of underftanding and religion, enough, I perfuade myfelf, thoroughly to believe, that fecond caufes have a wife director, and that none of our calamities are the effect of chance. This thought, I doubt not, you purfue through all its juft confequences, fuch as may work in you a true chriftian refignation to God's afflicting Providence, and render you contented under your lofs, nay even thankful for it, not only on account of the lives which have been faved, but alfo of the excellent fruits this affliction may, and I hope will, produce, by your improvement of it. For furely humbling one's felf under the Almighty's hand; fuch a dread of his power and juftice as may increafe the fear of offending him; lefs affection for, and no manner of truft in, the enjoyments of this world; and a more eager defire and endeavour after thofe in a better ftate, of which we may reft fecure that they cannot be taken from us, are very natural and becoming confequences of fo fad and fudden a calamity. You, God be praifed, have the comfort of being far from the condition of thofe wretches, whom the world have reafon to think marked out for vengeance. But each of us, who looks into himfelf, will find more than enough there, to juftify the fevereft difpenfations toward him. Or, if it were not fo, which yet always will be fo, the beft are not above the improvement of their

virtues,

virtues, of which great adverfities are an eminent exercife and proof. The poft waits; and I muft haften. My
heart bleeds for your poor wife. God fanctify this trouble
to you both: and give you the piety and the reward of thofe
faints, who *take joyfully the fpoiling of their goods, knowing
in themfelves that they have a better and more enduring fubftance in heaven!* I am your fincere friend and fervant,

Lewifham,
Jan. 31, 1712.   GEO. STANHOPE."

At the fame time Mr. *Bowyer* received the following letter:

" DEAR SIR,   *Jan.* 31, 1712.

I mourn for your misfortune; I hope our loving God will
fanctify it to you, and that your great lofs will in the
end be your great gain. I don't queftion but you are more
a Chriftian than not to bear this, or any other worldly lofs,
with fuch patience as becomes our holy profeffion, and
the difciples of our bleffed Lord and Redeemer. I pray
God blefs you and your family; and bleffed be his holy
name who faved you from perifhing!* The bearer, Mr.
Brydon, is my good friend and benefactor; and knowing
him to be a real honeft man, I recommend him to you, to
ferve you in what he propofes, which I hope will be for
your advantage. My wife and I give our humble fervice
to you and your worthy fpoufe. I pray God comfort you

---

* By a memorial prefented to lord chancellor *Harcourt* by Mr. *Bowyer,* confirmed by
oath, it appears that " the fire broke out between three and four, by accident unknown,
" in the working-rooms directly over his lodging chambers, and, burning with great
" violence, forced him with his wife and children to fave their lives by flight from their
" beds, with only fuch a fmall part of their common wearing apparel as could on the
" fudden be taken with them, though not fufficient to cover them, leaving behind them
" a gentleman of their family†, who perifhed in the flames, and was burnt to afhes."

† Mr. *Charles Cock;* for whom Mr. *B.* had a mourning-ring with this motto, " *C. C.* Paffé par
" Feu au Ciel, 30 *Jan.* 1712, agé 76."

C   both.

both. I am, upon your account, dear Sir, your forrowful, but fincerely loving friend and humble fervant, R. ORME*."

The *Saxon* types, which had been ufed in 1709, for printing St. *Gregory's* Homily, having been burnt with the reft of Mr. *Bowyer's* printing materials; Lord Chief Juftice *Parker* was fo munificently indulgent as to be at the expence of cutting a new fett of *Saxon* types for Mrs. *Elizabeth Elftob's*† *Saxon* Grammar; the punches and matrices of which were afterwards prefented to the Univerfity of *Oxford*, as will appear in the courfe of thefe memoirs.

To

* A Nonjuring Divine, of fingular eminence. He died *Jan.* 14, 1733.—Mr. *Orme* appears to have been a violent oppofer of government during the reign of *George* the firft, and was the perfon charged with abfolving at *Tyburn James Shepherd*, a boy under 18 years old, who was execured there for high treafon, *March* 17, 1717-18; an offence for which Mr. *Orme* was taken into a meffenger's cuftody *March* 21. The whole ftory, too long to be here abridged, may be feen in the Political State, vol. XV. On this oecafion a pamphlet was publifhed, intituled " A General Claim to Allegiance, Atheifts and " Tories excluded; with Arguments and Reflecti ns upon the late Conduct of Mr. *Orme*, " a Nonjuring Parfon, abfolving Mr. *Shepherd* from the crime of Murder unrepented."

† " This learned lady, daughter of *Ralph Elftob* merchant at *Newcaftle*, was born in 1683. Her mother, to whom fhe owed the firft rudiments of her extraordinary education, dying when fhe was but eight years old, her guardians difcouraged her progrefs in literature, as improper for a perfon of her fex; and after her brother's death fhe met with fo little patronage, and fo many difappointments, that fhe retired to *Evefham* in *Worcefterfhire*; whe e, having with difficulty fubfifted fome time by a fmall fchool, fhe was at laft countenanced by Mr. *George Ballard**, and the wife of the Reverend Mr. *Capon*, who kept a boarding-fchool at *Stanton* in *Gloucefterfhire*; and raifed for her, among her friends, an annuity of 21*l.* which the late Queen *Caroline* was pleafed to continue to her own death: after which this lady, miftrefs of eight languages befides her own, was taken into the family of the duchefs dowager of *Portland*, as governefs to her children, 1739; in which fhe died, *May* 30, 1756, and was buried at St. *Margaret's*, *Weftminfter*, having publifhed a tranflation of Madame *Scudery's* " Effay on Glory;" and a *Saxon* Grammar, in 1715, 4°. The Homily on St. *Gregory's* day, publifhed by her brother, in the *Saxon* language, 1709, 8vo. has her *Englifh* tranflation befides his *Latin* one. She affifted him in an edition of *Gregory's* Paftoral, intended probably to have included both the original and *Saxon* verfion, and had tranfcribed all the Hymns from an ancient MS.† in *Salifbury*

* Author of " Memoirs of *Britifh* Ladies who have been celebrated for their Writings or Skill in " the Learned Languages, Arts and Sciences, 1752," 4to and 8vo; reprinted in 8vo, 1775. He was originally a ftay-maker; but, being taken notice of for his learning and abilities by the gentlemen in his neighbourhood, they generoufly raifed for him an annuity of a hundred pounds, which enabled him to profecute his ftudies. He had afterwards a fmall poft given him in *Magdalen College*, *Oxford*, which he enjoyed till his death.

† Amongft other MSS. which fhe tranfcribed for her diverfion was a *Saxon* tranflation of *Athanafius's* C eed, firft printed in the *Confpectus* which in 1708 Dr. *Wotton* gave to the world of Dr. *Hickes's* valuable *Thefaurus*.

cathedral.

To enumerate all the works which paſſed through the preſſes of this able printer, would be almoſt as endleſs as it is unneceſſary. The following articles, however, between 1715 and 1720, deſerve to be at leaſt thus curſorily mentioned: Dean *Prideaux's* "Connection of the Hiſtory of the Old "and New Teſtament," 1715 and 1718, folio; Mr. *Pope's* Works, in folio and quarto, 1717; *Maittaire's* "Hiſtoria "Typographorum aliquot Pariſienſium, Vitas & Libros "complectens*, 1717," 8vo; St. *Cyprian's* Works, tranſ-lated by *Marſhall*, 1717; Dr. *Fiddes's* "Body of Divi-"nity,"

cathedral. She had undertaken, by the encouragement of Dr. *Hickes*, a *Saxon* Homilarium, with an *Engliſh* tranſlation, notes, and various readings; and five or more of the Homi-lies were actually printed off at *Oxford*, in folio.—Her brother [*William*], the famous *Saxoniſt*, was born in 1673, educated at *Eton*, admitted at *Catharine Hall, Cambridge*; but the air of that country not agreeing with him, he removed to *Queen's College, Oxford*; and was afterwards choſen Fellow of *Univerſity College*, where he was joint tutor with Dr. *Clavering*, afterwards Biſhop of *Peterborough*. He was rector of the united pariſhes of *St. Swithin* and *St. Mary Bothaw, London*, 1702, where he died in 1714. He tranſlated into *Latin* the *Saxon* Homily of *Lupus*, dated 1701, with notes for Dr. *Hickes*; and into *Engliſh* Sir *J. Cheke's Latin* tranſlation of *Plutarch* "De "Superſtitione," printed at the end of *Strype's* Life of *Cheke*, out of the MS. of which *Ob. Walker*, when Maſter of *Univerſity College*, had cut ſeveral leaves containing *Cheke's* remarks againſt Popery. He was author of an Eſſay on the great affinity and mutual agreement of the two profeſſions of Law and Divinity, *London*, ——, 8vo. with a pre-face by Dr. *Hickes*, and of two ſermons on public occaſions, 1704. He publiſhed *Aſcham's Latin* Letters, *Oxford*, 1703, 8vo; compiled an Eſſay on the *Latin* Tongue, its hiſtory and uſe, in which he was a very great proficient; collected for a Hiſtory of *Newcaſtle*; alſo the various proper names formerly uſed in the North; but what is be-come of theſe MSS. is not known. His moſt conſiderable deſign was an edition of the *Saxon* Laws, with great additions, and a new *Latin* Verſion by *Somner*, notes of various learned men, and a prefatory hiſtory of the origin and progreſs of the *Engliſh* Laws down to the Conqueror, and to Magna Charta. He intended alſo a tranſlation, with notes, of *Alfred's* paraphraſtic verſion of *Oroſius*, of which his tranſcript, with colla-tions, is in Mr. *Pegge's* hands; and another, by Mr. *George Ballard*, with the latter's large preface on the uſe of *Anglo-Saxon* literature, was left by the late Biſhop of *Carliſle* to the Society of Antiquaries library. A ſpecimen of Mr. *Elſtob's* deſign was actually printed at *Oxford*, 1690." Two of Mrs. *Elſtob's* letters to the earl of *Oxford*, dated 1713 and 1713-14, and one of her brother's, are among the *Harleian* MSS. Memoirs of Mr. *Elſtob* and his ſiſter, communicated to the Society of Antiquaries by the Rev. Mr. *Pegge*, 1768; and printed in their Archæologia, vol. I. p. xxvi.—The verſion of *Oroſius* has ſince been given to the publick, with an *Engliſh* tranſlation, by a very worthy friend and patron of Mr. *Bowyer's*, the Hon. *Daines Barrington*, 1773, 8vo.

* The concluſion of the Preface to this volume is too honourable to Mr. *Bowyer* to be omitted: "Quicquid in hâc editione fuerit peccatum, id à me ortum in me totum

"tranſlatum

" nity,"[*] 1717; *Chaucer's* Works, by *Urry*; 1718 and 1721;
Echard's " Hiftory of *England*," 1718, *Burchet's* " Naval
" Tranfactions," 1719; *Lefley's* " Theological Works," 2
vols. 1720; all in folio; *Le Neve's* " Monumenta Anglicana,"
1718-19, 4 vols. 8vo.

At a proper age young Mr. *Bowyer* was placed under the
care of Mr. *Ambrofe Bonwicke*, a Nonjuring clergyman of
great piety and learning, at *Headley*†, near *Leatherbead* in
Surrey; where he made fuch advances in literature as
reflected the higheft credit both on himfelf and his preceptor; for whofe memory, to his lateft years, he entertained
the fincereft refpect; and to whofe family he always remained
an ufeful friend. The attachment, indeed, was mutual.

One inftance of the good fchool-mafter's benevolence,
which made an indelible impreffion on the mind of his
pupil, appeared in the following letter, written a few days
after the dreadful fire which deftroyed the whole property
of the elder Mr. *Bowyer*:

" MY GOOD FRIEND, *Headley,*
Feb. 6, 1712-3.

" I heard of the fad calamity, it has pleafed God to try
" you with, laft *Monday*; but concealed it from your fon‡

" tranflatum velim. Omni prorfus culpâ Typographum libero, optimæ fidei & induf-
" triæ (ut quifquam eft alius) hominem, qui unà cum viro reverendo[*] doctoque quem
" operis typographicis præfecit egregiam navavit operam, ut hoc opus pro materiæ
" dignitate prodiret; typographique, quorum defcribitur hiftoria, fe dignum nancif-
" cerentur typographum. Tales nunc dierum refpublica literaria typographos, tales
" defideret ἰταχορθώτας; quibus nil deeft, nifi, quales olim typographis Parifienfibus
" contigerint, patroni."

* See an account of Dr. *Fiddes* (whom Dr. *Jortin* emphatically calls " a Proteftant
" Papift") in the *Supplement to Swift.*

† The poet *Fenton* was then ufher at that fchool.

‡ This circumftance Mr. *Bowyer* ufed frequently to mention with the higheft gratitude: as he did another in which the fame delicacy was fhewn to him. When the *brief*
was to be read in *Headley* church, Mr. *Bonwicke* contrived that he fhould be kept at
home, without affigning the reafon for it. The writer of thefe memoirs accompanied
him to that village fo lately as 1774, when Mr. *Bowyer*, with great fatisfaction, repeated
the above and many other particulars of his younger years.

* Mr. *Bowyer's* corrector of the prefs was ufually a clergyman; the one here alluded to was probably either Mr. *Blackburne* or Mr. *Linafay.*

" till

" till I had the account from yourself, and then broke it
" to him as gently as I could: he could not forbear shed-
" ding some tears; but that was no more than some of
" your friends here had done for you before, and it would
" be some comfort to them if their sharing in it might
" lessen your grief. We have in *Job* a noble example of
" patience and resignation under even a severer trial than
" this of yours; for, God be praised, though you have
" lost a worthy friend*, your children are alive, and one†
" of them providentially disposed of a little before, the
" news of which proved a happy mixture in your melan-
" choly letter; and though you began with it, I made it
" the close of my narrative to your son.   And when we
" *have seen the end of the Lord,* as St. *James* expresses it,
" we shall find that he is *very pitiful, and of tender mercy,*
" as he was to his servant *Job,* whose losses in the end were
" abundantly repaired; and since he is still the same God,
" if our behaviour be conformable, we may humbly hope
" for the like treatment.   As an earnest of which, I must
" tell you, that he has already put it into the heart of a
" certain person, upon hearing of your great loss, to pay
" the whole charges of your son's board, *&c.* for one
" year ‡; the person desires to be nameless, that the thanks
" may be returned to God only.   My wife, who truly
" condoles with you, gives her service to yourself and Mrs.
" *Bowyer,* to whom pray give mine also, and to my good
" friend Mr. *Ross:* our service likewise, with hearty wishes
" of much joy (notwithstanding this melancholy beginning)

---

* Mr. *Cock.*   See p. 9.

† Mr. *Bowyer's* daughter (by a former wife).   She had just before been married to
Mr. *James Bettenham,* a printer, of no small eminence in his profession, which he pursued with unabated industry and reputation till the year 1766, when he retired from business; and died *Feb.* 6, 1774, of a gradual decay, at the advanced age of 91.

‡ It may be unnecessary to mention, that this friend was Mr. *Bonwicke* himself.

4   " to

" to the new-married gentlewoman. Your fon fpeaks for
" himfelf in the inclofed, which he juft now brought to,
" Sir, your condoling friend, and faithful fervant,
" AMBR. BONWICKE*."

The following fhort Letter, written to Mr. *Wanley* †, is
here printed, in order to introduce the note which accom-
panies it ‡, relative to Mr. *Wanley's* defign of an edition of
fome

* This confcientious Divine (fon of the Rev. *John Bonwicke* ‖, rector of *Mickleham*
in *Surrey*) born *April* 29, 1652, and educated at *Merchant Taylors School*, was elected to
St. *John's College, Oxford*, in 1668, where he was appointed librarian in 1670; B. A.
1673; M. A. *March* 18, 1675; was ordained deacon, *May* 21, 1676; prieft, *June* 6
(*Trinity Sunday*), 1680; proceeded B. D. *July* 21, 1682; and was elected mafter of
Merchant Taylors School, June 9, 1686. In 1689, the college of St. *John's* petitioned
that he might continue mafter of the School (which is a nurfery for their College) for
life; but at *Chriftmas* 1691 he was turned out for refufing to take the oath of allegiance. I have a curious correfpondence of his with Mr. *Blechynden*, on this occafion,
in MS. with many of his college excrcifes, and letters to his father. By his wife (*Elizabeth Stubbs)* Mr. *Bonwicke* had twelve children.

† [An eminent adept in the *Saxon* antiquities, and the fcience of diftinguifhing the
different forts of writing, of which laft he intended to publifh fpecimens. He drew up
a Supplement to *Hydes* Catalogue of the *Bodleian* MSS. which Mr. *Hearne* publifhed.
He travelled over *England*, at the defire of Dr. *Hickes*, in queft of *Saxon* MSS. of which
he gave the account in the Doctor's Thefaurus; and intended an edition of the Bible in
Saxon. In the Society of Antiquaries is an original picture of him by Mr. *Thomas Dhall*,
1711, Archæologia, vol. I. p. 36. He was librarian to *Robert* earl of *Oxford*; and continued in the fame employment under earl *Edward*, from whom he received a handfome
penfion till his death, which happened *July* 6, 1726, æt. 55.

‡ " The copy I fhewed Mr. *Bowyer* confifted of thefe treatifes following; viz.
Chronicon Dunftapliæ; tranfcribed from the *Cottonian* MS. by mine own hand.
Benedicti Petroburgenfis Abbatis Chronicon; tranfcribed from the *Cottonian* MS. by
myfelf, and collated with the other.
Annales de Lanefcroft, tranfcribed from the *Cottonian* MS. for me by Mr. *Elphinftone.*
The late lord vifcount *Weymouth* put me upon the defign of publifhing thefe, or any
other of our old Hiftorians or Chronicles which I might like better: and, for the labour
and charge of copying the fame, gave me 100 *l.* intimating further, that when they
fhould be publifhed, he would give me another, as a reward for my Dedication. More-
over, his lordfhip promifed to take off fifty of the printed copies; and afterwards was
pleafed to extend this promife to 100 copies. I own that I was not willing the work
fhould be hurried, becaufe I would compare thefe treatifes with others. I was willing
to have large notes, illuftrating the whole, with charters, feals, monuments, epitaphs,
buildings, and as much other unprinted matter as would fall in my way properly, and
always pertinent to my fubject: not forgetting an *Index Nominum Propriorum &*

‖ " Hic pofitæ funt Reliquiæ JOHANNIS BONWICKE, SS. T. B. & iftius Ecclefiæ per annos XXIX
" Rectoris; qui natus eft Nov. 3, 1622; fepultus Nov. 5, 1698." *Epitaph in Mickleham Church.*

Materiarum,

fome of our antient hiftorians, on a plan worthy his fkill in *Englifh* Antiquities, and which ought to be adopted in fuch particulars. Both letter and note are tranfcribed from the *Harleian* MSS. N° 3778.

" Sir, I have computed the copy you fhewed me on
" *Monday* laft by the fpecimen Mr. *Sare** fince fhewed
" me; and I believe it will make about 205 fheets, con-
" taining 62 lines in each page, and about 64 letters each
" line. Your moft humble fervant, W. BOWYER."

In *June* 1716 young Mr. *Bowyer* was admitted as a fizar at *St. John's College, Cambridge*; of which College Dr. *Robert Jenkin*† was at that time mafter. The Doctor had been

a bene-

Materiarum, and a Gloffary. But it being thought that thefe things would take up too much time, I was ordered to publifh, as foon as poffible, even the naked text; and it was then alledged, that what elfe I had propofed might be printed in another volume at mine own leifure. I then brought Mr. *Sare*, Mr. *Wyat*, Mr. *Knaplock*, Mr. *Tooke*, and Mr. *Cowfe*, bookfellers, and all honeft men, together; propofed the matter to them, difclaimed all reward or other confideration for copy-money, and promifed to procure more than fifty fubfcriptions. Afterward, Mr. *Bowyer* came to me, and caft over the copy, as above is noted. In other meetings, I promifed fubfcriptions for more than 100 copies, and fhewed from whom they would proceed. We agreed with Mr. *Bowyer* about the paper, &c. the volume, letter, &c.; and were ready to enter upon mutual articles; when, to our great furprize, that noble peer deceafed [*July* 28, 1714], in very old age, without having fhewn the leaft regard to this work. Hereupon I got the bookfellers to meet me again; who, underftanding that our common patron was departed this life, and no money left for payment of the copies his lordfhip intended to buy, would by no means enter into any further deliberation or covenant about printing the book, but flew off from it utterly. When I found this, I thought myfelf likewife difcharged from it. This is a true account, why the treatifes above mentioned did not fee the light, as I intended. HUMFREY WANLEY."

* See Mr. *Sare's* character, p. 2. He died *Feb.* 4, 1723, æt. 68.

† Son of *Thomas Jenkin*, Gentleman, of *Minfter*, in the *Ifle of Thanet*, where he was born *Jan.* 1656; and bred at the King's School at *Canterbury*. He entered as fizar at St. *John's College, Cambridge*, *March* 12, 1674, under the tuition of Mr. *Francis Roper*; and became a Fellow of that Society *March* 30, 1680; Mafter *Apr.* 9, 1711 ‡; and held alfo the office of Lady *Margaret's* Profeffor of Divinity. Dr. *Lake*, being tranflated from the fee of *Briftol* to that of *Chichefter*, in 1685, made him his chaplain, and collated him to

‡ On the death of Dr *Humfrey Gower*; who left him a country feat at *Thriploe*, worth 20*l. per ann.* on the death of Mr. *Weft*, his nephew and heir; and 500*l.* to buy a living for the College, to which fociety he alfo left two exhibitions of 10*l.* each, and all his books to their library.

the

a benefactor to the elder Mr. *Bowyer* in the feafon of his calamity; and the fon, at the diftance of fixty years, had the

the præcentorfhip of that church, 1688. Refufing to take the oaths at the Revolution, he quitted that preferment, and retired to his Fellowfhip, which was not fubject then to thofe conditions, unlefs the bifhop of *Ely*, the vifitor, infifted on it. And he [the bifhop] was by the college-ftatutes not to vifit, unlefs called in by a majority of the Fellows. By this means he and many others kept their Fellowfhips. Upon the acceffion of King *George* I. an act was paffed, obliging all who held any poft of 5*l*. a year to take the oaths, by which Dr. *Jenkin* was obliged to eject thofe Fellows that would not comply, which gave him no fmall uneafinefs †; and he funk by degrees into childhood. In this condition he removed to his elder brother's houfe at *South Rungton* in *Norfolk*, where he died *April* 7, 1727, in his 70th year; and was buried (with his wife *Sufannah*, daughter of *William Hatfield*, efq. alderman and merchant of *Lynne*, who died 1713, aged 46, his fon *Henry*, and daughter *Sarah*, who both died young 1727) in *Holme* chapel, in that parifh of which his brother was rector. Another daughter *Sarah* furvived him. A fmall mural monument was erected to his memory, with this infcription:

S. M.	Ornamentum fuit illuftre;
Reverendi admodum ROBERTI JENKIN,	Exemplar venerabile,
Sanctæ Theologiæ pro Domina Margareta	Vindex fideliffimus,
in Academia Cantabrigienfi Profefforis,	Et ufque vixit
Omni laude digniffimi,	Monumentum perpetuum.
Et Collegii Divi Johannis Evangeliftæ Præfecti	Ob. 7 Die Aprilis,
Vigilantiffimi, fpectatiffimi;	Anno Domini 1727,
Qui doctrinæ, pietatis, religionis,	Æt. 70.

He publifhed, 1. " An Hiftorical Examination of the Authority of General Councils, " 1688."—2. " A Defence of the Profeffion which Bifhop *Lake* made upon his Death-" bed."—3. "Defenfio *S. Auguftini* adverfus *Jo. Phereponum*, 1707."—4. " An *Englifh* " tranflation of the Life of *Apollonius Tyaneus*, from the *French* of *Tillemont*."—5. " Re-" marks on Four Books lately publifhed; viz. *Bafnage's* Hiftory of the *Jews*; *Whifton's* " Eight Sermons; *Locke's* Paraphrafe and Notes on St. *Paul's* Epiftles; and *Le Clerc's* " Bibliotheque Choifie;" and was alfo author of, 6. " The Reafonablenefs and Certainty " of the Chriftian Religion;" of which a *fifth* edition, corrected, appeared in 1721.

Dr. *Jenkin* had an elder and a younger brother, *Henry* and *John*.

John was a Judge in *Ireland*, under the duke of *Ormond*; upon whofe going abroad, he became and died a Nonjuror, leaving a fon—what is become of the fon, and whether he had iffue or no, is unknown.

Henry, elder brother of the mafter, was vicar of *Tilney*, in *Norfolk* ‡, and rector of *South Rungton cum Wallington*, where he died in 1732, and had three fons, *Thomas*, *William*, and *Robert*.

Thomas, the eldeft, was the Mafter's proper fizar, and left two fons: the eldeft fettled in *Lincolnfhire*; the youngeft was in 1770 with his pupil Lord *Milfington*, eldeft fon to the earl of *Portmore*.

† The true account of the ejection is this: The ftatutes of that college require the Fellows, as foon as they are of that ftanding, to take the degree of B. D. But the oath of allegiance is required to be taken at every degree: fo that, after the Revolution, 24 of the Fellows not coming in to the oath of allegiance, and the ftatutes requiring them to commence B. D. they were conftrained to part with their fellowfhips. As to thofe who had taken that degree before the Revolution, there was nothing to eject them upon till their refufal of the abjuration-oath, which was exacted upon the acceffion of King *George* I. *Anonym.*

‡ See Dr. *Brett's* Life of Mr. *Johnfon* of *Cranbrook*.

William

the happiness of returning the favour to a relation of the worthy master, in a manner by which the person obliged was totally ignorant to whom he was indebted for the present he received, as will appear in Mr. *Bowyer's* last will.

Our young printer assisted his father in correcting Mr. *Maittaire's* excellent edition of the " *Batrachomyomachia*, " 1721," 8vo; Dr. *Wilkins's** " Leges *Anglo-Saxonicæ*;" the " Inscriptio *Sigæa*" by Mr. *Edmund Chishull**, folio; and the *Latin†* Life of Dr. *Barwick*, 8vo, the same year. He continued, however, at college till *June* 1722, under the tuition, first of the Rev. Dr. *Christopher Ansley‡*, and afterwards under the Rev. Dr. *John Newcome*||; during which time, it is probable that he took the degree of batchelor of arts. In 1719 he wrote what he called " Epistola pro Sodalitio à " Reverendo Viro *Francisco Roper* mihi legato;" which led to a supposition that he had been a candidate for a Fellowship. On recollection, however, he had not then

---

William left no issue.—*Robert*, the 3d son of *Henry*, was in the same station as his brother *Thomas*, under the Master; was a minor-canon of *Canterbury*, and possessed of the living of *Westbeere*, worth about 90 *l.* a year. He died *Oct.* 8, 1778.—Mr. *Austen*, of *St. Martin's*, *Canterbury*, married into the family of *Jenkin*, and has a long pedigree of it.—The Master, either by deed of gift or last will, gave all to his nephew *Thomas*.

* Some particulars of Dr. *Wilkins* and Mr. *Chishull* will accompany these memoirs.

† Published *anonymously* by the Rev. *Hilkiah Bedford*, who was also editor of the *English* Life of Dr. *Barwick* in 1724. He was prosecuted, and suffered imprisonment, in 1713, for fathering " The Hereditary Right of the Crown of *England* asserted," which was written by his friend Mr. *Harbin*. See the *Supplement to Swift*.—Mr. *Bedford* was born *July* 23, 1663; and died *Nov.* 26, 1724.

‡ Dr. *Ansley*, fellow of *Jesus*, was for some time a tutor; and, having entered into a matrimonial engagement, accepted of a very small college living, *Brinkley* in *Cambridgeshire*, a few miles north of *Newmarket*. Some years before his death he retired to an estate which he had at *Trompington*. He was father to the author of " The *Bath* Guide."

|| Afterwards master of the college, Lady *Margaret's* professor, and dean of *Rochester*. A Sermon of his, at an Ordination held at *St. Paul's*, *March* 13, 1719, was printed by Mr. *Bowyer* senior; and another, before the House of Commons, *Jan.* 30, 1744, is also in print. Dr. *Newcome* died *Jan.* 10, 1765; his lady some little time before him. She published " An Enquiry into the Evidences of the Christian Religion," 1728 and 1731; a work which, in an age when female authors were not so frequent as at present, conferred on her a greater share of literary reputation than many of her contemporaries were willing to allow. The late bishop *Squire* was her nephew.

D   been

been of long standing enough in the college to have stood
for a fellowship; and it since appears (see p. 32), that it was
an Exhibition of Mr. *Roper's* which occasioned Mr. *Bowyer's*
thanks; of which a copy is printed below, from his own
hand-writing *. Among his college-bills is a memorandum of receiving six pounds, " Mr. *Roper's* Legacy," 1719.
The following Poem is a specimen of his College Exercises:

" *Nequicquam sapit, qui sibi ipsi non sapit.*

" A GOODLY parson once there was,
  To 's maid would chatter *Latin*
(For that he was, I think, an ass,
  At least the rhyme comes pat in).
One day the house to prayers were met
  With well-united hearts:
Below, a goose was at the spit,
  To feast their grosser parts.
The godly maid to prayers she came,
  If truth the legends say,
To hear her master *English* lame,
  Herself to sleep and pray.
The maid, to hear her worthy master,
  Left all alone her kitchen:
Hence happen'd much a worse disaster
  Than if she'd shut the bitch in.
      Nov. 29, 1719.

While each breast burns with pious flame,
  All hearts with ardours beat,
The goose's breast did much the same,
  With too malicious heat.
The Parson smelt the odours rise;
  To 's belly-thoughts gave loose;
And plainly seem'd to sympathize
  With his twice-murder'd goose.
He knew full well self-preservation
  Bids piety retire;
Just as the *salus* of a nation
  Lays obligations higher.
He stopt, and thus held forth his *clerum*;
  While him the wench did stare at,
*Hoc faciendum; sed altérum
Non negligendum erat.*
  Parce tuum Vatem sceleris damnare!"

Not-

* " Rev'de Præses, est profectò in agendis gratiis nescio quid adeò suave & jucundum,
ut animo non prorsùs degeneri difficile sit eas non persolvere. Hinc quanquam nostri
Beneficii beatus Author ex hisce oculis longiùs amoveatur, incumbit tamen eadem grata
necessitas; & aliquid referendum est, ne pectus quasi immemori beneficio laboret. Quibus verò potiùs referendum est, quàm iis quibus acceptum tulimus? Sic quoties ministri
cælitùs delabuntur, qui humanis miseriis suppetias afferant, summo cultu reveremur, &
periculum est, ne nimiâ religione Numinis vicarium prosequamur.

Quoties de Angelis, de Cœlis, sit mentio, ignosce mihi, si defuncti amici † subeat
recordatio. Eheu! insandus renovatur dolor, & vulnera nostra planè recrudescunt. At,
at, simul ac Tecum mihi esse sermonem intueor, spes aliqua lætior effulget: ignosce
etiam mihi, si pro amico abrepto in vivis alter præsens esse videatur.

Hoc sane ingens mihi præbet solatium: tandem quadriennii ferè labores hìc exantlati
satis superque mercedis receperunt. Jam licèt nostrum nomen titulis illis, quos ab almâ
matre plerique ejusdem ordinis filii solent expetere, non sit insigniendum, mihi tamen
facilis erit assuetæ gloriæ jactura, tam novis, tam insolitis honoribus cumulato.

† Mr. *Roper's* death is here alluded to with peculiar propriety, as he had been the Master's tutor.
He was of very long standing in the College; where he was admitted Fellow, *Apr.* 2, 1666.

Jam

Notwithſtanding an habitual ſhyneſs of diſpoſition, which was unfavourable to him at firſt appearance, the regularity of his conduct and his application to ſtudy procured him the eſteem of many very reſpectable members of the univerſity. It was in this ſeminary of learning that he formed an intimacy with Mr. *Jeremiah Markland**,

one

Jam quaſcunque terrarum partes licebit videre, ubicunque enim ſpiritum hunc traxero, gratè perpetuò ſum prædicaturus, iis ædibus me vixiſſe, apud quas, ex aliorum exemplis, confirmare poſſum nè maxima quidem merita ſuis præmiis carere, & ex mei ipſius exemplo, nè minima quidem carere pluſquàm ſuis.

Non potes, Rev'de Præſes, non animo advertere, quantum me reprimam ne tuas laudes aggrediar; nolo enim nunc primùm id mihi indulgere quod tibi diſpliceat: liceat tamen hoc ſi non in tuum nomen, ſaltem in reverendi viri decus proferri, ipſum, plus quàm duplici dono nos cohoneſtâſſe, quibus legavit non ſolùm largitionem amplam, verùm etiam patronos ampliſſimos.

Extabit olim hinc aliquis qui defunctum ſuum patronum, te vivum amicum, pulchriore forſan oratione, non gratiore animo, ſit elaturus: utcunque tamen dicendo felix ſit. Hoc ſaltem invidebit; dum ipſe patroni dona ſolum participat, nos tanti patroni conſuetudinem ſæpiùs participâſſe. De hâc gloriâ ego quidem ſerio triumpho; de eloquentiâ ſuâ triumphet ille. Quòd ſi inſuper patrocinio tuo, Reverende Præſes, nos dignatus fueris, non erit quod futuro cuiquam Ciceroni invideam.

Ut igitur nos, quod facis, amplectaris, foveas, per inſitam tibi benevolentiam, per ſacros præclariſſimi viri manes, petit, orat, obteſtatur, favoris tui ſtudioſiſſimus & cultor devotiſſimus   GUIL. BOWYER, 1719."

* I have ſo juſt a regard for the memory and character of Mr. MARKLAND, that I hope to ſtand excuſed in enlarging on his article. The materials I draw from are in general new to the world, and undoubtedly authentic. He was one of the twelve children of the Rev. *Ralph Markland*, author of " The Art of Shooting flying;" was born *Oct.* 29, 1693; educated in *Chriſt's Hoſpital*; and thence ſent to *Peter-houſe*; of which, at his death, he was ſenior fellow. A *Latin* copy of verſes by him appeared in the " *Cambridge* Gratulations, 1714;" and in 1717 he ably vindicated the character of Mr. *Addiſon*, againſt the Satire of Mr. *Pope*, in an *Engliſh* copy of verſes inſcribed to the Counteſs of *Warwick**. But he became firſt diſtinguiſhed in the learned world by his " Epiſtola Critica, 1723," addreſſed to Bp. *Hare*, in which he gave many proofs of extenſive erudition and critical ſagacity. He publiſhed an edition of " *Statius's Silvæ*, 1728," 4to; Notes on "*Maximus Tyrius*, 1740;" a valuable volume of " Remarks on the Epiſtles of *Cicero* to *Brutus*, and of *Brutus* to " *Cicero* †. In a Letter to a Friend. With a Diſſertation upon Four Orations aſcribed

* On the ſtrength of theſe verſes (which are preſerved in *Gent. Mag.* for *July* 1779), and of a tranſlation of the " Friar's Tale" from *Chaucer* (printed in *Ogle's* edition 1741), our learned Critic was not unfrequently introduced into the multifarious publications of *Curll*, under the name of Mr. JOHN *Markland*, of St. *Peter's College*, in *Cambridge*. See the Court Poems, 1726; the Altar of Love; the Progreſs of Dulneſs; &c. and particularly " *Cythereia*, or Poems upon Love and In- " trigue, printed for *T. Payne*, 1723 " In the laſt mentioned collection (which I have never ſeen), *Curll* ſays, Mr. *Pope's* Satire, with Mr. *Markland's* Anſwer, firſt appeared. Both, however, were printed ſo early as 1717. Perhaps this circumſtance may furniſh a clue to what has been in part ſo ably diſcuſſed in the new edition of the Biographia Britannica, article *Addiſon*.

† Extracts from ſome of Mr. *Markland's* letters on this and other ſubjects will be inſerted hereafter.

one of the moſt learned and penetrating critics of the age, and

" to *M. Tullius Cicero*; viz. 1. Ad *Quirites* poſt Reditum; 2. Poſt Reditum in Senatu;
" 3. Pro Domo ſua, ad Pontifices; 4. De Haruſpicum Reſponſis. To which are added,
" ſome extracts out of the notes of learned men upon thoſe Orations, and Obſervations on
" them, 1745;" 8vo. attempting to prove them all ſpurious and the works of ſome ſophiſt *.
An excellent little treatiſe under the title of "De *Græcorum* Quintâ Declinâtione Impariſyl-
" labicâ, & inde formatâ *Latinorum* Tertiâ, Quæſtio Grammatica †, 1761," 4to. No
more than forty copies having been printed, which were all given away; it was annexed,
in 1763, to an admirable edition of the " Supplices Mulieres" of *Euripides*, in 4to.
Why this was publiſhed anonymouſly, a letter from him to Mr. *Bowyer* will explain :
" As to the compliments of ſcholars, I believe you do not ſet any great value upon
" them, and I believe I ſet as little; to avoid which myſelf, and to excuſe others the
" neceſſity of making them right or wrong, were two reaſons why no name is put to
" this edition." The following curious memorandum is taken from his own hand-
writing (in 1764) in a copy of that book: " This was printed at the expence of Dr.
" *Heberden* ‡, A. D. 1763. There were only 250 copies printed, this kind of ſtudy
" being at that time greatly neglected in *England*. The Writer of the Notes was then
" old and infirm; and having by him ſeveral things of the ſame ſort, written many
" years before, he did not think it worth while to reviſe them; and was unwilling to
" leave them behind him as they were, in many places not legible to any body but
" himſelf; for which reaſon he deſtroyed them‖. Probably it will be a long time (if
" ever) before this ſort of learning will revive in *England*; in which it is eaſy to fore-
" ſee that there muſt be a diſturbance in a few years, and all public diſorders are ene-
" mies to this ſort of literature §." Fortunately, however, for the world of letters, the

* When a pamphlet was publiſhed againſt theſe Remarks (which will be taken notice of under
the year 1745), Mr. *Clarke* told Mr. *Markland* of it, and would have had him read it; but he took
a pen, and wrote upon the pamphlet, "*April* 4, 1745. *I never looked into this Book.* Jer. Markland."
† Mr. *Markland* appears to have taken up this ſubject in conſequence of Mr. *Bowyer's* edition of
Kuſter. See under the year 1750. It was inſcribed, " Amiciſſimo Viro *W. H.* [*William Hall*] ar-
" migero; non ut patrono cliens, ſed ut amico amicus, quæ multo optabilior eſt neceſſitudo."
‡.This volume (inſcribed by Mr. *Markland*, *Tiberio Hemſterhuſio* & *Petro Weſſelingio* Viris doctiſ-
" ſimis, & ſumme inter ſe amicis,") is introduced by the following advertiſement: " Hæ notæ ple-
" ræque multis abhinc annis ſcriptæ erant, quas poſtquam ſcripſiſſet auctor, nactus eſt hujus dramatis,
" et utriuſque *Iphigeniæ* collationem cum tribus codicibus ex Bibliotheca Regia *Pariſienſi*, qui hic
" notantur literis A. B. C Hæc omnia editioni parata erant. Quum autem rure degens, valetudine
" infirmiſſimâ, et ſenectute jam ingruente, inſuper obſervaſſet quanto in neglectu a pleriſque fere ha-
" beretur lingua *Græca* et totum hoc literaturæ genus, ſtudiis hominum alio, ut fit, converſis; maluit
" has notas non edere, et eas mihi donavit, qui exemplaria aliquot hujus dramatis et notarum edenda
" jam curavi. Addita ſunt præcipua, quæ viri eruditi in hanc fabulam notarunt; quatenus ad no-
" titiam Auctoris pervenerunt. Effeci quoque, ut opuſculum de *Græcorum* Quintâ Declinatione Im-
" pariſyllabicâ &c. *Londini* editum duobus abhinc annis, cujus exemplaria erant pauciſſima, denuo
" recuſum, his ſubjiceretur. Abſente auctore, vicem ejus ad prelum ſuſcepit vir doctiſſimus
" *Joannes Fortinus* S. T. P cujus eruditæ curæ multum debere hanc editionem profitetur commen-
" tator. Ne fierent indices, obſtitit auctoris oculorum infirmitas, et arthritis ſæviſſima. Vale. *W. H.*
‖ " I hear with infinite concern of his having deſtroyed the two plays which you mention. If
" there remains any thing of his now undeſtroyed, I muſt add a wiſh, and that a very hearty one,
" *Parcant Fata ſuperſtiti!*" *Letter from Dr. Foſter to Mr. B. July* 1, 1766.
§ In the ſame dejected ſpirit Mr. *Markland* ſpeaks, in 1772, of the edition of *Euripides* lately publiſhed: " The *Oxonians*, I hear, are about to publiſh *Euripides* in 4to; two volumes I ſuppoſe. Dr.
" *Muſgrave* helps them with his collections, and perhaps conjectures. In my opinion, this is no time
" for ſuch works; I mean, for the undertakers."

notes.

and not more valued for his univerfal reading, than beloved
for

notes on the two " *Iphigeniæ*" were preferved *, and prefented, in *Feb.* 1768, " Doctiffimo,
" &, quòd longè præftantius eft, Humaniffimo Viro *Wilhelmo Heberden*, M. D. arbitratu
" ejus vel cremandæ vel in publicum emittendæ poft obitum fcriptoris: eâ tamen lege,
" ut fi Editione dignæ ab illo cenfeantur, quemadmodum olim judicabat in *Supplicibus*,
" exftet fimul hæc pagina, quæ teftetur animum memorem beneficiorum ab eo col-
" latorum in Annotatorem dum in vivis erat." They were in confequence given to the
world † in 1771, in 8vo; and the " Supplices Mulieres " with the " Quæftio Grammatica"
were re-printed in that fize for *Eton* fchool in 1775. Mr. *Markland* affifted Dr.
Taylor in his editions of *Lyfias* and *Demofthenes*; Dr. *Mufgrave* in his *Hippolytus*
1755; and Mr. *Bowyer* in an edition of feven plays of *Sophocles* ‡ 1758; by the notes
which he communicated to the refpective editors. The like fervice he conferred
on Mr. *Arnald* ||, in the fecond edition of his " Commentary on the Book of Wifdom."
His very happy elucidations of many paffages in the New Teftament may be found
in Mr. *Bowyer's* " Conjectures," marked in the 8vo edition with an *R.* In 1746,
he talked at a diftance of publifhing " the reft of *Statius* §;" and in one of his letters
dated

* " I am going on apace with the two plays, have finifhed one and one third of the other, heartily
" wifhing that it might be agreeable to Dr. *H.* to make it a pofthumous work, if he approves of the
" notes; or to deftroy them (it will give no pain) if he does not; either of which will make it very
" eafy to him, and defirable to me. In the mean time he fhall have them in lefs than a month.
" Pleafe to let him know that I with this moft fincerely, and on that fuppofition have written a
" dedication to him, as if I was a dead man." *Letter to Mr. B. Jan.* 28, 1768.—" Happy is it that
" Mr. *Markland's* fpirits and his tafte are as high and as keen as ever. *Euripides* may fave him; and
" I am glad that he has faved his notes, which, when I faw him laft, he had condemned to the flames."
Mr. *Clarke to Mr. B. Feb.* 12, 1768.

† " On the 5th of this month I received from Dr. *H.* a Bank note of 20*l.* with notice of fome wine
" and chocolate he had fent me. In my letter of thanks, I took the opportunity of telling him, " I
" have for fome time been in fear of your generofity; which was the reafon of my being glad to put
" off the publication of *Euripides* till after my death, becaufe I apprehended that you defigned the
" whole advantage of the edition (for the printing of which you had already paid, befide the 50*l.*
" Bank note you had fent) fhould be mine; which I thought was unjuft in me to take, and unreafon-
" able. If you can be prevailed upon (which I greatly wifh) to fuffer the expence of the printing to
" be repaid you out of the fale of the book, I will write to Mr. *Bowyer* immediately to reprint the
" firft half-fheet, and to ftrike out the words *poft obitum fcriptoris* and *dum in vivis erat*, and to ad-
" vertife it forthwith under my name. If you have any objection, you need only to fay that you had
" rather things fhould continue as they are." *Letter to Mr. B. June* 14, 1771.

‡ Of this edition an account will be given under the year 1758.

|| To whom he gives the character of a very worthy and pious man, and a very good fcholar. In
1758, he defires Mr. *Bowyer* " to inquire whether the letters *A B.* which are fubfcribed to the *London*
" edition of *Sophocles*, 1722, do not fignify *Auguftin Bryan*, who publifhed *Plutarch's* Lives; I was
" acquainted with him at *Cambridge*, and have heard Dr. *Hare* fay that had he lived he would
" have made a great man; though *Dorville*, I remember, fomewhere fpeaks of his unfkilfulnefs in
" *Greek.* But he was but a young man when he died; and there are very few who know any thing
" of *Greek* in comparifon with *Dorville.*" See Memoirs of the latter in *Burmann's* Funeral Oration
for him at the end of his " *Siculo, Amft.* 1764," fol.

§ The following obfervations, in a letter of *September* 9, 1746, are fhrewd and intelligent:
" I thank you for the pains you have taken about the *Statius*; but I wifh you would go no fur-
" ther with the perfon you mention, becaufe I would much rather have them difpofed of another
" way (which I will mention to you by and by) than to a Bookfeller. My reafon for it is this: If
" the perfon who buys them underftands his own bufinefs, the firft thing he will do will be to pro-
" cure fome operator to publifh an edition of the reft of *Statius*, fuitable to the form of his 200 copies.
" There are already pretty good materials for fuch an edition publifhed in the *Dutch* Mifcell. Obfer-
" vationes [*Amft.* 1736, 13 vols. 8vo.]; and the next ftep will be to apply to me to communicate my
" Collations, or what I have obferved upon the author, which I do not fee how I can refufe; and
" thus I fhall contribute to the Bookfeller's getting off his 200 copies at perhaps feven or eight
" fhillings

for the excellence of his heart, and primitive simplicity of manners.

dated 1771 he mentioned a work * as being in forwardness, under the title of " *Quæf-* " *tiones Venufinæ ad Horatii Carmina,*" &c. having " got as far as Serm. I. 3. in " the tranfcription." But, about the year 1774, he deftroyed almoft all his MSS. He began at *Cambridge* an edition of part of *Apuleius,* of which feven fheets were printed off, from *Morell's French* edition ; but, on Dr. *Bentley's* fending him a rude meffage concerning his having left out a line that was extant in one of the MSS. he ftopt fhort, and went no farther. Part of the impreffion was for many years in Mr. *Bentham's* hands ; but Mr. *Bowyer* (who would have carried on the work) could never obtain a copy of it.

Of the early period of Mr. *Markland's* life little is now known. In common with many learned and good men, whofe memories will not be difgraced by mentioning this trifling circumftance, and amongft whom might be named the great Dr. *Samuel Clarke* †, he fometimes was fond of relaxing from feverer ftudies by playing at Whift. It appears by a letter to Mr. *Bowyer,* dated *Sept.* 19, 1748, that he once won what muft have been efteemed a large fum of money. He fays, " The Paralytick you men- " tion, to whofe cafe that of *Horace* is applicable, *Mergus profundo fortior exfilit,* was " formerly my acquaintance and great benefactor, for I won an hundred pounds of him " at Whift, and got it every farthing. The moral of the ftory, if I take it right, is, *Vexatio dat intellectum* ‡ :"

After he obtained a fellowfhip, he was a tutor at *Peter-Houfe,* and once vifited *France*‖ ; in 1743, he refided at *Twyford* § ; from 1744 to 1752 at *Uckfield* in

" fhillings a volume, which he bought of me for half a crown apiece ; and he will make his edition " to confift of 500 copies, becaufe thofe who already have bought the *Silvæ* will be glad to com- " pleat the author. This is fo very obvious and feafible, that it occurs even to me who am no " fchemer : fo that if you chance to have any more difcourfe with Mr. —— about this matter, you " may tell him that I do not care to difpofe of them, becaufe I am not yet certain but that I may " fome time or other publifh the reft of *Statius,* which is very true, though between ourfelves it is " an hundred to one I never fhall. But the way I could wifh you would take with them is to deftroy " all the copies (except about 20 or 30) by fire or water, or any other annihilating way, that of wafte- " paper excepted ; and the fame courfe to be taken with the Epiftola Critica. This fhall be your war- " rant ; and you will do me a great pleafure if you will comply with it, without mentioning it to " any body. I know your old objection, that fomething is better than nothing ; which I allow to be " a good argument in a cafe of prefent neceffity and a want of the fum the books would fetch ; " where that is not the cafe, it appears to me to be one of thofe things which are *perinde ut quifque* " *putat,* and I am pretty certain that I fhall change my opinion herein "—On the 2d of *May,* 1757, he thus repeated his injunction : " I hereby empower you to burn or deftroy, in what manner you " pleafe, the printed copies of any books you may have in your hands belonging to me."

* This work was compleated, and, I believe, is ftill in being.

† Dr. *Clarke,* though he hufbanded his time in fuch a manner that he always carried books in his pocket that he might lofe no opportunity of reading, yet would fpend hours in playing at cards. For this anecdote I have the authority of his fon.

‡ The fame expreffion occurs in another letter, *July* 12, 1767 : " I fancy it would have been of " fervice to you to have feen and experienced part of the diftreffes which I have undergone here ; for " *vexatio dat intellectum,* that is, fpirits."—" *Markland* is a Hero, it is true ; and would be a Martyr, " upon conftitution. He is braced to bear almoft any thing ; and you would fink quite down with a " quarter of what he is to undergo." Mr. *Clarke* to Mr. B. *March* 10, 1768.

‖ In 1774, he mentions " buying *Fell's* edition of the *Greek* Teftament in *France,* above 40 years " ago."—" The life of fcholars is generally fedentary, and therefore cannot contain many facts : he in- " deed was in *France* fome little time with Mr. *Strode,* particularly in *Languedoc* ; but I know of " nothing interefting on that head, though I have heard him relate a few laughable particulars. " Bp. *Hare* would have provided for him, if he would have taken orders ; but *rou jaxa nudis furdiora* " *navitis.*" Mr. E. *Clark,* Letter to J. N. Nov. 10, 1777.

§ Here, in *June* 1743, he talks of the gout as an old companion with him ; *Feb.* 28, 1743-4, calls himfelf " a poor ruftic, who has been putting out his eyes in two very different employments, tran- " fcribing his own writings, and reading over thofe of *Cicero* once more ;" and, *April* 7, 1744, fays, " I intend to leave off ftudy, and addict myfelf to animal life."

Suffex ;

manners. Here alſo he formed many of thoſe connexions
which

Suſſex *; and from that year till his death he boarded in a farm-houſe at *Milton*,
near *Dorking*, in *Surrey*; where he deſcribed himſelf, in 1755, to be " as much
" out of the way of *hearing*, as of *getting*. Of this laſt (he adds) I have now
" no deſire; the other I ſhould be glad of." In this ſequeſtered ſituation he ſaw
as little company as poſſibly he could, and his walks were almoſt confined to the narrow limits of his garden.. What firſt induced him to retire from the world is not
known. It has been ſuppoſed to have proceeded from diſappointment; but of what
nature it is not eaſy to imagine. He was certainly diſintereſted to an extreme.. Money
was never conſidered by him as a good, any further than it enabled him to relieve
the neceſſitous; and in 1765 he had a freſh opportunity of indulging his benevolence
to the fulleſt extent, by diſtreſſing himſelf † to ſupport the widow with whom he
lodged, againſt the injuſtice and oppreſſion of her ſon, who, taking the advantage of
maternal weakneſs, perſuaded her to aſſign over to him almoſt the whole of her little
property.. The conſequence was a law-ſuit ‡, which, after an enormous expence to
Mr.

* Here he firſt formed an intimacy with Mr. *Clarke*, whoſe ſon was placed under his tuition —
" I have had the pleaſure of ſeeing him twice, and ſhould doat upon him if it was not for two things;
" I could wiſh he had a little better ſpirits, and would not walk ſo violently in queſt of them, which I
" am ſure is not the way to find them. I wiſh this for my own ſake as well as his; and I muſt teach
" him to ride, that I may have more of his company." *Mr. Clarke to Mr. B. April* 1744.

† His whole fortune, *May* 28, 1767, conſiſted of 500l. Three *per Cent*. Reduced Annuities, of which
he thus writes : " Any time before the end of *June*, be ſo kind as to order your broker to ſell an
" 100l. of my ſtock. I know the ſtocks are at preſent very low; but I fancy they will be much lower
" in a little time, and never higher while I live; and what name would you give a man who ſuffers
" himſelf to want money which he has in his pocket? Probably you will offer me your purſe, but
" that will not be near ſo ſatisfactory to me as the other; which I mention before-hand, to prevent
" giving you offence by a refuſal." *Aug.* 21, he requeſted Mr. *Bowyer* to ſell 200l. In anſwer to
a letter ſent him on this buſineſs, he ſays, " You aſk why I ſell out, and why 200l.? I anſwer,
" becauſe I cannot help it, and becauſe I ſhall want it; otherwiſe I would not ſell at ſuch a
" diſadvantage. Your hundred, for which I am greatly obliged to you and thank you, will not
" do my buſineſs; or if it would, and were two, I ſhould not take it at preſent, no more than I
" would refuſe it if I had none of my own, in which partly ſeems to conſiſt the difference be-
" tween a *knave* and *fool*; the former will take your money when he does not want it, the other
" will refuſe it when he does; ἕκαϛος τῷ ἰδίῳ νοῒ πληροφορείσθω. You may, if you pleaſe, ſend
" me your 100l. but I tell you before-hand I ſhall make no uſe of it — You would have me
" ſell my books; I wonder you ſhould ſay ſo to me, whoſe magnanimity (which you call *pride*
" and *folly*) you know. I do not care a ruſh for them, and yet I would much rather burn them
" than ſell them for the ſake of 30 or 40l. perhaps leſs, at moſt for a ſum which would be of no
" manner of uſe to me; but the thing would be an indelible ſcandal to my rich acquaintance,
" yourſelf in particular, and to ſcholars in general." *Letter to Mr. B. Nov.* 1, 1767.—' The ſtock
" muſt be ſold, and it will be the greateſt pleaſure you can give me in the world at preſent, if you
" can ſend me word next week that the money for it is in your hands, ready for me to be diſpoſed
" of. The difference of five or ten pounds, more or leſs, I do not value at ten pins, in compariſon
" of the anxiety I have been under leſt I ſhould be taken off before I have ſatisfied myſelf concern-
" ing thoſe whom I may be able and ought to aſſiſt. Mr. *S's* kindneſs to me, in all probability,
" ſecures me from want all my life, which is a very valuable thing to my caſe of mind; but it
" does not at all help me at preſent with regard to others, for whom I am chiefly concerned."
Ibid. Jan. 28, 1768.—The whole was accordingly ſold.

‡ " My engaging in a law matter was much contrary to my nature and inclination, and owing to
" nothing but *compaſſion* (you give it a ſuſpicious name when you call it *tenderneſs*, ſhe being in her
" 63d year, and I in my 74th) to ſee a very worthy woman oppreſſed and deprived by her own ſon
" of every farthing ſhe had in the world, and nothing left to ſubſiſt herſelf and two children but
" what ſhe received from me for board and lodging, and this too endeavoured by ſeveral bad and ridi-
" culous methods to be taken from her, and myſelf forced hence, that they might compel her into
" their

which introduced him into general esteem.   But the greatest
share

Mr. *Markland*, was terminated against the widow.   His whole fortune after that event
was expended in relieving the distresses of this family.   Whatever sums he could command were constantly disposed of in their support.   Yet it was with difficulty he could
be prevailed on to accept the pecuniary assistance which many of his friends were desirous of affording him.   From a worthy friend *, for whom he justly entertained the
highest regard, and whose benevolence he repeatedly experienced, he not without hesitation received a present in *August* 1766; and in the same month refused a handsome
offer of Archbishop *Secker* †.   In the *October* following, he declined even entering into a
correspondence with an old acquaintance who wished to serve him.   On the receipt of a
handsome sum from Dr. *Barnard*, he wrote thus to Mr. *Bowyer* ‡, *July* 12, 1767: " I
" received yours this morning, together with that of Dr. B. which I have not yet open-
" ed, nor shall: I mean as to the bill part; but this must not be mentioned for the
" world, for fear of giving offence.   One thing you may mention, as you please, that
" I am greatly satisfied with his not writing to me; it looks as if he did not like to be
" thanked; which to me is a sure mark of a noble mind."   Early in 1769, he condescend-
ed

" their unjust measures, not to mention the lesser injuries, indignities, and insolences, which were
" used towards her.   Could I run away, and leave an afflicted good woman and her children to
" starve, without the greatest baseness, dishonour, and inhumanity?   Poor as I am, I would rather
" have pawned the coat on my back than have done it.   I speak this in the presence of God; and I
" appeal to him, before whom I must soon appear, that this is the *true* and *only* reason of my acting in
" this matter; and though I know that the consequence of it will incommode me greatly, and almost
" ruin me, yet I am sure shall never repent of it.—I am greatly obliged to the humanity of Mr.
" *Barrington*, and am the more pleased with it, because it is owing to the regard of his old friend
" Mr. *Hall*.   It may be said of him, *Et colit exequias.*"   *Letter to Mr. B. Feb.* 19, 1767.
* " Whatever reasons I might have for not taking it before, yet it was always very clear that
" the Doctor's intention was kind and friendly, and there was all the reason in the world that I should
" acknowledge it.   Something of the same kind is to be said concerning the Archbishop's proposal,
" made by Dr. *Burton*; though that indeed affects me *ut lippum pictæ tabulæ*; for an editor who,
" through old age, has no eyes to read, and no hands to write with, must needs be a very absurd
" creature, or, what somebody in *The Tempest* calls *Caliban, a strange fish*.   Be so kind as to make
" my acknowledgements to his Grace when you see the Doctor."   *Letter to Mr. B. Aug.* 4, 1766.
† " If you did not write last night to the person who wanted to know my direction, please to add
" (as from yourself) to what you intended, That Mr. M. is very old, being within a few days of 73,
" with weak eyes and a shaking hand, so that he can neither read nor write without trouble; that he
" has scarce looked into a *Greek* or *Latin* book for above these three years, having given over all lite-
" rary concerns; and therefore it is your opinion that he had much better not write to Mr. M. which
" will only distress him; but that you are very sure he will not now enter into any correspondence of
" learning.   Any thing like this.—As to the other matter we talked of, the two plays and the 600 L
" I repent of what I said, and wish it unsaid; that is, I with nothing had been said on the subject.
" You may remember I told you that a certain person [the Abp.] was expected in this neighbour-
" hood soon.   I have been putting the supposition, whether if this person should offer (which God
" knows is impossible) the whole sum, I should be glad to take it of him; and I can say with great
" truth and sincerity, that I had much rather not.   I repeat it, that I had much rather not.   It is a
" matter of private wish only, not of necessity, and my reasons to myself are much stronger against it
" than for it."   *Letter to Mr. B. Oct.* 7, 1766.
‡ This is rendered more intelligible by the following extracts: " I wish you would be more
" explicit in telling the Provost and me in what *manner* and *how far* Mr. M. may be served."
Dr Foster to Mr. B. July 5, 1767.—" I will explain to you a little piece of business of late.   Mr.
" *Hetherington*, one of our Fellows (now probably the richest Clergyman in *England*), and for-
" merly Mr. *Markland*'s pupil at College, on hearing lately Mr. M's case, expressed a desire of
" assisting him; this was between the *Provost* and Mr. H.   The Provost took from him for Mr. M.
" 20l.; and that, with 20l. of *his own*, 20l. of mine, 20l. advanced by him for Mr. *Townshend*,
" made up what Mr. M. hath greatly obliged us with accepting.   This concerning Mr. H. is to *you*,
" not to Mr. M. for obvious reasons.   The Provost has much at heart the affair of a pension; and
" I should

fhare of his intimacy was with Mr. *Markland* and Mr.
William

ed to accept from a gentleman, to whom he had been tutor *, an annuity of 100*l.* which, with the dividends arifing from his fellowfhip, was from that year the whole of his income.

" I fhould not wifh an affair of that, or indeed of any fort, in the hands of a better folicitor." *Ib. July* 23.
—" I have a tale to tell you, that comes to me from that mafter of anecdotes Mr. *Gerifon,* and I dare fay
" is fpread by him among all his acquaintance. His account is this :—That Mr. —— told him,
" that Mr. *Markland* had dropped to Dr. *Earnard,* mafter of *Eton,* fome complaints, that he had
" been neglected, the world had ufed him ill, &c. That Dr. *B.* replied, If it would be agreeable to
" him, he would procure ten gentlemen that fhould fubfcribe twenty guineas *per annum* for his ufe,
" or twenty that fhould fubfcribe ten; to which Mr. *M* returned no anfwer, and confequently re-
" fufed. This whole affair, the complaint, the offer, the manner of conducting it, &c. furprized
" me. And, talking of it to a gentleman, who had likewife feen Mr. ——; his account was, that
" Mr. *M.* had complained a little; that the public had taken very little notice of him in the late pub-
" lication (as he might truly fay); and that Dr. *B.* in return fhould fay, if he would publifh any
" thing, he would procure (as above) ten gentlemen for twenty, or twenty for ten guineas fubfcrip-
" tion. This, I think, is the more likely account. Mr. *M.* might make fuch a complaint, and Dr. *B.*
" anfwer it in that manner; but I think the other utterly incredible." *Mr. Clarke to Mr. B. Sept.* 11, 1767.
 * The following extracts are fo extremely honourable to all the parties they relate to, that it would be
ungenerous to fupprefs them. On the 15th of *November,* 1767, Mr. *Markland* wrote to Mr. *Bowyer:*
" Mr. *Bl's* gratitude and good-will are very agreeable and commendable. As to the reft, I can fay
" nothing till I hear farther from or concerning Mr. *S.* who has been greatly misinformed; for I am
" under no other obligations than thofe of humanity."—" You have been an excellent and ufeful
" friend to me for above thefe 30 years; and I am always as certain of your good intention as I am
" that I now write this; but when you fay, " that you have informed Mr. *S.* of my ill ftate of health,
" and of my *worfe fituation;*" I think you do not fhew fo much juftice to him as kindnefs to me;
" becaufe, in reality, what you fay of my *worfe fituation* is not fo, though you may think fo; for
" my 440*l.*† when difpofed of (as it fhall be) with regard to others and to myfelf too, will make me as
" eafy and contented as if it were four millions; I mean on this fuppofition, that no man ought to be
" uneafy becaufe he cannot do more than he can do; this fhall be done at *Lady-day* without fail, if I
" be, or if I be not, worth fo much at that time, which article I am in fome pain about, as depending
" upon the *French* and *Spaniards*; but a man who fuffers mifery which he can prevent, deferves it;
" and this (though you do not) muft be my cafe till I difpofe of the ftock; I mean, unlefs fome un-
" forefeen event greatly alters my prefent circumftances before that time. I readily and without dif-
" pute allow you to be the beft and the only competent judge of your own affairs; do I require any
" thing unreafonable, when I defire that I may have the fame liberty in mine? *Ne dixeris.*"
 Letter from Mr. *S.* to Mr. *Bowyer:* " I was forry to find that my enquiry after Mr. *Markland* had
" been the occafion of fo much trouble to his friend; and fhould not have taken the liberty of making
" it at your houfe, had I known any other equally refpected by him, or where I could be equally
" informed of his fituation. You muft fuffer me to exprefs myfelf much obliged to you for the par-
" ticulars you have fent me, and to add my concern for the ill ftate of health you are in. I muft be
" free enough to fay, Sir, that I have much lamented that Mr. *Markland* withdrew himfelf from his
" friends. Retirement he was very well fuited to; but this he might have enjoyed without excluding
" himfelf thofe many comforts his friends might have adminiftered. Some few days ago I folicited
" leave to make him a vifit but of an hour on the fpot at prefent in difpute; but I received with many
" expreffions of kindnefs an abfolute denial. The time I was fortunate enough to pafs with him
" (though very early days with me) will always make me deeply interefted in every event which may
" concern him; and the recollection of it has ever furnifhed a regret, that it was not at a more ad-
" vanced period, when I might have profited more effentially of his inftructions and example. I fhall
" do myfelf the pleafure of calling on you very foon after my return to town; and fhall have an opportu-
" nity of expreffing more fully how much you have obliged your obedient humble fervant,   W. S."
  " I have juft received your letter with the inclofed, which I read with great pleafure, as it feemed
" to exprefs the mind of a perfon very different from what I expected. It is now 16 years, I think,
" fince I have feen or heard any thing of Mr. *S.* except what Dr. *Burton* and Dr. *Fofter* told me of
" him two months ago. I always looked upon him as a *modern* young man of good fortune: and now
" that I have fome reafon to think otherwife, I have nothing to offer but the dregs of an old life of

† Mr. *Markland* valued his 500*l.* ftock at 83*l. per Cent.* the price it then was worth.

William Clarke, a polite and accomplished scholar; two friends

come. In 1769 the disposal of his books became to him a matter of serious concern †. He at that time wished them to be in the hands of the friend to whom he presented the greater part of them in his life-time ‡, and the remainder at his death §. In 1771 he was agreeably gratified by the news of Mr. *Bowyer's* proffered legacy ‖, not for his own advantage, but for a sister's who in some degree depended on him for support. On the 10th of *November*, 1775, he tells Mr. *Bowyer*, " Mr. *Nichols* writes, you are indebted " to me 52*l*. 5*s*. 9*d*. which is more than I apprehended, and above the sum which I

" 75, charged with many infirmities; but if his view is my advantage, so much the better for us both. " I venture to say *us both*, because, in my opinion, no man does good to another, but he does a greater " to himself, according to the reverse of old *Hesiod*:

" Ὁ αὐτῷ κακὰ τεύχει ἀνὴρ, ἄλλῳ κακὰ τεύχων.

" This is carrying the system of self-love a great way, and many will deny it, but it is true for all " that; and I myself, and you, and every man who does a kindness to another, knows it to be so. and " it is necessary that it should be so. If I live ever to see Mr. *S.* I will shew to him, that what I did " in refusing his visit here, was necessary both for him and myself.

" The stock must every farthing be sold, to make me easy : this I had determined upon before I " knew any thing of Mr. *S.* and now I can do it with much greater confidence. The distress I have " been in on account of it is unspeakable ; for God's sake bring me out of it as soon as possible. I " thank you a thousand times for the Nest-egg, but at present I do not see the least probability of " wanting it ; if I do, I shall make as little scruple of asking for it, as I do now of refusing it." *Mr.* *M. to Mr. B. Nov.* 19, 1767.

" Mr. *S's* behaviour is truly laudable and meritorious ; more, I believe, than you imagine. When " he left Mr. *Markland*, something happened in old Mr. *S's* behaviour that gave Mr. *Markland* great " disgust. This the young gentleman had no hand in, and could not possibly prevent. After the " death of his father, Mr. *S.* thought Mr. *Markland* would see him as formerly. He desired that " favour, and made several applications, which Mr. *Markland* refused to comply with. I think, " after this, Mr. *S's* present behaviour is truly admirable, and even greater than his friend's, as he " acts with more judgement, and as great generosity. It is a happy event, which Providence has pro-" vided to soften the difficulties and discomforts of a valuable life." *Mr. Clarke to Mr. B. Dec.* 4, 1767.

† " As to the disposal of the *Greek* and *Latin* books we were mentioning, it now seems to me most " adviseable not to say a word concerning them The great point with me, is, to avoid giving of-" fence, which is preferable to all the books in the *Vatican* ; but if a man is in danger of offending " while he is wishing and endeavouring to shew his gratitude, this is very grievous, and by all " means to be avoided." *Letter to Mr. B. June* 22, 1769.

‡ In *December* 1769, he describes himself as " packing up his books at the age of 77 ;" and four years after, as ' having no books, nor much memory.'

§ " My books and papers I leave to Dr. *William Heberden* of Pall-Mall. Every thing else which " belonged to me (all which together is scarce worth mentioning) I leave to Mrs. *Martha Rose* of " *Milton*, whom I believe to be one of the most worthy persons, and know to be one of the greatest " objects of humanity and Christian compassion, I ever was acquainted with in a long life; whom " therefore I make my sole Executrix." *Mr. Markland's last Will, dated Oct.* 19, 1775.

‖ " I have taken three or four days to answer part of your last letter, because I was desirous to con-" sider by what method I could make your seasonable and unusual legacy (of a man *alive*) most useful " to my sister and self, and least burthensome to the living legator. What occurs to me and I foresee " at this distance, is this : About *Michaelmas* fifty pounds will be of service; twenty of this I would " send to my sister in a draught upon you; the other thirty, for mine own use here. I call it *season-* " *able* above, because you must know I receive nothing from *Midsummer* to *Christmas*. On second " thoughts, and considering what a comfort it will be to my sister, to know that she has a friend whom " she little thought of ; the sooner you can conveniently write to me the better it will be. I will ac-" quaint her immediately. She has been for some time in a very bad way, so that I am afraid she will " not long enjoy your good-will. Every occasion of joy, though never so small, is valuable to a person " in her bad state of health ; and, *Bis dat, qui cito dat*, is not less applicable to agreeable news, than " to donations of another kind. I do not mean this last as any *hint* ; for if left to my own choice, I " had rather stay till *Michaelmas* before I receive any money. One line, that you approve of what I " propose, will be sufficient. I have not yet determined whether I shall let her know the person to " whom she is so much obliged ; there may be reasons against it, as well as for it." *July* 7, 1771.

" have

friends with whom he regularly maintained a correspondence

" have long proposed to have always *in your or his hands* (40*l.*) *for* MY BURIAL." That
he was minutely exact in his accounts, is plain from his letters. In his connexions with
Mr. *Bowyer*, however, he had so implicit a confidence in the punctuality of his friend, as
never to require a voucher.

If ambition had been Mr. *Markland's* aim, he might have gratified it; there being
a positive proof under his own hand that he twice declined the *Greek* professorship, a
station where abilities like his would have been eminently displayed. On the 28th of
February, 1743-4, he tells Mr. *Bowyer*, " I suppose you have heard that the *Greek* Professor
" at *Cambridge** is dying. I am invited very kindly to accept of it by several
" friends, who have given me information, and advised me to be a candidate. Ἀλλ᾽
" ἐμὸν ὅποι θυμὸν ἐπὶ στήθεσσιν ἴπασαν, to speak in the language of a *Greek* Professor;
" and instead of going an hundred miles to take it, I would go two hundred the other
" way to avoid it." Again, *Feb.* 27, 1749-50, " I have lately had two letters from the
" Vice-chancellor (Dr. *Keene*, our Master), who wishes me to take the *Greek* Professor-
" ship, which is about to be vacant again. You, who know me, will not wonder that
" I have absolutely refused to be a candidate for it. This, perhaps, is a secret at pre-
" sent, and therefore do not mention it to any body." There is a traditionary report,
that he once received a munificent proposal from Dr. *Mead*, to enable him to travel, on
a most liberal plan, in pursuit of such literary matters as should appear eligible to himself; and that his retirement arose from a disgust his extreme delicacy occasioned him
to take during the negotiation. For great part of his life, and particularly during the
last twenty years of it, he was much afflicted with the gout, which he held to be " one
" of the greatest prolongers of mortality in Nature's store-room, as being so great an
" absorbent of all other maladies." In *June* 1767 he had an attack of the *St. Anthony's
Fire*; in *August* was afflicted with the yellow jaundice†; in *April* 1772 had an attack of the stone in his kidney; and in *October* 1773, he thus describes himself: " My
" complaints are the same as yours, owing to the same cause, much sitting still. Forty
" years ago I drank nothing but water for several years; but Dr. *Boerhaave* told me
" that when I grew old I must come to wine, which I find to be true; so that now I
" have bid adieu to water and all its works, except chocolate, which with eggs and
" milk are my chief support: one bottle of wine serves me four or five days." He
continued to correspond with Mr. *Bowyer* till within a few weeks of his death; when he
was prevented by a severe attack of the gout, attended with a fever, which put an end
to his existence in this world *July* 7, 1776. On a brass plate in *Dorking* church is
the following epitaph, by Dr. *Heberden:*

"JEREMIAH MARKLAND, A. M.
Was born the 29th of *October*, 1693;
Educated in the School of *Christ's Hospital, London*;
And elected Fellow of *St. Peter's College, Cambridge*.

---

* Dr. —— *Taylor*, fellow of *Trinity College*, who died *Feb.* 25, 1743-4; and was succeeded by
William Fraigneau, fellow of the same college; who resigned the professorship 1750, and died
vicar of *Battersea* in 1778.

† This disorder began with an excessive diarrhœa. " If this does not stop," says he, " it will soon
" carry off an old man. I am under no uneasiness, having made my will." *Letter to Mr. B. Aug.* 5, 1767.

Unambitious

ence throughout life*. Both thefe friends he furvived; and
fympa-

Unambitious of the rewards and honours which his abilities and application might
have obtained for him in the learned profeffions, he chofe to pafs his life in a liberal
retirement. His very accurate knowledge of the *Greek* and *Latin* languages was employed in correcting and explaining the beft ancient authors, and more particularly in
illuftrating the Sacred Scriptures. To thefe rational purfuits he facrificed every worldly
view; contented with the inward pleafure refulting from fuch ftudies, and from the
public and private affiftance which they enabled him to communicate to others. But,
above all, his uncommon learning confirmed in the higheft degree his hopes of a happier life hereafter. He died at *Milton*, in this parifh, the 7th day of *July*, 1776."
The following infcription was written foon after his death by Mr. *Edward Clarke*, the very
ingenious author of the "Letters concerning the *Spanifh* Nation, 1763."

"Memoriæ Sacrum
JEREMIÆ MARKLANDI:
Qui, quanquam fplendidiores eum
Et literæ et virtutes ornaverant,
Semper modeftiffimè fe geffit :
Omnes benignè, doctos urbanè,
Et, quod mirere magis,
Etiam indoctos fine fupercilio excepit.
In reftituendis et explicandis
Græcis et Latinis Poetis,
Statio, Euripide, Horatio, Juvenale,
Et præcipuè Novi Fœderis libris,
Cautus, acutus, felix,
Et, fi quando audacior,
Tamen non inconfultus :
In edendis Maximo Tyrio et Demofthene
Cum Davifio & Tayloro conjunctus
Utrifque et auxilio et ornamento fuit.

Sequantur alii Famam,
Aucupentur Divitias,
Hic illa oculis irretortis contemplatus
Poft terga conftanter rejecit.
A cœtu tandem et communione omnium
Per hos triginta annos proximè elapfos
In folitudinem fe recepit,
Studiis excolendis et pauperibus fublevandis,
Unicè intentus.
Memoriæ viri fibi amiciffimi,
Et præceptoris et parentis loco,
Viri candore, humanitate, modeftiâ, doctrinâ,
Religione demum ornatiffimi,
Dat, Dicat, Dedicat,
Olim Difcipulus.
Obiit prope *Dorking*, in comitatu *Surriæ*,
Julii 7°, 1776,
Annum agens octogefimum tertium."

* Mr. WILLIAM CLARKE was born at *Haghmon Abbey* in *Shropfhire*, 1696; educated
under Mr. *Loyd* at *Shrewfbury-fchool*; elected fellow † of *St. John's*, *Jan.* 22, 1716-17.
He was chaplain to Dr. *Adam Ottley*, Bifhop of *St. David's*; who died in 1723. The
rectory of *Buxted*, *Suffex*, was given to him by Abp. *Wake* in 1724. He was afterwards
domeftic chaplain to *Thomas Holles* Duke of *Newcaftle*; refidentiary and chancellor of
the church of *Chichefter* in *June* 1770; and in *Auguft* vicar of *Amport*, which he did not
long enjoy, dying *Oct.* 21, 1771. He married *Anne*, daughter of the celebrated Dr.
Wotton, by whom (befides fome children who died young) he had a fon (*Edward* mentioned above, to whom he refigned *Buxted* in the year 1768) and a daughter, He wrote
a learned Preface to Dr. *Wotton's* Collection of the *Welfh* Laws. But his principal
printed work is "The Connexion of the *Roman*, *Saxon* and *Englifh* Coins," which will be

† "This election of Fellows was in confequence of a removal of feveral Nonjuring Fellows, in
"virtue of an act of parliament. The ordinary election of Fellows is always in *Lent.*" Dr. TAY-
LOR, MS.—*Leonard Chappelow*, *Whitley Heald*, *Edward Wilmot*, *Henry Fetherftonhaugh*, and three
other gentlemen, were elected at the fame time. The Seniors were, Mr. *Bowtell*, Mr. *Foulkes*, Dr.
Edmondfon, Mr. *Chefter*, and Mr. *Hall*. BAKER's MSS.

fympathetically lamented their lofs.   Many of their letters are ftill extant; a treafure of polite literature and found criti-cifm, as will fufficiently appear from the extracts exhibited in thefe memoirs.

Two letters of Mr. *Vere Fofter*, a Fellow of *St. John's**, one of them to Mr. *James Bonwicke*, the other to Mr. *Bowyer*, may here not improperly be referred to; they are both printed in *The Gentleman's Magazine*, 1779, p. 250.

The beft apology for inferting the following letter is, that it would be an injury to the world to fupprefs the fentiments

particularly noticed under the year 1767.   He left behind him a confiderable number of MSS. particularly fome volumes of excellent Sermons, which the world may at fome time expect from his fon, who wrote the following epitaph :

" Memoriæ Sacrum
WILHELMI CLARKE, A. M.
Cancellarii et Canonici Ecclefiæ Ciceftrenfis :
Quem Pietate, Literis, Moribus urbanis,
Humanitate et Modeftia ornatum
Concives et Familiares fui
Uno ore ubique confeffi funt;
Et fi ipfi filiiffent,
Teftarentur ipfius Scripta :
In communi Vitâ comis, lætus, utilis,
Facile omnes perferre ac pati promptus,
Ingenui Pudoris, magni et liberalis Animi :
In Ecclefiâ fuadens, facundus Concionator,
Ut non folum in Aures fidelium,
Sed etiam in Animos
Veridica ftillaret Oratio :
Precibus offerendis fervidus et profluens,
Ut, tanquam fanctior Flamma,
In Cœlos afcendere viderentur :
In Parochiâ Paftor vigil, Laborum plenus,
Indoctis Magifter, Ægris Solamen,
Abjectis Spes, Pauperibus Crumena :
Tamen Eleemofynas fuas adeo occultè,
Adeo latè diffeminavit,
Ut illas non nifi Dies ultima Judicii ultimi
Revelare potuerit.
Natus eft anno 1696 in Comitatu Salopienfi
et Cœnobio de *Haghmon* :

Primis Literis imbutus in Salopiæ Scholâ;
Collegii Sti. Johannis, Cantabrigiæ, Socius :
Primo *Adamæ Ottley*, Menevenfi Epifcopo,
Poftea Duci Novo-Caftrenfi, *Thomæ Holles*,
A Sacris Domefticis :
Tandem ad Rectoriam de *Buxted* inter Regnos
A *Wilhelmo Wake*, Archiepifcopo Can-
tuarienfi,
Propter fua et egregia Soceri fui
Wilhelmi Wottoni Merita,
Sine Ambitu collatus.
Obiit Ciceftriæ, Oct. 21, A. D. 1771."

Sepulcrale Marmor,
Quo fubjacet Ciceftriæ,
Virente adhuc viridi Senectâ,
Mente folida et ferenâ, fic infcripfit :
" Depofitum
" Gulielmi Clarke, A. M.
" Canonici et Cancellarii
" Hujus Ecclefiæ :
" Qui obiit . . . . . .
" A. D. . . . . . ætatis . . . .
" Uxorem Annam,
" Gulielmi Wottoni, S. T. P.
" Et Annæ Hammondi Filiam;
" Et Liberos duos
" Superftites reliquit."

* *Vere Fofter*, Bachelor of Divinity, was the fon of a Clergyman in *Gloucefterfhire* ; chofen Fellow of *St. John's College, Cambridge, April* 4, 1720 ; became Vicar of *Barrow upon Soar*, in *Leicefterfhire*, about 1732 (a College living) ; and died there about 1755.

of the amiable Divine who wrote it.　The circumſtance which occaſioned it is ſufficiently explained by the letter:

　　" Good Mr. *Bowyer*,　　　　　　　*Lewiſham,*
　　　　　　　　　　　　　　　　　　April 28, 1722.

　　" I underſtand *Hugh Mattiſon*, the Bookſeller in *Lin-*
" *coln's Inn Fields*, is under ſome trouble on account of
" books ſtolen from you, and afterward bought by him.
" I think myſelf in juſtice bound to acquaint you, that for
" about ten years he hath been known (as my pariſhioner)
" and dealt with by me all that time; and that I always
" thought I had reaſon to believe him not only an exceed-
" ing careful and induſtrious, but a very honeſt poor man.
" The particulars of this affair I am not perfectly informed
" of, but I would fain hope he is not greatly to blame; or
" if he be, that this danger will render him more cautious
" for the future.　And ſince his reputation is all his de-
" pendence, the kindneſs I have for him moves me to re-
" queſt of you, that as little blemiſh may lye upon that,
" and your proceedings againſt him may be managed with
" as much tenderneſs as can conſiſt with juſtice and the
" nature of the thing.　I have not been already, nor ſhall
" I be hereafter, wanting in either reproofs or good counſel,
" as occaſion requires, and particularly in letting him know,
" that by any indirect or unfair ways of ſeeking to leſſen
" his wants, and make his family eaſy, he will not only
" defeat all hopes of bettering his condition, but certainly
" loſe the countenance and friendſhip of, Sir, your true
" friend and faithful ſervant,　　GEORGE STANHOPE*."

　　　　　　　　　　　　　　　　　　　　　　In

---

* I find, ſince the account in p. 7, was printed, that Dean *Stanhope* † was once preacher of the *Tueſday's* lecture at *St. Lawrence Jewry*, where, on his reſignation in 1708, he

† His grandfather *George Stanhope*, D. D. was Chaplain to *James* I. and *Charles* I. had the chaunterſhip of *York*, where he was alſo a canon-reſidentiary, held a prebend, and was rector of *Whel-drake* in that county.　He was, for his loyalty, " driven to doors with eleven children," and died in 1644.　See *Walker's* Sufferings of the Clergy, Part II. p. 83.

In *June* 1722, Mr. *Bowyer* left college, and entered into the printing bufinefs with his father; who received that year another teftimonial⁂ of his abilities, in a preface to Mr. *Maittaire's* " Mifcellanea *Græcorum* aliquot Scriptorum " Carmina, cum Verfione *Latina* & Notis," 4to.—In 1722, they printed in conjunction the " Firma Burgi" of Mr. *Madox* †, fol. Dr. *Thirlby's* ‡ edition of *Juftin Martyr*, fol. and Mr.

was fucceeded by Dr. *Mofs*. This lecture, though but moderately endowed as to profit, had long been reputed a *poft of honour*; having been poffeffed by a fucceffion of the moft able and celebrated preachers, of whom Abp. *Tillotfon* was one; and having been ufually attended by a refort of perfons of note and eminence, and particularly by numbers of the clergy, not only of the younger fort, but by feveral of long ftanding and eftablifhed characters. See Preface to Dean *Mofs's* Sermons.—To the reft of Dr. *Stanhope's* publications may be added, " The Sieur de *Charron's* Three Books of Wifdom, " written originally in *French*, with an Account of the Author, made *Englifh* by George " *Stanhope*, 1697; ' of which a third edition appeared in 1729, 3 vols. 8vo. In the *London Mag.* 1758, p. 163, is a curious correfpondence between Bifhop *Atterbury* and Dean *Stanhope*, on the increafing neglect of Public Baptifm.

⁂ " Quoniam *Græcarum* præ cæteris editionum nitor impenfe mihi femper placuit, " me cepit illas aliquatenus imitandi defiderium. Nactus itaque typographeum luculen- " tum, necnon artificem tam probum qu m folertem, peridoneumque (quod eft in arte " typicâ maximi momenti) correctorem, lepidum Batrachomyomachiæ poemation edidi : " neque fpes, quam de mei conaminis eventu conceperam, me fefellit, nec defecit ami- " corum gratia. Quamobrem primo non infeliciter experimento defunctum (nam menti " ftimulos addit fuccefsus) in ipfo quafi limine laborum ceffare puduit; et ultrà nihil, " quod incoeptis erectum mag s quàm feffum me teftaretur, moliri."

† The learned Exchequer Antiquary and Hiftoriographer Royal, who publifhed Formulare *Anglicanum*, 1702, f.; the Hiftory of the *Exchequer*, 1711, f. reprinted 1769, 2 vol. 4to. Firma Burgi, 1726, f.; Baronia *Anglicana*, 1741, f.; and left 40 volumes of Collections for a Hiftory of the Feudal Law, now in the *Harleian* Library, to which they were prefented by his widow.

‡ Styan *Thirlby*, LL.D. fon of Mr. *Thirlby*, vicar of *St. Margaret's* in *Leicefter*; and born, it is fuppofed, about 1692. He publifhed " An Anfwer † to Mr. *Whifton's* " Seventeen Sufpicions concerning *Athanafius*, in his Hiftorical Preface, by *Styan* " *Thirlby*, A. B. of *Jefus College*, 1712." In 1723, he was editor of *Juftin Martyr* ‡, the Dedication to which has always been confidered as a mafterly production, in ftyle particularly.

† " Written by one very young, and, he may add, at fuch broken hours as many neceffary " avocations and a very unfettled ftate of health would fuffer him to beftow upon them." *Preface.*— It appears by another tract in this controverfy that Mr. *Thirlby* was then " about 20 years old."

‡ " The learned Mr. *Thirlby*, fellow of *Jefus* college, is publifhing a new edition of *Juftin Mar-* " *tyr's* two Apologies, and his Dialogue with *Trypho* the *Jew*. The *Greek* text will be printed exactly " according to R. *Stephen's* edition. The verfion is *Langus's*, corrected in innumerable places. On " the fame page with the text and verfion are printed the notes and emendations of the Editor, with " felect notes of all the former editors, and of *Scaliger, Cafaubon, Salmafius, Cappellus, Valefius*, and " other learned men. The moft fufpected places have been collated with the MS from which R. *Ste-* " *phea's* edition was taken, and the variations are inferted in their proper places. At the end are " Bifhop *Pearfon's* notes from the margin of his book, and Dr. *Davies's* notes upon the firft Apology; " both

Mr. *Jebb's* Bibliotheca Literaria*, 4to; and in the following year Mr. *R. Gale's* † "Regiſtrum Honoris de *Richmond*," Mr.

.particularly. The late learned Dr. *Jortin*, who was one of his pupils, was very early in life recommended by him to tranſlate ſome of *Euſtathius's* notes for the uſe of *Pope's Homer*; (ſee a letter of Mr. *Fenton's* in the Additions to *Pope*, vol. II. p. 106.) He left College many years before his death, and reſided in *London*, firſt at Sir *Edward Walpole's*, and afterwards in private lodgings. He was fond of the common law, and ſtudied it; and after he came to *London*, had thoughts of being entered at one of the Inns of Court, and being called to the bar; but that ſcheme he afterwards dropped, and lived very retired, ſeeing only a few of his friends. Dr. *Thirlby* once had a deſign to publiſh *Shakſpeare* ‡; and Dr. *Jortin* undertook to read over that Poet, with a view to mark the paſſages where he had either imitated *Greek* and *Latin* writers, or at leaſt had fallen into the ſame thoughts and expreſſions. Dr. *Thirlby* dropt his deſign; but left a *Shakſpeare*, with many marginal notes and corrections, which is at preſent in the poſſeſſion of Sir *Edward Walpole*, to whom he bequeathed all his books and papers. He was appointed a king's waiter ‖ in the port of *London*, in *May*, 1741, a ſinecure place worth about 100*l. per annum*, which Sir *Edward Walpole* got for him. He died *Dec.* 19, 1753.

* Of this valuable work ten numbers only were publiſhed; in which are interſperſed the obſervations of *Maſſon*, *Waſſe*, and other eminent ſcholars of the time. The learned editor, who practiſed phyſic at *Stratford* by *Bow*, publiſhed in two folio volumes, 1725, "De Vita & Rebus geſtis *Mariæ Scotorum* Reginæ, *Franciæ* Dotariæ;" and "The "Hiſtory of the life and reign of *Mary* queen of *Scots* and dowager of *France*, extracted "from original records and writers of credit. *London*, 1725," 8vo.; an edition of *Ariſtides*, with notes, 1728, 2 vols. 4to.; and in 1733, an edition of *Bacon's* "Opus "Majus," folio, "neatly and accurately printed for *W. Bowyer* §." [See more, under 1733.]

† *Roger Gale*, Eſq. F. R. and A. S. the eldeſt ſon of that eminent antiquary and critic Dr. *Thomas Gale* Dean of *York* ** and of *Barbara* his wife, was poſſeſſed of a conſi-

"both now firſt printed." Mr. BOWYER, *in Bibliotheca Literaria*, No. I. p. 47.—"I think ſomebody "has told me, that *Juſtin Martyr's* Apology has been lately publiſhed from Dr. *Aſhton's* papers; "by whom I know not. If you know of ſuch a book, and it gives you no trouble to ſend it to me, I "ſhould be glad of it. His *Hierocles* ſhews, that *Needham* was not quite equal to that work: Has "this the ſame view with regard to *Thirlby*? That man was loſt to the republick of letters very ſur- "prizingly; he went off, and returned no more." Mr. *Clarke*, *Letter to Mr. B. March* 10, 1768.
‡ In the laſt edition of *Shakſpeare*, Dr. *Thirlby's* name occurs early in the liſt of commentators.
‖ The great Dr. *Clarke's* ſon enjoyed a ſimilar office.
§ Biog. Brit. *Bacon*, note D.
** Born at *Scruton* 1636, admitted at *Trinity College Cambridge*, and elected Fellow there; A. B. 1658; A. M. 1662; B. and D. D. 1675; *Greek* Profeſſor at *Cambridge* 1666, which he reſigned 1672, on being choſen head maſter of *St. Paul's* School; prebendary of *St. Paul's* 1676, F. R. S. inſtalled Dean *Sept.* 16, 1697. He died at *York*, *April* 8, 1702, æt. 68. See his epitaph in the middle of the choir of *York Minſter*, Drake's Ebor. p. 514. He publiſhed, 1. Opuſcula Mythologica, *Greek* and *Latin*, *Cantab.* 1671, 8vo.; reprinted at *Amſterdam* 1688, 8vo. with great improvements. 2. Hiſtoriæ Poe-ticæ Antiquæ Scriptores, *Paris*, 1676, 8vo. 3. *Jamblichus* de Myſteriis, *Oxon.* 1678, f. 4. Pſalterium juxta exemplar *Alexandrinum*, *Greek* and *Latin*, *Oxon.* 1678. 5. *Herodotus*, *Greek* and *Latin*, *London*, 1679, f. 6. An edition of *Cicero's* works, reviſed by him, printed at *London* 1681, 1684, 2 vols. f. 7. Hiſtoriæ *Anglicæ* Scriptores, *Oxon.* 1687, f. 8. Hiſtoriæ *Britannicæ*, *Saxonicæ*, *Anglo-Danicæ* Scriptores V. *Oxon.* 1691, f. Theſe two laſt were a continuation of the Rerum *Anglicanarum* Scrip-tores, publiſhed by Mr. *Fulman* and Biſhop *Fell*, *Oxon.* 1684, f. He left in MS. *Origenis* Philocalia, variis manuſcriptis collata, emendata, & nova verſione donata; *Jamblichus* de vita *Pythagoræ*; and *Antonini* Itinerarium *Britanniæ*. His Sermons preached on public occaſions were publiſhed 1704, 8vo. after his death. His ſecond ſon *Charles*, rector of *Scruton*, died 1738, having married *Cordelia*, daughter of Mr. *Thomas Thwaits* of *Eurrel*, who died 1721, leaving four ſons; the eldeſt, *Charles*, ſucceeded in the rectory. His name is ſubſcribed to a *Greek* copy of verſes in the "Epicedia *Cantabrigienſia*, "1691," as "Taxator Academiæ Sen. Coll. *Trin.*"

derable

Mr. *Joseph Sparke's* edition of " Hiftoriæ *Anglicanæ* Scripto-
" res,"

derable eftate at *Scruton, Yorkfhire,* now in the poffeffion of his grandfon *Roger Gale,*
Efq. He was for fome time Commiffioner of the Excife, afterwards one of the Reprefentatives in Parliament for *North Allerton,* the firft Vice Prefident of the Society of
Antiquaries, and Treafurer to the Royal Society. Though he was confidered as one of
the moft learned men of his age, he only publifhed the following books; *viz.* 1. His father's Commentary on *Antoninus's* Iter *Britanniarum, Lond.* 1709, 4to. 2. The Knowledge
of Medals, by *F. Jobert,* tranflated by him from the *French* without his name, *Lond.*
1715, 12mo. 3. Regiftrum Honoris de *Richmond**, fol. *Lond.* 1722. His difcourfe on
the four *Roman* Ways in *Britain* is printed in the fixth volume of *Leland's* Itinerary ;
his Remarks on a *Roman* Infcription found at *Lanchefter,* in the Philofophical Tranfactions, No. 357, p. 823; and extracts of two of his letters to Mr. *Peter Collinfon,* F.R.S.
concerning the vegetation of melon feeds 33 years old, and of a foffil fkeleton of a
man, dated in 1743 and 1744, in vol. XLIII. p. 265. He died at *Scruton, June* 25,
1744; and left all his MSS. by will to *Trinity College, Cambridge,* of which he was once
Fellow, and his coins to the public library at *Cambridge.* His correfpondence included
all the eminent Antiquaries of his time ; and Mr. *George Allan* of *Darlington* is poffeffed,
by gift of his grandfon, of a large collection of letters to and from him, which, if printed,
would make a valuable addition to antiquarian literature. He married *Henrietta* daughter of *Henry Roper,* of *Ealing,* efq. who died 1720, by whom he had *Roger-Henry,*
born 1740, who by *Catharine,* daughter of *Chriftopher Crow,* of *Kipling,* efq. left iffue
Catharine, born 1741; *Roger,* born 1743; and *Samuel,* born 175 ...

SAMUEL, his younger brother, was born in the parifh of *St. Faith,* near *St. Paul's,*
London, Dec. 17, and baptized *Dec.* 20, 1682; *Samuel Pepys†,* Efq. being one of his
godfathers. He was educated at *St. Paul's* fchool, and intended for the Univerfity ;
but his elder brother *Roger* being fent to *Cambridge,* and Dr. *Gale,* his father, dying
1702, *Samuel* was provided for in the Cuftom-houfe, *London,* and at the time of his
death was one of the Land Surveyors there. He was one of the revivers of the Society
of Antiquaries in 1717, and their firft Treafurer. On refigning that office, 1739-40, he
was prefented by them with a filver cup, value ten guineas, made by Mr. *Dingley,* and
infcribed

SAMUELI GALE, ARM.

OB QUAESTURAM

AMPLIUS XXI ANNOS

BENE ET FIDELITER GESTAM

SOCIETAS ANTIQUARIORUM

LONDINENSIS, L. D. D.

He was a man of great learning and uncommon abilities, and well verfed in the Antiquities of *England,* for which he left many valuable collections behind him ; but printed
nothing, except " A Hiftory of *Winchefter* Cathedral, *London,* 1715," begun by
Henry earl of *Clarendon,* and continued to that year, with cuts ; and his Effay on
Ulphus's Horn at *York,* in the Archæologia, vol. I. N° 39. He died of a fever, ætat.
72, univerfally efteemed, at his lodgings the *Chicken-Houfe* at *Hampftead, Jan.* 10,
1754; and was buried *Jan.* 14, by Dr. *Stukeley,* in the new burying ground near the
Foundling Hofpital (belonging to *St. George's* parifh, *Queen Square,* of which Dr.
Stukeley was rector). His very valuable library, and fine collection of prints by *Hol-*

---

* Of this, fee " *Britifh* Topography," vol. II. p. 414.

† This gentleman gave his library, containing a number of ancient and modern political tracts, particularly thofe relating to the Admiralty, of which he was Secretary, to *Magdalen College, Cambridge.*

lar,

" res*," Bishop *Burnet's* " History of his own Times†;" the
" Castrations of the last edition of *Holinshed's* Chronicle, both
" in the *Scotch* and *English* parts; containing 44 sheets,
" printed with the old types and ligatures, and compared
" literatim by the original;" Sir *Henry Spelman's English*
Works‡; and an edition of *L'Estrange's Josephus*; all in folio.

On the death of Mr. *Bonwicke* (*Oct.* 20, 1722), his grateful scholar had an opportunity of requiting in some measure the obligations he had received, by officiating for a time in the capacity of a school-master, for the benefit of the family. When he had discharged this act of kindness, he applied diligently to the management of the printing office, in conjunction with his father. To prevent the necessary repetition of the elder and younger Mr. *Bowyer*, I shall from this period in general speak of them as of one person; the principal attention to the mechanical part of the business devolving on the father, the correcting of the press to the son. In 1724 they printed Dr. *Mead's* " *Harveian* Oration" de-

lar, Caliot, &c. were sold by auction in 1754 by Mr. *Langford*. Mr. *Gale* dying a batchelor and intestate, administration of his effects was granted to his only sister *Elizabeth*, who in 1739 became the second wife of Dr. *Stukeley*, who outlived her. By that means all her brother's MSS. papers, &c. fell after her death into Dr. *Stukeley's* hands; since whose decease Dr. *Ducarel* hath (by the generosity of Mrs. *Fleming*, Dr. *Stukeley's* daughter by his first wife) been favoured with some few of Mr. *Samuel Gale's* MSS. which are now, 1779, in his possession; among these are, Mr. *Gale's* History of *York* Cathedral in folio, often mentioned by Mr. *Samuel Drake*; his Tour through many parts of *England* in 1705; his account of some antiquities at *Glastonbury*, and in the cathedrals of *Salisbury, Wells,* and *Winton*, 1711; his account of *Sheperton, Cowey Stakes,* &c. 1748; Observations upon *Kingsbury* in *Middlesex*, 1751; Account of *Barden, Tunbridge Wells,* &c. with a list of the pictures at *Penshurst*; account of a journey into *Hertfordshire, Bucks,* and *Warwickshire,* with a list of the fine portraits and pictures in Lady *Bowyer's* gallery at *Warwick Priory*, in a letter to Dr. *Stukeley*, 1720; also Mr. *Roger Gale's* Tour into *Scotland*, 1739; all in 4to.

* An early member of the Society of Antiquaries, and register of *Peterborough*.

† Some curious extracts from the margin of Mr. *Bowyer's* copy of this book, formerly the Rev. *J. Blackbourn's*, may be seen in *Swift's* Works, 4to. vol. IX. part ii. p. 217.

‡ This edition, which was published by Bishop *Gibson*, contains the Author's Life; his *English* works as published by himself; and his posthumous writings relating to the laws and antiquities of *England*. The original subscription price was 1l. 4s. 3d; the large paper (of which only 50 were printed) 2l. 8s. 6d.

livered

,livered 1723; with an appendix, by Mr. *Chishull* *, under the
title

* *Edmund Chishull*, son of *Paul Chishull* †, was born at *Eyworth* in *Bedfordshire*; admitted scholar of *Corpus Christi College, Oxford*; took the degree of M. A. *Feb* 27, 1693; became fellow of the college; and, having a grant of the Traveller's place from that society, sailed from *England Sept.* 12, 1698, and arrived on the 19th of *November* following at *Smyrna*, where he was chaplain to the *English* Factory till *Feb.* 10, 1701-2. He took the degree of B. D. *June* 16, 1705; was presented *Sept.* 1, 1708, on the death of Mr. *James Barker*, to the vicarage of *Walthamstow* in *Essex*; in 1711 was appointed chaplain to the queen; and in 1731 presented to the rectory of *South Church* in *Essex*. He published, "*Gulielmo* Tertio terræ marique Principi invictissimo in *Gallos* pugna " navali nuperrime devictos, Carmen heroicum. *Oxon.* 1692," folio; " In obitum au-" gustissimæ & desideratissimæ Reginæ *Mariæ* Carmen Pastorale." Mus. *Angl.* vol. III. p. 234. " Inscriptio *Sigea* antiquissima ΒΟΥΣΤΡΟΦΗΔΟΝ exarata. Commentario eam " Historico-Grammatico-Critico illustravit *Edmundus Chishull*, S. T. B. Regiæ Ma-" jestati à sacris, 1721," folio; which was followed by " Notarum ad Inscriptionem Si-" *gæam* Appendicula; additâ a *Sigeo* alterâ, *Antiochi Soteris* Inscriptione," folio, 15 pages, *no date*. Both were incorporated in his " Antiquitates ‡ *Asiaticæ* Christianam Æram ante-" cedentes; ex primariis Monumentis *Græcis* descriptæ, *Latinè* versæ, notisque & com-" mentariis illustratæ. Accedit Monumentum *Latinum Ancyranum* ‖. Per *Edmundum* " *Chishull*, S. T. B. Londini, Typis *Guil. Bowyer* 1728 **, folio;" being a collection of inscriptions made by Consul *Sherard*, Dr. *Picenini*, and Dr. *Lisle* (afterwards archdeacon of *Canterbury*, warden of *Wadham College*, and bishop of *St. Asaph*) in their travels 1705 and 1709, and deposited in Lord *Oxford's* library ††, where it remains in the *British*

† Bible clerk of *Queen's College, Cambridge*, where *Wood* supposes him to have taken the degree of B. A. He was admitted M. A. at *Pembroke College, Oxford, June* 18, 1634.

‡ Proposals for this book were published in 1724. Mr. *Bowyer's* copy of it (which was rendered more valuable by his MS. notes) was presented after his death (agreeably to his directions when living) to the Right Hon. *Edwin* Lord *Sandys*.—A letter to Mr. *Wasse* (concerning a passage in the *Sigæan* Inscription, &c.) by Mr. *Barker* is printed in the *Bibliotheca Literaria*, N° X.

¶ " Sequitur erudita & singularis Commentatio ad *Marmor Bosporanum Jovi Urio sacrum*. Eam " utique debes ingenio & humanitati *Aristarchi Cantabrigiensis*, quo nemo alius hac ætate sanctior, " nemo literis diviniis humanisque exercitation, aut ab omni laude felicior." Pref. to Comment. in *Leg. Decemvir*. Of Mr. *Chishull*, whom he styles " vir celeberrimus ingenii acumine & literarum " peritia, quibus excellebat maxime," Dr. *Taylor* speaks in the highest terms.—" Is this *Aristarchus* " *summè eruditus Cantab*. in Mr. *Chishull's* supplemental half-sheet, Dr. *Gooch?* If it be, every reader " will transfer the compliment to Dr. *Bentley*." Mr. *Clarke* to Mr. B. *Aug.* 14, 1729."—" The re-" storing and settling to a tittle the inscription to *Jupiter Ourios*, as printed in *Chishull's* cancelled " page, and by Dr. *Taylor*, was by Dr. *Ashton* of *Jesus*. *Chishull* never submitted completely. Dr. " *Taylor* by no means speaks highly of *Chishull* on this occasion. The wonder is, how *Wheler* and " *Spon* could vary so much in copying so few, so large and so plain letters; especially as it is not " probable that it was placed out of distinct sight." *T. F.*

** The first part contains (besides the title and five introductory leaves) 208 pages;—and a supplement, eight pages, including a correct edition § of his Conjectanea de nummo ΕΚΛΗ inscripto," and the " *Iter Asiæ* Poeticum," addressed to the Rev. *John Horn*. Another leaf was added in 1731, with a head of *Homer* (of which only 50 copies were printed); and a second leaf, on the inscription of *Jupiter Ourios*, dated " *Sept.* 29, 1731." The stone was then come into Dr. *Mead's* possession, and there is an exact engraving of it, a little larger than Dr. *Taylor's*. He submits, but without paying the least compliment, or even mentioning Dr. *Ashton*. Towards the printing of this book, Dr. *Mead* paid fifty-one guineas; Dr. *William Sherard* twenty guineas; and Dr. *Lisle* five guineas.

†† Prefixed to this curious MS. is the following letter, dated *Magdalen College, Oxford, Dec.* 16, 1776: " The inclosed paper contains some information which will be of use to any person who may " have occasion to consult the Earl of *Oxford's* copy of *Chishull's* Inscriptions, now in *The British* *Museum*, Catalogue N° 7509; to which I have often referred in my collection published not long " since. Inscriptiones Antiquæ, pleræque nondum editæ, in *Asia Minori & Græcia*, præsertim *Ath-" nis*, collectæ. *Oxon.* 1774," My request is, that you will insert it in the beginning or at the end of that MS. R. CHANDLER."

" Extract from an account of Mr. *Chishull's* papers, drawn up by Professor *Ward*, and now in the possession of *John Loveday*, Esq; of *Caversham* near *Reading*.

" The Earl of *Oxford's* copy.—This book contains 84 pages of inscriptions.—All the inscriptions from p. 1, to the end of p. 71, are found in book I. II. III. of Mr. *Chishull*.—Most of the inscriptions

§ First published under the title of " Dissertatio de nummo ΕΚΛΗ inscripto Dissertatio."

from

title of " Diſſertatio de Nummis quibuſdam à *Smyrnæis* in
" Medicorum

Muſeum, Harl. MSS. 7500. It was publiſhed by ſubſcription for one guinea (royal paper at two guineas) ; and a larger volume, under the title of " Antiquitates *Aſiaticæ*. Pars " altera diverſa, diverſarum urbium inſcripta marmora complectens," was intended to have been publiſhed by him for another guinea ; and 12 pages were printed : but the author's death put a ſtop to the progreſs of the volume ; and it does not appear what became of his MSS. Mr. *Chiſhull* was author of " A Charge of Hereſy maintained againſt Mr. *Dodwell's* " late Epiſtolary Diſcourſe concerning the Mortality of the Soul, by way of addreſs to the " Clergy of the Church of *England* ; laying open his oppoſition to the received creeds, and " his falſification of all ſacred and profane Antiquity *. *London*, 1706," 8vo ; and publiſhed ten ſingle Sermons †. And in 1747 the learned Dr. *Mead* publiſhed his " Travels in *Tur-* " *key*, and back to *England*; *London*, printed by *W. Bowyer*," folio. He was, jointly with *Francis Heywood*, jun. Eſq; of *Oxford*, executor to the laſt will of Dr. *Turner*, who died *April* 29, 1714; and wrote the *Latin* Inſcription on " A Monument ſacred to the Church " of *England*, and to the Memory of Dr. *Thomas Turner*, Preſident of *Corpus Chriſti* " *College* in the Univerſity of *Oxford*, erected in the Church of *Stowe*, in the County of " *Northampton*, on occaſion of the manor and eſtate of *Stowe* being purchaſed by the " executors of that pious public benefactor, together with other lands, to be ſettled, as " his will directs, on the Governors of the charity for relief of poor widows and children " of Clergymen, in the year of our Lord 1716 ; the whole eſtate at *Stowe*, and that from p. 72, to the end, are found in Book IV. of Mr. *Chiſhull*; ſome in book I. II. III ; and ſome in none of Mr. *Chiſhull's* books ; viz. Not found : *Smyrna*, p. 72, N° 2 ; p. 74, N° 5 ; p. 75, No. 10; p. 76, N° 2 ; p. 77, N° 7 ; ..... *biſar*, p. 78, 79, 80, N° 12.—Some inſcriptions in B. I. II. III. IV. of Mr. *Chiſhull* are not found in this.—In B. I. II. III. IV. of Mr. *Chiſhull*, I have referred to the page in this book, where each inſcription is found, for the greater eaſe in collecting them.—Some few inſcriptions in this book are twice written in different places ; the reading of ſeveral varies from that in Mr. *Chiſhull's* books ; ſome of the inſcriptions are longer than they are in thoſe books ; and the diviſion of the inſcriptions ſometimes differs.—The diſpoſition of the inſcriptions under the ſeveral places where they were found ſeems not always ſo regular as in Mr. *Chiſhull's* books.—I have put a ſmall croſs in the margin of the pages, againſt the beginning of each inſcription, which I found in Mr. *Chiſhull's* books ; ſo that when there is no croſs, ſuch inſcription was not found.
    " The places of the inſcriptions are not mentioned in the Earl of *Oxford's* copy ; but by Mr. *Chiſhull's* books are found to be in the following order :

Aphrcdiſias, now *Geyra*, 1. 29. 81. 84.	*Miletus*, now *Balot* or *Palatſba*, 63, 64.	*Smyrna*, 71. 78.
Teos, now *Bodrum*, 30. 45.	*Tyria*, 64.	*Iſſiclaerkoi*, 75.
Tralles, now *Guzal-biſar*, 45, 46.	*Metropolis*, now *Cixil-biſar*, 64.	*Durguthli*, 78.
Arab-biſar, 46, 47.	*Hierapolis*, 65, 66, and 83.	*Epheſus*, 78, 79.
Stratonicea, now *Eſki-biſar*, 47. 54.	*Thyatira*, now *Ak-biſar*, 66, 67.	*Angora*, 78.
Milaſa, now *Mileſſo*, 58.	*Kirk-agatch*, 67.	*Neapolis*, *Scala Nova* or *Cuſadaſi*, 78.
Iaſſus, now *Aſſinkulaſſi*, 58.	*Philadelphia*, 68, 69, and 78 and 83.	*Derrikiei*, 80, 81.
Branchidæ, now *Ieran*, 59. 63.	*Sardes*, 70, 71, and 81.	*Pergamus*, 83.

* For the hiſtory of this controverſy, ſee the Biographia *Britannica*, article *Dodwell*.
† 1. A Sermon on Pſalm cvii. 23, 24. before the *Levant* Company, 1698, 4to.—2. " The great " danger and miſtake of all new uninſpired Prophecies relating to the end of the world. Being a " Sermon preached on *November* 23d, 1707, at *Serjeants-Inn-Chapel*, in *Chancery-Lane*. With an " Appendix of hiſtorical collections applicable to all ſuch Prophecies as are condemned in this diſ- " courſe, and to thoſe which are now venting in the World, 1708," 4to.—3. " The Orthodoxy of " an *Engliſh* Clergyman conſidered, as to four heads, viz. The received Creeds ; The Thirty-nine " Articles ; The Supremacy of the Crown ; The Eſtabliſhed Liturgy of the Church. Being a Ser- " mon preached in the Chapel of *Rumford*, at the Viſitation there held on the 4th of *May*, 1711, by " the Rev. Dr. *Aiſton*, Archdeacon of *Eſſex*." 4to.—4. " Modeſty and Moderation, or the true rela- " tive duty of the tolerated and eſtabliſhed parties in any ſociety of men ; being a Sermon preached " at the Aſſizes at *Hertford*, on *March* the 3d, 1711-12," 8vo. 1712.—5. " The Duty of good ſub- " jects in relation to public peace. Being a Sermon preached at the Aſſizes at *Hertford*, on *Auguſt* " 11, 1712. Publiſhed at the requeſt of Mr. High Sheriff and the Grand Jury." 8vo.—6. " Againſt " Duelling. A Sermon preached before the Queen in the Royal Chapel at *Windſor Caſtle* on *No-* " *vember* the 23d, 1712. Publiſhed by her Majeſty's ſpecial command, 1712," 8vo.—7. " The " excellency of a proper charitable relief, a Sermon preached before the Sons of the Clergy, 1714," 4to.—8. " The Subject minded of his Duty. Tit. iii. 1. 1716," 8vo.—9. and 10. Two Aſſize Ser- mons in 1718, 8vo.

" at

" Medicorum honorem percuffis *;" a work which occafioned
a controverfy † of a very interefting nature to the profeffors
of

" at *Weft Wratting* in the county of *Cambridge*, amounting to fomewhat more than
" one thoufand pounds a year." A plate of this monument, executed in marble by
T. Stayner, is engraved by *J. Sturt*. Mr. *Chifhull* died at *Walthamftowe*, May 18,
1733. Mr. *Clarke*, in a letter to Mr. *Bowyer*, *July* 14 that year, fays, " I was very
" forry for Mr. *Chifhull's* death as a public lofs. Who would be folicitous about a cha-
" racter in the papers, when you may have as fine a one as is poffible for five fhillings?
" Your public prints are in that refpect like your old marbles, the great ufe of them
" was to preferve the names of little men; characters below hiftory muft look out for
" other fupports. I hope Mr. *Chifhull's* papers will fall into fome proper hand, that
" his defign and the few thoughts he has left might not be intirely loft."

* Both were reprinted 1725, 8vo. ex officina *Bouteftaniana*.

† The fubject of this controverfy was, whether the phyficians of antient *Rome* were
not in general vile and defpicable flaves, or whether there were not fome among them
at leaft who enjoyed the privileges of a free condition, and the honour due to their fervices. The following learned treatifes take their rife from Dr. *Mead's* Oration: 1.
" *Middletoni* Differtatio de ftatu Medicorum apud veteres *Romanos*, 1726;" tranflated
" and publifhed in 8vo. 1734. 2. " Notæ breves in eam per *P. W.* M. D. 1726."
3. " Ad *Middletoni* Differtationem Refponfio *J. W.* ‖ 1727." 4. " In Differtationem
" Animadverfio brevis, 1727." 5. " *Middletoni* Differtationis fuæ Defenfio, 1727."
6. " Defenfio fupradicta examinata §," 1728. 7. " Effay on the ftate and condition of
" phyficians among the ancients, occafioned by a late differtation of Dr. *Middleton*.
" By *Charles La Motte*, A. M. chaplain to the duke of *Montague*, and F. A. S. 1728,"
8vo. 8. " *Shacheri* Differtatio de Honoribus Medicorum apud veteres. Lipfiæ, 1732,"
4to. 9. " *Schlægeri* Hiftoria litis de Medicorum conditione. *Helmftad.* 1740." 4to.
10. " Differtationis de fervili Medicorum conditione Appendix, feu Defenfionis Pars Se-
" cunda. Cui accedit ad Dominum *La Motte* Epiftola Apologetica, *Anglice* confcripta.
" Auctore *Conyers Middleton*, S. T. P. Protobibliothecario Academiæ *Cantabrigienfis*,
" 1761 ‡."

‖ *John Ward*, Profeffor of Rhetoric at *Grefham College*; of whom fee under the year 1766.
§ Some afcribe this to Dr. *Letherland*, others to profeffor *Ward*; the latter, from the printer and
type, feems moft probable; and is confirmed by this quotation from Dr. *Maty*: " Dr. *Mead's* caufe was
" defended by the learned *Ward*, whofe anfwer to *Middleton's* reply feems to have difarmed this re-
" doubted enemy of the phyficians. There is reafon however to believe the Doctor would either have
" qualified or confirmed his thefis, had he been able to finifh a *Latin* work which was to have been
" entitled *Medicina vetus collectitia, ex auctoribus antiquis non Medicis*, for he had a greatnefs of
" mind that would not fuffer him knowingly to perfift in his errors." *Life of Mead*, p. 39.—" Not-
" withftanding the heat with which this controverfy was managed, Dr. *Middleton* every where expreffes
" the greateft regard for Dr. *Mead*; and many years after, when he had occafion to mention his name
" in his book of the *Greek* and *Egyptian* Antiquities, on account of an ancient piece of painting in
" the Doctor's poffeffion, he draws his character in fuch expreffions, as I cannot forbear tranfcribing.
" *Meadius* nofter, artis Medicæ decus, qui vitæ revera nobilis, vel principibus in republica viris,
" exemplum præbet, pro eo, quo omnibus fere præftat, artium veterum amore, alias poftea quafdam
" (imagines) et fplendidiores, opinor, Roma quoque deportandas curavit."
‡ The learned reader cannot but be gratified with the following Advertifement, prefixed by its editor
Dr. *Heberden* to this curious little treatife: " Triginta & quinque anni jam elapfi funt, ex quo *Middletonus*
" impugnavit *Meadi* fententiam de conditione medicorum *Romæ* degentium. Inter viros doctos, qui
" a *Meadi* partibus fteterunt, fuit *Wardus* profeffor rhetorices *Grefhamenfis*, qui uno & altero fcripto
" auctori noftro refpondit. Contra primum horum fe tueri cœperat *Middletonus* edita defenfionis parte
" prima, quæ in omnium manibus eft. Partem fecundam jamjam vulgaturus erat, cum ad villam
" *Harleii* Comitis *Oxonienfis* prope *Cantabrigiam*, in quâ tum forte aderat *Middletonus*, *Meadus* etiam
" arceffitus

of this useful science, and to the learned world in general*.

I am

* The acknowledgements of Dr. *Mead* to Mr. *Chishull* are thus elegantly expreffed in a preface introducing the Differtation: " Cum inter multos ac varios
" honores, quos medicis olim tributos fuiffe in Oratione mea ‖ oftendi, fingularis cujuf-
" dam, quem a *Smyrnaeis* acceperunt, ut nomina illorum in nummis ponerentur, men-
" tionem fecerim ; quo res ifta magis foret perfpicua, nummos aliquot ejufmodi e mul-
" tis aliis, quos apud me confervo, aere incifos, cum fingulorum explicatione hic adji-
" cere volui. Ex medicorum enim nominibus, tantis laudibus apud veteres celebratis ;
" deorumque falutarium imaginibus, fymbolis artis fuae inftructis, quae in his nummis
" confpiciuntur ; *Smyrnacos*, quo medicae artis profefforum famae ac dignitati confu-
" lerent, eos percuffiffe, omnes, opinor, aequi rerum aeftimatores mecum agnofcent.
" Fatendum eft fane magiftratuum nomina tam in *Smyrnaeorum*, quam in aliarum
" *Graeciae* civitatum nummis haud paucis comparere ; unde viri eruditi, & rei numma-
" riae fcientiffimi, fi qui forte id genus nummi, de quibus hic agimus, in manus eorum
" devenerint, magiftratibus ftatim adfcribentes, inter alios ejufdem (ut ipfi cenfuerunt)
" claffis in fcriniis hactenus collocarunt. Attamen fi rem paulo accuratius intueamur,
" nummos, in quibus magiftratuum nomina leguntur, alia numina, aut aliis faltem in-
" fignibus, cum re medica nihil commune habentibus, ornata exhibere percipiemus.
" Primus autem, quod fciam, *Seguinus* nummi alicujus *Smyrnaei* ectypum protulit,
" cui ulla omnino cum noftris fimilitudo effe videatur. Is quidem inter alios *Smyr-*
" *nacorum* nummos unum edidit, in cujus altera parte caput *Hygiae* noftrae perfimile
" adfpicitur, quod ipfe tamen *Apollinis* effe ftatuit ; in altera imago fedens, fed velata,
" & brachiis tranfverfis, nec reliqua adfunt fymbola ; ni forfan in lineamentorum ductu,
" quae temporis injuria evanida fuiffent & confufa, fculptor hallucinatus fuiffe exifti-
" metur. Imaginem autem *prytanis*, hoc eft fummi apud *Smyrnaeos* magiftratus, fe-
" dentis effe autumat †. Neque ab illuftriffimo *Spanhemio*, neque a *Vaillant*, in iis
" quae ad opera illius fcripferunt, hic diverfum aliquid affertur ; unde eos nihil certius
" habuiffe, quod de nummo ifto proponerent, manifefto conftat. Alter quoque num-
" mus ab eodem *Seguino* adducitur, qui hinc *Matris Deorum Sipylenae*, quae *Smyr-*
" *nae* colebatur, caput ; illinc ftantis *Ifidis* fimulacrum repraefentat ‡ : de quo in

" arceffitus effet, ut inviferet comitis filiam aegrotantem. *Harleius*, hâc oblatâ occafione, ut erat utri-
" que eorum amiciffimus, facile eos redegit in gratiam. Quapropter *Midaletonus* unicum, quod ha-
" buit, defenfionis exemplar in nobilis hofpitis fui manus ultro tradidit, pluris faciens *Meadi* amici-
" tiam, quam famam, quæ ex hujufmodi victoria, vel faltem ex ingenio fperari poterat. *Harleiani*
" codices MSS. poftea in Mufeum *Britannicum* devenerunt, et una cum his hoc ipfum defenfionis ex-
" emplar auctoris manu magna ex parte defcriptum. Quod proinde ex legibus Mufei omnibus ade-
" untibus patet, & quodammodo publici juris factum eft ; neque fane, fi penes privatum effet, ulla
" fubeft caufa diutius premendi hoc opufculum, *Middletono*, & *Meado*, et *Wardo* jam fato functis, et
" confopitâ omni illa animorum contentione, quâ hæc quæftio fuerat agitata. Quamobrem vifum eft
" id prælo committere, ut et commodius, et a pluribus evolvi poffit. Qui antiquitatis ftudio tenentur
" non inviti legent quod reliquum erat ad hanc difputationem penitus abfolvendam ; nonnullos forfan,
" de quæftione ipfa unice fecuros, fola ftili jucunditas fatis delectabit. Epiftola *Anglica*, quæ poft
" mortem auctoris inter chartas ejus reperta fuit, propterea fubjungitur, quia in eodem verfatur argu-
" mento. Vale."
‖ " The fyftem which the learned *Chishull*, and after him Dr *Mead*, grounded upon fome medals
" found at *Smyrna*, about a college of phyficians fettled in that city from the moft ancient times, and
" diftinguifhed by the privilege of celebrating annual games in honour of *Aefculapius*, and of *Hygeia*
" the goddefs of health, was at leaft very ingenious ; but whether Mr. *Wife* has fhewn it to be only
" ingenious, and has more happily accounted for thefe medals, by referring them to *Homer*, whom he
" thinks a *Smyrnaean*, muft be left to the decifion of the learned. See his *Nummorum antiquorum*
" *fcriniis Bodleianis reconditorum Catalogus*, p. 145, &c." *Maty*, Life of *Mead*, p. 57.
† Seguin. Select. Numm. Ant. p. 33. ‡ Seguinus, p. 32.
6 " Notis

I am indebted to the industry of Mr. *Bowyer* for copies of
two letters from Mr. *Chishull* to Dr. *Mead*, in relation to
some medals struck at *Smyrna* in honour of Physicians,
which are more fully illustrated in his Dissertation subjoined to the Doctor's oration.   They were copied from a
rough draught of Mr. *Chishull's* own hand; and the first of
them seems to be designed to furnish Dr. *Mead*, at his own
request, with some proofs of the honour paid to Physicians
by the ancient *Grecians* :

I.

" Honoured Sir,   [Copy without date.]

" It is with the greatest pleasure that I find myself ho-
" noured with any command of yours; and I shall be truly
" glad if any thing noted under the following heads may
" fall-in with your design.

" Notis ad Differtationem plura dicendi locus dabitur *.   Vir igitur reverendus, *Ed-*
" *mundus Chishull*, S. T. B. cujus eximia antiquitatis, omnifque adeo elegantioris doc-
" trinae cognitio ex egregiis illius, tum *in nummum* CKΩΠI *inscriptum*, tum etiam in
" *Sigaeam inscriptionem Commentariis*, orbi erudito diu jam innotuit, hos nummos pri-
" mus feliciter explicavit, & quasi postliminio recuperatos medicis restituit.   *Smyrnae*
" enim largior eorum provenit meffis, postquam terra circa *Aesculapii* templum coepta
" est dimoveri.   Qua occasione etiam erutum fuit, & luci redditum, caput marmoreum,
" in quo inscribitur, MAPKOC MOΔIOC IATPOC MEΘOΔIKOC; item nummus *Aristotelis*
" nomen exhibens; ut etiam *Hermogenis* medici, qui septuaginta septem volumina edi-
" derat, inscriptio.   Dum *Smyrnae* itaque commoratus est, plures hujusmodi nummos
" comparavit; quos attentiori cura expendens, ex nominibus & figuris inter se collatis
" ad rem medicam pertinere cito deprehendit.   Cum in patriam autem reversus fuit,
" sermone de medicinae antiquitatibus forte inter nos incepto, pro ea necessitudine,
" quae diu mihi cum eo fuerat, mentem suam de his nummis mihi statim aperuit; nec
" id tantum, sed & nummos ipsos, una cum quibusdam in eos observationibus, se dono
" mihi promisit missurum; quod & haud ita pridem amicissime praestitit.   Illius igitur
" beneficio nova haec ad rei nummariae scientiam accessio prorsus debetur.   Cujus etiam
" de republica literaria optime merendi studio & industria, si vivat modo & valeat, mag-
" num *Graecarum antiquitatum*†, aliorumque veteris aevi monumentorum *Corpus*, non-
" dum publici juris factum; doctissimis etiam Commentariis, tantoque thesauro dignis,
" locupletatum, antiquitatis studiosis expectare licebit.   Vale."

 * Vid. Differt. p. 4e, note *o*.
 † This appeared in 1728, under the title of " Antiquitates *Afiaticæ*," &c.   See p. 35.

" I.

" I. The chief honours and rewards given to fome emi-
" nent *Greek* Phyficians are at once noted by *Pliny*, l. vii. c. 37.

" II. Thofe beftowed on *Hippocrates* may more particu-
" larly be noted in the Δόγμα Ἀθηναίων among his Epiftles,
" and his life from *Serranus* ; and the hiftory as to that
" matter is the fame whether thofe pieces be genuine or not.

" III. Befides thefe, *Erafiſtratus* was in great honour in
" the court of *Seleucus* and *Antiochus Soter*, upon his dif-
" covering the diftemper of the latter; which fee in *Plu-
" tarch*, Life of *Demetrius*, and *Appian* in *Syriacis*. The
" reward of a hundred talents mentioned by *Pliny*, l. xxvi.
" c. 1. was for curing the fame *Antiochus* of another dan-
" gerous illnefs. The fcarcity of inftances of this fort has
" been owing to this, that Phyfic was not anciently pro-
" feffed as now-a-days in the nature of a liberal fcience,
" but was always joined with Pharmacy and Chirurgery,
" and fo practifed in great meafure by illiterate perfons.

" IV. From hence a ready anfwer may be given to thofe
" fevere fatires of *Cato* and *Pliny* againft *Medici* and *Medicina*,
" l. xxvi. c. 1. as alfo from the virtuous and pious princi-
" ples of the oath of *Hippocrates*, particularly the obligation
" to teach ἄνευ μιϑᾶ, and ἀγνῶς καὶ ὁσίως διατηρῆσαι βίον, κ. τ. λ.

" V. The fame calumny may be anfwered from the
" contrary character of *Pliny*, l. xxv. c. 2.——*Pythagoras* and
" *Ariftotle* both much addicted to this noble ftudy. The
" former was the firft that wrote of the virtue of herbs,
" *Plin.* xxv. 2. He kept it a fecret, as he did his other
" attainments. But the latter, fays *Ælian*, l. v. c. 9. *Athen.*
" l. viii. c. 13. φαρμακοπώλης ἀνεφάνη, was a profeffed apothe-
" cary. If he condefcended to a fhop according to the
" cuftom of thofe times, he yet fhewed himfelf above it
" by

" by his work, entitled Ἰατρικὰ, befides what he wrote con-
" cerning Plants and Anatomy.

" VI. It was this character that firft endeared *Ariftotle*
" fo much to *Alexander the Great,* whom, upon his firft
" coming to him, he cured of a great illnefs; and becaufe
" he enjoined him to ufe much ambulation for the con-
" firming of his cure, this by fome has been taken to be the
" reafon of *Ariftotle's* being furnamed the *Peripatetic. Laertius.*

" VII. *Alexander* himfelf learned of *Ariftotle* to ftudy
" and even to practife Phyfic (*Plut.* in vit. *Alex.* c. 13.
" p. m. 668.) δοκᾶ δέ μοι χ̧ τὸ φιλιατρεῖν Ἀλεξάνδρῳ προςρίψασθαι μᾶλ-
" λόν ἑτέρων Ἀριςοτέλης· ἐ γὰρ μόνον τὴν θεωρίαν ἠγάπησεν, ἀλλὰ χ̧ νοσᾶσιν
" ἐϐοήθει τοῖς φίλοις, χ̧ συνέτατ]ε θεραπείας τινὰς χ̧ διαίτας.

" VIII. The hiftorian has well expreffed it μᾶλλον ἑτέρων:
" for it was ufual with *Alexander* to beftow the greateft
" marks of efteem and honour on other Phyficians: Wit-
" nefs the ftory of his cure by *Philip* of *Acarnania,* and the
" fignal honour paid to that Phyfician, as by the King him-
" felf, fo by his whole army. *Alexander* fhewed him,
" fays *Arrian,* (l. ii. c. 4.) ὅτι πιςός ἐςιν αὐῖῷ φίλος· and the
" whole army, fays *Curtius,* l. iii. c. 6. *grates habebant*
" *tanquam præfenti Deo.*

" IX. *Herophilus* and *Erafiftratus,* l. xxix. c. 1. were thofe
" who firft made learning neceffary to Phyfic; which being
" a thing of great expence and pains, *Pliny* tells us, the
" fchool of *Herophilus* did not long fubfift. *Deferta deinde*
" *et hæc fecta, quoniam neceffe erat in ea fcire literas.* Of
" his fchool, fee *Plin.* l. xxvi. c. 2.

" X. But we learn from *Strabo,* at the end of Book xii.
" that the fchool both of the one and the other flourifhed
" till about his time in *Afia,* the one near *Laodicea,* and the
G " other

" other at *Smyrna*. He there names as mafters of thefe;
" *Zeuxes, Alexander*, and *Hicefius*. And *Athenæus* often
" mentions the fame Ἰκέσιος as an author, and l. ii. c. 18.
" Μειόδωρος Ἐρατιςρατείας Ἱκεσία φιλος. *Pliny, Hicefio non parvæ*
" *authoritatis medico*. The faces and characters of all thefe
" we have ftill preferved in coins at *Smyrna*, with many
" others brought by Mr. *Sherard*, and now repofited in the
" Duke of *Devonfhire's* cabinet; which city allowed that
" particular honour to thofe profeffors. They are found
" with their faces ftampt on one fide, and their profeffion
" noted on the other; by figures in a fitting pofture, with
" the finger advanced to their lips in token of that filence
" which the profeffion was enjoined by the oath of *Hippo-*
" *crates*. And before the face of fome is an Afterifk, of
" others a Thunderbolt; the meaning of which marks is
" told us by *Laertius* in the life of *Plato*, viz. κεραύνιον imply-
" ing τὼ ἀγωγὴν τῆς φιλοσοφίας, and ἀςέρισκος τὴν συμφωνίαν τῶν
" δογμάτων.

" This Phyfic School at *Smyrna* was adjoining moft pro-
" bably to the temple of *Æfculapius*, the ruins of which
" are ftill extant near a large fountain of extreme cold
" water, called *Arco-bafcar*, fituate, as is mentioned by
" *Paufanias*, near the fea, (*Paufan*. l. ii. c. 26.) In this
" place was dug up about thirty years ago, and fold by Sir
" *Philip Jackfon* then refident at *Smyrna* to Monf. *Galland*,
" and by him repofited in the gallery of *Verfailles*, a fine
" buft infcribed,

" ΜΑΡΚΟΣ ΜΟΔΙΟΣ ΙΑΤΡΟΣ ΜΕΘΟΔΙΚΟΣ*.
" The word Μεθόδικος intimating the fect of *Modius*, as
" ἰήτηρ Μεθόδα does the like in another printed infcription.

* There is a buft of him at *Wilton* with the fame infcription on the pedeftal, and on
the breaft thefe lines in capitals: (engraved for Dr. *Stukeley's* Itinerary, vol. II. pl. 103.)
ΙΗΤΗΡ ΜΕΘΟΔΟΥ ΑΣΙΑΤΙΚΗ ΠΡΟΣΤΑΤΑ ΧΑΙΡΕ.
ΠΟΛΛΑ ΜΕΝ ΕΣΘΛΑ ΠΑΘΩΝ ΦΡΕΣΙ ΠΟΛΛΑ ΔΕ ΛΥΓΡΑ.

" What

" What it was is explained by *Celfus*, l. i. c. 1. *Harum*
" *obfervationum medicinam effe* ..... *quam* μέθοδον *Græci*
" *nominant*, &c. Among the Δειπνοσοφιςαὶ of *Athenæus*, *in*
" *argumento operis*, are regiftered with great honour the
" characters of *Daphnus* of *Ephefus*, as well as the renown-
" ed *Galen*, ἱερὸς τὼ τέχνην, κ. λ.

" XII. Another infcription found in the fame place and
" engraven under a head, now loft, is as follows:

" ΗΕΡΜΟΓΕΝΗΣ ΧΑΡΙΔΗΜΟΥ κ. τ. λ."

II.

" Honoured Sir,   *Nov.* 13, 1723.

" I am heartily glad to underftand that we are like to
" have the happinefs of feeing your oration public. The
" medals are not yet in books. Some have taken them to
" be fo many magiftrates of *Smyrna*; but that they are Philo-
" fophers and Phyficians, is luckily a difcovery of my own.
" I hit upon the thought by obferving, that Phyficians are
" often cited with the addition of Ἡροφίλειος and Ἐρασιςράτειος,
" as by *Erotian in voce* Ἄμεην. Στράτων μὲν ὁ Ἐρασιςράτειος, Ζήνων
" δ᾽ ὁ Ἡροφίλειος. After this that there was a fchool of each
" according to *Strabo*, l. xii. Διδασκαλεῖον Ἡροφίλειοι ἰατρῶν μέγα
" ὑπὸ Ξεύξιδος καθάπερ ..... ἐν Σμύρνῃ τὸ τῶν Ἐρασιςρατείων ὑπὸ
" Ἰκεσίυ. Upon this foundation we are at no lofs for the
" explication of the following medals:

1. " *Caput laureatum fine epigraphe.*
" Rev. ΣΜΥΡΝΑΙΩΝ ΞΕΥΞΙΣ: *figura virilis fedens, ma-*
" *nu dextra ad os levata: ante faciem* κεραύνιον *nota in-*
" *ftitutionis philofophiæ.*

2. " *Caput laureatum fine epigraphe.*
" Rev. ΣΜΥΡΝΑΙΩΝ ΙΚΕΣΙΟΣ: *figura eadem.   Vide*
" *Numifmata Kempiana*, p. 82.

G 2   3. " *Caput*

3. " *Caput laureatum sine epigraphe.*
   " Rev. ΣΜΥΡΝΑΙΩΝ ΕΥΚΛΗΣ : *fig. eadem*; *ante faciem*
   " ἀϛερίσκος *nota* συμφονίας τῶν δογμάτων, *cum monogram-*
   " *mate urbis Smyrnæ**.

4. " *Caput laureatum sine epigraphe.*
   " Rev. ΣΜΥΡΝΑΙΩΝ ΠΑΣΙΚΡΑΤΗΣ : *fig. eadem cum du-*
   " *plici monogrammate*, *Smyrna urbis et sectæ Herophi-*
   " *leæ uno, ac sectæ Erasistrateæ altero, i. e.* ΕΡΑ.

" *Horum* Ξεῦξις *cum tota ipsius schola*; *i. e.* τοῖς περὶ τὸν Ξεῦξιν
" *laudatur ab Erotiano in voce* Καμμάρω. *Hicesius a Plinio*,
" l. xxvii. c. 4. *ut non parvæ auctoritatis medicus. Pasi-*
" *crates Menodoro adjungitur in inscriptione Dousaná. Meno-*
" *dorus vero Hicesio apud Athenæum*, I. iii. c. 9. Μηνοδῶρος ὁ
" Ἐρασιϛράτειος Ἰκεσίᾳ φίλος.

" Of these medals the first, third, and fourth, are now
" before me, with about twenty others of the same type
" and character. Being mistaken for unknown magistrates,
" they were esteemed the refuse of Dr. *Sherard's* medals.
" However many of a fairer stamp and better preserved were
" by him reposited in the cabinet of his Grace the Duke of
" *Devonshire*; particularly an Ἰκέσιος, and, if I mistake not,
" an Ἀλέξανδρος, being the other master mentioned by *Strabo*.
" I hope to be introduced by Dr. *Sherard* to the favour of
" consulting them in his Grace's rich collection. In the
" mean time these, Sir, with myself, are absolutely yours;
" and being obliged to be in town for waiting at Court on
" *Friday*, I will attend you with them at your house at
" what time you please to command me, by a line directed
" to, &c.   E. Chishull."

---

* This coin is not mentioned in Dr. *Mead's* Dissertation. Lord *Winchelsea* shewed
the Society of Antiquaries, 1723, a coin of *Smyrna*, with the same types as above-mentioned, and ΣΜΥΡΝΑΙΩΝ ΠΑΤΟΥΡΙΟΣ.

In

In 1724 Mr. *Bowyer* printed for Dr. *John Freind*, the physician, an Index to *Aretæus*; and for his brother Dr. *Robert Freind*, the master of *Westminster* school, a translation of *Cicero*'s Orator*.

In *January* 1724-5, Mr. *James Bonwicke*, Mr. *Bowyer*'s worthy schoolmaster, knowing his integrity and friendship, appointed him executor to his will, and bequeathed to him a small cabinet of medals†. The same cabinet, somewhat augmented, Mr. *Bowyer* afterwards left to a friend for whom he had the sincerest regard.

Of the publications from his press in 1725, it may be proper to mention the second volume of "*Breval*'s Travels," (of which he had printed the first volume in 1723) folio‡; and the "Histoire de la Peinture Ancienne extraite de l'Hist. "Naturelle de *Pline*, liv. XXV. avec le Texte *Latin*, corrigé "sur les MSS. de *Vossius* & sur la 1 ed. de *Venise*, & éclairci "par des Remarques nouvelles||," in folio, an anonymous publication of M. *Durand*; and an excellent edition of *Anacreon***, in 4to. to which the following memorandum is

---

* See some particulars of these learned brothers under the year 1761.

† "I leave my cabinet of medals to my dear friend Mr. *William Bowyer* Junior."—
Mr. *J. Bonwicke*'s Will.

"I give to Dr. *William Heberden* my little cabinet of coins."—Mr. *Bowyer*'s Will.

‡ Both volumes were reprinted for Mr. *Lintot* in 1728.

|| " A whole translation of such a valuable work as the Natural History of *Pliny*, at-" tended with such Remarks, would be a very useful performance, and very acceptable " to the publick." *New Memoirs of Literature*, 1725, vol. II. p. 252; where see a full and particular account of this entertaining book.

** "We are indebted to Mr. *Maittaire* for this beautiful edition of *Anacreon*. He gives us the *Greek* text such as it was printed in 4to. by *Henry Stephens*. He has translated LXI Odes into *Latin* verse: as for the other odes, fragments, and epigrams, they are translated into prose according to the best interpreters. Perhaps it were to be wished that Mr. *Maittaire* had been contented to publish a translation in prose of all the Odes of *Anacreon*. He has added his own notes, and short remarks taken from *Henry Stephens*, Mr. *De Longepierre*, Madam *Dacier*, *Tanaquill Faber*, Mr. *De la Fosse*, Mr. *Desmarais*, Mr. *Barnes*, and Mr. *Baxter*. Next to those notes, the readers will find an index of all the words of *Anacreon*, interspersed with many passages out of antient authors, which may give some light to the text of that

is fubjoined by Mr. *Maittaire* :—" Hujus editionis *Anacreon-*
" *ticæ* centum fola excufa funt exemplaria ; in quibus om-
" nibus errata graviora meâ ipfe manu expungi : reliquis
" veniam ut indulgeat, lector benevolus oratur*."

Amongft other capital works which received the benefit
of Mr. *Bowyer's* correction at this period, was the complete
edition of † *Selden,* in three volumes folio. This edition

was

that poet ; and then an account of the life, writings, ftyle, dialect, and metres of
Anacreon ; with a collection of epigrams upon *Anacreon*, and a catalogue of the
editions of his works confulted by Mr. *Maittaire*, and of the authors quoted by
him. Many curious perfons will be forry to hear that Mr. *Maittaire* has only publifhed a hundred copies of this valuable edition. He has taken no notice of fome emendations of Dr. *Bentley* upon the XIIIth ode of *Anacreon*. They were printed at *Rotterdam* in 1712, in a tranflation of *Anacreon's* odes into *French* verfe, and are alfo to be
found in the former " Memoirs of Literature," vol. IV. p. 286. *New Memoirs of Literature,* 1725, p. 253.

* Of this fmall impreffion 93 copies were difpofed of to fubfcribers, of whom a lift is
printed, with this infcription, " Horum Fautorum fubfidiis & fumptibus procurata eft
" hæc *Anacreontis* editio : quam ipfis igitur folis propriam dicavi ; qualecunque grati
" erga tam generofos meorum in re philologicâ conatuum adjutores animi monumen-
" tum." To this volume is annexed a colophon : " Huic editioni finis impofuit *Guli-*
" *elmus Bowyer* Typographus in vico vulgò vocato **White Fryars**, *Londini*, Anno Do-
" mini millefimo feptingentifimo vicefimo quinto ; undecimo kalendas Quintiles."

† *John Selden,* the famous Antiquary, was defcended from a good family, and born
Dec. 16, 1584, at *Salvinton* in *Suffex* ; educated at *Chichefter* free-fchool, and admitted
of *Hart-Hall, Oxon.* in 1598 ; removed to *Clifford's Inn* in 1602, to ftudy the law ; admitted of the *Inner Temple* in *May* 1604 ; and drew up a Treatife of the Civil Government of this Ifland in 1606. His firft friendfhips were with Sir *Robert Cotton,* Sir *Henry
Spelman, Camden,* and *Ufher,* all of them learned in antiquities ; which was alfo Mr.
Selden's favorite object. In 1610, he began to diftinguifh himfelf by publications in this
way, and put out two pieces that year ; Jani *Anglorum* facies altera ; and Duello, or the
Original of fingle Combat. In 1612 he publifhed notes and illuftrations on the firft
eighteen fongs in *Michael Drayton's Poly-Olbion,* and the year after wrote verfes in
Greek, Latin, and *Englifh,* upon *Browne's Britannia's* Paftorals ; which, with divers
poems prefixed to the works of other authors, occafioned Sir *John Suckling* to give him
a place in his Seffion of the Poets. Purfuing fuch ftudies, he foon acquired fuperior
eminence. Mr. *Selden,* though not above three and thirty years of age, had fhewn
himfelf a great philologift, antiquary, herald, and linguift ; and his name was fo wonderfully advanced, not only at home, but in foreign countries, that he was actually
then become, what he was afterwards ufually ftyled, the great dictator of learning to
the *Englifh* nation. In 1618, when he was in his 34th year, his " Hiftory of Tithes"
was printed in 4to. in the preface to which he reproaches the clergy with ignorance and
lazinefs, with having nothing to keep up their credit, but beard, title, and habit, their
ftudies not reaching farther than the breviary, the poftils, and polyanthea ; in the work
itfelf he endeavours to fhew, that tithes are not due under chriftianity by divine right,

though

was begun in 1722, and finished in 1726, very highly to though he allows the clergy's title to them by the laws of the land. This book alarming the clergy, and offending king *James* I; it was suppressed, and the author forced to make public submission. He again offended that monarch in 1621 by an opinion he gave against the crown as counsel in the house of lords, and was committed into the custody of the sheriff of *London*; but was released in five weeks by the favour of the lord keeper *Williams*. He was chosen member for *Lancaster* that year; but neglected all public business to apply himself to study. In 1624 he was appointed by the *Inner Temple* reader at *Lyon's Inn*, but refused to accept that office. In 1625 he was chosen burgess for *Great Bedwin, Wiltshire*, and again in 1626, when he was an active manager against the duke of *Buckingham*. In 1627, he was counsel for Mr. *Hampden*, and in the third parliament of king *James* was again elected for *Lancaster*, and had a considerable hand in the Petition of Rights. After the prorogation in *June*, retiring to *Wrest* in *Bedfordshire*, he finished his Commentaries on the *Arundelian* Marbles. In the next session he warmly opposed the court, and was committed to the *Tower*, and had his study sealed up, *March* 24, 1628. He was closely confined three months, but magnificently supported at the king's expence; and being afterwards allowed the use of such books as he desired, he proceeded in his studies. In Hilary Term, 1629, declining to give security for his good behaviour (as unwarrantable by law), he was committed to the *King's Bench* prison. He was released the latter end of the year, though it does not appear how; only that the parliament in 1646 ordered him 5000*l.* for the losses he had sustained on that occasion. In 1630, he was again committed to custody, with the earls of *Bedford* and *Clare*, Sir *Robert Cotton*, and Mr. *St. John*, being accused of having dispersed a libel, intitled, " A Proposition for his Majesty's service to bridle the impertinency of Parliaments;" but it was proved, that Sir *Robert Dudley*, then living in the duke of *Tuscany's* dominions, was the author. All these various imprisonments and tumults gave no interruption to his studies; but he proceeded, in his old way, to write and publish books. In 1640 he was chosen member of parliament for the university of *Oxford*; and though he was against the court, yet in 1642 the king had thoughts of taking the seal from the lord keeper *Littleton*, and giving it to him. In 1643, he was appointed one of the lay-members to sit in the assembly of divines at *Westminster*, in which he frequently perplexed those divines with his vast learning. About this time, he took the covenant; and the same year, 1643, was by the parliament appointed keeper of the records in *The Tower*. In 1644, he was elected one of the twelve commissioners of the Admiralty; and the same year was nominated to the mastership of *Trinity College* in *Cambridge*, which he did not think proper to accept. In the beginning of 1653, his health began to decline; and he died the 30th of *November* that year at the *Friary House* in *White-Friars*, where he had resided for some years, being possessed of it in the right of *Elizabeth* countess dowager of *Kent*, who had appointed him executor of her will, having before, from the first of her widowhood, committed the management of her affairs to him. He was buried in the *Temple* church, where a monument was erected to him; and archbishop *Usher* preached his funeral sermon. He left a most valuable and curious library to his executors, *Matthew Hale, John Vaughan*, and *Rowland Jewks*, esqrs; which they generously would have bestowed on the society of the *Inner Temple*, if a proper place had been provided to receive it; but, this being neglected, they gave it to the university of *Oxford*. Mr. *Selden* was immensely learned, and skilled in *Hebrew* and oriental languages beyond any man: *Grotius* styles him " the glory of the *English* nation." He was knowing in all laws, human and divine, yet did not greatly trouble himself with the practice of law: he seldom or never appeared at the bar, but sometimes gave council in his chamber. A chronological list of his writings, as published by Dr. *Wilkins*, is printed in Mr. *Bowyer's* Miscellaneous Tracts, p. 39.

the

the credit of Dr. *Wilkins** the laborious editor; and Mr.
Bowyer's

* *David Wilkins*, F.S.A. by birth a *German Swiss*, was appointed keeper of the archiepiscopal library at *Lambeth* by Archbishop *Wake*, and drew up a very curious catalogue
of all the MSS, and printed books in that valuable library in his time, which remains
there to this day. As a reward for his industry and learning, Archbishop *Wake* gave him
the following preferments. He was collated to the rectory of *Mongham Parva*, *April*
30, 1716.; and to that of *Great Chart*, *Aug.* 20, 1719, being then S.T.P.; to the
rectory of *Hadleigh*, *Nov.* 17, 1719; constituted chaplain to his Grace, *Nov.* 24, 1719;
collated to the rectory of *Monks Eleigh*, *Nov.* 25, 1719; appointed his Grace's Commissary of the deanry of *Bocking*, jointly and severally with *W. Beauvoir*; rector of
Bocking, *Nov.* 25, 1719; collated to a prebend of *Canterbury*, *Dec.* 27, 1720; presented to his Grace's option of the archdeaconry of *Suffolk*, *May* 16, 1724. He published, 1. "Novum Testamentum *Copticum*, *Oxon.* 1716," 4to. 2. A fine edition of
"Leges *Anglo-Saxonicæ* † ecclesiasticæ & civiles; accedunt Leges *Edvardi Latinæ*,
"Gulielmi

† This was the completion of the plan mentioned above, p. 11: "Hoc *Gulielmus Elstob*, in literis
"*Anglo-Saxonicis* versatissimus, præstare instituerat. Hinc *Wheloci* vestigia premens Leges, quas
"editio ejus exhibit, cum MSS. *Cantabrigiensibus*, *Bodleiano*, *Roffensi*, & *Cottonianis* contulerat, ver-
"sioneque nova adornare proposuerat, ut sic Leges antea jam publici juris factæ, ejus opera & studio
"emendatiores prodiissent. Verum morte immatura præreptus, propositum exequi non potuit."
Wilkins, Preface.—I shall add to this account an extract from an undated letter of Dr. *Hickes*, recommending this ingenious *Saxonist* to Mr. *Harley*: "You may be sure the person who wrote the in-
"closed is at a great loss for friends, when he made application to me, who have no friend and patron
"but yourself to whom I can speak for myself or others. It is in confidence that I may still take
"my usual liberty of addressing you, that I now appear in behalf of Mr. *Elstob*, whose modesty hath
"made him an obscure person, and ever will make him so unless some kind patron of good learning
"will bring him into light. He is rector of *St. Swithin's* church by *London Stone*, and hath set him-
"self to give the world a new edition of the *Saxon* Laws, towards which he hath made a considerable
"collection, which you may see at any time when you are pleased to have an account of his whole
"design. I doubt not but that my Lord Keeper hath a domestic chaplain of his own, to whom he will
"think fit to give the preferment mentioned in the inclosed; but however, if you think fit to make his
"name known to his lordship, and his learned design relating to the Laws, it might be of use to him
"against another time. He is a man of good learning, and very great diligence and application, and
"equal to the work he is upon; and the least countenance and encouragement from so great a judge
"and patron of learning as you, would make him proceed in it with all chearfulness, as once it did
"animate me in another undertaking. I am sure he would be confounded if he knew I had commu-
"nicated his letter to you, which is written *à la negligence*, as well as in confidence to a friend. G. H."
The munificent patron of literature encouraged this design; and, *April* 11, 1711, we find Mr. *Elstob*
thus acknowledging his obligations: " I am deeply sensible of the great honour you are pleased to do
"me, in permitting me the use of Judge *Hale's* History and Analysis of the Common Law of *England*.
"I think myself obliged inviolably to observe the conditions enjoined, of not making a transcript, to
"which I shall adhere with all fidelity and thankfulness. I hope this will find your Honour confirmed
"in that state of health, which all who love their country, and understand the interest of it, must
"needs think necessary for the public good. As no private person could be more sensible of the shock
"which the whole nation received in the hazard of your person, so no one can have a more hearty sa-
"tisfaction in the good progress of your recovery, and the increase of your power and glory! My sister
"desires she may have the happiness of acknowledging with me the great and undeserved services with
"which you have made her your debtor, as also your Honour's most obedient and devoted humble
"servant, W. E."—"The book shall be returned with all possible speed. If your Honour will
"be pleased by Mr. *Wanley* to limit the time, I shall be glad to be confined, that I may not transgress."
These letters are copied from the originals in the *Harleian* MSS. No. 7524; where are likewise
three letters from Mrs. *Elstob* to the Lord Treasurer, by which it appears that he solicited and obtained for her the Queen's bounty towards printing the *Saxon* Homilies; and Mr. *Bowyer* in 1713
printed for Mrs. *Elstob* "Some Testimonies of learned men in favour of the intended Edition of the
"*Saxon* Homilies, concerning the learning of the Author of those Homilies, and the advantages to
"be hoped for from an Edition of them. In a letter from the Publisher to a Doctor in Divinity."

Mrs.

Bowyer's great attention to it appeared in his drawing up the Epitome of the treatise "De Synedriis," and the several memorandams from "The Privileges of the Baronage," and "Judicature in Parliament," &c. which are printed at the beginning of his "Miscellaneous Tracts."

In 1726, the learned world was indebted to him for a "View of a Book, entitled, *Reliquiæ Baxterianæ.* In a Letter to a Friend;" a single sheet, 8vo; an admirable sketch of the learned *William Baxter's* * Glossary of *Roman*

" *Gulielmi* Conquestoris *Gallo-Normannicæ,* & *Henrici* I. *Latinæ*; subjungitur Do-
" mini *Henr. Spelmanni* Codex Legum Veterum Statutorum Regni *Angliæ,* quæ ab in-
" gressu *Gulielmi* I. usque ad annum nonum *Henr.* III. edita sunt. Toti operi præ-
" mittitur Dissertatio Epistolaris admodum Rev. Domini *Guilielmi Nicolsoni* Episcopi
" *Derrensis* de jure feudali veterum *Saxonum.* Cum Codd. MSS. contulit, notas, ver-
" sionem & glossarium adjecit *David Wilkins,* S. T. P. Canonicus *Cantuariensis,* Reve-
" rendissimo in Christo Patri ac Domino Domino *Gulielmo* Divina Providentia Archie-
" piscopo *Cantuariensi,* &c. &c. a sacris domesticis & Biblioth. *Lond.* 1721," folio.
3. *Jo. Selden's* Works, folio, 1726. 4. "Peutateuchus *Copticus,*" *London,* 1731, 4to.
5. "Concilia *Magnæ Britanniæ,*" &c. 4 vols. folio, 1736. He died *Aug.* 6, 1740, aged
62. For these particulars I am indebted to the kind communication of Dr. *Ducarel.*
—Dr. *Wilkins's* "Præfatio Historiam literariam *Britannorum* ante *Cæsaris* adventum,
" Bibliothecæ hujus Schema, *Bostonum Buriensem,* aliaque scitu non indigna complectens,"
was prefixed to Bishop *Tanner's* Bibliotheca *Britannico-Hibernica,* 1748.

* This eminent grammarian and writer was born in 1650, at *Llanlugan* in the diocese of *St. Asaph,* and county of *Salop.* His education was much neglected in his younger years, for at the age of eighteen, when he went to the school at *Harrow on the Hill,* in *Middlesex,* he knew not one letter in a book, nor understood one word of any language but *Welsh :* but he soon retrieved his lost time, and became a man of great learning. He applied chiefly to the study of antiquities and philology, in which he composed several books. In 1679, he

Mrs. *Elstob* is described by Mr. *Rowe Mores,* Diss. on Letter-founders, p. 28, as "the *indefessa comes*
" of her brother's studies, a female student in the university." She was " a Northern lady of an an-
" tient family and a genteel fortune ; but she pursued too much the drug called learning, and in that
" pursuit failed of being careful of an one thing necessary. In her latter years she was tutoress in the
" family of the duke of *Portland,* where we have visited her in her sleeping-room at *Bulstrode,* sur-
" rounded with books and dirtiness, the usual appendages of folk of learning. But if any one desires
" to see her as she was when she was, the favourite of Dr. *Hudson* and the *Oxonians,* they may view
" her portraiture in the initial G of *The English Saxon homily on the birth-day of St. Gregory :* the
" countenance of St. *Gregory* in the *Saxon* Ᵹ is taken from Mr. *Thwaites,* and both were engraved by
" *Gribelin,* though *Mich. Burghers* was at that time engraver to the University." Of *Burghers,* Mr.
Mores says, " He lived in a tenement belonging to *The Queen's College,* and called *Shoppa sexta,* which
" with the rest of the *shoppæ* in number ten is now taken into the scite of the college, the front wall
" of which stands upon the foundations of the *decem shoppæ.* We knew his niece *Dutch*-built and in
" mean condition ; she ironed for us—so likewise one *Fanny,* a niece of *Anth. Historiograph.* was our
" bed-maker. More we could mention contemporaries, and of the race of contemporaries, in their
" time in literary estimation ; but a concern for the literary offices to which fortune had subjected
" them imposes silence."

H   *published*

Roman Antiquities. Of this View Mr. *Clarke*, in a letter without date, fays, " Your account of *Baxter's* Glof-
" fary has pleafed the Doctor [Dr. *Wotton**] exceedingly ;
" and

publifhed a Grammar on the *Latin* tongue ; and in 1695, an edition of *Anacreon* with
notes, which was afterwards reprinted in 1710, with confiderable improvements. In 1701,
his edition of *Horace* made its appearance ¶, *Typis J. L*; and in 1719, his Dictionary of the
Britifh Antiquities † was publifhed by the Rev. Mr. *Mofes Williams*. His Gloffary, or
Dictionary of the *Roman* Antiquities, which goes no farther than the letter A, was publifhed in 1726, by Mr. *Williams* ‡, who added an Index of all the words occafionally explained in it, as he had before done in the *other* Gloffary ; and in 1731, he put out
propofals for printing his notes on *Juvenal* §. Mr. *Baxter* had alfo a fhare in the
Englifh tranflation of *Plutarch* by feveral hands. He was a great mafter of the ancient
Britifh and *Irifh* tongues ; was well fkilled in the *Latin* and *Greek* as well as the Northern
.and Eaftern languages ; and kept a correfpondence with moft of the learned men of his
time, efpecially with the famous antiquary Mr. *Edward Lhwyd*, fome of his letters
to whom are publifhed in his Gloffarium Antiquitatum Romanarum. There are
likewife in the Philofophical Tranfactions two letters of his to Dr. *Harwood*, one No.
306 concerning the town of *Veroconium* or *Wroxeter* in *Shropfhire*, and the other No.
461 concerning the hypocaufts of the ancients; and another No. 311 to Dr. *Hans Sloane*,
fecretary to the Royal Society, containing an abftract of Mr. *Lhwyd's* Archæologia *Britannica*. Mr. *Baxter* fpent moft of his life in the ufeful though irkfome employment of
teaching youth; for fome years he kept a boarding-fchool at *Tottenham High-crofs* in
Middlefex, where he remained till he was chofen mafter of the Mercers fchool in *London*.
In this fituation he continued above twenty-years, but refigned before his death, which
happened on the 31ft of *May*, 1723, in the feventy-third year of his age.

* Born *Aug.* 13, 1666. His genius for learning languages, at an age almoft incredible, was fo remarkable, as to be fet forth by his father, in a pamphlet, dedicated to
king *Charles* II. intituled, " An Effay on the Education of Children in the firft rudi-
" ments of learning; together with a narrative of what knowledge *William Wotton*,
" a child of fix years of age, hath attained unto, upon the improvement of thofe ru-

¶ The fecond edition was finifhed by him but a few days before his death, and publifhed by his
fon *John*, under this title : " *Q. Horatii Flacci* Eclogæ, una cum fcholiis perpetuis, tam veteribus
" quam novis. Adjecit etiam, ubi vifum eft, et fua, textumque ipfum plurimis locis vel corruptum,
" vel turbatum reftituit *Willielmus Baxter*, 1725, *Londini*, Typis *Gul. Bowyer*, 1725," octavo.

† Under the title of " Gloffarium Antiquitatum *Britannicarum*, five Syllabus Etymologicus Antiqui-
" tatum veteris *Britanniæ* atque *Iberniæ*, temporibus *Romanorum*. Auctore *Willielmo Baxter*, *Cor-
" navio*, Scholæ Merciariorum Præfecto. Accedunt Viri Cl. D. *Edvardi Luidii*, Cimeliarchæ *Afbmol.*
" *Oxon.* de fluviorum, montium, urbium, &c. in *Britanniá* nominibus Adverfaria Pofthuma.
" *Londini*, typis *W. Bowyer*, octavo ; dedicated to Dr. *Mead* : reprinted in 1733 ; with a new in-
fcription to Dr. *Mead*, figned " *Joannes Baxter*, Auctoris filius," and an additional leaf called
" Notæ breves, per virum reverendum *Gul. Stukeley*, R. S. S." which may be feen in Mr. *Bowyer's*
Mifcellaneous Tracts, p. 57.

‡ It was publifhed under the title of " Reliquiæ *Baxterianæ*, five *Willielmi Baxteri* Opera Pofthuma.
" Præmittitur eruditi Autoris vitæ a feipfo confcriptæ fragmentum. *Londini*, ex Officii â *G. Bowyer*,
" Sumptibus Editoris."—In 1731 this new title was printed for 50 remaining copies, " Gloffarium An-
" tiquitatum *Romanarum*, a *Willielmo Baxter*, *Cornavio*, Scholæ Merciariorum Præfecto. Accedunt
" eruditi Autoris vitæ a feipfo confcriptæ fragmentum, et felectæ quædam ejufdem Epiftolæ." *Lond.*

§ Under this title, " *Gulielmi Baxteri* quæ fuperfunt enarratio et notæ in D. *Junii Juvenalis* Saty-
" ras. Accedit Rerum et Verborum Obfervatione digniorum, quæ in iifdem occurrunt, Index locu-
" pletifli mus. Accurante *Gulielmo Mofe*, A. M. R. S. Soc."

7

" diments ;

" and it is his opinion that we fhall fee your own prefs
" produce nothing better than what you put into it.

" It

" diments; in the *Latin, Greek,* and *Hebrew* Tongues. By *Henry Wotton,* of *Corpus*
" *Chrifti College, Cambridge*; and Minifter of *Wrentham* in *Suffolk*;" re-printed in
8vo, 1752. He was admitted of *Catharine Hall, Camb idge,* under ten years old;
took the degree of B. A. in 1679; obtained afterwards a fellowfhip at *St. John's*; commenced B. D. in 1691; and was made chaplain to the earl of *Nottingham,* fecretary of
ftate; who in 1693 gave him the rectory of *Milton* in *Bucks.* The next year he publifhed
" Reflections upon Ancient and Modern Learning." A fecond edition came out in 1697,
with Dr. *Bentley's* Differtation annexed to it; on account of which, Mr. *Wotton,* although
he took no part in the controverfy, received fome very fevere treatment from Dr. *Bentley's* opponents: yet Mr. *Boyle* allows, that " he is modeft and decent, fpeaks generally
" with refpect of thofe he differs from, and with a true diftruft of his own opinions.
" His book has a vein of learning running through it, where there is no oftentation
" of it." Falling under the lafh of Dr. *Swift,* he wrote " A Defence," &c. printed
with a correct edition of the Reflections in 1705. In 1701 appeared " The Hiftory of
" *Rome,* from the Death of *Antoninus Pius,* to the death of *Severus Alexander,* by
" *W. Wotton,* B. D." 8vo. His firft publication as a Divine was a Sermon againft
Tindal's " Rights" in 1706; and in 1707 he obtained his Doctor's degree. His
next work was " Linguarum Vett. Septentrionalium Thefauri Grammatico-Critici
" & Archæologici, Auctore *Georgio Hickefio,* Confpectus Brevis per *Gul. Wotto-*
" *num,* S. T. B. Cui, ab antiquæ Literaturæ Septentrionalis Cultore, adjectæ ali-
" quot Notæ accedunt; cum Appendice ad Notas. *Londini,* Typis *Gul. Bowyer,*
" 1708," 8vo; a tranflation of which by Mr. *Shelton* will occur under the years 1735
and 1737. In 1709 he publifhed " *Bartlemy Fair,* or an Enquiry after Wit," occafioned
by Col. *Hunter's* celebrated " Letter on Enthufiafm." In 1714, the difficulties he was
under in his private fortune (for he had not a grain of œconomy) obliged him to retire
into *South Wales*; where, though he had much leifure, he had few books. Yet, being
too active in his nature to bear idlenefs, he drew up, at the requeft of *Browne Willis,*
efq. who afterwards publifhed them, the Memoirs of the Cathedral Church of *St. David's* in 1717, and of *Landaff* in 1719. Here he alfo wrote his " Mifcellaneous Dif-
" courfes relating to the Traditions and Ufages of the Scribes and Pharifees in our
" bleffed Saviour *Jefus Chrift's* time *; *London,* printed by *W. Bowyer,* 1718," 2 vols.
8vo. and in 1719 he publifhed a Sermon on *Mark* xiii. 32, to prove the divinity of the
Son of God from his omnifcience. Here alfo he acquired fuch fkill in the *Welfh* language, as enabled him to undertake the publication of the " Laws of *Hoel Dha*;"
which he did not live to finifh, dying *Feb.* 13, 1726-7, at *Buxted* in *Suffex.* He preached and printed a *Welfh* Sermon in 1722, being perhaps the firft *Englifhman* who ever
attempted to preach in that language; and, *May* 10, 1723, drew up an account of Mr.
R. Gale's " Regiftrum Honoris de *Richmond,*" and alfo of the " Record of *Caernarvon,*"
a MS. in the *Harleian Library,* which were printed in the Bibliotheca Literaria, p. 17.

---

* The firft of thefe volumes contains, 1. " A Difcourfe of the Nature, Authority, and Ufefulnefs
" of the *Mifna.*" 2. " Table and Contents of all the Titles of the *Mifna.*" 3. " A Difcourfe of the
" Recital of the *Shema, Phylacteries,* and *Schedules of Gates* and *Door-Pofts.*" 4. " Texts relating to
" the religious Obfervation of one Day in Seven. With Annotations." The fecond contains " *Shab-*
" *bath*; a Title of the *Mifna* concerning the *Sabbath. Eruvin*; a Title of the *Mifna,* concerning
" the Mixtures practifed by the *Jews* in *Jefus Chrift's* time, to ftrengthen the Obfervation of the *Sab-*
" *bath.* In *Hebrew* and *Englifh.* With Annotations."

٢٣.

" It is exactly to his taſte; and books which have
" the greateſt variety of matter, require the greateſt judg-
" ement to give a proper view of them. After his opi-
" nion, you need not aſk, nor can I think it worth the
" while to mention, my own : this is the firſt view which
" you have given the publick of yourſelf; the only fault I
" find with it is, that it is not ſo large as the life; the
" more we ſee of it, the better we ſhall like it." Very few
copies were printed, and thoſe having been given as preſents, it is ſeldom found with the Gloſſary. It is preſerved
with additions among Mr. *Bowyer's* Miſcellaneous Tracts.

In this year he printed the ſecond volume of *Tillotſon's*
Sermons, folio (in 1728 a ſecond edition of them, and a
third volume in 1734); the firſt *Engliſh* edition of *Gulliver's*
Travels, 8vo : and in 1727 a volume of Mr. *Locke's* works;
Vertot's Hiſtory of the Knights of *Malta*, two volumes,
folio; the Rev. *John Lindſay's* tranſlation of " *Maſon's* Vin-
" dication of the Church of *England*," folio; the " Comi-
" tia *Weſtmonaſterienſia*," 8vo; and the ſecond edition of
Mr. *Collier's* " Supplement, or vol. III. to the great Hiſto-
" rical, Genealogical, and Poetical Dictionary," (to which
he had printed an " Appendix," or vol. IV. in 1721,) all

28. " A Diſcourſe concerning the Confuſion of Languages at *Babel*, &c. by the late
" learned *William Wotton*, D. D." was publiſhed in 1730; and his " Thoughts con-
" cerning a proper method of ſtudying Divinity," with a Preface by Dr. *Gally*, in 1730,
and 1734. He was likewiſe the author of five anonymous pamphlets : 1. " A Letter to
" *Euſebia*. 1707." 2. " The caſe of the preſent convocation conſidered. 1711."
3. " Reflections on the preſent poſture of affairs. 1712." 4. " Obſervations on the
" ſtate of the nation. 1713." 5. " A Vindication of the earl of *Nottingham*. 1714."
What diſtinguiſhed Dr. *Wotton* from other men was chiefly his memory : his ſuperiority
ſeems to have lain in the ſtrength of that faculty: for, by never forgetting any thing,
he became immenſely learned and knowing; and what is more, his learning (as one expreſſes it) was all in ready caſh, which he was able to produce at ſight. He lived at a
ſeaſon when a man of his learning would have been better preferred than he was : but it
is ſuppoſed that his behaviour and conduct, which were very exceptionable, particularly
with regard to the fair ſex, prevented it.

in

in folio; Mr. *Browne Willis's* " Survey of the Cathedrals of
" *York, Durham, Carlisle, Chester, Man, Litchfield, Hereford,*
" *Worcester, Gloucester,* and *Bristol,*" 4to; and twenty copies
of a Catalogue of the late Duke of *Kingston's* Library*, 77
sheets, folio..

On the 20th of *December* 1727, he lost an affectionate
mother; and received on that occasion the following consolatory letter from Mr. *Chishull*:

" S I R,   *Christmas-day,* 1727.

" I would not trouble you with any business of mine
" yesterday, having too great a fellow-feeling of your case,
" and knowing how heavily you must then go, as *one that*
" *mourneth for his mother.* It is now your turn, as it once
" was mine, to experience the divine rhetorick of that ex-
" pression, in the fewest and lowest words, the fullest and
" highest that can be made : but withal, *sunt verba &*
" *voces quibus hunc lenire dolorem—possis*; I mean that ir-
" resistible consolation of St. *Paul,* 1 *Thess.* iv. 13, 14.

" I doubt not but this, and many like Christian com-
" forts, occur of themselves to you, with all the advan-
" tage of reflection. Providence, when I was under the
" same disconsolate circumstances, the very day after I
" received the afflicting news, led me to *Westminster Abbey,*
" and there first fed, and then alleviated my sorrow, by a
" *Greek* inscription :

Μνημονεύων τῆς σῆς ἀγαθότη]Θ-, &c.
Αἰάζω σε καλλίςη, καὶ λυπῦμαι σφόδρα.
Ἀλλ' ἐκ ὡς ἀγνοῶν, &c.
Τὴν γὰρ ἀνάςασιν νεκρῶν
Πιςεύω βεβαιῶς, καὶ προσδοκῶ.

* This has *no title*, and is adorned with views of his Grace's house.

                                              " The

" The melancholy occaſion will, I hope, be ſo far from
" hindering, that it will rather incline you to retire hither,
" and to fly a little from the place, though you cannot fly
" from the time of mourning. If he could find it conve-
" nient, I ſhould be very glad to ſee your father with you;
" and, in the mean time, with my hearty prayers for the
" conſolation of both him and you, I remain your aſſured
" friend and humble ſervant,   EDM. CHISHULL."

The principal works printed by Mr. *Bowyer* in 1728,
were *Maittaire's* edition of the " Marmora *Oxonienſia*;" *Bacon's* Works; Biſhop *Kennet's** Regiſter and Chronicle, Eccleſiaſtical and Civil, &c.; a ſecond edition of the " Comitia
" *Weſtmonaſterienſia*;" and the ninth, fifteenth, and ſix-
teenth, volumes of *Rymer's*† Fœdera; all in folio; with
Markland's

---

*. Dr. *White Kennet*, born at *Dover*, *Aug.* 10, 1660, was entered at *Edmund Hall*,
Oxford, in *June* 1678; M. A. 1683; B. D. 1685; D. D. 1699; archdeacon of *Huntingdon*, 1701; dean of *Peterborough*, 1707; conſecrated biſhop of that dioceſe, *Nov.*
9, 1718; died *Dec.* 19, 1728. This learned Divine commenced writer in politicks ſo
early as 1680; and in 1701 engaged againſt Dr. *Atterbury* in convocation diſputes. In
1705, ſome bookſellers having undertaken to print a collection of the beſt writers of the
Engliſh hiſtory, as far as to the reign of *Charles* I. in two folio volumes, prevailed with
Dr. *Kennet* to prepare a third volume, which ſhould carry the hiſtory down to the then
preſent reign of queen *Anne*. This, being finiſhed with a particular preface, was publiſhed with the other two, under the title of, " A complete Hiſtory of *England*, &c."
in 1706. The two volumes were compiled by Mr. *Hughes*, who wrote alſo the general
preface, without any participation of Dr. *Kennet:* and, in 1719, there was publiſhed the
ſecond edition with notes, ſaid to be inſerted by Mr. *Strype*, and ſeveral alterations and
additions. Not long after this, he was appointed chaplain to her majeſty; and, by the
management of biſhop *Burnet*, preached the funeral ſermon on the death of the firſt
duke of *Devonſhire*, on the fifth of *September* 1707. This ſermon gave great offence,
and made ſome ſay, that " the preacher had built a bridge to heaven for men of wit
" and parts, but excluded the duller part of mankind from any chance of paſſing it."
Biſhop *Kennet's* death put an end to his collections for the " Regiſter and Chronicle,"
which, as far as it extends, is a work of great utility.

† Mr. *Thomas Rymer*, born in the North of *England*, was an excellent Antiquary
and Hiſtorian. On quitting the Univerſity, he became a member of *Gray's Inn*; and
ſucceeded Mr. *Shadwell* as hiſtoriographer to king *William* III. Some of his pieces relating to our Conſtitution are very good; and his valuable collection of the " Fœdera"
in 20 volumes continued from his death by Mr. *Sanderſon*, reprinted at *The Hague* 1739
in ten volumes, will be a laſting monument of his induſtry and abilities. It was abridged
by M. *Rapin* in *French* in *Le Clerc's* Bibliotheque, and a tranſlation of it by *Stephen
Whatley*,

Markland's " *Statius* ;" the *notes only* to the second volume of Dr. *Jebb's Ariflides* *, in 4to; and an edition of Mr. *Spinckes's* † " Devotions," 8vo.

Deeply as he was enamoured of Science, he was not infenfible to the power of Beauty. Very highly to his own and his father's fatisfaction, he entered into the marriage ftate, in 1728 ‡, with *Ann Prudom*, his mother's niece. His happinefs, however, with this accomplifhed woman, lafted but little more than three years. Of two fons whom he had by her, *William* (born *Oct.* 8, baptized *Oct.* 29, 1729 ‖) was buried at *Low-Leyton, Feb.* 6, 1729-30; and *Thomas* (born *Sept.* 5, baptized *Sept.* 24, 1730) furvived

Whatley, printed in 4 vols. 8vo. 1731. He wrote " The *Englifh* Monarch," an heroic tragedy, 1678; feveral poems and tranflations; and " A View of the Tragedies of the laft Age," which occafioned thofe admirable remarks preferved in the preface to Mr. *Colman's* edition of *Beaumont* and *Fletcher*, and fince by Dr. *Johnfon* in his " Life of *Dryden*," p. 316. Mr. *Rymer* died *Dec.* 14, 1713.—Some fpecimens of his poetry are preferved in the firft volume of " A Select Collection of Mifcellany Poems, 1780."

* The text was printed at *Oxford*; the firft vol. publifhed in 1722, the fecond in 1730.

† Of whom, fee the Appendix, p. 533.

‡ He was married at *St. Clement's Danes, Oct.* 9, 1728. *Parifh Register.*—The arms ufed by Mr. *Bowyer* after this marriage were Party-per-pale, Or, a bend vaire Argent and Azure, between two bars Gules, *Bowyer*—quartered with Azure, 3 Lions heads arrefted, Argent, *Prudom.*—Creft, a demy blackmoor, drawing a bow with the right arm ftretched; Dart, Or.

‖ " I am refolved to be as early in my compliments as poffible, and lofe no opportunity
" of wifhing you and Mrs. *Bowyer* joy of your fon. I am forry that I cannot furprize
" you with a vifit, as I did laft winter, and fee how the joy and gravity of the father be-
" comes you; I imagine I fhould find you at breakfaft in an elbow chair, fet out in full
" ftate with a groupe of your female acquaintance wondering and rejoicing round you,
" *Tantum te potuiffe tantulum.* I hope you will every year be more fenfible of the fa-
" vour I did you §, find new and continued bleffings, and *have your quiver full of them.*
" In a few months, when you are quite wearied with ftudy and bufinefs, you will have
" the ftories of the nurfery to divert you.—I can almoft fancy that I fee Mr. *Bowyer*
" carrying his grandfon up ftairs to you:
            " ————— Aderit querenti
        " Placidum ridens Pater, et remiffo
        " Filius arcu.
" I defire that you would make my compliments to him upon this occafion, and with
" that he may have as much comfort in his grandfon **, as he has had in the father.
" My wife too wifhes you and Mrs. *Bowyer* all the joy imaginable, and fays Mrs. *Bow-*
" *yer's* is the prettieft way of keeping wedding-days than can be ††, and admires your
" learning, that you fhould know already the proper wifhes for married women." *Mr.*
Clarke to Mr. Bowyer, Oct. 13, 1729.

§ Mr. *Bowyer* was married by Mr. *Clarke.*

** A *Spanifh* nobleman being told that he was a grand-father, faid, " There my enemy has got
" an enemy." Old people delight more in their grand-children than in their children.

†† This is explained by the *date* of the marriage.

him

him. She was far advanced in her pregnancy of a third
fon, and died almoft fuddenly, of a premature labour, on
Sunday morning *Oct.* 17, 1731, when the greater part of
the family was at church.

On the death of his wife, Mr. *Bowyer* received this very
affectionate letter from Mr. *Clarke* :

"DEAR SIR, *Buxted, Oct.* 25, 1731.

" I was very much fhocked at your melancholy letter;
" and am wholly at a lofs what to fay or think upon fo
" forrowful an occafion. The repeated afflictions which
" you have fo often had of late, in parting with perfons very
" dear to you, feem only to have been preparing the way
" for this, the greateft you can ever fuffer. Thefe are trying
" circumftances; and there is no way of finding relief, but
" by feeking it from that hand which fent them. When
" fuch inftances of fubmiffion to the Divine Will are de-
" manded of us, there is no doubt but as extraordinary
" affiftances will be ready for our fupport.

" But I can fay nothing upon this fubject that you are a
" ftranger to. I would choofe rather to give your thoughts
" another turn, and perfuade you to try how the folitude
" of the country fuits with them : here you will have
" fewer objects to keep up the impreffions of forrow, and at
" this feafon need not fear any interruptions that will oc-
" cafion you the leaft ceremony. The time of vifiting in
" the country is now over : and Mr. *Lloyd*, who is now in
" town, has a man and two horfes to come down on *Satur-*
" *day*. He is going with his fon to *Cambridge*, and lodges
" (I think) at *The Bull* in *Bifhopfgate*. If you have leifure
" enough to take fuch a ride, it will be a convenience to him.
" I cannot poffibly ftir from home, now Mr. *Canon* has the
" care of two churches : but fhould think that a little change
" of air, and the company of your more diftant friends, can-
" not be improper upon fuch an occafion. I am, dear Sir,
" moft affectionately yours, W. CLARKE."

Mr.

Mr. *Chifhull* alfo again condoled with him, in terms be-coming the man of letters, the friend, and the Chriftian :

" GOOD SIR,   *Walthamflowe, Feb.* 9, 1731-2.

" From the fhadow and vale of death, in which I have
" fat above three months, I come now, though late, yet
" moft fincerely, to condole the unfpeakable lofs that you
" fuftained, when it pleafed God to take away from you
" the delight of your eyes by a ftroke. Yet I hope you
" have not mourned, at leaft do not ftill mourn, exceffively;
" but confidered, that He who gives us all good things, re-
" ferves always his right of refumption; more efpecially
" in the cafe of matrimony, which is never contracted with-
" out the exprefs mention of being parted by death.   The
" furvivor, therefore, muft look upon his term of happi-
" nefs as expired by God's overruling providence ; yet not
" without the continuance of his favour, if we receive the
" mighty change with fubmiffion and contentment.

" It was a moving circumftance in your letter, not read
" without the tears of all our family, in that fhe defigned
" us a vifit for thofe, which proved her laft, hours; and it
" fhall ever remain upon us as a debt to her pious me-
" mory.   You, I hope, will fulfill her kind intention, by
" feeing us now as foon, and afterwards as often, as you can;
" which to my children, who all mournfully falute you, as
" well as to myfelf, will be efteemed the greateft favour.
" I am, Sir, your moft compaffionate friend and fervant,

" EDM. CHISHULL.

" My fervice waits on your good father; with wifhes
    " for his and yours and the little orphan's health,
    " this and many following new-years."

In 1729 Mr. *Bowyer* compleated Mr. *Samuel Drake's*＊ edi-tion of Archbifhop *Parker's* " Antiquitates Eeclefiæ *Britan-*

＊ Who re-publifhed in 1713 " *Balthazaris Caftilicnis* Comitis Libri IV. de Curiali five
" Aulico ex *Italico* fermone in *Latinum* converfi, Interprete *Bartholomæo Clerke.*"

I   " *nica,*"

" *nicæ*," folio, which had been nine years in the prefs*; and printed " Hiftoire Naturelle de l'Or & de l'Argent, extraite " de *Pline* le Naturalifte, par *David Durand*†," folio; Two editions (10500 copies) of *Gay's* " Polly," 4to; Mr. *Browne Willis's* " Notitia Parliamentaria," two volumes 8vo; a tranflation of " *Sophocles*," by Mr. *Adams*, two volumes 8vo; and a little collection of " Select Poems from *Ireland*," 8vo.

The fame year he ufhered into the world a curious treatife, under the title of " A Pattern for young Students in " the Univerfity, fet forth in the Life of Mr. *Ambrofe Bon-* " *wicke*, fome time Scholar of *St. John's College, Cam-* " *bridge*." This little volume was generally afcribed to our learned printer, though it was in reality the production of *Ambrofe's* father, and came into Mr. *Bowyer's* hands as executor to *James Bonwicke*. This affertion is confirmed by a letter under the author's hand, addreffed to his wife, and found unopened at his death; in which he particularly bequeathed *two guineas* to his fon, for the trouble he would have in the tafk enjoined him. But, as the Preface to this little tract is not unlikely to be Mr. *Bowyer's*, it is here tranfcribed: " I need not apologize, I hope, for communi- " cating to the publick the life of a perfon fo little known " to it. The virtues of a private life, though they appear

---

* " The Rev. Mr. *Drake*, Fellow of *St. John's* College, is reprinting Archbifhop " *Parker's* work, De Antiquitate *Britannicæ* Ecclefiæ, & Privilegiis Ecclefiæ *Cantua-* " *rienfis*, cum Archiepifcopis ejufdem LXX. The Archbifhop's own edition, publifhed " by himfelf in 1572, will be exactly followed, in which is contained not only the lives " of the Archbifhops, but alfo a catalogue of the Chancellors, Vice-Chancellors, " Proctors, and Commencers in the univerfity of *Cambridge*, from the year 1500 to 1571, " with many other matters relating to that univerfity. The copies of the Archbifhop's " edition almoft all varying from one another, the correcteft will be made the text, and " the variations of the reft will be taken notice of. To make this edition beautiful, " copper-plates will be taken by the beft hand of all the arms, frontifpieces, and other " decorations, which are found in the edition of 1572." Mr. BOWYER, *in Bibliothecâ Literariâ*, 1722, Nº I. p. 46.

† See above, p. 45; and again under the years 1740 and 1778.

" not

" not to the world with all the advantage that thofe of a
" public one do, yet are of more ufe for its imitation, and
" perhaps not lefs difficult to be attained to in a remarkable
" degree. An appearance in the heavens contrary to the
" ufual courfe of nature may ftrike us with furprize, and
" convince us of a power more than human: but fuch a
" power is not lefs fhewn in the conftant motion of the
" planets, and the filent regularity of the world. Our
" reafon may be affected as much by the one, as our ima-
" gination is by the other. Every one, from a view of fuch
" a character as *Cicero* defcribes, and is here exemplified,
" will draw the fame conclufion. Ergo, fi quis, judices,
" hoc robore animi, atque hâc indole virtutis ac continentiæ
" fuit, ut refpueret omnes voluptates, omnemque vitæ fuæ
" curfum in labore corporis atque in animi contentione con-
" ficeret; quem non quies, non remiffio, non æqualium
" ftudia, non ludi, non convivia delectarent; nihil in vitâ
" expetendum putaret nifi quod effet cum laude & cum
" dignitate conjunctum: hunc meâ fententiâ divinis qui-
" bufdam bonis inftructum atque ornatum puto. *Pro M. Cœlio.*"

The *Cambridge* Mufes were not wanting in their condolance on this promifing young man's death. Several copies
of verfes were tranfmitted to his father. One, by *Lawrence
Jackfon**, A. B. is printed, with an epitaph by the fame
writer, at the end of the Life. Another by *L. Newton*,
B. A. is here firft exhibited to the publick:

* Author of, 1. " Occafional Letters on feveral Subjects;" 2. " An Examination of a
" Book, intitied, The True Gofpel of Jefus Chrift afferted, by *Thomas Chubb*; and alfo
" of his Appendix on Providence: To which is added, A Differtation on Epifcopacy,
" fhewing in one fhort and plain view the grounds of it in Scripture and Antiquity.
" By *Lawrence Jackfon*, B. D. fometime Fellow of *Sidney College* in *Cambridge*, 1739,"
8vo; and, 3. " A Letter to a young Lady, concerning the principles and conduct of the
" Chriftian Life. By *Lawrence Jackfon*, B. D. Prebendary of *Lincoln*. Addreffed to
" the Society for propagating Chriftian Knowledge."

ODE on the Death of AMBROSE BONWICKE.

I.

Dearest of all my friends, and best of men,
Accept the offering of a grateful pen.
Somewhat extremely kind I fain would say:
But, through the tumult of my breast
With too officious love opprest,
My feeble words want strength to force their
                              way.
But why this formal speech from me?
If I am eloquent in sighs,
      It will suffice
Thee my friend, my better part;
Partner of every secret of my heart.

II.

Unhappy youth! what shall I say?
Shall I intreat relentless Fate in vain?
      Shall I complain
That thou art immaturely snatcht away?
      Alas! what have I said?
In virtue thou'rt mature, though not in age:
And blessed are the dead:
Blessed it is to quit this earthly stage.
I'm the unhappy, who remain
Fast link'd to earth with a corporeal chain.

III.

      I, who groveling lie
      In darkness and obscurity:
Whilst thou, let loose, dost roam the
      realms above,
And view'st in brightest day the wondrous
     works of Jove.   [are,
   Those things from thee no longer hidden
Which rack the brain of the Philosopher.
      Oh! what discoveries
      Make thy enlighten'd eyes!
Thou now those riddles art able to explain,
Which thou and I have found too hard for
     mortal man.
Thou now canst understand, how God
Created heaven and earth, and all things
     with a nod.

IV.

     Thou now canst understand,
How all events are rul'd by the Almighty hand.
      Thou pity'st, when I try
      To fathom deep Eternity.
     Alas! too deep the pit,
For Reason's plummet, and the line of Wit:
Too light the plummet, and too short the line,
To search into the Power and Will Divine.

V.

      Thou shalt no more
Be lost upon the boisterous seas
     Of trouble and of woe,
     Common to all below:
Thou'rt safely landed on the shore
Of everlasting happiness and ease.
     Thou with a pitying eye
      Shalt see
Thy friends wade through a vale of misery.
     Thus a happy mariner
     (The Gods have seal'd for good)
Brought safe to shore by some propitious star,
Beholds his comrades sinking in the flood.

VI.

     But art thou for ever gone?
Must thy dear flesh be eaten by the worm?
     Will neither prayers nor tears atone
      For thy return?
      And must thy head,
With arts and learning so well furnished,
     No distinction have,
     But moulder in the grave,
Together with the vile and ignominious slave?
Shall I no more converse with thee?
     Shall we no more dispute?
Shall we no more the subtle *Locke* confute
Shall I no more partake of thy philosophy?
Yes, we shall meet again, my friend,
In a far more happy state,
Where our joys shall know no end,
Where Death shall have no power to separate.
                  L. N. B. A.

Mr. *Clarke*, in a letter, dated *Aug.* 11, says, " Dr. *Har-*
" *grave** was so pleased with *your pamphlet* against the Se-

* Dr. *Horgrave* had the living of *Hoadley* in *Sussex*, just by the duke of *Newcastle's*
seat at *Halland*, whose tutor he had been at *Cambridge*. He was afterwards Dean of
Chichester.

                                    " paratists,

" paratifts, that he carried it off by force, and I muft beg
" another upon any terms." What this was, is not at prefent recollected:

Through the friendfhip of the Right Honourable *Arthur
Onflow*, he was appointed Printer of the Votes of the Houfe
of Commons in 1729; and continued in that employ *,
under three fucceffive Speakers, for almoft fifty years.

In 1730 he printed " A Chronicle of the Kings of *Eng-*
" *land* from the Time of the *Roman* Government to the
" Death of King *James* the Firft. By Sir *Richard Baker* †,
" knight; with a Continuation to the year 1660, by *E.*
" *Phillips*; whereunto is added in this edition a fecond Con-
" tinuation, containing the Reigns of King *Charles* the Se-
" cond from his Reftoration, King *James* the Second, King
" *William* the Third and Queen *Mary* the Second, Queen
" *Anne*, and King *George* the Firft, by an Impartial Hand,"
folio; a very beautiful edition of the *Coptic* Pentateuch by
Dr. *David Wilkins* ‡ (an impreffion of 200 only); Dr. *R.*
Grey's ‖ " Memoria Technica, or a new method of arti-
" ficial Memory, applied to, and exemplified in, Chronology,
" Hiftory, Geography, Aftronomy; alfo *Jewifh*, *Grecian*, and
" *Roman* Coins, Weights, and Meafures, &c. with Tables
" proper to the refpective Sciences, and memorial lines
" adapted to each Table," 8vo; a fecond collection of

---

* Soon after his appointment, it was fuggefted to Mr. *Onflow*, that there was an impro-
priety in giving the Votes to be printed by a Nonjuror § ; but the worthy Speaker
treated the hint with the contempt it deferved, and faid, he was convinced he had employed an honeft man.

† The Hon. *Daines Barrington* has obferved, that *Baker* is by no means fo contemptible a writer as he is generally fuppofed to be; and that the ridicule on this Chronicle arifes
from its being part of the furniture of Sir *Roger de Coverley's* hall in the Spectator. Obfervations on the more antient Statutes, p. 113.—Probably fome of the ridicule may have been
kept up from the manner in which it is mentioned in *Jofeph Andrews*, Book I. Ch. 3.

‡ Of whom fee an account in pp. 48. 91.

‖ Of whom fee hereafter, p. 210.

§ A Lift of all the printers in *London*, diftinguifhed by their political principles, had juft before
been publifhed. See hereafter, p. 535.

I 3 " Select

" Select Poems from *Ireland*," 8vo; and " A Letter from
" the West," 6 copies only.

A Music-speech by Mr. *John Taylor* *, his contemporary

* Born about 1703 at *Shrewsbury*, where his father was a tradesman; received the
early part of his education at the public grammar-school of that town; was admitted of
St. John's College, Cambridge, A. B. 1730, and chosen fellow. One of the earliest, if
not the first, of his publications, was " Oratio † habita coram Academia *Cantabrigiensi* in
" Templo Beatæ *Mariæ*, die solenni martyrii *Caroli* primi regis, A. D. 1730, à *Joanne*
" *Taylor*, A. M. collegii D. *Joannis* Evangelistæ socio. *Lond.* Typis *Gul. Bowyer*
" Sen. & Jun. ‡ 1730, 8vo. This was followed the same year by " The Music-speech
" at the publick commencement in *Cambridge, July* 6, 1730. To which is added,
" An Ode, designed to have been set to music on that occasion ||." Mr. *Taylor* was
appointed Librarian § in *March* 1732 (an office he held but a short time.**), and was
afterwards

† *Thomas Bentley*, an aukward imitator of his uncle *Richard*, attacked the *Latinity* of this oration,
criticising anonymously in a news-paper the first sentence, as an unusual construction, without two
infinitive moods after *fore*; which the Doctor vindicated in conversation, by authorities both ancient
and modern. He was abused in the same channel for saying the *Scots* sold their king; a fact well attested. Mr. BOWYER, MS.—*Thomas Bentley* published *Cicero De Finibus* in 1718, and *Cæsar's* Commentaries in 1742. He also published a *Callimachus*; and not his *truly great Uncle*, to whom it is
ascribed in the first edition of the " Biographia *Britannica*."
‡ I have found no other title-page with the names of the father and son in it.
|| Having in a former edition of these Anecdotes suggested a doubt whether this speech was actu-
ally delivered in the Senate-house, as I find that Dr. *Long's* Music-speech was printed in the same
year; I was favoured with the following anonymous information : " Your doubt concerning Dr.
" *Taylor's* Music-speech is easily cleared up : many now living heard it spoken in the Senate-house,
" on the Commencement-day; among them the writer of this, one of the Doctor's earliest friends,
" who also recollects that the delivery of the verses was universally and very justly admired ; and
" what is more of an anecdote, that they were not finished many hours before they were heard in
" publick. Dr. *Long's* Music-speech was spoken at a former publick commencement."—Dr. *Long's*,
I since find, was first published in 1714, under the title of " The Music-speech, spoken at the public
" Commencement in *Cambridge, July* 6, 1714, by *Roger Long*, M. A. Fellow of *Pembroke-Hall*."
§ " There are at present two, a principal librarian and a librarian. The fact is, there never was
but the latter till Dr. *Middleton's* time, whose friends, taking the advantage of the accession of Bishop
Moore's books, created an entire new place to give the Doctor 50l. *per annum*, and to plague Dr.
Bentley; and he took an early opportunity in a publication to style himself Protobibliothecarius; but
the place has not the least superiority over the old one. Luckily this sounding title did not occasion
the same animosities as that of Protovates, assumed by *Whittington*, did between him and *Herman* and
Lilly. The two librarians jointly examine every book yearly, beginning the *Monday* after the Commencement. The under librarian is always in the way at proper hours, to deliver out books to the
members of the Senate that send for them, and shew the place to strangers who give him a fee." I
owe this remark to a friend of Dr. *Taylor*; to whom I am indebted for much useful information in
the progress of this volume.
** Either whilst he was librarian, or rather before, and perhaps after, he took great pains, as did
some others, before booksellers were obliged to be called in, in classing the noble present of *George* I.
to the University, consisting of 30,000 volumes of the best books, besides MSS. formerly belonging to
Bishop *Moore*. The catalogue of the Bible class, which is so large as to form a moderate folio, is still
preserved in his neat hand-writing, and affords full proof of his industry and knowledge in that branch
of learning, in which he particularly excelled and delighted. I have often heard him say, that he
would undertake to shew the library to the best scholar in *Europe*, or a girl of six years old. Even
this dull and laborious employ furnished him with some pleasant stories ; for among his many other
good qualities, that of telling a story well was too remarkable to be entirely omitted here. He used to
say, that, throwing the books into heaps for general divisions, he saw one whose title-page mentioned
somewhat of *height*, and another of *salt* ; the first he cast among those of mensuration, the other to those
of chemistry or cookery ; that he was startled, when he came to examine them, to find that the first was
" *Longinus* de Sublimitate," and the other " A Theological Discourse on the Salt of the World, that
good Christians ought to be seasoned with." One day shewing the library to the late lord *B*. who was
recommended to him, but of whose understanding the reports were unfavourable, he began by producing

porary at *St. John's*, was printed by Mr. *Bowyer* in 1730, under

afterwards Regiſtrar. In the year 1732 appeared the Propoſals for his *Lyſias* * ; on which Mr. *Clarke* writes thus to Mr. *Bowyer* : " I am glad Mr. *Taylor* is got into your " preſs : it will make his *Lyſias* more correct. I hope you will not let him print too " great a number of copies. It will encourage a young Editor, to have his firſt attempt " riſe upon his hands. I fancy you have got him in the preſs for life, if he has any to- " lerable ſucceſs there ; he is too buſy a man to be idle." It was publiſhed, under the title of " *Lyſiæ* Orationes & Fragmenta, *Græcè* & *Latinè*. Ad fidem Codd. Manuſcrip- " torum recenſuit, Notis criticis, Interpretatione nova, cæteroque apparatu neceſſa- " rio donavit *Joannes Taylor*, A. M. Coll. D. *Joan. Cantab.* Soc. Academiæ olim a " Bibliothecis, hodie a Commentariis. Accedunt Cl. *Jer. Marklandi*, Col. D. *Pet.* Soc. " Conjecturæ †. *Londini*, ex Officinâ *Gulielmi Bowyer*, in aedibus olim Carmeliticis, " 1739." Of this work, which is now become ſcarce, no more than 300 copies were printed on demy paper, 75 on royal paper, and 25 on a fine writing royal. The Doctor always entertained a fond hope of reprinting it, like his *Demoſthenes*, with an equal quantity of notes to both pages. It was in part republiſhed at *Cambridge*, in 8vo. 1740, under the title of " *Lyſiæ Athenienſis* Orationes *Græcè* & *Latinè* ex Interpreta- " tione & cum brevibus Notis *Joannis Taylori* in uſum ſtudioſæ Juventutis." At the end of this volume were advertiſed, as juſt publiſhed, " Propoſals for printing by Sub- " ſcription, a new and correct edition of *Demoſthenes* and *Æſchines*, by *John Taylor*, " A. M. Fellow of *St. John's College*, and Regiſtrar of the Univerſity of *Cambridge*.— " N. B. On or before the twenty-fourth day of *December* next will be publiſhed (and " delivered to Subſcribers if deſired) Oratio contra *Leptinem*, which begins the third " volume of the above-mentioned work." The Dedication to Lord *Carteret*, intended for the firſt volume (which Dr. *Taylor* did not live to publiſh) is dated *Dec.* 3, 1747 ;

ducing ſuch articles as might be moſt likely to amuſe ſuch a perſon ; but, obſerving him very attentive, though ſilent, he ventured to go a little further, and at laſt, as the jewel of the whole, put *Beza's* MS. of the Goſpels into his lordſhip's hands. and began telling his ſtory ; but in the midſt of it his lordſhip broke his long ſilence, by deſiring to know whether they were then in the county of *Cambridge* or *Hertford*. The doctor added, that he ſnatched the MS. from him, and was very glad when it was in its proper place, as thinking it not unlikely but that it might have got toſſed out of the window the next minute." *From the ſame authority as the foregoing note.*

* About the ſame time came out propoſals for a new edition of *Robert Stephens's Latin* Theſaurus (which was publiſhed in four volumes folio, 1734). " If Mr. *Taylor* (ſays Mr. *Clarke*, May 5, 1733) " is the author of the propoſals for the new Theſaurus, I am truly ſorry for him. I have by accident " ſeen *The Grub*, which I don't at preſent take in, being engaged deeper in the *Dutch* Gazette and " politicks. The ambition of being in the preſs, or the little advantage that can be ſqueezed from it, " ſpoils many hopeful young fellows. He muſt now be under a neceſſity of doing ſomething hand- " ſomely to recover his credit. I reckon you have him now, a ſure preſs-man. By what *The Grub* " ſays, the propoſals are not only ill writ, but the work very ill executed." The editors were, Meſſ. *Taylor*, *Johnſon* of Magdalen, *Hutchinſon* of *Trinity*, and *Law* of *Chriſt's*. The propoſals were attacked by an anonymous writer in *The Grub-Street Journal* ; and the anonymous editors defended themſelves in *The Weekly Miſcellany*. The controverſy is preſerved among Mr. *Bowyer's* Miſcellaneous Tracts

† " *Reiſke*, when he is finding fault with the *Engliſh* editors of *Demoſthenes* in partnerſhip, ſays, that *Markland* is continually running away from his author to *St. Paul's* Epiſtles, which was owing to his being a Clergyman. Could he make this miſtake from Cl. prefixed to his name ? One cannot wonder that the ſame perſon ſhould blame in Dr. *Taylor* his frequent digreſſions to explain other authors, gems, or inſcriptions ; to us theſe form the very nectar and ambroſia of his writings. Let any body read his own edition at large of his Elements of Law, and the late abſtract of it, and then judge. I apprehend that if it had been intended to give a favourable repreſentation of the Doctor's learning, the direct contrary practice ſhould have been obſerved ; *i. e.* the digreſſions ſhould have been preſented to the reader by themſelves." *From the authority before cited.*

the

under the following title: " The Music Speech at the Public
" Com-

the third volume, 1748; and the second, 1757. Earl *Granville*, then lord *Carteret*, had before this time intrusted to his care the education of his grandsons, lord viscount *Weymouth* and Mr. *Thynne*; and, as Dr. *Taylor* informs us, at the same time laid the plan, and suggested the methods, of their education. In consequence of this nobleman's recommendation, " to lay out the rudiments of civil life, and of social duties; to inquire " into the foundations of justice and of equity; and to examine the principal obliga- " tions which arise from those several connections into which Providence has thought " proper to distribute the human species," Dr. *Taylor* was led, as he says, to " the " system of that people, who, without any invidious comparison, are allowed to have " written the best comment upon the great volume of nature." These researches after- wards produced his " Elements of the Civil Law," printed in 4to, 1755 and 1769; and this latter work, it is well known, occasioned a learned, but peevish, preface to the third volume of the " Divine Legation." In 1742 he published " Commentarius ad Legem Decemviralem " de inope debitore in partes dissecando: quem in Scholis Juridicis *Cantabrigiæ Junii* 22, " 1741, recitavit, cum pro gradu solenniter responderet, *Johannes Taylor*, LL. D. Collegii " D. *Joannis* Socius. Accedunt a viris eruditissimis confectæ, nec in lucem hactenus editæ, " Notæ ad Marmor *Bosporanum Jovi Urio* Sacrum. Dissertatio de voce *Yonane*. Ex- " plicatio Inscriptionis in antiquo marmore *Oxon*. De Historicis *Anglicanis* Commen- " tatio." 4to. In 1743, " Orationes Duæ, una *Demosthenis* contra *Midiam*, altera " *Lycurgi* contra *Leocratem*, *Græcè* & *Latinè*; recensuit, emendavit, notasque addidit " *Joannes Taylor*, LL. D. Coll. D. *Johan*. Soc." In the next year, " Marmor *Sand-* " *vicense*, cum Commentario & Notis *Joannis Taylori*, LL. D." being a Dissertation on a marble brought into *England* by lord *Sandwich* in 1739; containing a most minute account of the receipts and disbursements of the three *Athenian* magistrates deputed by that people to celebrate the feast of *Apollo* at *Delos*, in the 101st Olympiad, or 374 before *Christ*, and is the oldest inscription whose date is known for certain. A Sermon preached at *Bishop Stortford* on the anniversary school-feast, *Aug*. 22, 1749: Another before the House of Commons, on the fast-day, *Feb*. 11, 1757.—He was admitted an advocate in *Doctors Commons*, *Feb*. 15, 1741; and succeeded Dr. *Reynolds*, as Chancellor of the diocese of *Lincoln*, in *April* 1744; but did not then think proper to enter into orders *. By a letter from Mr. *Clarke* to Mr. *Bowyer*, without date, but written probably in 1742, when lord *Carteret* was secretary of state, the former says, " If he (Dr. " *Taylor*) still persists in not going into orders, though an Archbishop would persuade " him to it, it is plain he is no great friend to the Church, though, as my lord *Halifax*

* " The fact is, the Doctor intended to be a Civilian; and to enable him to keep his fellowship, without going into orders, as all are obliged to do at *St. John's*, except two Physicians and two Civi- dians, he was nominated to a faculty fellowship on the Law line: but continuing in College to su- perintend his edition of *Demosthenes*, he probably saw that, in order to make the figure he could wish in that profession, he should have devoted himself to the practice of it earlier; and the prospect of a College living becoming now near and valuable, he took orders, and the living of *Lawford* being va- cant, he claimed it: this was a new case then, and has never happened since; it was thought by many of the Society at least hard, that a person should be excused all his time from reading prayers, preach- ing, and other ecclesiastical duties in College and the University, which must be performed in person, or another paid for doing them; and then, when the reward of all this long service seems within reach, that another, who has not borne any part of the heat and burthen of the day, should step in be- fore you and carry off the prize. The Doctor was however so lucky, as he generally was, as to carry his point, but not without much difficulty. His friends indeed, who kept up the credit of the house for punning, said from the first, that the Doctor would certainly go to Law for't.' *From the same authority*.

" said

" Commencement in *Cambridge, July* 6, 1730.   To which
" is

" faid when he kept Mr. *Addifon* out of it, I believe it is the only injury he will ever
" do it.   I heartily wifh he may be more agreeably, he will fcarce be more ufefully,
" employed.   Suppofing, which I am in hopes of, from his Grace's recommendation,
" that my lord *Carteret* fhould make him one of the Under-Secretaries, what will be-
" come of all the orators of the ages paft ? Inftead of publifhing the fentiments of an-
" tient Demagogues, his whole time will be engroffed in cooking up and concealing the
" many fineffes of modern politicks.   But, however, I fhould rejoice to fee him fo
" employed, and hope there is fome prospect of it."   His preferments, after he entered
into orders, were, the Arch-deaconry of *Buckingham* ; the Rectory of *Lawford* in *Effex*,
in *April* 1751 ; the Refidentiaryfhip of *St. Paul's*, in *July* 1757, fucceeding Dr. *Terrick*,
who is faid to have been raifed to the fee of *Peterborough* exprefsly to make the vacancy* ; and the office of prolocutor to the lower houfe of convocation the fame year.
He was alfo commiffary of *Lincoln* and of *Stowe* ; was a valuable member both of
the Royal and Antiquarian Societies, his name being diftinguifhed in the publications of
each ; and was appointed Director of the latter, *April* 23, 1759, and at the next
meeting one of their Vice-prefidents.   He was efteemed one of the moft difinterefted
and amiable, as he was one of the moft learned, of his profeffion ; and died, univerfally
lamented and beloved, *April* 4, 1766.   At the time of his death, an octavo edition of
his *Demofthenes*, in two volumes, was juft finifhed at the Univerfity prefs† ; and four
fheets only of an " Appendix to *Suidas* ‡."—Some Remarks of Dr. *Taylor's* (and alfo
of Mr. *Markland's*) were inferted in Mr. *Fofter's* " Effay on Accent and Quantity, 1763."
Two *Englifh* poems, and one in *Latin*, by Dr. *Taylor*, are printed in *The Gentleman's
Magazine*, 1779, p. 149. 250. 365.   No monument has yet been erected to his memory ;
but the following infcription, by Mr. *Clarke*, was printed in 1778 :

" Plorate, Linguarum, Artium, Scientiarum,   Hic Lepos Atticus,
      Vos O doctiffimi Cultores !   Hic Dorices ψιθύρισμα,
   Quotquot huic Marmori funereo   Hic fuave Mel Ionicum.
         Aliquando accefferitis,   Scriptores Græciæ veteris et Latii numerofos,
    Defiderio quærentes lacrumabili   Jus Civile, Urbanum, Municipale,
   Quale quantumque Corpori caduco   Leges, Ritus, Ceremonias, Mores,
       Hic fit fuperftes NOMEN :   Reconditiffimæ Antiquitatis,
   Quippe hic jacet Hellas propria,   Quis illi par fic unquam expedivit ?

* " One would imagine that Dr. *Terrick*, who afterwards got *Durham*, could not have got *Peterborough*, but that Dr. *Taylor* might get the Refidentiaryfhip ; but, if *Taylor* was the only perfon to be
ferved, there was no occafion for difturbing *Terrick*, as *Taylor* would certainly have had no objection
to ftepping over his head into the Bifhopric.   Will you fay that Dr. *Terrick* would not have got *Peterborough* if there had been no fuch perfon as Dr. *Taylor* ?   I own, it was part of the arrangement.
Such language was ufed when Dr. *Law* was made bifhop of *Carlifle*, as if it was for the fake of making
Dr. *Rofs* prebend of *Durham*.—A better ftory from the Doctor himfelf.   When the Earl of *Granville*
afked the King for it, the King faid, that he had never heard of Dr. *Taylor*, and that he underftood it
was a good piece of preferment, and was ufually given to a fcholar of note.   The artful ftatefman took
the hint, and faid, the Doctor's fame for learning was celebrated all over *Germany*.   There was no
occafion to fay more."   *From the fame authority.*

† The notes only were wanting.   Thefe were afterwards added, and the book publifhed in 1769.
Without drawing an invidious comparifon between the typographical labours of the Two Univerfities,
Dr. *Taylor's* editions of the *Greek* Orators, fhould they be its laft productions (*quod avortat Deus !*), will
do immortal honour to the *Cambridge* prefs.

‡ It was thus advertifed at the end of the 8vo *Lyfias*, 1741 : " In the Univerfity Prefs, and fhortly
" will be publifhed, Appendix Notarum in *Suidæ* Lexicon, ad paginas Edit. *Cantab.* A. 1705, ad-
" commodatarum : colligente, qui & fuas etiam aliquammultas adjecit, *Joanne Taylor*, A. M.
" Coll. *Jean.* Sec."

" is added an Ode designed to have been set to musie on
" that

Te sublato! mancus, debilis semper jacet,	Hic situs est
Ille tuus Demosthenes παιάνυς,	JOHANNES TAYLORUS Salopiensis.
Imperfecta restant τὰ Æschinis σε΄ζομενα,	Ecclesiæ Lincolniensis Cancellarius,
Solus integer et superstes Lysias.	Sancti Pauli Canonicus,
Hæc solummodo qui legerit	Obiit annum agens sexagesimum tertium,
Nemo non possit non exclamare,	4° Aprilis, 1766 *."

Having shewn the preceding part of this note to the friend of Dr. *Taylor*, to whom I am already so much obliged, I was favoured with the following curious particulars : " You have mentioned that Dr. *Taylor* was too busy a man to be idle. This is too shining a particular in the Doctor's temper and abilities not to be a little more insisted upon. If you called on him in College after dinner, you were sure to find him sitting at an old oval walnut-tree table entirely covered with books, in which, as the common expression runs, he seemed to be buried : you began to make apologies for disturbing a person so well employed ; but he immediately told you to advance, taking care to disturb, as little as you could, the books on the floor ; and called out, " *John, John*, bring pipes and glasses ;" and then fell to procuring a small space for the bottle just to stand on, but which could hardly ever be done without shoving off an equal quantity of the furniture at the other end ; and he instantly appeared as chearful, good-humoured, and *degagé*, as if he had not been at all engaged or interrupted. Suppose now you had staid as long as you would, and been entertained by him most agreeably, you took your leave and got half way down the stairs ; but, recollecting somewhat, that you had more to say to him, you go in again ; the bottle and glasses were gone, the books had expanded themselves so as to re-occupy the whole table, and he was just as much buried in them as when you first broke in on him. I never knew this convenient faculty to an equal degree in any other scholar. He loved and played well at cards ; was fond of carving, which he did with much elegance ; an agreeable practice, but which, notwithstanding what Lord *Chesterfield* says, some persons who have frequented good tables all their life-time cannot do, though they can blow their nose passing well. He always appeared handsomely in full dress as a clergyman, was grand in his looks, yet affable, flowing, and polite ; latterly he grew too plump, with an appearance of doughy paleness, which occasioned uneasiness to those who loved him, whose number, I think, must be considerable. His voice to me, who know nothing of music, appeared remarkably pleasing and harmonious, whether he talked or read *English*, *Latin*, or *Greek* prose, owing to his speaking through his lips much advanced, which always produces softness : this practice, or habit, I believe, he learnt from a speaking-master, to whom he applied to correct some natural defect ; for which purpose he always kept near him an ordinary small swing-glass, the use of which was unknown to his friends ; but in preaching, which he was fond of, one might perceive a shrillness or sharpness that was not agreeable ; perhaps he could not speak so loud as was required,

* " So much praise is lavished by this panegyrist on the Doctor, that one would think that *Salmasius, Scaliger*, and *Bentley* might have been glad to have exchanged learning and fame with him : yet, if we believe *Reiske*, who has published the text of *Demosthenes* since, and had all Dr. *Taylor's* papers put into his hands, the latter knew so very little of the matter, that he could adopt only five of his emendations in so large a work. He allows him indeed a little knowledge of *Attic* law ; but that, he says, was very easy after *Petit*. &c. It would not be difficult to give *Reiske* a trimming for the fault he finds with Dr. *Taylor* for the mode of his edition. His making a parson of Mr. *Markland*, and, as such, accounting for, and excusing, his frequent remarks on St *Paul's* Epistles, have been already noticed. *Reiske* slights all, but treats *Jurin* best ; thinks he might have done somewhat well, if he had not died young ; which, it is believed, was not the case. If other people had a right to be angry or sorry, *Reiske* was the last man in the world that should have uttered a syllable ; but I have not the least desire to provoke his *manes*, or enter into a dispute with his learned relict." *From the Friend I have so often cited.*

and

"that occasion. By *John Taylor*, M. A. Fellow of *St John's*
" *College.*

and at the same time keep his lips advanced and near together, as he had learnt to do
for common conversation. He understood perfectly, as a gentleman and scholar, all that
belongs to making a book handsome, as the choice of paper, types, and the disposition of
text, version, and notes. He excelled in many small accomplishments : wrote a large, fair,
elegant hand; was a perfect master of Dr. *Byrom's* short-hand, which he looked upon as
barely short of perfection, and which he taught to as many as chose to learn, for the benefit
of his friend. He never made a blot in his writing : always, beside his *Adversaria*, kept
a proper edition of most books for entering notes in their margin, as the *Louvre Greek*
Testament in folio. These were what Dr. *Askew* was intitled to by his will, besides his
common-place books, which, I think, in his open way of writing, for he never spared
paper, amounted before he left College to forty volumes in folio ; in those he had put
down a vast variety of philological learning, without neglecting matters of pleasantry ;
and I should think it must be impossible, if one that knew his manner and short-hand
had liberty to examine them, but that they must furnish an excellent *Tayloriana*. I
don't remember that he had any ear for music ; no more had the excellent Dr. *Powell*,
late master of *St. John's*, nor the justly celebrated *Linnæus*, and a thousand others whose
organs were in other respects happily formed and arranged. He was also of remarkable
sang-froid in very trying cases. Once being got into a coach and four with some friends,
for a scheme as we call it, the gentleman driver, the late Rev. *Roger Mostyn*, who was
remarkably short-sighted, picked up the reins as he thought, but left those of the leaders
below, who being smartly whipped to make them go off at an handsome rate, soon found
that they were at liberty, and went off with a speed beyond what the rest of the party could
desire. They proposed to the Doctor to jump out, who replied with the utmost coolness, " Jump out ! why jump out ? have not I hired the coach to carry me ?" This looks
more like the language of *Jack Tar*, than of one bred in the softer shade of *Academus'*
grove, yet I have little doubt of its being literally true, as he used much the same language to
me when the fore wheel of the post-chaise came off twice in one stage. He also told me
himself, that when the last of the two earthquakes at *London* happened (I mean that at six
in the morning), he was waked by it, and said, " This is an earthquake !" turned himself,
and went to sleep instantly. Yet nothing of this appeared in his common behaviour ; but
all was soft and placid. When we used to joke with him on the badness of his furniture,
which consisted of the table aforesaid, and three or four ordinary chairs, and they always
filled with books, he used to say that his room was better and more expensively furnished
than any of ours ; which was most certainly true, as he sat in the midst of an excellent
library, containing a very fine collection of philological, classical, and juridical books,
which formed the proper furniture of a scholar's room, though I cannot say that it is the
usual or fashionable furniture of the times. This fine and large collection he increased greatly
after he got to *London*, as all those, who knew it in *Amen Corner*, will bear me witness.
This was the more necessary for him to do, as he no longer had the command of the
well-furnished libraries of *Cambridge* ; and, as it was his taste and passion to do so, he
was enabled to gratify them by his goodly income, which had he lived, would have been
very sufficient, even though it had received no further increase. His testamentary disposition of this valuable library gave me less satisfaction than any other act of his life.
The general fault consisted in not keeping them together, thereby depriving his admirers of the suite and connexion of his ideas, as he had put them down in different books,
but with references backwards and forwards. It is plain that he could not be actuated
by the low fears and policy of *Cujacius*, who, to prevent this, ordered his books to be
sold separately ; because the Doctor entrusted the compleat sett with Dr. *Askew*,

where

" *College.* *London*, printed by *William Bowyer*, Jun. some-
where any thing of this kind might be practifed with more likelihood of fuccefs and fecrecy, than if depofited in a public library, where every perfon that confulted them would
know the ufe that was made of them by others. He probably meant well, and thought
that the fureft way of keeping them together for a long time was to place them in his
learned friend's princely collection. But the futility of this provifion quickly appeared;
and it would have much the fame whether the hammer had founded over them immediately on his death, or in the very few years after* when it did. The folio *Terentianus
Maurus* †, *Mediolani* 1497, which coft the Doctor four guineas out of the *Harleian* collection, and which, I dare fay, long before he was in eafy circumftances, an hundred would not
have got from him, was purchafed for twelve guineas by Dr. *Hunter*, and is for the prefent at leaft fafely lodged in that noble repofitory of curiofities all kinds. Nor do I much
more approve of his difpofal of the other part; had he given one, two, or three fets of
the moft ufeful Claffics, with Dictionaries, &c. to the fchool, this would have remained a teftimony of his gratitude, and been very ferviceable to the mafters, fcholars,
and neighbourhood, without any prejudice to the Univerfity, which is well fupplied with
thefe writers; not fo with the many curious articles that he had picked up fingly at a
great expence from foreign parts as he could hear of them. Thefe are not likely to be
of much fervice in the country; but might probably have been looked into in the Univerfity, which alfo would have been the proper place for diftant Literati to have inquired
for them, where accefs would be remarkably eafy and agreeable. Upon this occafion one can hardly help mentioning, that when he heard of Dr. *Newcome's* death,
whom he did not love (and, as we hope his averfions were not many, they might be
the ftronger) he inquired how he had difpofed of his books; and though it was a very
good one, he received the account with an air of contempt; upon which one of the company faid, " Then, Doctor, do you now take care to do better;" upon which he funk into
ferioufnefs, and faid foftly, " I wifh I may!" He was filent in large companies, but
fond of dealing out his entertainment and inftruction before one, two, or three perfons.
He entertained his friends with an hofpitality and generofity that bordered upon munificence, and enjoyed himfelf in the convivial hours. It may be a means of prolonging
fome worthy man's days, to mention, that he fhortened his own by a modefty or fhynefs
that prevented him from making his cafe fully known, and fubmitting himfelf to the
direction of a phyfician, though he was intimately acquainted with feveral of the moft eminent in the profeffion. He one day mentioned to me with fome pevifhnefs, that he was
coftive; I afked him why he would not confult Dr. *H.* He faid, " How can I do fo? he
will not take any thing." I replied, that he would certainly give him the beft advice out
of friendfhip and regard; but that there were others to whom he might apply, who might
not have the fame delicacy. The misfortune was, that he had applied to three, and
fmuggled a receipt for a purge from each, and ufed them all alternately and almoft without intermiffion, at leaft in a manner they never intended; I think there were 175 charged in the Apothecary's bill for the laft year. This calamity had hardly happened, had he
lived in a family, I mean with friends and relations about him, and not fervants only, as
the former could never have confented to his treating himfelf in fuch a ftrange manner."

† Dr. *Askew's* magnificent library produced, at the fale by auction, about 4000l.—His Majefty was
a purchafer to the amount of about 300l.; Dr. *Hunter*, about 500l.; and M. *De Bure* (who had commiffions to the amount of 1500l.) about 500l. Some valuable articles were bought by Dr. *Maty* for
the Truftees of *The British Mufeum.* J. N.

† In this book is the following MS note: " This is judged to be the only copy of this edition in
" *England*, if not in the whole world. If fo, it is worth any money.—Dr. *Askew* could find no copy
" in his Travels over *Europe*, though he made it his earneft and particular fearch in every Library which
" he had an opportunity of confulting. JOHN TAYLOR, *Cantabrig.*" J. N.

" time-

" time Student of the fame College, 1730:" a particularity I have not obferved in any other book that he printed.

In 1731 he printed " *Humfredi Llwyd,* Armigeri, *Bri-* " *tannicæ* Defcriptionis Commentariolum: necnon de *Monâ* " Infulâ, & *Britannicâ* Arce five Armamentario *Romano* " Difceptatio Epiftolaris*. Accedunt Æræ *Cambro-Britan-* " *nicæ.* Accurante *Mofe Gulielmo,* A. M. R. S. Soc." The fame year he took part in a controverfy occafioned by " The Traditions of the Clergy deftructive of Religion; " with an Enquiry into the Grounds and Reafons of fuch " Traditions: a Sermon [on *Matth.* xv. 6.] preached at the " Vifitation held at *Wakefield* in *Yorkfhire, June* 25, 1731, " by *William Bowman,* M. A. Vicar of *Dewfbury*†." This per- formance (which was charged with containing fome of the fentiments that had been advanced by Dr. *Tindal* in his " Rights of the Chriftian Church‡," and by Mr. *Gordon* in his " Independent Whig,") excited no fmall degree of offence; and feveral anfwers were written to it, and ftric- tures made upon it, both of a ferious and ludicrous nature ‖.

* " I made my compliments to Mr. *Williams* for his prefent of *H. Lhwyd,* and took " the liberty to mention that he had left fome miftakes in his author, which he fhould " have fet right in the notes, particularly that the *Britifh church obferved Eafter in the* " *fame way as the Afiatic churches, quarta decima lunæ*; when it is very plain from *Bede* " that the difpute between the *Britains* and *Saxons* was of another kind. Mr. *Smith* " has put that beyond all controverfy." Mr. *Clarke* to Mr. *B. Dec.* 16, 1731.

† In *Yorkfhire.* Mr. *Bowman* had alfo the vicarage of *Aldborough* in that county.

‡ See a comparifon of *Bowman* and *Tindal* in " Grub-ftreet verfus *Bowman,* being a " full and proper anfwer to the vicar of *Dewfbury's* late Sermon againft the Church and " Clergy of *England.* Publifhed in the *Grub-ftreet Journals,* Nº 85 and 87; With " large Additions. 1771." Againft this charge, however, Mr. *Bowman* defends himfelf in his Preface. In thofe books, he fays, " there are many things incomparably well faid, " and much juft and demonftrative reafoning;" yet profeffes that he no otherwife made ufe of them, than as the fame thoughts naturally occurred to him, without a defign of copying. The Sermon, which he publifhed to vindicate himfelf from the cenfures and mifreprefentations of fome of its Reverend Auditors, was " the refult of an impartial en- " quiry into the nature of a Chriftian Church, which was defigned as the foundation " of a much larger work." See the Preface to the Sermon; and fee alfo " A full Juf- " tification of the Doctrines contained in Mr. *Bowman's* Sermon, &c."

‖ See Gent. Mag. I. 333. 349. 366. 408. 414. 419. 462. II. 622. 781. 960.

Mr.

Mr. *Bowyer*, upon this occasion, printed a pamphlet, called,
" The Traditions of the Clergy NOT deſtructive of Religion.
" Being Remarks on Mr. *Bowman's* Viſitation Sermon; ex-
" poſing that Gentleman's Deficiency in *Latin* and *Greek*, in
" Eccleſiaſtical Hiſtory and true Reaſoning. By a Gentleman
" of *Cambridge**.*" Mr. *Clarke*, in a letter dated *Dec.* 1731,
ſays, " I believe I never thanked you for the ſeaſonable
" correction you have given the Vicar of *Dewſbury*. It is
" neceſſary that all ſuch writers ſhould receive ſome ani-
" madverſions: though I find the man has more judge-
" ment than I at firſt imagined he could poſſibly be maſter
" of. He could not reſiſt the vanity of being an author;
" but is wiſe enough to think that there is no neceſſity of
" defending every thing that he may take a fancy to print:
" it will be impoſſible to provoke him to an anſwer. Mr.
" *Canon* † is retiring to his cloyſter to ſpend ſome few years
" more with his old *Gamaliel* Dr. *Thirlby*." In another
letter, dated *Oct.* 15, 1732, the ſame gentleman ſays,
" I am not diſpleaſed with finding that my brother *Bow-*
" *man* is like to have ſome demands upon you. His
" anſwer, which has been long threatened, will, perhaps,
" like *Thuanus* ‡, appear at laſt: and it may poſſibly give
" you the ſame ſort of employment §; you may find *ſome-*
" *thing to correct in every ſheet*. I was indeed, though a
" ſtranger to his perſon ‖, at firſt ſomething prejudiced in
" favour

---

* Reprinted in the volume of " Miſcellaneous Tracts," p. 59.

† Afterwards Dr. *Canon*, one of the chaplains to *Charles* duke of *Somerſet*. He is
often mentioned in the Memoirs of Mr. *Whiſton*.

‡ Mr. *Buckley's* propoſals for *Thuanus*, and various ſpecimens of the work, were
printed by Mr. *Bowyer* in 1729. The whole was publiſhed in 1733.

§ He was then printing ſome very difficult parts of *Thuanus*, to which Mr *Clarke* alluded.

‖ " I loſt an opportunity of ſeeing Mr. *Bowman*, by not being at *Halland* the laſt
" public day: he made there a chearful appearance in a ſmall ſynod of the neighbour-
" ing clergy, who were ſo complaiſant as not to mention one word of the miniſtry.
" The firſt account of his Sermon was from you; and you ſay you mention ſome parts
" of it, *becauſe I would not allow you that the Preſbyterian opinion was the prevailing one.*

" But

" favour of his difcretion ; that he was at leaft wife enough
" to retire from more danger ; and that I might fay of him,
" as

" But fure there is nothing in Mr. *B's* fermon in favour of their principles, any more than
" ours. They are as ftrict in their way, as we are [in ours], and as far from brother *B's*
" latitude : they would not admit of minifters without their own ordination, nor talk
" fo lightly of it. But whatever faults may be in the fermon, I fuppofe your friend Mr.
" *Auften** thinks it the very beft that ever he printed. There is nothing that diverts me fo
" much in the whole performance, as his being called an *Eraftian*; as if fo much ill
" language could arife only from an untoward difpofition in his brethren towards calling
" names; for my part, I look upon it as a compliment, which he fhould have lefs reafon
" to be offended with, becaufe he has received fo few upon this occafion. *Beza* (who
" was one of *Eraftus'* adverfaries) faid of him, that he was *In facris literis diligenter*
" *verfatus, et qui egregiam operam ad Heidelbergenfis ecclefiæ inftaurationem navavit*: I
" doubt whether Mr. *B.* will ever be fo much honoured with the applaufe either of his
" adverfaries or his friends. His (*Eraftus's*) theological works were firft printed at *London*
" by the Archbifhop's [*Whitgift's*] licence; but why, or with what defign, is a fecret that I
" cannot find out; none of our ecclefiaftical hiftorians, that I have feen, taking notice of it.
" He was a phyfician of *Heidelberg*; and in a public difputation in that city, A. D. 1568,
" oppofed Dr. *George Withers*, an *Englifhman*, in a queftion about excommunication.
" His arguments were afterwards drawn up at large; but never printed in his life-
" time; and if brother *B.* had in this refpect been an *Eraftian*, I don't think it would
" have been any injury to his character. He permitted indeed fome of his friends to
" take copies of his reafons, and fo the queftion was privately controverted between
" him and his correfpondents. He died in 1583, and fix years after his book was
" printed with this remarkable title: Explicatio graviffimæ quæftionis, utrum Excom-
" municatio, quatenus Religionem intelligentes et amplexantes a facramentorum ufu
" propter admiffum facinus arcet, mandato nitatur divino, an excogitata fit ab homi-
" nibus. *Pefclavii apud Baocium Sultacceterum*, A. 1589. This, Mr. *Selden* (to whom I owe
" this account lib. I. de Synedriis, p. 1016), fays fhould be, *Londini, apud Joannem Wol-
" fium.* The common methods of excommunication will certainly admit of very ftrong
" objections; though how far *Eraftus* carried that point, I cannot fay, having never
" feen this book; but for fome years *Eraftianifm* has been a name for an utter rejec-
" tion of all chriftian difcipline; whether juftly or not, feems a queftion which I fhould
" be glad to be informed of. The account which is given of this fect in Dictionnaire
" Royale de l'Academie is furprizing: *Eraftiens—forte d'Heretiques qui firent une*
" *faction pendant les troubles d'Angleterre, &c.* They feem willing to allow us the
" honour of being the authors of all herefy, when we are only the importers. But I
" have troubled you fufficiently with *Thomas Eraftus*, and fhould, if I had room, fay
" as much of Prolegomena ad N. T. &c. The author [*Wetftein*] is a foreigner; and a
" friend of the great *Bentley*; and in my opinion difpofes the account of his MSS.
" in a very aukward manner ‡. I am almoft tempted to think of him, what *Thirlby*

* Mr. *Stephen Auften*, the bookfeller, who publifhed Mr. *Bowman's* Sermon; which paffed through
at leaft fix editions.
† In the Hall-book of the Company of Stationers is this entry: " 10 *Junii* 1589, *John Wolf* en-
" tered for his copy a treatife of *Thomas Eraftus, De Excommunicatione*, reprinted by M. *Fortefcue*, to
" be allowed by the Archbifhop of *Canterbury*."
‡ " There is an aukwardnefs in the difpofal of the MSS. but perhaps it is owing to enumerating
them firft for the Gofpels and then for the Epiftles; and perhaps he had not feen them all, when he
wrote his firft account, which occafioned fupplemental mention. Surely now the work itfelf is publifhed, Mr. *Clarke's* opinion of *Wetftein's* abilities is hardly juft, certainly not candid." *Anonym.*

" fays

" as *Horace* does of a nation* not well acquainted with the
" art of war,

    " Laxo meditatur arcu
   " Cedere campis.

" But, if he has a mind to try his fortune once more in
" *Paul's Church-yard†*, whatever I may think of his
" courage, I shall have no great opinion of his conduct.
" As for you, I am sure it can never be your business to
" drop a controversy in which you have nothing to fear.
" Make the most of him; and, in the style of the Votes,
" *call him to order.*" This threatened answer, I believe,
never appeared ‡; but the Vicar was anonymously defended
in " A full Justification of the Doctrines contained in Mr.
" *Bowman's* Sermon, &c." probably a production of his own.
And indeed it is generally supposed, that his insignificant
work was by no means deserving the notice which was taken
of it from so many different quarters. Besides nine or ten
pamphlets, the papers of the times abound with strictures on
a performance which would of itself have " sunk into waste
paper and oblivion §." Some poetical squibs, which it gave
birth to, are preserved at the end of Mr. *Bowyer's* Remarks ||.

" says of poor *Grabe*, Neque ingenio, neque judicio, neque si verum dicere licet doc-
" trina satis ad eam rem instructus." *Mr. Clarke to Mr. B.* Sept. 22, 1731.—" *Thirlby*
" passed the same self-sufficient censures on Dr. *Bentley*, in p. 18 of his edition of *Justin*
" *Martyr*, and in his preface. He treated *Meric Casaubon* and *If. Vossius* in a manner
" not much different." *MS. Letter from Dr. Charles Ashton to Dean Moss.*

 * The *Scythians*, 3 Carm. viii. 22.

 † Mr. *Austen* lived there. See p. 71.

 ‡ In 1740, it appears that Mr. *Bowyer* printed, for Mr. *Hutton*, a pamphlet called
" A Reply to Mr. *Bowman's* Letter to the Inhabitants of *Dewsbury*."

 § The usual fate," says *Swift*, " of common answerers to books which are allowed
" to have any merit. There is indeed an exception when any great genius thinks it
" worth his while to expose a foolish piece. To answer a book effectually, requires
" more pains and skill, more wit, learning, and judgement, than were employed in
" writing it." *Apology prefixed to the Tale of a Tub.*—Nobody but *Voltaire* could reply
to dull answerers, without losing by it ; he replied to all, and succeeded wonderfully.

 || Miscellaneous Tracts, p. 76. The whole was humourously burlesqued under the
title of " Mr. *Bowman's* Sermon preached at *Wakefield* in *Yorkshire* versified, by *Chris-
" topher Crambo*, Esq. 1731."

In

In 1730 (which ſhould have been mentioned in p. 61)
he printed " *Cyfreithjeu Hywel Dda ac Eraill*, ſeu Leges
" *Wallicæ* Eccleſiaſticæ & Civiles *Hoeli* Boni & aliorum
" *Walliæ* Principum, quas ex variis Codicibus Manuſcriptis
" eruit, Interpretatione *Latina*, Notis & Gloſſario illuſtra-
" vit *Gulielmus Wotton**, S. T. P. juvante *Moſe Gulielmio†,
" A. M.

* In the account given of this learned writer, in p. 50, r. " his genius for learning
" languages, when hardly paſt infancy." His Memoirs of *St. David's*, (ſee p. 51)
are ſubſcribed " *M. N.*" the two finals of both his names; the ſignature he
alſo made uſe of in his Letter to " The Guardian," Nᵒ 93; which letter will appear to
be his, on comparing it with his " Miſcellaneous Diſcourſes," vol. I. p. 95.—In the laſt
line of p. 51, refer to " Bibl. Lit. Nᵒ VI. p. 15—28;" and in p. 52, r. " better pro-
" vided for than he was."—In memory of his wife, who died in 1719, Dr. *Wotton* compoſed the following epitaph:

H. S. E.
Anna Wottona, Gul. Hammondi
St. Albanerſis Cantiani Arm. filia,
Job. Marſhami eq. aur. et bar. magni
Antiqq. *Ægypt.* ſtatoris ex filia neptis,
Rob. Marſhami baronis de *Romney*
Conſobrina, rariſſimi exempli et
Heroici animi fæmina; quæ per
XXIII annos et in ſecundis et in
Adverſis rebus virum aſſidue comitata,
Fatali tandem et improviſo morbo
Correpta, placide in Domino requievit,

Triſte et nunquam intermoriturum
Sui deſiderium ſuis omnibus relinquens.
Ob. VIII kal. *Octob.* A. D. MDCCXIX.
Vixit ann. XLVIII. menſ. IX. dies XVIII.
Anna filia unica relicta tuperſtite.
Gul. Wottonus, S. T. P. merentiſſimæ
Et incomparabili conjugi hoc ultimum
Amoris ſui monumentum
Moerens animo
P. C.
Functa jaces hic; ſed vivis, viveſque marito,
Anna, tuo; debent nec benefacta mori.

† Mr. *Moſes Williams*** was editor of " *Baxter's* Gloſſary," (ſee p. 49, 50);
and of " *H. Llwyd's* Commentariolum," (ſee p. 69).

** Mr. *Williams's* well-ſelected library was purchaſed by *William Jones*, eſq. one of the laſt of thoſe
genuine mathematicians, admirers, and contemporaries of *Newton*, who cultivated and improved the
ſciences in the preſent century. Mr. *Jones* was a teacher of the mathematicks in *London* under the patronage of Sir *Iſaac*, and had the honour of inſtructing the late earl of *Hardwicke* in that ſcience; who
gratefully enabled him to lay aſide his profeſſion, by beſtowing on him a ſinecure place of about 200l
a year; and afterwards obtaining for him a more beneficial office in his Majeſty's Exchequer, which he
enjoyed for the laſt twenty years of his life. The lord chancellor *Macclesfield* and his ſon (who was
afterwards preſident of the Royal Society) were alſo among the number of reſpectable perſonages who
received from him the rudiments of the mathematicks. The friendſhip of Sir *Iſaac Newton* he obtained
by publiſhing, when only twenty-ſix years old, the " Synopſis Palmariorum Matheſeos," a maſterly and
perſpicuous abſtract of every thing uſeful in the ſcience of number and magnitude. Some papers of *Collins*
falling afterwards into his hands, he there found a tract of *Newton's*, which had been communicated by
Barrow to *Collins*, who had kept-up an extenſive correſpondence with the beſt Philoſophers of his age.
With the author's conſent and aſſiſtance, Mr. *Jones* uſhered this tract into the world, with three other
tracts on analytical ſubjects; and thus ſecured to his illuſtrious friend the honour of having applied the
method of *infinite ſeries* to all ſorts of curves, ſome time before *Mercator* had publiſhed his quadrature
of the *hyperbola* by a ſimilar method. Theſe admirable works, containing the ſublimeſt ſpeculations
in geometry, were very ſeaſonably brought to light in the year 1711, when the diſpute ran high between *Leibnitz* and the friends of *Newton*, concerning the invention of Fluxions; a diſpute which this
valuable publication helped to decide. Mr. *Jones* was author of " A new Epitome of the Art of Prac-
" tical Navigation;" and of ſeveral papers which appeared in the Philoſophical Tranſactions. The
plan of another work was formed by this eminent mathematician, intended to be of the ſame nature
with the *Synopſis*, but far more copious and diffuſive, and to ſerve as a general introduction to the

Sciences.

" A. M. R. S. Soc. qui & Appendicem* adjecit," folio. And in 1731, part of the eighteenth volume of " *Rymer's* " Fœdera†," folio; [" fifty-six sheets and a half, print- ed

* The preface to this work (as has been already mentioned p. 28) was written by Mr. *Clarke*, who married Dr. *Wotton*'s only daughter.

† Compiled by *Robert Sanderson*, esq. F. A. S. usher of the court of chancery, and clerk of the chapel of the rolls. He had assisted Mr. *Rymer* in publishing the former volumes of the Fœdera, which he continued after Mr. *Rymer*'s death‡ (see p. 54) be-ginning with the sixteenth volume (the title page of which expresses " Ex schedis *Thomæ* " *Rymer* potissimùm edidit *Robertus Sanderson*, 1715") and ending with the twentieth, which is dated *Aug.* 21, 1735. He died *Dec.* 25, 1741.—Mr. *Rymer*'s first warrant (signed " *Marie* R." the king being then in *Flanders*), empowering him to search the public offices for this undertaking, is dated *Aug.* 26, 1693; was renewed by King *Wil-liam*, *April* 12, 1694; and again by Queen *Anne*, *May* 3, 1707, when Mr. *Sanderson* was joined to him in the undertaking. A similar warrant was issued *Feb.* 15, 1717, with the name of " *Robert Sanderson*, esq." only in it, who published the seventeenth volume in 1717. The first impression of these seventeen volumes being all disposed of (probably to subscribers and public libraries), a new edition of them was published in 1727, ex-pressed in the title to be " Editio secunda, ad originales chartas in Turri *Londinensi* " denuo summa fide collata & emendata, studio *Georgii Holmes*;" and there is also, fronting the title, the King's licence to *Tonson*, for reprinting *Rymer*, " which book is " now printed in seventeen volumes folio, and published by *Thomas Rymer* and *Robert*

Sciences, or, which is the same thing, to the mathematical and philosophical works of *Newton*, whose name, by the consent of all *Europe*, is *not so much that of a man, as of Philosophy itself*. A work of this kind had long been a *desideratum* in literature, and it required a geometrician of the first class, to sustain the weight of so important an undertaking; for which, as M. *d'Alembert* justly observes, *the combined force of the greatest Mathematicians would not have been more than sufficient*. The inge-nious author was conscious how arduous a task he had begun; but his very numerous and respectable acquaintance, and, particularly, his intimate friend, the late earl of *Macclesfield*, to whom he left by will his invaluable library, never ceased importuning and urging him to persist, till he had finished the whole work, the result of all his knowledge and experience through a life of *near seventy years*, and a standing monument, as he had reason to hope, of his talents and industry. He had scarce sent the first sheet to the press, when a fatal illness obliged him to discontinue the impression; and a few days before his death, he intrusted the manuscript, fairly transcribed by an amanuensis, to the care of Lord *Macclesfield*, who promised to publish it, as well for the honour of the author, as for the benefit of his family, to whom the property of the book belonged. The earl survived his friend many years; but the *Introduction to the Mathematicks* was forgotten or neglected; and, after his death, *the manu-script was not to be found*; whether it was accidentally destroyed, which is hardly credible, or whether, as hath been suggested, it had been lent to some geometrician, unworthy to bear the name either of a philosopher or a man, who has since concealed it, or possibly burned the original for fear of de-tection. This was a considerable loss not only to men of letters, but to the publick in general; since the *improvement of science* is a subject, in which their security and their pleasures, their commerce, and, consequently, their wealth, are deeply concerned; and, it may be added, the glory of the nation has suffered not a little by the accident; for, if the work of Mr. *Jones* had been preserved, the au hors of the *French Encyclopedia* would not have ventured to reproach us, that since the death of *Newton*, *our advancement in the Mathematicks has not satisfied the expectations of Europe*.—I have seen the large and splendid library, which fills up one whole side of the convenient gallery appropriated to that use in *Shirburn Castle*; and the original library of the *Macclesfield* family is placed on the opposite side of the gallery.—Mr. *Jones* was father to *William Jones*, esq. of *The Middle Temple*, barrister at law; a gentleman not less distinguished by his zeal for science in general, than by his own great pre-eminence in many important branches.

‡ Mr. *Rymer* wrote the *Latin* inscriptions on Mr. *Waller's* tomb at *Beaconsfield*.

" *Sanderson*."

ed to supply the castrated sheets;" Mr. Bowyer, MS.]
the fourth and fifth volume of " The Abridgement of the
" Philosophical Transactions*," 4to; " Sermons on several
" occasions, in three volumes, by the late Rev. *Nathanael*
" *Marshall*†, D. D. Canon of *Windsor*, and Chaplain in Or-
" dinary to his Majesty‡," 8vo; Mrs. *Newcome's*‖ " Evi-
" dences of the Christian Religion," 8vo; and several editions of " *Voltaire's* Life of *Charles* XII. King of *Sweden*,"
both in *French* and *English*¶.

" *Sanderson.*" In a dedication of the eighteenth volume, 1726, to King *George* I. Mr.
Sanderson acknowledges " his felicity, in having had the honour of serving under three
crowned heads for more than thirty years, in an employment declared by the three
greatest Potentates in the world as a work highly conducing to their service and the honour of their crown." This volume was republished, with castrations**, as is mentioned
above, in 1731. The nineteenth, published in 1732, is inscribed to King *George* II;
and Mr. *Sanderson* calls it " a collection containing so vast and rich a fund of useful and
instructive learning, in all transactions, whether foreign or domestic, as, I will adventure to say, no other nation ever did, nor is able to produce the like. The collection
is drawn from the pure and unadulterate fountain of your Majesty's *Sacra Scrinia*,
which gives the firmest sanction to the veracity, and the surest proof to the authority." The twentieth volume is dated 1735. There is another edition, printed at
The Hague, 1739, in which the twenty volumes are brought into ten.

* From the year 1700 to 1720. This was the part abridged by *Henry Jones*, M. A.
and fellow of *King's College* in *Cambridge*. It is inscribed to the lord chancellor *Macclesfield*, and bears the *Imprimatur* of Sir *Isaac Newton*, as President of the Royal Society. A third edition of this abridgement, with the *Latin* papers translated, was published in 1749.

† " I don't know whether I must be allowed to say any thing for myself, till my
" wife's compliments, for lending her Dr. *Marshall*, are presented in form; they are
" delightful Sermons, and a man must be very much out of humour with religious sub-
" jects, that is not pleased with them." *Mr. Clarke to Mr. B. Sept.* 22, 1731. Dr.
Marshall published " The genuine Works of St. *Cyprian*, Archbishop of *Carthage*, and
" Primate of all *Africa*; who suffered martyrdom for the Christian Faith in the year
" of our Lord 258. Together with his Life, written by his own Deacon *Pontius*.
" All done into *English* from the *Oxford* edition, and illustrated with divers Notes, by
" *Nathanael Marshall*, LL.B. rector of the united parishes of St. *Vedast* (alias *Fosters*)
" and St. *Michael Le-Querne*, *London*, and Chaplain in Ordinary to his Majesty, 1717,"
folio: and was, at the time of his death, lecturer of St. *John the Evangelist*. He left
behind him eight children, the eldest of whom was then rector of St. *John's* aforesaid.
He was buried at St. *Pancras*.

‡ Inscribed to the Queen, by the editor Mrs. *Margaret Marshall*, the author's widow.
‖ Wife to the master of St. *John's*. See above, p. 17.
¶ Translated probably by himself. An *eighth* edition, " with a compleat Index,"
was printed by him in 1755.

** What these were, might easily be seen, by comparing the two editions.

Early

Early in 1732 he completed for Mr. *Maittaire* " Mar-
" morum *Arundellianorum, Seldenianorum,* aliorumque Aca-
" demiæ *Oxoniensi* donatorum*; una cum Commentariis
" & Indice, Editio secunda†," folio; which he began in
1728.

* See the history of these donations in *Maittaire's* edition, and in "British Topogra-
" phy," vol. II. p. 128, & seqq.

† " The Marmora *Arundelliana* were first published by the great *Selden,* in
" 1628**. In the year 1676, the Marmora *Oxoniensia* came out, which, besides
" the *Arundel* Marbles, contained such as had been presented to the University by
" Mr. *Selden* and several other munificent benefactors. The learned Mr. *Maittaire* has
" now published a second edition of that work, which will doubtless be very acceptable
" to all the learned world, particularly to all lovers of antiquity; that gentleman's great
" abilities for such an undertaking being universally known and acknowledged††. In
" this edition the reader will find first of all the *Greek* inscriptions, together with the ap-
" pendix, then the *Latin,* and afterwards four *Hebrew,* all in large capital letters.
" After this, there is the *Greek* text again in a less character, with a *Latin* translation by
" *Selden, Prideaux,* and *Price,* page 1 to 99. In the next place, follow entire Disser-
" tations or Comments of learned Men, all apart by themselves ; as, 1. *Selden's* Com-
" mentaries, from page 99 to 197. 2. *Price's* Notes on the third Marble, from page
" 197 to 200. 3. *Palmerius's* Notes and Supplements to the first Marble, from page
" 200 to 222. 4. *Lydiat's* Annotations upon the same, from page 222 to 295. 5.
" *Marsham's* Commentaries on the fifty-eight first *Epochas* of the same Marble, from
" page 295 to 309. 6. *Prideaux's* perpetual Commentary on the Marbles, from page
" 309 to 509. 7. Some Notes of *Reinesius* upon the Marbles, from page 509 to 524.
" 8. *Sponius's* Notes on some of the Marbles, from page 524 to 527. 9. *Chishull's*
" Notes on the third Marble, from page 527 to 532. 10. Corrections from *Smith's*
" Epistle concerning the Seven Churches of *Asia,* from page 532 to 533. 11. Other
" Corrections, from *Bentley's* Dissertation on *Phalaris's* Epistles, from page 533 to 540.
" 12. *Maffei's* Translation of the first and second Marbles into *Italian,* with Notes,
" from page 540 to 549. Lastly, *Dodwell's* Chronological Tables on the first Marble,
" from page 549 to 553. After such various comments, by so many learned men, our
" editor thinks he might very well have put an end to the work here, and been excused
" from any further trouble ; but, having engaged himself by promise in his proposal, he
" has given us some conjectures and remarks of his own, as well upon the comments of
" those learned men before-mentioned, as upon the marbles themselves, from page 553
" to 605. Besides which, he has added a very copious Index, both of things and words,
" with short notes frequently interspersed, from page 605 to 667. As to the order in

** " My copy of *Selden* has, Typis & impensis *Guilielmi Stanesbeii,* MDCXXVIII. Others have
Apud *Joannem Billium,* 1629. That a single edition of such curious matters, which too were rare
then, should not be bought up greedily at home and abroad, doth no great honour to the taste and
learning of times which we are apt to admire. There is certainly another edition in the third volume
of the magnificent edition of his works in 1726, perhaps without any additions, which is extraordinary, as one should think the learned author would keep improving his copy. This quarto edition is
a poor mean blind one in 181 pages, including errata, &c. and by no means equal in typographical
execution to the merit of the subject." *Dr. Taylor's Friend.*

†† " This might be said by a complimenting Reviewer; but what can we think of an Editor that
would not pay one single visit to them all together at *Oxford?*" *Dr. Taylor's Friend.*

" which

1728. This beautiful volume, of which only 300 copies
were

" which the marbles are placed in this edition, our editor has not thought it neceſſary
" to keep to the ſame that was obſerved in the *Oxford* edition, where they were placed
" according to the order in which they ſtood in their repoſitory near the Theatre ; but
" ſince they have been removed from thence to a more commodious place, he judges it
" beſt to come, as near as poſſible, to the method uſed by *Selden, Gruter*, and others,
" who have ſhewed their ſkill and dexterity in recovering and adjuſting curioſities of this
" kind. Our editor further informs us, that both in the *Greek* and *Latin* marbles,
" where there are ſtatues or figures, either with or without inſcriptions, they are all
" placed laſt ; and thoſe ſtatues and figures are engraved anew, with the addition of
" two that were before omitted." *Preſent State of the Republick of Letters*, vol. IX.
p. 139.—" I thank you much for my copy of the *Oxford marbles* ; I am pleaſed with it, and
" believe there is no great danger of a new impreſſion**. Mr. *Maittaire* has ſhewn a
" great deal of modeſty and diligence, as well as learning in the work ; I don't ſee how
" ſuch a heap of Commentaries can be otherwiſe diſpoſed of than in the manner he
" has placed them ††. There is a note, at the bottom of the firſt page of his Pre-
" face, that I was a little in doubt about. He tells you that *Colomeſius* in the year
" 1665 had heard of a larger Commentary of *Selden's* ‡‡, and ſeen one of *M. de Grente-*
" *meſnil*

** " Yet there has been new a impreſſion, though without notes, by Dr. *Chandler*. An anonymous writer (Gent. Mag. 1779, p. 297), in a liberal epiſtle on the *Arundel* collection, expreſſes a wiſh
that the Univerſity would give a fac-ſimile of the *Parian* marble ; which was alſo the wiſh of that old
ſoldier and good *Grecian Jac. Palmerius à Grentemeſnil*, who publiſhed an excellent philological work in
1668, containing notes and corrections on thirty capital *Greek* authors (reckoning the *Arundel* Marbles for
one), in above 800 quarto pages ; his firſt work, when he was 80 years old, and had been a ſoldier from
20, till diſabled by age and the ſtone. His own ſhort preface is worth reading, and perhaps reprinting. I cannot help obſerving, that 30 or 40 years ago this book ſold for 4s. and that now it
generally goes for 2s. To be ſure, later editions of ſeveral of theſe authors have, ſo far as they
have gone, lowered the value of our truly honeſt critic ; but as, like the Sibyls leaves, there is enough
in conſcience ſtill left for the money, I am apt to think that theſe ſtudies are fallen one eighth in
price : I wiſh they may have taken a better turn." *Dr. Taylor's Friend.*—" The upper part of the
Parian chronicle, containing forty-five lines, is ſuppoſed to be worked-up in repairing a chimney.
Lydiat, while confined in the *King's Bench* for a debt of ſuretyſhip for his brother, wrote annotations
on this chronicle, which were firſt publiſhed by *Prideaux*. *Wood* ſays, he criticized ſeverely on *Selden's*
remarks, and inſtead of calling him a moſt judicious author, only ſtyled him an induſtrious one,
which *Selden* was weak enough to reſent ſo highly, as to refuſe to contribute towards his releaſe.
(Ath. Ox. II. 89.) This ſeems to be a piece of mere tittle-tattle ; for in the printed notes, p. 13, he
calls him *Induſtrius & eruditus amicus noſter Seldenus*. This ſtone ſhould have been engraved in the
Marmora *Oxon.* like the Marmor *Sandvicenſe*. This copy has ſome faults, beſides not giving the
true idea of the length of the gaps, or the true poſition of the letters on the ſtone in more than one
ſingle line, which alone happens to be perfect, as *Palmerius* complained long ago." *Britiſh Topogra-*
phy, vol. II. p. 129.
†† They might have been diſpoſed of in the manner of the *Variorum* edition of the Claſſics.
‡‡ It is not improbable but that *Selden* himſelf might have enlarged his Commentary.—" A perſon
was employed to prepare a new edition of *Selden's* Commentary, which had been found very incorrect,
and to inſert the additional marbles. This being delayed three years, biſhop *Fell* employed *Prideaux*,
who publiſhed them under the title of " Marmora *Oxonienſia*, ex *Arundellianis, Seldenianis*, aliiſque
" conflata ; recenſuit, & perpetuo commentario explicavit, *Humphridus Prideaux*, ædis Chriſti alumnus,
" appoſitis ad eorum nonnulla *Seldeni & Lydiati* annotationibus. Acceſſit *Sertorii Urſati Patavini* de
" notis *Romanorum* commentarius. *Oxon.* 1676," folio. Many inſcriptions in *Selden's* book, which
never got to *Oxford*, were thrown with others into an appendix. This book growing ſcarce, Mr.
Pearce of Edmund-Hall undertook 1721 to reprint it, with leave of the author now advanced in years ;
who recommended it to him to correct the many errors occaſioned by his own youth and the hurry of
the preſs ; but, on his declining this, Dr. *David Wilkins* undertook it in 1726, intending to add the
Pomfret and *Pembroke* collections. *Maittaire* performed the firſt part of the deſign in 1732, inſerting
the

were printed, was publifhed by fubfcription*. The fame year he printed, The fecond volume of *Churchill's* "Collection " of Voyages,' folio; " Acta Regia," Mr. *Whatley's* tranflation of *Rapin's* Abridgement of *Rymer*, folio; Dean *Moss's*† "Ser-

" mefnil**, &c. then adds at laft, *Nulla autem illius commentarii*, which is ambi-
" guous††, though to be fure he means *Selden's*. Every reader does not know im-
" mediately that *M. de Grentemefnil* is the gentleman that follows at N° 3." *Mr.*
Clarke to Mr. B. July 12, 1733.

* It appears by an advertifement, that 150 fheets were wrought-off in *Auguft* 1729; and that, though the work contained at leaft half as many more fheets as were at firft propofed, the price to fubfcribers (which was two guineas and a half) was not increafed. To others, it was raifed to three guineas.

† *Robert Mofs* was born at *Gillingham* in *Norfolk* 1666; admitted fizar at *Corpus Chrifti College, Cambridge*, 1682; A. B. and Fellow 1685; B. D. 1690; acquired great reputation both as a difputant and preacher; was a candidate for the place of Public Orator, which he loft by a very few votes; preacher at *Gray's Inn*, 1698; affiftant preacher to Dr. *Wake* at *St. James's*, 1699; chaplain in ordinary to king *William*; created D. D. 1705 when queen *Anne* vifited the univerfity of *Cambridge*. Upon the refignation of Dr. *Stanhope* 1708, the parifhioners of *St. Lawrence Jewry* invited him to accept their *Tuefday* lecture ‡‡; and on the death of Dr. *Roderick* the Queen nominated him to the deanry of *Ely*, in *May* 1712; and, it is fuppofed, would have advanced him to the bifhoprick had fhe furvived bifhop *Moore*. This was the higheft, but not the laft, promotion he obtained in the church; for in 1714 the rectory of *Glifton*, or *Geddlefton*, in *Hertfordfhire*, was given him by Dr. *Robinfon*, bifhop of *London*. He died, aged 63, *March* 26, 1729, totally debilitated by the gout and other infirmities, and was buried in the prefbytery of his own cathedral under a plain ftone with a fimple infcription. His character may be feen in the preface to the eight volumes of his fermons, drawn by their editor Dr. *Snape*, Provoft of *King's College*. Befides thefe, he is fuppofed to have been author of " The report vindicated from mif-reports; being a defence of my " lords the bifhops, as well as the clergy of the lower houfe of convocation, in a letter " from a member of that houfe to the prolocutor, concerning their late confultations " about the bifhop of *Bangor's* writings; with a poftfcript, containing fome few re-" marks upon the letter to Dr. *Sherlock*, 1717." (*Mafters's* Hiftory of *Corpus Chrifti College*, p. 347.) His nephew *Charles Mofs* (fon of his third brother *Charles*, phyfician at *Kingfton on Hull*) was educated at *Caius College*, where he was afterwards fellow and D. D. archdeacon of *Colchefter*, refidentiary of *Salifbury*, rector of *St. James's* and *St. George's Hanover Square*, bifhop of *St. David's* 1766, *Bath* and *Wells* 1774.

the conjectures and corrections of various learned men, but never once confulted the marbles themfelves, and totally omitted *Wheler's* monuments." *Britifh Topography*, vol. II. p. 131.—" *Corfini's* excellent account of the *Greek* Siglæ would now make a much more fuitable and interefting Supplement." *Dr. Taylor's Friend.*

** Or, as he is called above, *Palmerius*, by which name he is moft commonly known.

†† " Dr. *Taylor* had pointed out to me *Maittaire's* ambiguous language.—To the account you have given of the Marmor *Sandvicenfe*, in p. 64, add, There was collected towards the expence. of the feaft or fhew, which confifted of mufic vocal and inftrumental, games and horferaces, from contributions, fines, rents, &c. nearly 1700l.; the fum total of the expences is loft, but parts are fpecified. I wonder how the three managers could contrive to fpend the money; fo with the whole had appeared. The very learned *Corfini* has commented excellently well on this marble, though, unluckily for the publick, he had feen only a very indifferent copy of it in *Nouv. Bibliotb.* tom. XVI. p. 238; he was undoubtedly the greateft mafter in this walk of latter times." *Dr. Taylor's Friend.*

‡‡ This lecturefhip was efteemed very honourable, as appears by what has been already faid, p. 30.

" mons

" mons and Difcourfes on Practical Subjects," four volumes,
8vo; "Differtationes duæ de viribus medicatis Olei Anima-
" lis in Epilepfia aliifque affectibus convulfivis," 8vo, two editions; A tranflation of "*Tully's* Offices, by *Thomas Cockman**,
" D. D." 12mo; " Apparatus ad Linguam *Græcam* ordine
" novo ac facili digeftus, &c. Auctore *Georgio Thompfon*,
" E. A. P†. Scholæque Grammaticæ apud *Tottenham Altæ*
" *Crucis* magiftro ;" a fecond edition of Dr. *Grey's* " Memoria
" Technica," 8vo; and a variety of mifcellanies by Dean *Swift*‡,
which

* Mafter of *Univerfity College.* Died *Jan.* 31, 1744. Mr. *Bowyer* printed another edition of this book in 1739.

† i.e. *Ecclefiæ Anglicanæ Presbyter.*—He was affifted by Mr. *Morland* mafter of *St. Paul's,* Mr. *Thomas Pilgrim* Greek Profeffor at *Cambridge,* Profeffor *Ward,* Dr. *Patrick,* and Dr. *S. Clarke.*

‡ The copy-right of a confiderable number of Dr. *Swift's* fugitive effays was conveyed to Mr. *Bowyer,* for a valuable confideration, by Mr. *Pilkington,* to whom they had been given by the Dean; as appears by fome of Mr. *Pilkington's* letters to Mr. *Bowyer,* in the Supplement to *Swift's* Works : " I have fent you fome of the pamphlets I promifed, in " as large a parcel as I could venture," fays Mr. *Pilkington* in one of thofe letters, dated *Aug.* 28, 1732. " The Dean has, with his own hands, made fome alterations in fome " of them. I will, by next poft, or next but one, fend you another pamphlet at leaft, " and a new affignment from the Dean. He received a letter from Mr. *Pope* and Mr. " *Motte*; but neither have been of the leaft difadvantage to my requeft. I cannot fay " but I am proud of the firmnefs of his friendfhip ** to me."—Mr *Pope* appears to have had an intention of *publifhing* a fecond collection of Mifcellanies by Dr. *Swift*; who tells him, " As to thofe papers of four or five years paft, that you are pleafed to re- " quire foon; they confift of little accidental things writ in the country, family amufe- " ments, never intended further than to divert ourfelves and fome neighbours: or fome " effects of anger on public grievances here, which would be infignificant out of this " kingdom. Two or three of us had a fancy three years ago to write a weekly paper, " and call it an *Intelligencer.* But it continued not long; for the whole volume (it was " reprinted in *London,* and, I find, you have feen it) was the work only of two, myfelf " and Dr. *Sheridan.* If we could have got fome ingenious young man to have been the " manager, who fhould have publifhed all that might be fent to him, it might have con- " tinued longer, for there were hints enough. But the Printer here could not afford

** By the Dean's recommendation, Mr. *Pilkington* was made chaplain to Alderman *Barber* in his mayoralty. And to Mr. *Pope* he thus fpeaks of him : " The Scheme of paying debts by a tax " on vices is not one fyllable mine, but of a young clergyman whom I countenance; he told me it " was built upon a paffage in *Gulliver,* where a projector hath fomething upon the fame thought. " This young man is the moft hopeful we have : a book of his Poems was printed in *London* [in 1730, " 8vo, by Mr. *Bowyer*] ; Dr. *Delany* is one of his patrons : he is married, and has children, and makes " up about 100l. a year, on which he lives decently. The utmoft ftretch of his ambition is, to gather " up as much fuperfluous money as will give him a fight of you, and half an hour of your pretence ; " after which he will return home in full fatisfaction, and in proper time die in peace."

" fuch

which involved him in a difpute with Mr. *Pope**, that ultimately tended to his advantage†, as it ferved to confirm
that good opinion of his abilities and integrity which Mr.
Pope had long before entertained.

In 1733, he printed the "Opus Majus" of Friar *Bacon*
for Dr. *Jebb*‡, folio; another edition of *L'Eftrange's* tranflation

" fuch a young man one farthing for his trouble, the fale being fo fmall, and the price
" one half-penny; and fo it dropt. In the volume you faw (to anfwer your queftions),
" the 1, 3, 5, 7, were mine. Of the 8th I writ only the verfes (very uncorreft, but
" againft a fellow we all hated); the 9th mine, the 10th only the verfes, and of thofe
" not the four laft flovenly lines; the 15th is a pamphlet of mine printed before with
" Dr. *Sheridan's* preface, merely for lazinefs not to difappoint the town; and fo was
" the 19th, which contains only a parcel of facts relating purely to the miferies of *Ire-*
" *land*, and wholly ufelefs and unentertaining. As to the other things of mine fince I
" left you; there are in profe, *A View of the State of Ireland*; *A Project for eating*
" *Children*; and *A Defence of Lord Carteret*: in verfe, *A Libel on Dr. Delany and Lord*
" *Carteret*; *A Letter to Dr. Delany on the Libels writ againft him*; *The Barrack* (a
" ftolen copy); *The Lady's Journal*; *The Lady's Dreffing-Room* (a ftolen copy); *The*
" *Plea of the Damn'd* (a ftolen copy); all thefe have been printed in *London*. (I for-
" got to tell you that the *Tale of Sir Ralph* was fent from *England*.) Befides thefe
" there are five or fix (perhaps more) papers of verfes writ in the North, but perfect
" family-things, two or three of which may be tolerable; the reft but indifferent, and
" the humour only local, and fome that would give offence to the times. Such as they
" are, I will bring them, tolerable or bad, if I recover this lamenefs, and live long
" enough to fee you either here or there." *Dr. Swift to Mr. Pope, June* 12, 1732.

* To this Mr. *Clarke* alludes, in a letter dated *Dec.* 18, 1732: " I hope the great
" affairs about property in *Irifh* wit are in a way of being amicably adjufted, and that
" Mr. *Pope* and you agree to divide the intereft of it. It is awkward dealing with a
" man who ftands foremoft in his profeffion and at fuch a diftance from the reft of them,
" efpecially if he be a wit or a critick; he then imagines himfelf abfolute in his own
" province, and that every thing he meddles with belongs to it. Difputing with him is
" touching his prerogative, and the way to fall under his refentment. Have you come
" off fafe from this dangerous controverfy? or is Mr. *Pope* lefs affuming fince he has
" drawn-off fuch a quantity of fpleen into the *Dunciad?*"

† On the 5th of *May*, 1733, Mr. *Clarke* again began a letter on this fubject: " I
" wifh you joy of the peaceful fituation you feem to be in at prefent, and hope your
" difputes are finifhed to your fatisfaction. I have heard that ladies of the firft rank
" begin to efpoufe your fide of the queftion, and fall upon your powerful adverfary;
" that Lady *Betty Germaine* particularly has written a moft fevere fatire upon him: I
" have not feen it, but wonder you fhould take no notice that the fair fex are not at all
" in his intereft. For my part, I generally prefer peace before victory, and your letters
" confirm me in thefe fentiments: you talk of the difpute with more candour than
" either the victors or the vanquifhed are ufed to do. But, whatever are the terms of
" your accommodation, I like the iffue of it extremely, as it gives you leifure to talk of
" it with your friends in the country."

‡ Dr. *Samuel Jebb*, who had been a member of *Peter-Houfe, Cambridge*, afterwards a Nonjuror, infcribes to that fociety his " Studiorum Primitiæ;" namely, " S.
" *Juftini*

tion of *Josephus*, and proposals for a new version by the Rev.
William Whiston ; a part* of the very beautiful and accurate
edition of " *Jac. Augusti Thuani* Historiarum sui temporis Tomi
" Septem †," folio; " Appendix ad Marmora *Oxoniensia*;
" sive

" *Justini Martyris* cum *Tryphone* Dialogus, *Lond.* 1719," 8vo. Besides the works mentioned in p. 32, he published a beautiful and correct edition of " *Joannis Caii*
" *Britanni* de Canibus *Britannicis* liber unus ; de variorum Animalium & Stirpium, &c.
" liber unus ; de Libris propriis liber unus ; de Pronunciatione *Græcæ* & *Latinæ* Linguæ,
" cum scriptione novâ, libellus ; ad optimorum exemplarium fidem recogniti ; à *S.*
" *Jebb*, M.D. *Lond.* 1729," 8vo ; and " *Humphr. Hodii*, lib. 2. de *Græcis* illustribus
" Linguæ *Græcæ* Literarumque humaniorum instauratoribus, &c. *Lond.* 1742," 8vo.
" Præmittitur de Vita & Scriptis ipsius *Humphredi* Dissertatio, auctore *S. Jebb*, M.D."
He wrote also the epitaph inscribed on a small pyramid between *Haut Buisson* and
Marquise, in the road to *Boulogne*, about seven miles from *Calais*, in memory of *Ed-*
ward Seabright, esq. of *Croxton*, in *Norfolk*, three other *English* gentlemen, and two
servants, who were all murdered *Sept.* 20, 1723 **. The pyramid, being decayed,
was taken down about 1751, and a small oratory or chapel erected on the side of the
road ††. Dr. *Jebb* was recommended to settle at *Stratford*, near *Bow*, by Dr. *Mead*,
and practised there with great success till within a few years of his death, when he
retired with a moderate fortune into *Derbyshire*, where he died *March* 9, 1772, leaving
several children, one of whom is the present Sir *Richard Jebb*, M.D. one of the physicians extraordinary to his Majesty. His brother Dr. *John Jebb*, who is now dean of
Cashell, married a sister of the late General *Gansell's*.

 * In the title-page of each of the seven volumes, the name of the bookseller only appears, " Excudi curavit *Samuel Buckley*, 1733." At the end of the first, stands " *Lon-*
" *dini* imprimebat *Henricus Woodfall*;" of the second, *Samuel Richardson* ; of the
third, *Jacobus Bettenham* ; of the fourth, *Jacobus Roberts* ; of the fifth, *Thomas Wood.*
No printer's name occurs either in the sixth or seventh ; but the eight first books of
vol. VII. were printed by Mr. *Bowyer* ; and the remainder, I believe, with the whole
of the sixth volume, by Mr. *Edward Owen.* These were all very excellent printers.

 " † Mr. *Carte*, who under the borrowed name of *Phil ips* resided in *France* in the
" year 1722, having collected there materials for an *English* translation of the History
" of *Thuanus*, our learned Physician quickly perceived that this plan might be enlarged.
" He looked on his country as too disinterested to desire to possess this foreign treasure

 ** See Political State, vol. XXVI. p. 323. 443; and " A Narrative of the Proceedings in *France*,
" for discovering and detecting the murderers of the *English* gentlemen," where there is a print of the
pyramid, with the inscription, of which this is a copy :

" Ad annum	Imparatum Adolescentem aderti Latrones
MDCCXXIII, *Sept.* XX°,	Privatum Pecuniis, vulneribus perfossum corpore,
Et quarta circiter post meridiem hora,	Vita tandem spoliavere : occubuerunt una
Dum fatali peregrinandi studio adductus	Longo & pio avorum stemmate præclarus
Ad *Lutetias* usque *Parisiorum* proficisceretur	HENRICUS MOMPESSON, Armiger,
EDWARDUS SEABRIGHT Armiger,	JOHANNES DAVIS & JOHANNES LOCK,
Illustrissimi THOMÆ SEABRIGHT	Generoso orti sanguine, & inferioris Subsellii duo,
Apud *Anglos* Baronetti Frater unicus,	*Anglus* alter & alter *Gallus*,
Septem hoc in loco inermem et	Inhonesto nimium fato correpti omnes."

Richard Spendelow, a servant of Mr *Seabright*, who was left for dead by the murderers, recovered,
and, being the only survivor, was a most material instrument in bringing the assassins to justice. He
afterwards became steward to earl *Gower*, in which capacity he died *July* 24, 1755 ; possessed of some
property, as appears by his will, proved *July* 29, 1755 ; in which he is styled " *Richard Spendelow*,
" of *St George, Hanover Square*, in the county of *Middlesex*, Gentleman."

 †† From the information of a gentleman who has been in the chapel, where mass, he was told,
is occasionally performed for the souls of the persons who were murdered.

M

" alone,

" five *Græcæ* trium Marmorum * recens repertorum Inſcrip-
" tiones," &c. folio; 250 copies of the "Notitia Parliamen-
" taria," ſo far as relates to the borough of *Windſor*, a ſingle
ſheet in folio; a catalogue of Mr. *Browne Willis's* gold coins †,
by Mr. *Vertue*, a ſingle ſheet, 4to.; an edition of the " *Pe-*
" *riegeſis* of *Dionyſius*," 8vo; " *Milner's* Journal of the
" Duke of *Marlborough's* Marches," for Colonel *Montague*,
8vo; a part only of " Memoirs of the Twentieth Century.
" Being original Letters of State under *George* the Sixth:
" relating to the moſt important Events in *Great Britain*
" and *Europe*, as to Church and State, Arts and Sciences,
" Trade, Taxes, and Treaties, Peace, and War: and Cha-
" racters of the greateſt Perſons of thoſe Times; from the
" middle of the Eighteenth, to the end of the Twentieth
" Century, and the World. Received and revealed in the
" year 1728; and now publiſhed, for the Inſtruction of all
" eminent Stateſmen, Churchmen, Patriots, Politicians, Pro-
" jectors, Papiſts, and Proteſtants. In ſix volumes ‡. *London*,
                                           " 1733,"

" alone, and was deſirous *England* might do for *Thuanus* more than *France* itſelf;
" by procuring for all *Europe* the firſt complete edition of this immortal hiſtory. He
" therefore ſatisfied Mr. *Carte* for the pains he had taken; and employed Mr. *Buckley*
" as an editor equal to ſuch a taſk, whoſe three letters written in *Engliſh* to the Doctor,
" contain many curious particulars concerning the hiſtory itſelf, and the plan of this
" new edition; to the perfection and beauty of which Dr. *Mead* ſo liberally contributed.
" Theſe letters were tranſlated into *Latin* by Mr. Profeſſor *Ward*, with an elegance
" worthy the place they hold in the front of the work." Dr. *Maty*, *Life of Mead*, p. 39.

* Theſe monuments were brought into *England* in *October* 1732, from a town ſituated
between *Smyrna* and *Epheſus*. The inſcriptions were carefully and exactly taken off in
paper by Mr. *Joſeph Ames*, and preſented to Sir *Hans Sloane*; and Mr. *Maittaire* undertook to communicate them to the publick, with a *Latin* tranſlation and notes. The firſt
of theſe, we are told in the preface, receives conſiderable light from ſome of the monuments preſerved in the gallery at *Oxford*, and particularly from one of thoſe publiſhed by
Mr. *Chiſhull*.

† Of this catalogue 200 copies were printed; but I have never ſeen one. The ſingle
ſheet of the " Notitia Parliamentaria" is now alſo become a curioſity. I have ſaid, under
1729, that Mr. *Bowyer* then printed the two octavo volumes: I ſince find that it was only
the firſt volume, which was then reprinted with large additions. An account of Mr. *Willis's*
coins is ſuppoſed to exiſt among the MS. papers he bequeathed to the *Bodleian* Library.

‡ There is ſomething myſterious in the hiſtory of this work, which was written
by Dr. *Samuel Madden*, the patriot of *Ireland*; who projected a ſcheme, in 1731, for
promoting learning in the College at *Dublin* by Premiums, and ſettled in 1740 an an-
                                                                        nual.

" 1733," 8vo; and had fome fhare in eftablifhing a news-
paper, called *The Weekly Mifcellany**.

This year was rendered remarkable in the literary world
by the brilliancy of the public act at *Oxford*. Mr. *Bowyer* was
highly pleafed with the whole ceremony, and printed
feveral of the little productions which it occafioned.
Among various others, I find mentioned a little poem
of his own, " The Beau and Academick, a Dialogue in
" imitation of the *Bellus Homo & Academicus* fpoken at
" the late Public Act at *Oxford*; addreffed to the Ladies †."

　　　　　　　　　　　　　　　　　　　　　　　　　　　　　　This

nual fum of 100l. to be diftributed, by way of premium, to the inhabitants of *Ireland*
only; viz. 50l. to the author of the beft invention for improving any ufeful art or manufacture; 25l. to the perfon who fhould execute the beft ftatue or piece of fculpture;
and 25l. to the perfon who fhould finifh the beft piece of painting either in hiftory or
landfcape, the premiums to be decided by the *Dublin* Society, of which Dr. *Madden*
was the inftitutor, and which proved of infinite fervice to that kingdom, by exciting a
laudable fpirit of emulation amongft their artifts and manufacturers. In the year 1729
he brought out a tragedy at *Lincoln's Inn Fields*, called " *Themiftocles*, the Lover of his
" Country;" about 1743 or 4, he publifhed a long Poem called " *Boulter's* Monu-
" ment;" and died *Dec.* 30, 1765. One volume only of the above-mentioned " Me-
" moirs" appeared; and whether any more were really intended, is uncertain. A thoufand copies were printed, with fuch very great difpatch, that three printers were employed
on it (*Bowyer, Woodfall*, and *Roberts*); and the names of an uncommon number of
reputable bookfellers appeared in the title-page. In lefs than a fortnight, however,
890 of thefe copies were delivered to Dr. *Madden*, and probably deftroyed. The current
report is, that the edition was fuppreffed on the day of publication. And that it is
now exceedingly fcarce, is certain. Mr. *Tutet*, who has a copy of it, never heard but of
one other, though he has frequently enquired after it.

　* Mr. *Clarke, July* 14, 1733, fays, " I wifh you much fuccefs in *The Weekly Mifcel-*
" *lany.* I have taken it in, in hopes of meeting now and then with one of your Lucu-
" brations. If it does fucceed, you muft enlarge the plan of it a little. The managers
" muft remember the proverb, That one ounce of mother-wit is worth a pound of
" clergy." In another letter that year, Mr. *Clarke* afks, " How fhall I fee your Effays,
" or know who voted *pro* and *con* about the Teft ** ?" The profeffed editor of *The Mif-*
cellany was *William Webfter*, D.D. The firft number was publifhed *Dec.* 16, 1732;
and it was continued till *June* 27, 1741.

　† " Bellus Homo & Academicus. Recitârunt in Theatro *Sheldoniano* ad Comitia
" *Oxonienfia* 1733, *Lodovicus Langton* & *Thomas Baber*, Collegii Div. *Magd.* Com-
" menfales. By *W. Hafledine*, of *Magdalen College*; who took the degree of M. A.
" *Oct.* 20, 1736. Accedit Oratio *Petri Francifci Courayer*††, S. T. P. habita in iifdem
" Comitiis, 5 Id. *Julii.*"

　** See fome fpecimens of thefe Effays in the Mifcellaneous Tracts.
　†† A feparate tranflation of this fpeech was printed, in 1734, under the title of " An Oration fpoken
" in the Theatre at *Oxford*, at the Public Act, 1733, by *Peter Francis Courayer*, D. D. Tranflated
" from the *Latin*, by a Gentleman of the Univerfity of *Oxford*," 8vo.—Dr. *Courayer* was a Roman
Catholic clergyman, remarkable for his moderation, charity, and temper concerning religious affairs;

This year alſo he wrote the following epigram, intended
to be placed under the head of *Gulliver*:

" Here learn, from moral Truth and Wit refin'd,
" How Vice and Folly have debas'd mankind;
" Strong Senſe and Humour arm in Virtue's cauſe;
" Thus her great Votary vindicates her laws:
" While bold and free the glowing colours ſtrike;
" Blame not the painter, if the picture 's like."

In

and was preſented by the Univerſity of *Oxford* with a Doctor's degree, on the 28th of *May*, 1772,
for his maſterly *Defence of Engliſh Ordinations*. The diploma and his excellent letter of thanks to the
Univerſity are preſerved in *The Preſent State of the Republick of Letters*, vol. I. p. 485. In the ſame
volume there is a copious and ſatisfactory account of his *Defence of Engliſh Ordinations*. This very
pious Divine was born at *Vernon* in *Normandy* in 1681. Whilſt canon regular and librarian of the
abbey of St. *Genevieve* at *Paris*, he applied to archbiſhop *Wake* for the reſolution of ſome doubts, concerning the epiſcopal ſucceſſion in *England*, and the validity of our ordinations; being encouraged thereto
by the friendly correſpondence which had paſſed between the archbiſhop and the late Dr. *Du Pin* of the
Sorbonne. The archbiſhop ſent him exact copies of the proper records, atteſted by a notary public;
and on theſe he built his defence of the *Engliſh* ordinations, which was publiſhed in *Holland* in the year
1727. The original papers, which the archbiſhop ſent over to *Courayer*, together with ſeveral letters
which paſſed concerning the terms of a projected reconciliation between the churches of *France* and
England, are now in the poſſeſſion of the Rev. *Oſmund Beauvoir*, maſter of the King's ſchool at *Canterbury*, whoſe father was chaplain to the *Engliſh* embaſſy at *Paris*, and through his hands the correſpondence with archbiſhop *Wake* was carried on. Some of the letters are publiſhed in *Biographia
Britannica*, article WAKE. The author of *The Confeſſional* attacks ſeverely the memory of the
archbiſhop for charitably treating with the Divines of the *Sorbonne*, as if he had formed a ſcheme
for yielding up the Proteſtant doctrines to the church of *Rome*: though this whole affair, on
the part of the archbiſhop, was conducted with all poſſible fidelity and reſolution; ſuch as will
do him honour with the lateſt poſterity. The reader may ſee him well vindicated by Dr. *Maclaine*,
in the third number of his appendix to " *Moſheim's* Eccleſiaſtical Hiſtory," where the original
correſpondence with Mr. *Beauvoir* is printed. The Cardinal *De Noailles*, being highly offended with Dr. *Courayer's* book, the marſhal *De Noailles*, his brother, endeavoured to pacify him,
and reſtore *Courayer* to his favour; but without ſucceſs. While the danger of a proſecution, or
rather a perſecution, was depending, it was thought moſt adviſable that he ſhould take refuge in
England: but he was in ſo little haſte on this occaſion, that he made a ſlow journey to *Calais* in a
ſtage coach; and was detained there ſome time by a contrary wind, ſo that he might eaſily have been
apprehended. However, he got ſafe to *England*, where he was well received; but he complained to
archbiſhop *Wake*, that it was a bad country for a religious man to reſide in, becauſe of the unhappy
differences in religion, by which mutual charity is deſtroyed; and the liberty which many take of
ſpeaking againſt the doctrines of chriſtianity, and corrupting the minds of the people. " His up-
" right fortitude in declaring his ſentiments," Dr. *Maclaine* ſays, " obliged him to ſeek an aſylum in
" *England*; and, notwithſtanding his perſuaſion of the abſurdities which abound in the church of
" *Rome*, he never totally ſeparated himſelf from its communion." The Marquis of *Blandford*, ſoon
after his arrival in *England*, made him a preſent of fifty pounds, by the hands of *Nicholas Mann*, eſq.
who was afterwards maſter of the *Charter-houſe*. With ſome difficulty he obtained a penſion of one
hundred pounds a year from the court; and, having tranſlated Father *Paul's* Hiſtory of the Council of
Trent into *French*, in two volumes folio, 1736, he dedicated it to queen *Caroline*, the munificent patroneſs of diſtreſſed merit, in the moſt elegant ſtrains of gratitude: " Exiled," he ſays, " into your
" Majeſty's dominions by theſe enemies which the love of truth alone procured me; and the defence
" of a church which you have ever honoured with your eſteem and protection: Your goodneſs has
" been my aſylum in diſgrace, ſuſtained me under my afflictions, relieved my neceſſities, and ſupplied
" all my wants; oft-times preventing and exceeding my occaſions; while, to crown the grandeur of
" your beneficence, you have ſcarce ſuffered me to thank you for thoſe favours you deemed inconſi-
" derable, though the weight of them overwhelmed me. Delighted with the conſciouſneſs of well-
" doing, more than with all the elogies that naturally attend your benevolence, you refuſe to admit
" even the juſteſt acknowledgments; and to ſave thoſe you ſuccour, as far as poſſible, the publiſhing
" their misfortunes, by the recital of your grace and clemency, you ſeek only the divine ſatisfaction
" of ſolacing the unhappy, without bartering your liberality for applauſe." The Queen increaſed his

4

penſion

In 1734 he printed a large impreſſion of the ſecond volume of Archbiſhop *Tillotſon's* Sermons, *Voltaire's* " Letters " on the *Engliſh* Nation," Mr. *Richardſon's* * Notes on *Milton*, and "*Parſons's* † Chriſtian Directory," Mr. *Jortin's* " Remarks " on *Spenſer's* Poems," all in 8vo; and a very conſiderable number of plays for Mr. *Tonſon* in 12mo.

* This was a joint publication of the two Mr. *Richardſons*, father and ſon; the latter of them the celebrated painter.

† Publiſhed by Dr. *Stanhope*, of whom ſee pp. 7. and 30. Another work of Dr. *Stanhope's* may be traced from " *Jo. Alb. Fabricii* Bibliotheca *Græca*, *Hamburgi*, 1723," vol. IV. p. 26; namely, " The Meditations of *Marcus Aurelius Antoninus*, the *Roman* " Emperor, 1699 **," 4to. with the addition of *Andrew Dacier's* remarks, tranſlated by him from the *French* into *Latin*; and the Emperor's Life by the ſame ††, but conſiderably enlarged and corrected. This was reprinted in 1707.

penſion to two hundred pounds; and, by the ſale of the work, he raiſed fifteen hundred pounds more. He gave ſixteen hundred pounds to lord *Feverſham*, for an annuity of one hundred pounds *per annum*; which he enjoyed for fifty years. Thus he roſe, by degrees, to very eaſy circumſtances; which were made ſtill more ſo by the reception which his agreeable and edifying converſation procured him among great people, with many of whom it was his cuſtom to live for ſeveral months at a time. He was occaſionally generous to ſome of his relations in *France*. He had two ſiſters who were nuns; and in 1776 had a brother living at *Paris* in the profeſſion of the law, to whom he gave a handſome gold ſnuff-box, which had been preſented to him by Queen *Caroline*. His works were many, and all in *French*.† He tranſlated *Sleidan's* Hiſtory of the Reformation; and wrote a ſecond defence in ſupport of his firſt, againſt the arguments of the Jeſuits, father *Harduin*, cardinal *Tencin*, &c. In diſcourſing about religious ſubjects, he was reſerved and cautious, avoiding controverſy as much as poſſible. He never had any good opinion of *Bower*, who came over hither to write his Hiſtory of the Popes: he accuſed him of pretending to collect from books which he had never ſeen; and ſaid he was a dark myſterious man, of a very ſuſpicious character. Soon after his retirement to *England* (it is ſaid) he went to a prieſt of the *Romiſh* church for confeſſion, and told him who he was. The prieſt dared not take his confeſſion, becauſe he was excommunicated; but adviſed him to conſult his Superior of St. *Genevieve*. What was the iſſue of this application, we know not; but it is certain, that when in *London*, he made it his practice to go to maſs; and, when in the country at *Ealing*, whither he frequently retired for privacy, he conſtantly attended the ſervice of the pariſh church, declaring, at all times, that he had great ſatisfaction in the prayers of the church of *England*. The Jeſuits were his worſt enemies; yet when that order was ſuppreſſed, his great humanity lamented the fate of many poor men, who were thrown out of their bread, and caſt, in a helpleſs ſtate, upon the wide world. He died *October* 17, 1776, after two days illneſs, at the great age of 95. At his own deſire, he was buried in the cloyſter of *Weſtminſter Abbey*, by Dr. *Bell*, chaplain to the princeſs *Amelia*. His will, dated *Feb.* 3, 1774, was proved at *Doctors-Commons*, *Oct.* 24, 1776. He therein declares, " that he dies a member of the Catholick " church, but without approving of many of the opinions and ſuperſtitions which have been intro- " duced into the *Romiſh* church, and taught in their ſchools and ſeminaries, and which they have in- " ſiſted on as articles of faith, though to him they appear to be not only not founded in truth, but " alſo to be highly improbable." He left 50l. to St. *Martin's* pariſh, and 20l. to the pariſh of St. *Margaret's*, *Weſtminſter*, in which he died; a handſome ſum of money to the poor of *Vernou*, in *Normandy*, where he was born; and, after many legacies to his friends in *England*, the reſt and reſidue to two nephews of his name at *Vernon*.—The principal part of this note is taken from " Obſervations in a Journey to *Paris*," an entertaining little work, in two volumes, ſmall 8vo. 1777. The account of Dr. *Courayer* was communicated to this intelligent traveller by *James Smyth*, eſq. of *Upper Groſvenor Street*.

** Tranſlated into *Engliſh* in 1701, under the following title: " The Emperor *Marcus Antoninus* " his Converſation with himſelf; together with the Preliminary Diſcourſe of the learned *Gataker*; as " alſo the Emperor's Life; written by Monſieur *Dacier*, and ſupported by the authorities collected " by Dr. *Stanhope*; to which is added the Mythological Picture of *Cebes* the *Theban*, &c. tranſlated " into *Engliſh* from the reſpective originals, by *Jeremy Collier*, M. A." Of this tranſlation a third edition was printed by Mr. *Bowyer* in 1726.

†† This Life had been tranſlated in 1690, with ſome ſelect paſſages of the Meditations, by Dr. *King* of the Commons.

I know

I know not the fecret hiftory of the two following poems, which appear to have been occafioned by Mr. *Bowyer* and Mr. *Cave* * having been joint ftewards at fome public entertainment

* " Mr. *Edward Cave*, born at *Newton* in *Warwickfhire, Feb.* 29, 1691, and educated at *Rugby* fchool under the Rev. Mr. *Holyock*, was at firft placed with a collector of the excife. He ufed to recount with fome pleafure a journey or two which he rode with him as his clerk, and relate the victories that he gained over the excifemen in grammatical difputations. But the infolence of his miftrefs, who employed him in fervile drudgery, quickly difgufted him, and he went up to *London* in queft of more fuitable employment. He was recommended to a timber merchant at the *Bank-fide*, and while he was there on liking, is faid to have given hopes of great mercantile abilities ; but this place he foon left, I know not for what reafon, and was bound apprentice to Mr. *Collins*, a printer of fome reputation, and deputy alderman. This was a trade for which men were formerly qualified by a literary education, and which was pleafing to *Cave*, becaufe it furnifhed fome employment for his fcholaftick attainments. Here therefore he refolved to fettle, though his mafter and miftrefs lived in perpetual difcord, and their houfe could be no comfortable habitation. From the inconveniences of thefe domeftick tumults he was foon releafed, having in only two years attained fo much fkill in his art, and gained fo much the confidence of his mafter, that he was fent without any fuperintendant to conduct a printing-houfe at *Norwich*, and publifh a weekly paper. In this undertaking he met with fome oppofition, which produced a publick controverfy, and procured young *Cave* reputation as a writer. His mafter died before his apprenticefhip was expired ; and, as he was not able to bear the perverfenefs of his miftrefs, he quitted her houfe upon a ftipulated allowance, and married a young widow, with whom he lived at *Bow*. When his apprenticefhip was over, he worked as a journeyman at the printing-houfe of Mr. *Barber*, a man much diftinguifhed and employed by the Tories, whofe principles had at that time fo much prevalence with *Cave*, that he was for fome years a writer in *Mift's Journal*, which (though he afterwards obtained, by his wife's intereft, a fmall place in the Poft-Office) he for fome time continued. But as intereft is powerful **, and converfation, however mean, in time perfuafive, he by degrees inclined to another party ; in which, however, he was always moderate, though fteady and determined. When he was admitted into the Poft-Office he ftill continued, at his intervals of attendance, to exercife his trade, or to employ himfelf with fome typographical bufinefs. He corrected the *Gradus ad Parnaffum*, and was liberally rewarded by the Company of Stationers. He wrote an account of the criminals, which had for fome time a confiderable fale; and publifhed many little pamphlets that accident brought into his hands, of which it would be very difficult to recover the memory. By the correfpondence which his place in the Poft-Office facilitated, he procured country newspapers, and fold their intelligence to a journalift of *London*, for a guinea a week. He was afterwards raifed to the office of clerk of the franks, in which he acted with great fpirit and firmnefs ; and often ftopped franks which were given by members of parliament to their friends, becaufe he thought fuch extenfion of a peculiar right illegal.

** " This is by no means confined to perfons that move in fuch humble fpheres. The appreciating author of the " Decline, &c." has not only told us, p. 81. c. III. n. 15, that " officers of the police " or revenue eafily adapt themfelves to any form of government ;" but, for fear left a doctrine, that adds fo little to the Dignity of Human Nature (on which modern Philofophs lay fo much ftrefs) fhould not be readily admitted, has even condefcended to furnifh an inftance of a perfon deep in the fchemes of oppofition one week, and the next taking his feat at the board of Trade and Plantations as a lord thereof." *Dr. Taylor's Friend.*

This

tainment of a fett of printers: but, finding them in Mr.
Bowyer's hand-writing, and having reafon to think that at
least

This raifed many complaints; and having ftopped, among others, a frank given to the
old Duchefs of *Marlborough* by Mr. *Walter Plummer*, he was cited before the Houfe, as
for breach of privilege, and accufed, I fuppofe very unjuftly, of opening letters to detect
them. He was treated with great harfhnefs and feverity; but declining their queftions
by pleading his oath of fecrecy, was at laft difmiffed. And it muft be recorded to his
honour, that when he was ejected from his office, he did not think himfelf difcharged
from his truft, but continued to refufe to his neareft friends any information about the
management of the office. By this conftancy of diligence and diverfification of employment, he in time collected a fum fufficient for the purchafe of a fmall printing-office, and
began the *Gentleman's Magazine*, a periodical pamphlet, of which the fcheme is known
wherever the *Englifh* language is fpoken. To this undertaking he owed the affluence in
which he paffed the laft twenty years of his life; and the fortune which he left behind him,
which, though large, had been yet larger, had he not rafhly and wantonly impaired it by
innumerable projects. Mr. *Cave*, when he formed the project, was far from expecting
the fuccefs which he found; and others had fo little profpect of its confequence, that
though he had for feveral years talked of his plan among printers and bookfellers, none
of them thought it worth the trial. That they were not reftrained by their virtue from
the execution of another man's defign, was fufficiently apparent as foon as that defign began to be gainful; for in a few years a multitude of Magazines arofe, and perifhed: only
The London Magazine, fupported by a powerful affociation of bookfellers, and circulated
with all the art and all the cunning of trade, exempted itfelf from the general fate to
Cave's invaders, and obtained, though not an equal, yet a confiderable fale*. *Cave* now
began to afpire to popularity; and being a greater lover of poetry than any other art,
he fometimes offered fubjects for poems, and propofed prizes for the beft performances.
The firft prize was fifty pounds, for which, being but newly acquainted with wealth,
and thinking the influence of fifty pounds extremely great, he expected the firft authors
of the kingdom to appear as competitors; and offered the allotment of the prize to the
Univerfities. But when the time came, no name was feen among the writers that had
been ever feen before; the Univerfities and feveral private men rejected the province of
affigning the prize. At all this Mr. *Cave* wondered for a while; but his natural judgment, and a wider acquaintance with the world, foon cured him of his aftonifhment, as
of many other prejudices and errors. Nor have many men been feen raifed by accident
or induftry to fudden riches, that retained lefs of the meannefs of their former ftate.
He continued to improve his Magazine, and had the fatisfaction of feeing its fuccefs pro-
portionate to his diligence, till in the year 1751 his wife died of an afthma: with which
though he feemed not at firft much affected, yet in a few days he loft his fleep and
his appetite; and, lingering two years, fell, by drinking acid liquors, into a diarrhoea,
and afterwards into a kind of lethargick infenfibility, in which one of the laft acts of
reafon he exerted, was fondly to prefs the hand which is now writing this little narrative. He died on *January* 10, 1754, æt. 63, having juft concluded the twenty-third
annual collection." Dr. JOHNSON, in *Gent. Mag.* 1754, p. 55—57.

* This was actually the cafe in 1754; but *The London Magazine* is now far from being the moft
confiderable rival. Another, to the difgrace of the age, without any pretence to favour except a
fcandalous chronicle unintelligible to many of its readers; and a third, lefs cenfurable, but more in-
fipid, which has the merit of furnifhing its purchafers with ufeful patterns of needle-work, have made
their way aftonifhingly. Yet it may ftill with juftice be faid, that *The Gentleman's Magazine*, after
a period of nine-and-forty years, ftands foremoft for literary reputation, as the refpectable correfpondence, it continues to enjoy, abundantly evinces.

I am

leaſt the ſecond of them is his own, and that they were never before printed, they are ſubmitted to the reader:

I am enabled, by the favour of Mr. *Willlam Cave,* of *Rugby,* to lay before my readers an inedited epitaph by Dr. *Hawkeſworth.* Mr. *Edward Cave* was buried at *St. James's Clerkenwell;* but the following inſcription is at *Rugby:*

" Near this place lies
The body of
JOSEPH CAVE,
Late of this pariſh,
Who departed this life *Nov.* 18, 1747,
Aged 79 years.
He was placed by Providence in a humble ſtation;
But
Induſtry abundantly ſupplied the wants of Nature,
And
Temperance bleſt him with
Content and Wealth.
As he was an affectionate Father,
He was made happy in the decline of life
By the deſerved eminence of his eldeſt Son
EDWARD CAVE;
Who, without intereſt, fortune, or connection,
By the native force of his own genius,
Aſſiſted only by a claſſical education,
Which he received at the Grammar-ſchool
Of this Town,
Planned, executed, and eſtabliſhed
A literary work, called
THE GENTLEMAN'S MAGAZINE,
Whereby he acquired an ample fortune,
The whole of which devolved to his Family.
Here alſo lies
The body of WILLIAM CAVE,
Second Son of the ſaid JOSEPH CAVE,
Who died *May* 2, 1757, aged 62 years;
And who, having ſurvived his elder Brother
EDWARD CAVE,
Inherited from him a competent eſtate;
And, in gratitude to his benefactor,
Ordered this monument, to perpetuate his
Memory.

He liv'd a Patriarch in his numerous race,
And ſhew'd in charity a Chriſtian's grace:
Whate'er a friend or parent feels, he knew;
His hand was open, and his heart was true;
In what he gain'd and gave, he taught mankind,
A grateful always is a generous mind.
Here reſt his clay! His ſoul muſt ever reſt.
Who bleſs'd when living, dying muſt be bleſt."

To Mr. RICHARDSON.
Monday, Jan. 1735.

THINK not my *Pegasus* is jaded,
Or laurels are by winter faded,
They a perpetual verdure share,
And mock th' inclemencies of air.
Blest be the bounties of the Nine ;
I've stores of verse, a MAGAZINE.
* A monthly course † these labours run
Attendant on their Parent Sun,
So regular, that rigid Time
May take his measures ev'n from mine.

First then, we thank you much in few words
For compliments to us your stewards,
For that great post how much unfit!
One tastes no wine ‡—and one no wit !
How in both characters you'd shine,
At once the God of Wit and Wine !

From you we'll not admit excuses,
Though offer'd by our sister Muses.
Lame as I am with gout, I'll meet,
Though brought upon poetic feet ;
For oft I mount the Muses' steed
And wing away with postboy speed
To distant *Berwick upon Tweed.*
Now, to supply you (no reproach),
Say but the word, I'll send the coach ;
I'll order *John* to put-to *Æthon*—
I run with distichs—t'other's *Phlegon* ;
For so in gratitude each horse
Is nam'd, procur'd by God of Verse.
Thus shall you ride in dignity,
Beyond yourself—and worthy me !
While city crowds shall wondering stare ye at,
And raise the envy of the Laureat.

I'll place two seats, whene'er you come,
This for your arms—and that your bum ;
Or you shall take the elbow chair,
And be for once the Peerless Peer.

* Other MSS. read thus :
" A constant course these labours run,
Attendant on their Parent Moon,
As regular as carriers horse,
Their burthen bear with music worse." *W. B.*

Bring, if you will, my brother *Johnian* §,
An honest merry simpletonian ;
With student's face, but shallow pate,
Ah ! what's the *College* to the *Gate*‖ !
But for the little man, I'll this say,
He's something still for being an ESSAY.

Verse can, they say, bring down the
moon,
Exalted in her midnight noon.
Oh ! could it gain your rosy face,
How the full orb the board would grace,
When flush'd with wine, and plump with
praise !
Diminish'd stars shall hide their head,
Twinkle a while, then drop to bed,
While you shine forth serenely bright,
Restore the day in midst of night,
And make us scorn e'en *Phœbus'* light.

Thou jovial bard, might I transfuse
The wit of thy harmonious Muse
Into my comprehensive paper,
I'd add your titles—to my wrapper.
For you, I think, print Journals Daily,
By names unknown to *Nathan Bailey* **.
I long to mix poetic rage,
Companions like, add page to page.
While from your springs your streams shall
run
Through my canals to *Helicon,*
How in its course will wit refine,
Rais'd to Celestial from Sublime !

I'll say no more ; the Muse invites
To sacred friendship's social rites.
Then come along, pretensions wave ;
Your humble servant,   EDWARD CAVE.

P. S. These lines, my friend, had sooner come,
But we were both engag'd at home ;
He in parliament addresses,
I in indulging spouse-caresses,
For *Saturday* at night, you know,
Though kings should want—wives have
their due ††.

† The Gentleman's Magazine.   See p. 83.
‡ In the latter years of his life Mr. *Cave* was afflicted with the gout, which he endeavoured to cure or alleviate, by a total abstinence both from strong liquors, and animal food.   From animal food he abstained about four years, and from strong liquors much longer ; but the gout continued unconquered, perhaps unabated.
§ Mr. *Bowyer.*   ‖ Mr. *Cave's* abode.
** Mr. *Richardson* printed, at that time, a Daily Journal : The allusion here is to an article in *N. Bailey's* Dictionary, where *Courant* is gravely explained to mean, " the Title of a News-paper."
†† This, it seems, was known before *Tristram Shandy's* time.

To Mr. RICHARDSON.

Feb. 2, 1735.

I HOPE you'll think it not a scoff is,
That, 'though I now am out of office,
Yet second thus my landlord's letter,
And summon you again in metre,
To meet upon th' accustom'd plain,
Bestrow'd with shields and heaps of slain;
There the little man * shall work ye,
Or spend his wiser rage on turkey;
His doughty arm shall sheath within
It's more than equal length of chine.
There ducks perhaps, a juicy food,
May sate his noble thirst for blood,
Of which, digested into gravey,
May'nt you partake for all *Delany* †?
Soft apple-pye at least, or tanzy,
May mollify the cruel frenzy.

But I had somewhat more to tell you
Besides the mere concerns of belly;
There are to whom our harmless letter
Appears than libel little better;
Who see throughout some deep design,
And *Cave* is read in every line.
To these I've drawn this formal answer,
If proper, judge;—and so read on, sir.

THIS night we've try'd to please by se-
　　cret ways,　　　　　　[bays;
Have bravely borne the birch to gain the
Such is, it seems, the modern lust—of
　　praise!
Conceal'd for once ourselves we satirize,
As some put on a masquerade disguise,
Themselves to cuckold, and debauch their
　　wives.
But now by what new arts will you commend?
Say, will you damn the poet—or the friend?

Or, if his picture 's with true judgment hit,
You'll all, I hope, to the young *Hogarth* sit,
Nor fear the midnight vigils of his wit.
Impassive sages, free from love or hatred,
Hold ridicule the test of all that's sacred.
So gold by mercury 's refin'd, the oar
With even face contemns the subtle power.
　　Our verse we've thus explain'd, to shun
　　　　offence;
No second-sight can now find double sense,
See tilting armies in the fields of air,
The angry prelude of a liquid war.
If such there are (indulge the gloomy vapour)
I fill my glass—*To the well staining paper.*
So the fell lion with severe delight, [fight.
Lashing his sides, provokes th' approaching
　　But hold, you cry, this ne'er can suit
　　Your dapper size—e'en drop a foot.
Well then, proceed we from the guest
To th' humble waiters on your feast.
Lo *Puss*, perhaps, when we are gone,
May act the part that I have done;
She may with furious leaps assail
In airy rounds her sportive tail.
In silent holes the mice survey,
With trembling hearts the monster's play,
Her spotted sides, her grinning jaws,
Her arch of back, extent of paws,
By nature taught this lesson sage,
If such her spirit, how keen her rage!
Blest sons of *Phœbus*, darlings of the Nine,
Henceforth through you how will the
　　Printers shine,
Who ne'er without the Muse shall meet
　　to sup or dine!
Blessings, say I, attend your rhiming pen,
No King *John's*, sure, e'er equal St. *John's*
　　men!

The following epigram is probably Mr. *Bowyer's:*

" In syllabam longam in voce *Vertiginosus* ‡ à D. *Swift* correptam.

　" Musarum antistes, *Phœbi* numerosus alumnus,
　　" Vix omnes numeros *Vertiginosus* habet.
　" Intentat charo capiti vertigo ruinam:
　　" Oh! servet cerebro nata *Minerva* caput.
　" *Vertigo* nimium *longa* est, divine poeta;
　　" Dent tibi *Pierides*, donet *Apollo*, brevem."

* Mr. *Bowyer.*

† The celebrated Dean of *Downe*, who had published in 1734 " The Doctrine of Abstinence from
" Blood defended, &c.;" a tract which drew much irony on its ingenious author.

‡ In the Dean's well-known epigram on his own deafness. Mr. *Bowyer* was of opinion, that the
false quantity rendered the line more expressive of the malady under which *Swift* laboured.

In

In 1735 he printed Mr. *Wesley's* * "Dissertationes in Librum
" *Jobi*", and the first edition of " *Whiston's Josephus*," folio;
" *Littleton's* Dictionary;" Mr. *Shelton's* " Translation of Dr.
" *Wotton's* Conspectus" (of which see more fully under 1737),
a " Psalter in *Hebrew*," 4to; and " Dr. *Clarke's* edition of *Homer*"
in 8vo. In 1736, "Concilia *Magnæ Britanniæ* et *Hiberniæ*,
" à Synodo *Verolamiensi* A. D. CCCCXLVI, ad *Londinensem*
" A. D. CIƆIƆCCXVII: accedunt Constitutiones et alia ad
" Historiam Ecclesiæ *Anglicanæ* spectantia à *Davide Wilkins* †,
" S. T. P. Archidiacono *Suffolciensi*, & Canonico *Cantuariensi*,

---

* *Samuel Wesley*, born at *Winterborn Whitchurch* in *Dorsetshire*, where his father was
vicar; and admitted of *Exeter College, Oxford*, 1684; was rector of *South Ormesby* and
Epworth, in the county of *Lincoln*; and died *April* 25, 1735. He was a very voluminous author; having published, besides other things, " Maggots, or Poems on se-
" veral subjects, 1685," 8vo.; " Elegies on Queen *Mary* and Archbishop *Tillotson*, 1695,"
folio; " The Life of Christ, an heroic Poem, 1693," folio; reprinted with large additions and corrections in 1697; " The History of the New Testament, in Verse, 1701,"
12mo.; " A Treatise on the Sacrament;" and "Dissertationes in Librum *Jobi*," for
which last proposals were circulated in 1729, and which was finished after his death, by
his son *Samuel*, 1735. His poetry, which is far from being excellent, incurred the
censure of *Garth*; but he made ample amends for it by the goodness of his life, and the
" Dissertationes upon *Job*." He left an exceedingly numerous family of children; four
of whom are not unknown in the annals of *English* literature: 1. *Samuel*, sometime
usher of *Westminster* school, author of an excellent Poem, called " The Battle of the
" Sexes," and several humourous tales, printed, together with other poems by him, in
4to. in 1736, and afterwards in 12mo. He died *Nov.* 6, 1739, being at that time head-
master of *Tiverton* school. 2. 3. *John* and *Charles Wesley*; the two celebrated Methodist
Preachers. 4. Mrs. *Wright*, authoress of several Poems printed in the sixth volume of
the Poetical Calendar.

† In the account of Dr. *Wilkins*, already given p. 48, I have called him a *German-
Swiss*. This mistake arose from his having been confounded with his immediate successor at *Lambeth*. The other particulars of him, which I was favoured with by Dr.
Ducarel, are authentic; and I am enabled to add to them, from the same respectable authority, that he succeeded *Benjamin Ibbot*, A. M. afterwards D. D. as librarian at *Lambeth*,
about 1715, being appointed to that office by Archbishop *Wake*. He finished his catalogues of the MSS. and printed books there in 1718; when resigning that office, the archbishop appointed for his successor *John Henry Ott*, born in the Canton of *Zurick*, where his
father resided, from whom his Grace had received many civilities in the younger part of life.
Mr. *Ott* having many children, Archbishop *Wake*, when he came to the see, remembering his former kindness, appointed this *John Henry* his librarian; ordained him deacon
and priest, and collated him, *June* 26, 1721, to the rectory of *Blackmanston, Kent*; *July*
28, 1722, to that of *East Horseleigh, Surrey*; *Dec.* 15, 1722, to the vicarage of *Bexhil*,
Sussex (an option); *March* 9, 1722-3, to a prebend of *Litchfield* (an option); *Sept.* 21,
1728, appointed him one of the six preachers in *Canterbury* Cathedral; and, *Nov.* 16, 1730,
a prebendary of *Peterborough*. He continued librarian till Archbishop *Wake's* death;
and understood coins and medals (of which he had a good collection) extremely well.

" collecta,"

" collecta," four volumes, folio; " Baronia *Anglica*; an
" History of Land-honors and Baronies, and of Tenure *in*
" *capite*; verified by Records. By *Thomas Madox**, esq. late
" his

---

* This excellent Antiquary died *Jan.* 13, 1727. A short note of his writings has
been given in p. 31; which deserve, however, to be farther enlarged on. "Mr. *Madox*,
with a most indefatigable industry, collected and explained, at different times, a vast
number of records relating to the ancient laws and constitution of this country; the
knowledge of which tends greatly to the illustration of *English* history. He has, by his
unwearied labours in this way, obliged the readers as well as the compilers of such history:
for whoever would succeed in writing a general history, should be intimately acquainted
with the minuter parts of which it consists, a competent knowledge of which is necessary
in every reader that seeks for more than bare amusement. Mr. *Madox*, in the treatises he published himself, and in this posthumous piece just now put into our hands,
has supplied both with a noble apparatus. It was in the year 1702 that he first distinguished himself in these toilsome researches; when, under the patronage of the
learned and polite lord *Somers*, he presented the early fruits of them to the world, in
*A Collection of antique Charters and Instruments of divers Kinds taken from the Origi-
nals, placed under several Heads, and deduced (in a Series according to the Order of Time)
from the* Norman *Conquest, to the End of the Reign of King* Henry VIII †. He was
prompted to this work, by considering that there was no methodical History or System of
ancient Charters and Instruments of this nation then extant; and that it would be acceptable to curious persons, and useful to the publick, if something were done for supplying that defect. Having entertained such a design, and being furnished with proper
materials from the archives of the late Court of *Augmentations*, he was encouraged to
proceed in it, especially by the above-mentioned lord; and thereupon prosecuted it with
so much application, that out of an immense heap of original charters and writings, remaining in that repository, he selected and digested the main of this volume. In 1711,
our author set forth a work of much greater dignity and importance than the foregoing.
It was " The History and Antiquities of the *Exchequer* of the Kings of *England*, in two
" Periods, viz. from the *Norman* Conquest, to the end of the Reign of King *John*;
" and from the end of the Reign of King *John*, to the end of the Reign of King *Ed-
" ward* II. Taken from Records. Together with a correct copy of the ancient Dia-
" logue concerning the *Exchequer*, generally ascribed to *Gervasius T.lburiensis*; and
" a Dissertation concerning the most ancient Great Roll of the *Exchequer*, commonly
" stiled *The Roll of Quinto Regis Stephani* ‡. This was dedicated to the late Queen;
but there is likewise prefixed to it a long prefatory epistle to the lord *Somers*; in which
he gives that illustrious *Mæcenas* some account of this great unprecedented undertaking.
He observes, that though some treatises had been written concerning the *Exchequer*, yet
no history of it had been yet attempted by any man. He tells his lordship, that he had
pursued his subject to those ancient times, to which, he thinks, the original of the *Exchequer* in *England* may properly be assigned. From thence he has drawn down an orderly account of it through a long course of years. And, having consulted, as well the
books necessary to be perused upon this occasion, as a very great number of records and
manuscripts, he had endeavoured all along to confirm what he offered, by proper vouchers

† Known by the title of *Formulare Anglicanum*. It is a folio of 441 pages. The Dissertation concerning *Ancient Charters and Instruments*, prefixed to this work, is replete with useful learning upon
that subject.

‡ A large folio, containing 588 pages.

fetched

" his Majesty's Historiographer," folio, (which was begun
March 25, 1730); and " *Eboracum*; or the History and
" Antiquities

fetched from thence; which vouchers are subjoined column-wise in each page, except
where their extraordinary length made it impracticable. The records which he here at-
tests were, as he adds, taken by his own pen from the authentic membranes, unless
where it appears by his references to be otherwise. He has contrived throughout the
whole (as far as the subject-matter would permit) to make use of such memorials, as
serve either to make known or to explain the ancient laws and usages of this kingdom.
For which reason, as he notes, this work may be deemed, not merely a History of the
Exchequer, but likewise a *Promptuary* towards a History of the ancient Law of *England*.
He afterwards acquaints his lordship in what method he began and proceeded in compiling this work. First, he made as full a collection from records as he could, of materials relating to the subject. Those materials being ranged orderly in several books of
Collectanea, he reviewed them, and weighing what they imported, and how they might
be applied, he drew from thence a general scheme of his design. When he had pitched
upon the heads of his discourse, he took materials for them out of the aforesaid fund,
and digested them into their proper rank and order. In doing this, it was his practice for
the most part to write down, in the draught of this book, the respective records or testimonies first of all; *i. e.* before he wrote his own text or composition; and from them
formed his history or account of things; connecting and applying them afterwards, as
the case would admit. At the end of this history (as we have expressed it in the title)
Mr. *Madox* has published a copy of the treatise concerning the *Exchequer*, written in
the way of dialogue, and generally ascribed to *Gervasius Tilburiensis*. This treatise is
certainly very ancient, and intrinsically valuable. Our author introduces it by an epistolary dissertation, in *Latin*, to the then lord *Halifax*. The dialogue is followed by
another epistolary dissertation, in the same language, addressed to the lord *Somers*, relating to the Great Roll of the *Exchequer*, commonly stiled The Roll of *Quinto Regis
Stephani*. No historical account has been given in this volume, of the records reposited
in the *Exchequer*. Mr. *Madox* thought that might be more properly done, if there was
occasion for it, hereafter, in a continuation of this work; which he seems to have had
some intention of performing himself, when he published this part; or hoped some other
hand would supply, if he did not. But the last chapter of the history is a list of the
Barons of this court from the first year of *William* the Conqueror to the 20th of *Edward*
II. The last work this laborious Historiographer published himself, was " The *Firma*
" *Burgi* †, or Historical Essay concerning the Cities, Towns, and Boroughs of *Eng-*
" *land*. Taken from Records." This treatise was inscribed to his late Majesty. The
author warns his readers against expecting to find any curious or refined learning in it;
in regard the matter of it is low. It is only one part of a subject, which however is
extensive and difficult, concerning which, he tells us, much has been said by *English*
writers to very little purpose, serving rather to entangle than to clear it. When he first
entered upon the discussion of it, he found himself encompassed with doubts, which it
hath been his endeavour, as he says, to remove or lessen as he went along. He has
throughout mixed history and dissertation together, making these two to strengthen and
diversify each other. However modestly Mr. *Madox* might express himself concerning
the learning of this work, it is in reality both curious and profound, and his enquiries
very laudable and useful. The civil antiquities of this country would, in all probability,
have been further beholden than they are, to this skilful and industrious person, if his

---

† A folio, consisting of 348 pages in the whole; printed for *R. Gosling*, father to the late alderman,
and to the present banker.

life

" Antiquities of the City of *York*, from its original to
" the prefent time; together with the Hiftory of the
" Cathedral Church, and the Lives of the Archbifhops
" of that See, &c. By *Francis Drake**, of the City of
" *York*, Gent. F. R. S. and member of the Society of An-
" tiquaries in *London*," folio; " Antiquæ Infcriptiones Duæ,"
by Mr. *Maittaire*, 4to.; " The Alliance between Church
" and State, or the Neceffity and Equity of an Eftablifhed
" Religion, and a Teft Law demonftrated, from the Effence
" and End of Civil Society, upon the fundamental princi-
" ples of the Law of Nature and Nations†," 8vo; a third
edition of " Dr. *Grey's* Memoria Technica," 8vo; and a new
edition of the four firft volumes‡ of Dean *Mofs's* Sermons, 8vo.

life had been of a fomewhat longer continuance; for it may be prefumed from two or three paffages in the prefaces of thofe books he publifhed himfelf, that he meditated and intended fome others to follow them, different from this pofthumous Hiftory of Baronies, which, I think, his advertifement of it fuggefts to be the only manufcript left finifhed by the author. This is compiled much in the manner of his other writings. In the firft book he difcourfes largely of Land Baronies: In the fecond book he treats briefly of Titular Baronies; and in the third of Feudal Tenure in Capite." *Prefent State of the Republick of Letters*, vol. XVII. *p.* 426.—Befides the works above enumerated, this laborious Antiquary made large hiftorical collections upon various fubjects, relating to the laws, cuftoms, and manners of *England*. About eighty volumes of MSS. nearly all in his own hand-writing (including thofe mentioned in p. 31), form a part of that invaluable national repofitory *The Britifh Mufeum*; others are in private hands. Thefe collections are an inexhauftible mine of treafure to the Hiftorian, the Lawyer, and the Antiquary.

* *Francis Drake*, F. R. and A. S. was a furgeon at *York*, an eminent Antiquary, and much efteemed by Dr. *Mead*, Mr. *Folkes*, the two Mr. *Gales*, and all the principal members of the Royal and Antiquary Societies. He publifhed the Hiftory and Antiquities of *York*, 1736, folio; a copy of which, with large MS additions by the author, is in the hands of his fon, the Rev. *William Drake*, F. A. S. late mafter of the free-fchool at *Felfted* in *Effex*, and now (1779) vicar of *Ifleworth, Middlefex*, who has diftinguifhed himfelf by feveral curious articles in the Archæologia, IV. 143, V. 137. 379. and would republifh his father's book if the plates could be recovered. A metzotinto print of Mr. *Drake*, by *Val. Green*, was publifhed in 1771, from a picture by *N. Drake*, with this infcription: " *Franc. Drake* Armiger, *Eboracenfis*, Reg. Soc. necnon Antiqu. Socius."

† This volume, which was publifhed anonymoufly, was the firft introduction of Mr. *Bowyer* to Mr. *Warburton*, its very learned author. It was pronounced, in " The " Prefent State of the Republick of Letters," vol. XVII. p. 471, to be the work of " a gentleman, whofe capacity, judgment, and learning, deferve fome eminent dignity " in the church, of which he is now an inferior minifter."

‡ Four more volumes were printed in 1738, but not by Mr. *Bowyer*.

In

In the month of *May* 1736, Mr. *Bowyer* was appointed Printer to the Society of Antiquaries; and began his work for them by " A Table of *English* Gold Coins from the eighteenth " year of King *Edward* III. when gold was firſt coined in " *England**, with their ſeveral weights and preſent intrinſic " value, by *Martin Folkes* †, Eſquire."

Mr. *Bowyer* was elected into that reſpectable body on the 7th of *July* following, and ſoon ſhewed himſelf to be a very uſeful member. It appears from the minute-books that he regularly attended their meetings (which were then held at *The Mitre Tavern* in *Fleet Street*, where they were continued till 1753, when the Society, after their incorporation, removed to their preſent houſe in *Chancery Lane*); and frequently entertained them with valuable communications.

Of the original revivers of the Society in 1717, a general account is given in the Introduction to the firſt volume of their Archæologia. Of thoſe original members there remained only the following perſons at the time of Mr. *Bowyer's* admiſſion; *viz.* Dr. *Stukeley* †, Mr. *Alexander* ‡, the two Mr.

---

* Of the catalogue which is mentioned in p. 82, I have ſince ſeen two copies, one of them in the collection of Dr. *Ducarel*, the other in Mr. *Tutet's*. Both theſe copies are in large folio, on which ſize 100 were printed, and 100 in a ſmaller folio. The title of it is, " A Table of the Gold Coins of the Kings of *England*. By *B. W.* Eſq. a Member " of the Society of Antiquaries." The two engraved plates of ſilver and gold coins had been publiſhed by the Society in 1732; and this Catalogue appears to have been drawn up by Mr. *Willis* to illuſtrate the plate of gold coins, and was printed at the expence of Mr. *Vertue*.

† Of Mr. *Folkes*, and Dr. *Stukeley*, an account will be given in the courſe of theſe Memoirs.

‡ *Edward Alexander*, eſq. admitted Proctor in *Doctor's Commons* in 1695; was many years Regiſtrar to the Commiſſary of *London* Dioceſe. He purchaſed the manor of *Ongar* in *Eſſex* about the year 1717; married *Levina* daughter of Sir *Levinus Bennet*, of *Baberham* **, in

---

** This eſtate was ſold to *Robert Jones*, eſq. a merchant of *London*, director of the *Eaſt-India* Company, one of the elder brethren of the *Trinity Houſe*, and member for *Huntingdon*. He died in 1773; leaving an only daughter his heireſs, though ſhe diſobliged him in marrying. He pulled down the old houſe; which was built in the *Italian* ſtyle, by Sir *Horatio Pallavicini*, with a gallery along the front of the ſecond floor, and built a moderate-ſized modern houſe. *Pallavicini's* other houſe at *Shelford*, which ſuffered the ſame fate a few years before, had a *loggia* in the centre front. It is remarkable that an *Italian*, at that time of day, ſhould build two houſes ſo near! Sir *Horatio* was one of the collectors of the Pope's dues in Queen *Mary's* time, which, (having pocketed in the time of Queen *Elizabeth*, and conforming to the church of *England*) enabled him to purchaſe two conſiderable eſtates in

Mr. *Gales* * (*Roger* and *Samuel*), Mr. *George Holmes* deputy

in *Cambridgeshire*; and died *October* 27, 1751, aged 80. His grandson, *Richard Henry Alexander Bennet*, esq. married *Elizabeth* eldest daughter of the late *Peter Burrel*, esq. and is F. A. S. Mr. *Alexander's* valuable library lay packed up, and spoilt by damp, at *Ongar*, till his heir came of age, when it was sold almost for nothing about 1757.

* Of these learned brothers, and of their no less learned father, I have given the best account I could, in p. 32 and 33; which I am now enabled to correct, and to enlarge. In the account of Dean *Gale's* publications, p. 32, read, 8. " Historiæ *Britannicæ, Saxonicæ,* " *Anglo-Danicæ & Anglicanæ* Scriptores XX. ex vetustis codd. MSS. editi operâ *Thomæ* " *Gale* **, S. Th. Pr. Præfatio ostendit ordinem. Accessit rerum & verborum Index lo- " cupletissimus. *Oxon.* 1691," folio; and add, 9. " Rhetores Selecti, Gr. Lat. *De-* " *metrius Phalereus* de Elocutione; *Tiberius Rhetor* de Schematibus *Demosthenis*; " *Anonymous Sophista* de Rhetorica; *Severi Alexandrini* Ethopœiæ. Demetrium emen- " davit, reliquos è MSS. edidit & *Latinè* vertit; omnes Notis illustravit *Tho. Gale*, " Sc. Co. M. *Oxon.* 1676," 8vo. 10. " Ars sciendi, sive Logica; nova methodo " disposita & novis præceptis aucta, opera & studio *T. G. M. A. V. D. M.* 1682," 12mo; and, 11. " A Discourse concerning the Original of Human Literature, both " Philology and Philosophy," Phil. Transf. vol. VI. p. 2231.—In p. 33, read, 1. " *Antonini* " Iter *Britanniarum* Commentariis illustratum *Thomæ Gale*, S. T. P. nuper Decani *Ebor.* " Opus posthumum revisit, auxit, edidit *R. G.* Accessit *Anonymi Ravennatis Britanniæ* " Chorographia, cum autographo Regis *Galliæ* M̃ſᵒ, & codice *Vaticano* collata: ad- " jiciuntur conjecturæ plurimæ, cum nominibus locorum *Anglicis*, quotquot iis assignari " potuerint. *Lond.* 1709," 4to. In the preface to this book, Mr. *R. Gale* very properly points out what parts of it were his father's, and what his own. He translated from the *French* " The Knowledge of Medals, by *F. Jobert*," of which two editions were published without his name; one of them in 1715, 12mo. Instead of " his coins, &c." l. 15, read, " his cabinet of *Roman* coins to the public library, with a compleat catalogue of them " drawn up by himself." In *Horsley's* " *Britannia Romana*," p. 332, &c. is published, " An account of a *Roman* inscription found at *Chichester*. By *Roger Gale*, Esq." It is there given from Dr. *Stukeley's* Itin. Curios. I." who took it from the Phil. Transf. Nᵒ 379. And in Phil. Transf. 1731, Nᵒ 420, is " An extract of a Dissertation, de stylis veterum " & diversis chartarum generibus, by *Roger Gale*, Esq."—In the Antiquary Society's " Rerum Elenchus," the third plate is, " Baptisterium in templo *D. Jacobi* apud *West-* " *monasterienses*, ex delineatione societati a *Samuele Gale* armigero, ejusdem quæstore, " exhibita."—At the bottom of p. 33, add, " *Pepys's* library contains every thing that is

in *Essex*, which came to his two sons, who were knighted in her reign, and in that of her successor *James* I. See *Morant's Essex*, vol. I p 8. and 26. He is mentioned in the first edition of Mr. *Walpole's* Anecdotes of Painting, vol. I. p. 160, as an " arras-painter;" and in the second edition of that entertaining work, the following epitaph is quoted from a MS. of Sir *John Crew* of *Utbington*:

" Here lies *Horatio Palavazene*,   •   Him Death wyth besome swept from *Babram*,
Who robb'd the Pope to lend the Queene.   Into the bosom of oulde *Abraham*:
He was a thief: a thief! thou lyest;   But then came *Hercules* with his club,
For whie? he robb'd but Antichrist. ·   And struck him down to *Belzebub*."

Mr. *Walpole* observes, that this Sir *Horatio* died *July* 6, 1600; and that *July* 7, 1601, his widow married a Mr. *Oliver Cromwell*, as appears by the parish register of *Baberham*.

** This work consists of three volumes, though Dr. *Gale* published but two. The first (containing *Ingulphus, Petrus Blesensis*, and three other writers) was compiled by Mr. *William Fulman*, under the patronage of Bishop *Fell*, 1684; the second by Dean *Gale*, in 1687; the third by the same learned editor, 1691. See an account of Dean *Gale*, as far as relates to his publishing a part of *Walter Hemingford*, in *Hearne's* Preface to *Hemingford*, p. xxiii. For his epitaph, I have already referred to *Drake's* Eboracum: it is also printed in Mr. *Popham's* " Illustrium Virorum Elogia Sepulchralia, 1778," p. 115.

wanting

puty keeper of the records in *The Tower**, Mr. *Becket*
a

wanting in the other libraries, so as to be their complement *+**. To instance in a small particular: in three or more volumes, according to their sizes, he has collected almost every writer on short-hand, with a compleat catalogue of all that he could ever hear of. His collection of Calligraphy is large: and all the articles are got together, and arranged and catalogued in a scientifical manner; so that nothing is wanting to make it very valuable, but the being able to see it without the presence of a Fellow; as the present mode, directed by the founder, occasions an unreasonable confinement to a good-natured resident-member of a small Society; and disposes many to decline the benefit of using it, rather than be troublesome." *Dr. Taylor's Friend.*

* Mr. *George Holmes* (born at *Skipton in Craven, Yorkshire*) became about 1695 clerk to *William Petyt*, esq. keeper of the records at *The Tower*; and continued near sixty years deputy to Mr. *Petyt*, Mr. *Topham*, and Mr. *Polhill*. Upon the death of Mr. *Petyt* ††, which happened *Oct.* 9, 1707, Mr. *Holmes* was, on account of his singular abilities and industry, appointed by Lord *Halifax* (then President of a Committee of the House of Lords) to methodize and digest the Records deposited in *The Tower*, at a yearly salary of two hundred pounds, continued to his death, in 1748, in the 87th year of his age. He married ———— daughter of Mr. *Marshall*, an eminent Sword-

** This reminds me of mentioning one curious article in it; a Collection of original letters of *Henry* VIII. *Edward* VI. Queen *Elizabeth*, and of many noblemen of those times, bound up in one volume; an abstract of which is given in the catalogue of that library; with a fac-simile, or apograph, of the names of the writers of those letters, drawn up with great exactness by one of Mr. *Pepys's* clerks. It would reflect great credit on *Magdalen College*, if this abstract was to be engraved at their expence; it being, I am informed, drawn out properly for that purpose.—Mr. *Pepys's* large collections of prints and drawings to illustrate the history of *London* (his native city) are likewise particularly worth notice. They were arranged by him in 1700 in two large folio volumes, under the following heads: Vol. I. maps, views, and plans—buildings, monuments, and churches—*Thames* and its views. Vol. II. Regalia and habits of the city—lord mayors shews—companies arms—sessions house, *Newgate*, &c—parliament and convocation—coronations and public entries—cavalcades and triumphal arches—processions—habits—cries—vulgaria, or miscellaneous articles. See British Topography, I 743.—Mr. *Pepys* was elected president of the Royal Society in 1680, and presided two years. He died *May* 26, 1703. See more of him in *Granger*, IV. 523; who describes two well-executed portraits of Mr. *Pepys*, both engraved by *R. White* from a painting of Sir *Godfrey Kneller.*

†† Whose history will be illustrated by his epitaph, from *Popham's Elogia Sepulchralia*:

" Hic juxta sitæ sunt Reliquiæ
WILHELMI PETYT, Armig.
Qui olim Medii Alumnus fuit,
Nuper Interioris Templi Socius, et Thesaurarius.
Rotulorum ac Archivorum in Turri
Londinensi remanentium
Custos fidelissimus,
Quamplurimis tam genere quàm doctrinâ
Viris insignibus bene notus,
Et in magnâ æstimatione habitus.
Omnia sua
Cum amicis habuit communia:
Neque sanè cuiquam literarum veterum studioso,
Vel operam suam,
Vel consilium unquam negabat;
Quod in pluribus eruditorum scriptis apparet.
Municipalia Patriæ jura,
Historiam, Antiquitates,
Monumenta, Actaque Parliamentaria
Optimè callebat:
Antiquæ Constitutionis
Legum ac Libertatum *Angliæ*

Strenuissimus erat assertor.
Et ne operam et oleum perderet,
Et evanescerent labores,
Mundo valedicturus omnia sua MSS.
(Quæ varia implent volumina)
Unà cum libris impressis, juridicis, historicis,
Atque antiquitatum et processuum
Parliamentorum monumentis
(Quæ magno labore, studio, et sumptibus
Sibi comparavit)
Amicis quibusdam melioris notæ,
In fidei committo ad servanda integra et illibata,
Ultimo suo Testamento
Publicæ utilitatis gratia,
Legavit.
Quapropter locum certum,
Qui illis visus fuerit maxime accommodatus,
Eos eligere voluit:
Et centum et quinquaginta libras
Bibliothecæ ædificandæ
Destinavit.
Obiit 1707, Ætat. 72."

His valuable MSS. are deposited in the library of *The Middle Temple*.

O

cutler

a gentleman of eminence in his profession as a surgeon*,
Mr. *Robert Sanderson* (already mentioned in p. 74), Mr.
William Nicholas† store-keeper in the office of ordnance,
Mr. *Maurice Johnson*‡ of *Spalding*, Dr. *Knight*||, Mr. *George*
Vertue,

cutler in *Fleet Street*, by whom he had an only son *George*, who died many years before him. She outlived her husband, and received of government 200l. for his MSS.
about the records, which were deposited and remain in his office to this day. He re-published (as has been already mentioned, p. 73) the first seventeen volumes ** of *Rymer's*
Fœdera, in 1727. His curious collections of books, prints, and coins, &c. were sold
by auction in 1749. His portrait was engraved by the Society of Antiquaries, with
this inscription: " Vera effigies GEORGII HOLMES generosi, R.S.S. et tabularii publici
in Turre *Londinensi* Vicecustodis ; quo munere annos circiter LX summa fide et diligentia
perfunctus, XIV kalend. Mart. A.D. MDCCXLVIII, ætatis suæ LXXXVII, fato demum
concessit. In fratris sui erga se meritorum testimonium hanc tabulam SOCIETAS ANTI-
QUARIORUM *Londini*, cujus commoda semper promovit, sumptu suo æri incidendum
curavit, MDCCXLIX. R. *Van Bleeck p.* 1743. G. *Vertue del. & sculp.*"—In *Strype's London*,
1754, vol. I. p. 746, is a fac-simile of an antique inscription over the little door next to
the cloister in the *Temple* church. It was in old *Saxon* capital letters, engraved within
an half circle ; denoting the year when the church was dedicated, and by whom, namely,
Heraclius the patriarch of the church of the Holy Resurrection in *Jerusalem* ; and to
whom, namely, the Blessed Virgin ; and the indulgence of forty days pardon to such
who, according to the penance enjoined them, resorted thither yearly. This inscription,
which was scarcely legible, and in 1695 was entirely broken by the workmen, having been
exactly transcribed by Mr. *Holmes*, was by him communicated to *Strype*.

  * Author of Essays " on the Antiquity of touching for the King's Evil, 1722," 8vo.
" on the Venereal Disease in *England* ;" and on other subjects in the Philosophical
Transactions, Nº 357. 365. 366. 383. He died *November* 25, 1738.

  † *William Nicholas*, esq. the youngest son of Sir *John Nicholas*, Knight of the Bath
(and grandson of Sir *Edward Nicholas*, Secretary of State to *Charles* I. and II.) was
brought up a *Turkey* merchant. He represented the borough of *Wilton* in 1705, and
was one of the revivers of the Society of Antiquaries in 1717. Having survived his two
brothers *John* and *Edward*, their large possessions in *London*, *Surrey*, *Wiltshire*, &c. descended to him. He was the last of his family, and died unmarried, immensely rich, at his
seat at *West Horsley* in *Surrey*, *Dec.* 26, 1749, aged 84, and was buried in that church.

  ‡ *Maurice Johnson*, Esq. counsellor at law, a native of *Spalding* in *Lincolnshire*, where
he had a considerable fortune, was steward of that manor, and founded an Antiquarian
Society there as a Cell to that in *London*, to which he from time to time communicated some of their minutes. He was a gentleman of great learning, well versed in the history and antiquities of this kingdom ; but published nothing in his life-time. He
resided principally at *Spalding*, where he died *Feb.* 8, 1755, in a very advanced age,
and with him the Society he had formed ; of which Dr. *Stukeley*, the two Mr. *Gales*,
Mr *Drake* of *York*, Mr. *Folkes*, Dr. *Ducarel*, Mr. *Vertue*, Mr *Peck*, Mr. *T. Martin*,
and many others, were honorary members. Some of the proceedings of this Society, from
Mr. *Johnson's* letters to Mr. *R. Gale*, may probably be communicated to the publick.

  || *Samuel Knight*, D.D. a native of *London* (where his father was free of the mercers
company), received the early part of his education at *St. Paul's* school ; and was thence

  ** Before this second edition, a sett of the seventeen volumes was sold for a hundred guineas. See
the Preface to the " Acta Regia, 1726," 8vo.

3   admitted

Vertue*, Mr. *Browne Willis**, and Dr. *Rawlinson*†. From these worthy Antiquaries Mr. *Bowyer* experienced both patronage and friendship, as he did from many others who may more properly be called his contemporaries.

Not

admitted of *Trinity College, Cambridge*; where having taken his degree of M.A. he became chaplain to *Edward* earl of *Orford*, who presented him to the rectory of *Borough-Green*, in *Cambridgeshire*, to which he was instituted *Nov.* 3, 1707. He afterwards was collated by Bp *Moore* to a prebendal stall in the church of *Ely*, *June* 8, 1714; and presented by him to the rectory of *Bluntesham* in *Huntingdonshire*, *June* 22 following; was made chaplain to his late majesty, 1729; and promoted by Bp *Sherlock* to the archdeaconry of *Berks*, 1735. He published the Lives of *Erasmus* and Dean *Collet*, 1724, 1726, 8vo; died *Dec.* 16, 1746, in the 72d year of his age; and was buried in the chancel of *Bluntesham* church, where a neat monument of white marble is erected to his memory, with an inscription written by his friend Mr. *Castle*, late dean of *Hereford*, who knew him well, and has given him a character, which all who remember Dr. *Knight* will readily allow to be a just one: " Hic juxta situs est *Samuel* " *Knight*, S.T.P. ecclesiæ *Eliensis* præbendarius, com. *Berkensis* Archidiaconus, et " hujus ecclesiæ rector: Rei Antiquariæ cujuscumque generis cultor studiosus; præ- " cipuè vero famæ virorum ingenii, virtutis et literarum laude maximè insignium, fautor " eximius; prout ea quæ scripsit de vitâ rebusque gestis celeb. *Erasmi* et *Coleti*, palàm " testatum faciunt. Concinando assiduus; rebusque gerendis sedulus, præsertim iis " quibus aut amorem inter amicos, locorum longinquitate dissitos, fovere, aut publicum " Ecclesiæ commodum promovere, aut quamplurimis prodesse potuerit: adeò ut pos- " teris jure commendetur, tanquam humano generi amicus. Laboribus, studiis, nego- " tiis, tandem confectus, in hoc loco placidam invenit quietem, beatam expectans re- " surrectionem. Ob. *Dec.* 10, 1746, ætat. 72. Hoc monumentum, reverentiæ et pie- " tatis ergo, posuit filius unicus." *Bentham's Ely*, p. 264.

* For Mr. *Vertue*, and Mr. *Willis*, see the places referred to in the Index.

† *Richard Rawlinson*, LL.D. F.R. and A.S.S. (third son of Sir *Thomas Rawlinson*, lord-mayor of *London* 1706, whose picture painted by *Kneller* was engraved by *Vertue*, and his monument in *St. Dionis Backchurch, Fenchurch-street*, by an anonymous hand) was chosen, *May* 14, 1727, a member of the Society of Antiquaries; to whom he bequeathed a small freehold and copyhold estate at *Fulham*, on condition that they did not, upon any terms, or by any stratagem, art, means, or contrivance howsoever, increase or add to their (then) present number of 150 members, honorary foreigners only excepted. He also made them a considerable bequest of antiquities; but, resenting some supposed want of deference to singularities and dictatorial spirit, and some reflections on his own and his friend's honour, in an imputation of libeling the Society in the public papers, he, by a codicil made and signed at their house in *Chancery-Lane*, revoked the whole, and excluded all fellows of this or the Royal Society from any benefit from his benefactions at *Oxford*, which, besides his *Anglo-Saxon* endowment, were extremely considerable; including, amongst other curiosities, a series of medals of the Popes, which Dr. *Rawlinson* supposed to be one of the most compleat collections in *Europe*; and a great number of valuable MSS. which he directed to be safely locked up, and not to be opened till seven years after his decease**. He died *April* 6, 1755; and

** Dr *Taylor* was persuaded that this precaution was taken to prevent the right owners' recovering their own. He supposed that Dr. *R.* made no scruple of buying all that was brought to him; and that, among the

Not to mention (as I well could do) the names of several gentlemen of the first confequence now living, I
will only enumerate thofe of his more immediate friends,
who were members of the Society either at the time of
his admiffion, or very foon after.　In this number he
was

and in the fame year was printed, " The Deed of Truft and Will of *Richard*
" *Rawlinfon*, of *St. John Baptift* College in *Oxford*, Doctor of Laws; concerning
" his Endowment of an *Anglo-Saxon* Lecture, and other Benefactions to the College
" and Univerfity."　To the college of *St. John the Baptift*, where he had been a gentleman commoner, the Doctor left the bulk of his eftate, amounting to near 700l. a year,
a plate of Archbifhop *Laud*, thirty-one volumes of Parliamentary Journals and Debates, a fet of the Fœdera, all his *Greek*, *Roman*, and *Englifh* coins not given to the
Bodleian Library, all his plates engraved at the Society of Antiquaries expence, his diploma, and his heart, which is placed in a beautiful urn againft the chapel wall, with
this infcription:

" Ubi thefaurus, ibi cor.
" RIC. RAWLINSON, LL. D. & ANT. S. S.
" Olim hujus Collegii fuperioris ordinis Commenfalis;
" Obiit VI *Apr.* MDCCLV."

His body (with counfellor *Layer's* ** head in his right hand) was buried in a vault (in
the north aile of *St. Giles's* church, *Oxford*) of which, with the infcription, he had a
plate engraved in his life time.　His library of printed books and books of prints was
fold by auction in the year 1756; the fale lafted 50 days.　There was a fecond fale of
pamphlets, books of prints, &c. in the following year, during 10 days; which was

the reft, the MS. and printed copy of *Demofthenes*, which was loft on the road, and the detainer of which
he had curfed fo claffically, would be found among the fpoil.　The MS. belonged to *James Harris*,
efq. of *Salifbury*, by whom it was fent to *Cambridge*; but, to ufe the words of Dr. *Taylor*, " in iti-
" nere, mala quorundam fide, interceptus eft, & ex eo tempore diu fruftraque a me quæfitus; five im-
" prudentia, five confilio & dedita opera fit difcerptus.　Hunc SI QUIS adhuc, nec prece noftra nec
" pretio delinitus, domi in PLUTEO CONCLUSERIT, vel quovis modo FRAUDEM FAXIT, DEÆ FIDEI
" SACER ESTO."　I quote this paffage, as I can contradict the fuppofition it has given rife to: "I remem-
" ber the note you refer to in *Taylor's Demofthenes*; it is the laft article of his Syllabus of the books and
" MSS. which he perufed for his edition of the third volume.　But I never could learn what became of
" Mr. *Harris's* MS. which was loft by the careleffnefs of a common carrier.　Sure I am that it never
" arrived at the *Bodleian* Library, either in Dr. *Rawlinfon's* or any other collection.　The papers, &c.
" which the Doctor defired might not be made public till feven years after his death, were Collections
" for a continuation of the *Athenæ Oxonienfes*, and *Hearne's* Diaries.　Thefe are now open for
" any one that wifhes to confult them.　As to the Doctor's mode of collecting, I have nothing to fay.
" It was over with him before I entered upon my bufinefs here.　We have a MS. catalogue of moft
" of his MSS. &c.; but when it will be printed, I cannot fay.　The revenue of our prefs, by fome late
" determinations in parliament, has funk very much, and will not admit our undertaking any unfale-
" able works.　Thus, I fear, our Catalogue will remain unprinted, at leaft for fome time."　*Letter*
from Mr. Price to Mr. Gough, Nov. 10, 1779.　*Hearne's* Diaries were purchafed by Dr. *Rawlinfon*
for 100 guineas, of the widow and executrix of Dr. *William Bedford*, to whom they were given by *Hearne*.
** The political principles of Dr. *Rawlinfon* are now merely matter of fpeculation; but may be
afcertained by this peculiar circumftance: When the head of *Layer* was blown-off from *Temple Bar*,
it was picked up by a gentleman in that neighbourhood, who fhewed it to fome friends at a public-
houfe; under the floor of which houfe, I have been affured, it was buried.　Dr. *R.* mean-time having
made inquiry after the head, with a wifh to purchafe it, was impofed on with another inftead of
Layer's; which he preferved as a valuable relique, and directed it to be buried in his hand.

immediately.

was particularly noticed by Mr. *Beaupré Bell**, Mr. *David Papillon*†, Mr. *James West* ‡, Mr. *Drake* of *York* (of whom some

* immediately fucceeded by a fale of the Doctor's fingle prints, books of prints, and drawings; and this lafted eight days. For fome part of this note, I am obliged to *Edward Umfreville* efquire, the only furviving executor of Dr. *Rawlinfon's* will.

* Of *Beaupré-Hall*, near *Wifbech*, in the *Ifle of Ely*, where he had a noble manfion-houfe built of ftone in the ftyle of the old colleges, with an infinite number of rooms, and a confiderable eftate about it. This eftate was held by his anceftors the *Beauprés* from the Conqueft to the reign of *Elizabeth*, when it came, by the marriage of an only furviving daughter, to Sir *Robert Bell*, Speaker of the Houfe of Commons, and Chief Baron of the Exchequer; whofe great-grandfon affuming the name of *Beaupré Bell*, it was continued in this gentleman, whofe youngeft fifter *Elizabeth* married *William Greaves*, efq. of *Fulborne* in *Cambridgefhire*, Commiffary in the court of the Vice-chancellor of *Cambridge* above 50 years, and many years auditor of *Trinity College*, both which he refigned 1778, and now enjoys the eftate. Mr. *Bell* was a moft learned and ingenious antiquary, intimate with Mr. *Baker* of *St. John's*, Mr. *Thomas Hearne*, the two Mr. *Gales*, and all the eminent antiquaries of his time. He was particularly curious in coins, and publifhed propofals for a medallic hiftory of Imperial *Rome*, for which the plates, or fome of them, were engraved; and at his death bequeathed feveral valuable books and MSS. to the library of *Trinity College, Cambridge*, of which he had been a member. He printed a tranflation of an eclogue of *Sannazarius*, called " The Oziers;" and had once a defign of publifhing *Chaucer*, for which he collected what materials he could; but laid it afide, and offered to affift any gentleman with his collations of the MSS**. He drew up the hiftory of *Outwell*, in *Norfolk*, for Mr. *Blomfield*; but was much better furnifhed with notices for *Cambridgefhire*, and offered an account of places in that county, or the *Ifle of Ely*, to Mr. *R. Gale*. (MS. Letter to *R. Gale*, 1733-4). Mr. *Hearne*, in his Preface to *Walter Hemingford*, p. clxxx. has inferted, " An Account of the Church of *Swafham* in *Norfolk*, extracted from a Letter " written to the Publifher by the ingenious *Beaupré Bell*, of *Beaupré Hall* in *Norfolk*, efq."

† *David Papillon* ††, efq. a gentleman of confiderable eftate at *Acryfe*, otherwife *Aukridge*, in *Kent*, where he had a feat; though he generally refided at another very capital houfe belonging to him at *Lee*, near *Lewifham*, in *Kent*, where he had a very good library ‡‡, being curious in antiquarian refearches. He was a warm fupporter of Sir *Robert Walpole*; and in one day was returned member of parliament both for *Dover* and *Hythe*, after a moft violent oppofition in both. He was elected member for *Romney* in *Kent* in 1722 and 1727; again returned for *Dover* in 1734; and appointed in *February* 1742 one of the Commiffioners of Excife (which, in *April* 1754, he refigned to his fon *David Papillon*, Efq. who at prefent enjoys that office, together with all the *Kentifh* eftates). He died at *Canterbury*, *Feb*. 2, 1762.

‡ *James Weft*, of *Alfcott*, in the county of *Warwick*, efq. M.A. of *Baliol College*, *Oxford* (fon of *Richard Weft*, faid to be defcended, according to family tradition, from *Leonard*,.

** Mr. *Tyrwhitt*, Preface to " *Canterbury* Tales," p. xxii. mentions two MSS. in *Trinity College*.
†† Son of *Thomas Papillon*, efq. member of parliament for *Dover* 1678 and 1688; and for *London* in 1695 and 1698. See in *Maitland's* Hiftory of *London* fome account of that gentleman, who is fo often mentioned as candidate for the Shrievalty of *London* in *Charles* the Second's time, when the difpute between the city and court was carried on fo warmly, and alfo in the reign of *W*. III. His brother *Philip Papillon*, efq. was member of parliament for *Dover* in 1701—2—5—8—10—13 and 14; and died at *Lee*, *Sept*. 10, 1739, at the age of 80.
‡‡ " I have been told that he contracted with *T. Ofborne* to furnifh him with a hundred pounds worth of books at three-pence a-piece. The only conditions were, that they fhould be perfect, and that

some account has been given in p. 94), Dr. *Richardson**
the

Leonard, a younger son of *Thomas West* lord *Delawar*, who died in 1525**), was representative in parliament for *St. Alban's* in 1741 ; and, being appointed one of the joint secretaries of the Treasury, held that office till 1762. In 1765 or 1766, his old patron the duke of *Newcastle* obtained for him a pension of 2000l. a year. He was an early member, and one of the vice-presidents, of the Antiquary Society ; and was first treasurer, and afterwards president, of the Royal Society. He married the daughter and heirefs of Sir *Thomas Stephens*, timber-merchant in *Southwark*, with whom he had a large fortune in houses in *Rotherhithe* ; and by whom he had a son, *James West*, esq. now of *Alscott*, one of the auditors of the land-tax, and sometime member of parliament for *Boroughbridge* in *Yorkshire* (who in 1774 married the daughter of *Christopher Wrenn*, of *Wroxhall*, in *Warwickshire*, esq.) and two daughters ; *Sarah*, married, in *July* 1761, to *Andrew* late lord *Archer*, and ———— unmarried. He died *July* 2, 1772. His large and valuable collections of MSS. were sold to the earl of *Shelburne*. His very valuable collection of books, including many with large MS. notes by that able antiquary Bishop *White Kennet*, was sold by auction by Mr. *Langford* from a catalogue digested by Mr. *S. Paterson* in 1773 : the sale began *March* 29, and lasted 24 days. His prints and drawings were sold in 13 days ; coins and medals in 7 ; plate and miscellaneous curiosities, in 7 ; pictures, framed prints, and drawings, in 4 days, the same year.

* *William Richardson*, son of *Samuel Richardson*, B. D. youngest son of Mr. *John Richardson* (vid. *Calamy*, vol. II. p. 451), was born at *Wilshamsted* in *Bedfordshire*, where his father was vicar, on *July* 23, 1698. He was educated at *Oakham* and *Westminster* schools, and at *Emanuel College*. In 1726 he published, from Mr. *Bowyer's* press, the " Prælectiones Ecclesiasticæ" of his learned uncle *John Richardson*, B. D. well known by his masterly " Vindication of the Canon of the New Testament," against the artifices of Mr. *J. Toland*, in his Amyntor. In 1730 he published four sermons on the neceffity of Revelation ; and in 1733 an occasional sermon preached at the consecration of the new parochial church of *St. John*, *Southwark*, being at that time lecturer of the parish church of *St. Olave*. There he married, in 1728, *Anne* only daughter and heir of Mr. *William Howe*, of an antient family in the county palatine of *Chester*, and *Elizabeth* his wife, only daughter and heir of Mr. *Humphrey Smith*, of *Walton upon Thames*, *Surrey*. Having undertaken, at the request of the Bishops *Gibson* and *Potter*, to publish a new edition of " Godwin de Præfulibus," he returned to *Cambridge* in 1734 for the convenience of the libraries, and in 1735 proceeded D. D. After the death of Dr. *Savage* in 1736, he was chosen master of *Emanuel College*, of which he had never been fellow, a rare and almost unprecedented compliment to a man of letters. He pub-

that there should be no duplicate. *Osborne* was highly pleased with his bargain ; and the first great purchase he made, sent him a large quantity ; that the next purchase, he found he could send but few, and the next still fewer ; that, not willing to give up, he sent books worth five shillings a piece ; and at last was forced to go and beg to be let off the contract. Eight thousand books would be wanted ; and it seems that though the books, which booksellers call *rums*, appear to be very numerous, because they come oftener in their way than they like ; yet that they are not really so, reckoning only one of a sort." *Dr. Taylor's Friend.*—I have heard the same account from other hands ; with an intimation that the expression *rum books* arose from *Osborne's* sending large assortments of unsaleable works to *Jamaica* in exchange for *rum*.—But I believe this etymology is erroneous See a large number of words connected with *rum* in *N. Bailey's* " Collection of canting words and terms." The *French*, who have words of authority for every thing, as *brocanteur* for a maker or dealer in false coins, have also *bouquins* for rums, and *bouquiniste* for the seller, as a dealer in old cloaths is an old cloaths man ; so *rum man*. At *Cambridge* such an one is called *Maps and Pictures*.

** Gr. V. xi. p. 332, in Coll. Arm.

learned master of *Emanuel College*, Dr. *Tanner* * Bishop of *St. Asaph*,

lished at *Cambridge* his valuable edition of *Godwin*, with a continuation to the present time, in 1743. He served the office of Vice-chancellor in 1738 and 1769. He became Præcentor of the cathedral church of *Lincoln* in 1760; that dignity being an option of his late learned friend and patron Archbishop *Potter*, which was recovered from his Grace's executor Dr. *Chapman*, by a decree of the house of lords, after the reversal of a decree of the lord keeper *Henley*. He was chaplain to their Majesties from 1746 to 1748, when he retired; but was called forth at an advanced period of life, by the friendship of Sir *John Cust*, to preach before the House of Commons, on *Jan.* 30, 1764; this sermon is also printed. He died *March* 14, 1775, and was buried in the same vault with his wife, under the litany desk in the chapel of his college. He was many years an honour to the Society of Antiquaries: and left in MS. many valuable collections relative to the constitution of the University of *Cambridge*; many biographical anecdotes preparatory to an *Athenæ Cantabrigienses*, which he once intended to publish, and an accurate alphabet in his own writing of all the graduates of the University from 1500 to 1735 inclusive. His only son *Robert Richardson*, D. D. F. R. S. and S. A. is now prebendary of *Lincoln*, rector of *St. Anne's, Westminster*, and of *Wallington, Herts*. He is also chaplain to the earl of *Gainsborough*, and the fourth of the five persons of his name, mentioned in this note, who have held that honourable connection with the family of *Noel*.

* This excellent Antiquary, son of a father of both his names, vicar of *Market Lavington* in *Wilts*, was born in 1674, became a student in *Queen's College, Oxford*, in *Michaelmas* term, 1689; admitted clerk in that house 1690; B. A. 1693; entered into holy orders at *Christmas* 1694; and became chaplain of *All Souls College* in *January* following; chosen Fellow of *Queen's*, 1697; Chancellor of *Norwich*, and rector of *Thorpe* near that city, 1701; installed Prebendary of *Ely, Sept.* 10, 1713 (which he quitted 1723); Archdeacon of *Norwich, Dec.* 7, 1721; Canon of *Christ Church, Feb.* 3, 1723-4; prolocutor of the lower house of convocation convened anno 1727, to which honour he was unanimously elected on account of his great abilities, however contrary to his own inclinations; consecrated Bishop of *St. Asaph, Jan.* 23, 1731-2; died at *Christ Church, Oxford, Dec.* 4, 1735; and was buried in the nave of that cathedral, near the pulpit; where a monument to his memory is affixed to one of the pillars, with this inscription:

"M. S.
THOMÆ TANNER, S.T.P.
Qui natus *Lavingtoniæ* in Agro *Wiltoniensi*,
In Collegium Reginense admissus,
Deinde Omnium Animarum Capellanus,
Mox Socius cooptatus est.
Optimarum ibi artium Cultor,
Antiquitatis præsertim studio ita trahebatur,
Ut in Patriæ fastis, monumentisque eruendis,
Nemo illo diligentior,
Nemo in explicandis peritior haberetur.
Hinc maturè avocatus

Ad munus Cancellarii Dioceseôs *Nordovicensis*,
Auctus est insuper Præbenda *Eliensi*.
Academiæ denuo restitutus,
Hanc Ædem Canonicus ornavit.
A Clero interim Prolocutor renunciatus,
Ad Episcopatum tandem evectus est *Asavensem*.
Vir erat
Ad omne officium summâ fide et diligentiâ,
Rarâ pietate,
Humanissimâ erga omnes voluntate,
Liberalitate in egenos effusissimâ.
Obiit 14 die *Decembris*, A. D. 1735, ætatis 62."

He published, before he was twenty-two years old, "Notitia Monastica, or a short History of the Religious Houses in *England* and *Wales*," 1695, 8vo. republished in folio, 1751, with great additions, (which he began to collect in 1715), by his brother Mr. *John Tanner*, Præcentor of *St. Asaph*, and rector of *Lowestoft, Suffolk*. His "Bibliotheca *Britannico-Hibernica*," which employed him forty years, was published in 1748, folio; with a posthumous preface by Dr. *Wilkins* (see p. 48). He left large collections for the county of *Wilts*, and large notes on *Richard Hegge's* Legend of *St. Cuthbert*, 1663.

Afaph, Mr. *Warburton* * *Somerfet* herald, Mr. *Anftis* † and Mr. *Leake*,

1663. His immenfe and valuable collections are now in the *Bodleian* library at *Oxford*. His portrait was engraved at the expence of the Society of Antiquaries.

Another infcription, and a tranflation of it, are here fubjoined, from *Gent. Mag.* 1736, p. 692:

"VICITNE tandem morbus & fenium grave
 Tannere, te patrum decus;
Fregitque nullis territum laboribus
 Suprema fors mortalium?
Luftrare facra fuetus olim rudera
 Fanorum & antiquas domos,
Nunc ipfe veterum pulveri admiftus cinis
 Sub æde veneranda jaces,
Quæ tot capaci præfules docto finu
 Ipfamque *Fridfwidam* ** tenet.
At tu fepulchri non eges honoribus,
 Noftrive laude carminis,
Tu, quem peritum Antiquitatis ultimæ
 Ventura dicent fæcula;
Nomenque *Pario* feripta fervabunt tua
 Perenniora marmore."

"AT length oppress'd by age and malady,
Muft *Tanner* here a common victim lie?
Whofe induftry no trouble could allay,
Muft he fubmit to Death's imperious fway?
Pride of his anceftors! Once wont to tread;
Where now with facred duft his afhes fpread
Within thefe walls, whofe bounds have clofe embrac'd
So many prelates, fpoil of ages paft!
Fridfwida's felf lies here!—But you nor need
The numerous honours for the dead decreed;
Nor the fmall tribute which my verfe affords,
The herald's blazon, nor the pomp of words;
Whom late pofterity fhall juftly praife,
Skill'd in the monuments of ancient days;
Whofe works more truly fhall confign thy fame,
Than *Parian* marble could preferve thy name."

* *John Warburton*, efq. *Somerfet* Herald, an eminent Antiquary, was fon of *Benjamin Warburton*, of *Bury*, in *Lancafhire*, by *Mary* his wife, eldeft daughter and at length heir of *Michael Buxton*, of *Buxton*, in the county of *Derby*; born *Feb.* 28, 1681; created *Somerfet* Herald *June* 18, 1720 (loco *Samuel Stebbing*, efq. deceafed, the publifher of the laft edition of *Sandford's* General Hiftory). He refided chiefly at the *Heralds Office*, where he had an amazing collection of MSS. books, prints, &c. relating to the Hiftory and Antiquities of *England*, which were fold by auction after his death, A. D. 1759. He publifhed, 1. "*London* and *Middlefex* Illuftrated, *London*, 1749," 8vo. juftifying the arms annexed to his map of *Middlefex*. 2. "Vallum *Romanum, London*, 1753," 4to. cuts; maps of *Middlefex, Hertfordfhire, Effex*, and *Yorkfhire*, and fome prints. He married two wives; by the latter of whom he had a fon of both his names, now living in *Ireland*, who married the fifter of the late eminent antiquary *Edward Rowe-Mores*; and a daughter married to *John Elphinfton*, efq. fometime vice-admiral and commander in chief of the *Ruffian* fleet. He died at his houfe in the College of Arms, *May* 11, 1759, aged 78, and was buried in the fouth ifle of *St. Bennet's* church, *Paul's Wharf, London*. (De Vitis Fecialium in Bibl. *J. C. Brooke*, de Coll. Arm. vol. I. fol. 96.)

† Born at *St. Neots* in *Cornwall, September* 28, 1669, being fon of *John Anftis*, of that place, by *Mary* his wife, daughter and coheir of *George Smith*. He was admitted at *Exeter College, Oxford*, 1685, and three years after at *The Middle Temple*; reprefented the borough of *St. Germans*, 1702, 1703, 1704, in parliament, where he diftinguifhed himfelf againft the bill for occafional conformity, for which he got ranked in the lift of the *Tackers*, printed about that time. He was appointed Deputy-General to the Auditors of the Impreft, 1703, which office he never executed; one of the principal Commiffioners of Prizes, 2 *Anne*; Garter King at Arms 13 *Anne* ††; in which place he

** *Fridfwida*, a *Saxon* Queen, foundrefs of part of the College, and buried in the cathedral there.
†† "I have a certain information that my affair [it does not appear what] would be ended forthwith if the Lord Treafurer would honour me by fpeaking to her Majefty at this time, which, in behalf of the Duke of *Norfolk*, I moft earneftly defire, and humbly beg your Lordfhip's affiftance therein. If it fhould be delayed for fome days, I fhall then be back as far as the delivery of my petition. I am obliged to attend this morning at the Exchequer, about the Tin affair, and thereby prevented from

Mr. *Leake**, who fucceffively enjoyed the office of Garter
king

died on *Sunday*, *March* 4, 1743-4; and was buried the 23d following, in a vault in the
parifh church of *Dulo* in *Cornwall*. He publifhed, in 1706, " A Letter concerning
" the honour of Earl Marfhal," 8vo ; in 1720, " The Form of the Inftallation of
" the Garter," 8vo ; in 1724, " The Regifter of the moft noble Order of the Garter,
" ufually called the Black Book, with a Specimen of the Lives of the Knights," 2 volumes
folio; and in 1725, " Obfervations introductory to an hiftorical Effay on the Knight-
" hood of the Bath," 4to. intended as an Introduction to the Hiftory of that Order, for
which the Society of Antiquaries had begun to collect materials. His " Afpilogiı, a dif-
" courfe on Seals in *England*," with beautiful draughts, almoft fit for publication, of which
Mr. *Drake* read an abftract to the Society in 1735-6, and two folio volumes of drawings of
Sepulchral Monuments, Stone Circles, Croffes, and Caftles, in the three kingdoms, were
purchafed, with many other curious papers, at the fale of Mr. *Anftis's* library of MSS.
1768, by *Thomas Aftle*, efq. F. R. and A. S. Befides thefe, he left in MS. two large
folio volumes on the Office, &c. of Garter King at Arms, and of Heralds in general;
memoirs of the *Talbot*, *Carew*, *Granville*, and *Courtney* families; the Antiquities of
Cornwall; " Collections relating to the parifh of *Coliton* in *Devonfhire*," containing
matters relative to the tithes of that church (of which his fon *George Anftis* was vicar),
in a difpute before the court of Exchequer in 1742, marked in the printed catalogue of
his MSS. N°62, and now (1780) in Dr. *Ducarel's* library; and alfo large collections
relative to *All-Souls College*, *Oxford*, by whom they were bought. Sixty-four pages of
his *Latin* anfwer to " The Cafe of Founders Kinfmen" were printed in 4to. with many
coats of arms. His " Curia Militaris, or a Treatife on the Court of Chivalry, in three
" books," of which Mr. *Reed* has the preface and contents, the whole poffibly which
was ever publifhed (if publifhed at all), was printed in 1702, 8vo. In an unpublifhed
letter of his to Mr. *Wanley*, dated *Eafter Sunday*, 1713, I meet with this memorandum : " What I mentioned to you about the probability of the author of the poem of
" the depofition of *R.* II. from the Annotations on the Hiftory of *Charles* VI. p. 746.
" *Berry* Herault de Roy *Charles* VII. efleu à Roy d'Armes des *Francois* a fort particu-
" lierement defcrit la depofition & mort de ce *Richard* Roy d'*Angleterre*. I do not
" remember whether your poem contains the depofition and death of the king." In an
epigram by Mr. *Prior* (*Englifh* Poets, vol. XXXI. p. 258) our Herald is thus introduced :

> " But coronets we owe to crowns,
> " And favour to a court's affection,
> " By Nature we are *Adam's* fons,
> " And fons of *Anftis* by election."

His eldeft fon *John Anftis*, efq. who had been educated as a gentleman commoner at
Corpus Chrifti College, *Oxford*, was, at the revival of the order of the Bath in 1725,
joined to his father in the office of Garter ; and had the additional office of genealogift and
regifter of the Bath. At the opening of Dr. *Radcliffe's* library, 1749, he was, with feveral
other members of that univerfity, created LL. D. He died a batchelor, *Dec.* 5, 1754;
and was fucceeded in his eftate by his brother *George* above mentioned, befides whom
he had another brother in holy orders. He poffeffed a well-chofen collection of books,
and numerous MSS. on heraldic fubjects by his father.

* *Stephen Martin Leake*, efq. (fon of Captain *Martin*) went through different ranks in
the *Heralds Office* till he came to be Garter. He was the firft perfon who wrote profeffedly
on our *Englifh* coins, two editions of his " Hiftorical Account" of which were publifhed by

from waiting on your Lordfhip. With all duty, I am your Lordfhip's moft obedient and faithful
humble fervant, JOHN ANSTIS." *MS. Letter to the Lord Treafurer, March* 14, 1711.

him

king at arms, Mr. *Folkes**, Mr. *Bridges**, Mr. *Lethieullier*†, *Henry Hare* baron of *Colerane*‡ in *Ireland*, Profeſſor *Ward*,

him with plates, under the title of " Nummi *Britannici* Hiſtoria," *London*, 1726, 8vo; the ſecond, much improved, *London*, 1745, 8vo. He printed, in 1750, " The Life of " Sir *John Leake*, knt. Admiral of the Fleet," &c; to whom he was indebted for a conſiderable eſtate; which the Admiral deviſed to truſtees for the uſe of his ſon for life; and upon his death to Captain *Martin* (who married Lady *Leake's* ſiſter) and his heirs: by which means it came to the Captain's ſon, who, in gratitude to the memory of Sir *John Leake*, wrote an accurate account of his life, of which only 50 copies were printed. In 1766 Mr. *Bowyer* printed for him 50 copies of " The Statutes of the Order of the " Garter," 4to. He died, at his houſe called *Leakes Grove*, at *Mile-End, Middleſex, March* 24, 1773; and was buried the 31ſt in his chancel in the pariſh church of *Thorp* in *Eſſex*, of which manor he was lord. (See *Morant*, vol. I. p. 482.)

* For Mr. *Folkes* and Mr. *Bridges*, ſee the pages referred to in the Index.

† *Smart Lethieullier*, eſq. gentleman commoner of *Trinity College, Oxford*, was the ſecond ſon of *John Lethieullier*, eſq. of *Aldersbrook* in *Eſſex*, where he had a noble collection of MSS. choice books, medals, and natural curioſities, which he had collected in his travels through *France*, *Italy*, and *Germany*. His father dying *Jan.* 1, 1736-7, and his elder brother being dead before, he became heir to the paternal eſtates, which were very conſiderable. He married, *Feb.* 5, 1725-6, *Margaret* daughter of *William Sloper*, Eſq. of *Woodhay* in *Berkſhire*; but died *Aug.* 27, 1760, æt. 59, without iſſue. See his epitaph in the 8vo Hiſtory of *Eſſex*, IV. 297. He was ſucceeded in his eſtates, to which he had added the manor of *Birch-Hall* in *Theydon Bois*, by *Mary* ** only daughter of his next brother *Charles Lethieullier*, LL. D. fellow of *All Souls College*, F. A. S. and counſellor at law, who died the year before him. He was an excellent ſcholar, a polite gentleman, and univerſally eſteemed by all the learned men of his time. Some papers of his are printed in Phil. Tranſ. N° 497. Arch. I. p. 26, 57, 73, 75, II. 291. His library was ſold by auction 1760. His couſin Col. *William Lethieullier*, who was alſo F. A. S. travelled into *Egypt*, and brought over a very perfect mummy, deſcribed by Mr. *Gordon* in a tract mentioned in p. 107, and now in *The Britiſh Muſeum* with moſt of the Colonel's collections, the reſt having been in Mr. *Smart Lethieullier's* hands.

‡ *Henry Hare* lord baron of *Colerane*, deſcended from *John*, younger brother to Sir *Nicholas Hare*, Baronet, Maſter of the Rolls, and Privy Counſellor to King *Henry* VIII. (both ſons to *Nicholas Hare* of *Homersfield* in the county of *Suffolk*, the elder branch being ſeated at *Stow Bardolph* in *Norfolk*) was born at *Blechingley*, in *Surrey*, *May* 10, 1693; educated at *Enfield*, under Dr. *Uvedale*, who had alſo the honour of educating, among many other eminent men, the late earl of *Huntingdon* and Sir *Jeremy Sambroke*, bart. After the death of his grandfather, *Hugh* lord *Colerane*, in 1708, he ſucceeded to the title, and was admitted a gentleman commoner of *Corpus Chriſti* College, *Oxford*, under the tuition of Dr. *Rogers*, who afterwards married *Lydia*, one of his lordſhip's ſiſters ††. A lyric poem by lord *Colerane* appeared in the " Academiæ *Oxonienſis* " Comitia Philologica, 1713." Dr. *Baſil Kennet*, who ſucceeded Dr. *Turner* in the preſidency of that Society, inſcribed an epiſtolary poem on his predeceſſor's death to his Lordſhip. He was a great proficient in the learned languages, particularly the *Greek*; and

** Married to *Edward Hulſe*, eſq. the eldeſt ſon of Sir *Edward Hulſe*.

†† See the account of Dr *Rogers* prefixed to his XIX Sermons, p. xxiii. lxi.—In the Introduction to the Archæologia, it is ſaid by miſtake that this lady was married to Dr. *Turner*, the preſident, who died a ſingle man, and gave 20000l. to the uſe of poor clergymens widows.—Another of Lord *Colerane's* ſiſters was married to Mr. *Knight*.

eminently

Ward*, Mr. *Henry Baker**, Dr. *Mangey**, Mr. *Gordon* †,

eminently verfed in Hiftory, both Civil and Ecclefiaftical. He made the tour of *Italy* three times; the fecond time with Dr. *Conyers Middleton*, about 1723, in which he made a noble collection of prints and drawings of all the antiquities, buildings, and pictures, in *Italy*; given after his deceafe to *Corpus Chrifti* College. The efteem in which he was held by the Literati procured him admittance into the *Republica Litteraria di Arcadia*, and the particular intimacy of the Marquis *Scipio Maffei*; who afterwards vifited him at his ancient manor and feat at *Tottenham* in *Middlefex*. His Lordfhip died at *Bath*, *Auguft* 4, 1749; and was buried in the family vault at *Tottenham*, built, with the veftry, by his grandfather. His very valuable collection of prints relative to *Englifh* Antiquities, with a portrait of him when a young man by *Richardfon*, were obtained after his death by Mr. *Henry Baker* for the Society of Antiquaries. His books were fold to *T. Ofborne*, who detained fome of the family papers, which were with difficulty recovered from him. The pictures, with the bronzes and other antiquities, were fold by auction, *March* 13 and 14, 1754. The coins, it is fuppofed, were difpofed of privately. His natural and only daughter *Henrietta Rofa Peregrina*, born in *Italy*, and afterwards naturalized, was married in 1764 to *James Townfend*, efq. Alderman of *Bifhopfgate* Ward, who in her right enjoys the extenfive manor of *Tottenham*, and has repaired the family feat, commonly called *Bruce Caftle* from having anciently belonged to the *Bruces* earls of *Huntingdon*, which had been confiderably modernized in the clofe of the laft century.

* For Mr. *Ward*, Mr. *Baker*, and Dr. *Mangey*, fee the Index.

† *Alexander Gordon*, A.M. a *Scotfman*, an excellent draughtfman, and a good *Grecian*, who refided many years in *Italy*, vifited moft parts of that country, and had alfo travelled into *France*, *Germany*, &c. He was Secretary to the Society for Encouragement of Learning; and afterwards to the *Egyptian* Club, compofed of gentlemen who had vifited *Egypt* (viz. Lord *Sandwich*, Dr. *Shaw*, Dr. *Pococke*, &c.) He fucceeded Dr. *Stukeley* as Secretary to the Antiquary Society, which office he refigned in 1741 to Mr. *Jofeph Ames*. He went to *Carolina* with Governor *Glen*, where, befides a grant of land, he had feveral offices, fuch as regifter of the province, &c.; and died a juftice of the peace, leaving a handfome eftate to his family. He publifhed, 1. " Itinerarium Septentrionale, or a " Journey through moft parts of the Counties of *Scotland*, in two parts, with 66 copper- " plates, *Lond.* 1726," folio. 2. " Additions and Corrections, by way of Supplement, " to the Itinerarium Septentrionale; containing feveral Differtations on, and Defcrip- " tions of, *Roman* Antiquities, difcovered in *Scotland* fince publifhing the faid Itinerary. " Together with Obfervations on other ancient Monuments found in the North of " *England*, never before publifhed. *Lond.* 1732 ‡." folio. 3. " The Lives of Pope " *Alexander* VI. and his fon *Cæfar Borgia*, comprehending the wars in the reign of " *Charles* VIII. and *Lewis* XII. Kings of *France*; and the chief Tranfactions and Revo- " lutions in *Italy*, from the year 1492 to the year 1516. With an Appendix of original " pieces referred to in the work. By *Alexander Gordon*, A. M. F. R. and A. S. " author of the Itinerarium Septentrionale, *Lond.* 1729," folio. 4. " A compleat " Hiftory of the ancient Amphitheatres, more particularly regarding the Architecture " of thefe Buildings, and in particular that of *Verona*, by the Marquis *Scipio Maffei*; " tranflated from the *Italian*, 1730," 8vo. afterwards enlarged in a fecond edition. 5. " An " Effay towards explaining the hieroglyphical figures on the Coffin of the ancient Mum- " my belonging to Capt. *William Lethieullier*. *Lond.* 1737," folio, with cuts. 6. " Twen- " ty-five plates of all the *Egyptian* Mummies, and other *Egyptian* Antiquities in *Eng-* " *land*," about 1739, folio.

‡ A *Latin* edition of the Itinerarium, including the Supplement, was printed in *Holland*, 1731.

Mr.

Mr. *Maittaire**, Sir *Peter Thompson*†, Mr. *Robert Ains-worth*‡ the induſtrious editor of the beſt *Latin* Dictionary, this

* Of whom, ſee under the year 1742.

† Sir *Peter Thompson*, knt. F.R. and A.S.S. third ſon of Captain *Thomas Thompſon*, of *Poole*, in the county of *Dorſet*, in which town Sir *Peter* was born, *Oct.* 30, 1698, and died *Oct.* 30, 1770. *James* his elder brother died at *Poole*, *March* 8, 1739-40. Sir *Peter* was engaged in mercantile buſineſs more than forty years, during which period he chiefly reſided in *Mill-ſtreet, Bermondſey*, in the county of *Surrey*, and was in the commiſſion of the peace. He was appointed high ſheriff for the ſaid county 1745; and, upon the breaking out of the rebellion in *Scotland*, preſented to the king a loyal addreſs and aſſociation from that county; and upon that occaſion received the honour of knighthood. He repreſented the borough of *St. Alban's* in parliament from 1747 to 1754. He made it his choice in 1763 to withdraw from the engagements of commercial affairs, that he might enjoy the pleaſures of ſtudious retirement and reflexion, and the converſation of his friends, in the place of his birth; where he lived reſpected by all ranks of people for his affability and benevolence; and where, in an agreeable ſituation, he had built a handſome houſe, and, at a great expence, formed a capital collection of books, manuſcripts, foſſils, and other literary curioſities. This valuable library and muſeum, by the bequeſt of Sir *Peter* in his laſt will, became the property of his kinſman and heir *Peter Thompſon*, eſq. now a Captain of the company of grenadiers in the *Surrey* militia: by whoſe indulgence, free acceſs to this collection is readily granted to his intimate friends, and any other gentlemen who may deſire ſatisfaction as to matters of hiſtory and antiquities. Sir *Peter* communicated much information relative to the hiſtory of *Poole* to Mr. *Hutchins* in his Hiſtory of *Dorſet*; which ſee, vol. I. p. 12. His materials for a life of Mr. *Ames* are in the hands of Mr. *Herbert* ** of *Cheſhunt*.

‡ *Robert Ainſworth*, born at *Woodyale*, in the pariſh of *Eccles*, four miles from *Mancheſter*, in *September* 1660, was educated at *Bolton* in that county, and afterwards taught ſchool in the ſame town. Some years after he came to *London*, and was maſter of a conſiderable boarding-ſchool at *Bethnal Green*, where in 1698 he wrote and publiſhed a ſhort treatiſe of grammatical inſtitution, inſcribed to Sir *William Huſtler*, and reprinted in 1736, 8vo. under the title of " The moſt natural and eaſy way of In-" ſtitution, by making a domeſtic Education leſs chargeable to Parents, and more eaſy " and beneficial to Children. By which method, Youth may not only make a very con-" ſiderable progreſs in Languages, but alſo in Arts and Sciences, in two years." Mr. *Ainſworth* ſoon after removed to *Hackney*, and ſucceſſively to other villages near *London*, where he taught with good reputation many years, when, having acquired a moderate fortune, he left off, and lived privately. About the year 1714 it having been ſuggeſted to ſome principal bookſellers, that a new Compendious *Engliſh* and *Latin* Dictionary, upon a plan ſomewhat ſimilar to *Faber's Theſaurus*, was much wanted, Mr. *Ainſworth* was thought of as a proper perſon to undertake ſo long and troubleſome a work; and how well he executed it, has been ſufficiently ſhewn by eight editions, and another now preparing. He was author of, 1. the grammatical treatiſe above mentioned, 1698, 1736. 2. " Monumenta Vetuſtatis *Kempiana*†† ex vetuſtis Scriptoribus " illuſtrata,

** See his Propoſals for a new edition of " *Ames's* Typographical Antiquities."

†† The greateſt part of this collection was originally made by Mr. *John Gailhard*, who had been governor to *George* the firſt lord *Carteret*, ſo created *Oct.* 12, 1681; and ſold to his lordſhip for an annuity of 200l. After the death of that lord, which happened *Sept.* 22, 1695, Mr. *John Kemp* bought

this kingdom hath ever yet produced, Mr. *Philip Carteret Webb*,

" illuftrata, eofque viciffim illuftrantia, in duas partes divifa : quarum altera mumias,
" fimulacra, ftatuas, figna, luces, infcriptiones, vafa, lucernas, amuleta, lapides,
" gemmas, annulos, fibulas, cum aliis veterum reliquiis ; altera nummos materia
" modoque diverfos continet. 1720," 8vo. 3. " Ισυον, five, ex veteris Monumenti
" *Ifiaci* Defcriptione *Ifidis* Delubrum referatum, 1729," 4to ; 4. " De Clipeo
" *Camilli* antiquo, operis elegantiffimi, & cum per tot fæcula duraverat, integritatis
" plane mirandæ, e reliquiis Mufei *Woodwardiani*, apud Cl. V. *Ric. King*, trib. mil.
" adfervato, Differtatio. Præmittitur ejufdem monumenti argumentique limbo in-
" fculpti defcriptio *, 1734," 4to. and 5. " Thefaurus Linguæ *Latinæ* compen-
" diarius : Or, a compendious Dictionary of the *Latin* Tongue, defigned chiefly
" for the ufe of the *Britifh* Nation †, 1736," 4to. He had likewife a turn both for
Latin and *Englifh* poetry, fome fingle poems of his having been printed in each of thofe
languages. In 1721 he communicated a curious grammatical obfervation to Mr. *Chifhull*,
who ftyles him " doctiffimus *R. Ainfworth*, amicus meus & vicinus, ob fingularem
" eruditionem

bought a confiderable part of the collection during the minority of *John* the late earl *Cranville*, and
more after his death. His lordfhip died *Sept.* 19, 1717 (aged about 52) ; and, by his will, directed
that *Robert* earl of *Oxford*, or his fon *Edward* lord *Harley*, or one of them, fhould have his whole
collection of antiquities, with the books belonging to them, for 2000l. But this propofal not being
accepted, that collection was fold by auction, at the *Phœnix Tavern* in *Pall Mall*, on the 23d, 24th, 25th,
and 27th of *March* 1721, in 293 articles, for 1090l. 8s. 6d. *Henry* earl of *Winchelfea* faw them in
Gailhard's hands at *Angiers* 1676, and afterwards improved at *Paris* 1682. Six antient infcriptions,
bought at Mr. *Kemp's* fale by Dr. *Rawlinfon*, are now at *Oxford*, and publifhed among the " Marmora
" Oxonienfia." Several others purchafed by *Ebenezer Muffel*, efq. were re-fold at the auction of his
curiofities 1765. See *Maty's* Life of *Mead*, and Britifh Topography, I. 671.
 * This article had before appeared at the end of " Mufeum *Woodwardianum*, or catalogue of the
" Doctor's library and curiofities fold by auction at *Covent Garden*, 1728," 8vo. See *Ward's* Lives of
the *Grefham* Profeffors, p. 291. " The latter part of this catalogue, or *mufeum*, was drawn up by
" Mr. *Ainfworth*, though the Doctor had himfelf defcribed moft of the ftatues, tablets, and vafes,
" and written large notes upon moft of them" *Ward*, MS. p. 300. See the hiftory of this famous
fhield, Britifh Topography, I. 720.—At the end of fome copies of " *Joannis Ker* Selectæ de lingua
" *Latina* Obfervationes, *Lond.* 1729," 8vo. occurs " An *Englifh-Latin* Table, &c." to which fmall-
tract Mr. *Ainfworth* has put the initials of his name.
 † " Whilft this work was preparing, the execution of it was attended with fo many difficulties,
" that it went on very flowly for a long time, and for fome years was entirely fuppreffed. But afterwards
" on account of Mr. *Ainfworth's* advanced age, and a diforder that affected his eyes, I was defired to
" affift in reviewing the copy ; and at his requeft, and the bookfellers concerned, accepted of it, after
" about a dozen fheets had been wrought off." *Preface to the fecond Edition* ; which was publifhed in
1746 by *Samuel Patrick*, LL. D. ufher to *The Charter Houfe* ; with many additions and improvements ;
to which Mr. *Ainfworth* himfelf contributed, as did alfo Dr. *Ward*, who had given his affiftance in
the firft edition. In the fecond edition, however, Mr. *Bowyer* in MS. has remarked, that " There are
" many grofs miftakes ; particularly interpreting *genæ* [cheeks] to fignify *the eye-lafhes*, from a law
" of the XII Tables, *Mulieres ne radunto genas.* And *projicit* [throws away, or lays afide] *ampullas*
" & *fefquipedalia verba*, Hor. Art. Poet. 97, he interprets *utters* and *makes ufe of*, contrary to the fenfe
" of the place, and of the conftant ufe of the word. So ριπτω in *Greek*." It is, however, the beft
work of the kind that has hitherto appeared.—Dr. *Patrick* dying foon after, a third edition was
fuperintended by Mr. *Kimber* in 1751, with little or no variation ; and in 1752 an edition, in two volumes
folio, much improved, by Mr. *William Young*, a genius far fuperior to either of the preceding editors ;
and whofe abilities, if he could have beftowed the proper application, would have enabled him to publifh
a better *Latin* Dictionary than any that has ever appeared. (Mr. *Young*, I may here obferve, was the real
Parfon *Adams* of *Fielding*.)—An edition in two volumes 8vo. was publifhed in 1758, under the infpection
of Mr. *Thomas* ; who corrected a fourth edition in 4to, 1761.—In 1773, the very learned Dr. *Morell*, at
the age of 70, corrected, *for the third time*, an edition of this Dictionary, as appears by his Letter to
Meffrs. *Longman* and *Johnfton* prefixed to it. " There are few names," he obferves, " fo great as to
" enhance the fale of any book whatever, if its own utility does not recommend it : and as to myfelf ;
" not

Webb*, Dr. *Borlase** the hiftorian of *Cornwall*, Mr. *Locker*†

many

" eruditionem & humanitatem inter paucos æftimandus ‡. A letter from him, exhibited at the Antiquary Society in 1779, fhews that he wrote an aftonifhingly neat hand. In the latter part of his life he ufed to employ himfelf very much in rummaging the fhops of obfcure brokers in every quarter of the town; by which means he often picked up old coins and other valuable curiofities at a fmall expence; and became poffeffed of a very fine collection of *Englifh* coins, which he fold fingly to feveral gentlemen a fhort time before his death, which happened at *London*, *April* 4, 1743, at the age of 83. He was buried, according to his own defire, in the cemetery of *Poplar*, under the following monumental infcription, compofed by himfelf:

" *Rob. Ainfworth* & Uxor ejus, admodum fenes,

Dormituri, veftem detritam hic exuerunt,

Novam, primo mane furgentes, induturi.

Dum fas, mortalis, fapias, & refpice finem.

Hoc fuadent manes, hoc canit *Amramides.*

To thy reflection, mortal friend,

Th' advice of *Mofes* I commend;

Be wife, and meditate thy end." Deut. xxxvii. 29.

There is a caricature etching by *Pond* in 1739 after *Ghezzi*, intituled, " Due fafimo " Antiquari," fuppofed to be intended for Sir *Andrew Fountaine* ‖ and *Ainfworth* ; or, as others conjecture, for Baron *Stofch* and *Sabbatini.*

* For Mr. *Webb* and Dr. *Borlafe*, fee the Index.

† *John Locker*, efq. F. S. A. He is ftyled by Dr. *Ward* " a gentleman much efteemed for his knowledge of polite literature;" and was remarkable for his fkill in the *Greek* language, particularly the *modern*, of which he became mafter by accident: Coming home late

" not being a dangler, or in any way importunate, by conftitution; fince, after frequent dedications, " by permiffion, by requeft, I can only fay with my late friend Dr. *Young*, *I have been fo long re-* " *membered, I am forgot*; I was induced to infcribe this work to you, with whom alone I can boaft " a mutual obligation." This was the fifth edition in 4to; and my venerable Friend, who alfo fuperintended an octavo edition in one volume 1774, is now (1780) again engaged in correcting another edition in 4to.—It appears by an authentic paper, intituled " An Account of the Expence of correct- " ing and improving fundry books," 1776, folio, that Mr. *Ainfworth* received for the firft edition of his Dictionary, 666l. 17s. 6d. For the fecond edition, his executors were paid 250l.; Dr. *Patrick* 101l. 11s. 9d.; and Dr. *Ward* 261l. 5s. Mr. *Kimber* had twenty guineas for correcting the third edition; and Mr. *Young* 184l. 10s. for his improvements in the folio. Befides thefe fums, 218l. 8s. had been paid by the bookfellers to Dr. *Morell* for correcting *Ainfworth*, and 261l. 18s. to Mr. *Thomas*. In the whole, 1730l. 10s. 3d.—By the fame paper it appears, that Dr. *Patrick* had been paid 40l. Mr. *Young* 50 guineas, and Dr. *Morell* 200 guineas, for correcting the *Greek* Lexicon of *Hederic*; and that, in the fpace of about 40 years (to the very great credit of the proprietors) nearly 12000l. had been paid to authors and editors of Dictionaries and other large works, over and above the original fum given to them for their copies.

‡ Infcriptio Sigea, 1721, p. 28. Antiq. Afiat. 1725. p. 22.

‖ Sir *Andrew Fountaine*, knt. whofe anceftors were feated at *Narford* in *Norfolk* fo early as the reign of *Henry* III. was educated as a commoner of *Chrift* Church in *Oxford*, under the care of that eminent encourager of literature, Dr. *Aldrich*. He at the fame time ftudied, under Dr. *Hickes*, the *Anglo-Saxon* language, and its antiquities; of which he publifhed a fpecimen in " *Hickes's* " Thefaurus," under the title of " N umifmata *Anglo-Saxonica* & *Anglo-Danica*, breviter illuftrata " ab *Andrea Fountaine*, eq. aur. & ælis Chrifti Oxon. alumno. Oxon. 1705," in which year Mr. *Hearne* dedicated to him his edition of *Juftin* the Hiftorian. He received the honour of knighthood from King *William*; and travelled over moft parts of *Europe*; where he made a large and valuable collection of pictures, antient ftatues, medals, and infcriptions; and, while in *Italy*, acquired

many years clerk to the Companies of Leatherſellers and
Clock-

late one evening, he was addreſſed in modern *Greek* by a poor *Greek* ſailor from *The
Archipelago*, who had loſt his way in the ſtreets of *London*. He took him to his houſe;
where he was his ſervant for five or ſix years, and by him was perfected in that language, ſo as to write it fluently. He married *Elizabeth* eldeſt daughter of Dr. *Stillingfleet*; and died, much reſpected, *May* 30, 1760. In the Preface to the complete edition
of *Bacon's* Works, by Dr. *Birch* and Mr. *Mallet*, in 5 volumes, 4to, 1765, the advantages
of that edition above all the preceding ones are ſaid to be " chiefly owing to two gentle-
" men, now deceaſed, *Robert Stephens* eſq. Hiſtoriographer Royal **, and *John Locker*
" eſq. Fellow of the Society of Antiquaries; both of whom had made a particular
" ſtudy of Lord *Bacon's* writings, and a great object of their induſtry the correcting

quired ſuch a knowledge of *virtù*, that the dealers in antiquities were not able to impoſe on him.
In 1709 his judgement and fancy were exerted in embelliſhing the " Tale of a Tub" with deſigns almoſt
equal to the excellent ſatire they illuſtrate. At this period he enjoyed the friendſhip of the moſt diſtinguiſhed wits, and of *Swift* in particular, who repeatedly mentions him in the Journal to *Stella* in terms
of high regard. In *December* 1710, when Sir *Andrew* was given over by his phyſicians, *Swift* viſited
him, foretold his recovery, and rejoiced at it; though he wittily ſays, " I have loſt a legacy by his
" living; for he told me he had left me a picture and ſome books, &c." Sir *Andrew* was vice-
chamberlain to Queen *Caroline* whilſt Princeſs of *Wales* and after ſhe was Queen, and tutor
to Prince *William*, for whom he was inſtalled (as proxy) Knight of the Bath, and had on that
occaſion a patent granted him, dated *Jan.* 14, 1725, for adding ſupporters to his arms, viz. On
either ſide a Lion Gules, with wings erected Or, with the old family motto of *Vix ea noſtra voco*, and
the ancient arms of *Fountaine*, Or, a feſs Gules, between three elephants heads Sable. Sir *Andrew*
likewiſe quartered the arms of 1. *Walſhe*; 2. *Harſicle*; 3. *Damme*; 4. *Briggs*; 5. *Beaupré*; 6. *St.
Omer*; *Elizabeth* his ſiſter married Col. *Clent* of *Knightwick* in *Worceſterſhire*. By his ſkill and judgment he furniſhed the moſt conſiderable cabinets of this kingdom, to his own no ſmall emolument;
being a perfect connoiſſeur in medals, antient as well as modern. In 1727 he was appointed warden
of the mint, an office which he held till his death, which happened *Sept.* 4, 1753. He was buried
at *Narford* in *Norfolk*, where he had erected an elegant ſeat, and formed a fine collection of old
china ware, a valuable library, and an excellent collection of pictures, coins, and many other rare
pieces of antiquity. Amongſt the portraits in the library, were thoſe of *Titian, Aretin, Inigo Jones,
Palladio, Laniere, Rembrandt, Cornelius Janſen, W. Shakſpeare, Ben Jonſon, Waller, Cowley, Butler,
C. Cotton*, Dr. *Aldrich*, Earl of *Montroſs, Guſtavus Adolphus*, Pope *Alexander* VII. Prince *Rupert*,
Sir *Kenelm Digby*, Sir *John Maynard*, Admiral *Blake*, Dr. *Prideaux*, Dr. *Pococke*, Cardinal *Maza-
rin*, Marſhal *Turenne*, Duke of *Devonſhire*, Archbiſhop *Tillotſon*, Earl of *Pembroke*, Doctor *Wallis*,
Mead, and *Radcliffe*. Among the antiquities was a *Roman* vaſe of bronze dug up in the hall-yard,
the *Romans* being ſuppoſed to have had a ſtation at *Narford*, where many of their bricks were found.
There were alſo two fine ſepulchral cheſts of white marble dug up at *Rome*, neatly carved, and inſcribed:

D. M.	D. M.
SERVILLIO.	FLAVIVS. CASTVS. CVRATOR. EQVES. SING.
FORTVNATO.	AVCENN. VIXIT. ANN. XXXVIII.....
SERVILLIA. ATTICILLA.	A...TI. CVST. SEVERINI. C. DOMITIVS,
PATRONO. B. M. FECIT.	ASCLEPIVS. H. B. M. F.

See *Blomefield's Norfolk*, III. 521.
Sir *Andrew* loſt many miniatures by a fire at *White's* original chocolate-houſe in *St. James's Street*
where he had hired two rooms for his collections (*Walpole's* Anecdotes of Painting, II. 21.)
A portrait of him, by Mr. *Hoare* of *Bath*, is in the collection at *Wilton Houſe*: and two medals of
him are engraved in *Snelling's* " Engliſh Medals, 1776;" one of them, ſtruck at *Florence*, inſcribed,
ANDREAS. FOVNTAINE. EQVES. AVRATVS. ANGLVS. 1715. Exergue, A. SELVI. F. The other,
at *London*, in 1744; on one ſide, his buſt finely executed, and inſcribed ANDREAS. FOVNTAINE. EQ.
AVRAT. On the Reverſe (in alluſion to his office in the mint) this ancient *Roman* legend,
A. A. A. F. F. III VIR. That is, Aere, Argento, Auro, flando, feriundo, Triumviri. Exergue,
J. A. DASSIER; a young Engraver, whom he employed at *The Tower*.
** Mr. *Stephens*, who was one of the early members of the Society of Antiquaries, ſucceeded Mr.
Madox as hiſtoriographer royal in 1727, and died in 1732. He publiſhed " Lives of *North*," &c. See
Introduction to Archæologia, p. xxxvii.

2

" from

Clockmakers, Mr. *F. Wise**, Mr. *George North*, from whose researches we had great reason to have expected a History of the Society of Antiquaries †, Mr. *Charles Compton* treasurer to

" from original or authentic manuscripts, and the earliest and best editions, whatever
" of his works had been already published, and adding to them such, as could be re-
" covered, that had never seen the light. Mr. *Stephens* dying in *November* 1732, his
" papers came into the hands of Mr. *Locker*, whose death prevented the world from
" enjoying the fruits of his labours, though he had actually finished his correction of
" the fourth volume of Mr. *Blackburne's* edition, containing the Law-tracts, Letters,
" &c. After his decease, his collections, including those of Mr. *Stephens*, were pur-
" chased by Dr. *Birch*."

* *Francis Wise*, B. D. and F. S. A. many years fellow of *Trinity College, Oxford*, was born *Oct.* 3, 1695, educated at *New College* school under Mr. *Badger*, admitted at *Trinity College* 1710-11, A. M. 1717, and assistant to Dr. *Hudson* in the *Bodleian* library; elected fellow of his college 1719, where he had the honour of having for his pupil 1721 the earl of *Guilford*, who appointed him his chaplain, and presented him to the vicarage of *Ellesfield***, in *Oxfordshire*, 1726; as did his college to the rectory of *Rother-field-Grays*, in the same county, 1745. He was appointed keeper of the Archives 1728, and in 1748 *Radcliffe* librarian. He published, 1. " Annales *Ælfredi* Magni, *Oxon.*
" 1722," 8vo. 2. " Letter to Dr. *Mead* ‡‡ concerning some antiquities in *Berkshire*.
" *Oxford*, 1738," 4to. 3. " Further observations upon the *White Horse* and other
" antiquities in *Berkshire*; with an account of *White eat-cross* in *Buckinghamshire*;
" as also the *Red Horse* in *Warwickshire*, and other monuments of the same kind.
" *Oxford*, 1742," 4to. In 1750, he published by subscription " Catalogus nummorum
" antiquorum in scriniis *Bodleianis* reconditorum, cum commentario," with plates of many of the coins, folio. In 1758, " Enquiries concerning the first inhabitants, lan-
" guages, &c. of *Europe*," 4to. In 1764, " Observations on the history and chro-
" nology of the fabulous ages;" 4to. After long struggles with the gout, he died at his favourite retreat at *Ellesfield*, *Oct.* 6, 1767, aged 72, universally beloved and esteem-ed on account of his great merit and learning ‡‡.

† *George North*, M. A. (son of *George North* citizen and pewterer of *London*, who ac-quired a competence by industry) was born in 1707, and received his education at *St.*

** A view of his house and grounds at *Ellesfield* forms a tail-piece to the Preface to his *Bodleian* Coins.

†† This letter was as rudely as sillily animadverted upon in a pamphlet called, " The Impertinence " and Imposture of Modern Antiquaries displayed, or a Refutation of the Rev. Mr. *Wise's* letter to " Dr. *Mead*, concerning the White Horse, and other Antiquities in *Berkshire*, in a familiar letter to " a Friend. By *Philalethes Rusticus*. With a preface by the gentleman to whom this letter was ad-" dressed. *Lond.*" 4to. said in a MS. note in Mr. *Wise's* own copy to be written by Mr. *Asplin*, vicar of *Banbury*, and the preface by his friend Mr. *William Bumpsted*, of *Upton*, supercargo of the *Prince Frederic South-Sea* ship (of whom there is much to be met with in some of the pamphlets concerning the *Assiento* contract carried on by the *South-Sea* Company). It was replied to by Mr. *North*, as men-tioned in p. 112. In canvassing for the office of *Radcliffe* librarian, Mr. *Wise* was much hurt by the en-deavours of the author of this pamphlet to represent him as disaffected to the government.—The pam-phlet was so universally disliked, that the author is said to have called it in very soon after publica-tion; it has therefore long been very scarce, and, like many a misbegotten brat, its parent could never be found with any certainty. Notwithstanding the general opinion that it was written by Mr. *Asplin*, well known by some pamphlets on a different subject; the late Mr. *Rowe-Mores* always asserted the author's name was *Aspinwall*; and others have attributed it to the Rev. Mr. *Bumpstead*, a clergyman in *Essex*.

‡‡ British Topography, I. 176.

to the Society*, Dr. *Cowper* a physician of eminence
at

Paul's School, from whence in 1725 he went to *Bennet College* in *Cambridge*, where he took
his degrees of Batchelor and Master of Arts. In 1729 he was admitted into Deacons
orders, and went to officiate as curate at *Codicote*, a small village near *Welwyn* in *Hertfordshire*; to the vicarage of which he was presented by the bishop of *Ely* in 1743. In 1741
he published without his name, " An Answer to a Scandalous Libel, intituled, The Imper-
" tinence and Imposture of Modern Antiquaries displayed." This publication recommended him not only to the notice and esteem of the gentleman whose cause he had so generously
espoused (to whom he was at that time a perfect stranger) and so ably defended, but also
of several dignified members of the Society of Antiquaries, into which Society he was
soon received as a fellow. In 1742 and 1755 he drew up catalogues of the earl of *Oxford's*
and Dr. *Mead's* coins, for the public sale of them. The Rev. *Charles Clarke*, late of *Baliol College*, *Oxford*, having published " Some Conjectures relative to a very antient
" piece of money lately found at *Eltham* in *Kent*, endeavouring to restore it to the place
" it merits in the cimeliarch of *English* coins, and to prove it a coin of *Richard* the first
" king of *England* of that name. To which are added, some remarks on a dissertation
" (lately published †) on *Oriuna* the supposed wife ‡ of *Carausius*, and on the *Roman*
" coins there mentioned. *Lond.* 1751," 4to. Mr. *North* in 1752 published " Remarks
" on some conjectures, &c. shewing the improbability of the notion therein advanced;
" that the arguments produced in support of it are inconclusive or irrelative to the
" point in question, *Lond.* 1752," 4to. In these remarks he considered at large
the standard and purity of our most antient *English* coins, the state of the mints, and
the beginning of sterling, from the public records. No man could be better qualified for
this task than Mr. *North*, who, by his intimacy with Mr. *Holmes* and Mr. *Folkes*, became
perfectly acquainted with the records and whole state and history of the *English* coinage.
He wrote " A Table of *English* Silver Coins from the Conquest to the Commonwealth,
" with Remarks;" a transcript of which, in the hand-writing of Dr. *Gifford*, is now,
1780, in the collection of Mr. *Tutet*. He also began remarks on the money of
Henry III. and actually engraved two plates for that work, which were never published, but proofs given amongst several of his friends. From his first taking orders
till his death he had resided principally at *Coddicote*, without any other preferment than
this small vicarage of about fourscore pounds a year, aided by a little additional income from a small patrimony. He died *June* 27, 1772, having just completed his 65th
year; and was buried at the east end of his church-yard at *Coddicote*, where he had indulged his disappointment, and lived in as much obscurity as his ashes now rest. He had prepared large materials for a history of the Society of Antiquaries; but in a fit of illness, whose
consequences he apprehended might be fatal, he burnt these among other valuable collections. He left his library and his collection of *English* coins to the late Dr. *Askew*.

* *Charles Compton*, Esq. of *Grendon* in *Northamptonshire*, succeeded *Samuel Gale*, esq.
as treasurer to the Antiquary Society about 1742; and died *Nov.* 21, 1761, at his house
in *Poland-street*. He was son of the late General *Compton*, nephew to Mr. *William
Nicholas*, and great nephew to Dr. *Compton*, Bishop of *London*.

† By Dr. *Kennedy*, who asserted that *Oriuna* was that Emperor's *guardian goddess*. Dr. *Stukeley*
in his Palæographia Brit. N° III. 1752, 4to. affirmed she was his *wife*; to which Dr. *Kennedy* replied
in " Further Observations, &c. 1756." 4to. and upon his antagonist's supporting his opinion in his
" History of *Carausius*, 1757, 1759," he abused him in a six-penny 4to. letter. Dr. *Kennedy*, who was
a native of *Scotland*, had resided some time at *Smyrna*; and died at an advanced age, *Jan.* 26, 1760. He
had a collection of about 200 pictures, amongst which were two heads of himself by *Kysing*; he had
also a very valuable collection of *Greek* and *Roman* coins, which, with the pictures, were sold by auction
in the year 1760. Amongst the *Roman* coins, were 256 of *Carausius*, nine of them silver, and 89 of
Allectus; these coins of *Carausius* and *Allectus* were purchased by P. C. *Webb*, esq. the 256 for 70l.
and the 89 for 16l. 10s They are now in the noble cabinet of Dr. *Hunter*, who has added to the
number very considerably.

‡ " *Oriuna*, on the medals of *Carausius*, used to pass for the moon: of late years it is become a
" doubt whether she was not his consort. It is of little importance whether she was moon or empress;

at *Chester**, Mr. *Hall*†, Dr. *Birch*‡ (with whom Mr.
Bowyer

* *William Cowper*, M. D. and F. S. A. practifed phyfic many years at *Chester* with
great reputation. He publifhed (without his name) 1. " A fummary of the life of St.
" *Werburgh*, with an hiftorical account of the images ** upon her fhrine, (now the
" epifcopal throne) in the choir of *Chcfter*. Collected from antient chronicles, and old
" writers. By a citizen of *Chefter*. Publifhed for the benefit of the charity-fchool,
" *Chefter*. 1749." 4to; and by this effay in antiquarianifm, which he is faid to have
ftolen from the MSS. of Mr. *Stone*††, raifed a great outcry againft himfelf. He
was alfo author of " Il Penferofo : an evening's contemplation in *St. John's* church-
" yard, *Chefter*. A rhapfody, written more than twenty years ago ; and now (firft)
" publifhed, illuftrated with notes hiftorical and explanatory. *Lond.* 1767." 4to; (addreffed, under the name of *M. Meanwell*, to the Rev. *John Allen*, M. A. fenior fellow
of *Trinity College, Cambridge*, and rector of *Torporley* in *Chefhire*) in which he takes a
view of fome of the moft remarkable places around it diftinguifhed by memorable perfonages and events. He died *Oct.* 20, 1767, while he was preparing a memorial of his
native city. He had alfo made collections for the county, which are now in the hands
of his brother, an attorney near *Chefter*, but confift of little more than tranfcripts
from printed books and minute modern tranfactions interweaving, with the hiftory of the
county and city, a great mafs of other general hiftory. See Brit. Topography, I. 249.
253. and *Gower's* " Sketch of Materials for a Hiftory of *Chefhire*."

† *William Hall*, efq. of *The Middle Temple* ; an excellent fcholar, and an intimate
friend of Mr. *Markland*‡‡, who infcribed to him his " Quæftio Grammatica," as mentioned above, p. 20. He went to *Bath* for his health in the autumn of 1766, where he
unhappily fell into a ftate of infanity, and died in *December* that year. Dr. *Akenfide*
has infcribed a beautiful Ode " To *William Hall*, Efq. with the Works of *Chaulieu*."
Englifh Poets, vol. LV. p. 265.

‡ This valuable hiftorical and biographical writer was born in the parifh of *St. John*,

" but how little muft we know of thofe times, when thofe land-marks to certainty, royal names, do not
" ferve even that purpofe ! In the cabinet of the king of *France* are feveral coins of fovereigns, whofe
" country cannot now be gueffed at." *Walpole, Preface to Hiftoric Doubts.*

** Reprefenting her family, &c. in number thirty, juft then repaired.

†† *William Stone*, minor-canon of the church of *Chefter*, who drew up two curious quarto volumes of church notes, &c. relative to the city and cathedral, which were prefented by his fon to the
cathedral library, and afterwards lent to Dr. *Gower*.

‡‡ Mr. *Markland's* anxiety, during the illnefs of his friend, will appear from the following fhort
extracts : " Your letter frees me from a fear I have been under this fortnight, during which I have
" looked firft under the article of the *Dead* in every paper. I believe you did not know that Mr.
" *Hall* has been extremely and dangeroufly ill, fomewhat in your way, from the ftrangury, though
" the caufe was different from yours." *Letter to Mr. B. March* 24, 1766.—" You told me he
" [Mr. *H.*] had had a relapfe, but was got well again, and would write to me foon. Not having
" heard from him fince, I am under fome concern about him, left he fhould have met with a fecond
" relapfe. This is to beg of you to let me know how it is with him, this being a dangerous time of
" the year to all, unlefs to thofe who ἀναιμωις εἰσι, ἢ ἀθανατα καλιονται. You will excufe this folicitude
" for a friend; confidering that, if you had been in fuch a precarious condition, I fhould have written
" in the fame manner to him." *Ibid. April* 13.—" Your heart-breaking letter of yefterday, which I
" received this morning [a letter which mentioned the death of Mr. *Hall*], has fuperfeded all paltry
" regards of money, which pleafe to put off till you hear from me again." *Ibid. Dec.* 21, 1766.—
" I fend you the inclofed, only to verify the wife man's obfervation, *Boaft not thyfelf of to-morrow ; for
" who knoweth what a day may bring forth ?* This was written on *Oct.* 4; and on *Oct.* 5, he was a
" mad-man." *Ibid. Feb.* 15, 1767.—" I am always uneafy when I do not fatisfy even your expecta-
" tions; which, when you expected to have a letter from me on to-morrow morning by the poft, was
" impoffible, for nobody here fends a letter on a *Friday*, becaufe the General Office in *London* is fhut
" up on a *Sunday*. I fuppofe if you fent a letter to *Darking* for *London* on *Saturday*, you would not
" be furprized if I did not receive it till *Monday*. I had your depofitions, &c. . . . . . . before a
" week paffes, I hope I fhall inform you better, for I have very ftrong appearances of being right
" again in two or three days." *Mr. Hall to Mr. Markland, Oct.* 4, 1766.

Clerkenwell,

Bowyer was affociated in a great variety of literary purfuits,
and

Clerkenwell, on the 23d of *November*, 1705. His parents were both of them Quakers;
and his father, *Joseph Birch*, was a coffee-mill-maker by trade. Mr. *Joseph Birch* endeavoured to bring up his fon to his own bufinefs; but fo ardent was the youth's paffion
for reading, that he folicited his father to be indulged in this inclination, promifing,
in that cafe, to provide for himfelf. The firft fchool he went to was at *Hemel-Hemfted*
in *Hertfordfhire*. It was kept by *John Owen*, a rigid Quaker, for whom Mr. *Birch*
afterwards officiated fome little while as an ufher. The next fchool was kept by one
Welby, near *Turnmill-freet*, *Clerkenwell*, who never had above eight or ten fcholars at a
time, whom he profeffed to inftruct in the *Latin* tongue in a year and a half. To him
Mr. *Birch* was, likewife, an ufher; as he alfo afterwards was to Mr. *Beffe*, the famous
Quaker, in *George's Court* in St. *John's Lane*, who publifhed the pofthumous works of
Claridge. It is farther faid, that he went to *Ireland* with Dean *Smedley**; but in what
year, and how long he refided with the Dean, cannot now be afcertained. He was indefatigable in his application, and ftole many hours from fleep to increafe his ftock of
knowledge. By this unremitting diligence, though he had not the happinefs of an univerfity education, he foon became qualified to take holy orders in the church of *England*,
to the furprize of his acquaintance. We do not precifely know when this event took
place; but it muft have been as early as in 1728. In the fame year he married the daughter of the Rev. Mr. *Cox*, to whom he was curate; but his felicity was of fhort duration, Mrs. *Birch* dying of a puerperal fever in lefs than twelve months after their mar-
riage†. In 1732 he was recommended to the friendfhip and favour of the late Lord High
Chancellor *Hardwicke*, then Attorney General; to which noble Peer, and to the prefent Earl of *Hardwicke*, he was indebted for all his preferments. The firft proof he
experienced of his patron's regard, was the living of *Ulting*, in the county of *Effex*,
in the gift of the crown, to which he was prefented 1732. In 1734, he was appointed
one of the domeftic chaplains to the unfortunate Earl of *Kilmarnock*, who was beheaded
1746. Mr. *Birch* was chofen a member of the Royal Society, *Feb.* 20, 1734-5; and of
the Society of Antiquaries, *Dec.* 11, 1735, of which he afterwards became Director till
his death. Before this the *Marifchal College* of *Aberdeen* had conferred on him, by
diploma, the degree of Mafter of Arts. In 1743, by the intereft of lord *Hardwicke*, he was prefented by the crown to the finecure rectory of *Landewy Welfrey* in-
the county of *Pembroke*; and in 1743-4, was preferred, in the fame manner, to the
rectory of *Sidington St. Peter's*, in the county and diocefe of *Gloucefter*. We find no
traces of his having taken poffeffion of this living; and, indeed, it is probable that he
quitted it immediately, for one more fuitable to his inclinations, and to his literary
engagements, which required his almoft conftant refidence in town; for on the 24th of
February, 1743-4, he was inftituted to the united rectories of St. *Michael*, *Wood-freet*,
and St. *Mary Staining*; and in 1745-6 to the united rectories of St. *Margaret Pattens*,
and St. *Gabriel*, *Fenchurch-freet* (by lord chancellor *Hardwicke*, in whofe turn the
prefentation then was). In *January*, 1752, he was elected one of the Secretaries of the
Royal Society, in the room of Dr. *Cromwell Mortimer*, deceafed. In *January*, 1753,

* Who publifhed in 1728 " A Specimen of an univerfal View of all the Eminent Writers on the Holy
" Scriptures; being a Collection of the differtations, explications, and opinions of learned men, in all
" ages, concerning the difficult paffages and obfcure texts of the Bible; and of whatfoever is to be met
" with, in profane authors, which may contribute towards the better underftanding of them." This
extenfive undertaking was intended to have been compofed in two large folio volumes. Had the plan
proceeded, it is no very far-fetched conjecture to fuppofe that Mr. *Birch* was to have been an affiftant.

† See Mr. *Birch's* pathetic " Verfes on the Death of a beloved Wife," in the " Select Collection of
" Poems, 1780," vol. V. p. 258.

the

and to whom I with gratitude acknowledge that I was early

the *Marifchal College* of *Aberdeen* created him Doctor of Divinity; and in that year the fame degree was conferred on him by archbifhop *Herring*. He was one of the truftees of *The Britifh Mufeum* *, for which honour he was probably indebted to the prefent Earl of *Hardwicke*; as he was for his laft preferment, the rectory of *Depden* † in *Effex*, to which he was inducted *Feb*. 26, 1761. In the latter part of his life he was chaplain to the Princefs *Amelia*. In 1765, he refigned his office of Secretary to the Royal Society, and was fucceeded by Dr. *Morton*. His health declining about this time, he was ordered to ride for the recovery of it; but being a bad horfeman, and going out, *Jan*. 9, 1766, he was unfortunately thrown from his horfe, on the road betwixt *London* and *Hampftead*, and died on the fpot, in the 61ft year of his age, to the great regret of the Doctor's numerous literary friends; and was buried in *St. Margaret Pattens*. Dr. *Birch* had, in his life-time, been very generous to his relations; and none, that were nearly allied to him, being living at his deceafe, he bequeathed his library of books and manufcripts, with his picture painted in 1735, and all his other pictures and prints not otherwife difpofed of by his will, to *The Britifh Mufeum*. He, likewife, left the remainder of his fortune, which amounted to not much more than five hundred pounds, to be laid out in Government Securities, for the purpofe of applying the intereft to increafe the ftipend of the three affiftant librarians: thus manifefting at his death, as he had done during his whole life, his refpect for literature, and his defire to promote ufeful knowledge. To the Royal Society he bequeathed his picture painted by *Wills* in 1737, being the original of the mezzotinto print done by *Faber* in 1741. His valuable publications are enumerated below ‡.—I am indebted to the new edition of the " Biographia Britannica" for

* This truft was an honour much coveted by Dr. *Taylor*, who faid it was the blue ribband of a fcholar; and certainly no man could be better qualified to figure in it than he was, from his general knowledge of books, medals, and antiques, and his liberal way of thinking on all fubjects; but, *Diis aliter vifum eft.*—Dr. *Taylor's Friend.*

† " *Depden* was in the poffeffion of Dr. *Cock*, and of his own patronage, who confented to an exchange for a living of lord *Hardwicke's* own, near *Colchefter*, which was out of diftance of Dr. *Birch's* city livings. This living was bought by Dr. *Cock's* father, an honeft man, who got a handfome fortune as a carrier at *Cambridge*. In 1736, before the mortmain act took place, *St. John's College* (of which the prefent Dr. *Cock* is a member) was defirous of buying the living at the price he gave, and would have allowed the fon the next turn; but this was not accepted, though it would have been a dear bargain to them. Dr. *Cock*, by confenting to the exchange, got a living in a much better country, and befides of more value than his own, (befides getting rid of the terror he had had from his houfe being robbed by a gang of difguifed perfons of notorious villainy), and alfo was fure of receiving *Depden* again, without any favour, whenever Dr. *Birch* fhould die, who was the much older perfon; accordingly he has held both ever fince that event, and refides on lord *Hardwicke's* living, where he has laid out a great deal of money in making the parfonage commodious and handfome." *Dr. Taylor's Friend.*

‡ 1. " The General Dictionary, hiftorical and critical;" including a new tranflation of Mr. *Bayle*, and interfperfed with feveral thoufand new Lives. Dr. *Birch's* affociates in this undertaking were the Rev. *John Peter Bernard*, Mr. *John Lockman*, and Mr. *George Sale*. The whole defign was completed in ten volumes folio; the firft of which appeared in 1734, the fecond and third in 1735, the fourth in 1736, the fifth in 1737, the fixth and feventh in 1738, the eighth and ninth in 1739, and the laft in 1741.—2. " Profeffor *Greaves's* Mifcellaneous Works, 1737," 2 vols. 8vo.—3. " *Thurlow's* " State Papers, 1742," 7 volumes, folio.—4. Dr. *Cudworth's* " Intellectual Syftem" (improved from the *Latin* edition of *Mofheim*); his difcourfe on the true notion of the Lord's Supper, and two fermons, with an account of his life and writings; 2 vols. 4to. 1743.—5. " The Life of the Hon. *Robert* " *Boyle*, 1744;" prefixed to an edition of that excellent philofopher's works, revifed by Dr. *Birch*.— 6. " The Lives of illuftrious perfons of *Great Britain*," annexed to the engravings of *Houbraken* and *Vertue*, 1747—1752.—7. " An Inquiry into the Share which King *Charles* the Firft had in the Earl of *Gla-* " *morgan*, 1747," 8vo. A fecond edition of this treatife was publifhed in 1756, under the title of " An In- " quiry

early in life indebted for his friendly patronage), Bishop
Pococke,

for the greatest part of this article; and the candid editor of that excellent work, I am
sure, will excuse my mentioning one slight mistake in it. Among other proofs of
Dr. *Birch's* industry, it is said, p. 303, "not to mention other instances, there
"are no less than *sixteen* volumes, in quarto, of *Anthony Bacon's* papers, *transcribed*
"*from the Lambeth Library.*" I have no doubt but Dr. *Birch* transcribed the number
of volumes here represented; though but a small part of them was taken from the
Lambeth Library. The fact is, there is but *one volume in folio* on the subject in that

"quiry into the Share which King *Charles* the First had in the Transactions of the Earl of *Glamorgan,*
"afterwards Marquis of *Worcester,* for bringing over a Body of *Irish* Rebels, to assist that King, in the
"years 1645 and 1646. In which Mr. *Carte's* imperfect Account of that Affair, and the Use of his MS.
"Memoirs of the Pope's Nuncio *Rinuccini,* are impartially considered. The whole drawn up from the
"best Authorities, printed and manuscript. The second Edition. To which is added an Appendix,
"containing several Letters of the King to the Earl of *Glamorgan,* from the Originals in the *Harleian*
"Collection of Manuscripts;" and it was a work which excited no small degree of attention.—
8. "An Historical View of the Negociations between the Courts of *England, France,* and *Brussels,* from
"the year 1592, to 1617; extracted chiefly from the MS. State Papers of Sir *Thomas Edmondes,* knt.
"Embassador in *France* and at *Brussels,* and Treasurer of the household to the Kings *James* I. and
"*Charles* I.; and of *Anthony Bacon,* esq brother to the Lord Chancellor *Bacon.* To which is added,
"a Relation of the State of *France,* with the Character of *Henry* IV. and the principal persons of
"that Court, drawn up by Sir *George Carew,* upon his return from his Embassy there in 1609, and
"addressed to King *James* I. Never before printed. 1749," 8vo.—9. "A Sermon on the Proof of the
"Wisdom and Goodness of God, from the Frame and Constitution of Man, preached before the Col-
"lege of Physicians, in consequence of Lady *Sadlier's* will, 1749."—10. An edition of "*Spenser's*
"Fairy Queen, 1751," 3 vols. 4to. with prints from designs by *Kent.*—11. "The Miscellaneous
"Works of Sir *Walter Raleigh;*" to which was prefixed the Life of that great, unfortunate, and injured man, 1751, 2 vols. 8vo.—12. "The theological, moral, dramatic, and poetical Works of Mrs.
"*Catherine Cockburn;* with an account of the Life of that very ingenious Lady, 1751," 2 vols. 8vo.—
13. "The Life of the Most Reverend Dr. *John Tillotson,* Lord Archbishop of *Canterbury.* Compiled
"chiefly from his original Papers and Letters, 1752," 8vo. A second edition, corrected and enlarged,
was prefixed to the Archbishop's Works, revised by Dr. *Birch,* in 1752; and printed separately in
1753.—14. "*Milton's* Prose Works, 1753," 2 vols. 4to. with a new Life of that great Poet and
Writer.—15. "Memoirs of the Reign of Queen *Elizabeth,* from the year 1581, till her Death. In
"which the secret Intrigues of her Court, and the Conduct of her Favourite, *Robert* Earl of *Essex,*
"both at home and abroad, are particularly illustrated. From the original Papers of his intimate
"Friend, *Anthony Bacon,* Esquire, and other Manuscripts never before published, 1754", 2 vols.
4to.—16. "The History of the Royal Society of *London,* for improving of Natural Knowledge, from
"its first Rise. In which the most considerable of those Papers, communicated to the Society, which
"have hitherto not been published, are inserted in their proper order, as a Supplement to the Philo-
"sophical Transactions, 1756 and 1757," 4 vols. 4to.—17. He corrected the "State Papers of
"Queen *Elizabeth,*" published by Mr. *Murden,* 1759, 2 vols. folio.—18. "The Life of *Henry* Prince
"of *Wales,* eldest son of King *James* I. Compiled chiefly from his own papers, and other manu-
"scripts, never before published, 1760," 8vo.—19. "Letters, Speeches, Charges, Advices, &c. of
"*Francis Bacon,* Lord Viscount *St. Alban,* Lord Chancellor of *England,* 1763," 8vo. A small Supplement was added to it in 1764; and the whole were in 1765 incorporated in a compleat edition of
the Chancellor's works, revised by Dr. *Birch* and Mr. *Mallet.*—20. "Letters between Col. *Robert*
"*Hammond,* governor of the *Isle of Wight,* and the Committee of Lords and Commons at *Derby House,*
"General *Fairfax,* Lieutenant-General *Cromwell,* Commissary-General *Ireton,* &c. relating to King
"*Charles* I. while he was confined in *Carisbrooke Castle* in that Island. Now first published. To
"which is prefixed a Letter from *John Ashburnham,* esq. to a Friend, concerning his deportment
"towards the King, in his attendance on his Majesty at *Hampton Court,* and in the *Isle of Wight,* 1764,"
8vo. These letters were the last publication Dr. *Birch* lived to print.—21. His last essay, "The Life
"of Dr. *Ward,*" (finished but a week before his death, from hints suggested by Dr. *Ducarel,* the
late Mr. *Henry Baker,* and other friends of the Professor) was published by Dr. *Maty* in 1766. His
numerous communications to the Royal Society may be seen in the Philosophical Transactions; and
his poetical talents are evident from the verses referred to in p. 115.

library;

Pococke*, Mr. *Collinſon*† the ingenious botaniſt whoſe researches

library (being the eighth volume of Biſhop *Gibſon's*‡ papers) containing only 282 pages
of *Anthony* and Lord *Bacon's* Letters, &c. That volume, which, by the favour of Dr.
Ducarel, I have had an opportunity of examining, was lent, by permiſſion of Archbiſhop
Secker, to Dr. *Birch*, out of which he ſelected all that had not been printed before, adding alſo ſeveral letters from the *Hatfield* collection, the *Harleian* MSS. &c. &c. and publiſhed the whole in one volume, 8vo, 1763.

* Of whom, ſee under the year 1743.

† I am furniſhed with materials to do juſtice to this excellent character, from a little
tract printed by his worthy friend Dr. *Fothergill*, 1770, under the title of " Some
" Account of the late *Peter Collinſon*, Fellow of the Royal Society, and of the Society
" of Antiquaries in *London*, and of the Societies of *Berlin* and *Upſal*. In a Letter to a
" Friend."—" The family of the *Collinſons* is of antient ſtanding in the North: *Peter*
and *James* were the great grandſons of *Peter Collinſon*, who lived on his paternal eſtate
called *Hugal-Hall*, or *Height of Hugal*, near *Windermere Lake*, in the pariſh of *Stavely*,
about ten miles from *Kendal* in *Weſtmoreland*. *Peter*, whilſt a youth, diſcovered his
attachment to natural hiſtory. He began early to make a collection of dried ſpecimens
of plants, and had acceſs to the beſt gardens at that time in the neighbourhood of *London*; and became early acquainted with the moſt eminent naturaliſts of his time; the Doctors *Derham*, *Woodward*, *Dale*, *Lloyd*, and *Sloane*, were amongſt his friends. Among
the great variety of articles which form that ſuperb collection, now (by the wiſe diſpoſition of Sir *Hans* and the munificence of parliament) *The Britiſh Muſeum*, ſmall was
the number of thoſe with whoſe hiſtory Mr. *Collinſon* was not well acquainted; he being
one of thoſe few who viſited Sir *Hans* at all times familiarly; their inclinations and pur-
ſuits in reſpect to natural hiſtory being the ſame, a firm friendſhip had nearly been eſtabliſhed between them. *Peter Collinſon* was elected a Fellow of the Royal Society on the 12th
of *December*, 1728; and perhaps was one of the moſt diligent and uſeful members, not
only in ſupplying them with many curious obſervations himſelf, but in promoting and
preſerving a moſt extenſive correſpondence with learned and ingenious foreigners, in all
countries, and on every uſeful ſubject. Beſides his attention to natural hiſtory, he mi-
nuted every ſtriking hint that occurred either in reading or converſation; and from this

‡ " Dr. *Teniſon*, who in 1674 had publiſhed the " Baconiana," bequeathed all his MSS. not before
" depoſited in *Lambeth* Library, to his chaplain Dr. *Edmund Gibſon*, then rector of *Lambeth*, and after-
" wards ſucceſſively biſhop of *Lincoln* and *London*, and to Mr. (afterwards Dr.) *Benjamin Ibbot*, who
" had ſucceeded Dr. *Gibſon*, as library-keeper to his grace. Dr. *Ibbot* dying *April* 11, 1725, many
" years before biſhop *Gibſon*, the whole collection of archbiſhop *Teniſon's* papers came under the diſ-
" poſition of that biſhop, who directed his two executors, the late Dr. *Betteſworth*, dean of the
" Arches, and his ſon, *George Gibſon*, eſq. to depoſit them, with the addition of many others
" of his own collecting, in the manuſcript library at *Lambeth*; and accordingly after his lordſhip's
" death, which happened on the 6th of *Sept.* 1748, all theſe manuſcripts were delivered by his ſaid
" executors to archbiſhop *Herring*, on the 21ſt of *October* of that year, and placed in the library on
" the 23d of *February* following. But as they lay undigeſted in bundles, and in that condition were
" neither convenient for uſe, nor ſecure from damage, his grace the preſent archbiſhop [*Secker*] di-
" rected them to be methodiſed and bound up in volumes with proper indexes, which was done by his
" learned librarian, *Andrew Coltee Ducarel*, LL. D. Fellow of the Royal and Antiquarian Societies,
" to whoſe knowledge, induſtry, and love of hiſtory and antiquities, the valuable library of manu-
" ſcripts of the archiepiſcopal ſee of *Canterbury* is highly indebted for the order in which it is now
" arranged; and by whoſe obliging and communicating temper it is rendered generally uſeful. Biſhop
" *Gibſon's* collection, including what is the chief part of it, that of archbiſhop *Teniſon* fills fourteen
" large volumes in folio. The eighth of theſe conſiſts merely of lord *Bacon's* papers." Dr. *Birch*,
Preface to Lord Bacon's Letters.

3   ſource

searches in natural hiſtory have immortalized his name,
Mr.

ſource he derived much information, as there were very few men of learning and ingenuity, who were not of his acquaintance at home ; and moſt foreigners of eminence in natural hiſtory, or in arts and ſciences, were recommended to his notice and friendſhip. His
diligence and œconomy of time was ſuch, that though he never appeared to be in a hurry,
he maintained an extenſive correſpondence with great punctuality ; acquainting the learned
and ingenious in diſtant parts of the globe, with the diſcoveries and improvements in natural
hiſtory in this country, and receiving the like information from the moſt eminent perſons in almoſt every other. His correſpondence with the ingenious *Cadwallader Colden*, eſq. of *New York*, and the juſtly celebrated Dr. *Franklin* of *Philadelphia*, furniſh
inſtances of the benefit reſulting from his attention to all improvements *. The latter of
theſe gentlemen communicated his firſt eſſays on electricity to Mr. *Collinſon*, in a ſeries of
letters, which were then publiſhed, and have been reprinted in a late edition of the Doctor's
ingenious diſcoveries and improvements. Perhaps, in ſome future period, the account procured of the management of ſheep in *Spain*, publiſhed in the Gentleman's Magazine for
May and *June*, 1764, may not be conſidered among the leaſt of the benefits accruing from
his extenſive and inquiſitive correſpondence. His converſation, chearful and uſefully
entertaining, rendered his acquaintance much deſired by thoſe who had a reliſh for natural hiſtory, or were ſtudious in cultivating rural improvements ; and ſecured him the
intimate friendſhip of ſome of the moſt eminent perſonages in this kingdom, as diſtinguiſhed by their taſte in planting and horticulture, as by their rank and dignity. He
was the firſt who introduced the great variety of ſeeds and ſhrubs, which are now the
principal ornaments of every garden ; and it was owing to his indefatigable induſtry,
that ſo many perſons of the firſt diſtinction are now enabled to behold groves tranſplanted from the Weſtern continent flouriſhing ſo luxuriantly in their ſeveral domains, as if
they were already become indigenous to *Britain*. He had ſome correſpondents in almoſt
every nation in *Europe* ; ſome in *Aſia*, and even at *Pekin* ; who all tranſmitted to him
the moſt valuable ſeeds they could collect, in return for the treaſures of *America*. The
great *Linnæus*, during his reſidence in *England*, contracted an intimate friendſhip
with Mr. *Collinſon*, which was reciprocally increaſed by a multitude of good offices, and
continued to the laſt. Beſides his attachment to natural hiſtory, he was very converſant in
the antiquities of our own country, having been elected a member of the Society of Antiquaries *April* 7, 1737 ; and he ſupplied them often with many curious articles of
intelligence and obſervations, reſpecting both our own and other countries. His perſon was rather ſhort than tall ; he had a pleaſing and ſocial aſpect ; of a temper open

* " In 1730, a ſubſcription-library being ſet on foot at *Philadelphia*, he encouraged the deſign by
" making ſeveral very valuable preſents to it, and procuring others from his friends : and as the li-
" brary-company had a conſiderable ſum ariſing annually to be laid out in books, and needed a
" judicious friend in *London* to tranſact the buſineſs for them, he voluntarily and chearfully under-
" took that ſervice, and executed it for more than thirty years ſucceſſively ; aſſiſting in the choice of
" books, and taking the whole care of collecting and ſhipping them, without ever charging or accepting
" any conſideration for his trouble. The ſucceſs of this library (greatly owing to his kind counte-
" nance and good advice) encouraged the erecting others in different places on the ſame plan : and it
" is ſuppoſed there are now upwards of thirty ſubſiſting in the ſeveral colonies, which have contri-
" buted greatly to the ſpreading of uſeful knowledge in that part of the world, the books he recom-
" mended being all of that kind, and the catalogue of this firſt library being much reſpected and fol-
" lowed by thoſe libraries that ſucceeded. During the ſame time he tranſmitted to the directors of the
" library the earlieſt accounts of every new *European* improvement in agriculture and the arts, and
" every philoſophical diſcovery ; among which, in 1745, he ſent over an account of the new *German*
" experiments in electricity, together with a glaſs tube, and ſome directions for uſing it, ſo as to re-
" peat thoſe experiments." *Letter from Mr. R. Franklin to Michael Collinſon, Eſq.*

and

Mr. *Nickolls**, Mr. *Edwards*† the moſt celebrated orni-
thologiſt

and communicative, capable of feeling for diſtreſs, and ready to relieve and ſympa-
thize. Excepting ſome attacks of the gout, he enjoyed, in general, perfect health,
and great equality of ſpirits, and had arrived at his 75th year; when, being on a viſit to
lord *Petre*, for whom he had a ſingular regard, he was ſeized with a total ſuppreſſion
of urine, which baffling every attempt to relieve it, proved fatal on the 11th of *Auguſt*,
1768. Mr. *Collinſon* left behind him many materials for the improvement of natural
hiſtory; and the preſent refined taſte of Horticulture, may in ſome reſpects be attributed
to his induſtry and abilities. The late lord *Petre*, the late duke of *Richmond*, and others
of the firſt rank in life and letters, were his friends, and he was continually urging them
to proſecute the moſt liberal improvements. An excellent portrait of him, by *Miller*, is
prefixed to Dr. *Fothergill's* Letter.

* Mr. *John Nickolls*, F. R. and A. SS. a Quaker, in partnerſhip with his father of the
ſame name, a capital mealman at *Ware* in *Hertfordſhire*, and of *Trinity* pariſh near
Queenhith, *London*. He was choſen F. A. S. *Jan.* 17, 1740; and poſſeſſed the eſteem of
a reſpectable number of friends, who were deprived of him by a fever at the age of 34,
Jan. 11, 1745. His remains were depoſited in the buryal ground at *Bunhill Fields*
on the 16th. Mr. *Nickolls* publiſhed "Original Letters and Papers of State, addreſſed
"to *Oliver Cromwell*, concerning the affairs of *Great Britain*, from the year 1649 to
"1658, found among the Political Collections of Mr. *John Milton*; now firſt publiſhed
"from the Originals **; 1743," folio. inſcribed to *Arthur Onſlow*, eſq. He was the
firſt †† REGULAR collector of *Engliſh* heads ‡‡. His noble collection of about 2000
heads, four volumes in folio, and ſix in quarto, neatly let-in (which furniſhed Mr. *Ames*
with his valuable catalogue), came ſoon after his death into the library of Dr. *Fothergill*,
who purchaſed it for eighty guineas. Dr. *Fothergill* purchaſed likewiſe a pretty large
collection of tracts which Mr. *Nickols* had picked up in his purſuit of heads, written
by thoſe of his own perſuaſion from their firſt appearance; which the benevolent poſſeſſor intends to leave to the Meeting to which he at preſent belongs, in *Peter's Court*,
Weſtminſter. Beſides theſe collections, he had ſeveral views by great maſters; ſome of
which fell alſo into the hands of Dr. *Fothergill*. The catalogue of his library, in his
own hand-writing (including 332 volumes of tracts in folio, 4to. and 8vo.) is in the
poſſeſſion of Mr. *Tutet*.

† *George Edwards* was born at *Stratford*, a hamlet belonging to *Weſtham* in *Eſſex*,
on the 3d of *April*, 1694. He paſſed ſome of his early years under the tuition of a cler-

** The originals of theſe Letters were long treaſured up by *Milton*; from whom they came into the
poſſeſſion of *Thomas Elwood*, a perſon who for many years was well acquainted with, and eſteemed by
Milton. From *Elwood* they came to *Joſeph Wyeth*, citizen and merchant of *London*; and from *Wyeth's*
widow, they were obtained by Mr. *Nickolls*; after whoſe deceaſe they were preſented by his father
to the Society of Antiquaries, as appears by their minutes.

†† *Anthony Wood*, in his account of E. *Aſhmole*, tells us, "In his library I ſaw a large thick paper
"book near a yard long, containing on every ſide of the leaf two, three, or more pictures or faces
"of eminent perſons of *England*, and elſewhere, printed from copper cuts paſted on them, which Mr.
"*Aſhmole* had with great curioſity collected; and I remember he has told me, that his mind was ſo
"eager to obtain all faces, that when he could not get a face by itſelf, he would buy the book, tear it
"out, paſte it in his blank book, and write under it from whence he had taken it." An admirable
portrait this of our modern portrait-collectors, who have ſent back many a volume to the bookſeller's
ſhop ſtript of its graven honours. A moſt noted Collector told a perſon at *Cambridge*, who now and
then ſells a head, "That his own collection muſt needs be large and good, as it reſted on ſix points:
"1. I buy; 2. I borrow; 3. I beg; 4. I exchange; 5. I ſteal; 6. I ſell."—Mr. *Aſhmole's* book was
conſumed with the reſt of his library.

‡‡ See the virulent cenſure of Mr. *Rowe Mores* on this ſpecies of collectors, Diſſertation on *Engliſh*
Founders, p. 85.

gyman,

thologist that ever adorned this country, Dr. *Charles Lyt-telton*

gyman, named *Hewit*, who was then master of a public school at *Laytonstone*, and after quitting the school, he was placed with another minister of the established church at *Brentwood*; and being designed by his parents for business, was put apprentice to a tradesman in *Fenchurch Street*. About the middle of his apprenticeship, Dr. *Nicholas*, a physician of eminence, and a relation of his master, died: and his books having been removed from *Covent Garden* to an apartment then occupied by our young naturalist, he availed himself of this unexpected incident, and passed all the leisure of the day, and, not unfrequently, a considerable part of the night, in turning over this large collection of natural history, arts, and antiquities. On the expiration of his time, he conceived a design to travel into foreign countries, to improve his taste, and enlarge his mind. In 1716 he spent a month in *Holland*. In 1718 he went to *Norway*, at the invitation of a gentleman, whose nephew was master of the vessel in which he embarked. In his excursion to *Frederickstadt*, he was not distant from the siege of *Frederickshall*; where *Charles* XII. lost his life. By this circumstance he was disappointed of visiting that country, as the *Swedish* army was particularly assiduous in confining strangers; and, notwithstanding all his precaution, he was confined by the *Danish* guard, who supposed him a spy. In 1719 he visited *France*, and during his stay there, he made two journies of one hundred miles each; the first to *Chalons* in *Champagne*, in *May* 1720; the second on foot to *Orleans* and *Blois*, in disguise to escape being robbed. An edict happened at that time to be issued, to secure vagrants, in order to transport them to *America*, to people the banks of the *Missisippi*; and Mr. *Edwards* narrowly escaped a western voyage. On his arrival in *England*, he closely pursued his favourite study of natural history, applying himself to drawing and colouring such animals as fell under his notice. Birds first engaged his particular attention; and the curious encouraged the young naturalist, by paying a good price for his early labours. Among his first patrons and benefactors may be mentioned *James Theobald*, esq. of *Lambeth*, F. R. and A. S. a gentleman zealous for the promotion of science. In 1731, with two of his relations, he made an excursion to *Holland* and *Brabant*, where he collected several scarce books and prints. In *December* 1733, by the recommendation of Sir *Hans Sloane*, bart. president of the College of Physicians, he was chosen their librarian, and had apartments in the college. This office was peculiarly agreeable to his taste. The first volume of his " History of Birds" was published in quarto, 1743; the subscribers to which exceeded even his most sanguine expectation; and a second volume appeared in 1747. The third was published in 1750, and in 1751 the fourth. This being the last he intended at that time, he seems to have considered it as the most perfect of his productions in natural history; and therefore with devout gratitude offered it up to the great God of nature. Our author, however, continued his labours under a new title, " Gleanings of Natural History," in 1758; another volume in 1760; the third part, which made the seventh and last volume of his works, in 1764. Thus, after a long series of years, the most studious application, and the most extensive correspondence to every quarter of the world, he concluded a work which contains engravings and descriptions of more than six hundred subjects in natural history, not before described or delineated. He likewise added a generical index in *French* and *English*, which is now perfectly compleated with the *Linnæan* names, by that great naturalist *Linnæus* himself, who frequently honoured him with his friendship and correspondence. Some time after Mr. *Edwards* had been appointed library keeper to the

R College

telton * afterwards bishop of *Carlisle* and president of the
Society

College of Physicians, he was, on St. *Andrew's* day, 1750, presented by the Royal
Society with the gold medal, in confideration of his natural hiftory juft then completed. A copy of this medal he had afterwards engraved and placed under the general
title in the firft volume of his Hiftory. He was a few years afterwards elected fellow of
that Society and of the Society of Antiquaries, and alfo a member of many of the
Academies of *Europe*. His collection of drawings, which amounted to upwards of
nine hundred, were purchafed by the earl of *Bute*, who would confer a favour on the
publick by caufing engravings to be made from them, as they contain a great number of
Englifh as well as foreign birds and other animals hitherto not accurately delineated or
defcribed. After the publication of the laft work, being arrived at his 70th year, and finding his fight begin to fail, he retired to a fmall houfe which he had purchafed at *Plaiftow* ;
previous to which, he difpofed of all his copies and plates of his works. Having
completed his 80th year, emaciated with age and ficknefs, he died *July* 23, 1773, defervedly lamented by a numerous acquaintance. His remains were interred in the
church-yard of *Weft Ham*, his native parifh, where his executors have erected an
infcription to his memory. The *Linnæan* Index, his papers from the Philofophical
Tranfactions, and Memoirs of his Life, were publifhed in 1776, in a proper fize to bind
with his other works. A print of him, engraved by *J. S. Miller* in 1754, after a
painting by *Dandridge*, is a moft ftriking likenefs. He left two fifters, to whom he bequeathed the fortune acquired by affiduous application to his favourite purfuits ; they
died lately, within a few hours of each other, and were buried together.

    * *Charles*, third fon of Sir *Thomas*, and brother to *George* firft lord *Lyttelton*, educated
at *Eaton*, went from *Univerfity College, Oxford*, to *The Inner Temple*, and became a barrifter at law ; but entering into holy orders, was collated by the venerable
Bifhop *Hough* to the rectory of *Alvechurch* in *Worcefterfhire*, *Aug.* 13, 1742. He took
the degree of LL.B. *March* 28, 1745, and LL.D. *June* 18, the fame year ; was appointed king's chaplain in *December* 1747, dean of *Exeter* in *May* 1748, and was confecrated bifhop of *Carlifle*, *March* 21, 1762. In 1754 he caufed the ceiling and cor-
nices of the chancel of *Hagley* church to be ornamented with fhields of arms in their
proper colours, reprefenting the paternal coats of his ancient and refpectable family. In
1765, on the death of *Hugh* lord *Willoughby of Parham* †, he was unanimoufly elected prefident of the Society of Antiquaries ; a ftation in which his diftinguifhed abilities were eminently difplayed. He died unmarried *Dec.* 22, 1768. His merits and good qualities are
univerfally acknowledged ; and thofe parts of his character which more particularly endeared him to the refpectable Society over which he fo worthily prefided, I will point out
in the words of his learned fucceffor ‡ : " The ftudy of antiquity, efpecially that
" part of it which relates to the hiftory and conftitution of thefe kingdoms, was one
" of his earlieft and moft favourite purfuits ; and he acquired great knowledge in it by
" conftant ftudy and application, to which he was led, not only by his natural difpofi-
" tion, but alfo by his ftate and fituation in life. He took frequent opportunities of
" improving and enriching this knowledge, by judicious obfervations in the courfe of

    † This ingenious and learned nobleman, who was elected vice-prefident of the Royal Society *Nov.*
30, 1752, accepted the prefidentfhip of the Society of Antiquaries *July* 26, 1754. His lordfhip
was alfo one of the truftees of *The Britifh Mufeum* ; prefident of the Society for equitable affurance on
lives and furvivorfhip, in *Nicholas Lane*, near *Lombard Street, London* ; and one of the vice-prefidents
of the Society for the encouragement of arts, manufactures, and commerce. He died *Jan.* 21, 1765.
    ‡ See the Speech of Dr. *Milles* Dean of *Exeter*, on fucceeding to the Prefidency, *Jan.* 12, 1769,
prefixed to the Archaologia, vol. I. p. xli—xliv.

    2

                                                 " feveral

Society of Antiquaries, Mr. *Fairfax* *, Mr. *Morant* the historian

" several journies which he made through every county in *England*, and through many
" parts of *Scotland* and *Wales*. The Society has reaped the fruits of thefe obfervations
" in the many valuable papers, which his lordfhip from time to time has communi-
" cated to us; which are more in number, and not inferior either in merit or import-
" ance, to thofe conveyed to us by other hands †. Bleft with a retentive memory,
" and happy both in the difpofition and facility of communicating his knowledge, he was
" enabled alfo to act the part of a judicious commentator and candid critic, explaining,
" illuftrating, and correcting, from his own obfervations, many of the papers which
" have been read at this Society. His ftation and connections in the world, which ne-
" ceffarily engaged a very confiderable part of his time, did not leffen his attention to
" the bufinefs and interefts of the Society. His doors were always open to his friends,
" amongft whom none were more welcome to him than the friends of literature, which
" he endeavoured to promote in all its various branches, efpecially in thofe which are
" the more immediate objects of our attention. Even this circumftance proved bene-
" ficial to the Society; for, if I may be allowed the expreffion, he was the center in
" which the various informations on points of antiquity from the different parts of the
" kingdom united, and the medium through which they were conveyed to us. His
" literary merit with the Society received an additional luftre from the affability of his
" temper, the gentlenefs of his manners, and the benevolence of his heart; which
" united every member of the Society in efteem to their Head, and in harmony and
" friendfhip with each other. A principle fo effentially neceffary to the profperity, and
" even to the exiftence of all communities, efpecially thofe which have arts and litera-
" ture for their object, that its beneficial effects are vifibly to be difcerned in the pre-
" fent flourifhing ftate of our Society, which I flatter myfelf will be long continued under
" the influence of the fame agreeable principles. I fhall conclude this imperfect fketch
" of a moft worthy character, by obferving, that the warmth of his affection to the So-
" ciety continued to his lateft breath; and he has given a fignal proof of it in the laft
" great act, which a wife man does with refpect to his worldly affairs; for, amongft the
" many charitable and generous donations contained in his will, he has made a very
" ufeful and valuable bequeft of manufcripts ‡ and printed books to the Society, as a
" token of his affection for them, and of his earneft defire to promote thofe laudable
" purpofes for which they were inftituted." The Society expreffed their gratitude and
refpect to his memory by a portrait of him engraved at their expence in 1770.

* *Brian Fairfax*, efq. F. S. A. uncle to the lord vifcount *Fairfax* of *Ireland*, and
one of the Commiffioners of the Cuftoms. He died *Jan.* 9, 1749, and bequeathed a very
confiderable fortune to the Hon. *Robert Fairfax*, who in one parliament was member
for *Maidftone*. His collection of *Greek*, *Roman*, and *Englifh* coins and medals, were
fold by auction, *April* 24, 25, and 26, 1751. Amongft other curiofities, Mr. *Fairfax*
poffeffed one part of the famous *Heraclean* Table ‖. In his very valuable library was
the

---

† Thefe are preferved in the Archæologia, vol. I. p. 9. 140. 213. 228. 310.

‡ Among thefe is a MS. hiftory of the building of *Exeter* cathedral, by himfelf; and his large collections towards a Hiftory of *Worcefterfhire*.

‖ In 1732 two large tables of copper were difcovered near *Heraclea*, in the bay of *Tarentum*, in
Magna Græcia; the firft and moft important of them, which was broken into two, containing, on
one fide, a *Greek* infcription relating to lands facred to *Bacchus*; on the other, a *Latin* infcription,
being part of a pandect or digeft of *Roman* municipal laws. Both thefe infcriptions were given to the
world in 1736 by Mr. *Maittaire*, as already mentioned in p. 94. The fecond table, engraved on one

historian of *Essex*[#], Dr. *Cromwell Mortimer*[*], Mr. *Frank*[†],

Mr.

the Bible printed by *Fust*, on vellum, 1462, and *Cicero's* Offices by the same printer, also on vellum, 1466. The whole library, being 2343 lots, was intended to have been sold by auction on *April* 26, 1756, and the 17 following days; but, after being advertised, was privately sold for 2000l. to *Francis Child*, esq. and the printed catalogues, except 20, were suppressed. Mr. *Child* sent the library to his seat at *Osterley*, *Middlesex*, where it remains in the possession of his younger brother and heir, *Robert Child*, esq. and makes part of the *superb and magnificently bound* library [**], of which a catalogue was drawn up, and only *twelve* copies printed, in 1771, in a *handsome* quarto. This latter catalogue is supposed to have been drawn up by Dr. *Morell*; but more probably by the Rev. Dr. *Winchester*, who had been tutor to these gentlemen, and collected many books for the eldest of them. Mr. *Fairfax's* pictures, statues, urns, and other antiquities, were sold by auction, *April* 6 and 7, and the prints and drawings, *May* 4—8, 1756.

[*] For Mr. *Morant* and Dr. *Mortimer*, see the pages referred to in the Index.

[†] *Richard Frank*, of *Campsal*, esq. F. R. S. recorder of *Pontefract* and *Doncaster*; a polite scholar, and a lover of antiquities. His valuable collections, including those of Dr. *Johnston* [††] (which came into his hands on the death of the author's grandson *Henry Johnston*),

side only, contained a *Greek* inscription relating to lands belonging to the temple of *Minerva*, nearly of the same antiquity with the first; but the inscription imperfect, the table being broken off at the lower end. The first part of the first table, soon after the discovery, was carried to *Rome*, and purchased there at a great price by *Francisco Ficoroni*, a celebrated antiquary. In 1715 it was brought by an *Italian* into *England*, where it was purchased by Mr. *Fairfax*; and at one of the public sales of his collection was bought for 42l. by *Philip Carteret Webb*, esq. who in 1760 obliged the world with a curious account of it, read by him before the Society of Antiquaries, *Dec.* 13, 1759. Mr. *Webb* presented the table, *March* 12, 1760, to the King of *Spain*, by the hands of the *Neapolitan* minister in *London*, to be deposited in the royal collection of antiquities at *Naples*, where the other half and the second table had been placed by purchase in 1748. The Commentaries of *Mazochius* on these tables, in 600 folio pages, were published at *Naples* in 1758. In return for the table, Mr. *Webb* received from his *Sicilian* majesty a present of a valuable diamond ring.

[**] In Mr. *West's* catalogue, N° 1920 (made up of old title pages of early printed books, &c.) contained a MS. list of "Books in Mr. *Child's* library at *Osterley*, printed before the year 1500;" and another such list, "before the year 1551."

[††] Dr. *Nathaniel Johnston*, physician at *Pontefract*, made large collections from *Dodsworth's* papers and other quarters, and communicated many particulars to bishop *Gibson*. Mr. *Drake* tells us, the Doctor's MSS. are in such an awkward scrawl as to be scarce legible, and that a subscription was proposed some few years since to lodge them in the Castle library, which might have made them more useful than they can be now. The Doctor gave out, he had spent thirty years in amassing materials, and proposed to write the antiquities of the county after *Dugdale's*, and the natural history after *Plott's* manner. *Wood* was informed he grew weary of the work. *Nicolson* has left this censure on his labours, that " only death prevented the publication of what its readers would have been weary of." The Proposals for printing them (published in 1722 by his grandson) are preserved in Mr. *Bowyer's* Miscellaneous Tract. He had written a history of the *Talbot* family from their *Norman* ancestor *Richard Talbot* to *Edward Talbot*, last earl of *Shrewsbury* of the house of *Sheffield*; an historical account of the reign of *Charles* I. after the breaking out of the civil war; and a short account of *Stephen's* reign. The first of these is in Mr. *Gough's* possession. His historical account of the family of *Bruce* is in the *Harleian* library, N° 3879. He had a copy of Domesday for *Yorkshire* transcribed in a common hand by himself. Dr. *Burton* (Pref. to his Monasticon) informs us, he had the use of above one hundred folio volumes relating to this county, collected by this indefatigable physician, and then in the hands of *Richard Frank*, esq. who had purchased as many as could be found, amounting to 97 volumes folio, and some bundles in 4to. after the death of the author's grandson, *Henry Johnston*. A catalogue of them and others in the Doctor's possession was published in the Cat. MSS. Angl. tom. ii. p. 99. Among the rest is mentioned a large volume of prospects of *York*, and other towns and castles, draughts of *Roman* and *Saxon* camps, and views of churches, abbies, and seats: others contain arms,

Mr. *Maitland** and Mr. *Tindal** the historians, Dr. *Middleton* †

the

Johnston ‡), are now, 1780, in the hands of *Bacon Frank* of *Campsal*, esq. nephew and heir to the Recorder.

* For Mr. *Maitland* and Mr. *Tindal*, see the pages referred to in the Index.

† This learned and ingenious Divine, son of a clergyman in *Yorkshire*, was born at *Richmond* in that county, on the 27th of *December*, 1683. His father, being possessed of an easy fortune besides his preferment in the church, gave him a liberal education; and at seventeen years of age, he was sent to *Trinity College* in *Cambridge*, of which in 1706 he was chosen fellow. In 1707 he commenced master of arts; and two years after joined with several other fellows of his college in a petition to Dr. *More*, then bishop of *Ely*, as their visitor, against the celebrated Dr. *Bentley* their master In the early part of his life, he was not thought to possess any very extraordinary talents; and his attention was more devoted to music than to study, at the time he engaged in the controversy with *Bentley*. This occasioned *Bentley* to call him in contempt a fidler; and probably to this sarcasm the world may be indebted for the many excellent works he afterwards produced. However, he had no sooner joined in the proceedings against *Bentley*, than he withdrew himself from his jurisdiction, by marrying Mrs. *Drake*, daughter of Mr. *Morris*, of *Oak-Morris* in *Kent*, and widow of counsellor *Drake* of *Cambridge*, a lady of ample fortune. After his marriage he took a small rectory in the *Isle of Ely*, which was in the gift of his wife; but resigned it in little more than a year, probably because he thought it not worth keeping. In *October* 1717, when king *George* I. visited the university of *Cambridge*, he was created, with several others, a doctor of divinity by mandate; and was the person who gave the first motion to that famous proceeding against Dr. *Bentley*, which made such a noise in the nation. Upon the great enlargement of the public library at *Cambridge*, by the addition of bishop *More's* books, which had been purchased by the king for 6000 guineas ‖, and presented to the university, the erection of the new office of principal librarian, was first voted, and then conferred upon Dr. *Middleton*, as I have already mentioned in p. 62 §. After the decease of his first wife, he travelled through *France*

into

arms, tombs, and monumental inscriptions, before the civil war. Dr. *Ducarel* informed the Society of Antiquaries, 1756, that Dr. *Johnston's* MSS. amounted only to ninety-seven volumes, and some quarto bundles, though in the Cat. MSS. Ang. they are a hundred and thirty-five; the rest were carried off by an amanuensis employed to copy such as related to the *Darcy* family, which, together with the originals, were burnt by an accidental fire in lord *Holdernejs's* house; but no volumes had been carried into *Suffolk*, and used as waste paper, as some of the members had reported: that the two volumes of drawings were brought by the amanuensis into that county, where they were pasted on the walls of the late chancellor's *Johnston's* house by children: that Mr. *Thomas Martin* had taken off many, and hoped to take off the rest, of which he promised an account. A volume of these drawings, with MS. notes, supposed to be one of those carried into *Suffolk*, was in the possession of Mr. *Astle*, who exchanged them with *John Hatfield-Kay*, of *Hatfield-hall*, *Yorkshire*, esq. Another volume of drawings was recovered by the means of Dr. *Ducarel*, and sent to the late Mr. *Franke*, in whose library (now his nephew's, 1780) they remain. See British Topography, II. 402—404.

‡ *Henry Johnston*, LL. D. rector of *Whilton*, *Northamptonshire*, and vicar of *Stow-Market*, *Suffolk*; afterwards chancellor of the diocese of *Landaff*, prebendary of *Lincoln*, and rector of *Stoke* and *Soham Monks*, in the county of *Lincoln*, at which place he died *Sept.* 19, 1755. See the family pedigree in Dr. *Ducarel's Anglo-Gallic* coins, p. 57.

‖ See *Bentham's Ely*, after *Richardson's* edition of *Godwin*.

§ " This was quite a party action, and pushed on by Dr. *Gooch* to plague *Bentley* by rewarding his opponent. The late worthy Dr. *Simonds* of *Bury* (father to the Professor of Modern History in *Cambridge*,) then fellow of *St. John's College*, with five or six more of that house, formed the whole number that had sense, honesty, and courage enough to vote against the creating an useless place on

such

the celebrated librarian of *Cambridge*, well known by his many

into *Italy*, and arrived at *Rome* early in the year 1724. Much leisure, with an infirm state of health, was the cause of his journey to *Italy*; where, though his character and profession were well known, he was yet treated with particular respect by persons of the first distinction both in church and state. The author of his life in the old " Biographia Britannica," relates, that on his first coming there, he got himself introduced in his character of principal librarian to his brother-librarian at *The Vatican*, who received him with great politeness; but, upon his mentioning *Cambridge*, said, he did not know before that there was any university in *England* of that name, and at the same time took notice, that he was no stranger to that of *Oxford*, for which he expressed a great esteem. Our new librarian took some pains to convince his brother not only of the real existence, but of the real dignity of his university of *Cambridge*. At last the keeper of *The Vatican* acknowledged, that he had indeed heard of a celebrated school of that name in *England*, where youth were prepared for their admission at *Oxford*; and Dr. *Middleton* left him at present in that sentiment *. But this unexpected indignity made him resolve to support his residence at *Rome* in such a manner, as should be a credit to his station at *Cambridge*; and accordingly he agreed to give 400l. per annum for a hotel, with all accommodations, fit for the reception of persons of the first rank in *Rome*; which, joined to his great fondness for antique curiosities, occasioned him to trespass a little upon his fortune. He returned through *Paris* in the year 1725. In *December* 1731 he was appointed *Woodwardian* professor; and in *July* 1732 published his inauguration speech. Reading lectures upon fossils was not an employment suited to his taste, or to the turn of his studies; and he resigned it in 1734. Soon after this, he married a second wife, *Mary*, the daughter of the Rev. *Conyers Place*, of *Dorchester*; and upon her death, a third, *Anne*, daughter of *John Powell*, esq. of *Boughroyd*, near *Radnor*. In 1735 he published " A Dissertation concerning the Origin " of Printing in *England*," of which I shall have occasion to speak further hereafter. In 1741 came out his great work, " The History of the Life of *M. Tullius Cicero*," in two volumes, 4to. published by subscription, and dedicated to lord *Hervey*, who was much the author's friend. In *December* 1748 he published his " Free Inquiry " into the Miraculous Powers, which are supposed to have subsisted in the Chris- " tian Church from the earliest Ages, through several successive Centuries." Innumerable answerers now appeared against him; two of whom, *Dodwell* and *Church*, distinguished themselves with so much zeal, that they were complimented by the university of *Oxford* with the degree of doctor in divinity. It does not appear that he originally intended to reply to any of them separately, for he was meditating a general answer to all the objections made against the Free Inquiry; but being seized with illness, and imagining he might not be able to go through it, he singled out *Church* and *Dodwell*, as the two most considerable of his adversaries, and employed

such an occasion; but so high did party run, and so low had it descended, that the very mob in the street hooted them all their way home. This particular respect shewed him [the library story], and his expence at *Rome* for the honour of *Cambridge*, are believed to have been mere puffs of the Doctor's when he came back, in order to induce the members of the senate to create this place for him, as an indemnification for the expences he had incurred in defence of their fame and honour. This may deserve attention, though it contradicts the story in the Biographia Britannica, which supposes him then actually librarian, and that he was to live and shew off like the Cardinal Protobibliothecarius of the Vatican." *Dr. Taylor's Friend.*

 * This story, it must be allowed, is highly improbable. How could *Cambridge* be unknown to any man of letters at *Rome*, when that University had produced, before the Reformation, so many persons of celebrity in the History of the *Romish* Church? And with regard to later times, was it likely that the name and writings of such a critic, for instance, as Dr. *Bentley*, had not reached *The Vatican*? If the Librarian was so ignorant as is represented, he was very ill qualified for his office.

himself

many excellent writings, Dr. *S. Chandler** the celebrated
Dif-

himfelf in preparing a particular anfwer to them. This, however, he did not live to
finifh, but died of a flow hectic fever and diforder in his liver, on the 28th of *July*, 1750,
in the 67th year of his age, at *Hilderfham* in *Cambridgefhire*, an eftate of his own purchafing. A little before his death, he thought it prudent to accept of a fmall living
from Sir *John Frederick*, bart. He publifhed a great variety of tracts on various learned
fubjects, too many and too well known to be here enumerated; all which, except the
Life of *Cicero*, were collected in 1752, and printed together in four volumes 4to. Befides
the mezzotinto print of him, which is a very good likenefs, a medal of him was caft
and repaired by *Giovanni Pozzo* at *Rome* in 1724, which fome years ago was copied in
London by Mr. *Stewart*, and has fince been engraved, as well as copied at an eafier expence by Mr. *Wedgwood*. Dr. *Middleton* fuperintended in his own houfe the education
of two or three young gentlemen of rank, among whom was the prefent Lord *Montford*,
for whofe father he purchafed a valuable library, fince difperfed by a bookfeller's marked
catalogue. The Doctor's antiques, which he defcribed in " Germana quædam Antiqui-
" tatis Monumenta," are in the cabinet of *Horace Walpole*, efq.

* *Samuel Chandler*, D. D. F. R. and A. S. eldeft fon of Mr. *Henry Chandler*, many
years minifter of a congregation of Proteftant Diffenters in *Bath*, was born *Sept.* 20, 1693,
at *Hungerford* in *Berks*, where his father was then minifter. He was defcended from
anceftors heartily engaged in the caufe of Nonconformity; his grandfather (a tradefman at *Taunton*) having much injured his fortune by his principles. His early genius
for learning was carefully cultivated; and he was placed under a mafter with whom he
made a great proficiency in claffical learning, and particularly in the *Greek* language. He
was fent with a view to the miniftry to the academy of the Rev. Mr. *John Moore* at *Bridge-
water*; whence he was foon removed to *Gloucefter*, under the tuition of the very
learned and ingenious Mr. *Samuel Jones*, who had the honour of educating Archbifhop
Secker, Bifhop *Butler*, and the late lord *Bowes* chancellor of *Ireland*. In this
feminary Mr. *Chandler* acquired a rich fund of literature and fcience, particularly of
critical, biblical, and oriental learning; and formed an acquaintance and friendfhip
with the great perfonages juft mentioned, which was continued with reciprocal inftances of efteem and regard to the end of life. He left the academy, and began to
preach about *July* 1714, with increafing reputation. The Prefbyterian congregation at
Peckham elected him their minifter in 1716. While he was employed there, he was
called upon to preach in conjunction with Dr. *Lardner*, for the winter half year,
a weekly evening lecture at *The Old Jewry*, on the evidences of natural and revealed
religion. When this lecture was dropped, another of the fame kind was fet up, which
was preached by Mr. *Chandler* alone. The fubftance of thefe fermons he publifhed in
his " Vindication of the Chriftian Religion, 1725," at which period he was a book-
feller** at *The Crofs Keys* in *The Poultry*, the fhop afterwards kept by Mr. *J. Gray* ††.

** Dr. *Chandler* was not originally brought up to that profeffion. It was in confequence of having
loft his wife's fortune in the *South Sea* bubble that he took it up; and he continued in it but two or
three years. His edition of " *Caffiodorus*" was printed " for *John Morley*, at the *Crofs Keys* in The
" *Poultry*," in the latter end of 1722. And the earlieft book that I have feen with the name of
S. Chandler is in 1725; in which year, befides his own work, he publifhed the " Mifcellanea Sacra" of
John lord vifcount *Barrington*. As he was elected affiftant paftor at *The Old Jewry* in 1726, he then
of courfe declined bufinefs. His " Reflexions on the Conduct of Modern Deifts, 1727," was pub-
lifhed by *J. Chandler*; and his " Vindication of *Daniel*" by *J. Gray*.

†† Mr. *Gray*, like his predeceffor, became a Diffenting minifter, and afterwards, upon his
complying with the terms of admiffion into the Church of *England*, rector of a living at *Rippon* in
Yorkfhire. In conjunction with *Andrew Reed*, he abridged the Philofophical Tranfactions from 1720 to
1732, in 2 vols. 4to. 1733. He alfo publifhed the *Elmerick* of *Lillo*, and, at the dying requeft of
the author, dedicated it to *Frederick* prince of *Wales*.

To

Diffenting Divine, Mr. *Hardinge* clerk of the Houſe of Commons,

To this, Archbiſhop *Wake* alludes, in the following extract from a MS. letter, dated *Lambeth Houſe*, *Feb.* 14, 1725, (which I tranſcribe from a copy of the " Vindication," once belonging to Dr. *Philip Furneaux*) : " I cannot but own myſelf ſurprized to ſee ſo " much good learning and juſt reaſoning in a perſon of your profeſſion, and do think it " pity you ſhould not rather ſpend your time in writing books than in ſelling them. " But I am glad, ſince your circumſtances oblige you to the latter, that you do not " wholly omit the former." After heartily commending the " Vindication," his Grace aſſures Mr. *Chandler*, that as to himſelf, " he was not only uſefully entertained, but " edified by it." The reputation gained by this publication made way for his being choſen, in 1726, aſſiſtant to Mr. *Thomas Leaveſley**, then paſtor to the congregation in *The Old Jewry*. He was ſoon after appointed co-paſtor with Mr. *Leaveſley*, and ſucceeded him as ſole paſtor 1728. In the courſe of this miniſtry he formed the deſign of a fund for the widows and orphans of Diſſenting miniſters, and received without ſolicitation the diploma of D. D. from the two univerſities of *Edinburgh* and *Glaſgow*. The high reputation which he had gained by his defences of the Chriſtian religion, procured him from ſome principal perſons of the eſtabliſhed church the offers of conſiderable preferments, and particularly of a living worth four hundred pounds a year, which he conſtantly declined. In the younger part of life he had been ſubject to frequent and dangerous fevers; but by the uſe of a vegetable diet twelve years, obtained ſo happy an alteration in his conſtitution, that he enjoyed an uncommon ſhare of vigour and ſpirits till 70; after which he experienced frequent returns of a moſt painful diſorder, which he bore with great reſignation till his deceaſe, *May* 8, 1766, in his 73d year. A chronological account of his writings, drawn up by Dr. *Flexman*, is annexed to his Funeral Sermon, which was preached at *The Old Jewry* by Dr. *Amory* †, *May* 18, 1766, and prefixed (with ſome corrections) to his Poſthumous Sermons, 1769. The moſt material of them are enumerated below ‡. We learn by the Preface to the Poſthumous Sermons, that Dr. *Chandler*, among other learned and uſeful deſigns, had begun a Commentary on the Prophets; and left behind him in an interleaved Bible a large number of notes for illuſtrating the ſacred writers. He alſo left in MS. many obſervations in the manner of *Elſner* and *Raphelius*, which Dr. *Furneaux* had taken ſome pains to digeſt, and which are now the property of Dr. *Kippis*, Mr. *Farmer*, Dr. *Price*, and Dr. *Savage*, and are intended to be publiſhed. I have much reaſon to regret that I cannot trace out the preſent poſſeſſor of a copy of the firſt edition of Mr. *Bowyer's* " Conjectures on the New Teſtament," 1763, which I am informed was filled with obſervations by Dr. *Chandler*, and ſold in 1766 by auction at Mr. *Baker's*. At the ſame time were ſold ſeveral other books with the Doctor's MS. notes; particularly, *Milton's* Paradiſe Loſt (bought by Mr. *Way* for 18 ſhillings); the New Teſtaments of *Schmidius* and *Curcellæus*; *Scapula's* Lexicon (bought by Dr. *Kippis*); and *Stockii* Clavis Ling. Sanctæ Vet. & Nov. Teſt. A portrait of Dr. *Chandler*, engraved by *T. Kitchin* from a painting by *Chamberlin*, is prefixed to his Poſthumous Sermons.

* Mr. *Leaveſley* was ſucceſſor, in 1724, to Mr. *Simon Browne*, an able and learned miniſter, of whom a good account is given in the Biographia Britannica, 1780, vol. II. p. 643.

† Who had been choſen aſſiſtant to Dr. *Chandler* in 1759, and ſucceeded him as paſtor in 1766. See more of him in Biog. Brit. 1779, vol. I. p. 175—180.

‡ " A Paraphraſe and critical Commentary on the Prophecy of *Joel*. 1735." 4to.—" A Vindi- " cation of the Chriſtian Religion, in Two Parts."—" Reflexions on the Conduct of modern Deiſts."— " A Vindication of the Antiquity and Authority of *Daniel's* Prophecies, and their Application to " Jeſus Chriſt; in Anſwer to the Objections of the Author of the Scheme of Literal Prophecy conſi- " dered;

Commons and one of the Secretaries of the Treasury*,
Mr.

* Nicholas Hardinge, esq. of Canbury, near Kingston in Surrey, (brother of Caleb Hardinge, M. D. grandson of Sir Robert Hardinge of King's Newton, in the county of Derby, knt. and father of George Hardinge, esq. of The Middle Temple, barrister, an eminent counsel, and of Henry vicar of Kingston) fellow of King's College, Cambridge, and member of parliament for Eye in Suffolk. He married in December 1738, Jane second daughter of Sir John Pratt of Wilderness in Kent (chief justice of the king's bench) and sister to the present lord Camden; and died April 9, 1758. His library was sold by auction in 1759. His " Dialogue in the Senate-house † at Cambridge," is preserved in the " Poetical Calendar," vol. IX. p. 92 ; and his " Denhilliad," a poem occasioned by the Hounds running through Lady Gray's gardens at Denhill in East Kent,

" dered; with a Preface containing some Remarks on the Nature, Design, and Application of Scrip-
" ture Prophesies. 1728." 8vo.—" Plain Reasons for being a Christian. 1730." 8vo.—" A Vindica-
" tion of the History of the Old Testament; in Answer to the Misrepresentations and Calumnies of
" Thomas Morgan, M. D. and Moral Philosopher. 1740." 8vo.—" A Defence of the Prime Mi-
" nistry and Character of Joseph: In Answer to the Misrepresentations and Calumnies of the late
" Thomas Morgan, M. D. and Moral Philosopher. 1742." 8vo. This treatise occasioned " A Vin-
" dication of the Moral Philosopher, against the false accusations, insults, and personal abuses, of
" Samuel Chandler, late Bookseller, and Minister of the Gospel. By Thomas Morgan, M. D."
" and was followed by " The Witnesses of the Resurrection of Jesus Christ, re-examined, and
" their Testimony proved entirely consistent. 1744." 8vo. This tract was occasioned by a pam-
" phlet, intitled, " The Resurrection of Jesus considered, by a Moral Philosopher, [Mr. Peter An-
" nett."]—" A Review of the History of the Man after God's own Heart; in which the Fals-
" hoods and Misrepresentations of the Historian [J. N.] are exposed and corrected. 1762."
8vo.—" A short and plain Catechism, being an Explanation of the Creed, Ten Commandments,
" and the Lord's Prayer; by way of Question and Answer. 1742." 12mo.—Two Tracts against
the Papists, 1735. 1745.—Several Miscellaneous Tracts in defence of Civil and Religious
Liberty, occasioned by disputes in which he was involved by his brethren as well as by the ministers
of the Church of England.—" The History of the Inquisition by Philip à Limborch, Professor of Di-
" vinity amongst the Remonstrants; translated into English; to which is prefixed, a large Introduction
" concerning the Rise and Progress of Persecution, and the real and pretended Causes of it. 1732."
2 vols. 4to. which he vindicated in three tracts from the remarks of Dr. Berriman.—" The History of
" Persecution, in Four Parts. 1. Among the Heathens. 2. Under the Christian Emperors. 3. Under
" the Papacy, and Inquisition. 4. Among Protestants; with a large Preface, containing Remarks
" on Dr. Rogers's Vindication of the Civil Establishment of Religion. 1736." 8vo. " The Case
" of Subscription to explanatory Articles of Faith, as a Qualification for Admission into the
" Christian Ministry, calmly and impartially reviewed. 1748," 8vo. Dr. Chandler wrote the
Dedication to King George 1. prefixed to the Works of John Howe, M. A. and also Prefaces
to the following pieces: " A Supplement to Plutarch; or the Lives of several eminent and
" illustrious Men, omitted by that Author; extracted from the Latin and Greek Historians; by
" Thomas Rowe. 1728." 8vo. He left prepared for the press (and all printed off except 5 sheets) " The
" Life of David," published in 2 vols. 8vo. 1766, in which the Psalms relating to him are explained;
and the Objections of Mr. Bayle, and others, against the Scripture Account of his Life and Character, examined and refuted; also four volumes of Sermons, since published by subscription 1760,
having printed 22 singly during his life. The Life of Mrs. Mary Chandler, his sister, inserted in " The
" Lives of the Poets of Great Britain and Ireland, by Mr. Cibber ‡ and other hands, 1753," was
written by Dr. Chandler. Besides the preceding Discourses and Treatises, he published " Cassiodori
" Senatoris Complexiones in Epistolas, Acta Apostolorum et Apocalypsin, e vetustissimis Canonico-
" rum Veronensium membranis nuper erutæ. Editio altera ad Florentinam fideliter expressæ, operâ
" et curâ Samuelis Chandleri. 1722." 12mo. and wrote about fifty papers in a Weekly Publication,
intitled " The Old Whig, or Consistent Protestant, in Defence of the Principles of Civil and Religious
" Liberty. 1735—1738." And two of his letters were printed so early as 1714, in a pamphlet of Mr.
Carte's, which will be mentioned under the year 1747.

† In this Dialogue, the BEADLE was James Burrough, esq. fellow of Caius College, afterwards
master, and knighted; well known at Cambridge as an architect. See p. 133.

‡ Without depreciating from the merit of these Lives, it may not be improper to observe that a double
literary fraud was here intended. Theophilus Cibber, who was then in The King's Bench, had ten guineas for the
use of his name, which was put ambiguously Mr. Cibber, in order that it might pass for his father's. The real
publisher was Mr. Robert Shiels, an amanuensis of Dr. Johnson, on whose authority I relate this anecdote, and
who gave to Shiels many particulars in the life of Samuel Boyse.

S

Mr. *Ames** Secretary to the Society of Antiquaries, Dr. *Par-*
*fons** (to whofe friendfhip I acknowledge repeated obligations), Mr. *Rowe Mores* †, and, laft, not leaft, by *Honeft Tom*
Martin

1747, in the fixth volume of the " Select Collection, 1780," p. 82. His *Latin* poems
(in every meafure and ftyle) are much admired. Two of them are in the " Mufæ An-
" glicanæ," and another in the " Select Collection," vol. VI. p. 87. He was a very
diligent and able officer in both his departments; and though one of the beft claffical
fcholars of his age, deeply verfed in the Hiftory, Laws, and Conftitution of *England,*
on which he could exprefs himfelf with the greateft precifion. He obliged his friends
with an engraving, by Mr. *Vertue,* of two views of the chapel of *St. Mary,* adjoining
to the fouth fide of the parochial church of *Kingfton upon Thames,* in the county of
Surry, in which feveral *Englifh Saxon* kings are faid to have been crowned, which was
ruined in 1730 by the falling down of one of the pillars and arch next the church **.

* For Mr. *Ames* and Dr. *Parfons,* fee the pages referred to in the Index.

† *Edward Rowe Mores,* defcended from an antient family at *Great Coxwell,* in the
county of *Berks,* (and allied by his mother to that of *Rowe* ††, of *Higham Ferrfield,* in
Walthamftow, in the county of *Effex*) was born about the year 1729, at *Tunftall* in *Kent,*
(where his father was rector for near 30 years ‡‡). He was educated at *Merchant Taylors*
School ‖‖; and afterwards became a commoner of *Queen's College, Oxford.* He early diftinguifhed himfelf as an excellent Scholar and Antiquary, by publifhing at *Oxford,* 1748, before he was twenty, " Nomina & Infignia gentilitia Nobilium Equitumque fub *Edvardo*
" primo rege militantium;" the oldeft treafure, as he ftyles it, of our nobility after Domefday and the Black Book of the Exchequer; and affifted *Jacob Ilive* §§ in correcting an
edition

** The firft view reprefents the antient form of the building, with the addition of a modern roof.
The other, the modern form of the building in 1726, when the draught of it was taken. The chapel
was demolifhed by digging a grave in *March* 1729-30; the fexton and his man were killed on the fpot,
his fon and daughter dug out alive. Britifh Topography, II. 268. There is a mezzotinto print of the fexton.

†† Four monuments of the *Rowe* family were engraved at the expence of Mr. *Mores.*

‡‡ For an account of him, fee the " Hiftory of *Tunftall,*" p. 58.

‖‖ Mr. *Mores* had made a few collections for a hiftory of this fchool, and lifts of perfons educated
there. A view of it is engraved by *Mynde,* for *Strype's* edition of " *Stowe's* Survey," infcribed " Scholæ
" Mercatorum Sciflorum *Lond.* facies orientalis. Negatam a Patronis D. Scholaris, *Edv. Rowe*
" *Mores,* arm. A. M. S. A. S.

§§ " *Jacob Ilive* *** was a printer, and the fon of a printer; but he applied himfelf to Letter-cutting
" [1730], and carried on a Foundery and a Printing-houfe together: in the year 1734 he lived in
" *Alderfgate-ftreet,* over againft *Alderfgate coffee-houfe.* Afterwards when *Calafio* was to be re-
" printed under the infpection of Mr. *Romaine,* or of Mr. *Lutzena* a *Portuguefe Jew,* who corrected
" the *Hebrew,* as we ourfelves did fometimes another part of the work, he removed to *London Houfe*
" (the habitation of the late Dr. *Rawlinfon*) where he was employed by the publifhers of that work.
" In 1751 Mr. *Ilive* publifhed a pretended tranflation of *The Book of Jafher,* faid to have been made
" by one *Alcuin* of *Britain.* The account given of the tranflation is full of glaring abfurdities; but
" of the publication this we can fay from the information of the only one who is capable of informing
" us, becaufe the bufinefs was a fecret between the two. Mr. *Ilive* in the night-time had conftantly
" an *Hebrew* Bible before him *(fed qu. de hoc)* and cafes in his clofet. He produced the copy for
" *Jafher,* and it was compofed in private, and the fame worked off in the night-time in a private
" prefs-room. Mr. *Ilive* was an expeditious compofitor; he knew the letters by the touch." *Diff. on*
Founders, p. 64.—*Ilive,* who was fomewhat difordered in his mind, was author of feveral treatifes on
religious and other fubjects. He publifhed in 1733 an Oration proving the plurality of worlds, that this
earth is hell, that the fouls of men are apoftate angels, and that the fire to punifh thofe confined to this
world at the day of judgement will be immaterial, written in 1729, fpoken at *Joiners Hall* purfuant to the will of his mother †††, who died *Aug.* 29, 1733; and a fecond pamphlet called " A Dia-

*** He had two brothers, *Abraham* and *Ifaac,* who were both likewife printers.

††† *Elizabeth* daughter of *Thomas James,* a benefactor to *Sion College* library, and defcendant of Dr. *Thomas*
James librarian of the *Bodleian.* She was born 1689, and died 1733, and held the fame fingular opinions in
divinity as her fon. See his Oration, p. 63.

" logue

Martin of Palgrave; whose lately published "History of *Thet-*
"*ford*"

edition of *Calasio's* Concordance, two years earlier*. He had printed, except notes
and preface, a new edition of *Dionysius Halicarnassensis* " de claris Rhetoribus," 8vo,
with vignettes engraved by *Green*; the few copies of which were sold after his death.
In 1752 he was elected a member of the Society of Antiquaries, and printed that in
half a sheet, 4to. some corrections made by *Junius* in his own copy of his edition of *Cædmon's Saxon* paraphrase of *Genesis*, and other parts of the Old Testament, *Amstelod.* 1655; and in 1754 he engraved 15 of the drawings from the
MS. in the *Bodleian* library. The title of these plates is " Figuræ quædam anti-
" quæ ex *Cædmonis* monachi paraphraseos in Genesim exemplari pervetusto in biblio-
" theca *Bodleiana* adservato deiineatæ; ad *Anglo-Saxonum* mores, ritus, atque aedi-
" ficia, seculi præcipue decimi, illustranda in lucem editæ. Anno Domini MDCCLIV."
These plates are now in the possession of Mr. *Gough*. Being intended for orders by
his father, he took the degree of M.A. *Jan.* 15, 1753; before which time he had
formed considerable collections relative to the Antiquities, &c. of *Oxford*, and particularly to those of his own college, whose archives he arranged, and made large
extracts from, with a view to its history. He had three plates of the Black Prince's
apartments there, since pulled down, drawn and engraved by that very ingenious artist
B. Green. Twenty-eight drawings by the same hand, at his expence, of antient gates,
halls, &c. since ruined or taken down, are now in the possession of Mr. *Gough*; as
also some collections for a history of *Godstow* nunnery, by Mr. *Mores*, for which a
plate of its ruins was engraved, and another of *Iffley* church†, *Oxfordshire*. After he
left the university he spent some little time abroad; and on his return to *London*, was
introduced by Mr. *Warburton* into the *Heralds College*, where he resided some years,
intending at that time to have become a member of that Society, for which he
was extremely well qualified by his great knowledge and skill in heraldic matters;
but altering his design, he retired about 1760 to an estate purchased by himself at
Low-Leyton, in which village he had resided some time before, was for some years
church-warden there, and greatly improved the church. Here he built a whimsical house
on a plan, it is said, of one which he saw in *France*. In 1759 he circulated queries for
a parochial history of *Berkshire*, but made no considerable progress. His collections on
that subject are now in the possession of Mr. *Gough*. In 1762 he applied himself to executing a design formed about six years before by Mr. *Dodson*, mathematical master at
Christ's Hospital, to establish a society for assurance on lives and survivorships by annuities
of 100 *l.* increasing to the survivors, in six classes of ages from 1 to 10—10 to 20—20 to
30—30 to 40—40 to 50—50 to the extremity of life. The deed of settlement, the declaration of trust, and the statutes of the society, were printed the same year; and in 1765
" A short Account of the Society." It was established by deed, and Mr. *Mores* was to be
perpetual director, with an annuity of 100l. a year. Before 1768 some dispute arose between Mr. *Mores* and the original members of this society, and he withdrew from them.
All his papers on this subject are now in the hands of Mr. *Astle*. The society still subsists
under the name of " The Equitable Society," and their office is in *Bride Street* near *Black-*

" logue between a Doctor of the Church of *England* and Mr. *Jacob Ilive*, upon the subject of the
" Oration, 1733." This strange Oration is highly praised in *Holwell's* third part of Interesting Events
relating to *Bengal*. For publishing " Modest Remarks on the late Bishop *Sherlock's* Sermons," he
was confined in *Clerkenwell Bridewell* from *June* 15, 1756, till *June* 10, 1758, during which period
he published " Reasons offered for the Reformation of the House of Correction in *Clerkenwell*, &c.
" 1757," and projected several other reforming treatises, enumerated in British Topography, vol. I.
p. 637. In the same volume, p. 597, is a memorandum, communicated by Mr. *Bowyer*, of *Ilive's*
attempt to restore the Company of Stationers to their primitive constitution. He died in 1763.

* It was published by Mr. *Romaine*, in 4 volumes, folio, 1747.

† Other plates engraved at Mr. *Mores'* expence were six for a history of *Great Coxwell*, four in
folio, besides several smaller, of antique seals, and two silver coins of silver of *John* and *Henry* found
in digging the foundation of the new town hall at *Oxford*.

friars

" *ford*" Mr. *Bowyer* lived to begin printing, but died before it was completed at the prefs *.

friars Bridge. In the latter part of life, Mr. *Mores* (who had long turned his thoughts to the fubject of early Printing) began to correct the ufeful publication of Mr. *Ames.* I have a tranfcript of his few corrections on that book. On the death of Mr. *John James* of *Bartholomew Clofe* (the laft of the old race of letter-founders) in *June* 1772, Mr. *Mores* purchafed all the curious parts of that immenfe collection of punches, matrices, and types, which had been accumulating from the days of *Wynkyn de Worde* to thofe of Mr. *James.* From thefe a large fund of entertainment would probably have been given to the curious, if the life of Mr. *Mores* had been prolonged. His intentions may be judged of from his valuable " Differtation on Typographical Founders and Founderies ;" a performance on which I have the lefs occafion to enlarge in this place, having ventured to give my opinion of it in a fmall Appendix to the work itfelf. As no more than 80 copies of it were printed, it will at leaft be confidered as a typographical curiofity. Mr. *Mores* was a moft indefatigable collector, and poffeffed great application in the early part of his life, but in the latter part gave himfelf up to habits of negligence and diffipation, which brought him to his end by a mortification in the 49th year of his age, at his houfe at *Low-Leyton, Nov.* 28, 1778. His large collections of curious MSS. and valuable library of books were fold by auction by Mr. *Paterfon* in *Auguft* 1779. Of the former his " Hiftory and Antiquities of *Tunftall* in *Kent*" were the only papers that were completed for the prefs ; and that Hiftory (for which he had engraved a fett of plates out of the many drawings taken at his expence) I purchafed at the fale, and have fince given to the publick as a fpecimen of parochial antiquities, which will fhew the ideas of this induftrious Antiquary, and his endeavour to make even the minuteft record fubfervient to the great plan of national hiftory. His MSS. relative to *Queen's College* fell into the hands of Mr. *Aftle* ; by whom they have fince been prefented to the Rev. Mr. *Price,* keeper of the *Bodleian* Library. His " Excerpta ex Regiftris Cur. Prerog. *Cantuar.*" three volumes, 8vo. written in his own neat hand † ; his collections about *All Souls College,* and for the Hiftory and Antiquities of the City of *Salifbury,* containing feveral curious particulars relating to *Salifbury,* and tranfcripts of records, &c. by him; an epitome of the regifters of the fee of *Canterbury* ; a catalogue of fome of the Court Rolls preferved in that library; fome fhort annals of the univerfity of *Oxford,* from 1066 to 1310; and a *Latin* MS. on the feveral eminent men of the name of *Ælfric,* which feems to have been intended for publication, are now, 1780, in the library of Mr. *Aftle.* Several books of *Englifh* antiquities, with his MS. notes, and the moft valuable part of fuch of the MSS. and fcarce tracts as relate to our local antiquities, were purchafed by Mr. *Gough,* and form no inconfiderable part of his valuable *Mufeum of Britifh Topography* at *Enfield.* Mr. *Mores* married *Sufannah* the daughter of Mr. *Bridgman* an eminent grocer in *Whitechapel,* who had married his father's widow. By this lady, who died in 1767, he had a daughter *Sarah,* who married in 1774 to Mr. *John Davis,* a houfe painter at *Walthamftow,* and died before her father; and a fon, *Edward,* married in 1779. His only fifter was married in 1756 to Mr. *John Warburton* (fon of the late antiquary and *Somerfet* herald, *John Warburton,* efq.) who has refided at *Dublin* many years, and is now purfuivant of the court of exchequer in *Ireland* ‡.

 * Mr. *Thomas Martin* was born at *Thetford, March* 8, 169⅚, in the fchool-houfe of *St. Mary's* parifh, the only remaining parifh of that town in *Suffolk.* His grandfather
William

---

† Vol. I. contains extracts from wills in the Prerogative office from 1385 to 1533; vol. II. extracts from 1533 to 1561; vol. III. extracts from 1592 to 1660. To the firft volume is prefixed a curious and learned differtation concerning the authority of the Prerogative Court, with the names of the feveral Regifters.

‡ For further particulars of Mr. *Mores,* the reader is referred to the Memoirs of him prefixed to the " Hiftory of *Tunftall.*"

I   I fhall

I shall return from this very long digression, if it can properly be so called, to the subject which introduced it.

William was rector of *Stanton St. John* in *Suffolk*, where he was buried in 1677. His father *William* was rector of *Great Livermere*, and preacher or curate of *St. Mary's* (and consequently minister of the school and hospital) in *Thetford*, both in the same county. He married *Elizabeth* only daughter of Mr. *Thomas Burrough*, of *Bury St. Edmunds*, and aunt to the late Sir *James Burrough*, master of *Caius College, Cambridge*; and dying 1721, aged 71, was buried in *Livermere* chancel, where his son *Thomas* erected a monument for him, his mother, and their children, then all dead except himself. *Thomas* was the seventh of nine children, and was probably educated at *Thetford*. In 1715 he had been some time clerk to his brother *Robert*, an attorney there, but soon grew weary of that employment. He was at an early period an assistant to Mr. *Le Neve*[*], in compiling his "Monumenta Anglicana, 1718-19." In 1722 he married *Sarah* widow of Mr. *Thomas Hopley* of *Thetford*, by whom he had eight children. She died *November* 15, 1731. He very soon, however, repaired this loss, by marrying *Frances*, the widow of *Peter Le Neve*, Norroy, who had not been long dead, and to whom he was executor. By this lady he came into the possession of a very valuable collection of *English* antiquities, pictures, &c. She bore him also about as many children as his former spouse, four of whom, as well as five of the others, arrived at manhood. He survived his second wife, and dying *March* 7, 1771, was buried, with others of his family, in *Palgrave* church porch, where no epitaph as yet records the name of that man who has so industriously preserved those of others. As an antiquary, he was most skilful and indefatigable. He had the happiest use of his pen, copying, as well as tracing, with dispatch and exactness, the different writing of every æra, and tricking arms, seals, &c. with great neatness. About the year 1736 he drew up with his own hand an accurate and compleat catalogue and index to all the ancient deeds, charters, records, &c. of *Eton College*, where they now (1780) remain. His collection of antiquities, particularly of such as relate to *Suffolk*, was very considerable, greater than probably ever were before, or will be hereafter, in the possession of an individual; their fragments have enriched several private libraries. His distresses obliged him to dispose of many of his books with his MS. notes on them in his life-time, 1769. A catalogue of his library was printed after his death at *Lynn*, in 8vo. 1771, in hopes of disposing of the whole at once. Mr. *Worth*, chemist, at *Diss*, F.S.A. purchased the rest, with all his other collections, for 600l. The printed books he immediately sold to *Booth* and *Berry* of *Norwich*, who disposed of them in a catalogue, 1773. The pictures and lesser curiosities Mr. *Worth* sold by auction at *Diss*; part of his MSS. in *London*, in *April* 1773, by Mr. *Samuel Baker*; and by a second sale there in *May* 1774, MSS. scarce books, deeds, grants, pedigrees, drawings, prints, coins, and curiosities. What remained on the death of Mr. *Worth*, consisting chiefly of the papers relating to *Thetford*, *Bury*, and the county of *Suffolk*, were purchased by Mr. *Hunt*, bookseller, at *Harleston*, who incorporated them into a marked catalogue, and sold the rest to private purchasers. The dispersion was completed by the sale of Mr. *Ives'* collection in *London*, *March* 1777. His "History of *Thetford*" was published by Mr. *Gough* in 1779.

* " Mem. That although my name (*Thomas Martin*, now of *Palgrave* in *Suffolk*, viz. anno 1722; but when these five volumes were published living at *Thetford* on the *Suffolk* side, the place of my nativity) be not mentioned in the three first books; yet the collector had the use of my MSS. from the beginning, through the hands of my worthy friend *Peter Le Neve*, esq. Norroy King of Arms, under whose name a great number of inscriptions transcribed out of several churches in the diocese of *Norwich*, &c. by my own hand, are printed; but afterwards I became intimately acquainted with Mr. *John Le Neve* himself, who declared the great helps he had from my collections." *This is copied from Mr. Martin's own hand-writing in his sett of Le Neve's "Monumenta Anglicana."*

It has been already obferved, that Mr. *Bowyer* was a regular attendant at the meetings of the Society of Antiquaries, and his communications contributed to the general ftock of entertainment. Among thefe was a letter to *Roger Gale*, efq. occafioned by an infcription on *Vitellius*, found at *Bath* in *Auguft* 1736; which, with fome notes on it by the great Antiquary to whom it was addreffed, is printed among the Mifcellaneous Tracts, p. 133——143. It was preferved in MS. among Mr. *Allan* of *Darlington's* curious " Collections re- " lating to the Antiquities of *Great Britain*, tranfcribed " from the manufcript papers of *Roger Gale*, Efq."

Some infcriptions at the earl of *Exeter's* feat at *Burleigh*, communicated to the Society by Mr. *Bowyer*, and his Differtation on the *Gule* or *Yule* of our *Saxon* anceftors (on which Dr. *Pettingal* has learnedly treated in the Archæologia, vol. II. p. 60.) remained in MS. till they were inferted in his Mifcellaneous Tracts, p. 152——160.

In the beginning of the year 1736 he was an active promoter of the Society for the Encouragement of Learning *. An original letter from their Secretary will beft explain the motives for inftituting this Society:

" To the Rev. Dr. *Richardfon*, mafter of *Emanuel College, Cambridge*.

" Rev. Sir,

London, Dec. 8, 1736.

" Not only your own character for promoting erudition, " but the experience we lately have had of the generous and " frank manner in which you fubfcribed to the Society for " the Encouragement of Learning lately eftablifhed, make " me prefume to addrefs you at prefent, and to give fome ac- " count of the progrefs and advancement of the faid So- " ciety. We are every day increafing, both in number " and in members, either confpicuous for their quality and

---

* On the few books undertaken by this Society, three printers were employed (I fuppofe from each author's having had the privilege to nominate his own printer); Mr, *Bowyer*, Mr. *Bettenham*, and Mr. *Richardfon*.

" ftation,

" ſtation, or learning and ingenuity *. Next, as I have the
" honour of ſerving them in the quality of their Secretary,
" I own I never ſaw any Committee better attended, nor
" more unanimity among any ſet of men. They have
" already entirely paved the way for the reception of au-
" thors, appointed bookſellers for their ſervice, ſettled the
" regulations concerning printers and the printing part ;
" being determined to ſpare neither pains nor charges in
" what they ſhall publiſh, ſo that it may be done in the
" moſt correct, elegant, and beautiful manner ; in fine,
" nothing is wanting but to ſet out with ſome author of
" genius and note, in order to give the public a ſpecimen
" of their deſire to ſerve them as well as the author. Se-
" veral authors have already applied, and ſome works are
" accepted ; but the committee have laid it down as a rule
" not to begin or ſet out but with the work of ſome man
" of genius and merit in *Engliſh* ; wherefore as the learn-
" ed and ingenious Dr. *Middleton*, of *Cambridge*, we hear,
" is about the Life of *Cicero*, and greatly advanced therein,
" I ſhould be obliged, if you would take an opportunity,
" or any of your friends who know him, to acquaint him,
" that if he does our Society the favour to let them pub-
" liſh it, I dare venture to aſſure him, that it will be re-
" ceived with honour and the higheſt approbation, with-

---

* Their ſtatutes were dated *May* 27, 1736. In *June* that year the number of the
members amounted to 102. The duke of *Richmond* was their preſident, and *Brian
Fairfax* eſq. vice-preſident ; Sir *Hugh Smithſon* (now duke of *Northumberland*), and
Sir *Thomas Robinſon* bart. truſtees for the year. The firſt committee of managers were,
earl of *Hertford*, earl of *Abercorn*, earl of *Oxford*, earl *Stanhope*, lord *Percival*, ſir
Brownlow Sherard, bart. the hon. *William Talbot*, Dr. *Richard Mead*, Dr. *Alexander
Stuart*, Dr. *Robert Barker*, Dr. *Addiſon Hutton*, the rev. Mr. *Thomas Birch, Charles
Frederick*, eſq. (now Sir *Charles*), *James Weſt*, eſq. Major *Edwards, Benjamin Mar-
tyn*, eſq. *George Lewis Scott*, eſq. *Paul Whitehead*, eſq. Mr. *John Ward*, profeſſor at
Greſham College, James Thomſon, eſq. *Samuel Strutt*, eſq. *Daniel Mackercher*, eſq.
George Sale, eſq. the rev. Mr. *George Watts* ; the auditors the hon. *John Talbot, Henry
Talbot, Henry Kenſall, Edward Stevenſon*, and *William Newland*, eſquires. See ſome
further particulars of this Society in Mr. *Bowyer's* " Miſcellaneous Tracts."

" out

" out the least formality : I shall add, that in point of in-
" terest, it will be a little estate to the author whose works
" they begin with, for every mortal will buy it. You have
" no doubt heard in what a discouraging way Dr. *Bentley*
" has used our Society ; for though his work of *Manilius*
" was ready to be printed, and he desired by several people
" to have it published by the Society, he not only raised
" such ill-grounded objections against the institution itself,
" but chose to throw it into the hands of a common book-
" seller, rather than in those of the Society, which has not
" only made several gentlemen of letters and high life ex-
" claim against the discouraging and ungenerous act, but
" will be recorded to the learned world perhaps when he is
" dead and rotten ; such men deserve fleecing from book-
" sellers, and I am mistaken if he, or his editors, won't
" meet with it, I am sure none will regret them ; but 'tis
" hoped, nay expected, from the excellent character Dr.
" *Middleton* bears in the world, that our Society will meet
" with other treatment from him ; for it is as much the
" duty of a great author, to lend a helping hand to en-
" courage and countenance so laudable an institution as is
" that of this Society, as 'tis for the Society to assist and
" encourage the author. The favour of your answer from
" him I shall greatly esteem, and the sooner you do me
" that honour the better, that it may be deposited, if fa-
" vourable, at the next General Meeting, which is the 3d
" day of *February*. My direction is at *Slaughter's Coffee-*
" *House* in *St. Martin's-Lane*. The works of any other in-
" genious friend or acquaintance, if recommended by you,
" will always be distinguishingly received, I dare say, by the
" committee, as will your commands at all times, by

" Rev. Sir, your most humble and obedient servant,

ALEX. GORDON."

However

However liberal the idea of such an inftitution might have been, the execution of it counteracted the intention of its founders.   It was in fact a direct attack on the bookfellers, who after all are certainly no bad rewarders of literary merit*;   and their affistance having been found indifpenfably neceffary to the undertaking, a contract was entered into, for three years, with *A. Millar*, *J. Gray*, and *J. Nourfe*.   In this period no more than four books were printed; " Differtatio de Structurâ & Motu Mufculari, Auc-" tore *Alexandro Stuart*, M. D. Sereniffimæ *Carolinæ Mag.* " *Brit.* &c. nuper Regin. Med. Ord. Coll. Rcg. Med. *Lond.* " & R. S. S." 4to†, 1738; Sir *William Keith's* " Hiftory of " *Virginia*," 8vo; " A Collection of Original Letters and Pa-" pers concerning the Affairs of *England* from the year 1641 " to 1660.   Found among the duke of *Ormond's* Papers. " In two volumes.   By *Thomas Carte*, M. A. 1739," 8vo; and Profeffor *Stuart's* " Neceffity of Revelation, 8vo," 1739; none of which were very large or expenfive.

In 1740 a new contract was entered into with fix other bookfellers (*G. Strahan*, *C. Rivington*, *P. Vaillant*, *J. Brindley*, *S. Baker*, and *J. Ofborn*, jun.); whofe profits on the bufinefs were fo injudicioufly retrenched, that the purpofes of the Society were entirely fruftrated.   On this plan two books only were publifhed; " The Negotiations of Sir

---

* " I fuppofe this Society for encouraging Learning alarms the Bookfellers; for it " muft be at laft a downright Trading Society, a mere CONGER ‖ (forgive me if I mif-fpell " fo myfterious a word).   I hope you will take care to be one of their printers, for they " will certainly be a Society for encouraging Printing; Learning perhaps may be too far " gone, and paft all private encouragement."   *Mr. Clarke to Mr. B. early in* 1737.
† Printed by Mr. *Richardfon*.

‖ A fett of reputable Bookfellers, who entered into a kind of partnerfhip to print fome expenfive works, under the firm of " The Printing Conger."   There was afterwards a fecond partnerfhip of the fame fort, called " The New Conger."—The word, I believe, was at firft applied to them invidioufly, alluding to the *Conger Eel*, which is fuppofed to fwallow the fmaller fry.

T   " *Thomas*

" *Thomas Roe*, on his Embaffy to the *Ottoman Porte**, from
" the year 1621 to 1628 inclufive, &c." folio, 1740†;
and " *Maximus Tyrius*" in 4to. the fame year.

In 1742, a third method was adopted, and the Society
chofe to become their own bookfellers. The experiment
was tried with *Ælian* " De Animalibus," 4to. in 1743.
A few months were fufficient to demonftrate the imprac-
ticability of the attempt; and before the year was at
an end, they again had recourfe to three bookfellers, on
a plan in fome degree enlarged. Thus circumftanced,
they publifhed Bifhop *Tanner's* " Notitia Monaftica," folio, in *January* 1743-4; and Profeffor *Stuart's English*
tranflation of Sir *Ifaac Newton's* " Quadrature of Curves" in
September 1745. But their finances were then become
almoft exhaufted, after having expended a fubfcription of
nearly two thoufand pounds. By " A Memorial of the
" prefent ftate of affairs of the Society, *April* 17, 1746‡,"
it appears they had incurred fo confiderable a debt as to
be deterred from proceeding any further. The " Biblio-
" theca *Britannica*" of Bifhop *Tanner* was, however, completed under their patronage in 1748.

On the 27th of *December*, 1737, Mr. *Bowyer* loft his
father at the age of 74; and it is evident, from his fcattered papers, that he feverely felt this affli&ion; applying
to himfelf the beautiful apoftrophe of *Æneas* to *Anchifes*.‖:

" Híc me, pater optime, feffum
" Deferis, heu! tantis nequicquam erepte periclis!"

* Propofals for publifhing five volumes of thefe Negotiations were circulated in 1730;
but the undertaking failing of encouragement, only this one volume was publifhed in
1740, fo that the moft curious and interefting part of his papers ftill remain in MS.
Biog. Brit. ROE, note L.

† Of this volume Mr. *Richardfon* was oftenfibly the editor as well as printer. He
infcribed to the King, in a fhort dedication, which does honour to the ingenious writer.

‡ Printed among Mr. *Bowyer's* Mifcellaneous Tra&s. ‖ Æn. iji. 710.

His

His friend Mr. *Clarke*, on this melancholy event, again addreffed to him a letter of fympathy and confolation:

"DEAR SIR, *Uckfield*, 1738.

"I faw lately, by mere accident, in the news-papers, "that Mr. *Bowyer* was dead*; and am very fenfible of the "great concern that you are under upon that account. It "is a natural, I believe I might fay a defirable, infirmity: "they who feel no affliction at the lofs of their friends, can "have had no pleafure in the enjoyment of them. A per- "fon, whom you have been fo long ufed to look upon "with love and reverence, muft, at bidding you farewell "for ever, raife fome forrowful fentiments, not to be eafily "fuppreffed. I wifh it was my good fortune to have an "opportunity of being with you upon this occafion. Not "that I could be of the leaft ufe, or could fay any thing "which you have not heard and thought-of in a much "better manner a thoufand times before. But I fhould

---

* By a former letter of Mr. *Clarke's*, dated *Dec.* 14, 1737, it appears that Mr. *Bowyer's* illnefs was of fome continuance: " Though I have faid nothing to you fince "your firft melancholy account of Mr. *Bowyer's* illnefs, yet I have been but too fenfi- "ble of the concern and anxiety it muft give you. My own fears have taught me, in a "nearer relation, what yours muft have fuggefted upon fuch an occafion. Mr. *Bowyer's* "complaints are fuch as are moft probably incurable; and at his age the ftrongeft of us "muft expect fomething that will place us among the incurables. Nor do I think that "alone, unlefs attended with great pain, to be one of the moft afflicting circumftances:
" For evils that are known,
" There's certain remedy; for doubt, there's none.
"When we are taking leave of our friends, we are apt to look upon them in the tendereft "light that our relation to them can place us: we confider the value of our lofs, without "reflecting upon the mercies we have had in not lofing it much fooner. It is good-na- "ture that makes us feel our afflictions much fharper; and it muft be good fenfe, or, "what is much better, good principles of religion, that muft teach us how to bear "them. Your friends will be perfuaded that you are already in the hands of the very "beft comforters; and I dare fay, if we fhould wifh that your fon fhould not lofe his "father till he was as well prepared for it, you would think it a very friendly and af- "fectionate wifh; and furely fuch an event as you think your fon ought not to make "too great an affliction of, fhould be looked upon with the fame evennefs-of mind by "you. I wifh all of you happy in one another while you ftay here; and I think then "we have nothing more to wifh, but to leave the reft to God."

T 2 "like

" like to find you fo much alone, to fee you planning out
" new fcenes of life, or pleafing yourfelf with the profpects
" of thofe that will fucceed when life is over.—*Pliny* has
" obferved, upon the lofs of one of his old friends (I don't
" remember whom), *That nothing that he had ever heard or*
" *read upon fuch occafions could give him any relief; his for-*
" *row was fuperior to all ufual confolations.*—Though I am
" always a little apt to fufpect the fentiments of fuch pro-
" feffed wits, as not quite fincere, rather delicate than juft;
" yet if the obfervation was true, it muft be carried no
" further than the firft natural impreffions; nothing new
" that could be faid could have more weight with him than
" what had been faid ten thoufand times over. I own there
" is fomething in the glitter of a new thought, like that of
" a new coin; it of courfe catches our attention for fome
" moments, and we view it perhaps in two or three dif-
" ferent lights; but when that is over, we lay no more
" value upon it, or believe that it has really any more
" weight, than the coins of former princes: it is juft fo
" with our thoughts; they may lofe fomething of their
" luftre, by being given and taken fo often upon common
" occafions; but their real value is the fame.

" I am writing this at Mr. *Lloyd's*; a vifit that of late al-
" ways gives me fome concern; he wears apace, declines
" vifibly; *i. e.* he is doing the very thing that we muft all
" of us foon do after him. His diftemper may perhaps
" let him live many years; but in fuch a manner as to be
" too fenfibly affected with the pains of living. If fuch
" afflictions are made truly ufeful to the interefts of an-
" other life, they are in that view defirable vifitations; but
" when that is done, their friends fhould not fhew any

4

" over-

" over-great impatience at parting with them.   I hope *Tom**
" is with you; he will be one of your beſt companions: I
" ſhould be pleaſed to ſee him, as no doubt he is a much
" greater philoſopher than his father; and that you may not
" leave him till you can do it with the ſame ſatisfaction that
" your father has now done, is what I truly wiſh, who am,
" with the greateſt ſincerity, your moſt affectionate, *W. C.*"

In 1737 Mr. *Bowyer* printed a Diſſertation " De Vitâ,
" Scriptis, & Ætate *Heſiodi*," by Dr. *Robinſon*, prefixed to
the *Oxford* edition of *Heſiod*, in 4to, 1737; " *Epicteti En-*
" *chiridion*; the Morals of *Epictetus* made *Engliſh*, in a
" poetical Paraphraſe, by *Ellis Walker*, M. A." 12mo; of
which his father had printed the firſt edition, 1716.

" An Enquiry into the Natural Right of Mankind to de-
" bate freely concerning Religion, wherein the Maxims ad-
" vanced by ſeveral late Writers upon this ſubject are examin-
" ed, by a Gentleman of *Lincoln's Inn*, 1737," 8vo. is mentioned by Mr. *Clarke* in ſuch a manner † as to ſhew that Mr.

---

* Mr. *Bowyer's* ſon, then only ſeven years old.

† " I did not apprehend by your former letter that I was to read this *Eſſay upon the*
" *Freedom of Debate* either as critick or corrector, and now I have not leiſure to ſet ſe-
" riouſly to it till after next week.   The author, whoever he is, is maſter both of him-
" ſelf and the ſubject; but general taſte is ſo uncertain a thing, who can judge of
" it ?   I think he is ſometimes too diffuſe, and ſometimes too methodical ; here keeping
" to the ſtrictneſs of demonſtration, and there leaving the argument for the ſake of or-
" naments.   Beſides, the good deſign of it will be no advantage to its ſale.   On the
" right ſide of the queſtion, a book muſt be excellently well written in all reſpects to be
" generally read ; when one with half the ſenſe or ſpirit on the other ſhall ſucceed much
" better.   I wiſh it much ſucceſs, and think it deſerves it.   There are ſome little parti-
" cularities in expreſſion, which I don't ſo well like ; p. 274, l. 3, " with ſome Index
" expurgatorius ;" ſcarce *Engliſh*.   Ibid. l. 7, " a book not near ſo bold as the Grounds
" and Reaſons and the Moderator."—I don't underſtand that ſentence clearly—I ſuppoſe
" it ſhould be, *or the Moderator* ; the comma is wanting.   P. 276, " The *Heidlebergh's*
" *Catechiſmus*,"—why not The *Heidlebergh Catechiſm* ?   The *Auſhurgh's Confeſſio* would
" ſound odd.—Who is your author ?"   *Letter to Mr. B.* 1737.—The copy-right of this
volume was regularly aſſigned over to Mr. *Bowyer* by the author (Mr. *Henry Anderſon*)
with an expreſs permiſſion to alter it as he thought proper ; a liberty which I believe Mr.
Bowyer exerciſed very liberally.

Bowyer

Bowyer had paid a particular attention to it. Nor muſt I omit " *Wotton's* Short View of *George Hickes's* Grammatical, " Critical, and Archeological Treaſury of the ancient " Northern Languages; with ſome Notes by a Lover of the " ancient Northern Literature, and an Appendix to the " Notes, faithfully and intirely tranſlated into *Engliſh* from " the *Latin* Originals, by *Maurice Shelton**, of *Barningham-* " *hall*

* " I am ſo much ſurprized at the atchievement of your friend in *Suffolk*, that I know " not what to ſay to it. He muſt ſurely have a great love for tranſlation, to think of un- " dertaking ſuch a work†; or perhaps he might imagine that it would give him a con- " ſiderable figure among his brethren of the quorum, and ſhew that he was acquainted " with our laws in their firſt original, and able to take them, as *Ralpho* did firſt matter, " *all alone, before one rag of form was on*. I believe Dr. *Wotton* never thought of making " any improvements to this work, and might poſſibly believe that it wanted none. He " made a preſent of it to Dr. *Hickes*, as a compliment for the great pains he had taken " in opening a way to the Northern Literature. I have ſome letters of Dr. *Hickes's* by " me; but I think none of them worth printing; beſides, they have all of them ſome " little private affairs not worth communicating to the publick. Dr. *Hickes* took care " of the impreſſion, and the notes (which I believe is a ſecret) are all his, except thoſe " upon the *Saxon* coins by Mr. *Thwaites*. This Dr. *Hickes* had no mind to have known, " that it might not look too much like puffing; and therefore they have been generally " quoted for Dr. *Wotton's*, as in *Waterland's* Hiſtory of the *Athanaſian* Creed, page 129, " ſecond edition. By this you will ſee, that Dr. *Wotton* could never think of any addi- " tions to this work: it was carefully examined by the author of the *Theſaurus*, and " made ſuch as he would have it; a little ſketch of his deſign, to raiſe the curioſity of the " reader to further inquiries, or (as you would ſay in the trade) to call-in cuſtomers. " It would be of no uſe to let your friend in *Suffolk* be acquainted with this ſecret, who " perhaps would like the work never the better for thinking Dr. *Hickes* had ſuch a " hand in it. As to the queſtion about juries, Dr. *Hickes* (as you know) had taken " much pains to ſhew that *compurgators* and *juries* did (as he expreſſes it) *toto cælo* " *differre*; and for no other reaſon that I can ſee, but becauſe *juries* were anciently uſed " in *Scandinavia*, and were in ſome reſpects differently modeled from the old compur- " gators; but I ſtill think, that the *Welſh* laws have a manifeſt agreement between " them in ſo many particulars, that the original of juries muſt be accounted for in that " manner. It is of no uſe to enquire, whether the cuſtom of uſing compurgators had " its original from the civil or the canon law. That, from the ſeventh century downwards " compurgators were univerſally made uſe of, wherever the feudal law prevailed, is " very evident from thoſe laws mentioned in *Ina's* laws 693, and in *Lothaire* and " *Edric's* 673; [ſee Feud. lib. I. tit. iv. ſect. 2. and tit. x. and tit. xxvi. ſect. 1.] And " what is more obſervable in theſe laws, the number of compurgators is expreſsly fixed

† " Mr. *Wotton's* " Conſpectus brevis" was tranſlated into *Engliſh* by Mr. *Shelton* for his own im- " provement, and publiſhed to ſhew that one of his majeſty's juſtices of the peace may have ſenſe and " a taſte for learning. Further uſe of the publication we know not; for thoſe who ſeek after this or " any other ſort of knowledge will have recourſe to the originals." *Mr. Rowe Mores.*

" to

" *hall* in the county of *Suffolk*, efq. one of his majefty's
" juftices of the peace for the faid county, &c.   To which
" are

" to twelve ; *Dabitur ei defenfio cum duodecim facramentalibus.*   And the fame number
" was frequently introduced among all thofe nations whofe laws were formed upon the
" feudal cuftoms, as *Lombards, Alemans,* &c.   But the *Saxons,* thinking it not fo
" reafonable that the fame number of compurgators fhould be neceffary in all cafes,
" ordered that the NUMBER *fhould* differ according to the NATURE and IMPORTANCE of
" the queftion controverted.   *Si quis regis miniftrum homicidii incufet, fi fe purgare au-*
" *deat, faciat hoc* XII *miniftris regis.   Si quis autem miniftrum incufet, qui minoris cogna-*
" *tionis* [*i. e.* conditionis] *fit quam minifter regis, purgabit fe per* XI *fui æquales, et*
" *unum regis miniftrum* [*i. e.* duodecim facramentalibus inferioris ordinis].   *Et ita in*
" QUALIBET LITE *quæ major eft quatuor mancutis,* (*i. e.* folidis 24.) Leg. Sax. p. 47.
" fect. 3.   If the thing in queftion, or the damage fuftained, was valued at above four
" marks, then twelve compurgators were neceffary ; if not, a lefs number were fufficient.
" And, to guard more effectually againft fraud and perjury, the *Saxons* introduced two
" forts of compurgators to determine the fame queftion, called *the greater and leffer oath.*
" How this was, is indeed not fully explained in what remains of the *Saxon* conftitu-
" tions ; but among the *Welfh,* who had the fame cuftom, it is very clear.   *The greater*
" *oath confifted of compurgators who were gentlemen ; the leffer oath of compurgators of*
" *ordinary condition.*   Their number was generally the fame, but the nature of their
" oath different ; the gentlemen were to fwear that the *defendant's oath appeared to them*
" *moft probable* ; the common people, that they *believed the defendant's true* ; and with
" this moft remarkable difference, that the *oath of the leffer compurgators,* unlefs all
" their number agreed in it, was of no force ; but the oath of the *greater compurgators*
" *was valid* if a majority of their number agreed in it.   There was therefore among thefe
" compurgators almoft every cuftom that is remarkable among our *grand* and *petty* juries.
" They were called fo, not from the *number of the jurors,* or the *nature of their office,*
" but from the *condition of the perfons* who ferved in them ; their *verdict or oath* was
" exactly correfpondent to that of the juries now in ufe ; for, in the verdict of a petty
" jury, all of them muft be agreed ; but the grand jury can accufe or acquit the party,
" *though all of them fhould not agree* in their opinion.   Why therefore muft the original
" of juries be afcribed to *William* the Conqueror? or what did he do that could intitle
" him to be the author of them ? Why he fixed them to the number XII, and not
" lefs ; for grand juries are now (I believe) always more than twelve.   [Delatoria
" excedat duodecim quoties Judici placuerit ; non autem deficiat, ut in quibufdam aliis
" *juratis inquifitoriis.*] Was not twelve (or more than twelve) frequently, though not con-
" ftantly, the number of compurgators in the *Saxon* times ? and was it not the original
" number in the old feudal laws? But the *Normans,* though by no means the authors of
" this cuftom, acted very politickly in the management of it ; compurgators (for any thing
" that appears to the contrary) might be any perfons of a proper rank, whom the de-
" fendant could procure to appear and fwear for him.   This did not fo well anfwer the
" *Norman* purpofes in their firft fettlements here ; the *Saxons* would have fucceeded
" much better in their civil difputes with them, than it was intended they fhould, if
" the old cuftom of the defendant's finding his compurgators had continued : they were
" therefore from this period placed in the *nomination of the crown,* and by that means
" the *Normans* had a greater influence upon them.   This I take to be the true ftate of
" the cafe with regard to juries.   What Dr. *Wood* fays may be very true, that he knows

" no-

" are added by the fame Tranflator other curious and pro-

" no law that *obliges a grand juror to be a freeholder*, yet I believe they are always gen-
" tlemen, though by no other law now, but ancient and perpetual ufage*. Juries in an
" affize upon a Writ of Right were always *liberi homines*. *Glanv.* l. ii. c. 11. l. ix.
" c. 7. vol. II. p. 71. But Dr. *Hickes's* account of them is certainly very wrong:
" *In ea maxime differunt* [i. e. compurgatores et juratores] *quod numerus compurgatorum*
" *incertus erat, ut qui augeri folebat pro rei vel caufæ quæ agebatur momento; & pro*
" *numero confacramentalium qui jurabant compurgatio majus vel minus facramentum*
" *dictum eft*. Diff. Epift. p. 35. The firft part of this account is plainly confuted by the
" *Saxon* laws, and the latter by the *Welfh*. And it is ridiculous to look for our cuftoms
" among the old planters of *Scandinavia*, where there is no fort of hiftory before the
" tenth century, when we can fo readily account for thefe cuftoms from the feudal
" laws. [Hialmar. And Feudal Laws firft written under *Fred.* I. A. D. 1158.] I
" think it is high time to difmifs the juries; but, before I have done with Dr. *Hickes*, I
" think you might take notice that his fixing the *Saxon* pound always at LX fhillings,
" and the fhilling always at V pence, is undoubtedly a miftake. Silver in the *Saxon*
" times was not always of the fame value: when it was the *higheft*, V *pence made a*
" *fhilling*, and XLVIII fhillings a pound; when it was *lower*, IV *pence made a*
" *fhilling*, and LX fhillings a pound. The weight of the penny was probably the fame
" in both cafes, but the value leffened in the latter; and as the weight of their *penny*
" was not diminifhed, there was no other method of accommodating it to the value of
" *filver*, but by raifing or leffening the value of the penny. Unlefs this different pro-
" portion of the penny to the fhilling be allowed of, the computations of money in the
" *Saxon* laws cannot be accounted for. Bifhop *Fleetwood* [Chron. Pret. p. 29], to re-
" move this difficulty, was for altering the text of the laws; but, without taking fo un-
" warrantable a liberty, altering the value of the penny clears all the difficulties. This
" might be another note upon p. 61, of the Confpectus." *Letter from Mr. Clarke to*
Mr. B. without date.

* " None of the gentlemen write with that clearnefs and precifion that they would do, if they had
really been right. As to gentlemen; I have been told that the late Sir *Gregory Page* had three *Eaft
India* bonds of 100,000l. each. I fuppofe if he had no title, nor an inch of freehold, but lived in
hired houfes fuited to his fortune, nobody would have queftioned his gentility, or doubted his fitnefs
for being on a grand jury; and as to freemen, they may be totally different from freeholders, though
the confufion of them is very common. The excellent Dr. *Burn*, (*Weftm.* p. 21) defcribing " a fet of
" tenants in *pure villenage*, who were bound to the lord, as members of, and annexed to, the manor,
" and ufually fold with the farm to which they belonged" (*cum eorum corporibus & eorum fequelis*
is the very term now applied only to cattle, as a mare or a cow with its follower, i. e. the young one),
adds, " It was in contradiction to thefe, that the others [tenants] were called *free*; which obfervation
ought efpecially to be noted, otherwife we fhall fall into great confufion in abundance of inftances; for
wherever *free* men, *free* tenants, or *free* holders are mentioned of *old time*, by thefe are not to be underftood what we now call *free* holders, but only that they were not villans or bondmen. All our
military anceftors within the feveral cuftomary manors are ftyled *free* tenants, but the lands were not
free hold [to them] according to the modern acceptation of the word." The fame learned writer,
p. 15, tranfcribes from *Littleton* the form of performing homage, which was the moft honourable [i. e.
the leaft difhonourable] fervice, and moft humble fervice of reverence, that a *free* tenant can do to his
lord, &c. &c. &c. Fealty was a much lower ceremony, and yet done by a *free* tenant, &c. &c. See
the form in the fame place. It is probable from the univerfality of thefe tenures formerly, that if thefe
free tenants (who had fworn fealty to their lord) had been thereby difqualified from appearing on grand
juries, that no grand jury could ever have been compofed, as people of all ranks hold under one
another. Witnefs the King of *Scotland* to our King, and our King to *France* for *Normandy*. We now
therefore fee that *homines* might be *liberi*, though they performed homage and fealty to others for
their lands, and might not neceffarily have an inch of freehold of their own; yet they were probably capable of being on juries of any kind. In general the *liberi homines* would poffefs the freehold land,
but they might be free tenants without it." *Dr. Taylor's Friend.*

" per

" per Notes for a further illustration of the Text*; a short
" Appendix of Notes of correction, &c. and a Dedication
" to the right honourable *James Reynolds*, esq. lord chief
" baron of his majesty's court of exchequer at *Westminster*.
" The second edition, with emendations and large additions,
" besides a Preface and a general Index, by the same Trans-
" lator," 4to. In the same year he printed " The present
" State of *Scotland*," 8vo ; " Carmen Epinicium Augus-
" tiffimæ *Russorum* Imperatrici sacrum," a small poem by
Mr. *Maittaire*, for private use ; and 164 pages of a History
of *Northamptonshire*, by that able antiquary *John Bridges*,
esq. of *Barton Seagrave*, near *Kettering*, who spent many
years in collecting materials, and spared no expence in sur-
veying every parish, &c. Seven thousand† copies of his
proposals for printing the book (which were on a whole
sheet, with red letters in the title-page) were circulated
in 1735, and sixteen hundred and fifty† more in 1737 ;
the subscription four guineas‡.

Among

* The following citation from a letter of Mr. *Clarke*, dated *Dec.* 9, 1737, relates to
what is printed from a former letter of his, in p. 143 : " *Juries* and *sacramentales* are
" not supposed to be exactly the same, but only as father and son, of one original ; and
" as to *Welsh* antiquities, they only help to clear some of our ancient customs with rela-
" tion to compurgators, and make us understand their office better ; they prove no-
" thing as to the point itself. *Spelman*'s observations about the different extent of
" power in grand and petty juries, is a mistake ; there is now no such difference, what-
" ever there was in his time. As to the compurgators being provided, or summoned
" by the defendant, it is of no moment ; they tried the cause, just as our juries do, *i.e.*
" it was determined by their oath or verdict."

† I mention the number of proposals that were printed, as an extraordinary circumstance ; and the more so, as scarcely any of them are now to be met with. After repeated inquiries, I have never seen one.

‡ Mr. *Bridges* dying *July* 30, 1741, only the hundreds of *Fawesley*, *Wardon*, and part
of *Norton*, were published in two numbers, containing 160 folio pages, with views of
Daventry church and priory (now both pulled down) and *Catesby* monastery. Four
pages more (containing the rectory of *Green's Norton*, alias *Norton Davy*, in the deanry of
Brackley) were printed off as the beginning of a third number. These, with all the papers
in Mr. *Bowyer*'s hands, were given up, *Dec.* 26, 1742, to Mr. *Gibbons*, a stationer near
the *Temple* church. Mr. *Bridges*, by will dated *August* 8, 1723, left all his books and MSS.
to be sold, and out of the sale 500l. to his brothers *Nathaniel* and *Ralph*. He ex-

U   cepted

Among the books of 1738 ſtand foremoſt two editions of a work of no ſmall conſequence in the typographical annals of Mr. *Bowyer*; the firſt* volume of "The Divine "Legation of *Moſes* demonſtrated, on the Principles of a "Religious Deiſt, from the omiſſion of the Doctrine of a "Future State of Rewards and Puniſhments in the *Jewiſh*

cepted ſuch MSS. as related to his intended hiſtory of *Northamptonſhire*, with all braſs plates, prints or draughts relating to that deſign, which were left as an heir-loom to his family, to be committed to ſuch perſon or perſons as ſhould be thought proper to carry on that deſign, and to be kept locked up in a diſtinct preſs and boxes. All the drawings which Mr. *Bridges* left behind him, made by the famous *Tillemans* (who was paid a guinea a day), with the map of the county, nearly finiſhed by *Thomas Eyre* of *Kettering*, were in 1749 in the poſſeſſion of his executor the Rev. Mr. *Bridges*, of *Sidney College*, *Cambridge*, rector of *Orlingbury*, near *Wellingborough*, *Northamptonſhire*; ſome other plates engraven for the work, and left in the hands of Mr. *Gibbons*, who became a bankrupt, were loſt. Dr. *Rawlinſon* purchaſed ten plates deſigned for the hiſtory, which are now in the *Bodleian* library. Mr. *New*, F. S. A. had 20 prints taken from Mr. *Bridges's* plates. Dr. *Ducarel* has ſixteen. Some views of *Peterborough* minſter, &c. were lately in the hands of Mr. *Bathurſt*, bookſeller, as ſpecimens. *Toms* the engraver had ſeveral of the plates. Dr. *Jebb* had in 1749 all Mr. *Bridges's* papers and MSS. relating to the county, which were purchaſed before 1754 by the late Sir *T. Cave*, bart. of *Stanford*. Theſe collections amounting to 40 volumes being put 1755 into the hands of a committee of twelve gentlemen of the county, with Sir *Thomas Cave* at their head, application was made to Mr. *Benjamin Buckler*, of *All Souls College*, *Oxford*, (now D. D. and keeper of the univerſity archives), to ſuperintend the publication of them; but he, after peruſing ſome of them, declined the buſineſs. They were afterwards put into the hands of the Rev. Mr. *Peter Whaley*, late fellow of *St. John's College*, *Oxford*, and maſter of the grammar ſchool of *Chriſt's Hoſpital*, who compiled from them an hiſtory of the county, continued to the preſent time. The pages printed by Mr. *Bridges* were reprinted in this edition, and compriſed in 150, excluſive of *Sutton* hundred introduced before that of *Norton*. The firſt volume appeared about 1762, containing the hundreds of *Faweſley*, *Wardon*, *Sutton*, *Norton*, *Towceſter*, *Cleyley*, *Wimerſley*, *Spelho*, *Newbottle*, and *Guilſborough*. The firſt part of the ſecond volume, publiſhed *April* 1769, contains the hundreds of *Rothwell*, *Orlingbury*, *Hamfordſho*, *Higham*, and *Huxlow*. The promiſed plates of buildings and ruins (even thoſe three delivered with the firſt publication) are reſerved for the ſecond, which has been long expected, ſince the compiler's retirement from his ſchool to the living of *Horley* in *Surrey* has left him at full leiſure to proſecute his deſign, and was actually promiſed at the cloſe of the year 1779. But the work has been ſtopped at the *Oxford* preſs upwards of two years: the gentlemen of the county not giving it due encouragement, the printer was obliged to deſiſt.

* This volume was firſt publiſhed in *January* 1737-8; and in *March* A "Vindication "of the Author of the Divine Legation of *Moſes*, &c. from the Aſperſions of the "Country Clergyman's Letter in the Weekly Miſcellany of *Feb.* 24, 1737."—"Faith "working by Charity to Chriſtian Edification, a Sermon preached at the laſt Epiſcopal "Viſitation for Confirmation in the Dioceſe of *Lincoln*: with a Preface, ſhewing the "reaſons of its publication; and a Poſtſcript, occaſioned by ſome Letters lately pub-"liſhed in The Weekly Miſcellany; by *W. Warburton*, A. M. Chaplain to his Royal "Highneſs the Prince of *Wales*," appeared in *June*, and a ſecond edition of "The Di-"vine Legation" in *November* 1738.

2   "Diſpenſation.

" Difpenfation. In Six Books. By *William Warburton*,
" A. M. Author of *The Alliance between Church and State**,*"
8vo. This volume contained the three firft books.

In 1738 he alfo printed the third and fourth volume of
Bifhop *Atterbury's* Sermons†, 8vo; " The prefent State of
" *Bromley College*," a fingle fheet, for Bifhop *Wilcocks*; " A new

* Of which, fee above, p. 94. Some particulars of this truly great Divine fhall be given under the year 1763.

† *Francis Atterbury*, born *March* 6, 1662, was educated at *Weftminfter*; and in 1680 was elected a ftudent of *Chrift-Church*. In 1693, he applied to the earl of *Nottingham*, to fucceed to his father's rectory of *Milton*; but, being unfuccefsful, came to *London*: where he was foon diftinguifhed, appointed chaplain to King *William*, and elected preacher at *Bridewell*, and lecturer of *St. Bride's*; which laft office he refigned in *December* 1698. In 1700, he was made archdeacon of *Totnefs*, by Sit *Jonathan Trelawney* bifhop of *Exeter*; and, entering deeply into the famous controverfy concerning the convocation againft Dr. *Wake*, dean of *Exeter*, was created doctor in divinity in a manner which did him fingular honour. On the acceffion of queen *Anne*, he was appointed one of her chaplains; in *October* 1704, dean of *Carlifle*; in 1707, canon refiden-tiary of *Exeter*; in 1706, preacher at *The Rolls*. In 1710, he was unanimoufly chofen prolocutor of the lower houfe of convocation; in 1711, made dean of *Chrift Church* **; in the beginning of *June* 1713, advanced to the bifhoprick of *Rochefter* and deanry of *Weftminfter*; and, if the queen had lived, would probably have arrived at *Canterbury*. He officiated, as dean, at the coronation of king *George* I; when he received from his majefty fome marks of perfonal diflike. This was probably owing to his having warmly efpoufed the caufe of *Sacheverell*, whofe defence he penned, in concert with Dr. *Smal-ridge*††, and from whom he afterwards received a legacy of five hundred pounds. In 1715, he refufed to fign the declaration publifhed by the Bifhops againft the rebellion, and was ever afterward in conftant oppofition to the court. He was apprehended on fufpicion of treafon, and committed to *The Tower*, *Aug.* 22, 1722. The bill to inflict pains and penalties on him received the royal affent *May* 27, 1723. It is faid, the king gave his affent to this bill with regret, from concern at being obliged to banifh a man of fuch eminent parts and learning. His fentence was fomewhat foftened, by his daughter's attending him on his travels; and Mr. *Morice*, her hufband, was permit-ted freely to correfpond with him. He left this kingdom on the 18th of *June*; and died at *Paris*, *Feb.* 17, 1731-2. His body was brought to *England*, and interred in *Weftminfter Abbey*‡‡. It is univerfally agreed that he was a man of uncommon abi-lities, perfectly fkilled in polite literature, and a moft accomplifhed writer. But his political character is ftamped with an indelible ftain, of which his letters to the pre--tender and his adherents in 1722 afford too glaring a proof. A portrait of him, en-graved by *T. Cook*, is prefixed to the Fifth Volume of the " Select Collection of Poems, " 1780," where his beautiful Imitations of *Horace* are preferved.

** His fpeech, as Dean of *Chrift Church*, in the Convocation at *Oxford*, on Lord *Harley's* receiving the degree of M. A. is in Gent. Mag. 1737, p. 548.
†† *Smalridge* followed *Atterbury* in many of his preferments, and was faid to carry water to quench the flames his predeceffor had raifed.
‡‡ See an admirable character of him as a Preacher in The Tatler; as a Poet, Gent. Mag. 1738, p. 522; and a very juft one, at large, (from *Bofwell's* Method of Study) in Gent. Mag. 1780, p. 113.

" and

" and eafy Method of learning *Hebrew* without Points.   To
" which is annexed, by way of praxis, the Book of Proverbs,
" divided according to the Metre; with the Maforetical read-
" ing in *Roman* letters, the interlinear verfion of *Santes Pag-*
" *ninus*, &c. a grammatical Analyfis, and fhort Notes critical
" and explanatory; the whole defigned for the more fpeedy
" and perfect attainment of the *Hebrew* tongue.   By *Richard*
" *Grey*, D. D. rector of *Hinton*, in *Northamptonfhire*," 8vo;
the third volume of " Sermons at *Boyle's* Lectures," folio;
" A Catalogue of the MSS. of the Mafter of the Rolls;"
" An Epiftle to Mr. *P*[*ope*] in Anti-heroicks.   Written in
" 1736." [By Lord *Paget*.] 8vo; and alfo a part of the
" Univerfal Dictionary of Arts and Sciences," on which fubject I find the following memorandum : " While the fecond
" edition of *Chambers's* Cyclopædia, the pride of bookfellers,
" and the honour of the *Englifh* nation, was in the prefs, I
" went to the author, and begged leave to add a fingle fyl-
" lable to his magnificent work; and that for *Cyclopædia*, he
" would write *Encyclopædia*.   To talk to the writer of a
" Dictionary is like talking to the writer of a Magazine;
" every thing adds to his parcel; and, inftead of contri-
" buting one fyllable, I was the occafion of a confiderable
" paragraph.   I told him that the addition of the prepo-
" fition EN made the meaning of the word more precife;
" that *Cyclopædia* might denote the inftruction OF a circle,
" as *Cyropædia* is the inftruction OF *Cyrus*; but that, if he
" wrote *Encyclopædia*, it determined it to be from the dative
" of *Cyclus*, inftruction IN a circle.   I urged, fecondly, that
" *Voffius* had obferved, in his book ' De Vitiis Sermonis,' that
" *Cyclopædia* was ufed by fome authors, but *Encyclopædia* by
" the beft.   This deferved fome regard, and he paid to it the
" beft he could; he made an article of his title to juftify

" it.

" it. *W. B.*"—Mr. *Bowyer* had conceived some extensive idea of improving this valuable Dictionary*, on a plan which does not appear to have been put in practice.

In the same year were published, from another press, the third and fourth volumes of " *Breval's* † Travels;" of which Mr. *Bowyer* printed the two former volumes in 1723 and 1725. (See p. 45.)

In 1739, he printed " The Earl of *Strafforde's* Letters " and Dispatches, with an Essay towards his Life by Sir " *George Radcliffe.* From the originals in the possession of " his great-grandson the right honourable *Thomas* Earl of " *Malton*, Knight of the Bath. By *William Knowler*, LL.D.

* " Your project of improving and correcting *Chambers* is a very good one; but alas! " who can execute it? You should have as many undertakers as professions; nay, per- " haps, as many antiquaries, as there are different branches of ancient learning." *Letter from Mr. Clarke to Mr. Bowyer.*

† " *John Durant Breval*, Esq. the celebrated traveller, was the son of *Francis Durant de Breval*, D.D. who became Prebendary of *Westminster*, *Nov.* 21, 1674, which dignity he enjoyed till his death in *Feb.* 1707. He was educated at *Westminster* school, from whence he went to *Trinity College, Cambridge*, where he was elected a Fellow about the year 1702; but, upon some disagreement between him and Dr. *Bentley*, then Master of that College, he soon after quitted or resigned his Fellowship ‡, and went into the army then in *Flanders*, as an ensign. The ease with which he acquired the *Flemish* and *German* languages, his great learning, his exquisite pencil, and genteel behaviour, were soon taken notice of by the Duke of *Marlborough*, who not only promoted him to the rank of Captain, but also employed him in divers negotiations with several *German* Princes, which he executed with great integrity, and very much to the satisfaction of his noble employer. He began his Travels about the year 1720; published the two first volumes in folio 1723 and 1725, and the third and fourth in 1738; and died, universally beloved, in *January* 1738-9." To these particulars (which were communicated to Dr. *Ducarel* many years since by the late worthy *Samuel Gale*, Esq. who was an intimate friend of Captain *Breval*) I may add, that he published in 1734, " The History of the House of " *Nassau*," 8vo; " The Hoop-Petticoat, a poem, 1716;" " The Art of Dress, an " Heroi-Comical Poem, 1717;" " *Mac Dermot*, or the *Irish* Fortune-hunter, a poem, " 1717;" " *Calpe*, or *Gibraltar*, a poem, 1717;" and in that year brought out a Comedy, called " The Play is the Plot," which not succeeding on the stage, he reduced it to a Farce, called " The Strollers," which met with more favour. In the year 1737 he brought out at *Covent-Garden* a Musical Opera called " The Rape of *Helen.*" He wrote also, under the character of *Joseph Gay*, " The Confederates, a Farce, " 1717," with a humorous caricature print of *Pope*, *Gay*, and *Arbuthnot*; " *Ovid* in " Masquerade;" and a Prologue on the revival of *Tartuffe*. And hence the Captain found a place in *The Dunciad*, II. 126, 238.

‡ Mr. *Breval* and Mr. *Miller* were the two Fellows expelled by Dr. *Bentley*, *April* 5, 1708.—*Breval*, speaking of the conduct of *Bentley* on this occasion, used the remarkable expression of " *Tantum non* " *jugulavit!* "

4

" Rector

"Rector of *Irthlingborough**;" "Jus Parliamentarium;" a
"*Spanish* and *English* Dictionary;" another part of "*Cham-*
"*bers's* Dictionary;" the first number of Dr. *Nathaniel*
Salmon's "Antiquities of *Essex*†," a *Latin* "Catalogue
"of the Antiquary Society's prints," all in folio; with "Que-
"ries relating to the County of *Dorset*," a single sheet, by
Mr. *Hutchins* ‡, whose History of that County Mr. *Bowyer*
printed in 1774; Dr. *Taylor's* celebrated edition of *Lysias* in 4to.
(mentioned in p. 63); Professor *Stuart's* "Necessity of a Di-
"vine Revelation," 8vo; another edition of "Dr. *Cockman's*
"*Tully*," 12mo; "Tabula exhibens Paradigmata Verbo-
"rum *Hebraicorum* regularium & irregularium, per omnes
"conjugationes, modos, tempora, & personas, plenius &
"accuratius excusa," a very large single sheet, by Dr. *R.*
Grey; for whom he also printed, in that year, "Historia

* Commonly called *Artleburrow*. It is between *Wellingborough* and *Higham Ferrers*, in the gift of the Earl.

† This was begun in *November* 1739; and the *nineteenth* number, with *title-page* and *subscribers* names, appeared in *February* 1740-41. The author (who was a Nonjuring Clergyman, and brother to the author of the Modern History) died *April* 2, 1742.

‡ Mr. *Hutchins*, a native of the county, rector of *Holy Trinity* in *Wareham*, began in 1737, while curate of *Milton-Abbas*, to collect materials for its history, which, after many difficulties, he lived to see put to press, at last supported by a very hand-some subscription. It was published under the title of, "The History and Anti-"quities of the county of *Dorset*, compiled from the best and most ancient hist-"torians, inquisitiones post mortem, and other valuable records and MSS. in the "public offices, libraries, and private hands; with a copy of Domesday-book and the "Inquisitio Gheldi for the county; interspersed with some remarkable particulars of "natural history, and adorned with a correct map of the county, and views of anti-"quities, feats of the nobility and gentry. In two volumes. *London*, 1774." folio. Mr. *Hutchins* was born in 1698 at *Bradford-Peverell*, where his father *Richard Hutchins* was curate, who died rector of *All Saints* in *Dorchester* 1734, having held it from 1693. He was educated at *Baliol College*, where he cultivated an acquaintance with Mr. *God-win* and Mr. *Sandford*: to the friendship of the former, who closed a long and worthy life about three years before him, he bears ample testimony in his preface. Upon his being presented to *Wareham*, he married *Anne*, daughter of the Rev. Mr. *Steevens*, rec-tor of *Pimpern*, whose grandfather had been steward to Mr. *Pitt's* family, who permitted Mrs. *Steevens* to present to the living for the next turn, in hopes of keeping it for her son; but the presentee, Mr. *Andrews*, dying within the year, she lost her turn. Mr. *Hutchins* was presented to *Swyre* 1729, to *Melcomb-Horsey* 1733, and to *Wareham* 1743; and, after a long combat with the infirmities of age and gout, and a severe loss by the fire at *Wareham*, 1762, died *June* 21, 1773, and was buried in *St. Mary's* church at *Wareham*, in the antient chapel under the South aile of the chancel. Brit. Topog. I. 319.

"*Josephi*

" *Jofephi* Patriarchæ, literis tam *Romanis* quam *Hebraicis*
" excufa, cum verfione interlineari S. *Pagnini*, & vocum
" indice analytico; præmittitur nova methodus *Hebraice*
" difcendi, diligentiùs recognita, & ad ufum fcholarum
" accommodata," 8vo.

In 1740 he purchafed a monument*, which he intended fhould ferve both for his father and himfelf. The ftone
was completed, except the infcription ; and in that ftate was
placed on the outfide of the mafon's houfe at *Hampftead*,
where it remained till after having been expofed to the
weather for 37 years it was unfit for ufe.

The principal books of 1740 were, " *Maximi Tyrii*
" Diſſertationes, ex recenfione *Joannis Davifii*, Coll. Regin.
" *Cantab*. Præfidis, Editio altera, ad duos codices MSS.
" locis quamplurimis emendata, notifque locupletioribus
" aucta; cui accefferunt viri eruditiffimi *Jer. Marklandi* Coll.
" D. *Petri Cantabrig*. Socii, Annotationes," 4to ; " A Col-
" lection of State Papers, relating to Affairs in the Reigns
" of King *Henry* VIII. King *Edward* VI. Queen *Mary*, and
" Queen *Elizabeth*, from the year 1542 to 1570. Tran-
" fcribed from Original Letters and other authentic Memo-
" rials, never before publifhed, left by *William Cecill* Lord
" *Burleigh*, and now remaining at *Hatfield Houfe*, in the
" library of the right honourable the prefent Earl of *Salif-*
" *bury*. By *Samuel Haynes*, A. M. Rector of *Hatfield* in
" *Hertfordfhire*," folio ; " *Examen* ; or an Enquiry into the
" Credit and Veracity of a pretended *Complete Hiftory* [Dr.
" *Kennet's*]; fhewing the perverfe and wicked defign of it,
" and the many falfities and abufes of truth contained in

---

* " *June* 13, 1740. Received of Mr. *William Bowyer* ten pounds, in part for a mo-
" nument to be erected at *Lowleyton*. By me *Rob. Scott*." Orig. Receipt.
" *Mem. Sept.* 7, 1740. Paid him more three pounds one fhilling ; and agreed with
" him for twenty pounds when it is put up." Mr. BOWYER, MS.

" it ;

" it ; together with some Memoirs occasionally inserted, all
" tending to vindicate the honour of the late King *Charles*
" the Second, and his happy Reign, from the intended
" *aspersions* of that *foul pen.* By the Hon. *Roger North**,
" 1740," 4to. published by Mr. *Mountagu North*; a second
edition of *Maittaire's* " *Anacreon*," 100 copies, and *six
only* on writing paper, 4to; " Psalmorum *Davidis* Para-
" phrasis Poetica. Auctore *Arturo Johnstono Scotto*†, cum
" Indice

---

* Sixth son of *Dudley* fourth lord *North*, and brother to *Charles* lord *North*, and *Francis* lord *Guilford*, with whom, after having studied at *The Middle Temple*, he spent the
greater part of his life. In the reign of *Charles* II. he was a counsellor of note, and in
that of *James* II. attorney-general. He has taken great pains in the " Examen" to vilify
Dr. *Kennet's* " Complete History of *England*;" and has, Mr. *Granger* says, " in se-
" veral instances contradicted facts founded upon antient records, and decried or ex-
" tolled the characters of persons whose merit or demerit is as well established as these
" facts." He was also author of, 1. " The Gentleman Accomptant, or an Essay to un-
" fold the Mystery of Accompts by way of Debtor and Creditor, commonly called Mer-
" chants Accompts, and applying the same to the Concerns of the Nobility and Gen-
" try of *England*, &c. done by a Person of Honour. 1714." 12mo. 2. " The Life
" of the Right Honourable *Francis North*, Baron of *Guilford*, Lord Keeper of the Great
" Seal under King *Charles* the Second, and King *James* the Second; wherein are insert-
" ed the characters of Sir *Matthew Hale*, Sir *George Jefferies*, Sir *Leoline Jenkins*, *Sidney*
" *Godolphin*, and other the most eminent Lawyers and Statesmen of that time. 1742,"
4to. 3. " The Life of the Honourable Sir *Dudley North*, Knight, Commissioner of
" the Customs, and afterwards of the Treasury, to his Majesty King *Charles* the Second.
" And of the Honourable and Reverend Dr. *John North*, Master of *Trinity College* in
" *Cambridge*, and *Greek* Professor, Prebend of *Westminster*, and some time clerk of
" the Closet to the same King *Charles* the Second. By the Honourable *Roger North*,
" esq. 1748." 4to. These three persons were brothers to their Biographer.

† *Arthur Johnston* was born at *Caskieben*, near *Aberdeen*, the seat of his ancestors,
an ancient family, frequently honoured with knighthood; and probably was educated
at *Aberdeen*, as he was afterwards advanced to the highest dignity in that University, which could hardly have happened had he not belonged in his youth to that learned
body. The study he chiefly applied himself to, was that of physick; and to improve
himself in that science, he travelled into foreign parts. He was twice at *Rome*, but the
chief place of his residence was *Padua*, in which University the degree of Doctor of
Physic was conferred on him in the year 1610, as appears by a manuscript copy of verses
in the Advocates' library in *Edinburgh*. After leaving *Padua*, he travelled through the
rest of *Italy*, and over *Germany*, *Denmark*, *England*, and *Holland*, and other countries, and at last settled in *France*; where he met with great applause as a *Latin*
poet. He lived there twenty years, and by two wives had thirteen children. At
last, after twenty-four years absence, he returned into *Scotland* in the year 1632. It
appears by the Council Books at *Edinburgh*, that the Doctor had a suit at law before
that court about that time. In the year following, it is very well known that King
Charles the First went into *Scotland*, and made Bishop *Laud*, then with him, a member
of

" Indice; Vocabulorum ;" accompanied with " The Pfalms
" of *David* according to the tranflation in the *Englifh* Bible,
" with

of that council; and by this accident, it is probable, that acquaintance began between
the Doctor and that Prelate, which produced the excellent work which gives occafion to
this note; for we find that in the fame year, the Doctor printed a fpecimen of his Pfalms
at *London*, and dedicated them to his Lordfhip, which is as plain a proof almoft as
can be defired that the Bifhop prevailed upon Dr. *Johnfton* to remove to *London* from
Scotland, and then fet him upon this work; neither can it be doubted but, after he had
feen this fample, he alfo engaged him to perfect the whole, which took him up four
years; for the firft edition of all the Pfalms was publifhed at *Aberdeen* in 1637, and at
London the fame year. In 1641 Dr. *Johnfton* being at *Oxford*, on a vifit to one of his
daughters, who was married to a divine of the church of *England* in that place, was
feized with a violent diarrhœa, of which he died in a few days, in the 54th year of his
age, not without having feen the beginning of thofe troubles that proved fo fatal to his
patron. He was buried in the place where he died, which gave occafion to the following
lines of his learned friend *Wedderburn* in his " *Sufpiria*" on the Doctor's death :

" *Scotia* mœfta, dole, tanti viduata fepulchro
" Vatis; is *Angligenis* contigit altus honos."

In what year Dr. *Johnfton* was made phyfician to the King, does not appear; it is moft
likely that the Archbifhop procured him that honour at his coming into *England* in
1633, at which time he tranflated *Solomon's* Song into *Latin* elegiac verfe, and dedicated it to his Majefty. His Pfalms were reprinted at *Middleburg*, 1642; *London*,
1657; *Cambridge*, ...; *Amfterdam*, 1706; *Edinburgh*, by *William Lauder* *,

---

* *William Lauder* was a *Scotchman*, educated at the univerfity of *Edinburgh*, where he finifhed his ftudies
with great reputation, and acquired a confiderable knowledge of the *Latin* tongue. He afterwards
taught with fuccefs in the clafs of Humanity † ftudents who were recommended to him by the Profeffor thereof. On the 22d of *May*, 1734, he received a teftimonial from the heads of the Univerfity,
certifying that he was a fit perfon to teach Humanity in any fchool or college whatever; and in 1742
was recommended by Mr. *Patrick Cuming* and Mr. *Colin Maclaurin*, Profeffors of Church Hiftory and
Mathematicks, to the Mafterfhip of the Grammar School at *Dundee*, then vacant. Whether he fucceeded in this application or not, is uncertain; but a few years afterwards we find him in *London*, contriving to ruin the reputation of *Milton*, an attempt which ended in the deftruction of his own. His
reafon for this attack probably fprung from the virulence of a violent party fpirit, which triumphed
over every principle of honour and honefty. He began firft to retail part of his defign in *The Gentleman's
Magazine*, 1747; and finding that his forgeries were not detected, was encouraged in 1751 to collect
them, with additions, into a volume, intituled " An Effay on *Milton's* Ufe and Imitation of the Mo-
" derns in his Paradife Loft," 8vo. The fidelity of his quotations had been doubted by feveral people,
and the falfehood of them was foon after demonftrated by Mr. (now Dr.) *Douglas*, in a pamphlet intituled " *Milton* vindicated from the Charge of Plagiarifm brought againft him by *Lauder*, Lauder
" himfelf convicted of feveral forgeries and grofs impofitions on the publick. In a Letter humbly ad-
" dreffed to the Right Honourable the Earl of *Bath*, 1751," 8vo. The appearance of this detection
overwhelmed *Lauder* with confufion. He fubfcribed a confeffion, dictated by a learned friend ftill
living, wherein he ingenuoufly acknowledged his offence, which he profeffed to have been occafioned
by the injury he had received from the difappointment of his expectations of profit from the publica-
cation of *Johnfton's* Pfalms. This misfortune he afcribed to the couplet in Mr. *Pope's* Dunciad cited in
the following note, and from thence originated his rancour againft *Milton*. He afterwards imputed his conduct to other motives, abufed the few friends who continued to countenance him; and
finding that his character was not to be retrieved, quitted the kingdom, and went to *Barbadoes*, where
he fome time taught a fchool. His behaviour there was mean and defpicable; and he paffed the remainder of his life in univerfal contempt. He died fome time about the year 1771, as my friend Mr.
Reed was informed by the gentleman who read the funeral fervice over him.

† So the *Latin* tongue is called in *Scotland* from the *Latin* phrafe *Claffis humaniorum Literarum*, the clafs or
form where that language is taught.

" with an Index of the words," in 4to, fmall 8vo, and
12mo ; " Academiques de *Ciceron*, avec le Texte *Latin*
" de l'edition de *Cambrige*, & des Remarques nouvelles, outre

1739 ; and laft on the plan of the *Delphin* claffics, at *London*, 1741, 8vo, at the expence of Auditor *Benfon* *, who dedicated them to his prefent Majefty, and prefixed to this
edition the memoirs of Dr. *Johnfton* (whence I have extracted this note), with the teftimonies of various learned perfons. A laboured comparifon between the two tranflations of *Buchanan* and *Johnfon* was printed the fame year in *Englifh*, in 8vo, intituled,
" A Prefatory Difcourfe to Dr. *Johnfton's* Pfalms, &c." and " A Conclufion to it."
His tranflations of the Te Deum, Creed, Decalogue, &c. were fubjoined to the Pfalms.
His other poetical works are his Epigrams, his Parerga, and his Mufæ *Anglicæ*,
or commendatory Verfes upon perfons of rank in Church and State at that time.

* Mr. *Benfon* was the fon of Sir *William Benfon*, formerly fheriff of *London*. He was born in
the year 1682; and in the reign of Queen *Anne* made a tour abroad, during which he vifited
Hanover and fome other *German* courts, and *Stockholm*. In 1710 he was high fheriff of *Wilts*,
and foon after wrote his famous letter to Sir *Jacob Banks of Minehead*, by birth a *Swede*, but naturalized; wherein he fet forth the miferies of the *Swedes*, after they had made a furrender of their liberties
to arbitrary power, which was then making great advances at home. Being fummoned for this letter
before the Lords of the Privy Council, he owned himfelf to be the author of it, in defiance of a profecution then ordered by the Queen's Attorney General, and put his name to all the fubfequent editions,
of which not lefs than 100000 copies were fold in our own and foreign languages. He was member
for the Borough of *Shaftefbury* in the firft parliament of *George* the Firft, who in the year 1718 made
him Surveyor General of his works, in the place of Sir *Chriftopher Wren*, by which he vacated his feat
in parliament. He refigned this poft not long after, to oblige the then minifter. The commentator
on the Dunciad, B. III. ver. 325, relates, that " Mr. *Benfon* gave in a report to the Lords, that their
houfe and the painted chamber adjoining were in immediate danger of falling; whereupon they met in
a committee to appoint fome other place to fit in while the houfe was taking down; but it being propofed to take the opinion of fome other builders, they found it in very good condition; upon this the
lords were going to addrefs the King againft *Benfon* for fuch a mifreprefentation; but the Earl of *Sunderland*, then fecretary of ftate, gave them affurance that his Majefty would remove him, which was done
accordingly. In favour of this man, proceeds the note, the famous Sir *Chriftopher Wren*, who had been
architect to the crown for above 50 years, built moft of the churches in *London*, laid the firft ftone of
St. Paul's, and lived to finifh it, had been difplaced from his employment at the age of near 90 years."
On the refignation of this office, Mr. *Benfon* received a fhort time after an affignment of a confiderable
debt due to the crown in *Ireland*, and alfo the reverfion of one of the two offices of Auditor of the Impreft, which he enjoyed after the death of Mr. *Edward Harley*. He attended King *George* I. in a
vifit which he made to his *German* dominions. and while there gave directions for that curious water-
work in the gardens of *Herenhaufen*†, which is known to excell the famous fountain of *St. Cloud* in
France. If we may compare fmall things with great, the water was laid into the town of *Shaftefbury*
from a farm at a mile diftance by an horfe engine erected at his expence; but the yearly profits not anfwering the fund and repairs, it failed in about four years, and was renewed again 1714 ‡. In the
prime of his life few perfons were more diftinguifhed by the characters of the fine gentleman,
the fcholar, the ftatefman, and the patriot; but in the latter part of it he lived very retired, chiefly at
Wimbleton in *Surrey*, where he died *February* 2, 1754. He was a great admirer of *Milton* and *John-
fon*; on which account, *Pope* mentions him in the Dunciad, B. 4. L. III.
" On two unequal crutches propt he came,
" *Milton's* on this, on that one *Johnfton's* name."
To do honour to *Milton*, he erected a monument to his memory in *Weftminfter Abbey*, employed Mr.
Tanner to engrave a medal of him, and paid Mr. *Dobfon* for tranflating the Paradife Loft into *Latin*.
His own publications were, " *Virgil's* Hufbandry, or an Effay on the Georgics; being the Second Book
" tranflated into *Englifh* Verfe : to which are added the *Latin* Text, and Mr. *Dryden's* Verfion, with
" Notes Critical and Ruftic. 1724," 8vo; and " Letters concerning Poetical Tranflations, and *Virgil's*
" and *Milton's* Arts of Verfe, &c. 1739," 8vo.

† Bifhop *Pococke*, in his Travels, vol. II. part ii. page 226, fays, " The gardens of *Herenhaufen* are defervedly
" admired; the *jet d'eau* is the fineft in the world, the waters being forced to it by machines which are well
" known, and are the invention of Mr. *Holland*, &c."
‡ *Hutchins's* " Hiftory of *Dorfet*," vol. II. p. 25.

4

" les

" les conjectures de *Davies* & de Monf. *Bentley*, & le Com-
" mentaire Philofophique de *Pierre Valentia*, Jurif. *Eſpag-*
" *nol.* par un des membres de la S. R." 8vo ; and " Aca-
" demica, five de Judicio erga Verum. Ex ipſis primis fon-
" tibus ; operâ *Petri Valentiæ Zafrenſis*, in extremâ Bæticâ.
" Editio nova emendatior ; *Typis Bowyerianis*," 8vo. both
by Mr. (afterwards Dr.) *Durand**, 8vo ; and " The Ana-
" tomy of the Human Body, by *William Cheſelden*, Surgeon
" to his Majeſty's Royal Hoſpital at *Chelſea*, Fellow of the
" Royal Society, and Member of the Royal Academy of
" Surgeons at *Paris*†," 8vo.

In 1741 he corrected, and put into a convenient form,
two very uſeful little ſchool-books, " Selectæ è Veteri Teſ-
" tamento Hiſtoriæ," and " Selectæ ex Profanis Scripto-
" ribus Hiſtoriæ." The Prefaces to both theſe volumes ‡
were

---

* See above, p. 58.—In the title-pages of theſe books, inſtead of an ornament, a
blank ſhield was printed, in which Mr. *Durand*, in many of the copies which he gave
away, wrote, in a remarkably neat hand, ſome little compliment to the friends to whom
he ſent the books.

† Of Mr. *Cheſelden*, an account ſhall be given hereafter. Two editions of his Anatomy had before paſſed through Mr. *Bowyer's* preſs in 8vo, 1730 and 1740; and a fine
edition of it in folio, 1734. He reprinted it in 8vo, 1750, 1756, and 1762.

‡ Both theſe works were firſt publiſhed at *Paris*, in 1726 and 1727, by Monſ.
Heuſet, profeſſor of *Beauvais College* in *Pàris*. The author of the " New Memoirs of
" Literature, 1727," by the following account of theſe little books, firſt gave Mr.
Bowyer the hint for reprinting them : " When children have made ſome proficiency
" in *Latin*, 'tis an uſual thing to make them explain authors leſs eaſy, that is, very dif-
" ficult, whom they underſtand as well as they can, and who are of no uſe to improve
" their mind, or their memory, becauſe they read them throughout, whereas they
" ſhould only read ſelect paſſages out of theſe authors, which might at the ſame time
" inſtruct and pleaſe them. Mr. *Heuſet*, being ſenſible of this inconveniency, has com-
" piled out of the beſt *Latin* writers thoſe paſſages that are moſt inſtructive and agree-
" able, and placed them methodically in a new collection, deſigned chiefly for the uſe
" of children, and yet uſeful to every body. He had two things in view, the clear-
" neſs of thoughts and expreſſions, and the uſefulneſs of the matters. With reſpect to
" clearneſs, he has frequently ſuppreſſed, in the maxims and hiſtories collected by him,
" thoſe thoughts that are either obſcure, or too ſubtil ; he has changed thoſe expreſ-
" ſions that are too nice and ſublime, into others more ſimple ; he has contracted thoſe
" phraſes that are too long, and preferred perſpicuity and eaſineſs to harmony. And
" becauſe the diſpoſition of words in the *Latin* tongue is the greateſt difficulty for be-
" ginners, he thought it proper to place them in a more natural order, and more like

" that

were tranflated by Mr. *Bowyer*, and are inferted in his
" Mifcellaneous Tracts." From his prefs appeared this
year the fecond volume (in two parts*, containing Books
IV. V. VI.) of " The Divine Legation ;" a fecond edition
of " The Alliance between Church and State," 8vo ; Dean
Stanhope's tranflation of " *Epictetus's* Morals," 8vo; " Epitres
" Morales, Lettres Philofophiques, & Traits Mathema-
" tiques," par M. *Silouette*; and an edition in *French* of
Mr. *Richardfon's* very celebrated *Pamela†*.

On

" that of the *French*, and other modern fanguages. The author reduces to Prudence,
" Juftice, Fortitude, and Temperance, all the maxims and hiftories which he has com-
" piled, in order to compofe a number of books equal to thofe moral virtues ; and he
" has prefixed to them a very fhort book concerning the Supreme Being, Religion, and
" the Nature of Man. This work will be very ufeful to young fcholars, and perhaps
" deferves to be reprinted in *England*.".

* To the end of Part II. was added, " An Appendix ; containing fome Remarks on
" a late Book, intituled, *Future Rewards and Punifhments believed by the Ancients*,
" *particularly the Philofophers*; *wherein fome Objections of the Rev. Mr.* Warburton, *in*
" *his* Divine Legation of Mofes, *are confidered*."

† Mr. *Samuel Richardfon*, who was born in 1689, had no acquaintance with the learned languages but what a common fchool-education afforded ; his mind, like that of
Shakfpeare, being much more enriched by nature and obfervation. He exercifed the profeffion of a printer, with the higheft reputation, for a long feries of years in *Salifbury Court*,
Fleet Street. Diffimilar as their geniufes may feem, when the witty and wicked Duke
of *Wharton* (a kind of *Lovelace*) about the year 1723 fomented the fpirit of oppofition
in the city, and became a member of the Wax Chandlers Company ; Mr. *Richardfon*,
though his political principles were very different, was much connected with, and favoured by him, and printed his " True Briton," publifhed twice a week. Yet he exercifed his own judgment, in peremptorily refufing to be concerned in fuch papers as
he apprehended might endanger his own fafety, and which accordingly did occafion
the imprifonment and profecution of thofe who were induced to print and publifh them.
He printed for fome time a news-paper called " The Daily Journal ;" and afterwards
" The Daily Gazetteer," which was for the moft part under the patronage of Sir
Robert Walpole ; but on that minifter's withdrawing his fupport, he declined it about
the year 1747, when it fell into other hands. Through the intereft of his friend Mr.
Speaker *Onflow*, he printed the firft edition of the Journals of the Houfe of Commons. He purchafed a moiety of the patent of law-printer at *Midfummer* 1760, and
carried on that department of bufinefs in partnerfhip with Mifs *Catherine Lintot* **.
By his firft wife *Martha Wilde*, daughter of Mr. *Allington Wilde*, printer, in
Clerkenwell, he had five fons and a daughter, who all died young. His fecond
wife (who furvived him many years) was *Elizabeth* fifter of the late Mr. *Leake*,
bookfeller of *Bath*. By her he had a fon and five daughters. The fon died young ;
but four of the daughters furvived him ; viz. *Mary*, married in 1757 to Mr. *Ditcher*,
an eminent Surgeon of *Bath* ; *Martha*, married in 1762 to *Edward Bridgen*, efq. F.R.
and A.SS.; *Anne*, unmarried ; and *Sarah*, married to Mr. *Crowther*, Surgeon, of *Bof-*

** After Mr. *Richardfon's* death, his widow and Mifs *Lintot* were for fome time joint patentees.

well

On the 8th of *November* 1741, died of an apoplexy Mr. *Fletcher Gyles*, bookseller in *Holborn*, treasurer of the charity school in *Hatton Garden*, and an intimate friend of Mr.

well Court, and since dead. His country retirement, first at *North End* near *Hammersmith*, and afterwards at *Parsons Green*, was generally filled with his friends of both sexes *. He was regularly there from *Saturday* to *Monday*, and frequently at other times, being never so happy as when he made others so, being himself, in his narrower sphere, the *Grandison* he drew; his heart and hand ever open to distress. His *Pamela*, which appears to have been written in three months †, first introduced him to the literary world; and never was a book of the kind more generally read and admired. It was even recommended not unfrequently from the pulpit, particularly by Dr. *Slocock*, late of *Christ Church, Surrey*, who had a very high esteem for it, as well as for its author. But it is much to be regretted that his improved edition, in which much was altered, much omitted, and the whole new-modeled, has never yet been given to the public, as the only reason which prevented it in his life-time, that there was an edition unsold, must long have ceased ‡.

By many family misfortunes, and his own writings, which in a manner realised every feigned distress, his nerves naturally weak, or, as *Pope* expresses it, " tremblingly alive " all o'er," were so unhinged, that for many years before his death his hand shook, he had frequent vertigoes, and would sometimes have fallen had he not supported himself by his cane under his coat. His paralytic disorder affected his nerves to such a degree for a considerable time before his death, that he could not lift a glass of wine to his mouth without assistance. This disorder at length terminating in an apoplexy, deprived the world of this amiable man and truly original genius, on *July* 4, 1761, at the age of 72. He was buried, by his own direction, with his first wife, in the middle aile, near the pulpit of *St. Bride's* church.

In a MS. of the late Mr. *Whiston* the bookseller, which fell into the hands of one of my friends, was the following passage: " Mr. *Samuel Richardson* was a worthy man alto- " gether. Being very liable to passion, he directed all his men, it is said, by letters; " not trusting to reprove by words, which threw him into hastiness, and hurt him, " who had always a tremor on his nerves." I have heard nearly the same account from some of his workmen. But this, I believe, was not the reason; though the fact was certainly true; it was rather for convenience, to avoid altercation, and going up into the printing-office; and besides, his principal assistant Mr. *Tewley* was remarkably deaf.

* Many of these he has particularly distinguished, in his last will, by the bequest of a ring; namely, " the kind Dr. *Heberden*," Dr. *Young*, Dr. *Delany*, the right honourable *Arthur Onslow*, Mr. *George* (now lord) *Onslow*, Miss *Talbot*, Miss *Lintot*, Mrs. *Millar* (now lady *Grant*), Mr. *Dyson*, Mr. *Poyntz*, Mr. *Yeates*, Mr. *Barwell*, Mr. *Hatsell*, Mr. *Stracey*, Mr. *Harper*, Mr. *S. Harper*, Mr. *Chapone*, Mr. *James Bailey*, Mr. *John Rivington*, Mr. *William Tewley* (his faithful overseer), and eleven other names which I do not recollect. In enumerating his friends, he appears to have been embarrassed by the multitude which occurred to him. " Had I given Rings," he says, " to all the Ladies " who have honoured me with their correspondence, and whom I sincerely venerate for their amiable " qualities, it would even in this last solemn act appear like ostentation."

† See *Aaron Hill's* Letters, in the second volume of his Works, p. 298.

‡ Since this article was written, Proposals have been circulated, " for printing and publishing a " correct, uniform, and beautiful edition of those celebrated and admired pieces, written by the late " Mr. *Samuel Richardson*, intitled, " *Pamela*, or Virtue Rewarded;" " The History of Miss *Clarissa* " *Harlowe*;" and " The History of Sir *Charles Grandison*." To which will be added anecdotes of " the author, with his head elegantly engraved, a critique on his genius and writings, and a collection " of letters written by him on moral and entertaining subjects, never before published. By *William* " *Richardson* [his nephew, and successor in the printing-office]." The whole is intended to be comprized in Twenty Volumes octavo, to be published monthly at Four Shillings a Volume.

Besides

Mr. *Bowyer*, in whofe hand-writing I find the original of
an undirected letter, which, though written in the character
of

Befides his three great works, he publifhed an edition of " *Æfop's* Fables, with
Reflections," and " Letters to and from feveral Perfons," and had a fhare in " The
" Chriftian's Magazine, by Dr. *James Mauclerc*, 1748 ;" and in the additions to the
fixth edition of *De Foe's* " Tour through *Great Britain*." " Six original letters upon
" Duelling" were printed, after his death, in " The Literary Repofitory, 1765," p. 227.
Nº 97, vol. II. of the Ramblers, it is well known, was written by Mr. *Richard-*
fon, in the preamble to which Dr. *Johnfon* ftyles him " an author from whom the age
" has received greater favours, who has enlarged the knowledge of human nature, and
" taught the paffions to move at the command of Virtue." He has been often compared
to *Rouffeau* ; and *Rouffeau* was one of his profeffed admirers. In his letter to *D'Alem-*
bert, fpeaking of *Englifh* romances, he fays, " Thefe, like the people, are either fublime
" or contemptible. There never has been written in any language a romance
" equal to, or approaching to *Clariffa*." But the efteem was not reciprocal ; Mr.
Richardfon being fo much difgufted at fome of the fcenes and the whole tendency of
the new *Eloifa*, that he fecretly criticifed the work (as he read it) in marginal notes,
and thought, with many others, that this writer " taught the paffions to move at the
" command of Vice." If this fecret cenfure of Mr. *Richardfon's* fhould be thought too
fevere or phlegmatic, let it be confidered, that admitting the tendency of *Rouffeau's*
principles to be better in the main than his more rigid readers allow, his fyftem is too
refined to be carried into execution in any age when the globe is not uniformly peopled
with philofophers.
Dr. *Johnfon*, in his Biographical Preface to *Rowe's* Poems, obferves, " The character
" of *Lothario* feems to have been expanded by *Richardfon* into *Lovelace*, but he has ex-
" celled his original in the moral effect of the fiction. *Lothario*, with gaiety which can-
" not be hated, and bravery which cannot be defpifed, retains too much of the fpectator's
" kindnefs. It was in the power of *Richardfon* alone to teach us at once efteem and de-
" teftation, to make virtuous refentment overpower all the benevolence which wit, and
" elegance, and courage, naturally excite ; and to lofe at laft the hero in the villain."
Mr. *Aaron Hill*, in a letter to Mr. *Mallet*, who fuppofed there were fome traces of
Hill's hand in *Pamela*, fays, " Upon my faith, I had not any (the minuteft) fhare in
" that delightful *nurfery of virtue*. The fole and abfolute author is Mr. *Richardfon* ;
" and fuch an author too he is, that hardly mortal ever matched him, for his eafe of
" natural power. He feems to move like a calm fummer fea, that fwelling upward,
" with unconfcious deepnefs, lifts the heavieft weights into the fkies, and fhews no fenfe
" of their incumbency. He would, perhaps, in every thing he fays or does be more
" in nature than all men before him, but that he has one *fault*, to an unnatural *excefs*,
" and that is MODESTY*." In a letter to Mr. *Richardfon*, after endeavouring to divert
him from a melancholy train of thought he had fallen into in 1748, from " the death
" of a relation emphatically *near*," Mr. *Hill* proceeds, " Are you to hope no end to
" this long, long nervous perfecution ? But it is the tax you pay your genius ! and I
" rather wonder you have fpirits to fupport fuch mixture of prodigious weights ! fuch
" an effufion of the foul, with fuch confinement of the body ! than that it has con-
" ftrained your nerves to bear your fpirits' agitation †." Many other of this gentleman's
letters are filled with commendations of Mr. *Richardfon* and his writings ; and from one
of them I fhall copy a complimentary epigram by this ingenious printer :

* *Hill's* Works, vol. II. p. 221. † Ibid. vol. II. p. 277.

" When

of Mr. *Gyles's* executor, is evidently Mr. *Bowyer's* compofition, and fhews that he wifhed at leaft to return by his kindnefs

to

> " When noble thoughts with language pure unite,
> " To give to kindred excellence its right,
> " Though unencumber'd with the clogs of rhyme,
> " Where tinkling founds, for want of meaning, chime,
> " Which, like the rocks in *Shannon's* midway courfe,
> " Divide the fenfe, and interrupt its force;
> " Well may we judge fo ftrong and clear a rill
> " Flows higher, from the Mufes facred HILL."

Mrs. *Sheridan*, on publifhing the " Memoirs of Mifs *Sidney Biddulph*," took an opportunity of " paying the tribute due to exemplary goodnefs and diftinguifhed genius, " when found united in one perfon, by infcribing thefe Memoirs to the Author of *Clariffa* " and Sir *Charles Grandifon*."

Dr. *Young* addreffed his " Conjectures on Original Compofition" to Mr. *Richardfon*; and the former part of " Refignation" was printing by Mr. *Richardfon* at the time of his death; in which the poet took occafion of paying the following affectionate compliment to his memory:

> " To touch our paffions fecret fprings   " Nature, which favours to the few
> " Was his peculiar care;   " All art beyond imparts,
> " And deep his happy genius div'd   " To him prefented, at his birth,
> " In bofoms of the fair;   " The key of human hearts."

The following epigram on *Clariffa*, by the late *David Graham*, efq. fellow of *King's College, Cambridge*, has all the fimplicity of the *Greek* epigrammatifts:

> " This work is Nature's; every tittle in't
> " She wrote, and gave it *Richardfon* to print."

Mrs. *Montagu's* elegant compliment, in Lord *Lyttelton's* " Dialogues of the Dead *," turns nearly on the fame thought. " It is pity he fhould *print* any work but *his own*," fays *Plutarch* to the Bookfeller, who had juft before obferved that in two characters drawn by a *printer*, that of *Clariffa* difplays " the dignity of heroifm tempered by the meek- " nefs and humility of religion, a perfect unity of mind, and fanctity of manners;" and that of Sir *Charles Grandifon*, " a noble pattern of every private virtue, with fenti- " ments fo exalted as to render him equal to every public duty."

Mrs. *Chapone*, in her " Ode to Health," has this apoftrophe:

> " Haft thou not left a *Richardfon* unbleft?
> " He woos thee ftill in vain, relentlefs maid;
> " Tho' fkill'd in fweeteft accents to perfuade,
> " And wake foft pity in a favage breaft:
> " Him Virtue loves, and brighteft Fame is his,
> " Smile thou too, Goddefs, and complete his blifs!"

The verfes annexed to the fourth edition of *Clariffa* were by the friend to whom I owe great part of this note.

In Dr. *Warton's* effay on *Pope's* Genius, p. 283, 284, is the following elogium: " Of " all reprefentations of madnefs, that of *Clementina* in the Hiftory of Sir *Charles Gran-* " *difon* is the moft deeply interefting. I know not whether even the madnefs of *Lear* " is wrought up, and expreffed by fo many little ftrictures of nature and genuine paf- " fion. Shall I fay it is pedantry to prefer and compare the madnefs of *Oreftes* in *Eu-* " *ripides* to this of *Clementina*?"

Mr. *Richardfon's* reputation is far from being confined to his own country. He has been read in many of the languages, and known to moft of the nations of *Europe*; and

---

* Dialogue XXVIII. between *Plutarch—Charon—*and a Modern Bookfeller.

to the furviving daughters the good offices he had conftantly experienced in bufinefs from their father :

" REV. SIR,

" Mr. *Bowyer* having at my requeft acquainted you of my
" brother *Gyles's* death, I think myfelf obliged to affure you
" of the fame honourable dealings from his family †, that

has been greatly admired, notwithftanding every diffimilitude of manners, or even difadvantage of tranflation. Several writers abroad, where no prepoffeffion in his favour
could poffibly take place, have expreffed the high fenfe which they entertained of the
merit of his works. M. *Diderot*, in his Effay on Dramatic Poetry, p. 96, mentions
Richardfon particularly as a perfect mafter of that art : " How ftrong," fays he, " how
" fenfible, how pathetic, are his defcriptions ! his perfonages, though filent, are alive
" before me ; and of thofe who fpeak, the actions are ftill more affecting than the words."
A portrait of him, by *Grignion*, is prefixed to an edition of *Grandifon*, 1770.

Since the verfes by Mr. *Bowyer* (in p. 90) were printed off, I have difcovered, that
the occafion of them was exactly what I had conjectured in p. 86. It happening to fall
to the turn of Mr. *Cave* and Mr. *Bowyer* to invite their brethren to a focial feaft, the
facetious perfon to whom the office of fummoning them was delegated thought proper
to fend it in rhyme :

" SIR,   Saturday, *Jan.* 17, 1735-6.
YOU're defir'd on *Monday* next to meet
At *Salutation Tavern, Newgate-Street.*
Supper will be on table juft at eight.
STEWARDS, One of *St. John's*, t'other of *St. John's Gate.*"

This fummons produced the following extempore anfwer, which I fhall tranfcribe,
as Mr. *Richardfon's* poetical productions are not very numerous :

" *Jan.* 17, 1735-6.

To Steward *St. John*, Steward *St. John's Gate*,
Who meet to fup on *Monday* night at eight.
DEAR fons of *Phœbus*, darlings of the Nine,
Henceforth, thro' you, how will the *printers*
 fhine,   [or dine !
Who ne'er, without the Mufe, fhall meet to fup
Bleffings, fay I, attend your rhyming pen,
No *king* John's fure, e'er equal'd *faint* John's men !
 But, tell me, friends, nor blufh, nor be afraid
To own the truth—had you no third man's aid ?
Speak out, like men—to make the verfe run fweeter,
Did not fome mild-beer bellman tag the metre ?
If fo, I pray, invite the honeft fellow,
Let him partake the *praife*, and make him mellow.

Perpetual ftewards may you voted be ;
No lefs fuch verfe deferves—*perpetual poet* he !
 For me, I'm much concern'd I cannot meet
" At *Salutation Tavern, Newgate Street.*"
Your notice, like your verfe (fo fweet and fhort !)
If longer, I'd fincerely thank'd you for't.
Howe'er, receive my wifhes, fons of verfe !
May every man who meets, your praife rehearfe !
May *mirth*, as *plenty*, crown your chearful board,
And ev'ry one part *happy*—as a lord !
That when at home (by fuch fweet verfes fir'd)
Your families may think you all infpir'd !
So wifhes he, who, pre-ingag'd, can't know
The pleafures that would from your meeting
 flow.   S. R."

On thefe verfes (printed in Gent. Mag. vol. VI. p. 51) Mr. *Cave* thus remarks : " Con-
" cerning this gentleman, the company obferved, that though the publick is often agree-
" ably entertained with his elegant difquifitions in profe, not one imagined that his ex-
" tenfive bufinefs would allow him the leaft leifure to invoke the Mufes ; without whofe
" aid, the *Johnians* infifted, he could not have returned fo poetical and fo fpeedy an
" anfwer :

" Their *Bellman*, hence, fhall emulation fire,
" To raife, with grateful thanks, the metre higher,
" To him, whofe genius makes one printer fhine,
" *Rich*—Son of *Phœbus*, darling of the Nine."

† Mr. *Gyles* left behind him two unmarried daughters.

                   " you

" you might have expected from him if living. For I
" should be very sorry to lose from it so good a friend, and
" one for whom my brother had such a particular esteem.
" I cannot pretend to judge of the value of books or copies;
" nor have I yet informed myself what profits have arose
" from yours*, a marked sale coming on so close upon my
" brother's death, that it has engaged the chief of my at-
" tention ; but if you will be pleased to favour me with a
" line to let me know what your expectations are for the
" impressions of your books that have been already sold,
" and for the right of copy of those that are now in the
" press, I have great reason to hope I shall comply with
" them. I wish this affair had been settled by my brother
" himself; but as it was not, I shall endeavour to repre-
" sent him in every respect, and be an executor not only of
" his will, but of his intention as far as I can discover it.

" COLLET MAWHOOD."

In 1742 he published " Lectures on Poetry, read in the
" Schools of Natural Philosophy at *Oxford*, by *Joseph Trapp*,
" A. M. Fellow of *Wadham College*, and Reader of Poetical
" Lectures lately founded in that University, by *Henry*
" *Birkhead†*, LL. D. sometime Fellow of *All Souls College*;
" translated

* Most probably intended for Mr. *Warburton.*—Mr. *Gyles* was the original publisher
of " The Alliance," and of " The Divine Legation."

† *Henry Birkhead*, born in 1617 near *St. Paul's* cathedral in *London*, after having
been educated under the famous *Farnabie*, was entered a commoner of *Trinity College*,
Oxford, in 1633; admitted scholar there *May* 28, 1635, and soon after was seduced to
become a member of the college of Jesuits at *St. Omers*. He soon, however, returned
to the church of *England*, and, by the patronage of Archbishop *Laud*, was elected
fellow of *All Souls* in 1638, being then B. A. and esteemed a good philologist. He proceeded in that faculty, was made Senior of the Act celebrated in 1641, and entered on
the law line. He kept his Fellowship during the time of the Usurpation ; but resigned
it after the Restoration, when he became registrar of the diocese of *Norwich*. This too
he resigned in 1684; and resided first in *The Middle Temple*, and then in other places, in
a retired and scholastic condition, for many years. " He was accounted," says *Wood*,
" an excellent *Latin* poet, a good *Grecian*, and well versed in all human learning."
His works are, 1. " Poemata in Elegiaca, Iambica, Polymetra, Antitechnemata &

X " Metaphrases,

" tranflated from the *Latin*, with additional Notes." This work appears, from various letters of Mr. *Clarke**, to have been a joint production with that gentleman. Each of them tranflated particular parts, and it was left to Mr. *Bowyer* to adopt fuch paffages from Mr. *Clarke* as he thought proper†. Let his own account of this work fpeak for itfelf :

" Metaphrafes, membranatim quadripartita, 1656," 8vo ; 2. " Otium Literarum ; five " Mifcellanea quædam Poemata, &c. 1656," 8vo. He alfo publifhed in 4to. with a Preface, 1652, fome of the philological works of his intimate friend *Henry Jacob*, who had the honour of teaching *Selden* the *Hebrew* language, or at leaft of improving him in it. Dr. *Birkhead* alfo wrote feveral *Latin* Elegies on the Loyalifts who had fuffered in the caufe of *Charles* the Firft, which are fcattered in various printed books, and many of them fubfcribed *H. G.*—*Henry Birkhead*, author of " *Colon's* Fury," a tragedy on the *Irifh* rebellion, was a different perfon. See *Athen. Oxon.* vol. II. p. 1006.

* " As to *Trapp*, I own I have been very negligent in tranflating ; both his matter " and my own interruptions have prevented me having any great tafte or opportunity for, " it ; but I fhall go through it time enough, I hope, for you to correct before it is in the " prefs. I would by no means have you drop it, but here and there befprinkle a few' " notes, to give it an advantage above the *Latin*." *Mr. Clarke to Mr. Bowyer, in* 1737.,

† " I would fain make this packet look as big as poffible, that you might receive it " with fome pleafure, though you read it with indignation. I am afhamed indeed to fend " fo fmall a part, when it has lain fo long by me ; but I muft confefs the truth : As fome " of your other journeymen can never work with a penny in their pocket, it is my mif- " fortune to be of their mind, as long as I have time to fpare. As to the work, I quef-, " tion much whether you will like this fample ; it may very probably not agree with yours ; " but then you have full power to do what you pleafe with it, and take here and there a' " line, where you approve of it moft ; and this perhaps may give you as much trouble as " doing the whole. That logical way of fifting and canvaffing definitions is not very " pleafant to read or tranflate. I think I have kept too clofe to the original, though I " have fometimes taken the liberty to add a few words when I thought them neceffary, " either to clear and explain a thought, or to give a little more ftrength to it ; I wifh I " had taken the fame liberty in retrenching now and then ; for the fame ideas are fome- " times purfued too far in different words, where our language will not bear the change, " or furnifh us with a proper variety fo well as the *Latin*. The connexion of his fen-' " tences is often extremely carelefs, but that is of no moment. As to poetry, I have tranf- " lated, or altered, or barely tranfcribed, juft as it pleafed my own humour. Some quo- " tations were not, that I know of, tranflated any where ; and others were fo done, that " the words which the quotation turned upon were quite dropped. It was neceffary to " make them fpeak in *Englifh* to the fame purpofe they were produced for in *Latin*, that " the *Englifh* reader might guefs why they came there. But I fhall trouble you no further " upon this bufinefs, but only to tell you, that I could not forbear adding three or four " notes ; you have laughed at one of them already, but I cannot forbear thinking the " author is miftaken in that point, till I fee more reafon to be of his opinion, and the reft " are mere trifles, only they are not very long ones. I own, that I think you do nothing, " unlefs you fcatter a few notes up and down, fomething that is not in the original, whe-

" ther

itfelf : " Whatever reafons have been given for tranflating
" *Virgil*, and writing an *Englifh* Comment on him, may be
" urged in behalf of thefe *Englifh* Lectures ; which, as
" they are an illuftration of Poetry in general, fo are they
" of *Virgil* in particular. The notes to this edition were
" chiefly added as it went through the prefs ; in which,
" though I fometimes differ from my ingenious author,
" yet I hope not with greater freedom than he has taken
" with others, and will pardon in me. I am well aware
" how eafy it is to let fome miftakes flip in the heat of
" compofition : and when thefe had once paffed the prefs,
" the author, I fuppofe, was not very folicitous to re-
" examine minutely the fubfequent editions ; fatisfied with
" the approbation he had received from that learned body,
" before whom his Lectures were firft delivered : an ho-
" nour which I fhall never wifh to fee diminifhed by any
" thing I can fay, or any one elfe ; and fhall now there-
" fore with much greater pleafure take this opportunity
" of repeating the teftimony of them from Mr. *Felton**.
" The feveral paffages cited from *Virgil* are printed in
" *Englifh* from Dr. *Trapp's* Verfion. The other Poetical

" ther right or wrong; 'tis true tafte in trade, whatever you may think of it ; but I am
" ill-furnifhed for fuch an undertaking. I have neither *Voffius*, nor *Scaliger*, nothing in
" that way. Who is this Father *Brumoy*, that *Theobald* mentions ? would he not now
" and then give you pretty hints ? Enquire about him." *Letter from Mr. Clarke, Dec.*
9, 1737. This gentleman, however, fpeaks very flightingly of the book in another
letter without date : " I now begin to think that your tranflation of *Trapp's Prælections*
" will *take* ; for it is really but a very fuperficial book. Though, for the future, I
" defire that we might always fay *Lectures*, in the modern ftyle ; *Prælections* will never
" do in town. He has offended me very much by affecting to find fault with *Voffius*
" upon every little occafion ; and therefore you muft excufe me if I now and then
" fpeak peevifhly of the Doctor. I have endeavoured to make *Ariftotle's* definition of
" Tragedy intelligible ; and I think I have taken the right fenfe of it, which perplexed
" us a little laft fummer. The *Monita, Notæ, &c.* which I have added to the tranf-
" lation you are to do juft what you pleafe with. I wrote the notes in a great hurry
" this morning ; and if they are not fenfe, or too long, or too fhort, or too infignifi-
" cant, alter them to your tafte, or deftroy them, as you think beft."
* See thefe in the Preface to *Felton's* Differtations, p. xxi.

Y 2   " Tranflations

" Tranflations without a name the Editor is to be account-
" able for ; though he wifhes he had as good a title to the
" excellence of two or three of them, as he has to the im-
" perfections of the reft."

In 1742 he alfo printed Dr. *Mangey's* * edition of " *Phi-*
" *lonis Judæi* Opera quæ reperiri potuerunt," two volumes,
folio ; " The Life of lord Keeper *North*," 4to, (already
mentioned in p. 148); the Firft and Fifth Volumes of
Birch's edition of "*Thurloe's* State papers," folio (fee p. 116);
Heifter's " Surgery," 2 vols. 4to; " Liber *Jobi* in Verficulos
" metricè divifus, cum Verfione *Latinâ Alberti Schultens,*

* *Thomas Mangey,* M. A. chaplain at *Whitehall,* and fellow of *St. John's College,*
Cambridge [afterwards D. D. F.S.A. and rector of *St. Mildred's, Bread Street*] was
early diftinguifhed by his " Practical Difcourfes upon the Lord's Prayer, preached before
" the Honourable Society of *Lincolns Inn* ; publifhed by the fpecial order of the Bench,
" 1716," 8vo. Thefe Difcourfes were printed by Mr. *Bowyer,* as were alfo the fecond
and third editions, in 1717 and 1721 ; and in 1718 " Remarks upon *Nazarenus* ; where-
" in the Falfity of Mr. *Toland's Mahometan* Gofpel, and his Mifreprefentations of *Ma-*
" *hometan* fentiments in refpect of Chriftianity, are fet forth ; the Hiftory of the old *Na-*
" *zaræans* cleared up, and the whole conduct of the firft Chriftians in refpect of the
" *Jewifh* Laws explained and defcribed." The author then ftyled himfelf " Rector of
" *St. Nicholas's* in *Guilford.*" In *January* 1718-19, Mr. *Bowyer* printed for him "Plain
" Notions of our Lord's Divinity," a Sermon preached on *Chriftmas-day* ; in *June,* 1719,
" The eternal Exiftence of our Lord *Jefus Chrift,*" a Vifitation Sermon ; in *October* that
year, " The Holinefs of Chriftian Churches," a Sermon preached at *Sunderland,* on con-
fecrating a new church there ; and in 1719-20, " The providential Sufferings of good
" men," a 30th of *January* Sermon before the Houfe of Commons. In 1719 Dr. *Man-*
gey wrote " A Defence of the Bifhop of *London's* Letter," 8vo ; and, befides the Sermons
already mentioned, publifhed five fingle ones, in 1716, 1726, 1729, 1731, and 1733. On
the 11th of *May,* 1721, he was prefented to a prebend † [the fifth ftall] in the cathedral
church of *Durham,* being at that time ftyled " LL. D. chaplain to Dr. *Robinfon* Bifhop
" of *London,* and vicar of *Yealing,* in the county of *Middlefex.*" He was advanced to
the firft ftall of *Durham, Dec.* 22, 1722; and was one of the feven Doctors in Divinity
created *July* 6, 1725, when Dr. *Bentley* delivered the famous Oration prefixed to his
Terence ; and at the end of 1726 he circulated propofals for an edition of *Philo Judæus,*
which he completed as above-mentioned in 1742. He died *March* 11, 1754-5. His
MS. remarks on the New Teftament came into the poffeffion of Mr. *Bowyer,* who extracted from them many fhort notes, which are printed in his " Conjectures" under the
fignature of *Anonym.*

† Mr. *Granger,* in his account of Bifhop *Crew* (Biog. Hift. 8vo. vol. IV. p. 285.) fays, " He gave
" Dr. *Mangey* a prebend of *Durham* for a flattering dedication prefixed to a *Sermon,* which, as Dr.
" *Richard Grey,* then his domeftic chaplain, affured Mr. *George Afhby,* he never read. He was fully
" fatisfied with the dedication."

" Notifque

" Notifque ex ejus Commentario excerptis ; quotquot ad
" divinum planè Poema illuftrandum (quoad vel argumenti
" materiam & filum, vel fenfuum pathos & fublimitatem,
" vel ftyli copiam & elegantiam) neceffariæ videbantur.
" Edidit, atque Annotationes fuas ad metrum præcipuè
" fpectantes, adjecit *Ricardus Grey*, S. T. P. Accedit Canticum
" *Moyfis*, Deut. XXXII. cum Notis Variorum," 8vo ; *Hody**,
" De *Græcis* Illuftribus," 8vo ; a third edition of the firft
volume of " The Divine Legation," and a fecond edition of
the fecond volume †, the whole corrected and enlarged,
and the work announced in the title-page to be " In
" NINE BOOKS," 8vo ; " A Critical and Philofophical Com-
" mentary on Mr. *Pope's* Effay on Man ; in which is con-

* *Humphrey Hody* was defcended from an antient family in *Somerfetfhire*, and born
1659 at *Odcombe* in that county, of which his father was rector. He was admitted at
Wadham College 1676, and fellow there 1684; and when he was barely turned of 20,
wrote againft *Arifteas'* hiftory of the LXX Interpreters. He publifhed feveral polemical
tracts againft the Nonjurors and about the Convocation, and in 1674 a learned *Latin*
work on the Original text and *Greek* and *Latin* Vulgate verfions of the Bible. The
piece above-mentioned (containing an account of thofe learned *Grecians* who retired to
Italy before and after the taking of *Conftantinople* by the *Turks*, and reftored the *Greek*
tongue and learning in the Weft) remained in MS. till it was publifhed by Dr. *S. Jebb* in
this year 1742 (fee before, p. 81). Dr. *Hody* died *Jan.* 20, 1706, and was buried in
the chapel of his college, in which he founded ten fcholarfhips of ten pounds each, five
for the ftudy of the *Greek*, and five for that of the *Hebrew* languages. Dr. *Jebb* prefixed to this book memoirs of its author in *Latin* from an *Englifh* life by himfelf.

† To this was alfo annexed a fecond edition of the Appendix ** already mentioned,
with a P.S. in anfwer to the " Principles and Connexions of Natural and Revealed Re-
" ligion, by *Arthur Afhley Sykes*, D. D." and a Letter to Bifhop *Smalbroke*, on his
new printed " Charge to the Clergy, 1741."

** A fhort Advertifement prefixed to this Appendix preferves a curious anecdote : " The Author
" of the Pamphlet here examined hath lately made a public confeffion of his Authorfhip, figned with
" his own *Name*; and thereby faved himfelf from all farther correction of this kind. For he who is
" fo loft to fhame, as a WRITER, to own what he before wrote, and fo loft to fhame, as a MAN,
" to own what he hath now written, muft needs be paft all amendment, the only reafonable view
" in *correction*. I fhall therefore but do, what indeed (were it any more than repeating what he him-
" felf hath difcovered to the Public) would be juftly reckoned the crueleft of all things, tell my
" reader the name of this Miferable, which we find to be J. TILLARD." The gentleman fo feverely
handled here had been bred in the mercantile profeffion, with a ftrong tincture of literature. *John
Tillard*, efq. died at his houfe in *Great James Street, Bedford Row*, in *December* 1773. His fon
Richard, vicar of *South Leverton*, in the county of *Nottingham*, publifhed " Thoughts concerning
" the fafety and expediency of granting relief to the clergy in matter of fubfcription, occafioned by
" Mr. *Wollafton's* Addrefs, 1773," 8vo; and fome Tract relative to *Hume's* Hiftory, 8vo.

" tained

" tained a Vindication of the faid Effay from the Mifrepre-
" fentations of Mr. *De Refnel*, the *French* tranflator, and
" of Mr. *De Croufaz*, Profeffor of Philofophy and Mathe-
" maticks in the Academy of *Laufanne*, the Commentator,"
8vo; and the additional Book of the *Dunciad*, in 4to, very
highly to the fatisfaction both of the Poet and of his learned
Commentator. " I thank you for all your care," fays Mr.
Pope* on this occafion.—And Mr. *Warburton** tells him,
" I am glad you have been printing for Mr. *Pope*. Don't
" mention to any, I beg of you, your fufpicion about the
" notes. Mr. *Knapton* has fent me the fpecimen of the
" Commentary on the Effay, which I like extremely well.
" I thank you for your obfervation on the quotations from
" the *Optics*. You are certainly right; they fhould be in
" *Englifh*. I don't know when I fhall be in *London* again :
" But I have never more pleafure there than when I loll and
" talk to you at my eafe *de quolibet ente* in your dining-room.
" You don't tell me how you like my improvements of
" the Commentary. Thank you for your care of commif-
" fions. I am glad the *Dunciad* has fuch a run. The
" *Greek*, I know, will be well printed in your edition,
" *notwithftanding the abfence of* SCRIBLERUS."

This was neither the firft nor the ftrongeft expreffion of
the regard entertained for Mr. *Bowyer* by Mr. *Warburton* ;
who had long before told him, " No one's thoughts will
" have a greater weight with me than your own, in whom
" I have experienced fo much candour, goodnefs, and
" learning." It is not however to be concealed, that a difference afterwards arofe, in which, as is not uncommon,
each party was confident that he was right. Mr. *B.* (who
either was, or at leaft thought himfelf, flighted) has not

* In letters (ftill in MS.) dated 1742.

unfrequently

unfrequently remarked, that, after the death of our *English Homer**, the letters of his learned friend " wore a dif-
" ferent complexion." But perhaps this may be one of
the many inftances, which occur through life, of the im-
propriety of judging for ourfelves in cafes which affect our
intereft or our feelings.

In 1742, he alfo printed the " Senilia" of his old
friend Mr. *Maittaire* † ; and was Editor of the feventh volume

---

* Mr. *Pope* died *May* 30, 1744.

† This eminent fcholar was born in 1668. Dr. *South*, canon of *Chrift Church*, made
him a *canoneer* ** or ftudent of that houfe, where he took the degree of M. A. *March* 23,
1696. From 1695 till 1699 he was fecond mafter of *Weftminfter School*; which was afterwards indebted to him for " *Græcæ* Linguæ Dialecti, in ufum Scholæ *Weftmonafterienfis,*
" 1706," 8vo. (a work recommended in the warmeft terms by Dr. *Knipe* to the fchool
over which he prefided, " cui fe fua omnia debere fatetur fedulus Author") and for
" The *Englifh* Grammar, applied to, and exemplified in, the *Englifh* tongue, 1712,"
8vo. In " Catalogus Librorum Manufcriptorum *Angliæ* & *Hiberniæ*, Oxon. 1697,"
t. ii. p. 27. isinferted "Librorum Manufcriptorum Ecclefiæ *Weftmonafterienfis* Catalogus.
" Accurante viro erudito *Michaele Mattærio.*" But before the volume was publifhed,
the whole collection amounting to 230, given by Bifhop *Williams*, except one, was deftroyed by an accidental fire in 1694 (*Widmore's* " Hiftory of *Weftminfter Abbey,*'
p. 164). In 1711, he publifhed " Remarks on Mr. *Whifton's* Account of the Convoca-
" tion's Proceedings with relation to himfelf: in a Letter to the right reverend Father
" in God *George* Lord Bifhop of *Bath* and *Wells*," 8vo ; and alfo " An Effay againft
" Arianifm, and fome other Herefies ; or a Reply to Mr. *William Whifton's* Hiftorical
" Preface and Appendix to his Primitive Chriftianity revived." 8vo. In 1709 he gave
the firft fpecimen of his great fkill in typographical antiquities, by publifhing " *Stepha-*
" *norum* Hiftoria, vitas ipforum ac libros complectens," 8vo ; which was followed in
1717 by " Hiftoria Typographorum aliquot *Parifienfium*, vitas & libros complectens,"
8vo. In 1719, " Annales Typographici ab artis inventæ origine ad annum M D. *Hagæ*
" *Com.*" 4to. To this volume is prefixed, " Epiftolaris de antiquis *Quintiliani* editioni-
" bus Differtatio, clariffimo viro *D. Johanni Clerico.*" The fecond volume, divided into
two parts, and continued to the year MDXXXVI, was publifhed at *The Hague* in 1702 ; introduced by a letter of *John Toland*, under the title of " Conjectura verofimilis de prima
" Typographiæ Inventione." The third volume, from the fame prefs, in two parts, continued to MDLVII, and, by an Appendix, to MDCLXIV, in 1725. In 1733 was publifhed
at *Amfterdam* what is ufually confidered as the fourth volume, under the title of " An-
" nales Typographici ab artis inventæ origine, ad annum MDCLXIV, operâ *Mich. Mait-*
" *taire*, A. M. Editio nova, auctior & emendatior, tomi primi pars pofterior." The
aukwardnefs of this title has induced many collectors to difpofe of their firft volume,
as thinking it fuperfeded by the fecond edition ; but this is by no means the cafe ; the
volume of 1719 being equally neceffary to complete the fet as that of 1733, which is a

** Commonly fo called as being brought in by a canon, and not elected from *Weftminfter fchool.*

I   revifion

lume of Dr. *Swift's* Miscellanies; an Author with whose
writings he had long been peculiarly conversant; many of
the

revision of all the former volumes. In 1741 this excellent work was closed at *London*,
by " Annalium Typographicorum Tomus Quintus & ultimus; indicem in tomos quatuor
" præeuntes complectens;" divided (like the two preceding volumes) into two parts.
The whole work, therefore, when properly bound, consists either of five volumes, or of
nine; and in nine volumes it was properly described in the catalogue of Dr. *Askew*,
whose elegant copy was sold to Mr. *Shaftoe* for 10l. 5s. I have deviated from chronological order to place the " Annales Typographici" in one view.—In the intermediate
years, Mr. *Maittaire* was diligently employed on various works of value. In 1713 he
published by subscription " Opera & Fragmenta Veterum Poetarum, 1713," two handsome volumes in folio, inscribed to Prince *Eugene*. The title of some copies is dated 1721;
but I believe there was no new edition. In 1714, he was editor of the *Greek* Testament,
2 vols. The *Latin* writers, which he published separately, most of them with Indexes,
came out in the following order: In 1713, *Christus Patiens* * ; *Justin*; *Lucretius*; *Phæ-
drus*; *Sallust*; and *Terence*. In 1715, *Catullus, Tibullus*, and *Propertius*; *Cornelius
Nepos*; *Florus*; *Horace*; *Juvenal*; *Ovid*, 3 vols. and *Virgil*. In 1716, *Cæsar's* Commentaries; *Martial*; *Quintus Curtius*. In 1718 and 1725, *Velleius Paterculus*. In 1719,
Lucan. In 1720, *Bonefonii* Carmina. And here he appears to have stopped; all the other
classics which are ascribed to him having been thus disclaimed, by a memorandum which I
have under his own hand, in the latter part of his life: " As the Editor of several classics
" some years ago printed in 12mo. at Mess. *Tonson* and *Watts'* press, thinks it sufficient
" to be answerable for the imperfections of those editions, without being charged with
" the odium of claiming what has been put out by Editors much abler than himself;
" he therefore would acquaint the publick, that he had no hand in publishing the fol-
" lowing books, which in some news-papers have been advertised under his name; viz.
" *Sophoclis* Tragœdiæ; *Homerii* Ilias; Musarum *Anglicanarum* Analecta; *Livii* His-
" toria; *Plinii* Epistolæ & Panegyricus; Conciones & Orationes ex Historicis *Latinis*.
" M. M." In 1721 he published " Batrachomyomachia *Græcè* ad veterum exempla-
" rium fidem recusa: Glossâ *Græcâ*; variantibus lectionibus; versionibus *Latinis*; com-
" mentariis & indicibus illustrata †," 8vo. At the end of this volume he added proposals
for printing by subscription *Musæus* in *Greek* and *Latin*, for half a guinea; and *Rapin's
Latin* works, for a guinea, both in 4to; *Musæus* to be comprised in twelve sheets,
Rapin in fifty. But neither of these were ever committed to the press, from want probably of sufficient encouragement. In 1722, " Miscellanea *Græcorum* aliquot Scrip-
" torum Carmina, cum versione *Latina* & Notis," 4to. In 1724 he compiled, at
the request of Dr. *John Freind*, (at whose expence it was printed,) an index to the works
of *Aretæus*, to accompany the splendid folio edition of that author which appeared
from the *Clarendon* press in 1723. The index is introduced by a short *Latin* preface.
In 1725 he published an excellent edition of *Anacreon* in 4to, of which no more than
100 copies were printed, and the few errata in each copy corrected by his own hand.
A second edition of the like number was printed in 1741, with six copies on fine
writing-paper. In 1726 he published " *Petri Petiti* Medici *Parisiensis* in tres priores

* An heroic poem by *Renè Rapin*, a Jesuit; first printed in 1674.
† In this beautiful and accurate edition, which has been already mentioned in p. 17, the Editor
corrected the Errata with a pen in every copy. Two hundred and four copies only were printed. Of
these one hundred and ninety-five were subscribed for, at half a guinea in sheets; eight were
reserved by the Editor for himself; and only one single copy remained for public sale.

" *Aretæi*

the Dean's separate tracts having originally passed through his hands, and some of them having been illustrated by his Notes. The seventh volume is thus introduced: "The " following sheets have been collected and published to " gratify the wishes of all people of taste, who have not " been furnished with the *Dublin* edition of Dean *Swift's* " Works. That edition was corrected and revised, as his " printer Mr. *Faulkner* intimates, by some of the Author's

" *Aretæi Cappadocis* Libros Commentarii, nunc primum editi," 4to. This learned Commentary was found among the papers of *Grævius*. From 1728 to 1732 he was employed in publishing " Marmorum *Arundellianorum, Seldenianorum*, aliorumque Aca- " demiæ *Oxoniensi* donatorum, una cum Commentariis & Indice, editio secunda," folio ; to which an " Appendix" was printed in 1733, of which see before under those years. " Epistola *D. Mich. Maittaire* ad *D. P. Des Maizeaux* in qua Indicis in An- " nales Typographicos methodus explicatur," &c. is printed in " The Present State of the " Republick of Letters," *August* 1733, p. 142. The life of *Robert Stephens* in *Latin*, revised and corrected by the author, with a new and complete list of his works, is pre- fixed to the improved edition of *R. Stephens's Thesaurus*, 4 volumes in folio, 1734 In 1736 appeared " Antiquæ Inscriptiones duæ," folio; being a commentary on two large copper tables discovered near *Heraclea*, in the Bay of *Tarentum*, as before mentioned in p. 123. In 1738 were printed at *The Hague*, " *Græcæ* Linguæ Dialecti in Scholæ Regiæ " *Westmonasteriensis* usum recogniti operâ *Mich. Maittaire*. Præfationem & Appendi- " cem ex *Apollonii Dyscoli* fragmento inedito addidit *J. F. Reitzius.*" Mr. *Maittaire* prefixed a Dedication of this volume to the Marquis of *Granby*, and the Lords *Robert* and *George Manners*, his brothers; and a new Preface, dated 3 cal. *Octob.* 1737. This was again printed at *London* in 1742. In 1739 he addressed to the Empress of *Russia* a small *Latin* poem; under the title of " Carmen Epinicium Augustissimæ " *Russorum* Imperatrici sacrum." His name not having been printed in the title-page, it is not so generally known that he was editor of *Plutarch's* " Apophthegmata, " 1741," 4to. The last publication of Mr. *Maittaire* was a volume of poems in 4to, 1742, under the title of " Senilia*, sive Poetica aliquot in argumentis varii generis " tentamina." It may be worth mentioning, that Mr. *Baxter's* dedication to his " Glossarium Antiquitatum *Britannicarum*" was much altered by Mr. *Maittaire*. He died *August* 7, 1747, aged 79. There is a good mezzotinto print of him by *Faber*, from a painting by *B. Dandridge*, inscribed, " *Michael Maittaire*, A. M. Amico- " rum jussu." His valuable library, which had been 50 years collecting, was sold by auction by Mess. *Cock* and *Langford* at the close of the same year, and the be- ginning of the following, taking up in all 44 nights. Mr. *Cock*, in his prefatory ad- vertisement, tells us, " In exhibiting thus to the publick the entire library of Mr. *Mait-* " taire, I comply with the will of my deceased friend, and in printing the catalogue " from his own copy just as he left it (though, by so doing, it is the more voluminous), " I had an opportunity not only of doing the justice I owe to his memory, but also of " gratifying the curious." I scarcely need add that the printing of it was com- mitted to the care of Mr. *Bowyer*; but shall take this opportunity of observing, that the present mode of compiling catalogues of celebrated libraries for sale, so much more laconic than that which obtained about 40 years ago, except when Mr. *Samuel Paterson* exerts that talent of cataloguing for which he is particularly distinguished, cannot possibly do equal justice with the antient mode, either in a literary or pecuniary view.

* It is a well-known but ill-natured joke of Dr. *Mead*, that these were rather " Anilia."

Z " friends;

" friends; or (in another place, perhaps more truly) by
" the Author himſelf; an advantage, as that Editor rightly
" remarks, which the *London* Bookſellers could not have.
" To that *Dublin* edition we are obliged for the following
" volume, ſome tracts excepted; ſuch as *A Propoſal to Par-*
" *liament for preventing the Growth of Popery*;—*Free*
" *Thoughts on the State of Affairs*, 1714;—*Apology to Lady*
" *Carteret, for not dining with her Ladyſhip*, &c.—All
" which have been univerſally aſcribed to our Author,
" though the *Iriſh* Editor has thought proper, or been
" commanded, to omit them.   Many of the following
" tracts are political, and once made what is called *a noiſe*
" *in the world*; they were univerſally eſteemed, even by
" thoſe of the oppoſite party, particularly that of *The Con-*
" *duct of the Allies*, which will remain for ever a light into
" the affairs then tranſacting in *Europe*; an æra not the
" leaſt remarkable in hiſtory.   It muſt be acceptable to the
" poſſeſſors of *Gulliver's* Travels, to have an opportunity
" to correct the text by our compariſon of the *Dublin* edi-
" tion with thoſe of *London*, which is to be found at the
" end of this volume*.   It is ſurprizing, that any one
" could have been ſo ſtupid as to interpolate any produc-
" tion of this inimitable writer.   The papers written by
" our author in *The Examiner* (which commence at N° 13,
" and end at 44†) gave, at the time of publication, a ge-
" neral pleaſure or pain, ſatisfaction or diſquiet, as people
" were inclined.   A ſpirit of liberty diffuſes itſelf through all

---

* Under the title of " Some particular Paſſages in *Gulliver's* Travels, compared
" with the *Dublin* Editions."   This compariſon, which I believe is to be found only in
the edition here noticed, will be found very uſeful whenever a complete edition of
Swift's Works ſhall be preſented to the publick.

† This is a ſlight miſtake. *Swift's* Examiners have been wrong numbered in all the
editions of his works.   His firſt was publiſhed *Nov.* 2, 1710; and in the original editions is marked N° 14.   His laſt, the firſt part of N° 46, dated *June* 14, 1711, which
had been omitted in former editions, I have reſtored in the " Supplement to his Works."
The wrong numbering aroſe from Mr. *Barber's* having omitted the original N° 13
(a paper on *Non-reſiſtance*), when he collected the *Examiners* into a volume.

" his

" his writings, and proves him, as the *Dublin* Editor has it,
" *an enemy to tyranny and oppreſſion in any ſhape whatever*."
In 1743 Mr. *Bowyer* printed the firſt volume of " Dr.
" *Pococke's** Travels through the Eaſt," folio; the " State
" Papers

* Dr. *Richard Pococke* (who was diſtantly related to the learned Orientaliſt Dr. *Edward Pococke*, being ſon of Mr. *Richard Pococke*, ſequeſtrator of the church of *All Saints* in *Southampton*, and head maſter of the free-ſchool there, by the only daughter of the Rev. Mr. *Iſaac Milles*, miniſter of *Highclere* in *Hampſhire* †) was born at *Southampton* in 1704. He received his ſchool learning there, and his academical education at *Corpus Chriſti College, Oxford*; took his degree of LL.B. *May* 5, 1731; and that of LL. D. (being then precentor of *Liſmore*) *June* 28, 1733; together with Dr. *Secker*, then rector of *St. James's*, and afterwards archbiſhop of *Canterbury*. He began his Travels into the Eaſt in 1737, returned in 1742, and was made precentor of *Waterford* in 1744. In 1743, he publiſhed the firſt part of thoſe Travels, under the title of " A Deſcription of the Eaſt, and of ſome other Countries, vol. I. Obſervations on " *Egypt*." In 1745 he printed the ſecond volume under the ſame title, " Obſervations on " *Palæſtine* or the *Holy Land, Syria, Meſopotamia, Cyprus*, and *Candia*," which he dedicated to the Earl of *Cheſterfield*, then made lord lieutenant of *Ireland*; attended his lordſhip thither as one of his domeſtic chaplains, and was ſoon after appointed by his lordſhip Archdeacon of *Dublin*. In *March* 1756 he was promoted by the Duke of *Devonſhire* (then lord lieutenant) to the Biſhoprick of *Oſſory*, vacant by the death of Dr. *Edward Maurice*. He was tranſlated by the King's letter from *Oſſory* to *Elphin* in *June* 1765, Biſhop *Gore* of *Elphin* being then promoted to *Meath*; but Biſhop *Gore*, finding a great ſum was to be paid to his predeceſſor's executors for the houſe at *Ardbracean*, declined taking out his patent, and therefore Biſhop *Pococke* in *July* was tranſlated by the Duke of *Northumberland* directly to the ſee of *Meath*, and died in the month of *September* the ſame year, ſuddenly, of an apoplectic ſtroke, whilſt he was in the courſe of his viſitation ‡.—See an elogium of his Deſcription of *Egypt* in " *Pauli Erneſti Jab-* " *lonſki* Pantheon Ægyptiorum, Præfat. ad part iii." He penetrated no further up the *Nile* than to *Philæ*, now *Gieuret Ell Hicreff*, whereas Mr. *Norden* in 1737 went as far as *Derri*, between the two cataracts. The two travellers are ſuppoſed to have met on the *Nile*, in the neighbourhood of *Eſnay*, in *January* 1738. (*Norden's* Travels, *Engl.* Edit. 8vo. p. 188.) But the fact, as Dr. *Pococke* told ſome of his friends, was, that being on his return, not knowing that Mr. *Norden* was gone up, he paſſed by him in the night, without having the pleaſure of ſeeing him. There is an admirable whole length of the Biſhop, in a *Turkiſh* dreſs, painted by *Liotard*, in the poſſeſſion of Dr. *Milles* Dean of *Exeter*, his firſt couſin. He was a great traveller, and viſited other places beſides the Eaſt. His deſcription of a rock on the Weſt ſide of *Dunbar* harbour in *Scotland*, reſembling *The Giants Cauſeway*, is in Phil. Tranſ. vol. LII. art. 17; and in Archæologia, vol. II. p. 32, his account of ſome antiquities found in *Ireland*. " When travelling through *Scotland* [where he preached ſeveral times to crouded con- " gregations], he ſtopped at *Dingwal*, and ſaid he was much ſtruck and pleaſed with

† Of Mr. *Iſaac Milles's* three ſons, the eldeſt, *Thomas*, was appointed *Greek* profeſſor at *Oxford*, 1706, and biſhop of *Waterford* and *Liſmore* 1708, where he died 1740, leaving his fortune to his nephew the preſent Dean of *Exeter*. The ſecond, *Jeremiah*, was fellow and tutor of *Baliol College*, who preſented him 1705 to the rectory of *Dulnmar Loo*, in *Cornwall*. The third, *Iſaac*, was treaſurer of *Waterford* 1714, and treaſurer of *Liſmore* cathedral 1717.

‡ His collection of antiquities and foſſils was ſold by Meſſ. *Langford, June* 5 and 6, 1766. Among theſe was a ſingular petrified echinus, found in a chalk pit in *Bovingdon* pariſh, in *Hertfordſhire*. Sir *Thomas Fludyer* bought it for three guineas; Mr. *Seymour* offered five guineas for it at his ſale; Mr. *Foſter* ſix guineas; and it ſold for ten.

" its

" Papers of *Oliver Cromwell*" (fee p. 120), folio; " *Ælian*
" de Animalibus," 4to. (fee p. 138); " The Life of Sir
" *Dudley North*," 4to, (fee p. 152); and " The Dunciad"
both in 4to and 8vo.

In 1744 he printed " Notitia Monaftica; or, an Ac-
" count of all the Abbies, Priories, and Houfes of Friers,
" heretofore in *England* and *Wales*; and alfo of all the
" Colleges and Hofpitals founded before A.D. MDXI. By
" the Right Reverend Doctor *Thomas Tanner**, late Lord
" Bifhop of *St. Afaph*. Publifhed by *John Tanner*, A.M.
" Vicar of *Loweftoft* in *Suffolk*, and Precentor of the Cathe-
" dral Church of *St. Afaph*," folio; " A Critical Commen-
" tary upon the Book of the Wifdom of *Solomon*, being a
" Continuation of Bifhop *Patrick* and Mr. *Lowth*; by
" *Richard Arnald†*, B.D." folio; two editions of " The
" Effay on Man," with the Commentary; " Remarks
" on feveral Occafional Reflections, in Anfwer to the

" its appearance; for the fituation of it brought *Jerufalem* to his remembrance, and he
" pointed out the hill which refembled *Calvary*." (*Cordiner's Letters on the North of*
Scotland, p. 64.) The fame fimilitude was obferved by him in regard to *Dartmouth*. He
preached a fermon in 1761 for the benefit of the *Magdalen* charity in *London*, and one
in 1762 before the Incorporated Society in *Dublin*, for promoting *Englifh* Proteftant
Working Schools in *Ireland*, both which were printed.

* See an account of Bifhop *Tanner* above, p. 103; where, l. 5, r. " chofen Fellow of
" the fame;" l. 7, " Archdeacon of *Norfolk*;" l. 13, " *Dec.* 14." This volume
was publifhed by *John Whifton*, *John Ofborn*, and *Francis Changuion*, the three bookfellers with whom the laft contract of the Society for the encouragement of learning
was made. See p. 138. The original plates belonging to this work are in the poffeffion
of the Rev. Dr. *Tanner*, prebendary of *Canterbury*, the fon of Bifhop *Tanner*. Mr.
Thomas Evans, bookfeller, in the *Strand*, has lately circulated propofals for a new edition
of it, but with what improvements does not appear. Our modern publifhers judge of
the value of books by their arbitrary price, and have been mifled, to their coft, to reprint
fome books, whofe whole merit is their fcarcity. This is by no means, however, the
cafe with the " Notitia Monaftica;" which is as valuable as it is fcarce, and, if reprinted with fuch improvements as it is in the power of feveral gentlemen to beftow on
it, would be an acceptable prefent to the publick. The Bifhop's portrait prefixed to
the " Notitia," is infcribed, " Reverendus admodum *Thomas Tanner*, *Afaphenfis*
" Epifcopus, Primævæ Antiquitatis Cultor. *G. Vertue fculp.* 1743." This print was
a copy of a larger, engraved 1736 by *Vertue*, at the expence of the Society of Antiquaries, with fome difference in the decoration, and this addition to the infcription:
" Hoc ectypum fratris fui digniffimi antiquis moribus ornati pofteris facratum effe voluit
" Soc. Ant. *Lond.* 1736."

† Of whom, fee under the year 1760.

4   " Rev.

" Rev. Dr. *Middleton*, Dr. *Pococke**, the Master of the
" *Charter-House†*, Dr. *Richard Grey*, and others; serving
" to explain and justify divers Passages in The Divine Lega-
" tion, objected to by those Learned Writers. To which is
" added, A General Review of the Argument of The Divine
" Legation, as far as it is yet advanced: wherein is consi-
" dered the Relation the several Parts bear to each other
" and the Whole. Together with an Appendix, in An-
" swer to a late Pamphlet‡, intituled, An Examination of Mr.
" *Warburton's* Second Proposition," 8vo; " Observations
" on the present Collection of Epistles between *Cicero* and
" *M. Brutus*, representing several evident marks of Forgery
" in those Epistles; and the true state of many important
" Particulars in the Life and Writings of *Cicero*: in An-
" swer to the late pretences of the Reverend Dr. *Conyers*
" *Middleton*. By *James Tunstall§*, B. D. Fellow of *St. John's*
" *College*, and Orator of the University of *Cambridge*. To
" which is added, a Letter from the Reverend Dr. *Chapman*
" on the antient Numeral Characters of the *Roman* Le-
" gions ||," 8vo; Mr. *Carte's* Account of his " Collection of
" Papers;"

* Whose account of hieroglyphics, and the relation they had to language, given in his Observations on *Egypt*, differed from what had been said about them in *The Divine Legation*.

† *Nicholas Man*, esq. ‡ By Dr. *Stebbing*. § Of whom, see under the year 1765.
|| To the 65th page of this work, the following unpublished letter from Mr. *Markland* to Mr. *Bowyer*, dated *June* 30, 1743, has reference: " When I had read yours,
" I looked for the foul copy (which I had accidentally kept) of that letter which I had
" written to Dr. *Chapman*, concerning the First Epistle of *Cicero* to *Brutus*. In my
" copy, instead of, *which was the case of C. Octavius, whom we commonly call Augustus*,
" I find, *which was Augustus's case*. Whether I altered it myself in the transcribing,
" or Mr. *T.* has done it for me, I cannot say, and it is no great matter; however
" it is more full and clear as it is printed. By your questions I perceive that you have
" not a perfect and distinct notion of this matter, and therefore, since you desire it, will
" endeavour to explain it to you; though I did not imagine that it would want any
" explanation, for indeed there is no difficulty in it either way, if a man has but the
" necessary *præcognita*, which I took for granted all scholars have. You know that the
" name of him whom we commonly call *Augustus*, was originally *Caius Octavius Thu-*
" *rinus*. The first was the *Prænomen*; the second, the *Nomen*, or *Gentile*, or name of
" the *family*; the third, the *Cognomen*, as was usual. Thus it stood till towards
" the 19th year of his age; when his uncle C. *Julius Cæsar* dying, appointed him his
" heir,

"Papers;" Mr. *Edwards's* "Letter to the Author of a late
"Epistolary Differtation, addreffed to Dr. *Warburton*," 8vo;
Dr.

"heir, and at the fame time ordered him to change his name, and to pafs out of the
"Octavian into the *Julian* family. Some of his friends (efpecially his father-in-law
"L. *Philippus*, who had married the widow his mother) thinking that he had not in-
"tereft and power enough to come at what *Cæfar* had left him, which was fallen into
"the hands of *M. Antony* chiefly, advifed him to be quiet, and not to take upon him
"the name of *Cæfar*. This deliberation took up (N. B.) fome time; but at laft *Octa-*
"*vius* determined to ftrike a bold ftroke, and to demand his inheritance, and to change
"his name, which he did with the accuftomed legal forms; and then, inftead of *C.*
"*Octavius Thurinus*, his name was *C. Julius Cæfar*, with the ufual addition of *Octa-*
"*vianus* to fhew that he came out of the family of the *Octavii*. Several years after,
"when he was fettled in the poffeffion of the empire, and had done great fervice to the
"ftate, the fenate refolved to compliment him with fome new title of honour; and after
"much confultation they agreed upon that of *Auguftus*; fo that then he was, *C. Julius*
"*Cæfar Octavianus Auguftus*. You now fee that the title (for it was no more) of
"*Auguftus* had nothing to do with the name of *Octavius*; and that if it be put as you
"would have it *, ' which was the cafe of *Auguftus* whom we commonly call *Octavius*,'
"it would have been unintelligible, and without argument. As to the feveral paffages
"from *Cicero*, wherein you fay he is called *Octavius*, look at them, and you will find
"every one of them written in the intermediate time (which was the reafon why I put
"in the N. B. above) between the death of *Julius Cæfar* and *Octavius's* changing his
"name, which was fome months; after which, you will find that *Cicero* from that
"time never calls him *Octavius*, but either *C. Cæfar*, or *Cæfar*, or *Octavianus*;
"which laft word you muft underftand is a noun adjective, and fignifies, belonging to
"the *Octavii*; that is, who was originally of the *Gens* or *Family* of the *Octavii*. This
"was always the cuftom in adoptions, to add the *Gentile* of their own family to that
"into which they paffed. So the famous *L. Aemilius Paullus*, who conquered *Perfes*
"king of *Macedonia*, gave one of his fons, *P. Aemilius Paullus*, to be adopted by one
"of the *Scipio's*, that is, into the *Cornelian* family: after which the young man, in-
"ftead of *P. Aemilius Paullus*, was called *P. Cornelius Scipio Aemilianus*. This was
"he who afterwards finally demolifhed *Carthage* in the third Punick war, in which you
"often meet with him by the name of *Scipio Aemilianus*. Thus if *M. Tullius Cicero*
"had adopted *Cn. Pompeius Magnus*, this latter would have been called *Cn. Tullius*
"*Cicero Pompeianus*; as, on the other hand, if *Pompey* had adopted *Cicero*, *Cicero*
"would have been *M. Pompeius Magnus Tullianus*. This is the original of moft of
"the proper names that end in *anus*, which are almoft as numerous as the family ones
"which end fimply in *us*; the reafon of which is evident, becaufe there was fcarce any
"family which had not, fome time or other, adoptions made out of it into fome other
"family; and then he who before was by family a *Calpurnius*, or *Titius*, or *Sempro-*
"*nius*, &c. became a *Calpurnianus*, *Titianus*, or *Sempronianus*. And now you per-
"ceive why *Lucilius Clodius* cannot fubfift in the fame perfon, viz. becaufe both *Luci-*
"*lius* and *Clodius* (or *Claudius*) are *Gentilia*, or the names of families; for if this *L.*
"*Clodius Marcellus*, whom I was fpeaking of in that letter, had been adopted into the
"*Lucilian* family, his name would have been from that time *L. Lucilius*, fomething
"(fuppofe *Longus*, or any other cognomen belonging to the *Lucilii*) *Clodianus*, not
"*Clodius*. You likewife perceive that you fpeak inaccurately (though Dr. *Middleton* I
"find does it, and fo do fome of the modern antients, if one may fo call them, *Florus*

* It ftands thus in Dr. *Chapman's* "Obfervations," p. 65.

"and

Dr. *Grey's* " Anſwer to Mr. *Warburton's* Remarks on ſe-
" veral Occaſional Reflections, ſo far as they concern the
" Preface to a late Edition of the Book of *Job*; in which the
" Subject and Deſign of that Divine Poem are ſet in a full
" and clear Light, and ſome particular Paſſages in it oc-
" caſionally explained, in a Letter to the Reverend Author
" of the Remarks."

Mr. *Markland*, in a letter dated *April* 17, 1744, tells
Mr. *Bowyer*, " Mr. *Clarke* ſent me Mr. *Taylor's* preſent*;
" wherein I did not expect to meet with any notes under
" my own name; and *your pamphlet*, in which I think I
" clearly ſee ſeveral things that are certainly the Biſhop's,
" and

" and *Appian*; but none of the more ſkilfull ones) when you call *Auguſtus*, *Octavius*
" *Auguſtus*; which is as if you ſhould call Sir *Robert Walpole*, Sir *Walpole Orford*;
" for while he was *Octavius*, he was not *Auguſtus*, nor till ſeveral years afterwards;
" and when he was *Auguſtus*, it would have been more than an affront to have called
" him *Octavius*, and nobody ever did do it, becauſe it would have been a kind of
" petty treaſon, and a verbal denial of his right to the name and inheritance of his
" uncle *Julius Cæſar*; and therefore the ſophiſt who forged theſe letters under the name
" of *Brutus* to *Cicero*, in the famous Epiſtle, the 22d, never calls him any thing but
" *Octavius*; or if he calls him *Cæſar* (as he does once), he does it in a ſneer, and
" adds the word *tuus* to it, YOUR *Cæſar*, p. 172. This is right, and conſiſtent with
" the character of *Brutus*. But alas! he could not go through with it; for p. 76, he
" forgets himſelf, and calls him ſimply *Cæſar*, which the true *Brutus* would have
" loſt his life ſooner than have done, had he once taken it into his head that it was
" wrong. But this by the bye. Now pleaſe to read over that part of the ſheet, and
" tell me whether it be clear to you."

* Probably the " Marmor Sandvicenſe."—Mr. *Clarke*, in a letter without date, but
written about the ſame time, ſays, " I thank you for the anſwer to the *Trial*, &c.
" which I had not ſeen, and have given to Mr. *Markland* according to your direction. I
" have had the pleaſure of ſeeing him twice, and ſhould doat upon him, if it was not
" for two things, *i.e.* I could wiſh he had a little better ſpirits, and would not walk ſo
" violently in queſt of them, which I am ſure is not the way to find them. I wiſh this
" for my own ſake as well as his, and I muſt teach him to ride, that I may have more
" of his company. He tells me the pamphlet is Mr. *Moſs's*; it is well done; he pre-
" ſerves, what I thought was ſcarce poſſible, the dignity of the ſubject in anſwering
" ſuch a trifler. I ſee your friend Mr. *Warburton* is ſtill a hero; he makes nothing
" of attacking whole battalions alone: though he gives me the moſt pleaſure of any body,
" I cannot but ſay I am in pain for him. Is there no keeping that fire and genius
" within proper limits? He will fall, as great men have done before him, by the
" things he deſpiſed moſt, Dr. *Sykes*, and the people. The Doctor has outdone him-
" ſelf, and I am perſuaded that he is right in his three firſt poſitions, The Exoteric
" Doctrines, The Senſe of the old Legiſlation, and the *Jewiſh* Theocracy; and I long

" la.

" and feveral that are certainly not fo. He has fent me
" likewife Mr. *Warburton's* anfwer to his opponents, and
" Dr. *Sykes's* Examination, &c. the former of which feems
" to me to have been publifhed chiefly with the defign of
" giving the General Review of the Argument of the Di-
" vine Legation, which is an ufeful thing ; and the latter
" (Dr. *Sykes's*) feems to be a fly one. I fhall be glad to fee
" an anfwer, a direct one, to fome parts of it." This pamphlet was probably *Bifhop Berkeley's on Tar Water*, which was
firft publifhed in *England* at the very time Mr. *Markland* dates
his letter. It was publifhed by *M. Cooper* ; but the fcheme
of reprinting it from the *Dublin* edition was Mr. *Bowyer's*,
and confequently it was no unufual expreffion to call it
his pamphlet. Mr. *Markland's* obfervation exactly fuits
Bifhop *Berkeley's* pamphlet, and could not well apply to
any original compofition of Mr. *Bowyer's*. Accordingly
too we find Mr. *Clarke* a year after faying, upon Mr.
Bowyer's publifhing *Julian*, " that it would not anfwer his
" purpofe fo well as *Tar-water* ;" which in fact he had frequently occafion to reprint. He is fuppofed to have written
a fmall pamphlet that year on " the prefent ftate of *Europe* ;"
taken principally from *Pufendorff*.

In 1745, he printed 250 copies of " Acts and Obferva-
" tions of the *Spalding* Gentlemen's Society in *Lincolnfhire*,
" illuftrated with Sculptures from Models, Drawings, and
" Sketches, made by the Members, and engraved by *George*
" *Vertue* a Member. With an Allegorical Device defigned

" to fee how the author of The Divine Legation will difengage himfelf, though I
" expect he fhould beat up his quarters, and bear down all before him. I wonder none
" of them turn his arguments from *Arthur* and *William* the Conqueror againft him ;
" they are certainly decifive, and prove the actions afcribed to *Ofiris* to be all imagi-
" nary ; for *Arthur's* are undoubtedly fo, and his hiftorian (as in the cafe of *Sefoftris*)
" had nothing fo ftriking to afcribe to him as what was borrowed from the Conqueror."

" by

" by *Maurice Johnson*[*], efq. and engraved by *Vertue*, 1746.
" *London*, printed by order of the Society by *William*
" *Bowyer* a Member, 1745," folio, intended as a title-
page to such of their minutes as might be printed; the se-
cond volume of " Dr. *Pococke's* Travels to the East," folio;
" A Table of *English* Silver Coins from the *Norman* Con-
" queſt to the preſent time, with their Weights, intrinſic
" Values, and ſome Remarks upon the ſeveral pieces. By
" *Martin Folkes*[†], eſq." 4to; and a new edition of the
" Table

---

* Of whom, ſee p. 98.—Two letters from Mr. *Johnſon*, one to Mr. *New* relating to
the Regiſters of the Biſhops of *Lincoln*, the other to Mr. *Bogdani* concerning an extraordinary interment in *Lincoln* cathedral, are in the firſt volume of the Archæologia,
p. 30, 31.—" Mr. *Johnſon's* death was announced in the provincial papers, with
" this remarkable paragraph, That he had endeavoured to *raiſe* a vaſt ſpirit of
" inquiry and knowledge, (or ſomewhat tantamount) in that *flat* country—as if it
" was much harder to *raiſe* knowledge in *Holland*, than *Switzerland*; but it ſeems
" to be an idea impreſſed on the minds of the natives, as I know that two of his Ma-
" jeſty's Juſtices of the Peace quarrelling, the one ſaid to the other, You muſt not
" think, in this *flat* country, to ſet yourſelf *above* every body elſe.—When Mr. *Johnſon*
" brought his ſon to be admitted at *St. John's College, Cambridge*, in *October* 1740, he was
" ſhewn the Public Library by Dr. *Taylor* himſelf, and among the reſt the *Paris* Bible of
" 1476, in which the date had been artfully altered to 1464, without having occaſioned
" any doubt. See *Clement*, Biblioth. Curieuſe[‖]. Mr. *Johnſon*, who to the abilities of a
" ſcholar and an antiquary joined the *coup d'œil* of a man of buſineſs, immediately
" cried out, A rank and palpable forgery! and from that moment Dr. *Taylor*, or any
" body elſe, never had the leaſt doubt, or could have; and ever ſince that time the two
" editions have lain together (I don't ſay they did not before, though the library was
" not in order, or opened till afterwards), and the Under Librarian now regularly tells
" the ſtory to all viſitors." *Dr. Taylor's* Friend.

† *Martin Folkes*, eſq. (ſon of *Martin Folkes*, eſq. bencher of *Grays Inn*, and *Dorothy* ſecond daughter[‡] and coheireſs of Sir *William Hovell*, knt. of *Hillington Hall* in
the county of *Norfolk*,) was born in the pariſh of *St. Giles in the Fields*, in the city of
Weſtminſter, *October* 29, 1690. He laid the foundation of that learning which rendered
him ſo conſpicuous in the republic of letters at *Clare Hall*, in the Univerſity of *Cambridge*,
where he was placed under the tuition of that eminent mathematician Dr. *Laughton*.
On the 29th of *July* 1714, he was elected a member of the Royal Society, and, about
eight years after, Vice-preſident of that learned body. Nor were theſe honours unjuſtly
beſtowed; for Mr. *Folkes* was not only himſelf indefatigable in obſerving the ſecret
operations and aſtoniſhing objects of nature, but alſo ſtudious to excite the ſame vi-
gilance in others. In 1723, ſoon after the death of that ſagacious obſerver of the minute
creation, the great *Anthony Van Leeuwenhoek*, who, after having been a valuable corre-

‖ See alſo *Maittaire*, Annales Typogr. t. V. par. ii. p. 565; and Origin of Printing, p. 106. 170. 276.
‡ *Clementia*, the eldeſt daughter, was married, firſt, to *Charles Stuart*, eſq. grandfather of the
preſent Sir *Simeon*; and, ſecondly, to Sir *Thomas Montgomery*. The youngeſt daughter, *Etheldreda*,
was married to Archbiſhop *Wake*. See *Blomefield's Norfolk*, vol. IV. p. 566.

A a   ſpondent.

" Table of Gold Coins," &c. (see p. 95;) " Remarks"
" on

spondent to the Royal Society above fifty years, bequeathed to them his cabinet of
microscopes, Mr. *Folkes* gave an account of that valuable legacy, inserted in the
Philosophical Transactions, N° 380, p. 446, and in the Abridgement by *Eames*
and *Martyn*, vol. VI. p. 129. Dr. *Jurin*, who in 1728 inscribed the thirty-fourth volume
of the " Philosophical Transactions" to Mr. *Folkes*, declares to him, " the motive of
" my doing so was the same, which induced the greatest man that ever lived, to single
" you out to fill his chair, and to preside in the assemblies of the Royal Society, when
" the frequent returns of his indisposition would no longer permit him to attend them
" with his usual assiduity. The motive, Sir, we all know, was your uncommon love
" to, and your singular attainments in, those noble and manly sciences, to which the
" glory of Sir *Isaac Newton*, and the reputation of the Royal Society, is solely
" and entirely owing." He was elected President of the Royal Society *November*
30, 1741; and, in the year 1742, a member of the Royal Academy of Sciences in *Paris*, in the room of the celebrated Dr. *Halley*. In the year 1746, he
was created Doctor of Laws by the University of *Oxford*; and, on the death of *Algernon*
Duke of *Somerset*, 1749-50, was chosen President of the Society of Antiquaries; who
having obtained a charter in 1751, he was confirmed President, conformably to that
instrument. But he did not long enjoy these honours; for, about the latter end of the
same year 1751, he was struck with a palsy, of which he never recovered; and, finding
his indisposition continually increase, he resigned his office as President of the Royal Society on *November* 30, 1753, but continued President of the Society of Antiquaries till
his death. On the 25th of *June*, 1754, he had a second paralytic stroke, and never
spoke afterwards, but died on the 28th of the same month; and was buried near his
father and mother in the chancel of *Hillington* church, under a black marble slab, with
no inscription but his name and the date, pursuant to the express direction of his last
will, dated in *September* 1751, by which (his only son *Martin* * having been dead many
years) he bequeathed to his wife *Lucretia* † (who had unhappily been for some time confined at *Chelsea*) four hundred pounds a year for life, in lieu of dower; to each of his
daughters twelve thousand pounds; to *Dorothy Rishton*, the eldest of them (who had
three children), his own portrait by *Gibson*, and one of herself in crayons by
Knapton; to *Lucretia* ‡ the youngest, his plate, pictures, busts, medals, coins ancient
and modern, and his valuable library. This lady was also appointed executrix and his
brother Mr. *William Folkes* ‖ executor of the will; by which he gave likewise an hundred
pounds to be laid out in rings for his friends; and two hundred pounds to the Royal So-

* He was admitted of *Clare Hall*; accompanied his father and mother to *Rome*, where he discovered
a most extraordinary taste for medallic knowledge; and went afterwards to finish his studies at an academy at *Caen* in *Normandy*, where he was thrown from his horse and killed on the spot.

† This lady appeared, under the name of Mrs. *Bradshaw*, at the theatre in *The Haymarket*, in 1707;
and at *Drury Lane* from 1710 to 1712, soon after which period she was married to Mr. *Folkes*. The
author of " The History of the *English* Stage, 1741," who calls her " one of the greatest and most
" promising genii of her time," says she was taken off the stage by Mr. *Folkes* " for her exemplary and
" prudent conduct;" and that " it was a rule with her, in her profession, to make herself mistress of
" her part, and leave the *figure* and *action* to Nature." From the characters in which I find her
name **, she must have been a handsome woman at least, had a good figure, and probably only second-
rate theatrical talents.

‡ Married in *May* 1756 to *Richard Betenson*, esq. (now Sir *Richard*). She died *June* 6, 1758,
aged 36. See her monument, in *Wrotham* church, in *Thorpe's* " Registrum Roffense," p. 832.

‖ This gentleman, who was a counsellor at law, and agent to the Duke of *Montague* in *Lancashire*,
married to his second wife a daughter of Sir *William Browne*, knt. whose estate is at present enjoyed
by his son, Sir *Martin Browne Folkes*, bart.

** *Sylvia*, in " The Double Gallant;" *Corinna*, in " The Confederacy;" *Arabella Zeal*, in " The Fair
" Quaker;" *Derinda*, in " The Stratagem;" *Arabella*, in " The *London* Cuckolds;" *Angelica*, in " The Con-
" stant Couple;" &c. &c. To " The Generous Husband" she spoke a prologue (about 1712) in boys cloaths.

ciety,

ciety, with his large cornelian ſeal ring, on which are engraved their arms, for the perpetual uſe of the Preſident. He alſo bequeathed to that learned body an original portrait of lord *Bacon*. It has been thought ſomewhat ſingular, that this gentleman, who at the time of his death was Preſident of the Society of Antiquaries, ſhould leave them not the ſmalleſt token of his regard. Mr. *Folkes* was a man of great modeſty, affability, and integrity; a friend to merit, and an ornament to literature. His capital work was his " View of the *Engliſh* gold and ſilver " coinage," which he meditated ſo early as 1731. In 1736 (ſee p. 95) he publiſhed a ſheet and a half, intituled " A Table of *Engliſh* Gold Coins," &c. This makes table XXXVIII. of the firſt volume of the Society's " Vetuſta Monumenta," and was reprinted by them in 1736 in eight pages 4to *. and 1767 in their book of coins. Mr. *Folkes* had himſelf reprinted it with ſome additions in 1745, and there was annexed to it a larger and more conſiderable work by him, intituled, " A Table of *Engliſh* Silver Coins from the " *Norman* Conqueſt to the preſent time, with their weights, intrinſic values, and " ſome remarks upon the ſeveral pieces. *London*, printed for the Society of Antiquaries," 4to. This alſo they reprinted 1763 in their work before-mentioned. In order further to illuſtrate his deſign, Mr. *Folkes* engraved 42 plates, containing near 480 coins, but not intirely filled up, and in 1745 exhibited it to the Society of Antiquaries. They then reſolved to complete it, and Mr. *Folkes* furniſhed the plan of plates, and letter-preſs for 50, offering his aſſiſtance, and to make up his own plates, and give them to the Society. Upon his death, they purchaſed his 44 plates and copy for 120l. the mere coſt of engraving! and Mr. *William Folkes* gave them ſome of his brother's MS. papers. Thus was Mr. *Folkes's* valuable deſign carried into execution by this learned Body, by republiſhing at their own expence his tables and plates, with explanations, in 4to. 1763. Many coins were added to his plates. Twenty additional plates were engraved, containing no leſs than 700 coins, including many not known to Mr. *Folkes*, together with ſix ſupplemental ones, conſiſting of coins omitted in their proper place; and as others have occurred ſince, the Society have it in contemplation ſtill to augment them. The coin of *Euſtace*, pl. I. fig. 2, engraved anew from the original in Dr. *Hunter's* cabinet, in Arch. vol. V. p. 481, is one proof of many that might be adduced of the inaccuracy with which this valuable deſign was conducted. As Mr. *Folkes's* book publiſhed in 1745 (excepting only an appendix containing the coins ſtruck in *Scotland* between the acceſſion of *James* I. and the union under queen *Anne)* related wholly to the Hiſtory of the *Engliſh* Mint, the Society ſubjoined a particular deſcription of the ſeveral coins, their weights, legends, &c. by Dr. *John Ward*, then director, who drew up great part of the letter-preſs for Mr. *Folkes*, and on his demiſe by Dr. *Andrew Gifford*. This new edition of both his pieces was completed from his corrected copy of his own edition, to which copy Profeſſor *Ward*, Dr. *Gifford*, Dr. *Ducarel*, and Mr. *Colebrook*, had in 1756 largely contributed their obſervations. Upon the deceaſe of Profeſſor *Ward*, the conduct of the new edition devolved on his coadjutor Dr. *Gifford*. The plates were begun to be completed by *James Green*, who had before been appointed engraver to the Society †, and on his reſignation of that office, on account of ill health, ſome of them were given to *Wood* the engraver. At length, at the deſire of the editor, the execution of the whole engraving was committed to *Francis Perry* (of whom ſee Brit. Top. vol. I. p. 164), who

---

* The full title was, " A Table of *Engliſh* Gold Coins, from the eighteenth year of King *Ed-*
" *ward* III. when gold was firſt coined in *England*, with their ſeveral weights and preſent intrinſic
" values. By *Martin Folkes*, eſq. *London*, printed for the Society of Antiquaries, 1736," 4to.

† For whom he executed only the ſeal of *Chriſt Church, Canterbury*, which had been imperfectly done by Mr. *Vertue* juſt before his death, and the old mantle-piece at *Walden*, in one plate. Mr. *Green* died in 1758, and was ſucceeded as engraver to the Society by Mr. *James Baſire*, whoſe *burin* will do credit to every individual or body of men who employ it.

finiſhed

"*Cicero:* In a Letter to a Friend. With a Differtation
" upon

finifhed his work in 1758, and received for it 39*l.* 11*s.* The explanations fubjoined, and the improved copy of Mr. *Folkes's* work, were not put to prefs till 1761, in which year the firft 15 fheets were printed in 14 weeks †. But unexpected delays arifing on the part of the conductor, the next 14 fheets took up 39 weeks to print; and the new edition was not publifhed till 1763, under the title of " Tables of *Englifh* Silver " and Gold Coins: firft publifhed by *Martin Folkes,* efq. and now reprinted, with " Plates and Explanations, by the Society of Antiquaries, *London,* 1763," 4to. The advertifement in two pages was drawn up by Dr. *Taylor,* then director. The fupplement in 40 pages, with a poftfcript of four more and fix plates, were by Dr. *Gifford.* During a long interval between the commencement and completion of this great work, the public was furprized, and the Society more fo, by the appearance of 44 plates of *Englifh* filver coins, engraved by *Francis Perry* above-mentioned, publifhed by the late Mr. *Thomas Snelling,* evidently copied from the Society's plates, though not continued beyond *Cromwell's* protectorate. Mr. *Folkes's* account of the ftandard measures preferved in the capitol at *Rome* is printed in the Phil. Tranf. N° 442. His obfervations on the *Trajan* and *Antonine* pillars at *Rome* (which he vifited with his lady) were read before the Society of Antiquaries, *Feb.* 5, 1735-6, and printed in their Archæologia, vol. I. p. 117. And in the fame volume, p. 122, are his obfervations on the brafs equeftrian ftatue at *Rome,* occafioned by a fmall brafs model of it found near *London;* which were read before the Society, *April* 7, 1736. He fhewed them the fame year a caft of the *Farnefe* fphere on the back of *Atlas,* fuppofed to be the moft exact reprefentation of it in antiquity. The colure paffes through thofe parts of the afterifms by which it is faid to have paffed in the days of *Hipparchus;* but the interfection of the equator and ecliptic is not at the colure, but at fome diftance, whence *Bianchini,* who intended a differtation on it, refers it to the time of the *Antonines.* The figures all turn their backs, becaufe the ancients fuppofed the conftellations looked on the earth, and fo they would appear to do, if viewed from without the ftarry fphere; and *Ptolemy,* defcribing their appearance on a celeftial globe, places them on the backs of the figures, which was not rightly underftood by fome moderns. A portrait of Mr. *Folkes* was painted in 1736 by *Vanderbank,* and the following year feraped in mezzotinto by *Faber;* again in 1741 by *Hogarth,* from which *Faber* alfo fcraped a mezzotinto plate in 1742; a third time by *Hudfon,* from which there is a mezzotinto print by *M'Ardell,* with the title of " Prefident of the Royal Society." *James Anthony Daffier* ftruck a medal of him in 1740, and two years after another was ftruck at *Rome.* The fale of his library in 1756 lafted forty-one days; his prints and drawings, eight; mathematical inftruments, gems, pictures, bufts, urns, &c. two; coins and medals, five. Mr. *Folkes* had, amongft other curiofities, two editions of *Pliny's* Natural Hiftory, printed at *Venice,* one by *Spire* ‡, 1469, and the other by *Jenfon,* 1472. Dr. *Afkew* bought them both, the former for eleven guineas, and the latter for feven guineas and a half; on the Doctor's deceafe they were again fold, the edition of 1469 (now in *The Britifh Mufeum*) for 43*l.* and the other for 23*l* ‖. Among the literati patronized by Mr. *Folkes,* was Mr. *Norden,* the celebrated *Danifh* traveller, whofe firft account of his travels to the public was a Letter addreffed to the Royal Society, giving an account of the ruins and coloffal ftatues at *Thebes* in *Egypt,* with drawings, 1742, 4to. afterwards incorporated into his fecond volume in folio. I the rather mention this learned foreigner here, becaufe his fubject is fo intimately connected with the preceding note.

† As was exactly ftated by Mr. *Bowyer,* in his letter to the Council, in *March* 1762, in anfwer to a charge of unneceffary delay brought againft him.

‡ This edition is fuppofed to have efcaped the obfervation of F. *Harduin.* See fome remarkable particulars of it in " The Origin of Printing," p. 45. 103.

‖ Mr. *Granger,* in his Biographical Hiftory of *England,* vol. IV. p. 325, obferves from *Ames's* Typographical Antiquities, that a copy of the " Spaccio della Beftia trionfante," by *Giordano Bruno*

(fee

" upon four Orations* afcribed to *M. Tullius Cicero*, viz.

" I. Ad

* Thefe Remarks were originally addreffed to Mr. *Bowyer* by his learned friend; from whofe Letters on this fubject I fhall tranfcribe fome extracts : " I believe I fhall " drop (as to the publick) this affair of thefe fpurious letters and the orations I men- " tioned ; for though I am as certain that *Cicero* was not the author of them as I am " that you were not, yet I confider that it muft be judged of by thofe who are already " prejudiced on the other fide; and how far prejudice will go, is evident from the " fubject itfelf; for nothing elfe could have fuffered fuch filly and barbarous ftuff as " thefe epiftles and thofe orations to pafs fo long and through fo many learned mens " hands for the writings of *Cicero*, in which view I confefs I cannot read them without " aftonifhment and indignation." *June* 30, 1743. " I fuppofe you are fo deeply en- " gaged in votes, addreffes, and the confutation of hereticks, that you cannot find " time to fend a line to a poor ruftic, who upon your account however has been putting " out his eyes in two very different employments, viz. tranfcribing his own writings, " and reading over thofe of *Cicero* once more. Had I made an end of this latter, I " would have fent you the former as far as I have gone; but having a few more days " reading to come, I intended to defer fending you the copy till fome time next month, " when my neighbour Mr. *Davis* goes to town, and I dare fay will convey it fafely. " When you have it, read it over; and if you think it worth your while to print it " when finifhed, much good may it do you! I fay when finifhed, becaufe I have done " nothing upon the third head, the Reafoning of the Author of the Epiftles; and I find " I fhall not be able to do any thing till the fummer when I get into *Suffex*; fo that if " you have faith, and will truft me for one part, you may in the mean time do what " you will with the other two, and put them either into the prefs or the fire, as you " fee moft proper; and if you choofe it, I will fend the copy before Mr. *Davis* comes, " whenever you appoint; for as I defigned it for you, it is proper you fhould have the " difpofal of it as you think fit. *Feb.* 28, 1743-4."—" As I intend to leave off ftudy, " and addict myfelf to animal life, I fhould be glad to be excufed drawing out the re- " mainder, or third fection, of the papers I fent you by Mr. *Davis*; I mean, unlefs you " think you fhall make fome advantage by them; in which cafe I will fet about it as foon as " ever I receive your letter, having all my neceffary tackle with me; but I imagine this bufy " time is not a proper feafon for writings of that kind, and I have no manner of incli- " nation to fcribble merely for fcribbling fake, efpecially upon a fubject of very little " confequence." *April* 17, 1744.—" Mr. *Davis*, by whom I fend this, will be in town " on *Thurfday* night, and on *Friday* you may have the papers; concerning which you " fhall do juft as you pleafe, either as to printing them, or otherwife, though I am of

(fee Spectator, N° 389), was fold in 1711 at the auction of the library of *Charles Bernard*, efq. for 28l. and purchafed by *Walter Clavel*, efq. This fame copy fucceffively came into the feveral col- lections of Mr. *John Nickolls*, Mr. *Jofeph Ames*, Sir *Peter Thompfon*, and M. G. *Tutet*, efq. who now poffeffes it. Dr. *Harwood*, in the firft preface to his " View of the various editions of Claffics," fays, that it is agreeable to inveftigate the hiftory of a fcarce book, and the different value it acquires in paffing through different hands. He gives an inftance in the firft edition of the *Greek* Pfalter, print- ed in 1481, which ftood in a bookfeller's catalogue marked at five fhillings; nobody afking for it, the price was reduced, and it was fold for four fhillings to a gentleman, who afterwards parted with it to the late Dr. *Afkew* for five guineas, at whofe fale this individual Pfalter fold for 16 guineas. To this obfervation of Dr. *Harwood* may be added, that Dr. *Mead* had the following books, which at his fale were purchafed by Dr. *Afkew*, and re-fold on the deceafe of the latter, at the following prices :

Cicero's Offices, printed by *Fuft* in 1465, — — 13l. 13s. fold again for 30l.
Olivet's edition of the works of *Cicero*, Paris, 1740, large paper, 14l. 14s. - - - 36l. 15s.
Salluft. Venet. apud *Vind. Spiram*, 1470, - - - - - - 5l. 17s. - - 14l. 3s. 6d.
Dr. *Mead* had alfo both the *Venice* editions of " *Pliny's* Natural Hiftory;" that of 1469 was bought, at eleven guineas, for the King of *France*; the edition of 1472, with fine illuminations, the copy par- ticularly noticed by *Maittaire*, was fold for eighteen guineas to Mr. *Willock*, a bookfeller.

" opinion

" 1. Ad Quirites post reditum; 2. Post reditum in Senatu.
" 3. Pro Domo sua, ad Pontifices; 4. De Haruspicum respon-
" sis.   To which are added, some Extracts out of the Notes
" of learned Men upon those Orations; and Observations on
" them.   By *Jeremiah Markland*, Fellow of *St. Peter's Col-
" lege, Cambridge*;" Mr. *Squire's** " Sermon at *St. Bridget's*;"
and his " Inquiry into the Foundation of the *English*
" Government," 8vo; Mr. *Whaley's*† " Original Poems and
" Translations," 8vo; " Remarks on several Occasional Re-
" flections, in Answer to the Rev. Doctors *Stebbing* and *Sykes*,
" serving to explain and justify the Two Dissertations in The
" Divine Legation, concerning the Command to *Abraham*
" to offer up his Son, and the Nature of the Jewish Theo-
" cracy, objected to by those Learned Writers‡." Part II.
and last‖, 8vo; and two Sermons by Mr. *Warburton*,

I. " A

" opinion you will print them, because you will see I have started in all probability an-
" other controversy concerning the Four Orations, which I will maintain to be spurious
" *contra mundum*. As to Mr. *Sherwin's* Testament **, I designed to give it you, if you
" will have it. I have read over Mr. *T[unstall]* twice more since I came hither, and
" am more and more confirmed that it can never be answered. The copy which I have
" sent you makes about 140 pages; and the Reasoning Section, which remains, may
" make perhaps 70 more, so that it will be but a small book, and consequently the loss
" in the printing it will be so much the less." *Letter without date.*

* Afterwards Bishop of *St. David's*; of whom more hereafter.

† *John Whaley*, M. A. fellow of *King's College, Cambridge*, and an ingenious poet.
He had published an earlier Collection of Poems, in one volume 8vo, 1732. To the
labours of Mr. *Whaley*, I am indebted for several articles in the " Select Collection
" of Miscellany Poems, 1780."

‡ ———— " Arcades ambo,
" Et cantare pares, & RESPONDERE parati."   VIRG.

‖ " I have bid a final adieu to controversy, unless some very great provocation draw
" me back." *Remarks*, p. 242.—The whole conclusion of this pamphlet is well worth
attending to.   " As to the manner in which I have answered some of my adversaries,"
says the learned Writer, " their insufferable abuse, and my own love of quiet, made it
" necessary. I had tried all ways to silence an iniquitous clamour; by neglect of it;
" by good words; by an explanation of my meaning; and all without effect. The first
" volume of this obnoxious work had not been out many days, before I was fallen upon

** The New Testament of Dr. *Gregory's* text, with notes by Mr. *Sherwin*, Dr. *Whitby* (whose copy
this had been), Mr. *Markland*, Mr. *Bowyer*, and others. Mr. *Markland* gave it to Mr. *E. Clarke*,
who is now possessed of it, enriched with many valuable notes by his father, and many by himself.

" by

1. " A faithful Portrait of Popery, by which it is feen to
" be the Reverfe of Chriftianity, as it is the Deftruction of
" Morality, Piety, and Civil Liberty; a Sermon preached
" at *St. James's* Church, *Weftminfter*, 1745," 8vo. 2. " A
" Sermon occafioned by the prefent unnatural Rebellion,
" &c. preached in Mr. *Allen's* chapel at *Prior Park*, near
" *Bath*, and publifhed at his Requeft, 1745," 8vo.

" by a furious ecclefiaftical news-writer, with the utmoft brutality. All the return I
" then made, or then ever intended to make, was a vindication of my moral character,
" wrote with fuch temper and forbearance as feemed affection to thofe who did not
" know that I only wanted to be quiet. But I reckoned without my hoft. The angry
" man became ten times more outrageous. What was now to be done? I tryed an-
" other method with him. I drew his picture; I expofed him naked; and fhewed the
" public of what parts and principles this tumour was made up. It had its effect; and I
" never heard more of him. On this occafion, let me tell the reader a ftory. 'As a *Scotch*
" bagpiper was traverfing the mountains of *Ulfter*, he was one evening encountered by a
" hunger-ftarved *Irifh* wolf. In this diftrefs, the poor man could think of nothing better
" than to open his wallet, and try the effects of his hofpitality. He did fo, and the
" favage fwallowed all that was thrown him with fo improving a voracity, as if his ap-
" petite was but juft coming to him. The whole ftock of provifion, you may be fure,
" was foon fpent. And now, his only recourfe was to the virtue of the bagpipe; which
" the monfter no fooner heard, than he took to the mountains with the fame precipi-
" tation that he had come down. The poor piper could not fo perfectly enjoy his deli-
" verance, but that, with an angry look at parting, he fhook his head, and faid, ' Ay!
" are thefe your tricks? Had I known your humour, you fhould have had your mufic
" before fupper.' But though I had the Caduceus of peace in my hands, yet it was only
" in cafes of neceffity that I made ufe of it. And therefore I chofe to let pafs, without
" any chaftifement, fuch impotent railers as Dr. *Richard Grey*, and one *Bate*, a zany
" to a mountebank. On the other hand, when I happened to be engaged with fuch
" very learned and candid writers as Dr. *Middleton* and the Mafter of the *Charter-houfe*,
" I gave fufficient proof how much I preferred a different manner of carrying on a con-
" troverfy, would my anfwerers but afford me the occafion. But alas! as I never *fhould*
" have fuch learned men long my adverfaries, and never *would* have thefe other my
" friends, I found that, if I wrote at all, I muft be condemned to a manner, which all,
" who know me, know to be moft abhorrent to my natural temper. So, on the whole,
" I refolved to quit my hands of them at once, and turn again to nobler game, more
" fuitable, as Dr. *Stebbing* tells me, to my clerical function, that peftilent herd of liber-
" tine fcriblers, with which the ifland is over-run; whom I would hunt down, as good
" king *Edgar* did his wolves; from the mighty author of ' Chriftianity as old as the
" creation †,' to the drunken blafpheming cobler, who wrote againft Jefus and the Re-
" furrection‡."

† *Tindal.*
‡ A pamphlet intituled " The Refurrection of Jefus demonftrated to have no Proof." On this
little tract Mr. *Warburton* thus wrote to Mr. *Bowyer:* " I am much obliged to you for fending me
" *Morgan's* book, for *Morgan's* it is every line fpeaks; and fuch execrable ftuff the fun never faw;
" and next to writing fo bad, would be anfwering fo bad a writer."

In.

In the fame year 1745, to oblige Mr. *Faulkner**, Mr. *Bowyer* wrote this fhort preface to a pofthumous pamphlet of Dean *Swift:* "The following treatife of *Directions to Servants* "was begun fome years ago by the Author, who had not "leifure to finifh and put it into proper order, being en- "gaged in many other works of greater ufe to his country, "as may be feen by moft of his writings. But, as the Au- "thor's defign was to expofe the villainies and frauds of "fervants to their mafters and miftreffes, we will make no "apology for its publication; but give it our readers in the "fame manner as we find it in the original, which may "be feen in the printer's cuftody. The few tautologies "that occur in the characters left unfinifhed, will make "the reader look upon the whole as a rough draught, with "feveral outlines only drawn. However, that there may "appear no daubing or patch-work by other hands, it is "thought moft advifeable to give it in the Author's own "words. It is imagined that he intended to make a large "volume of this work; but, as time and health would not "permit him, the reader may draw, from what is here "exhibited, means to detect the many vices and faults to "which people in that kind of low life are fubject. If "gentlemen would ferioufly confider this work, which is "written for their inftruction (although ironically), it "would make them better œconomifts, and preferve their "eftates and families from ruin. It may be feen, from "fome fcattered papers (wherein were given hints for a de- "dication and preface, and a lift of all degrees of fervants), "that the Author intended to have gone through all their

---

* " As you are famous for writing Prefaces, pray help me to one for *Advice to Ser-* "*vants.*" *Mr. Faulkner to Mr. B. Nov. 8,* 1745.

" characters.

" characters. This is all that need be said as to this treatife,
" which can only be looked upon as a fragment."

In 1746 Mr. *Bowyer* projected (what during his whole
life he had in view) a regular edition of *Cicero's* Letters *,
in chronological order, on a plan which it is to be lamented
that he did not complete; as an uniform feries thus properly arranged would have formed a real hiftory of *Tully's*
life, and thofe which cannot be dated might be thrown to
the end without any inconvenience. In that year he
publifhed " The Life of the Emperor *Julian*," tranflated
from the *French* of F. *La Bleterie*, and improved with
twelve pages of curious notes, and a genealogical table.
The notes were not entirely Mr. *Bowyer's*, but were drawn
up in part by Mr. *Clarke* and other learned men. This
tranflation (by Mifs *Anna Williams*†, a blind lady, affifted
by two fifters of the name of *Wilkinfon*) was made under
his immediate infpection, and was revifed by Mr. *Markland* and Mr. *Clarke*‡. His advertifement is here exhibited:

" The

※ Mr. *Markland*, *Dec.* 16, 1746, fays, " *Macte tuâ induftriâ*, as to *Cicero*; but I
" fear you will find reafon to be tired of it upon two accounts; one, becaufe fuch a
" work as this will require the whole man and his attention, at leaft for fome confiderable
" time; and another, becaufe fuch an editor fhould either have of his own, or have the
" command of, a library in which are to be found all the *literatores*; not to mention a
" third, that when you have taken all thefe pains, the book perhaps may hang upon
" your hands."

† Mifs *Williams*, who is ftill living, publifhed a volume of " Mifcellanies in Profe
" and Verfe, 1766," 4to, by the kind affiftance of Dr. *Johnson*, who wrote feveral
pieces contained in that volume. She is the daughter of *Zachariah Williams*, who
publifhed a pamphlet printed in *Englifh* and *Italian*, intituled, " An Account of
" an Attempt to afcertain the Longitude at Sea, by an exact Theory of the Variation
" of the Magnetical Needle. With a Table of Variations at the moft memorable
" Cities in *Europe*, from the year 1660 to 1860, 1755," 4to. The *Englifh* part of
this was, I am told, written by Dr. *Johnson*, the *Italian* by Mr. *Baretti*.

‡ " I like your fpecimen of *Julian* very well, and fancy it will anfwer your purpofe;
" not indeed fo well as Tar-water, but better than any other holy water you could give
" us. I fuppofe you don't finifh your fheets off, till Mr. *Markland* has read them. It
" is worth while to ftay for their return; for he fweeps all at a fingle reading, and can
" tell by memory, whether *Ablarius* or *Ablavius* is the true name of a Conful that
" fcarce any body ever heard of. You muft take care that your *fair tranflators* don't
" keep rather too clofe to the *French*; it is pardonable in their fex, but will not pafs
" fo well in yours; though I faw little to complain of. The *French* fpelling of the
" proper names *they* muft always follow. They have too, *Mafter of Julian*, for what

B b
" is

" The following piece was recommended to me by an
" eminent Writer*, who has had the good fortune to
" pleafe the world; and is therefore beft entitled to judge
" of its tafte.   I found it, in many refpects, agreeable to
" my own.   By authority therefore and inclination I was
" led to communicate it to the public.   It appears, per-
" haps, under fome difadvantage, becaufe the Author has
" not thought proper to put his name to it; which has
" precluded the Editor likewife from the pleafure of adding
" his, being obliged not to come behind his *French* original
" in point of delicacy.   I truft it to make its way in the
" world by its own merit, without any other recommenda-
" tion.   That the *Englifh* edition, however, might receive
" fome advantage, I have added *a plate of coins,* and *fome*
" *notes* †, to illuftrate the hiftory, fometimes perhaps to bring
" in frefh matter to it.   Thofe who have no relifh for the
" knowledge of medals, will find themfelves interefted
" enough in the narrative, and may leave the fhowy part
" of the entertainment to other readers.   The motives
" which led *Julian* to quit the Chriftian religion will be
" always matter of enquiry; for one Apoftate upon princi-
" ple raifes our fpeculation more than thoufands without
" principle, or againft principle.   Among other reafons

" is eafier with us, *Julian's Mafter :* and in another place, to employ in doing good
" *that liberty* ; more expreffive, *both the liberty,* &c. But thefe are trifles. I fancy
" that moft of the difficulties you find in medals are of the Antiquaries' own making,
" in laying down general rules, which are precarious. *Cæfars* were fometimes fent
" into provinces, as *Julian* was, with full powers; and the mints in thofe provinces
" might compliment them with the diadem, as knowing it would not difpleafe the Em-
" peror. In others, the fame perfon might go without it. *F. Jobert* feems to be
" clear in this : " On feroit voir de fimples *Cefars* couronnez de laurier, ou parez du
" diademe—on montreroit avec la meme facilité plufieurs medailles d'Empereurs—ou
" leur tete fe trouve toute nuë." What will you think then of *Valefius's* affertion of
" *never* appearing with a coronet ? This muft be for the fake of an hypothefis ; unlefs
" he had feen all the medals of *Julian,* there is no afferting it." *Mr. Clarke to Mr. B.*
in a letter without date.

* Suppofed to be Mr. *Warburton,* whofe mafterly Difcourfe, under the title of
" *Julian,*" Mr. *Bowyer* printed in 1750.

† Which may be feen in the volume of his Mifcellaneous Tracts.

" which

" which arise from a view of his life, I would suggest, the
" early prejudices he must have conceived against the
" cruelty of *Constantius*; the reigning vice, I may say, of
" that family. We imbibe in our youth the principles of
" our guardians in proportion only to our veneration
" for them. Perhaps our own Queen's *Mary's* attachment
" to Popery might be accounted for from a like cause; a
" short reign, like *Julian's*——and Christianity, as the Refor-
" mation, first established by a long reign, recovered the
" faster for a little opposition to it. But I will detain the
" reader no longer from the history, and his own reflections."

The following letter was sent by Mr. *Bowyer* on this occasion to *The London Courant* :

" It is one of the hardest things in nature to give an
" enemy the praise which is due to him. I was led into
" this reflection on a double account, from reading a most
" entertaining piece, " The Life of the Emperor *Julian*;"
" the author of it a *Frenchman*; the subject, an Apostate
" from the Christian Religion. A writer of our own had
" heretofore attempted somewhat of the same kind, the
" celebrated Mr. *Johnson**, a man of wit, and a sprightly
" controversialist. But very different talents are requisite
" to make a good historian : an extensive view of the
" times he writes of; a methodical disposition of his work;
" a clear narration of facts, varied according to the different
" scenes that occur in it, and carried on throughout with
" a politeness becoming an attendant on a Prince; and,
" above all, a true knowledge of human nature, which
" traces out the springs of action, whether actuated by
" prejudice, passion, or policy, are qualities which the

* Chaplain to Lord *Russel*, in the time of *Charles* II.—His inflexible patriotism involved him in frequent dangers; particularly, in 1692, his life was attempted by seven assassins, who beat him in his bed, and one of them cut his head with a sword. He lived till *May*, 1703. All his treatises were collected in 1713, in one folio volume, with some memorials of his life.

" *English*

" *English* writer wanted, and so remarkably distinguish
" the *French*, that a man would scarce think he was read-
" ing the same period of time in both. Then for the sub-
" ject, the very name of an Apostate carries with it so
" frightful an idea, that we think it is inconsistent with
" every virtue, and presently conclude, that the man who
" has deserted Christianity, has abandoned humanity like-
" wise. Others take a contrary turn : and, having found
" a Prince of distinguished sense, whose mind was not
" open to the conviction of revelation, magnify every ex-
" cellence in *him*, to the discouragement of *that*. Both
" extremes this Author hath happily avoided. The reader
" will find here an agreeable contrast of very different pro-
" perties ; an Emperor and a Philosopher, intrepid in war,
" and yet superstitiously fearful of omens ; credulous, and
" yet an infidel ; persuaded of the truth of miracles, and
" yet rejecting the evidence of them ; a hero, and yet a
" bigot in religion ; and in that too of forbearing princi-
" ples, and yet intent upon establishing his own ; a ra-
" tional enquirer, and yet devoted to priests and sophists ;
" a satirist, and yet good-natured ; in short, an assemblage
" (as the Author expresses it) of eminent qualities ill sorted,
" which, with the variety of incidents and advantages that
" attended him, give the history of his Life, founded on
" the strictest truth, all the surprize of fiction *."

---

* Mr. *A. V. Desvoeux*, a clergyman in *Ireland*, and chaplain to his majesty's regiment
of carabineers, not knowing of Mr. *Bowyer's* intention, had published proposals at *Dublin*
for printing a translation of the same work, with " An Appendix, containing several
" Dissertations on points relating to *Julian's* History." I have the titles of these Dissertations in the Author's hand-writing ; but have never seen a printed copy of his translation.—Mr. *Desvoeux* published " A philosophical and critical Essay on *Ecclesiastes*.
" *London*, 1760," 4to. dedicated to the primate of *Ireland*. This work is well spoken
of by Bishop *Lowth* in his 24th Prælection, " De Sacra Poesi *Hebræorum*." See the
author's preface ; and in p. 501 of the work : " I have shewn in another work," says
he, on which words his note is : " See our *Julian's* life and character illust. Diss. VII."

It

It has been suggested to me that Mr. *Bowyer* was the author of " A Dissertation : in which the Objections of a late " Pamphlet * to the Writings of the Antients, after the Manner of Mr. *Markland*, are clearly answered : those passages in *Tully* corrected ; on which some of the Objec- " are founded. With Amendments of a few Pieces of Cri- " ticism in Mr. *Markland's* Epistola Critica. 1746." 8vo. It was certainly printed by him ; and if he did not write it himself (which is extremely probable), he was at least an assistant in it.

Two other single sermons by Mr. *Warburton* were printed by him in 1746†. 1. " The Nature of National Offences " truly stated ;" preached on the general Fast-day, *Dec.* 18, 1745 ; and 2. " A Sermon preached on the Thanksgiv-

---

* The *late Pamphlet* was written by Dr. *Ross* (the present worthy and learned Bishop of *Exeter*), then only just A. M. who thus early declared that esteem, which he ever afterwards professed for Dr. *Middleton's* elegant taste in literary accomplishment, by hazarding this elegant *bijou* against one of the Doctor's most formidable antagonists. To Bp. *Ross* also the publick is indebted for a valuable edition of *Cicero's* Epistolæ ad Familiares, 1749, 8vo. But whoever considers, that these were both very early productions, and knows that the Bishop has confined himself, through 30 years of the prime of a life uncommonly abstemious, to an unceasing reading of the very best books only on the most important subject, will find that his admiration of them increases his regret, that any reasons should have prevented his receiving more ample fruits of this Prelate's learning and judgment. How much cause of regret would the republic of letters have had, if any considerations had induced Bishop *Lowth* to withhold a late work from them, that, for the multiplicity and importance of its discoveries, has perhaps not been equalled since the publication of the Sacred Authors themselves ! Happy indeed it is for the christian world, when men of these gigantic abilities condescend to instruct us, and thereby lessen our sorrow for the loss of a *Sherlock*, or a still greater *Secker !*

† In a letter to Mr. *Bowyer*, dated *Jan.* 20, 1745-6, Mr. *Warburton*, after giving some little commissions " in confidence that his friend had survived and got the better of " the alarms for the constitution, and frights from the *Highlanders*, that lately filled the " country with confusion," tells him, " I have subscribed 30*l.* to the *Lincolnshire* Asso- " ciation (which is more than any of the clergymen in the county) ; and I have published " three sermons. Have not I fairly contributed my quota both in temporals and spi- " rituals ? I will neither be a civil nor an ecclesiastical slave ; but don't be surprized if " I soon submit to the *vinc'la jugalia.* To offer up my freedom to one of the finest " women in *England*, is being more than free. In the mean time, whether bond or " free, depend upon my being always yours."—Mr. *Warburton* was married to Miss *Tucker* on the fifth of *September* 1745.

" ing

" ing appointed to be obſerved the 9th of *October*, for the
" Suppreſſion of the late unnatural Rebellion." Of theſe,
and of the two ſingle Sermons mentioned in p. 183, there
were ſeveral editions in 8vo. In this year alſo Mr. *Bowyer*
printed Mr. *Warburton's* " Apologetical Dedication to the
" Rev. Dr. *Henry Stebbing*, in anſwer to his Cenſure and
" Miſrepreſentations of the Sermon preached on the General
" Faſt-day appointed to be obſerved *Dec.* 18, 1745," 8vo; and
the firſt volume of " A New Method of learning with greater
" Facility the *Greek* Tongue*; containing Rules for the De-
" clenſions, Conjugations, Reſolution of Verbs, Syntax,

---

* In a copy of this book Mr. *Bowyer* has left the following memorandum : " When the
" firſt edition of this Grammar was tranſlated into *Engliſh*, as I printed one volume and
" Mr. *Bettenham* the other, I thought it would be a means of recommending myſelf to
" the proprietors, Meſſ. *Nourſe* and *Hawkins*, if I ſuggeſted to them to add *Lowe's Col-*
" *lection of Ligatures* new engraved and improved. The engraver executed his part
" very ill, as the reader will ſee; but for the firſt edition it was to paſs. When a ſe-
" cond edition was going to the preſs, I renewed my application to print one of the
" volumes, as I had done before, and reminded the proprietors that the plate ſhould be
" new engraved. I was rejected with ſcorn ‡; and Mr. *Hawkins* told me, *I ſhould not*
" *print a letter of it: That my brother Bettenham ſhould print the whole.* The faults in
" the plate are monſtrous; and two ligatures are omitted, which I had introduced into
" it from *H. Stephens's Epiſtola ad quæſdam amicos, &c.* printed in *Theodorus Janſſo-*
" *nius ab Almeloveen*, p. 192, 193, in which he complains of the people's want of ability
" even to read *Greek* in ſome of *Aldus's* editions, particularly ȷ̃ for ἐςι, and S for καὶ.
" It is very remarkable, that when *Maittaire* reprinted this epiſtle in his *Stephanorum*
" *Hiſtoria*, p. 331, 332, ed. *Lond.* 1709, he has omitted to exemplify theſe two liga-
" tures. By *H. Stephens The Art of Printing* complains ‖ of being a ſufferer; now a
" Printer, W. BOWYER."

‡ That Mr. *Bowyer* not only frequently experienced this ſpecies of mortification, but too ſeverely felt
it, is apparent from various teſtimonies of his own. In the margin of a copy of *Homer*, in which are
many of his corrections and obſervations, is the following memorandum : " The copy-right of print-
" ing the Odyſſey was bought at Mr. *Knapton's* ſale by Mr. *Millar*, who, upon its being knocked
" down to him, ſaid publickly, *I bought it with a view to your printing it, Mr.* Bowyer; *therefore*
" *wiſh you would buy a copy in 4to. of Mr.* Knapton, *from which you may print.* I did ſo, and ac-
" quainted Mr. *Millar* of it. He then told me, he had altered his mind, and intended Mr. *Bettenham*
" ſhould print the firſt volume, and I ſhould print the ſecond volume. Afterwards, he ſaid, Mr.
" *Bettenham* having urged that he had a careful corrector, he ſhould print both volumes, and
" bade me deliver them to him; he would make me amends in ſomewhat elſe. I never printed
" a line of *Homer* ſince. I would have given him theſe MS. additions, if he had kept to his promiſe;
" but I have been, by Mr. *Bettenham* and other bookſellers, treated many times in the ſame manner,
" particularly in the *Greek* Grammar, by Meſſ. *de Port-Royal*, for *Nourſe* and *Hawkins*, printed a ſe-
" cond time by *Bettenham*; and in the book of Surgery [*Heiſter's*] printed lately by me the firſt edi-
" tion; afterwards only one volume."

‖ *Artis Typographicæ Querimonia*, the title of ſome verſes there.

" Quantity,

" Quantity, Accents, Dialects, and Poetic Licence. Digested
" in the cleareft and concifeft Order. With Variety of ufeful
" Remarks, proper to the attaining a complete Knowledge
" of that Language, and a perfect Underftanding of the
" Authors who have writ in it. Tranflated from the *French*
" of the Meffieurs *De Port Royal*. In two Volumes." 8vo.

On the 21ft of *Auguft*, 1747, Mr. *Bowyer* entered a
fecond time into the matrimonial ftate, with a moft benevolent and worthy woman, Mrs. *Elizabeth Bill*, by whom
he had no children.

In that year he printed " A General Hiftory of *England*,
" volume I.* containing an account of the firft inhabitants
" of the country and the tranfactions in it from the earlieft
" times to the death of King *John*, A. D. 1216, by *Thomas*
" Carte†, an *Englishman*," folio; his friend Mr. *Chifhull's*
" Travels

* Of the firft volume of this Hiftory, 150 copies were printed on royal paper, 850 on
a fecond fize, and 2000 on fmall paper. Of the fucceeding volumes, 100 only were
printed on royal paper, and 650 on fmall paper.

† Mr. *Thomas Carte*, fon of the Rev. *Samuel Carte*‡, M. A. of *Magdalen College*,
Oxford, prebendary of *Litchfield*, vicar of *St. Martin's*, *Leicefter*, and rector of *Eaftwell*
in

‡ Who publifhed two Sermons, in 1694 and 1705 **; " Tabula chronologica archiepifcopatuum
" & epifcopatuum in *Anglia* & *Wallia*, ortus, divifiones, tranflationes, &c. breviter exhibens; una
" cum indice alphabetico nominum, quibus apud authores infigniuntur; concinnata per *Sam. Carte*,
" vic. *S. Martini*, *Leiceftr*. & explicata per eundem." fol. without date. Part of a letter of his to
Humphrey Wanley, dated *Aug*. 7, 1710, concerning a teffellated pavement found about 1670, near *All*
Saints church at *Leicefter*, with a drawing of it by *B. Garland*, is in Phil. Tranf. N° 331, p.
324. And his account of that town, in anfwer to fome queries of *Browne Willis*, efq. is frequently referred to by Mr. *Throfby*, in his " Memoirs of the Town and County of *Leicefter*, 1777," 12mo. as
among the MSS. in the *Bodleian* Library ††. His affiftance to Mr. *Willis* is gratefully acknowledged in
the

** He is faid in *Letfome's* " Preacher's Affiftant" to have been vicar of *St. Mary's*, and in Phil. Tranf. is
mifcalled vicar of *St. Margaret's*. Of the laft of thefe mifnomers he has himfelf taken notice in one of his
MSS. which was fhewn to Mr. *Cole* by the prefent Mafter of *Emanuel College*; and the other muft have been likewife a miftake, for I am told, by a friend who knew *Leicefter* in 1726, that Mr. *Fox*, then vicar of *St. Mary's*,
was an old man, and had probably enjoyed it for 30 or 40 years.

†† I am affured that the MS. which is handed about under the title of " *Carte's* Antiquities of *Leicefter*" is
a very trifling thing; the greater part of it being taken up with the changes made in the power and conftitution
of the corporation, from their abfolute fubjection to the earl of *Leicefter*, to the prefent time; and that it contains very little of local antiquities, though it may furnifh ufeful hints to an antiquary. *Thomas Staveley*, efq.
of *Cuffington* in *Leicefterfhire*, (who, from *Peter Houfe*, *Cambridge*, was admitted of *The Inner Temple*, *July* 2, 1647, and
called to the bar *June* 12, 1654; who, in 1674, when the Court efpoufed the caufe of Popery, and the prefumptive
Heir to the Crown openly profeffed himfelf a Roman Catholic, difplayed the enormous exactions of the Court of
Rome, by publifhing " The Romifh Horfeleech") fucceeded *John Oneby*, efq. as fteward of the court of records at
Leicefter in 1662, and was intimately acquainted with its early hiftory. Some years before his death, which happened
1683, he retired to *Belgrave* near *Leicefter*, and, paffing the latter part of his life in the ftudy of *Englifh* hiftory, acquired a melancholy habit, but was efteemed a diligent, judicious, and faithful Antiquary. He had a brother, who
refided at *Medburn* in *Leicefterfhire*. Their fifter or next relation was married to Mr. *Brudenel*, by whom fhe had two
daughters,

" Travels in *Turkey* and back to *England*," folio (of which à
particular

in that county, was born at *Clifton upon Dunsmoor* in *Warwickshire*, where his father
was at that time vicar; and was baptized there by *immersion*, *April* 23, 1686. We
have no account of the place where he received his grammar learning; but his academical education was in *University College*, *Oxford*, where he was admitted 1698. He
took his batchelor's degree in 1702; was afterwards incorporated at *Cambridge*, and
took his master's degree there in the year 1706. Upon his entering into holy orders,
he was appointed reader of the abbey church at *Bath*; and preaching there on the
thirtieth of *January* 1714, he took occasion in his sermon to vindicate king *Charles*
the First with regard to the *Irish* massacre, which drew him into a controversy on that
subject

the Preface to the second volume of " Mitred Abbeys;" and to him Dr. *Stukeley* inscribes his plan of
Roman Leicester *, plate 92 of his Itinerary, vol. I. The time of his death, with some traits of his
character, will appear from the following inscription on a stone in the floor of the chancel of *St.
Martin's* church:

<table>
<tr><td>

" The remains of
SAMUEL CARTE, M. A. many years
Vicar of this parish. He was a person
of great learning, exemplary life
and conversation, strict piety,
sound judgement, orthodox principles,
and a zealous and *able* defender † of the
doctrine of the Holy Trinity.
He died *April* 16th, 1740,

</td><td>

in the 87th year of his age, in full
assurance of a joyful resurrection.
Near this place lie interred
Ann ‡ wife and *Elizabeth* daughter
of the said *Samuel Carte*.
Here lieth the body of *Sarah Carte*, daughter
of the Rev. *Samuel Carte*, who died *March*
6th, 1773, in the 72d year of her age."

</td></tr>
</table>

Mr. *Carte* at one time assisted the celebrated *Jeremiah Collier*, who preached to a Nonjuring congregation up two pair of stairs in a house in *Broad Street*, *London*.—I shall take this opportunity of
adding here, that Dr. *Samuel Jebb*, before-mentioned, p. 32 and 51, was librarian to Mr. *Collier*, born
at *Nottingham*, and married a relation of the wife of Mr. *Dillingham*, apothecary, in *Red Lion Square*,
under whom he took lectures in Pharmacy and Chemistry. To the list of his writings may be added
a translation of " *Martin's* Answer to *Emlyn*," 8vo, which was printed by Mr. *Bowyer* in 1718, and
again in 1719.

daughters, one of whom died a maiden, and the other was married to Mr. *George Alcox*, rector of *Langton*, who
died at *The Bath* without issue. Besides the " History of Churches," which first appeared in 1712, Mr.
Staveley left some papers on the history and antiquities of *Leicester*, which Dr. *Farmer* (who calls him *William*
by mistake) proposed to publish. The younger Mr. *S. Carte*, who had a copy of these papers, says of them,
in a MS. letter to Dr. *Ducarel*, *March* 7, 1750, " His account of the earls of *Leicester*, and of the great abbey,
" appears to have been taken from *Dugdale's* Baronage and Monasticon; but as to his sentiments in respect to
" the borough, I differ with him in some instances. By the charter for erecting and establishing the court of
" records at *Leicester*, the election of the steward is granted to the mayor and court of aldermen, who likewise
" have thereby a similar power in respect to a bailiff for executing their writs. But afterwards, viz. *Dec.* 20,
" 7 *Jac.* I. the great earl of *Huntingdon* having been a considerable benefactor to *Leicester*, the corporation came
" to a resolution of granting to him and his heirs a right of nominating alternately to the office of steward and
" bailiff, and executed a bond under their common seal, in the penalty of one thousand pounds, for enforcing
" the execution of their grant. And as *John Major*, esq. was elected by the court of aldermen to succeed Mr.
" *Staveley* [in *December* 1684], I infer that *Staveley* was nominated by the earl of *Huntingdon*, and confirmed by
" the aldermen, in pursuance of the grant above-mentioned."—Copies of *Staveley's* MSS. and of *Carte's* are
supposed to be among the collections of the late Sir *Thomas Cave*. *Throsby* had the use of both; and from
these and printed books made up his meagre volumes.

* An intelligent friend informs me, that the whole of this plan must be a mere figment. The plan of
Leicester as it stood before its demolition in *Henry* the Second's time, on the rebellion of earl *Robert*, is every
where to be traced. There are the vestiges of two *Roman* works, and no more; viz. the mount near the river
(as was their custom), and the ruins of a bath near *St. Nicholas church*. Two tessellated pavements have been
found, the one already mentioned to have been described by Mr. *Carte*; the other, much larger, about thirty
years ago, now covered with earth again.—" A view of the *Rialto Bridge*, over which King *Richard* III. was
" carried into *The Gray Friars* to be buried," was engraved for *Peck's* " Desiderata Curiosa."

† This will be illustrated by his conduct to Mr. *Jackson*; of whom see under the year 1752. It is somewhat
extraordinary that the word " able" is an interlineation on the stone.

‡ She is supposed to have died young.

particular account has been already given in p. 36);
" Bibliotheca

fubject with Mr. afterwards the celebrated Dr. *Chandler*. He immediately publiſhed a
pamphlet in 4to, intituled, " The *Iriſh* maſſacre ſet in a clear light, wherein Mr. *Baxter's*
" account of it in the hiſtory of his own life, and the abridgment thereof by Dr. *Calamy,*
" are fully conſidered ; together with two letters from Mr. *Chandler*, reviving the afore-
" ſaid account, to the Rev. Mr. *Thomas Carte*, at *Bath*; with his two replies to Mr
" *Chandler*." This is inſerted in *Somers's* tracts. On the acceſſion of the preſent royal
family, he refuſed to take the oaths to the government, and put on a lay habit. I know
not what ſhare he took in the rebellion of 1715; but am well aſſured, that at the cloſe of
it he was concealed at *Coleſhill*, from the ſearch of the king's troops, in the houſe of Mr.
Badger, then curate of that town and of *Over Whitaker*, chaplain to the earl of *Ayles-
ford*, and afterwards rector of *Bedworth* in *Warwickſhire*. Mr. *Carte* officiated ſome
time as curate at *Coleſhill*; and is ſaid to have acted as ſecretary to biſhop *Atterbury,*
before his troubles. In the year 1722 he was accuſed of high treaſon; and a
proclamation was iſſued, *Aug.* 13, offering a reward of 1000l. for apprehending
him. He fled, and reſided ſome time in *France*, under the borrowed name of
Philips; and being introduced to moſt men of learning and family in that country, he
gained acceſs to all libraries, public and private, and collected large materials for illuſtrating an *Engliſh* tranſlation of *Thuanus*; which was in ſuch forwardneſs in 1724, that
he conſulted the munificent Dr. *Mead* on the mode of publication ; who perceiving that
the plan might be made more extenſively uſeful, obtained Mr. *Carte's* materials, *pretio
haud exiguo*, and engaged Mr. *Buckley* in the noble edition*, in ſeven volumes folio,
which has been already deſcribed in p. 81. Whilſt this was carrying on, Queen *Caroline*, the univerſal patroneſs of learned men, having received ſome favourable im-
preſſions of Mr. *Carte*, obtained leave for him to return home in ſecurity, which
he did ſome time between 1728 and 1730. In 1735 he publiſhed the third volume of
his " Life of the Duke of *Ormonde*," which he completed by the publication of the
two firſt volumes in 1736. In this work he appears to have profited by the inſtruc-
tions he had received from Dr. *Swift*; to whom, in a letter dated *Aug.* 11, 1736,
he communicated his plan for writing a Hiſtory of *England* †. In an unpubliſhed letter
to

* It may naturally enough be aſked, why Mr. *Carte* himſelf was not allowed to ſuperintend this
edition of *Thuanus*. He probably would have been the principal editor, but that he was then abroad in
exile. The *Latin* addreſs to Dr. *Mead*, prefixed to the work, and dated from *The Inner Temple*, 7 kal.
Jan. 1733, was ſigned *Thomas Carte*, but probably received ſome corrections from Profeſſor *Ward*,
who tranſlated into elegant *Latin* the three introductory Letters of Mr. *Buckley*; whoſe particular acknowledgements are made to Mr. *Carte*, for having communicated his numerous collections from MSS.
and printed copies ; for correcting the orthography of proper names ; for his uſeful explanatory notes ;
for reviſing the life of *Thuanus*, and compiling the indexes. But Mr. *Buckley* ſhall ſpeak for himſelf :
" Variantes lectiones ex MSS. cunctiſque editionibus collectas, & nominum propriorum interpreta-
" tiones, *Cartius* in exemplari, quod prelo erat parandum, accurate deſcripſit. In quem finem dum
" totum opus evolvit, plurima quoque in utraque *Genevenſi* editione errata typographica correxit, notis
" etiam brevioribus in extrema pagina adſcriptis multa explicuit, & quædam emendavit. Ad hæc in-
" gentem numerum propriorum nominum, quæ a *Puteano* prætermiſſa erant, ex auctoribus ipſis, unde
" narrationes ſuas hauſerat *Thuanus*, aliiſque illius ævi ſcriptoribus, interpretatus eſt. Qua in re de
" omnibus ſane eruditis, atque adeo de *Thuano* ipſo, optime meritus eſſe videtur. . . . . . Simile quoque
" ſtudium & induſtriam in vitâ auctoris recenſendâ idem vir doctus poſuit : quæ & in ſex hiſtoriæ
" tomorum, vitæque in ſeptimo tomo, indicibus quos conficere ſuſcepit, eum adhibiturum pariter expec-
" tare licebit." Mr. *Buckley's* firſt letter is dated " ipſis kalend. *Jan* 1728;" the ſecond, " 7 id. *Dec.* 1728;"
the third, " ipſis kal. *Oct.* 1730." His Dedication to K. *George* II. is dated " 7 kal. *Jan.* 1733."

† " Having at laſt, after a long application and in the midſt of ſharp rheumatic pains, the effects of
" a ſedentary life, finiſhed my hiſtory *of the Life of the firſt Duke of* Ormonde, *and of the Affairs of*
" *Ireland in his Time*, I here ſend you a copy of that work, of which I beg your acceptance. I have

C c   " endeavoured

" Bibliotheca *Radcliviana*; or, a short Description of the
                                                    " *Radcliffe*

to Dr. Z. *Grey*, dated *May* 14, 1736, he says, " I was laid up four months this winter
" by the gravel and a lumbago, caught by coming to town in *December*, and lying one
" night at Alderman *Barber's* in a bed not lain in since the *May* before. I thank God
" it is at last over; but it has hindered my other two volumes from being printed before
" this time. They will be finished in ten days more, there being only about six sheets
" more to print, and will be delivered in the beginning of *June*. However I send you
" now six copies of the letters, and shall be obliged to you for disposing of them. I
" suppose you have read that volume, and seen there the letters relating to the earl of
" *Glamorgan*, who certainly forged every commission he pretended to from the king.
" I give you his character in the history very justly, but yet too tenderly drawn, because
" I am naturally unwilling to lay a load on any man's memory, except I am absolutely

" endeavoured to follow the instructions you gave me, and hope I have done so in some measure. If
" it have your approbation in any degree, it will be so much to my satisfaction. It hath been a long
" subject of complaint in *England*, that no history has yet been wrote of it upon authentic and proper
" materials; and even those who have taken notice of the military actions of our ancestors, have yet
" left the civil history of the kingdom (the most instructive of any) untouched, for want of a proper
" knowledge of the antiquities, usages, laws, and constitution, of this nation. *Rapin de Thoyras*, the
" last writer, was a foreigner, utterly ignorant in these respects; and, writing his history abroad, had
" no means of clearing up any difficulties that he met with therein. He made, indeed, some use of
" *Rymer's Fœdera*; but his ignorance of our customs suffered him to fall into gross mistakes, for
" want of understanding the phraseology of acts, which have reference to our particular customs.
" Besides, *Rymer's* collection contains only such treaties as were enrolled in *the Tower*, or in the
" rolls of Chancery: he knew nothing of such as were enrolled in the Exchequer, and of the public
" treaties with foreign princes enrolled in this latter office. I have now a list of above four hundred
" by me. *Rymer* never made use of that vast collection of materials for an *English* history, which is
" preserved in the *Cotton* Library *: nor ever consulted any journal of our privy council; whenever he
" refers to any, still quoting Bishop *Burnet* for his author. He never read the rolls of parliament,
" nor any journal of either house, where the chief affairs within the nation are transacted; and did
" not so much as know there was such a place as the Paper-office, where all the letters of the *English*
" ambassadors abroad, and all the dispatches of our secretaries of state at home, from the time of *Ed-
" ward* the Fourth to the Revolution (since which the secretaries have generally carried away their
" papers) are kept in a good method, and with great regularity; so that he wanted likewise the best
" materials for an account of our foreign affairs. These defects have made several of our nobility and
" gentry desire a new history to be wrote, in which the above mentioned, and other materials, as au-
" thentic as they, may be made use of. They have proposed it to me: and my objections regarding
" the vastness of the expence as well as labour, that, to satisfy myself, I must have all materials by
" me; not only copies out of our records, journals, &c. in *England*; but even copies of negotiations
" of foreign ambassadors at this court (*e. g.* of the *French*; all the negotiations and letters of which,
" for two hundred years past, I knew where to have copied); they have proposed a subscription of a
" thousand a year, for as many years as the work will require, to defray this expence. The subscrip-
" tion is begun, and will (I believe) be compleated this winter; and then that work will employ all
" my time. One advantage I already find from the very talk of this design, having been offered several
" collections and memoirs of particular persons, considerable in their time, which I did not know were
" in being, and which would else no part of them ever see the light; and the manner of the history's
" being carried on will probably make every body open their stores. This is one reason, among many
" others, which makes me very desirous of having your judgement of the work I have now published,
" and that you would point out to me such faults as I would fain correct in my designed work. It
" will be a very particular favour to a person who is, with the greatest esteem and respect, Sir, your
" very obliged and obedient servant,   THOMAS CARTE."

* Many of the assertions in this letter are erroneous. Whoever will be at the pains of consulting that valuable treasure called *Rymer's* Fœdera, will find, that numberless treaties and other materials were collected from
the records of *The Exchequer*, since removed into *The Chapter House*; and also from the *Cotton* Library. Mr. *Carte*
seems also to have been unacquainted with the condition of the *State Papers*, which were formerly kept in the
old gateway at *Whitehall*, but which are now deposited within the buildings of *The Treasury*.

" forced

" *Radcliffe* library at *Oxford*, &c. folio, by *James Gibbs*,
" architect,

" forced to it. I intimate (so strongly that no body of common sense can mistake the
" thing) that he forged letters and commissions without number, and I could have
" produced the compiler of the Nuncio's memoirs in evidence, (who had all those com-
" missions before his eyes, and all the papers signed by *Glamorgan* to the Nuncio) to
" prove the commissions and letters he pretended to from King *Charles*, absolutely
" forged; for he says he was perfectly acquainted with *Glamorgan's* secretary, and knew
" his hand-writing as well as his own; and all those commissions and letters were wrote
" in the hand of an *Irish* priest who was *Glamorgan's* secretary. I considered that it is
" a delicate thing to say in express terms that such a writing is forged; forgery is a
" charge to a great nobleman as little to be used as the word *lie* to a gentleman; other
" words are to be used to express the same meaning in both cases. I have done so in
" *Glamorgan's* case, and I can very truly tell my friends the duke of *Beaufort* and lord
" *Noel Somerset*, that I have treated their ancestor tenderly; though I really believe
" no man that reads my book will think that I have done so, besides myself, who know
" what I have omitted to say. I have done the same in other cases; but if any will
" think fit to dispute that measure of iniquity which I assign to any one man in my
" history, (which I only do for the sake of doing justice to the king or some other in-
" jured person) I am ready to make up his full accompt, which my tenderness to him
" made me decline, till I should be forced to it. I shall write something more to you
" on this subject when I write less in a hurry than I do now." Mr. *Carte's* residence
was then at Mr. *Awnshaw's*, *Red Lion Court, Fleet Street*. In a subsequent letter,
Jan 18, 1736-7, he adds, " I am ashamed of being so long silent since my return from
" *Bath* in *November* last, and know not whether you will admit the following relation
" for a just excuse: I was called thence to take measures for preventing a piratical im-
" pression of my work in *Ireland*, undertaken there by some *Dublin* booksellers. No
" friend I had in *London*, nor any bookseller I was acquainted with could suggest to me
" any method of relief; but at last calling to mind an order of the House of Lords,
" made in 1721, upon *Curll's* printing the duke of *Buckingham's* life, and pirating his
" works, I consulted the Parliament-office, and found it full for my purpose, declaring
" that whosoever should presume to print any account of the life, the letters, or other
" works of any deceased Peer, without the consent of his heirs or executors, should be
" punished as guilty of a breach of privilege of that House. I carried an attested copy
" of this order to lord *Arran*, and his lordship sent it to his agent in *Dublin* to serve
" upon the booksellers concerned in that design, and discharge them in his name from
" proceeding therein. This, I hope, has stopped their printing; but as it is a remedy
" only in my case, and arising from the particular nature of my work, there is still an
" absolute necessity for a new act of parliament to secure the property of authors in their
" works; and I should hope that your University should petition this session for such an
" act, of which lord *Cornbury*, at the instance of *Oxford*, has a draught already made,
" which has been approved by the Speaker, and will cause me a good deal of attendance
" in town this session. The hurry of that affair was not quite over, when going out of
" town sooner than I intended one night in *December* to *Winchmore Hill*, where all my
" books and papers are, and getting up at six in the morning (the servants being all in
" bed), and coming down in the dark into the parlour where I usually sit and keep the
" papers I am using for the time, I found it on fire, and about three foot in breadth of
" the top of the wainscot burnt. This was occasioned by a beam being put close under

C c 2

" the

" architect, F.R.S." probably the same person who is mentioned

" the hearth of a chamber above. Had I not discovered it in time, the whole house
" would have been burnt. As it was, all my papers were hurried away, and put into
" a terrible confusion ; and though I have looked several times for your last letter, I
" could not find it till this moment that I sit down to answer it. My book has been
" entirely printed ever since *July* last, when I advertised that my subscribers might
" have it at my printer's. It will not be published till next week after the meeting of
" the parliament ; but if the subscribers you were so kind as to procure for me at *Cam-*
" *bridge* would have their books sent down, and will tell me how, I will take care to
" send them. I fancy, after it comes to be generally read, we shall hear no more of
" accusations or reflections on the king, with regard to the rebellion of *Ireland*. I have
" cleared all that affair so much to the satisfaction of the most considerable men of all
" parties, that I have received from both Whigs and Tories such compliments and ex-
" pressions of esteem, that I know not whether I deserve, but I am sure I did not expect.
" All I shall say of it is, that no book was ever wrote with more integrity and impar-
" tiality ; and if all the load and odium of the *Irish* rebellion, encouragement of the
" rebels, and faint prosecution of the war, is laid upon the parliament ; I could not
" help it, and wrote what I found, what I can support by undeniable evidence, and
" what I was in conscience obliged to write. This *Glamorgan's* secretary was an *Irish*
" priest, bred up with the digester of the memoirs. I shew in my history that *Glamorgan*
" had left *Oxford*, had put to sea, and had like to have been taken in the *Irish* channel
" before *April* 30 ; and though he did escape into the North of *England*, yet nobody at
" *Oxford* knew afterwards where he was, nor could any letters (especially such as that
" to the Pope) be sent to him. In fine, I have not the least doubt, but that *Glamorgan*
" forged every pretended power or commission he had ; and all of them so fully express
" his vanity, and are so adapted to his present views (views which in most cases could
" not arise till after he was in *Ireland*), that they could have no other author but him-
" self. I must observe to you, that this letter being directed to the Nuncio, is the only
" original of the king's writing among his papers (for *Glamorgan* only gave him copies
" translated of the others *) ; and whatever commission or other powers, instructions or
" letters, *Glamorgan* pretended to the Nuncio to have from the King, must be in a
" hand agreeable to that which the Nuncio had as an original." And in a third letter,
Feb. 22, 1736-7, says, " I will endeavour to do what you recommended to me in a less
" volume than the work I have now published, that so it may come into the hands of all
" the world. It shall be done some way or other. But I must first make some searches,
" which I shall have an opportunity of doing in a short time. For though I am entirely
" satisfied the lord *Herbert* assumed of himself the title of earl of *Glamorgan*, and never
" had any *fiant* for it, nor any privy seal, nor any grant under the signet, much less
" under the broad seal ; yet my exactness will not let me assert a thing positively, till I
" have searched into every thing that can give any light into the subject. Sir *William*
" *Dugdale*, who had gone through almost all our records, at least such as relate to our
" nobility, takes no notice in his Baronage of any such title. There is among his
" MS. papers in the *Bodleian* library at *Oxford*, a list of all the fiants, grants under
" the signet for honours and offices, whilst the king was at *Oxford*, with the date of
" each *fiant*, warrant, and grant. There is no such thing mentioned in that catalogue.
" But I propose likewise to search the signet or secretaries office here, the privy seal,
" and the paper office, to see if there be any mention of such a grant or warrant to lord

* If *Glamorgan* only gave copies translated of the other commissions, it is no great wonder that they
should be written in his Secretary's hand.

" Herbert ;

" *Herbert** ; for if there was none fuch, nobody can difpute but that all his pretended
" commiffions directed to him as earl of *Glamorgan* were meer forgeries." In *April* 1738
he publifhed, on a feparate fheet †, " A general Account of the neceffary materials for an
" Hiftory of *England*, the Society and Subfcriptions propofed for defraying the Ex-
" pences thereof, and the Method wherein Mr. *Carte* intends to proceed in carrying on
" the fame work." Of his progrefs in this bufinefs, he thus wrote to Dr. *Grey*, dated
from Mr. *Ker's*, at *The Golden Head*, in *Great Newport Street*, *Oct.* 4, 1738. " When
" I received the favour of your letter of *July* 26, I intended to have fet out the week
" following for *Maddingley*, and to have had the pleafure of waiting on you at *Houghton*
" *Conqueft* in my way ; but an unwelcome fummons from *Warwickfhire* calling me
" thither to appeal againft being raifed in the land-tax, broke my defign, and indeed
" my journey, becaufe I concluded Sir *J. H. Cotton* would be gone to *Oxford* before I
" could get to his houfe, when my appeal was over. However I wrote to Mr. *Bettenham*
" that I would take and difpofe of ten copies of your Anfwer to *Neale's* fourth volume,
" as I did of your late Anfwer. I have fince fent for them, but have not had them,
" I fuppofe becaufe they are not yet publifhed, or (as my bookbinder tells me from Mr.
" *Bettenham's* fervant when I fent for them) becaufe Mr. *Bettenham* does not print the
" book. I judge this laft is a miftake of my bookbinder ; but if Mr. *Bettenham* fhould
" not print it, I beg of you to fend me word who does. I believe *Oxford* will fill by
" the end of this month, and then I believe about fifteen of the colleges will fubfcribe
" towards my undertaking. As foon as that is done, I propofe to try what thofe of
" *Cambridge* will do, in which I promife myfelf your good offices. I have fent one of
" my propofals to your neighbour Mr. *Ongley* (who I am told is a very honeft gentle-
" man, of an ample fortune, and generous fpirit) and have wrote to him on that
" fubject. I do not know him perfonally, but he will confider the reafon of the thing
" what is faid in my letter, which poffibly, with your reafoning with him thereon,
" may induce him to fubfcribe. I have now 600*l.* a year either fubfcribed or promifed
" me by gentlemen at a diftance, who will fign their names to the inftrument when
" they come to town ; fo that I am in little doubt but the work will go on ; and nothing
" troubles me but the delay in compleating the fubfcription, that I may get a meeting
" of the contributors, and fall to executing my fcheme. 'Tis a large fum to be raifed
" by private perfons ; public bodies will, I hope, follow the example of the chapter of
" *Durham*, who fubfcribed their 20 guineas a year, and make up the reft." Soon after
the date of this letter, he was at *Cambridge*, collecting materials for fuch purpofe from the
Univerfity and other libraries. His head quarters were at *Madingley*, with the late
Sir *John Hynde Cotton*, bart. whofe great collection of pamphlets publifhed between
1640 and the Reftoration he methodized, and had bound in a great number of volumes
now in the library there. *March* 8, 1744, a caufe was determined in his favour in
chancery, in which he was plaintiff, and his brother and fifter *Samuel* ‡ and *Sarah* defendants,

---

* If *Herbert* never was *Glamorgan*, to be fure no commiffion could come to him as fuch ; but 'tis
wonderful that he fhould forge fuch a patent, becaufe if any commiffion or letter came to him from
the king, it would inftantly deftroy all the commiffions he had before pretended to. That bold forgeries, intended to produce important confequences, were practifed at that time is certain, witnefs the
inftrument that brought the *Scotch* into *England* at the beginning of the rebellion, &c.

† Reprinted in Gent. Mag. that year, p. 227. 364.

‡ *Samuel Carte* was admitted fcholar of *Trinity Hall, Cambridge, May* 5, 1704, and proceeded
LL.B. He was afterwards a member of *Symonds Inn*, practifed as a folicitor in chancery

in.

who died in a very advanced age, and in great obscurity, at
Rotherhithe;

fendants, occasioned by a doubt in their father's will. By the report in this case (*Atkyns* III. 174.) it appears that Mr. *Samuel Carte* the elder had made *Thomas* his eldest son executor and residuary legatee; but in a clause added in 1739, it was provided, " that " if he should be molested and prosecuted by the government, by which he might incur " a forfeiture, or could not be his executor," then *Samuel* and *Sarah* were to be executors,

in 1708, was eminent in his profession, and a learned Antiquary. Most of his MSS. and antiquarian papers (it is believed) were sold by his widow all together to the late learned Antiquary Sir *Thomas Cave*, bart. (whose large collections * for *Leicestershire*, including six or eight copies of *Burton's* History †, with notes by the author and other persons, the natural history by *Peck* ‡, with the MSS. of *Staveley* ‖, and both the *Cartes*, are now the property of his grandson who is a minor.) Mr. *S. Carte* assisted Dr. *Jackson*, schoolmaster of *Coventry*, in his " Account of the Benefactions and Cha- " rities belonging to that city, particularly that of Sir *Thomas White*. Lond. 1733," 8vo §. He also, though his name does not appear, was the editor of " Collectanea Ecclesiastica, by *Samuel* " *Brewster*, esq. 1752," 4to. and added many learned notes to that curious work. In the latter part of life he had chambers in *Symonds Inn*, but resided opposite to Dr. *Stukeley* in the passage which leads from *Queen's Square* to *Southampton Row*. He was alive in 1760, but died not long after. Dr. *Ducarel* has some valuable letters ** of his in MS. on various matters of antiquity; particularly on ancient fonts and seals, on the peculiar of *Bockley*, on a tradition of some subterraneous passages at *Leicester*, and on the chancellors of *Winchester*.—His brother *John* was admitted of the same Hall *Jan.* 9, 1707, where he took the degree of LL B. He was chaplain to *William* the fifth lord *Digby*; and was presented by his father (who possessed the advowson in right of his prebend) to the vicarage of *Tachbroke*, in the county of *Warwick*; and afterwards, by the dean and chapter of *Westminster*, to that of *Hinckley*, in *Leicestershire*, where he was inducted *Dec.* 20, 1720, and resided till his death, *Sept.* 17, 1735. He seldom failed to preach twice every *Sunday* in the church at *Hinckley*, and once in *Stoke* church, of which he enjoyed the rectory as annexed to the vicarage of *Hinckley*. The last time he preached was the Funeral Sermon of his Clerk *James Merry*, after which he never more was able to attend the duties of the church. The Sermon at his own funeral was preached by Dr. *Jackson* above-mentioned to a crowded congregation at *Hinckley*, where Mr. *Carte* was buried in the chancel near the communion table, and where no other memorial remains to his memory than an inscription on a gallery, that it was erected in 1723, whilst he was vicar; though his surviving parishioners still speak of his learning, his probity, his simplicity of manners, and his unaffected piety, with a degree of veneration. He was a most zealous assertor of the rites and ceremonies of the church of *England*, which, he justly observed, were equally remote from the extremes of Popery and Fanaticism; and his opinions were founded on the firm basis of Scripture, with which he was so intimately acquainted, as to be able to repeat the greater part of the Bible. A favourite book of his was " *Bysse's* Beauty of Holiness," which, he said, was worth its weight in gold.—*Moses Emanuel*, a *Jew* of uncommon learning, well known in that part of the country as a travelling pedlar, received always much pleasure from the conversation of Mr. *Carte*, who in return took amazing pains to convince him of the truths of Christianity. Their friendly altercations were long and frequent, and turned principally upon the fifty-first and fifty-third chapters of *Isaiah*.—His absence of mind is recollected in many remarkable particulars. Some years before his death he paid his

* Of these, the hundred of *Guthlaxton* only is prepared for the press.

† Mr. *Gough* has the printed copy, with numerous notes and many pedigrees, which once belonged to *Robert Fisher*, and afterwards to Mr. *West*; Dr. *Ducarel* has another, with many notes by the late Dr. *Vernon*, rector of St. *George*, *Bloomsbury*; a third is in *Jesus College* Library, *Cambridge*, with large emendations and additions by *Gascoigne*; a fourth in the *Harleian* Library.

‡ Of *Burton* and *Peck* some account shall be given in the Appendix.

‖ Since what is said of Mr. *Staveley* in p. 191 was printed off, I find that he married *Mary* the fourth daughter of Mr. *Oneby* (see Gent. Mag. 1777, p. 316.) by whom he had several sons, who all died without issue; he had also four daughters, one of which *(Anne)* was married to the father of the poet *Welsted*; another *(Mary)* to the Mr. *Brudenell* already mentioned, by whom she had a son and two daughters.—Mr. *Fox* (see p. 191.) was vicar of St. *Mary's* from 1688 till his death in 1736 or 1737.

§ MS note by Dr. *Richardson*, communicated by the Rev. Mr. *Cole*, Brit. Top. II. 304.

** In one of these, dated *July* 30, 1753, he says, " there was in my time a cross patée fitchée over the cover " of a font in *Leicester*: it was (in no long time) altered, and a carved dove set at the top of the cover, instead " of the cross."

7

addresses

Rotherhithe; " The Evangelical History and Harmony. By
" *Matthew*

'cutors, and to poſſeſs what was given to *Thomas.* On the 9th of *May* 1744, he was diſcharged out of cuſtody, into which he had been taken (with Mr. *Garth)* on the ſuſpen-
ſion of the Habeas Corpus act * ; and on the 18th of *July* that year, the court of common council of the city of *London* agreed " to ſubſcribe fifty pounds a year for ſeven
" years to Mr. *Carte,* towards defraying the charges of his writing the Hiſtory of *Eng-*
" *land.*" " A Collection of the ſeveral Papers publiſhed by Mr. *Carte,* in relation to
" his Hiſtory of *England,*" 8vo. (ſee p. 172) was printed in *Auguſt.* On the 18th of
October, the company of goldſmiths voted " twenty-five pounds a year, for ſeven years,
" towards the charge of tranſcripts of records, negotiations, &c." and in *December* the
companies of grocers and vintners ſubſcribed twenty-five pounds a year each for the ſame
purpoſe. Propoſals for printing the work were circulated in 1746; the firſt volume
was completed in *December* 1747; and unluckily the credit of the whole was overthrown by a ridiculous note upon the cure of *the king's evil* † ; which in reality was not
his own, but which he was over-perſuaded to inſert after the ſheet in which it was
printed

---

addreſſes to Miſs *Dugdale,* of *Blyth Hall* near *Coleſhill* (a lineal deſcendant of the illuſtrious Antiquary), and the wedding-day was fixed; but he actually forgot to go till the day after that
which was agreed on, when the lady with indignation refuſed her hand, and the match was
broken off. Perpetually abſorpt in thought, he was careleſs in his dreſs, and totally deſtitute of
œconomy. He even carried his careleſſneſs in money matters to ſuch a degree, that when the
inhabitants of *Stoke* have brought to him the tithes, which he never took the trouble to aſk for,
he has not uncommonly (if he chanced to be engaged with a book) requeſted them to come at
a future time, though perhaps the next hour he was obliged to borrow a guinea for ſubſiſtance.
The parſonage houſe adjoins to the church-yard; yet he was frequently ſo engaged in ſtudy, that
the ſermon-bell rang till the congregation were weary of waiting, and the clerk was under
the neceſſity of reminding him of his duty.—During the fifteen years in which he was vicar of
Hinckley, he neglected to make any demand for tithes of the hamlet of *Hide* in that pariſh; which
his adminiſtrator diſcovering after his death, made a claim on the inhabitants of that hamlet
for tithes in kind; and, to recover them, filed a bill in chancery, which came to a hearing in *Eaſter*
term 1747. The defendants inſiſted that the vicarage was never endowed, and that a contributory payment of ſeventeen ſhillings which had formerly been made was in lieu of all tithes; and that tithes
in kind were not paid within memory of man. Mr. *Carte,* being obliged to prove the endowment,
as his brother was only vicar, and not rector, procured from the abbot of *Lyra* in *Normandy,*
to which abbey *Hinckley* had formerly been appendant as an alien priory, a grant in 1209 to the vicar
of that pariſh. The certificate however having been unluckily ſigned by the abbot, and not by
the regiſtrar of the abbey, it was not admitted to be read in evidence; and as the impropriators
(the Dean and Chapter of *Weſtminſter)* did not think proper to diſclaim their right to the tithes,
which might have put an end to the queſtion in favour of Mr. *Carte,* an iſſue was directed, " to try
" whether the vicar of *Hinckley* is intitled to tithes in kind for the hamlet of *Hide,* in the pariſh of
" *Hinckley.*" (*Atkyns's* Reports, III. 426.) This iſſue was afterwards tried; when the jury found
that the vicar in his life-time was not intitled to tithes in kind, and on *July* 17, 1749, the bill was
diſmiſſed with coſts. The arrears of the *modus,* however, were adjudged to Mr. *Carte.* (*Vezey's*
Reports, I. 3.)

* I am told that, whilſt under examination, the Duke of *Newcaſtle* aſked him if he was not a Biſhop."
" No, my Lord Duke," replied Mr. *Carte;* " there are no Biſhops in *England* but what are made
" by your Grace; and I am ſure I have no reaſon to expect that honour."—In the *Weſtminſter* Journal
of *May* 12, 1744, it was inſinuated that Mr. *Carte* " was confined for he knew not what; and diſcharg-
" ed he knew not why."

† See this note at length, with remarks on it, in Gent. Mag. 1748, p. 13, 14. See alſo " Verſes
" from the Jacobite Journal, addreſſed to the immortal Mr. *Carte,*" in the ſame Magazine, p. 135.—
Three pamphlets were in a few days occaſioned by this note: 1. " Remarks on Mr. *Carte's* general
" Hiſtory of *England;*" 2. " A Letter to the Jacobite Journaliſt, concerning Mr. *Carte's* Hiſtory, by
" *Duncan Mac Carte,* a Highlander;" and 3. " Some Specimens of Mr. *Carte's* Hiſtory of *England,*
" with Remarks thereon, by *Donald Mac Carte.*"—Mr. *Barrington* has preſerved an anecdote
which he heard from an old man who was witneſs in a cauſe with reſpect to this ſuppoſed
miraculous

" *Matthew Pilkington*, LL. B. Vicar of *Stanton* in the county
" of

printed was actually committed to the pre∫s *. This imprudence was fatal to his intere∫t. The corporation of *London* (in con∫equence of a motion made by Sir *William Calvert* one of his earlie∫t ∫ub∫cribers, and ∫econded by Sir *John Barnard*) unanimou∫ly re∫olved to withdraw their ∫ub∫cription † in *April* 1748; and the Hi∫tory fell into almo∫t total negle&ct. The fir∫t volume (∫ee p 189) was printed in 1747, and ∫old by *J. Hodges* on *London Bridge*; it was in∫cribed, " To the Duke of *Beaufort* Pre∫ident, " and to the Society of Noblemen and Gentlemen; the Chancellor, Ma∫ters and " Scholars of the Univer∫ity of *Oxford*, with the Societies of *New, Magdalen, Brazen-* " *no∫e*, and *Trinity* Colleges; the Lord Mayor, Aldermen, and Common Council of " the City of *London*, and the wor∫hipful Companies of Grocers, Gold∫miths, and " Vintners; by who∫e generous encouragement the work was undertaken." The ∫econd (containing an account of all public tran∫actions from the acce∫sion of *Henry* III. A. D. 1216, to the death of *Henry* VIII. *April* 21, 1509) was publi∫hed in 1750; and the third (containing an account of all public tran∫actions from the acce∫sion of *Henry* VIII. A. D. 1509, to the marriage of the Ele&ctor Palatine with the Prince∫s *Eliza-* *beth* daughter of *James* I. in A. D. 1613) in 1752, both printed for the author, at his hou∫e in *Dean's Yard, We∫tmin∫ter*. In the preface to the ∫econd volume, he vindicates the obnoxious note in the fir∫t, and a∫∫erts his own accuracy. To the third al∫o a Pre-

miraculous power of healing. " He had, by his evidence, fixed the time of a fa&ct, by Queen " *Anne*'s having been at *Oxford*, and touched him, whil∫t a child, for the evil: when he had " fini∫hed his evidence, I had an opportunity of a∫king him whether he was really cured? Upon " which he an∫wered with a ∫ignificant ∫mile, that he believed him∫elf to have never had a com- " plaint that de∫erved to be con∫idered as the evil; but that his parents were poor, *and had no* " *obje&ction to the bit of gold.*" The learned and honourable writer very properly ob∫erves on this occa- ∫ion, " that this piece of gold, which was given to tho∫e who were touched, accounts for the great " re∫ort upon this occa∫ion, and the ∫uppo∫ed afterwards miraculous cures." *Fabian Philips*, in his Treati∫e on Purveyance, p. 257, a∫∫erts, " that the angels i∫∫ued by the kings of *England* on the∫e oc- " ca∫ions amounted to a charge of three thou∫and pounds *per annum*;" and Queen *Elizabeth* was ∫o tired of touching tho∫e who de∫ired to be cured for the evil, that in *Glouce∫ter∫hire*, during one of her progre∫∫es, ∫he told tho∫e who were pre∫∫ing on her, that God only could relieve them from their com- plaints. By a proclamation, *March* 25, 14 *James* I. it appears that the kings of *England* would not permit ∫uch patients to approach them during the ∫ummer; and by another proclamation, *June* 18, 1626, it is ordered, that no one ∫hall apply for this purpo∫e, who does not bring a proper certi- ficate that he was never touched before; a regulation which undoubtedly aro∫e from ∫ome ∫uppo∫ed patients, who had attempted to receive the bit of gold more than once. Sir *Kenelm Digby* informed Mon∫. *Moncon∫s*, that if the per∫on had lo∫t the piece of gold, the complaint immediately returned. *Gemelli* (the famous traveller) gives an account of 1600 per∫ons being pre∫ented for this purpo∫e to *Louis* XIV. on *Ea∫ter Sunday*, 1686. The words u∫ed were, *Le Roy te touche, Dieu te gueri∫∫e*. Every *Frenchman* received 15 ∫ous, and every foreigner 30. *Ob∫ervations on the Statutes*, 1775, p. 107, 108.—Dr. *Ducarel* has informed me, that being in 1746 on a vi∫it to the Rev. Mr. *Bu∫s*, then (and ∫till, 1780) vicar of *Wadhur∫t* in *Su∫∫ex*, he was ∫hewn in the regi∫ter book of that pari∫h certi- ficates for divers per∫ons to recommend them for the touch in the reign of *James* II. ∫igned by the vicar and church-wardens, ∫etting forth that they verily believed *A. B.* was affli&cted with the King's evil, and that *he had never been touched before*; by which it ∫eems to have been under∫tood ∫o late as the clo∫e of the la∫t century, that they could be pre∫ented but once to the King on that account.—*Charles* II. touched 92107 per∫ons between *May* 1661 and *April* 1682. See *Brown's* " Chari∫ma Ba∫ilicon," 1684, 8vo

* In the conclu∫ion of the note, Mr. *Carte* declares him∫elf to have been " an infidel on that head, " till convinced of his mi∫take by the late Mr. *An∫tis*, Garter King of Arms, who furni∫hed him with " tho∫e proofs out of the *Engli∫h* records, which atte∫t the fa&cts, and are printed in *Tooker's* treati∫e on " that ∫ubje&ct," publi∫hed in 1597.

† On a petition from Mr. *Carte* to the court of common-council, *Oct.* 11, 1750, fifty pounds were paid him for the year which was nearly elap∫ed when the ∫ub∫cription was withdrawn.

face

" of *Derby*, and chaplain to his grace the duke of *Cleveland*," folio;

face is prefixed. Twenty-two copies of the three volumes were sent in 1752 to Monf. *De Lemoignon*, Grand Chancellor of *France*. The fourth volume (containing an account of all public transactions from the marriage of the Elector Palatine with the Princefs *Elizabeth*, A. D. 1613, to A. D. 1654, about five years before the Reftoration) was publifhed after the author's death, in 1755, by *W. Ruffel**, at *Horace's Head*, without *Temple Bar*. His defign was to have brought the hiftory down to the Revolution, for which purpofe he had taken great pains in copying every thing valuable that could be met with in *England, Scotland, Ireland*, &c. At the conclufion is the following fhort apolcgy: " The author pro-" pofed to have carried on this volume to the Reftoration; but death unhappily put a pe-" riod to it fooner." He died at *Caldecot* Houfe, near *Abingdon* in *Berkfhire, April 2*, 1754; having publifhed, 1. " The *Irifh* Maffacre, fet in a clear light, 1714," a pamphlet in 4to.—2. " *Thuani* Hiftoria fui temporis, 1733," 7 vol. folio (in conjunction with Mr. *Buckley*, fee p. 81).—3. " The Hiftory of the Life of *James* Duke of *Ormonde*, " from his birth in 1610, to his death in 1688; by *T. C. A. M.* 1735, 1736," 3 vol. folio, dedicated to the Earl of *Arran*, who delivered to him 153 bundles of his grandfather's papers.—4. " A Collection of original Letters and Papers concerning the " Affairs of *England*, from 1641 to 1660—1739," 2 vol. 8vo.—5. " The Hiftory " of the Revolutions of *Portugal†*, from the Foundation of that Kingdom to the year " 1567, with Letters of Sir *Robert Southwell*, during his Embaffy there, to the Duke " of *Ormond*; giving a particular account of the depofing Don *Alfonfo*, and placing " Don *Pedro* on the Throne, 1740," 8vo.—6. " A full Anfwer to the Letter from " a By-Stander, 1742," a pamphlet, 8vo.—7. " A full and clear Vindication " of the full Anfwer‡ to a Letter from a By-Stander, 1743," a pamphlet, 8vo.— 8. " Catalogue des Rolles § *Gafcons, Normans*, et *Francois*, confervés dans les Archives

* Son of a Nonjuring Clergyman, who was educated at *St. John's College, Cambridge*, and kept a boarding-houfe in *Weftminfter* for young fcholars whofe parents were Nonjurors. In 1732 the father was editor of " *Marci Hieronymi Vidæ, Cremonenfis, Albæ* Epifcopi, Poemata quæ extant omnia; " quibus nunc primum adjiciuntur ejufdem Dialogi de reipublicæ dignitate; ex collatione optimorum " exemplarium emendata, additis indicibus accuratis," 2 vols. 12mo. infcribed (in a poetical dedication) " *Alexandro Pope* armigero, Poetarum inter *Anglos* celeberrimo." And in 1746 he was editor of " S. S. Patrum Apoftolicorum Opera genuina, &c. Curâ *Richardi Ruffel*, A. M." 2 vols. 8vo.—The bookfeller failed in bufinefs, became afterwards an itinerant in that profeffion, and was principally fupported by Mr. *Jennens* of *Gopfal* in *Leiceftershire*, of whom I fhall have occafion to fpeak hereafter as an editor of *Shakfpeare*. Another fon was *James Ruffel*, the author of " Letters from a " young Painter in *Italy*, 1748," 2 vols. 8vo. This gentleman, who is fuppofed to have made no great figure in his profeffion, refided at *Rome*, and fupported himfelf by acting as *Cicerone* to the *Englifh* gentlemen who vifited that immenfe repofitory of antient and modern *virtù*. He died there, probably about 15 years ago.

† Though Mr. *Carte* forgot to mention this work in his " Vindication of the full Anfwer to a " Letter from a By-Stander," where he gives a lift of his writings; I can venture to call it his on good authority. The letters of Sir *Robert Southwell* were amongft the papers he received from the Earl of *Arran*.—At Dr. *Campbell's* fale, Mr. *Reed* bought a copy of Sir *Robert Southwell*, with the language of the book corrected by that gentleman, feemingly with a view to a new edition.

‡ *Corbyn Morris*, efq. commiffioner of the cuftoms, who died *Dec.* 24, 1779, wrote the " Letter " to the By-Stander."

§ The titles only of thefe Rolls make two folio volumes; it would certainly, however, be a work deferving the encouragement of all learned men throughout *Europe*, to print thefe inftruments at length; the fame may be faid with regard to the records in the *Bermingham* tower at *Dublin*, fome of which go as far back as the time of *Edward* I. Obfervations on the Statutes, p. 109, n. The utility indeed of fuch publications is fo obvious, that it is really wonderful that neither of the great nations who are interefted fhould have engaged in them.

" de

folio; " *Demofthenis* Selectæ Orationes: Ad Codices MSS.
" recenfuit,

" de la Tour de *Londres*; tiré d'après celui du Garde defdites Archives : Et contenant
" la precis et le fommaire de tous les titres qui f'y trouvent concernant la *Guienne*, la
" *Normandie*, et les autres Provinces de la *France*, fujettes autrefois aux Rois d'*Angle-*
" *terre*, &c. *Par*. 1743," 2 vol. folio, with two moft exact and correct indexes of places
and perfons. This valuable collection, being calculated for the ufe of the *French* *, is preceded by a preface in that language.—9. " A Preface to a tranflation, by Mrs.
" *Thompfon*, of the Hiftory of the memorable and extraordinary Calamities of *Mar-*
" *garet* of *Anjou*, Queen of *England*, &c. by the Chevalier *Michael Baudier* †, *London*,
" 1736," 8vo.—10. " Advice of a Mother to her Son and Daughter, tranflated from
" the *French* of the Marchionefs de *Lambert*, *London*," feveral editions.—11. " Further
" Reafons, addreffed to the Parliament, for rendering more effectual an Act of Queen
" *Anne*, relating to the vefting in Authors the Right of Copies, for the Encourage-
" ment of Learning, by *R. H.*" [about 1737; fee his letter in p. 195.]—12. " Hiftory
" of *England*," 4 volumes in folio ‡. A tranflation of this Hiftory into *French* was
intended by feveral hands; the firft book was undertaken by M. L'Abbé *Delacroix*; the
fecond and fixth by Pere *Peter* of *Dublin*; the third by Pere de *Monchelon*; the fourth
by M. *Goffort*; the fifth by M. de *Lavirotes*. This tranflation, I believe, was never
finifhed; but Dr. *Ducarel* has the fecond and fifth books complete, and the greater
part of the third and fifth books, in the hand-writing of the tranflators.—At Mr. *Carte's*.

* Dr. *Ducarel* informs me, that the authority of the records in *The Tower*, fo far as relates to *Nor-*
mandy and other provinces in *France* formerly belonging to the *Englifh*, have always, and to his knowledge within thefe laft forty years, been admitted as evidence in the courts of judicature, where exemp-
tions from the quartering of foldiers on their eftates, or any other privileges formerly granted, have
been received as evidence; the inftruments being duly authenticated by the keeper of the records.—
Mr. *Barrington* has alfo obferved, that on an alarm occafioned by an edict iffued by Cardinal *Fleury* at
the latter end of his adminiftration, the *French* inhabitants of thofe provinces, which formerly belonged to the crown of *England*, were furnifhed in feveral inftances with evidence of their titles to
franchifes from our records.

† The original of this work is preferved in MS. in the library of the abbey of *St. Germain des Prez*
at *Paris*, with a Hiftory by the fame writer (in *French*) of " the Adminiftration of Cardinal *Wolfey*,"
of which latter work Dr. *Ducarel* has a fair tranfcript.

‡ He had, as he himfelf fays, p. 43, of his Vindication of the full Anfwer to a Letter from a By-
Stander, " read abundance of collections relating to the time of King *Charles* II. and had in his power
" a feries of memoirs from the beginning to the end of that reign; in which all thofe intrigues and
" turns at court, at the latter end of the king's life, which bifhop *Burnet*, with all his gout for tales,
" of fecret hiftory, and all his genius for conjectures, does not pretend to account for, are laid open
" in the cleareft and moft convincing manner; by the perfon who was moft affected by them, and had
" the beft reafon to know them." In the fecond volume of this hiftory there is a very clear account
of the conftitution of our parliament, and of the time when cities and boroughs firft came to be reprefented; fhewing the difference between the king's council in parliament, and the parliament itfelf; in
which he has removed the miftakes of writers, who had confounded them. In the early part of the *Eng-*
lifh hiftory Mr. *Barrington* prefers the authority of *Carte* to any other hiftorian. As he was indefatigable in his refearches, having dedicated his whole life to them, fo was he moft exact in his authorities, many of which were new ones. He was affifted, in what relates to *Wales*, by the labours
of Mr. *Lewis Morris*, of *Penryn*, in *Cardiganfhire*, (vol. I. p. 33.) His political prejudices cannot be fuppofed to have had any bias in what relates to a tranfaction 500 years ago, and which has
nothing to do with the royal touch for the cure of the king's evil. But perhaps the beft account of this
work is that given by Monf. *D'Eyverdun*, in a note to his critique on Mr. *Walpole's* " Hiftoric
" Doubts," in his " Memoires Litteraires de la *Grande Bretagne* pour l'an 1768. *Lond*. 1769," 8vo,
p. 24. " Mr. *Carte* a donné une hiftoire generale de l'*Angleterre* en 4 volumes en folio, dans le deffein
" de l'oppofer à celle de *Rapin*. Il eft mort avant d'avoir achevé ce grand travail, qu'il a pouffé
" jufqu'au Protectorat de *Cromwell*. Ce fcavant ouvrage, d'ailleurs affez mal ecrit, eft rempli de
" recherches fort utiles, et de prejuges qui ne ie font gueres."

death.

" recensuit, Textum, Scholiasten, & Versionem plurimis
" in locis castigavit, Notis insuper illustravit *Ricardus*
" *Mounteney*,

death, all his papers came into the hands of his widow *, who afterwards married Mr.
Jernegan, (whose father *Henry*, a goldsmith in *Russel Street*, made the curious silver
cistern which was disposed of by Lottery about 40 years ago, and who lies buried in
Covent Garden church-yard, with an epitaph by *Aaron Hill*. See his Works, vol. III.
p. 162.) a gentleman intended for orders in the *Romish* church, though he declined taking
them after having received an education for that purpose. She left them to her second
husband for his life, and after his death to the university of *Oxford*, where they are
now lodged in the *Bodleian* library, having been delivered to the University in the life-
time of Mr. *Jernegan*, for a valuable consideration, in 1778. While they were in Mr.
Jernegan's possession, the present earl of *Hardwicke* paid 200l. for the perusal of them.
Mr. *Macpherson* also obtained the use of them, by a present of 300l. made by his publisher to the proprietor; and out of these and other papers compiled his History and
State Papers †, 1775. Besides his collections for his History of *England*, Mr. *Carte* left
behind him, in manuscript, " A Vindication of King *Charles* the first, with regard to
the " *Irish* massacre ‡." He was a man of strong constitution, laborious and indefatigable in his studies. Dr. *Mangey* ‖, who was universally allowed to be a man of

* This lady was a daughter of Colonel *Brett's*.—I have mentioned above, that Mr. *Carte* was
originally of *University College*; but have been since told that he afterwards removed to *Brazen Nose*.

† " The *Stuart* papers contained in these volumes consist of the collection of Mr. *Nairne*, who was
" under secretary, from the Revolution to the end of the year 1713, to the ministers of King *James*
" II. and to those of his son. The extracts from the Life of King *James* II. consisting of more than
" thirty sheets of print, were partly taken by the late Mr. *Carte*, and partly by the editor, in a jour-
" ney he made for that purpose to *France*. Mr. *Nairne's* papers came into the possession of Mr.
" *Carte* some time before his death." MACPHERSON.

‡ In 1747 Dr. *Birch* published " An Enquiry into the Share which King *Charles* I. had in the
" Transactions of the Earl of *Glamorgan*," asserting in opposition to Mr. *Carte* that the King was privy
to the negotiations of that nobleman. Mr. *Walpole* observes, that seven years elapsed without Mr.
Carte's reply; but that two months before he died he was supposed to be the author of an advertisement, promising an answer. In 1758 a work appeared, which was written and designed for the press
in 1748, and was announced in the news-papers in 1754, intituled, " The case of the Royal Martyr
" considered with candour;" part of which contains strictures upon Dr. *Birch's* work. In the preface
the author ** mentions his obligations to Mr. *Carte*, who favoured him with a great many letters upon
the subject, and observes, that " Mr. *Carte's* great learning and critical skill in our history will al-
" ways have its due weight with men of sense and unprejudiced minds, and as to his peculiar notions
" of government, they chiefly affected himself." He seldom, proceeds this gentleman, " troubled
" his friends with any thing of that kind. During a correspondence with him for many years, I can
" truly say that I could never have guessed at his political principles by any one single hint or notice in
" all his letters;" and he concludes, " he was a credit to every one who had the pleasure of his ac-
" quaintance, and I esteem it my peculiar happiness that I have this opportunity of paying a grateful
" respect to the memory of a man, who did honour to literature while he lived, and at his death left
" a monument of his abilities behind him, which bids fair to outlive the malice of *Scotish* criticism, the
" noisy, the virulent efforts of ignorance and prejudice, if not the force of time.
" *Eheu! Britannia!*
" *Quando ullum invenies parem?*
" *Multis ille quidem flebilis occidit;*
" *Nulli flebilior quam tibi, Britannia.*"

‖ The Doctor acknowledges himself obliged to him for many communications out of the King of
France's library, for his edition of *Philo Judæus*, and calls him " Vir præclaræ industriæ, eruditionis,
" & ingenii."

** *John Boswell*, M. A. of *Taunton*, author of " A Method of Study, or a useful Library, 1738," 8vo;
and of two pamphlets called " Remarks on the Free and Candid Disquisitions," 1750 and 1751.

great

" *Mounteney**, Coll. Regal. apud *Cantabrigienses* haud ita
" pridem Socius. Præfiguntur Obfervationes† in Com-
" mentarios vulgò *Ulpianeos*, & Tabula antiquæ *Græciæ De-*
" *moſtheni* accommodata," 8vo ; " Letters on various fub-
" jects, by the late Sir *Thomas Fitzoſborne*, bart." 8vo.
[by *William Melmoth*‡, efq.] A third Edition of " The
" Alliance between Church and State," 8vo ; " A Letter
" from an Author to a Member of Parliament, concern-
" ing Literary Property" [by Mr. *Warburton*] 8vo ; " Cri-
" tical Notes on fome paſſages of fcripture ||," [by Mr. *Manne*,
of whom fee p. 173] 8vo ; " A Critical Enquiry into the
" opinions and practice of the antient Philofophers, con-
" cerning the nature of the foul and a future ftate [by Mr.
" *Towne*]; with a Preface by the author of *The Divine Le-*

great learning, faid, that he always thought he could fit as long at his ftudies as any
man, till he came to live in the fame houfe with Mr. *Carte*, who, he faid, ufed to write
or read from early in the morning till night, only allowing himfelf time to take a difh or
two of tea, or fomething of that kind ; fo that, faid the doctor, I could not keep pace
with him at all. When his ftudies of the day were over, he would eat heartily ; and when
he was in company, was very chearful and entertaining, without the leaft tincture of
morofenefs or referve, but extremely negligent of propriety and neatnefs in externals.

* This gentleman, who in 1725 went from *Eton* to *King's College* where he became a
Fellow, publifhed the firft edition of his *Demoſthenes* in 1731. He was a barrifter of the
Inner Temple, afterwards became one of the barons of the exchequer in *Ireland*, when,
in 1743 there came on in that court the famous trial between *James Annefley*, efq. and
Richard earl of *Anglefey* ; in which this judge made a moft refpectable figure. He was
the author of " Obfervations on the probable Iffue of the Congrefs," printed by Mr.
Bowyer in 1748, 8vo. And in the fame year appeared " Baron *Mounteney*'s celebrated
" dedication of the felect orations of *Demoſthenes*, to the late Sir *R. Walpole*, with
" notes, &c."

† Thefe were by Dr. *John Chapman*, the prefent archdeacon of *Sudbury*, well known
by many learned publications.

‡ The excellent Tranflator of " Letters of *Pliny* the Conful, with occafional Remarks,
" 1746," 2 vols. 8vo ; of which a fecond edition, corrected, appeared in 1747 ; and alfo
of " Letters of *Marcus Tullius Cicero* to feveral of his friends, with Remarks, 1753," 3
vols. 8vo ; and of *Cicero's* " Effays on Old Age and Friendfhip," 2 vols. 8vo. 1773 and 1778.

|| In the fame year came out an 8vo. pamphlet, by *E. Langford*, M. A. " Objections
" to a pamphlet lately publifhed, intituled, *Critical Notes*, &c. in a letter to the author."

" *gation*,

" *gation*," two editions, 8vo; Mrs. *Cockburn's* * " Remarks
" upon the Principles and Reasoning of Dr. *Rutherforth's*
" Essay on the Nature and Obligations of Virtue, in vindi-
" cation of the contrary principles and reasonings inforced
" in the Writings of the late Dr. *Samuel Clarke*," 8vo;
" Answer to Dr. *Rutherforth's* Determinatio Quæstionis The-
" ologicæ, by *Joseph Edwards* †, M. A. Vice-principal of
" *Magdalen Hall, Oxford*," 8vo; and two editions of " A Sup-
" plement ‡ to Mr. *Warburton's* edition of *Shakespeare*," 8vo.

In

---

* Of this ingenious lady see an account under the year 1751.—" Dr. *Rutherforth's* Essay,
which was published in *May* 1744, soon engaged her thoughts; and, notwithstanding
an asthmatic disorder, which had seized her many years before, and now left her small
intervals of ease, she applied herself to the confutation of that elaborate discourse; and
having finished it with a spirit, elegance, and perspicuity, equal, if not superior, to
all her former writings, transmitted her manuscript to Mr. *Warburton*, who published
it with a Preface of his own." BIRCH.

† Author of four single Sermons, in 8vo. 1731, 1736, 1743, 1749. See *Letsome's*
" Preacher's Assistant."

‡ By *Thomas Edwards*, esq; reprinted next year under the title of " Canons of Cri-
" ticism."—Mr. *Edwards*, though a younger brother, became possessed of a good paternal estate at *Turrick* in *Bucks*; and was the last of his family, as appears by his
5th Sonnet in *Dodsley's* Collection of Poems, vol. II. p. 326, where he pathetically laments the loss of four brothers and as many sisters. He was an excellent scholar, having
been thoroughly grounded in the Classicks at *Eton School*, whence he went to *King's*
College, Cambridge. He afterwards studied the law at *Lincoln's Inn*, his father and
grandfather having been of that profession. He spent the latter part of his life principally at *Turrick*; died on a visit at his friend Mr. *Richardson's* at *Parson's Green*, the
3d of *Jan*. 1757, aged 58; and was buried in the church-yard of *Ellesborough* in *Buckinghamshire*, with the following inscription:

" Under this stone are deposited the remains of
Thomas Edwards, esq. of *Turrick* in this parish,
where he spent the last seventeen years.
of a studious, useful life.
He was sincere and constant in the profession and
practise of Christianity, without narrowness or superstition;
steadily attached to the cause of liberty,
nor less an enemy to licentiousness and faction;
in his poetry simple, elegant, pathetic;
in his criticism exact, acute, temperate;
affectionate to his relations, cordial to his friends,
in the general commerce of life obliging and entertaining.

He

In 1748, Mr. *Bowyer* endeavoured to relieve himself from the fatigues of business, by an occasional retirement to *Knightsbridge*, where he appears to have promised himself the satisfaction of prevailing on Mr. *Markland* to accompany him*. The principal books printed by him this year were " The History and Antiquities of *Colchester*, in " three books, collected chiefly from MSS. with an appen-" dix of records and original papers," folio, by Mr. *Morant*, reprinted with improvements in his " History of *Essex*," 1768; Bp. *Tanner's* " Bibliotheca *Britannico-Hibernica*," folio (see p. 138); " A critical Commentary upon the

He bore a tedious and painful distemper with a patience, which could only arise from a habit of virtue and piety; and quitted this life with the decent unconcern of one whose hopes are firmly fixed on a better.

He died on the third day of *January*, MDCCLVII, aged LVIII;
and this stone is inscribed to his memory,
with the truest concern and gratitude,
by his two nephews and heirs, *Joseph Paice* and *Nathaniel Mason*."

These nephews were his sister's sons. Mr. *Edwards* was equally distinguished for his genius and the goodness of his heart. His " Canons of Criticism" did him great credit, both as a critic and as a scholar, and of course provoked the vengeance of Dr. *Warburton*, which he wreaked very illiberally in a note on the Dunciad (IV. 567); of which Mr. *Edwards* was more susceptible than the circumstance required, deeming his rank in life impeached by the words " *a gentleman*, as he is pleased to call himself, of *Lincoln's* " *Inn*, but, in reality, a gentleman only of the Dunciad," &c. The gentleman, whose assistance Mr. *Edwards* acknowledges in the preface, was Mr. *Roderick*, Fellow of *Magdalen College* in *Cambridge*, and of the Royal and Antiquarian Societies. He died *July* 20, 1756, not long before his friend, bequeathing to him such of his papers as related to the " Canons of Criticism." Thirteen of his Sonnets are printed in *Dodsley's* Collection, eight in *Pearch's*, and four in the " Select Collection," 1780. Twenty-seven others may be seen in the last edition of his " Canons of Criticism, 1765."—He was also author of a pretty *jeu d'esprit*, called " The Trial of the Letter Υ, alias Y," which is printed with his " Canons of Criticism;" and of a pamphlet called " Free and candid " Thoughts on the Doctrine of Predestination." See Dr. *Akenside's* and Mrs. *Chapone's* Odes to him.

* " I approve of your *Knightsbridge* scheme very much, not upon my own account " (though perhaps your kindness to me looks upon that as an article in the purchase), " but as a good bargain. If you were about to leave off business, I think there would " be some difference in the case, for then I imagine you would get a little farther from " *London*. For my own part, I must get somewhere near the sea side, for the sake " of bathing and riding, which is commonly good upon the coast; for of all places in " the world, *London* is the worst for an infirm person, who has nothing to do in the " business of it, and very little in the pleasures." *Mr. Markland to Mr. Bowyer*, *Oct.* 22, 1748.

3

" Book

" Book of the Wifdom of *Jefus*, the Son of *Sirach* *,
" being a continuation of Bp. *Patrick* and Dr. *Lowth*, by *R.*
" *Arnald*, B. D." folio ; " A Voyage round the World in the
" years 1740, 1, 2, 3, 4, by *George Anfon*, efq. compiled
" from his papers and materials, by *Richard Walter* †, M. A.
" chaplain of his Majefty's fhip *The Centurion* in that Expe-
" dition," 4to ; " Lufus Poetici, Editio tertia, emendatior,"
by Mr. *Jortin*, 4to; a Second edition of " *Fitzofborne's*
" Letters," 8vo. " *Ifocratis* opera omnia, *Græcè* & *Latinè*,"
publifhed by Dr. *Battie*, 2 vols. 8vo. " *Bath*, a Poem," 4to ;
Mr. *Edwards's* " Canons of Criticifm," 8vo ; a fourth
edition of " The Effay on Man ;" and " Poems on feveral
" occafions, by *Edward Cobden* ‡, D. D." 8vo, [for the benefit of his Curate's Widow].

An

* In this volume is " A Difcourfe concerning the Two *Sirachides*, one the Author,
the other the *Greek* Tranflator, of the Book of *Ecclefiafticus*.

† This volume, though commonly afcribed to Mr. *Walter*, whofe name appeared in
the title-page, and who had taken-in fubfcriptions, was the production of the late *Benjamin Robins*, efq. of whom a good account is given by Dr. *Wilfon*, in his introduction
to the works of Mr. *Robins*, 2 vols. 8vo, 1761.—The fifth edition of the " Voyage,"
in 1749, was revifed by Mr. *Robins* himfelf, who defigned, if he had remained in *England*, to have written a fecond part of it.—The *French* affect to call this *chef d'œuvre*
in its way a romance ; and we muft certainly give the writer credit for fome of the things,
to the honour of his hero, which he would have us believe ; as he would almoft perfuade
us that the abilities of the Commander were fuch, that we might fancy he planned the
taking the *Acapulco* fhip before he left *England*. However, the account, from its grand
divifions, &c. is a mafter-piece of compofition, and certainly has not been equalled
(unlefs by Dr. *Robertfon's* Hiftories) in thefe enchanting particulars.—A lift of the original writers on the fubject of this voyage may be feen in Gent. Mag. 1780, p. 322.
Mr. *Walter* is ftill living, and is chaplain of *Portfmouth* Dock-yard.

‡ *Edward Cobden*, D. D. chaplain in ordinary to King *George* the Second, was early
in life chaplain to Bp. *Gibfon*, to whofe patronage he was indebted for the following
preferments ; *viz.* the united rectories of *St. Auftin* and *St. Faith* in *London*, with that
of *Acton* in *Middlefex*, a prebend in *St. Paul's*, another at *Lincoln*, and the archdeaconry of *London*, in which laft he fucceeded Dr. *Tyrwhit* in *July* 1742. His earlieft
publication was, " A Letter from a Minifter to his Parifhioner, upon his building a Meet-
" ing-houfe," 8vo. " A fhort Character of Mrs. *Jeffop*, widow of the late Rev. Mr.
" *Jeffop* of *Temsford* in *Bedfordfhire*, and mother of Mrs. *Cobden*," is printed in his Works.
Seven of his Sermons are enumerated in *Letfome's* " Preacher's Affiftant ;" and " A
" Charge to the Clergy of *London*, *April* 22, 1746, with a fhort character of Dr. *Roper*,"

An extract from a letter which he sent this year to a very near relation may here be not improperly introduced. It shews that gratitude to his father's benefactors was always a leading feature of his mind:

" You have heard all the circumstances of the late dread-
" ful fire* which I can tell you, and I shall be glad if you
" have prevented me in all the reflections upon it which
" I can suggest to you.   Your grandfather, you know,
" suffered a like calamity; WE, therefore, from experience,
" ought more particularly to have a fellow-feeling with the
" sufferers in this—

" Non *ignara mali*, miseris succurrere disco.

" You are not capable of contributing to their relief;
" but when you reflect upon the kind support he then
" met with (the effects of which you now enjoy), what
" humility should it excite in you, what zeal and resolution,
" to repay by a useful life the obligations you lie under,
" and to become a helpful member to society, to which you
" are so much indebted! Many are entitled to the favours
" of the world, from the merit of their ancestors ; on the
" contrary, the world has a right to demand good actions
" from US, for the very subsistence we owe to it, who are
" but the children of Providence and human beneficence."

was printed by Mr. *Bowyer* in 1747. The last Sermon which he published was preached before the King at *St. James's*, *Dec.* 11, 1748, and was intituled, " A " Persuasive to Chastity." In an advertisement the Doctor observes, " that it having " given occasion to some unjust censures, he thought proper to publish it, hoping that " nothing in the sentiment or expression will be found unworthy of the sacred function " of a preacher of the Gospel, or of the serious attention of a Christian assembly." In 1755 he published a pamphlet, intituled, " An Essay tending to promote Religion," 8vo. in the title-page to which he stiles himself " lately Chaplain above twenty-two years to " his Majesty ;" and in 1756 " A Poem sacred to the memory of Queen *Anne*, for her " bounty to the Clergy," 4to. His whole works were collected by himself, in 1757, in two volumes, 4to. He died *April* 22, 1764, aged more than 80. Mrs. *Cobden* died *Jan.* 8, 1762.

* Which happened in *Cornhill*, *March* 25, 1748.

In

In 1749 he printed the firſt edition of Mr. *Weſt's** tranſlation of " *Pindar's* Odes," 4to; a large impreſſion of Lord
Bolingbroke's " Idea of a Patriot King;" the eighteenth edition of his old friend Mr. *Nelſon's* work on the " Feaſts
" and Faſts of the Church of *England*;" " A Deſcription
" of the Machine for the Fireworks, with all its orna-
" ments, and a detail of the manner in which they are
" to be exhibited in *St. James's Park, Thurſday, April* 27,
" 1749, on account of the General Peace†," 4to; " The laſt

---

* *Gilbert Weſt*, eſq. ſon of the reverend Dr. *Weſt* and of a ſiſter of Sir *Richard
Temple* afterwards lord *Cobham*, was educated at *Eton* and at *Oxford*, with a view to
the church; but obtaining from his uncle a commiſſion either in a regiment of dragoons
or dragoon guards, entered into the army, where he continued till his appointment into the
office of lord *Townſhend*, ſecretary of ſtate, with whom he attended the king to *Hanover*.
He was nominated clerk-extraordinary of the privy council in *May* 1729; ſoon after
which he married, and ſettled at *Wickham* in *Kent*, where he devoted himſelf to learning, and to piety. For his " Obſervations on the Reſurrection," which appeared in
1747, he received from *Oxford*, by diploma, the degree of LL.D. *March* 30, 1748.
He was very often viſited by *Lyttelton* and *Pitt*, who, when they were weary of faction
and debates, uſed at *Wickham* to find books and quiet, a decent table, and literary
converſation ‖. There is at *Wickham* a walk made by *Pitt* ‡; and, what is of far more
importance, at *Wickham Lyttelton* received that conviction which produced his " Diſ-
" ſertation on *St. Paul*." Mr. *Weſt's* income was not large; and his friends endeavoured, but without ſucceſs, to obtain an augmentation. It is reported, that the education
of the young prince was offered to him, but that he required a more extenſive power of
ſuperintendance than it was thought proper to allow him. In time, however, his revenue was improved; he lived to have one of the lucrative clerkſhips of the Privy
Council in 1752, and Mr. *Pitt* at laſt had it in his power to make him treaſurer of *Chelſea
Hoſpital*. He was now ſufficiently rich; but wealth came too late to be long enjoyed;
nor could it ſecure him from the calamities of life: he loſt his only ſon in 1755, and
on the 26th of *March*, 1756, a ſtroke of the palſy (to uſe the words of the incomparable writer from whom I have borrowed the greater part of this note) " brought to the
" grave one of the few poets to whom the grave needed not to be terrible."

† This was printed under the inſpection of *Gaetano Ruggeri* and *Giuſeppe Sarti*, who
ſuperintended this buſineſs by direction of the Board of Ordnance.

‖ Mr. *Upton's* " Letter concerning a new edition of *Spenſer's* Fairie Queen, 1751," 4to, was inſcribed to Mr. *Weſt*.

‡ " Lord *Chatham*, to the ſublimer qualities of a great miniſter of ſtate, joined in an extraordinary
" degree the rare and pleaſing talent of dreſſing or ornamenting a country, which, though ſlightingly
" ſpoken of by Dr. *Johnſon* in his account of *Shenſtone*, will probably be more eſteemed for ages to
" come, than the *Pindarics*, &c. of many of the writers he holds out to public notice. Unluckily for
" many of this order, Mr. *Granger* has juſtly obſerved, that their head prefixed ſells now for as much
" as the whole work, or rather that the latter would not ſell at all but for the former. It was at
" one of the lodges on *Enfield Chace* that Mr. *Pitt* early in life diſplayed his great taſte this way. The
" ſpot was only fifty acres, given by government; it ſtill ſubſiſts and is admired, though Mr. *Pitt*
" ſold it, and afterwards exerciſed his genius at *Hayes*. The ſlighteſt particulars of ſo great a perſonage
" deſerve to be recorded. When he ſaw the aſtoniſhing ſpot at *Ilam* in *Derbyſhire*, belonging to Mr.
" *Port*, he ſaid, The ground rolls and tumbles finely here." *Dr. Taylor's Friend*.

E e   " words

" words of *David*, divided according to the metre, with Notes
" critical and explanatory, by *Richard Grey**, D. D." 4to;
" Liberty †, a Poem," by *J. Brown* ‡, M. A. folio; " the Songs
" in

* Mr. *Richard Grey*, of *Lincoln College*, *Oxford*, took the degree of M. A. *Jan.* 16, 1718-19. He early in life obtained the rectory of *Kilncote* in *Leicestershire*, and afterwards that of *Hinton* in *Northamptonshire*, and a prebend in *St. Paul's*. He was also (1746) official and commissary of the archdeaconry of *Leicester*. He published at *Oxford* a visitation sermon in 1730. In the same year appeared his " Memoria Tech-" nica," (already noticed in p. 61); and also his " System of *English* Ecclesiastical Law, " extracted from the *Codex Juris Ecclesiastici Anglicani* of the Right Reverend the Lord " Bishop of *London*, for the use of young Students in the Universities who are designed " for Holy Orders," 8vo. For this work ‖ (which was printed in 1732 and 1736, and again in 1743 with the addition of marginal references to the pages in the " Codex") the University gave him a Doctor of Divinity's degree by diploma, *May* 28, 1731. In 1732 he published " The Great Tribunal, an Assize Sermon;" and a second edition of his " Memoria Technica;" and a third edition of the latter in 1735. He was in 1736 the undoubted author of a large anonymous pamphlet, under the title of " The miserable " and distracted State of Religion in *England*, upon the downfall of the Church " established," 8vo; and printed that year another Visitation Sermon. In 1738 he published his " New and easy Method of learning *Hebrew* without Points" (see p. 147); in 1739, " Historia *Josephi*," and " Paradigmata Verborum," &c. (see p. 150); in 1742 " Liber *Jobi*," &c. (see p. 157); in 1744 his " Answer to Mr. *Warburton's* Re-" marks," (see p 160); and a " Sermon for the benefit of the *Northampton* Infir-" mary," with an Appendix, containing a particular account of the charity, and a plan of the building; in 1749, " The last words of *David*, &c." (as above); in 1751, " Nova Methodus *Hebraice* discendi diligentius recognita, & ad usum Scholarum ac-" commodata. Adjicitur (praxeos exercendæ gratiâ) Historia *Josephi* Patriarchæ li-" teris tam *Romanis* quam *Hebraicis* excusa, cum Versione interlineari S. *Pagnini*, & " Vocum Indice Analytico," 8vo; in 1753, an *English* translation of Mr. *Hawkins Browne's* fine poem " De Animi Immortalitate;" and in 1756 a fourth edition of his " Memoria Technica." He died *Feb.* 28, 1771, in his 78th year.

† The date of this poem is not settled in the " Biographia."

‡ This elegant, ingenious, and unhappy author (who at the time of printing this poem, and long after, lived in habits of intimate friendship with Mr. *Bowyer*, from whose press such part of his writings as made their first appearance in *London* were produced) was born at *Rothbury*, in the county of *Northumberland*, November 5, 1715. The family from which he was descended were the *Browns* of *Colstown*, near *Haddington* in *Scotland*. His father *John Brown* was a native of *Scotland*, and, at the time of his son's birth, was curate to Dr. *Thomlinson*, rector of *Rothbury*. He afterwards was collated to the vicarage of *Wigton* in *Cumberland*. To this place he carried his son, who there received the first part of his education. From thence he was removed to the university of *Cambridge*, 1732, and entered of *St. John's College* under the tuition of Dr. *Tunstall*.

‖ This was at least the ostensible reason. But I have been told that Dr. *Grey*, who had been Secretary, &c. to Lord *Crew* (Bishop of *Durham* from 1674 to 1722) was of great use to the university in the information he gave them, as to what he had heard the Bishop say were his intentions in his bene-factions there, which were left much at large in his will. This information was a great satisfaction to the university, and, together with the personal character of *Grey*, contributed much to procuring him the honour above-mentioned.

After

" in *Jack* the Giant Queller," a dramatic piece by *Henry Brooke*; and a second volume of " *Fitzosborne's* Letters," 8vo. with a new edition of both volumes in one, 8vo.

In 1750, a prefatory critical diſſertation, and ſome valuable notes*, were annexed by Mr. *Bowyer* to *Lud.* " *Kuſterus* de vero Uſu Verborum Mediorum, eorumque " Differentiâ

* After taking the degree of batchelor of arts with great reputation, he returned to *Wigton*, and was ordained by Dr. *Fleming*, biſhop of *Carliſle*. His firſt preferment was to a minor canonry and lectureſhip of that cathedral. He remained in obſcurity at that city ſeveral years till the rebellion 1745, when he acted as a volunteer at the ſiege of the caſtle, and behaved with great intrepidity. In 1739, he took the degree of M. A. and ſome time after was preſented to the living of *Morland*, in the county of *Weſtmorland*. He reſigned his preferment in the cathedral of *Carliſle* in diſguſt. On Mr. *Pope's* death, he wrote " The Eſſay on Satire," addreſſed to Dr. *Warburton*, who immediately introduced him to his friend Mr. *Allen* and others, and by his intereſt with lord *Hardwicke* procured him the living of *Great Horkeſley* in *Eſſex*. He took his degree of D. D. in 1755 †. In 1757, he publiſhed his celebrated " Eſtimate of " the manners and principles of the times," a work which was run down by popular clamour, but not anſwered. Obtaining the vicarage of *St. Nicholas*, *Newcaſtle*, he reſigned his living in *Eſſex* to Lord *Hardwicke*, between whom, as well as Dr. *Warburton* and him, there had ſome time before been a coolneſs. He received no higher preferment, which to a perſon of Dr. *Brown's* ſpirit muſt have been a great mortification. In the latter part of life, he had an invitation from the empreſs of *Ruſſia* to ſuperintend a grand deſign which ſhe had formed of extending the advantages of civilization over that great empire. He accepted the offer, and actually prepared for his journey; but finding his health in too precarious a ſtate to admit of his fulfilling his intention, he was obliged to relinquiſh it. This and other diſappointments were followed by a dejection of ſpirits which he had often been ſubject to. In an interval of deprivation of reaſon, he was prompted to do violence to himſelf, and on the 23d of *September*, 1766, cut his throat in the fifty-firſt year of his age. Such of his writings as were printed by Mr. *Bowyer* will be mentioned under their ſeveral years.

* Mr. *Markland*, in a letter, dated *Oct.* 21, 1749, ſays, " The ſpecimen of *Kuſter* " I like very well, and your Annotations; in which I have taken the liberty to fill up " ſome of the abbreviations, to which I am a great enemy, as cauſing obſcurity." Before this little volume was publiſhed, a copy of it was ſent for the inſpection of Mr. *Markland*, who, *Feb.* 27, 1749-50, ſays, " The reaſon why you have not heard from me, is, be- " cauſe I really have not had time ſo much as to look into the *Kuſter* as yet, another " part of the parcel you ſent having taken up all the time I could ſpare, and given me " more trouble and perplexity than I think I ever yet experienced in the literary way; " if you know, or can gueſs, what I mean, I need not ſay any more, but it is probable " you will know more of it hereafter, which perhaps is as ænigmatical as the former ſen- " tence; however, I made an end of it to my great joy yeſterday, and then intended to " read *Kuſter*; but laſt night about one o'clock I waked in great diſorder, and putting

† " *Brown*, the antagoniſt of Lord *Shaftesbury*, is now in College, and has taken his Doctor's " degree. He preached a Sermon here, which many people commended; it was to prove that Ty- " ranny was productive of Superſtition, and Superſtition of Tyranny; that Debauchery was the cauſe " of Free-thinking, and Free-thinking of Debauchery. His concluſion was, that the only way of " keeping us from being a *French* province, was to preſerve our conſtitutional liberties, and the purity " of our manners." MS. *Letter to Mr. B. from a* Cambridge *Friend*, 1755.

" my

" Differentiâ à Verbis Activis & Paſſivis*;" a new edi-
tion of which work, with further improvements, appeared in 1773. The Diſſertation was likewiſe adopted by
Mr. *Holwell*, in 1766, in his curious edition of " Selecti
" *Dionyſii Halicarnaſſenſis* de Priſcis Scriptoribus Tractatus
" *Græcè* & *Latinè*," with this polite acknowledgment :
" Hanc Diſſertationem ſuæ *L. Kuſteri* de vero Uſu Verbo-
" rum Mediorum, &c. edit. 1750, præfixit *Guil. Bowyer*,
" Typographus. Eandem, auctior quidem, ut hanc noſ-
" tram Select. *Dion. Hal.* Tractat. editionem ornaret, im-
" petravi : quo nomine, Viro optimè de republicâ literariâ
" merito, gratias ago." About the ſame time Mr. *Bowyer*
wrote a *Latin* Preface to the " Veteres Poetæ citati ad Pa-
" tris *Philippi Labbei* de ancipitum *Græcarum* Vocalium in
" prioribus Syllabis Menſurâ (ubi confirmanda eſſet) con-
" firmandam ſententiam. Necnon ad indicandum quibus
" Vocibus licet corripere Vocalem longam ante alteram in ea-
" dem dictione. Operâ & Curâ *Edwardi Leedes*, in Scholâ
" *Burienſi* ad acuendos adoleſcentium animos, erga Poeſeûs
" ſtudium (cum ipſe Poëta non ſit) cotis vice fungentis."

In 1750 he printed Mr. *Vertue's* " Catalogue of King
" *Charles* the Firſt's Pictures," 4to; " Officia Religionis
" Chriſtianæ, metricè enumerata a *Ben. Culm*†, S. T. B." 4to;

" my watch to my ear, I found I could not hear. This diſorder and deafneſs ſtill con-
" tinues, but not in ſo great a degree as it was at firſt, which makes me hope that it is
" nothing but a cold, or ſome temporary malady which will ſoon go off; but at preſent
" I am no more able to read any thing with attention than I am to command an army ;
" ſo that if you are in haſte for *Kuſter* or the looſe leaves, let me know by the next poſt,
" and I will ſend them forthwith." What the *literary* communication was with which
Mr. *Markland* was ſo perplexed does not appear. His remarks on " the looſe leaves"
are printed in Mr. *Bowyer's* " Miſcellaneous Tracts," p. 150.

* Mr. *Clarke*, who communicated ſuch remarks on *Kuſter* as had occurred to him,
ſays on this occaſion, " I am always rejoiced when the preſs gives you the pleaſure, as
" well as the trouble of attention; and it would always do that, if you would keep
" ſome ſcheme of your own on foot. This book will certainly do ; and the more liber-
" ties you take with it, I ſhall like it the better."

† Fellow of *St. John's*, and rector of *Freſhwater*. See Gent. Mag. 1779, p. 249.

" *Julian*,

" *Julian*, or a Difcourfe concerning the Earthquake and
" Fiery Eruption which defeated that Emperor's attempt to
" rebuild the Temple at *Jerufalem*; in which the reality of
" a divine interpofition is fhewn; the objections to it are
" anfwered; and the nature of that evidence which de-
" mands the affent of every reafonable man to a *miraculous*
" fact is confidered and explained. By the Rev. Mr. *War-*
" *burton*, Preacher to the Hon. Society of *Lincoln's Inn*,"
8vo; Mr. *Jortin's* " Remarks on Ecclefiaftical Hiftory,"
8vo; a new edition of Mr. *Chefelden's** " Anatomy of the
" human body," 8vo; " An Account of the Doctrine, Man-
" ners,

---

* This work has been already mentioned in p. 155.—The firft edition of it appeared
fo early as 1713, and was infcribed to Dr. *Mead*, to whom Mr. *Chefelden* acknowledges
himfelf entirely indebted for the kind reception his induftry had met with, " particularly
" in that feat of learning [*Oxford*] which with diftinguifhed honours rewarded the
" merit of Dr. *Mead*;" and in the Preface acknowledges his obligations to Dr. *Douglas*,
to " his honoured friend Mr. *Green*, furgeon to the Hofpital of *Chrift Church* and that
" of *St. Bartholomew*;" and to " his late worthy mafter Mr *Ferne*, furgeon to *St. Tho-*
" *mas's Hofpital*." To this volume was added, " Syllabus, five Index humani corporis
" partium Anatomicus†, in xxxv Prælectiones diftinctus. In ufum Theatri Anatomici
" *Willielmi Chefelden* Chirurgi, S. R. S. Editio fecunda."—This incomparable Lithotomift
and Anatomift, who was Surgeon to *St. Thomas's* and *Chelfea Hofpitals*, was born at *Bur-*
row on the Hill, in the county of *Leicefter*, defcended from an antient family in the county
of *Rutland*, whofe arms and pedigree are in *Wright's* " Hiftory of *Rutland*." He received the rudiments of his profeffional fkill at *Leicefter* ‡; and married *Deborah Knight*,
a citizen's daughter, by whom he had iffue one daughter, *Williamina Deborah*. (This
lady was married to *Charles Cotes*‖, M. D. of *Woodcote* in *Shropfhire*, member of
parliament for *Tamworth* § in *Staffordfhire*, who died *March* 21, 1748, without iffue.
She furvived her hufband, and died fome years fince at *Greenhith*, in the parifh of
Swanfcombe, in *Kent*.) Mr. *Chefelden* publifhed " A Treatife on the high Operation for
" the Stone, 1723," 8vo. and was one of the earlieft of his profeffion who contributed by
his writings to raife it to its prefent eminence. The following verfes were addreffed to him,
in 1733, " on his many dextrous and fuccefsful operations:"

† Mr. *Highmore*, the celebrated painter, who had attended the lectures of Mr. *Chefelden* to improve
himfelf in Anatomy, made afterwards feveral drawings from the real fubjects at the time of diffection,
two of which were engraved for Mr. *Chefelden's* " Anatomy," and appear, but without his name, in
Tables XII. and XIII.
‡ I have reafon to believe that he was a pupil of Mr. *Wilkes*, a furgeon of the firft reputation in
Leicefter; where Mr. *Chefelden* had a near relation, of his own name, a phyfician; and another, more
diftant, fucceeded Mr. *Wilkes* as a furgeon. Mr. *Wilkes* had a brother, a lockfmith, at *Wolverhampton*.
‖ Son of Dr. *Digby Cotes*, rector of *Colefhill*, *Warwickfhire*, prebendary of *Litchfield*, and principal
of *Magdalen Hall*, *Oxford*, where he had been public orator. He died *Jan.* 11, 1745. Another of
his fons was in 1745 a lieutenant-colonel of a regiment of foot in *Flanders*.
§ *Tamworth* ftands in two counties, *Staffordfhire* and *Warwickfhire*; but properly belongs to the former.

" Oh.

" ners, Liturgy, and Idiom of the *Unitas Fratrum*, &c. by
" the

" Oh wondrous Artiſt! (ſurely given,
By the peculiar grace of Heaven,
As a new Saviour to mankind,
The lame to cure, relieve the blind,
And, by thy ever happy knife,
To eaſe, and lengthen human life!)
How doſt thou grace that noble art,
Which owes to you its nobleſt part!
How well deſerve the general praiſe
Your univerſal fame does raiſe!
How juſt your merit, for the place
Conferr'd on you by royal grace!
Well might the care alone be thine,
To tend on gracious *Caroline*,
Since all allow your ſkill divine.

No more let *France* her artiſts boaſt,
To you but ſmatterers at moſt.
Their *Charité*, or *Hotel Dieu*,
Ne'er ſaw ſuch cures as done by you ;
Aware of this, with utmoſt ſpeed,
Their NEW ACADEMY * decreed
You all their honours, and, to grace
Their liſt, therein gave you a place :
From ſuch a member they receive
A greater honour than they give.
Long may you live, and bleſs the land
With your unerring ſkill and hand.
May this ne'er fail, that never warp ;
And may they both deſcend to *Sharp!*"

In the beginning of 1736 he was thus honourably mentioned by Mr. *Pope*: " As
" ſoon as I had ſent my laſt letter, I received a moſt kind one from you, expreſſing
" great pain for my late illneſs at Mr. *Cheſelden*'s. I conclude you was eaſed of
" that friendly apprehenſion in a few days after you had diſpatched yours, for mine
" muſt have reached you then. I wondered a little at your quære, who *Cheſelden* was.
" It ſhews that the trueſt merit does not travel ſo far any way as on the wings of poetry :
" he is the moſt noted and moſt deſerving man in the whole profeſſion of chirurgery ;
" and has ſaved the lives of thouſands by his manner of cutting for the ſtone †." He
appears to have been on terms of the moſt intimate friendſhip with Mr. *Pope*, who frequently, in his Letters to Mr. *Richardſon*, talks of dining with Mr. *Cheſelden*, who then
lived in or near *Queen Square*. I have accidentally the original of an unprinted letter to
him, which, for its ſingularity, is worth tranſcribing : " Dear Sir, You know my laconic
" ſtile. I never forget you. Are you well? I am ſo. How does Mrs. *Cheſelden*? Had
" it not been for her, you had been here. Here are three cataracts ripened for you
" (Mr. *Pierce* aſſures me). Don't tell your wife that ***********. Adieu.
" I don't intend to go to *London*. Good night ; but anſwer me. Yours, A. POPE.
" *Bath, Nov.* 21.—Shew this to Mr. *Richardſon* ; and let him take it to himſelf—and
" to his ſon—he has no wife ‡." Another proof of this intimacy ariſes from a poem of
the younger Mr. *Richardſon*, ſent to Mr. *Pope* at *Twickenham*, after his being declared
out of danger by his phyſicians, where we are told that
" — *Cheſelden*, with candid wife,
" Detains his gueſt ; the ready Lares ſmile.
" Good *Chiron* ſo, within his welcome bower,
" Receiv'd of Verſe the mild and ſacred Power ;
" With anxious ſkill ſupply'd the bleſt relief,
" And heal'd with balms and ſweet diſcourſe his grief."
In *February* 1737, Mr. *Cheſelden* was appointed ſurgeon to *Chelſea* Hoſpital. " The
" Operations of Surgery of Monſ. *Le Dran*, ſenior Surgeon of the Hoſpital of *La Cha-
" rité*, &c. tranſcribed by *Thomas Gataker*, Surgeon ; with Remarks, Plates ‖ of the

---

* The " Royal Academy of Surgery at *Paris*," of which Mr. *Cheſelden* was an Aſſociate.
† Letter to Dr. *Swift, March* 25, 1736.
‡ Mrs. *Richardſon* died in 1725, on her birth-day, aged 51, after having been married thirty-three years.
‖ Many of theſe were drawn by Mr. *Cheſelden* himſelf, whoſe " Oſteography" was in 1749 adver-
tiſed as " ſoon to be had, in a large folio, for four guineas in ſheets ; the plates were then broken, and
" but few of the books left."

I

" Operations,

" the Rev. *John Gambold* * ;" two editions of the " Canons
" of

" Operations, and a fett of Inftruments, by *William Chefelden*, Efq. furgeon to the
" Royal Hofpital at *Chelfea*, and Member of the Academy of Surgery at *Paris*," were publiſhed in 1749, 8vo. Mr. *Chefelden*, as a governor of *The Foundling Hofpital*, ſent a benefaction of 50*l.* to that charity, *May* 7, 1751, incloſed in a paper with the following lines :
" 'Tis what the happy to th' unhappy owe ;
" For what man gives, the gods by him beſtow." POPE.
He died at *Bath*, *April* 11, 1752, of a diſorder ariſing from drinking ale after eating hot
buns. Finding himſelf uneaſy, he ſent for a phyſician, who adviſed vomiting immediately ;
and if the advice had been taken, it was thought his life might have been ſaved. By his
own direction, he was buried at *Chelfea*.—In Phil. Tranſ. N° 333, are dimenſions of ſome
very large human bones found at *Old Verulam*, by Mr. *Chefelden*.—Dr. *Stukeley's* proſpect
of *Vernometum*, or *Burrow Hill*, from the *Leiceſter* road, Sept. 8, 1722, is inſcribed
" *Will'o Chefelden*, " Chirurgo peritiſſimo, Amico."—" The Grateful Patient †, inſcribed
" to Mr. *Chefelden* by Mr. *Richard Yeo*, a Lad of twelve years of age," is in Gent. Mag.
1732, p. 769. And in the London Mag. 1742, p. 563, are ſome verſes " On the recovery
" of a young Gentleman Commoner [Mr. *Wynne*] of *Jeſus College, Oxford*, from whom
" Mr. *Chefelden* extracted a large ſtone after uſing *Stephens's* medicines to no purpoſe."

* This truly primitive Chriſtian, to whoſe memory I am happy in having this opportunity
of gratefully acknowledging my regard, was born near *Haverford Weſt* in *South Wales*, and
became a member of *Chriſt Church College, Oxford*, where he took the degree of M.A. *May*
30, 1734; and was afterwards vicar of *Stanton Harcourt*, in *Oxfordſhire*, where, in 1740,
he wrote " The Martyrdom of *Ignatius*, a Tragedy," publiſhed after his death by the Rev.
Benjamin La Trobe, with the Life of *Ignatius*, drawn from authentic accounts,
and from the Epiſtles written by him from *Smyrna* and *Troas* in his way to *Rome*,
1773, 8vo. A Sermon, which he preached before the Univerſity of *Oxford*, was
publiſhed under the title of " Chriſtianity, Tidings of Joy, 1741," 8vo. In 1742 he
publiſhed at *Oxford*, from the univerſity-preſs, a neat edition of the *Greek* Teſtament,
but without his name, " Textu per omnia *Milliano*, cum diviſione pericoparum & in-
" terpunctura *A. Bengelii*," 2 vols. 12mo. Joining afterwards the Church of the
Brethren, eſtabliſhed by an Act of Parliament ‡ of the year 1749, and known by the name
of *Unitas Fratrum*, or, *The United Brethren*; he was, for many years, the regular
miniſter of the congregation ſettled at *London*, and reſided in *Neville's Court, Fetter
Lane*, where he preached at the Chapel of the Brethren. In the year 1754, he was conſecrated a Biſhop of the Brethren's Church. Soon after he had joined the Brethren, he
publiſhed a treatiſe, which he had written whilſt at *Stanton Harcourt*, and which proves
his ſteady attachment to the Church of *England*, entirely conſiſtent with his connexion
with, and miniſtry in, the Church of the Brethren. The title of it is, " A ſhort Sum-
" mary of Chriſtian Doctrine, in the way of Queſtion and Anſwer; the Anſwers being
" all made in the ſound and venerable words of the Common-prayer-book of the Church
" of *England*. To which are added, Some Extracts out of the Homilies. Collected
" for the Service of a few perſons, Members of the Eſtabliſhed Church; but imagined
" not to be unuſeful to others." I know not the exact date of this treatiſe; but a ſecond
edition of it was printed in 1767, 12mo. Mr. *Gambold* alſo publiſhed " Maxims and
" Theological Ideas, collected out of ſeveral Diſſertations and Diſcourſes of Count *Zin-
" zendorf*, from 1738 till 1747." His " Hymns for the uſe of the Brethren" were
printed by Mr. *Bowyer* in the years 1748, 1749, and 1752; ſome Hymns, and a ſmall

† " The Grateful Patient of 12 years" ſeems to be too old for the ſtory that is told to Mr. *Chefelden's*
praiſe. Being to cut a child, and having tied him to avoid his making any efforts to move, he told
him, if he would lie quite ſtill, he would give him ſome ſugar-plumbs. The operation was performed
ſpeedily, and, as we may preſume, happily and eaſily; for the child (who muſt be ſuch from the bribe) immediately demanded the plumbs. Perhaps too it may be reckoned an inſtance of the operator's good ſenſe,
who knew the advantage to both parties that might be expected from the patient's mind being amuſed.

‡ The " Petition of the Brethren" on this occaſion, moſt probably drawn up by Mr. *Gambold*, was
printed by Mr. *Bowyer*. It is preſerved in the " Journals of the Houſe of Commons," vol. XXV. p. 727.
Hymn-

" of Criticifm," 8vo; and " Epiftola* ad *Edw. Bentham,*
" S. T. P. a *Johanne Burton* †, S. T. B. Coll. *Eton.* Soc."

In

Hymn-book for the children belonging to the Brethren's congregations, were printed entirely by Mr. *Gambold's* own hand in *Lindfey-houfe* at *Chelfea.* A Letter from Mr. *Gambold* to Mr. *Spangenberg, June* 4, 1750, containing a concife and well-written character of the Count of *Zinzendorf*,* was inferted in Mr. *James Hutton's* " Effay towards " giving fome juft ideas of the perfonal character of Count *Zinzendorf,* the prefent Ad-" vocate and Ordinary of the Brethren's Churches, 1755," 8vo. In 1752 he was editor of " Sixteen Difcourfes on the Second Article of the Creed, preached at *Berlin* by the " Ordinary of the Brethren," 12mo. In *June* 1753 appeared " The Ordinary of the " Brethren's Churches his fhort and peremptory Remarks on the way and manner " wherein he has been hitherto treated in Controverfies, &c. Tranflated from the *High* " *Dutch,* with a Preface, by *John Gambold,* Minifter of the Chapel in *Fetter Lane.*" In the fame year he publifhed, from Mr. *Bowyer's* prefs, " Twenty-one Difcourfes, or " Differtations, upon the *Augfburg* Confeffion, which is alfo the Brethren's Confeffion " of Faith; delivered by the Ordinary of the Brethren's Churches before the Seminary. " To which is prefixed a Synodical Writing relating to the fame fubject. Tranflated " from the *High Dutch,* by *F. Okeley,* B. A." In 1754 he was editor of " A modeft " Plea for the Church of the Brethren, &c." 8vo; with a Preface by himfelf. In the fame year, in conjunction with Mr. *Hutton,* Secretary to the Brethren, he alfo drew up " The Reprefentation of the Committee of the *Englifh* Congregations in union with the " *Moravian* Church," addreffed to the Archbifhop of *York;* and alfo " The plain Cafe " of the Reprefentatives of the People known by the name of the *Unitas Fratrum,* from " the year 1727 till thefe times, with regard to their conduct in this country under mif-" reprefentation." And in 1755 he affifted in the publication of " A Letter from a Mi-" nifter of the *Moravian* Branch of the *Unitas Fratrum;* together with fome additional " notes by the *Englifh* Editor, to the Author of the *Moravians* compared and detected;" and alfo of " An Expofition, or true State of the matters objected in *England* to the " people known by the name of *Unitas Fratrum;* by the Ordinary of the Brethren; " the Notes and Additions by the Editor." In the year 1756 he preached at *Fetter Lane* chapel, and printed afterwards, a Sermon upon a public Faft and Humiliation, fetting forth " The Reafonablenefs and Extent of religious Reverence." He was not only a good fcholar, but a man of great parts, and of fingular mechanical ingenuity. It was late in both their lives before Mr. *Bowyer* was acquainted with his merits; but he no fooner knew them, than he was happy in his acquaintance, and very frequently applied to him as an occafional affiftant in correcting the prefs; in which capacity Mr. *Gambold* fuperintended (amongft many other valuable publications) the beautiful and very accurate edition of Lord Chancellor *Bacon's* Works in 1765; and in 1767 he was profeffedly the editor, and took an active part in the tranflation from the *High Dutch,* of " The Hiftory of *Greenland;* con-taining a " Defcription of the Country and its Inhabitants; and particularly a Relation of " the Miffion, carried on for above thefe thirty years by the *Unitas Fratrum* at *New* " *Herrnhut* and *Lichtenfels* in that country, by *David Crantz;* illuftrated with Maps " and other Copper Plates: printed for the Brethren's Society for the Furtherance of " the Gofpel among the Heathen," 2 vols. 8vo. In the autumn of 1768 he retired to his native country, where he died, at *Haverford Weft,* univerfally refpected, Sept. 13, 1771.

* Annexed to his " Epiftola Critica ad *Joh. Gul. Thompfon,* Dialogi *Platonis,* qui *Par-*" *menides* infcribitur, editorem. Accedit Elogium memoriæ facrum *Johan. Rogers.*"

† Of whom a mafterly account appeared in 1771, in a *Latin* Epiftle, intituled, " De " Vitâ & Moribus *Johannis Burtoni,* S. T. P. *Etonenfis,*" of which an epitome was given in the Gent. Mag. 1771, p. 305; which I would have tranfcribed, but that

* The compiler of this Noble Bifhop's Life in the " Biographia Britannica, 1766," acknowledges his obligation to Mr. *Gambold,* for fome perfonal information on that fubject.

I have

In 1750 also, having been employed to print an edition of *Bladen's* * translation of *Cæsar's* Commentaries; that work received considerable improvements from his hands†, and the addition of such notes‡ in it as are signed TYPOGR. In the subsequent editions of this work, though printed by another person, and in Mr. *Bowyer's* life-time, the same signature, contrary to decorum, and even justice, was still

I have had the pleasure of seeing it already printed, with improvements, in the *third* volume of the " Biographia Britannica ;" where it is properly followed by a well-written life of his intimate friend Dr. *Edward Bentham.*—It is very well observed by Dr. *Kippis,* that Dr. *Burton,* who was born at *Wembworth* in *Devonshire* in 1698, and died *Feb.* 11, 1771, was " an able divine, a sound scholar, and an excellent academic ; and " set an useful example to university-men, whether as fellows, tutors, officers, or edi- " tors ;" and that Dr. *Bentham,* who was born in the College at *Ely, July* 23, 1707, and died *Aug.* 1, 1776, was " a distinguished ornament of the University of *Oxford,* " of the Church of *England,* and of the general cause of Religion and Literature."

* *Martin Bladen,* esq. of *Abury Hatch,* in the county of *Essex,* was an officer in the army, bearing the commission of a lieutenant-colonel in queen *Anne's* reign, under the duke of *Marlborough,* to whom in 1705 he dedicated this translation ‖. In 1714, he was made comptroller of the Mint, and, in 1717, one of the lords commissioners of trade and plantations. In the same year he was appointed envoy extraordinary to the court of *Spain,* in the room of —— *Brett,* esq. ; but declined it, chusing rather to keep the post he already had, which was worth a thousand pounds *per annum,* and which he never parted with till his death, which happened *February* 14, 1746. He was a re- presentative in parliament successively for the boroughs of *Stockbridge, Malden,* and *Portsmouth. Coxeter* hints that he was secretary of state in *Ireland,* but in this he seems not absolutely certain, making a query in regard to the time when, which how- ever must, if at all, have been in queen *Anne's* reign ; for from the third year of *George* I. to the time of his death, he held his place at the board of trade, and probably was not out of *England.* He wrote two dramatic pieces, both of which (for the one is only a Masque introduced in the third act of the other) were printed in the year 1705, with- out the author's consent. Their names are, 1. " *Orpheus* and *Eurydice,*" a masque ; 2. " *Solon,*" a tragedy.

† Mr. *Markland,* whom he consulted on a particular passage in this translation, re- plies, " I think in all my life I never saw such a translation as that you have sent me of " these lines. If I were in your place, I would leave it just as it is. You will have an " infinite deal of trouble, without any reward, or so much as thanks from those whose " affair it is : perhaps, just the contrary. I repeat it again, do not meddle with it."

‡ These, with several additional ones from his interleaved copies of *Bladen's* and *Duncan's* translations, will be preserved among his " Miscellaneous Tracts."

‖ *Bladen* dedicates to the Duke of *Marlborough,* who was his school-fellow at a little school in the country ; neither of them great scholars ; though the Duke, from a polished behaviour, rose to the greatest dignities, from the station of page of the back stairs, to the post of first general in the world.

retained ;

retained; a circumstance which he always mentioned with no small degree of diffatisfaction.

In the difpute between Dr. *Burton* of *Eaton* and Dr. *King* of *St. Mary Hall* (occafioned by the " Remarks*" of the former on the *Latinity* of a well-known " Ora-" tion†" of the latter) he had the honour of fharing with Dr. *Burton* in the invectives moft liberally beftowed by Dr. *King*, in his " Elogium famæ inferviens *Jacci Eto-*" *nienfis*, five Gigantis; or, the Praifes of *Jack of Eaton*, " commonly called *Jack the Giant*‡; collected into *Englifh* " metre, after the manner of *Thomas Sternbold*, *John Hop-*" *kins*, *John Burton*, and others. To which is added, a " Differtation on the *Burtonian* Style. By a Mafter of Arts, " 1750."

The illiberality which generally attends a controverfy of this kind, and which, from the ftanza quoted below, it will be feen the prefent had its full fhare of, is certain (after the warmth which produced it ceafes) to fink, and very properly, the whole into oblivion. Let any reader perufe the following ftanza, which is here given only to introduce Mr. *Bowyer's* defence, and afterwards determine whether Dr. *King* was defenfible in fuffering fuch lines as the following to fall from his pen :

" Some, loudly as the nightbirds fcreech,
" Profefs diflike; fome hint it;
" And little Bowyer damns the fpeech,
" Becaufe he did not print it."

* " Remarks on Dr. *King's* Speech before the Univerfity of *Oxford*, at the Dedica-
" tion of Dr. *Radcliff's* Library, on the 13th of *April*, 1749. By *Phileleutherus*
" *Londinenfis*."

† " Oratio in Theatro *Sheldoniano* habita idibus *Aprilis*, MDCCXLIX, die dedicatio-
" nis Bibliothecæ *Radclivianæ*."

‡ From his fize and bulk, which exceeded the common ftandard.

" Be.

"Be it known (fays Mr. *B.*) that, for having *hefitated* in
" *private converfation*, and with the *greateft deference*, fome
" doubt concerning the Latinity of an eminent Orator and
" Poet, I have felt the effects of his double talent of fiction
" and colouring, and have been thus figured and disfigured
" by his magifterial hand ; *A little man, but of great fuffi-*
" *ciency* ;—*as foon as* Dr. King's *fpeech was publifhed, took*
" ALL OCCASIONS *to abufe the Doctor*—*Is it not in the power,*
" he goes on, *of a fcavenger or chimney-fweeper, as you pafs*
" *by him in the ftreets, to fpoil your cloaths* * ? Yes, againft
" the laws of decency and good-manners. But, within
" thefe bounds, in the republic of letters we are all CAPITE
" *cenfi*, and need no other qualification to give a vote. I
" fay, within the laws of *decency*; for he has fhewn, that
" barbarity is not confined to bad *Latin*, and, I hope, not
" annexed to any particular profeffion. I will ftill then
" prefume to be an advocate for freedom, while he is reft-
" lefs for dominion, crying out,

" *Quid domini faciant, audent fi talia fures?*
" In *Englifh* thus,
" *Gods! fuch enormity for vengeance calls,*
" *If* Printers *dare to cenfure* Principals!"

The above-cited remarks of Mr. *Bowyer* were intended
for the conclufion of his preface to *Montefquieu's* " Re-
" flexions, &c." but were omitted in confequence of this
hint from Mr. *Clarke:*

" DEAR SIR, *Aug.* 29, 1751.
" You feem to afk what is the rule of prudence to a man
" of bufinefs in points of refentment. Reclufes are no ca-
" fuifts in fuch cafes: your men of bufinefs are the beft

---

* The words in *Italic* are literally quoted from Dr. *King's* notes.

F f 2 " judges :

" judges: for my part, I think, very few things are
" worth refenting; either the perfon or the infult makes
" them contemptible; and yet every perfon who offers a
" public outrage deferves correction; and it is neceffary to
" make fome examples for the fake of the public, and treat
" them as you do other criminals. I fhould probably
" think Dr. *King* a perfon that deferved no quarter; though
" I am not very much pleafed with the laft leaf of your
" preface: I fhould either fupprefs or alter it. The terms
" *hefitate, private converfation, greateft deference,* look as if
" you fet about this bufinefs of felf-defence with fome fort
" of diffidence. Make no apologies, and enter into no par-
" ticulars. I fhould be for new cafting the whole from the
" middle of page xxxiv. and draw the Baron's character for
" humanity and learning to as much advantage as I could;
" and then contraft it with Dr. *King's*—as the very re-
" verfe—without mentioning your cafe at all."

In 1751 he printed *Montefquieu's* " Reflexions on the
" Caufes of the Rife and Fall of the *Roman* Empire;"
tranflated the Dialogue between *Sylla* and ~~Socrates~~; made
feveral corrections to the work, from the Baron's " Efprit
" des Loix;" and improved it with his own notes. A new
edition, with many alterations, was printed in 1759.
The preface, with fome additional notes, may be feen in
his " Mifcellaneous Tracts."—In the fame year he introduced to the publick the firft tranflation that was made of
Roußeau's paradoxical Prize Oration, which announced that
fingular genius to the attention and admiration of *Europe.*
It was printed under the title of " The Difcourfe which
" carried the Premium at the Academy at *Dijon* in 1750.
" On this Queftion propofed by the faid Academy, Whether
" the

" the re-eftablifhment of *arts* and *fciences* has contributed
" to the refinement of manners?" The Preface to this
pamphlet was his own, and will appear in his " Mifcella-
" neous Tracts;" the tranflation was made under his direction. A fecond tranflation of it was printed, by *W.*
Richardfon, 1779, 12mo.

Among the other books of 1751 were " Obferva-
" tions on the paft growth and prefent ftate of the City of
" *London*, &c. By the author of a letter from the By-
" Stander," [*Corbyn Morris*, efq.] folio; " De Principiis
" Animalibus Exercitationes*, a *Gulielmo Battie*, M.D." 4to;
" A hiftory of the church of *Weftminfter Abbey*, chiefly from
" MS. authorities; by *Richard Widmore*†, M. A. librarian
" to the dean and chapter," 4to; " The Works of *Alex-*
" *ander Pope*, efq. in nine volumes complete‡. With his
" laft corrections, additions, and improvements, as they
" were delivered to the Editor a little before his death; to-
" gether with the Commentaries and Notes of Mr. *Warbur-*
" *ton*," large 8vo; " The Works of Mrs. *Catharine Cock-*
" *burne* ‖, Theological, Moral, Dramatic, and Poetical;
" fome

---

* Delivered as part of the *Lumleian* Lecture. See an account of Dr. *Battie* in p. 231.

† For whom in 1743 Mr. *Bowyer* had printed, " An Enquiry into the time of the
" firft foundation of *Weftminfter Abbey*, as difcoverable from the beft authorities now
" remaining, both printed and MS. To which is added, an account of that church," 4to.

‡ "The Public has here a complete edition of his Works; executed in fuch a manner
" as, I am perfuaded, would have been to his fatisfaction. The Editor hath not, for
" the fake of profit, fuffered the Author's name to be made cheap by a *fubfcription*;
" nor his Works to be defrauded of their due honours by a vulgar or inelegant impref-
" fion; nor his memory to be difgraced by any pieces unworthy of his talents or virtue.
" On the contrary, he hath, at a very great expence, ornamented this edition with all
" the advantages which the BEST ARTISTS in Paper, Printing, and Sculpture, could
" beftow upon it." WARBURTON's *Advertifement*, p. iv.

‖ This remarkable inftance of an extraordinary genius for literature in the female fex
was the daughter of Captain *David Trotter*, a native of *Scotland*, and a fea commander
in the reign of King *Charles* II. She was born in *London*, *Aug.* 16, 1679, and baptized
in the Proteftant church, according to which fhe was bred up in her infancy a Proteftant;
but,

" fome of them now firft printed ; revifed and publifhed,
" with

but, being a fprightly, ingenious, and beautiful child, fhe was particularly careffed by
fome confiderable families among the Papifts. This favour naturally wrought a good opinion
of fuch friends ; and entering into an intimacy with them as fhe grew up, fhe became an eafy
conqueft to their faith, in which fhe continued many years. In the mean time her genius
ripened apace, and fhot forth proofs of her talents for poetry, even before fhe had paffed
her childhood. In her 17th year fhe produced a tragedy called *Agnes de Caftro*, which
was acted in 1695. This performance, and fome verfes addreffed to Mr. *Congreve* upon
his *Mourning Bride* in 1697, brought her into the acquaintance of that gentleman.
Thus encouraged in her firft attempt, her Mufe brought upon the ftage three plays more,
before the death of Mr. *Dryden* in 1701, to whofe memory fhe joined with feveral other
ladies in paying a tribute of verfe. However, poetry and dramatic writing was not the
moft diftinguifhed of Mifs *Trotter's* talents ; fhe had a remarkable philofophic turn, and
capacity equal to fuch refearches. Mr. *Locke's* Effay on Human Underftanding came out
during this interval : that famous philofopher had dreffed out logick and metaphyficks in
fuch a new mode as was very agreeable to the tafte of the fex in general, and particularly
engaged the attention and admiration of our young authorefs. She had begun to project
a defence of the effay againft fome remarks of Dr. *Burnet* of *The Charter Houfe*, which
was finifhed fo early as the beginning of *December* 1701. She had but lately paffed the
22d year of her age ; and the mafterly way in which the piece was drawn muft needs have
given fingular pleafure to her great champion, who accordingly expreffed his fatisfaction by
a prefent of books to his fair defendrefs. Philofophy fojourns in the neighbourhood of religion ; thefe philofophic reveries would naturally lead a thoughtful mind to that fubject ;
and taking into her confideration the tenets of her prefent faith, fhe began to difcover
their indefenfible grounds ; fhe therefore refolved to renounce it, and publifhed a vindication of her change in 1707 ; and returning to the eftablifhed church of *Scotland*, fhe
changed her condition likewife the next year 1708, and was married to Mr. *Cockburne*,
a learned divine of that church. The duties of a wife and mother called Mrs. *Cockburne* from her books and pen many years ; and domeftic cares engaging her attention, we hear nothing of her as a writer till 1726, when her zeal for Mr. *Locke's*
opinions drew her again into public light. She exercifed her pen afterwards as occafion offered ; and in 1739 fhe entered into the controverfy concerning the foundation
of moral duty and obligation. In that controverfy fhe wrote two treatifes, the firft of
which fhe tranfmitted in manufcript to Mr. afterwards Dr. *Warburton*, the late bifhop of
Gloucefter, who publifhed it, with a preface of his own, in 1747. Mrs. *Cockburne* furvived this publication two years only. She died in 1749, and was interred at *Long
Horfley*, near her hufband, who died the year before her, with this fhort fentence upon
the tomb, *Let their works praife them in the gates*, Prov. xxx. 31. Her works were
collected * and publifhed in 1751, in two volumes, 8vo. with an account of her life pre-

* " This collection is an inconteftible proof of the author's genius. But her abilities as a writer will
not be feen without attending to the peculiar circumftances in which her writings were produced : her
early youth, for inftance, when fhe wrote fome ; her very advanced age, and ill ftate of health, when
fhe drew up others ; the uneafy fituation of her fortune during the whole courfe of her life ; and an
interval of near twenty years, in the vigour of it, fpent in the cares of a family, without the leaft leifure
for reading or contemplation ; after which, with a mind fo long diverted and encumbered, refuming
her ftudies, fhe inftantly recovered its entire powers ; and, in the hours of relaxation from domeftic
employments, purfued to the utmoft limits fome of the deepeft refearches the human underftanding is
capable of." BIRCH.

fixed,

" with an account of the Life of the Author, by *Thomas*
" *Birch*, M. A." 2 vols. 8vo; Dr. *Stanhope's* " Paraphrafe on
" the Four Gofpels," 8vo; Mr. *Brown's* " Effay on the
" Characteriftics," 8vo; " *Q. Horatii Flacci* Epiftola ad *Au-*
" *guftum*, with an *Englifh* Commentary on the Epiftle
" to *Pifo*," [by Mr. *Hurd*, now Bifhop of *Litchfield* and
Coventry,] 8vo; " The Opinion of an eminent Lawyer
" [Lord *Hardwicke*] concerning the right of appeal from
" the Vice-chancellor of *Cambridge* to the Senate; fupported
" by a fhort hiftorical account of the jurifdiction of the
" Univerfity. By a Fellow of a College," [the excellent
Editor of the preceding article]; the Bifhop of *Clogher's*
" Effay on Spirit," 8vo; and a fhort Defcription of a Print
of Sir *Watkin Williams Wynne*.

I cannot but take notice under this year how facred the
copy-right of books was then efteemed. Mr. *Bowyer's*
ideas on that fubject will appear from his claim* to a fhare
in

fixed, to which I am obliged for the fubftance of this note. Her character is that
of a moft uncommon lady, no lefs celebrated for her beauty in her younger years, than
for her genius and accomplifhments. She was fmall of ftature, but had a remarkable
livelinefs in her eyes, and a delicacy of complexion which continued to her death.

* I fhall give this claim in his own words, from a letter to a refpectable bookfeller,
dated *Dec.* 3, 1751: " I am quite concerned to underftand that you have forgot ever
" feeing *Brabazon Aylmer's* affignment of *Barrow's* ' Sermon on the Trinity ;' and the
" more fo, becaufe, as fpirits have grown warmer fince, I have been told I was to blame
" for acquiefcing fo tamely in not having a fhare in the laft edition of *Barrow's* Works.
" Perhaps Mr. *Hitch*, when he is well, may help you to remember fome circumftance
" relating to it, who told me (and I think from your refearches) that my affignment
" was good for nothing, becaufe the Sermon was affigned over before. He add-
" ed, ' That I need not doubt the honour and veracity of the reporters.' I had be-
" fore been told, that the Sermon was left out in the edition preceding yours, and
" would be fo again. The more you have forgot the affignment, the more defirous am
" I of recovering it. I wifh you would look among your papers, though I own it is not
" likely you fhould be folicitous to preferve a claim which interfered with yours. I
" would advertife for *Aylmer's* executors to help me; but I think Mr. *Hitch* faid he died
" poor. You will pleafe to obferve, it is not a matter of indifference even now. My
" father printed the Sermon, and it is now to be feen. If he had not a right to do fo
" from

in the Works of Dr. *Barrow*, in confequence of his father's having been poffeffed of an affignment to a fingle Sermon.

On the publication of the third edition of Lord *Orrery's* " Remarks on the Life and Writings of Dr. *Swift*," in 1752, he wrote and printed, but never publifhed, " Two Letters " from Dr. *Bentley* in the Shades below, to Lord *Orrery* in " a Land of Thick Darknefs." The notes figned *B.* in the *ninth* quarto volume of *Swift's* works are extracted from thefe letters; which are reprinted at large among his " Mifcellaneous Tracts."

In 1752 he printed " A critical Commentary upon " the Books of *Tobit*, *Judith*, *Baruch*, the Hiftory of *Su-* " *fannah*, and *Bel* and the Dragon; to which are added, " Two Differtations on the Books of *Maccabees* and *Efdras**; " being a Continuation of Bifhop *Patrick* and Mr. *Lowth*, " by *R. Arnald*, B. D." folio; a confiderable part of *Ainf-* *worth's* " *Latin* Dictionary," 4to; " *Antonii Alfopi* Ædis " Chrifti olim Alumni Odarum Libri duo †," 4to; " A Pa- " raphrafe, with Critical Annotations, on the Epiftles of " St. *Paul* to the *Romans* and *Galatians*; to which is pre- " fixed, an analytical fcheme of the whole. By *Timothy*

" from *Aylmer*, he invaded fome one's property. Lay your hand on your heart, and " tell me whether you would fo quietly give up your property firft, and fecondly your " reputation (if fuch a thing there be) by letting the affignment be forgot, forgot by " the very perfons whofe intereft it is to forget it."

* In this volume there is alfo " A Differtation on the Dæmon *Afmodæus*, tranflated " from *Calmet*."

† This little volume was publifhed by Mr. *Bernard* (afterwards Sir *Francis*). He was bred to the law, and practifed at the bar for many years; was governor of *Maffa-* *chufett's Bay* at the time the ftamp act was paffed, and on his return to *England* was created a baronet, with peculiar marks of royal favour, *April* 5, 1769. His " Cafe before the " Privy Council" was printed by Mr. *Bowyer* in 1770; and two editions of his " Select " Letters" in 1774. He died *June* 16, 1779.

5

" *Edwards*,

"*Edwards**, A. M.*" 4to; Mr. *Jackson's* † "Chronological
                                             "Antiquities;

* This Paraphrase was published, after the death of the author, by *Maniſter Barnard*,
A. M. rector of *Whitcſtone, Devon*. Of Mr. *Edwards* I know no more than what his
editor informs us; that he was vicar of *Okehampton* in *Devonſhire*; was eſteemed a
perſon of great learning and ſound judgment, and perfectly underſtood the original text;
that he for many years made Divinity his chief ſtudy, and particularly applied himſelf to
the explanation of theſe Epiſtles, on which he beſtowed great part of his time, and if
he lived, intended to have gone through all *St. Paul's* Epiſtles.

† This learned philoſopher and divine, eldeſt ſon of the Rev. *John Jackſon* (firſt
rector of *Senſey* near *Thirſk*, and afterwards rector of *Roſſington* and vicar of *Doncaſter* in *Yorkſhire*), was born at *Senſey*, in that county, *April* 4, 1686; and educated at *Doncaſter* ſchool under the famous Dr. *Bland* (afterwards head maſter of *Eton*
ſchool, dean of *Durham*, and from 1732 to 1746 provoſt of *Eton College*); who, obſerving his proficiency, often left the inſtruction of the younger ſcholars to his care. Thus
accompliſhed, he was entered of *Jeſus College, Cambridge*, towards the end of 1702; and
from his reſidence at *Midſummer* following proſecuted the academical ſtudies with diligence,
and learned *Hebrew* under the celebrated Orientaliſt *Simon Ockley* ‡. He proceeded A. B.

at

‡ Born at *Exeter* in 1678; and educated at *Queen's College, Cambridge*. He took the degrees in arts
and that of B. D. and entered into holy orders; was ſkilled in all the Oriental languages, and well
acquainted with moſt of the modern ones, particularly *French, Spaniſh*, and *Italian*. By marrying
early in life, he precluded himſelf from a fellowſhip. In 1705 he was preſented, by *Jeſus College*, to
the vicarage of *Swaveſey* in *Cambridgeſhire*; and in 1711 was choſen *Arabic* Profeſſor, and appointed
chaplain to the earl of *Oxford*, after whoſe diſgrace in 1714, having a numerous family, and being a
bad œconomiſt, he became ſo much embarraſſed in his circumſtances as in the ſummer of 1717 to be
thrown into priſon in *Cambridge Caſtle* for debt; from which he was however diſcharged before his death,
which happened at *Swaveſey, Auguſt* 9, 1720. The firſt volume of his principal work, " The Hiſ-
" tory of the *Saracens*," was printed in 1708, 8vo, and inſcribed to Dr. *Aldrich*, Dean of *Chriſt Church*.
To the ſecond volume, which appeared in 1718, inſcribed to *James* earl of *Caernarvon*, were annexed
" Sentences of *Ali*, Son-in-law of *Mahomet*, and his fourth ſucceſſor," inſcribed to *Thomas Freke*, eſq.
In the Introduction to that volume, dated " *Cambridge Caſtle, Dec.* 2, 1717," Mr. *Ockley*, after a
handſome encomium on the great application of M. *Petit de la Croix*, the famous Oriental Interpreter to
Louis XIV, obſerves, " My unhappy condition hath always been widely different from any thing that
" could admit of ſuch an exactneſs. Fortune ſeems only to have given me a taſte of it out of ſpight, on
" purpoſe that I might regret the loſs of it. Though perhaps I may accuſe her wrongfully for befriend-
" ing me with an excuſe for thoſe blemiſhes, that would have admitted of none had I been furniſhed
" with all thoſe aſſiſtances and advantages, the want of which I now bewail. If that was her mean-
" ing, ſhe hath been very tender of my reputation indeed, and reſolved that my adverſaries ſhould have
" very little reaſon to accuſe me of the loſs of time. The firſt volume coſt me two journies to *Oxford*, each
" of them of ſix weeks only (incluſive of the delays upon the road, and the difficulty of finding the books
" without any other guide than the catalogue, not always infallible). But my chief buſineſs lying
" then in one author [*Alwákidi*], it was ſo much the eaſier to make a quick diſpatch; becauſe it is of
" no ſmall moment in affairs of this nature to be once well acquainted with the hand of the manuſcript,
" and the ſtyle of the author. But in my ſecond undertaking I found a quite different appearance of
" things in more reſpects than one. Either my domeſtick affairs were grown much worſe, or I leſs
" able to bear them, or, what is more probable, both. What made me eaſy as to my journey and
" charges during my abſence, was the liberality of the Worſhipful *Thomas Freke* of *Hannington, Wilts*,
" eſq. to whom the world is indebted for whatſoever is performed at preſent in this ſecond volume; I
" mean with regard to the expences of it: which ſtill would not have anſwered the end, if I had not
" been indulged all poſſible conveniences of ſtudy, firſt by the favour of my much honoured friend,
" the incomparable Dr. *Halley*, who, with the conſent of his learned colleague Dr. *Keill*, allowed me
" the keys of the *Savilian* ſtudy; and in the next place by the Reverend and learned Dr. *Hudſon*,
" chief library-keeper of the *Bodleian*; who, according to his wonted humanity, permitted me to take
" out of the library whatſoever books were for my purpoſe; otherwiſe, though I had five months time,
G g   " much

" Antiquities; or, the Antiquities and Chronology of the
                                                   " moſt

at the uſual period; and leaving the univerſity in 1707, was appointed tutor to the children of Mr. *Simpſon*, at *Renſhaw* in *Derbyſhire*. In the mean time the rectory of *Roſſington* having been reſerved from the death of his father for him by the corporation of *Doncaſter**, he took Deacon's orders in 1708; and in 1710 was ordained prieſt, and entered into the

" much could not have been done, conſidering the variety and difficulty of the manuſcripts; beſides
" that I was forced to take the advantage of the ſlumbers of my cares, that never ſlept when I was
" awake; and if they did not inceſſantly interrupt my ſtudies, were ſure to ſucceed them with no leſs
" conſtancy than night doth the day. Though it would be the height of ingratitude in me not to ac-
" knowledge that they were daily alleviated by the favours and courteſies which I received from per-
" ſons of the greateſt dignity and merit in that noble univerſity; too numerous to be all here inſerted,
" and all too worthy (ſhould I mention any one of them) to be omitted. Some ſuch apology as this
" will always be neceſſary for him that undertakes a work of this nature upon his own bottom without
" proper encouragement. If any one ſhould pertly aſk me, Why then do you trouble the world with
" things that you are not able to bring to perfection? Let them take this anſwer of one of our famous
" *Arabian* authors; ' What cannot totally be known, ought not to be totally neglected; for the know-
" ledge of a part is better than the ignorance of the whole.' The only way that I know to remedy
" theſe misfortunes, is that which I propoſed before, the encouragement of our youth. They will
" hardly come in upon the proſpect of finding leiſure in a priſon to tranſcribe thoſe papers for the
" preſs which they have collected with indefatigable labour, and oftentimes at the expence of their
" reſt, and all the other conveniences of life, for the ſervice of the publick. No; though I were to
" aſſure them from my own experience, that I have enjoyed more true liberty, more happy leiſure,
" and more ſolid repoſe, in ſix months here, than in thrice the ſame number of years before. Evil is
" the condition of that hiſtorian who undertakes to write the lives of others, before he knows how to
" live himſelf. But if there be no encouragement given, perhaps thoſe learned gentlemen whom the
" world hath ſo liberally obliged *gratis*, will think themſelves bound in honour to make ſome return;
" unleſs their loathneſs to quit that impregnable fortreſs againſt envy (that always attends the merit of
" the virtuous) into which they are ſo happily retreated, ſhould reſtrain them. Not that I ſpeak this,
" as if I thought I had any juſt reaſon to be angry with the world: I never ſtood in need of its aſſiſt-
" ance in my life, but I found it always very liberal of its advice; for which I am ſo much the more
" beholden to it, by how much the more I did always in my judgment give the poſſeſſion of wiſdom the
" preference to that of riches." A third edition, to which the late Dr. *Long*, Maſter of *Pembroke Hall*,
prefixed a Life of *Mahomet*, was, by the permiſſion of Mr. *Lintot*, proprietor of the copy-right, printed
in 1757 at *Cambridge*, in 2 vols, 8vo. " for the ſole benefit of Mrs. *Anne Ockley*," the author's daughter, and a very deſerving woman, for whom a handſome ſubſcription was by this means made.—His
other publications were, 1. " Introductio ad Linguas Orientales, &c. 1706," 8vo.—2. " The Hiſtory
" of the preſent *Jews* throughout the World. Tranſlated from the *Italian* of *Leo Modena*, a *Vene-
" tian* Rabbi, 1707," 12mo.—3. " The Improvement of Human Reaſon, exhibited in the Life of *Hai
" Ebn Yokdhan*, written in *Arabick* above 500 years ago, by *Abu Jaafar Ebn Tophail*. In which is
" demonſtrated, by what methods one may, by the meer Light of Nature, attain the Knowledge of
" things natural and ſupernatural, more particularly the Knowledge of God and the affairs of another
" Life. With an Appendix; in which the poſſibility of Man's attaining the true Knowledge of God,
" and things neceſſary to Salvation without Inſtruction, is briefly conſidered, 1708, 1711."—4. " A
" Sermon on the Divinity and Authority of the Chriſtian Prieſthood, preached at *Ormond* chapel [now
" *St. George's* church] 1710."—5. " A new Tranſlation of the Second Apocryphal Book of *Eſdras*,
" from the *Arabic* Verſion of it, as that which we have in our common Bibles is from the *Latin*
" Vulgar," about 1712.—6. " An Account of *South Weſt Barbary*, containing what is moſt remark-
" able in the Kingdoms of *Fez* and *Morocco*. Written by a perſon who had been a Slave there a con-
" ſiderable time, and publiſhed from his authentic manuſcript, 1713."—7. " The Neceſſity of In-
" ſtructing Children in the Scriptures. An Anniverſary Sermon preached on *Whitſun Tueſday* (*May*
" 26, 1713) at *St. Ives*, *Huntingdonſhire*, founded by Dr. *Robert Wilde* (author of *Iter Boreale*), who
" gave ſix Bibles yearly to the Poor Children of that Pariſh, 1713."—There is a manuſcript letter of
his to Dr. *William Wotton*, dated *June* 25, 1714, now in the hands of Dr. *Owen*, and given him by
his friend Mr. *Bowyer*. It is an anſwer to ſome queries relating to the *Confuſion of Tongues*, and contains ſome curious obſervations on the conſtruction, &c. of the *Eaſtern* languages.

  * The corporation might do ill or well on this occaſion, in reſerving their living for a minor, as it
ſhould happen; however, againſt his death, they ſold the next turn for 800*l.* and with the money
paved the long ſtreet of their town, that forms part of the great North road.

                                                            full

" moft ancient Kingdoms,   from the Creation of the World,
                                        " for

full poffeffion of that rectory.   But the parfonage-houfe being gone to decay, he boarded
at *Doncafter*, and in 1712 married *Elizabeth* daughter of *John Cowley*, efq. collector of
excife there.   On this marriage, he entirely rebuilt the parfonage houfe at *Roffington*,
and went to refide in it.   He commenced author in 1714, by publifhing three anonymous letters in defence of Dr. *S. Clarke's* " Scripture Doctrine of the Trinity." He was
not at that time perfonally acquainted with Dr. *Clarke*; but met with him foon after at
Lynne Regis in *Norfolk*.   Mr. *Tonfon* the bookfeller, intending in 1726 to publifh a Bible
with paraphrafe and notes by feveral hands, applied to him, by Dr. *Clarke*, to undertake
the comment upon the Prophets, propofing a handfome gratuity; but he declined the
offer, and the fame year engaged in the caufe of his friend againft Dr. *Waterland**.   In
the fame year alfo there paffed feveral letters between him and Mr. *Whifton*, on the fubject
of infant-baptifm.   In 1718 he went to *Cambridge*, to take his degree of M. A.; but finding fuch an oppofition raifed againft it as he was unable to remove, he defifted from the
purfuit.   Prefently after his return, he received a confolatory letter from Dr. *Clarke*, who
alfo procured for him the confraterfhip of *Wigfton's Hofpital* † in *Leicefter*, to which he
was prefented in 1719 by lord *Lechmere*, in whofe gift it was as then Chancellor of the
dutchy of *Lancafter*, and to whom Dr. *Clarke* had been the year before indebted for the
mafterfhip of that hofpital.   On this promotion Mr. *Jackfon* left *Roffington*, and removed
to *Leicefter*, where, as confrater, he was alfo afternoon preacher or lecturer of *St. Martin's Church*; but conftantly vifited his flock at *Roffington* for two or three months every
year during his life.   *May* 30, 1720, he took out a licence from his diocefan Dr. *Gibfon*,
bifhop of *Lincoln*, to qualify him for afternoon preacher at *St. Martin's* aforementioned.
In 1721 and the following year feveral prefentments were lodged againft him in the Bifhop's
court, as alfo in that of Dr. *Trimnel*, archdeacon of *Leicefter*, for preaching erroneous doctrines ‡; but he fo ftrenuoufly vindicated himfelf, as to defeat the profecutions.   Yet,
after the cafe of the *Arian* fubfcription was publifhed by Dr. *Waterland*, he refolved, with
Dr. *Clarke*, never to fubfcribe the articles any more, by which refolution he loft, about
1724, the hopes of a prebend of *Salifbury*, which Bifhop *Hoadly* refufed to give him with-
out fuch fubfcription ||.   The Bifhop's denial was the more remarkable, as he had fo often
intimated his own diflike of all fuch fubfcriptions.   However, he had been prefented
before by Sir *John Fryer* to the Private Prebend of *Wherwell* in *Hampfhire*, where no
fuch qualification was requifite.   In 1723 Mr. *Jackfon* publifhed " The Duty of Subjects
" towards their Governors; a Sermon preached before the Hon. *Charles Churchill's*
" Regiment of Dragoons, at their Camp near *Leicefter*, *Auguft* 1723;" and in 1728,
" The Duty of a Chriftian fet forth and explained in feveral Practical Difcourfes, being

---

* Nine treatifes by Mr. *Jackfon* on this controverfy, from 1716 to 1738, are enumerated in the
Supplementary Volume [vol. VI. part 2.] of the Biographia Britannica, 1776, p. 107.

† The confraterfhip of *Wigfton's Hofpital* is held (for life) by patent from the chancellor of the
dutchy of *Lancafter*, and was particularly acceptable to Mr. *Jackfon*, as it requires no fubfcription to
any article of religion.   *Chillingworth* had it, who alfo refufed (for a time) to fubfcribe.   *Neal* (Hift.
of Puritans, vol. III. chap. II. p. 101. 8vo.) fays, *Chillingworth* was perfuaded to fubfcribe for the
two preferments he before mentioned, viz. the chancellorfhip of *Sarum* and the mafterfhip of *Wigfton's
Hofpital*.   Both thefe are held by patent, and require no fubfcription.   But *Chillingworth* was not
chancellor of the diocefe, but of the church of *Sarum*, which ftall undoubtedly requires fubfcription,
as much as any fimple prebendal ftall in a cathedral.

‡ Complaint was made to Bp. *Gibfon* that Mr. *Jackfon* did not read the *Athanafian* Creed in the
chapel of the Hofpital; to which Mr. *Jackfon* replied, that the chapel was not in the Bifhop's jurifdiction, and that the ftatutes of this houfe directed the Apoftles' Creed to be read, and no other.

|| See a letter of Mr. *Jackfon's* on this occafion, Biog. Brit. p. 108.

" an

" for the fpace of 5000 years, &c. To which are added
" proper

" an Expofition of the Lord's Prayer; to which is added, a Difcourfe on the Sacrament
" of the Lord's Supper, for the Ufe of Families." On the death of Dr. *Clarke*, in *May*
1729, he fucceeded, by the prefentation of the Duke of *Rutland*, chancellor of the
dutchy of *Lancafter*, to the mafterfhip of *Wigfton's* Hofpital, which office he held till
his death. He repaired and made feveral additions to the mafter's houfe; repaired the
hofpital, and by degrees augmented the ftipend of the poor to 3s. a week. In 1730, he
was denied the ufe of the pulpit at *St. Martin's* *; and publifhed that year " A Defence
" of human-liberty, in anfwer to the principal arguments which have been alledged
" againft it, and particularly to *Cato's* Letters on that fubjeCt, &c. The fecond edition,
" to which is added, A vindication of human liberty, in anfwer to a differtation on li-
" berty and neceffity, written by *Anthony Collins*, efq," 8vo. And in that and the following year, he publifhed four traCts in defence of human reafon, occafioned by Bifhop
Gibfon's " Second Paftoral Letter." In 1731 he attacked *Tindal's* " Chriftianity
" as old as the Creation;" in 1733 he publifhed an anfwer to " Things divine
" and fupernatural, conceived by analogy with Things natural and human," a work
attributed to Bifhop *Browne* of *Corke*; in 1734, " The exiftence and unity of God
" proved from his nature and attributes, &c. To which is added an appendix,
" wherein is confidered the ground and obligations of morality," which led him into
a controverfy with Mr. *W. Law* and other writers †; in 1735, " A Differtation on
" Matter and Spirit, with fome Remarks on a book, intituled, *An inquiry into the na-
" ture of the human foul*" [by Mr. *Baxter*]; and in 1736 " A Narrative of the Cafe of
" the Rev. Mr. *Jackfon's* being refufed the Sacrament of the Lord's Supper at *Bath*;"
which had been done in a very public manner by Dr. *Coney*. In 1742 he had an epiftolary debate with his friend *W. Whifton* concerning the order and times of the high priefts.
In 1744 he publifhed " An Addrefs to the Deifts, being a proof of Revealed Religion,

* *Henry* earl of *Huntingdon* fettled by deed, 18 *Elizabeth*, a ftipend of 30l. a year ‡ on the confrater of
Wigfton's Hofpital, on condition he fhould preach certain Sermons in *St. Martin's* church (one of
which was to be on *Sunday* in the afternoon), if the pulpit fhould be then vacant, he having no power
to thruft out the vicar. On the firft of *November*, 1730, Mr. *Jackfon* being then mafter of the hofpital, and intending to officiate in the place and at the defire of Mr. *Hacket* the confrater, Mr. *Carte*
(then vicar), without fending Mr. *Jackfon* notice, fet the facriftan at the bottom of the pulpit ftairs
to refufe him admittance to the pulpit, alledging he would preach himfelf; which he did, having
firft of all thus publickly affronted Mr. *Jackfon*; who immediately removed the Sermon from *Sunday*
to *Friday*, alledging he had a power to do fo by the Earl's deed. Some of the parifhioners on this filed
a bill (which is always in the nature of a petition) againft him in the Dutchy Court. The chancellor,
OCtober 23, 1731, decreed the Sermon fhould be on *Sunday*, according to the former ufage; but difmiffed the other complaints in the bill, which were indeed fpiteful and frivolous. Mr. *Jackfon* lived
to fee fome of thofe who figned the petition and were moft violent againft him fo reduced, as to be glad
of a place among the poor in *Wigfton's Hofpital*, which with a true chriftian temper he beftowed upon
them, without hefitating or reproaching them for their former behaviour. This account is taken
from a copy of the bill (or petition) filed againft *Jackfon*; *Jackfon's* anfwer; and the duke of *Rutland's*
determination. Mr. *Ludlam* has a copy of the ftatutes of *Wigfton's Hofpital*, drawn up by *Henry* earl
of *Huntingdon*, Sir *Ralph Sadler* chancellor of the dutchy of *Lancafter*, and *George Bromley* attorney-
general, in virtue of letters patent 14 *Elizabeth*; and alfo the aCt of parliament confirming the fame,
and the deed of gift of *Henry* earl of *Huntingdon*, OCt. 11, 18 *Elizabeth*; the deed declaring the ufes
of the faid gift. The original of thefe are in the room called the Evidence-room of *Wigfton's Hofpital*,
with innumerable leafes (for lives) of lands belonging to the fame, terriers, &c. and in the utmoft
dirt and diforder.   † Of which the particulars may be feen, Biog. Brit. p. 109.

‡ The earl made a rent-charge on certain lands (parcel of the poffeffions of the late diffolved abbey of *St.
Mary de Pratis*) of fixty pounds a year, payable to the Mafter of *Wigfton's Hofpital*. Of this, the Confrater
receives thirty pounds; the reft is for two exhibitions to two fcholars of *Leicefter* fchool, and other ufes.

" from

"proper Indexes," three volumes, 4to; Two editions of
Mr.

" from Miracles and Prophecies, in anfwer to a Book, intituled *The Refurrection of*
" *Jefus confidered by a Moral Philofopher*," 8vo; and in 1745 entered the lift againft
Mr. *Warburton*, in " The Belief of a future State proved to be a fundamental
" Article of the Religion of the *Hebrews*, and held by the philofophers; the heathen
" theology explained, and the time of *Job*; with remarks on Mr. *Lardner's* fifth
" volume, &c. 1745," 8vo. On this production Mr. *Warburton* not unpleafantly
remarked, that all its objections, even to the very blunders, had been long ago
obviated or anfwered. " But I would recommend," he fays, " Mr. *Jackson's* pam-
" phlet to the reader's perufal, as a fpecimen of that illuftrious Band in which he has
" thought fit to inlift; and which indeed would have been imperfect without this *An-*
" *fwerer General*; and, after having written againft the *Inquiry into the Nature of the*
" *Human Soul*, does me too much honour to be overlooked." Mr. *Jackson* either publifhed a fecond part of his " Belief of a future ftate," or added an appendix to his former
part, " occafioned by fome fevere reflections on the author and his writings, contained
" in the fecond part of Mr. *Warburton's* Remarks," which appeared in 1746. Mr.
Warburton in *March* 1747 replied, in a Preface to Mr. *Towne's* " Critical inquiry into
" the opinions and practice of the ancient philofophers, &c." Mr. *Jackson* immediately
purfued the fubject in " A further defence of the ancient philofophers, againft the mif-
" reprefentations of a critical enquiry, prefaced by Mr. *Warburton*, 1747;" and by
" A Treatife on the improvement made in the Art of Criticifm, collected out of the
" writings of a celebrated hypercritic; by *Philocriticus Cantabrigienfis*, 1748." Mr.
Warburton having made fome remarks on this treatife, the controverfy clofed by
" A defence of a late pamphlet called, A treatife on the improvement made in the
" Art of Criticifm, being an anfwer to fome remarks made upon it, 1749." Mr. *Jack-*
fon's next work was, " Remarks on Dr. *Middleton's* free inquiry into the miraculous
" power fuppofed to have fubfifted in the Chriftian Church after the days of the
" Apoftles." From this time he does not appear to have publifhed any thing till 1752,
when his laft and capital work, " Chronological Antiquities *," &c. came out in
three volumes, 4to. He afterwards made many collections and preparations for printing an edition of the New Teftament in *Greek*, with Scholia in the fame language,
and would have inferted all the various readings, had not the infirmities of age,
which he felt fome years before his death, prevented him from finifhing the defign †. His bodily ftrength declining, and the faculties of his mind gradually decreaf-
ing (of which he feemed but too fenfible), he became incapable of clofe application to
ftudy ‡; but retained his thirft after knowledge till his death, which happened *May* 12,
1763. By his wife, who died before him, he had twelve children; of whom one fon and
three daughters were living in 1764.—I have been furnifhed with the following hints of
Mr. *Jackson's* character by a friend, who was acquainted with him from the year 1750:
" He always feemed to me rather a man of induftry than genius, at leaft fuch genius as

* In a quarter of a fheet of the " Additions" to this work, is an anfwer to a note printed at the
end of a new edition of the firft volume of " The Divine Legation."
† An account of the materials he had collected for this intended edition, with notes containing
alterations, corrections, and additions to his Chronology, are inferted in an appendix to " Memoirs of
" the Life and Writings of the late Rev. Mr. *John Jackson*, &c. London, 1764, [by Dr. *Sutton* of
" *Leicefter*]," 8vo. whence this note is principally extracted. There are many particulars relating
to Mr. *Jackson* in *Whifton's* Life of Dr. *Clarke*.
‡ He had publifhed thirty-fix feparate books and pamphlets. And in " The Old Whig," N° 33
and N° 39, were his productions.

" is

Mr. *Mason's* "*Elfrida*, a dramatic poem, written on the
"model

"is neceffary to reconcile the inconfiftent accounts of antient writers, and make out a
" clear fyftem of antient chronology. He certainly took all that he has faid about hiero-
" glyphics and myfteries from *Warburton*; but fo totally forgot or overlooked it (as
" was his cuftom on other occafions), that he verily thought it all his own; nor did he
" underftand any of the Eaftern languages, except a little *Hebrew*. He was a ftrict
" follower and ftrenuous defender of Dr. *Clarke*. He was much offended at Dr. *Concy*
" (and would have been at any one) for faying that he denied the divinity of the Son.
" But then he would not on any account give the Son the appellation of felf-exiftent,
" neceffarily-exiftent, &c. or any of thofe metaphyfical titles. His being fo early a de-
" fender of Dr. *Clarke*, and his political zeal for the *Hanover* family, got him his pre-
" ferment; and his earlieft writings, efpecially his " Plea for Human Reafon," appear
" to have been his beft."—To this account I fhall not fcruple to annex a letter, though
compounded of infolent egotifm and meannefs, on a fubject where inexperience in typographical mechanifm mifled Mr. *Jackfon* to fuppofe himfelf unhandfomely treated.
However trifling the fubject may appear, Mr. *Bowyer's* anfwer will vindicate himfelf, and
give fome degree of inftruction to thofe who are not converfant with the prefs.

"S I R,　　　　　　　　　　　　　　　　　　　*July* 4, 1752.
" I received your letter with your account, but find you have out-reckoned me about
" a fheet and half, befides 15s. 6d. in odd matters not fit to be allowed. I paid
" 1l. 8s. for a copper-plate; and you charge 5s. for printing it, when you had no letters
" to fet, and charge me alfo for the printed page. Sure this is wrong. Next you
" charge me 5s. 6d. for cutting a few *Greek* characters in wood, which I fuppofe is not
" ufual to be done; and you undertook to print all but what was on the copper-plate.
" You alfo charge me 5s. for printing a little bit of a page, and charge me for the
" whole page printing befides. This is very wrong. But you was to charge thefe ex-
" traordinaries towards paying Mr. *Noon*, which I wonder you fhould do, confidering
" I dealt fo honourably with you. I am not willing to pay this overcharge, which I
" think is an impofition, all efpecially but the wooden characters, and this *may* be fo
" too. The fheets of the volumes printed are as follow: 1ft volume, 531 pages or 66
" fheets and ⅔ths; 2d volume, 505 pages, 66 fheets, ¼th; 3d volume, 373 pages, 46
" fheets, ⅝ths; fo in all 176 fheets ⅛th. In this account I have reckoned fome half
" pages, or lefs, for whole pages; but you have reckoned mere blank paper as if printed.
" I am going into the country, and fhall not return to *Leicefter* till the week after
" *Michaelmas*. But I write by this poft to Mr. *Noon* to take the 3l. 3s. for his trouble,
" and to pay you 38l. 6s. on my account, in full of all demands for printing (errors ex-
" cepted, if there be any either on your fide or on mine). Your ftrictnefs in reckon-
" ing the printing will make me more careful how I agree again, if I fhould have occa-
" fion. I had no meaning but to pay for fo many pages as fhould be actually printed,
" and wonder you fhould reckon a fheet and more of mere blank paper that has not a
" letter upon it. I will fend to Mr. *Noon* your account of the paper ufed, fo that if
" there be any error it may be amended. Your very humble fervant, J. JACKSON."
On this impertinent letter, a friend of Mr. *Jackfon*, who has lately feen it, remarks,
" He was extremely ignorant of every thing but books. No wonder he did not under-
" ftand the art of printing, nor that he could not be convinced of the reafonablenefs
" of what is the univerfal cuftom. All printing is eftimated and contracted for by the
" fheet. But if there muft be a deduction for every piece of white paper in a page, no
" accompt could ever be fettled."

Mr.

" model of the ancient *Greek* tragedy," 4to. and 8vo ; A

Mr. *Bowyer's* modeſt anſwer was this:

" Had you, Sir, been an Author of a lower claſs, one of thoſe who are paid by the ſheet,
" you would more eaſily have digeſted it, that no deductions ſhould be made for a blank
" page; that titles, dedications, and the like, though of a larger letter, ſhould be
" paid for at the ſame rate as the body of the book. And it is the more reaſonable the
" printer ſhould be paid ſo, becauſe he pays the very ſame price to the workman. He
" contracts with him at ſo much a ſheet one with another; and if there are any blanks,
" the advantage is divided between the author who gets his living by his brains, and
" the journeyman who picks it up by his fingers ends; nay, the proprietor or bookſel-
" ler receives an advantage likewiſe, the blank pages go to the buyer for full ones, and
" help to make up the number of ſheets. But what a world ſhould we have, if every
" thing was brought to mathematical nicety; if every ſubſcriber was to cavil at a blank
" page, and complain he had paper impoſed on him inſtead of print! The copper-plate
" you mention was printed off at the rolling-preſs, another branch of buſineſs; and the
" money I charged is what I paid for working it. Aſk Mr. *Whiſton*, who prints *Boyle's*
" head in moſt of his title-pages, and is the ſon of a mathematician, and himſelf a phi-
" lomath. The few letters I paid for cutting in wood are ſuch as no printer has in
" town, viz. the *Epiſemon Vau, Koppa,* and *Sanpi,* and two or three more. I fur-
" niſhed *Latin, Greek,* and *Hebrew*; and I told you (though you have forgot it) that
" I ſhould be obliged to get a few letters cut in wood, which would come to a very ſmall
" matter extraordinary. I called upon Mr. *Noon* with my bill the day after you went
" out of town, and left it with him ſoon after, in whoſe hands it lay till I told him I
" would clear his *demand* of three guineas. He then gave it me, and ſaid I might
" ſend it to you. But I find my honour is a ſnare to me, and my compliance with his
" demand only makes me ſuſpected by you. Hard fate, whichſoever way I turn myſelf;
" but I attribute it all to your inexperience in printing; and am, Sir, your moſt humble
" ſervant,   W. BOWYER."

To *another* Author, a moſt worthy Divine, for whom Mr. *Bowyer* had a very high regard,
but who thought himſelf aggrieved where in reality there was no cauſe of complaint,
the following letter was addreſſed:

" REV. SIR,

" I am ſorry you are not ſenſible of the openneſs of my dealing, and that I have
" taken no advantage of my own propoſal or yours. Your queſtion at firſt was, ' Whether
" quotations in *Greek*, and ſome printing in 𝕭𝖑𝖆𝖈𝖐 𝖑𝖊𝖙𝖙𝖊𝖗, would not add to the expence?'
" It would, you was told; but how much it would add to the expence could not be
" determined till I ſaw what quantity of *Greek* there was. You tell me, *March* 6,
" 1742-3, ' As to the *Greek* of any ſort that may occur, it muſt be charged hereafter
" according to the quantity or the extraordinary trouble occaſioned by it. I promiſe
" myſelf that OTHERWISE the charge will not exceed in *London* the propoſal from our
" univerſity preſs. The firſt nine ſheets,' you obſerve, ' have very little *Greek* in
" them.'—I have charged the whole, as if they had little or none. I have not ſtood for
" a word or two, though of accents and ſubſcripts I mended hundreds. I would further
" obſerve, that I paid as much to the compoſitor for the firſt nine ſheets as I did
" for the reſt, and even for the dedication, though in ſo large a letter. It is ſome
" ſmall advantage allowed to him from the invention of printing. Reduce every thing
" to the poor workman to the hardeſt ſtandard, what tyranny would be exerciſed! The
" mower agrees for ſo much an acre; perhaps a ſhower comes, and his taſk is eaſier:
" ſhall he make a deduction for it?   W. B."

second part of Dr. *Battie's** Lectures " De Principiis Ani-
" malibus,

* *William Battie* was born in *Devonshire* in 1704.   He received his education at
Eton, where his mother refided after her hufband's death in order to affift her fon
with thofe little neceffary accommodations which the narrownefs of her finances
would not permit her to provide in any other form.   Here he was fo very diligent
and laborious, and his mother was fo bufy and anxious for his advancement, that fhe
once expreffed herfelf very freely to Dr. *Snape*, for ftopping a remove, as fhe thought,
for two or three days, on the accidental illnefs of the fcholar who was his immediate
fenior.   In the year 1722 he was fent to *King's College, Cambridge*, to which place alfo
his mother accompanied him.   On a vacancy of the *Craven* fcholarfhip by the refignation of Mr. *Titley* of *Trinity College*, he offered himfelf as a candidate, and was fuccefsful.   The circumftance of his getting the fcholarfhip, as I have it from one of his
competitors on that occafion, are as follows : The candidates on the day of election
being reduced to fix, the provoft Dr. *Snape* examined them altogether, that they might,
as he faid, be witneffes to the fuccefsful candidate.   The three candidates from
King's College were examined in *Greek* authors without *Latin* verfions, and the provoft difmiffed them all with this pleafing compliment, that, being not yet determined in
his choice, he muft trouble them to come again.   Dr. *Bentley* (whofe fon was one of the
candidates) and the other electors examined them feparately, but one of them (Mr. *Pilgrim* †, the *Greek* Profeffor) being abfent, the other fix were fo divided, as after a year
and a day, to let the fcholarfhip lapfe to the Donor's family, when Lord *Craven* gave it
to *Battie*.   Probably the remembrance continued with him ; and induced him to make
a fimilar foundation in the fame college, with a ftipend of 20*l. per annum*, and the fame
conditions, for the benefit of others, which is called Dr. *Battie's* foundation.   He nominated to it himfelf while living, and it is now nominated to by the fame perfons who
fill up the *Craven* fcholarfhips.   His fituation at College may be judged from the
following extract of a letter written by him to a friend, and dated *March* 28, 1725:
" When I received yours, I little thought of being able to anfwer a queftion in
" it fo much to my fatisfaction as I do now ; I mean about the Univerfity Scho-
" larfhip, which I was yefterday upon my Lord *Craven's* recommendation, by
" means of Dr. *Snape*, admitted to, after having for fome time given over all
" thoughts of it.   I fhall now begin to live agreeably, and have, I hope, got through
" the worft part of my life ; for, with this addition, it will be no hard matter to live on
" a Fellowfhip agreeably to myfelf, and to the fatisfaction, I am fure, of all my friends ‡.
" There is only one piece of trouble likely to lye upon my hands for fome time, which
" is a fpeech next 29th of *May* ; after which I defign to read Sir *Ifaac Newton* with
" Profeffor *Saunderfon*, and make that, our *Englifh* and Modern Hiftory, and fome fmall

† Afterwards prefented by the Univerfity to the valuable living of *Standifh* in *Lancafhire*, where
he died.
‡ " Dr. *Stewart*, who in his ' Effay on the Riches of Nations,' hazards more paradoxes than
" perhaps any other writer, and yet is generally in the right, feems to be worfe informed about the
" univerfities (though he has refided at one for fome time) than upon any other fubject.   He feems
" to think that all or moft of the emoluments are confined to Students in Divinity, and that that occa-
" fions an overflow of labourers in that vineyard.   The fuccefs of Dr. *Battie* and many others may ferve
" to fhew that this is not the cafe.   The fact is, that little or no notice is taken of a lad's future in-
" tentions, provided he feems difpofed to take a Bachelor of Arts degree.   Afterwards, indeed, by
" the ftatutes of feveral colleges, all perfons (a few only excepted) muft take orders within fix
" years after they are M. A. in about 13 or 14 years after firft admiffion ; but this, I fuppofe, is
" not what Dr. *Stewart* meant.   That more clergy are wanted than phyficians or counfellors ; and
" that the Univerfities are the only regular places for educating the former ; whereas the latter are,
" and may be, completed elfewhere, will fufficiently account for the difparity in the numbers." *T. F.*

5   " matters

" malibus, Exercitationes in Coll. Reg. Medicorum *Lond.*"
8vo.

" matters of law, my study for some time." His own inclination prompted him to the profession of the law; but feeling how unequal he was, independent of other assistance, to the expence attending that course of study, he made known his intention, and his inability to accomplish it, to two old batchelors his cousins, both wealthy citizens, whose names were *Coleman.* Of them he solicited the loan of a small allowance, that might qualify him to reside at one of the Inns of Court, where he was assured he could pursue his profession on a more contracted plan of expence than any other young man called to the bar; with a positive engagement to indemnify them for their kindness if ever his future success should furnish him with the means: but they declined interfering in any respect with his concerns. This disappointment diverted his attention to physic, and he first entered upon the practice at *Cambridge*, where in 1729 was printed, " *Isocratis* Orationes Septem & Epistolæ. Codicibus MSS. nonnullis, " & impressis melioris notæ Exemplaribus collatis; Varias Lectiones subjecit, Versio-" nem novam, Notasque, ex *Hieronymo Wolfio* potissimùm desumptas, adjecit *Gul.* " *Battie*, Coll. Regal. *Cantab.* Socius." These orations were contained in a single octavo volume, in the preface to which he promises, " si modo hoc primum non displicuerit " conamen, ut reliqua Oratoris nostri opera nitidiore saltem vestitu donentur *." In this undertaking he regularly tasked himself to get through a stated portion every day. It was about this period the *Colemans* retiring from business settled in some part of the country near enough to admit of the Doctor's accepting a general invitation to their house, which he was encouraged to make use of whenever the nature of his business allowed him the leisure; this he did with no small inconvenience to himself, without the least prospect of advantage, not to mention the wide disproportion between their political principles, the old gentlemen being genuine city Tories, and the Doctor a staunch Whig, though both parties afterwards reversed their opinions; and the Doctor was one whom no consideration of advantage in the greatest emergencies of life could ever prevail on to swerve from what he conscientiously believed to be truth. A fair opening for a physician happening at *Uxbridge*, induced Dr. *Battie* to settle in that quarter. At his first coming there, the provost of *Eton*, Dr. *Godolphin*, sent his coach and four for him, as his patient; but the Doctor sitting down to write a prescription, the Provost raising up himself, said, " You need not trouble yourself to write: I only sent for " you to give you credit in the neighbourhood." His skill being attended with some fortunate events, he was quickly enabled to realize five hundred pounds. With his money in his pocket, he again paid a visit to his relations in the country, requesting their advice how to dispose of his wealth to the best advantage. This solid conviction of the young man's industry and discretion fired them with equal pleasure and astonishment, and from that hour they behaved towards him with the firmest friendship. He then removed to *London*, where the established emoluments of his practice produced him a thousand pounds *per annum*. In the year 1738 or 1739, he fulfilled by marriage a long attachment he had preserved for a daughter of *Barnham Goode* †, the under-

---

* This expression occasioned some humourous verses in the *Grub Street* Journal of 1730.

† The same person who was honoured with an extraordinary couplet ‡ by Mr. *Pope*, in whose notes *Goode* is said to be " an ill-natured critic, who wrote a satire on *Pope*, called The Mock *Æsop*, " and many anonymous libels in news-papers for hire."—Mr. *Goode* had two other daughters, one of whom was married to Mr. *Harvest*, an eminent brewer at *Kingston* (father to *George Harvest*, M. A. fellow of *Magdalen College, Cambridge*, and perpetual curate of *Thames Ditton, Surrey*, who died

‡ " Lo sneering *Goode*, half malice and half whim,
" A Fiend in glee, ridiculously grim."   DUNCIAD, iii. 153.

Dec.

8vo. (fee p. 221); "ΟΔΟΙΠΟΡΟΥΝΤΟΣ ΜΕΛΕΤΗΜΑΤΑ,
" five Iter *Surrienfe* & *Suffexienfe*; præmittitur, De Linguæ
" *Græcæ*

der-mafter of *Eton* fchool, againft whom the *Colemans* at all times expreffed the moft
inveterate political antipathy; they however behaved to the wife with the utmoft civility,
and when they died they left the Doctor thirty thoufand pounds *. In 1749 he obliged
the learned world with a correct edition of his favourite *Ifocrates*, from Mr. *Bowyer's*
prefs, in two volumes 8vo. In the difpute which the College of Phyficians had with Dr.
Schomberg about the year 1750, Dr. *Battie*, who was at that time one of the cenfors,
took a very active part againft that gentleman, and in confequence of it was thus (perhaps too feverely) characterized in a poem called *The Battiad* †:

" Firft BATTUS came, deep read in worldly art,	Then at his club behold him alter'd foon,
Whofe tongue ne'er knew the fecrets of his heart:	The folemn Doctor turns a low Buffoon:
In mifchief mighty, though but mean of fize,	And he, who lately in a learned freak
And like the Tempter, ever in difguife.	Poach'd every Lexicon, and publifh'd *Greek*,
See him, with afpect grave, and gentle tread,	Still madly emulous of vulgar praife,
By flow degrees, approach the fickly bed:	From *Punch's* forehead wrings the dirty bays."

By fuccefsfully mimicking this character, however, Dr. *Battie* is faid to have once faved a
young patient's life. He was fent for to a gentleman now alive, but then only 14 or 15, who
was in extreme mifery from a fwelling in his throat; when the Doctor underftood what the
complaint was, he opened the curtains, turned his wig, and acted *Punch* with fo much
humour and fuccefs, that the lad (thrown into convulfions almoft from laughing) was fo
agitated as to occafion the tumour to break, and a compleat cure was the inftantaneous
confequence. Had fuch a ftory been told of *Hippocrates*, it would probably have been
confidered as a great inftance of his fagacity, good fenfe, and good nature. For if the reftoration to health be the phyfician's aim, how could this defirable effect be obtained
fooner or more effectually? In 1751 he publifhed " De Principiis Animalibus Ex-
" ercitationes in Coll. Reg. Medicorum, *Lond.*" in three parts, which was followed
next year by a fourth. About the year 1756, on application from an intimate
friend to folve the appearance of certain confequences fuggefted by a paffage in
the beginning of Mr. *Locke's* " Reafonablenefs of Chriftianity," which implies
the eternity of that death all the race of *Adam* were expofed to by his tranfgreffion
until redeemed by *Chrift*; which redemption depends upon the terms delivered
by him to mankind in the difpenfation of the Gofpel; the Doctor applied himfelf
clofely to the illuftration of this point. It was 14 years before he communicated
the refult of his reflections, which he then read over to his friend in MS. This
tract, with certain others, was printed fome time before his death; but, not having
been publifhed, will at prefent admit of no further difcuffion. In 1757, being then

Dec. 24, 1780); the other to *Edward Littleton* ‡, LL. D. fellow of *Eton College*, and vicar of
Maplederham, *Oxfordfhire*, (who died *Nov.* 16, 1733); and, after his deceafe, to his immediate
fucceffor at *Maplederham*, the benevolent and learned Dr. *John Burton*.

* The elder *Coleman*, I have been fince informed, lived at *Bury*; and *Battie* going to vifit him,
from *Cambridge* juft after an election, Mr. *Coleman* afked him, whom he would have voted for, if
he had a vote? *Battie* having declared for the oppofite party, fo offended Mr. *Coleman*, that they
parted abruptly, and never met again. I know not when *Coleman* died; but *Battie*, now at *Uxbridge*,
made court to the other brother, a cheefemonger in the city; and always took care to pay his vifits
in a chariot.—Mr. *Coleman* was fo proud of him, as to tell his neighbours, " That was his kinfman's
" chariot, Dr. *Battie*, an eminent phyfician at *Uxbridge*;" and when he died, gave him the bulk of
his fortune.

† Said to be written by *Mofes Mendez*, *Paul Whitehead*, and Dr. *Schomberg*; and of which two
cantoes were publifhed, and fince reprinted in " THE REPOSITORY, a Collection of Fugitive Pieces,
" of Wit and Humour, 1776," 2 vols. 8vo, publifhed by *Dilly*.

‡ See Dr. *Morell's* Life of Dr. *Littleton*, prefixed to his Sermons, which were publifhed by fubfcription for the
benefit of his widow and children, in two volumes 8vo, 1735.

" *Græcæ* inftitutionibus quibufdam Epiftola Critica." By
Dr. *Burton*.

In

physician to *St. Luke's Hospital*, and superintendant * of a private mad-house near *Wood's
Close* in the road to *Islington*, he published in 4to, " A Treatise on Madness," in which
having thrown out some censures on the medical practice formerly used in *Bethlem Hospital*, he was replied to, and severely animadverted on, by Dr. *John Monro*, in a pamphlet
called " Remarks on Dr. *Battie's* Treatise on Madness," published the next year. This
reply contained a defence of the author's father, who had been lightly spoken of in the
fore-mentioned Treatise. In 1762 he published " Aphorifmi de cognofcendis & curandis
" morbis nonnullis ad principia animalia accommodati;" on which see some strictures in
Gent. Mag 1763, p. 20. In *February* 1763 he was examined before a Committee of the
House of Commons, on the State of the Private Madhouses in this Kingdom; and received
in their printed Report a testimony very honourable to his abilities †. In *April* 1764, he
resigned the office of physician to *St. Luke's Hospital*. In 1767, when the disputes ran
high between the College of Physicians and the Licentiates, Dr. *Battie* wrote several
letters in the public papers in vindication of the College. In 1776, he was seized with
a paralytic stroke, which carried him off *June* 13, that year, in his 75th year. The
night he expired, conversing with his servant, a lad who attended on him as a nurse, he
said to him, " Young man, you have heard, no doubt, how great are the terrors of death.

* Or, more properly speaking, master of it; though, to avoid the possibility of a personal profecution, it passed under some other name. Of this house he had a lease, which he bequeathed to his
family.

† " Your Committee being desirous of obtaining every degree of assistance and information which
" might enable them more perfectly to obey the orders of the House, they desired the attendance of
" Dr. *Battie* and Dr. *Monro*, two very eminent physicians, distinguished by their knowledge and
" their practice in cases of lunacy. Dr. *Battie* gave it as his opinion to your Committee, that the
" private madhouses require some better regulations; that he hath long been of this opinion; that
" the admission of persons brought as lunatics is too loose and too much at large, depending upon
" persons not competent judges; and that frequent visitation is necessary for the inspection of the
" lodging, diet, cleanliness, and treatment. Being asked, If he ever had met with persons of sane
" mind in confinement for lunacy? He said, it frequently happened. He related the case of a wo-
" man perfectly in her senses, brought as a lunatic by her husband to a house under the Doctor's di-
" rection, whose husband, upon Dr. *Battie's* insisting he should take home his wife, and expressing
" his surprize at his conduct, justified himself by frankly saying, he understood the house to be a
" sort of Bridewell, or place of correction. The Doctor related also the case of a person whom he
" visited in confinement for lunacy, in *Macdonald's* house, and who had been, as the Doctor be-
" lieves, for some years in this confinement; upon being desired by *Macdonald* to attend him, by the
" order, as *Macdonald* pretended, of the relations of the patient, he found him chained to his bed,
" and without ever having had the assistance of any physician before; but some time after, upon being
" sent for by one of the relations to a house in the city, and then told, *Macdonald* had received no
" orders for desiring the Doctor's attendance; the Doctor understood this to be a dismission, and he
" never heard any thing more of the unhappy patient, till *Macdonald* told him some time after, that
" he died of a fever, without having had any farther medical assistance, and a sum of money de-
" volved upon his death to the person who had the care of him." *Journals of the House of Commons,
vol.* XXXIX. *p.* 448. In consequence of this inquiry, a bill was ordered to be prepared for the regulation of private madhouses, which was not then carried into execution, though the few cases
which were examined into by the Committee were pronounced " sufficient to establish the reality of
" the too great abuses complained of in the present state of private madhouses; the force of the
" evidence, and the testimony of the witnesses, being at the same time so amply confirmed, and
" materially strengthened, by the confessions of persons keeping private madhouses, and by the au-
" thority, opinions, and experience of Doctor *Battie* and Dr. *Monro*." In 1772, on occasion of
some fresh abuses, a bill was again ordered to be prepared, but to as little purpose as the former.
A third ineffectual attempt to obtain an act was made in 1773. But the abuses continuing to increase,
the subject was more successfully resumed by parliament in 1774, when an act for the better regulation of private madhouses received the royal assent; and, happily for a sett of beings who are undoubtedly entitled to every possible alleviation of their misery, the power of licensing the keepers
of such houses is vested in the College of Physicians.

" This

In 1753, when the nation was in a ferment at the indulgence proposed to be granted to the *Jews*, Mr. *Bowyer* published, in 4to, "Remarks on a Speech made in Common Council, "on the Bill for permitting Persons professing the *Jewish* "Religion to be naturalized, so far as Prophecies are supposed to be affected by it." The design of this sensible little tract, which was written with spirit, and well received by those who were superior to narrow prejudices, was to shew, that, whatever political reasons might be adduced against the Bill, Christianity would in no degree be prejudiced by the indulgence proposed to be granted to the *Jews*. It is printed with his "Miscellaneous Tracts."

In the same year some of his notes were annexed to "A "Journal from *Grand Cairo* to *Mount Sinai*, and back again *, "translated

---

"This night will probably afford you some experiment; but may you learn, and may "you profit by the example, that a conscientious endeavour to perform his duty "through life, will ever close a Christian's eyes with comfort and tranquillity." He soon departed without a struggle or a groan. He was buried, by his own direction, at *Kingston* in *Surry*, "as near as possible to his wife, without any monument or memorial "whatever." He left three daughters, *Anne*, *Catharine*, and *Philadelphia*, of whom the eldest (the only one who remained single at the time of Dr. *Battie's* death) was married to *George Young*, esq. a captain in the royal navy, and sold her father's house and estate at *Marlow*, called *Court Garden* †, to *Richard Davenport*, esq. an eminent surgeon in *Essex Street*, in *The Strand*; one of the younger brothers of *Davies Davenport*, of *Capesthorne*, in the county of *Chester*, esq. The second daughter was married to *Jonathan Rashleigh*, esq. of *Penquite*, in *Cornwall*, by whom she has several children; the third to *John Call*, esq. lately engaged in the service of the *East India* Company. Dr. *Battie*, by his will, gave 100*l.* to *St. Luke's Hospital*, 100*l.* to the corporation for relief of widows and children of clergymen, and 20 guineas to Lord *Camden*, "as a small token of regard "for his many public and private virtues." His books and papers, whether published or not, he gave to his daughter *Anne*.

* To the Society of Antiquaries, to whom this book was inscribed, Bishop *Clayton* observed, that as the Journal particularly describes many places in the wilderness, where great numbers of antient characters are hewn in the rocks; if a person was sent to live some time among the *Arabs*, he might get copies of the characters, and some helps, by which the antient *Hebrew* characters now lost, may be recovered. He added, "I don't "know whom to apply to, more properly to look out for a suitable person. As to the "expence, I am willing to bear any proportion you shall think proper, in order to have

† This house was built under the direction of the Doctor, who lived in it to his death. He is said to have forgot the stair-case, and all the offices below were constantly under water. A favourite scheme of his for having the barges drawn up the river by horses instead of men, however well meant and useful, rendered him extremely unpopular. He narrowly escaped from being tossed over the bridge by the bargemen. In this scheme he is said to have sunk 1500*l.*

"this

" tranflated from a manufcript written by the Prefetto of
" *Egypt*, in company with fome miffionaries *de propagandâ*
" this defign effected." [The Bifhop propofed to have given 100*l.* per annum for five
years.] The Prefetto of *Egypt* had with him perfons acquainted with the *Arabic, Greek,
Hebrew, Syriac, Coptic, Latin, Armenian, Turkifh, Englifh, Illyrican, German,* and
Bohemian languages, yet none of them had any knowledge of the characters which were
cut in the faid rock 12 and 14 feet high with great induftry *. The Bifhop declared,
that he did not make this propofal as a matter of curiofity, but as it might be of great
fervice to the Chriftian revelation, by corroborating the hiftory of *Mofes.*

* An excellent Antiquary, in a letter on this fubject, (Gent. Mag. 1753, p. 331,) fays, " I hope
the gentlemen addreffed will pay a proper regard to the propofal of the Bifhop of *Clogher*, and will
fend fome qualified perfon to take an exact copy of that very antique infcription on the rock at
Mount Sinai. It may feem very daring in any one, whilft we have fo few *data*, and while little more
is known relating to this infcription, but that it exifts, to adventure any conjecture concerning it, and
yet I think one may guefs fomething, from analogy, about the fubject-matter of it. I believe it will
prove to be hiftorical, fince I have obferved that fuch ancient memorials have been preferved in that
manner. " That the moft ancient people," fays Mr. *Wife*, " before the invention of books, and before
" the ufe of fculpture upon ftones, and other fmaller fragments, were wont to reprefent things great
" and noble, upon entire rocks and mountains, feems fo natural, that it is eafily imagined, and af-
" fented to by all. And that the cuftom was not laid afide for many ages after, is plain from hiftory.
" *Semiramis*, to perpetuate her memory, is reported to have cut a whole rock into the form of herfelf.
" *Hannibal*, long after the invention of books, engraved characters upon the *Alpine* rocks, as a tefti-
" mony of his paffage over them; which characters were remaining about two centuries ago, if we
" may believe *Paulus Jovius.* But, what is moft to our purpofe, it appears to have been particularly
" the cuftom of the Northern nations, from that remarkable infcription, mentioned by *Saxo*, and fe-
" veral ages after him delineated, and publifhed by *Olaus Wormius.* This was infcribed by *Harold*
" *Hyldetand* to the memory of his father; it was cut on the fide of a rock in *Runic* characters, each
" letter of the infcription being a quarter of an ell long, and the length of the whole 34 ells." (Mr.
Wife's letter to Dr. *Mead.*) Thefe Northern examples are indeed the moft for this learned author's purpofe, who contends that the *white horfe*, in the vale of that name in *Berkfhire*, is a monument of this
fort, and was intended to perpetuate the remembrance of a fignal victory obtained by the *Saxons*
at *Afhdown*, under the conduct of King *Ælfred*, over the *Danes.* But the cuftom was Eaftern as well
as Northern, as appears from that very remarkable inftance which we have in Capt. *Hamilton's* Account
of *The Eaft Indies.* The author, after giving a fhort hiftory of that fuccefsful attack, which the *Dutch*
made upon the ifland of *Amoy* in *China*, A. D. 1645, adds, " This hiftory is written in large *China*
" characters, on the face of a fmooth rock that faces the entrance of the harbour, and may be fairly
" feen as we pafs out and in to the harbour." This is but of late date compared with the monument at
Mount Sinai; but as the Eaftern people in general are extremely tenacious of their antient cuftoms, as
appears from the travels both of Dr. *Pococke* and Dr. *Shaw*, the conjecture is not the lefs probable, that
this *Arabian* infcription will be found to afford us fome hiftorical fact."—It would have been a fenfible
difappointment to our worthy prelate, had he lived to fee that, after an attentive examination by the late
Mr. *Wortley Montagu* in 1765, thefe characters appear to be nothing more than the work of Chriftian
converts, Pilgrims to Mount *Sinai.* They approach neareft to the *Hebrew* of any character, and are
intermixed with figures of men and beafts. Mr. *Montagu's* defcription of the holes in the rock ftruck
by *Mofes* bears ample teftimony to the fcripture hiftory. See Phil. Tranf. vol. LVI. article 8, and
Gent. Mag. 1765, p. 374 401.—The laft account which we have of thefe written monuments is by
Mr. *Niebuhr.* " The infcriptions, fays he, on the road from *Suez* to Mount *Sinai*, do not anfwer
" the idea formed of them. I faw no rocks covered with characters for half a league together each;
" but very different infcriptions which *Pococke* copied before, and Mr. *Montagu* after me. As they
" are all engraved on very unequal and rough furfaces, my copies of them could not be more diftinct
" than thofe taken by the travellers before-mentioned. They appeared to me nothing more than the
" names of perfons who have paft that way. Yet as they are unknown in *Europe*, I fhall give fome
" of them in the account of my travels, with divers well-written hieroglyphics which I found in thefe
" defarts." *Defcription de l'Arabie, Copenh.* 1773, *p.* 85.—Thofe who reflect on the fatigue of caravan-
travelling in thefe parched countries, fo feelingly detailed in Mr. *Irwin's* late journey over land from
Suez to *Cairo*, may perhaps think it very extraordinary that Pilgrims fhould confume the little leifure
fuch journeys afford in attaching themfelves to a rock (even the fhady fide) at the height of 12 or 14
feet, to carve letters, which while they are defcribed to approach neareft to the *Hebrew* of any known
character, are intended to be reprefented as having no more meaning than the fcrawls of children with
chalk on a wall.

" *fide*.

" *fide* at *Grand Cairo:* To which are added, Remarks on
" the Origin of Hieroglyphics, and the Mythology of the an-
" cient Heathens. By the Right Rev. *Robert* Lord Bifhop of
" *Clogher**." This benevolent and very learned prelate highly
efteemed the friendfhip of Mr. *Bowyer,* honoured him with
a regular

* Dr. *Robert Clayton,* advanced to the bifhoprick of *Killala, Jan.* 23, 1729, was
tranflated to the fee of *Corke, Dec.* 19, 1735, and to that of *Clogher, Aug.* 26, 1745. He
was Fellow of the Royal and Antiquarian Societies; was always confidered as a prelate of
great learning, and of diftinguifhed worth and probity; and died, much lamented, *Feb.*
25, 1758. His publications are, 1. A letter in the Philofophical Tranfactions, N° 461,
p. 813, giving an account of a *Frenchman* 70 years old (at *Inifhanan,* in his diocefe of
Cork) who faid he gave fuck to a child.—2. " The Chronology of the *Hebrew* Bible vin-
" dicated; the facts compared with other ancient Hiftories, and the difficulties ex-
" plained, from the Flood to the Death of *Mofes*; together with fome Conjectures in
" relation to *Egypt,* during that period of time; alfo two Maps, in which are attempted
" to be fettled the Journeyings of the Children of *Ifrael,* 1751," 4to.—3. " An impar-
" tial Enquiry into the Time of the Coming of the Meffiah; together with an abftract
" of the evidence on which the Belief of the Chriftian Religion is founded; in two
" Letters to an eminent *Jew,* 1751," 8vo.—4. " An Effay on Spirit; wherein the Doc-
" trine of the Trinity is confidered in the Light of Nature and Reafon; as well as in the
" Light in which it was held by the ancient *Hebrews*; compared alfo with the Doctrine
" of the Old and New Teftament; together with fome Remarks on the *Athanafian* and
" *Nicene* Creeds, 1751;" 8vo.—5. " A Vindication of the Hiftories of the Old and New
" Teftament, in anfwer to the Objections of the late Lord *Bolingbroke*; in Two Letters
" to a young Nobleman, 1752," 8vo. reprinted in 1753.—6. " A Defence of the Effay
" on Spirit, with Remarks on the feveral pretended Anfwers; and which may ferve as
" an Antidote againft all that fhall ever appear againft it, 1753," 8vo.—7. " A
" Journal from *Grand Cairo* to *Mount Sinai,* and back again, &c. 1753," as above;
two editions, 4to. and 8vo. It was foon after this publication that his lordfhip became (in
March 1754) a Fellow of the Society of Antiquaries.—8. " Some Thoughts on
" Self-love, Innate Ideas, Free-will, Tafte, Sentiments, Liberty and Neceffity, &c.
" occafioned by reading Mr. *Hume's* Works, and the fhort Treatife written in *French*
" by Lord *Bolingbroke* on Compaffion, 1754," 8vo.—9. " A Vindication of the Hif-
" tories of the Old and New Teftament, Part II. Wherein the Mofaical Hiftory of
" the Creation and Deluge is philofophically explained; the Errors of the prefent The-
" ory of the Tides detected and rectified; together with fome Remarks on the Plura-
" lity of Worlds. In a Series of Letters to a young Nobleman. Adorned with feveral
" Explanatory Cuts, 1754," 8vo.—10. " Letters † between the Bifhop of *Clogher* and
" Mr. *William Penn,* concerning Baptifm, 1755," 8vo.—11. " A Speech made in the
" Houfe of Lords in *Ireland,* on *Monday, Feb.* 2, 1756, for omitting the *Nicene* and
" *Athanafian* Creeds out of the Liturgy, &c. Taken in fhort-hand at the time when
" it was fpoken, by *D. S.* 1756," 8vo. third edition 1774.—12. " A Vindication,
" Part III. Containing fome Obfervations on the Nature of Angels, and the Spiritual
" Account of the Fall and Redemption of Mankind. In a Series of Letters to a
" young Nobleman, 1758," 8vo. The three parts of the " Vindication," with the

† " Having fome years ago been indulged with a copy of the following Letters, after fome impor-
" tunity I have at length obtained a permiffion for their publication; which I was the more defirous
" of, as I apprehend it may be of fervice to have a friendly debate on one of the Sacraments of the
" Church of *England* made known; where the reader, whatever he fhall determine, will receive a
" pleafure at leaft in feeing a difpute, concerning fo important an article of Religion, carried on with-
" out a breach of its effential characteriftics, Charity and Candour." *Advertifement of Mr. Bowyer,*
prefixed to the Letters.

" Effay

a regular and not unfrequent correfpondence*, and prefented him with the copy-right of all his valuable writings.

In 1753 alfo he printed " Medals, Coins, Great Seals,
" Impreffions from the elaborate works of *Thomas Simon*†,
" Chief Engraver of the Mint to King *Charles* the Firft, to
" the Commonwealth, the Lord Protector *Cromwell*, and
" in the reign of King *Charles* the Second, to MDCLXV. By
" *George Vertue*‡," 4to; a new edition of *Horace's* "Epiftola ad
" *Auguftum*,"

" Effay on Spirit," were reprinted by Mr. *Bowyer*, in one volume, 8vo, 1759; with
fome additional notes, and an Index of Texts of Scripture illuftrated or explained.

* That Bifhop *Clayton's* confidence was not mifplaced, will appear by the following
Letter, which was fent by Mr. *Bowyer* to Dr. *Bradley*, the celebrated Aftronomer Royal:
" REV. SIR, *Nov.* 9, 1758.
" Before the Bifhop of *Clogher* died, he fell under the cenfure of fome Aftronomers,
" for having afferted† that the Moon kept the fame face to the Earth without turning on
" its own centre. In vindication of himfelf, he fent me the inclofed letter to print, if I
" thought proper. As I would not publifh any thing *now* under his name, which fhould
" be thought a manifeft abfurdity; and as I am not a proper judge how far what he has
" here advanced is fo, I would humbly beg the favour of you to let me know if you think
" it barely plaufible. I do not prefume to afk your decifion on the queftion; but only to
" fay whether what he hath produced hath the appearance of probability, which is the
" chief object of the prefs, and in general the utmoft attainment of human inquiries.
" I have further to afk pardon, if my regard to his character hath made me exceed my
" own, when I fubfcribe myfelf, Reverend Sir, your moft humble fervant, W. BOWYER."
I know not what anfwer was returned by Dr. *Bradley*, or whether his advancing infir-
mities‡ prevented his returning any; the Bifhop's letter, however, did not appear in print.

† A new and improved edition of this work, with an Appendix by Mr. *Gough*, and
two additional Plates finely engraved by *Bafire*, was printed by *J. Nichols* in 1780.

‡ *George Vertue*, an eminent engraver and diligent collector of Antiquities relative
both to his Art and the Hiftory of *England*, and no lefs diftinguifhed by the amiable fincerity and integrity of his heart, was born in the parifh of *St. Martin in the Fields*, 1684.
After an apprenticefhip of about four years with one mafter, who failed and quitted the
kingdom, and a feven years engagement with *Vandergucht* § the father, he began to work
for himfelf in 1709; became one of the firft members of the Academy of Painting inftituted
in 1711; and, under the patronage of *Kneller*, lord *Somers*, and the earls of *Oxford* and
Winchelfea, diftinguifhed himfelf by engraving portraits ‖. He was early in life diftinguifhed

† In the Second Part of his " Vindication of the Old and New Teftament."
‡ Dr. *Bradley* died *July* 15, 1762, in his feventieth year. There is a full account of him in the
new edition of the " Biographia Britannica," vol. II. p. 556.
§ *Gerard Vandergucht's* pictures and bronzes were fold by *Chriftie* in 1777.
‖ His prices for them may be partly learnt from his anfwer to a queftion from Dr. *Z. Grey, July* 19,
1737: " Mr. *Weft* is a gentleman fo much my friend, that I can't forgett eafily any recommendation
" from him, and on his account (if it was not my own inclination) I fhoud ufe every one civilly. What
" you propofe to have done I can't juftly be certain as to the expence of engraving; becaufe for octavo
" plates,

" *Augustum*," &c. 8vo. (see p. 222); Bp. *Hoadly's* " Sermons

guished by Mr. *Prior*, who, in his lines on *Tom Britton*, joins *Vertue* with Sir *Godfrey Kneller*. He was appointed engraver to the Society of Antiquaries on their revival in 1718, and continued to execute their prints till his death. He engraved the *Oxford* Almanacks from 1723 to his death, and embellished them by views of public buildings and historic events. The visits he paid to most of the galleries of the nobility, and to the universities, in search of *English* portraits, suggested a design of engraving a great variety of them, as well as of historic prints. The death of his last patron the late Prince of *Wales*, and a declining state of health, put a period in 1756 to a life of unremitted industry and zeal for tracing out and preserving *British* antiquities. Mr. *Vertue* was buried in the cloisters of *Westminster Abbey*, where there is a marble monument to his memory, with the following inscription, perfectly characteristic of its subject:

" Here lies the body of GEORGE VERTUE,

Late Engraver,

And Fellow of the Society of Antiquaries.

He was born in *London*, 1684;

And departed this life on the 24th of *July*, 1756.

With manners gentle, and a grateful heart,

And all the genius of the graphic art;

His fame will each succeeding artist own,

Longer by far than monuments of stone."

The Rev. Mr. *Gilpin*, in his " Essay upon Prints," says of *Vertue*, that " he was an " excellent antiquarian, but no artist; he copied with painful exactness in a dry, dis- " agreeable manner, without force or freedom: in his whole collection of heads we can " scarce pick out half a dozen which are good." This character seems scarcely, or but little, overcharged, especially when it is considered that *Vertue* applied so much to portrait engraving; and as we have upwards of 500 portraits by him, it might therefore have been expected he should have made a greater progress in his art. His sketches and notes were purchased by the Hon. *Horace Walpole*, whom they furnished with the outlines of his Anecdotes of Painting and Engravings in *England*, and Memoirs of the Artist himself. A list of his works, much too long to be inserted here, may be seen in those Memoirs, which were abstracted in the Supplement to the " Biographia Britan- " nica." His books, prints, and drawings, were sold by auction in *March* 1757; as were his pictures, models, plaister and wax impressions, limnings, coins, and medals, in *May* the same year. His widow presented the Society of Antiquaries with a number of his plates of *English* antiquities; and they purchased of her his large historic plates, all which they have republished. On Mrs. *Vertue's* death, the remainder of his plates and prints were sold by Mr. *Langford* in 1776 and 1777. Mr. *Ford* in the *Haymarket* sold by auction, in 1766, the drawings of his brother *James*, who had followed the profession of a painter at *Bath*, where he then died.

" plates, the head only of any person, I have had different prices, as the dificulty or labour is more " or less. The general prices I have had for such works, has been 10 guineas, 8 guineas, and 6 the " lowest, from pictures, paintings being done—indeed, when from a print bigger or lesser that is al- " ready engraved, it may cost a fourth or fifth part less, or near thereabouts. In respect to a print, if it " be any noted one, I can soon send you a certain answer if you please to let me know your intention, " and shall think it no trouble if you please to direct a line as before to,

" Sir, your respectful servant, G. VERTUE."

The prices of some of his earliest peformances for the Society of Antiquaries were as follows:

			l.	s.
1718.	Richard II. in *Westminster Abbey*, copper-plate included, - - -		21	0
1719.	*Ulphus's* Horn, - - - - - - - - - -		2	0
1721.	Shrine of *Edward* the Confessor (the Society found the plate), - -		15	15
	Waltham Cross, including paper and working off, - - - -		5	0

" on

" on the Terms of Acceptance," 8vo; and the firſt* volume
of " The Principles of Natural and Revealed Religion occa-
" ſionally opened and explained; in a courſe of Sermons
" preached before the honourable Society of *Lincoln's Inn,*
" by the Rev. Mr. *Warburton,* Preacher to the Society."

In 1754, with a view to exonerate himſelf from fatigue,
he entered into partnerſhip† with Mr. *James Emonſon,* who
was a relation to his father. As, in conſequence of ſome
diſagreements not material to mention, this connexion was
not of long ſubſiſtence‡, I ſhall purſue the hiſtory of Mr.
Bowyer's preſs as before.

In that year (1754) he printed " The Life of Pope *Sixtus*
" the Fifth (one of the moſt remarkable and entertaining Lives
" that is to be met with in Ancient or Modern Hiſtory); in
" which is included the State of *England, France, Spain,*
" *Italy, The Swiſs Cantons, Germany, Poland, Ruſſia, Sweden,*
" and *The Low Countries,* at that time; with an account of
" *St. Peter's,* the Conclave, and manner of chuſing a Pope;
" the *Vatican* Library, the many grand obeliſks, aque-
" ducts, bridges, hoſpitals, palaces, ſtreets, towns, and
" other noble edifices, begun or finiſhed by him. The

* The ſecond was printed in 1754. In a prefatory inſcription to the worſhipful Maſters of the Bench, Mr. *Warburton* very handſomely acknowledges his obligations for the honour done him, at the laſt vacancy, on the generous offer of the Preacherſhip of the Society. Another volume was printed in 1767, but *not* by Mr. *Bowyer,* under the title of " Sermons and Diſcourſes on various ſubjects and occaſions, volume the third. " By Dr. *William Warburton,* Lord Biſhop of *Glouceſter.*"

† Having taken on this occaſion a houſe in *Great Kirby Street, Hatton Garden;* Mr. *Clarke* ſays, " I wiſh Mrs. *Bowyer* joy of eſcaping into a freer and ſweeter air. She muſt " read *Cowley's* poem on Gardening with ten times the pleaſure, when ſhe ſees her own " works blooming round her. I wiſh I could ſend her a rood or two that here lies " almoſt neglected. How it would flouriſh in her hands!"

‡ On their ſeparation, in *July* 1757, Mr. *Emonſon* opened a printing-office in *St. John's Square,* with a new evening paper, under the title of " *Lloyd's* Evening Poſt." After carrying on buſineſs with reputation more than twenty years, having ſurvived an only ſon, he retired with an eaſy competence, and died *June* 6, 1780.

H h 4 " whole

" whole interfperfed with feveral curious incidents and
" anecdotes not to be met with in any other Author.
" Tranflated from the *Italian* of *Gregorio Leti*, with a Pre-
" face, Prolegomena, Notes, and Appendix, by *Ellis*
" *Farneworth*, M. A. fometime of *Jefus College, Cambridge,*
" and Chaplain to feveral of his Majefty's Ships during the
" late war," folio *; an edition of " *Ecton's* Thefaurus," improved by *Browne Willis*, efq. 4to; Mr. *Cooke's* † " Enquiry
" into Patriarchal Temples," 4to.; " The Dignity of Hu-
" man Nature ‡, or, the means to attain the true end of
" our exiftence," by Mr. *Burgh* §, 4to; Dr. *Grey's* tranflation
of Mr. *Hawkins Browne's* poem " De Animi Immortalitate,"

4to;

* " It would be ungrateful in me here to omit my thanks to the Printer, to whom I
" am much obliged for many ufeful hints in the profecution of this work, and for the
" care he has taken in the typographical part of it." *Author's Preface.*—An anonymous
tranflation of this valuable work had been printed in 8vo, 1704.—See an account of Mr.
Farneworth under the year 1762.

† *William Cooke*, M. A. chaplain to the earl of *Suffolk*, rector of *Oldbury* and *Didmarton* in *Gloucefterfhire*, and vicar of *Enford* in *Wiltfhire*, at which laft place he died
Feb. 25, 1780, after having enjoyed the vicarage more than 40 years. He publifhed an
Abridgement of Dr. *Stukeley's Stonehenge* and *Abury*, tinctured with *Hutchinfoniafm*; and
alfo circulated Propofals for a Medallic Hiftory of Imperial *Rome*, with plates of coins,
which, I am informed, was left in the prefs at his deceafe, and is now completing by his fon.

‡ Of this volume, 25 copies only were printed on fine paper.

§ This ingenious Moralift and Philofopher, who at one time was an affiftant to Mr.
Bowyer in correcting the prefs, was afterwards for many years mafter of an academy,
firft at *Stoke Newington*, and then at *Newington Green*. His fituation in the firft period
of his life is unknown; but in the preface to " Youth's Friendly Monitor," he fays,
that a feries of misfortunes in the earlier part of life had determined him to bring his
mind to retirement and a very moderate income. His firft effay in authorfhip was " *Britain's*
" Remembrancer, 1746," 8vo. Of this pamphlet five large editions were fold in *England*; and it was reprinted in *Scotland, Ireland*, and *America*. It was afcribed to fundry Bifhops; was quoted both by the Clergy and Diffenting Minifters in their pulpits;
and was univerfally allowed to be a feafonable and ufeful tract. A fixth edition was publifhed in 1766 for *George Freer*, in *Bell Yard, Temple Bar*. If this was a true picture
of the times 40 years ago, how little addition to the colouring would adapt it to the prefent! By " The Dignity of Human Nature," which was publifhed in *April* 1754, and
infcribed to the Princefs Dowager of *Wales*, whofe " gracious condefcenfion voluntarily
" fhewn to the author on various occafions" is gratefully acknowledged, he acquired
much

4to; "Queries to the Gentlemen of *Great Britain*," for

much reputation as a writer. In 1756 "Youth's Friendly Monitor," of which a sur-
reptitious copy had been printed * under a disguised puffing title, was published by
himself in 12mo†; and in the conclusion of an address to the reader, p. xii. he says,
" The character of an author is not what I aim at; that of a faithful educator of youth
" is my utmost ambition. I have never taken the pen in hand, but when I have been
" desired or prompted to it; and if I have got ten pounds by all I have published, I have
" got a thousand. I have given an account above of some of the writings which have
" been drawn from me; and how I came to trouble the public with them; and the case
" is the very same with the others; as one or two small tracts on the destructive grievance
" of low-prized spirituous liquors, published at the time when that affair was under con-
" sideration in parliament; a sort of Paraphrase in verse on the civth Psalm, to which
" were added a few papers in prose, intituled, An Idea of the Creator from his Works,
" which was printed for the benefit of an orphan, and raised him a very pretty sum;
" and some periodical moral-essays in the papers, of which I did not, when I projected
" the design, imagine that any considerable weight would be left upon me. I am sorry
" it is so necessary for me to declare, in this public manner, that my own employment
" is my supreme pursuit, and that it is not an itch of scribbling that has occasioned my
" being so often in the press; but that I have been partly drawn and partly dragged
" into it; and that now I have reason to hope I have nearly done with that most irk-
" some and unprofitable labour." In 1758 he printed a pamphlet under the title of
" Political Speculations;" and the same year "The Rationale of Christianity," though
he did not publish this last till 1760; when he printed a kind of *Utopian* Romance, intituled, "An Account of the First Settlement, Laws, Form of Government, and Police,
" of the *Cessares*, a people of *South America*; in Nine Letters, from Mr. *Vander Neck*,
" one of the Senators of the Nation, to his Friend in *Holland*, with Notes by the
" Editor," 8vo. In 1765 he published an excellent volume of essays, in 12mo, under
the title of " *Crito*;" and a second volume of the same work in 1767; in which year
a new edition of " The Dignity of Human Nature" appeared, in 2 vols. 8vo. Mr.
Burgh wrote " Proposals (humbly offered to the public) for an Association against the
" Iniquitous Practices of Engrossers, Forestallers, Jobbers, &c. and for reducing the
" Price of Provisions, especially Butchers Meat, 1766," 8vo. His literary labours were
closed in 1774 by a compilation, intituled " Political Disquisitions; or, An Enquiry
" into publick Errors, Defects, and Abuses, illustrated by, and established upon, Facts
" and Remarks extracted from a variety of Authors ancient and modern, 1774," 3
vols. 8vo. This work was executed, as far as it went, while the author was in so bad
a state of health, that it was with difficulty he finished as much as is already published.
His design, for which he had collected materials, was to have extended to many more
books of equal size; but finding himself declining, he stopped when three volumes were
finished. He died *August* 26, 1775.

* A thousand copies had been printed about the year 1753, for the purpose of distributing them
among his pupils; and some of them, by the desire of Dr. *Hales*, were presented to Dr. *Hayter*, then
Bishop of *Norwich*, for the use of the younger part of the children of the Princess Dowager of *Wales*;
which, says Mr. *Burgh*, " was what gave occasion first to my being taken notice of by that most amiable
" and illustrious Princess, in a manner far enough above what I could have thought of or expected."
† The full title of this edition was, " Youth's Friendly Monitor; being a Set of Directions, pru-
" dential, moral, religious, and scientific; first drawn up for a Farewell Present by the Master of an
" Academy near *London*, to his pupils on their removing from under his care. To which is prefixed,
" an account of the extraordinary proceedings of some persons, which occasioned the publication of
" this tract, contrary to the author's original intentions; together with *Theophilus*, a Character worthy
" of Imitation."

I i the

the Society of Antiquaries *; the second volume of Mr.
Warburton's " Sermons at *Lincoln's Inn*," (see p. 239);
with " An Appendix, containing three Sermons preached
" on the occasion of the late Rebellion in 1745 †, and a
" Discourse on the Nature of the Marriage Union ‡," 8vo;
" A View of Lord *Bolingbroke's* Philosophy, in two Letters
" to a Friend," [by Mr. *Warburton*] 8vo. (completed in
the following year by two more Letters, and a new edition
of these); " *Barbarossa*, a tragedy," by Mr. *Brown* ||, 8vo;
Dr. *Armstrong's* § " Art of preserving Health, a didactic
" Poem," 8vo; " An Account of a Spiritual Court Pro-
" secution of a certain Bishop against a Clergyman of his
" Diocese," 8vo; another edition of *Mounteney's* " Demos-
" thenes," 8vo; Dr. *Gally's* ** " Dissertation on Pronouncing
" the *Greek* Language," 8vo; " Poll for the County of
" *Hertford*," 8vo; " The principal Charters which have
" been granted to the Corporation of *Ipswich* in *Suffolk*
" translated ††," 8vo; and a neat edition of " *Anacreon*,"
in 12mo, with notes which Mr. *Bowyer* himself collected.

In

* See these, enlarged, in the first number of " Bibliotheca Topographica Britannica,"
1780.

† Large impressions of these were printed separately, by Mr. *Bowyer*, at the time they
were preached. See above, p. 183. 189.

‡ At Mr. *Allen's* Chapel, printed also separately. See p. 189.

|| Of whom, see above, p. 210.—In the " Biographia Britannica," it is said that
this tragedy was produced on the stage in the beginning of 1755. It was acted *Dec.* 17,
1754, and published the same month. It first introduced its author to the acquaintance and friendship of Mr. *Garrick*, who wrote both the prologue and epilogue to it,
and spoke himself the prologue in the character of a country boy. With the following
passage in the epilogue,
" Let the poor devil eat, allow him that, &c."
the author was much disgusted, as it represented him in the light of an indigent person.
Vanity was undoubtedly one of the most prominent features in the character of Dr. *Brown*.

§ Of whom, see under the year 1758.

** Of whom, see hereafter, p. 250.

†† By Mr. *Canning*, minister of *St. Laurence*; who had published in 1747, " An Ac-
" count of the Gifts and Legacies that have been given and bequeathed to charitable
" uses

In 1754 died Mr. *James Gibbs**, the celebrated architect, concerning whom, in p. 195, I have made an erroneous conjecture, which the fourth volume of Mr. *Walpole's* elegant publication enables me to rectify.

In

" uses in the town of *Ipswich*, with some account of the present state and management,
" and some proposals for the future regulation of them," 8vo. In 1755 Mr. *Bowyer*
printed for him " An Address to the Freemen of *Ipswich*," half a sheet, folio.

* This ingenious architect was born at *Aberdeen* in 1683, and studied his art in
Italy. Mr. *Gwynne*† says of him, that " no architect since Sir *Christopher Wren* ever
" had a better opportunity of displaying his genius in the great style of architecture. He
" was employed in building and repairing several of the principal churches in *London*,
" and he has acquitted himself upon the whole tolerably well. *St. Martin's in the Fields*
" is esteemed one of the best in the city, though far from being so fine as it is usually
" represented. The New Church in *The Strand* is an expensive rich design, without the
" least appearance of grandeur. He also designed *St. Bartholomew's Hospital*, and a
" great number of houses for persons of distinction; but there appears nothing uncom-
" mon or new in them, and he was rather a mannerist in things of that kind. He made
" designs for three sides of the quadrangle of *King's College, Cambridge*, in a modern
" style, without any regard to the part already built, though he confesses the chapel is
" the finest *Gothic* pile he ever saw. This custom of mixing *Gothic* and modern architecture
" in the same pile of building has also been practised in the University of *Oxford* with great
" success, and serves to shew that very little attention is paid to taste and elegance in a
" place where one would expect to find hardly any thing else ‡. Another instance of this
" erroneous practice he has given at *Derby*, where he has added to a fine rich *Gothic* steeple
" [tower] a church of the *Tuscan* order, which, in his account of the work, he expressly
" says is suitable to the old steeple [tower]."—" About the year 1720 (I now use the words
" of Mr. *Walpole*) he became the architect most in vogue, and the next year gave the
" design of *St. Martin's* church, which was finished in five years, and cost thirty-two
" thousand pounds. His likewise was *St. Mary's in the Strand*, a monument of the
" piety more than of the taste of the nation. The new church at *Derby* was another of
" his works; so was the new building at *King's College, Cambridge*, and the senate-
" house there, the latter of which was not so bad as to justify erecting the middle building
" in a style very dissonant. The *Ratcliffe* Library § is more exceptionable, and seems to
" have sunk into the ground; or, as *Sarah* duchess of *Marlborough* said by another
" building, it looks as if it was making a curtsy. *Gibbs*, though he knew little of
" *Gothic* architecture, was more fortunate in the quadrangle of *All Souls*, which has
" blundered into a picturesque scenery, not void of grandeur, especially if seen through
" the gate that leads from the schools. The assemblage of buildings in that quarter,
" though no single one is beautiful, always struck me with singular pleasure, as it
" conveys such a vision of large edifices, unbroken by private houses, as the mind is

† *London and Westminster Improved*, p. 44—46.
‡ It rather shews that modern architects do not understand *Gothic*, or prefer their own vagaries to it.
Both these observations are too true.
§ At the opening of the Library, *Gibbs* was complimented by the University with the degree of
M. A. He soon after published " A Description of the Library."—Mr. *Walpole* observes, that
" *Gibbs*, like *Vanbrugh*, had no aversion to ponderosity; but, not being endued with much invention,
" was only regularly heavy. His praise was fidelity to rules; his failing, want of grace."

" apt

In 1755 Mr. *Bowyer* fent a literary prefent (I know not of what value) to the cathedral library at *Chichefter**. The principal books printed by him in that year were, " The " Hiftory and Antiquities of the Town, Hundred, and " Deanry of *Buckingham*, by *Browne Willis*, efq †. LL.D."

4to ;

" apt to entertain of renowned cities that exift no longer. In 1728 *Gibbs* publifhed a " large folio of his own defigns, which I think will confirm the charaƈer I have given of " his works. His arched windows, his ruftic-laced windows, his barbarous buildings for " gardens, his cumbrous chimney-pieces, and vafes without grace, are ftriking proofs of " his want of tafte. He got 1500*l.* by this publication, and fold the plates afterwards " for 400*l.* more. His reputation was however eftablifhed ; and the following compli- " ment, preferved by *Vertue*, on his monument of *Prior* in *Weftminfter Abbey*, fhews " that he did not want fond admirers ‡ :

" While *Gibbs* difplays his elegant defign,
" And *Ryfbrack*'s art does in the fculpture fhine,
" With due compofure and proportion juft,
" Adding new luftre to the finifhed buft,
" Each artift here perpetuates his name,
" And fhares with *Prior* an immortal fame.   *T. W.*

" There are three prints of *Gibbs* ; one from a piƈture of *Huyffing*, another from " one of *Schryder*, a *Swifs*, who was afterwards painter to the King of *Sweden*, and the " third [a mezzotinto by *MacArdell*] from *Hogarth*. *Gibbs* was affliƈted with the " gravel and ftone, and went to *Spa* in 1749, but did not die till *Auguft* 5, 1754. He " bequeathed an hundred pounds to St. *Bartholomew*'s *Hofpital*, of which he was archi- " teƈt and governor, the fame to *The Foundling Hofpital*, and his library and prints to " the *Ratcliffe* Library at *Oxford*, befides charities, and legacies to his relations and " friends." Anecdotes of Painting, 1780, vol. IV. p. 44—47.

✶ " In your generous difpofition, I hear that you are inclined to think of our Li- " brary. Poverty is importunate. I afk every body that I decently can, and fhould be " proud of your name among our benefaƈtors. But come and fee it ; and then you will " fay, that fo fine a room will excufe this liberty." Mr. *Clarke* to Mr. *B. Aug.* 15, 1755.

† *Browne Willis*, efq. LL.D. was born *Sept.* 14, 1682, at *St. Mary Blandford*, in the county of *Dorfet*. He was grandfon of Dr. *Thomas Willis* ‖, the moft celebrated phyfician of his time, and the eldeft fon of *Thomas Willis*, efq. of *Bletchley*, in the county of *Bucks*. His mother was daughter of *Robert Browne*, efq. of *Frampton*, in *Dorfetfhire*. He had the firft part of his education under Mr. *Abraham Freeftone* at *Bechampton*, whence he was fent to *Weftminfter* fchool, and at the age of feventeen was

---

‡ " It fhews at leaft that this fingle fpecimen of *Gibbs*'s fkill had one admirer ; but who is *T. W.* " and what is his weight on this occafion ? It is certain that *Gibbs* was much employed, and that is " no contemptible commendation for an artift, and looks as if there were no better at the time. He " fucceeded to a very bad period of architeƈts." Dr. *Taylor*'s *Friend.*

‖ Mr. *Vertue*'s " Weft Profpeƈt of St. *Martin's Church in the Fields, Weftminfter*," his native pa- rifh, is infcribed, " To *Browne Willis*, efq. whofe grand-father, Dr. *Thomas Willis*, the celebrated phy- " fician, was many years an inhabitant of this parifh ; and he bequeathed to it a perpetual Curacy for " early Morning Prayers, and in the Evening."

4   admitted

4to; the fourth (and laſt) volume of Mr. *Carte's* "General
"Hiſtory

admitted a gentleman commoner of *Chriſt Church College, Oxon,* under the tuition of
the famous geographer *Edward Wells,* D.D.* When he left *Oxford,* he lived for
three years with the famous Dr. *Wotton*† (of whom ſee before, p. 51.). In 1702 he proved
a conſiderable benefactor to *Fenny Stratford,* by reviving the market of that town. In 1705
he was choſen member of parliament for the town of *Buckingham,* in the room of Sir
Richard Temple, bart. who had made his election for the county of *Bucks;* and during the
ſhort time he was in parliament, he was a conſtant attendant, and generally upon committees. In 1707 he married *Catharine,* daughter of *Daniel Elliot,* eſq. of a very ancient family in *Cornwall,* with whom he had a fortune of 8000l. and by whom he had a numerous iſſue ‡. She died *October* 2, 1724. Between the years 1704 and 1707 he contributed very largely towards the repairing and beautifying *Bletchley* church, of which
he was patron, and to which he gave a ſet of communion plate. In 1717-18 the Society
of Antiquaries being revived, Mr. *Willis* became a member of it. *Aug.* 23, 1720, the
degree of M.A. and 1749 that of LL.D. were conferred on him, by diploma, by the univerſity of *Oxford.* At his ſolicitation, and in concurrence with his couſin Dr. *Martin
Benſon,* afterwards biſhop of *Glouceſter,* rector of this pariſh, a ſubſcription was raiſed
for building the beautiful chapel of *St. Martin's* at *Fenny-Stratford.* A remarkable
circular letter on this occaſion (moſt probably written by Mr *Willis)* is printed in the
Political Regiſter, 1725, vol. XXX. p. 596. The chapel was begun in 1724 §, and conſecrated by Dr. *Richard Reynolds,* Biſhop of *Lincoln, May* 27, 1730. A dreadful fire
having deſtroyed above 50 houſes and the church at *Stony-Stratford, May* 19, 1746, Mr.

* Amongſt Mr. *Browne Willis's* numerous publications is a little tract, intituled, "Reflecting Ser-
"mons conſidered; occaſioned by ſeveral Diſcourſes delivered in the Pariſh Church of *Bletchley,* in
"the county of *Bucks* (of which Dr. *Willis* was patron), by Dr. *E. Wells,* rector, and Mr. *E. Wells*
"(his nephew), curate," one ſheet, 8vo. No date.
† Mr. *Willis* always uſed to mention this friend of his by the ſtyle of *William Wotton Bachelor of
Divinity,* that he might teſtify his proteſt againſt degrees given at *Lambeth;* for *W. Wotton* was in
reality a *Lambeth Doctor,* and was conſequently a titular *Doctor* at leaſt. BOWYER, MS.
‡ He had four daughters, the two eldeſt (who were twins) outlived their father, and died unmarried; one is now the widow of the late Dr. *Eyre,* F.R. and A.S.; the other was married to the
Rev. Mr. *Harvey,* fellow of *New College.*
§ In an unprinted letter to Dr. *Snape,* Maſter of *King's College,* dated *Dec.* 22, 1727, Mr. *Willis* thus
deſcribes the progreſs of the chapel: "Honoured Sir, I have now received from Dr. *Grey* the good
"news of the generoſity of your College to *Stratford* chapel. I cannot enough acknowledge your
"friendſhip herein, which I wiſh it was in my poor power to make any return for. We have, I
"thank God, filled our roof with the arms deſigned, which are of ſix *Oxonians* and three *Cambridge*
"Colleges, beſides *Eaton;* but have made proviſion for four coats more over our altar, the firſt of
"which ſhall be yours. Two gentlemen have already contributed, and paid us their reſpective ten
"guineas; and now your College has condeſcended to ſubſcribe, we only wait for a fourth bene-
"factor, which I hope ſoon to obtain, being applying to ſome friends, and then we deſign to put them
"all four up together. It is an unſpeakable pleaſure to me, now we have got your arms, to reflect
"that all the places relating to the county wherein I live, and where I have had my education, have
"been our benefactors, and are enrolled among our founders. As *Eaton* and *King's Colleges, Weſt-
"minſter College,* at which ſchool I was bred, *Chriſt Church* and *Trinity Colleges* belonging thereto,
"*New College,* which is impropriator, and *Wadham,* and *Wincheſter College* appendant to that, beſides
"the town of *Bucks,* our county town; and to theſe I may reckon *Windſor,* which has a good eſtate
"in *Bucks,* and where we have alſo partook of your bounty; but I will not be farther troubleſome
"than to requeſt you will be ſo kind as to put into Dr. *Grey's* hands, or his order, the charity you
"ſo nobly beſtow on a moſt miſerable poor place, which is ever bound to pray for you, as is, Ho-
"noured Sir, your moſt devoted and obliged ſervant to command, B. WILLIS."—Mr. *Baker* of *St.
John's* contributed a magnificent common-prayer-book to this chapel.—Mr. *Willis* engraved the North
Eaſt proſpect of the chapel in one plate, and its fine cieling in another, with the arms of its benefactors.
Willis,

" Hiſtory of *England*," of which ſee above, p. 201; " A
" Letter

Willis, beſides collecting money among his friends for the benefit of the unhappy ſufferers, repaired, at his own expence, the tower of the church, and afterwards gave a lottery ticket towards the rebuilding of that church, which came up a prize. In 1741 he preſented the univerſity of *Oxford* with his fine cabinet of *Engliſh* coins, at that time looked upon as the moſt complete collection in *England*, and which he had been upwards of forty years in collecting; but the Univerſity thinking it too much for him, who had then a large family, to give the gold ones, purchaſed them for 150 guineas, which were paid to Mr. *Willis* for 167 *Engliſh* gold coins, at the rate of four guineas *per* ounce weight; and even in this way, the gold coins were a conſiderable benefaction. This cabinet Mr. *Willis* annually viſited upon the 19th of *October*, being *St. Frideſwide's* day, and never failed making ſome addition to it. He alſo gave ſome MSS. to the *Bodleian* Library, together with a picture of his grand-father, Dr. *Thomas Willis*. In 1752 he laid out 200l. towards the repairs of the fine tower at *Buckingham* church *, and was, upon every occaſion, a great friend to that town. In 1756, *Bow Brickhill* church, which had been diſuſed near 150 years, was reſtored and repaired by his generoſity. In 1757 he erected, in *Chriſt Church*, *Oxford*, a handſome monument for Dr. *Iles*, Canon of that Cathedral, to whom his grandfather was an exhibitioner †; and in 1759 he prevailed upon *Univerſity College* to do the ſame in *Bechampton* church for their great benefactor Sir *Simon Benet*, bart. above 100 years after his death: he alſo, at his own expence, placed a ſquare marble ſtone over him, on account of his benefactions at *Bechampton*, *Buckingham*, *Stoney-Stratford*, &c. Mr. *Willis* died at *Whaddon-hall*, *Feb.* 5, 1760, and was buried in *Fenny-Stratford* chapel, *Feb.* 11. The following inſcription (drawn up by himſelf) on a white marble tablet ſet in a black frame is put over him;

" Hic ſitus eſt	Hæc capella exiguum monumentum eſt,
Browne Willis, Antiquarius,	Obiit 5° Die *Feb.* A. D. 1760,
Cujus avi cl^{mi}. æternæ memoriæ,	Ætatis ſuæ 78.
Thomæ Willis,	O Chriſte, ſoter et judex,
Archiatri totius *Europæ* celeberrimi,	Huic peccatorum primo
Defuncti die Sancti *Martini*, A. D. 1675,	Miſericors et propitius eſto."

He gave to his eldeſt grandſon and heir (whom he appointed his ſole executor) all his books, pictures, &c. except " *Rymer's* Fœdera" in 17 folio volumes, which he bequeathed to *Trinity College*, *Oxford*, and the choice of one book to the Rev. Mr. *Francis Wiſe*, and ordered his manuſcripts to be ſent within a quarter of a year to the univerſity of *Oxford*. In 1710, when Mr. *Gale* publiſhed his " Hiſtory and Anti-
" quities of *Wincheſter* Cathedral," Mr. *Willis* ſupplied him with the Hiſtory of *Hyde Abbey*, and Liſts of the Abbots of *Newminſter* and *Hyde*, therein publiſhed. In 1712, he publiſhed " Queries for the Hiſtory and Survey of the County of *Buck-*
" ingham," in one ſheet in folio. In 1715 and 1716 his " Notitia Parliamentaria, or an
" Hiſtory of the Counties, Cities, and Boroughs in *England* and *Wales*," 2 vols. 8vo.

---

* This tower fell down about three years ago, juſt as Mr. *Pennant* was gone out, and ſo completely ruined the church, that it was neceſſary to take it down; and being rebuilt on the Caſtle Hill, it exhibits a fine view from Lord *Temple's* gardens at *Stowe*.—This inſtance, however it may ſhew *Browne Willis's* church-munificence, ſhould yet make us cautious how we raiſe ponderous additions to old and decayed buildings. Who can ſay that the original builders here, and in many other places, might not ſtop ſhort in deſpair of compleating their deſigns with ſafety? It ſhould ſeem from the tradition of the inhabitants that the fall of this tower was not altogether unexpected.

† One who contributes towards the expences of a perſon at the Univerſity.

" Letter to a Friend in *Italy*, and Verfes occafioned on
" reading

to which he added a third in 1750. The firft volume was reprinted in 1730, with addi-
tions ; and a fingle fheet, fo far as relates to the borough of *Windfor*, in folio, 1733.
In 1717 a fmall abridgement of " The Whole Duty of Man," 12mo. was printed at his
expence, intended as a prefent to the poor. In the " Antiquities of the Cathedral
" Church of *Worcefter*," written by *Thomas Abingdon*, efq. and publifhed by Dr.
Rawlinfon in 8vo. *London*, 1717, at page 116 is a lift of the Priors of *Worcefter*, by
Browne Willis, efq. In 1717 he publifhed " A Survey of the cathedral church of *St.*
" *David's*, and the edifices belonging to it, as they ftood in the year 1715," 8vo ; in 1718
and 1719, " An Hiftory of the Mitred Parliamentary Abbies and Conventual Cathedral
" Churches*," 2 vols. 8vo ; in 1719, 1720, 1721, " Surveys of the Cathedral Churches of
" *Landaff*, *St. Afaph*, and *Bangor*, and the edifices belonging to each," 8vo. with cuts.
In 1720 he affifted Mr. *Strype* in an edition of *Stowe's* Survey of *London* ; in 1729, he
publifhed " A Prayer, &c." 8vo ; in 1727, 1730, 1733, " Survey of the Cathedrals of *Eng-*
" *land*, with *Parochiale Anglicanum*, illuftrated with Draughts of the Cathedrals," 3 vols.
4to ; " A Table of the gold coins of the Kings of *England*, by B. W. † efq. a member
" of the Society of Antiquaries, *London*, 1733," in one fheet folio, making plate XL.
of their " Vetufta Monumenta," was of his compiling ‡ ; as were the feries of Principals
of Religious Houfes, at the end of Bifhop *Tanner's* " Notitia Monaftica" in folio, 1744,
fent by him 1743 to Mr. *John Tanner*, editor of that work. In 1749 he publifhed
" Propofals for printing a Journal of the Houfe of Commons ;" about 1750, an
" Addrefs to the Patrons of Ecclefiaftical Livings," without name or date, in one fheet,
4to ; in 1754, an improved edition of " *Ecton's* Thefaurus Rerum Ecclefiafticarum,"
4to. His laft publication was the " Hiftory and Antiquities of the Town, Hundred,
" and Deanry of *Buckingham*, *London*, 1755," 4to. His large collections for the whole
county are now among his MSS. in the *Bodleian* Library. His friend the Rev. Mr. *Cole*, of
Milton, *Cambridgefhire*, has tranfcribed and methodized, in two volumes folio, his " Hif-
" tory of the hundreds of *Newport* and *Cotflow*," from the originals, in four volumes,
which Mr. *Willis* delivered to him a few weeks before his death, with an earneft requeft
that he would prepare them for publication, for which they are now ready. It is
much to be lamented that this part of the labours of that moft induftrious Antiquary,
from 1712 to his death 1760, fhould be loft to the public who derive fo much advantage
from fuch of them as are publifhed.—I am indebted for great part of this note to the
" Account of Mr. *Willis*," which was read before the Society of Antiquaries in 1760,
by Dr. *Ducarel*, who thus fums up the character of his friend : " This learned Society,
" of which he was one of the firft revivers, and one of the moft induftrious members,
" can bear me witnefs, that he was indefatigable in his refearches ; for his works were
" of the moft laborious kind. But what enabled him, befides his unwearied diligence, to
" bring them to perfection, was, his being bleffed with a moft excellent memory. He
" had laid fo good a foundation of learning, that though he had chiefly converfed with
" records, and other matters of antiquity, which are not apt to form a polite ftyle, yet
" he expreffed himfelf, in all his compofitions, in an eafy and genteel manner. He was,
" indeed, one of the firft who placed our ecclefiaftical hiftory and antiquities upon a firm,

---

* A recommendatory letter by Dr. *Wotton* is prefixed to the fecond volume of this work.
† In fome copies it is printed " *W. B.* efq."
‡ This in p. 82 has been mifcalled " A Catalogue of Mr. *Willis's* gold coins," which has been in-
advertently confounded with it in p. 95.

" bafis,

" reading *Montfaucon*," [by the Rev. Mr. *Edward Clarke**,
Fellow

" bafis, by grounding them upon records and regifters; which, in the main, are unex-
" ceptionable authorities. During the courfe of his long life he had vifited every cathe-
" dral in *England* and *Wales*, except *Carlifle*; which journies he ufed to call his *pilgri-*
" *moges*†. In his friendfhips, none more fincere and hearty; always communicative,
" and ever ready to affift every ftudious and inquifitive perfon. This occafioned an ac-
" quaintance and connexion between him and all his learned contemporaries. For his
" mother, the univerfity of *Oxford*, he always expreffed the moft awful refpect and the
" warmeft efteem. As to his piety and moral qualifications, he was ftrictly religious,
" without any mixture of fuperftition or enthufiafm, and quite exemplary in this refpect:
" and of this, his many public works, in building, repairing, and beautifying of churches,
" are fo many ftanding evidences. He was charitable to the poor and needy; juft and
" upright towards all men. With regard to himfelf, he was remarkably fober and tem-
" perate; and often faid, that he denied himfelf many things, that he might employ
" them better. And, indeed, he appeared to have had no greater value for money,
" than as it furnifhed him with opportunities of doing good. In a word, no one ever
" deferved better of the Society of Antiquaries; if induftry and an inceffant applica-
" tion, throughout a long life, to the inveftigating the antiquities of this national
" church and ftate, is deferving of their countenance." To this judicious portrait I
fhall take the liberty to annex a fportive falley of a female pen, the late Mifs *Talbot*,
who, in an unprinted letter to a lady of firft-rate quality (dated from the rectory-houfe
of *St. James's* parifh, *Jan.* 2, 1738-9) very humouroufly characterizes Mr. *Willis* and
his daughters ‡.

* Son of the fo often-mentioned rector of *Buxted*, who got leave a little before his
death to refign in his favour. See above, p. 28.

† " Among the innumerable ftories that are told of him, and the difficulties and rebuffs he met with
in his favourite purfuits, the following may fuffice as a fpecimen. One day he defired his neighbour, Mr.
Lowndes, to go with him to one of his tenants, whofe old habitation he wanted to view. A coach driving
into the farm-yard, fufficiently alarmed the family, who betook themfelves to clofe quarters; when
Browne Willis, fpying a woman at a window, thruft his head out of the coach, and cried out, " Woman,
" I afk you if you have got no *arms* in your houfe." As the tranfaction happened to be in the rebellion
of 1745, when fearches for arms were talked of, the woman was ftill lefs pleafed with her vifitor, and
began to talk accordingly. When Mr. *Lowndes* had enjoyed enough of this abfurdity, he faid, " Neigh-
" bour, it is rather cold fitting here; if you will let me put my head out, I dare fay we fhall do our
" bufinefs much better." So the late Dr. *Newcome* going in his coach through one of the villages
near *Cambridge*, and feeing an old manfion, called out to an old woman, " Woman, is this a *religious*
" *houfe*?" " I don't know what you mean by a religious houfe," retorted the woman, " but I be-
" lieve the houfe is as honeft an houfe as any of yours at *Cambridge*." *Dr. Taylor's Friend*.

‡ " You know *Browne Willis*, or at leaft it is not my fault that you do not; for when at any
" time fome of his oddities have peculiarly ftruck my fancy, I have writ you whole volumes about
" him. However, that you may not be forced to recollect how I have formerly tired you, I will repeat,
" that with one of the honefteft hearts in the world, he has one of the oddeft heads that ever dropt out
" of the moon. Extremely well verfed in coins, he knows hardly any thing of mankind; and you may
" judge what kind of education fuch an one is likely to give to four girls, who have had no female
" directrefs to polifh their behaviour, or any other habitation than a great rambling manfion-houfe in
" a country village. As by his little knowledge of the world he has ruined a fine eftate, that was,
" when he firft had it, 2000l. *per annum*; his prefent circumftances oblige him to an odd-headed kind
" of frugality, that fhews itfelf in the flovenlinefs of his drefs, and makes him think *London* much
" too extravagant an abode for his daughters; at the fame time that his zeal for Antiquities makes
" him think an old copper farthing very cheaply bought with a guinea, and any journey properly
" undertaken that will bring him to fome old Cathedral on the Saint's-day to which it was dedicated.
" As, if you confine the natural growth of a tree, it will fhoot out in a wrong place—in fpite of his
" expenfivenefs,

Fellow of *St. John's College, Cambridge,*] 4to; three volumes of Mr. *Whiston's* translation of *Josephus,* 8vo; " Oeconomia

" expensiveness, he appears saving in almost every article of life that people would expect him other
" wise in; and in spite of his frugality, his fortune, I believe, grows worse and worse every day.
" I have told you before, that he is the dirtiest creature in the world; so much so, that it is
" quite disagreeable to sit by him at table; yet he makes one suit of cloaths serve him at least two
" years; and then his great-coat has been transmitted down, I believe, from generation to generation,
" ever since *Noah.* On *Sunday* he was quite a beau. The Bishop of *Gloucester* is his idol; and if
" Mr. *Willis* were Pope, *St. Martin,* as he calls him, would not wait a minute for canonization. To
" honour last *Sunday* as it deserved, after having run about all the morning to all the *St. George's*
" churches whose difference of hours permitted him, he came to dine with us in a tie-wig, that exceeds in
" deed all description. 'Tis a tie-wig (the very colour of it is inexpressible) that he has had, he says,
" these nine years; and of late it has lain by at his barber's, never to be put on but once a year in honour
" of the Bishop of *Gloucester's* [*Benson*] birth-day.—But, you will say, what is all this to my engage
" ment this morning? Why, you must know, *Browne* distinguishes his four daughters into the *Lions*
" and the *Lambs.* The Lambs are very good and very insipid; they were in town about ten days, that
" ended the beginning of last week; and now the Lions have succeeded them, who have a little spirit
" of rebellion, that makes them infinitely more agreeable than their sober sisters. The Lambs went
" to every church *Browne* pleased every day; the Lions came to *St. James's* Church on *St. George's*
" day. The Lambs thought of no higher entertainment than going to see some collections of shells;
" the Lions would see every thing, and go every where. The Lambs dined here one day, were
" thought good awkward girls, and then were laid out of our thoughts for ever. The Lions dined
" with us on *Sunday,* and were so extremely diverting, that we spent all yesterday morning, and are
" engaged to spend all this, in entertaining them, and going to a Comedy, that, I think, has no ill-
" nature in it; for the simplicity of these girls has nothing blameable in it, and the contemplation of
" such unassisted nature is infinitely amusing. They follow Miss *Jenny's* rule, *of never being strange*
" *in a strange place;* yet in them this is not boldness. I could send you a thousand traits of them, if
" I were sure they would not lose by being writ down; but there is no imitating that inimitable
" *naïveté* which is the grace of their character. They were placed in your seat on *Sunday.* (Alas!
" I was used to seeing it filled with people that were quite indifferent to me, till seeing you in it once
" has thrown a fresh melancholy upon it!) I wondered to have heard no remarks on the Prince and
" Princess; their remarks on every thing else are admirable. As they sat in the drawing-room before din
" ner, one of them called to Mr. *Secker, I wish you would give me a glass of sack!* The Bishop of *Oxford*
" [*Secker*] came in; and one of them broke out very abruptly, *But we heard every word of the Ser*
" *mon where we sat; and a very good Sermon it was,* added she, with a decisive nod. The Bishop of
" *Gloucester* gave them tickets to go to a play; and one of them took great pains to repeat to him, till
" he heard it, *I would not rob you; but I know you are very rich, and can afford it; for I ben't co ve*
" *tous, indeed I an't covetous.* Poor girls! Their father will make them go out of town to-morrow;
" and they begged very hard that we would all join in entreating him to let them stay a fortnight, as
" their younger sisters have done; but all our entreaties were in vain, and to-morrow the poor Lions
" return to their den in the stage-coach. Indeed, in his birth-day tie-wig he looked so like the Father
" in the Farce Mrs. *Secker* was so diverted with, that I wished a thousand times for the invention of
" *Scapin,* and I would have made no scruple of assuming the character, and inspiring my friends with
" the laudable spirit of rebellion. I have picked out some of the dullest of their traits to tell you.
" They pressed us extremely to come and breakfast with them at their lodgings four inches square in
" *Chapel Street,* at eight o'clock in the morning, and bring a Stay-maker and the Bishop of *Gloucester*
" with us. We put off the engagement till eleven, sent the Stay-maker to measure them at nine, and
" Mrs. *Secker* and I went and found the ladies quite undressed; so that, instead of taking them to
" *Kensington Gardens* as we promised, we were forced, for want of time, to content ourselves with
" carrying them round *Grosvenor Square* into the Ring, where, for want of better amusement, they
" were fain to fall upon the basket of dirty sweetmeats and cakes that an old woman is always teizing
" you with there, which they had nearly dispatched in a couple of rounds. It were endless to tell
" you all that has inexpressibly diverted me in their behaviour and conversation. I have yet told you
" nothing; and yet I have, in telling that nothing, wasted all the time that my heart ought to have
" employed in saying a thousand things to you, that it is more deeply interested in. I wanted to ex
" press a thousand sentiments; but I hope you know them already, and at present my time is all spent.
" If you have a mind to a second part (which I assure you will far exceed the first) of the Memoirs of
" the Lions, tell me so, and you shall have it when you please; for there is no fear of my forgetting
" what is fixed on my memory by such scenes of mirth. Yours most faithfully, C. TALBOT."

K k " In

" Oeconomia Naturæ in morbis acutis & chronicis glan-
" dularum. Auctore *R. Ruſſell*, M.D. F.R.S." 8vo;
an *Engliſh* tranſlation of Dr. *Ruſſell's* ".Oeconomy," 8vo;
a ſecond edition of Dr. *Gally's* * treatiſe on *Greek* Accents ;
" *Boerhaave's*

* Dr. *Henry Gally*, born at *Beckenham*, in *Kent*, in *Auguſt* 1696, was admitted Penſioner of *Ben'et College*, under the tuition of Mr. *Fawcett*, *May* 8, 1714, and became
Scholar of the Houſe in *July* following. He took the degree of M. A. in 1721, and was
upon the King's Liſt for that of D. D. (to which he was admitted *April* 25, 1728) when
his Majeſty honoured the Univerſity of *Cambridge* with his preſence. In the year 1721
he was choſen lecturer of *St. Paul's, Covent Garden*, and inſtituted the ſame year to the

" In the ſummer of 1740, after Mr. *Baker's* death, his executor came to take poſſeſſion of the
" effects, and lived for ſome time in his chambers at College. Here *Browne Willis* waited upon him
" to ſee ſome of the MSS. or books; and after a long viſit, to find and examine what he wanted, the
" old bed-maker of the rooms came in; when the gentleman ſaid, " What noiſe was that I heard juſt
" as you opened the door?" (he had heard the ruſtling of ſilk)—"Oh !" ſays *Browne Willis*, " it is only
" one of my daughters that I left on the ſtaircaſe."— Once, after long teizing, the young ladies
" prevailed on him to give them a *London* jaunt; unluckily the lodgings were (unknown to them) at
" an undertaker's, the irregular and late hours of whoſe buſineſs was not very agreeable to the young
" ladies; but they comforted themſelves with the thoughts of the pleaſure they ſhould have during
" their ſtay in town; when, to their great ſurprize and grief, as ſoon as they had got their break-
" faſt, the old family coach rumbled to the door, and the father bid them get in, as he had done
" the buſineſs about which he came to town." T. F.—It may be worth mentioning, that " The
" Court Regiſter, or Stateſman's Remembrancer," publiſhed by *William Sliford* in 1743, 8vo, is inſcribed, " To that learned and induſtrious Antiquary *Browne Willis*, eſq." to whom, and to *John
Bridges*, eſq. of *Barton Segrave*, the author had been an amanuenſis. Mr. *Sliford* was alſo aſſiſted
in that work by Sir *Juſtinian Iſham*, baronet, *Roger Gale*, eſq. and *James Weſt*, eſq.
I cannot reſiſt the temptation to increaſe the immoderate length of this note by an extract of a letter
from an accompliſhed and valuable friend (the Rev. *John Kynaſton*, M. A. Fellow of *Braſen Noſe College, Oxford*), who has ſeen the preceding paragraphs :
* * * * * * * * * * " *Hot Wells, Briſtol, Feb.* 7. 1781.
" Your Anecdotes of the *Lions* and the *Lambs* have entertained me prodigiouſly, as I ſo well knew
" the grieſly Sire of both. *Browne Willis* was indeed an original. I met with him at Mr. *Cart-
" wright's*, at *Aynho*, in *Northamptonſhire*, in 1753, where I was at that time chaplain to the family,
" and curate of the pariſh. *Browne* came here on a viſit of a week that ſummer. He looked for all
" the world like an old portrait of the æra of Queen *Elizabeth*, that had walked down out of its frame.
" He was, too truly, the very dirty figure Miſs *Talbot* deſcribes him to be; which, with the anti-
" quity of his dreſs, rendered him infinitely formidable to all the children in the pariſh. He often
" called upon me at the parſonage houſe, when I happened not to dine in the family; having a great, and,
" as it ſeemed, a very favourite point to carry, which was no leſs than to perſuade me to follow his ex-
" ample, and to turn all my thoughts and ſtudies to *venerable Antiquity*; he deemed that *the ſummum
" bonum*, the height of all human felicity. I uſed to entertain Mr. and Mrs. *Cartwright* highly, by
" detailing to them *Browne's* arguments to debauch me from the purſuit of polite literature, and ſuch
" ſtudies as were moſt agreeable to my turn and taſte; and by parcelling out every morning after
" prayers (we had daily prayers at eleven in the church) the progreſs *Browne* had made the day be-
" fore in the arts of ſeduction. I amuſed him with ſuch anſwers as I thought beſt ſuited to his hobby-
" horſe, till I found he was going to leave us; and then, by a ſtroke or two of ſpirited raillery, loſt
" his warm heart and his advice for ever. My egging him on, ſerved us, however, for a week's ex-
" cellent entertainment, amid the dullneſs and ſameneſs of a country ſituation. He repreſented me, at
" parting, to Mr. *Cartwright*, as one incorrigible, and loſt beyond all hopes of recovery to every
" thing truly valuable in learning, by having unfortunately let ſlip that I preferred, and feared I ever
" ſhould prefer, one page of *Livy* or *Tacitus, Salluſt* or *Cæſar*, to all the Monkiſh writers (with
" *Bede* at the head of them)
" ———— quot ſunt, quotve fuerunt,
" Aut quotquot aliis erunt in annis.
" *Sic explicit hiſtoriola de* Brownio Williſio !" * * * * * * * * * * * * * *

rectory

" *Boerhaave's* Aphorifms," 8vo; Dr. *Maty's* " Authentic
" Memoirs of the Life* of *Richard Mead†*, M.D." 8vo;
" Mufeum

rectory of *Wavenden,* or *Wanden,* in *Buckinghamfhire.* The lord chancellor *King* appointed him his domeftick chaplain in 1725, preferred him to a prebend in the church of
Gloucefter in 1728, and to another in that of *Norwich* about three years after. He prefented him likewife to the rectory of *Afhney,* alias *Afhton,* in *Northamptonfhire,* in 1730;
and to that of *St. Giles's in the Fields,* in 1732; his majefty made him alfo one of his
chaplains in ordinary in 1735. Dr. *Gally* died *Auguft* 7, 1769. He was the author
of, 1. " Two Sermons on the Mifery of Man, preached at *St. Paul's, Covent Garden,*
" 1723," 8vo.—2. " The Moral Characters of *Theophraftus,* tranflated from the *Greek,*
" with Notes, and a Critical Effay on Characteriftic Writing, 1725," 8vo.—3. " The
" Reafonablenefs of Church and College Fines afferted, and the Rights which Churches
" and Colleges have in their Eftates defended, 1731," 8vo. This was an anfwer to a
pamphlet‡ called " An Enquiry into the Cuftomary Eftates and Tenants of thofe who
" hold Lands of Church and other Foundations by the tenure of three Lives and twenty-
" one Years. By *Everard Fleetwood,* efq." 8vo.—4. " Sermon before the Houfe of
" Commons upon the Acceffion, *June* 11, 1739," 4to.—5. " Some Confiderations upon
" Clandeftine Marriages, 1750," 8vo. This was much enlarged in a fecond edition the
year following.—6. The pamphlet on *Greek* Accents, taken notice of above.

* Another, but far lefs interefting, Life of Dr. *Mead,* by Sir *Tanfield Leman,*
bart. M. D. appeared in 1749, 8vo.

† This great phyfician (whofe abilities and eminence in his profeffion, united with his
learning and fine tafte for thofe arts which embellifh and improve human life, long rendered him an ornament, not only to his own profeffion, but to the nation and age
in which he lived) was born at *Stepney, Aug.* 11, 1673 ‖, and received the early part
of his education under his father *Matthew Mead,* a celebrated Nonconformift Divine,
who, with the affiftance of Mr. *John Nefbitt,* fuperintended the education of thirteen
children. In 1688 he was placed under the care of Mr. *Thomas Singleton*; and in 1689 under
Grævius, at *Utrecht.* In 1692 he removed to *Leyden* §, where he attended for three years
the lectures of *Herman* and *Pitcairn,* and applied himfelf moft fuccefsfully to the ftudy of
phyfic.. In company with *Samuel* his eldeft brother, *David Polhill,* efq. and Dr. *Thomas
Pellet,* he vifited *Italy,* and luckily difcovered at *Florence* the *Menfa Ifiaca,* which had
been many years given over as loft. He took his degree of Doctor of Philofophy and
Phyfic at *Padua, Aug.* 16, 1695; and paffed fome time afterwards at *Naples* and *Rome.*
On his return, about *Midfummer* 1696, he fettled in the very houfe where he was born, and
practifed in his profeffion there for feven years with great fuccefs. In 1702 he publifhed his
" Mechanical Account of Poifons." Thefe Effays, however juftly efteemed on their
firft appearance, did their author ftill more honour in the edition he publifhed of them
more than forty years afterwards. He became Fellow of the Royal Society in 1704, in
1706 was chofen one of their Council, and in 1717 a Vice-prefident. He was chofen
phyfician to *St. Thomas's Hofpital, May* 5, 1703, when he removed from *Stepney* to

‡ Befides the anfwer to this Pamphlet by Dr. *Gally,* there were two others by Dr. *Roger Long* and
Dr. *William Derham.*

‖ In the church-yard of *Ware* in *Hertfordfhire,* on the fouth fide of the church, is an altar-monu-
ment to " *William Mead,* M. D. who died *Oct.* 28, 1652, aged 148 years and 9 months." Q. if
of this family?

§ He was there contemporary with *Boerhaave,* with whom he afterwards maintained the moft
friendly intercourfe through life.

Crutched

" Muſeum *Meadianum*, ſive Catalogus Nummorum, veteris
" ævi Monumentorum, ac Gemmarum, cum aliis quibuſ-
" dam

Crutched Fryars; where having reſided ſeven years, he removed into *Auſtin Fryars*; and about the ſame time was appointed by the Company of Surgeons to read the anatomical lectures in their hall. In the mean time, *Dec.* 4, 1707, he was honoured by the univerſity of *Oxford* with the degree of Doctor of Phyſic by diploma *. On the laſt illneſs of Queen *Anne*, he was called into a conſultation, and ventured to declare that " ſhe " could not hold out long." He opened his mind freely on this ſubject to his friend and protector Dr. *Radcliffe*, who made uſe of that friendſhip to excuſe his own attendance. *Radcliffe* ſurviving the Queen but three months, *Mead* removed into *his* houſe, and reſigned his office in *St. Thomas's Hoſpital*. Uninfluenced by prejudices of party, he was equally the intimate of *Garth*, *Arbuthnot*, and *Freind*. He was admitted Fellow of the College of Phyſicians *April* 9, 1716; and executed the office of Cenſor in 1716, 1719, and 1724. In 1719, on an alarm occaſioned by the fatal plague at *Marſeilles*, the Lords of the Regency directed Mr. *Craggs*, then Secretary of State, to apply to Dr. *Mead*, to give the beſt directions for preventing the importation of the plague, or ſtopping its progreſs. His opinion was approved; and quarantine directed to be performed. Of his " Diſcourſe con- " cerning Peſtilential Contagion †," no leſs than ſeven editions were printed by Mr. *Bowyer* in 1720; the eighth, which appeared in 1722, and again in 1743, was enlarged with many new obſervations, and tranſlated into *Latin* ‡ by Profeſſor *Ward*, whoſe ſervices to Dr. *Mead*, on occaſion of the *Harveian* Oration of 1723, I have already mentioned in p. 35. By order of the Prince of *Wales*, Dr. *Mead* aſſiſted, *Auguſt* 10, 1721, at the inoculation of ſome condemned criminals: the experiment ſucceeding, the two then young princeſſes, *Amelia* and *Caroline*, were inoculated *April* 17, 1722, and had the diſtemper favourably. On the acceſſion of their royal father to the throne in 1727,

---

* It ſeems irregular that he ſhould have practiſed in *London* before he obtained a diploma.

† This Diſcourſe is ſaid to have greatly hurt his practice, for a time at leaſt, not for any medical, but political reaſons, as it was ſuſpected to be intended to prepare the way for barracks, &c. at a time of day when the nation were more jealous of a ſtanding army than now.

‡ The firſt edition had been tranſlated into *Latin* by Mr. *Maittaire*, of whom ſee p. 167; where I ſhould have obſerved, that late in life he was tutor to the earl of *Cheſterfield's* ſon. I might alſo have added Dr. *Jortin's* too laconic character of him, *Life of Eraſmus*, vol. I. p. 35. After mentioning the " Annales Typographici," he adds, " I have occaſion often to cite *Maittaire*, who was a uſeful com- " piler, *and nothing more*."—" With due deference to Dr. *Jortin's* judgement, the words *and nothing* " *more* are illiberally applied. Had *Maittaire* been perfectly ignorant, and had he never written a " word, he would have eſcaped all cenſure; as it is, he has publiſhed five large quarto volumes (I " throw in the lives of the *Stephens'* and the *Paris* Printers), which muſt have coſt him infinite trouble, " and has ſaved as much to ſuch great geniuſes as theſe, who are glad to avail themſelves of his com- " pilations; but why cannot they uſe the bridge without ſpeaking ſlightingly of it? Are not more " people glad to uſe *Maittaire*, than moſt original compoſers? When *Maittaire* compiled his firſt volume, " it muſt have occaſioned him much trouble, however incomplete; of this nobody could be more ſenſi- " ble than himſelf, witneſs his going over that period again in the latter part of his life. Since his time, " owing undoubtedly to his labours and diſcoveries, vaſt additional information on this ſubject has come " in from all quarters; and it is probable, that a gentleman now would be thought to do good ſervice to " literature that would melt *Maittaire's* two volumes into one, and incorporate into them the improve- " ments that *Germany*, *Italy*, and *France* afford in ſuch quantity. Since Mr. *Maittaire's* time, many " juridical pieces have been diſcovered, that throw great light on the origin of printing; upon which " ſubject nobody can be qualified to write now, that is not perfectly acquainted with theſe, and they, " and the authors that argue from them, are numerous. This would be additional matter, that " could not be known to Mr. *Maittaire*, and probably would be new to moſt *Engliſh* ſcholars." *Dr.* *Taylor's Friend*.—The late Dr. *Aſkew* thought very differently of *Maittaire* from Dr. *Jortin*.

Dr.

" dam Artis recentioris & Naturæ operibus, quæ vir cla-
" riffimus *Ricardus Mead*, M. D. nuper defunctus com-
" paraverat,"

Dr. *Mead* was appointed physician in ordinary to his Majesty, and had afterwards the satisfaction of seeing his two sons-in-law (Dr. *Edward Wilmot* and Dr. *Frank Nicholls)* his associates in the same station. Being desirous of retirement, he declined the presidentship of the College of Physicians, which was offered him *Oct.* 1, 1734; but was elected honorary member of that at *Edinburgh, Oct.* 6, 1745. Mr. *Bowyer* printed the improved edition of his " Account of Poisons" in 1744; his treatise " De Imperio Solis ac Lunæ," &c. in 1746; " De Morbis Biblicis" in 1749; and " Monita Medica" in 1750. This was the last, and perhaps the most useful of all his works *: with a candour and simplicity so characteristical of a great man, he freely communicates in it all the discoveries that his long practice and experience had opened to him with regard to different diseases and their several cures. The world was deprived of this eminent physician *Feb.* 16, 1754; and on the 23d he was buried in the *Temple* church, near his brother *Samuel*, a counsellor at law, to whose memory the Doctor had caused an elegant monument to be placed, with his bust, and the following inscription :.

M. S.
SAMVELIS MEAD IC.
MATTHAEI CELEBRIS THEOLOGI FIL.
HVIVS SOCIETATIS ALVMNI,
INTER HOSPITII VERO LINCOLNIENSIS
ADSESSORES COOPTATI;
QVI HONESTAM ET ANTIQVAM FAMILIAM,
EX QVA IN AGRO BVCKINGENSI ORTVS EST,
NON SPLENDIDIS TITVLIS,
SED EGREGIIS SVIS VIRTVTIBVS
ET PRAECLARIS ANIMI DOTIBVS ORNAVIT,
PIETATE, INTEGRITATE VITAE,
PRVDENTIA, MORVMQVE GRAVITATE,
SVMMAE FACILITATI CONIVNCTA CONSPICVVS;
NON VNIVERSI TANTVM IVRIS PERITVS,
SED ET OMNI LITERARVM GENERE EXCVLTVS,

INTERQVE DOCTISSIMOS HVIVS SAECVLI
MERITO NVMERATVS;
OB AMOREM IN SVOS, FIDEM ERGA AMICOS,
LIBERALITATEM IN PAVPERES,
QVORVM PATRONVS ERAT CERTISSIMVS,
BENEVOLENTIAM ERGA OMNES,
CARITATEM DENIQVE IN PATRIAM,
VSQVE IN EXEMPLVM CLARVS,
OBIIT XIII KAL. APRIL. A. D. MDCCXXXIII.
ÆTATIS SVAE QVAM COELIBEM EGERAT LXIII.
VIRO INCOMPARABILI FRATRI SVO GERMANO
NATV MAXIMO, DE SE OPTIME MERITO,
AFFECTVS ET HONORIS CAVSA,
RICARDVS MEAD ARCHIATER
HOC MONVMENTVM MOESTISSIMVS POSVIT.

To Dr. *Mead* there is no monument in the *Temple*; but an honorary one was placed by his son in the North aile of *Westminster Abbey.* Over the tomb is the Doctor's bust; at his right hand a wreathed serpent, darting its sting, and on his left several books. Below the bust are his arms and crest. The inscription, which was written by Dr. *Ward*, is as follows :

M. S.
V. A. RICARDI MEAD ARCHIATRI,
ANTIQVA APVD BVCKINGENSES FAMILIA NATI,
QVI FAMAM HAVD VVLGAREM MEDICINAM FACIENDO
IN PRIMA IVVENTVTE ADEPTVS,
TANTA NOMINIS CELEBRITATE POSTEA INCLARVIT,
VT MEDICORVM HVIVS SAECVLI PRINCEPS HABERETVR.
IN AEGRIS CVRANDIS LENIS ERAT AC MISERICORS,
ET AD PAVPERES GRATVITO IVVANDOS SEMPER PARATVS,
INTER ASSIDVAS AVTEM ARTIS SALVTARIS OCCVPATIONES
OPERIBVS NON PAVCIS DOCTE ET ELEGANTER CONSCRIPTIS,
QVAE INGENIO PERSPICACI ET VSV DIVTVRNO NOTAVERAT
IN GENERIS HVMANI COMMODVM VVLGAVIT,

LITERARVM

* His " Medical Works" were collected and published in one volume, 4to. 1762.

" paraverat," 8vo; " Mufei *Meadiani* pars altera, &c."
8vo.

LITERARVM QVOQVE ET LITERATORVM PATRONVS SINGVLARIS,
BIBLIOTHECAM LECTISSIMAM OPTIMIS ET RARISSIMIS LIBRIS
VETERVMQVE ARTIVM MONVMENTIS REFERTAM COMPARAVIT,
VBI ERVDITORVM COLLOQVIIS LABORES LEVABAT DIVRNOS,
ANIMO ITAQVE EXCELSO PRAEDITVS, ET MORIBVS HVMANIS
ORBISQVE LITERATI LAVDIBVS VNDIQVE CVMVLATVS,
MAGNO SPLENDORE ET DIGNITATE VITA PERACTA,
ANNORVM TANDEM AC FAMAE SATVR PLACIDE. OBIIT
XIV. KALENDAS MARTIAS A. D. MDCCLIV, AETATIS SVAE LXXXI:
ARTIVM HVMANIORVM DAMNO HAVD FACILE REPARABILI,
QVIBVS IPSE TANTVM FVERAT DECVS ET PRAESIDIVM.
BIS MATRIMONIO IVNCTVS,
EX PRIORI DECEM SVSCEPIT LIBEROS,
QVORVM TRES TANTVM SVPERSTITES SIBI RELIQVIT,
DVAS FILIAS VIRIS ARCHIATRORVM HONORE ORNATIS NVPTAS,
ET VNVM SVI IPSIVS NOMINIS FILIVM,
QVI PIETATIS CAVSA PATRI OPTIME DE SE MERITO
MONVMENTVM HOC PONI CVRAVIT.

The following infcription (which I found in Mr. *Bowyer's* hand-writing) was likewife propofed for his monument in *February* 1754:
" Here reft the remains of a truly learned and truly great man,
RICHARD MEAD, M. D.
A polite fcholar, a fuccefsful phyfician, a beneficent patron.
His knowledge untainted by pedantry, his tafte without any affectation,
His ear impervious to flattery, his foul fuperior to avarice.
He maintained the honour of his profeffion fteadily,
And rendered, by honeft arts, extenfive his fame, his merit more extenfive,
Both, fuperior to envy, without the aid of marble fhall refift the teeth of time.
His generous Mind to lateft ages known
From others' works, his Learning from his own."

The Doctor was twice married. By his firft lady he had ten children (of whom three furvived him, two daughters married to Dr. *Wilmot* and Dr. *Nicholls*, and his fon *Richard* heir to his father's and uncle's fortunes); by the fecond lady, he had no iffue. During almoft half a century he was at the head of his profeffion, which brought him in one year upwards of feven thoufand pounds, and between five and fix for feveral years. The clergy, and in general all men of learning, were welcome to his advice; and his doors were open every morning to the moft indigent, whom he frequently affifted with money; fo that, notwithftanding his great gains, he did not die very rich. He was a moft generous patron of learning and learned men, in all fciences, and in every country; by the peculiar magnificence of his difpofition, making the private gains of his pro-feffion anfwer the end of a princely fortune, and valuing them only as they enabled him to become more extenfively ufeful, and thereby to fatisfy that greatnefs of mind which will tranfmit his name to pofterity with a luftre not inferior to that which attends the moft diftinguifhed character of antiquity. To him the feveral counties of *England*, and

6   our

8vo. " An Eſſay towards a new *Engliſh* Verſion of the Book
" of

our colonies abroad, applied for the choice of their phyſicians. No foreigner of any learning, taſte, or even curioſity, ever came to *England* without being introduced to Dr.
Mead; and he was continually conſulted by the phyſicians of the continent. His large
and ſpacious houſe in *Great Ormond Street* became a repoſitory of all that was
curious in nature or in art, to which his extenſive correſpondence with the Learned in all parts of *Europe* not a little contributed. The king of *Naples* ſent to
requeſt a collection of all his works; preſented him with the two firſt volumes of Sig.
Bajardi, and invited him to his own palace: and, through the hands of M. *de Boze*,
he frequently had the honour of exchanging preſents with the king of *France*.
He built a gallery for his favourite furniture, his pictures and his antiquities. His
library, as appears by the printed catalogue * of it, conſiſted of 6592 numbers, containing upwards of 10000 volumes, in which he ſpared no expence for ſcarce and ancient editions. It is remarkable that many of his books ſold for much more than they
had coſt him; the *advanced prices* of ſome in particular I have already mentioned in
p. 181. His pictures alſo were choſen with ſo much judgement, that they produced
3417*l.* 11*s.*; about ſix or ſeven hundred pounds more than he gave for them. Nor did he
make this great collection for his own uſe only, but freely opened it to public inſpection.

* The ſale of the firſt part of this collection, conſiſting of 3280 articles, began *Nov.* 18, 1754, and
laſted 28 days. The ſecond ſale, containing 3461 articles, beſides ſome out of the catalogue, began
April 7, 1755, and laſted 29 days †. The Prints and Drawings were ſold in 14 nights, beginning
Jan. 13, 1755. The Gems, Bronzes, Buſts, and Antiquities, in five days, from *March* 11; and the
Coins were ſold in eight, from *February* 11 to 19, 1755.

			l.	*s.*	*d.*
His collection produced, 57 days ſale of books, including 19*l.* 6*s.* 6*d.* for 15 book-caſes			5518	10	11
3 - - - pictures	- -	-	3417	11	0
14 - - - prints and drawings	-	-	1908	14	6
8 - - - coins and medals	-	-	1977	17	0
5 - - - antiquities, &c.	-	-	3246	15	6
			16069	8	11

As a very ſmall ſpecimen of the whole collection, he ordered by his will to be preſerved in his family
an antient *Greek* inſcription to *Jupiter Urius* (ſee before, p. 35), an antique Painting of *Auguſtus* beſtowing a crown on a perſon kneeling (engraved and explained in " Three Diſſertations by *G. Turn-*
" bull, 1740," 4to, tranſlated from four elegant *French* writers, and dedicated to Dr. *Mead*; alſo in
the *Engliſh* tranſlation of *Rollin's* Hiſtory of the Arts and Sciences of the Antients, I. 137.); *Bartoli's* 60
drawings from all the antient paintings at *Rome* bought out of Cardinal *Maſſini's* ſale; and a few other
articles. He had parted with in his life-time to the late *Frederick* Prince of *Wales* ſeveral miniature
pictures of great value‡ by *Iſaac Oliver* and *Holbein*, which are now in his Majeſty's collection; all
his *Greek* MSS. to Dr. *Aſkew* for 500*l.*; and the entire ſeries of *Greek* Kings (eighteen coins excepted)
part to Mr. *Angel Carmey*, a dealer, and part to Dr. *Kennedy*; which conſequently do not appear in the
catalogue. Prints of ſeveral of his antiquities, and alſo a view of his gallery, were engraved in his life-time
by *Baron, Baſire, T. R.* and *A. L.* The bas-relief of *Demoſthenes* dying (purchaſed by Mr. *White* for
14*l.* 14*s.*) is engraved for *Barton's* edition of *Plutarch's* Lives of that Orator and *Cicero*; the *Roman* Re-
tiarius (found at *Cheſter* 1738, and now in the poſſeſſion of *M. C. Tutet*, eſq.) by the Society of Antiquaries. The Mummy and ſome other *Egyptian* antiquities were engraved and illuſtrated by *Alex-*
ander Gordon, in a folio diſſertation, 1737; (ſee before, p. 107). The buſt of *Homer* was purchaſed
for 136*l.* 10*s.* by the Earl of *Exeter*, who preſented it to *The Britiſh Muſeum*; that of *Antinous* by the
Marquis of *Rockingham*, for 241*l.* 10*s.*; *Xenocrates* (for 19*l.* 8*s.* 6*d.*) and *Theophraſtus* (for 12*l.* 12*s.*)
by Dr. *Niſbet*, at whoſe ſale in 1762 they were again diſpoſed of.

† The 29th day's ſale is wanting in moſt copies of the catalogue, having been printed ſeparately afterwards,
and delivered by itſelf.
‡ *Walpole*, Anecdotes, vol. I. p. 165.

Ingenious

" of *Job*, from the original *Hebrew*, with some Account

Ingenious men were sure of finding at Dr. *Mead's* the best helps in all their undertakings *; and scarcely any thing curious appeared in *England* but under his patronage : the encouragement he gave to the edition of *Thuanus* has been noticed in p. 81. By his singular humanity and goodness, " he conquered even Envy itself ;" a compliment which was justly paid him in a dedication, by the editor of Lord *Bacon's* Works, in 1730. He constantly kept in pay a great number of scholars and artists of all kinds, who were at work for him, or for the publick. He was the friend of *Pope*, of *Halley*, and of *Newton* ; and placed their portraits in his house, with those of *Shakspeare* † and *Milton*, near the busts of their great masters the ancient *Greeks* and *Romans*. A marble busto of Dr. *Harvey*, done by an excellent hand, from an original picture in his possession, was given by him to the College of Physicians, with this inscription :

HANC MAGNI ILLIVS GVLIELMI HARVEII,
SENIS OCTOGENARII, IMAGINEM,
QVI SANGVINIS CIRCVITVM PRIMVS MONSTRAVIT,
MEDICINAMQVE RATIONALEM INSTITVIT,
AD PICTVRAM ARCHETYPAM QVAM IN SVO SERVAT MVSEO EFFICTAM,
HONORIS CAVSA HIC PONENDAM CVRAVIT
RICARDVS MEAD, MEDICVS REGIVS. A. D. MDCCXXX.

A marble bust of Dr. *Mead*, by *Roubilliac*, was presented to the College in 1756, by the late Dr. *Askew*. A portrait of him was etched by *Pond*, another by *Richardson* ; a mezzotinto by *Houston*, from a painting of *Ramsay* ; and an engraved portrait by *Baron*. There was also a medal of him struck in 1773, long after his decease, by *Lewis Pingo* ; legend, RICARDVS MEAD, MED. REG. ET S.R.S. His bust, profile to the left, under it L. PINGO F. Reverse, LABOR EST ANGVES SVPERARE. A young *Hercules* strangling a serpent ; above, the Sun and Moon.—Exergue, N. AP. XI. MDCLXXIII. O. F. XVI. MDCCLIV. with the Doctor's arms.

Dr. *Thomas Burnet* of *The Charterhouse* had written a treatise *De Statu Mortuorum & Resurgentium*, of which he had a few copies printed for the use of himself and his friends. One of these, after the author's death, happened to fall into Dr. *Mead's* hands ; who, not knowing the author, but liking the book, had 25 copies handsomely printed in 4to ; *Maittaire* revising the press, who made many blunders by inserting manuscript notes and additions from the author's interleaved copy into improper places of the text. Mr. *Wilkinson* of *Lincoln's Inn*, who was executor to Dr. *Burnet*, lent Dr. *Mead* afterwards a corrected copy, of which Dr. *Mead* was at the expence of printing 50 copies, with a caution prefixed to those chosen few on whom the book was bestowed, not to suffer it to be translated, or reprinted, and published ; but this did not prevent a bad translation and a spurious edition soon after getting abroad. So, to do justice to the author's memory, Mr. *Wilkinson* himself caused an octavo edition to be printed and published, as well of this book as of another, intituled *De fide et officiis Christianorum*, of which Lord Chancellor *Macclesfield* had prevailed on him to suffer as many copies to be printed, and in the same size, as Dr. *Mead's* edition of the *De Statu Mortuorum & Resurgentium*. These gentlemen, with *Maittaire*, are the three persons whom *Wilkinson* means, but does not name, in the preface to his octavo edition of these two books in 1727.

---

* See Mr. *Edwards's* character of Dr. *Mead*, in the Appendix to these Anecdotes.
† *Shakspeare, Milton*, and *Pope*, were the production of *Scheemaker*.—*Shakspeare* was purchased by Mr. *Skinner* for 16l. 16s. ; *Milton* by Mr. *Duncombe* for 11l. 11s. ; *Pope* by Gen. *Campbell* for 18l. 7s. 6d. ; *Newton* by Mr. *Burrel* for 5l. 5s. ; *Halley* does not appear in the catalogue. A bust of *Cromwell* by *Cibber* was sold to Gen. *Campbell* for 3l. 7s. 6d.

3

" of his Life, by *Thomas Heath* *, Efq. of *Exeter*," 4to; " Six
" Differtations on different fubjects, by *John Jortin* †, D. D."
8vo;

* This gentleman was an alderman of *Exeter*, and father of *John Heath*, efq. one
of the Judges of the Common Pleas. His brother *Benjamin* was a lawyer of eminence,
and town clerk of *Exeter*. *Benjamin* was likewife an author, and wrote, 1. " An Effay
" towards a demonftrative Proof of the Divine Exiftence, Unity, and Attributes; to
" which is premifed, a fhort Defence of the Argument commonly called *à Priori*, 1740."
This pamphlet was dedicated to Dr. *Oliver* of *Bath*, and is to be ranked amongft the
ableft defences of Dr. *Clark's*, or rather Mr. *Howe's*, hypothefis; for Dr. *Clark*
appears to have taken it from *Howe's* " Living Temple." 2. " The Cafe of the
" County of *Devon* with refpect to the Confequences of the new Excife Duty on Cyder
" and Perry. Publifhed by the direction of the Committee appointed at a General
" Meeting of that County to fuperintend the Application for the Repeal of that Duty,
" 1763," 4to. To this reprefentation of the circumftances peculiar to *Devonfhire* the
repeal of the act is greatly to be afcribed. The piece indeed was confidered as fo well
timed a fervice to the public, that Mr. *Heath* received fome honourable notice on account
of it at a general meeting of the county. 3. " Notæ five Lectiones ad Tragicorum *Græ-*
" *corum* veterum, *Æfchyli*, &c. 1752," 4to. A work which places the author's learning and critical fkill in a very confpicuous light. A principal object of this publication
was to reftore the metre of the *Grecian* Tragick Poets. It is much to be regretted
that the diftafte for ancient learning, which for fome years paft hath prevailed in this
country, fhould have left it for foreigners to appreciate this work according to its intrinfic value. The fame folidity of judgment apparent in the preceding, diftinguifhed the
author's laft production; 4. " A Revifal of *Shakefpear's* Text, wherein the Alterations
" introduced into it by the more modern Editors and Critics are particularly confidered,
" 1765," 8vo. It appears from the lift of *Oxford* graduates, that Mr. *Benjamin Heath*
was created Doctor of Civil Law by diploma, *March* 31, 1762.

† Dr. *John Jortin* was born in the parifh of *St. Giles in the Fields*, *London*, *October*
23, 1698. His father *Renatus* ‡ was a native of *Bretagne*, in *France*; his mother,
Martha, was daughter of *Daniel Rogers* §, of *Haverfham*, in *Bucks*. He was brought
up as a day fcholar at the *Charter Houfe* fchool in *London*; and boarded with his mother, who, having no other child, lived for that purpofe in the neighbourhood. He
learned *French* at home, and fpoke it well. Having compleated his fchool education
when he was about 15, he remained at home about a year, and perfected himfelf in
writing and arithmetic. By this means he always wrote a very fair hand, and was fo
far advanced in arithmetic, that foon after he went to the univerfity he entered on mathematicks under Dr. *Saunderfon*, the blind profeffor. He was admitted a penfioner in
Jefus College, *Cambridge*, *May* 16, 1715, being then about 17; and his mother re-

‡ This gentleman was a ftudent at *Saumur*; and his teftimonial from that academy, dated in
1682, is ftill in the hands of his family. He came over a young man to *England*, with his father,
uncle, two aunts, and two fifters, when the Proteftants fled from *France*, about 1687. He was
made one of the gentlemen of the privy chamber to King *William* III. in 1691; became afterwards fecretary to Lord *Orford*, to Sir *George Rooke*, and to Sir *Cloudefley Shovel*; and was caft
away with the latter, *Oct.* 22, 1707.

§ Defcended from Mr. *Rogers*, fteward to one of the earls of *Warwick*, whofe refidence was at
Lees, near *Chelmsford*, in *Effex*, temp. *H.* VIII. and produced many clergymen of note in that
county.

moved

8vo; " Remarks on Sir *Charles Grandifon*," by Dr. *Free*
(80 copies only printed); Remarks on the same Book,
by

moved to *Cambridge*, to be near him. Whilft he was an under-graduate there, he tranflated for Mr. *Pope* fome of *Euftathius's* Notes on *Homer*. How he came to be employed
in that work, is related below *, from a manufcript written by himfelf not long before his
death.

* " When I was a foph at *Cambridge*, *Pope* was about his tranflation of *Homer's* Ilias, and had
" publifhed part of it. He employed fome perfon (I know not who he was) to make extracts for
" him from *Euftathius*, which he inferted in his Notes. At that time there was no *Latin* tranflation
" of that commentator. *Alexander Politi* (if I remember right) began that work fome years after-
" wards, but never proceeded far in it. The perfon employed by Mr. *Pope* was not at leifure to go
" on with the work; and Mr. *Pope* (by his bookfeller I fuppofe) fent to *Jefferies*, a bookfeller at
" *Cambridge*, to find out a ftudent who would undertake the tafk. *Jefferies* applied to Dr. *Thirlby*,
" who was my tutor, and who pitched upon me. I would have declined the work, having (as I
" told my tutor) other ftudies to purfue, to fit me for taking my degree. But he, *qui quicquid*
" *volebat valdè volebat*, would not hear of any excufe; fo I complied. I cannot recollect what
" Mr. *Pope* allowed for each book of *Homer*; I have a notion that it was three or four guineas. I
" took as much care as I could to perform the tafk to his fatisfaction; but I was afhamed to defire
" my tutor to give himfelf the trouble of overlooking my operations; and he, who always ufed to
" think and fpeak too favourably of me, faid that I did not want his help. He never perufed one
" line of it before it was printed, nor perhaps afterwards. When I had gone through fome books
" (I forget how many), Mr. *Jefferies* let us know that Mr. *Pope* had a friend to do the reft, and
" that we might give over. When I fent my papers to *Jefferies*, to be conveyed to Mr. *Pope*, I in-
" ferted, as I remember, fome remarks on a paffage, where Mr. *Pope*, in my opinion, had made a
" miftake; but as I was not directly employed by him, but by a bookfeller, I did not inform him
" who I was, or fet my name to my papers. When that part of *Pope's Homer* came out, in which
" I had been concerned, I was eager, as it may be fuppofed, to fee how things ftood, and much
" pleafed to find that he had not only ufed almoft all my notes, but had hardly made any alteration
" in the expreffions. I obferved alfo, that in a fubfequent edition, he corrected the place to which
" I had made objections. I was in hopes in thofe days (for I was young) that Mr. *Pope* would
" make inquiry about his *coadjutor*, and take fome civil notice of him; but he did not, and I had
" no notion of obtruding myfelf upon him; I never faw his face." *Dr.* JORTIN, *MS.*—" So all
" *Pope's* coadjutors complain of him; probably they had fome reafon for thinking that he was
" too well paid, and they too poorly. As *Jortin* was confeffedly a fcholar, *Pope's* incuriofity or
" incivility is reprehenfible. I once faw an *original* letter of *Pope's*, in which he fairly owned, that
" he did not underftand *Greek*, which was probably very true. The perfon at firft employed, per-
" haps, was *Broome*; the fecond friend, *Fenton*. This hiftory of *making a book* is worth detailing,
" and one man's running away with all the credit." *T. F.*—" The hiftory of the notes has
" never been traced. *Broome*, in his preface to his poems, declares himfelf the commentator
" *in part upon the Iliad*; and it appears from *Fenton's* letter, preferved in *The Mufeum*, that *Broome*
" was at firft engaged in confulting *Euftathius*; but that after a time, whatever was the reafon,
" he defifted: another man of *Cambridge* was then employed, who foon grew weary of the work; and
" a third was recommended by *Thirlby*, who is now difcovered to have been *Jortin*, a man fince well
" known to the learned world, who complained that *Pope*, having accepted and approved his perform-
" ance, never teftified any curiofity to fee him. The terms which *Fenton* ufes are very mercantile:
" ' I think at firft fight that his performance is very commendable, and have fent word for him to finifh
" the 17th book, and to fend it with his demands for his trouble. I have here enclofed the fpeci-
" men; if the reft come before the return, I will keep them till I receive your order.' *Broome* then
" offered his fervice a fecond time, which was probably accepted, as they had afterwards a clofer
" correfpondence. *Parnell* contributed the life of *Homer*, which *Pope* found fo harfh, that he took
" great pains in correcting it; and by his own diligence, with fuch help as kindnefs or money could
" procure him, in fomewhat more than five years he completed his verfion of the *Iliad*, with the
" notes. He began it in 1712, his twenty-fifth year, and concluded it in 1718, his thirtieth year."
Dr. Johnson.—I have been informed that the Rev. Mr. *Brooke Bridges*, rector of *Orlingbury* in *North-*
amptonfhire, has, or had, fome original letters of *Pope* to his uncle the Rev. Mr. *Ralph Bridges*, then
chaplain

by Mr. *Plumer* (26 only printed); and a neat and correct edition of the Works of *Pindar*, 12mo. (of which he was himself

death. On the 16th of *January* 1718-19, his grace was passed for the degree of B. A. He was soon after chosen fellow of his college ; his grace for M. A. was passed *Jan.* 13, 1721-2 ; and he completed his degree at the following commencement. At *Michael-mas* 1722 he was appointed moderator, and taxer the year following. In this year he published a few *Latin* poems, in a thin quarto, under the title of " Lusus Poetici," with a *Latin* preface *. He was admitted to Deacon's orders by Dr. *Kennet*, Bishop of *Pe-terborough*, Sept. 22, 1723 ; ordained priest by Dr. *Greene*, Bishop of *Ely*, *June* 14, 1724 ; and was presented by his college to the living of *Swavesey*, near *Cambridge*, *Jan.* 20, 1726-7. About the 15th of *February* following he married *Anne* the daughter of Mr. *Chibnall*, of *Newport Pagnell*, *Bucks*. In the " Republick of Letters," 1729, vol. IV. p. 142, is a poem " De Motu Terræ circa Solem," by Mr. *Jortin*. He resigned the living of *Swavesey*, Feb. 1, 1730-1 ; came to *London* ; and was soon after appointed reader and preacher at a chapel belonging to the parish of *St. Giles in the Fields*, then in *New Street*, near *Great Russel Street*, *Bloomsbury*. This duty he continued in till about the year 1746. He learned music after he came to *London*, and was a good player of thorough-bass on the harpsichord. Mr. *Petit*, a *Frenchman*, was his master ; an excellent player of *Corelli's* music on the violin. In 1730 he published, in 12mo, " Four " Sermons † on the Truth of the Christian Religion." In 1731 Mr. *Jortin* was editor of " Miscellaneous Observations upon Authors ancient and modern," 2 vols. 8vo. There is no name to this work ; nor is the whole of it his own, there being se-veral observations in it that were communicated by his friends ‡. There is a preface
by

chaplain to Dr. *Compton*, Bishop of *London*, and afterwards incumbent of *South Weald* in *Essex* ; in which *Pope* plainly acknowledges his " own want of a critical understanding in the original beau-" ties of *Homer*." But this was in 1708, when *Pope* prepared the first specimen of his Version for *Tonson's* Miscellanies. He was afterwards much obliged to this Mr. *Bridges* (whose mother was Sir *William Trumbull's* sister) for large corrections in his subsequent translation ; which are still pre-served in *The British Museum*.—The letter to Mr. *Bridges*, alluded to above, has been since given to the publick in Dr. *Johnson's* Life of *Pope*.

* A second edition of these poems came out in 1724, in a small 8vo. A third edition in 4to. (see p. 207) was printed by Mr. *Bowyer* in 1748, with additional poems, but without a preface. The author did not put his name to the two last editions. They were not sold. He printed them to give away to his friends.

† The substance of this little work was re-published in the " Six Discourses," &c. 1746.

‡ This work was first published in 24 six-penny numbers. Among the signatures of the disserta-tions *A*. and *R*. denote, if I am not misinformed, Bishop *Pearce* ; *Cantabrigiensis*, and a letter (without a name) called *Animadversiones in Luciani Asinum*, Dr. *Taylor* ; L. T. Mr. *Theobald* ; J. M. *Masson* ; B. G. *Brampton Gurdon* ; B. C. G. Dr. *Robinson*, the editor of *Hesiod* ; S. B. Mr. *Samuel Baxter* ; Ω Dr. *Thirlby* ; J. U. Mr. *Upton* ; T. R. Mr. *Rud* (editor of *Symeon Dunelmensis*, 1732) ; D. Mr. *Wasse* ; a hand, J. *Walker*. The other signatures have not been explained. It is much to be regretted that this critical work was not continued. It was republished in " Miscellaneæ Obser-" vationes in Auctores veteres & recentiores ; ab eruditis *Britannis* anno 1731 edi cœptæ, cum " Notis & Auctario variorum virorum doctorum. *Amst.* 1732—1734," 4 vols. divided each into three parts, and published every two months. When Mr. *Jortin* declined the *English* publication, the foreign one was still continued by the editor *Jac. Phil. D'Orville*, assisted by the learned *Bur-man*, under the title of " Miscellaneæ Observationes criticæ in auctores-veteres & recentiores ; ab " eruditis *Britannis* inchoatæ, & nunc a doctis viris in *Belgio* & aliis regionibus, continuatæ ;" and a number of it appeared, at first once in three months, then once in four months, till the tenth was completed in 1739. Three more were afterwards occasionally published, in nine parts, 1741—

1745 ;

himself the Editor), with a *Latin* Verfion from the *Oxford* edition in folio of 1697.

The

by Mr. *Jortin* to each volume, and the fecond is infcribed to the late duke of *Rut-land*. In 1734 he publifhed, without his name, from Mr. *Bowyer's* prefs (fee p. 85), " Remarks on *Spenfer's* Poems," 8vo ; at the end of which are fome Remarks on *Milton*. In *Auguft* 1734, his " Remarks on *L. Annæus Seneca*" appeared in a work called " The " Republick of Letters." In 1737 the earl of *Winchelfea* gave him the rectory of *Eaft-well* in *Kent* ; but he foon after quitted it, the air of that place not agreeing with his health. On the 20th of *March*, 1746-7, Dr. *Pearce*, then rector of *St. Martin's in the Fields*, appointed him afternoon preacher at one of the chapels of eafe belonging to that parifh, in *Oxendon Street*, in the room of the Rev. Mr. *Johnfon*, then deceafed, where he continued preacher till 1760. In 1746 he publifhed " Six Difcourfes on the Truth " of the Chriftian Religion," of which a fecond edition came out in 1747, a third in 1752, and a fourth in 1768. In 1747 he preached occafionally at *Lincoln's Inn* for Mr. *Warburton*, then preacher there, and afterwards Bifhop of *Gloucefter* ; and con-tinued to be his affiftant about three years. On Dr. *Pearce's* promotion to the bifhopric of *Bangor*, the confecration fermon was preached by Mr. *Jortin*, at *Kenfington, Feb.* 21, 1747 ; and publifhed (in 8vo) by order of Archbifhop *Herring*. The late earl of *Burlington*, at the requeft of Archbifhop *Herring* and Bifhop *Sherlock*, appointed him preacher of *Boyle's* Lecture, *Dec.* 26, 1749 ; which he held for three years, but did not publifh any of the Sermons preached on that occafion. In *May* 1751 Archbifhop *Herring* gave him, unfolicited, the rectory of *St. Dunftan in the Eaft*, London * ; and in *Auguft* that year he paid a fhort vifit to his friends at *Cambridge*, where he had not been before from the time of his quitting the univerfity. He publifhed in 1751 the firft volume of his " Remarks on Ecclefiaftical Hiftory †," which is infcribed to the then earl of *Burlington* ; and the fecond volume, in 1752, infcribed to Archbifhop *Herring*. He alfo wrote in 1752 a few mifcellaneous Remarks on the Sermons of Archbifhop *Tillotfon*, which he gave to his friend Dr. *Birch*, who printed them in his Appendix to the Life of that Prelate, N° III. p. 442. In 1753 he wrote an ingenious and learned letter to Mr. *Avifon*, the author of an " Effay on Mufical Expreffion," concerning the Mufic of the Antients, and fome paffages in claffic writers relating to that fubject. This letter is add-ed, without his name, to a fecond edition of that Effay which was printed in 1753 ; but

1745 ; and in the year 1751 an entire volume at once, with a preface by *D'Orville*, who had re-fumed the work upon a fomewhat different plan, and propofed to continue it, but was prevented by his death, which happened that very year. In the fifth volume, p. 47—54, is a Differtation " De " Originibus *Neapolitanis*," figned *R . . nolds*, which, as appears vol. X. p. 444, was by Mr. *Rey-nolds*, on whom a handfome elogium is beftowed by *D'Orville*.—In my copy of this work, Mr. *Jortin's* fhare of it (with that of moft of the aforementioned writers) is pointed out in MS. by Mr. *Bowyer*.

* Of this preferment the following anecdote is related : That in the fpring of the year 1751 Mr. *Jortin* dined at a feaft of the Sons of the Clergy, where Archbifhop *Herring* was prefent ; and, on being told the Archbifhop was defirous of renewing his acquaintance with him, he prepared for going to the upper end of the room, by looking at the lower end amongft a great number of hats that were laid on a table in a confufed manner, for his own ; his friends told him that the hat was by no means neceffary, he therefore waited on the prelate without it. The Archbifhop complimented him on his talents and writings, and ended the converfation by giving him, in the prefence of the clergy, a prefentation to the rectory of *St. Dunftan*, which he had purpofely brought in his pocket. Mr. *Jortin* then returned to his feat, telling his friends, " I have loft my hat, but I have got a living."

† Mr. *Warburton* had, in 1750, announced to the publick " his learned friend's curious Differ-" tations on Ecclefiaftical Antiquity ; compofed, like his life, not in the fpirit of *controverfy*, nor " what is ftill worfe, of *party*, but of *truth* and *candour*." *See Julian, p.* 316.

4

is

The following letter, on a subject of much delicacy, will perhaps be thought worth preserving, though it does not appear to whom it was addressed:

" I was

is appropriated to him in a third edition, 1775. In 1754 came out the third volume of " Remarks on Ecclefiaftical Hiftory," with an infcription to Archbifhop *Herring*. In a preface to the " Six Differtations on different fubjects, 1755," is a compliment to his patron the Primate, who conferred on him that year the degree of D. D. The friendfhip the Archbifhop had for him, and the reafons why he accepted this degree from him, will appear by the following extract from a MS. of his own:

" Archbifhop *Herring* and I were of *Jefus College* in *Cambridge*; but he left it about " the time when I was admitted, and went to another. Afterwards, when he was " preacher at *Lincoln's Inn*, I knew him better, and vifited him. He was at that time, " and long before, very intimate with Mr. *Say* *, his friend and mine, who lived in *Ely* " *Houfe*; and Mr. *Say*, to my knowledge, omitted no opportunity to recommend me " to him. Afterwards, when he was Archbifhop of *York*, he expected that a good " living would lapfe into his hands; and he told Mr. *Say*, that he defigned it for me. " He was difappointed in his expectation; fo was not I; for I had no inclination to go " and dwell in the North of *England*. Afterwards, when Mr. *Say* died, he afked me, " of his own accord, whether I fhould like to fuceeed him in the queen's library. I " told him that nothing could be more acceptable to me; and he immediately ufed all " his intereft to procure it for me; but he could not obtain it †. Afterwards the Arch- " bifhop affured me of his affiftance towards procuring either the preacherfhip or the " mafterfhip of *The Charter Houfe*, where I had gone to fchool. This project alfo fail- " ed; not by his fault. He likewife, in conjunction with Bifhop *Sherlock*, procured for " me the preaching of *Boyle's* lecture. He alfo offered me a living in the country; and " (which I efteemed a fingular favour) he gave me leave to decline it, without taking it " amifs in the leaft, and faid he would endeavour to ferve me in a way that fhould be more " acceptable. He did fo, and gave me a living in the city. Afterwards he gave me a " Doctor's degree. I thought it too late in life, as I told him, to go and take it at " *Cambridge*, under a Profeffor, who, in point of academical ftanding, might have " taken his firft degree under me when I was Moderator. I was willing to owe this " favour to him; which I could not have afked, or accepted, from any other Arch- " bifhop. That fome perfons, befides Mr. *Say*, did recommend me to him, I know, " and was obliged to them for it; but I muft add, that on this occafion they did " σπεύδοντα ὀτρύνειν, fpur a free courfer, and that he would have done what he did without " their interpofition."

* " *Francis Say*, efq. librarian to Queen *Caroline*, and fecretary to five fucceeding Bifhops of *Ely*, with whom he lived beloved and honoured, gained great reputation early in life, and preferved it unblemifhed to his death. He was religious without fhew, and learned without pedantry; an exact critic, yet without ill-nature; a judge both of himfelf and others, without partiality. He had complaifance without flattery, and humanity without weaknefs; was condefcending, but not abject; generous, but not profufe; wife without feverity, communicative without vanity, and chearful without levity; benevolent as became a good man, and charitable as became a good chriftian. Thefe good qualities were accompanied with a fingular modefty, that caft a beauty and becomingnefs over them, and made his, as far as it might be, a perfect character. He was juft to all the world, and the world was juft to him; for he had not an enemy in it. He died *Sept.* 10, 1748." The above character, inferted in the public papers, is fuppofed to have been drawn up by Archbifhop *Herring*, who was firft acquainted with *Frank Say* in Bifhop *Fleetwood's* family.

† The office was beftowed on *Archibald Bower*.

In

Sept. 20, 1755.

" I was laſt night informed that it was reported I had
" adviſed taking out a ſtatute againſt you.   As no one, I
                                                    " am

In 1758 Dr. *Jortin* publiſhed the firſt volume of his " Life of *Eraſmus* *," in 4to ;
which was printed by Mr. *Edward Say*, brother to his friend already mentioned.   The
ſecond volume, containing Remarks on the Works of *Eraſmus*, and an Appendix of extracts from *Eraſmus* and from other authors, was printed by Mr. *Bowyer*.   A copy of
this work having been ſent to Dr. *Sherlock*, then Biſhop of *London*, Dr. *Jortin* ſoon after
received the following letter :

" REV. SIR,   *Fulham, Oct.* 13, 1760.

" This letter ſhould have waited on you long ſince, and it then would have appeared
" as a letter of thanks for the great favour done me by the preſent of the Life and Doc-
" trines of *Eraſmus* ; but it had lain by me ſo long, that it has changed its form, and
" now appears as an excuſe.   And, to prepare the way for the better reception of this
" apology, I will tell you what the truth of the matter is.   When I received the firſt
" part, and found that it was printed for *J. Whiſton*, I was in doubt whether it came
" from the printer, or from the author ; the author would expect nothing but thanks ;
" the bookſeller might probably expect to be paid.   What further delay there was in
" this affair is to be attributed to my ill health, and to Mr. *Whiſton's* frequent avoca-
" tions in the country.   But, Sir, that this fault may go no further, I deſire you to ac-
" cept my ſincere acknowledgments for the acceptable preſent of the account of *Eraſmus*,
" and for the diſtinction ſhewed me upon this occaſion.   I am, Sir, your affectionate
" brother, and very humble ſervant,   THOMAS, *London*."

                        To this letter he returned the following anſwer :

" MY LORD,

" You are very courteous and condeſcending to give yourſelf the trouble of ſending
" me your written thanks for a ſmall acknowledgment of reſpect and gratitude which I
" made to you.   I could not poſſibly forget your Lordſhip, who is one of thoſe very few
" amongſt my ſuperiors, to whom I have obligations.   Beſides, *Eraſmus* waited upon
" you, to pay, in ſome meaſure, the debt of an *Author* to an *Author* ; for I had re-
" ceived the four volumes of your *Diſcourſes*, which I have peruſed attentively, and
" twice over.   More than this, concerning them, it becomes not a perſon in my ſta-
" tion to ſay to a perſon in yours ; but it becometh me to return you my thanks for
" that and for other favours ; and to acknowledge myſelf, my Lord, your Lordſhip's
" moſt obliged, &c."

On the 9th of *January*, 1762, died Dr. *Hayter*, then Biſhop of *London*, for whom
Dr. *Jortin* had a great eſteem.   His friend Dr. *Oſbaldeſton* the Biſhop of *Carliſle* ſucceeded in this ſee ; and on the 10th of *March* appointed him domeſtic chaplain ; and at
the end of that month made him prebendary of *Harleſton*, in the cathedral church of
London.   This Biſhop alſo, in *October* 1762, gave him the living of *Kenſington*, where he
ſoon after went to reſide, and gave up his town houſe in *Hatton Garden*.   In 1763 he
aſſiſted Mr. *Markland* in correcting the proof ſheets of the " Supplices Mulieres," as
has been already mentioned in p. 20.   In *April* 1764 he was appointed Archdeacon of

* The late Biſhop of *Lincoln*, Dr. *Green*, meditated ſuch a work while he was at *St. John's College* ;
but his election to the maſterſhip of *Ben'et*, and the ſatisfaction he felt on knowing that it was undertaken by Dr. *Jortin*, put a ſtop to his deſign.

                                                                London

" am perfuaded, hath a deeper fenfe of obligations to you,
" or feels more for your prefent troubles, I was fhocked at
" this

London *. His kind patron died *May* 13, 1764. In 1766 he fent Dr. *Neve*, in a letter, fome
few remarks on *Philipps's* Hiftory of the Life of Cardinal *Pole*, which were added to Dr.
Neve's animadverfions on that hiftory, in an appendix, N° I. In 1767 a fecond edition
of his three volumes of " Remarks on Ecclefiaftical Hiftory" was publifhed, but printed
clofer, fo as to be brought into two volumes, 8vo; a circumftance which was not very
pleafing to the author. On the 27th of *Auguft*, 1770, he was taken ill of a diforder in
his breaft and lungs, and was bled feveral times for it, but without fuccefs. He continued growing worfe, till he died on the 5th of *September* following, in his 72d
year. His illnefs was not attended with much pain, and he was fenfible to the laft †.
He

* I have been told, but cannot afcertain the fact, that on the death of Dr. *Samuel Nichols*, in *No-*
vember 1763, the living of *St. James's* was offered to Dr. *Jortin* by Bifhop *Osbaldefton*, which he
declined accepting.

† " A review of the life of the late Dr. *Jortin* (fays an elegant writer, who is defervedly a fa-
" vourite with the publick) cannot but fuggeft the moft pleafing reflections. As a poet, a divine,
" a philofopher, and a man, he ferved the caufe of religion, learning and morality. There are,
" indeed, many writers whofe reputation is more diffufed among the vulgar and illiterate, but few
" will be found whofe names ftand higher than Dr. *Jortin's* in the efteem of the judicious. His
" *Latin* poetry is claffically elegant. His difcourfes and differtations, fenfible, ingenious, and ar-
" gumentative. His remarks on Ecclefiaftical hiftory, interefting, and impartial. His Sermons,
" replete with found fenfe and rational morality, expreffed in a ftyle, fimple, pure, and attic. Sim-
" plicity of ftyle is a grace, which, though it may not captivate at firft fight, is fure in the end to
" give permanent fatisfaction. It does not excite admiration, but it raifes efteem. It does not
" warm to rapture, but it fooths to complacency. Unfkilful writers feldom aim at this excellence.
" They imagine, that what is natural and common, cannot be beautiful. Every thing in their
" compofitions muft be ftrained, every thing affected: but Dr. *Jortin* had ftudied the antients,
" and perhaps formed himfelf on the model of *Xenophon*. He wrote on fubjects of morality, and
" morality is founded on reafon, and reafon is always cool and difpaffionate. A florid declama-
" tion, embellifhed with rhetorical figures, and animated with pathetic defcription, may indeed
" amufe the fancy, and raife a tranfient emotion in the heart, but rational difcourfe alone can con-
" vince the underftanding, and reform the conduct. The firft efforts of genius have commonly
" been in poetry. Unreftrained by the frigidity of argument, and the confinement of rules, the
" young mind gladly indulges the flights of imagination. *Cicero*, as well as many other antient phi-
" lofophers, orators, and hiftorians, is known to have facrificed to the Mufes in his earlier pro-
" ductions. Dr. *Jortin* adds to the number of thofe who confirm the obfervation. In his *Lufus*
" *Poetici*, one of the firft of his works, are united claffical language, tender fentiment, and har-
" monious verfe. Among the modern *Latin* poets, there are few who do not yield to Dr. *Jortin*.
" His Sapphics, on the ftory of *Bacchus* and *Ariadne*, are eafy, elegant, and poetical. The little
" ode, in which the calm life of the philofopher is compared to the gentle ftream gliding through a
" filent grove, is highly pleafing to the mind, and is perfectly elegant in the compofition. The
" Lyrics are indeed all excellent. The poem, on the Immortality of the Soul, is ingenious, poe-
" tical, and an exact imitation of the ftyle of *Lucretius*. In fhort, the whole collection is fuch as
" would fcarcely have difgraced a *Roman* in the age of an *Auguftus*. Time, if it does not cool
" the fire of imagination, certainly ftrengthens the powers of the judgement. As our author ad-
" vanced in life, he cultivated his reafon rather than his fancy, and defifted from his efforts in poe-
" try, to exert his abilities in the difquifitions of criticifm. His obfervations on one of the Fathers
" of *Englifh* poetry, need but to be more generally known, in order to be more generally approved.
" Claffical productions are rather amufing than inftructive. His works of this kind are all juvenile,
" and naturally flowed from a claffical education. Thefe however were but preparatory to his higher
" defigns, and foon gave way to the more important enquiries which were peculiar to his profeffion.
" His difcourfes on the Chriftian religion, one of the firft fruits of his theological purfuits, abound
" with that found fenfe and folid argument, which entitle their author to a rank very near the cele-
" brated *Grotius*. His differtations are equally remarkable for tafte, learning, originality, and in-
" genuity.

" this charge of ingratitude and inhumanity. I knew, with
" the reſt of the world, that your good-nature only had
" brought

He left the following direction in writing for his funeral : " Bury me in a private manner
" by day-light at *Kenſington* in the church, or rather in the new church-yard, and lay
" a flat ſtone over the grave. Let the inſcription be only this ;

" *Joannes Jortin*
" Mortalis eſſe deſiit
" Anno Salutis ——
" Ætatis ——." He

" genuity. His life of *Eraſmus* has extended his reputation beyond the limits of his native country,
" and eſtabliſhed his literary character in the remoteſt Univerſities of *Europe*. *Eraſmus* had long
" been an object of univerſal admiration, and it is matter of ſurprize, that his life had never been
" written with accuracy and judgment. This taſk was reſerved for Dr. *Jortin*, and the avidity
" with which the work was received by the learned, is a proof of the merit of the execution. It
" abounds with matter intereſting to the ſcholar ; but the ſtyle and method are ſuch as will not
" pleaſe every reader. There is a careleſſneſs in it, and a want of dignity and delicacy. His Re-
" marks on Eccleſiaſtical Hiſtory, are full of manly ſenſe, ingenious ſtrictures, and profound erudition.
" The work is highly beneficial to mankind, as it repreſents that ſuperſtition which diſgraced hu-
" man nature, in its proper light, and gives a right ſenſe of the advantages derived from religious
" reformation. He every where expreſſes himſelf with peculiar vehemence againſt the infatuation
" of bigotry and fanaticiſm. Convinced, that true happineſs is founded on a right uſe of the reaſon-
" ing powers, he makes it the ſcope of all his religious works, to lead mankind from the errors of
" imagination to attend to the dictates of diſpaſſionate reaſon. Poſthumous publications, it has
" been remarked, are uſually inferior in merit to thoſe which were publiſhed in an author's life-
" time. And indeed the opinion ſeems plauſible, as it may be preſumed, that an author's rea-
" ſon for not publiſhing his works, is a conſciouſneſs of their inferiority. The ſermons of Dr.
" *Jortin* were however deſigned, by their author, as a legacy to mankind. To enlarge on their va-
" lue, would only be to echo back the public voice. Good ſenſe and ſound morality appear in them,
" not indeed dreſſed out in the meretricious ornaments of a florid ſtyle, but in all the manly force,
" and ſimple graces, of natural eloquence. The ſame caprice, which raiſes to reputation thoſe
" trifling diſcourſes which have nothing to recommend them but a prettineſs of fancy, will again
" conſign them to oblivion : but the ſermons of Dr. *Jortin* will continue to be read with pleaſure
" and edification, as long as human nature ſhall continue to be endowed with the faculties of reaſon
" and diſcernment *. The tranſition from an author's writings to his life, is frequently diſadvanta-
" geous to his character. Dr. *Jortin*, however, when no longer conſidered as an author, but as a
" man, is ſo far from being leſſened in our opinion, that he excites ſtill greater eſteem and applauſe.
" A ſimplicity of manners, an inoffenſive behaviour, an univerſal benevolence, candour, modeſty,
" and good ſenſe, were his characteriſtics. Though his genius, and love of letters, led him to
" chooſe the ſtill vale of ſequeſtered life, yet was his merit conſpicuous enough to attract the notice
" of a certain primate, who did honour to epiſcopacy. He was preſented, by Archbiſhop *Herring*,
" to a benefice in *London* †, worth 200 pounds a year, as a reward for his exertions as a ſcholar
" and a divine. Some time after, he became chaplain to a late Biſhop of *London*, who gave him the
" vicarage of *Kenſington*, and appointed him Archdeacon of his dioceſe. This was all the prefer-
" ment he had, nor had he this till he was advanced in life. He did not however repine. Thus
" he ſpeaks of himſelf. ' Not to his erudition—but to his conſtant love and purſuit of it—he owes
" a ſituation and a ſtation, better than he expected, and as good as he ought to deſire.' While per-
" ſons of inferior attainments were made biſhops, a man who had been uncommonly eminent in the
" ſervice of learning and religion, was left to pine in the ſhade of obſcurity. Many who were
" thought to have little more than the ſhadow of piety and learning, have had the ſubſtantial reward
" of them, if ſecular advantages could beſtow it. *Jortin* was acknowledged to poſſeſs true virtue
" and real knowledge, but was left to receive his recompence in the ſuggeſtions of a good conſcience,
" and the applauſe of poſterity. The writer of this eulogium, as it has been called, is not con-

* It is ſurpriſing that a late learned and elegant diſſertator [Mr. *Mainwaring*] ſhould not have noticed and ap-
plauded the Sermons of Dr. *Jortin*, as well as thoſe of Biſhops *Secker* and *Hurd*, and Dr. *Powell*.
† In tranſcribing this ſentence from Mr. *Knox*, a few words have been neceſſarily altered.

" ſcious

" brought you into your prefent difficulties, and that your
" affliction under them arofe more from the inconveniencies
" you brought on others, than on yourfelf. It muft add
" not a little to your difquiet, to think you have a monfter
" among your creditors : but I owe it both to you and them
" to teftify that you can have but *one*; for I never heard
" any of them propofe taking a ftep which might ill fuit
" your inclinations ; or, what was more tender, your
" credit. If a ftatute was ever mentioned, it was feared
" only from the intricacy of your affairs, not fuggefted

He was accordingly buried, about nine o'clock in the morning, in the new church-yard at *Kenfington*, and the above infcription put on his grave-ftone. He left a widow (who died *June* 24, 1778, and was buried in the fame grave); and two children, *Rogers Jortin*, efq. of the Exchequer-office in *Lincoln's-Inn*; and *Martha*, married to the Rev. *Samuel Darby*, late fellow of *Jefus College, Cambridge*, and now rector of *Whatfield*, near *Hadleigh, Suffolk*. They are both living; and to Mr. *Jortin* I am to return thanks for the greateft part of the information contained in this note.

Dr. *Jortin* compleated in his life-time his " Remarks on Ecclefiaftical Hiftory," ending with the year 1517, the time when *Luther* began the Reformation. Thefe "Re-" marks were printed by Mr. *Bowyer* in 1773, as the fourth and fifth volumes, in 8vo. He left alfo fome manufcript Remarks on Authors, interfperfed with many critical and biographical anecdotes (which it is to be hoped may be communicated to the publick) ; fome other Mifcellaneous Pieces ; correct copies of fuch of his Sermons as might be publifhed, of the " Doctrine of a future State as it may be collected from the Old Tefta-" ment," and of Four Charges delivered by him as Archdeacon. His fon, foon after his death, in 1771, at the folicitation of many of the parifhioners of *St. Dunftan in the Eaft* and of *Kenfington*, publifhed four volumes of his Sermons in 8vo. with the following dedication :

" To the Parifhioners of *St. Dunftan in the Eaft*, and of *Kenfington*, thefe Sermons
" of his Father, printed at their requeft, are infcribed as a teftimony of refpect
" by *Rogers Jortin*.
" *Lincoln's Inn*, *Jan.* 1, 1771."

Thefe being favourably received by the public, a fecond edition of them was publifhed in 1772 ; with three additional volumes of Sermons, the " Doctrine of a future " State," and the four Charges. All thefe were printed by Mr. *Bowyer*. A portrait of Dr. *Jortin* has been engraved for private ufe by *John Hall*, from a painting by *E. Penny*, with the fame infcription as on his tomb.

" fcious of exaggeration. He owns, however, that he entertained a favourable prepoffeffion con-" cerning this liberal and laborious fcholar at a very early age. When a fchool-boy he had the ho-" nour to be feveral times in his company, and always looked up to him with a degree of veneration " natural to a young mind ftrongly attached to letters. He is happy to find that the unprejudiced " coincide with him in his maturer judgment." *Effays Moral and Literary, by Vicefimus Knox, A. M.* vol. I. 2d Ed. p. 115—123.

M m " from

" from the malevolence of any heart. I fay this, to clear
" others, not myfelf; for it is too much for me to think
" that fuch an imputation fhould live, and be carried to
" your ear. My heart, Sir, will ever wifh you happinefs;
" but for fear it fhould fall under any mifconftruction of
" it after fo bad a reprefentation of it, I muft beg you will
" give me leave to renounce the office of being one of your
" truftees, in which it will be impoffible for me after this
" to act with freedom, though I intend ever fo uprightly.
" I know not whether another truftee muft be chofen in
" my place; but, if there muft, whatever additional ex-
" pence that may occafion, I will thankfully defray. I
" would further beg, that no inquiry may be made who
" propagated the ftory of me; for as I fufpect no one
" perfon, fo I would continue to harbour no ill thoughts
" of any particular; and I will reft fatisfied in the perfua-
" fion you will ever retain your good ones, of, Sir, your
" fincere friend and moft humble fervant, W. B.

 " I would have waited on you with the inclofed renun-
 " ciation, but that I am haftening into the country."

The following year (1756) produced from Mr. *Bowyer's*
prefs two valuable tracts in the Antiquarian line, by *Philip*
Carteret Webb*, efq. which proved a prelude to the publication of the " Archaeologia." They were both read at
the public meetings of the Society of Antiquaries, and were
printed by their order; viz. 1. " A fhort Account of fome
" Particulars concerning *Domefday Book*, with a view to
" promote its being publifhed," 4to; and, 2. " A fhort
" Account of *Danegeld*; with fome further Particulars re-
" lating to *William* the Conqueror's Survey," 4to. In the

  * Of whom, fee under the year 1760.

fame

fame year alfo he printed Dr. *Patrick Brown's* "Natural
"Hiftory of *Jamaica*," folio; "A Series of Differtations on
"fome elegant and very valuable *Anglo-Saxon* Remains: 1.
"A Gold Coin in the *Pembrochian* Cabinet, in a Letter to
"*Martin Folkes*, efq. 2. A Silver Coin of Mr. *John White's*;
"3. A Gold Coin of Mr. *Simpfon's* of *Lincoln*, in a Letter to
"Mr. *Vertue*; 4. A Jewel in the *Bodleian* Library; 5.
"Second Thoughts on Lord *Pembroke's* Coin, in a Letter
"to Mr. *Ames**. Alfo the Coins engraved on a Copper-
"plate, with a Preface, wherein the Queftion, Whether
"the *Saxons* coined any Gold or not, is candidly debated
"with Mr. *North*. By *Samuel Pegge*, A. M." 4to; Dr.
Kennedy's† "Further Obfervations on *Caraufius*, Emperor
"of *Britain*, and *Oriuna*, fuppofed by fome to be a real
"perfon. With Anfwers to thofe trifling Objections made
"to the former Difcourfe. Together with fome new
"Thoughts concerning his Succeffor, *Allectus*, Emperor
"alfo of *Britain*; and particularly on that Gold Coin of
"*Allectus*, fent to *France* from the fame hand. Illuftrated
"with twelve extraordinary Coins of *Caraufius*, not hither-
"to publifhed‡," 4to; Mr. *John Wefley's* Tranflation of, and
notes on, the New Teftament, 4to; Mr. *Towne's* "Free and
"Candid Examination of the Bifhop of *London's* Sermons,
"wherein the commonly received fyftem concerning the
"Jewifh and Chriftian difpenfations is particularly confider-

* Secretary to the Society of Antiquaries.

† Some account of Dr. *Kennedy* has been already given in p. 113.

‡ This was foon followed by a plate, neatly engraved by *Perry*, intituled, "Numif-
"mata felectiora *Allecti* & *Caraufii Britanniæ* Imperatorum, è Mufæo *Kennediano*,"
and a fingle leaf of "Explanatory Notes on the Plate of *Allectus*, Emperor of *Britain*,
"with thofe of *Caraufius*;" and foon afterwards by "A Letter to the Rev. Dr.
"*Stukeley*, on the Firft Part of his *Medallic Hiftory of Caraufius, Emperor of Britain*,
"his ill-grounded Opinions and moft extraordinary Affertions therein contained;"
which was the "fix-penny 4to. letter" alluded to in p. 113.

"ed,"

" ed*," 8vo; " A ſhort Hiſtory of the *Iſraelites*, with an Ac-
" count of their Manners, Cuſtoms, Laws, Polity, and Religion;
" being an uſeful Introduction to the Reading of the Old Teſ-
" tament. Tranſlated from the *French* of Abbé *Fleury*, by *Ellis*
" *Farneworth*†, M. A." 8vo; " Collateral Bee-boxes, or a
" new, eaſy, and advantageous Method of managing Bees, in
" which part of the Honey is taken away in an eaſy and plea-
" ſant manner, without deſtroying or much diſturbing the
" Bees; early ſwarms if deſired are encouraged, and late ones
" prevented, by *Stephen White*‡, M. A. rector of *Holton* in

* The deſign of this piece is to ſhew that the common ſyſtem which makes redemption and a future ſtate a popular doctrine among the antient *Jews*, abounds with abſurdities and inconſiſtencies. The author warmly eſpouſes Dr. *Warburton's* ſcheme
upon the ſubject, and his principal view ſeems to be to get the queſtion thoroughly examined, and the *Jewiſh* law freed from the many perplexities in which thoſe who plead
for the received ſyſtem have involved it.

† Of whom, ſee under the year 1762. This little piece of the learned Abbé had
been before tranſlated by R. G. 1750, 8vo.

‡ This gentleman, who was a member of *St. John's College***, *Cambridge*, was
founder of a charity ſchool at *Holton* in *Suffolk*, on which he expended a conſiderable
ſum of his own, beſides what he collected by ſubſcription from his friends. He publiſhed, for the benefit of this ſchool, a ſermon, under the title of " A Diſſuaſive from
" Stealing, 1747," and 1769, 12mo, and a collection of " Pſalms; ſet to Muſic by Mr.
" *Riley*," 12mo, 1769. His treatiſe on Bees was reprinted by Mr. *Bowyer* in 1758,
and again in 1764.—" Mr. *White* had the ſingular faculty of being a ruminant. He
" maſticated a ſecond time his ſupper at chapel the next morning. I kept my bees by
" his books; but I believe his ſcheme never made it's fortune. See The Practical Bee-
" maſter by *John Keys*. *London*. No date, but probably 1780, 8vo. where he talks of
" inconveniencies, which I never found when I practiſed the methods, but his own was
" to be recommended at the expence of others." *T. F.*

** Contemporary with *John White*, B. D. fellow of that college, and vicar of *Oſpringe*, *Kent*.
We mention this becauſe theſe two writers have been ſometimes miſtaken for each other. The publications of Mr. *John White* were, 1. " A Letter to a Gentleman of the Diſſenting Perſuaſion con-
" cerning the Lives of Churchmen and Diſſenters, 1743," 8vo; 2. " A Second Letter to a Diſſent-
" ing Gentleman, 1745," 8vo; which was the ſame year followed by, 3. " A Third Letter."
Theſe Letters were ſo well received, that they were ſeveral times reprinted, in 1745, 1746, and
1747, and again (collected into one volume) in 1748. Mr. *J. White* was alſo author of 4. " A
" Sermon on the Fall, *Dec.* 18, 1745," printed in 1746, 8vo; 5. " A Defence of the Letters to a
" Diſſenting Gentlemen, 1746," 8vo. reprinted in 1748 and 1749; 6. " A Second Defence, 1748
" and 1749," 8vo; 7. " A Letter to Mr. *Chandler*, 1749," 8vo; 8. " A Diſcourſe againſt the
" Diſſenters, 1750," 12mo; 9. " Appendix to the Controverſy between the Rev. Mr. *White* and
" the Diſſenting Gentlemen, 1750," 8vo; 10. " The Proteſtant Diſſenter guided to the Church of
" *England*, 1750," 8vo; 11. " An Anſwer to the Free and Candid Diſquiſitions, 1751," 8vo;
12. " The Proteſtant *Engliſhman* guarded againſt the Arts and Arguments of *Romiſh* Papiſts
" and Emiſſaries, 1753," 8vo; and ſome other controverſial treatiſes, in 1755.

" *Suffolk*,"

" *Suffolk*," 8vo ; *Athelſtan**, a tragedy, by Dr. *Brown*, 8vo ; Mr. *Palairet's* † Notes on the New Teſtament, and Specimen of a *Dutch* Concordance ; Catalogues of the Libraries of Mr. *Folkes* and Dr. *Rawlinſon*; and " Certifi- " cates and Receipts, in *Latin* and *Engliſh*, for the ſuperan- " nuated Scholars of Merchant Taylors School," drawn up by Mr. *Edward-Rowe Mores* ‡.

Under the year 1757 I find the following memorandum on the back of a note for 50*l*. (lent *April* 8, 1755) : " If I die " before this note of hand is diſcharged, I order it to be re- " leaſed and given up to my friend who ſigned it. Witneſs " my hand, *Feb.* 3, 1757. W. BOWYER."—He had a con- ſiderable number of ſuch notes for ſmaller ſums, many of them in like manner releaſed, and ſome of more than fifty years date.

The principal books of 1757 were " Memoirs of the " Marquis of *Clanricarde*, lord lieutenant of *Ireland*, and " commander in chief of the forces of *Charles* I. in that " kingdom, during the rebellion," folio;" " Travels or " Obſervations relating to ſeveral Parts of *Barbary* and " *The Levant*. Illuſtrated with Cuts. The ſecond edi- " tion, with great improvements. By *Thomas Shaw* ‖,
" D. D.

---

* Mr. *Garrick* performed a principal part in this play, and wrote the epilogue. Dr. *Brown* did not give his name to the world either with *Barbaroſſa* or *Athelſtan*.

† Preacher of the *Dutch* chapel at *St. James's*, and author of ſeveral treatiſes on the learned languages. He publiſhed at *Leyden*, in 1752, " Obſervationes in ſacros Novi " Fœderis libros ;" and at *London*, in 1754, " *Eliæ Palairet*, Eccleſiæ *Gallicæ Torna-* " *cenſis* Paſtoris, Specimen Theſauri Critici Linguæ *Græcæ* ; in quo ſpeciales vocabu- " lorum ſignificationes indicantur, ellipſes ſupplentur, pleonaſmi evolvuntur, & ex " Scholiis antiquis illuſtrantur, cum indicibus neceſſariis," 4to. In 1756 he corrected for Mr. *Bowyer* the *Ajax* and *Electra* of *Sophocles*, for an edition which will be no- ticed under the year 1758. He died *Jan.* 2, 1765.

‡ Of this eccentric Genius ſome account has been given, p. 130—132 ; to which I ſhall, under the year 1761, take an opportunity of adding ſome further particulars.

‖ This learned traveller, ſon of Mr. *Gabriel Shaw*, was born at *Kendal* in *Weſtmore- land* about the year 1692. He received his education at the grammar ſchool of that
place ;

" D. D. F. R. S. Regius Profeſſor of *Greek,* and Princi-
" pal of *St. Edmund Hall,* in the Univerſity of *Ox-*
" *ford,*" 4to ; " Diſcourſes and Eſſays, in Proſe and Verſe,
" by

place ; was admitted batchelor at *Queen's College, Oxford, Oct.* 5, 1711, where he took
the degree of A. B. *July* 5, 1716 ; A. M. *Jan.* 16, 1719 ; went into holy orders, and
was appointed chaplain to the *Engliſh* factory at *A'giers.* In this ſtation he continued
ſeveral years, and from thence took opportunities of travelling into ſeveral parts. During
his abſence, he was choſen fellow of his college, *March* 16, 1727 ; and at his return in
1733 took the degree of doctor in divinity, *July* 5, 1734, and in the ſame year was elected F. R. S. He publiſhed the firſt edition of his travels at *Oxford* in 1738 ; beſtowed on the univerſity ſome natural curioſities, and ſome ancient coins and buſts *,
which he had collected in his travels. On the death of Dr. *Felton,* 1740, he was nominated by his college principal of *St. Edmund Hall,* which he raiſed from a ruinous
condition by his munificence ; and was preſented at the ſame time to the vicarage of
Bramley in *Hants.* He was alſo regius profeſſor of *Greek* at *Oxford* till his death, which
happened on the 15th of *Auguſt,* 1751. For a more particular account of his character,
I ſhall ſubjoin the epitaph on his monument in *Bramley* church, written by his friend Dr.
Browne, provoſt of *Queen's College, Oxford:*

" Peregrinationibus variis
Per *Europam, Africam, Aſiamque*
Feliciter abſolutis,
Et exuviis mortalibus hic loci
Tandem depoſitis,
Cœleſtem in Patriam remigravit
THOMAS SHAW, S. T. P. et R. S. S.
Gabrielis Fil. *Kendalienſis :*
Qui
Conſulibus *Anglicis* apud *Algerenſes*
Primùm erat a Sacris ;
Mox *Coll. Reginæ* inter Socios aſcriptus ;
Aulæ dein *Sancti Edmundi* Principalis,
Ac ejuſdem munificus Inſtaurator ;
Linguæ demum *Græcæ* apud *Oxonienſes*
Profeſſor Regius.
De literis quantum meruit auctor celebratus,
Edita uſque teſtabuntur opera,

Pyramidibus ipſis, quas penitiùs inſpexerat,
Perenniora forſan extitura.
Hic, ſtudiis etſi ſeverioribus indies occupatus,
Horis tamen ſubſecivis emicuit
Eruditus idem et facetus conviva.
Optima quanquam mentis indole
Et multiplici ſcientia inſtructus,
Literatorum omnium, domi foriſque,
Suffragiis comprobatus ;
Magnatum, procerumque popularium,
Familiari inſignitus notitiâ ;
Nec ſummis in eccleſiâ dignitatibus impar ;
Fato tamen iniquo† evenit,
Ut *Bramleyenſis* obiret *parœciæ*
Vicarius penè ſexagenarius
XVIII. cal. *Sept.* A. D. 1751.
Uxor JOANNA, *Ed. Holden* arm. conſulis
Algerenſis olim conjux, bis vidua, M. P."

His travels were tranſlated into *French,* and printed in quarto 1743, with ſeveral notes
and emendations communicated by the author. Dr *Pococke,* afterwards biſhop of *Oſſory,*
having attacked thoſe travels in his " Deſcription of the Eaſt," our author publiſhed a
ſupplement by way of vindication in 1746. In the Preface to the " Supplement," he
ſays the intent and deſign of it is partly to vindicate the Book of Travels from ſome objections that have been raiſed againſt it by the Author of " The Deſcription of the
" Eaſt, &c." He publiſhed " A further Vindication of the Book of *Travels,* and the
" *Supplement* to it, in a Letter to the Right Reverend *Robert Clayton,* D. D. Lord

---

※ Three of theſe are engraved among the *Marmora Oxonienſia,* 1763, Nº lxxiv. lxxvi. lxxviii.
† " As the circumſtances of *Bramley* vicarage are not explained, one doth not readily ſee the
" misfortune of dying vicar of it. If it had been called a *moderate* or *ſmall* College-living, we
" ſhould have known at once, that a man of his well-known good character got only very trifling
" preferment, and that too from his College, who perhaps muſt have given it to him had he had
" no character at all." *T. F.*

5

" Biſhop

" by *Edward Cobden*, D. D. Archdeacon of *London*, and
" lately Chaplain to his Majesty King *George* II. above
" Twenty-two Years, in which Time most of these Dis-
" courses were preached before him. Published chiefly for
" the use of his Parishioners," one large 4to. volume,
divided in two parts*; " A Natural History of Fos-
" sils,

" Bishop of *Clogher*." This letter consists of six folio pages, and bears date in 1747.
After the Doctor's death, the above-mentioned second edition of his travels came out
in 1757. The contents of the supplement are interwoven in this edition; and the improvements were made, and the edition prepared for the press, by the author himself,
who expressly presented the work, with these additions, alterations, and improvements,
to the public, as an essay towards restoring the ancient geography, and placing in a
proper light the natural and sometimes civil history, of those countries where he travelled.

* Of this volume 250 copies only were printed, 50 of which were appropriated to
a charitable use. The first part of it contains twenty-eight Discourses preached on various occasions between the years 1720 and 1754†; inscribed to the parishioners of
Acton, and of the united parishes of *St. Austin* and *St. Faith*, for whose service they
were chiefly composed. " As age and infirmities," he tells them, " have even almost
" disabled me from instructing you in the pulpit (after fifty years constant discharge of
" that duty); it is my desire, to preach to you somewhat longer from the press; that
" those things you have formerly heard, may be fixed deeper in your memories, and
" copied out in your conduct. I am in hopes, the interesting relation we bear to each
" other, will engage you to read them with candour, and consider them with atten-
" tion. I can truly affirm that I have given you no other directions than what I have
" myself wished, and endeavoured to follow." The second part of the volume is a re-
publication (with additions) of the poems already mentioned in p. 207. It contains also
" An Essay sacred to the Memory of Queen *Anne*, for her Bounty to the Clergy;" and
" An Essay tending to promote Religion; inscribed to Sir *John Barnard*, in token of
" respect for his integrity in a corrupted age." This Essay, the Author says, " is
" of a miscellaneous nature, consisting partly of verse and partly of prose, and contains
" some queer antiquated notions concerning the disposal of ecclesiastical preferments."
The immediate cause of it was the Author's being disappointed of a Canonry of
St. Paul's, to which he had " no other pretensions but Duty, Justice, and Reason, un-
" less it were the exceeding convenience" of that preferment, as he had most of *Pater
Noster Row* already under his care. " Another reason," he says, " is, that as it is
" attended with riches, it would at this time be very agreeable to let into my barren pas-
" tures‡ a small rivulet from the stream of plenty; and, as my little Prebend in that

† Among these is his " Concio ad Clerum, xi. cal. *Maii*, 1752," and three Sermons preached
after the noted one mentioned in p. 208. The last time he preached before the King was *Dec.* 8,
1751. He resigned his warrant for chaplain *Nov.* 23, 1752; after having delivered into his Majesty's hands his reasons in writing for so doing.
‡ " His income, he says, was but moderate (all his preferments together not exceeding 350*l. per
annum* clear, which he would often say was as much as he desired, and more than he deserved.
" This income, frugality and moderation converted into plenty, and contentment into happiness.)
" And about this time he met with losses amounting to above 2000*l.* which reduced his substance very
" low."

" church

" fils, by *Emanuel Mendez da Cofta**, Fellow of the
" Royal and Antiquarian Societies of *London*, and mem-
" ber of the Imperial Academy *Naturæ Curioforum* of
" *Germany*, vol. I. Part I." 4to; Mr. *Farneworth's* tranflation of " *Davila's* Hiftory of *France*," 2 vols. 4to; two
editions of Dr. *Powel's* " Commencement Sermon," 4to;
a fecond edition of Dr. *Brown's* " Eftimate of the Manners
" and Principles of the Times," 8vo; Bifhop *Hoadly's*
" Sixteen Sermons," 8vo; his " Letter to *Clement Che-*
" *vallier* †, Efq." 8vo; a fourth edition of Dr. *Grey's* " Me-
" moria Technica," 8vo; " Letters concerning Tafte (the
" third edition, with additions) by the Author of the

" church affords me fome money for Bread, this would amply fupply me with Butter.
" The laft I fhall mention is, that, as Archdeacon of *London*, my place in the Choir is
" next to that of our worthy Dean ; and when Striplings are made Refidentaries, they are
" ftill pufhing for precedence, which they think they have a right to (and I never con-
" tefted) as moft Money includes moft Honour. Now the uniting a Canonry with the
" Archdeaconry would prevent all difputes, and make matters quite eafy, which
" would be an excellent thing in a Cathedral : for Clergymen, as well as others, have
" a fpice of ambition."

* Librarian to the Royal Society, and member of the Botanic Society in *Florence*.
He publifhed, in 1776, " Elements of Conchology, or an Introduction to the Knowledge
" of Shells, with fome plates, containing Figures of every Genus of Shells," 8vo. and in
1778 " *Britifh* Conchology, &c." in 4to. Propofals for printing his " Foffils" by fubfcription were circulated in 1752 ; and in the Preface, Mr. *Du Cofta* declares, that
" he then publifhed fo much of the work as the affiftance he had received would enable
" him to do; and that the reft was ready for the prefs, and would be publifhed with
" fpeed proportioned to the generofity of thofe who think fuch refearches worthy of
" encouragement."

† This letter was occafioned by the villainous attempt of one *Bernard Fournier*, by
a forged note over a frank of Bifhop *Hoadly*, to defraud him of no lefs a fum than 8,800*l.*
The Bifhop, it is well known, was obliged to call *Fournier* and his note into Chancery,
where he obtained a judgement in his favour. A full account of this iniquitous tranfaction may be feen in Dr. *Hoadly's* Life of the Bifhop, p. xxiii. The Letter to Mr.
Chevallier was an aftonifhing performance of a Divine turned of eighty-one years of age ;
and he received many compliments on that account from fome of the greateft lawyers of
the age. Mr. *Walpole* humouroufly faid, " The Bifhop had not only got the better
" of his adverfary *(Fournier)*, but of old age."—I may add, that this fmall pamphlet
appears to have undergone fo many revifals and corrections, that the mere typographical
alterations coft the Bifhop 40*l.*

" Life

"Life of *Socrates* *," 8vo; and "Travels in *Egypt* and
"*Nubia*,

* *John Gilbert Cooper*, efq. of *Thurgarton*, in *Nottinghamfhire*, was the fon of a gentleman of fortune and family. After paffing through *Weftminfter* fchool under Dr.
Nichols, along with the late Lord *Albemarle*, Lord *Buckinghamfhire*, Major *Johnfon*,
and the Gentleman diftinguifhed in thefe Memoirs by the fignature *T. F.* he became fellow commoner of *Trinity College, Cambridge*, and refided two or three years. Soon afterwards he married Mifs *Wright*, daughter to the Recorder of *Leicefter*, and fettled at
his family feat. He died in *April* 1769, after fuffering a long and excruciating illnefs
arifing from the ftone. Befides the " Life of *Socrates*," (which may be confidered as
his *magnum opus*, and in compiling which he was fupplied with authorities by his
learned friend Mr. *Jackfon* of *Leicefter*, of whom fee p. 225), Mr. *Cooper* was author of
" Curfory Remarks on Mr. *Warburton*'s new Edition of Mr. *Pope*'s Works; occafioned
" by that modern Commentator's injurious Treatment, in one of his Notes upon the
" Effay on Criticifm, of the Author of the Life of *Socrates* †. In a Letter to a Friend,
" 1751," 8vo. He wrote fome numbers of the periodical paper called " The World;"
was author of " *Ver Vert* ‡, or the Nunnery Parrot, an Heroic Poem in Four Can-
" tos, infcribed to the Abbefs of D*****; tranflated from the *French* of Monfieur

† " As Ignorance, when joined with Humility, produces ftupid admiration, on which account
" it is fo commonly obferved to be the mother of Devotion and blind homage; fo, when joined with
" Vanity (as it always is in bad Critics) it gives birth to every iniquity of impudent abufe and
" flander. See an example (for want of a better) in a late worthlefs and now forgotten thing, called
" the *Life of Socrates*; where the head of the Author (as a man of wit obferved, on reading the book)
" has juft made a fhift to do the office of a *camera obfcura*, and reprefent things in an inverted order,
" himfelf *above*, and *Sprat, Rollin, Voltaire*, and every other Author of reputation *below*." I have
tranfcribed the learned Commentator's note, to introduce Mr. *Cooper's* account of this tranfaction:
" I have undergone," fays he, " young as I am, too many difappointments in life, to wonder much
" at many things which the mob of mankind call extraordinary; otherwife I might be furprifed that
" almoft a total retirement from the world would not fhelter me from the injuries of it, efpecially
" too at an age when few have had any concerns with it. I thought I might have enjoyed an un-
" envied obfcurity in the moft undifturbed peace and tranquillity, and that CALUMNY was too bufy
" about the names of thofe who were candidates for fame, to find time to vifit the recefs of one,
" whofe contempt of every advantage of life, but what conduced to quiet, fhould, it was hoped,
" protect him from the poifonous breath of that daughter of ENVY. But I was greatly miftaken, it
" feems, in my humble expectations; for I had fcarcely begun to feel the calm comforts which the
" abfence of contention yields to a thinking creature, before I was informed by letters from fome
" friends in town, that Mr. *Warburton* had, with his ufual humanity and good manners, very com-
" pendioufly anfwered the *Life of Socrates* in the tail of one note, by the free ufe of thofe appella-
" tions he has indifcriminately thrown out upon, not only all thofe who have ever had any contro-
" verfy with him, but upon all others too whom he ever fufpected to have the rafhnefs to contra-
" dict any of his opinions. Howfoever this would have alarmed me heretofore, as an author, from
" the pen of any other perfon, it had no effect upon me then from the writer it came from, and I fat
" down contemptuoufly contented, without fo much as being folicitous to know what abufe he had
" conferred upon my writings. I fay, abufe, for he never fpeaks of an opponent without it. But
" as indifferent as I was about my character as a writer, I can't fay I was quite fo eafy when I was
" afterwards told that he had attacked it as a man. Upon this I wrote to him, that I thought he
" had ufed me very ill, and fhould take a proper notice of him for it in publick; in anfwer to which
" he tells a friend of mine, ' That he was furprifed I fhould think myfelf ill-ufed, for that he had
" never mentioned my name or writings in publick, or in converfation, but with honour, till I had
" wrote a book wherein I had treated him through the whole with a fcurrility worfe than *Billingfgate*,
" and that he had now taken no other revenge than the cafual mention of the Author of the *Life of*
" *Socrates* (without the mention of my name) with a flight joke.' I will afk any impartial reader,
" if there is the leaft reflection through the whole *Life of Socrates*, or the notes, upon Mr. *W*'s
" morals? whether I have not confined my criticifm to his practice as an author? and whether
" every thing therein advanced cannot be proved over and over again by citations from the *Divine*
" *Legation*, and his other tracts? At the fame time I defire one part of the difpute betwixt us may
" be finifhed by an anfwer to thefe queftions: Is not calling a guiltlefs man an impudent flanderer,
" calumny? and quite a different revenge than a flight joke? and has not Mr. *Warburton* done that
" in the note in queftion?" *Curfory Remarks*, p. 3—6.
‡ Reprinted in the firft Volume of *Dilly's* Repofitory, 1777.

" *Greffet*;"

"*Nubia*, by *Frederick Lewis Norden**," folio and 8vo.

"*Gresset*;" and published a volume of "Poems ‡ on several Subjects," 1764, 8vo; and an ingenious "Project for raising an Hospital for decayed Authors," reprinted in "the second volume of *Dodsley's* Fugitive Pieces." His elegant *Latin* epitaph on an infant son, who died the day after he was born 1749, is printed in Gent. Mag. 1778, p. 486, with a whimsical poetical translation. On the first appearance of the "Letters on "Taste" it was observed, that Mr. *Cooper's* "genius seemed to shine more in descrip-"tion than in definition; that he had more of imagery than of speculation; that his "imagination was the strongest talent of his mind, and that, if he had not attempted to "offer any thing new on the subject of Taste, he was always so entertaining, spirited, "and splendid in his diction, that the reader who is not instructed by him, cannot fail "of being pleased and diverted." See *Literary Magazine*, 1757, p. 134.

* Born at *Gluckstadt* in *Holstein*, October 22, 1708. His father was a lieutenant colonel of artillery, and himself was bred to arms. Being intended for the sea service, he entered in 1722 into the corps of cadets, a royal establishment in which young men are instructed in such arts and sciences as are necessary to form good sea-officers. Here he is said to have made a great progress in the mathematics, ship-building and drawing, especially in the last. He copied the works of the greatest masters in the art, to form his taste and acquire their manner; but he felt a particular pleasure in drawing from nature. The first person who took notice of this rising genius, was M. *De Lerche*, knight of the order of the elephant, and grand master of the ceremonies. This gentleman put into his hands a collection of charts and topographical plans, belonging to the king, to be retouched and amended, in which Mr. *Norden* shewed great skill and care; but, considering his present employment as foreign to his profession, M. *De Lerche*, in 1732, presented him to the king, and procured him, not only leave, but a pension to enable him to travel; the king likewise made him, at the same time, second lieutenant. It was particularly recommended to him to study the construction of ships, especially such galleys and rowing vessels as are used in *The Mediterranean*. Accordingly he set out for *Holland*, where he soon became acquainted with the admirers of antiquities and the polite arts, and with several distinguished artists, particularly *De Reyter*, who took great pleasure in teaching him to engrave. From *Holland* he went to *Marseilles*, and thence to *Leghorn*, staying in each place so long as to inform himself in every thing the place furnished relating to the design of his voyage. At this last port he got models made of the different kinds of rowing vessels, which are still to be seen at the chamber of models at the *Old Holm*. In *Italy* he spent near three years in perfecting his taste, and enlarging his knowledge. Here his great talents drew the attention of persons of distinction, and procured him an opportunity of seeing the cabinets of the curious, both in antiquities and medals, and of making his advantage of the great works of painting and sculpture, especially at *Rome* and *Florence*. At the latter city he was made a member of the drawing academy, and in this city he received an order from the king to go into *Egypt. Christian* VI. was desirous of having a circumstantial account of a country so distant and so famous, from an intelligent man, and one whose fidelity could not be questioned; and no one was thought more proper than Mr. *Norden*. He was then in the flower of his age, possessed of great abilities, of a fine taste, and a courage equal

‡ Many of Mr. *Cooper's* little poems, originally printed in "The Museum," and in "*Dodsley's* "Collection," are collected in this volume.—These poems, says Mr. *Dodsley*, having been very favourably received by the publick when they first appeared, at different times, in detached pieces, the author has been prevailed upon to permit me to collect them into this small volume. When I requested him to give me a preface, he replied, "That to those whom such trifles afforded pleasure, "a formal introduction would be unnecessary; that he wrote most of them when he was very young, "for his own amusement, and published them afterwards for my profit; and, as they had once an-"swered both those ends, was very little sollicitous what would be the fate of them for the future."

originally written in *French*, and tranflated by Dr. *Peter Templeman**.

The

to every danger or fatigue; and, to crown all, a ftrong defire of examining, upon the fpot, the wonders of *Egypt*, before he received the order of his mafter. How he acquitted himfelf in this bufinefs appears in his "Travels." He ftayed in thefe countries about a year, during which the king further promoted him, and at his return, when the count of *Dannefkiold-Samfoe*, who was at the head of the marine, prefented him to his majefty, the king expreffed himfelf greatly pleafed with the mafterly defigns he had made in his travels, and defired he would draw up an account of them. At this time he was made captain-lieutenant, and foon after captain of the royal navy, and one of the commiffioners for building fhips. When the war broke out between *England* and *Spain*, count *Dannefkiold Samfoe* propofed to the king, that feveral of the officers of his majefty's navy fhould go as volunteers into the fervice of the powers at war; and chofe Mr. *Norden*, in particular, to accompany his own nephew, count *Ulric Adolphus*, then a captain of a man of war, in fuch expeditions as the *Englifh* fhould happen to undertake. On their arrival in *London*, Mr. *Norden*, whofe fame had preceded him, was received with diftinguifhed favour; feveral of the moft confiderable men at court, and even the prince of *Wales*, hearing of the drawings he had made in *Egypt*, were curious to fee them, and fhewed him great kindnefs. The following fummer he accompanied the count on an expedition under Sir *John Norris*; and in 1740, he again went on board the fleet deftined to *America*, under the command of Sir *Chaloner Ogle*, with a defign to reinforce Admiral *Vernon*. After this, Mr. *Norden* fpent about one year in *London* in great efteem, and was admitted a member of the Royal Society. On this occafion he gave the publick †, under the patronage of Mr. *Folkes*, an idea of fome ruins and coloffal ftatues, intituled, "Drawings of fome Ruins and Coloffal Statues, at *Thebes* in *Egypt*; "with an Account of the fame, in a Letter to the Royal Society, 1742." This effay, with the plates belonging to it, gained him new applaufe, and heightened the defire that the publick had before conceived of feeing that work entire, of which this made only a fmall part. About this time he found his health declining, and propofed to the count to take a tour to *France*, and to vifit the coafts and ports of that kingdom, in hopes that a change of climate might have been a means of eftablifhing his health; but he died at *Paris* in 1742, much regretted by his acquaintance, as a perfon who had done honour to his country, and from whom the world had great expectations.

* Son of *Peter Templeman*, an eminent attorney at *Dorchefter* in the county of *Dorfet* (by *Mary* daughter of *Robert Haynes*, a gentleman who was bred at *Wadham College*, *Oxford*, and became a merchant at *Briftol*, but when advanced in years quitted bufinefs and retired to *Yeovil* in *Somerfetfhire*), who died 1749, and his widow 19 years after him, aged 93. Dr. *Templeman* was born *March* 17, 1711, and was educated at *The Charterhoufe* (not on the foundation), from whence he proceeded to *Trinity College*, *Cambridge*, where he took his degree of Bachelor of Arts with diftinguifhed reputation. During his refidence at *Cambridge*, by his own inclination, in conformity with that of his parents, he applied himfelf to the ftudy of divinity, with a defign to enter into holy orders; but after fome time, from what caufe we know not, he altered his plan, and applied himfelf to the ftudy of phyfic. In the year 1736 he went to *Leyden*, where he attended the lectures of Dr. *Boerhaave*, and the Profeffors of the other branches of medicine in that celebrated Univerfity, for the fpace of two years or more. About the beginning of 1739 he returned to *London*, with a view to enter on the practice of his profeffion, fupported by a handfome allowance from his father. Why he did not fucceed in that line,

† See above, p. 180.

was

The moſt material books of 1758 were, "A Report
"from the Committee appointed to enquire into the
"original

was eaſy to be accounted for by thoſe who knew him. He was a man of a very liberal
turn of mind, of general erudition, with a large acquaintance amongſt the learned of
different profeſſions, but of an indolent, inactive diſpoſition; he could not enter into
juntos with people that were not to his liking; he could not cultivate the acquaintance
to be met with at tea-tables; he could not intrigue with nurſes, nor aſſociate with the
various knots of pert, inſipid, well bred, impertinent, good humoured, malicious goſ-
ſips, that are often found ſo uſeful to introduce a young phyſician into practice: but
rather choſe to employ his time at home in the peruſal of an ingenious author, or to
ſpend an *Attic* evening in a ſelect company of men of ſenſe and learning. In this he re-
ſembled his brother *Armſtrong*, whoſe limited practice in his profeſſion was owing to the
ſame cauſe. In the latter end of the year 1750 he was introduced to Dr. *Fothergill* (by
the friend whom I am to thank for the information in this note) with a view of inſti-
tuting a Medical Society, in order to procure the earlieſt intelligence of every improvement in phyſic from every part of *Europe*. An extract from one of his letters * will give
ſome idea of this plan, which never took effect. At the ſame period he tells his friend,
"Dr. *Mead* has very generouſly offered to aſſiſt me with all his intereſt for ſucceeding
"Dr. *Hall* at *The Charterhouſe*, whoſe death has been for ſome time expected. In-
"ſpired with gratitude, I have ventured out of my element (as you will plainly per-
"ceive), and ſent him the following Ode:

"Ad virum celeberrimum, RICARDUM MEAD, M. D. &c.

Horrenda ſcribant prælia cæteri,
Martiſque lauros ſanguine roſcidas;
 En civicam nectit coronam
  Teque cupit celebrare Muſa!

Seu tu Patronus nobilis artium
Audis, benignus ſive ſalutifer
 Morbos levare; idemque clarus
  Artibus excoluiſſe vitam.

Ritu *Herculis* prima eſt tibi gloria
Angues domare et lurida toxica;
 Tu fraudibus lethi retectis
  Expedies per acuta corpus.

Cum peſte languet *Gallia* livida,
Te quiſque poſcit ſollicitâ prece;
 Et te docente artes fugandi,
  Diva Salus tua dicta firmat.

Monſtrare leges, queis mare turgidum,
Newtonus audet; fortiter adjuvans

Monſtras eaſdem nos regentes
 Corporibus peperiſſe morbos:
O corda fratrum! lucida ſidera!
Ut vos amicè lumina jungitis!
 Externa *Newtonus* retexit;
  Ipſe homini interiora pandis.

Non mille proſint, queis tua pectora
Implentur; heu rapit omnia
 Sors dura! Divinum Senemque
  Poſtera te celebrabit ætas.

Tecum vetuſtas marmora condidit,
Vultuſque fictos undique colligis;
 At mox tua infixi nepotes
  Ora magis pretioſa ducent.

Jam fata ſemper vincere pertinax,
Præcepta tradis fida medentibus;
 Sic tu brevi vitæ ſuperſtes
  Eſto Opifer venientis ævi."

Dr. *Templeman*'s epitaph on Lady *Lucy Meyrick* (the only *Engliſh* copy of verſes of his
writing that we know of) is printed in the Eighth volume of the "Select Collection of Miſ-
"cellany Poems, 1781." In 1753 he publiſhed the firſt volume of "Curious Remarks and
"Obſervations in Phyſic, Anatomy, Chirurgery, Chemiſtry, Botany, and Medicine, ex-
"tracted

* "I ſpent the whole afternoon yeſterday with Dr. *Fothergill* in ſettling the plan of our deſign,
"which in ſhort is this: By a ſettled regular correſpondence in the principal cities of *Europe*, to
"have the moſt early intelligence of the improvements in chemiſtry, anatomy, botany, chirurgery,
"with accounts of epidemical diſeaſes, ſtate of the weather, remarkable caſes, obſervations and
"uſeful medicines. A ſociety to be formed here in town, to meet regularly once a week, at which
"meeting all papers tranſmitted to be read, and ſuch as are approved of to be publiſhed in the *Engliſh*
"language,

" original Standard of Weights and Measures in this King-

" tracted from the History and Memoirs of the Royal Academy of Sciences at *Paris*;"
and the second volume in the succeeding year. A third was promised, but I believe never
printed. It appears indeed that if he had met with proper encouragement from the
publick, it was his intention to have extended the work to twelve volumes, with an additional one of Index, and that he was prepared to publish two such volumes every year*.
The above-mentioned translation of *Norden* appeared in the beginning of the year 1757;
and in that year he was editor of " Select Cases and Consultations in Physic, by Dr.
" *Woodward*," 8vo. On the establishment of *The British Museum* in 1753, he was
appointed to the office of Keeper of the Reading-room, which he resigned on being
chosen, in 1760, Secretary to the then newly instituted Society of Arts, Manufactures,
and Commerce. In the year 1762 he was elected a corresponding member of the
Royal Academy of Sciences of *Paris*, and also of the Oeconomical Society at *Berne*.
Very early in life Dr. *Templeman* was afflicted with severe paroxysms of an asthma†,
which eluded the force of all that either his own skill, or that of the most eminent physicians then living, could suggest to him; and it continued to harrass him till
his death, which happened *Sept.* 23, 1769. He was esteemed a person of great learning,
particularly with respect to languages, spoke *French* with great fluency, and left the
character of a humane, generous, and polite member of society‡. Of his two brothers,
Giles is now rector of *Winborn St. Giles* and of *Chessilborn*, in the county of *Dorset*, to
which he was presented by the Earl of *Shaftesbury* and Lord *Rivers*. *Nathaniel*, solicitor of *Lincoln's Inn*, one of the sixty clerks in Chancery, and one of the commissioners
of hackney coaches, died *Dec.* 21, 1774. Dr. *Templeman's* uncle *William* was also an
attorney, and was clerk of the peace for the county of *Dorset* from the accession of *George*
II. to the time of his death in 1754. He married *Elizabeth* daughter of *Andrew Purchase*, alderman of *Dorchester*, and great grand-daughter to Bishop *Ironside*, by whom he
had four sons, now living: *William*, steward to the late Prince of *Wales* for *Dorset* and
Somerset for several years to the time of the Prince's death, and now one of the Commissioners of the Lottery; *Nathaniel*, rector of *Almer* and *Loders* 1753-4, and of *The Holy
Trinity* and *St. Peter* in *Dorchester*, 1781; *Richard*, rector of *St. James*, *Shaftesbury*,
and of *Compton Abbas* or *West Compton*; and *John*, an attorney-at-law in *Dorchester*.

" language, in the manner of our Philosophical Transactions; a pamphlet of 2s. or 2s. 6d. once in
" three months. In a dearth of new things on each of those heads, to extract out of the *French*
" Memoirs, *German* Ephemerides, &c. such things as shall appear to the Society to be useful dis-
" coveries or observations, and not sufficiently known or attended to. The greatest difficulty lying
" on us is the choice of proper persons to execute this design; some being too much taken up in bu-
" siness, and others justly exceptionable as being untractable, presumptuous, and overbearing.
" The men of business, however, will be of some use to us, in communicating remarkable cases
" and occurrences. Such a work will require a great number of hands; and besides good abilities,
" it will be necessary they should be good sort of men too." *MS. Letter.*
* This circumstance is taken from one of his own letters, in which he adds, " All my golden
" dream is at an end; for though I have the satisfaction to have the applause of those whose judge-
" ment I value, yet the generality of the world do not give me such encouragement as even to
" pay my expences. I could rail heartily; but it signifies nothing for poor *Bayes* to fume, when
" the upper gallery is disposed to hiss and pelt." *MS. Letter.*
† In 1745 he mentioned this disorder to a medical friend as returning more violently and frequently than ever, and in regular attacks like an ague. His friends thought him in a galloping
consumption; and by their advice he went to *Hampstead* to drink asses milk. " After lodging
" there," he says, " to no manner of purpose more than a month, I returned to town, and now
" began to think I had nothing else to do but to apply to quackery, and hesitated a little betwixt
" *Ward* and the Bishop of *Cloyne*. I concluded, however, that the first place was due to the Church,
" and accordingly entered upon Tar-water." *MS. Letter.*
‡ It may not be improper to distinguish Dr. *Templeman* from Mr. *Thomas Templeman*, the author of
" Engraved Tables, containing Calculations of the number of square Feet and People in the several
" Kingdoms of the World;" who was a writing-master in the town of *St. Edmund's Bury*. Both are
often confounded, and the latter often appears in quotations with the Doctor's degree of the former.
There was no consanguinity betwixt the Doctor and this man's family,

" dom, and the Laws relating thereto ; with the Proceed-
" ings of the House of Commons thereupon ; publiſhed by
" their Order※," folio ; " The *Roman* Antiquities of *Diony-*
" *ſius Halicarnaſſenſis*, tranſlated into *Engliſh*, with Notes
" and Diſſertations†, by *Edward Spelman*‡, eſq." 4 vols.
4to ; *Vertue's* " Catalogue of King *James* the Second's Col-
" lection of Pictures, Buſts, Statues, &c." 4to ; " A State

* " This report deſerves to be more known. Though it produced no effect, yet it
" diſplayed ſuch a ſpirit of enquiry, and ſuch a thorough knowledge of ſo nice and im-
" portant a ſubject, that it would have done honour to the Royal Society, with Sir *Iſaac*
" *Newton* at their head. The late Lord *Carysfort* was Chairman of the Committee. I
" think I have ſeen an article in the *Encyclopedie*, that *Alfred* (or ſome other
" monarch) obliged all *England* to uſe the ſame weights and meaſures, which they
" gravely obſerve to be a very proper and deſirable practice. But *Engliſhmen* often like
" better to ſuffer the inconveniences of following their own fancies, than ſubmit to be-
" neficial reſtraints." *T. F.*

† Namely, " A Diſſertation concerning the Arrival of *Æneas* in *Italy*;" and " A
" Fragment‡‡ out of the Sixth Book of *Polybius* ; containing a Diſſertation upon
" Government in general, particularly applied to that of the *Romans* ; together with
" a Deſcription of the ſeveral powers of the Conſuls, Senate, and People of *Rome*,
" tranſlated from the *Greek*, with notes ; to which is prefixed a Preface, wherein the
" Syſtem of *Polybius* is applied to the Government of *England* ; and to the abovemen-
" tioned Fragment concerning the Powers of the Senate is annexed a Diſſertation upon
" the Conſtitution of it."

‡ Of *High Houſe*, near *Rougham*, *Norfolk* ; a lineal deſcendant of the famous Sir
Henry Spelman, who was his great great grandfather. Mr. *Spelman* was alſo the
tranſlator of *Xenophon's* " Expedition of *Cyrus*, 1740 ‡‡," 2 vols. 8vo ; which he
dedicated to Lord *Lovell*, whom he celebrates for his learning and great taſte. Mr.
Spelman died *March* 12, 1767.—" I happened to fall in with him once for a ſhort time
" at Dr. *Taylor's*, in *Amen Corner*. When I ſaw the Doctor next, he told me that
" *Spelman* aſked him who I was ; and being told that I was fellow of a college, he ſaid,
" ' Good God, doth any fellow of a college know any thing of *Greek* ?' It happened that
" I had attempted to ſet him right in a paſſage that he had totally miſtaken. His ſpeech
" was certainly a curious one, as Dr. *Taylor* had been of the order reprobated almoſt all
" his life. I ſhould have thought it rude to have ſaid the ſame of country gentlemen,
" though they are not obliged to underſtand *Greek*, which can hardly be ſaid of gownſ-
" men without affront, yet I underſtand the ſpeech was intended as a compliment to
" me." *T. F.*

‡‡ Originally publiſhed in 1743 without a name. " I had my reaſons," ſays Mr. *Spelman*, " for
" not putting my name to the book, though my bookſeller thought fit to annex my name, or ſome-
" thing like my name, to what he called a ſecond edition, without my knowledge, and to add to it
" a moſt impertinent thing of his own." What the " moſt impertinent thing" added by the bookſeller was, or whether there really was a ſecond edition, I have not been able to diſcover.—Mr.
Bowyer afterwards printed for Mr. *Spelman* a few copies of " A Diſſertation on the Preſence of the
" Patricians in the *Tributa Comitia*," 4to, which were given to his friends.
‡‡ The original publiſher was R. *Wellington*. It was reprinted in one volume 1776.

" of

" of Facts in Defence of his Majesty's Right to certain Fee
" Farm Rents in the County of *Norfolk*," 4to. by *P. C.*
Webb *, esq. (only 100 copies); "A Letter to Dr. *Stukeley*;"
" *Kymber* †, a Monody, to Sir *Armine Wodehouse*, bart. by
" Mr. *Potter* ‡," 4to ; " Imitations of *Horace*, by *Thomas*
" *Nevile* ‖, M. A. Fellow of *Jesus College, Cambridge*," 8vo ;
two editions of " Sketches, or Essays on various subjects,
" by *Launcelot Temple*, Esq." [Dr. *John Armstrong* §]; a
seventh

* Of whom, see under the year 1760.

† A panegyric on Sir *Armine* and his ancestors.

‡ Who has since favoured the publick with elegant translations of *Æschylus* and of a considerable part of *Euripides*.

‖ In 1767 this excellent Poet obliged the world with a translation of "The Georgics
" of *Virgil*," from the *Cambridge* press ; and in 1769 completed " his design of fami-
" liarising to the young Reader the *Roman* Satire consistently with the more immediate
" aim of delineating present manners," by his Imitations of *Juvenal* and *Persius*.

§ This gentleman, who was born in *Castleton* parish, *Roxburghshire*, where his father and brother were ministers, compleated his education in the university of
Edinburgh, where he took his degree in physic, *Feb.* 4, 1732, with much reputation ; and published his Thesis, as the forms of that University require ; the
subject was " De Tabe purulenta." In 1735 he published a little humourous fugitive pamphlet in 8vo. printed for *J. Wilford*, intituled, " An Essay for abridging
" the Study of Physick ; to which is added a Dialogue betwixt *Hygeia, Mercury,*
" and *Pluto*, relating to the Practice of Physick, as it is managed by a certain illustrious
" Society. As also an Epistle from *Usbek* the *Persian*, to *Joshua Ward*, esq." The
dedication runs thus : " To the Antacademic Philosophers, to the generous Despisers of
" the Schools, to the deservedly-celebrated *Joshua Ward, John Moor*, and the
" rest of the numerous Sect of Inspired Physicians, this little work is humbly in-
" scribed, by their most devoted servant, and zealous Admirer." This piece contains
much fun and drollery ; in the dialogue, he has caught the very spirit of *Lucian*. It is
not marked with his name, but I can, on the best authority, assert that he was the author
of it. In 1737 he published " A Synopsis of the History and Cure of Venereal Diseases,"
8vo, inscribed, in an ingenious dedication, to Dr. *Alexander Stuart*, as to " a person who
" had an indisputable right to judge severely of the performance presented to him."
This was soon followed by the " Oeconomy of Love," a poem which has much merit,
but, it must be confessed, is too strongly tinctured with the licentiousness of *Ovid*. Let
me add, however, that his maturer judgement expunged many of the luxuriances of youthful fancy, in an edition " revised and corrected by the author" in 1768. It appears by
one of the Cases on Literary Property that Mr. *Millar* paid fifty guineas for the copy-
right of this poem, which was intended as a burlesque on some didactic writers. It
has been observed of Dr. *Armstrong*, that his works have great inequalities, some of
them being possessed of every requisite to be sought after in the most perfect composition,
while others can hardly be considered as superior to the productions of mediocrity. The
" Art of preserving Health," his best performance, which was published in 1744, and
which will transmit his name to posterity as one of the first *English* writers, has been
honoured with the following testimony of a respectable critic : " To describe so difficult a
" thing,

seventh edition of Dr. *Brown's* " Eftimate ;" and a very
large

" thing, gracefully and poetically, as the effects of a diftemper on the human body,
" was referved for Dr, *Armftrong* ; who accordingly hath nobly executed it at the end of
" the third book of his Art of preferving Health, where he hath given us that pathetic
" account of the fweating ficknefs. There is a claffical correctnefs and clofenefs of ftyle'
" in this poem that are truly admirable, and the fubject is raifed and adorned by num-
" berlefs poetical images *." On this work I fhall alfo tranfcribe a beautiful elogium
from an eminent phyfician † : " Of all the poetical performances on this fubject, that
" have come to my hands, Dr. *Armftrong's Art of preferving Health* is by far the
" beft. To quote every charming defcription and beautiful paffage of this poem, one
" muft tranfcribe the whole. We cannot, however, expect new rules, where the prin-
" cipal defign was to raife and warm the heart into a compliance with the folid pre-
" cepts of the ancients, which he has enforced with great ftrength and elegance. And,
" upon the whole, he has convinced us, by his own example, that we ought not to
" blame Antiquity for acknowledging
         " One power of phyfic, melody, and fong."
In 1746 Dr. *Armftrong* was appointed one of the phyficians to the Hofpital for Lame
and Sick Soldiers behind *Buckingham Houfe.* In 1751 he publifhed his poem " on
" Benevolence," in folio ; and in 1753, " Tafte, an Epiftle to a young Critic."
In 1758 appeared " Sketches, or Effays on various fubjects, by *Launcelot Temple,* efq. in
" two parts." In this production above-mentioned, which poffeffes much humour and
knowledge of the world, and which had a remarkably rapid fale, he is fuppofed to
have been affifted by Mr. *Wilkes.* In 1760 he had the honour of being appointed
phyfician to the army in *Germany* ; where in 1761 he wrote a poem called " Day,
an Epiftle to *John Wilkes,* of *Aylefbury,* efq." In this poem, which is not collected in his works ‡, he wantonly hazarded a reflection on *Churchill* §, which drew
on him the ferpent-toothed vengeance of that fevereft of fatirifts ||, whofe embalming

* Dr. *Warton's* " Reflections on Didactic Poetry," annexed to his edition of *Virgil,* vol. I. p. 329.
† Dr. *James Mackenzie's* " Hiftory of Health, &c." third edition, *Edinburgh,* 1760, p. 227, 228.
‡ It is preferved in *Almon's* " New Foundling Hofpital for Wit, 1772," vol. V. p. 110.

§ " Efcap'd from *London* now four moons, and more,   What news to-day ?—I afk you not what rogue,
I greet gay *Wilkes* from *Fulda's* wafted fhore,   What paltry imp of fortune's now in vogue ;
Where cloath'd with woods a hundred hills afcend,   What forward blundering fool was laft preferr'd,
Where nature many a paradife has plann'd :   By mere pretence diftinguifh'd from the herd ;
A land that, e'en amid contending arms,   With what new cheat the gaping town is fmit ;
Late fmil'd with culture, and luxuriant charms;   What CRAZY SCRIBLER reigns the prefent WIT ;
But now the hoftile fcythe has bared her foil,   What ftuff for winter the Two Booths have mixt ;
And her fad peafants ftarve for all their toil.   What bouncing Mimick grows a ROSCIUS next."

|| In almoft the laft lines of poetry which *Churchill* lived to write, after referring thofe who hinted
that he would " run his ftock of genius out" to fome writers who had obtained what he thought
unmerited celebrity, he thus pointedly concludes the catalogue with Dr. *Armftrong* :

" Let them, with ARMSTRONG, taking leave   A deep revenge, when, by Reflection led,
    of Senfe,   She draws his curtains, and looks Comfort dead,
Read mufty lectures on *Benevolence,*   Let every Mufe be gone ; in vain He turns
Or con the pages of his gaping *Day,*   And tries to pray for fleep ; an *Ætna* burns,
Where all his former fame was thrown away,   A more than *Ætna,* in his coward breaft,
Where all, but barren labour was forgot,   And Guilt, with vengeance arm'd, forbids him
And the vain ftiffnefs of a *Letter'd* SCOT ;   reft.
Let them with ARMSTRONG pafs the term of light,   Tho' foft as plumage from young Zephyr's wing,
But not one hour of darknefs ; when the night   His couch feems hard, and no relief can bring.
Sufpends this mortal coil, when Memory wakes,   INGRATITUDE hath planted daggers there,
When for our paft mifdoings Confcience takes   No good man can deferve, no brave man bear."

I make no apology for this citation ; as it will never obfcure the character of a humane, benevolent, kindly affectioned man of genius, who was incapable of the crime with which he is charged.

large impreffion of a fecond part of that popular publication, which was followed by " An Explanatory Defence"
of

or corrofive pen could deify or lampoon any man, according as he acquiefced with, or
diffented from, his political principles. It may be here obferved, that nothing appears
fo fatal to the intercourfe of friends as attentions to politicks. The cordiality which
had fubfifted between Dr. *Armftrong* and Mr. *Wilkes* was certainly interrupted, if not
diffolved, by thefe means. In 1770 Dr. *Armftrong* publifhed a collection of " Mifcel-
" lanies" in two volumes ; containing, 1. " The Art of preferving Health ;" 2. " Of
" Benevolenee, an Epiftle to *Eumenes* ;" 3. " Tafte, an Epiftle to a young Critic,
" 1753 ;" 4. " Imitations of *Shakefpeare* and *Spenfer* ;" 5. " The Univerfal Almauac,
" by *Noureddin Ali* ;" 6. " The Forced Marriage, a Tragedy ;" 7. " Sketches." In
an advertifement to thefe volumes, Dr. *Armftrong* fays, he " has at laft taken the trou-
" ble upon him to collect them, and to have them printed under his own infpection ;
" a tafk that he had long avoided ; and to which he would hardly have fubmitted him-
" felf at laft, but for the fake of preventing their being, fome time hereafter, expofed
" in a ragged mangled condition, and loaded with more faults than they originally had :
" while [when] it might be impoffible for him, by the change perhaps of one letter, to
" recover a whole period from the moft contemptible nonfenfe. Along with fuch pieces as
" he had formerly offered to the public, he takes this opportunity of prefenting it with
" feveral others ; fome of which had lain by him many years. What he has loft, and
" efpecially what he has deftroyed, would, probably enough, have been better received
" by the great majority of readers, than any thing he has publifhed. But he never
" courted the public. He wrote chiefly for his own amufement ; and becaufe he found
" it an agreeable and innocent way of fometimes paffing an idle hour. He has always
" moft heartily defpifed the opinion of the mobility, from the loweft to the higheft : and
" if it is true, what he has fometimes been told, that the beft judges are on his fide, he
" defires no more in the article of fame and renown as a writer. If the beft judges of
" this age honour him with their approbation, all the worft too of the next will favour
" him with theirs ; when by heaven's grace he'll be too far beyond the reach of their
" unmeaning praifes to receive any difguft from them." In 1771 he publifhed " A
" fhort Ramble through fome Parts of *France* and *Italy*, by *Launcelot Temple* ;" and in
1773, in his own name, a quarto pamphlet, under the title of " Medical Effays ;" towards the conclufion of which, he accounts for his not having fuch extenfive practice as
fome of his brethren, from his not being qualified to employ the ufual means, from a
ticklifh ftate of fpirits, and a diftempered excefs of fenfibility. He complains much of
the behaviour of fome of his brethren, of the herd of criticks, and particularly of the
Reviewers. He died in *September*, 1779 ; and, to the no fmall furprife of his friends,
left behind him more than 3000l. faved out of a very moderate income arifing princ.pally
from his half-pay. By the favour of a refpectable Phyfician, whom I am proud to call
my friend, I am enabled to add fome further traits to the character of this ingeni us
writer : " I was early acquainted with Dr. *Armftrong*, have vifited him at his lodgings,
" knew many of his intimates, have met him in company, but from my having vifited
" the metropolis fo feldom fince my refidence in *Dorfetfhire*, I was not fo well ac-
" quainted with him as I fhould otherwife have been, or wifhed to be. He always ap-
" peared to me (and I was confirmed in this opinion by that of his moft intimate friends)
" a man of learning and genius, of confiderable abilities in his profeffion, of great bene-

O o   " violence

of it; *Walker's* " Narrative of the Siege of *Londonderry*," republished by Dr. *Brown*, who did all he could to reform and revive us, " as a useful lesson to the present times, " with a prefatory address to the public," 8vo; " Lec- " tures concerning Oratory, delivered at *Trinity College*, " *Dublin*, by *John Lawson**, D. D." 8vo; and an edition of " *Cicero's Tusculan* Disputations," 8vo. In the same year a collection was published, intituled, " *Sophoclis* " Tragœdiæ Septem Scholiis Veteribus illustratæ: Cum " Versione & Notis *Thomæ Johnsoni*. Accedunt Variæ " Lectiones, & Emendationes Virorum doctorum unde- " cunque collatæ. Duobus Voluminibus." Four † only of these Plays were printed by Mr. *Bowyer*; but in those the publick are indebted to him for more than barely the manual operation, as is evident from the introduction ex- tracted below‡. I have his copy of the Seven Plays, im-

proved

" volence and goodness of heart, fond of associating with men of parts and genius, but " indolent and inactive, and therefore totally unqualified to employ the means that usu- " ally lead to medical employment, or to elbow his way through a crowd of competitors. " An intimate friendship always subsisted between the Doctor and the Author of *The* " *Seasons*, as well as with other gentlemen of learning and genius; he was intimate " with, and respected by, Sir *John Pringle*, to the time of his death."

 * Dr. *Lawson* died *January* 9, 1759.

 † *Ajax Flagellifer*; *Electra*; *Antigone*; *Trachiniæ*. The other three, which were printed by Mr. *Pote* at *Eton*, are *Oedipus Tyrannus*, or rather *Rex Oedipus*, *Philoctetes*, and *Oedipus Coloneus*.

 ‡ " Typographus Lectori S. Ex septem *Sophoclis* Tragœdiis *Ajacem* et *Electram* " edidit *Johnsonus*, A. D. 1705, quibus versionem, notas, et variantes lectiones adjecit: " Dein *Antigonen*, et *Trachinias* cum notis, sed absque variis lectionibus, A. D. 1708. " Hæ quatuor fabulæ junctim recusæ sunt A. D. 1746, quibus tres cæteræ accessere cum " versione itidem *Johnsoni*, et scholiaste in *Oedipo* non ante vulgato. Neve in hac quasi " posthuma editione tribus fabulis sua deessent notarum adjumenta, vir quidam ingenio " et doctrina solertissimus plurimas congessit, unde *Johnsoni* operam in hac parte lenius " desideraremus. Ea vero editione jam divendita, et nova flagitata, me rogat bibliopola, " ut aliquem commendarem, qui talem moliretur. Cumque nemo inveniretur, nisi qui " esset aut impar oneri, aut mercedi plusquam par, me tandem hortatur, ut ipse pro " officio aliquem pannum attexerem, ne liber gratiâ novitatis penitus destitueretur. " Dum schedæ igitur sub prelo properantur, imo sub duobus prelis, variantes lectiones,

" quas

proved throughout with marginal obfervations; the *Ajax*, in particular, is accurately corrected in the hand-writing of Mr. *Markland**. In revifing the *Ajax* and *Electra*, Mr. *Bowyer* had the affiftance of Mr. *Palairet†*. The pains,

" quas *Johnfonus* ad finem duarum fabularum appofuerat, fuis paginis fubjeci, quo fa-
" cilius oculos allicerent, et effent ad ufum promptiores. Tres tabulas, duos fcilicet
" *Oedipos* et *Antigonen*, vir doctiffimus *Joannes Burtonus, Etonenfis, S. T. P.* edidit, di-
" cam, an editurus eft, aut alius quifpiam fub ejus aufpiciis. Inde lectiones in *Anti-*
" *gonen* tranftuli; in aliis utrifque idem facturus, nifi quod, cum fub alio prelo effent
" elaboratæ, nollem arroganter nimis falcem in alienas fegetes immittere. Verfionem
" in quibus plerifque lccis *Johnfonus* refingendam admonuit, refinxi; quod non in om-
" nibus, fatendum eft non bene provifis confiliis id deberi. In hac parte fperabam
" aliquid auxilii ex editione *Londinenfi,* A. D. 1722, in 12°. cujus dedicationi fubfcri-
" buntur literæ initiales *A. B.* Sed in *Ajace* et *Electra* verfionem *Johnfoni,* quæ in
" lucem tum prodierat, arripuit, in cæteris *Winfemii.* Hanc κατὰ πόδας fequitur editio
" *Glafguenfis,* A. D. 1745, nifi quod *Johnfoni* notulas in quatuor tragœdias ad finem
" adjunxerit; et tamen collectanea, quæ ad cæteras acceffere, omifit. Emendationes
" in textum et fcholia undecunque potui, κατὰ κτῆσιν τȣ καιρȣ, conrafi, et meffem, quam
" vir doctus ad duos *Oedipos* et *Philoctetem* contulerat, manipulo auxi. In cæteris tra-
" gœdiis notæ, quæ *T. J.* nomine non funt infignitæ, nunc primum acceffere. Inter
" has quædam loca in fcholiis ad *Ajacem* videbis feliciter reftituta a viro docto anony-
" mo; unde facile fenties quam multa reftant reftituenda. Dudum conqueftus eft *Hen-*
" *ricus Stephanus* in *Schediafmate* II. c. 13, errores quamplurimos ex compendiaria
" MSStorum fcriptura effe ortos. Quales quidem non nifi eodem fonte, ex quo pro-
" fluxere, funt diluendi. Ex utroque prelo novi errores accrevere, quos petimus ut
" æquo animo feras, memor nos aliquam materiam futuro editori fuffeciffe, et paulu-
" lum incuriæ tumultuaria quadam diligentia compenfaffe."

* In a Letter to Mr. *Bowyer,* dated *March* 6, 1758, Mr. *Markland* fays, " I fee you
" have altered the order of the Plays in *Sophocles,* and put *Antigone* in the third place,
" inftead cf *Oedipus Tyrannus.* I fuppofe this was done by the command of my lords
" the bookfellers; and the *Trachiniæ* I fhould judge to be the laft in your edition, by
" the *Finis,* and the *Addenda* out of *Sam. Petit,* who, though an excellent fcholar, had
" juft as much tafte of the Poets as a cow has of a leg of mutton. I would fend you a
" gallant correction of that place in the *Trachiniæ,* v. 1176. Πρὸς τῶν φυιόντων, &c.
" which puzzled *Johnfon* fo much, and fo juftly; but it is troublefome to me to write,
" having the gout in both hands and both feet, and not able to ftir out of my chair to
" get at any book."

† I fhall prefent the reader with a fhort correfpondence on this fubject: *June* 29, 1756.
" Doleo te, vir doctiffime, adverfa valetudine uti; et vehementer vereor ne aliquis
" accedat morbi tui fomes ex fchedis *Sophoclis* perlegendis: Imprefentiarum ut parcas
" tibi rogo & obteftor, & ut mihi remittas fchedam, quam habes, inemendatam. Ipfe
" eam relegam, & tuæ opis, quantum potero, vicem præftabo. Ut Deus falutem tibi
" reftituat orat ex animo   G. BOWYER."

" Cariffime vir, melius me habeo; correxi fchedam, et hodie poftmeridiem per penni-
" poftam tibi remifi. Ut profpera valetudine utaris ex animo apprecor. Vale, meque
" tui ftudiofum amare perge.   PALAIRET."

however,

however, beftowed on this edition were moft ungracioufly acknowledged by a fubfequent editor * in 1775.

Towards the clofe of the year 1758, a report was circulated that Mr. *Bowyer* was about to retire from bufinefs; a report which gave rife to the following correfpondence with the celebrated *Englifh Rofcius*. The letters, I believe, will not be thought a difcredit to the memory of either of them.

1. To D. GARRICK, Efq. in *Southampton Street, Covent Garden*.

" SIR,   *Nov.* .... 1758.

" The laft time I faw you, I had the honour of your
" hand.   I am fince furprifed to underftand that you have
" carried to the Speaker the intereft of your heart, in behalf
" of another, to print the Votes for him.   You did fo, I
" doubt not, on a report that I was to print them no more;
" a report raifed without the leaft foundation, and propa-
" gated by many who wifh it true.   But might not I have
" expected from your humanity, from your knowledge of
" the world, may I add, from the knowledge you were pleafed
" to exprefs of me, that you would have inquired into the
" truth of the report, even at the fhop where I had the
" pleafure of feeing you, before you took fuch a ftep, how-
" ever undefignedly, againft me ?

" As you did not defign me an injury, fo it will be faid
" you have done me none.   Sir, I have heard of a perfon

* " In textu *Græco* exhibendo, editionem *Johnfonianam* fecuti fumus.... Vix
" dici poteft quam infinita SCHOLIORUM farrago in poftrema editione, quæ prodiit
" *Lond.* 1758, in duobus voluminibus, 8vo. apparuit. Omnia ita vitiata & tranf-
" pofita erant, ut rudis indigeftaque potius vocum moles, quam *Sophoclis* expofitio,
" viderentur. Hæc jam fub incudem revocata, & maximo cum labore recenfita, nunc
" primùm ad fuam paginam proprio magis juftoque ordine difponuntur. In reliquis
" expurgandis longiùs quidem elaboraviffemus, fi temporis anguftiæ aliæque curæ non
" impediviffent. *J. T.*" This quotation needs no comment. If this editor had taken
the text of *Bowyer* for his copy inftead of that of *Johnfon*, he would have faved himfelf
the trouble of weeding out *many* of the typographical blunders he complains of.

" who

" who was blinded while he was blooded, which has been
" pretty much my cafe.   The ftanders-by cried out in con-
" cern for him, *He is fainting, he is dying* ; till at length
" the poor man died in reality.   This remains to be my
" cafe.   If it fhould be fo, I fubmit it to you, whether
" you would not be acceffary to the legal death of, Sir,
" your moft obedient humble fervant,   W. BOWYER."

2. Mr. GARRICK's * anfwer, without date, but received *Nov.*
29, 1758.

" SIR,
" I have been in the country, and did not receive your
" letter till laft night.   I was much furprifed at it indeed ;
" and

---

* This excellent actor, whofe name will be ever held in refpect by the admirers of
theatrical reprefentations, was the fon of *Peter Garrick*, a captain in the army, who
generally refided at *Litchfield*.   He was born at *Hereford*, where his father was on a
recruiting party, and baptized *February* 20, 1716, as appears by the church regifter of
the parifh of *All Souls* in that city.   His mother's maiden name was *Clough*, daughter
to one of the vicars in *Litchfield* cathedral.   At the age of ten years he was put under
the care of Mr. *Hunter*, mafter of the grammar-fchool at *Litchfield* ; and very early
fhewed his attachment to dramatic entertainments, having in the year 1727 reprefented
the character of Serjeant *Kite* in *The Recruiting Officer* with great applaufe.   From fchool
he went to *Lifbon* to vifit his uncle, but ftayed only a fhort time there before he returned
to *England*, on which he went again to Mr. *Hunter*, and in 1735 became the pupil of
Mr. *Samuel Johnfon*, who about that time undertook to teach the claffics to a certain
number of young gentlemen.   But even under this moft able tutor, the vivacity of his
character unfitted him for ferious purfuits, and his attention to the drama prevailed over
every other object.   After a time, Mr. *Johnfon* grew tired of teaching ; and Mr. *Garrick* being defirous of a more active life, the tutor and pupil took the refolution to
quit *Litchfield*, and try their fortunes in the metropolis.   They accordingly fet
out together on the 2d of *March*, 1736 ; and on the 9th of the fame month,
Mr. *Garrick* was entered of *Lincoln's Inn*, it being then intended that the law
fhould be his profeffion.   Having had a recommendation from Mr. *Walmfley* to Mr.
Colfon, mafter of the fchool at *Rochefter*, he, on the death of his uncle, about 1737,
went directly thither, with a view to finifh his education.   In the company of fo rational
a philofopher as Mr. *Colfon*, he was imperceptibly and gradually improved in the talent
of thinking and reafoning ; nor were the example and precepts of fo wife a man vainly
beftowed on a mind fo acute as that of *Garrick*.   His father died foon after, and was not
long furvived by his mother.   He then engaged in the wine trade, in partnerfhip with
his brother *Peter Garrick* ; but this connection lafting but a fhort time, he refolved to

try

" and think you have not well confidered the matter, or
" you would not have been fo warm in your expoftulations.

" The

try his talents on the ftage, and in the fummer of 1741 went down to *Ipfwich*, where he acted with great applaufe under the name of *Lyddal*. The part which he firft performed was that of *Aboan* in the tragedy of *Oroonoko*. After a fummer fpent in the country, he determined to venture on the *London* ftage. He had now effayed his powers, and confidered himfelf as worthy to appear in an high form on any theatre; but it is generally faid, that the then directors of *Drury Lane* and *Covent Garden* could not be induced to entertain the fame fentiments. He was therefore obliged to accept the offer of Mr. *Giffard*, mafter of *Goodman's Fields* play-houfe, who engaged him; and he made his firft appearance there on the 19th of *October*, 1741, with great fuccefs, in the character of *Richard* the Third*. The feeing a young man, in no more than his twenty-fourth year, reaching at one fingle ftep to that height of perfection which maturity of years and long practical experience had not been able to beftow on the then capital performers of the *English* ftage, was a phænomenon which could not but become the object of univerfal fpeculation, and as univerfal admiration. The theatres towards the court-end of the town were on this occafion deferted, perfons of all ranks flocking to *Goodman's Fields*, where Mr. *Garrick* continued to act till the clofe of the feafon, when, having very advantageous terms offered him for performing in *Dublin* during fome part of the fummer, he went over thither, where he found the fame juft homage paid to his merit, which he had received from his own countrymen. In the enfuing winter, however, he engaged himfelf to Mr. *Fleetwood*, manager of *Drury Lane* playhoufe, in which theatre he continued till the year 1745, in the winter of which he again went over to *Ireland*, and continued there through the whole of that feafon, being joint manager with Mr. *Sheridan* in the direction and profits of the theatre royal in *Smock Alley*. From thence he returned to *England*, and was engaged for the feafon of 1746 with the late Mr. *Rich*, patentee of *Covent Garden*. This was his laft performance as an hired actor; for in the clofe of that feafon, Mr. *Fleetwood's* patent for the management of *Drury Lane* being expired, and that gentleman having no inclination farther to purfue a defign by which, from his want of acquaintance with the proper conduct of it, or fome other reafons, he had already confiderably impaired his fortune, Mr. *Garrick*, in conjunction with Mr. *Lacy*, purchafed the property of that theatre, together with the renewal of the patent, and in the winter of 1747, opened it with the beft part of Mr. *Fleetwood's* former company, and the great additional ftrength of Mr. *Barry*, Mrs. *Pritchard*, and Mrs. *Cibber*, from *Covent Garden*. In this ftation Mr. *Garrick* continued until the year 1776, with an interval of two years, from 1763 to 1765, which he devoted to travelling abroad; and, both by his conduct as a manager, and his unequalled merit as an actor, from year to year, added to the entertainment of the public, which with an indefatigable affiduity he confulted. Nor were the publick by any means ungrateful in returns for that affiduity.

---

* It appears by *Davies's* " Life of *Garrick*," that the audience at firft were totally at a lofs whether to clap or hifs, &c. This deferves to be infifted on, as it fhews how little qualified people are to judge *of any thing* at firft. Afterwards, when half a dozen people had thought proper to declare their approbation, then fervility, fafhion, &c. followed of courfe, and joined the cry. I know nothing of mufic; but it is certain that the merit of the *Italian* mufic, which, like their painting, is undoubtedly the beft in the world, was not only not perceived in *England* at firft (and in *France* not yet), but fuch people as *Addifon* endeavoured publickly to decry it as bad. *T. F.*

6

By

" The fact is this—I was told by a man whom I regard and
" would serve with justice, that the *person* who printed the
" Votes

By the warm and deserved encouragement which they gave him, he was raised to that state of ease and affluence to which it must be the wish of every honest heart to see superior excellence exalted. After his return from his travels, Mr. *Garrick* declined the performance of any new character; but continued to appear every season in some of his favourite parts until the year 1776, when, satisfied with the wealth he had acquired and the fame which he had established, in familiarity with many of the most respectable persons of the kingdom, he retired to the enjoyment of repose from the fatigues of his profession, and quitted the stage on the 10th day of *June*, 1776, after performing the character of *Don Felix*, in Mrs. *Centlivre's* comedy of *The Wonder*. At this period the stone, a disorder to which he had been long subject, began to make such inroads on his constitution, that the happiness which he expected from retirement was often interrupted, and sometimes destroyed, by the violence of the pain he endured. He had been used to try the effects of quack medicines, to relieve him from the torments which he suffered, and it has been thought that his health received much injury from this injudicious mode of tampering with his malady. At *Christmas* 1778 he visited earl *Spencer* at *Althorpe*, where he was taken ill, but recovered sufficiently to return to *London*, and died at his house in *The Adelphi*, after a few days illness, on the 20th of *January* 1779. His body was interred with great funeral pomp in *Westminster Abbey*, on the 1st of *February* following. Mr. *Garrick* in his person was low, yet well-shaped, and neatly proportioned; and, having added the qualifications of dancing * and fencing to that natural gentility of manner which no art can bestow, but with which our great mother Nature endows many even from infancy, his deportment was constantly easy, natural, and engaging. His complection was dark, and the features of his face, which were pleasingly regular, were animated by a full black eye, brilliant and penetrating. His voice was clear, melodious, and commanding; and, although it might not possess the strong overbearing powers of Mr. *Mossop's*, or the musical sweetness of Mr. *Barry's*, yet it appeared to have a much greater compass of variety than either; and, from Mr. *Garrick's* judicious manner of conducting it, enjoyed that articulation and piercing distinctness, which rendered it equally intelligible, even to the most distant parts of an audience, in the gentle whispers of murmuring love, the half-smothered accents of infelt passion, or the professed and sometimes awkward concealments of an aside speech in comedy, as in the rants of rage, the darings of despair, or all the open violence of tragical enthusiasm.

Were it our office to record the failings of Mr. *Garrick*, we could only persuade ourselves to observe that they were chiefly such as are overlooked in characters of less distinguished opulence and celebrity. We forbear therefore to violate his fame by a safe but ungenerous recapitulation of petty errors; adding only in excuse for his well-known vanity, that perhaps no man who had been fed with such excess of praise, would have exhibited fewer marks of self-approbation. We hope, indeed, we may be forgiven, if we dwell longer on a singular inconsistence in his character, which has been often mentioned, but never fairly stated. He has been loudly praised for liberality, and as loudly censured on the score of avarice. Perhaps the alternate predominance of qualities, so opposite in their natures, may be thus accounted for. In any exigence that presented itself on a sudden, he was readily generous, because he knew benevolence was the most

* I am told that he had no ear for music, though he observed perfect time in dancing.   T. F.

popular.

" Votes had refigned it. Upon which, I wrote to Mr. *George*
" *Onflow*, the Speaker's fon, to recommend a perfon, *if the*
" *fact*

popular of virtues, and that the exertion of it would be expected from the poffeffor of a
fortune extenfive as his own. But this hafty impulfe was occafionally blafted by intermediate reflection. During the interval that fometimes neceffarily paffed between the
promife and the act of difburfement, the tedious procefs by which he had acquired a fum
equal to that he was expected to part with, impreffed itfelf forcibly on his imagination.
It was not till then that his difpofition inclined to parfimony *. This ungraceful narrownefs, this inglorious repentance, is often detected among thofe in whofe thoughts their
own gradual advance towards wealth is almoft uppermoft; and the frequent occurrence
of an idea, like this, to Mr. *Garrick*, will affift us in reconciling the contradictory tales
of his deficiency and excefs of bounty; for to deny that he was fometimes magnificent
in his donations, would be to refufe his memory a tribute that can only be withheld as
the expence of notoriety and truth. Such, however, was the fate of his pecuniary favours, that he often forfeited the gratitude due to them, through his backwardnefs in
yielding what he had pledged himfelf to beftow, and did beftow at laft. By fome, indeed, he has been charged with raifing hopes of relief, and finally difappointing them.
This charge however, if true, can be imputed only to a ftronger and lefs refiftible operation of the caufe already mentioned. In the mean time, his example ferves to fhew
us how refolutely we ought to feize the moment that difpofes our wavering natures
to benevolence, as fecond thoughts are not always propitious to the interefts of humanity. We may conclude by adding, that deliberation, fo ufeful on many occafions, in
refpect to poetry and charity, exerted a fatal influence over *Akenfide* and *Garrick*. It
unftrung the lyre of the one, and contracted the heart of the other.

To Mr. *Garrick's* reputation as an actor, the concern of the public at having loft
him, bears a ftronger teftimony than panegyrick, in any other form, could fupply. As
to his particular *forte* or fuperior caft in acting, it would be perhaps as difficult to determine it, as it would be to defcribe minutely his feveral excellences in the very different
parts in which he at different times thought proper to appear. Particular fuperiority
was fwallowed up in his univerfality; and fhould it even be contended, that there have
been performers equal to him in their own refpective *fortes* of playing, yet even *their*
partizans muft acknowledge, that there never exifted any one performer that came near
his excellence in fo great a variety of parts. Every paffion of the human breaft feemed
fubjected to his powers of expreffion; even Time itfelf appeared to ftand ftill, or advance,
as he would have it. Of this no one can be ignorant who ever faw him in the feveral
characters of *Lear* or *Hamlet*, *Richard*, *Dorilas*, *Romeo*, or *Lufignan*; in his *Ranger*,
Bays, *Drugger*, *Kitely*, *Brute*, or *Benedict*. During the courfe of his management,
the publick were much obliged to him for his indefatigable labour in the conduct of,

* There can be little doubt of his avarice, from the general charge; at leaft it is up-hill work
to prove fuch an one's generofity. Generofity is of too great notoriety to be queftioned. The Marquis of *Granby* might be unjuft in the exercife of it, preferably to paying his debts; but nobody
makes a doubt whether he was avaricious. The Duke of *Marlborough* paid his debts, yet it is not a
queftion whether he was generous or no. The fact is, *Garrick* died worth 140,000*l.* all of his own
getting, in lefs than 40 years. Suppofe he had died worth only 130,000*l.* would not that have
been enough to *have left behind him?* and no doubt 10,000*l.* properly beftowed, muft have eftablifhed his or *Marlborough's* fame. I don't fay *Garrick* was obliged to do this. But neither is the
world obliged to admire his generofity, if he had it not: it is plain they were willing enough to applaud the merit he undoubtedly poffeffed. *T. F.*

" *fact was true.* Now, Sir, upon my honour, I did not
" know that *you* were the printer of the Votes; and more-
" over,

the theatre, and in the pains he took to difcover and gratify their tafte ; and, though the fituation of a manager will perpetually be liable to attacks from difappointed au- thors and undeferving performers ; yet, it is apparent, from the barrennefs both of plays and players of merit for fome years at the oppofite theatre, that Mr. *Garrick* cannot have refufed acceptance to many of either kind, that were any way deferving of the town's regard. In fhort, notwithftanding this is not the age of either dramatic or theatrical genius, the pains he took in rearing many tender plants, added feveral valuable performers to the *Englifh* ftage, whofe firft bloffoms were far from promifing fo fair a fruit as they have fince produced :—and among the feveral dramatic pieces which made their firft appearance on the theatre in *Drury Lane*, there are very few, whofe authors have not acknowledged themfelves greatly indebted to Mr. *Garrick* for ufeful hints or advantageous alterations, to which their fuccefs has in great meafure been owing. Add to this the revival of many pieces of the more early writers ; pieces poffeffed of great merit, but which had, either through the neglect or ignorance of other managers, lain for a long time unemployed and unregarded. But there is one part of theatrical conduct which ought unqueftionably to be recorded to Mr. *Garrick's* honour, fince the caufe of virtue and morality, and the formation of public manners, are very confiderably depen- dent on it, and that is, the zeal with which he ever aimed to banifh from the ftage all thofe plays which carry with them an immoral tendency, and to prune from thofe which do not abfolutely on the whole promote the interefts of vice fuch fcenes of licen- tioufnefs and libertinifm, as a redundancy of wit and too great livelinefs of imagination have induced fome of our comic writers to indulge themfelves in, and to which the fympa- thetic difpofition of an age of gallantry and intrigue had given a fanction. The purity of the *Englifh* ftage was certainly much more fully eftablifhed during the adminiftration of this theatrical minifter, than it had ever been during preceding managements : for what the public tafte had itfelf in fome meafure begun, he, by keeping that tafte within its proper channel, and feeding it with a pure and untainted ftream, feemed to have completed ; and to have endeavoured as much as poffible to adhere to the promife made in the Prologue above quoted, and which was fpoken at the firft opening of that theatre under his direction,

" Bade fcenic virtue form the rifing age,
" And truth diffufe her radiance from the ftage."

His fuperiority to all others in one branch of excellence, however, muft not make us overlook the rank in which he is entitled to ftand as to another ; nor our remembrance of his having been the *firft actor* living, induce us to forget, that he was far from being the *laft writer*. Notwithftanding the numberlefs and laborious avocations attending on his profeffion as an actor, and his ftation as a manager, yet ftill his active genius was perpe- tually burfting forth in various little productions both dramatic and poetical, whofe merit cannot but make us regret his want of time for more extenfive and important works. Of thefe he has publicly avowed himfelf the author of thirty-five *, fome of which are originals, and the reft tranflations or alterations from other authors, with a defign to adapt them to the prefent tafte of the public. Befides thefe, Mr. *Garrick* was

* See thefe enumerated in an improved edition of the " Companion to the Play-houfe, 1781," to which I owe the greater part of this note.

the

" over, if you had been my brother, I could not have act-
" ed with more juſtice or delicacy towards you. If the fact
" had been true, I ſhould have been willing to ſerve a per-
" ſon I regarded ; as it was not, there was no harm done,
" and you have not in the leaſt been injured. Though I am
" always deſirous to aſſiſt the man I like, and do it zealouſ-
" ly ; yet I would not knowingly do the leaſt injury, I own,
" to one who had injured me, and much leſs to Mr.
" *Bowyer*. This, I flatter myſelf, is my real character
" among thoſe who know me ; and you are really miſtaken
" if you think otherwiſe of me. I cannot poſſibly anſwer
" the laſt paragraph of your letter, becauſe I don't under-
" ſtand it * ; but if you think my letter to Mr. *Onſlow* has in
" the leaſt affected your intereſt, let me know, and I ſhall
" as readily repair the miſchief, as I have moſt ignorantly
" done it. I am, Sir, your moſt obedient humble ſervant,
" D. GARRICK.

" P. S. I write in great hurry, and you muſt excuſe it."

3. " To DAVID GARRICK, Eſq.

" SIR, *Dec.* 7, 1758.

" As I before acquitted you of any intention to do me an
" injury, ſo I acknowledge your kind readineſs to repair
" one, if you had unwittingly done me any ; I do ſo hearti-
" ly, and the rather, becauſe you have heightened my ob-

---

the author of an Ode on the death of Mr. *Pelham*, which, in leſs than ſix weeks, ran
through four editions. The Prologues, Epilogues, and Songs, which he wrote, are almoſt innumerable, and poſſeſs a conſiderable degree of happy conception and execution.
It would be in vain to attempt any enumeration of them ; and it is the leſs neceſſary, as
we cannot doubt but ſome one of his ſurviving friends will take care to give a complete
edition of his works, in ſuch a manner as will do honour to his memory.

* Mr. *Garrick's* obſervation requires ſome apology to be made for Mr. *Bowyer* ; who
evidently wrote in haſte, and meant perhaps that Mr. *G.* would in law be reckoned an
acceſſary to his death.

" ligations

" ligations with that perfonage to whom you applied,
" where I would moft wifh to have them placed.

" On the other hand, you will excufe me, I hope, for
" remonftrating *clofely* perhaps, but not *warmly*, againft
" fuffering your weight and confequence to be made ufe of,
" without having a true ftate of circumftances laid before
" you. But I find my fentiments were too cold, what-
" ever my expreffions were ; and that your heart, in the
" caufe of friendfhip, will not ftay to weigh minute confi-
" derations. Convinced, I humbly bow to that virtue
" which in your breaft fcarce knows excefs ; and if it has
" any weaknefs, is, like a complexion from fairnefs, the
" more amiable for it. I truft then to the influence of it,
" as *it believeth all things*, that you will now place me in the
" number of your moft obliged humble fervants,

" W. BOWYER."

In 1759 he printed an edition of " *Theocritus*," 8vo;
" Chronographiæ *Afiaticæ* & *Egyptiacæ* Specimen ; in quo,
" 1. Origo Chronologiæ LXX Interpretum inveftigatur ; 2.
" Confpectus totius operis exhibetur," 8vo, [by *Charles Hayes*＊,
Efq.];

* This induftrious and learned gentleman, who was known as an author only to his
intimate friends, and whofe remarkable modefty guarded his great erudition from the too
common foible of oftentation, was born in the year 1678; and in 1704 became diftinguifhed by his much efteemed " Treatife of Fluxions," printed that year in folio with his
name, the only publication to which he ever fuffered it to appear. In 1710 came out a
fmall pamphlet of his, of nineteen pages in 4to, intitled, " A New and Eafy Method to
" find out the Longitude, from the obfervation of the altitudes of the cœleftial bodies ;"
and in 1723, he publifhed in *Englifh*, in 8vo, " The Moon, a Philofophical Dialogue ;"
written in the moft genteel and polite language, and tending to fhew, that the Moon is
not a mere dark and opake body, but is miftrefs of no inconfiderable fhare of light of her
own. During a long courfe of years the management of the late *Royal African Company*
lay in a manner wholly on Mr. *Hayes* (he being chofen annually either Sub-governor, or
Deputy-governor) ; yet, in the midft of thefe important avocations, he fpent much time
and labour in making philofophical experiments, and in gratifying his thirft after general
knowledge. To his fkill in ancient and modern languages he added the knowledge of the

Hebrew;

Efq.]; " Dialogues on Sincerity, Retirement, the Golden
" Age

Hebrew; and applied himfelf affiduoufly to the ancient hiftorians, and with more particular
attention to the Sacred Writings. Endeavouring to folve the difficulties which had perplexed the Learned, he laid a plan to reduce all into chronological form, according to
what he thought to be the true order of time. He much admired that tranflation of
the Scriptures into *Greek*, which bears the name of the Septuagint: and critically examined the hiftory of that verfion compofed by *Arifteas*, which had been looked upon
by many perfons of great worth and learning as no better than a forged ftory; and
when he had completed his enquiries on this head, in 1736, he publifhed, in 8vo. " A
" Vindication of the Hiftory of the Septuagint" from the mifreprefentations of its opponents. His next work was a learned piece of criticifm, intituled, " A critical Exami-
" nation of the Holy Gofpels according to St. *Matthew* and St. *Luke*, with regard to
" the Hiftory of the Birth and Infancy of our Lord *Jefus Chrift*, 1738," 8vo. He
now returned to his favourite ftudy, the fettling of times; and, in 1741, came out
his " Differtation on the Chronology of the Septuagint: With an Appendix, fhew-
" ing, that the *Chaldean* and *Egyptian* Antiquities, hitherto efteemed fabulous, are
" perfectly confiftent with the Computations of that moft ancient Verfion of the Holy
" Scriptures," 8vo; a work of great labour and fagacity, in which the ages of
the Patriarchs, and the variation there is in this particular, between the *Hebrew*,
Septuagint, and *Jofephus*, are largely confidered; a pious regard is always retained both for the *Hebrew* and *Greek* text, and fome conjectures modeftly offered for
the integrity of them both; and thofe who read this tract will in the Appendix find
matter fufficient to fatisfy a learned curiofity, and to make them view the *Chaldean* and
Egyptian hiftories in another light than that in which they have hitherto appeared. Not
contented with going thus far, in 1757, he printed, in the fame fize, " A Supplement" to
the laft mentioned Differtation; in which he gives a complete feries of the kings
of *Argos* and *Athens* from *Inachus*, to the firft year of the firft Olympiad; and
likewife of the old Emperors of *China*, from *Fohi* to the birth of *Chrift*; and
at the fame time fhews, that the chronology of all thefe nations perfectly agrees
with the *Septuagint*. Thefe (excepting fome occafional tracts in defence of the
Royal African Company) are all the *Englifh* works of this learned and indefatigable author. A period being put to the affairs and exiftence of the *Old African Company*, 1752, Mr. *Hayes* found himfelf happily exonerated from that burden, which,
though he had long fupported it, yet was not altogether fuitable to his inclinations.
He had juft before this purchafed a pretty retirement at *Down* in *Kent*, and withdrawing
thither, gave himfelf up wholly to his beloved ftudies. He had now leifure to look over
his papers, and revife them; and to confider what materials he had already provided for
his grand defign: and, as appears by the date on the manufcript, which he did not live
to publifh, he began in *May* 1753, to compile, in *Latin*, his " Chronographia *Afiatica* &
" *Ægyptiaca*." This was a laborious undertaking for a perfon of 75 years of age; but
it pleafed God, notwithftanding his reclufe and fedentary life, to blefs him with tolerable
health, and to preferve his intellects clear and ftrong till within a few days of his death.
The laft date annexed to this *Latin* manufcript is 1756; fo that probably he finifhed it
in that year, or foon after. In *Auguft* 1758, he left his houfe in *Kent*, and for the fake
of his health, and of fome more agreeable converfation than that retired place could afford him, being now about 80 years of age, took chambers in *Gray's-Inn*; and there,
in 1759, he fhewed, as he faid, that he had not led an indolent life in the country, by
                                                                        acquainting

"Age of *Elizabeth*, and the Conſtitution of the *Engliſh*
"Government,"

acquainting the learned world with what he had done, in a *Latin* piece, intituled, "Chro-
"nographia, &c." [as above]. Under the firſt part he ſhews, that both the Seventy In-
"terpreters, and *Joſephus*, took their ſyſtem of chronology from ſeveral ancient writings (diſtinct from the ſacred books of the Old Teſtament), which had for many ages
been carefully preſerved by the prieſts, in the library belonging to the temple of *Jeruſalem* *. The ſecond is a ſummary view of the whole great work, which he left behind
him in manuſcript, in a large folio ſize, all written with his own hand, and that a ſur-
priſingly fair and clean one, which neither diſcovers any weakneſs of nerves, nor any of
thoſe tremors incident to advanced age. This work, in the preface to his ſpecimen, he
ſays he hath happily finiſhed † ; and gives the title of it in the following manner :
"Novum

* *Joſephus*, who wrote to the Heathens, might take his authority from whence he would : but
the *Septuagint*, who were only tranſlators of a *Sacred* Book, how could they dare to ſubſtitute different numbers than their original ? And why would *Jewiſh* Prieſts *preſerve* with care in the
Temple writings that claſh with the Bible, when they hardly *preſerved* that ? The *Mahometan* General ſaid better, that the MSS. in the *Alexandrian* Muſeum either agreed with, or contradicted,
the Coran ; in the firſt caſe they were uſeleſs, in the laſt hurtful, and therefore in either caſe to be
burnt. *T. F.*

† "When he preſented me with the printed ſpecimen," ſays the anonymous Letter-writer, " I
" was thereby furniſhed with a proper opportunity of preſſing him to begin the publication of the
" large work, telling him it could never come out with equal advantage from any other hands, but
" thoſe who compoſed and wrote it. It is no wonder if the weighty labour of attending the preſs.
" did, at his time of life, deter him from undertaking it : But he was ſo far from neglecting this va-
" luable performance, that he enjoined his worthy executor to put all his papers on this ſubject into
" the hands of one who ſhould either uſher them into the world, or collect them together, reviſe
" them, and put the book into ſuch a condition as it might not be thought an inſignificant preſent
" to a public library in one of the univerſities. In ſhort, after the death of my friend, the papers were
" recommended to my care, however unequal to the taſk, and were carefully read over by me : But
" as they conſiſted moſtly of looſe quires, and partly of looſe ſheets, and ſome of theſe were by him
" copied over more than once, it was no little trouble to collate them, and required ſome judgement
" to diſtinguiſh which of thoſe copies (which were not complete duplicates, for they varied from each
" other) ſhould ſtand as a part of the work : and this I was to determine, ſometimes from the date,
" where there was one annexed, which diſcovered which was his laſt thought ; and ſometimes from
" other intrinſic conſiderations. I often met with corrections and additions on the back of a ſheet,
" which I thought would be much more authentic and ſatisfactory, if they were left ſtanding there
" in the author's own hand-writing, than to tranſcribe and inſert them in their proper places : And
" I was very cautious of letting my hand appear in the work, except where correcting a miſtaken
" letter or word, tranſcribing of ſome ſlip of paper, or adding a few lines by way of connection,
" required it. This elaborate work conſiſts of two parts ; the former, which is much the largeſt,
" is a kind of *Introduction* or *Prolegomena* to the ſecond. The ſecond is ſtyled, *Canon Chronicus Ge-
" neralis.* Theſe chronological tables, in collateral columns, ſhew in one view the ſeveral contempora -
" ry monarchs, and the times in which they lived. The firſt part of it begins with the creation of the
" world, and ends at the founding of the temple of *Jeruſalem* by *Solomon.* The ſecond extends
" from thence to the ſeventh year of *Artaxerxes Longimanus*, King of *Perſia.* And here the author's
" manuſcript leaves off ; and the chronology of 455 years is wanting to complete the deſign, which
" was to have been brought down to the year of the world 5500 ; in which he fixes the birth of
" *Chriſt.* This deficiency I have endeavoured to ſupply, as well as I could, according to the au-
" thor's ſyſtem, and have bound it up at the end of the manuſcript. In that part of the chronology
" in the author's writing, are ſeveral valuable notes, for explaining difficulties which occurred,
" Having thus diſcovered the true author of the abovenamed treatiſes, and made it known that the
" original manuſcript copy of this elaborate work, of near three hundred pages in a large folio, is
" now in being, and in ſafe hands, in the condition before related, I think it time to conclude my
" long letter with one obſervation concerning the uſefulneſs of it to the curious ſearchers after the
" true doctrine of times. The variation in the two computations is very great, and learned men
" have

" Government," [by Mr. *Hurd*,] 8vo ; " An Eſſay on Taſte*,
" by *Alexander Gerard*, M. A. Profeſſor of Moral Philoſophy
" at *Aberdeen*, with three Diſſertations on the ſame ſub-
" ject, from the *French* of M. *De Voltaire*, M. *D'Alembert*,
" F. R. S. and M. *De Monteſquieu*," 8vo ; a " Treatiſe on
" Fluxions, by *Iſrael Lyons*†, jun." 8vo ; " A Review of
" a free

" Novum aggreſſi ſumus opus ; quod jam, auxiliante Deo, feliciter abſolvimus ſub
" hoc titulo :—Chronographia *Aſiatica* & *Ægyptiaca* ab orbe condito ad Chriſtum natum
" per annos 5500, ad fidem ſcriptorum vetuſtiſſimorum reſtituta & illuſtrata." The
learned author did not long ſurvive the publication of this ſpecimen, dying at his chambers in *Gray's-Inn*, *Dec.* 18, 1760, in his 82d year. I owe this account of Mr. *Hayes*
to a letter from an anonymous friend of his, who had been indulged with a peruſal of
moſt of his writings before they were ſent to the preſs, with the liberty of imparting his
ſentiments on them. " If I differed in any thing from him (ſays this friend), as I could
" not eſpouſe all his opinions, and never made him a compliment of my own, he would
" reply in ſo mild a manner, that I never left him without admiring his great fund of
" learning, the clear method in which he explained his mind, and his ſedate and ſerene
" temper."
* This Eſſay was corrected through the preſs by the celebrated *David Hume*.
† Mr. *Lyons* was ſon of a *Poliſh Jew* ſilverſmith and teacher of *Hebrew* at *Cambridge* ; where he was born 1739. In his earlieſt youth he ſhewed a wonderful inclination to learning, particularly mathematics ; but though Dr. *Smith*, late maſter of
Trinity College, offered to put him to ſchool at his own expence, he would go only a day
or two, ſaying, he could learn more by himſelf in an hour than in a day with his maſter.
He began his ſtudy of Botany in 1755, which he continued to his death ; and could remember not only the *Linnæan* names of almoſt all the *Engliſh* plants, but even the
ſynonyma of the old botaniſts, which form a ſtrange and barbarous farrago of great bulk ;
and had large materials for a Flora *Cantabrigienſis*, deſcribing fully every part of each
plant from the life, without being obliged to conſult, or being liable to be miſled by,
former authors. In 1758 he publiſhed a treatiſe on Fluxions, dedicated to his patron, Dr.
Smith ; and in 1763 " Faſciculus plantarum circa *Cantabrigiam* naſcentium quæ poſt
" *Raium* obſervatæ fuere," 8vo. Mr. *Banks* (now Sir *Joſeph Banks*, bart. and preſident
of the Royal Society), whom he firſt inſtructed in this ſcience, ſent for him to *Oxford* about
1762 or 1763, to read lectures ; which he did with great applauſe to at leaſt ſixty pu-

" have taken different ſides in determining the important queſtion. What my ſentiments are in this
" point is not material, nor need I ſay which of the ſides is now more generally eſpouſed : But as
" both of them are attended with no inconſiderable difficulties, thoſe who take part with the *Greek*
" chronologiſts will here meet with the objections of their opponents coolly ſifted into, and all the
" arguments in favour of the Septuagint account ſet in a ſtrong and clear light : and thoſe who re-
" ceive the *Hebrew* computation, will perhaps find ſomething, before new to them, urged againſt
" their opinion, which they will think worthy of their conſideration, if not of an anſwer. A third
" ſort, who are unwilling to enter into a controverſy of this nature, will here meet with a greater
" ſtore of *Eaſtern* and *Egyptian* hiſtory and antiquities, laid down in a conciſe and maſterly way, and
" founded on ſubſtantial authority, than any other book of this bulk will afford them." *Gent. Mag.*
1761, *p.* 543.

6

pils;

" a free Inquiry into the Origin of Evil," [by the Rev. Mr. *Shepherd*,] 8vo; and " The *Norfolk* Dumplin-eater," [by the Rev. Mr. *Stona*] 8vo.

In 1760 Mr. *Bowyer* superintended a second edition of Mr. *Arnald's* † " Critical Commentary upon the Book of the " Wisdom of *Solomon*," and enriched it with the remarks of Mr. *Markland*; of which let us take his own account :
" In this edition, the reader will observe that the many
" additions communicated to the author by a very learned
" friend ‡ are included in hooks, which he designed to have
" melted down into the body of his work, and to have ac-
" knowledged, no doubt, his obligations to the person that
" sent them. But he had executed this design in part only,
" the observations being transcribed no further than Chap.
" IX. and the original copy of them not found among his

pils; but could not be prevailed upon to make a long absence from *Cambridge*. He had a salary of 100*l.* *per annum* for calculating the " Nautical Almanac," and frequently received presents from the Board of Longitude for his own inventions. He could read *Latin* and *French* with ease, but wrote the former ill; had studied the *English* history, and could quote whole passages from the monkish writers verbatim. He was appointed by the Board of Longitude to go with Capt. *Phipps* (now Lord *Mulgrave)* to the North Pole in 1773, and discharged that office to the satisfaction of his employers. After his return, he married and settled in *London*, where he died of the measles in about a year. He was then engaged in publishing some papers of Dr. *Halley*. His " Calculations in Spherical Trigonometry abridged," were printed in Phil. Transf. vol. LXI. art. 46.

* See under the year 1761.

† *Richard Arnald*, B. D. fellow of *Emanuel College, Cambridge*, by which Society he was presented to the rectory of *Thurcaston*, four or five miles North of *Leicester*. He married the daughter of Mr. *Wood*, rector of *Wilford* near *Nottingham*, and published two Sermons at *Cambridge*, 1726, and 1737; a third, at *London*, under the title of " The Parable of the Cedar and Thistle, exemplified in the Great Victory at *Culloden*, " 1746," 4to; the first edition of the " Commentary on *Wisdom*" in 1744 (see p. 172); a " Commentary on *Ecclesiasticus*" in 1748 (see p. 107.); and the " Commentary on " *Tobit*," &c. in 1752 (see p. 224). It is seldom an agreeable circumstance to a clergyman or his family to have a successor; but it was otherwise in the present case, as Mr. *Hurd* (now Bishop) patronized the son, a fellow of *St. John's College*, who, by his favour and recommendation, became sub-preceptor to his Royal Highness the Prince of *Wales*, canon of *Windsor*, and archdeacon of *Litchfield*.

‡ Mr. *Markland.*

" papers.

" papers. This lofs has, by good fortune, been fupplied
" by another friend*, through whofe hands the obferva-
" tions were tranfmitted to him, and who was indulged the
" liberty of taking a copy of them for himfelf; from
" whence they are now given to the publick. They cor-
" rect often miftakes of the author; which it was thought
" proper to continue as he left them, that the reader might
" the better judge of the force of the remarks, and that a
" liberty might not be taken after his death, which him-
" felf only, while alive, had a right to make ufe of."

The other books of 1760 were " The Ceremonial of the
" Funeral of King *George* the Second," folio ; " The Actor,"
a poem by *Robert Lloyd*‡, M. A. 4to ; " Ancient and Modern
" *Rome*,

---

* Mr. *Bowyer.*

† Son of Dr. *Pierfon Lloyd*, fecond mafter of *Weftminfter* fchool ‡, where *Robert* was
educated, and whence he was admitted of *Trinity College, Cambridge,* and took the degree of M. A. At the Univerfity, as at *Weftminfter*, he diftinguifhed himfelf by his
poetical genius and (forry I am to add) by his irregularities. He was for fome time
employed as one of the ufhers of *Weftminfter* fchool, where he wrote the poem
which gave occafion to this note, which not only gave proofs of great judgment in
the fubject he was treating of, but had alfo the merit of fmooth verfification and great
ftrength of poetry. In the beginning of the Poetical War, which for fome time raged
among the wits of this age, and to which the celebrated *Rofciad* founded the firft charge,
Mr. *Lloyd* was fufpected to be the author of that poem. But this he honeftly difowned
by an advertifement in the public papers; on which occafion the real author, Mr.
Churchill, boldly ftepped forth, and in the fame public manner declared himfelf;
and drew on that torrent of *Anti-Rofciads, Apologies, Murphiads, Churchilliads,
Examiners,* &c. which for a long time kept up the attention and employed the
geniufes of the greateft part of the critical world. After Mr. *Lloyd* quitted his place
of ufher of *Weftminfter* fchool, he relied entirely on his pen for fubfiftence; but,
being of a thoughtlefs and extravagant difpofition, he foon made himfelf liable to debts
which he was unable to anfwer. In confequence of this fituation he was confined in the
Fleet Prifon, where he depended for fupport almoft wholly on the bounty and generofity of his friend *Churchill*, whofe kindnefs to him continued undiminifhed during all his
neceffities. On the death of this liberal benefactor, Mr. *Lloyd* funk into a ftate of
defpondency, which put an end to his exiftence on the 15th of *December*, 1764, in lefs

‡ Afterwards chancellor of *York*, and portionift of *Waddefdon, Bucks*; whofe learning, judgement,
and moderation endeared him to all who partook of his inftructions, during a courfe of almoft 50
years fpent in the fervice of the publick at *Weftminfter School.* He had a penfion from his Majefty
of 400*l*. a year for his own life, and that of his now widow ; and died *Jan.* 5, 1781.

than

" *Rome*, a poem, written at *Rome* in 1755, by *George Keate*,
" efq." 4to; " De Solis ac Lunæ Defectibus, Libri V. P.
" *Rogerii Bofcovich** Societatis *Jefu*, ad Regiam Societatem
" *Londinenfem*. Ibidem autem & Aftronomiæ Synopfis &
" Theorema Luminis *Newtoniana*, & alia multa ad Phyfi-
" cam pertinentia, verfibus pertractantur; cum ejufdem
" Auctoris Annotationibus," 4to; " An Account of a Cop-
" per Table, &c. by *Philip Carteret Webb*†, efq." 4to; " The
" *Latin* Infcription on the Copper Table, difcovered in
" the

than a month after he was informed of the lofs of Mr. *Churchill*. Mr. *Wilkes* fays, that
" Mr. *Lloyd* was mild and affable in private life, of gentle manners, and very engaging
" in converfation. He was an excellent fcholar, and an eafy natural poet. His peculiar
" excellence was the dreffing up an old thought in a new, neat, and trim manner. He
" was contented to fcamper round the foot of *Parnaffus* on his little *Welch* poney,
" which feems never to have tired. He left the fury of the winged fteed, and the daring
" heights of the facred mountain, to the fublime genius of his friend *Churchill*." A partial collection of his poetical works was made by Dr. *Kenrick* in two volumes 8vo, 1774;
and a good imitation by him, from " The Spectator," may be feen in the Seventh Volume
of the " Select Collection of Mifcellaneous Poems, 1781," p. 223. He was alfo the
Author of " The Capricious Lovers," a comic opera, 1764, 8vo; and of four other dramatic works. His imitation of *Theocritus*, on the King's going to the Houfe, deferves
much praife.

＊ In this work the judicious author's learning and genius (to ufe an expreffion of Dr.
Johnfon) have laboured Science into Poetry, and have fhewn, by explaining Aftronomy,
that Verfe did not refufe the ideas of Philofophy. This poem was written at various
periods; a part of it having been publicly recited at *Rome* in 1735.

† This diftinguifhed Antiquary, born in 1700, was regularly bred to the profeffion
of an attorney, which profeffion he followed for many years in *Budge Row, London*,
and afterwards removed to *Great Queen Street, Lincoln's Inn Fields*. He was peculiarly
learned in the Records of this kingdom, and particularly able as a parliamentary and con-
ftitutional lawyer. In 1751 he affifted materially in obtaining the charter of incorporation for the Society of Antiquaries, remitting in that bufinefs the cuftomary fees which
were due to him as a folicitor; and on many other occafions proved himfelf a very ufeful
member of that learned body. Purchafing a houfe and eftate at *Busbridge*‡, near *Godel-
ming*, in *Surrey*, where he refided in the fummer, it gave him an influence in the borough
of *Haflemere* ‖, for which he was chofen member in 1754, and again in 1761. He
became, under the patronage of Lord Chancellor *Hardwicke*, fecretary of bankrupts in
the Court of Chancery, and was appointed one of the joint folicitors of the Treafury in
1756. In *July* 1758 he obtained a filver medal from the Society of Arts, for having
planted a large quantity of acorns for timber. In 1760 (as has been mentioned already,
p. 124) he had the honour of prefenting the famous *Heraclean* table to the king of *Spain*,
by the hands of the *Neapolitan* minifter, from whom he received in return (in *November*
that year) a diamond ring, worth 300*l*. In *April* 1763, the period of Mr. *Wilkes's*

‡ Since purchafed by Sir *Robert Barker*, bart.
‖ The contefted election in 1754 is well known and remembered by the humorous ballad, intituled, " The Cow of *Haflemere*," attributed to Dr. *King* of *Oxford*, and printed that year in folio.

being

" the year 1732, near *Heraclea*, in the Bay of *Taren-*
" *tum*, in *Magna Græcia*, and publifhed by *Mazochius*
" at

being apprehended for writing *The North Briton*, N° 45, Mr. *Webb* became officially
a principal actor in that memorable profecution, but did not altogether approve of the
feverity with which it was carried on. He held the office of folicitor to the Treafury
till *July* 1765, and continued fecretary of bankrupts till Lord *Northington* quitted the feals
in 1766. He died at *bufbridge*, *June* 22, 1770, aged 70 ; and his library (including that of
*John Godfrey**, efq. which he had purchafed entire) was fold, with his MSS. on vellum, *Feb.*
25, and the 16 following days, 1771. A little before his death he fold to the Houfe of
Peers thirty MS. volumes of the Rolls of Parliament. His MSS. on paper were fold,.
by his widow and executrix, to the Earl of *Shelburne*. The coins and medals were
fold by auction the fame year, three days fale. In this fale were all the coins and medals
found in his collection at the time of his deceafe, but he had difpofed of the moft valuable part to different perfons. The feries of large brafs had been picked by a nobleman.
The noble feries of *Roman* gold (among which were *Pompey*, *Lepidus*, &c.) and the
collection of *Greek* kings and towns had been fold to Mr. *Duane*, and now form part of
the immenfe collection of Dr. *Hunter*. The ancient marble bufts, bronzes, *Roman*
earthenware, gems, feals, &c. of which there were 96 lots, were fold in the above year.
On the death of the late Mrs. *Webb*, the remainder of the curiofities was fold by Mr.
Langford. Mr. *Webb's* publications were, 1. " A Letter to the Rev. Mr. *William War-*
" *burton*, M. A." occafioned by fome paffages in his book intituled " The Divine Legation
" of *Mofes* demonftrated. By a Gentleman of *Lincoln's Inn*, 1742," 8vo. 2. " Remarks
" on the Pretender's Declaration and Commiffion, 1745," 8vo. 3. " Remarks on the
" Pretender's Son's fecond Declaration, dated the 10th of *October* 1745, by the Author
" of the Remarks on his firft Declaration, 1745," 8vo. 4. " Excerpta ex Inftrumentis
" publicis de *Judæis*," confifting of feven pages fmall 4to. 5. " Short, but true State of

* Son of *Benjamin Godfrey*, efq. of *Norton Court*, near *Feverfham* in *Kent*, whom he fucceeded in
that eftate. He was very corpulent, through indolence or inactivity, and a great epicure, which
fhortened his life. Mr. *Godfrey* (who was related to Sir *Edmondbury*) was a perfon of learning, and had a good collection of antiquities ; and alfo of coins and medals, which, after his
death, were fold by auction. His library (containing about 1200 valuable volumes) was bought
for 100*l*. by *T. Osborne*, who fold the whole again to Mr. *Webb* before it was unpacked.
Mr. *Godfrey* contributed the plate of *Roman* antiquities in p. 248 of Dr. *Harris's* Hiftory of
Kent, and was a good friend and benefactor to Dr. *Harris*, who ufed to fpunge upon him ;
and, though a prebendary of *Rochefter*, with other good preferments, died infolvent, at *Norton
Court*, and was buried in the parifh church at Mrs. *Godfrey's* expence. After Mr. *Godfrey's* death
(about 1741) his widow retired to her native county (*Staffordfhire*, it is fuppofed) and carried with
her the valuable MSS. which Dr. *Harris* had collected for the fecond volume of his Hiftory of
Kent, which he never publifhed. The late Dr. *Thorpe* and other gentlemen made what enquiries
they could how fhe difpofed of them, or what became of them after her death, but could never get
the leaft intelligence. Mrs. *Anne Godfrey* (who died about 1746, and was buried with her hufband at
Norton) was a vain talkative woman, and would often, when her hufband was chatting with
a friend on antiquarian matters, interrupt him on the fubject, and expofe her ignorance. Her
maiden name was *Gough* ; her father was an exchange broker in *London* ; her brother, who
was bound apprentice to an apothecary, but did not ferve out his time, married fhortly after
Anne, daughter of *George Mafon*, efq. and great grand-daughter of *John Oneby*, efq. (whofe
epitaph fee in *Gent. Mag.* 1777, p. 316). This lady had a handfome fortune, which young *Gough*
loft in the *South Sea* bubble, and was afterwards in fome degree dependent on Mr. *Godfrey*, after
whofe death Mrs. *Godfrey* impoverifhed herfelf in the affiftance of her brother, fo as to be unable to
pay her own debts. Mr. *Gough* died at *Camberwell* about 1755 ; and his widow in *May* 1771. On the
death of the latter, her effects were fold by auction ; and the editor of this work purchafed the original portraits of Mr. and Mrs. *Godfrey*, a curious old plan of *Norton Court* (mentioned in Brit.
Topog. vol. I. p. 497*), two miniature paintings of perfons unknown, and fome other curiofities.

6

" Facts

" at *Naples* in the year 1758, more particularly confi-
" dered and illuftrated; by *John Pettingal**, D. D. read
" at the Meeting of the Society of Antiquaries the firft
" of *May*, 1760, and ordered to be printed," 4to; the
fecond volume† of Dr. *Jortin's* " Life of *Erafmus*," 4to;
" An Enquiry into the Beauties of Painting, and the Me-
" rits of the moft celebrated Painters‡, by *Daniel Webb*, efq."

" Facts relative to the *Jew* Bill, fubmitted to the Confideration of the Publick," three pages
fmall 4to. 6. " Five Plates of Records relating to the *Jews*, engraven at the expence
" of *Philip Carteret Webb*, efq." 7. " The Queftion whether a *Jew* born within
" the *Britifh* Dominions was, before the making the late Act of Parliament, a
" Perfon capable by Law to purchafe and hold Lands to him and his Heirs, fairly
" ftated and confidered. [To which is annexed an " Appendix, containing copies of
" public Records relating to the *Jews*."] By a Gentleman of *Lincoln's Inn*, 1753," 4to.
Printed for *Roberts*, price 2s. 6d. " A Reply" to this, in the fame fize and at the
fame price, written, as it is fuppofed, by Mr. *Grove*, author of the Life of Cardinal
Wolfey, was printed for *Robinfon*, *Woodyer*, and *Swan*. 8. " A fhort Account of
" fome Particulars concerning *Domefday Book*, with a view to promote its being publifh-
" ed, 1756," 4to. 9. " A fhort Account of *Danegeld*, with fome further Particulars
" relating to *William* the Conqueror's Survey, 1756," 4to. 10. " A State of Facts, in
" Defence of his Majefty's Right to certain Fee-Farm Rents in the County of *Norfolk*,
" 1758," 4to. 11. " An Account of a Copper Table, containing two Infcriptions in
" the *Greek* and *Latin* Tongues; difcovered in the year 1732, near *Heraclea*, in the
" Bay of *Tarentum*, in *Magna Græcia*." By *Philip Carteret Webb*, Efq. Read at a
Meeting of the Society of Antiquaries the 13th of *December*, 1759, and ordered to be
printed 1760, 4to. 12. " Some Obfervations on the late Determination for difcharging
" Mr. *Wilkes* from his Commitment to *The Tower of London*, for being the author and
" publifher of a feditious Libel called *The North Briton*, Nº 45. By a Member of the
" Houfe of Commons, 4to. 1763." He alfo printed a quarto pamphlet, containing a
number of General Warrants iffued from the time of the Revolution, and fome other
political tracts, particularly at the time of the rebellion in 1745, on the clofe of which
his abilities, as folicitor on the trials in *Scotland*, proved of eminent fervice to the publick.
Mr. *Webb* was twice married, and by his firft lady (who died *March* 12, 1756) left one
fon of his own name, admitted of *Ben'et College, Cambridge*, 1755, under the private
tuition of the Rev. *John Hodgfon* ‖; removed to *The Temple* 1757; married Mifs *Smith*,
of *Milford, Surry*, 1763, by whom he has a fon born 1764, and a daughter fince dead.
His fecond wife was *Rhoda*, daughter of *John Cotes*, efq. of *Dodington*, in *Chefhire*, by
Rhoda one of the daughters and coheirs of Sir *John Huborn*, bart. of *Warwickfhire*;
but by her he had no iffue.

* See under the year 1763.

† To this volume Mr. *Bowyer* made an Index as it paffed through the prefs, which
will be inferted among his " Mifcellaneous Tracts."

‡ Remarks on fome paffages in this work [by the late Mr. *Highmore*] are in the
Gent. Mag. 1766, p. 353.

‖ Mr. *Hodgfon* came on this occafion from *Queen's College, Oxford*; and took his degree of
M. A. at *Cambridge* 1756. He was alfo F. S. A. and private tutor, at the fame college, to the
prefent earl of *Maffareene*. The differtation on an antient Cornelian, in the poffeffion of *John Law-
fon*, efq. in Archæologia, II. p. 42, was written by him. He was prefented by Mr. *Webb's* intereft
to a living in *Barbadoes*, where he died 1761. The author of this fhort note is forry he cannot do
greater juftice to the character of this mild, unaffected, excellent fcholar.

8vo;

8vo; "Dialogues Moral and Political," [by Mr. *Hurd*,] 8vo; "An additional Dialogue of the Dead," [between *Aristides* and *Pericles*,] by Dr. *Brown**, 8vo; "De Ratione Inter- "pungendi, Auctore *J. Ward*†, P. P. C. G." 8vo; "The "Honour and Dishonour of Agriculture, translated from "the *Spanish* [of Father *Feijoo*‡, Disc. 13. vol. VIII.], by "a Farmer in *Cheshire* ‖," 8vo; "Observations on *Miscella-* "*nea Analytica*," by Dr. *Powell*, 8vo; "A Letter from "Baron *Montesquieu* to Dr. *Warburton*," prefixed to the Let- ters on *Bolingbroke*, 8vo; "Emendationes in *Suidam*, Pars "I." by Mr. *Toup*, 8vo; and "Lady *Catesby's* Letters," from the *French*, by Mrs. *Brooke*, 12mo. It

* This pamphlet is said to have been occasioned by an unintentional affront given to Dr. *Brown* by Lord *Lyttelton*. That nobleman in a numerous and mixed company neg- lected to take notice of our author in so respectful a manner as he thought he deserved, and in resentment of it he composed the above-mentioned dialogue.

† The learned Professor; of whom an account shall be given hereafter.

‡ See *Hughes's* Letters, vol. III. p. 49.

‖ Of this little volume the ingenious Mr. *Benjamin Stillingfleet* was the editor, if not the translator. He was grandson to the Bishop of *Worcester*, and equally distinguish- ed as a naturalist and a poet, the rare union so much desired by the ingenious Mr. *Aickin*. Both the Bishop and our author's father were fellows of *St. John's College* in *Cambridge*. The latter was also F. R. S. M. D. and *Gresham* professor of phy- sic; but, marrying in 1692, lost his lucrative offices, and the Bishop's favour; a misfortune that affected both him and his posterity. He took orders § however, and obtained, by his father's patronage, the rectory of *Newington Butts*, which he immediately exchanged for those of *Wood-Norton* and *Swanton* in *Norfolk*. He died in 1708. *Benjamin*, his only son, was educated at *Norwich* school, which he left in 1720, with the character of an excellent scholar. He then went to *Tri- nity College, Cambridge*, at the request of Dr. *Bentley*, the master, who had been private tutor to his father, domestic chaplain to his grandfather, and was much indebted to the family. Here he was admitted *April* 14, 1720; took the degree of B. A. and became a candidate for a fellowship; but was rejected, by the master's in- fluence. This was a severe and unexpected disappointment; and but little alleviated af- terwards by the Doctor's apology, that it was a pity that a gentleman of Mr. *Stillingfleet's* parts should be buried within the walls of a college. Perhaps, however, this ingratitude of Dr. *Bentley* was not of any real disservice to Mr. *Stillingfleet*. He travelled into *Italy*; and, by being thrown into the world, formed many honourable and valuable connexions. The present Lord *Barrington* gave him, in a very polite manner, the place of master of the barracks at *Kensington*; a favour to which Mr. *Stillingfleet*, in the dedication of his "Calendar of *Flora*" to that nobleman, 1761, alludes with great politeness, as well

§ This is exactly the case of Archbishop *Potter* and son; the latter, marrying to the dislike of the father, was cut off by him from any of the fortune; he got however, or gave him, 2000*l. per annum* in church preferments; as if a man might be very deserving of that, who was not fit to receive his paternal fortune. *T. F.*

as

It was a peculiarity, if it might be so called, in the character of Mr. *Bowyer*, that his engagements as a man of
business never were sufficient to divest him of those sensi-
bilities, which men conscious of their superiority in respect
to literary abilities sometimes experience to be not among
the blessings of a learned education. As he knew himself

the

as the warmest gratitude. His "Calendar" was formed at *Stratton* in *Norfolk*, in
1755, at the hospitable seat of Mr. *Marsham*, who had made several remarks of
that kind, and had communicated to the publick his curious "Observations on the
Growth of Trees." But it was to Mr. *Wyndham*, of *Felbrig* in *Norfolk*, that he
appears to have had the greatest obligations. He travelled abroad with him; spent
much of his time at his house; and was appointed one of his executors; with a
considerable addition to an annuity which that gentleman had settled upon him in
his life-time. Mr. *Stillingfleet's* genius led him principally to the study of natural
history, which he prosecuted as an ingenious philosopher, an useful citizen, and a
good man. Mr. *Gray* makes the following favourable mention of him, in one of his
letters dated from *London*, in 1761: " I have lately made an acquaintance with this
" philosopher, who lives in a garret in the winter, that he may support some near rela-
" tions who depend upon him. He is always employed, consequently (according to my
" old maxim) always happy, always chearful, and seems to me a worthy honest man.
" His present scheme is to send some persons, properly qualified, to reside a year or two
" in *Attica*, to make themselves acquainted with the climate, productions, and natural
" history of the country, that we may understand *Aristotle*, *Theophrastus*, &c. who have
" been Heathen *Greek* to us for so many ages; and this he has got proposed to Lord
" *Bute*, no unlikely person to put it in execution, as he is himself a botanist." An epistle
by Mr. *Stillingfleet*, in 1723, is printed in the " Poetical Magazine, 1764," p. 2 24. He
published, about 1733, an anonymous pamphlet, intituled, " Some Thoughts concern-
" ing Happiness;" and in 1759 appeared a volume of " Miscellaneous Tracts,"
chiefly translated from essays in the " Amœnitates Academicæ," published by *Lin-*
næus, interspersed with some observations and additions of his own. In this volume he shews a taste for classical learning, and entertains us with some elegant
poetical effusions. He annexed to it some valuable " Observations on Grasses," and dedicated the whole to *George* Lord *Lyttelton*. A second edition of it appeared in 1762; a
third in 1775. Mr. *Stillingfleet* likewise published " Some Thoughts occasioned by the
" late Earthquakes, 1750," a poem in 4to; " Paradise Lost," an Oratorio, set to
Music by *Stanley*, 1760, 4to; and " The Principles and Powers of Harmony, 1771,"
4to. a very learned work, built on *Tartini's* " Trattato di Musica secondo la vera scienza
" dell' Armonia." These, and his " Essay on Conversation, 1757," in the first
volume of *Dodsley's* Collection of Poems, entitle him to no small degree of rank among
our *English* Poets. The " Essay" is addressed to Mr. *Wyndham* with all that warmth
of friendship which distinguishes the author. As it is chiefly didactic, it does not
admit of so many ornaments as some compositions of other kinds. However, it contains
much good sense, shews a considerable knowledge of mankind, and has several passages
that, in point of harmony and easy versification, would not disgrace the writings of our

most:

the firſt in his profeſſion, he diſdained the ſervility of ſolicitation ; but, when he ſaw himſelf neglected, or another
preferred where friendſhip gave him a claim, he did not
ſuppreſs the impulſes of reſentment, which he felt on ſuch
occaſions.   Many inſtances of this might be produced.
They did not, however, ariſe from avarice ; nor was the
article of profit that which acted with the greateſt force
upon him.   The moſt trifling conſideration would produce
as warm an expoſtulation as one of the greateſt.   As an
inſtance, the following ſhall be produced, to ſhew how
ſenſibly he felt himſelf hurt on ſuch an occaſion.

His friend the Dean of *Briſtol** having preached before
the Houſe of Commons, on the General Faſt-day, *Feb.* 1 3,
1761 ;

moſt admired poets. Here more than once Mr. *Stillingfleet* ſhews himſelf ſtill ſore from
Dr. *Bentley's* cruel treatment of him ; and towards the beautiful and moral cloſe of this
poem (where he gives us a ſketch of himſelf) ſeems to hint at a mortification of a more
delicate nature, which he is ſaid to have ſuffered from the other ſex. This too may perhaps account for the aſperity with which he treats the ladies in the " Verſes" printed in
the ſixth volume of the " Select Collection of Poems, 1781." To theſe diſappointments
it was perhaps owing that Mr. *Stillingfleet* neither married, nor went into orders. His
London reſidence was at a Sadler's in *Piccadilly*, where he died in 1771, aged above 70,
leaving ſeveral valuable papers behind him. To theſe Mr. *Pennant* alludes in a beautiful elogium on him, prefixed to the fourth volume of the " *Britiſh* Zoology," when he
ſays, " I received the unfiniſhed tokens of his regard by virtue of his promiſe ; the only
" papers that were reſcued from the flames to which his modeſty had devoted all the
" reſt." He was buried in *St. James's* church, without the ſlighteſt monument of his
having exiſted. A portrait of him is in the poſſeſſion of Mr. *Torriano*. Mr. *Stillingfleet's* eldeſt ſiſter, *Elizabeth*, was married to Mr. *Locker*, a gentleman " eminent for
" curioſity and literature †," who has been already mentioned in this volume, p. 110.

* Dr. *Samuel Squire*. This learned Divine, the ſon of an apothecary, was born at
Warminſter in *Wiltſhire*, in 1714, and was educated at *St. John's College, Cambridge*, of
which he became a Fellow. Soon after, Dr. *Wynn* Biſhop of *Bath* and *Wells* appointed
him his chaplain, and collated him to the Archdeaconry of *Bath*. In 1748, he was preſented
by the King to the rectory of *Topsfield* in *Eſſex*; and, in 1749, when the Duke of *Newcaſtle*
(to whom he was Chaplain, and private ſecretary ‡ as chancellor of the univerſity)

† Such is the character of him given by Dr. *Johnſon*, to whom Mr. *Locker* communicated a collection of examples ſelected by *Addiſon* from the writings of *Tillotſon*, with an intention of making
an *Engliſh* Dictionary. *Life of Addiſon, p.* 65.

‡ In this character, from an unlucky ſimilitude of names, he was ridiculed in the famous *Fragment* by the appellation of " Dr. *Squirt*, apothecary to *Alma Mater's* (or the old lady's) Steward."
His dark complexion procured him in college converſation, and in the ſquibs of the time, the nick
name of " The Man of *Angola*."

1761; Mr. *Bowyer* of courfe expected to print the Sermon. The profit attending fuch a fmall article, it will be eafily fuppofed

was inftalled Chancellor of *Cambridge*, he preached one of the commencement fermons, and took the degree of D. D. In 1750, he was prefented by Archbifhop *Herring* to the rectory of *St. Anne, Weftminfter* (then vacant by the death of Dr. *Pelling*), being his Grace's option on the fee of *London*, and for which he refigned his living of *Topsfield* in favour of a relation of the Archbifhop. Soon after, Dr. *Squire* was prefented by the King to the vicarage of *Greenwich* in *Kent*; and, on the eftablifhment of the houfhold of the Prince of *Wales* (his prefent Majefty), he was appointed his Royal Highnefs's Clerk of the Clofet. In 1760, he was prefented to the Deanry of *Briftol*; and in 1761 (on the death of Dr. *Ellis*) was advanced to the Bifhoprick of *St. David's*, the revenues of which were confiderably advanced by him *. He died, after a fhort illnefs, occafioned by his anxiety concerning the health of one of his fons, *May* 7, 1766. As a parifh minifter, even after his advancement to the mitre, he was moft confcientioufly diligent in the duties of his function; and as a prelate, in his frequent vifits to his fee (though he held it but five years), he fought out and promoted the friendlefs and deferving, in preference, frequently, to powerful recommendations, and exercifed the hofpitality of a Chriftian Bifhop. In private life, as a parent, hufband, friend, and mafter, no man was more beloved, or more lamented. He was a Fellow of the Royal and Antiquary Societies, and a conftant attendant upon both. He married one of the daughters of Mrs. *Ardefoif* †, a widow lady of fortune (his parifhioner) in *Soho Square*. Some verfes to her " on making a pin-bafket," by Dr. (now Sir *James) Marriott*, are in the fourth volume of *Dodfley's* collection. *Ifaac Akerman*, efq. and *Matthew Howard*, efq. married her two other daughters. Mrs. *Squire*, an excellent woman, by whom the Bifhop left two fons and a daughter, ftill living, did not long furvive him. A fermon, entitled " Mutual Knowledge in a future State, &c." was dedicated to her, with a juft elogium on his patron, by Dr *Dodd* ‡ in 1766. In this, the occafion of the Bifhop's death, already mentioned, is thus alluded to, " Alas ! Madam, " we think with anxious concern of the exquifite fenfibility of his affectionate heart." Befides feveral fingle fermons on public occafions, Bifhop *Squire* publifhed the following pieces : 1. " An Enquiry into the Nature of the *Englifh* Conftitution; or, an Hiftorical Effay " on the *Anglo Saxon* Government, both in *Germany* and *England*." 2. " The ancient " Hiftory of the *Hebrews* vindicated; or, Remarks on the third volume of the Moral " Philofopher. *Cambridge*, 1741." 3. " Two Effays. I. A Defence of the ancient " *Greek* Chronology. II. An Enquiry into the Origin of the *Greek* Language. *Cambridge*. 1741." 4. " *Plutarchi* de *Ifide* & *Ofiride* liber; *Græcè* & *Anglicè*, *Græca*

* Thefe improvements of the eftates of bifhopricks, colleges, and other ecclefiaftical revenues happening by fits and ftarts, make them the more noticed; but in the main they are not more extraordinary than thofe held in lay hands.

† Mrs. *Ardefoif* had alfo a fon, who, after being apprenticed to a merchant in the city, went into the army, and died young.

‡ Chaplain to the Bifhop, from whom he received a prebend of *Brecon*. In *Dodd's* Poems is " A Sonnet, occafioned by reading the Truth and Importance of Natural and Revealed Religion;" " Gratitude and Merit," an epigram on Bifhop *Squire*; and " An Ode written in the Walks at " *Brecknock*," expreffive of gratitude to his friendly patron. Of Bifhop *Squire*, Dr. *Dodd* alfo fays, in his " Thoughts in Prifon," Week IV.

    —— " And ftill more, when urg'd, approv'd,
    " And blefs'd by thee, *St. David's* honour'd friend;
    " Alike in Wifdom's and in Learning's fchool
    " Advanc'd and fage, &c." [See p. 73. ed. 1781.]

    " refenfuit,

ſuppoſed, could be no material object. But the indelicacy of the tranſaction drew from him the following expoſtulatory epiſtle :

" REV.

" recenſuit, emendavit, Commentariis auxit, Verſionem novam *Anglicanam* adjecit *Samuel*
" *Squire,* A.M. Archidiaconus *Bathonienſis* ; acceſſerunt *Xylandri, Baxteri, Bentleii,*
" *Marklandi,* Conjecturæ & Emendationes, *Cantab.* 1744." 5. " An Eſſay on the Ba-
" lance of Civil Power in *England,* 8vo. 174..;" which was added to the ſecond edition of the Enquiry, &c. in 1753. 6. " Indifference for Religion inexcuſable * , or, a
" ſerious, impartial, and practical Review of the certainty, importance, and harmony of
" natural and revealed Religion. *London,* 1748," again in 12mo, 1759. 7. " Re-
" marks upon Mr. *Carte*'s Specimen of his General Hiſtory of *England,* very proper to
" be read by all ſuch as are Contributors to that great Work, 1748," 8vo. 8. " The
" Principles of Religion made eaſy to young Perſons, in a ſhort and familiar Catechiſm.
" Dedicated to (the late) Prince *Frederick. London,* 1763." 9. " A Letter to the
" Right Hon. the Earl of *Hallifax* on the Peace, 1763," 8vo. by Dr. *Dodd,* received
great aſſiſtance from Biſhop *Squire.* He alſo left in MS. a *Saxon* Grammar compiled by himſelf. The following juſt character of one of his patrons, prefixed to his Grace's Seven Sermons, was written by this prelate : " Archbiſhop *Herring*'s perſon was tall and comely ;
" his conſtitution, from his tendereſt youth, weak and delicate ; his addreſs eaſy, en-
" gaging, and polite. He was generous without prodigality, magnificent without pro-
" fuſion, and humble without meanneſs. His diſtinguiſhed application to the buſineſs
" of his function, his learning, his warm attachment to the conſtitution in church and
" ſtate, and his pathetic eloquence in the pulpit, having recommended him to the early
" notice of the great, he ever afterwards maintained himſelf in the poſſeſſion of their fa-
" vour, eſteem, and affection, by his ingenuous converſation, and by his ſingular can-
" dour, temper, and moderation. Every new preferment, by rendering both his pub-
" lic and private virtues more known and conſpicuous, convinced the world that he was
" ſtill worthy of ſomething higher ; till, unſoliciting and unexpecting, he was called by
" his ſovereign, with the univerſal approbation, to the moſt exalted dignity of the
" church. So kind and obliging was his Grace's manner in conferring favours, that it
" added a double pleaſure to the receiver. He felt the anxiety of the doubtful petitioner,
" and removed his ſuſpenſe as ſoon as poſſible ; and, when forced to deny a requeſt, he
" always ſeaſoned the refuſal with every circumſtance of benevolence, which might ren-
" der the diſappointment leſs grievous. His religion was of that pureſt and nobleſt kind
" which true Chriſtianity inſpires : It was piety without ſuperſtition, devotion without
" hypocriſy, and faith which worketh by love. Conſcious of the uprightneſs of his own
" heart, and of the ſincerity of his belief of the doctrines and precepts of the Goſpel,
" he was willing to think the beſt of other people's principles, and to live the friend of
" mankind. Having no ſelfiſh views, nor private intereſts of his own to ſerve, he was

* Of this work Mr. *Sack†,* jun. now at *Magdeburg,* thus expreſſed himſelf in a MS letter to
the Rev. Mr. *Duncombe :* " Biſhop *Squire's* ' Indifference for Religion inexcuſable,' is extremely
" well tranſlated, and very much eſteemed by every one who loves his religion more than his party's
" opinions. You know that is not the caſe with every divine. My father in particular is extremely
" pleaſed with the method the Biſhop employs in defending the Chriſtian religion, it being ſo much
" the ſame with that he made uſe of in his ' Defence of the Chriſtian Faith,' that one would think
" the two works had but one author. I am ſorry I had but once the honour to viſit him."

† The late Rev. Mr. *Sack,* firſt chaplain to the King of *Pruſſia.*

" always

" REV. SIR,

" I underſtand I am not to have the favour of printing
" your Sermon; which gives me reaſon to fear that I have
" behaved in ſuch a manner as to forfeit a friendſhip which
" was founded on a natural, I may ſay, a *trading* principle,
" conſidering I was a pupil of Dr. *Newcome*. Your tutor,
" ſay my brethren, muſt have a mean opinion of you, ſince
" he could not make a printer of you fit to print for him-
" ſelf* or his nephew †. Let me know wherein I have of-
" fended, that I may endeavour to make myſelf more ac-
" ceptable to the world, the college, or at leaſt to you, Sir;
" who am, your moſt humble ſervant, W. BOWYER."

This was not the only inſtance in which he ſtrongly expreſſed his feelings at what he thought a ſlight put upon him
from a quarter where he imagined he had a natural claim
to favour. In a letter, dated *Jan.* 11, 1767, to a living
Dignitary of the Church, ſpeaking of *Cambridge*, he ſays,
" My father (good man!) ſent me thither, to qualify me,
" by a new kind of experiment, for a printer. But it
" ſerved only in trade to expoſe me to more affronts, and
" to give me a keener ſenſibility of them. Time and old
" age are at laſt our beſt inſtructors; and I ſhould have
" made an ill uſe of the documents of nature, if I had not
" learnt to take conſolation from my approach to that ſtate
" where the great and little will be equal."

" always ready to ſacrifice his preferments, his fortune, and even his life to the ſafety of
" his Majeſty's perſon, to the eaſe and ſucceſs of his adminiſtration, and to the perpe-
" tuity of the Proteſtant eſtabliſhment; looking on that eſtabliſhment as the only ſupport
" of the Church of *England*, as the bulwark of our civil liberty, and the ſureſt defence
" of the independency of *Europe*."
  * " The ſquib is better than the ſermon," ſaid Mr. *B.* to a friend on this occaſion.—
" Dr. *Newcome* printed once a Sermon; and carried it to *Cambridge*, becauſe he could
" not print it in *London* decently unleſs with *W. B.*"
  † Biſhop *Squire* was nephew to Mrs. *Newcome*. See above, p. 17.

R r   Let

Let us now turn to a more pleafing trait in the character of Mr. *Bowyer*, by perufing a letter dictated at once by gratitude and manly liberality of fentiment:

" To the Right Hon. the Earl of MACCLESFIELD.

" MY LORD, *July* 4, 1761.

" I have no pretence to your Lordfhip's patronage, but " from what your noble father fhewed to mine; which I " have prefumed to perpetuate by the inclofed letter*, re- " pofited, I fuppofe, in the Univerfity of *Oxford*. I little " thought of making it a ftep to introduce myfelf to your " Lordfhip; but Mr. *Richardfon's* † death, which you will " fee

---

* Which will be printed in p. 313.

† To what has been already faid of this original Genius in pp. 89. 138. and 156. I fhall take the prefent opportunity of adding a few further particulars and remarks. It appears by the original edition of *The True Briton* (fee p. 156), that Mr. *Richardfon* printed no more than *fix numbers*; and it feems highly probable that *the fixth (June* 21, 1723) was written by himfelf, as it is much in *his* manner. What is faid in p. 157, on the authority of Mr. *Hill*, that " *Pamela* was written in three months," is to be underftood of the firft and fecond volumes only, of which *five* editions were fold in one year. The *French* tranflation of it (fee p. 156) was undertaken by the confent of Mr. *Richardfon*, who furnifhed the tranflator ‡ with feveral corrections. It was in two volumes, 12mo, of which only the firft was printed by Mr. *Bowyer*.—In the enumeration of his writings, p. 158, l. 2. read " A Volume of Familiar Letters to and from feveral " perfons, upon Bufinefs and other fubjects." He was alfo the editor of Sir *Thomas Roe's* Letters (fee p. 138); he publifhed, or rather printed, a large fingle fheet relative to the Married State, intituled, " The Duties of Wives to Hufbands;" and was under the difagreeable neceffity of publifhing " The Cafe § of *Samuel Richardfon*, of " *London*,

---

‡ His *Clariffa* was tranflated into *Dutch* by the Rev. Mr. *Stinftra*, author of " A Paftoral Letter " againft Fanaticifm," tranflated into *Englifh* by Mr. *Rimius*. With this learned foreigner Mr. *Richardfon* afterwards carried on a correfpondence (Mr. *Stinftra* writing in *Latin*, which was interpreted to Mr. *Richardfon* by fome of his literary friends), and invited him to *England*, which his attendance on an aged mother obliged Mr. *Stinftra* to decline. See in the collection of Mr. *Hughes's* Letters, vol. II. p. 2. a letter from Mr. *Duncombe* to Mr. *Richardfon*, who is very juftly ftyled by the editor " The great mafter of the heart, the *Shakfpeare* of Romance."

§ I fhall, without apology, lay the whole of this cafe, as a fingular curiofity, before the reader of thefe Memoirs : " The Editor of ' The Hiftory of Sir *Charles Grandifon*' had intended to fend the " volumes of it, as he did thofe of ' The Hiftory of *Clariffa Harlowe*,' to be printed in *Ireland*, be- " fore he publifhed them himfelf in *London*. Accordingly, when he had printed off fo confiderable " a part of the work, as would have conftantly employed the prefs to which he purpofed to con- " fign them, he fent over 12 fheets of the firft volume to Mr. *George Faulkner*; intending to follow " it with the reft, as opportunity offered. He had heard an *Irifh* bookfeller boaft, fome years ago, " That he could procure, from any printing-office in *London*, fheets of any book printing in it, while " it was going on, and before publication; and Mr. *Faulkner* cautioning him on this fubject with

" regard

" see mentioned in the public papers, has incited me to
" hope

" *London*, Printer, on the Invasion of his Property in the History of Sir *Charles Gran-*
" *dison.*

" regard to this work, he took particular care to prevent, as he hoped, the effects of such an infa-
" mous corruption, as it must be called ; since it could not be done but by bribing the journeymen
" or servants of the *London* printer. He gave a strict charge, before he put the piece to press, to all
" his workmen and servants, as well in print (that it might the stronger impress them), as by word
" of mouth, to be on their guard against any out-door attacks. This was the substance of the
" printed caution which he gave to his workmen, on this occasion : ' A bookseller of *Dublin* has
" assured me, that he could get the sheets of any book from any printing-house in *London*, before
" publication. I hope I may depend upon the care and circumspection of my friends, compositors
" and press-men, that no sheets of the piece I am now putting to press be carried out of the house ;
" nor any notice taken of its being at press. It is of great consequence to me. Let no stranger be
" admitted into any of the work-rooms. Once more, I hope I may rely on the integrity and care of
" all my workmen—And let all the proofs, revises, &c. be given to Mr. *Tewley* [his foreman] to
" take care of.' He had no reason to distrust their assurances ; most of them being persons of expe-
" rienced honesty ; and was pleased with their declared abhorrence of so vile a treachery, and of all
" those who should attempt to corrupt them. Yet, to be still more secure, as he thought, he or-
" dered the sheets, as they were printed off, to be deposited in a separate warehouse ; the care of
" which was entrusted to one, on whom he had laid such obligations, as, if he is guilty, has made
" his perfidy a crime of the blackest nature *. Having three printing-houses, he had them com-
" posed, and wrought, by different workmen, and at his different houses ; and took such other pre-
" cautions, that the person to whose trust he committed them, being frequently questioned by him
" as to the safety of the work from pirates, as frequently assured him, That it was impossible the
" copy of any complete volume could be come at, were there persons in his house capable of being
" corrupted to attempt so vile a robbery. What then must be his surprise, when intelligence was
" sent him from *Dublin*, That copies of a considerable part of his work had been obtained by three
" different persons in that city ; and that the sheets were actually in the press ? The *honest* men pub-
" lished their own names, in three different title-pages stuck up, in *Dublin*, in the following
" words : ' *Dublin*, *Aug.* 4, 1753. Speedily will be published, The History of Sir *Charles Gran-*
" *dison.* In a series of Letters published from the Originals, by the Editor of *Pamela* and *Clarissa.*

* " *Peter Bishop*, whose business was to read proofs to the corrector, and to employ his leisure hours in the
" warehouses ; and who (and no other person) being entrusted with the sheets of Sir *Charles Grandison*, as
" wrought off ; and to lay-by three sheets of each of the twelves edition, and one of the octavo, for Mr. *Richard-*
" *son's* sole use ; had an opportunity which no other man, however inclined, could have, to perpetrate this base-
" ness. Mr. *Richardson*, on suspicions too well-grounded, dismissed *Bishop* from his service ; and, after he was
" gone, having reason to suspect *Thomas Killingbeck*, one of the compositors, as the confederate of *Bishop*, and by
" whose means, he having worked some years in *Ireland*, it was easy for him to manage this piece of treachery ;
" and *Killingbeck*, on examination, giving him cause to strengthen his suspicions ; yet asserting his innocence ;
" he proposed to him the said *Killingbeck* to draw up himself such an affidavit as he thought he could safely take,
" to exculpate himself. *Killingbeck* made poor excuses and pretences ; but, at last, took till the next morning
" to draw it up. The next morning he told Mr. *Richardson*, that he was advised not to draw up such an affida-
" vit ; and gave such evasive reasons, as induced every body to believe him guilty. Upon this, Mr. *Richardson*
" discharged him from his service. He left his house, pretending he would draw up something, as desired ;
" but never since came near it ; and is now applying for work elsewhere. Since writing the above, Mr.
" *Richardson* has received a letter from *Bishop*, on occasion of some friend of his advising him to an ample con-
" fession ; and to depend on that forgiving temper which he had before experienced ; in which, among other
" avowals of his innocence, he thus expresses himself :—' I never gave Mr. *K.* one sheet of *Grandison* ; and
" he must have stole them out of the warehouse ; for, upon recollection, the key of the bridge warehouse [in
" which were the five first volumes], for the conveniency of *Arthur* [the principal warehouse-keeper], who
" keeps his cloaths there, hung upon a nail, in the one pair of stairs warehouse ; and any person putting his
" arm through an opening in the wainscot, and standing on the stairs, may easily reach it [a great negligence,
" at least, in *Bishop*, after such warning, and repeated caution] : And 'tis not impossible but Mr. *K.* might see
" me take the key from thence, and make use of it at a proper opportunity. If he proves to be the villain (adds
" *Bishop*), as I have great reason to think he will, by his refusing to take an oath, I hope proper care will be
" taken to hinder his escape, &c.'—If *Bishop* should be innocent (against other presumptions, from which he
" will hardly be able to clear himself) it cannot but be observed, that the cause given to suspect unguilty persons
" is not one of the least mischiefs that attends the baseness of such cruel and clandestine invaders."

" In

" hope for that family friendſhip renewed to me in my de-
" clining years, which filled me with ſentiments of grati-
" tude

" diſon, before publication, by certain Bookſellers in *Dublin*;" which bears date
Sept.

" In ſeven Volumes. *Dublin*: Printed by and for *Henry Saunders*, at the corner of *Chriſt Church*
" *Lane.*' The ſecond :—' *Aug.* 4th, 1753. In the Preſs, The Hiſtory of Sir *Charles Grandiſon*'
" (as in the other). ' *Dublin*: Printed by *John Exſhaw*, on *Cork Hill.*' The third :—' *Dublin*,
" *Aug.* 4th, 1753. In the Preſs, and ſpeedily will be publiſhed, The Hiſtory of Sir *Charles Gran-*
" *diſon*' (as in the two others). ' *London*: Printed for *S. Richardſon*:' [vile artifice!] ' *Dublin*:
" Reprinted for *Peter Wilſon*, in *Dame Street.*' The editor had convincing proofs given him, that
" one of theſe men had procured a copy of a conſiderable part of the work in octavo; another in
" duodecimo; and that they were proceeding to print it at ſeveral preſſes. Terms having been
" agreed upon between Mr. *Faulkner* and the editor, in conſideration of the preference to be given
" him (one of which related to the time of publiſhing the *Dublin* edition, that it might not interfere
" with the appearance of the *London* one) Mr. *Faulkner*, in conſequence of the ſucceſsful corrup-
" tion, ſignified to the editor, that it was needleſs to ſend him any more than the 12 ſheets he had
" ſent him; and that he had obtained a fourth ſhare of theſe *honourable* confederates: But that (to
" procure this grace, as is ſuppoſed) he had been compelled, as he calls it, to deliver up to them,
" to print by, the copy of the 12 ſheets aforeſaid, which had ſome few corrections in them, which
" occurred on a laſt reviſal; but which are of no moment with regard to the hiſtory: Though poſ-
" ſibly this *worthy* confederacy may make uſe of thoſe few corrections in thoſe 12 ſheets, in order to
" recommend their ſurreptitious edition as preferable to that of the proprietor. Of what will not
" men be capable, who can corrupt the ſervants of another man to betray and rob their maſter?
" The editor, who had alſo great reaſon to complain of the treatment he met with in his *Pamela*,
" on both ſides the water, cannot but obſerve, that never was work more the property of any man,
" than this is his. The copy never was in any other hand: He borrows not from any other author:
" The paper, the printing, entirely at his own expence, to a very large amount; returns of which
" he cannot ſee in ſeveral months: Yet not troubling any of his friends to leſſen his riſque by a ſub-
" ſcription: The work, thus immorally invaded, is a moral work: He has never hurt any man;
" nor offended theſe: They would have had benefits from the ſale, which the editor could not
" have, being not a bookſeller; and he always making full and handſome allowances to bookſellers.
" But nothing leſs, it ſeems, would content theſe men, than an attempt to poſſeſs themſelves of his
" whole property, without notice, leave, condition, or offer at condition; and they are haſtening
" the work at ſeveral preſſes, poſſibly with a view to publiſh their piratical edition before the lawful
" proprietor can publiſh his. And who can ſay, that, if they can get it out before him, they will
" not advertiſe, that his is a piracy upon theirs? Yet theſe men know, that they have obtained the
" parts of the work they are poſſeſſed of, at the price of making no leſs than 40 workmen, in the
" editor's houſe, uneaſy, and ſome of them ſuſpected: Of making an innocent man unſafe in his
" own houſe: Of diſhonouring him in the opinion of his employers (who, probably, may not
" chooſe to truſt their property in the hands of a man, who cannot ſecure his own from inteſtine
" traitors): And to the ruin of as many as he ſhall diſcharge, as ſuſpectable of the baſeneſs; and
" whom, in that caſe, no other maſter will care to employ. Theſe, among others that might be
" enumerated, are the miſchiefs to which this vile and rapacious act of clandeſtine wickedneſs will
" ſubject an innocent man. Since the above was written, Mr. *Richardſon* has been acquainted, that
" his work is now printing at four ſeveral printing-houſes in *Dublin*, for the benefit of the confede-
" racy; viz. two volumes at Mrs. *Reiley's*; one at Mr. *Williamſon's*; one at Mr. *Powell's*; one at
" Mr. *M'Culloch's*; and that they hope at Mrs. *Reiley's* to get another volume to print; and are
" driving on to finiſh their two volumes for that purpoſe. The work will make ſeven volumes in
" twelves; ſix in octavo; and he apprehends, from the quantity he himſelf had printed when the
" fraud was diſcovered, that the confederacy have got poſſeſſion of five entire volumes, the greateſt
" part of the ſixth, and of ſeveral ſheets of the ſeventh and laſt; but the work being ſtopped when
" the wickedneſs was known, they cannot have the better half of the concluding volume. He is
" further aſſured, that theſe worthy men are in treaty with bookſellers in *Scotland*, for their print-
" ing his work, in that part of the united kingdom, from copies that they are to furniſh; and alſo,
" that they purpoſe to ſend a copy to *France*, to be tranſlated there, before publication; no doubt
" for pecuniary conſiderations; and in order to propagate, to the utmoſt, the injury done to one,
" who never did any to them; and who, till this proceeding, he bleſſes God, knew not that there
" were ſuch men in the world; at leaſt, among thoſe who could look out in broad and open day.
" It

" tude in my childhood; and that I may have the honour
" of

Sept. 14, 1753 *.   " A Collection of the Moral Sentences in *Pamela, Clarissa*, and
" It has been customary for the *Irish* booksellers to make a scramble among themselves who should
" first entitle himself to the reprinting of a new *English* book : and happy was he, who could get
" his agents in *England* to send him a copy of a supposed saleable piece, as soon as it was printed,
" and ready to be published.   This kind of property was never contested with them by authors in
" *England*; and it was agreed among themselves (*i. e.* among the *Irish* booksellers and printers) to
" be a sufficient title; though now and then a *shark* was found, who preyed on his own kind; as the
" news-papers of *Dublin* have testified.   But the present case will shew to what a height of base-
" ness such an undisputed licence is arrived.   After all, if there is no law to right the editor and
" sole proprietor of this new work *(new* in every sense of the word), he must acquiesce; but with
" this hope, that, from so flagrant an attempt, a law may one day be thought necessary, in order to
" secure to authors the benefit of their own labours: Nor does he wish, that even these invaders of
" his property in *Ireland* may be excluded from the benefit of it, in the property of any of the works
" to which they are, or shall be, fairly and lawfully entitled.   At present, the *English* writers may
" be said, from the attempts and practices of the *Irish* booksellers and printers, to live in an age of
" *liberty*, but not of *property*.
" N. B. This is not a contention between booksellers of *England* and *Ireland*, and on a doubtful
" property; but between a lawful proprietor of a new and moral work—and
" Let Messieurs *Wilson, Exshaw*, and *Saunders*, reflecting upon the steps they have taken, and
" making the case their own (for they no doubt have servants)—fill up the blank."
　* The *Gray's Inn Journal* of *October* 13, 1753, enumerates the pains, inconveniencies, and hardships of eminent authors; the variety of anguish and distress to which the extreme sensibility of the
minds of men of genius renders them liable, the fatigue of intense study and painful vigils, the care
and anxiety attendant on composition, their dissatisfaction with their own performances, even after
they have pleased every body else; and then justly observes, what an additional load of affliction it
must bring upon them, to have their property invaded, and to lose, in a great measure, the benefit of
their labours.   The author then relates the case of Mr. *Richardson*, and, after observing, that a greater
degree of probity might be expected from booksellers, on account of their occupation in life, and
connexions with the learned, he goes on thus : " What then should be said of Mess. *Exshaw, Wilson*,
" and *Saunders*, booksellers in *Dublin*, and perpetrators of this vile act of piracy ? They should all
" be expelled from the republic of letters, as literary *Goths* and *Vandals*, who are ready to invade
" the property of every man of genius.   Had the *Sosii*, who were booksellers in *Rome*, been guilty
" of such sordid dealings, I am persuaded, they would have been mentioned with infamy by *Horace*;
" and it is recent in every body's memory, that *Curll* underwent many severe corrections for con-
" duct of the same nature with that already mentioned.   I am sorry that the laws of the land have
" not sufficiently secured to authors the property of their works; until that is done, the courts of *Par-
" nassus* are in the right to take cognizance of this flagrant unpoetic licence, by the following order :
" To the Students of TRINITY COLLEGE in *Dublin*.
　" Trusty and well beloved,
" Whereas *Peter Wilson, John Exshaw*, and *Henry Saunders*, booksellers in your city, have, by
" the arts of bribery and corruption, obtained the greatest part of ' The History of Sir *Charles*
" *Grandison*,' to the great detriment of our favourite son, Mr. *Samuel Richardson*, to whom we have
" imparted a large portion of our etherial fire, and to whom we have opened the secrets of the hu-
" man heart, with full commission to describe all the feelings of the same; and whereas we are
" moved with the highest indignation at such an unjustifiable deed; we do hereby enjoin our young
" collegians, in a collective body, to march to the respective houses of the said *Peter Wilson, John*
" *Exshaw*, and *Henry Saunders*, their bodies to seize, and in solemn procession to proceed with the
" same to the place where *William Wood*, hardwareman, was executed in effigy, and then and there
" the said persons in a blanket to toss †, but not till they are dead; and of this you are not to fail
" under our highest displeasure.   Given on *Parnassus* this 10th of *October*, in the year of the *Home-
" rican* æra, two thousand seven hundred and fifty-three.   By order of *Apollo*,
" *Jonathan Swift*, Secretary."

　† It is a constant practice (we are informed) in *Germany, France, Holland*, and *Switzerland*, to publish a description of such traitors, with their pictures engraved, and send them to all the printing offices, to prevent
masters being imposed upon by them, and the journeymen and apprentices will not converse with such nefarious
villains, nor suffer their dead carcases to be interred.   Pity, indeed, it is, that some signal and exemplary punishment cannot be inflicted upon the encouragers of this vile treachery, as well as upon the perpetrators, who
ought to be contemned as the discouragers of publick instruction and entertainment, the persecutors and op-
pressors of genius, and the plunderers of the republick of literature.

" *Grandison*,"

" of being recommended by your Lordſhip to print for the
" Royal Society, if that office ſhall be removed to any other
" printing-houſe.   But, whatever ſhall be the event, your
" Lordſhip

" *Grandiſon*," was printed in 12mo, 1755. To the elogiums on Mr. *Richardſon*, in
pp. 158, 159, may be added this by the Earl of *Corke:* " Mr. *Richardſon* draws tears
" from every eye. It is impoſſible to take up his works without quitting the thoughts
" of every thing elſe, and travelling with him wherever he pleaſes to carry us *." Dr.
Dodd, in his " Day on Vacation" mentions him thus:

" Ah ! *D[uncombe]*, now where art thou ? Bleſt indeed
" In converſe with the man † the world admires."

And Mrs. *Pilkington*, in her Memoirs, vol. II. p. 238, having been directed to the
houſe of Mr. *Richardſon*, to receive a ſmall ſum of money, thus gratefully deſcribes the
viſit: " As I had never formed any great idea of a printer by thoſe I had ſeen in *Ire-
" land*, I was very negligent of my dreſs, any more than making myſelf clean; but was
" extremely ſurpriſed, when I was directed to a houſe of a very grand outward appear-
" ance, and had it been a palace, the beneficent maſter deſerved it. I met a very civil
" reception from him ; and he not only made me breakfaſt, but alſo dine with him and
" his agreeable wife and children.   After dinner he called me into his ſtudy, and ſhewed
" me an order he had received to pay me twelve guineas, which he immediately took
" out of his eſcrutore, and put into my hand; but when I went to tell them over, I
" found I had fourteen, and ſuppoſing the gentleman had made a miſtake, I was for
" returning two of them; but he, with a ſweetneſs and modeſty almoſt peculiar to him-
" ſelf, ſaid, he hoped I would not take it ill, that he had preſumed to add a trifle to
" the bounty of my friend. I really was confounded, till, recollecting that I had read
" *Pamela*, and been told it was written by one Mr. *Richardſon*, I aſked him, whether he
" was not the author of it ? He ſaid, he was the editor : I told him, my ſurprize was
" now over, as I found he had only given to the incomparable *Pamela* the virtues of
" his own worthy heart.   When he reads theſe lines, as read them I am certain he
" will, even for the writer's ſake, let him reflect, that at leaſt his bread was not ſcattered
" on the water." And Mr. *Sherlock*, the celebrated *Engliſh* Traveller, beſtows whole
letters ‡ in commendation of *Clariſſa*, of which the Preface to the Firſt Edition was written by the learned Mr. *Warburton*. In his private character Mr. *Richardſon* was a ſilent
plain

* From a MS. Letter to Mr. *Duncombe*.
† " Every reader will confeſs the propriety of what is ſaid of this gentleman, when I tell them
" the perſon here meant is the truly amiable author of *Clariſſa*." Dr. *Dodd*.
‡ " The greateſt effort of genius that perhaps was ever made was forming the plan of *Clariſſa*
" *Harlowe*." . . . . . " *Richardſon* is not yet arrived at the fulneſs of his glory." . . . . . " *Richard-
" ſon* is admirable for every ſpecies of delicacy; for delicacy of wit, ſentiment, language, action,
" every thing." . . . . . " His genius was immenſe. His miſfortune was that he did not know the
" ancients. Had he but been acquainted with one ſingle principle, ' Omne ſupervacuum pleno de
" pectore manat,' (all ſuperfluities tire) ; he would not have ſatiated his reader as he has done.
" There might be made out of *Clariſſa* and Sir *Charles Grandiſon* TWO works, which would be both
" the moſt entertaining, and the moſt uſeful, that ever were written. . . . . His views were grand.
" His ſoul was noble, and his heart was excellent. He formed a plan that embraced all human
" nature. His object was to benefit mankind. His knowledge of the world ſhewed him that hap-
" pineſs was to be attained by man, only in proportion as he practiſed virtue. His good ſenſe then
" ſhewed him that no practical ſyſtem of morality exiſted ; and the ſame good ſenſe told him that
" nothing but a body of morality, put into action, could work with efficacy on the minds of youth.
" Sermons

" Lordſhip will pardon me in taking this opportunity of
" unburthening my heart of thoſe ſenſations which time
" cannot

plain man, who ſeldom exhibited his talents in mixed company.   He heard the ſentiments
of others ſometimes with attention, and ſeldom gave his own ; rather deſirous of gaining
your

" Sermons and eſſays, experience ſhewed him, were ineffectual.   The manner of them was dry and
" uninteresting to young people ; and arguments addreſſed to what is weakeſt in youth, to their un-
" derſtandings, he clearly perceived, were without effect.   He ſaw farther, that example was the
" great point which formed the young ; and he ſaw that man was compoſed of paſſions and imagi-
" nation as well as of underſtanding.   Thoſe were his general principles ; and upon thoſe principles
" he reaſoned thus : Mankind is naturally good, for it is rare to meet young people with bad hearts.
" A young man then coming into the world wiſhes to be perfect.   But how ſhall he learn ?   The
" world is a bad ſchool ; and precepts ſcattered up and down in books of morality are of little uſe.
" An example would form him ; but where is it to be found ? None exiſts.   I will then create one
" for him.   I will ſet before him a model of perfection.   The more he imitates it, the more perfect
" he will be ; the more perfect he is, the happier he will be.   As he reaſoned upon man, ſo he
" reaſoned upon woman.   He aimed at no leſs than beſtowing felicity on the generation he ſaw
" riſing before him, and on every one that was to ſucceed it.   And had he not had powers to ac-
" compliſh this aim, his wiſh was ſo grand, ſo noble, and of ſuch a ſuperior order of benevolence,
" that that alone would have entitled him to immortality ; I had almoſt ſaid canoniſation.   But
" ſuch is the perverſeneſs and weakneſs of mankind, that what conſtitutes *Richardſon's* greateſt merit,
" is conſidered by many as a capital defect in his conception.   They object that ſuch a woman as
" *Clariſſa*, and ſuch a man as Sir *Charles Grandiſon*, having never exiſted, the author has created
" palpable chimæras, and conſequently his creations are uſeleſs and unaffecting.   How conſiſtent
" are the reaſonings of men !   Century after century, and country after country, have vied with
" each other in praiſing the work and the author of the *Venus of Medici*.   Yet this work muſt be
" univerſally allowed to be farther from nature than *Richardſon's Clariſſa*.   No woman ever came
" near the beauty of this ſtatue ; yet, has that diminiſhed the merits of the author ? Has he not
" always been, and is he not hourly and juſtly admired for the ingenuity of his idea, though this
" idea is totally barren of profit to the world ?   Not ſo with *Clariſſa* : ſhe muſt profit every female
" that beholds her.   Though the whole of theſe two imaginary beings did evidently never exiſt,
" yet ſo great has been the maſtery of theſe uncommon artiſts, that there is not a particle in the
" compoſition of the ſtatue, nor a trait in the character or conduct of the heroine, that can be ſaid
" to deviate in the minuteſt degree from the preciſe line of nature and of truth.   *Richardſon* has
" done no more than animate the *Venus of Medici*.   The *Grecian* ſculptor had *created, of every crea-
" ture's beſt*, a marble body : the *Engliſh* writer created equally, *of every creature's beſt*, a ſoul, a
" mind, a genius for that body.
" . . . . . The writers of *England* excel thoſe of all other nations in the pathetic ; and *Richardſon*
" in this point is, I think, ſuperior to all his countrymen.   He makes one cry too much : and by a
" very ſingular talent, peculiar to himſelf alone, he fills our eyes almoſt as often by elevated ſenti-
" ments, as he does by tender ones.   He abounds with ſtrokes of greatneſs, ſometimes in the
" actions and ſometimes in the ſentiments of his characters, which raiſe the reader's ſoul, and
" make the tear of generoſity ſpring into his eye he knows not whence.
" . . . . . It is injuring *Richardſon* to quote a trait of pathos from him, when he has whole vo-
" lumes which it is impoſſible to read without crying and ſobbing from beginning to end.   I feel for
" the injuſtice that is done this author, who, I will venture to aſſert, is ſecond to no man that ever
" wrote.   It is aſtoniſhing, however, how many men of parts I have met with who ſpeak of him
" with contempt.   Moſt of them, it is true, have condemned him without reading him ; and they
" have condemned him becauſe he is a writer of *Novels* or *Romances*.   What is a name ? What ſig-
" nifies how a work is called ; whether it is a romance, a novel, a ſtory, or a hiſtory ? No matter
" for the title ; examine the work.   Does it grapple the attention (to uſe *Shakſpeare's* expreſſion)
" with hooks of ſteel ? does it move, does it elevate, does it enlighten, does it amuſe ?   Theſe are
" the points to be enquired into, and not how it is called.   I have known many other clever people,
" who have dipped into *Clariſſa*, and who hold it and it's author very cheap.   Some of theſe men
" have gone through a volume or two, others have read a number of letters here and there, have
" then formed their opinions of it's merits, and thrown away the book.   *Richardſon's* object was not
" to

" cannot efface ; and which will remain while I fhall be
" able to fubfcribe myfelf, your Lordfhip's moft dutiful
" and obedient humble fervant, W. BOWYER."

The application was fuccefsful. The noble Lord condefcended to patronife a fon of the printer his father had generoufly contributed to fupport ; and recommended him
effectually to the very learned Society over which he with
fo much dignity prefided. And Mr. *Bowyer* had the fatisfaction of continuing in that employment till his death, under
the friendfhip and patronage of five fucceffive prefidents＊.

your friendfhip by his modefty than his parts. His turn of temper led him to improve
his fortune with mechanical affiduity; and having no violent paffions, nor any defire of
being triflingly diftinguifhed from others, he at laft became rich, and left his family in
eafy independence; though his houfe and table, both in town and country, were ever
open to his numerous friends. Two of them, viz. Mr. *Edwards* and a Mifs *Dutton*,
died much about the fame time at his houfe on *Parfon's Green*. In *Dodfley's* Collection, vol. V. p. 296, are fome verfes on an alcove there by Mrs. *Bennet*, fifter to Mr.
Bridgen. Mr. *Richardfon* was mafter of the Company of Stationers in 1754, during the
mayoralty of Mr. *Janffen*, when the arms in the Company's Hall were new painted.
The following memorial infcription is copied from a flat ftone in the body of *St. Bride's*
church :

" Here lyeth interred the body of
MARTHA
the beloved wife of
SAMUEL RICHARDSON,
who departed this life
January the 25th, 1730-31.
Here alfo lie the bodies of
WILLIAM and SAMUEL two of their fons,
Who died { WILLIAM the 12th day of *May*, 1730.
{ SAMUEL the 5th day of *October*, 1730.
Here alfo lyeth interred the body of
THOMAS VERREN RICHARDSON,

the beloved and hopeful fon of
WILLIAM RICHARDSON, and nephew of the faid
SAMUEL RICHARDSON, who departed this life
November the 8th, 1732,
In the fixteenth year of his age.
Alfo here lyeth the body of
Mr. SAMUEL RICHARDSON of this parifh,
who died *July* the 4th, 1761, aged 72 years.

Mrs. ELIZABETH RICHARDSON
Died the 3d of *November*, 1773,
Aged 77 years."

His picture by Mr. *Highmore*, a ftriking likenefs, from which *Mac Ardell* fcraped a mezzotinto, with Mr. *Edward's* fonnet engraved under it, is now in the poffeffion of his fon-
in-law *Edward Bridgen*, efq. F. R. and A. SS.

＊ The earls of *Macclesfield* and *Morton*, Sir *James Burrow*, *James Weft*, efq. and
Sir *John Pringle*.

" to write a volume, or a letter; it was to make. If the entire work be not examined, it is im-
" poffible to judge it. He built a palace. The ftair-cafe is too high : if it had fewer fteps, it
" would be better. One tires fometimes before one gets to the head of it. But go on ; enter into
" the apartments; obferve their diftribution, their proportion, their effect; fee their *enfemble*;
" examine their whole ; and then anfwer if ever there was an edifice equal to it for beauty, gran-
" deur, fublimity, and magnificence ? There never was in any country. The introduction into
" the ftory of *Clariffa* is a *leetle* too long ; but when you pafs that, there never was a ftory equally
" interefting, or equally affecting ; and I affert, without dread of being contradicted by any man of
" tafte and talents who reads it through, that there does not exift, in the univerfe, a work equal to
" it for WIT, SENTIMENT and SENSE." See *Sherlock's* Original Letters, vol. I. *paffim*.

The

The letter to the earl of *Macclesfield* gives me an opportunity of clearing up a transaction to which it alludes. The *Saxon* types, which were used in printing *St. Gregory's* Homily, having been burnt, as has been already mentioned in p. 10, Lord Chief Justice *Parker* was at the expence of cutting a new *Saxon* type from *fac similes* by Mrs. *Elstob*; the punches and matrices of which Mr. *Bowyer's* son presented, by the hands of *Edward-Rowe Mores**, esq. to the University of *Oxford*, with the following letter:

" To

* To what has been said of Mr. *Mores* in p. 130, may be added, that his father † was in 1709 curate at *Low Leyton*, to Mr. *John Strype* the Historian; that the late Mr. *Mores* took the degree of B.A. *May* 12, 1750, and of M.A.‡ *Jan.* 15, 1753; and that he was one of the governors of *Bridewell* and *Bethlem* Hospitals. In 1750 he was one of a committee for examining the Minute-books of the Society of Antiquaries, with a view to the selecting from thence of papers proper for publication ‖. The edition of *Dionysius*, which he had nearly finished in 1749, has been published in 1781, with the short preface transcribed below §. By his intimacy with the late Mr. *St. Eloy*, one of the registers of the prerogative court, he got access to that office, and had thereby an opportunity of drawing up his learned dissertations on the authority of that court. It has been suggested that he entered into deacons orders ** in the church of *Eng-*

† That the rector of *Tunstall* was of a litigious disposition, appears not only from the squabble with his parishioners recorded in his son's history of that parish, but from a perusal of several of his original letters to Mr. *Strype*, a man of a quiet, humane, and meek disposition, with whom Mr. *Mores* had disputes; and from his own letters his boisterous and wrangling nature may easily be discovered.

‡ The late Mr. *Scott* of *Wolstan Hall* observes of him, in a MS. memorandum, that he had a distinguished character for literature at *Oxford*.

‖ A more numerous committee was appointed for the same purpose in 1762. But still the publication lingered till 1770, when the first volume of the Archæologia appeared.

§ " Quæ sequitur *Dionysii* Commentariorum Editio est a manu viri doctissimi *Edvardi-Rowe* " *Mores*, armigeri, nuper defuncti. Eam typis jam olim mandatam fuisse, ex pagina 161 perspicies. " Quo minùs in publicum tunc prodiret, in causâ erat annotationum desiderium, quas in animo " habebat vir eruditus conficere: modo per negotia inopinata licuisset. Annotationibus tamen " assiduè meditabatur hanc suam editionem cumulare; quod consilium per mortem tandem irritum " factum est. Etenim, cum ex hæredibus statim quæsitum esset, utrùm ejusmodi quidquam inter " scripta ejus extaret, re solicitè exploratâ verè nimis compertum est, nihil omnino superesse; nisi " fortasse suo editionis *Hudsonianæ* exemplari ab editore nostro notæ quædam adscriptæ fuerint: " quod exemplar, cujus in manus jam inciderit, non liquet. Cum itaque frustra expectarent bib-" liopolæ, si quis illius messi falcem suam vellet inserere; maluerint libellum inchoatum in lucem " emittere, quàm juventutis academicæ, hanc editionem jam diu efflagitantis, votis æquissimis non " obsequi."

** He was at one time in treaty for the advowson of the rectory of *Bradwell juxta mare*, in *Essex*, which he intended for his son; who being then very young, Mr. *Mores* talked to his friends of going into orders himself, that he might be able to hold it. The annual profits of this living are said to exceed 700l. It was held till his death 1771, by Dr. *Roger Long*, Master of *Pembroke Hall*, *Cambridge*. The advowson of it, with immediate resignation, was sold in 1781 for 1500l.

land,

" To *Edward-Rowe Mores*, Efq. at *Low Leyton*.

" SIR, *Dec.* 4, 1753.

" I make bold to tranfmit to *Oxford*, through your
" hands, the *Saxon* punches and matrices, which you were
" pleafed

land, with a view to exempt himfelf from ferving civil offices; but at what time, or
by which of the bifhops his ordination was conferred, we have not been happy enough
to difcover. In the original warrant for letters of adminiftration granted to his fon, on
his dying inteftate, and in the bond given on that occafion (which I have feen in the
Prerogative-office), he is ftyled " The *Reverend* Edward-Rowe Mores, late of the pa-
" rifh of *Leyton*, in the county of *Effex*, *Doctor in Divinity*." When, where, or how,
he came by this degree, is extremely unaccountable; nor would this have been inferted,
had I not been affured by a very intimate friend of his, that Mr. *Mores* received the *honorary* title of D. D. in confequence of a literary favour which he had conferred on fome
foreign *Roman* Catholic Ecclefiaftics *, who wifhed to repay him by a pecuniary acknowledgement, which he politely declined accepting. Mr. *Mores* was as ambitious of
fingularity in religion as in other purfuits; and if he could be faid to be a member of
any particular church, it was that of *Erafmus*, whom he endeavoured to imitate. He
thought the *Latin* language peculiarly adapted to devotion, and wifhed, for the
fake of *unity*, that it was univerfally in ufe. He compofed a creed in it, with a kind
of mafs on the death of his wife, of which he printed a few copies, in his own houfe,
under the difguifed title of " Ordinale Quotidianum, 1685. Ordo Trigintalis." Of
his daughter's education he was particularly careful. From her earlieft infancy
he talked to her principally in *Latin*. The gentleman from whom I received this
information dined with Mr. *Mores* when his daughter was not more than two years
old. Among other articles they had foup, with which the child had foiled her lip.
Abfterge labium, faid the father. The child underftood the *Latin*, and wiped her

---

* From what Univerfity in particular this degree was received, though I have inquired wherever I
thought it likely to gain intelligence, I cannot at prefent afcertain. It was imagined that he was
indebted for it to the Society of the *Sorbonne*. But, on application to our very learned countryman
Dr. *Hooke*, who has long done honour to the Profeffor's chair of Aftronomy in that illuftrious Body,
I have been favoured with this moft fatisfactory anfwer: " It never was cuftomary in the *Sorbonne*
" to beftow the degree of Doctor on any perfon, who had not ftudied in *Paris*, and taken all the
" inferior degrees according to the ftatutes of the Univerfity; nor is there upon record one example
" to the contrary. Befides, I can atteft, that for thefe forty years paft there has been no literary
" correfpondence between the Society of *Sorbonne*, and the Rev. Mr. *Rowe Mores*; for, having never
" been abfent during all that time from the faid Society, I fhould certainly have been privy to it."
MS Letter, dated *Paris, à la Bibliotheque Mazarine, ce* 13 *Avril*, 1781.—To counterbalance this
weighty teftimony, let me quote a few lines from the letter of my original informant: " At this
" diftance of time I cannot fay pofitively, who were the Ecclefiaftics whom Dr. *Mores* obliged, or
" by what Society the degree was conferred; but this I am pofitive of, that Dr. *Mores* affured me
" that the degree conferred was a Doctor's in Divinity, and that it was procured for him by the
" intereft of thofe gentlemen with whom he had held a literary correfpondence. I remember,
" when he told me of this affair, he added, ' I could fhew you my diploma, but,' fays he, fmil-
" ing, ' I queftion whether I could do it fafely, for I do not know whether there are not fome
" things in it which might fubject me to a *pramunire*.' The difcourfe unluckily happened to take
" another turn, which prevented my requefting to fee it. I heartily wifh that you could meet
" with the diploma itfelf; and that a matter of this confequence fhould not be delivered to pofte-
" rity upon hearfay evidence. I dare to fay the correfpondence which paffed between him and thofe
" gentlemen is preferved, which would throw further light on this matter."

6

" pleafed to intimate would not be unacceptable to that
" learned body. It would be a great fatisfaction to me, if
" I could

upper lip. *Inferius*, faid Mr. *Mores*, and fhe did as he meant fhe fhould. She
was fent to *Rouen*, for education; but without the leaft view to her being a *Roman* Catholic: on the contrary, he was much difpleafed when he found fhe had been
perverted. Two original letters to the Superior of the Houfe under whofe care fhe was
placed, which are printed below *, contain a fufficient refutation of the report of his
being himfelf a member of the church of *Rome*. They are carefully tranfcribed from
an original copy delivered by Mr. *Mores* himfelf to the gentleman who communicated
them to me, without any material alteration even in the punctuation.

* I. " Matronæ venerabili Præfidenti domûs monialium S. Josepho dicatæ in civitate Rotho-
   " magenfi, Edoardus-Rowe Mores S.
" Filiam meam unicam tutelæ veftræ committimus: eo quidem lubentius quod præter arctam domûs
" veftræ difciplinam nullas apud vos noftræ gentis impræfentiarum commorari intelligimus. Judicio
" fatis acuto, ingenio facili, et indole non infuavi eft prædita; tractabilis, docilis, fed orbata matre,
" quæ vivens quidem diutino conflictata eft morbo, et a me nimis amata, et in plurimis ultra infantiles
" annos evecta, & præ cæteris ætatis fuæ fexûfque plerumque pollens, omne præter meum detrec-
" tavit imperium; cui variis districto negotiis curandi recognofcendique et defuit et deeft otium.
" Ad te autem venit, Matrona venerabilis, in paternis ab incunabilis enutrita ædibus, non e fchola
" noftrarum aliqua (quas omnes refpuo faftidioque) aut labem aut maculam in fanctarum tuarum
" gregem invectura; fed pura, munda, et a fæculi flagitiis innoxia; in puritate, munditia, & innocen-
" tia, mox, fi fic Deo placuerit, nobis reddenda. De operibus acu conficiendis, et quantum in iifdem
" exerceri oporteat, utpote quæ ad me minus pertineant, loquantur quæ comites funt fœminæ. Utilia
" funto, non nugatoria: ad rem domefticam accommodata. De iis quæ ad me magis attinent—fcri-
" bendi, delineandique, et arithmetices artibus imbuta prodeat. In fuperiori commenfalium or-
" dine collocamus, neutiquam vero ut habenæ remittantur inertiæ, aut ut arctiffima domûs veftræ re-
" laxetur difciplina; quamvis in ordine fuperior, in ditione fit quafi infima, quamvis laica ut reli-
" giofa: non prætextu quovis obambulet oppidum, neque mœnia tranfmeet cœnobii; nec ullis nifi
" domûs veftræ fanctimonialibus familiaritate conjuncta fit. Cum iis una prandeat, una cœnet, et
" ea re fodalis efto. inter provectiores etenim hactenus ordinatam ad parvulas migrare nolumus.
" ecclefiæ diligenter peragat officia, matutinum fcilicet et vefpertinum—mature furgat—mature fe ad
" lectum conferat,—deftinatis negotiis fedulo navet operam—et quanto magis in his exegeritis obfequi-
" um tanto magis apud nos, reverenda, in exiftimatione et honore eritis. Epiftolas a puellula affig-
" natas mihi, et epiftolas a me puellulæ affignatas, inapertas tranfire vellem. de cæteris fi quæ fint
" (quod vix crediderim) aperiantur, legantur, et pro libitu difponantur veftro. de libris quos fecum
" affert, idem fere poftulandum eft, ut in fecretis legat fas efto. religionem fpectant nulli nifi biblia.
" Huc ufque, Matrona fpectatiffima, locutus et te et filiam meam divino præfidio commendarem.
" præterire vero non poffum quod cum ipfe, ecclefiæ alienæ theologus, tutamini veftro meam com-
" miferim filiam, eandem mihi detur fperare fiduciam quam præftarem ipfe, fi tuam mihi filiam cre-
" didiffes ipfa, mandatis tuis votifque ftudiofe obtemperaturo. et cum eidem uterque confecrati
" fimus fervitio, Omnipotentis gloriæ & animarum faluti, præ oculis efto affinitatis conjunctio: et
" me tuum perinde refpicias fratrem, ac ipfe te meam fororem in Domino. ad eandem uterque col-
" lineamus metam, etfi parum difcrepet infequendi ratio.—Pax Dei omnipotentis adfit vobis cœtui·
" que veftro! Amen.
" *è Leytonâ in comitat. Effexiæ die decollationis S. Joh. bapt. 1768.*"
   II. " Matronæ venerabili fororum hofpitalar. fodalitatis S. Josephi, in civitate Rothomagenf.
   " Superiori Edoardus-Rowe Mores S.
" Lætabar admodum et gratias rependo maximas, infigniffima Matrona, quod filiam meam pere-
" grinam, ignoti parentis prolem, ex defideriis meis in fodalitium cooptare veftrum dignata es.
" Adaugetur mihi mentis oblectatio quod in camera Superiori vicina novitia diverfetur hofpes—
" quanto magis vicinia tibi propinqua fir, Reverenda, tanto magis in literatura propinqua fit, et in mo-
" ribus, et in virtute omni. Tot inter verfata pietatis exemplaria fieri vix poteft ut in delictum
" cadat: advena autem cum fit, et externæ gentis, et exteris affuefacta moribus, infcite labefcenti con-
" cedatur delicti venia. fin autem hofce fupergrediatur limites, et vel apud te, vel apud aliquam, in of-
" fenfu

" I could by this means perpetuate the munificence of the
" noble donor, to whom I am originally indebted for them,
" the late Lord Chief Juftice *Parker*, afterwards Earl of
" *Macclesfield*, who, among the numerous benefactors
" which my father met with, after his houfe was burnt in
" 1712-13, was fo good as to procure thofe types to be
" cut, to enable him to print Mrs. *Elftob's* * *Saxon* Grammar.
" *England* had not then the advantage of fuch an artift in
" letter-cutting as has fince arifen†: and it is to be lament-
" ed,

* " This type Mifs *Elftob* ufed in her grammar, and in her grammar only. In her
" capital undertaking, the publication of ' The *Saxon* Homilies,' begun and left un-
" finifhed, whether becaufe the type was thought unfightly to politer eyes, or whether
" becaufe the Univerfity of *Oxford* had caft a new letter that fhe might print the work
" with them, or whether (as fhe expreffes herfelf in a letter to her uncle Dr. *Elftob)*
" becaufe ' women are allowed the privilege of appearing in a richer garb and finer or-
" naments than men,' fhe ufed a *Saxon* of the modern garb; but not one of thefe rea-
" fons is of any weight with an antiquary, who will always prefer the natural face
" to ' richer garb and finer ornaments;' and on his fide is reafon uncontrovertible.
" The fount of Mifs *Elftob*, though approaching nearly to the old *Saxon*, has yet fome
" tincture of the innovations brought by King *Alfred* from *Rome*, and by King *Edward*
" *the Confeffor* from *Normandy*; all which coalefcing formed the *Englifh* hand." *Diff.*
on Founders, p. 29, 30.—Some account of this learned lady has been already given in
p. 11. and 48. The copies of the unfinifhed " Homilarium" have been lately purchafed
among the remnants of an old bookfeller's fhop, by Mr. *Prince* of *Oxford*.

† Mr. *William Cafton*, born in that part of the town of *Hales Owen* which is fituated in
Shropfhire, in 1692, and who is juftly ftyled by Mr. *Rowe-Mores* " the *Coryphæus* of
" Letter-founders," was not trained to that bufinefs; " which is a handy-work, fo con-
" cealed among the artificers of it," that Mr. *Moxon*, in his indefatigable refearches on that
fubject, " could not difcover that any one had taught it any other; but every one that had
" ufed it learnt it of his own genuine inclination ‡." He ferved a regular apprenticefhip
to an engraver of ornaments on gun-barrels; and was taken from that inftrument to an em-

" fenfu magis fit, ut certior fim factus obfecro; neque paterna deerit ad corrigendum auctoritas.
" Lætitiam vero meam nonnihil diluit, Rev. epiftolium futile fatis et ineptum W *** meæ, vobis
" veftrifque jure devinctiffimæ, (datum ab enthea quadam noftræ gentis ut conjicere eft) infciente
" te dictitatum: veftram etenim veftrafque alias effe cenfeo quam quæ fic inepte blaterarent. exinde
" difcimus de religione cum puellula fuiffe actum. ægre profecto fero, et præter fidem mihi præ-
" ftitam arbitror, quod in meffem meam alter ingerat falcem: ægriùs, quod cum tutiffimæ natam
" meam fidei commiffam crederem, fpreta fentire videar præcepta mea. ex votis erat meis ut de rebus
" hujufmodi ætati teneræ minus idoneis omnino conticeretur, ex mandatis vero ut cum Anglicis
" fociaretur nullis. idem repetimus votum; mandatum iteramus idem.—ut in iis edoceatur quæ fta-
" tuimus olim, Rev. exorare liceat. Cætera mihi curæ funto.
                                    " Valeas, et (ignotum licet) ames me.
    " è Leytonâ in com. Effex. poftridie concept. 1768."
    ‡ Differtation upon *Englifh* Typographical Founders and Founderies, p. 17.

                                                            ployment

" ed, that the execution of thefe is not equal to the inten-
" tion

ployment of a very different tendency, *the propagation of the Chriſtian faith.* In the year 1720 (the year in which his eldeſt ſon was born) the Society for promoting Chriſtian knowledge, in conſequence of a repreſentation made by Mr. *Salomon Negri,* a native of *Damaſcus* in *Syria,* well ſkilled in the Oriental languages, who had been profeſſor of *Arabic* in places of note for a great part of his life, deemed it expedient to print for the uſe of the Eaſtern churches the New Teſtament and Pſalter in the *Arabic* language, for the benefit of the poor Chriſtians in *Paleſtine, Syria, Meſopotamia, Arabia,* and *Ægypt ;* the conſtitution of which countries allowed of no printing ; and Mr. *Caſlon* was pitched upon to cut the fount, which in his ſpecimens is diſtinguiſhed by the name of *Engliſh Arabic.* Mr. *Caſlon,* after he had finiſhed his *Arabic* fount, cut the letters of his own name in *Pica Roman** , and placed the name at the bottom of a ſpecimen of the *Arabic ;* and Mr. *Palmer* (the reputed author of *Pſalmanazar's* " Hiſtory of Printing") ſeeing this name, adviſed Mr. *Caſlon* to cut the whole fount of Pica. Mr. *Caſlon* did ſo ; and as the performance exceeded the letter of the other founders of the time, Mr. *Palmer,* whoſe circumſtances required credit with thoſe who, by this advice, were now obſtructed, repented of having given the advice, and diſcouraged Mr. *Caſlon* from any further progreſs. Mr. *Caſlon,* diſguſted, applied to Mr. *Bowyer,* under whoſe inſpection he cut in 1722 the beautiful fount of *Engliſh* which was uſed in printing *Selden's* Works, 1726 ; and the *Coptic* types which were uſed for Dr. *Wilkins's* edition of the Pentateuch. He was encouraged to proceed by Mr. *Bowyer* and Mr. *Bettenham ;* and Mr. *Caſlon* always acknowledged Mr. *Bowyer* as his maſter, and that he had taught him an art, in which, by diligence and unwearied application, he arrived to that perfection, as not only to free us from the neceſſity of importing types from *Holland,* but in the beauty and elegance of thoſe made by him ſo far ſurpaſſed the beſt productions of foreign artificers, that his types have not unfrequently been exported to the continent ; and it may with great juſtice and confidence be aſſerted, that a more beautiful ſpecimen than his is not to be found in any part of the world. Mr. *Caſlon's* firſt foundery was in a ſmall houſe in *Helmet Row* in *Old Street ;* he afterwards removed into *Ironmonger Row ;* and about the year 1735 into *Chiſwell Street,* where the foundery was carried on at firſt by himſelf †, and afterwards in conjunction with *William* his eldeſt ſon, whoſe name firſt appeared in the ſpecimen of 1742. His ſecond ſon, *Thomas,* is a bookſeller of eminence in *Stationers Court.* In or about the year 1750, Mr. *Caſlon* was put into the commiſſion of the peace for the county of *Middleſex ;* and retired from the active part of buſineſs to a houſe oppoſite *The Nag's Head* in the *Hackney* road, whence he removed to another houſe in *Water Gruel Row,* and afterwards to *Bethnal Green,* where he died *Jan.* 23, 1766, at the age of 74, and was buried in the church-yard ‡ of *St. Luke, Middleſex,* in which pariſh all his different founderies were ſituated. Of the modern ſtate of this undoubtedly moſt capital foundery in the world, the particulars are given by Mr.

* This circumſtance has lately been verified by the *American* Dr. *Franklin,* who was at that time a journeyman under Mr. *Watts,* the firſt printer that employed Mr. *Caſlon.*

† It appears by the Diſſertation of Mr. *Mores,* p. 86, that Mr. *Caſlon* had a brother named *Samuel,* who was his mould-maker, and afterwards lived with Mr. *George Anderton,* of *Birmingham,* in the ſame capacity.

‡ A handſome monument is erected to his memory, with this ſlight inſcription :
" W. CASLON, Eſq. ob. 23 Jan. 1766, Æt. 74.
" Alſo, W. CASLON, Eſq. (ſon of the above)
" Ob. 17 Aug. 1778, æt. 58 years."

Mores,

" tion of the noble donor; I now add, to the place in which
" they are to be repofited. However, I efteem it a pecu-
" liar happinefs, that as my father received them from a
" great patron of learning, his fon configns them to the
" greateft feminary of it, and that he is, Sir, your moft
" obliged friend, and humble fervant,   W. BOWYER."

                                              Among

Mores, with fome attempts at pleafantry. His ridicule, however, before the publication of his book, had loft its fting by the death of the *fecond* of the *Caflons*. That
artift, who had certainly great merit, though not equal to his father, is fucceeded in
bufinefs by a fon, to whom we cannot recommend a better model than his grandfather,
who was univerfally efteemed as a firft-rate artift, a tender mafter, and an honeft, friendly, and benevolent man. One particular in his character is thus excellently defcribed
by Sir *John Hawkins*: " Mr. *Caflon*, meeting with encouragement fuitable to his
" deferts, fettled in *Ironmonger Row* in *Old Street*; and, being a great lover of mufic,
" had frequent concerts at his houfe, which were reforted to by many eminent
" mafters; to thefe he ufed to invite his friends, and thofe of his old acquaint-
" ance, the companions of his youth. He afterwards removed to a large houfe in
" *Chifwell Street*, and had an organ in his concert-room; after that he had ftated
" monthly concerts, which, for the convenience of his friends, and that they might
" walk home in fafety when the performance was over, were on that *Thurfday* in the
" month which was neareft the full moon, from which circumftance his guefts were
" wont humouroufly to call themfelves *Lunatics*. In the intervals of the performance
" the guefts refrefhed themfelves at a fideboard, which was amply furnifhed; and when
" it was over, fitting down to a bottle of wine, and a decanter of excellent ale, of Mr.
" *Caflon*'s own brewing, they concluded the evening's entertainment with a fong or
" two of *Purcell*'s fung to the harpfichord, or a few catches; and about twelve re-
" tired *." There is a metzotinto print of him by *J. Faber*, from a painting by *F.
Kyte*, infcribed *Gulielmus Caflon*. The original picture is in the poffeffion of his grandfon; who has alfo a painting of his father, from which he intends to have an engraving.
    It is but common juftice to mention in this place the names of *Cottrell* † and *Jackfon*,
as letter-founders trained up under the aufpices, and purfuing with commendable induftry the fteps, of Mr. *Caflon* their excellent inftructor.

    * Hiftory of Mufic, vol. V. p. 127.
    † " Mr. *Thomas Cottrell* is in order *à primo proximus*. He was in the late Mr. *Caflon's* houfe, an
" apprentice to *dreffing*, but not to *cutting*. This part he learned, as Mr. *Moxon* terms it, ' of his
" own genuine inclination.' He began in the year 1757 with a fount of *Englifh Roman*;" [and has
fince cut a fount of *Norman* intended (but not ufed) for *Domefday-book*]. " He lives in *Nevil's Court*
" in *Fetter Lane*; obliging, good-natured, and friendly; rejecting nothing becaufe it is out of the
" common way, and is expeditious in his performances.—Mr. *Jofeph Jackfon* was in Mr. *Caflon's*
" houfe too, an apprentice to the whole art, into which he launched out for himfelf upon the fame
" principle as did Mr. *Cottrell*; for, actuated by the fame motives, they both flew off together. Mr.
" *Jackfon* lives in *Salifbury Court*, in *Fleet Street*; he is obliging and communicative, and his fpeci-
" men will, *adjuvante numine*, have place amongft the literate fpecimens of *Englifh* letter-cutters."—
Of Mr. *Jackfon* Mr. *Mores* would have faid more, if he had known him in 1781. The labour of
eight fucceffive years has been diligently exerted fince Mr. *Mores* defcribed his foundery in 1773.
He too, after cutting a variety of types for the Rolls of Parliament (a work which will ever reflect
                                                           honour

Among the specimens of the University types, these
Saxon characters are preserved, under the following title :
" Characteres *Anglo-Saxonici* per eruditam fœminam *Eliz.*
" *Elstob* ad fidem codd'. mss. delineati : quorum tam instru-
" mentis cusoriis quam matricibus Univ. donari curavit
" *E. R. M.** è Collegio *Regin.* 1753.

 " Cusoria majuscula 42.—desunt Λ et Ƿ.
 " Matrices majusculæ 44.
 " Cusoria minuscula 37.—desunt ę et ƿ.
 " Matrices minusculæ 39."   In

* On the first face of this business there is at least an unhandsome suppression of Mr.
Bowyer's name. The following short series of letters will set the matter in a clearer light :
 I. " To the Rev. Mr. SHEPHERD, Fellow of *Corpus Christi College*, *Oxon.*
 " REV. SIR,   *Dec.* 24, 1760.
 " A letter, of which the inclosed is a copy †, was sent agreeably to the date of it,
" *Dec.* 4, 1753, with the *Saxon* puncheons and matrices mentioned in it, to *Edward-*
" *Rowe Mores*, esq. at *Low Leyton*, in *Essex*, who soon after put them into the hands
" of Mr. *Caslon*, letter-founder, to repair, and render them more fit for use. Mr.
" *Caslon* having kept them for four or five years without touching them, Mr. *Bowyer*
" removed them into the hands of Mr. *Cottrell*, another letter-founder, from whom
" Mr. *Bowyer* received them fitted up, and delivered them a second time to Mr. *Mores*,
" in the year 1758, together with 15lb. of letter fresh cast from those matrices, and
" with them a copy of Mrs. *Elstob's Saxon* Grammar, bound and lettered, the book for
" which they were originally cut ; all which are said by Mr. *Mores* to have been deli-
" vered to the University of *Oxford*, agreeably to the design of the inclosed letter. Mr.
" *Bowyer* looks on his donation as of no moment in itself ; but somewhat remarkable for
" the history attending it ; and, having had no authentic testimony of the University's
" receipt of it, would be glad if you would give him any information about it. Perhaps
" Dr. *Randolph*, who was at that time Vice-chancellor, as he thinks, and to whom he
" hath the honour to be known, would assist you in it. I am, Sir, your most obliged
" humble servant,   W. BOWYER.
 " P. S. I need not have gone back in my narrative further than to the year 1758, if
" it were not to account for the early date of my letter, *December* 1753."

honour on the good taste and munificence of the present reign), has employed his talents on
Domesday, and in a manner more successful than his fellow labourer. I have the pleasure of in-
forming the publick, that the larger volume of that valuable record is quite finished at the press,
and the small one in great forwardness, on a plan which I had the honour of projecting, and
Mr. *Jackson* the skill to execute. To his *Occidentals* may also be added a beautiful Pica *Greek*,
which he cut under the express direction of Mr. *Bowyer*, who used to say, the types in common
use were ' no more *Greek* than they were *English*.' And (under the direction of *Joshua Steele*,
esq. the ingenious author of " Prosodia Rationalis, an Essay towards establishing the Melody and
" Measure of Speech,") Mr. *Jackson* hath augmented the number of musical types by such as
represent the emphasis and cadence of prose. *See Diss. on Founders*, pp. 82, 83. 97.
 † The letter printed above, p. 313.

                          II.

In 1761, appeared, " Verſes on the Coronation of their " late Majeſties King *George* II. and Queen *Caroline*, *October*
" 4,

II. " To *Edward-Rowe Mores*, Eſq. *Low Leyton*, *Eſſex*.
" SIR, *White Fryars*, *Jan.* 13, 1761.
" I deſired you laſt week, or before, by letter, to let me know to whom you ſent the
" matrices and punches of the *Saxon*, deſtined to *Oxford*. I now again earneſtly intreat
" that favour, becauſe I am to ſend an anſwer to be laid before the Vice-chancellor. I
" am, Sir, your very humble ſervant, W. BOWYER."

III. " To Mr. *Bowyer*.
" DEAR SIR, *Leyton*, *Jan.* 19, 1761.
" The puncheons and matrices are very ſafe at my houſe; they came one day too
" late for me to take them the laſt time I went to *Oxford*; I have therefore kept them
" with intent to carry them the enſuing ſpring, when I hope to ſpend a little time there.
" I am, dear Sir, your very humble ſervant, EDWARD-ROWE MORES."

IV. " To the Rev. Dr. *Randolph*.
" REV. SIR, *Jan.* .... 1761.
" I am aſhamed I have given you ſo much trouble about a very trifle in itſelf, but
" which ceaſes to be ſo to me when the Univerſity does me the honour of accepting it.
" Mr. *Mores's* letter, which I have now received and have here incloſed, will teſtify
" what my intentions long ſince were, and what his are againſt the enſuing ſpring.
" I am, Sir, your humble ſervant, W. B."

V. " To Mr. *Bowyer*.
" DEAR SIR, *Jan.* 10, 1773.
" I am heartily obliged to you for that which I have this moment received, and I muſt
" acknowledge it as a reproach to myſelf, for I too well remember what I promiſed;
" yet, as the beſt excuſe I can make, be pleaſed to take this. The day after I had the
" pleaſure of being with you, a pleaſure which I long to enjoy again, I met with an old
" acquaintance of the ſtock of *Iſrael* juſt returned from parts abroad, who had brought
" with him a volume of almanacks for years to come, written in *Portugueſe* *; he was to
" bring it for me the next day to his houſe in *London*, which I dare ſay he did; but
" your life and my life are pretty ſimilar, and I have not been in *London* ſince. As I
" write immediately, I cannot tell whether you have had occaſion for it or not, that
" pleaſure I propoſe to myſelf *craſtino primo diluculo*. I ſhall take it as a ſingular fa-
" vour if you will oblige me with the anecdote of the *French Polyglott* and Cardinal
" *Richlieu*, inſerted in the margin of your *Palmer*†. Now, Sir, to give a further proof
" that you are not out of my thoughts, permit me to trouble you with what I intend to
" ſay in defect of the Vice-chancellor of *Oxford*, the late Dr. *Browne* ‡, Provoſt of
" *Queen's*, a moſt worthy gentleman, and not to be blamed upon this occaſion, becauſe
" I believe that he did not fully comprehend the matter.

* Mr. *Bowyer* had it at that time in contemplation to print a *Hebrew* calendar, to anſwer the purpoſe of a modern almanack. He intended alſo to have printed a calendar ſhewing the holidays of
old *Rome*. I have the copy of both, which he had begun to prepare for that purpoſe.
† This anecdote is inſerted in Diſſ. on Founders, p. 11.
‡ The matrices were not depoſited at *Oxford* till the 4th of *October* 1764, when Dr. *Browne*, who
died in that year, was quite incapable of attending to buſineſs.

I

" She

" 4, 1727; ſpoken by the ſcholars of *Weſtminſter School*
" (ſome of them now the ornaments of the nation), on
" *January* 15 following, being the day of the inauguration
" of Queen *Elizabeth,* their foundreſs; with a tranſlation of
" all the *Latin* copies: the whole placed in the order of
" the tranſactions of that important day. Adorned with
" the coronation medals of the Royal Pair, and a buſt of
" our preſent King. To which is ſubjoined, the Ceremo-
" nial of the auguſt proceſſion, very proper to be com-
" pared with the approaching one *; and a catalogue of the
" coronation medals of the kings and queens of *England* †."
The original part of this pamphlet was entirely Mr. *Bowyer's*;
the

" She [Mrs. *Elſtob*] procured a fount of *Engliſh Saxon* to be cut according to her
" own delineation from the manuſcripts of the times; they were cut by Mr.
" *Robert Andrews,* at the expence of the Earl of *Macclesfield*; ſhe uſed them in
" her grammar only. The punches and matrices are now in the *Clarendonian,*
" a preſent made at the inſtance of one who would gladly ſhew a greater in-
" ſtance of affection and duty, by Mr. *William Bowyer,* a fellow of the Society
" of Antiquaries of *London,* a typographer of the *Stephanian* age, a ſon of *Alma*
" *Cant.*; but a letter of Mr. *Bowyer's* will ſpeak better than we can ſpeak for
" him, and we inſert it with the greater pleaſure, as it mentions with honour
" thoſe who live in our eſteem.
" And now, dear Sir, be pleaſed to correct what I have ſaid, and make it agreeable to
" yourſelf; there ſhould be no ceremonies betwixt us: add what you pleaſe, but I can
" abate nothing. The letter cannot be altered ‡, for it is at *Oxford.* Dear Sir, I am
" yours affectionately,   EDWARD-ROWE MORES."
    * That of their preſent Majeſties.
    † The following account of this pamphlet was given anonymouſly by Mr. *Bowyer,*
in the " Gentleman's Magazine," 1761, p. 422:
    " Among the numerous forms of the proceeding at a coronation, which are in ge-
neral but a liſt of dignities, and a new arrangement of the court calendar, I am not a
little pleaſed to ſee one which gives life to the ſplendid ſhew; and, while the eye is entertained, affords reflection for the underſtanding; I mean, the epigrams ſpoken by the
Weſtminſter ſcholars upon the coronation of his late Majeſty; which are now very ſeaſonably revived, and appear new to the preſent generation. The editor has ranged
them in order of the proceſſion; by which means, as he obſerves, the buſineſs of the day
gradually opens before us, and we ſhall be improved, as well as entertained, ſpectators.
.....In ſhort, we are enraptured with genuine gold, dazzling gems, and ſparkling wit,
throughout the ceremony. After this, it is but juſt we ſhould give the reader a ſpeci-

    ‡ It is printed in his Diſſertation on Founders, p. 28.
men-

the *Latin* verfes were tranflated, partly by him, but principally by the perfon who now infcribes thefe Anecdotes to
his memory. The advertifement to this pamphlet, which
was entirely his own, is a curiofity: " Two things, we
" truft, the great names fubfcribed to thefe epigrams will
" pardon; the one, that we have not obferved the method
" in which they were delivered; which being in an *extem-*
" *pore* manner, a neglect of order was then becoming;
" but, as they defcribe a ceremony long fince paft, and
" now to be revived, it was more natural to place them in
" the order of the proceffion, that the reader might fee the
" bufinefs of the day gradually open before him, and be
" again a fpectator at it. He will recall the folicitude
" of *Chloe*, rifing by candle-light; the laying afide of
" hoops, and putting on favours; the eager expectation
" of the people; the opening of the proceffion with the
" herb-woman; the importance of the beadle of *Weftmin-*
" *fter*, by the help of his ftaff; kettle-drums, organ-blowers,

men of one or two of the epigrams; and fhall leave him under the pleafing uncertainty of determining which are originals, and which tranflations.

On the Favours*.

Thy name, great prince, infcrib'd in filk behold,
On glittering favours rough with woven gold.
The man erect difplays it on the creft,
The fofter fair one wears it at her breaft.
Thus *Britain* her united wifh imparts;
Thine are the wifeft heads, and trueft hearts.

On the Opening of the Proceffion †.

Firft in proceffion of the pompous day,
With fragrant flowers a matron marks the way:
Next trumpets, kettle-drums, a various band;
Too hard, too many, in a verfe to ftand:
Then peers, earls, dukes, their different lights
And laft both majefties—meridian day: [difplay,
To fmall beginnings what great things we owe,
Since one old woman leads up fuch a fhow!

On the Diamonds and Coronets ‡.

In mimic fcenes, where counterfeits will pafs;
The crowns are tinfel, and the diamonds glafs;
No fictions here prophane the facred roof,
The heroes virtues and their gold are proof.
Nobles and gems difplay a flood of light:
Their blood unftain'd, as is their water bright.

On the Sceptre borne by the Queen §.

See *Caroline* fuftain the ivory dove,
An emblem not of greatnefs, but of love;
Confcious that facred vows, and beauty's fmiles,
Make fweets of power fuperior to its toils.
More proud her monarch's heart than throne to
  fhare;
Let the queen-confort ftill be regent there.

* An original by the prefent Duke of *Leeds*.
† A tranflation by *J. Nichols*.   ‡ A tranflation by Mr. *Bowyer*.
§ An original by the Hon. *Spencer Cowper*, afterwards Dean of *Durham*.

" beef-

" beef-eaters; the charms of peereffes, and maids of ho-
" nour; fictitious dukes; the dazzling profufion of fincere
" gold and real diamonds; the attractive majefty of Queen
" *Caroline*; the ftrength of *Britifh* forces, and the antiquity
" of the *Englifh* monarchy; the bifhop bearing the trea-
" fure of divine truths; the King, the enfigns of royalty;
" the Queen, of love and harmony; the crofs on his
" crown, and the fpurs on his feet; the venerable chair,
" brought from *Scotland*, A. D. 1296; the people's con-
" cern for the abfence of prince *Frederick*, and gratitude
" for the prefence of duke *William*; the act of crowning
" proclaimed by cannons, and beaming forth with the
" concentered blaze of coronets; the medals of the king
" and queen, ennobled lefs from their metal than their
" impreffes; the toil of the day; the narrownefs of the
" hall; the leveling of the law courts; the king's majeftic
" feat between them; the fumptuoufnefs of the prefent
" tables, and the frugality of the ancient; the fmall-beer
" fee; the tribute of three maple cups; the pyramids of
" fweetmeats; the terror of the champion; the ill-timed
" flumber of an over-tired fpectator; the candles touched
" into light; the rapine of the vulgar; no abatement of
" the univerfal joy from an unhappy accident; the king,
" in his turn, a partaker of the lord mayor's pomp, having
" firft contemplated it in the peaceful manfion of a Quaker,
" &c. On each particular the reader will find fome re-
" flexion, which will prevent his being, in the enfuing
" proceffion, an unimproved fpectator.

" For another particular we have more reafon to apolo-
" gife, that, though in the tranflations [which are diftin-
" guifhed by being included in crotchets] we have in ge-

" neral

" neral kept close to the originals, yet in some few instances
" we have deviated from them, when we thought the
" point of the epigram might be somewhat sharpened,
" without any injury to the scope of it.   This we have spa-
" ringly done, and, whenever we have taken that liberty,
" have marked it out by *Italic* characters.

" As the poets here have been prophets, the reader will
" with pleasure compare the events with their predictions.
" We have seen our venerable Monarch go down to the
" grave full of years and honours; and though it was some
" abatement to the comfort of them, that his laurels were
" earned with toil amidst destructive wars, we may pro-
" mise ourselves that Heaven hath reserved the blessings,
" which were wanting to him, to be accumulated upon his
" Grandson; in whom the hearts of his subjects are united
" beyond what history can parallel, or poetry itself can
" paint.   Duty and affection in all orders of men seem to
" flow in such uninterrupted streams, that he will want
" but the exercise of one of his royal virtues, that of for-
" giveness."

A copy of these verses was sent, by Mr. *Bowyer*, with the
following letter:

" To the Rev. Dr. MARKHAM, Master of *Westminster school.*
   " REV. SIR,   *April* ... 1761.
" My father being honoured with the friendship of Dr.
" *Freind**, he owed to him these verses on the last corona-
                                                    " tion.

* Dr. *Robert Freind*, born at *Croton* in *Northamptonshire*, where his father was
rector, was sent early to *Westminster school*, and elected thence to *Christ Church*,
Oxford, where he appears to have been a student at the time of the inauguration of
K. *William* and Q. *Mary*. He proceeded M. A. *June* 1, 1693; became second master
of *Westminster school* in 1699; and accumulated the degrees of B. and D.D. *July* 7,
1709. In 1711 he drew up the preamble to the earl of *Oxford's* patent of peerage;
                                                                        and

" tion, fpoken in *Weftminfter fchool*. As at the time they
" were printed they were thought no difcredit to it, fo I
" truft they will now again be received with frefh appro-
" bation from the publick. As it is long fince they were
" printed, you may poffibly not have a copy of them. I
" thought it my duty, therefore, to fend you one. If
" you want more, you may command them from, Sir,
" your moft obedient humble fervant, W. BOWYER."

The principal articles printed by Mr. *Bowyer* in 1761
were, " Propofals for printing Mr. *Morant's* * Hiftory of
" *Effex,*"

and in that year fucceeded *Duke* the poet in the valuable living of *Witney* in *Oxford-fhire*; and alfo became head-mafter of *Weftminfter fchool*. He publifhed, from Mr. *Bowyer's* prefs, in 1724, an edition of *Cicero's* " Orator;" and obtained a prebend of *Weftminfter* in 1731. In 1734 he was defirous of refigning *Witney* to his fon, after-wards Dean of *Canterbury*. This could not be done without permiffion from Bifhop *Hoadly*, which he had little reafon to expect. On application, however, to that Pre-late, through Queen *Caroline* and Lady *Sundon* †, he received this laconic anfwer, " If Dr. *Freind* can afk it, I can grant it ‡." On fucceeding to a canonry of *Chrift Church* ||, he refigned his ftall at *Weftminfter* in favour of his fon in 1744. He died April 15, 1745.

* *Philip Morant*, M. A. and F. S. A. a learned and indefatigable Antiquary and Bio-grapher, fon of *Stephen Morant*, was born at *St. Saviour's* in the Ifle of *Jerfey*, Oct. 6, 1700; and, after finifhing his education at *Abingdon* fchool, on the 16th of *December* 1717 was entered at *Pembroke College, Oxford*, where he took the degree of B. A.

† This lady, more known by the name of Mrs. *Clayton*, was the bed-chamber woman and inti-mate friend of Queen *Caroline*; and for a confiderable time fole arbitrefs of church preferments. Se-veral of Bp *Hoadly's* Letters to her, from 1715 to 1734, are preferved in his Works. In one of them he fays, " I do not follow great precedents, and write on the outfide, or in the front, *To the much* " *efteemed, To the much refpected. To the highly honoured Mrs. Clayton*. But it is writ within, in laft-" ing characters. Your own virtues have writ it. Your other accomplifhments are great and un-" common; but it is your fincerity and goodnefs which make the deepeft impreffion, which manage " the others, and gave them their agreeablenefs."—On the bufinefs of the living of *Witney*, Bp *Hoadly* tells this Lady, " I had no defign in my neglect of avoiding to give all the affurances that " you yourfelf ever defired about Mr. *Freind*. If you and I continue together upon this dirty pla-" net, you yourfelf fhall be fatisfied of the truth of what I have faid to you; and I fay this the ra-" ther, becaufe, if you are not fatisfied in what I do, I am very fure I fhall not be fo myfelf. You " have done more in two or three words, when you tell me, *You fhall efteem it as done to yourfelf*, to " move and engage me (if I had not been already engaged to it) than all the oratory of all others could " have done. And if that cafe fhould happen which you once put; but which my heart will not " fuffer me to repeat; Friendfhip and Honour fhall moft certainly act a part, which if your fpirit " could then look out and fee, it would fay, *This is exactly as it would have been, had I been ftill* " *there.*"

‡ " Dr. *Freind* could afk any thing. All his letters to Lady *Sundon* are ftill exifting; they are trifling and low beyond conception; yet Dr. *Freind* was a fcholar that *Bentley* would confult." T. F.
|| See *Widmore's* Hiftory of *Weftminfter Abbey*, p. 226.

June

" *Effex*," folio ; " Memoirs of the Life of *Roger de Wefc-*
" *ham*, Dean of *Lincoln*, and Bifhop of *Coventry and*
" *Litchfield*, favourite of *Robert Groffetefte*, Bifhop of *Lin-*
" *coln* ;

June 10, 1721, and continued till *Midfummer* 1722; when he was preferred to the office of Preacher of the *Englifh* church at *Amfterdam*, but never went to take poffeffion. He took the degree of M. A. in 1724, and was prefented to the rectory of *Shellow Bowells*, *April* 20, 1733 ; to the vicarage of *Bromfield*, *Jan.* 17, 1733-4 ; to the rectory of *Chicknal Smeley*, *Sept.* 19, 1735 ; to that of *St. Mary's*, *Colchefter*, *March* 9, 1737 ; to that of *Wickham Bifhop's*, *Jan.* 21, 1742-3 ; and to that of *Aldham*, *Sept.* 14, 1745. All thefe benefices are in the county of *Effex*. In 1748 he publifhed his " Hiftory of *Colchefter*," of which only 200 copies were printed, at the joint expence of himfelf and Mr. *Bowyer*, who confequently interefted himfelf very much in the embellifhment of the book, as well as in earneftly recommending it to fubfcribers *. The engravings were by *Vertue* † and *Mynde*. In 1751 Mr. *Morant* was elected a member of the Society of Antiquaries ‡ ; and from that time till his death continued a regular

---

* " I have applied to Mr. *Browne Willis* for leave to dedicate a plate to him. He fays, he has juft
" married his children, and in acting the part of a father he has reduced himfelf fo low that he
" knows not how to be a patron. What think you of Dr. *Mead?* Mr. *Vertue* is better, and will
" expedite your plates, he fays, with care. I did not fee the fheet G before it was fent to you; if I
" had, I fhould have propofed one or two alterations. I have prefumed to add a word or two to
" note H. *Spanheim* has fo fully proved the law that laid open the citizenfhip of *Rome* to belong to *Ca-*
" *racalla*, that it would be unpardonable to let the miftake, though heretofore fupported by great
" names, be perpetuated. Strange, that the Bifhop of *London* [*Gibfon*] fhould not take notice of fo
" material a point of learning ! *Spanheim's* book was printed firft in *London*, and afterwards taken
" into *Grævius's Thefaurus*. P. 25, a complete province, not governed by proconfular deputies, but
" accounted præfidial, and appropriated to the emperors, as being annexed to the empire, after the
" divifion of the provinces by *Auguftus*, &c. This is expreffed, as if *South Britain* was annexed to
" the empire by *Auguftus*, which you do not mean. What then do you mean ? That præfidial
" provinces, in diftinction to the proconfular, were annexed to the empire ? Rather the contrary is
" true. In the firft divifion under *Auguftus*, ten prætorian and two confular provinces were al-
" lotted to the people's fhare, *i. e.* to the empire ; the reft the Emperor kept under his own govern-
" ment. The governors of the people's provinces were called generally provincials ; thofe of the
" Emperor never fo ; but either *legati confulares*, or *proprætores*, or *legati prætorii*, or *legati im-*
" *peratoris pro prætore*, whether they had gone through the office of prætor or conful, or not. See
" *Salmaf.* Hift. *Aug.* Script. vol. I. p. 200. 374. vol. II. p. 346, &c. But the Antiquaries will
" not regard this branch of learning, becaufe it looks too claffical ; they are more critical about
" things that are more *Gothic* or more Monaftical." *Mr. B. to Mr. Morant, May* 3, 1748.

† The Ichnography, infcribed to Mr. *Yorke*, coft five guineas ; the plate given by Mr. *Folkes*
three guineas ; and one was given by the Society of Antiquaries.

‡ " I don't know much of the fteps which the Society of Antiquaries have lately taken. If you
" are chofen, you would have been called on for the money, a guinea at entrance, and a fhilling a
" month afterwards. But they have lately been much engaged in planning fchemes for a charter,
" which may coft a good deal of money, and I doubt whether it will be of great benefit. I imagine
" fome perfons want fome new places to be made, and falaries annexed to them. In all focieties,
" the advantages of the publick are moft talked of when there are the greateft private views. As to
" *Effex*, I think, to fpeak fincerely, you had better begin again with it. If you undertake it, I
" doubt the fuccefs of it. *Tindal* began it in 4to, and was forced to drop it. You do me much ho-
" nour in afcribing ' *Pompey* the Little **' to me. I am obliged to you ; and fhall be glad never
" to be fufpected of a worfe thing." *Mr. B. to Mr. Morant. Aug.* 1, 1751.

** This was written by the ingenious Mr. *Coventry*, rector of *Edgware, Middlefex*, and author of *Penfhurf,*
&c. in *Dodfley's* Collection. He died, of the fmall pox, about the year 1759.

6

" *coln* ; being intended as a Prelude to the Life of the
" laſt mentioned excellent Prelate ; wherein the Errors
" of former Antiquaries are carefully conſidered. By *Sa-*
" *muel*

correſpondence with Mr. *Bowyer* *. In *February* 1768 he was appointed by the lords
ſub-committees of the houſe of peers to ſucceed Mr. *Blyke* † in preparing for the preſs
a copy of the Rolls of Parliament ; a ſervice, to which from my own knowledge I can
ſay he diligently attended till his death, which happened *Nov.* 25, 1770, in conſequence of a cold caught in returning by water from *The Temple* to *Vauxhall* in his
way to *South Lambeth*, where he reſided for the convenience of attending to his parliamentary labours ; a work for which, as a native of *Jerſey*, and excellently ſkilled
in the old *Norman French*, he was particularly well qualified ; and which, after his
death, devolved on *Thomas Aſtle*, eſq. F. R. and A. SS. who had married his only
daughter ; and by whoſe favour I am able to lay before the reader an exact account
of Mr. *Morant's* writings, from a liſt of them drawn up by himſelf. 1. " An Intro-
" duction to the Reading of the New Teſtament, being a Tranſlation of that of Meſſ. de
" *Beauſobre* and *Lenfant*, prefixed to their edition of the New Teſtament. Printed for
" *S. Chandler* and *J. Batley*," 1725, 1726, 4to.—2, " The Tranſlation of the Notes
" of Meſſ. de *Beauſobre* and *Lenfant* on *St. Matthew's* Goſpel. *Lond.* 1727," 4to.

* " My intention, for ſome months paſt was, to have been in *London* either this week or the
" next ; but an afflicting loſs that has happened in my family the beginning of this year hinders me
" from coming at preſent. Within the compaſs of three days I was ſo unhappy as to loſe my only
" brother and ſiſter-in-law ; the former on the 9th, and the latter on the 11th of *January*. My good
" brother indeed died at a diſtance, and I could but ſeldom have the pleaſure of ſeeing him ; but
" my ſiſter-in-law lived with us, and had been a conſtant and inſeparable companion to my good
" wife for above 50 years, and was withal a perſon of the moſt amiable qualities, and the moſt
" faithful friend, ſo that her loſs is irreparable. It has ſo affected my good wife, that my abſence
" even for a day ſinks her ſpirits to that degree, that I find I cannot leave her at preſent ; but I
" hope time, and the chearful weather that is coming, will recruit her ſpirits. In the mean time I
" ſhould be obliged to you, if you would be ſo kind as to diſpoſe of the copy of my Hiſtory of *Col-*
" *cheſter*, and the plates ; you have yourſelf the beſt right to it, if you will be pleaſed to allow me
" ſomething for it that is reaſonable ; and I include therewith ſuch corrections and additions as I
" have made to the work ſince publication. If it ſhould no way ſuit you, Dr. *R. Rawlinſon* is a
" great collector, and will very probably like it beyond any body elſe. Or, if you know any other
" perſon whom it would ſuit, be pleaſed to do for me as you would do for yourſelf. I ſhall come to
" town as ſoon as the inconveniencies above-mentioned are a little worn out by time ; and poſſibly
" we may come together, my good wife and I ; for motion, and change of place, are ſome cure to
" melancholy ; though it is full as bad when you return to your wonted habitation, and miſs your
" friend." *Mr. Morant to Mr. Bowyer*, May 1, 1752.—" I propoſed to Dr. *Rawlinſon* your offer
" on *Thurſday* laſt, and ſhall ſee him again next *Thurſday*. He deſires to know what you aſk for the
" plates, and the copy of your book, *i. e.* as I apprehend, a fair copy corrected by your own hand,
" with a liberty of reprinting it, if he will ; but of this there is no probability, ſince we have ſeve-
" ral ſtill remaining. We will ſay then, a copy corrected, and the ſeveral plates you ſell for. . . .
" I am ſorry for the melancholy ſituation of your family ; but objects, I hope, will be leſſened to the
" memory by the diſtance of time, as they are to the eye by the diſtance of ſpace." *Mr. Bowyer to*
Mr. Morant, May 9, 1752.—" I had the favour of your letter, and am obliged to you for what you
" have done to ſerve me. The plates coſt above thirty guineas, beſides the copy ; and therefore I
" ſhould have been obliged to you, if you had been ſo kind as to make the beſt bargain with Dr.
" *Rawlinſon*, or any body elſe, as if it had been for yourſelf. However, as you ſeem to expect
" that I ſhould ſet a price, I think fifteen pounds is very moderate, for a copy corrected, and the
" ſeveral plates." *Mr. Morant to Mr. Bowyer*, May 12, 1752. The treaty with Dr. *Rawlinſon*
broke off, and the book was afterwards judiciouſly incorporated with the " Hiſtory of *Eſſex*."
† *Richard Blyke*, eſq. F. R. and A. SS. of whom ſee under the year 1774.

- N. Tindal.

" *muel Pegge*, Prebendary of *Litchfield*," 4to; " Truth in
" Rhyme," a poem by Mr. *Mallet**, 4to; " Concio ad
" Clerum,"

N. Tindal tranflated the text printed therewith.—3. " The Cruelties and Perfecutions
" of the *Romifh* Church difplayed, &c. *Lond.* printed for *J. Knapton*, 1728," 8vo.
tranflated into *Welfh* by *Thomas Richards*, curate. of *Coychurch* in *Glamorganfhire*,
1746, with the approbation of Dr. *Gilbert*, then Bifhop of *Landaff.*—4. " I epitomifed
" thofe Speeches, Declarations, &c. which *Rapin* had contracted out of *Rufhworth* in
" the Life of King *James* I. King *Charles* I. &c." 1729, 1730.—5. " Remarks on the
" 19th chapter of the fecond book of Mr. *Selden's* Mare Claufum. Printed at the end
" of Mr. *Falle's* Account of *Jerfey*," 1734.—6. " I compared *Rapin's* Hiftory with the
" 20 volumes of *Rymer's Fœdera*, and *Acta Publica*, and all the ancient and modern
" Hiftorians, and added moft of the Notes that were in the folio edition," 1728. 1734.
This is acknowledged at the end of the preface in the firft volume of *Rapin's* Hiftory.—
7. " Tranflation of the Notes in the fecond Part of the *Othman* Hiftory, by Prince
" *Cantemir*," folio, 1735.—8. Revifed and corrected " The Hiftory of *England*, by
" way of Queftion and Anfwer, for *Thomas Aftley*," 1737, 12mo.—9. Revifed and
corrected " *Hearne's* Ductor Hiftoricus," and made large Additions thereto, for *J.*
Knapton.—10. " Account of the *Spanifh* Invafion in 1588, by way of Illuftration to
" the Tapeftry Hangings in the Houfe of Lords and in the King's Wardrobe. Engraved
" and publifhed by *J. Pine*," 1739, folio.—11. " Geographia Antiqua & Nova; taken
" partly from *Dufrefnoy's* Methode pour étudier la Geographie; with *Cellarius's* Maps.
" Printed for *J.* and *P. Knapton*," 1742, 4to.—12. " A Summary of the Hiftory of
" *England*," folio; and " Lifts at the end of Mr. *Tindal's* Continuation of *Ra-*
" *pin's* Hiftory, in vol. III. being 55 fheets. Reprinted in three volumes," 8vo.—13.
" The Hiftory and Antiquities of *Colchefter*," folio, *London*, 1748; fecond edition
1768.—14. " All the Lives in the Biographia Britannica marked C." 7 vols. folio, 1739.
1760. I alfo compofed *Stillingfleet*, which hath no mark at the end.—15. " The Hif-
" tory of *Effex*," 2 vols. folio, 1760—1768†.—16. " I prepared ‡ the Rolls of Parliament
" for the Prefs."—Other works in MS. 1. " An Anfwer to the firft Part of the Dif-
" courfe of the Grounds and Reafons of the Chriftian Religion, in a Letter to a Friend,
" 1724. Prefented in MS to *Edmund Gibfon*, Bifhop of *London*." Never printed.
N.B. This was the beginning of Mr. *Morant's* acquaintance with the Bifhop, who gave
him feveral livings in the county of *Effex.*—2. " The Life of King *Edward* the Con-
" feffor."—3. About 150 Sermons.

* The following account of Mr. *Mallet* is chiefly collected from Dr. *Johnfon's* life of
him. " He was by original one of the *Macgregors*, a clan that became about fixty years
ago, under the conduct of *Robin Roy*, fo formidable and fo infamous for violence and
robbery, that the name was annulled by a legal abolition; and when they were all to
denominate themfelves anew, the father, I fuppofe, of this author, called himfelf *Mal-*
loch. David Malloch was by the penury of his parents compelled to be *Janitor* of the
high fchool at *Edinburgh*; a mean office, of which he did not afterwards delight to

† In the Preface, dated *Jan.* 2, 1768, Mr. *Morant* fays, " All that remains for me to do is, to
" exprefs my heartieft acknowledgments and gratitude to the great Author of my life and happinefs,
" who hath enabled me to go through this and other laborious employments. I can look back with
" inexpreffible fatisfaction upon a life not fpent in idlenefs or indolence, or in fruitlefs amufements;
" but in a conftant endeavour to do all the good in my power. I muft beg leave to add, that if the
" world is benefited by my labours, the praife is due to my only Patron good Bifhop *Gibfon*."

‡ Mr. *Morant* prepared the Rolls of Parliament as far as the 16th year of the reign of K. *Henry* IV.

hear.

"Clerum," by Dr. *Freind**, Dean of *Canterbury*, 4to; Mr.
Markland's

hear. But he furmounted the difadvantages of his birth and fortune; for when the
duke of *Montrofe* applied to the college of *Edinburgh* for a tutor to educate his fons,
Malloch was recommended; and with his pupils made afterwards the tour of *Europe*;
nor is he known to have difhonoured his credentials. Having cleared his tongue from
his native pronunciation fo as to be no longer diftinguifhed as a *Scot*, he feemed inclined
to difincumber himfelf from all adherences to his original, and took upon him to change
his name from *Scotch Malloch* to *Englifh Mallet*, without any imaginable reafon of preference which the eye or ear can difcover. What other proofs he gave of difrefpect to
his native country, I know not; but it was remarked of him, that he was the only *Scot*
whom *Scotchmen* did not commend." Our biographer might have added, that he was the
only one whom they did not lament. The news of his death was followed by no encomiums on his writings or his virtues. *April* 6, 1734, he obtained the degree† of M. A. at *St.
Mary Hall, Oxford*. "In 1740, when the prince of *Wales* had a feparate court, he made
Mallet his under-fecretary; and when it was found that *Pope* had clandeftinely printed
an unauthorifed number of the " Patriot King," *Bolingbroke* employed *Mallet* (1749)
as the executioner of his vengeance. *Mallet* wanted either virtue, or fpirit, to refufe
the office; and was rewarded, not long after, with the legacy of lord *Bolingbroke's*
works, which were publifhed with fuccefs very inadequate to our editor's expectation. In
confequence of a thoufand pounds left by the dutchefs of *Marlborough*, he undertook to
write the life of the duke her hufband. From the late duke he had likewife a penfion to
promote his induftry. He talked much of the progrefs he had made in this work, but
left not, when he died, the fmalleft veftige of any hiftorical labour behind him. In the
political difputes which commenced at the beginning of the prefent reign, Mr. *Malloch*
took part with his countryman lord *Bute*, to ferve whom he wrote his tragedy of
" *Elvira*," and was rewarded with the office of keeper of the book of entries for fhips
in the port of *London*, to which he was appointed in the year 1763. He enjoyed alfo a
confiderable penfion, which had been beftowed on him for his fuccefs in turning the
public vengeance upon *Byng*, by means of a letter of accufation under the character of
a " Plain Man." Towards the latter end of his life, he went with his wife to *France*;
but after a while, finding his health declining, he returned alone to *England*, and died
in *April* 1765. He was twice married, and by his firft wife had feveral children. One
of his daughters has diftinguifhed herfelf as a dramatic writer. His fecond wife was the
daughter of a nobleman's fteward, who had a confiderable fortune, which fhe took care
to retain in her own hands. Mr. *Malloch's* ftature was diminutive, but he was regularly
formed. His appearance, till he grew corpulent, was agreeable, and he fuffered it to
want no recommendation that drefs could give it. His converfation was elegant and
eafy. The reft of his character may, without injury to his memory, fink into filence."
See, however, his letter to *Derrick*, publifhed in a collection, 2 vols. 12mo. 1767, vol.
II. p. 21. " As a writer," fays Dr. *Johnfon*, perhaps a little too contemptuoufly, " he
" cannot be placed in any high clafs. There is no fpecies of compofition in which he
" was eminent. His dramas had their day, a fhort day, and are forgotten. His life
" of *Bacon* is known, as it is appended to *Bacon's* volumes, but is no longer mentioned."
The titles of his plays are enumerated in " The Companion to the Playhoufe," vol. II.
p. 296, ed. 1781, whence moft of the circumftances not mentioned by Dr. *Johnfon* are
here extracted.

* *William Freind*, D. D. fon of the learned Mafter of *Weftminfter fchool*, already
mentioned in p. 324. He fucceeded, as has been there faid, to the valuable rectory

† See the Catalogue of *Oxford* Graduates. His name alfo as " M. A." is fubfcribed to his
" Verfes prefented to the Prince of *Orange* on vifiting *Oxford* in the year 1734."

of

Markland's " Quæstio Grammatica," 4to, (see p. 20); " A
              " Vindication

of *Witney* in 1734; and held also that of *Islip*, in the same county, given him by the
Dean and Chapter of *Westminster*. He obtained a prebend of *Westminster*, *Oct.* 17,
1744; which he quitted for a canonry of *Christ Church*, *Oxford*, in 17 ; and was appointed Dean of *Canterbury* in 1760. He married one of the sisters of the late Sir *Thomas Robinson*, bart. and the present Primate of *Ireland*, by whom he left three sons,
viz. Robert, barrister at law, and student of *Christ Church* (since deceased); *William*
and *John*, both in orders; and a daughter, *Elizabeth*, married to Capt. *Duncan Campbell*, of the *Chatham* division of Marines. Dean *Freind* was appointed Prolocutor of the
Lower House of Convocation in 1761, in which character he preached the elegant
" Concio" above-mentioned. He died at *Witney*, *Nov.* 28, 1766. He had a valuable
library and collection of prints, both which were sold by auction in 1767. On receiving a
proof of the " Concio ad Clerum," he told Mr. *Bowyer*, " You have been so correct
" and exact in printing, that you have left me little to alter, except what arises, I fancy,
" from a blunder of my own." *MS. Letter.*—Against the South wall of the chancel at
Witney is a tablet of white marble, with an inscription to the memory of " Dr. *Robert*
" *Freind*, son of *William*, rector of *Croton* in *Northamptonshire*, who died *August* 9,
" 1754, aged 84. He was head-master of *Westminster school*, rector of *Witney*, preben-
" dary of *Westminster* and *Windsor*, and, on resigning the former, canon of *Christ*
" *Church*. He married *Jane*, daughter of —— *Delancle*, one of the pastors of the re-
" formed church of *Charenton*, who taking refuge in *England* became a prebendary of
" *Westminster*. She died *Feb.* 3, 1758, aged 81. Dr. *William Freind*, his son, dean
" of *Canterbury*, rector of *Witney*, died *Nov.* 28, 1766, aged 55. *Charles Freind* died
" *July* 16, 1736, aged 16, leaving his parents and only brother surviving." A slab on
the floor has this inscription: " By the consent of *Benjamin* lord bishop of *Winchester*,
" and *Thomas* lord bishop of *Oxford*, the burial vault underneath was appropriated to
" the sole use of Dr. *Freind* and family, 1753."—This inscription enables me to correct
the note in p. 324. Dr. *Robert Freind* (who obtained his prebend at *Windsor* in *April*
1729) died *Aug.* 9, 1754. A specimen of his poetry, both in *Latin* and *English*, may be
seen in the " Select Collection of Miscellany Poems," vol. VII. p. 122. He wrote also
the Dedication to Queen *Caroline*, prefixed to the Medical Works of his brother Dr.
John Freind.—*John*, who was also of *Westminster school*, was elected to *Christ Church*
in 1690; and, under the auspices of dean *Aldrich*, undertook, with Mr *Foulkes*, to publish two orations, one of *Æschines*, the other of *Demosthenes*, which were well received;
and was also prevailed upon to revise an edition of *Ovid's* Metamorphoses, 1696, which
Dr. *Bentley* severely reprehends. He was " director of the studies" to Mr. *Boyle*; wrote
the Examination of Dr. *Bentley's* Dissertation on *Æsop*; and, says the great critic, " was
" of the same size for learning with the late editor of the *Æsopean* Fables [Mr. *Anthony*
" *Asop*]. If they can make but a tolerable copy of verses, with two or three small
" faults in it, they must presently set up to be authors." But, whatever may be thought
of those juvenile performances, in his professional capacity he was a masterly writer. He
proceeded M. A. *April* 12, 1701; B. M. *June* 1, 1701; and, after having published
several curious medical treatises, was chosen professor of chemistry at *Oxford* in 1704;
and the next year attended lord *Peterborough* on his *Spanish* expedition, of which Dr.
Freind published an account in 1707. He was created M. D. by diploma, *July* 12, that
year; was elected a member of the Royal Society in 1712; and attended the duke of
Ormond into *Flanders*. After his return, residing chiefly at *London*, he gave himself up
                                         wholly

" Vindication * of the New Calendar Tables, and Rules an-
" nexed to the Act for regulating the Commencement of the
" Year, &c." 4to; Dr. *Armstrong's* " Day, an Epistle to *John*
" *Wilkes*, Esq." 4to; the first edition of Mr. *Dodsley's* ex-

wholly to the cares of his profession. He was elected a burgess for *Launceston* in 1722; and, being suspected of having a hand in *Layer's* plot, was committed to *The Tower*, *March* 17, 1722-3, where he continued a prisoner till the 21st of *June* following. Soon after he obtained his liberty, he was made physician to the prince of *Wales*: and, upon that prince's accession to the crown, became physician to queen *Caroline*, who honoured him with a share of her confidence and esteem. He did not enjoy this office long; dying *July* 26, 1728, in his 52d year. Bishop *Atterbury*, in an unpublished letter now in my possession, says, " You have heard of the death of Dr. *Freind*; a public loss, in more
" respects than one! for I dare say, notwithstanding his station at court, he died of
" the same political opinions in which I left him. He is lamented by men of all parties
" at home, and of all countries abroad; for he was known every where, and confessed
" to be at the head of his faculty." Their majesties, in consideration of his great merit, settled a pension upon his widow. His celebrated " History of Physic," the first part of which was printed in 1725, was translated into *Latin* by Dr. *Wigan*, and published, with the *Latin* works of Dr. *Freind*, at *London*, in folio, 1753; which were reprinted at *Paris*, in 4to, 1735. An original portrait of Dr. *John Freind* is in the possession of Mrs. *Parsons*.—There appears also to have been a third brother, of whom the facetious Mrs. *Pilkington*, describing her situation in *The King's Bench*, thus writes: " We had a
" sort of a chapel belonging to the jail, where Dr. *Freind*, a clergyman, brother to Dr.
" *Freind* the physician, obliged us with divine service every *Sunday*. This gentleman
" was himself a prisoner in *The King's Bench*, and after all the grandeur he had once
" lived in, was now so low reduced, as even to be beholden to such an unfortunate crea-
" ture as I for six-pence; which, unfortunate as I was, I could not refuse to so fine an
" orator. a gentleman! and by all accounts, only undone by boundless generosity and
" hospitality. The first day I heard him preach I was charmed with his elocution, but
" the rest of the congregation, mad and drunk, bade him hold his tongue;—he indeed,
" like *Orpheus*, played to wolves and bears; nor were they half so obliging to him, as
" the storms were to *Arion*; neither could he, though uttering dulcet and harmonious
" sounds, make the rude crowd grow civil with his song. This fine gentleman I often
" invited to my lonely mansion—he was not a little surprised to hear my mournful story;
" and indeed it somewhat alleviated my sorrow to find such a companion:—Poor gentle-
" man! Death has released him; I am sure I should have done it, had the Almighty
" given me a power equal to my inclination to serve him." This was the Dr. *Freind* who died *April* 15, 1745.

* By *Peter Daval*, esq. of *The Middle Temple*, a Barrister at Law, afterwards Master in Chancery, and at the time of his death, *January* 8, 1763, Accomptant General of that Court. He at an early period of life translated the Memoirs of Cardinal *De Retz*, which were printed in 12mo, 1723, with a dedication to Mr. *Congreve*, who encouraged the publication. He was Fellow of the Royal Society, and an able Mathematician. In the dispute concerning Elliptical Arches, at the time when *Black Fryers Bridge* was built, his opinion on the subject was applied for by the Committee. See his answer, *London Mag. March* 1760.

cellent

cellent Collection of " Fugitive Pieces," by Mr. *Spence* *,
Lord

---

* *Joseph Spence*, M. A. This ornament of polite literature was fellow of *New College, Oxford*, where he took the degree of M. A. *Nov.* 2, 1727; and in that year became first known to the learned world by " An Essay on *Pope's* Odyssey; in which some " particular *beauties* and *blemishes* of that work are considered, in two parts," 12mo. " On the *English* Odyssey," says Dr. *Johnson*, " a criticism was published by *Spence*, a " man whose learning was not very great, and whose mind was not very powerful. His " criticism, however, was commonly just, what he thought, he thought rightly; and " his remarks were recommended by his coolness and candour. In him *Pope* had the " first experience of a critick without malevolence, who thought it as much his duty to " display beauties as expose faults; who censured with respect, and praised with alacrity. " With this criticism *Pope* was so little offended, that he sought the acquaintance of the " writer, who lived with him from that time in great familiarity, attended him in his " last hours, and compiled memorials of his conversation. The regard of *Pope* recom- " mended him to the great and powerful, and he obtained very valuable preferments " in the church." He was elected, by the University, Professor of Poetry *July* 11, 1728, succeeding the Rev. *Thomas Warton*, B. D. father to Dr. *Joseph Warton*, now master of *Winchester school*, and Mr. *Thomas Warton*, author of " The " History of *English* Poetry," and poetry professor; each of which three professors were twice elected to their office, and held it for ten years, a period as long as the statutes will allow. Mr. *Spence* wrote an account of *Stephen Duck*, which was first published, as a pamphlet, in 1731, and said to be written by " *Joseph Spence*, esq. " Poetry Professor." From this circumstance it has been supposed that he was not then in orders. But this is a false conclusion, as he was ordained in 1724; and left this pamphlet in the hands of his friend Mr. *Lowth* †, to be published as soon as he left *England*, with a *Grub-street* title, which he had drawn up merely for a disguise, not choosing to have it thought that he published it himself. It was afterwards much altered, and prefixed to *Duck's* poems. He travelled with the present duke of *Newcastle* (then earl of *Lincoln)* into *Italy*, where his attention to his noble pupil did him the highest honour ‡. In 1736, at Mr. *Pope's* desire, he republished § " *Gorboduc*," with a preface containing an account of the author, the earl of *Dorset*. He never took a doctor's degree; but quitted his fellowship on being presented by the Society of *New College* to the rectory of *Great Horwood* in *Buckinghamshire*, in the year 1742. As he never resided upon his living, but in a pleasant house and gardens lent to him by his noble pupil, at *Byfleet* in *Surrey* (the rectory of which parish he had obtained for his friend *Stephen Duck*), he thought it his duty to make an annual visit to *Horwood*, and gave away many sums of money to the distressed poor, and placed out many of their children as apprentices. In *June* 1742, he succeeded Dr. *Holmes* as his Majesty's Professor of Modern History, at *Oxford*.

† The present Bishop of *London*; who, with that obliging condescension for which his Lordship is eminently distinguished, has honoured me with much useful information on the subject of this note.

‡ The mortification which Dr. *Goddard* the present Master of *Clare Hall*, his Grace's *Cambridge* tutor, felt by this appointment, probably occasioned the extraordinary Dedication to the Duke, prefixed to his " Sermons," 1781, 8vo.

§ In a malignant Epistle from *Curll* to Mr. *Pope*, 1737, our author is introduced as an early patron of the late ingenious Mr. *Dodsley*:

    " 'Tis kind indeed a Livery Muse to aid,
    " Who scribbles Farces to augment his trade :
    " Where *You* and *Spence* and *Glover* drive the nail,
    " The Devil's in it if the plot should fail."

2

Lord *Whitworth* (who had been employed on a moſt important

His " Polymetis, or an Enquiry concerning the Agreement between the Works of the
" *Roman* Poets, and the Remains of the ancient Artiſts, being an Attempt to illuſtrate
" them mutually from each other," was publiſhed in folio in 1747. Of this work
of acknowledged taſte and learning, Mr. *Gray* has been thought to ſpeak too con-
temptuouſly in his Letters. His chief objection is, that the author has illuſtrated
his ſubject from the *Roman,* and not from the *Greek,* Poets; that is, that he has not
performed, what he never undertook; nay, what he expreſsly did not undertake. A
third edition appeared in folio in 1774, and an Abridgement of it has been frequently
printed in octavo. I have ſeen a pamphlet with *Spence's* name to it in MS. as the author,
called " Plain Matter of Fact, or, a ſhort Review of the Reigns of our Popiſh Princes
" ſince the Reformation ; in order to ſhew what we are to expect if another ſhould hap-
" pen to reign over us. Part I. 1748," 12mo. He was inſtalled prebendary of the
ſeventh ſtall at *Durham, May* 24, 1754; and publiſhed in that year, " An Account of
" the Life, Character, and Poems, of Mr. *Blacklock,* Student of Philoſophy at *Edin-*
" *burgh,*" 8vo; which was afterwards prefixed to his Poems. The proſe pieces which
he printed in " The Muſeum" he collected and publiſhed, with ſome others, in a pamphlet called " MORALITIES, by Sir *Harry Beaumont,* 1753." Under that name he
publiſhed " *Crito,* or a Dialogue on Beauty," and " A particular Account of the Em-
" peror of *China's* Gardens near *Pekin,* in a Letter from *F. Attiret,* a *French* Miſſionary
" now employed by that Emperor to paint the apartments in thoſe gardens, to his
" Friend at *Paris;*" both in 8vo. 1752, and both re-printed in *Dodſley's* " Fugitive
" Pieces." He wrote " An Epiſtle from a *Swiſs* Officer to his friend at *Rome,*" firſt
printed in " The Muſeum;" and ſince in the third volume of *Dodſley's* Collection. The
ſeveral copies publiſhed under his name in the *Oxford* Verſes are preſerved in the
" Select Collection, 1781." In 1758 he publiſhed " A Parallel, in the Manner of
" *Plutarch,* between a moſt celebrated Man of *Florence (Magliabecchi),* and one
" ſcarce ever heard of in *England (Robert Hill,* the *Hebrew* Taylor)," 12mo.
Printed at *Strawberry Hill.* In the ſame year he took a tour into *Scotland,* which
is well deſcribed in an affectionate letter to Mr. *Shenſtone,* in a collection of ſeveral letters publiſhed by Mr. *Hull* in 1778, vol. I. p. 238. In 1763 he communicated to Dr. *Warton* ſeveral excellent remarks on *Virgil,* which he had made
when he was abroad, and ſome few of Mr. *Pope's.*—*Weſt Finchale Priory* (the
ſcene of the holy *Godric's* miracles and auſterities, who, from an itinerant merchant, turned hermit, and wore out three ſuits of iron cloaths) was now become
Mr. *Spence's* retreat, being part of his prebendal eſtate. In 1764 he was well pourtrayed
by Mr. *James Ridley,* in his admirable " Tales of the *Genii,*" under the name of " *Pheſoi*
" *Ecneps* (his name read backwards) Derviſe of the Groves;" and a panegyrical letter
from him to that ingenious moraliſt, under the ſame ſignature, is inſerted in " Letters of
" Eminent Perſons," vol. III. p. 139. In 1764 he paid the laſt kind office to the remains of his friend Mr. *Dodſley,* who died on a viſit to him at *Durham.* He cloſed his
literary labours with " Remarks and Diſſertations on *Virgil*; with ſome other claſſical
" Obſervations ; by the late Mr. *Holdſworth.* Publiſhed, with ſeveral Notes and ad-
" ditional Remarks, by Mr. *Spence,*" 4to. This volume, of which the greater part was
printed off in 1767, was publiſhed in *February* 1768 ; and on the 20th of *Auguſt* following, Mr. *Spence* was unfortunately drowned in a canal in his garden at *Byfleet* in *Surrey.*
Being, when the accident happened, quite alone, it could only be conjectured in what
manner it happened ; but it was generally ſuppoſed to have been occaſioned by a fit
while he was ſtanding near the brink of the water. He was found flat upon his face, at
the

portant embaſſy to *Ruſſia*, which his Lordſhip there deſcribes), Mr. *Burke*[*], Mr. *Clubbe*[†], Mr. *William Hay*,[‡]

Mr.

the edge, where the water was too ſhallow to cover his head, or any part of his body. The duke of *Newcaſtle* poſſeſſes ſome MS. volumes of anecdotes of eminent writers, collected by Mr. *Spence*, who in his life-time communicated to Dr. *Warton* as many of them as related to *Pope*; and, by permiſſion of the noble owner, Dr. *Johnſon* has made many extracts from them in his " Lives of the *Engliſh* Poets."

* The tract by this maſterly writer is called " A Vindication of Natural Society, " written in the Character of a late noble Author [Lord *Bolingbroke*]." It was firſt printed in 1756; 8vo.

† " The Hiſtory and Antiquities of the ancient Villa of *Wheatfield*, in the County of " *Suffolk*," firſt printed in 1758, 4to. was written by the Rev. *John Clubbe*; author alſo of a treatiſe on Phyſiognomy, 1763, 4to. He (like Mr. *Spence)* was unfortunately drowned in a moat that ſurrounded his own garden, *March* 2, 1773. His works were collected ſoon after his death, and printed at *Ipſwich* in 2 vols. 8vo. no date.

‡ This good-humoured agreeable writer was born at *Glenburne*, near *Lewes*, in the county of *Suſſex*, probably about the beginning of the preſent century, and was educated under Mr. *Bonwicke*[||] at *Headley ſchool*. In the year 1730 he publiſhed a poem called " *Mount Caburn*," dedicated to the Dutcheſs of *Newcaſtle*, in which he deſcribes the beauties of his native country, and celebrates the virtues of his friends and relations. On Lord *Hardwicke's* being called up to the Houſe of Lords, his ſeat in parliament for the Borough of *Seaford* was vacated, and Mr. *Hay* was choſen to fill it in the month of *January* 1734, and continued to repreſent the ſame place during the reſt of his life, being re-choſen in the new parliament *June* 1734, and again in 1741, 1747, and 1754. As a ſenator he ſupported the meaſures of Sir *Robert Walpole*, and is imagined to have been the author of a pamphlet on the miniſterial ſide, intituled " A Letter to a Freeholder on the late " Reduction of the Land Tax to One Shilling in the Pound, 1732," 8vo. Being convinced that the laws concerning the poor were inſufficient to anſwer the purpoſes for which they were deſigned, he took great pains to new model and improve them; in conſequence whereof, he publiſhed a pamphlet in 1735, on the ſubject, intituled, " Re- " marks on the Laws relative to the Poor, with Propoſals for their better Relief and Em- " ployment," 8vo. no date; and about the ſame time brought in a bill (which however was not proceeded on) to correct the abuſes which had crept into the adminiſtration of thoſe laws. In *May* 1738 he was appointed a Commiſſioner of the Victualling Office, and in 1747 brought in a bill for the better relief of the poor by voluntary charities, which paſſed the Houſe of Commons; but, for reaſons which do not appear, was loſt in the upper aſſembly. In 1751 the late *Henry Fielding* having again drawn the attention of the publick towards the ſame object, Mr. *Hay* republiſhed his pamphlet with additions, but without producing any effect; though Dr. *Burn*, in his Hiſtory of the Poor Laws, p. 183, ſays, that it contains many things worthy of obſervation. In 1753 appeared " Religio Philoſophi, or the Prin- " ciples of Morality and Chriſtianity, illuſtrated from a view of the Univerſe, and of " Man's ſituation in it," 8vo; which was followed in 1754 by the ingenious " Eſſay

|| In 1766, Mr. *Bowyer*, having mentioned to an intimate friend the uneaſineſs he laboured under from the violent attacks of gravel and ſtone, was adviſed to turn to his " old ſchoolfellow " *Hay's*" Eſſay on Deformity, at the end of which the author had added his own caſe, very ſimilar to Mr. *Bowyer's*, and inſerted the regimen by which he was conſtantly relieved.

" on

Mr. *Cooper,* Dr. *Lancaster**, Dr. *Hill*†, and other elegant
writers,

" on Deformity," in which he has treated what might be apprehended a barren
subject with great spirit, vivacity, and good-humour; indeed he has drawn so amiable
a picture of his mind, that it may be concluded he was amply recompensed by Providence
for those defects of his body which he rallies with so much liveliness. " Bodily Defor-
" mity," he observes, " is very rare. Among 558 gentlemen in the House of Com-
" mons, I am the only one that is so. Thanks to my worthy Constituents, who never
" objected to my person, and I hope never to give them cause to object to my behaviour."
In the same year he translated Mr. *Isaac Hawkins Browne's* admired poem " De Im-
" mortalitate Animi," and printed it in 4to; and likewise was appointed Keeper of the
Records in *The Tower.* His attention and assiduity during the few months he held that
office were eminently serviceable to his successors. In 1755 he gave the publick a translation of " *Martial,*" of which two editions were printed the same year. He survived
this publication but a short time, dying *June* 19, 1755. He left a son, who inherited the
imperfections of his father's person. This gentleman went into the service of the *East
India* Company, where he acquired rank, fortune, and reputation; but, being one of those
who opposed *Cossim Ally Kawn,* was so unfortunate as to fall into the hands of that ruffian,
who caused him to be murdered, with several other gentlemen, at *Patna Oct.* 5, 1763.

* " The Essay on Delicacy was the production of Dr. *Nathaniel Lancaster,* many
" years rector of *Stanford Rivers,* near *Ongar,* in *Essex,* uncle to the Editor of these
" Letters ‡. He was a man of strong natural parts, great erudition, refined taste, and
" master of a nervous, and at the same time, elegant style, as is very obvious to every
" one who has had the happiness to read the Essay here spoken of. His writings were
" fewer in number than their author's genius seemed to promise to his friends, and his
" publications less known than their intrinsic excellence deserved. Had he been as so-
" licitous, as he was capable, to instruct and please the world, few prose-writers would
" have surpassed him; but in his latter years he lived a recluse, and whatever he com-
" posed in the hours of retired leisure he (unhappily for the public) ordered to be
" burned, which was religiously (I had almost said irreligiously) performed. He was a
" native of *Cheshire;* and, in his earlier years, under the patronage and friendship of
" the late earl of *Cholmondeley,* mixed in all the more exalted scenes of polished life,
" where his lively spirit, and brilliant conversation, rendered him universally distinguish-
" ed and esteemed; and even till within a few months of his decease (near 75 years of
" age) these faculties could scarce be said to be impaired. The Essay on Delicacy (of
" which we are now speaking), the only material work of his which the editor knows
" to have survived him, was first printed in the year 1748, and has been very judici-
" ously and meritoriously preserved by the late Mr. *Dodsley,* in his Fugitive Pieces."
Notwithstanding Mr. *Hull's* assertion that his uncle wrote nothing but the " Essay," a
Sermon of his, under the title of " Public Virtue, or the Love of our Country," was
printed in 1746, 4to. He was also author of a long anonymous rhapsodical poem, called
" The Old Serpent, or Methodism Triumphant," 4to. The Doctor's imprudence involved him so deeply in debt, that he was some time confined for it, and left his parson-
age house in so ruinous a condition, that his successor Dr. *Beadon* was forced entirely to
take it down. He died *June* 20, 1775, leaving two daughters, one of whom married to
the Rev. *Thomas Wetenhall,* of *Chester,* chaplain of a man of war, and vicar of *Walthamstow, Essex,* from 1759 till his death 1776.

† The celebrated botanist, afterwards Sir *John Hill.* The history of this *Proteus*
in literature is too well known to need recital here, where he is only mentioned as

‡ I use in this note the words of Mr. *Hull,* in a note on " Select Letters between the late
" Dutchess of *Somerset,* Lady *Luxborough,* &c. &c." 1768, 2 vols. 8vo.

writers, 2 volumes, 8vo; 200 copies of " Mr. *Smith's* *
" Will," for the ufe of the Truftees, 8vo; " The *Englifh*
" Verb, a Grammatical Effay in the Didactive Form†,"
8vo; a Tranflation of the " Elegies of *Tyrtæus*," 8vo; two
new editions of Mr. *Webb's* " Inquiry into the Beauties of
" Painting," 8vo; " A Conference between a *Myftic*, a
" *Hutchinfonian*, a *Calvinift*, a *Methodift*, and a Member of
" the Church of *England*, and others; wherein the Tenets
" of each are freely examined and difcuffed," by Dr. *Dodd*‡,
8vo;

author of *Lucina fine Concubitu.* He was born in or about the year 1716; and, after
figuring as an author in almoft every poffible department of literature, had the honour
of being made a Knight of the Polar Star by the King of *Sweden*, and died in *November* 1755.

* Commonly known by the name of *Dog Smith.* His charities in the county of
Surrey are generally known. See an Abftract of them in *Rudder's* " New Hiftory of
" *Gloucefterfhire*," p. 535.

† By Mr. *James White*, a fchool-mafter in *Cecil Street* in *The Strand.* He publifhed
a tranflation of " The Clouds" of *Ariftophanes* in 1759.

‡ This unfortunate Divine, eldeft fon of the Rev. *William Dodd*, many years
vicar of *Bourne*, in *Lincolnfhire*, was born *May* 29, 1729. He was fent, at the age
of fixteen, to the univerfity of *Cambridge*, and admitted, in the year 1745, a fizar of
Clare Hall. In 1749-50 he took the degree of B. A. with great honour, being upon
that occafion in the lift of wranglers. Leaving the univerfity, he imprudently married
a Mifs *Mary Perkins* in 1751, was ordained a deacon the fame year, prieft in 1753, and
foon became a celebrated and popular preacher. His firft preferment was the lecturefhip
of *Weft Ham.* In 1754 he was alfo chofen lecturer of *St. Olave's, Hart Street*; and in
1757 took the degree of M. A. at *Cambridge.* On the foundation of the *Magdalen Hofpital* in 1758, he was a ftrenuous fupporter of that charity, and foon after became preacher
at the chapel of it. By the patronage of Bifhop *Squire*, he in 1763 obtained a prebend
of *Brecon*, and by the intereft of fome city friends procured himfelf to be appointed one
of the king's chaplains; foon after which he had the education of the prefent earl of *Chefterfield* committed to his care. In 1766 he went to *Cambridge*, and took the degree of
L L. D. At this period, the eftimation in which he was held by the world was fufficient to
give him expectations of preferment, and hopes of riches and honours; and thefe he
might probably have acquired, had he poffeffed a common portion of prudence and difcretion. But, impatient of his fituation, and eager for advancement, he rafhly fell
upon means, which in the end were the occafion of his ruin. On the living of *St. George,
Hanover Square*, becoming vacant, he wrote an anonymous letter to the Chancellor's
lady, offering 3000 guineas if by her affiftance he was promoted to it. This being traced
to him, complaint was immediately made to the king, and Dr. *Dodd* was difmiffed with
difgrace from his office of chaplain. From this period he lived neglected, if not defpifed;
and his extravagance ftill continuing, he became involved in difficulties, which tempted
him to forge a bond from his late pupil lord *Chefterfield*, *Feb.* 4, 1777, for 4200*l.* which
he

8vo; Dr. *Brown's* " Sermon at *Bath*," 8vo ; *Johnson's*
" Epigrammatum Delectus," 12mo ; a part of two editions
of Mrs. *Sheridan's* * " *Sidney Biddulph*," 12mo; " The Life
" of the Chevalier *Taylor*," two volumes, 12mo; and "The
" Hiftory of *James Lovegrove*, efq." by Mr. *James Ridley* †.

Bifhop *Warburton's* " Divine Legation" (a work of fome
confequence in the Typographical Annals of Mr. *Bowyer*)
appears by the very learned Prelate's Letters‡ to have received no fmall advantage from his corrections; and this
even in an edition which (in the courfe of Mr. *B's* firft
partnerfhip) was of neceffity given to another prefs.——In
1762 he was employed to print his Lordfhip's " Doctrine

he actually received; but, being detected, was tried at the *Old Bailey*, found guilty,
and received fentence of death; and, in fpite of every application for mercy, was executed at *Tyburn, June* 27, 1777. Dr. *Dodd* was a voluminous writer, and poffeffed confiderable abilities, with little judgement and much vanity. An accurate lift of his various writings is prefixed to his " Thoughts in Prifon," ed. 1781.

* Mrs. *Frances Sheridan*, wife to *Thomas Sheridan*, M. A. was born in *Ireland* about
the year 1724, but defcended from a good *Englifh* family which had removed thither.
Her maiden name was *Chamberlaine*, and fhe was grand-daughter of Sir *Oliver Chamberlaine*. The firft literary performance by which fhe diftinguifhed herfelf was a little
pamphlet at the time of a violent party difpute relative to the theatre, in which Mr.
Sheridan had newly embarked his fortune. So well-timed a work exciting the attention
of Mr. *Sheridan*, he by an accident difcovered his fair patronefs, to whom he was
foon afterwards married. She was a perfon of the moft amiable character in every
relation of life, with the moft engaging manners. After lingering fome years in a
very weak ftate of health, fhe died at *Blois*, in the South of *France*, in the year 1767.
Her " *Sydney Biddulph*" may be ranked with the firft productions of that clafs in ours, or
in any other language. She alfo wrote a little romance in one volume, called, *Nourja-
bad*, in which there is a great deal of imagination productive of an admirable moral.
And fhe was the authorefs of two comedies; " The Difcovery" and " The Dupe."

† This ingenious writer was the eldeft fon of Dr. *Glofter Ridley*. He was the author
of " The Tales of the Genii, 1764," 2 vols. 8vo; a humourous paper called " The
" Schemer," firft printed in " The *London* Chronicle," and fince collected into a volume; and fome other literary performances.

‡ " *March* 3, 1739. I efteem myfelf exceeding happy in fuch a learned Printer, but
" much more in fo candid a friend. Your very ingenious obfervations are, and always
" will be, an extreme pleafure to me."—Mr. *B.* himfelf fays, in one of the letters
alluded to in p. 338, " The firft, fecond, and third volumes of your Divine Legation,
" from the year 1737, were printed under my infpection only, without your Lordfhip read-
" ing a fingle proof. Fame followed them as faft as you could wifh; and I do not know
" that you felt any abatement of it from the inaccuracy of the Printer. I pretend not to
" be faultlefs; but the editions were printed as correctly, I hope, as books ufually are."

X x   " of

" of Grace ;" a work which, as might have been expected, sold rapidly. A second edition being soon wanted, and Mr. B. not having been intrusted with the care of it, he thought it neceſſary to vindicate himſelf from reflections that might ariſe on this apparent change in his Patron's ſentiments. With this view, he prepared a ſeries of letters to the Biſhop; of which, together with a few he had formerly received from that great writer, he afterwards printed *twelve** *copies*. But on this ſubject it is the more unneceſſary to enlarge, as I can aſſert, on the beſt authority, that, not-withſtanding any little altercations which had happened, Biſhop *Warburton* always continued to retain a ſincere re-gard for Mr. *Bowyer*.

In the ſame year, 1762, he was Editor of the Thirteenth and Fourteenth octavo volumes of Dr. *Swift's* Works. For theſe volumes his own advertiſement will account :

" The pleaſure Dean *Swift's* Works have already afford-
" ed will be a ſufficient apology for communicating to the
" Reader, though ſomewhat out of ſeaſon, theſe additional
" volumes ; who will be leſs diſpleaſed that they have been
" ſo long ſuppreſſed, than thankful that they are now at
" laſt publiſhed. We have no occaſion to apologiſe for the
" pieces themſelves ; for as they have all the internal
" marks of genuineneſs, ſo, by their further opening the
" Author's private correſpondence, they diſplay the good-
" neſs of his heart, no leſs than the never-ceaſing ſallies of
" his wit. His anſwer to *The Rights of the Chriſtian Church*
" is a remarkable inſtance of both ; which, though un-
" finiſhed, and but the ſlight proluſions of his ſtrength,

* Two copies only of theſe Letters were given away by Mr. *Bowyer* ; the others have been ſince deſtroyed by the writer of this note.

" ſhew

" fhew how fincere, how able a champion he was of reli-
" gion and the church. So foon as thefe were printed in
" *Dublin*, in a new edition of the Dean's works, it was a
" juftice due to them to felect them thence, to complete the
" *London* edition. Like the Author, though they owe
" their birth to *Ireland*, they will feel their maturity in
" *England* * ; and each nation will contend which fhall re-
" ceive them with greater ardour. In the laft volume is
" added, an Index to ALL the WORKS ; wherein are ranged
" the *bon-mots* fcattered throughout them under the article
" SWIFTIANA, by which their brightnefs is collected, as it
" were, into a *focus*, and they are placed in fuch open day,
" that they are fecured, for the future, from the petty
" larceny of meaner wits."

The other books of 1762 were the firft † part of Mr.
Morant's "Hiftory of *Effex*," folio; Mr. *Farneworth's* ‡ tranflation

* The following Epigram, occafioned by this thought, was written by the Compiler
of thefe Anecdotes :
  " Which gave the DRAPIER *Birth* two Realms contend :
  " And each afferts her Poet, Patriot, Friend :
  " Her Mitre jealous BRITAIN may deny ;
  " That Lofs IERNE's Laurel fhall fupply ;
  " Through Life's low Vale, fhe, grateful, gave him Bread ;
  " Her vocal Stones fhall vindicate him dead."

† A fecond part came out in 1763 ; a third in 1766. Thefe three parts are all contained in the fecond (though firft-publifhed) volume. In 1768 the firft volume (containing a new edition of the Hiftory of *Colchefter*) was publifhed complete.

‡ *Ellis Farneworth*, M. A. and rector of *Rofthern* in *Chefhire*, was fon of Mr. *Farneworth*, rector of *Bontefhal* in *Derbyfhire*, and, I believe, was born there. He was bred
firft at *Chefterfield* fchool under the celebrated Mr. *William Burrow*, and afterwards was
removed to *Eton*. He was admitted of *Jefus College, Cambridge* ; and matriculated
Dec. 17, 1730. He was prefented by Dr. *James Yorke*, Dean of *Lincoln*, to the rectory of *Carfington*, in *Derbyfhire*, at the folicitation of the late *William Fitzherbert*, of
Tiffington, efq. and was inftituted *Oct.* 6, 1762 ; but he did not enjoy his benefice long,
as he died *March* 25, 1763. He was author, it is believed, of that ludicrous and pleafant account of *Powell*, the fire-eater, in Gent. Mag. 1755, p. 59, figned *Philopyrphagus*
Afhburnienfis ; and was curate to the Rev. *John Fitzherbert*, vicar of *Afhbourne*,
brother of *William* above-mentioned. His publications from the prefs of his old

friend

lation of "*Machiavel*," 4to; Mr. *Shepherd's* * " Odes Moral
" and

friend Mr. *Bowyer* † were, 1. " The Life of Pope *Sixtus* V." translated from
the *Italian*, folio (see p. 240). 2. " A short History of the *Israelites* ‡," from the
French of Abbé *Fleury*, 1754, 8vo. (see p. 268). 3. " *Davila's* " History of the
" Wars of *France*," translated from the *French*, 1757, 2 vols. 4to. (see p. 272). 4.
A translation of the Works of *Machiavel*; " illustrated with Notes, Annotations, Dis-
" sertations, and several new Plans on the Art of War," 2 vols. 4to. 1761 ; reprinted
in 4 vols. 8vo. 1775.

* *Richard Shepherd*, B.D. Fellow of *Corpus Christi College*, *Oxford*; where he took
the degree of M. A. *Jan.* 14, 1757, and that of B. D. *Jan.* 28, 1765. This gentleman
has been already mentioned in p. 295. He published " The Nuptials, a Didactic poem,"

† " Poor *Farneworth*, though obliged to hawk his *Machiavel* round the town, yet tacked me
" every where to the conditions of sale. *Stackhouse* **, while under the pay of a bookseller, refused
" his lord and master, *T. Cox*, to deliver his copy to any one but the printer he befriended, though
" *Cox* urged the necessity of coming out before the season was passed. These heroes knew how to
" set a value not only on themselves, but on their friendships too." *MS Letter of Mr. B.* 1762.

‡ By the following letter to Mr. *Bowyer*, dated *Compton*, near *Ashbourne*, *Derbyshire*, it
appears that Mr. *Farneworth* was *not* the translator of this useful little book : " Mr. *Farneworth*
" has left his poor sister in woeful circumstances, a very worthy gentlewoman, in the decline of life,
" and of an infirm constitution. She will be so just to the creditors as to give up all his effects to
" any one who will administer, and depend upon Providence, and the benevolence of her friends
" and other charitable people, for her future subsistence.' I was sorry *Fleury's* little useful book was
" so unsuccessful ; it was I that put it into his hands, both the original and translation that had
" lain by me many years, in hopes that it would have raised him fifteen or twenty pounds, knowing
" that both he and his sisters, for then he had another living, were low at that time. Your very
" humble servant, THOMAS BEDFORD."
The writer of the preceding letter was second son of the famous *Hilkiah Bedford* ††, who was taken
up and imprisoned as author of " The Hereditary Right of the Crown of *England* asserted," though
he was not the author. He was of *Westminster school* ; afterwards admitted of *St. John's College, Cambridge* ; became master's sizar to Dr. *Robert Jenkin*, the master ; and was matriculated, *Dec.* 9, 1730 ;
Being a Nonjuror, he never took a degree ; but going into orders in that party, officiated amongst
the people of that mode of thinking in *Derbyshire*, fixing his residence at *Compton* near *Ashbourne*, where he became much acquainted with *Ellis Farneworth*, and was indeed a good scholar.
Having some original fortune, and withal being a very frugal man, and making also the most of his
money for a length of years, Mr. *Bedford* died rich at *Compton*, in *February* 1773, where he was
well respected. As soon as he took orders, he went chaplain into the family of Sir *John Cotton*, bart.
then at *Angiers* in *France*. From thence, having a sister married to *George Smith*, esq. near *Durham*
(who published his father Dr. *John Smith's* fine edition of *Bede*), Mr. *Bedford* went into the
North, and there prepared his edition of " *Symeonis* monachi *Dunhelmensis* libellus de exordio atque
" procursu *Dunhelmensis* ecclesiæ ;" with a continuation to 1154, and an account of the hard usage
Bishop *William* received from *Rufus* ; which was printed by subscription in 1732, 8vo. from a very
valuable and beautiful MS. in the cathedral library, which he supposes to be either the original, or
copied in the author's life-time. He was living at *Ashbourne* 1742, and about that time published
an " Historical Catechism," containing, in brief, the sacred history, the doctrines of christianity,
and an explanation of the feasts and fasts of the church, the second edition corrected and enlarged.
The first edition was taken from Abbé *Fleury* ; but as this second varied so much from that author,
Mr. *Bedford* left out his name.

** *Thomas Stackhouse*, M.A. vicar of *Benham*, *Berks*, author of the famous treatise " on the Miseries of the
" inferior Clergy, 1722," 8vo ; " Memoirs of Bishop *Atterbury*, from His Birth to his Banishment, 1723,"
8vo ; " A Funeral Sermon on the Death of Dr. *Brady*, 1726," 8vo ; " The Complete Body of Divinity," &c.
1729, folio ; " A new History of the Bible, from the Beginning of the World, to the Establishment of
" Christianity, 1732, and 1742," 2 vols. folio ; a Sermon on the 30th of *January*, 1736, 8vo ; a " Sermon
" on the Decalogue," 1743, folio ; and " A New and Practical Exposition of the Apostles Creed, 1747,"
folio. He died *Oct.* 11, 1752.

†† Of whom see a particular account in *Brit. Top.* vol. I. p. 337.

4

" and Allegorical," 4to; " The Cub at *Newmarket*, a poem*,"
4to; Mr. *Hoole's*† " Tranflation of *Taffo*," 2 volumes, 8vo;
Mr. *Hurd's* " Letters on Chivalry and Romance," two editions, 8vo; a new edition of Mr. *Chefelden's*‡ " Anatomy
" of

8vo, in 1763; and collected his " Mifcellanies," in two volumes, 8vo, *Oxford*, 1775.
In 1779 he publifhed " Reflections on the Doctrine of Materialifm, &c." 8vo. Since
the former part of this note were written, Mr. *Shepherd* has publifhed " A brief Examina-
" tion of the *Socinian* Expofition of the prefatory verfes of *St. John's* Gofpel, 1781," 8vo.

* This was one of the early productions of *James Bofwell*, efq. the celebrated Hiftorian of *Corfica*.

† By this gentleman, who is auditor of accompts at the *Eaft India* houfe, the publick
have been favoured with three tragedies, and alfo with a tranflation of *Taffo*, part of
Ariofto, and fix of the operas of *Metaftafio*.

‡ While the particulars of this excellent Anatomift in p. 213, & feq. were printing,
I was informed that there was an eloge on Mr. *Chefelden* in the Memoirs of one of
the *French* Academies, which I fought after with fruitlefs inquiries, but have fince
found in the " Memoires de l'Academie Royale de Chirurgerie, 1757," tome VII. 12mo.
p. 168; and am happy to find that my account of him (collected from various fources
of information) is no way materially erroneous. The Memoirs however (for which the
materials were furnifhed by his family) will fupply fome additional facts. Mr. *Chefelden*,
it there appears, was born in 1688, at *Somerby* § in *Leicefterfhire*. After receiving a
claffical education, he was placed, about the year 1703, under the immediate tuition of
Cowper, the celebrated anatomift, in whofe houfe he refided, and ftudied furgery under
Mr. *Ferne*, head furgeon of *St. Thomas's Hofpital*, whom he afterwards fucceeded for
19 years. In 1711 Mr. *Chefelden* was elected fellow of the Royal Society At the
early age of 22, he read lectures on Anatomy, of which the Syllabus was firft printed
in 4to, 1711; and afterwards (as already mentioned) annexed to his 8vo volume in
1713. Such lectures were not then very common in *England*, having been firft intro-
duced by M. *Buffiere* ||, a *French* refugee, a furgeon of high repute in the reign of
Queen *Anne*. Till then, popular prejudice had run fo high againft the practice of
diffection, that the civil power could not without difficulty accommodate the furgeons
with proper fubjects. Their pupils therefore were under the unavoidable neceffity of
attending the univerfities **, or other public feminaries of medicine and furgery; the
anatomift who wifhed to inveftigate the fubject more intimately being unable to gratify his inclination. Mr. *Chefelden* continued his lectures for twenty years, and in
that period obliged the publick with many curious and fingular cafes, which are printed in the Philofophical Tranfactions, the Memoirs of the Academy of Surgery at
Paris, and in other valuable repofitories. His " Ofteography," infcribed to Queen
Caroline, was publifhed by fubfcription, in a handfome folio, in 1733. A peevifh critique
on that work was printed by Dr. *Douglas* in 1735, under the title of " Remarks on

§ I had before faid at *Burrow on the Hill*, fomewhat more exactly; but both are right, *Burrow
on the Hill* being part of the parifh of *Somerby*.

|| This was the furgeon who attended Mr. *Harley* after the wound he had received from *Guifcard*;
he attended alfo that affaffin after his commitment to *Newgate*. M. *Buffiere* lived to be called in to
the confultation on the laft illnefs of Queen *Caroline*. The notorious *St. André* (of whom fee Memoirs in Gent. Mag. 1781, p. 320) was another very early lecturer in anatomy.

** At *Cambridge* bodies were then with difficulty, if at all, procured.

" that

" of the Human Body," 8vo; Mr. *Webb's* " Remarks on
" the

" that pompous book, the Osteography of Mr. *Chefelden*." It received a more judicious censure from the famous *Haller*, who with great candour pointed out what was amiss in it, yet paid Mr. *Chefelden* the encomium which he so well deserved. *Heister* also, in his " Compendium of Anatomy," has done justice to his merit. In his several publications on Anatomy, Mr. *Chefelden* never failed to introduce select cases in surgery; and to the work of M. *Le Dran* (see p. 214), annexed twenty-one useful plates; and a variety of valuable remarks, some of which he had made so early as whilst he was a pupil of Mr. *Ferne*. Guided by consummate skill, perfectly master of his hand, successful in resources, he was prepared for all events, and performed every operation with remarkable dexterity and coolness: fully competent to each possible case, he was successful in all. But the study to which he more particularly devoted his attention, was the operation of cutting for the stone. In 1722 he gained great applause by his successful practice in this line; and in the following year published his " Treatise on the high Operation for the Stone" (see p. 213), which was soon followed by an anonymous pamphlet, called " *Lithotomus castratus*, or an Examination of the " Treatise of Mr. *Chefelden*;" and accusing our Anatomist of plagiarism. He had not only, however, in his preface, acknowledged his obligations to Dr. *Douglas* *, but annexed to his own work a translation of what had been written on the subject by *Franco*, who published " Traité des Hernies," &c. at *Lyons* in 1561; and by *Rosset* in his " Cæsarei, Partus Assertio Historiologica, *Paris*, 1590." The whole business was more candidly explained in 1724, by a writer who had no other object than the interest of mankind, in a little work, called " Methode de la Taille au haut appareile re- " cueillie des Ouvrages du fameux Triumvirat †;" these were *Rosset*, to whom the honour of the invention was due; *Douglas*, who had revived it after long disuse; and *Chefelden*, who had practised the operation with the most eminent success and skill ‡. In 1729

* " In the year 1717-18, Dr. *James Douglas* presented a paper to the Royal Society, in which " he demonstrated from the anatomy of the parts, that the high operation for the stone might be " performed safely; and though most were convinced of it, yet either no one understood which way " to do it, or cared to venture his reputation upon it, till his brother Mr. *John Douglas*, a good " anatomist, and formerly a pupil in *St. Thomas's Hospital*, performed it; his method is nearly the " same with *Rosset's* (vid. Mr. *Douglas's* treatise called Lithotomia *Douglassiana*), though, as he de- " clares, he had never heard of that author at that time. He performed his operations with suc- " cess, and if he may not be called the inventor, he was surely the first man that ever practised it " this way upon living bodies (his operation and *Franco's* differing as much as the ways by the " greater and lesser apparatus), for which the Company of Surgeons (forward to encourage every " improvement in surgery) have presented him with his freedom, with an exemption from several " expensive offices. In my own account of this operation I have fairly set down every thing that I " judged most material to be known, with out the least disguise or partiality to myself; and that the " reader might see what had been before done, and that I might not be suspected of arrogating to " myself any part of this operation, which was not my own invention (which I confess is very " little), I have added to it a translation of what had been writ upon the subject by several authors." Mr. *Chefelden, in the Preface to his Treatise above-mentioned.*

† I quote this title from the *Eloge*; not knowing the exact title of the book, nor in what language it was written.

‡ The surgeon and anatomist will find much satisfactory information on this subject in the *Eloge* which furnishes this note. The writer of it was present at many of Mr. *Chefelden's* operations, one of which was performed in so small a time as 54 seconds; and received from him the particular detail of his method, on the single condition of not communicating it to any person till it had been laid before the Royal Academy of Sciences at *Paris*. That Academy defrayed the expences of the gentleman's journey, returned their thanks to Mr. *Chefelden*, and began a correspondence with him.

5

he

" the Beauties of Poetry," 8vo ; and " Innocence, a Poe-
" tical

he was elected a corresponding member of the Royal Academy of Sciences at *Paris* ; and
almost on the institution of the Royal Academy of Surgery in that city, 1732, had the honour of being the first foreigner associated to their learned body.   A man aspiring most
eagerly to fame might have rested here.   So partial a reputation was not sufficient for Mr.
Cheselden, who in 1728 again immortalized himself by giving fight to a lad near fourteen
years old, who had been totally blind from his birth *, by the closure of the iris without
the least opening for light in the pupil.   His fame was now so fully established, that, on
Mr. *Ferne's* retiring from business, he was elected head surgeon of *St. Thomas's Hospital*,
and was esteemed the first man in his profession.   At two other hospitals, *St. George's* and
the *Westminster Infirmary*, he was elected consulting surgeon ; and had also the honour of
being appointed principal surgeon to Queen *Caroline* †, who had a great esteem for him.
Having now obtained his utmost wishes as to fame and fortune, Mr. *Cheselden* sought for
that most desirable of blessings, a life of tranquillity ; which he found in 1737 in the appointment of Head Surgeon to *Chelsea Hospital*, which he held with the highest reputation till his death.   In 1738 Mr. *Sharpe* dedicated his " Treatise on the Operations
" of Surgery" to Mr. *Cheselden* ; to whom he acknowledges himself " chiefly indebted
" for whatever knowledge he can pretend to in surgery ;" calls him " the ornament
" of his profession ;" and says, " To Mr. *Cheselden* posterity will be ever indebted for
" the signal services he has done to surgery."   In the latter end of the year 1751, he
was seized with a paralytic stroke, from which, to appearance, he was perfectly recovered ; when, on the 10th of *April*, 1752, a sudden stroke of apoplexy hurried him
to the grave, at the age of 64.   Amongst the other good qualities of Mr. *Cheselden*,
tenderness for his patients was eminently conspicuous.   His eulogist relates a remarkable
contrast between him and a *French* surgeon of eminence.   Whenever *Cheselden* entered
the Hospital on his morning visits, the reflection of what he was unavoidably to perform impressed him with uneasy sensations ‡ ; but in the afternoon he would frequently
amuse himself as a spectator at the fencing-school.   The *Frenchman*, astonished at what
he thought a weakness in our great Surgeon's behaviour at the Hospital, was persuaded
to accompany him to the fencing-school, where he could not bear the fight, and was
taken ill.   The adventure was the subject of conversation at court.   Both were praised
equally for goodness of heart.   In fact, however different the occasions, each was
affected by similar sentiments of humanity.   Mr. *Cheselden* had an only daughter, who
(as has been already said) was married to Dr. *Cotes* ‖.   His intimacy with Mr. *Pope* has
been

* The particulars of this operation are related at large by the Eulogist of Mr. *Cheselden*, who was
a witness to the performance, and received from him as a present the invaluable instrument invented by Mr. *Cheselden* on the occasion.   Mr. *Cheselden* drew up a particular account of the whole
process, and the various observations made by the patient after he had recovered his fight.   See
Phil. Transf. vol. XXXV. p. 451.   Abridgement, vol. VII. p. 493.

† By a letter from Mr. *Ford* to Dr. *Swift*, Nov. 22, 1737, it appears that her Majesty, by an injudicious delicacy, hastened her death.   She had a rupture which she would not discover ; and the
surgeon who opened her navel [most probably Mr. *Cheselden*] declared, " if he had known it two
" days sooner, she should have been walking about next day."   By the Queen's concealing her
distemper, they gave her strong cordials for the gout in her stomach, which did great mischief.

‡ Mr. *Cheselden*, I have heard, was generally sick with anxiety before he began an operation, but
during it he was quite himself and self-collected.

‖ My good friend Mr. *Kynaston* has enabled me to correct a capital error in what is said on Dr.
Cotes in p. 213, which I cannot do better than in the words of his obliging letter, dated *June* 20,
1781 : " You have told us he was the son of *Digby Cotes*, Principal of *Magdalen Hall*, and formerly-
" Public

" tical Effay, by Mr. *Abraham Portal* *," 8vo ; and an
" *Italian* Grammar," by Mr. *Lates*, of *Oxford*, 8vo.

In 1763 Mr. *Bowyer* publiſhed an excellent edition of the
Greek Teſtament, in 2 volumes, 12mo. under the title of "No-
" vum Teſtamentum *Græcum*, ad fidem *Græcorum* ſolùm
" Codicum MSS. nunc primùm expreſſum, adſtipulante
" *Joanne Jacobo Wetſtenio*, juxta ſectiones *Jo. Alberti Ben-
" gelii* diviſum ; & novâ Interpunctione ſæpius illuſtratum.
" Acceſſère in altero volumine Emendationes conjecturales
" Virorum doctorum undecunque collectæ." This edition
was ſold with great rapidity† ; though announced to the
publick

been mentioned in p. 214, where the following circumſtance might have been added : In 1742, in a converſation with Mr. *Pope* at *Dodſley's*, Mr. *Cheſelden* expreſſed his
wonder at the folly of thoſe who could imagine that the fourth book of the *Dunciad*
had the leaſt reſemblance in ſtyle, wit, humour, or fancy, to the three preceding
books. He was much mortified when his friend undeceived him, by ſaying, that
" he was ſorry Mr. *Cheſelden* did not like the poem, as he [*Pope*] was the author of it."
A friend ſaying to Mr. *Cheſelden* at dinner that as he was the beſt anatomiſt in *England*,
he ought to be the beſt carver, he anſwered ; " I am."

* Son of a clergyman, preferred in *Eſſex*. He was lately a goldſmith and jeweller on
Ludgate Hill, and now (1781) keeps a ſtationary and muſic warehouſe in *The Strand*,
and has this year collected his Poetical Works in one octavo volume.

† Mr. *Markland*, *April* 11, 1763, tells him, " I am really glad that your N. T. is
" likely to turn out ſo much better than you expected : which, I can tell you, is owing
" to the notes being written in *Engliſh*. And if the Notes on this Play [the *Supplices Mu-
" lieres* of *Euripides*] had been written in that language, I do not doubt but twice the num-

" Public Orator of the Univerſity of *Oxford*. He moſt certainly was not. I knew his brother well,
" *Shirley Cotes*, late rector of *Wigan*. He was educated at *Magdalen Hall*, under *Digby Cotes*, whom
" I take to have been his uncle, a younger brother of the father of *Charles* the phyſician, and
" my friend *Shirley*. There were ſix brothers in all ; one you have mentioned, who was a Lieute-
" nant Colonel. *This* was the eldeſt. The next was, I think, *Charles* the phyſician. The third,
" I apprehend, *Thomas Cotes*, the admiral. The fourth, *Waſhington Cotes*, an *Iriſh* Dean. The
" fifth. my worthy friend *Shirley*, late rector of *Wigan* ; and the youngeſt, *Humphry Cotes*, wine
" merchant, and candidate for *Weſtminſter*. I am very clear the father of theſe ſix ſons was the poſ-
" ſeſſor of the family eſtate at *Woodcote* in *Shropſhire* (now inherited by the eldeſt ſon of *Shirley*‡ ;)
" but whether *Digby*, the Principal of *Magdalen Hall*, was in ſo near a relationſhip to him as bro-.
" ther, I am not quite clear ; though I think I have heard my much-eſteemed friend, the late
" rector of *Wigan*, ſay, that he was. *Digby's* family lived in *Oxford*, in my time. Three daugh-
" ters and one ſon, who was upon the foundation of *Trinity College*, and afterwards vicar of *Sher-
" borne* in *Dorſetſhire*." Edward Cotes, vicar of *Sherborne*, 1773 ; rector of *Biſhops Caſtle*, 1748 ;
and vicar of *Haydon*, 17 ; all in the county of *Dorſet*, died *July* 18, 1780.

‡ " *John Cotes*, eſq. educated at *Eton*, and removed thence to *Magdalen College*, *Oxford*, where he reſided ſome
" years, a Gentleman Commoner, under the care of the Rev. Dr. *Wheeler*, at that time principal Tutor of the
" College, now Canon of *Chriſt Church*, and King's Profeſſor of Divinity. Mr. *Cotes*, at his return from making
" the tour of *Europe*, married in 1779 the honourable Miſs *Courtenay*, ſiſter of Lord Viſcount *Courtenay*."

" ber

publick in a light, perhaps, not the moſt captivating to a
purchaſer; to the advertiſements in the public papers Mr.
Bowyer having ſubjoined a ſomewhat ſingular remark;
" This edition boaſts neither elegance of type nor paper*,
" but truſts to other merits." The conjectural emendations
are a very valuable addition to the *Greek* Teſtament, and
were extremely well received by the Learned †.

The other books of 1763 were, " A Report from the
" Committee appointed on the 27th of *January* 1763, to

" ber would have been ſold; for I think it is plain that we are haſtening to the ſetting aſide
" *Latin* and *Greek*; and if the ſetting them aſide, in our Schools, for *Engliſh*, *French*, *Ita-*
" *lian*, *Spaniſh*, &c. were to come to the vote, I fancy the moderns would carry it by a
" great majority.—I ſhall not be ſurpriſed or ſorry to hear that you differed with the perſon
" you mention ‡, rather than be inſtrumental in expoſing him. On the contrary, I
" ſhall think you have acted very honourably in ſo doing. The plea, of another perſon's
" undertaking it, if you do not, is nothing to you. You mention a *Dedication*, but do
" not ſay of *what*; I hope, not of the *Muſe*—which would be ridiculous in one of his
" degree and ſtation, at any age; but at 80 is intolerably abſurd. It would be very
" fortunate for him, if, when you refuſe to be concerned in it, you would plainly and
" honeſtly tell him the reaſon. I know he would like it. Probably he does not think
" of that circumſtance, *Non decet*. I have known him deſiſt from improper things for a
" ſingle hint. Heaven preſerve us from hobby-horſes at eighty!"
 * It was an edition more particularly accommodated to the uſe of ſchools.
 † " We may allow illiterate witlings and half-learned poets to call perſons engaged
" in grammatical ſtudies by the opprobrious title of word-catchers and point-ſetters;
" but we cannot but be concerned to hear any one, who really is, or pretends to be,
" a man of learning, join with them in the cry. To convince all ſuch deſpiſers how
" much depends even upon the minutiæ of grammar, I would offer this remark, that
" the conjunction και has upwards of ten meanings, not only in the Bible (on account of
" its anſwering to that extenſive *Hebrew* particle Vau), but alſo in the beſt profane au-
" thors; and that it has been above twenty times wrongly tranſlated in the New Teſta-
" ment, ſo as to deſtroy, if not the ſenſe of thoſe paſſages, at leaſt their force and
" elegance, which is not likely to be reſtored to them by perſons who know no other
" meaning of και but one. I would have them too obſerve, that the leaving out the
" definitive article (*the*) where it is expreſſed in the *Greek*, and inſerting it where it is
" not expreſſed, has perverted the meaning of ſome important paſſages of Holy Writ.
" I would alſo recommend it to them to look into a *Greek* Teſtament lately publiſhed by
" Mr. *Bowyer*, a printer, whoſe erudition not only ſets him on a par with the beſt
" ſcholars among the early printers, but would do credit to perſons of high rank even
" in the learned profeſſions. They may there ſee how much has been done by punc-
" tuation, parentheſis, proper ſection, and other contemptible articles, towards illuſtrat-
" ing a book, which, as of all books it moſt deſerves our reading, claims our greateſt
" care that it be truly pointed and juſtly tranſlated." *Two Grammatical Eſſays, &c.* 1769.

‡ Dr. *Cobden*; of whom ſee pp. 207. 271.

" enquire

" enquire into the State of Private Madhouſes, with the
" Proceedings of the Houſe of Commons thereupon, pub-
" liſhed by their Order," folio ; " Tracts on the Liberty, Spi-
" ritual and Temporal, of Proteſtants in *England*," by Bp.
*Ellys**, 4to; a new edition of "*Ecton's* Theſaurus," 4to ; the
firſt volume of Dr. *Warner's†* " Hiſtory of *Ireland*," 4to ;
Mr.

* A ſecond part was publiſhed in 1765 ; under which year an account will be given
of Bp. *Ellys.*

† *Ferdinando Warner*, LL. D. rector of *St. Michael, Queenhithe, London*, and of
Barnes in *Surrey*, a celebrated preacher, and author of 1. " A Sermon preached before
" the Lord Mayor *January* 30, 1748." 2. " A Sermon preached before the Lord
" Mayor on *September* 2, 1749." 3 " A Syſtem of Divinity and Morality, contain-
" ing a ſeries of Diſcourſes on the principal and moſt important points of natural and
" revealed Religion ; compiled from the Works of the moſt eminent Divines of the
" Church of *England*, 1750," 5 vols. 12mo. This was reprinted in 4 vols. 8vo. 1756.
4. " A Scheme for a Fund for the better Maintenance of the Widows and Children of
" the Clergy, 1753," 8vo. 5. " An Illuſtration of the Book of Common Prayer and
" Adminiſtration of Sacraments, and other Rites and Ceremonies of the Church of *Eng-*
" *land*, &c. 1754," folio. In this year he took the Degree of LL. D. 6. " *Bolin-*
" *broke*, or a Dialogue on the Origin and Authority of Revelation, 1755," 8vo.
7. " A free and neceſſary Enquiry whether the Church of *England* in her Li-
" turgy, and many of her learned Divines in their Writings, have not by ſome unwary
" Expreſſions relating to Tranſubſtantiation and the real Preſence, given ſo great an
" Advantage to Papiſts and Deiſts, as may prove fatal to true Religion, unleſs ſome
" Remedy be ſpeedily ſupplied ; with Remarks on the Power of Prieſtly Abſolution.
" 1755," 8vo. 8. In 1756 he publiſhed the firſt volume of his " Eccleſiaſtical Hiſtory
" to the eighteenth Century," folio ; the ſecond volume in 1757. 9. " Memoirs of
" the Life of Sir *Thomas More*, Lord High Chancellor of *England* in the reign of
" *Henry* VIII. 1758," 8vo. This is dedicated to Sir *Robert Henley*, afterwards Lord
Chancellor *Northington*, who is complimented for the favours he had conferred on him
on his receiving the ſeals ; probably for the rectory of *Barnes*, which was given him in
1758, and with which he held *Queenhithe* and *Trinity the Leſs*. 10. " Remarks on the
" Hiſtory of *Fingal* and other Poems of *Oſſian*, tranſlated by Mr. *Macpherſon*, in a Letter
" to the Right Hon. the Lord L———[*Lytteſton*] 1762," 8vo 11. " The Hiſtory of *Ire-*
" *land*, vol. I. 1763," 4to. He publiſhed no more of this, being diſcouraged by a diſappointment in his expectations of ſome Parliamentary aſſiſtance. 12. " A Letter to the Fel-
" lows of *Sion College*, and to all the Clergy within the Bills of Mortality, and in the
" County of *Middleſex*, humbly propoſing their forming themſelves into a Society for
" the Maintenance of the Widows and Orphans of ſuch Clergymen. To which is added,
" a ſketch of ſome Rules and Orders ſuitable to that purpoſe, 1765," 8vo. 13. " The
" Hiſtory of the Rebellion and Civil War in *Ireland*, 1767," 4to. For collecting materials for his Hiſtory of *Ireland*, he went over to that kingdom about 1761. 12. " A full
" and plain Account of the Gout, from whence will be clearly ſeen the folly or the
" baſeneſs of all Pretenders to the cure of it, in which every thing material by the beſt

5

" writers

Mr. *Folkes's* * " Tables of *English* Silver and Gold Coins,"
2 vols. 4to. (fee p. 180); " A Differtation upon the *Taf-*
" *cia* †, or Legend, on the *Britifh* Coins of *Cunobelin* and
" others, by *John Pettingal* ‡, D. D. Read at the Society of
" Antiquaries, and ordered to be printed," 4to ; Mr. *Mark-*

" writers on that fubject is taken notice of, and accompanied with fome new and im-
" portant inftructions for its relief, which the author's experience in the gout above
" thirty years hath induced him to impart, 1768," 8vo. He died *Oct.* 3, 1768, and
thereby deftroyed the credit of the remedy which he recommended for the gout, and the
reputation of his book, which inftantly funk into oblivion. He had the living of *Wandf-*
worth when he died. His fon *John* is D. D. and vicar of *Weft Ham, Effex.*

* Dr. *Birch's* MSS. have enabled me to add a few circumftances to what is faid of
Mr. *Folkes* in p. 177—180. He was born in *Queen Street*, near *Lincoln's Inn Fields* ;
and received a private education till he went to *Clare Hall, Cambridge*, where he took
the degree of M. A. and was afterwards admitted *ad eundem* at *Oxford*. There alfo
he was made LL. D. and admitted *ad eundem* at *Cambridge*. A remark on Father
Hardouin's amendment of a paffage in *Pliny*, relating to the gnomon of *Ancona*, Nat.
Hift. lib. ii. § 74. ed. *Parif.* by *Martin Folkes*, efq. Pr. R. S. is in Phil. Tranf. vol.
XLIV. p. 365.—In p. 178, l. 30, r. " a fon and two daughters ;" and in the laft
line of the note read, " fhe fpoke an epilogue." His portrait by *Hogarth* is in the
meeting-room of the Royal Society. Mr. *Hearne*, the celebrated Antiquary, in a letter
to the Earl of *Oxford, Aug.* 28, 1732, fays, " As for Mr. *Martin Folkes* (an ingenious
" Gentleman) his defign upon our *English* Coins (in which is not much erudition,
" however the fubject be curious) I never heard of it before. I remember Sir *Andrew*
" *Fountaine*, many years ago, told me more than once he had fuch a work in view,
" by way of continuation of his *Saxon* Coins ; but what progrefs he made I never heard,
" though I prefume confiderable with refpect to fuch a Collection, unlefs he parted
" with all or moft to Lord *Pembroke.*"—Since p. 180 was printed off, I have been
favoured by a friend with the following remark : " The plates of *English* filver coins,
" publifhed by *Snelling*, were only 17, and not 44 as here afferted. It is alfo
" an error to fay that they were not continued beyond the protectorate of *Crom-*
" *well*, as they were brought down to the reign of the late king ; and it is too harfh
" to fay in general terms 'evidently copied from the Society's plates,' as himfelf has
" given the names of feveral gentlemen who lent him rare and valuable coins for the ex-
" prefs purpofe of being engraven in his work, befides feveral in his own poffeffion which
" he has fpecified, and many others which are well known to have been put into his
" hands, but the poffeffors names were not mentioned on account of the coins not being
" of any great rarity. There is alfo a proof of *Snelling* having publifhed feveral coins
" totally unknown to the editor of the Society's plates, the latter having frequently re-
" ferred to the ' View of the *English* Silver Coin.' What *Snelling* was to blame for is
" in having availed himfelf fomewhat unhandfomely of the Society's *unpublifhed* plates ;
" whence, however, he copied only a very fmall number of coins, the originals of which
" were not then to be got at, and thofe few are wrong engraven by both editors ; there-
" fore *fiat juftitia!*"

† The reward offered for difcovering ftealers of cattle in the Highlands is called
Tafcal money. See " Letters from the North," vol. II. p. 243.

‡ Minifter of the chapel in *Duke Street, Weftminfter.*

land's

land's edition of the " Supplices Mulieres" of *Euripides,* 4to.
(see p. 20); " Epiſtolæ ſex," by Mr. *Waterhouſe*,"* 4to; Dr.
Brown's " Cure of *Saul,"* and his " Diſſertation on the Riſe,
" Union, and Power, the Progreſſions, Separations, and
" Corruptions of Poetry and Muſic," 4to; " *Telemachus,* a
" Maſque, by *George Graham†,"* M. A. 4to; " The *Alps,* a
" poem," by Mr. *Keate‡,* 4to; " *Elvira,* a tragedy," by
Mr. *Mallet,* 8vo; Dr. *Gally's* " Second Diſſertation § againſt
" pronouncing the *Greek* Language according to Accents,
" in anſwer to Mr. *Foſter's* Eſſay on the different nature of
" Accent, and Quantity," 8vo; " Faſciculus Plantarum,"
&c. by Mr. *Lyons,* 8vo, (see p. 294); " An Introduction
" to *Engliſh* Grammar," by Dr. *Lowth* (ſince Biſhop of *London*) which he very frequently reprinted, 8vo. and 12mo;
" A View of the Internal Policy of *Great Britain,"* 12mo;
and " *Julia Mandeville,"* 12mo. by Mrs. *Brooke.*

In 1763 Mr. *Bowyer* attended the aſtronomical lectures of
Mr. *Ferguſon‖,* and not unfrequently conſulted him on that
ſubject.   A letter to him on the paſchal full moons is inſerted below **.   In *September* this year he paid a viſit to his
friend

---

* The Rev. *Benjamin Waterhouſe,* rector of *Hollingbourne,* near *Maidſtone,* in *Kent.*

† This gentleman, the younger ſon of a clergyman, was educated at *Eton* ſchool, and
from thence elected, in 1746, to *King's College, Cambridge.* He afterwards became one
of the aſſiſtants at the ſchool already named, and died in *February* 1767. He was author of a tragedy, which was refuſed by Mr. *Garrick,* and has not hitherto appeared in
print. His elder brother, *David,* alſo fellow of *King's,* and a barriſter at law, has
likewiſe been dead ſome years.

‡ This elegant writer's poetic works are now (1781) collected in two volumes, 8vo.
He is equally diſtinguiſhed as a painter.

§ Which may be added to the liſt of his publications in p. 250. Dr. *Gally* was made
king's chaplain in *October* 1735.

‖ Of whom an account will be given under the year 1767.

** " Sɪʀ, It was a great entertainment to me to hear you direct your aſtronomical
" lecture to the confirmation of hiſtory, but eſpecially of ſo important a part of it, as to
" fix the exact year of the Paſſion of *Jeſus Chriſt.* This is a point in which every
" Chriſtian is intereſted. All will thank you for the reſult of your inquiries, though
" they may not have patience to accompany you in your progreſs through them. It

" may

friend Mr. *Clarke* at *Buxted*, where change of liquor occasioned

" may look like ill-nature in me, to endeavour to abate of the satisfaction you took in
" finding, from your computation, that in the whole course of twenty years †, *viz.* from
" A. D. 21, to A. D. 40, there was but one Paſſover Full Moon that fell on a *Friday*; and
" that one was in the 33d year of our Saviour's age, not including the year of his birth.
" It may ſeem untoward in me to leſſen this confirmation of the ſacred hiſtory, or abate of
" your pleaſure in diſcovering it; but as ſome learned writers have been lately involved
" in difficulties on this head, which you probably are not aware of, I will lay them be-
" fore you, that you may have a freſh ſatisfaction in removing them. I will lead you
" into the labyrinth, and truſt to your aſtronomical ſkill to conduct me out of it. *Jo-*
" *ſeph Scaliger*, a great maſter in chronology, as well as every branch of critical learn-
" ing, made the ſame computation which you have done, but with a different reſult;
" for he found two years in ſeven produced a Paſſover day on a *Friday*, and was in ſome
" doubt. The accurate Mr. *Mann*, who is lately dead, took up this examination again,
" and, having adopted *Scaliger's* calculation, found reaſon, as he thought, to place the
" Paſſion of *Jeſus Chriſt* on the firſt of thoſe years, in which the Paſſover fell on a
" *Friday*, A. D. 27; ſeven years ‡ more early than that which you and our preſent Divines
" adopt, of A. D. 33. Another great Chronologer between theſe two made tables like-
" wiſe for the ſame purpoſe, the celebrated Mr. *Dodwell*, in his book *De Cyclis*, which
" ſerve but the more to embarraſs the ſubject, his calculations differing from the other
" two. Mr. *Mann* ſhould, in juſtice to his ſubject, have detected Mr. *Dodwell's* errors,
" if they are ſuch; but, truſting wholly to *Scaliger's* computations, he did not heſitate
" about *Dodwell's*, becauſe about a year before his death, when I hinted to him the
" difference, he ſaid he would examine it; and I loſt, by not waiting on him, as he de-
" ſired I would, the reſult of his examination §. Yours, &c. *W. B.*"
To the learned Father *Boſcovich* ‖ he thus addreſſed his thoughts on the ſame ſubject:
" Vir doctiſſime, Aſtronomus noſtras, cui nomen *Ferguſon*, ut definiat annum ipſiſſimum
" quo Chriſtus paſſus eſt, computavit quibus annis plenilunium paſchale in feria ſexta
" hebdomadis inciderit per viginti annorum limites, intra quos omnes conſentiunt

---

† See Mr. *Ferguſon's* Brief Deſcription of the Solar Syſtem, p. 15.

‡ " It is very remarkable, and much in favour of this ſyſtem, that *Magnan*, who probably never
" heard a ſyllable of it, concludes from medals alone, that the vulgar æra is ſeven years too late.
" I think he ſays ſeven or eight; but that depends on a ſmall matter, even whether you place the
" birth in *December* or *January*; which though it makes in reality but a few days difference, yet in
" dating is a whole year." *J. F.*

§ Mr. *Bowyer*, after this, collected the ſeveral computations of the Paſchal full moons, by *Roger Bacon*, *Joſeph Scaliger*, Sir *Iſaac Newton*, Mr. *Manne*, Mr. *Ferguſon*, and F. *Lamy*, which are all printed in his " Conjectures on the New Teſtament," 4to. p. 149.

‖ The learned Jeſuit, whoſe elegant *Latin* poem has been mentioned in p. 297; the printing of which was undertaken, at the ſolicitation of Dr. *Morton*, by Mr. *Dodſley*. But Dr. *Morton*, appre-hending perhaps that Mr. *Dodſley* might run too great a riſk in printing it on his own ſingle ac-count, applied to Mr. *Hollis* to prevail with Mr. *Millar* to take a part with Mr. *Dodſley* in the publi-cation. To this Mr. *Millar* agreed; and thus this poem, " which," ſays Mr. *Hollis*, " however " important in itſelf to all lovers of aſtronomy, or honourable on many accounts for the *Britiſh* na-" tion, was in danger otherwiſe of being ſuppreſſed by diſguſt, or of being printed abroad," was given to the publick by the means of an *Engliſh* preſs. Since this tranſaction, Father *Boſcovich's* abilities have been better known to the world, which has done juſtice to his merit on ſeveral occa-ſions. See " Memoirs of Mr. *Hollis*," p. 98.

" eum

fioned a flight diforder, of which both Mr. *Clarke* and Mr. *Markland* take notice in their letters*.

" eum crucifixum effe. Deprehendit vero tale plenilunium accidiffe folummodo, A.D.
" 33. Per. Jul. 4746. Facile affenfum præberem viro in arte fua præftantiffimo, nifi
" alii viri doctiffimi aliud juberent; præfertim *Nicolaus Mann* ex *Scaligeri* et fua compu-
" tatione probare velit plenilunium fuiffe *Judeæ* etiam feria fexta, A.D. 26. Per. Jul.
" 4739. Martii 22. At fi *Dodwelli* tabulas rectè intelligo, ne femel quidem per decem
" annos, ab A.D. 26, ad A.D. 35, in fexta feria pafchale novilunium cecidit; imo nec
" in tabulis *Rogeri Bacon*, quamvis in eum finem tabulas compofuerit. ' Multi,' inquit,
" in aftronomia periti laboraverunt hic, ut has oppofitiones folis & lunæ invenirent, &
" non potuerunt invenire annum paffionis a xxx ad xxxv, ubi in Martio effet oppofitio
" in die Veneris, nec dies ante oppofitionem nec proximus poft, ita ut quod cum paf-,
" fione concorderet. Nec EGO POTUI INVENIRE adhuc.' Per cyclos quofdam credo,
" *Baconem, Scaligerum*, & *Dodwellum* computaffe, *Ferguson* forfan per inftrumentum
" Horarium. Sed unde fit, rogo, ut omnes iftos computiftas adeo inter fe diftare, ut
" ex tabula † ifta ex illis omnibus confecta videre licet ?"

* " I am forry that you have not been fo well fince you left *Suffex*. Believe
" me, it was not the air, but the beer, that difagreed with you. We could do very well
" with you in the country, air and exercife would certainly be an advantage to you, if we
" could furnifh you with proper liquor. I doubt the inconveniences of bufinefs may contri-
" bute fomething, and occafion part of the attrition that fo fenfibly affects your infide.
" But thefe are maladies you will never get rid of. *Aliter non fit, Avite, liber.*" Mr. *Clarke*
to Mr. *B.* dated *All Souls*, 1763.—" What befel you at *Buxted* is a common cafe, owing to
" a great relaxation of the fashionable nervous fyftem. The late Duke of *Marlborough*
" (*Churchill*) had it to a great degree, infomuch that the hero often cried like a child ‡.
" I fuppofe this was the cafe of *Heraclitus* too, who, it is faid, always wept when he went
" out of doors. They give it a philofophical turn, and fay, that he wept at the follies of
" mankind. But then I do not fee why he fhould not have wept within doors as well as
" without. *Juvenal's* remark on it is droll enough, ' Mirandum eft, unde ille oculis fuffe-
" cerit humor.' I often wifh, however, that we had a collection of the fragments of this
" crying philofopher; for from what I have feen of his, he feems to have been a
" ftrange, fenfible, out-of-the-way man, and very much fuperior to his brethren the
" ancient philofophers. The weather, I fancy, will foon break, as I judge from the
" barometer; fo that I do not much expect to fee you, and will compound with you if
" you will fend me the two emendations on the *Supplices* and that on *Clemens Alexandri-*
" *nus.* You need only to mention what Mr. *Toup* reads, without giving yourfelf the
" trouble of fending the reafons or proofs. He has a conjecture on *Iphigenia in Aulide*,
" which is confirmed by two very good MSS. and is moft certainly wrong; and yet, were
" I to publifh that play, I would publifh it as he has conjectured, though I know it to
" be falfe; but it has the authority of MSS. and it is *Greek*, which the vulgar read-
" ing is not. He finds fault with Mr. *Pierfon*, who I believe is right, and who knew
" what he was about; and yet Mr. *T's* conjecture, which was obvious enough, and
" I do not doubt was feen by Mr. *Pierfon*, could not be true, had it been confirmed
" by twenty MSS. But Mr. *T.* has not gone far enough in the old tragedians to
" know that; Mr. *Pierfon* had."

† This table is printed in the " Conjectures," &c. as already mentioned in p. 349.
‡ " From *Marlborough's* eyes the tears of dotage flow." Dr. *Johnfon's Vanity of Human Wishes.*

In

In 1764 Mr. *Bowyer* printed Dr. *Tunstall's* [*] " Lectures
" on

* *James Tunstall*, D. D. Fellow of *St. John's College*, *Cambridge*, and one of the two
principal tutors of that Society, was instituted to the rectory of *Sturmer*, in *Essex*, in
December 1739, and elected public orator † (on the resignation of Dr. *Williams*) in October 1741, after a smart opposition from Mr. *Philip Yonge*, of *Trinity College*, now Bishop
of *Norwich*, and who was afterwards chosen when Dr. *Tunstall* resigned upon being made
chaplain to Archbishop *Potter*. This primate had only four chaplains whilst he held the
see of *Canterbury*; and of these Dr. *Tunstall* was the junior. He was created D. D. at
the Commencement at *Cambridge*, *July* 10, 1744; was collated by the Archbishop to
the rectory of *Great Chart* in *Kent*; and to the vicarage of *Minster* in the Isle of *Thanet*,
175 , both of which he quitted for the valuable vicarage of *Rochdale* in *Lancashire*, in *November* 1757, given him by Archbishop *Hutton* who married Mrs. *Tunstall's*
aunt. The exchange, from many untoward circumstances, did not answer his expectation. He died *March* 28, 1772. Dr. *Tunstall* distinguished himself as one intimately acquainted with *Tully's* works and the history of those times, by a learned and
spirited attack upon that classical work of Dr. *Middleton's*, so much admired in *Italy*,
the " Life of *Marcus Tullius Cicero*," by questioning the genuineness of *Tully's*
Epistles to *Brutus*, in his " Epistola ad virum eruditum *Conyers Middleton*, Vitæ
" *M. T. Ciceronis* Scriptorem; in quâ, ex locis ejus operis quamplurimis recen-
" sionem *Ciceronis* Epistolarum ad *Atticum* & *Quintum Fratrem* desiderari osten-
" ditur, &c. *Cantabrigiæ*, 1741 ‡." His other publications were, 1. " Observa-
" tions on the present Collection of Epistles between *Cicero* and *M. Brutus* §," &c.

† " I am persuaded by my friends to offer myself for the Orator's place, as soon as Dr. *Williams*
" resigns, and promise myself the continuance of your favour. The Doctor does not resign this
" year; and I am thus forward, lest you should have applications from other hands. Mr. *Yonge*
" of *Trinity* is the only competitor who has yet declared." *MS. Letter of Dr. Tunstall to Dr. Z.
Grey, April* 7, 1740.

‡ " As the Doctor had made great use of these materials in his Life of *Tully*, he would probably
much rather have seen the genuineness of the Four Gospels called in question. Accordingly he
had recourse to every expedient to save a sinking cause; descended so low, as to say the Public
Orator's language was not intelligible, and would have been very glad to have proved it. I
could name a well-known patriotic Duke, who has lately not only read over the whole controversy (which is neither short nor slight), but declares his astonishment that any body could have
any doubts about the merits of the cause. Yet Dr. *Middleton* was much the more fashionable
man, and many superficial gentry would have taken the wrong side with such a popular writer.
Dr. *Tunstall's* death was rather premature, occasioned either by family uneasinesses or disappointment
of preferment‖; yet he was a person of such equal civility, if not humility of deportment, that it was
said of him for some time after he had left *Lambeth*, that many a man came there, as chaplain,
humble; but that none ever went thence so, except Dr. *Tunstall*." *T. F.*—who was not his pupil,
but, in the language of college, belonged to the other side or line, yet willingly pays this mark of
respect to a learned and virtuous character.

§ " I cannot help mentioning that Mr. *Cumberland* informed me, that in the Library of the
Escurial are 20 *Greek* Letters, from *M. Brutus* to the *Greek* Cities; exacting contributions from
them. Such is the illiberality of *Spain*, that he could only procure one. They are in *Greek*, which
may occasion a speculation, how far it is likely that a *Roman* General could write in that language on a public business. From the only word I have heard, viz. καταπαρα, I presume that
he threatened them, in case of non-compliance, with as severe a fate as he inflicted on the brave
Xanthians. One may wonder too that 20 such detached Orders should any how be got together
" and preserved." *T. F.*—It is more probable they are the manufacture of some Sophist.

‖ The cause above assigned contributed to it. *Rochdale* was reputed worth 700l. per annum; but fell greatly
short of it. Dr. *Tunstall* left several daughters, some of them most unfortunately circumstanced in their health,
to whom their uncle, the Rev. Mr. *Dodsworth* Treasurer of *Salisbury* (who superintended the publication of the
" Lectures") has been a father. Mrs. *Tunstall* did not long survive her husband. D.

(see

"on Natural and Revealed Religion," 4to; Mr. *Evans's*
"Specimens

(see p. 176); 2. "A Sermon before the House of Commons, *May* 29, 1746."
3. "A Vindication of the Power of the State to prohibit Clandestine Marriages
"under the pain of absolute nullity; particularly the Marriages of Minors made
"without the consent of their Parents and Guardians, &c. 1755," 8vo. 4. "Mar-
"riage in Society stated; with some Considerations on Government, the different
"kinds of Civil Laws, and their distinct Obligations in Conscience, in a second Letter
"to the Rev. Dr. *Stebbing*, occasioned by his Review, &c. 1755," 8vo. 5. "Aca-
"demica: Part the first, containing several Discourses on the certainty, distinction, and
"connection of Natural and Revealed Religion, 1759," 8vo. This contains "Concio
"ad Clerum habita in templo beatæ *Mariæ* in Academia *Cant*. pro gradu S. T. B.
"anno 1738;" the Thesis read when he took his Doctor's degree in 1744, and some
Sermons. The second part was to have consisted of Lectures, 1. On the Being, Perfection,
and Providence of God; 2. On the Laws of Universal Benevolence; 3. On a State of future Existence; and was, I suppose, the work published after his death, under the title of
"Lectures on Natural and Revealed Religion, read in the Chapel of *St John's College*,
"*Cambridge*, by *James Tunstall*, D. D. sometime chaplain to Dr. *Potter*, Archbishop
"of *Canterbury*, and Vicar of *Rochdale* in *Lancashire*," 4to. These Lectures were
begun by the Author when a Tutor in *St. John's*, but he was prevented from finishing the comprehensive plan laid down in the beginning of them, by being called from
that employment in College to the service of Archbishop *Potter*. They were, however,
so nearly completed, that the Author, had he lived, intended to have published them
himself, and they were faithfully printed from his MS. without the least addition or
correction. A very large and respectable list of subscribers is prefixed to these Lectures,
of which 1500 copies were printed, and *eight* only on large paper. Some critical Annotations by Dr. *Tunstall* are annexed to the first edition of Mr. *Duncombe's Horace*. In 1740
he obtained for Dr. *Grey* Mr. *Warburton's* remarks on *Hudibras*, as is publickly acknowledged in the Preface to that work, and is confirmed by the following quotation from a
unpublished letter of Mr. *Tunstall* to Dr. *Grey*: "Immediately after your favour came to
"hand I applied to Mr. *Warburton*, who answers in these words: 'I can deny you
"nothing. Dr. *Grey* shall have my Remarks on *Hudibras*, and I will depend upon his
"honour †. I had thoughts (as I had considered this author pretty much) to have given
"an edition of him, and had mentioned it to an eminent bookseller. But I will think
"no more of it, as this matter will oblige you. But I cannot possibly set about tran-
"scribing them for the Doctor till after *Lady-day*, because of my second volume.'
"Thus far Mr. *Warburton*, whom I had told that he might depend upon your doing
"him justice in the notes he communicated, for I knew I could safely promise it ‡."
Among

---

† Yet Dr. *Grey*, two years after, shot some arrows at this *Colossus*.
‡ From the readiness with which Dr. *Warburton* supplied *Grey* with his remarks on *Hudibras*, and
the grateful acknowledgment with which they were received (see Preface to *Hudibras*, p. 35), the
rudeness of that Author's mention of the edition to which he had contributed is difficult to be accounted for. Speaking of criticks in his preface to *Shakspeare*, he introduces Dr. *Grey's Hudibras*
in the following manner: "I hardly think there ever appeared, in any learned language, so execra-
"ble a heap of nonsense under the name of Commentaries, as hath been lately given us on a certain
"satyric poet of the last age by his Editor and Coadjutor." For this attack Dr. *Grey* took his revenge
in some pamphlets mentioned under his article, and in 1754 again noticed his antagonist in the following terms: "The first to whom I am indebted is the Rev. Mr. *Smith*, of *Harleston*, in *Nor-
"folk*,

" Specimens of *Welsh* Poetry," 4to ; Mr. *Costard** on the Fall of the Stone in *Ægospotamos*, 4to ; " The Ruins of *Netley* " *Abbey*," a poem, by Mr. *Keate*, 4to ; " An Account of the " First Settlement of the *Cessares*, a people of *South America*," 8vo. (see p. 241) ; two editions of " Thoughts on Foreign " Travel," by Mr. *Hurd*, 8vo ; " A Letter to Dr. *Leland*," in vindication of Bishop *Warburton*, 8vo ; Mr. *Shenstone's†* " Essays on Men, Manners, and Things," being the first volume of his works, 8vo ; Dr. *Owen's* " Observations on " the Four Gospels," 8vo ; Dr. *Akenside‡* " De Dysen- " teriâ,"

Among Dr. *Birch's* MSS. in *The British Museum* is a Collection of MS. Letters from Dr. *Tunstall* to the Earl of *Oxford*, in 1738 and 1739, on *Ducket's* Atheistical Letters, and the Proceedings thereon ; there is also a Letter to Dr. *Birch*, dated " *Great Chart*, " *Nov.* 21, 1744," communicating an original letter from *Meric Casaubon*, his prede-cessor as vicar of *Minster*, whence it appears that Dr. *Tunstall* was *then* possessed of the livings of *Minster* and *Chart*.

* This very learned writer (well known by his many valuable publications) was formerly fellow and tutor of *Wadham College, Oxford* ; and is now vicar of *Twick-enham, Middlesex*. Mr. *Bowyer* had always a very high regard for him, and greatly esteemed his writings.

† Of Mr. *Shenstone*, besides the Life by Dr. *Johnson*, a good account has been given, from authentic information, in Dr. *Nash's* " History of *Worcestershire*," vol. I. p. 531—534.

‡ To the Life of Dr. *Akenside* which has appeared in the first volume of the " Biogra- " phia," and the additions prefixed to the second, I shall add, from Dr. *Johnson*, that the Discourse on the Dysentery " was considered as a very conspicuous specimen of " *Latinity*, which entitled him to the same height of place among the Scholars, as he " possessed before among the Wits."—The following circumstances, which are extracted from *Brand's* " Observations on Popular Antiquities, 1777," 8vo. p. 113, are omitted by

" *folk*, the most friendly and communicative man living, who was greatly assistant to Sir *Thomas* " *Hanmer* in his edition of *Shakespeare*, as he was to me in *Hudibras*, for which he has been spitefully " called my Coadjutor, but by a gentleman whose slander stands for nothing with every candid and " ingenuous person." *Grey's* Commentary on *Hudibras*, notwithstanding Dr. *Warburton's* censure, will, generally, be viewed with favour. Trifling and insignificant as the books he quotes are allowed to be, they were such as *Butler* himself saw, referred, and alluded to, and therefore were the proper sources to consult for materials to explain him. As Mr. *Warton* has ob-served of *Shakspeare*, " If *Butler* is worth reading, he is worth explaining ; and the researches " used for so valuable and elegant a purpose merit the thanks of genius and candour, not the " satire of prejudice and ignorance." It may be remarked that the multiplicity of authors quoted in the Commentary on *Hudibras* always impresses a superficial reader in the same manner. *Fielding*, whose writings shew to what an excellent purpose he applied his reading, and who did not attempt to conceal what he obtained from books (little as it was, owing to business and dissipation), appears to have been struck in the same manner as many others of Dr. *Grey's* readers. " If we should carry on the " analogy between the traveller and the commentator, it is impossible to keep one's eye a moment " off from the laborious much-read Doctor *Zachary Grey*, of whose redundant notes on *Hudibras* I " shall only say, that it is, I am confident, the single book extant in which above five hundred au-"thors are quoted, not one of which could be found in the collection of the late Dr. *Mead*." *Pref.* to *Voyage to Lisbon*.

Dr.

" teriâ," 8vo; " The Song of *Solomon*, newly tranflated
" from the original *Hebrew*, with a Commentary and An-
" notations," [by Dr. *Percy*, fince Dean of *Carlifle*,] 8vo;
and the fecond edition of Dr. *Grey's** *Hudibras*.

In

Dr. *Kippis*. " Dr. *Akenfide* was born at *Newcaftle upon Tyne*, and received the firft
" principles of his education at the very refpectable grammar-fchool there; his father a
" reputable butcher of the town. A halt in his gait, occafioned when a boy, by the
" falling of a cleaver from his father's ftall, muft have been a perpetual remembrancer
" of his humble origin. I mention this, becaufe, from the biographical account of
" him prefixed to the pofthumous edition of his works (an outline with which he muft
" have furnifhed his friends), one is inclined to believe that he was afhamed of his
" birth. We regret, on perufing it, the omiffion of thofe pleafing and interefting little
" anecdotes ufually given of the firft indications of genius. His townfmen have many
" other reafons that lead to the confirmation of this fufpicion. Taking this for granted,
" it was a great and unpardonable foible in one of fo exalted an underftanding. Falfe
" fhame was perhaps never more ftrongly exemplified. The learned world" (I continue
to ufe Mr. *Brand's* words) " will forgive me for attempting in this note to defeat his
" very narrow purpofe (for I can call it by no fofter name), the wifhing to conceal from
" pofterity a circumftance that would by no means have leffened his fame with them. I
" flatter myfelf it is compatible with the refpect we owe to the dead, and even to the
" memory of him, who on other accounts deferved fo highly of his country."

* Dr. *Zachary Grey* was of a *Yorkfhire* family, originally from *France* †. He was admitted
a penfioner in *Jefus College, Cambridge*, *April* 18, 1704, but afterwards removed to *Trinity
Hall*, where he was admitted fcholar of the houfe, *Jan.* 6, 1706-7; and though he was
never Fellow of that College, yet being LL. D. in 1730, he was elected one of the truftees
for Mr. *Ayloffe's* benefaction to it. He was rector of *Houghton Conqueft* in *Bedfordfhire*,
and vicar of *St. Peter's* and *St. Giles's* parifhes in *Cambridge*, where he ufually paffed the
winter, and the reft of his time at *Ampthill*, the neighbouring market town to his living.
He died *Nov.* 25, 1766, at *Ampthill*, in the 79th year of his age, and was buried at *Houghton
Conqueft*. He was of a moft amiable, fweet, and communicative difpofition; moft friendly
to his acquaintance, and never better pleafed than when performing acts of friendfhip and
benevolence. He had one brother (*George* ‡, born in 1680) a chamber counfellor at *Newcaftle*. Dr. *Grey* was twice married; his firft wife was a Mifs *Tooley*; and by his fecond
lady

† " The *Greys* or *Grays*," fays *Rapin*, " came from *Gray*, a town in *Franche Comté*, and had
" probably lands given them by the Conqueror or his immediate fucceffors, among other *Normans*
" and *Frenchmen* who made the poffeffions of the former inhabitants their prey." Several noble families of this name appeared very early, and they have continued pretty prolific, great numbers of
them being difperfed all over the kingdom both in high and low life. And fee a letter to Dr. *Grey*
on the fubject from the late *Charles Gray*, efq. in Bibl. Topog. Brit. Nº II. p. 171.

‡ I have a number of this gentleman's MS. letters to Dr. *Grey*, by which it appears that they
both were very induftrious in collecting memorials of their family, which, with an ample pedigree,
were in the hands of Mr. *George Grey* ‖; who often mentions his " brother and fifter *Hindmarfh*" and

‖ Mr. *Reed* has a collection of records, pedigrees, &c. of the family (bought out of the *Northampton* Catalogue, mentioned p. 356), with fome curious particulars of the *Greys* earls of *Kent*; amongft others, " Summons
" to Parliament of the Lords *Grey of Codnover, Wilton, Ruthyn*, and the other Lords of that name, collected out
" of *Rymer's* volumes and *Dugdale's* Summons;" and alfo " My Lord's expences for his houfhold in feven weeks
" ended 5 *April* 1593; diftinguifhed under the refpective articles of " Buttry and Pantry," " Seller," " Spy-
" cery," " Ewery," Wood and Cole," " Accator of Store," " Prefents," and " Redy Money."

" brother

In *December*, 1764, Mr. *Bowyer* prefented a copy of Mr.
Folkes's

lady (who was related to Dean *Mofs*, and whom he married in 1720) had two daughters, one of whom was married to the Rev. Mr. *William Cole* of *Ely*, Fellow of *St. John's College*, *Cambridge*, and now rector of *Alberghe* near *Harlefione* and *Bungay* in *Norfolk*; the other to the Rev. Mr. *Lepipre*, rector of *Afpley Guife* in *Bedfordfhire*. The Doctor was often at *Wimple* in the time of *Edward* Earl of *Oxford*, from whom he received many marks of friendfhip, particularly a prefent of a noble filver cup and ewer. By feveral letters which are in my poffeffion, from the late Duke of *Bedford*, Lord *Trevor*, Lord *St. John*, and others of the Nobility and Gentry of *Bedfordfhire*, it appears, that, being in the commiffion of the peace, and a man of refpectable character, he was much courted for his interest in elections. He was not, however, very active on those occasions, preferring literary retirement. The number of his publications were fo great, that Bifhop *Warburton* infults him for them. Amongft them were, 1. " A Vindication of the Church of *England*, in two parts, 1720," 8vo. 2. " Prefbyterian Prejudice difplayed, 1722," 8vo. 3. " A Pair of clean Shoes and Boots " for a Dirty Baronet, or an Anfwer to Sir *Richard Cox*, *London*, 1722," 8vo. 4. " A " Letter of Thanks to Mr. *Benjamin Bennet*, *London*, 1723," 8vo. 5. " A Caveat " againft Mr. *Benjamin Bennet*, *London*, 1724," 8vo. 6. " A Defence of our ancient and " modern Hiftorians againft the frivolous Cavils of a late Pretender to Critical Hiftory, in " which the falfe Quotations and unjuft Inferences of the anonymous Author are confuted " and expofed in the manner they deferve. In two parts. 1725." 8vo 8. In 1732 he wrote the Preface to his relation Dean *Mofs's* Sermons *, faid to be " by a Learned Hand †." 9.

" brother *Warcop*." In feveral of his letters he obferves, that their father died at the age of fixty, and that he did not himfelf expect to exceed that age. He lived, however, to be at leaft 65. In one letter he fays, " As to our family you have a particular account in *Dugdale's* Baronage, vol. I. p. 710, " viz. ' *Henry* Lord *Grey of Codnover* gave to *Nicholas*, his fecond fon, the Manor of *Barton* in *Yorkfhire*, about 2 *Edward* II.' The pofterity of *Nicholas* enjoyed it till the reign of Queen *Elizabeth*, " and my great grandfather was a fon of that family, and I believe was father to him who fold the " eftate. Our arms are the original arms of that; for when I firft went to *London*, I applied to one " of the Heralds of my acquaintance to get me a feal cut, and he told me it was the arms of the " *Codnover* family; and that family, as appears by *Dugdale*, is the original of all the *Greys*." The following little circumftance, in another of his letters, dated *July* 30, 1731, may be worth preferving: " I had a letter lately from aunt *Milton*, who is very well, and lives at *Namptwich*. There " were THREE widow *Miltons* there, viz. the POET's widow, my aunt, and another. The Poet's " widow died laft fummer."—In another letter he fays, " My Grandfather *Cawdrey*, after he loft " his fellowfhip, went to live with one Dr. *Mafon*, who was mafter of requefts to King *Charles* the " Firft; but I cannot find who this Doctor was."

* " Sermons and Difcourfes on Practical Subjects, by *Robert Mofs*, D. D. late Dean of *Ely*, and " Preacher to the Hon. Society of *Gray's-Inn*. Publifhed from the originals at the Requeft of the " faid Society; with a Preface, giving fome account of the author, by a Learned Hand. 1732." Of thefe a fecond edition corrected appeared in 1736.—Vol. V. was publifhed in 1733; Vol. VI. and VII. in 1736; Vol. VIII. in 1738; and a new edition of the four laft volumes in 1746.

† I am aware that this " learned hand" has been always fuppofed to be Dr. *Snape*, (fee above, p. 78.) and it is afcribed to him by the Rev. Mr. *Mafters* in his "Hiftory of *Corpus Chrifti College*," *Cambridge*, p. 349. I now transfer the credit of it to Dr. *Grey* on the authority of the following letter from his brother: " I received the favour of your kind letter, and alfo of the Dean's valuable Sermons, for " which I return a great many thanks. When I read them, I remember the extraordinary pleafure " I had in hearing moft of them delivered from the pulpit by that admirable orator; and muft beg " an account of the day and place each of them was preached, having feveral memorandums or notes " by me, and the day when I heard them at *Gray's Inn*. YOUR PREFACE I think a very good one, " and think you fhould have put your name to it." Mr. G. *Grey* to Dr. *Grey*, May 14, [1732.]— Dr. *Snape* was poffibly the editor of the Sermons, but the Preface was by Dr. *Grey*.

" The

Folkes's "Table of Gold and Silver Coins" to the Cathedral Library

" The Spirit of Infidelity detected, in anfwer to *Barbeyrac*, with a Defence of Dr. *Water-*
" *land*. London, 1735," 8vo. 10. " *Englifh* Prefbyterian Eloquence, *London*, 1736," 8vo.
11. " Examination of *Chandler's* Hiftory of Perfecution, *London*, 1736," 8vo. 12.
" The true Picture of Quakerifm, &c. *London*, 1736," 8vo. 13. " Caveat againft the
" Diffenters, *London*, 1736," 8vo. 14. " An impartial Examination * of the fecond †
" volume of Mr. *Daniel Neal's* Hiftory ‡ of the Puritans, 1736." That on the third
" volume was printed in 1737. That on the fourth in 1739. 15. " An Examination
" of the fourteenth chapter of Sir *Ifaac Newton's* Obfervations upon the Prophecies of
" *Daniel*; in which that Author's Notion of the Rife and Caufes of Saint-Worfhip in
" the Chriftian Churches is carefully confidered and difproved, 1736," 8vo. 16.
" Schifmatics delineated from authentic Vouchers, in reply to *Neal*, with *Dowfing's*
" Journal, &c. 1739," 8vo. 17. " A Review of Mr. *Daniel Neal's* Hiftory of the Pu-
" ritans, with a Poftfcript." The Poftfcript is a Defence of the Bifhop of *Worcefter's*
" Vindication of the Church of *England*, &c." This is an 8vo. pamphlet of 82 pages,
" *Cambridge*, 1744." 18. An edition of *Hudibras*, 1744, 2 vols. 8vo. 19. " Ad-
" drefs to Lay Methodifts, 1745," 8vo; 20. " Popery in its proper colours, with a Lift
" of Saints invocated in *England* before the Reformation, 17..," 8vo; 21. " Re-
" marks upon a late edition of *Shakefpeare*, with a long ftring of emendations borrowed
" by the celebrated editor from the *Oxford* edition without acknowledgment. To
" which is prefixed, a Defence of the late Sir *Thomas Hanmer*, Bart. addreffed to the
" Rev. Mr. *Warburton*, preacher of *Lincoln's-Inn*," 8vo. No date. (about 1745) 22.
" A Word or two of Advice to *William Warburton*, a Dealer in many Words. By a
" Friend. With an Appendix, containing a tafte of *William's* fpirit of railing,
" 1746," 8vo. 23. " A free and familiar Letter to that great Refiner of *Pope* and
" *Shakefpeare*, the Rev. Mr. *William Warburton*, Preacher at *Lincoln's Inn*. With
" Remarks upon the Epiftle of Friend *W. E.* In which his unhandfome Treatment
" of this celebrated Writer is expofed in the manner it deferves. By a Country Curate.
" 1750." 8vo. 24. " A Supplement to *Hudibras*, 1752," 8vo. 25. " Critical, Hif-
" torical, and Explanatory Notes § on *Shakefpeare*, with Emendations of the Text and
" Metre, 1755," 2 vols. 8vo. 26. " Chronological Account of Earthquakes." 1757, 8vo.
In 1756 he affifted Mr. *Whalley* in his edition of *Ben Jonfon*. In the preface to that
work is the following acknowledgment : " I am likewife obliged to the learned Dr. *Za-*
" *chary Grey*, who communicated to me fome claffical imitations he had obferved in

* For this work Dr. *Grey* received the thanks of many Divines of the firft eminence, particularly
of Dr. *Gibfon* then Bifhop of *London*, and Dr. *Sherlock* Bifhop of *Salisbury*. The laft-mentioned
Prelate fays, " It is happy that Mr. *Neal's* account appeared, when there was one fo well verfed in
" the hiftory, and fo able to correct his miftakes and his prejudices. The fervice you have done,
" muft be confidered as a very important one by all the friends to the conftitution of the church of
" *England*." MS. Letter to Dr. *Grey*, April 5, 1739.
† The firft part of *Neal* had been examined by Bifhop *Maddox*.
‡ In the library of the cathedral church at *Durham* is a copy of *Neal's* " Hiftory," with the Mf. remarks of Bp *Warburton* in the margin. When Dr. *Warburton* came to *Durham* as Prebendary, he.
found *Neal* in the Library, but not one anfwer. This difgufted him ; and provoked him to make
the lively remarks already mentioned. A tranfcript of them is in the hands of Mr. *Prince* of *Oxford*.
§ On this work Dr. *Johnfon* has obferved, that " *Grey's* diligent perufal of the old *Englifh*
" Writers has enabled him to make fome ufeful obfervations. What he undertook, he has well
" enough performed ; but as he neither attempts judicial nor emendatory criticifm, he employs ra-
" ther his memory than his fagacity. It were to be wifhed that all would endeavour to imitate his
" modefty, who have not been able to furpafs his knowledge." *Preface to Shakfpeare*.

" *Jonfon* ;

Library at *Chicheſter* *, with the following inſcription :

HAS. NVMMORVM. ANGLICORVM. TABVLAS.

VETERIS. AMICITIAE. MONVMENTVM.

CVM. VIRO. REVERENDO. GVILIELMO. CLARKE.

CANONICO. CICESTRENSI.

AVRO. ARGENTO. AERE.

PVRIORIS. PRETIOSIORIS. STABILIORIS.

IN. BIBLIOTHECA.

EIVSDEM. ECCLESIAE. CATHEDRALIS.

REPONI. VOLVIT.

GVILIELMVS. BOWYER. TYPOGRAPHVS.

In

" *Jonſon;* and who hath pointed out ſome alluſions to the times with that exact know-
" ledge which he hath ſhewn in clearing up the various references of the like kind
" which abound in *Hudibras.*" Dr. *Grey* correſponded regularly with Mr. *Peck*; and
furniſhed him with ſeveral articles for the ſecond volume of his " Deſiderata Curioſa," and
alſo that annexed to his Life of *Cromwell.* I have ſeveral of Mr. *Peck's* † Letters to
him, from 1732 till his death.—Some materials towards a Life of Mr. *Thomas Baker,*
the celebrated *Cambridge* Antiquary, were prepared by Dr. *Grey*; and the MS. has ſince
been digeſted and improved by a gentleman who had an intention of printing it. Some
particulars of Mr. *Baker* will appear in the Appendix to theſe Anecdotes, from the papers of Dr. *Grey,* after whoſe death I bought them in 1778 out of a bookſeller's catalogue at *Northampton,* together with the following MSS. 1. " A Life of Dean *Moſs,*"
which may poſſibly be printed. 2. " Memoirs of *Robert Harley,* Earl of *Oxford.*"
3. " Notes on *Hudibras,*" many of them unpubliſhed; and 4. A large collection of
original Letters from ſeveral eminent perſons to Dean *Moſs* and Dr. *Grey.*—Some few
MS. volumes, which were in Dr. *Grey's* collection, relating to miſcellaneous articles, are
in the poſſeſſion of his ſon-in-law Mr. *W. Cole* of *Ely.*

* He had before made ſome occaſional preſents to their library; one of which has
been mentioned in p. 244. Another is thus acknowledged by Mr. *Clarke* (who appears
to

† A few extracts will, perhaps, not be diſagreeable to the reader: " I ought ſooner to have
" thanked you for civilities and the promiſe of your correſpondence, which you made me at *Cam-*
" *bridge.* I am ſettling materials for a third volume of *Deſiderata Curioſa;* becauſe, when I print
" the ſecond, I muſt give the contents of the third at the end of it, according to the method laid down
" in my firſt. I remember you ſaid you had a copy of the Exerciſe performed at the entertainment
" in 1564 ‡, and Dr. *Boyce's* Life, both from Mr. *Baker's* papers: and you was ſo kind as to ſay,
" with Mr. *Baker's* leave, I ſhould be welcome to them. I beg therefore you will preſent my moſt
" humble ſervice and beſt reſpects to my ſaid honoured friend and benefactor, and aſk his leave to
" ſend them; which if you can obtain, be pleaſed to direct for me to be left at Dr. *Stukeley's* in
" *Stamford.*" Mr. *Peck* to Dr. *Grey, Nov.* 4, 1732.—" This epiſtle waits upon you with the moſt
" grateful acknowledgements for the great pains you have been at in tranſcribing the papers I re-
" queſted of Dr. *Williams.* I beſeech you to tell the Doctor I am greatly obliged to him for per-
" mitting thoſe tranſcripts to be made, as alſo for his many other civilities. There is a little thing
" in *Benet College* Library, which I ſhould be very thankful for a copy of. In Dr. *Stanley's* copy
" it is thus ſet down: M. XIV. 98. Teſtimonium quod *Henrici* IV. Corpus fuit in *Thameſin*.

‡ See " the Triumphs of the Muſes; or the grand reception and entertainment of Queen *Elizabeth* at *Cam-*
bridge, 1564," (tranſcribed principally by Dr. *Grey*) in *Peck's* " Deſiderata," vol. II. Nº XV. and alſo in the
Gent. Mag. 1772, pp. 450. 625 and 1773. p. 21.

" projectum,

In confequence of overtures from a few refpectable friends at *Cambridge*, Mr. *Bowyer* had fome inclination, towards the latter

to have had the augmenting of it very much at heart) : " I thank you for remembering " the fpital. Every addition is fomething to our little library. We take in all, like " a real hofpital, the poor, the maimed, and the blind. But I cannot think of con- " cealing your name under fuch a cover. Who can reach 8 or 9 feet high, to fhew the " favour he has received? Let me have a *folio* of fome fort or other, that I may put " my hand upon it as I walk by, and fay, ' Here's Mr. *Bowyer!*' What would you " have from public libraries? If people do not read, that is no more the fault of the " library, than their not praying in publick is of the church. But is there no pleafure " in furveying fuch ftructures, though we do not ufe them?" *Mr. Clarke to Mr. Bow- yer, March* 14, 1759.—On the receipt of Mr. *Folkes's* book, Mr. *Clarke* fays, " How " much am I obliged to you for a moft elegant and agreeable prefent to our church " library, which I received on *Tuefday* morning! It gave me the more pleafure, as it " was opening the new year fo aufpiciously, with a book that will be as much looked " into as any in the library; and upon a fubject that does not feem to admit of many " more improvements. I am likewife commiffioned by the Dean and the reft of our " body, to make their very grateful acknowledgements for the favour you have done " them. You may be fure that I had not the leaft fcruple about *terms* or *ceremonies* in " ordering the loofe leaf to be prefixed. It was making me a compliment that I ought

" projectum, & non tumulatum *Cantuariæ* *. Perhaps Mr. *Baker* can give you fome account of it. " I fhall always remember you when I meet with any old deeds or hands worth your acceptance." *Ibid. Dec.* 3, 1734.—" When I was at *Cambridge*, you fhewed me an humourous defcription of a " ftorm, by a Clergyman then on fhipboard. I wifh you would beftow a copy of that paffage on " me; adding the name of the fhip, whither bound, and the dates. The MS. I think was your " own." *Ibid. Dec.* 9, 1734.—Several other acknowledgements occur in fubfequent letters; and in the Preface to the fecond volume Mr. *Peck* fays, " Neither may I forget thanks to the reve- " rend *Zachary Grey*, LL.D. rector of *Houghton Conqueft*, who kindly lent me his hand to copy fe- " veral things, which I had not time to tranfcribe when I was laft fummer at *Cambridge*." The correfpondence goes on after the publication of the *Defiderata*. " I thank you for your kind pre- " fent of your two laft pieces, which I received from Mr. *Bettenham*. I make no queftion but you " will have encouragement enough to print your Anfwer to *Neal's* third volume fpeedily. I want " much to know what your *other Squibs* are (as you call them) which you have in the prefs. I " pray you to give my humble fervice and thanks to Mr. *Bernard*, and wifh him to fend the account " of *S. Peter's* Gild, which fhall be very fafely returned." *Mr. Peck to Dr. Grey, May ult.* 1736.—" I " heartily condole with you upon the lofs of our mutual friend, the late very reverend and learned " Mr. *Thomas Baker*. His death (after that of Mr. *Cowper*) hath been a great concern to me." *Ibid. fans Date.* " Mr. *Benfon* (I dedicate to) [the Auditor] is the fame gentleman you mention, " and a gentleman, I affure you, of exceeding good fenfe and learning and candour. For my part, " I do not fee how *Weftminfter* Abbey is profaned by a Cenotaph in honour of *Milton*, confidered only " as a poet. His politics I have nothing to fay to. You or I may write of *Milton* and *Cromwell*, " and ftill think as we pleafe." *Ibid. Dec.* 15, 1739. " I had the favour of yours, and the paper " about *Richard Cromwell* and *Durham*, came in time, and is very *a-propos*, and I heartily thank " you for it. I am juft going to the Antiquarian Society." *Ibid. London, Jan.* 10, 1739.—" I am " favoured with yours, and as foon as I can find the book you mention, will fend it directed for " you at *Cambridge*, affuring you that it is very much at your fervice. My father's books lie at " prefent in great diforder, and it will take fome time to look them over; but as you are now in " great want of the book, upon receipt of a line from you, I will make immediate fearch for it." *Mr. F. Peck (the fon) to Dr. Grey, July* 17, 1745.

* This is printed in Defid. Cur. vol. II. 6, 7. n. 2.

" to

latter end of 1765, to have undertaken the management of the Univerſity Preſs, by purchaſing a leaſe of their excluſive privileges; and actually went thither for that purpoſe*.
The

" to be pleaſed with, and therefore from a principle of ſelf-love willing to perpetuate;
" though at preſent it puts me under ſome diſadvantages: I cannot ſhew the book with
" ſo much freedom as I ſhould otherwiſe do. You have certainly diſpoſed of it in theſe
" two volumes to the moſt advantage you could. The coins and the explanations are
" much the better for being ſeparate, and may be turned to with more eaſe. The word
" *ſhilling* was uſed very ſoon after the Conqueſt for the twentieth part of a pound ſter-
" ling; the Engliſh, fond of their own language, applied it to the Norman *ſolidus* or *ſolt*,
" and *called their own ſhilling the groat*, which was, agreeably to the *Roman* cuſtom,
" the *tremiſſis* of the ſhilling." *Ibid. Jan.* 3, 1765.—In a ſubſequent letter he ſays,
" Your volatile ſpirits often put me in mind of *Hudibras's* ſword, which worked its
" way through the ſcabbard—it was ſo manful. Your zeal for your friend *Markland*
" is not at all in the ſtrain of the *Supplices*—You treat univerſities and heads of houſes
" with an air of a viſitor, as if they had no taſte, no regard for learning, becauſe they
" don't do the new edition of the *Supplices* the honour of a funeral in their libraries.
" To prevent your indignation from turning more immediately to this quarter, I deſire
" to do the office of an undertaker, and beg you would ſend down a copy of the *Supplices*,
" handſomely bound, to be decently interred in our library. He ſhall have all the ho-
" nours of the place, the ſame that ſages, ſaints, and criticks, have had before—kept
" ſacred from any interruption by the unburied dead, who never moleſt the manes of
" theſe good authors, that take ſanctuary among us." And in another letter, *Nov.* 20,
1767, Mr. *Clarke* ſays, " We have juſt put a ticket into the lottery for our library;
" for we find that nothing but the wheel of Fortune will give it a tolerable appearance."

* To the Compiler of theſe Anecdotes, whom he afterwards ſent to *Cambridge* as a Ne-
gotiator with the Vice-Chancellor, he thus writes in *September* 1765: " According to Dr.
" *Powell's* diſcourſe with me, I underſtood the Univerſity would not proceed upon
" making the moſt *pecuniary* bargain, but on making ſuch an one as ſhould be conſiſtent
" with ſafety and their own credit. I think he ſaid that 400*l. per annum* † would ſatisfy,
" if they had reaſonable ſecurity. But be that as it may, and as a computation of the
" returns ſhall anſwer. I ſuppoſe an abſolute bargain will hardly be ſtruck till I ſee
" you; though I think I could leave myſelf to your direction. A bookſeller joining
" with me might, as you obſerve, extend the trade very much. Even ſo, it is much
" better to be propoſed to him, when we have made a bargain, than before. But I al-
" moſt dread the thought, from the example of **** and *******. The former was ad-
" viſed to take ******* partner in the law-patent. The conſequence was, they never
" ſettled accounts during the whole partnerſhip; and at laſt they were ſo intricate,
" that upon arbitration each was to be content with what he had received. Mr. *Arch-
" deacon*, as you obſerve, muſt be a leading perſon, and there is ſome delicacy neceſſary
" to be ſhewn to him. But you muſt be my right hand, or indeed both hands; for I
" would hope from this plan, if it ſhould take, to have leſs trouble than I have now
" with authors and bookſellers. Beſides, my pride will be to ſee you come forward,

† For ſeven years preceding 1765, the Univerſity had cleared 1500*l.* annually by the profits of
their preſs.

" and

The treaty, however, was fruitlefs; and he did not much regret the difappointment. Mr. *Clarke, Sept.* 4, 1765, wrote thus upon this fubject: "What to fay about the "Univerfity affair, I do not well know—it is certain that "you have more bufinefs already than does you good; and "fuch a fortune as will anfwer all the rational purpofes of "life, that you need not wifh for more. If you were "younger, and ambitious of raifing a greater fortune, I "could tell what to fay. But there are certainly two ob-"jects in view in this propofal, which, if thefe objections "did not lie in the way, would to me be great induce-"ments. The thoughts of *governing the bookfellers*, either "for gain or glory, would give me a greater pleafure, than "any other object in trade. In that refpect, I think juft "as you do. But *Tanti non eft*; the laurel is fcarce worth "the labour. Happinefs and eafe are greater acquifitions "than victory.—Befides, the honour of putting the Uni-"verfity in a way to get fomething befides credit, would "be a means of enrolling you among her Benefactors; "and that not for a temporary, but a perpetual Dona-"tion.—But you had better relinquifh all thefe honours, "unlefs you quit bufinefs and think of doing nothing elfe."

Mr. *Markland,* to whom he communicated what had "paffed, tells him, "The fubject of your journey to *Cam-*"*bridge* I am no judge at all of; but I underftand your

"and in the way to make a figure like the ****** and the ********* ; much. "greater than, good *John*, your fincere friend and well-wifher, W. Bowyer.

"I have heard not a word more of *Cambridge* affairs fince you went. I have worked "hard to-day, and hope to give a good account of myfelf. I have read your conclufion "of the Novel *, which is admirable, but too good for the place. It is like a new piece "of cloth fewed into an old garment."

* The work here alluded to was a trifling production called "The Amours of *Lais*;" which ending abruptly in the original copy, a few pages were added to it by *J. N.*

5 "practical

" practical inference at laſt, which ſays, that you are too
" old to live out a leaſe ; and I think you conclude right,
" it not being worth while to put out to ſea again, not even
" if you were ſure of making a proſperous voyage.   I have
" received another letter from Mr. ———, who tells me that
" he intends to lay out fifty pounds in books, and deſires
" me to recommend to him fifty pounds worth of Theo-
" logy and Claſſics.   I have thought of it, and find my-
" ſelf in the condition of *Simonides*, when he was aſked
" about the Deity, deſiring more time to conſider of it.
" But I believe I ſhall not anſwer it at all ; for it ſeems to me
" as difficult as to make a pair of breeches for a man you
" never ſaw."

In 1765, at the requeſt of the munificent Mr. *Hollis*[*],
he wrote the ſhort *Latin* preface to " *Joannis Walliſii* Gram-
" matica

---

[*] " Some time in the ſpring of the year 1765 Mr. *Hollis* ſeems to have propoſed to
" Mr. *Millar* the reprinting Dr. *Wallis's Latin* Grammar of the *Engliſh* tongue ;
" concerning which Mr. *Millar* was deſireus of having the opinion of the Rev. Dr.
" ***** [*Lowth*], who, at the bookſeller's requeſt, was conſulted by Mr. *Bowyer* on
" the ſubject.   The Doctor returned for anſwer, that in his opinion the reprinting of
" this Grammar would be for the benefit of natives, as well as of foreigners.   The deſign
" of reprinting Dr. *Wallis's Latin* Grammar of the *Engliſh* tongue undoubtedly origi-
" nated with Mr. *Hollis* ; without any other view than to promote the knowledge of
" the *Engliſh* language among foreigners, who could not otherwiſe be made acquainted
" with the value and excellence of many of our *Engliſh* writers, of whoſe works the
" ſpirit and ſentiments were often erroneouſly, and always imperfectly, repreſented in
" tranſlations.   With this patriotic view, to the honour of his country, he propoſed
" the reprinting of this Grammar to Mr. *Millar,* whoſe buſineſs it was to conſider what
" might be expected from the ſale of it ; and relying upon the judgment of the reverend
" Divine abovementioned, he requeſted Mr. *Bowyer,* who had a literary connection with
" the Doctor, to procure it for his farther information.   The anſwer to Mr. *Bowyer's*
" application encouraged Mr. *Millar* to undertake the new edition ; and the ſame anſwer
" having ſuggeſted to Mr. *Hollis* the advantage it would be to the book, to have the
" approbation cf ſo learned and eminent a man more diſtinctly and publicly expreſſed, he
" endeavoured, by the interceſſion of Mr. *Bowyer,* to prevail with the Doctor to honour
" the republication of *Wallis's* Grammar with a preface of his own writing.   Why this
" favour was refuſed, no particular reaſon appears.   The Doctor was certainly at his
" liberty, and no man had a right to know his motives for declining a little labour in his
" own walk, from which he might have derived ſome little honour, if not to his emi-

" nent

" matica* Linguæ *Anglicanæ*;" and a larger *English* Preface†, intended for that work. He sent some copies of this book to Mr. *Clarke* when abroad, to be given to the *Spanish* Literati‡. In the same year he had many consultations with Mr. *Hollis*, on a projected edition of *Marvell's* Works; and from thence to 1767 very frequently turned his thoughts on that subject, consulted Dr. *Birch* concerning various parts of *Marvell's* writings, and communicated to Mr. *Hollis* the result of his various enquiries §.

The

" nent talents, yet certainly to his benevolence in promoting a work where party and
" controversy were out of the question. But to say the truth, Mr. *Hollis* was not, in
" those days, fit company for orthodox Divines. It was well known that he was con-
" cerned in this new edition of *Wallis's* Grammar; and no less that he was at that
" time procuring a new edition of *Locke's* Letters concerning Toleration, on which sub-
" ject it appeared afterwards that the ruling theology was not in perfect accord with
" the doctrine of those letters. But, leaving speculation, let us return to fact. Mr.
" *Bowyer* was prevailed with to write the short elegant preface which now stands be-
" fore this last edition of Dr. *Wallis's* Grammar, wherein his learned and reverend
" friend had this advantage, that a sort of justice was done to his merit, which he could
" not decently have done for himself, had he obliged Mr. *Hollis* with a preface of his
" own.—*Jan.* 7, 1765, *Wallis's* Grammar being printed off, and ready for publication,
" Mr. *Hollis* made Mr. *Bowyer* a present [of twenty pounds] for writing the preface."
See " Memoirs of Mr. *Hollis*," pp. 232, 234, 264.

* Mr. *Markland*, in answer to a letter from Mr. *Bowyer* about this Grammar,
says, " I wonder you should think of printing a *Latin* book on that subject, which at
" present would not be read (I had almost said *could* not) even in *English*; but I sup-
" pose it is not your own choice. I would as soon write Lectures on *Taste* as any thing
" on the *Digamma*."

† Which will appear among his Miscellaneous Tracts.

‡ An hundred copies were purchased by Mr. *Hollis* for this purpose; which were sent
to *Spain*, *Portugal*, *Italy*, &c.

§ On this subject I shall transcribe from the Biographer of Mr. *Hollis*: " The 23d of
" *April* [1767] Mr. *Hollis* and Mr. *Baron* met by appointment, and had much discourse
" concerning the part Mr. *Baron* should take in a new edition of *Andrew Marvell's*
" works. If there is no mistake in the date, Mr. *Hollis* had thought of this republica-
" tion near two years before, as appears by the following memorandum found among his
" papers: ' *September* 3, 1765. Busied in the morning looking over *Andrew Marvell's*
" works, and papers relating thereto, preparatory to a conversation with Mr. *Bowyer*,
" concerning the new edition of them.—4. With Mr. *Bowyer*, with whom I had a full
" conversation relating to the new edition of *Andrew Marvell's* works, to the printing
" of which he seemed reluctant, from the difficulties that will attend it; animated him
" all I could to that end; and we are to talk farther concerning it.'—It does not how-
" ever appear, from any thing we have seen, that they had farther talk on the subject,
" till

The principal books of 1765 were Dr. *Maclaine's** tranſ-

"till the ſpring of 1767, when Mr. *Hollis* propoſed to engage Mr. *Baron* as an aſſiſtant.
" The reſult was, that the new edition was to be in one volume quarto, to be printed
" by *Millar* and *Cadell*; Mr. *Baron* to correct the preſs for the proſe, and Mr. *Bowyer*
" for the poetical and *Latin* parts. Mr. *Hollis* and Mr. *Baron* met on the 29th of
" *April*, and had a long converſation on the ſubject; when it appeared in the end, that
" *Baron*, not thinking himſelf equal to the taſk, for want of anecdotes, did not ſeem
" inclined to undertake it. Hence it appears, that Mr. *Hollis* expected ſomething more
" from *Baron* than juſt to correct the preſs. *Baron* was a great collector of the works,
" and hiſtorical accounts, of the defenders of liberty, civil and religious. *Marvell*, in
" that department, was a hero; but it is probable Mr. *Baron* had not ſucceeded in ſearch-
" ing for materials relating to the hiſtory of this conſummate patriot, or ſuch as were
" neceſſary to illuſtrate ſome paſſages in his works, which wanted explanation; and
" here, in all probability, the project dropped. With reſpect to Mr. *Bowyer*, a looſe
" paper has been communicated to us, importing, that ' he refuſed to be concerned in
" the republication of *Marvell's* works, upon any account.' What were Mr. *Bowyer's*
" reaſons † for this refuſal does not appear. We may venture to ſay, that party-con-
" ſiderations had no ſhare in his reluctance; for this worthy and learned printer made
" no ſcruple to print other works ‡ publiſhed about this time, which were, in their con-
" tents, no leſs obnoxious to the ruling powers than the revival of *Marvell's* principles
" and ſtrictures would have been. The want of two ſuch able co-operators as *Baron* and
" *Bowyer* put an end to Mr. *Hollis's* project of republiſhing *Marvell's* works. They
" have been, however, ſince republiſhed in 1776, in three volumes quarto, by Captain
" *Edward Thompſon*, who acknowledges his obligations to Mr. *Hollis's* collections,"
(ſee *Memoirs of Mr. Hollis*, pp. 361, 362.) and, in order to magnify *Marvell*, has defamed
his own contemporaries as plagiaries. Perhaps a more ridiculous and ill-founded charge
was never made than that which Captain *Thompſon* has ventured to exhibit againſt *Addiſon*, *Watts*, and *David Mallet*, in the Preface to this Work. That the ſame MS. ſhould
fall into the hands of theſe three gentlemen, and that each of them ſhould be tempted to
ſteal different parts of it, would be too groſs an improbability to merit any belief, even if
the characters of the accuſed did not exempt them from ſuch a ſuſpicion. Of the two
former ſeveral defences have been already produced to the publick; but the latter has yet
been without an advocate. It may be therefore candid to obſerve, that the imputation
on his reputation may be clearly wiped away to the ſatisfaction of every impartial perſon.
The ballad which Mr. *Mallet* is charged with purloining, was originally printed about
the year 1724, and was inſerted in THE PLAIN DEALER, *July* 24, 1724. Whoever will
compare that copy with the preſent which is given to *Marvell*, will find variations in
almoſt every Stanza, which would ſurely not have been made, as they are in general for
the worſe, had the Ballad originally ſtood as it is now read in *Mallet's* Works. In the
ſame paper, *Auguſt* 28, 1724, is a Letter from Mr. *Mallet*, wherein he gives the Hiſtory
of the Lady who was the ſubject of the Ballad; whence it appears that the circumſtances
of the tranſaction were founded on facts. The alterations were evidently made by him
afterwards; and there is little room to doubt but that the MS. was written after the publication of the improved copy.

* Dr. *Maclaine* is now miniſter of the *Engliſh* church at *The Hague*; which office he
has long filled with the higheſt reputation.

† It was from an apprehenſion they would not ſell ſufficiently to defray the expence, and not
from any diſlike to the works of *Marvell*, that Mr. *Bowyer* declined the undertaking: that he was
in no reſpect prejudiced againſt the writer, appears from his having contributed his advice and perſonal aſſiſtance in collecting the ſcarcer tracts. *J. N.*

‡ *e. g.* " The Confeſſional," Dr. *Harris's* " Hiſtory of *Charles* II." &c. &c.

lation

lation of " *Mosheim's* Ecclesiastical History," 2 vols. 4to;
the *Latin* Works of Lord *Bacon,* being the fourth and
fifth volumes in 4to. of the best * edition of that illustrious
writer; *Du Port* " De Signis Morborum," 4to; A second part of Bishop *Ellys's* † " Tracts on Spiritual and Tem-

---

* It was corrected throughout by the learned and industrious Mr. *Gambold*, and the *Latin* volumes were accurately revised by Mr. *Bowyer.*

† Dr. *Anthony Ellys* was born in the year 1693, and educated at *Clare Hall, Cambridge,* of which Society he became a Fellow. After taking orders, he in 1724 became vicar of *St. Olave Jewry,* and rector of *St. Martin, Ironmonger Lane,* which is united to the former. In 1725 he was presented by Chancellor *Macclesfield,* to whom he is said to have been chaplain, to a prebendal stall at *Gloucester*; and on the 25th of *April* 1728, when King *George* the Second went to *Cambridge,* was favoured with the degree of Doctor of Divinity, being one of those named in the Chancellor's list on that occasion. In 1736 he published " A Plea for the Sacramental Test, as a just Security to the Church " established and very conducive to the welfare of the State," 4to. In 1749 he published a Sermon preached before the House of Commons on the 30th of *January*; and in *October* 1752 was promoted to the See of *St. David's,* and consecrated *Jan.* 28, 1753. This preferment he owed to the recommendation of Archbishop *Herring,* and held it with his prebend and city living *in commendam.* He was also vicar of *Great Marlow, Bucks.* About the same time he published anonymously a pamphlet called "Remarks on " an Essay concerning Miracles, published by *David Hume,* esq. amongst his Philosophical " Essays," 4to, no date. In 1754 he published a Sermon preached before the House of Lords, *Jan.* 30; and in 1759 another preached before the Society for the Propagation of the Gospel in foreign parts. He died at *Gloucester, Jan.* 16, 1761, and was buried in the South aile of the Cathedral there, where a neat pyramidal monument was erected to his memory with the following epitaph on a tablet of white marble supported by a cherub :

" Near this place
Lieth the body of
Anthony Ellys, D.D.
Minister of the united parishes of
St. Olave Old Jewry, and *St. Martin's Ironmonger Lane,* in the City of *London,* 38 years;
Prebendary in this church 37 years;
Consecrated Bishop of *St. David's* 28 *Feb.* 1753;
Who departed this life 17 *Jan.* 1761,
Aged 68 years.
A person truly excellent,

Learned, just, benevolent, pious,
To whose rare virtues and abilities
Adulation cannot add,
Envy cannot deservedly take from.
He married *Anne* the eldest daughter,
Of Sir *Stephen Anderson,* of *Eyworth,*
In the county of *Bedford,* bart.
Whom he left, with only one daughter,
To lament the common loss
Of one of the best of
Mankind."

He left behind him ready for the press the above-mentioned " Tracts on the Liberty Spiri- " tual and Temporal of Protestants in *England,* addressed to *J. N.* esq. at *Aix la Chapelle*;" the first part whereof was printed in 1763, and the second in 1765. The editors of this posthumous work say, " He was not only eminent for his fine parts, extensive know- " ledge, and sound judgement, jewels truly valuable in themselves; but they were set in " him to the highest advantage, by a heart so overflowing with benevolence and candour, " as never even to conceive terms of acrimony or reproach towards the opinions or per- " sons of those who differed from him. This Christian temper of his is discoverable in " all the parts of these tracts that are taken up on controversy, for he always thought a " person, though on the right side of the question, with principles of persecution, to be a " worse man than he that was on the wrong." Some verses on his death, by Dr. *Dodd,* are printed in the Christian's Magazine, 1761, p. 89. and in his Poems.

3

" poral

" poral Liberty," (fee p. 346,) 4to ; " An Harmony of
" the Four Gofpels, fo far as relates to the Hiftory
" of our Saviour's Refurrection, with a Commentary
" and Notes, by Dr. *Parry**," 4to ; " The *Temple Stu-*
" *dent*," a poem, by Mr. *Keate*, 4to ; Mr. *Hurd's* " Dia-
" logues Moral and Political," 3 vols. 8vo ; the fecond edition of " A Letter† to the Right Reverend Author of the
" Divine Legation of *Mofes* demonftrated ; in anfwer to the

---

* *Richard Parry*, D. D. rector of *Wichampton* in *Dorfetfhire*, and preacher at *Market*
Harborough in *Leicefterfhire*, for which latter county he was in the commiffion of the
peace. He was a ftudent of *Chrift Church, Oxford*, and took the degree of M. A. *March*
31, 1747; B. D. *May* 25, 1754; and D. D. *July* 8, 1757. He was a very learned Divine; and an able, active, magiftrate. He died miferably poor, at *Market Harborough*,
April 9, 1780, fcarce leaving fufficient to defray the charges of his funeral ‡. His publications were, 1. " The Chriftian Sabbath as old as the Creation, 1753," 4to ; (he was
then chaplain to Lord *Vere*.) 2. " The Scripture Account of the Lord's Supper. The
" Subftance of three Sermons preached at *Market Harborough* in 1755, 1756," 8vo.
3. " The Fig Tree dried up ; or the Story of that remarkable Tranfaction as it is related
" by *St. Mark* confidered in a new light explained and vindicated. In a Letter to .....
" ...... efq. 1758," 4to. 4. " A Defence of the Lord Bifhop of *London's* [*Sherlock*]
" Interpretation of the famous Text in the Book of *Job*, ' I know that my Redeemer
" liveth,' and againft the Exceptions of the Bifhop of *Gloucefter* [*Warburton*], and the
" Examiner of the Bifhop of *London's* Principles; with occafional Remarks on the Ar-
" gument of the Divine Legation, fo far as this point is concerned with it," 1760, 8vo.
5. " Differtation on *Daniel's* Prophecy of the Seventy Weeks," 1762, 8vo. 6. " Re-
" marks on Dr. *Kennicott's* Letter, &c. 1763," 8vo. 7. " The Cafe between *Gerizim*
" and *Ebal*, &c. 1764," 8vo. 8. " The Harmony," &c. above mentioned, 1765, 4to ;
9. " The Genealogy of *Jefus Chrift*, in *Matthew* and *Luke*, explained ; and the *Jewifh*
" Objections removed, 1771," 8vo. 10. He wrote one of the anfwers to Dr. *Heathcote's*
pamphlet on the *Leicefterfhire* election in 1775. See Brit. Top. vol. I. p. *518.

† Of this Letter, whofe author was the prefent worthy and learned bifhop of *London*, there
was an extremely rapid fale. The firft edition had been printed at *Oxford*. The fecond
(of which there was a large impreffion) appeared in *November* 1765 ; a third in *February*
1766 ; to which immediately fucceeded a fourth, with the addition of " A Letter to the
" Rev. Dr. *Brown*." In the courfe of this controverfy many fquibs were thrown out on
both fides in the news-papers ; and among others were fome by Mr. *Bowyer*. In " The
" St. *James's* Chronicle," *June* 25, 1766, were fome queries which Mr. *Markland* fuppofed to have been his ; but which I believe were by a different writer. Some letters
on the fubject I know he wrote, particularly *one* (if not *two)* in anfwer to *Il Moderato*,
in the above-mentioned news-paper of *April* and *May* 1766.

‡ It appears from an advertifement in the news-papers, *July* 17, 1781, that Dr. *Parry* poffeffed three numbers in the Affurance-office at *Serjeants Inn*, each of which produced 193*l.* to his
nominee or executor. Thefe numbers, however, as a friend obferves to me, prove his poverty, not
the contrary, as they were probably fecurity for money he had borrowed, or debts he owed.

" Appendix

" Appendix to the fifth volume of that work; with an
" Appendix, containing a former Literary Correspondence.
" By a late Professor in the University of *Oxford*," 8vo;
" The Way to Things by Words, and to Words by Things,"
by Mr. *Cleland**, 8vo; " Thoughts on Civil Liberty, Licen-

* This publication was followed, in 1768, by " Specimens of an Et*i*mological † Voca-
" bulary, or Essay, by means of the Anal*i*tic † Method, to retrieve the ancient *Celtic*;"
with " A View of a Literary Plan, for the Retrieval of the ancient *Celtic*; in aid of an
" Explanation of various Points of Antiquity in general, and of the Antiquities of *Great*
" *Britain* and *Ireland* in particular," and Proposals for publishing by subscription ‡, in
two volumes quarto, " The *Celtic* Retrieved, by the Anal*i*tic † Method, or Reduction to
" Radicals ; illustrated by a Glossary of various, and especially *British* Antiquities," and
in 1769 by " Additional Articles to the Specimen," &c. In these curious publications
Mr. *Cleland* has displayed a large fund of ingenuity and erudition, not unworthy the education he received in *Westminster-school*, where he was contemporary with Earl *Mansfield*. Mr. *Cleland* is the author of some Plays, and a great number of fugitive performances. He is much better known, however, as the reputed author of a book too infamous to be here mentioned. His " Memoirs of a Coxcomb" have great merit, though
they also are too licentiously written. His father was a colonel, and the friend and correspondent of *Pope*.

† " The Writer's *Celtic*," an ingenious friend observes, " has swallowed up his *Greek*."
‡ " As to this recourse to a subscription, I have no apology to make for it, but one, which is,
" that it is necessary, as being the only one. Not that I am insensible of there being many and just
" objections to this method, but the candour of a liberal construction will hardly rank among them
" its being liable to an abuse. This is no more than what it has in common with the best of things.
" Whoever considers the vast comprehensiveness of this plan, and the aids of all kinds which it
" must, to have justice done to it, indispensably and implicitly require, will easily allow the under-
" taking to be not only impossible to a small private fortune; but, even where there might be a
" large one, the work itself to imply so much of proposed utility to the public, as not to be without
" some right to solicit the assistance of the public. It was the failure of that assistance, that, pro-
" bably, lost to it one of presumably the most useful and valuable works that any language or any
" nation could have had to boast of, the second part of *The British Archæologia*, of one of our greatest
" and solidest antiquaries, *Edward Lhuyd*, who, or suppressed, or dropped, or, at least, did not effec-
" tually carry it on, from his disgust or discouragement, at his having been forced to publish the first
" part at his own heavy expence: a loss this to the *British* republic of letters hardly reparable !
" Need I mention the celebrated Dr. *Hyde's* boiling his tea-kettle, with almost the whole impression
" left on his hands, of that profoundly learned treatise of his, *De Religione Veterum Persarum*, ad-
" mired by all literary *Europe*, and neglected at home : so low was the taste for literature, in this
" country, already sunk ! For the republication of this work, we have now, however, the obligation
" to the public spirit of Dr. *Sharpe*, that patron and promoter of literature, of which himself is at
" once an ornament, a judge, and a support, with the greater merit for his not deserting it in its pre-
" sent state of disgrace. With so cold, so unpromising a prospect before me, and very justly consci-
" ous of not only an incomparably less title to favourable opinion, but of having much more to
" apologise for, than of any merit to plead, I have only, in extenuation of my presumption to ad-
" dress the public under such disadvantages, one solemn and unaffected truth to offer; and this it
" is, Finding this retrieval of the *Celtic* (that language actually existing no where as a language,
" and every where as the root of all or most of the languages in *Europe*, dead or living, modern or
" ancient, and entering into the composition of almost every word that we now, at this instant, use in
" common conversation) ; finding, I say, the retrieval of this elementary, or mother-tongue, at least
" included in proposals from *more than one* foreigner, I have thought it my duty to form a wish, that
" it might not be my fault, if the *British* public was not, as early as other countries, in possession of
" the benefit of such a retrieval, for the satisfactory elucidation of some of the most interesting *Bri-
" tish* antiquities. But how far I may find the public disposed to second that wish, or to enable me
" to fulfil it, must remain entirely at the discretion of that public." CLELAND.

" tiousness,

." tioufnefs, and Faction," by Dr. *Brown,* 8vo ; and the firft volume of Mr. *Burgh's* " *Crito*, or Effays on various " fubjects," 12mo.

In the beginning of the year 1766, by engaging in a partnerfhip with the Writer of thefe Memoirs, Mr. *Bowyer* was again enabled to withdraw, in fome degree, from that clofe application which had begun to be prejudicial to his health. His new affociate, whilft an apprentice, had been intrufted with a confiderable fhare of the management of the printing-office ; and the connexion was fuch as, I am proud to fay, was highly fatisfactory to Mr. *Bowyer.* To his partner, it was all that a young man could poffibly have hoped for ; it was an introduction to a number of refpectable friends, whofe patronage was equally honourable and advantageous. The good-natured reader will pardon the vanity of this paragraph ; it is meant as a tribute of gratitude to a Benefactor, whofe memory the writer cannot but revere.

In the fucceeding annals of Mr. *Bowyer's* life, the mode hitherto adopted will be obferved. The productions of the prefs will be confidered as his, without encumbering the narrative with the unneceffary diftinction of a partnerfhip.

In the year laft mentioned (1766) he wrote an excellent *Latin* Preface * to " *Joannis Harduini*, Jefuitæ, ad " Cenfuram Scriptorum Veterum Prolegomena. Juxta Au- " tographum." In this Preface is a diftinct account of the

---

* " I was glad to fee your Preface ; it is perhaps all I fhall ever read of the book. " *Swift* fays, that he never knew but two or three good lyars in his life. You have " fhewn how evidently the moft artful of them are detected, by fhifting their fails, and " not abiding by their own decifions. Surely your friend the Bookfeller, whom you are " obliging with a Preface, is, as ufual, a little hard upon authors, and more dictatorial " than ufual, when he won't let you write, to puff off his work *gratis*." *Mr. Clarke, MS.*

nature

nature of the work, as well as of the mode in which it was preferved " in naufragio fortunarum fuarum, quod tota " familia Jefuitica nuper fecit."—" Hoc vero fragmentum," fays Mr. *Bowyer*, " quafi ex undis ereptum, & in manus " *P. Vaillant* bibliopolæ traditum, noluit ille orbi literario " invidere. Paradoxa enim per fe cum novitate fua delec- " tant, tum longe magis *Harduini* artificio exornata, qui " tam belle novit dare obfcuris nitorem, lucidis umbram, " fictis probabilitatem, omnibus denique fpeciem, prout " velit, & gratiam. Iftud, igitur, quicquid eft, fideliter " imprimendum curavit: autographumque ipfum in *Mufeo* " *Britannico* reponendum, tanquam votivam tabulam, pof- " teritati confecravit. Paucula hæc, quæ raptim prælibavi, " erudito colloquio, quo vir reverendus *Cæfar De Miffy** me " honeftavit, accepta debent referri. Si quid imprudentér " dictum fit, meæ tribuendum eft infcitiæ; fi quid quod " non difpliceat, ejus laudi; qui mox, ut fpero, plura fu- " per hac re publica luce dignabitur."

Mr. *De Miffy's* remarks on the celebrated Jefuit's extra-ordinary production accordingly appeared about the fame time, under the title of " De *Joannis Harduini* Jefuitæ " Prolegomenis cum Autographo collatis, Epiftola, quam " ad amiciffimum virum *Wilhelmum Bowyerum*, iifdém " nondum proftantibus, fcripferat *Cæfar Miffiacus* [vulgò " *C. De Miffy*] Reg. Mag. *Brit.* à Sacris *Gallicè* peragendis." Both thefe works were printed in 8vo.

In the fame year Mr. *Bowyer* printed a complete and very elegant edition of the Works of Dr. *Harvey*, in 4to. The liberality with which this publication was conducted by the College of Phyficians is a lafting monument of honour to

+ * Of whom, fee under the year 1774.

themfelves,

themselves, and to the great Author whose invaluable writings were thus collected. The other books of that year were, " Observations on the Statutes," by the Hon. *Daines Barrington*, two editions, 4to; Mr. *Pegge's* " Essay on the " Coins of *Cunobelin*," 4to; Mr. *Keate's* poem " On the " Death of Mrs. *Cibber*," 4to; " *Hogarth** Moralised," by Dr. *John Trusler*, 8vo; " An Account of the Life† of *John* " *Ward;*

* Of this great, this inimitable artist, I had collected some materials with a view to an article in this volume. But my intelligence was so greatly extended beyond the limits of a note, that I have been under the necessity of forming from them a separate publication, intituled, " Biographical Memoirs of *William Hogarth*," &c. to which I take the liberty to refer my readers.

† *John Ward*, son of a dissenting minister of the same name‡, was born in *London* about 1679. His father died *Dec.* 28, 1717, in his 82d year; his mother (*Constancy* §) in *April* 1697. He was for some years a clerk in the Navy-office; and at leisure hours pursued his studies with great diligence, under the guidance of *John Ker*, M.D. ‖ author of "Selectarum de linguâ *Latinâ* observationum libri II." who kept an academy, first at *Highgate*, and afterwards in *St. John's Square, Clerkenwell*. He continued in his employment in the Navy-office till the summer of 1710, when, finding no other means of gratifying his zeal for the acquisition of knowledge, he was induced to undertake the education of a certain number of the children of his friends; chusing rather, as he expressed himself in a letter to a friend, " to converse even with boys upon subjects of literature, than to transact the ordinary affairs of life among men." For this purpose he opened a school in *Tenter Alley* in *Moorfields*, which he kept for many years. In 1712, he became one of the earliest members of a society, formed by a set of gentlemen, divines, and lawyers, in *London*, who agreed to meet together once a week, or as often as their affairs would permit, to prepare and read discourses, each in his turn, upon the civil law, as also upon the law of nature and nations, for their mutual entertainment and improvement. This society, with some occasional interruptions, was kept up till *Michael-*

‡ He was interred in a church in *Worcester*; the following epitaph being written upon him by his son: " H. S. E. *Joannes Ward, Tysoe* in agro *Warwicensi* natus, civis vero *Londinensis*; vir antiquis " moribus magnaque pietate præditus; qui, si quis alius, variam et incertam humanæ vitæ condi- " tionem expertus, sibi similis et constans semper permansit; multa enim integritatis, multa religio- " nis causâ perpessus, omnia fortissimo et excelso animo sustinuit, utpote qui felicitatem non tam in " externa rerum specie, quam in mente recti sibi conscia collocavit. In matrimonio habuit *Constan-* " *tiam Rayner, Londinatem*, feminam virtute ac sanctimonia præstantem, studioque in omnes bonos, " dum vixit, singulari, quæ liberos XIV ei peperit, quorum duo tantum superstites *Joannes* et *Abi-* " *gail*. Post vitam autem annis et laboribus exhaustam, terrenas res diu pertæsus, cœlumque sus- " pirans, in *Christo* placide obdormivit, v. kal. *Jan.* A. D. MDCCXVII. ætatis suæ LXXXII."

§ " *Caleb's* spirit paralleled, in a sermon preach'd at the funeral of the late Mrs. *Constancy Ward*, " of *East Smithfield, London*, at the Meeting-house in *Devonshire Square, April* 7, 1697. By *Walter* " *Crosse*, M. A. Lond. 1697." 4to.

‖ He took that degree at *Leyden, March* 5, 1696-7, as appears from his Thesis printed there in 4to, and intituled " Disputatio physico-medica inauguralis de secretionis animalis efficiente causâ et " ordine." In the title-page, Dr. *Ker* styles himself *Scoto-Hibernus*.

mas

" *Ward*, LL. D. Profeſſor of Rhetoric in *Greſham College*;
" F.R.S. and F.S.A.   By *Thomas Birch*, D.D. Sec. R. S.
                                                    " and

mas term, 1742. Several of the members have been perſons of diſtinguiſhed character both in church and ſtate; and Mr. *Ward* continued highly eſteemed among them, while the ſociety ſubſiſted. In the ſame year, 1712, he publiſhed a ſmall piece in *Latin*, of 39 pages in 8vo. printed at *London*, with the title of " De ordine, ſive " de venuſta et eleganti tum vocabulorum, tum membrorum ſententiae collocatione. " His quædam adjiciuntur de vitiis ordinis: item de variis modis, quibus, pro ver- " borum numero, ordo ſententiae tranſponi poteſt." Mr. *Ainſworth* having drawn up the elaborate account of Mr. *Kemp's* antiquities, which has been mentioned in p. 109, was furniſhed by his friend and neighbour Mr. *Ward*, not only with the de- ſcriptions and explanations of the ſtatues and lares in the collection, but likewiſe with the diſcourſe " de vaſis et lucernis, de amuletis, de annulis et fibulis," and par- ticularly the learned " Commentarius de aſſe et partibus ejus," which had been printed in 1719, 8vo. Mr. *Ward* became ſo eminent for his knowledge of polite literature, as well as antiquity, that on the 1ſt of *September*, 1720, he was choſen Profeſſor of Rhetoric in *Greſham College*, and on the 28th of *October* following made his inaugural oration there, " de uſu et dignitate artis dicendi." The ſame year Dr. *Mead* having publiſhed at *London*, in 8vo. his diſcourſe of the plague, Mr. *Ward* gave the public, in 1723, a *Latin* tranſlation of the eighth edition, the doctor not approving the tranſlation of the firſt edition by Mr. *Maittaire*, which was never printed. *November* 30, 1723, Mr. *Ward* was elected F. R. S. and was often choſen afterwards into the council of that reſpectable body, and at laſt, in 1752, appointed one of their Vice Preſidents, in which office he was continued till his death. In 1724, he ſubjoined to an edition of *Gerard John Voſſius's* " Elementa Rhetorica," printed at *London*, an excellent piece " de ra- " tione interpungendi," containing a ſyſtem of clear and eaſy rules with regard to point- ing, ſuperior to whatever had before been publiſhed on that ſubject. Dr. *Conyers Mid- dleton* having, in 1726, publiſhed at *Cambridge*, in 4to. a *Latin* diſſertation " de medi- " corum apud veteres *Romanos* degentium conditione;" Mr. *Ward*, in *February* 1726-7, publiſhed an anſwer * to it in 8vo. under the title of " Ad viri Reverendi *Con. Middle- " toni*, S. T. P. de medicorum apud veteres Romanos degentium conditione diſſertatio- " nem, qua ſervilem atque ignobilem eam fuiſſe contendit, reſponſio." Dr. *Middleton* publiſhed a defence of his diſſertation in 1727, to which. Mr. *Ward* replied in a piece, printed at *London* in 1728, in 8vo. intituled, " Diſſertationis V.R. *Con. Middletoni*, " S. T. P. de medicorum *Romae* degentium conditione ignobili et ſervili defenſio exami- " nata: ubi omnia, quæ contra reſponſionis auctorem diſſeruit, infirmata ſunt et refu- " tata †." In 1728 Mr. *Ward* aſſiſted in preparing *Thuanus* for the preſs; and tranſlated

* See what is ſaid on this head in p. 37, which this article of Dr. *Ward* will illuſtrate.
† " Dr. *Middleton* finiſhed an anſwer to this laſt piece of Dr. *Ward's*; but, meeting *Mead* at Lord " *Oxford's*, he was prevailed on to deliver up the MſF. to Lord *Oxford*. After all the parties were " dead, Dr. *Heberden* preſumed there could be no harm in publiſhing a few copies of a mere piece of " literature in 1761, to be given away only." *T. F.*—The Author of " Breves Notæ" on *Middleton's* Diſſertation, 1726, was Dr. *P. Wigan*, a *Scotchman*. Dr. *Middleton* anſwered it as his. See p. 23, of his laſt publication, where he calls him *medicus noſter*. *Middleton* ſeldom wrote but out of pique. The preſent controverſy aroſe on his part from a converſation at *Cambridge*, where having compli- mented the modern profeſſors of phyſic at the expence of the ancient, he found himſelf called upon by the company to maintain his opinion againſt Dr. *Mead*, who publicly aſſerted the contrary. See *Middleton* 2, 3.

" and F. S. A." from hints fuggefted by feveral learned
friends (as has been already mentioned in p. 117), and
finifhed

from Mr. *Buckley's Englifh* the dedication to the King, and his three letters to
Dr. *Mead* (fee p. 81), concerning the new edition ; which tranflations were prefixed to it in
1733 ; in the month of *Auguft* of which year, he took a journey through *Holland* and *Flanders* to *Paris*, whence he returned in *October* following.   In 1732, he was employed by the
bookfellers, who were patentees for printing *Lilly's* grammar of the *Latin* tongue, to give
a correct edition of it, purged of the numerous errors which had crept into all the former.
This he executed with great accuracy *, and added in the preface an accurate and curious
hiftory of that grammar.   In that year he affifted Mr. *George Thompfon*, Mafter of the
Grammar School at *Tottenham High Crofs*, in his " Apparatus ad Linguam *Græcam* ordine
" novo ac facili digeftus," 8vo.   In the fame year, the " *Britannia Romana*" of *John
Horfley* †, M. A. and F. R. S. being publifhed at *London* in folio, there was printed in
it an " Effay on *Peutinger's* Table fo far as it relates to *Britain*," by Mr. *Ward* ; who
had revifed that elaborate work of Mr. *Horfley* in manufcript, and communicated to him
many important remarks for its improvement.   On the 5th of *February*, 1735-6, Mr. *Ward*
was chofen a member of the Society of Antiquaries, of which he was elected director, on
the 15th of *January*, 1746-7, on Dr. *Birch's* refignation of that office.   And in *April*,
1753, the Profeffor was appointed Vice-prefident of that fociety, and continued fo till his
death.   In 1736 Mr. *Ainfworth* was again indebted to him for literary affiftance (fee p.
109) ; as were Mr. (afterwards Dr.) *Patrick* and Mr. *Young* in the fucceeding edition of
Ainfworth's Dictionary.   In the fame year (1736) he was chofen one of the firft committee of the Society for the Encouragement of Learning (fee p. 134), as he was of
feveral fubfequent ones during the fubfiftence of that fociety ; who printed, among other
works at their expence, two which do honour to Profeffor *Ward* ; the prefatory dedication to the new and beautiful edition of *Maximus Tyrius* being written by him, who had
the care of the edition ; and in the preface to the edition of *Ælian* " De Animalibus," the
editor, *Abraham Gronovius*, is full of acknowledgements to Mr. *Ward* for his affiftance
in that work, and has alfo teftified his regard by infcribing to him, in a long dedication,
his edition of *Pomponius Mela*, 12mo, *Leyden*, 1743.   In *December*, 1740, his " Lives
" of the Profeffors of *Grefham College* ‡" were publifhed at *London* in folio, a work
which is a confiderable addition to the hiftory of learning in our country.   In 1741
he tranflated into *Latin* the Life of Dr. *Johnfton* prefixed to Auditor *Benfon's* edi-

---

* The Rev. and learned author of " A Letter to his Grace the Lord Archbifhop of *Canterbury*,
" containing a Propofal for the Improvement of *Latin* fchools, London, 1748, 8vo. remarks, p.
20, that " we are certainly in debt to the laft editor of *Lily's* Grammar, Mr. *Ward*, Profeffor of
" *Grefham College*, for many valuable improvements of this Grammar.   I am forry," adds the author, " that this learned gentleman fhould think of patching up another's performance, and not ra-
" ther give us one of his own."

† Who was educated in the public grammar fchool at *Newcaftle*, ftudied afterwards in one of the
Scotch colleges, where he took a degree, and died paftor of a diffenting congregation at *Morpeth*, in
Northumberland, 1732, a little before the publication of his book ; which might be greatly enlarged
from fucceeding difcoveries, taken notice of in the late edition of the " *Britifh* Topography," and
ftill later ones not known to the publick.   The plates of the *Britannia Romana* were lately purchafed of
one of the author's fons-in-law for twenty guineas by Dr. *Gifford*, for *The Britifh Mufeum*.   A copy of
it, with confiderable additions by Dr. *Ward* (of which Mr. *Gough* has a tranfcript) is in the fame
library.

‡ A copy of this work alfo, with confiderable additions by the author, is in *The Britifh Mufeum*.

tion

finished for the press after the death of Dr. *Birch*, by his intimate friend and executor Dr. *Maty*, in 8vo; " 2 *Hora-*
" *tii*

tion of that author's version of the Psalms. In the Gentleman's Magazine for 1740, pp. 30, 31, is preserved Mr. *Ward's* explanation of a *Roman* altar found at *Cast Steeds* in *Cumberland*; and in the Magazine for 1743, p. 528 & seq. occurs a specimen of the candid spirit of the writer, in his defence of his assertion, in his Lives of the Professors of *Gresham College*, that the works of the famous Dr. *Sydenham* were composed by him in *English*, and translated into *Latin* by Dr. *Mapletoft* and Mr. *Havers*. This piece of his is no where else to be met with. In 1751, Dr. *Wishart*, principal of the university of *Edinburgh*, published a new edition of " *Florentius Volusenus*, or *Wilson*, de, " animi tranquillitate," with a *Latin* letter to the editor from Mr. *Ward*, dated ipsis idibus *Novemb.* 1750. On the 20th of *May*, 1751, the professor was honoured by the university of *Edinburgh* with the degree of LL. D. Upon the establishment of *The British Museum* in 1753, Dr. *Ward* was on the 11th of *December* elected one of the trustees of it; in which office he was singularly useful, by his assiduous attendance, advice, and assistance in forming that establishment, and settling rules for rendering it of benefit to the public. In *July* of the year following, he published an edition of " Institutio " *Græcæ* grammatices compendiaria, in usum scholæ *Westmonasteriensis*," compiled by *Camden* while master of *Westminster school*. In this edition Dr. *Ward* carefully corrected the errors of the former, and made several very considerable improvements in the grammar itself. The last work published by himself was his " Four Essays upon the " *English* Language, by *John Ward*[*], D.LL. *R. P. G. C.* F. R. and A. SS. and *T. B. M.*" which he gave the world in the month of *June* 1758, preceding his death, the preface being dated *May* 24. He died in the 80th year of his age, at his apartments in *Gresham College*, on *Tuesday*, *October* 17, 1758, having gone well to bed; but he waked between three and four in the morning with a complaint of a coldness in his head, and soon after expired. His body was interred on the 24th of the same month in the burying-ground in *Bunhill Fields*. He had written an epitaph for himself in 1752 (seeming then to be apprehensive that his death might be nearer than it really proved to be); which, with the alteration only of dates, and the addition of the four lines printed in *Italic*, was afterwards adopted for him by his friend Dr. *Chandler*.

" Hic requiescit
Quod mortale fuit
JOHANNIS WARD, LL. D.
In collegio *Greshamensi*
Per ann. XXXVIII Rhetor. Profess.
Ob. ann. Salut. Human. MDCCLVIII,
Ætatis suæ LXXX.

Bonus, ut melior vir,
Aut doctior, non alius quisquam;
Imbutusque anima, qualem neque candidiorem
Terra tulit.
Item
Dilectæ ejus sororis
ABIGAILIS WARD [†]."

His executors were Mr. *John Ward*, bookseller in *Cornhill*, a very distant, if any relation, who died soon after the Doctor, and Mr. *Thomas Treadway*, late glover in *Leadenhall Street*, an ingenious man of a literary turn, who died about two years ago. The Doctor had a valuable library, which was sold by auction *March* 19, 1759, and the fourteen following days. He had prepared for the publick his " System of " Oratory, delivered in a course of Lectures publickly read at *Gresham College*,

[*] The meaning of these strange capitals may not at first sight be obvious. Those in Roman are well known; the others are, " Rhetorick Professor in Gresham College," and " Trustee of *The* " *British Museum*."
[†] Mrs. *Abigail Ward*, the Doctor's sister, died at his apartments in *Gresham College*, on *Tuesday*, *Sept.* 10, 1745.

7

" *tii Flacci* Epistolæ ad *Pisones*, & *Augustum*; with an
" *English* Commentary and Notes: To which are added
" Critical

" *London,*" which were, in pursuance of his intention, printed at *London* in 1759,
in 8vo, in two volumes. Another posthumous work of his, published at *London* in
1761, in 8vo, was intituled " Dissertations upon several Passages of the Sacred Scrip-
" tures *," which he had selected out of many others in manuscript, and of which
" he had actually caused a fair copy to be transcribed for the press. A second volume
of these. " Dissertations" came out in 1774; which, though not, as the former, transcribed for the press, were equally designed for it by the author. The papers written by
him, and communicated to the Royal and Antiquarian Societies, are enumerated below †.
He communicated to Mr. *Vertue,* when he published upon two large sheets, " A
" Draught of a *Roman Mosaic* Pavement, found in *Littlecote Park,* in the parish of
" *Ramsbury, Wiltshire,*" a large account of it, engraved on one of the plates; with
the

* In 1762 the late Dr. *Nathaniel Lardner* published at *London,* in 8vo. " Remarks upon the
" late Dr. *Ward's* Dissertations upon several Passages of the sacred Scriptures;" and observes, that
" Dr. *Ward's* intimate acquaintance with antiquity, and his uncommon skill in all parts of literature,
" are well known; his sincere piety and respect for the sacred Scriptures were as conspicuous;"
" and his Dissertations, though posthumous, have been well received by the public." Of the
second volume, which is not very easily to be met with, see Gent. Mag. 1775, p. 127.

† 1. A *Latin* dissertation de equuleo, or the wooden horse of the antient *Romans,* Phil. Transf.
N° 412, p. 23-14. 2. " Remarks upon an ancient date, found at *Widgel Hall,* near *Buntingford,* in
" *Hertfordshire,* on an oaken plank," N° 439, p. 120. 3. " Remarks upon an ancient Date, over
" a Gateway, near the Cathedral at *Worcester,*" N° 439, p. 136. 4. " An Account of a Disserta-
" tion published in *Latin* by Dr. *Weidler,* concerning the vulgar Numeral Figures; as also some Re-
" marks upon an Inscription, cut formerly in a window belonging to the parish church of *Rum-
" sey* in *Hampshire.* Read *June* 7, 1744." N° 474, p. 79. 5. " An Explication of a *Roman* In-
" scription found not long since at *Silchester* in *Hampshire.* Read *December* 13, 1744." N° 474,
p. 200. 6. " A Brief Enquiry into the reading of two dates in *Arabian* figures, cut upon stones
" found in *Ireland.*" Read *February* 28, 1744-5. N° 475, p. 283. 7. " An Attempt to explain
" some Remains of Antiquity lately found in *Hertfordshire.*" Read *April* 4, 1745. N° 476, p.
349. 8. " A Brief Account of a *Roman* Tessera." Read *March* 3, 1747-8. N° 486, p. 224.
9. " A Description of the Town of *Silchester* in its present state; with a short account of an antient
" date in *Arabian* figures at *Shalford* farm, adjoining to *Wasing,* in the parish of *Brimpton,* near
" *Aldermarston* in *Berkshire.*" Read *December* 22, 1748, N° 490, p. 603. 10. " Remarks upon an
" ancient *Roman* Inscription found in *Italy,* erected to the Goddess *Flora.*" Read *January* 11,
1749-50, N° 494, p. 293. 11. " An Abstract of a Discourse on the Medals of *Pescennius Niger,*
" and upon some circumstances in the history of his life; written in *French* by Monf. *Claude Gros de*
" *Boze.* Read *May* 31, 1750, N° 495, p. 452. 12. " An Attempt to explain an ancient *Greek*
" Inscription on a bronze cup, published with a draught of the cup by Dr. *Pococke,* in his Descrip-
" tion of the East, vol. II. part 2, p. 207." Read *June* 28, 1750, N° 495, p. 488. 13. " An
" Account of a *Roman* Altar, with an Inscription upon it, lately found at *York.*" Read *February*
1, 1753, vol. XLVIII. p. 33. 14. " An Abstract of a Discourse intituled, the History of the Em-
" peror *Tetricus,* explained and illustrated by medals; written in *French* by Monf. *Claude Gros de*
" *Boze.*" Read *April* 5, 1753, vol. XLVIII. p. 124. 15. " An Attempt to explain an ancient,
" *Roman* Inscription, cut upon a stone lately found at *Bath.*" Read *November* 22, 1753, vol.
XLVIII. p. 332. 16. " An Account of a *Roman* Inscription found at *Malton* in *Yorkshire,* in the
" year 1753." Read *March* 20, 1755, vol. XLIX. p. 69. 17. " An Account of four *Roman* In-
" scriptions, cut upon three large stones, found near *Wroxeter* in *Shropshire,* in the year 1752."
Read *May* 15, 1755, vol. XLIX. p. 196. 18. " An Attempt to explain two *Roman* Inscriptions,
" cut upon two Altars, which were dug up some time since at *Bath.*" Read *December* 11, 1755,
vol. XLIX. p. 285. 19. " Some Considerations on a Draught of two large pieces of lead with
" *Roman* inscriptions upon them, found several years since in *Yorkshire.*" Read *July* 1, 1756, vol.
XLIX. p. 686. " Among the " Vetusta Monumenta" of the Society of Antiquaries were published,
two.

" Critical Differtations. By the Reverend Mr. *Hurd.* In
" three volumes. The fourth edition, corrected and
" enlarged," 8vo; Dr. *Harris's** " Life of King *Charles*
" the Second," 2 vols. 8vo; the large " *Greek* Grammar,

the initial letters of his name. He was likewife the author of the dedications, preface, and notes, in the edition of *Horace* engraved by *Pine.* He wrote many epitaphs;
admired for their elegance and propriety, on his friends, and other perfons of diftinction
in the republic of letters; and particularly that upon his excellent friend, Dr. *Mead,*
(fee p. 253.) His piety was fincere and unaffected, and his profeffion as a Chriftian was
that of a Proteftant Diffenter, with a moderation and candour which recommended him
to the efteem of thofe members of the eftablifhed church who had the pleafure
of his acquaintance or friendfhip. His knowledge of antiquity was extenfive and
accurate; and he was remarkably well fkilled in the *Roman* law, which was of no
fmall advantage to him in his refearches into the conftitution, cuftoms, and hiftory
of the *Roman* empire. His modefty was equal to his learning, and his readinefs
to contribute to any work of literature was as diftinguifhed as his abilities to do it.
Among other learned men, to whom he communicated what lights occurred to him on
the fubjects in which they were engaged, Dr. *Lardner* was obliged to him for his remarks,
inferted in the firft volume of that excellent writer on the credibility of the gofpel hiftory, and for a conjecture publifhed in part II. vol. VII. p. 350. In the works of Dr.
George Benfon are likewife three differtations of Mr. *Ward,* but without his name. "The
" Manner of St. *Paul's* two Confinements at *Rome* confidered," is printed in the Appendix to *Philemon,* in 1752. That " concerning the perfons to whom St. *Paul* wrote
" what is called the Epiftle to the *Ephefians,*" is printed in the Hiftory of the firft
Planting of the Chriftian Religion, vol. II. p. 342, in 1755. And that called " A Poftfcript to the aforegoing Differtation," in form of a letter, in vol. III. p. 55, in 1756.

    * The Rev. *William Harris,* a Proteftant Diffenting Minifter of eminent abilities and
character, at *Honiton* in *Devonfhire.* On the 20th of *September,* 1765, the degree of
D. D. was conferred on him by the univerfity of *Glafgow,* by the unanimous confent of
the members of that body. " He publifhed an hiftorical and critical account of the
" lives of *James* I. *Charles* I. *Oliver Cromwell,* in five volumes, 8vo. after the man-
" ner of Mr. *Bayle.* He was preparing a like account of *James* II. He alfo wrote
" the life of *Hugh Peters;* befides many fugitive pieces occafionally, for the public
" prints, in fupport of liberty and virtue. All his works have been well received ‡; and
                                                          " thofe

two difcourfes of his, viz. " De codice *Genefeos Cottoniano* differtatio hiftorica," in 1744, and
" A brief Account of the Court of Wards and Liveries," in 1747. See alfo vol. II. Nᵒ 15. 19.
His other communications to that Society, are, 1. " Copy of a Letter from Mr. Profeffor *Ward* to
Mr. Vice-prefident *Folkes,* relating to an Infcription found at *Chichefter,*" three pages, read Oct.
9, 1740. 2. " A Brief Enquiry into the Antiquity of an ancient Map of *London* and *Weftminfter,*
" contained in fix fheets; as alfo fome account of feveral ancient prints of *The Royal Exchange,*
" built by Sir *Thomas Grefham.*" Read *July* 15, 1742. 3. " Extracts from the Accompts of the
" Church-wardens of the Parifh of St. *Helen's,* in *Abingdon, Berkfhire;* from the firft of *Philip* and
" *Mary,* to the 34th of Queen *Elizabeth* (now in the poffeffion of Mr. *George Benfon)* with fome
" obfervations by Mr. Profeffor *Ward.* Read *Nov.* 24, 1743," printed in Archæol. vol. I. p. 11.
4. A Difcourfe on Beacons, *April* 13, 1749, Ibid. p. 1.
    ‡ Dr. *Harris's* works were differently thought of by the authors of the " Critical Review." See
their account of The " Life of *Charles* II." in *March* 1766.—Induftry was their principal
characteriftic. They certainly have none of the vivacity which infpired *Bayle;* and in the judgement of difpaffionate readers impartiality is frequently violated.

                                                                 " for

" for the ufe of *Weftminfter fchool*," 8vo ; " The Life of
" *Mæcenas*, by *Ralph Schomberg**, M. D." the " Hiftory
" of *Greenland*," publifhed by Mr. *Gambold*†, (fee p. 216);
" The Confeffional‡," 8vo ; " A larger Confutation of
" Bifhop

" those who differ from him in principle, ftill value him in point of induftry and faith-
" fulnefs." I give this character in the words of his munificent patron Mr. *Hollis*, who
had prefented him with many valuable books in reference to the fubjects of his hiftories ;
and was at the expence of procuring his Doctor's degree. Dr. *Harris* died at *Honiton*,
Feb. 4, 1779.

* This writer's character has been lately difplayed, in *glaring* colours, in " The Com-
" panion to the Playhoufe," vol. I. p. 394.

† Since the account of Mr. *Gambold* has been given in p. 215, the publication of a
hiftory of the *Moravian* church has furnifhed a few additional circumftances. " Mr.
" *Gambold's* connexion with the Brethren commenced in 1738, when *Peter Boehler* vi-
" fited *Oxford*, and held frequent meetings with *John* and *Charles Wefley* for the edi-
" fication of awakened people, both learned and unlearned." His difcourfes were in
" *Latin*, and were interpreted by Mr. *Gambold*." His " Maxims, Theological Ideas,
" and Sentences, &c." appeared in 1751, 8vo. " He was confecrated a bifhop at an
" *Englifh* provincial Synod held at *Lindfey Houfe* in Nov. 1754, and was greatly efteemed
" for his piety and learning by feveral *Englifh* Bifhops, who were his contemporaries
" in the Univerfity of *Oxford*. In 1765 a congregation was fettled by Bifhop *Gambold*,
" at *Coothill*, in *Ireland*." I fhall alfo take the opportunity of annexing a fhort account
of this pious Divine, by a friend who knew him in the early part of life : " Mr. *Gam-
" bold* was a fingular, over-zealous, but innocent Enthufiaft. He had not quite fire
" enough in him to form a fecond *Simeon Stylites*. He was prefented to *Stanton Har-
" court* by Bifhop *Secker* ||, I think in 1739, but cannot be certain. He had been only
" Chaplain of *Chrift Church*, not a Student (the term given to the Fellows) of that
" royal foundation. He deferted his flock in 1742, without giving any notice to his
" worthy diocefan and patron, to affociate with people, among whom, though he might
" be innocent, have been fome monftrous characters. When he was young, he had
" nearly perifhed through difregard to his perfon. At this time he was kindly relieved
" by his brother collegian in the fame department, Dr. *Free*, a perfon well known in
" *London*; but the tale is not worth gaining." *Letter from Mr. Daniel Prince to J. N.*

‡ The anonymous Author of this celebrated performance was obliged to Mr.
Bowyer for fome ufeful hints in its progrefs through the prefs, and for feveral improvements towards a new (and much enlarged) edition. This affiftance was thus handfomely
acknowledged :

" WORTHY SIR,   *Nov.* 16, 1766.

" Though Mr. *Millar* has not perhaps acquainted you with all my fcruples concern-
" ing another edition of *The Confeffional*, yet I can have no objection to be determined
" by the confiderations you lay before me with fo friendly a view to the common benefit
" of my Brethren, and the credit of the book, which however exhibits nothing more
" than every Clergyman ought to know without it. I am obliged to you greatly for fug-

|| Dr. *Secker* fucceeded Dr. *Potter*, as Bifhop of *Oxford*, in 1737, and probably prefented Mr.
Gambold (for the living is in the bifhop of *Oxford's* gift) in 1739.

" gefting

" Bishop *Hare's* System of *Hebrew* Metre ; in a Letter to
" the Rev. Dr. *Edwards*, in answer to his *Latin* Epistle.

" By

" gesting the particulars concerning the articles. The history of the clause, passed in
" the Lords House, and rejected by the Commons, did not escape me. But it was
" made use of in a pamphlet published by Mr. *Millar* against Dr. *Powell's* subscription
" sermon some years ago ; and I was aware, that if the Author of *The Confessional*
" should ever come to be known, it would at the same time be known, that the same
" person was the author of that pamphlet ; and to repeat that circumstance, might be
" called pillaging his own works, which somebody calls the worst kind of plagiarism.
" However, as it is so much to the purpose, I will try if it may decently be put into a note
" at the place you mention. The terms of the limited subscription in the 13th *Eliza-*
" *beth*, I had noticed in *Selden* and elsewhere ; but own I had overlooked the double sub-
" scription in the act of uniformity, and am obliged to you for reminding me of it.
" With regard to the canonical subscription, my opinion is exactly the same with yours.
" But the case with me was this : I had the late Lord *Hardwicke's* opinion in MS. long
" before it was printed, from the late Mr. *Erskine's* papers ; and as I supposed it con-
" clusive as to the Clergy, I did not meddle with the limited subscription, as that might
" give advantage to an adversary, the point being certainly problematical. I own I
" differ with his Lordship as to the obligation of the canons, even upon the clergy, in
" this matter of subscription. I cannot see how canonical obedience, which is retained
" to things lawful and honest, can be extended to an ordinance enjoining unlimited
" subscription, contrary to law. But the point was rather too delicate for me to handle
" in the light it appears to me, and, as I now perceive, it appears likewise to you. Some
" years ago I had occasion to ask a leading man in *Cambridge* by what authority they
" required subscription for degrees, and had for answer, it was by virtue of an injunc-
" tion from *James* I. under his own royal hand. The *Cambridge* people have dropped
" subscription at Matriculations, though I imagine both you and I subscribed at Ma-
" triculation, perhaps both at the very same time ; for I remember you at St. *John's*
" of my own year, and to have once drunk tea with you at a friend's room in your own
" college. I suppose you take my judgement of the forgery of the controverted clause of
" the 20th article, from a note, p. 294, of *The Confessional*. But if you please to read
" the note again, you will see I decide nothing concerning the authenticity of the clause
" as passed or not passed in Convocation ; but consider the authenticity, &c. to depend
" upon the question, Whether the imprinted book referred to 13 *Elizabeth* had the
" clause ? I think it next to demonstrable it had not ; and whether *Hales* thought it un-
" authentic for the same reason or not, he certainly paid no regard to it, if he wrote
" that letter. When I say, that *Laud* stopped that gap, I do not mean that he then
" first inserted it ; for undoubtedly it was in many printed editions long before *Laud*
" figured in the world. What I meant was, that he took care to have it inserted in all
" future editions ; but in this I find since I was mistaken, for it had been inserted in all
" the *English* editions published after 1628, when the articles were printed with his
" Majesty's declaration before them. I have not *Collier's* Ecclesiastical History, nor
" would it be easy to meet with it in the country ; but I have the book from whence he
" is said to have taken his materials, viz. ' Vindication of the Church of *England*
" against Priestcraft in Perfection.' I have likewise Dr. *Bennet* on the same argument ;
" but it is impossible these should leave any impression on me (I will not say on any im-

" partial

" By *Robert Lowth*, D. D. F. R. S. S. *Lond.* and *Goetting.* and

" partial reader), after having read ' An Historical and Critical Essay on the Thirty-nine
" Articles of the Church of *England*,' printed for *R. Francklin* 1724, and ascribed to
" Mr. *Collins*, and which was written in answer to them, and leaves not in my mind
" the least remains of a doubt but that the clause was a forgery, that *Laud's* record
" was perhaps not much better, and that the MSS. in *Benet College* library are the true
" originals of the articles passed in the Convocations of 1562 and 1571 respectively.
" N. B. I never saw an answer to the Historical and Critical Essay. With respect to
" *Collier*, he says, ' And hereby in particular I have answered every thing urged in the
" Ecclesiastical History of Mr. *Collier*, who is but a mere abridger of the *Vindicator*. I
" think the Curators of the Church will do great honour to the author of *The Confes-*
" *sional*, by appointing so able and dignified a Veteran to enter the lists with him. But
" if the other person you name should undertake the same task, it is great odds but they
" run foul of each other. I am, worthy Sir, your much obliged humble servant."
In a second letter to Mr. *Bowyer*, dated *Dec.* 23, 1766, the author says, " I think
" myself highly obliged to you for your favour of the 16th instant, as it rid me of a
" doubt concerning the Uniformity Act; for I had been assured from another hand, that
" the copies varied, which I was inclined to think might be true, as I had observed some-
" thing like a various reading in Dr. *Nichols* *, which I had not then at hand to consult.

" I really

---

* *W. Nichols*, son of *John Nichols*, of *Donington* in *Bucks*, born in 1664, became a Batler or Commoner of *Magdalen Hall, Oxford*, in 1679; removed afterwards to *Wadham College*, and as a member
thereof took the degree of B. A. *Nov.* 27, 1683; was admitted probationer-fellow of *Merton Col-*
lege in *October* 1684; M. A. *June* 19, 1688; and about that time taking holy orders, became chaplain to *Ralph* earl of *Montagu*, and in *September* 1691 rector of *Selsey*, near *Chichester*, in *Sussex*;
was admitted B. D. *July* 2, 1692; and D. D. *Nov.* 29, 1695. After a life entirely devoted to piety
and study, we find him, in the close of it, thus pathetically describing his situation, in a letter to
Robert Earl of *Oxford*:

" May it please your Lordship, *Smith Street, Westminster, Aug.* 31, 1711.
" I was in hopes, that her Majesty would have bestowed the Prebend of *Westminster* upon me,
" being the place where I live, and that I might be nearer to Books, to finish my Work on the
" Liturgy and Articles, for which she was pleased to tell to me, with her own mouth, she would
" consider me. My good Lord, I have taken more pains in this matter than any Divine of our
" Nation, which I hope may bespeak the favour of a Church-of-*England* Ministry. Therefore I
" most humbly beseech your Lordship for your interest for the next Prebend of that Church (if this
" be disposed of) that shall be void; for, if I had merited nothing, my circumstances want it. I
" am now forced on the drudgery of being the Editor of Mr. *Selden's* Books, for a little money to
" buy other Books to carry on my Liturgical Work. I have broken my constitution by the pains
" of making my Collections myself throughout that large Work, without the help of an Amanu-
" ensis, which I am not in a condition to keep, though the disease of my stomach (being a con-
" tinual colic of late, attended by the rupture of a vein) might plead pity, and incline my Su-
" periors not to suffer me all my days to be a *Gibeonite* in the Church without any regard or relief.
" Pray, my Lord, represent my case to the good Queen; and I shall never be wanting to make my
" most ample acknowledgement for so great a favour. I could long since have made my way
" to preferment without taking all this pains, by a noisy cry for a Party: but as this has been
" often the reproach, and once the ruin, of our Clergy, so I have always industriously avoided
" it, quietly doing what service I could to the Church I was born in, and leaving the issue there-
" of to God's Providence, and to the kind offices of some good man, who some time or other
" might befriend me in getting some little thing for me to make my circumstances easy: which
" is the occasion that your Lordship has the trouble of this application from, my Lord,
" Your Lordship's most dutiful, most obedient, and most humble servant, WILL. NICHOLS."
His publications were, 1. " An Answer to an heretical Book, called *The naked Gospel*, which was con-
" demned and ordered to be publickly burnt by the Convocation of the University of *Oxon*, 19
" *Aug.* 1690, with some Reflections on Dr. *Bury's* new Edition of that Book, 1691," 4to. 2.
" A short History of Socinianism," printed with the answer before-mentioned; and dedicated to

Chaplain in ordinary to his Majesty [since successively Bishop
of *St. David's, Oxford,* and *London,*]" 8vo; " The Second Part

" I really am concerned that I cannot agree with your supposition, that *Mosheim* was
" mistaken in ascribing the project to *Wake*. After a serious and deliberate examination
" of circumstances, I think *Mosheim* and the Biographer perfectly reconcileable. If
" you will read over the article *Wake* in the latter attentively, together with the re-
" marks, you will readily see, that the project did not take its rise from the Commo-
" nitorium ; and that some circumstances relating to the forming of it are artfully kept
" out of sight by the Biographer. I dare say you know from the signature P. [Dr. *Philip*
" *Nichols*] who compiled that article, as well as I do. Some of his artifices I have detected in
" other articles. And if you will read *Wake's* Letters to *Courayer*, which follow, you will
" find to what length he carries church-matters, even to tread upon the heels of Popery.
" As to his former defences of Protestantism, there perhaps have been few such rene-
" gados to good principles as he was ; and I for my part can wonder at nothing such men

his patron the Earl of *Montagu*. 3. " A Practical Essay on the Contempt of the World, 1694,"
8vo, inscribed to " Sir *John Trevor*, Master of the Rolls," to whom the author acknowledges his
obligations for " a considerable preferment bestowed in a most obliging and generous manner." 4.
" The Advantages of a learned Education," a Sermon preached at a School Feast, 1698," 4to.
5. " The Duty of Inferiors towards their Superiors, in Five Practical Discourses ; shewing, I.
" The Duty of Subjects to their Princes. II. The Duty of Children to their Parents. III. The
" Duty of Servants to their Masters. IV. The Duty of Wives to their Husbands. V. The Duty
" of Parishioners and the Laity to their Pastors and Clergy. To which is prefixed a Dissertation
" concerning the Divine Right of Princes, 1701," 8vo. 6. " An Introduction to a devout Life,
" by *Francis Sales*, Bishop and Prince of *Geneva* ; translated and reformed from the Errors of the
" *Romish* Edition. To which is prefixed a Discourse of the Rise and Progress of the Spiritual Books
" in the *Romish* Church, 1701," 8vo. 7. " A Treatise of Consolation to Parents for the Death of
" their Children. Written upon the occasion of the Death of the Duke of *Gloucester* ;" and addressed " to the most illustrious Princess *Anne* of *Denmark*, 1701," 8vo. 8. " God's Blessing on
" Mineral Waters ; a Sermon preached at the Chapel at *Tunbridge Wells*, 1702," 4to. 9. " A
" Conference with a Theist ; in five parts ; dedicated to the Queen's most excellent Majesty, 1703,"
8vo ; of which a third edition, " with the addition of Two Conferences, the one with a *Machiave-*
" *lian*, the other with an Atheist, all carefully revised and prepared for the press by the Author,"
was published in 2 vols. 8vo, 1723. 10. " A Practical Essay on the Contempt of the World ; to
" which is prefixed a Preface to the Deists, and vicious Libertines of the Age, 1704," 2d Ed. 8vo. 11.
" The Religion of a Prince ; shewing that the Precepts of the Holy Scriptures are the best Maxims
" of Government, 1704," 8vo. 12. " Defensio Ecclesiæ *Anglicanæ*, 1707," 12mo. 13. " A Pa-
" raphrase on the Common Prayer, with Notes on the Sundays and Holidays, 1708," 8vo. 14.
" Afflictions the Lot of God's Children, a Sermon on the Death of Prince *George*, 1709," 8vo.
15. " A Comment on the Book of Common Prayer, and Administration of the Sacraments, &c.
" 1710," folio. 16. " A Supplement to the Commentary on the Book of Common Prayer, 1711,"
folio. In the Preface to this Supplement Dr. *Nichols* mentions " a long fit of illness with which
" God had pleased to visit him, and a very unestablished state of health both before and after it."
This illness appears soon to have ended in his death. 17. " Historiæ Sacræ Libri VII. Ex *Axtonii*
" *Cocceii Sabellici* Encadibus concinnatum, in usum Scholarum, & Juventutis Christianæ, 1711,"
12mo. 18. " A Commentary on the first fifteen, and part of the sixteenth Articles of the Church of
" *England*, 1712," fol. 19. " A Defence of the Doctrine and Discipline of the Church of *England* ; first
" written in *Latin* for the Use of Foreigners by *William Nichols*, D.D. and translated into *English*
" by himself, 1715," 12mo — A volume of letters written by and to Dr. *Nichols* in *Latin* (by
Jablonski, Osterwald, Wetstein, &c.) was presented by his widow *Catherine Nichols* to the Archbishop of *Canterbury*, Oct. 28, 1712, to be deposited either in *Lambeth* or *St. Martin's Library*.
They are accordingly preserved among the valuable MSS. at *Lambeth*, N° 676.—It may not be
improper to distinguish this pious Divine from his name-sake *William Nicols*, M. A. and rector of
Stockport in *Cheshire*, who was a student of *Christ Church, Oxford*, and published, 1. " De Literis
" inventis libri sex ; ad illustrissimum Principem *Thomam Herbertum, Pembrokiæ* Comitem, &c.
" 1711," 8vo. 2. " Oratio coram venerabili Societate pro promovendâ Religione Christianâ ha
" bita *Londini, Decemb.* 29, 1715," 12mo ; and, 3. " ΠΕΡΙ ΑΡΧΩΝ Libri Septem. Accedunt Li-
" turgica, 1717," 12mo.

" can.

" of a Literary Correspondence, between the Bishop of *Glou-*
" *cester*

" can do. The case standing thus, I am obliged to leave the text just as it is, so far as
" concerns *Mosheim* and *Wake*, excepting some little modification with respect to Mr.
" *Maclaine*, whom I had cited before inaccurately, and shall therefore be more exact
" and more cautious in some expressions ; but have no manner of occasion to meddle
" with any with whom he might correspond in *England*, as he puts down the
" note as his own. With your leave, therefore, I will add a note in this part of the
" text, giving my reasons for thinking *Mosheim* was not mistaken, and for the rest leave
" the public to judge. If I mistake not, Dr. *Lardner* discovered *Mosheim's* mistake of
" one King for another, and made mention of it in one of his late books of *Jewish* and
" Heathen testimonies. I think the subscription at Matriculation was dropped at *Cam-*
" *bridge* since you and I were admitted. If you recollect the names of two scholars,
" contemporaries at *St. John's* with you, *Mearson* and *Fidler*, you will know how to
" account for my particular remembrance of you. I must not omit to return you my
" thanks for your notes upon the *Greek* Testament, and particularly for the excellent
" Preface before them. They have been of great use to me and others on several occa-
" sions, and I wish we had more such collections by equally able hands.—A correspon-
" dent I have *abroad*, mentioned to me not long ago, a design to put The *Confessional*
" into a *French* dress ; in which he, with some other of his friends, as he said, were con-
" cerned. I have prevailed with him to drop the design at least till another edition
" come out. He is a man of great knowledge, though young ; and capable of doing
" justice to any subject he thinks fit to undertake, and ought not to be employed in the
" drudgery of *translating*. If Mr. *Millar* can make any use of this hint, you may com-
" municate it, and he will let me know. I suppose I am to expect some smart strictures
" from Mr. *Maclaine* : but there are such things as *Reprisals* in due time and place.
" I have been ill for ten days or a fortnight, and quite disabled from business ; and am
" not yet thoroughly recruited. But hope to send some copy of the additions and cor-
" rections by next post. *Piget me unum tantum eruditum Typographum in Angliâ superesse,*
" *et illum annum agentem primum supra sexagesimum.* The words are not mine, but I
" sincerely join in the lamentation ; and am, worthy Sir, Your much obliged humble
" servant.—I wish Mr. *Maclaine* had given some account of Dr. *Mosheim*, as it would
" have recommended his book in this country."

Mr. *Bowyer's* answer is worth preserving :

" REVEREND SIR, *Jan.* 11, 1767.

" The *Latin* compliment your last brought me, is enough to swell the glowing tide of
" vanity, were not my life at a lower ebb than my encomiast imagines, being advanced
" to the LXVIIIth year ; which makes me something doubt, whether I am the person
" whom you remember at College, admitted in the year 1716, and who came away in the
" year 1722. My father, good man, sent me thither * to qualify me by a new kind of ex-
" periment

* Mr. *Bowyer* has frequently lamented to me the great hardships which he experienced at College, where " the commons of the sizers," he said, " were in his time (1716—1722) miserably poor,
" though since much mended." His father, though in every other respect a generous man, used in
company to talk of " the great expence he was at in keeping his son at the University." This being
repeated to the son, he determined to live there at the lowest expence possible ; his tutor's bills (which
I have now before me) not amounting, board included, to twenty pounds a year. To this circumstance
his old friend Mr. *Clarke* thus alludes : " I now find that nobody is so proper to converse with Mr.
" *Markland* as you are ; who had almost starved yourself upon a principle of honour. This indeed
" was in you only a sally of youth ; but he is now as young as you were at 17, and would do it at.

" any

" *cefter* and a late Profeſſor of *Oxford:* Accurately printed
" from an authentic copy.   To which are added the Notes
" of the firſt Editor, with Notes upon Notes, and Remarks
" on the Letters," 8vo. (only 75 copies were printed;)
" Delectus Epigrammatum *Græcorum**, in uſum Scholæ *Eto-*
" *nenſis*," 8vo; *Rhazes* " De Variolis †," 8vo; *Martin's*

" periment for a printer. But it ſerved only in trade to expoſe me to more affronts,
" and to give me a keener ſenſibility of them. Time and old age are at laſt our beſt
" inſtructors, and I ſhould have made an ill uſe of the documents of nature, if I had not
" learnt to take conſolation from my approach to that ſtate, where the great and little
" will be equal. I have been led into theſe reflections from an incident that has juſt hap-
" pened from the little connections between us ‡.....I thought it neceſſary to lay
" this before you, that I might not claim the merit, or ſuffer for the defects, of any
" other typographical operator; and, that I may not ſeem to act clandeſtinely, I ſend Mr.
" *Millar* a copy of this. I am, Sir, your very obliged humble ſervant, W. BOWYER.
        " P. S. I wiſh you the compliments of the ſeaſon: *Multos & felices.*
        The next " good wiſh is, *Sin infelices, paucos.*"
  * " Mr. *Pote* tells me that you are to reprint for him our *Selecta ex Poetis Græcis,*
" which gives me pleaſure with the proſpect of its being more correctly and reputably
" done than we could expect it to be any where elſe. The copy, which he ſays he has
" given you to print from, is corrected with a pen in a few places, but thoſe *very few*
" compared with others ſtill uncorrected; as you will ſee, and (I truſt) amend. I ſin-
" cerely condole with you on the loſs of our friend, that excellent man and ſcholar,
" Dr. *Taylor." MS. Letter of Dr. Foſter to Mr. Bowyer, Apr.* 17, 1766.
  † That I may not be accuſed of decking Mr. *Bowyer* with borrowed plumes, it
will be proper to mention, that this volume was printed, with Mr. *Bowyer's Arabic*
types, in the office of Mr. *William Richardſon.*

" any time. It is a little too much to have a man's virtues reduce him to a mere ſkeleton; you
" were wiſe enough to take up in time, and he will, I hope, at laſt.—You never paid a proper de-
" ference to your father's judgement. How long did he live in trade, beloved and careſſed by the
" whole fraternity of bookſellers, and how little was done in compariſon of what you have accom-
" pliſhed! Make but a man talked of in trade for any excellence in his way, and it will do his bu-
" ſineſs. To be *in ore vulgi* is all he wants. You are not beholden to the world, but yourſelf:
" for that many-headed monſter the World is, in its collective capacity, juſt as ſelfiſh as the indivi-
" duals that compoſe it." *MS. Letter, Jan.* 26, 1768.
  ‡ This alludes to a private miſunderſtanding, not worth relating; but which two ſhort letters
will ſufficiently illuſtrate:
  " Though I underſtand you have diſſolved that friendly connexion which was commenced be-
" tween the author of *The Confeſſional* and me, I do not neglect to put into your hands what he ſug-
" geſted for the benefit of his book and *Moſheim*, in a letter I received from him, ſince you went to
" *Bath*, and which I here ſend you. I thought myſelf obliged to lay before him a narration of my
" conduct, which I hope he will look upon as a ſufficient juſtification of it. Be pleaſed to return
" me the letter incloſed, for the ſake of the compliment, which I am to live upon." *Mr. Bowyer*
to Mr. Millar, Jan. 12, 1767.
  " I received yours of the 12th two days ago, but had not time to anſwer it. If you have any
" cauſe to regret this tranſaction, you certainly have only yourſelf to blame. Your complaining to
" the author is abſurd in my opinion, as you never had a warmer friend than, yours, &c. I incloſe
" you the author's letter as you deſired. Praiſe will feed none of us, though it may pleaſe us for
" a time. You have your merit, but none of us are without faults; and perhaps we think our-
" ſelves of too much importance in our own ideas." *Mr. Millar to Mr. Bowyer, Jan.* 17, 1767.

                                                " Diſſer-

" Differtation * on the Blafphemy, &c. againft the Holy
" Ghoft," 8vo; Mr. *Holwell's* " Selecti *Dionyfii* Tracta-
" tus," (already mentioned in p. 212,) 8vo; *Toup's* " Emen-
" dationes in *Suidam*, Pars III." 8vo; Mr. *Elphinftone's* † " Prin-
" ciples of *Englifh* Grammar," 12mo; and " The Great Impor-
" tance of a Religious Life ‡," 12mo, of which valuable little
book he afterwards lived to print many large impreffions.

* Printed at the expence of the munificent Mr. *Jennens* of *Gopfal*; of whom fee
under the year 1772.

† Schoolmafter at *Kenfington*, Author of feveral literary Works, and well known as
the tranflator of *Martial's* Epigrams.

‡ It is a fomewhat fingular circumftance that the real author of this moft admirable
treatife fhould never yet have been publicly known ‖, and the more fo, as it is plainly
pointed out in the following " Short Character" prefixed to the book itfelf " It may
" add weight, perhaps, to the reflections contained in the following pages to inform the
" reader, that the author's life was one uniform exemplar of thofe precepts, which,
" with fo generous a zeal and fuch an elegant and affecting fimplicity of ftyle, he endea-
" vours to recommend to general practice. He left others to contend for modes of
" faith, and inflame themfelves and the world with endlefs controverfy : it was the wifer
" purpofe of his more ennobled aim, to act up to thofe clear rules of conduct which
" Revelation hath gracioufly prefcribed. He poffeffed by temper every moral virtue ;
" by religion every Chriftian grace. He had a humanity that melted at every diftrefs ;
" a charity which not only thought no evil, but fufpected none. He exercifed his
" profeffion with a fkill and integrity, which nothing could equal but the difinterefted
" motive that animated his labours, or the amiable modefty which accompanied all his
" virtues. He employed his induftry, not to gratify his own defires; no man indulged
" himfelf lefs : not to accumulate ufelefs wealth ; no man more difdained fo unworthy
" a purfuit ; it was for the decent advancement of his family, for the generous affiftance
" of his friends, for the ready relief of the indigent. How often did he exert his dif-
" tinguifhed abilities, yet refufe the reward of them, in Defence *of the Widow, the Fa-
" therlefs, and him that had none to help him !* In a word, few have ever paffed a more
" ufeful, not one a more blamelefs life ; and his whole time was employed either in
" doing good, or in meditating it. He died on the 6th day of *April* 1743, and lies
" buried under the Cloifter of *Lincoln's Inn* Chapel. MEM. PAT. OPT. MER. FIL. DIC."
The following Epitaph, infcribed on a ftone under the Cloifter above referred to, will
clearly point out the Author of the above performance :

" Here lies the Body of
WILLIAM MELMOTH, Efq;
Late one of the Senior Benchers
of this Hon. Society, Who died
April the 6th, 1743, in the 77th
Year of his Age."
Let Mr. *Melmoth's* name therefore be handed down to pofterity with the honour it fo emi-

‖ It has been fo commonly attributed to the firft Earl of *Egmont*, particularly by Mr. *Walpole*
in his Catalogue, that I have without hefitation afcribed it to that Nobleman in the " Supplement
" to *Swift* ;" an error which I here readily retract.

nently

In 1767 he was appointed to print the Rolls of Parliament and the Journals of the House of Lords. He was principally indebted for this appointment to the Earl of *Marchmont*; and his gratitude to that noble peer is testified in the inscription which he left behind him, to be placed in *Stationers-Hall*, which will appear at the end of these Memoirs.

The want of sufficient room now compelled him, though not without reluctance *, to exchange *White Fryars*, where he was born and had resided nearly 67 years, for *Red-Lion Passage, Fleet Street*; where he opened his new office with the sign of his favourite *Cicero's* head; under which was inscribed,

" M. T. CICERO, A QUO PRIMORDIA PRELI,"

in allusion to the well-known early editions of *Tully's Offices*.

In that year he printed, for his old and valuable friend Mr. *Clarke*, " The Connexion of the *Roman*, *Saxon*, and
" *English* Coins †; deducing the Antiquities, Customs, and
" Manners, of each People to Modern Times; particularly
" the Origin of Feudal Tenures, and of Parliaments: il-
" lustrated throughout with Critical and Historical Remarks
" on

nently deserves; let the author of the " Short Character" have his share of the honour due to the worthy Son of a worthy Sire; and let it be mentioned, to the credit of the age, that, notwithstanding many large editions had before been circulated, 36000 copies of this useful treatise have been sold in the last 15 years.—In conjunction with Mr. *Peere Williams*, Mr. *Melmoth* was the publisher of *Vernon's* Reports, under an order of the Court of Chancery. He had once an intention of printing his own Reports; and a short time before his death advertised them at the end of those of his coadjutor *Peere Williams*, as then actually preparing for the press. They have, however, not yet made their appearance. The younger Mr. *Melmoth* has been already mentioned, as the celebrated Translator of *Pliny* and *Cicero's* Letters, and Author of those which pass under the name of Sir *Thomas Fitzosborne*.

* As there were few steps of any consequence in which he did not consult Mr. *Markland*, he wrote to him of course on this event, which to him was an important one. " Far from condemning you (says Mr. *Markland*) in what you have done as to the " printing-house, I agree with you entirely, provided you agree with yourself, for, if a " man (who is not a madman or an idiot) does not know at our time of life what is " proper for him to do, the condition of mortality is certainly on a worse footing than " Providence designed it."

† In the Preface to this work, Mr. *Clarke* thus handsomely acknowledges the assistance he received from Mr. *Bowyer:* " Many errata, which escaped me in examining the

3 " sheets

" on various Authors, both Sacred and Profane*. By *Wil-*
" *liam Clarke,* A. M." " The appearance of this work from
" the prefs," Mr. *Clarke* fays, " was entirely owing to the
" difcovery made by the late *Martin Folkes,* Efq; of the
" old *Saxon* pound."

" fheets from the prefs, Mr. *Bowyer* has done me the favour to correct; and if others
" have paffed him unobferved, he may well be excufed, from the nature of this work,
" and the multiplicity of other bufinefs. I am obliged to him for more material ob-
" fervations. As for myfelf, I fhall not think it neceffary to apologife for the leffer
" typographical errors, efpecially at fuch a diftance from the prefs, and at a time of
" life when a clofe attention to very minute particulars is much impaired." And, in a
private letter, he fays, " I am greatly obliged to you for all the trouble you have
" taken; for every hint, caution, alteration, correction, you have fuggefted. I believe
" I fhall adopt them all.—That your friend the late Speaker † fhould give fo much at-
" tention to thefe dry difquifitions is more than I could have imagined. I fuppofe his
" favourite fubject, the Houfe of Commons, excited his curiofity."—Again, " I thank
" you for printing this work fo handfomely, both as to the types and paper: It will
" make it look a little more fignificant; and as the notes are large, they will be read in
" fo large a type without difficulty. But I am ftill more obliged to you for altering,
" or correcting, any inaccuracies in the language, which, I fancy, you have done in fe-
" veral places; though, as I have nothing but a rough copy by me, I have nothing but
" memory to afcertain it. Pray go on, and ufe your own judgement. I fhould have
" read it over with that view, but could not find an appetite fufficient for that purpofe."
Some of Mr. *Bowyer's* notes are interfperfed with the Author's throughout the volume.
Part of the Differtation on the *Roman* Sefterce is his production: and the Index (a peculiarly good one, and on which he not a little prided himfelf) was drawn up entirely
by him. " Of all your talents," fays Mr. *Clarke,* " you are a moft amazing man at
" Indexes ‡. What a flag too do you hang out at the ftern! You muft certainly perfuade
" people that the book overflows with matter, which (to fpeak the truth) is but thinly
" fpread. But I know all this is fair in trade; and you have a right to expect that the
" publick fhould purchafe freely, when you reduce the whole book into an epitome for
" their benefit; I fhall read the Index with pleafure."—The fending of the prefents
was left to Mr. *Bowyer's* management; on which occafion Mr. *Clarke* writes, " I
" like all that you have done very well; the fooner I get quit of all this parade the
" better. But don't fay a word to any body of what prefents I have made, left by tak-
" ing air it might give others a pretence for being offended.—I find the Archbifhop
" [*Secker*] and you are intimate; he trufts you with fecrets: but I could tell you a fecret,
" which nobody knows but my wife, that if our Deanry fhould be ever vacant in my
" time (which is not likely) I would not accept it—I would no more go into a new
" way of life, furnifh new apartments, &c. than Mrs. *Bowyer* would go to a lord-
" mayor's ball. I have learnt to know that at the end of life thefe things are not worth
" our notice." *April* 8, 1767.

* The title-page in feveral copies is only, " The Connexion of the *Roman, Saxon,* and
" *Englifh* Coins, deduced from Obfervations on the *Saxon* Weights and Money." The
title as above quoted was an after-thought.

† Mr. *Onflow* perufed the work in MS. and honoured Mr. *Clarke* with fome ufeful hints and
obfervations.

‡ I have feveral in MS. which Mr. *Bowyer* drew up, for his own ufe, to various books. *J. N.*

Ih

In the same year Mr. *Bowyer* completed the first and second volumes of Lord *Lyttelton's* " History * of the Life and Reign " King *Henry* the Second," 4to; which had been ten years in the press. He also printed " Remains of *Japhet*; being " Historical Enquiries into the Affinity and Origin of the *Eu-* " *ropean* Languages, by *James Parsons* †, M. D. Member of

" the

* Of which see more particulars under the year 1771.

† This excellent physician and polite scholar was born at *Barnstaple*, in *Devonshire*, in *March*, 1705. His father, who was the youngest of nine sons of Colonel *Parsons*, and nearly related to the baronet of that name, being appointed barrack-master at *Bolton* in *Ireland*, removed with his family into that kingdom ‡ soon after the birth of his then only son § *James*, who received at *Dublin* the early part of his education, and, by the assistance of proper masters, laid a considerable foundation of classical and other useful learning, which enabled him to become tutor to Lord *Kingston*. Turning his attention to the study of medicine, he went afterwards to *Paris* ||, where (I now use his own words) " he followed the " most eminent professors in the several schools, as *Astruc*, *Dubois*, *Lemery*, and others ; " attended the Anatomical Lectures of the most famous [*Hunaud* and *De Cat*]; and Che- " micals at the King's Garden at *St. Come*. He followed the Physicians in both hospitals " of the *Hotel Dieu* and *La Charité*, and the Chemical Lectures and Demonstrations of " *Lemery* and *Boulduc* ; and in Botany, *Jussieu*. Having finished these studies, his Professors

‡ In the Preface to the Memoirs of *Japhet*, he says, " I spent several years of my life in *Ireland*, " and there attained to a tolerable knowledge in the very ancient tongue of that country, which ena- " bled me to consult some of their manuscripts, and become instructed in their grammatical institutes. " Afterwards I became acquainted with several gentlemen from *Wales*, well versed in their own " history and language ; men of sense and liberal learning ; who, in many conversations upon such " subjects, gave me such satisfaction and light, in matters of high antiquity, as to occasion my ap- " plication to the study of the *Welsh* tongue also : in which I had equal pleasure and surprize, when, " the more I enquired, the more nearly related the *Irish* and *Welsh* languages appeared. When I " was sent abroad to study the medicinal art, I frequently conversed with young gentlemen from " most parts of *Europe*, who came to *Paris*, and followed the same masters, in every branch of the " profession, with me ; and my surprize was agreeably increased in finding that, in every one of their " native tongues, I could discover the roots of most of their expressions in the *Irish* or *Welsh*."
§ He had afterwards another son (a surgeon) and a daughter, who were born in *Ireland*.
|| " Several great masters then gave lectures at that place on the several branches of physic, who " drew after them a great concourse of pupils of every nation. Mr. *Hunaud* read in Anatomy and " Surgery ; *Astruc* and *Dubois* in Physic ; *Lemery* and *Boulduc* taught Chemistry ; and the learned " *Jussieu* shewed the plants in the botanical garden, then one of the best stocked in *Europe*. Dr. " *Parsons* followed the courses of these eminent men, and contracted a friendship with most of them. " Forty years have made a great change in the state of the balance between our neighbours and " ourselves : *England*, and *London* in particular, formerly tributary to that kingdom for the education " of a multitude of young gentlemen, might now with greater right expect a return from that " country, being furnished with better opportunities, and surely not inferior professors in these dif- " ferent branches. It was undoubtedly during the course of these occupations that Dr. *Parsons* " imbibed his taste for Natural History. This amiable and interesting study, so congenial with " human curiosity, so proportioned to human abilities, so necessary to human wants, is besides so " intimately connected with physick, that it is almost impossible to cultivate the latter with any " success, without having at least some tincture of the former. In order to derive greater advan- " tages from the several curiosities which passed under his eyes, Dr. *Parsons* applied himself to the " art of drawing, and became so well versed in it, that ever after he was not obliged to have recourse " to any other hand but his own to illustrate his descriptions." Dr. *Maty*.

" gave

" the College of Physicians, and Fellow of the Royal and
" Antiquary

" gave him honourable attestations of his having followed them with diligence and industry,
" which entitled him to take the degrees of Doctor and Professor of the Art of Medicine,
" in any University in the dominions of *France*. Intending to return to *England*, he
" judged it unnecessary to take degrees in *Paris*, unless he had resolved to reside there ; and
" as it was more expensive, he therefore went to the University of *Rheims*, in *Champaign*,
" where, by virtue of his attestations, he was immediately admitted to three examina-
" tions, as if he had finished his studies in that academy ; and there was honoured with
" his degrees *June* 11, 1736. In the *July* following he came to *London*, and was soon
" employed by Dr. *James Douglas* to assist him in his anatomical works, where in some
" time he began to practise. He was elected a member of the Royal Society in 1740 ;
" and, after due examination, was admitted a Licentiate of the College of Physicians,
" *April* 1, 1751 ; paying college fees and bond stamps of different denominations to the
" amount of 41*l.* 2*s.* 8*d.* subject also to quarterage of two pounds *per annum*. In 1755
" he paid a farther sum of 7*l.* which, with the quarterage-money already paid, made up
" the sum of 16*l.* in lieu of all future payments." *Thus far from his own MS.*—On
his arrival in *London*, by the recommendation of his *Paris* friends, he was introduced to the
acquaintance of Dr. *Mead*, Sir *Hans Sloane*, and Dr. *James Douglas*. This great anatomist
made use of his assistance, not only in his anatomical preparations, but also in his representations of morbid and other appearances, a list of several of which was in the hands of his
friend Dr. *Maty*; who had prepared an Eloge on Dr. *Parsons*, which was never used, but
which, by the favour of Mrs. *Parsons*, I am enabled to preserve *. In 1738, by the
interest

* " Though Dr. *Parsons* cultivated the several branches of the profession of physic, he was princi-
" pally employed in the obstetrical line. He not only soon became an eminent practitioner in that
" way, but likewise read Lectures on the Structure of the Pelvis and Uterus, Generation, the Nutrition
" of the Fœtus, Hermaphrodites, Monstrous Births, the Diseases of Women in general before and
" after Delivery, the art of Midwifry, with all its necessary operations, explained by proper Anato-
" mical Preparations from Dr. *Douglas's* Collection. The first specimen (for we don't reckon his
" Syllabus to these Lectures, intituled ' Elenchus Gunaico-Pathologicus') which Dr. *Parsons* gave
" of his abilities and medical erudition, was occasioned by a pretended Hermaphrodite brought
" over to *London* from the Coast of *Angola*. The existence of human beings uniting in them the
" perfect characters and powers of both sexes is an opinion conceived in ages of darkness and super-
" stition, and supported by interest and imposture. In fact, none of them has hitherto stood the
" test of careful examination ; and so far from being, like some insects and most plants, furnished
" with double organs, they have universally proved vitiated men or women. This is, and was long
" known to anatomists ; yet as the vulgar, and amongst them perhaps people that ought to know
" better, may, or feign to be caught by the same appearances and impositions that seduced their
" ancestors, the attempt our author made to undeceive them, was by no means ill-judged. His
" treatise was intituled, ' A Mechanical and Critical Enquiry into the Nature of Hermaphrodites,
" by *James Parsons*, M. D. F. R. S. *London*, 1741,' in 8vo ; with several figures engraved from his
" own drawings. This subject has been since treated by other writers, who have added but little
" to the Historical and Anatomical part of our Author's Treatise. A short account of it, drawn
" up by himself, was inserted in the Philosophical Transactions of the Royal Society, of which some
" time before† he was become a member. In one of the subsequent volumes ‡ he described another

† In *May* 1740
‡ " A Letter to the President, concerning an Hermaphrodite shewn in *London*, 1750," Phil. Transf. Vol. XLVII.
" p. 142. Part ii. We likewise refer here to two other papers from our Author : " A Letter from Dr. *James Parsons*
" to *Martin Folkes*, Esq; President, containing an Account of a Præternatural Conjunction of two Female Children,
" with Observations on Monstrous Productions ; with copper-plates ; the Figures designed from the subject by the
" Doctor," Phil. Transf. N° 489. p. 526 ; and " An Account of a Sheep having a monstrous Horn hanging from his
" Neck," Phil. Transf. Vol. XLIX. Part i. p. 183. Our Author seems to have collected many facts relative to
" Monsters, with a view of obliging the world with a new treatise ; but we have found nothing sufficiently
" finished on that or any other subject." Dr. *Maty*.

" subject

" Antiquary Societies of *London*;" the laft publication of an old
and

intereft of his friend Dr. *Douglas*, he was appointed phyfician to the public Infirmary
in *St. Giles's*. In 1739 he married, at the parifh church of *St. Andrew; Holborn*, Mifs
Elizabeth Reynolds, by whom he had two fons and a daughter, who all died young.
Dr.

" fubjeft fhewn in *London* as an Hermaphrodite, but which he proved to have been but an imperfeft.
" female. To his medical abilities our late friend added a fcrupulous integrity and inflexible
" firmnefs when he thought he was right. This he fhewed, in refpeft to the celebrated Monf. *Le*
" *Cat* of *Rouen*, whofe Treatife upon the Senfes he analyfed for the Royal Society. Phil. Tranf.
" N° 466. p. 264. But Authors, like Beauties, are feldom perfeftly pleafed; for though the ac-
" count of the faid Treatife was upon the whole flattering, yet as fome miftakes were pointed out,
" efpecially with regard to the *Newtonian* Syftem of Colours, the *French* Anatomift wrote to the
" Doftor fome hafty and angry letters, which he anfwered in a decent but firm manner; and
" without giving up his judgement becaufe he was the friend of the gentleman he had ventured to
" find fault with. The fame love of truth engaged him, at the very time that Mrs. *Stephens's* me-
" dicines made the greateft noife, and met both with medical approbation and national reward, to
" refift the torrent, examine the evidence given in their favour, and produce feveral inftances in
" which they failed. This book was publifhed in the year 1742[*]; and, befides the polemical
" part, contained a new defcription, and figures of the bladder and urinary paffages. Dr. *Parfons*
" was introduced to the Royal Society as a Naturalift, in 1743, by their Prefident, the great *Martin*
" *Folkes*, Efq. That gentleman chofe our friend to help him in repeating the curious and nice Ex-
" periments of Monf. *Trembley* on the Frefh Water Polype; an account of which, drawn by his
" mafterly hand, was inferted in the Philofophical Tranfaftions. He failed not to make the moft
" honourable mention of his affiftant; and paffed a juft encomium upon the elegant drawings made
" to illuftrate his account[†]. Two curious papers delivered the fame year by Dr. *Parfons* had a place
" in that volume; the firft related to the fea calf, a fpecies of the Phoca[‡]; another fpecies of
" which he defcribed ten years after[§]. His fecond paper was a defcription of the Rhinoceros[||].
" His figure of this animal was particularly well received, as hitherto no good print of it had been
" publifhed[**]. The horn of the Rhinoceros is extremely remarkable, both on account of its pofi-
" tion upon the nofe, and a variety hinted at in the following line of *Martial*.
" *Namque gravem gemina cornu fic extulit urfum.*
" The reading indeed of this paffage has been correfted by fome learned commentators, who, in-
" ftead of fuppofing a bear to have been toffed up by a double horn, contended that two bears or
" two bulls were thrown up by a fingle one. But from a figure in the *Præneftan* Pavement, a medal
" of *Domitian*, a paffage in *Paufanias*, and the teftimony of *Kolbe*, who faw a Rhinoceros at the *Cape*
" *of Good Hope*, as well as from the infpeftion of fome double horns in Sir *Hans Sloane's* and other
" gentlemens' Mufeums, our Author afcertained the matter of faft, and ingenioufly, at leaft, ac-
" counted for it. In his opinion, the Rhinoceroffes known to the *Romans* came all from
" *Africa*, and were double-horned; whereas moft of thofe which have been from time to time fhewn
" in *Europe* were *Afiatics*, and fingle-horned. This explanation was adopted by Sir *Hans Sloane* him-
" felf; but, after all, we as yet know too little of this ftupendous animal, to determine pofitively
" whether this variety be due to the climate, the age, or any other particular of his life[††]. The ho-

---

[*] Speaking of Mrs. *Stephens's* remedy for the ftone, Dr. *Mead* fays, " Upon this fubjeft, I refer the reader to
" a very ufeful book, publifhed fome years fince by a fkilful anatomift and phyfician; in which both the mif-
" chiefs done by this medicine, and the artifices employed to bring it into vogue, are fet in a clear light."
[†] " Dr. *Parfons* likewife defigned the figures for the plate of Mr. *Freke's* Ambe for fetting Shoulder-bones,
" Phil. Tranf. N° 470. Tab. 4."
[‡] " Some Account of the Phoca, Vitulus Marinus, or Sea Calf, fhewed at *Charing-Crofs*, in *Feb.* 1742-3;
" Phil. Tranf. N° 469. with figures."
[§] " A Differtation upon the Clafs of Phocæ Marinæ. Phil. Tranf. Vol. XLVII. Part ii. p. 109.
[||] " A Letter from Dr. *Parfons* to *Martin Folkes*, Efq; Prefident of the Royal Society, containing the Natural
" Hiftory of the Rhinoceros. Read *June* 9, 1743, Phil. Tranf. N° 470, p. 523, with Figures." This being
controverted in Gent. Mag. vol. XXXVIII. p. 208, the Doftor replied to it in the fame volume, p. 268.
[**] Mrs. *Parfons* has ftill (1781) the beautiful painting of this animal, by the Doftor's hand; another painted
b him was in Dr. *Mead's* colleftion. *J. N.*
[††] Not to mention that double horns from *The Eaft Indies* are now aftually exifting in *England*.

" nour

and esteemed friend, for whom Mr. *Bowyer* had a very high
regard

Dr. *Parsons* resided for many years in *Red-Lion Square*, where he frequently enjoyed the
company and conversation of Dr. *Stukeley*, Bp. *Lyttelton*, Mr. *Henry Baker*, Dr. *Knight*, and
many

" nour which Dr. *Parsons* received on being appointed, by the Royal Society, to read the *Crounian*
" Lectures for several years, induced him to venture his Conjectures upon Muscular Motion *. Af-
" ter having overthrown the opinions of those who had gone before him (a task in this, as well as
" in many other physiological researches, by much the easiest) he endeavours to establish his own.
" This consists in attributing to the air, or an ethereal fluid, the inflation of the smallest muscular
" fibres, which he attempts to prove to be small tubes, running parallel with the nervous hollow
" fibrillæ, replete with that air, and discharging it into the muscular cells at the command of the
" will. This hypothesis, like all others, labours under many difficulties, and wants the support of
" facts. Our author was himself sensible of this defect, and ingenuously confessed the invention of
" any more such systems to be a labour as much in vain as the punishment of *Sisyphus*. The publick
" were however obliged to him, for having added to his theory a good description of the womb,
" illustrated with some figures from his own dissections. Besides these Muscular Lectures, the vo-
" lume for the year 1745 was enriched with three shorter, though perhaps not less curious, com-
" munications. The first contained a Specimen of his Researches into the Structure of Vegetable
" Seeds †; the second described some Curious Pebbles, or Crystals, from *Gibraltar*, cut in irre-
" gular forms, and exquisitely polished by the hands of Nature ‡; and the third presented a View
" and accurate Description of an *East Indian* Deer §, called the Biggel ‖. The next year was still
" more fruitful in interesting productions. Dr. *Parsons* seems to have been the first in *London* who
" gave musk with a liberal hand at the close of a fever long neglected, and attended with the worst
" symptoms. And his account of the case ** encouraged other practitioners to follow his example.
" He likewise imparted to the publick some judicious Observations on the Danger of burying Infected
" Cows ††, as was then the practice, with Quick Lime ‡‡. He philosophically, as well as anatomical-
" ly, accounted in a third paper for the Phænomenon of the Woman who partly preserved the power
" of speaking, though deprived of a great part of her Tongue §§. But his principal performance at

* " The *Crounian* Lectures on Muscular Motion for the Years 1744 and 1745. Read before the Royal
" Society; being a Supplement to the Philosophical Transactions for those Years, 1745," 4to.
† Phil. Transf. N° 466. p. 264.
‡ " An Account of certain perfect minute double-pointed Crystals, brought from the cloven rocks of
" *Gibraltar*, with a Figure by Dr. *Parsons*. Phil. Transf. N° 476, p. 463."
§ " An Account of a Quadruped brought from *Bengal*, and now to be seen in *London*, in *January*, 1745, by
" Dr. *James Parsons*, with a Figure of the Animal drawn by himself from the Life. Phil. Transf. N° 476,
" p. 465."
‖ Indostan Antelope. *Pennant*, Synops. Quadruped. 20, p. 29. " Dr. *Parsons*," says the Author of this
" excellent work, " to whom we are of late years obliged for the best Zoologic Papers in the Phil. Transf. is the
" only Writer who has described this animal."
** " A singular case of a malignant fever cured by administering musk in a considerable quantity. Phil. Transf.
" N° 478, p. 75. That his researches in Natural Philosophy did not prevent his taking notice of curious ob-
" servations in the different branches of his art, likewise appears from the following paper: An Account of
" some very extraordinary Tumors upon the head of a young labouring man in *Bartholomew's Hospital*, with
" Figures drawn by the Doctor from the life. Phil. Transf. Vol. L. Part i. p. 396." Mrs. *Parsons* has still
the fine original drawing by the Doctor's own hand.
†† It was a remark of Dr. *Parsons*, at a meeting of the Royal Society, " that the cattle in the high grounds
" about *Highgate*, *Hampstead*, *Millhill*, and *Hendon*, remained free from the infection, which had spread all about
" in the lower ground."
‡‡ " An Account of the Effects from burying Cows with Quick Lime, which died of the Distemper among
" horned Cattle, with Observations. Phil. Transf. N° 480, p. 224. In the following Number, Dr. *Parsons* il-
" lustrated a paper from a friend with one of his drawings, being two figures of an extraordinary schirrous Ute-
" rus, illustrating Dr. *Templeman's* Account of the Patient he attended in the Infirmary of *St. Andrew's* Work-
" house, drawn from the subject by Dr. *Parsons*. Phil. Transf. N° 481. p. 285. He likewise obliged the late
" Bishop of *Carlisle* with two views of a beautiful Nautilus, inserted in the Phil. Transf. N° 487. p. 320."
§§ " A Physiological Account of the Case of *Margaret Cutting*, who speaks distinctly, though she has lost
" the Apex and Body of her Tongue, with Explanations of the Phænomenon, addressed to the Royal Society,
" by *James Parsons*. Phil. Transf. N° 484. p. 627." Much has been said lately of this woman in Gent. Mag.
for 1781.

" that

regard, and to whofe memory I am happy to infcribe a
biogra-

many other of the moſt diſtinguiſhed members of the Royal and Antiquarian Societies, and
that of Arts, Manufactures, and Commerce ; giving weekly an elegant dinner to a large but
ſelect

" that time was his ' Human Phyſiognomy explained, in the *Crounian* Lectures on Muſcular Motion
" for the year 1746, printed as a Supplement to the Tranſactions of that year, 4to, 1747. This
" Eſſay has the merit of originality, being an attempt to ſhew by what mechaniſm the ſeveral
" muſcles of the face impreſs upon it the various ſentiments of the ſoul, and moſtly leave inde-
" lible traces of the reigning paſſions. It was favourably received abroad ; and the celebrated
" *Buffon*, after having made an honourable mention of the author, borrowed from him his figures
" and his thoughts upon the ſubject. One of the papers which I mentioned before gave riſe to a
" new work, intituled, ' Microſcopical Theatre of Seeds,' 1745 *, in 4to. Theſe Seeds, which, to a
" naked eye, appear, except in colour and ſize, not very different one from another, exhibit,
" when magnified, the richeſt diſplay of variety and grandeur ; no two are found exactly ſimilar ;
" and the elegance of the forms, multiplicity of the internal parts, variety of ſubſtance lodged ſepa-
" rately in the inſide, ſhew how inexhauſtible the fund is from which Nature draws her patterns.
" As Dr. *Parſons* was very particular in his deſcription and repreſentation of theſe minute objects,
" he furniſhed not only a ſource of entertainment to thoſe who know how to beſtow their admira-
" tion, but likewiſe the means of diſtinguiſhing genuine and ſcarce ſeeds from thoſe that may be
" either ſpurious or ſpoiled. I could have wiſhed, that, contented with the merit which was en-
" tirely his own, he had not added to each deſcription, under the title of *Uſes*, the farrago of pro-
" perties attributed to them by various authors, without ſufficiently diſtinguiſhing the reſults of
" experience from the effects of imagination ; which poſſibly hindered this valuable work from meet-
" ing with ſufficient encouragement to induce the author to complete his plan. He indeed, before
" his death, intended to reſume it ; and being then come to an age in which the little glory ariſing
" from extenſive reading had loſt much of its influence, he probably would have rendered his Trea-
" tiſe more univerſally pleaſing, by reducing it within the bounds of his own obſervations. The
" ſurpriſing variety of branches, which Dr. *Parſons* embraced, and the ſeveral living as well as
" dead languages he had a knowledge of, qualified him abundantly for the place of Aſſiſtant Se-
" cretary for foreign correſpondences, which the Council of the Royal Society beſtowed upon him
" about the year 1750. He acquitted himſelf to the utmoſt of his power of the functions of this
" place, till a few years before his death, when he reſigned in favour of his friend, who now grate-
" fully pays this laſt tribute to his memory. Dr. *Parſons* joined to his academical honours thoſe
" which the Royal College of Phyſicians of *London* beſtowed upon him, by admitting him, after due
" examination, Licentiate, on the firſt day of *April*, 1751. The diffuſive ſpirit of our friend was
" only equalled by his deſire of information. To both theſe principles he owed the intimacies
" which he formed with ſome of the greateſt men of his time. The names of *Folkes, Hales, Mead,*
" *Stukeley, Needham, Baker, Collinſon,* and *Garden,* may be mentioned on this occaſion ; and many more
" might be added. Weekly meetings were formed, where the earlieſt intelligence was received and
" communicated of any diſcovery both here and abroad ; and new trials were made to bring to the teſt
" of experience the reality or uſefulneſs of theſe diſcoveries. Here it was that the Microſcopical Animals
" found in ſeveral infuſions were firſt produced ; the propagation of ſeveral inſects by ſection aſcer-
" tained ; the conſtancy of Nature amidſt theſe wonderful changes eſtabliſhed. In order to deſtroy the
" concluſions deduced from the phænomena of the Polypes in favour of Materialiſm, Dr. *Parſons*
" compoſed his ' Philoſophical Obſervations on the Analogy between the Propagation of Animals
" and that of Vegetables †, *London*, 1752,' in 8vo. Our author places the firſt rudiments either of

* " The Microſcopical Theatre of Seeds, being a ſhort view of the particular marks, characters, con-
" tents, and natural dimenſions of all the Seeds of the Shops, Flower and Kitchen Gardens, with Copper
" Plates of the Figures of the Seeds of an intelligible ſize, publiſhed in numbers, in the year 1744. 4to. Vo-
" lume the firſt only."

† This volume was inſcribed to Dr. *Sherlock,* Biſhop of *London,* who tells him, in a letter from *The Temple,*
Dec. 16, 1751, " I am very ſenſible of the honour you intend me, by inſcribing your book to me : the ſubject
" of which is not only curious, but of great importance to the defence of religion ; and will, I doubt not,
" appear with great advantage coming from your hand. I am forced to make uſe of another hand in writing,
" therefore will ſay no more, but I ſhall be very glad of any opportunity of ſeeing you, and if conſiſtent with
" your buſineſs, I ſhall be very much obliged to you if you would give me the pleaſure of ſeeing you here. I
" am, Sir, your very humble ſervant, THOMAS, LONDON."

7   " plants

biographical note, related on his own authority, and that of his friends and family.

select party. He enjoyed also the literary correspondence of *D'Argenville, Buffon, Le Cat, Beccaria,*

" plants or animals in the seeds or eggs, which he supposes by the intervention of the masculine
" vivifying spirit to be brought into action, and rendered capable of producing new individuals in a
" successive chain, according to the immutable laws impressed by the Creator upon each species.
" But, to own the truth, this book, though abounding in good and useful hints, seems still to want
" something in point of order, clearness, and philosophical precision. We view Dr. *Parsons* with
" more pleasure when he is describing natural objects, or occupied in communicating valuable ob-
" servations. Thus his description of one of the smallest Monkeys *; the Syah Gush †, or *Persian*
" Mountain Cat; a new Salamander ‡; his Accounts of the Formation of Crabs Shells § and Co-
" rallines ‖; of an unknown Species of the Echinus petrified **; of Fossil Fruits ††; a singular Shell
" Fish piercing the hardest Stones, and lodging itself in them ‡‡; and even his Observations and
" Thoughts on a White Negroe §§; on Amphibious Animals ‖‖; the Construction of the Aspera
" Arteria in Cranes ***, &c. afford a still greater satisfaction than his well-meant efforts to pry into
" the mysteries of generation, or to ascertain the migration of the first inhabitants of the world.
" The book I have in view was published in 1767, in one large volume in 4to, under the
" title of ' Remains of *Japhet*, being Historical Enquiries into the Affinity and Origin of the
" *European* Languages.'—It is a most laborious performance, tending to prove the antiquity
" of the first inhabitants of these islands, as being originally descended from *Gomer* and
" *Magog*, above 1000 years before *Christ*, their primitive and still subsisting language, and its affinity
" with some others. It cannot be denied but that there is much ingenuity as well as true learning
" in this work, which helps conviction, and often supplies the want of it. But we cannot help thinking
" that our friend's warm feelings now and then mislead his judgement, and that some at least of his
" conjectures, resting upon partial traditions, and poetical scraps of *Irish* Filids and *Welsh* Bards,
" are less satisfactory than his Tables of Affinity between the several Northern Languages, as de-
" duced from one common stock. Literature, however, is much obliged to him for having in this,
" as well as in many of his other works, opened a new field of observations and discoveries. In
" enumerating our learned friend's Dissertations, we find ourselves at a loss whether we should fol-
" low the order of subjects, or of time; neither is it easy to account for their surprising variety and
" quick succession. The truth is, that his eagerness after knowledge was such, as to embrace almost
" with equal facility all its branches, and with equal zeal to ascertain the merit of inventions, and
" ascribe to their respective, and sometimes unknown, authors, the glory of the discovery. Many

* " An Account of the Cagui Minor, a very small Monkey communicated to *Martin Folkes*, Esq; President
" of the Royal Society, with the figure. Phil. Trans. Vol. XLVII. Part ii. p. 146."
† " Siah-Ghush, or Black Ear: *Pennant*, Synops. Quadruped. 137. p. 189. Le Caracal de *Buffon*, Tab. IX.
" p. 262. Tab. XXIV."
‡ " Some Account the Animal sent from *The East Indies* by General *Clive* to his Royal Highness the Duke of
" *Cumberland*, with a figure from the life, drawn in the Town of *London*, by Dr. *Parsons*. Phil. Trans.
" Vol. XLVII. Part ii. p. 684."
§ " Observations upon the Shells of Crabs, &c. in a Letter to Mr. *Peter Collinson*. Phil. Trans. Vol. XLVII.
" Part ii. p. 439."
‖ " A Letter to the Rev. Dr. *Birch*, upon the Formation of Corals, Corallines, &c. Vol. XLVII. Part ii.
" p. 505.
** " On a petrified Echinus, shewed to the Royal Society by Dr. *Pocock*. Phil. Trans. Vol. XLIX.
" Part ii. p. 155."
†† Dr. *Parsons* gave a particular account of several fossil fruits and other bodies of *Shepey Island*, with two
copper plates designed by himself, in the fiftieth volume of the Phil. Trans. Part i. p. 396, mentioned lately by
Mr. *Jones* in his " Physiological Disquisitions," p. 381.
‡‡ " Dr. *Parsons's* Letter to *Martin Folkes*, Esq; LL.D. President of the Royal Society, containing some ob-
" servations upon certain shell fish (lodged in a large stone brought from *Nichon* Harbour, by Mr. *Samuel More*,
" purser of the *Sterling Castle* man of war.) Phil. Trans. Nº 485. p. 44. called by the Doctor *M. ulus cylin-*
" *droides*, or *Mytulus Dactyliformis*."
§§ " Phil. Trans. Vol. LV. p. 45.   ‖‖ Ibid. Vol. LVI. p. 194.   *** Ibid. p. 208.

" operations,

" operations, which the ancients have transmitted to us, have been thought fabulous, merely from
" our ignorance of the art by which they were performed. Thus the burning of the ships of the
" *Romans* at a considerable distance, during the Siege of *Syracuse*, by *Archimedes*, would, perhaps,
" still continue to be exploded, had not the celebrated M. *Buffon* in *France* shewn the possibility
" of it, by presenting and describing a Model of a Speculum, or rather Assemblage of Mirrors, by
" which he could set fire at the distance of several hundred feet. In the contriving indeed, though
" not in the executing of such an apparatus, he had in some measure been forestalled by a writer
" now very little known or read. This Dr. *Parsons* proved in a very satisfactory manner* ; and he
" had the pleasure to find the *French* Philosopher did not refuse to the Jesuit his share in the invention;
" and was not at all offended by the liberty he had taken. Another *French* discovery, I mean a
" new kind of painting fathered upon the ancients, was reduced to its real value, in a paper †which
" shewed our Author was possessed of a good taste for the fine arts : and I am informed, that his
" skill in music was by no means inferior, and that his favourite amusement was the flute. Richly,
" it appears from these performances, did our Author merit the honour of being a member of the
" Antiquarian Society, which long ago had associated him to its labours. To another Society,
" founded upon the great principles of humanity, patriotism, and natural emulation, he undoubted-
" ly was greatly useful ‡. He assisted at most of their general meetings and committees ; and was
" for many years chairman to that of Agriculture ; always equally ready to point out and to pro-
" mote useful improvements, and to oppose the interested views of fraud and ignorance, so insepa-
" rable from very extensive associations. No sooner was THIS SOCIETY ‖ formed, than Dr. *Parsons*
" became a member of it. Intimately convinced of the nobleness of its views, though from his station
" in life little concerned in its success, he grudged neither attendance nor expence. Neither ambi-
" tious of taking the lead, nor fond of opposition ; he joined in any measure he thought right; and
" submitted chearfully to the sentiments of the majority, though against his own private opinion.
" The just ideas he had of the dignity of our profession, as well as of the common links which ought
" to unite all its members, notwithstanding the differences of country, religion, or places of education,
" made him bear impatiently the shackles laid upon a great number of respectable practitioners; he
" wished, fondly wished, to see these broken ; not with a view of empty honour and dangerous
" power, but as the only means of serving mankind more effectually, checking the progress of de-
" signing men and illiterate practitioners, and diffusing through the whole body a spirit of emula-
" tion. Though by frequent disappointments he foresaw, as well as we, the little chance of a

* " Observations on Father *Kircher's* Opinion concerning the burning the Fleet of *Marcellus* at *Syracuse*.
" Phil. Transf. Vol. XLVIII. part ii. p. 628."
† " Observations on the Count *de Caylus's* Opinion concerning Encaustic Painting. Phil. Transf. Vol. XLIX.
" Part II. p. 655."
‡ " The Society for the Encouragement of Arts, Manufactures, and Commerce. He likewise was associated to
" the Oeconomical Society at *Bern*, Dec. 26, 1763. The letter he received on this occasion, dated *Jan.* 2, 1764,
" was conceived in these very honourable terms : ' Le choix que l'illustre Societé dont vous etes un si digne mem-
" bre a fait de vous pour vous mettre à la tête d'un departement aussi interessant & aussi etendu que l'est celui de
" l'Agriculture, a guidé notre Societé, qui en fait l'object principal de ses recherches & de ses travaux,
" quand elle vous associa à elles. Recevèz ce Diplome c'y joint, Monsieur, comme une marque des sentiments
" qu'elle donne à ceux qui se distinguent parmi les hommes, par leurs vertus & leurs labours ; ce sont des pa-
" triotes qui d'un choix libre s'associent tous ceux qui comme eux sacrifient leurs vies au bonheur de la patrie &
" de l'humanité. La Societé a cru ne pouvoir mieux faire que de vous associer Monsieur *Wyche*, votre illustre
" frere, qu'une mort premature vient, à ce que j'apprens, enlever à sa patrie, à votre Societé, & à ses amis. J'ai
" l'honneur d'etre, &c.   N. E. TSCHARNE, Secrétaire de la Societé."
" Dr. *Parsons's* answer, dated *Feb.* 28, 1764, was this : ' A l'instant que j'ai eu l'honneur de recevoir votre
" agreable Lettre, avec le Diplome de votre illustre Societé, je ne me laissois pas d'etre frappé d'une gratitude, &
" des sentiments tres vifs, en etant distingué d'une marque de son estime aussi glorieuse qu' interessante à mon
" gré. C'est un fait, Monsieur, que j'estimerai toujours encore un des plus heureux accidents de ma vie : c'est
" un honneur qui augment beaucoup le caractere & la reputation que chacun doit souhaiter qui aime l'huma-
" niné, & qui voudroit bien rendre service au publique. Ayez donc la bonté, Monsieur, de me faire la grace de
" temoigner à l'illustre Societé de Berne ma reconnoissance pour ce grand honneur qu'elle vient de me faire,
" & dont l'impression ne me sera jamais effacé. J'ai l'honour d'etre, &c.
                " J. PARSONS, President dans les department de l'Agriculture de la Societé des Arts; Membre
                        " de la Societé Royale & Antiq. de London, & du College Royal de Med."
‖ A Medical Society instituted by Dr. *Fothergill* and other respectable Physicians, Licentiates, in vindication
of their privileges.

" speedy

others of the moſt diſtinguiſhed rank in ſcience *. As a practitioner, he was judicious, careful, honeſt, and remarkably humane to the poor ; as a friend, obliging and communicative ; chearful and decent in converſation ; ſevere and ſtrict in his morals, and attentive to fulfil with propriety all the various duties of life. In 1769, finding his health impaired

"ſpeedy redreſs, he nobly perſiſted in the attempt; and, had he lived to the final event, would un-
"doubtedly, like *Cato*, ſtill have preferred the conquered cauſe to that ſupported by the Gods. Af-
"ter having tried to retire from buſineſs and from *London*, for the ſake of his health, and having
"diſpoſed of moſt of his books with that view, he found it inconſiſtent with his happineſs to forſake all
"the advantages which a long reſidence in the capital, and the many connexions he had formed, had
"rendered habitual to him. He therefore returned to his old houſe, and died in it, after a ſhort
"illneſs, *April 4*, 1770. The ſtyle of our friend's compoſitions was ſufficiently clear in deſcription,
"though in argument not ſo cloſe as could have been wiſhed. Full of his ideas, he did not always
"ſo diſpoſe and connect them together as to produce in the mind of his readers that conviction
"which was in his own. He too much deſpiſed thoſe additional graces which command attention
"when joined to learning, obſervation, and ſound reaſoning. Let us hope that his example and
"ſpirit will animate all his colleagues; and that thoſe practitioners who are in the ſame circum-
"ſtances will be induced to join their brethren, ſure to find amongſt them thoſe great bleſſings of
"life, freedom, equality, information, and friendſhip. As long as theſe great principles ſhall ſub-
"ſiſt in this Society, and I truſt they will out-laſt the longeſt liver, there is no doubt but the mem-
"bers will meet with the reward honeſt men are ambitious of, the approbation of their conſcience,
"the eſteem of the virtuous, the remembrance of poſterity."

* Mrs. *Parſons* has ſtill ſeveral letters ſubſcribed by the illuſtrious names above-mentioned; and one from Dr. *Garden* ſhall be here inſerted: "Though I have not the honour of your perſonal
"acquaintance, yet it is with great pleaſure and gratitude that I can acknowledge an acquaintance
"with your learned and ingenious works, to which I have been indebted for many uſeful things,
"and have peruſed ſuch of them as have fallen in my way with no leſs pleaſure than profit. What
"I have yet had the pleaſure of ſeeing are ſome papers in the Transactions, and *The Analogy of*
"*Animals and Vegetables*. This was a performance I had long wiſhed to ſee, and lately was
"ſo lucky as to meet with it. Since which time, I could not help reſolving to addreſs the
"Learned Author, and humbly beg the favour of his correſpondence, that I might have an oppor-
"tunity from time to time of laying open my difficulties in any enquiries of that kind to him, and
"begging his aſſiſtance and advice At the ſame time I muſt own I am but poorly qualified to make
"proper and ſuitable returns for ſuch a favour; but if any accounts of any of our Vegetable, Ani-
"mal, or Mineral Productions would be acceptable, I ſhould take the greateſt and moſt ſenſible
"pleaſure to procure or make out ſuch as might be agreeable of ſuch things as may fall under my
"notice. It is now about three years and an half ſince I firſt arrived in *South Carolina*, where I
"have practiſed Phyſic ever ſince, and employed every ſpare hour in Botany; but my progreſs has
"been much retarded for want of the proper books and aſſiſtances. There is only my learned and
"ingenious friend the Honourable Dr. *Bull*, who knows the leaſt Iota of Botany or any part of
"Natural Hiſtory here, which, with my ſmall Botanical Library (which only conſiſted of *Tourne-*
"*fort*, *Ray*, and *Lin. Fund. Botan.* with the *Flora Virgin. Gron.*), was a great hindrance and loſs to a
"beginner. I have lately had a copy of all *Linnæus's* Works, except the late performance of the
"*Species Plantarum*, which I have only juſt heard of in a Letter from a *German* Correſpondent.
"This laſt year I was obliged to leave *Carolina*, and go to the Northern Colonies, in ſearch of a
"cooler and freer air, on the account of health; and as ſoon as my health and ſtrength would per-
"mit; I travelled over moſt of the adjacent countries in ſearch of their Vegetable Productions, and
"met with many curious things, ſome of which we have not here. In the Province of *New York*
"I met with the Honourable *Cadwallader Colden*, a truly great Philoſopher and very accurate and
"ingenious Botaniſt; as witneſs his Philoſophical performances, and his Genera Plantarum; publiſhed
"in the *Acta Upſalienſa*. I could not help being greatly pleaſed, and at the ſame time chagrined, at
"the account which he gave me of Dr. *Kalm* the *Swede*, who is juſt now publiſhing his Collections,
"made in our Colonies, in the *Swediſh* Language, by the particular deſire of his King. This will
"not only give them the glory and honour of ſuch public undertakings, but the ſole advantage of
"what obſervations he may have made. This looks as if we muſt be obliged to ſtrangers to point
"out our own richneſs, and ſhew us the advantages of what we ourſelves poſſeſs. Something ſi-
"milar to this will ſoon be ſeen in Dr. *Loefling's* Voyage to our Iſlands and the *Spaniſh* Main, eſpe-
"cially while he is to be ſupported by the Royal Bounty. And have not we lands that would
"produce moſt of theſe vegetables that the *Spaniards* juſt now reap ſuch advantage from ? Yes,
"ſurely we have; but as we are ignorant of the proper method of curing and manufacturing them,
"our

paired, he proposed to retire from business and from *London*, and with that view disposed of a considerable number of his books and fossils, and went to *Bristol.* But he returned soon after to his old house, and died in it after a week's illness, on the 4th of *April,* 1770, to the inexpressible grief of his afflicted wife and sister-in-law, and many of his intimate friends, to whom his memory will always be precious. By his last will, dated in *October*, 1766, he gave his whole property to Mrs. *Parsons*; and, in case of her death before him, to Miss *Mary Reynolds*, her only sister, " in recompence for her " affectionate attention to him and to his wife, for a long course of years, in sickness and " in health." It was his particular request, that he should not be buried till some change should appear in his corpse ; a request which occasioned his being kept unburied 17 days, and even then scarce the slightest alteration was perceivable. He was buried at *Hendon*, in a vault which he had caused to be built on the ground purchased on the death of his son *James*, where his tomb is thus inscribed :

" Here,
Taken from his sorrowing Family and Friends
By the common lot of frail Humanity,
Rests JAMES PARSONS, M.D.
Member of The College of Physicians,
and F. R. S. and S. of A.
A Man,
In whom the most dignifying Virtues were united
with Talents the most numerous and rare.
Firm and erect in conscious conviction,
No consideration could move him
To desert Truth, or acquiesce to her Opponents.
Physick, Anatomy, Natural History, Antiquities,
Languages, and the fine Arts,
Are largely indebted to his skill and industry
in each ;

For many important Truths discovered in their
Support,
Or Errors detected with which they were obscured.
Yet, though happy beyond the general Race of
Mankind in mental endowments,
The sincere Christian, the affectionate Husband,
The generous and humane Friend,
Were in him superior to the sage Scholar and
Philosopher.
He died *April* 4th, 1770,
in the 66th year of his age.

Here also lies the Body of JAMES PARSONS,
Son of the above named Dr. PARSONS,
who died *Dec.* 9. 1750,
in the ninth Year of his Age."

A portrait of Dr. *Parsons*, by Mr. *Wilson*, is now in *The British Museum* ; another, by *Wells*, in the hands of his widow, with a third unfinished ; and one of is son *James*; also a family piece, in which the same son is introduced, with the Doctor and his lady, accompanied by her sister. Among many other portraits, Mrs. *Parsons* has fine ones of the illustrious *Harvey*, of Bp. *Burnet*, and of Dr. *John Freind*; a beautiful miniature of Dr. *Stukeley*; some good paintings, by her husband's own hand, particularly the Rhinoceros, which he described in the Philosophical Transactions. She is also possessed of his Mss. and some capital printed books ; a large folio volume, intitled, " Figuræ " quædam Miscellaneæ quæ ad rem Anatomicam * Historiamque Naturalem spectant ;
" quas

" our people are deterred from running the risk of losing money, labour, or time, in this slow " way of getting knowledge of them by experiment, while they have some other commodities that " answer tolerably well in the mean time.—Mr. *Clayton* in *Virginia*, and *John Bartram* in *Pensyl-* " *vania*, are the only Botanists or Naturalists that I know of, besides Mr. *Colden* on the Continent. " And I doubt not but you are well acquainted with the character and genius of both these men. " Mr. *Bartram* is certainly a most surprising man, who, without any assistance of conversation or of " books, (he understands a very little botanical *Latin*), should have arrived at so great a knowledge " of Plants, especially in a systematical way. It is a great pity that he does not understand Mr. " *Loefling's* Dissertation on Gems ; for I am fully persuaded he is amongst the best-qualified men to " improve that part of the science. How often have I been pleased, delighted, and instructed, by " many of his lively and strong natural thoughts on Gems, as to their *structure, use, time*, and pro- " perties ! I shall not detain you longer, but again beg leave to request the favour of your corre- " spondence, and your forgiveness for this trouble. I am, with great esteem, Sir, your most obedient " and very humble servant,
ALEXANDER GARDEN.
" *Charles Town, South Carolina*, May 5, 1755."

The

The other books of 1767 were the third volume of Mr.
Hooke's * " *Roman* Hiftory," 4to ; the feventh, eighth, and
ninth

" quas propriâ adumbravit manu *Jacobus Parfons*, M. D. S. S. R. Ant. &c." another,
called " Drawings of curious Foffils, Shells, &c. in Dr. *Parfons's* Collection, drawn
" by himfelf † ;" a fett of the fine prints engraved at the expence of Mr. *Hollis* ‡, whofe
character Dr. *Parfons* has thus briefly depicted :

" Memorabilium quorundam Monumenta, quæ curâ & fumptibus eximii viri *Thomæ*
    " *Hollifii* Armigeri nuper prodierunt ; quæque mihi grato animo dono dedit.
    " Tanti autem viri munera mihi fanè funt gratiffima : qui dum vitam placidè
    " inter ftudia politiora atque humano generi utiliffima, femper trahit, non majo-
    " ribus affentator fervilis, nec inferioribus eft arrogans ; omnibus tamen gratus,
    " neque unquam abfentem rodit amicum.   *J. P.* 18 *Julii*, 1764."

Mrs. *Parfons*, I can add with certainty, if properly applied to, is ready to give, either
to the Royal or Antiquarian Society, a portrait of her worthy hufband, and a fum of
money to found a lecture to perpetuate his memory, fimilar to that eftablifhed by his
friend Mr. *Henry Baker*.

* The great abilities of Mr. *Hooke*, and the high rank he juftly holds in the Republick of
Letters, demand a much more particular account of him than I am able to fupply.
The earlieft particulars of his life that I have met with are furnifhed by himfelf, in a
modeft, but manly, addrefs to the Earl of *Oxford*, dated *Oct.* 17, 1722, which I believe
has never before been publifhed : " My Lord, The firft time I had the honour to wait
" upon your Lordfhip fince your coming to *London*, your Lordfhip had the goodnefs to
" afk me, what way of life I was then engaged in ; a certain *mauvaife honte* hindered
" me at that time from giving a direct anfwer. The truth is, my Lord, I cannot be
" faid at prefent to be in any form of life, but rather to live extempore. The late epi-
" demical diftemper feized me §, I endeavoured to be rich, imagined for a while that I
" was, and am in fome meafure happy to find myfelf at this inftant but juft worth nothing.
" If your Lordfhip, or any of your numerous friends, have need of a fervant, with the
" bare qualifications of being able to read and write, and to be honeft, I fhall gladly

† I have been indulged with a fight of thefe valuable drawings. Amongft other curiofities, is
an exact delineation of a human fœtus, which was the fubject of an extraordinary impofture,; the
upper part being well made, and in good proportion, the lower extremities monftrous. It was inclofed in a glafs-cafe, and fhewn at *The Heathcock, Charing Crofs*, as " a furprifing young Mermaid
" taken on the coaft of *Acapulco*." This figure the Doctor drew ; and caufed the fhow-man to
be turned out of town.

‡ Dr. *Parfons* having fent Mr. *Hollis* fome prefent in return for thefe valuable prints, received
a reply, dated *Auguft* 21, 1764, which is worth preferving, as characteriftic of the writer : " I return
" you my thanks for a curious and obliging prefent, which was received this day, and is already de-
" pofited amidft my other choiceft virtù. A number of the prints from the plates in my poffeffion
" having been lately ftricken off, and the laft fet having feemed not unacceptable to you, I have
" taken the liberty to fend you another fet of them, for, if you pleafe, a friend. My time, I con-
" fefs, has been greatly engaged, and even fineffed on to certain purpofes, honeft ones it is hoped,
" for years paft ; but thofe purpofes will have their end before it is long, and then I fhall be able
" to partake again, happily, in the fociety of my friends, and of wife and good men. I am, with
" unfeigned and deep refpect, Sir, your moft obedient humble fervant,   T. HOLLIS."
I fhall add to this letter a fhort extract from the biographers of Mr. *Hollis* : " Paid four guineas, the
" full fubfcription for fix copies of the Remains of *Japhet*, by Dr. *James Parfons* ; burnt five of the
" fubfcriptions. We give this memorandum juft as we find it, being uncertain whether a friendly
" partiality for the author, or the fubject, was the motive of this generous fubfcription. It is cer-
" tain, that there are pofitions in that book from which, we apprehend, Mr. *Hollis* would diffent."
Memoirs, p. 495.
§ The *South Sea* infatuation.

E e e

" under-

ninth volumes of the same excellent work in 8vo; " The

" Natu-

" undertake any employments your Lordship shall not think me unworthy of. I have
" been taught, my Lord, that neither a man's natural pride, nor his self-love, is an
" equal judge of what is fit for him; and I shall endeavour to remember, that it is not
" the short part we act, but the manner of our performance, which gains or loses us the
" applause of him who is finally to decide of all human actions. My Lord, I am just
" now employed in translating, from the *French*, a History of the Life of the late Arch-
" bishop of *Cambray*; and I was thinking to beg the honour of your Lordship's name
" to protect a work which will have so much need of it. The original is not yet pub-
" lished. 'Tis written by the Author of the ' Discourse upon Epic Poetry,' in the new
" edition of *Telemaque*. As there are some passages in the book of a particular nature,
" I dare not solicit your Lordship to grant me the favour I have mentioned, till you
" first have perused it. The whole is short, and pretty fairly transcribed. If your
" Lordship could find a spare hour to look it over, I would wait upon your Lordship
" with it, as it may possibly be no unpleasing entertainment. I should humbly ask your
" Lordship's pardon for so long an address in a season of so much business. But when
" should I be able to find a time in which your Lordship's goodness is not employed?
" I am, with perfect respect and duty, my Lord, your Lordship's most obliged, most
" faithful, and most obedient humble servant, NATHANIEL HOOKE." The translation
here spoken of was afterwards printed in 12mo, 1723. From this period till his death
Mr. *Hooke* enjoyed the confidence and patronage of men not less distinguished by
virtue than by titles. In 17... he published a translation of *Ramsey's* Travels of *Cyrus*,
in 4to; in 1733 he revised a translation of " The History of the Conquest of *Mexico*
" by the *Spaniards*, by *Thomas Townsend*, Esq;" printed in 2 vols. 8vo *; and in the same
year he published, in 4to, the first volume † of " The *Roman* History, from the building
" of *Rome* to the ruin of the Commonwealth; illustrated with maps and other plates."
In the dedication to this volume, Mr. *Hooke* took the opportunity of " publicly testifying
" his just esteem for a worthy friend ‡ to whom he had been long and much obliged," by
telling Mr. *Pope* that the displaying of his name at the head of those sheets was " like
" hanging out a splendid sign, to catch the traveller's eye, and entice him to make trial of
" the entertainment the place affords. But," he proceeds, " when I can write under my
" sign that Mr. *Pope* has been here, and was content, who will question the goodness of the
" house?" The volume is introduced by " Remarks on the History of the Seven *Roman*
" Kings, occasioned by Sir *Isaac Newton's* Objections to the supposed 244 years duration §
" of the Royal State of *Rome*." His nervous pen was next employed in digesting " An
" Account of the Conduct of the Dowager Dutchess of *Marlborough*, from her first com-
" ing to Court, to the Year 1710. In a Letter from Herself to Lord ——. 1742." 8vo. His
reward, on this occasion, was considerable; and the reputation he acquired by the per-

* First printed in 1724. fol.
† A *third* edition of this volume was printed in 1757.
‡ This friendship extended to the close of our *English Homer's* life. " *Pope*," says Dr. *Johnson*,
" expressed undoubting confidence of a future state. Being asked by his friend Mr. *Hooke*, a papist,
" whether he would not die like his father and mother, and whether a priest should not be called,
" he answered, *I do not think it essential, but it will be very right; and I thank you for putting me in*
" *mind of it*." Mr. *Hooke*, on this occasion, told Dr. *Warburton*, " that the priest, whom he had
" provided to do the last office to the dying man, came out from him, penetrated to the last degree
" with the state of mind in which he found his penitent; resigned and wrapt up in the love of
" God and man."
§ Though Sir *Isaac* objected to the Seven Kings of *Rome* lasting 244 years, yet the reign of the
seven last kings of *Spain*, from 1516 to 1758, lasted nearly as long: (*viz. Charles* I. 39; *Philip* II. 43;
Philip III. 23; *Philip* IV. 44; *Charles* II. 35; *Philip* V. 45; *Ferdinand* VI. 13; 242 years.) T. F.

7

" formance

" Naturalift's Journal," by the Hon. *Daines Barrington*, 4to;

" Critica

formance much greater. The circumftances of the tranfaction are thus related by Dr. *Maty* [*] : " The Relict of the great Duke of *Marlborough* being defirous of fubmitting to " pofterity her political conduct, as well as her Lord's, applied to the Earl of *Chefterfield* " for a proper perfon to receive her information, and put the memoirs of her life into " a proper drefs. Mr. *Hooke* was recommended by him for that purpofe. He accord- " ingly waited upon the Dutchefs, while fhe was ftill in bed, oppreffed by the infirmities " of age. But, knowing who he was, fhe immediately got herfelf lifted up, and conti- " nued fpeaking during fix hours. She delivered to him, without any notes, her account " in the moft lively as well as the moft connected manner. As fhe was not tired herfelf, " fhe would have continued longer the bufinefs of this firft fitting, had fhe not perceived " that Mr. *Hooke* was quite exhaufted, and wanted refrefhment as well as reft. So " eager was fhe for the completion of the work, that fhe infifted upon Mr. *Hooke's* not " leaving her houfe till he had finifhed it. This was done in a fhort time; and her " Grace was fo well pleafed with the performance, that fhe complimented the author " with a prefent of five thoufand pounds, a fum which far exceeded his expectations. " As foon as he was free, and permitted to quit the houfe cf his benefactrefs, he haft- " ened to the Earl, to thank him for his favour, and communicated to him his good " fortune. The perturbation of mind he was under, occafioned by the ftrong fenfe of " his obligation, plainly appeared in his ftammering-out his acknowledgements; and he, " who had fucceeded fo well as the interpreter of her Grace's fentiments, could fcarcely " utter his own." The fecond volume [†] of his " *Roman* Hiftory" appeared in 1745;

[*] See his " Memoirs of Lord *Chefterfield*," 4to, vol. I. p. 116.—As *Ruffhead's* account of this tranfaction is fomewhat different, it may be pleafant to compare it with Dr. *Maty's*: " This gen- " tleman [*Hooke*] feems to have poffeffed no fmall fhare of Mr. *Pope's* efteem and friendfhip. His " folicitude to do him fervice is ftrongly exemplified in the following anecdote: The firft Dutchefs " of *Marlborough* was defirous of having an account of her public conduct given to the world. " Mr. *Hooke*, a Roman Catholic in the myftic way, and compiler of the *Roman* Hiftory, was, " by Mr. *Pope* and others, recommended to her Grace, as a proper perfon to draw up this account, " under her infpection; and, by the affiftance of the papers fhe communicated to him, he performed " this work fo much to her Grace's fatisfaction, that fhe talked of rewarding him largely, but " would do nothing till Mr. *Pope* came to her, whofe company fhe then fought all opportunities to " procure, and was uneafy to be without it. He was at that time with fome friends, whom he was " unwilling to part with, a hundred miles diftant. But at Mr. *Hooke's* earneft folicitation, when " Mr. *Pope* found his prefence fo effentially concerned in his friend's intereft and future fupport, he " broke through all his engagements, and in the depth of winter, and ill ways, flew to his affift- " ance. On his coming, the Duchefs fecured to Mr. *Hooke* five thoufand pounds; and by that " means attached him to her fervice. But foon after fhe took occafion, as was ufual with her, to " quarrel with him.
" Her every turn by violence purfu'd,
" Nor more a ftorm her hate, than gratitude.
" Thus Mr. *Hooke* reprefented the matter. The reafon fhe gave of her fudden diflike of him, was " his attempt to pervert her to Popery. This is not without probability: for he, finding her Grace " (as appears from the Account of her conduct) without any religion, might think it an act of " no common charity to give her his own."—Speaking of Mr. *Hooke*, who had then lately been promoted, Mr. *Pope* fays, " He begins to feel the effects of a court-life, the dependance on the " great, who never do good, but with a view to make flaves." And in a letter to Mr. *Allen*, he tells him, " I can never enough thank you, my dear and true friend, for every inftance of your kind- " nefs. At prefent. I am loaded with them, but none touch me more fenfibly, than your attempts " for Mr. *Hooke*; for I am really happier in feeing a worthy man eafed of the burthen which for- " tune generally lays fuch men under, as have no talents to ferve the bad and the ambitious; " than in any pleafures of my own, which are but idle at beft." In his laft will, he gave five pounds to Mr. *Hooke*, to be laid out in a ring, or any other memorial. See *Ruffhead's* Life of *Pope*.

[†] A fecond edition of this volume was printed in 1756.

when

" Critica *Hebræa*, or, a *Hebrew-English* Dictionary without
" Points,

when Mr. *Hooke* embraced the fair occasion of congratulating his worthy friend the Earl of *Marchmont*, on " that true glory, the consenting praise of the honest and the wise," which his Lordship had so early acquired. " To those whom you distinguish by parti-
" cular marks of your good opinion," says the Dedicator to his Patron, " you give
" reputation ; and I have happily experienced, that reputation, so derived, is not mere
" air and fruitless. Through that warmth of good-will which your Lordship on all oc-
" casions expresses for me, I have profited, greatly profited, by *your* glory. You, my
" Lord, can be no stranger to this truth ; yet, I trust, you will forgive me, if, to draw
" still more advantage from your fame, I here take the liberty to tell your Lordship in
" print, for the information of others, what you knew before : As a player, taken
" alone on the stage, speaks aloud to himself, that he may be heard by those who fill
" the theatre. I would, by this dedication of my book to your Lordship, publish, as
" far as by such means I can, that you, my Lord, are my patron and my friend ; and
" that I am, with the greatest respect, esteem, and gratitude, your Lordship's most faith-
" ful and most humble servant." [The Writer of this Note confesses that he has a view
to himself in transcribing this last passage. He wishes, at the distance of near forty
years, to add his feeble testimony to the " fair fame" of the Earl of *Marchmont* ; whose
" patronage and friendship" he is proud to have experienced.] To the second volume
Mr. *Hooke* added " The *Capitoline* Marbles, or Consular Calendars, an ancient Monu-
" ment accidentally discovered at *Rome* in the year 1545, during the Pontificate of
" *Paul* III*." In 1758, Mr. *Hooke* published " Observations on, I. The Answer of M:
" l'Abbé de *Vertot* to the late Earl *Stanhope's* Enquiry, concerning the Senate of *Ancient*
" *Rome*: dated *December* 1719. II. A Dissertation upon the Constitution of the
" *Roman* Senate, by a Gentleman: published in 1743. III. A Treatise on The *Roman*
" Senate, by Dr. *Conyers Middleton*: published in 1747. IV. An Essay on the *Roman*
" Senate, by Dr. *Thomas Chapman*: published in 1750;" which he with great propriety inscribed to Mr. Speaker *Onslow*. Mr. *Hooke* here requests the reader, " That he
" will not, from the seemingly quarrelsome humour of the Observator, conclude him,
" insensible of the superior abilities of those learned men, whose works he criticises ;
" or so wrong-headed, as to think that a writer's happening sometimes to reason weakly.
" and inconclusively, is any proof of his not being an able reasoner, or a person of true
" and extensive learning." The Observations, he adds, he wishes not to be considered
as " a critique or censure on those pieces only which are mentioned in the title-page,
" but on all the Accounts of the Regal State of *Rome*, and the first Settlement of the
" *Roman* Commonwealth, which have been given by other modern writers, who have
" taken *Dionysius* of *Halicarnassus* for their chief and most trusty guide." He concludes the Preface with the following anecdote : " A very great man (in all senses) said
" to the author, after doing him the honour to read his Remarks on the History of the
" Seven *Roman* Kings, and his Dissertation on the Credibility of the History of the first
" 500 years of *Rome*, ' I believe you are right, but I don't care whether you are or
" no ; Why don't you give us the *third* volume ?' To prevent the like rebuke from
" any reader of the following Observations, I take this occasion to signify, that, though
" the said third volume was never promised, and is not finished, and though the author
" has little hope of ever finishing it in such a manner as to satisfy either the publick or
" himself, yet it is his purpose to do his best to please those persons who desire a third

* Since so beautifully engraved by *Piranesi* in his " Lapides *Capitolini*, sive Fasti Consulares,
" Triumphalesque *Romanorum* ab urbe conditâ usque ad *Tiberium Cæsarem*."

" volume ;

" Points, in which the feveral Derivatives are reduced to
" their

" volume; of which no inconfiderable part (already written and revifed) will probably
" be fent to the prefs before the end of the approaching fummer. It is poffible, that
" fome perfons, of a teafing difpofition, may afk, Why the author did not finifh the
" third volume, inftead of lofing time in improving his firft volume, and writing critical
" obfervations? To this if any confiderate and pacific friend of the author were to
" anfwer, he would probably fay, That granting the time and labour, fpent in improving
" the firft volume, and in writing critical obfervations, to have been fufficient for the
" work of a third volume, the author may neverthelefs be excufed, if he judged,
" That to thofe readers, who read with a defire to fee what is true or probable, the
" improvements and obfervations aforefaid would be more acceptable than a third vo-
" lume without thefe; becaufe, in his opinion, they may, in fome meafure, conduce to
" clear up feveral obfcurities in the hiftory, not only of the earlier but of the later ages
" of Rome. In the fecond edition of the firft volume, the hiftory of the 42 years from
" the Secefffion to the Decemvirate (in which interval Sp. Caffius made the firft propofal
" of an Agrarian law; and the Tribune Volero prevailed to have Comitia Tributa intro-
" duced) was, in great part, a new compofition, which placed things in a very different
" light from that in which they had before been prefented. (The character and conduct
" of Caffius are vindicated.) And, in the third edition of that volume, fome confider-
" able changes and additions (improvements, it is hoped) were made in the hiftory of the
" Romans, from A. U. 357, when they took Veii, to the year 370, when Marcus Manlius
" (who preferved the Capitol, after the Gauls had burnt the City of Rome) was affaffi-
" nated. An examination is made into the true caufe of that implacable hatred which
" the Senate and Camillus bore to Manlius; and into the manner of his death." I
have in Mf. an excellent Index to this volume of Mr. Hooke, drawn up by Mr. Bowyer,
which may perhaps find a place amongft his " Mifcellaneous Tracts." The volume was
followed by " A Short Review * of Mr. Hooke's Obfervations, &c. concerning the Roman
" Senate, and the character of Dionyfius of Halicarnaffus, 1758," 8vo; an anonymous
pamphlet, but written by Edward Spelman, Efq; (of whom fee p. 278) The third volume of Mr. Hooke's " Roman Hiftory," to the end of the Gallic war, was printed under

* " Mr. Hollis, whenever his attention to public liberty was required, was a faithful centinel,
" never off duty. On Mr. Hooke's Roman Hiftory he has this note: ' See a curious tract, written
" by Mr. Spelman, intituled, A Short Review of Mr. Hooke's Obfervations, &c. in which the biaffes
" of that yet refpectable gentleman, Mr. Hooke, a Romanift, are fet forth. In the year above-men-
" tioned, Mr. Hooke publifhed ' Obfervations on the accounts given by Vertot, Middleton, and Chap-
" man, on the Roman Senate; in which he treated Dionyfius as a mere writer of romance, &c. and
" the above-mentioned authors, particularly Dr. Middleton, with a difrefpect for which the fubject
" gave no occafion, and which the Monthly Reviewers afcribe to the Doctor's offenfive letter from
" Rome.' Mr. Spelman had then publifhed, or was about to publifh, his excellent tranflation of this
" fame Dionyfius's Hiftory; and on that, and other accounts, thought it neceffary to obviate the pre-
" judices which might be inftilled into fome part of the public by thefe obfervations in the fhort
" Review above-mentioned. In this little piece he fails not to vindicate his Hiftorian, though
" briefly, yet, as competent judges have determined, very effectually. Mr. Hooke's paffion for the
" defpotic form of government appeared by an anecdote communicated to us by a gentleman who
" was an eye and ear witnefs of the tranfaction. In the year 1746, Mr. Hooke, in company with
" fome gentlemen of refpectable characters, took out of his pocket a pamphlet, written by Mr.
" Warburton (afterwards Bp. of Gloucefter) juft then publifhed; from which he reads a paffage to
" the following effect: When God in his juftice weighs the fate of nations, he confiders all arbitrary
" governments as paper and packthread in the fcale! ' What! faid Mr. Hooke, does Mr. Warburton
" imagine, that GOD ALMIGHTY confiders the great monarchies of France and Spain only as paper
" and packthread?' No one in the company made any reply, and the converfation dropped. But,
" we may fuppofe, they took the fairnefs of the citation for granted. The paffage alluded to is in
" a pamphlet, intituled, ' Apologetical Dedication to the Reverend Dr. Henry Stebbing, &c. 1746.'"
Memoirs of Mr. Hollis, p. 497.

his

" their general Roots," &c. by the Rev. *Julius Bate**, 4to;
" *Edge-Hill*, a Poem," by Mr. *Jago* †, 4to; " Partridge Shoot-
" ing, an Eclogue," by *Francis Fawkes*‡, M. A. 4to; Mr.
Toup's " Epiſtola Critica ad celeberrimum virum *Gulielmum*
" Epiſcopum *Glocestriensem*," 8vo; " Tracts and Tables in

his inſpection before his laſt illneſs, but did not appear till after his death, which happened in 1764. The fourth and laſt volume was publiſhed in 1771. Mr. *Hooke* left two
ſons; of whom, one is a Divine of the Church of *England*; the other, a Doctor of *The
Sorbonne*, and Profeſſor of Aſtronomy in that illuſtrious Seminary.

   * Of whom an account will be given in the Appendix.

   † *Richard Jago*, M. A vicar of *Snitterfield* in *Warwickſhire*, and rector of *Kimcote* in
Leiceſterſhire, obtained a large ſubſcription for the above-mentioned poem in 1767. He
was the intimate friend and correſpondent of Mr. *Shenſtone*, contemporary with him at
Oxford, and, it is believed, his ſchool-fellow; was of *Univerſity College*; took the
degree of M. A. *July* 9, 1739; was author of ſeveral poems in the 4th and 5th volumes
of *Dodſley's* Poems; publiſhed a ſermon, in 1755, on the Cauſes of Impenitence conſidered, preached *May* 4, 1755, at *Harbury* in *Warwickſhire*, where he was vicar, on occaſion of a converſation ſaid to have paſſed between one of the inhabitants and an appari-
tion in the church-yard there; and was alſo author of " Labour and Genius, 1768," 4to;
of " The Blackbirds," a beautiful elegy in the Adventurer (ſee Dr. *Johnſon's* Life of
Weſt); and of many other ingenious performances. He died *May* 28, 1781.

   ‡ This ingenious poet, a native of *Yorkſhire*, had his ſchool education at *Leeds*, under
the care of the Rev. Mr. *Cookſon*, vicar of that pariſh, from whence he was tranſplanted
to *Jeſus College, Cambridge*, where he took the degrees in arts. Entering early into holy
orders, he ſettled firſt at *Bramham* in *Yorkſhire*, near the elegant ſeat of that name (Mr.
Lane's), which he celebrated in verſe ‖, in 1745, in a 4to. pamphlet, anonymous. His firſt
poetical publications were *Gawen Douglas's* " Deſcriptions of May and Winter moderniſed."
Removing afterwards to the curacy of *Croydon* in *Surrey*, he recommended himſelf to the
notice of Archbiſhop *Herring*, then reſident there on account of his health, to whom
(beſides other pieces) he addreſſed an Ode on his recovery in 1754, printed in Mr. *Dodſley's* Collection. In conſequence, his Grace collated him in 1755 to the vicarage of *Or-
pington* with *St. Mary Cray*, in *Kent*; and Mr. *Fawkes* lamented his patron's death in
1757 in a pathetic Elegy ſtyled *Aurelius*, firſt printed with his Grace's " Seven Sermons,"
in 1763. He married about the ſame time Miſs *Purrier* of *Leeds*. In *April* 1774, by the
late Dr. *Plumptre's* favour, he exchanged his vicarage for the rectory of *Hayes*. He was
alſo one of the chaplains to the Princeſs Dowager of *Wales*. He publiſhed a volume of
Poems by ſubſcription in 8vo, 1761; the " Poetical Calendar, 1763," and " Poetical
" Magazine 1764," in conjunction with Mr. *Woty*; " Partridge-ſhooting (above-menti-
" oned) an Eclogue, to the Honourable *Charles Yorke*, 1767," 4to. and a " Family
" Bible," with Notes, in 4to, a compilation. But his great ſtrength lay in tranſlation,
in which, ſince *Pope*, few have equalled him. Witneſs his fragments of *Menander* (in
his Poems); his " Works of *Anacreon, Sappho, Bion, Moſchus*, and *Muſæus*," 12mo,
1760; his " Idylliums of *Theocritus*," by ſubſcription, 8vo, 1767; and his " Argo-
" nautics of *Apollonius Rhodius*," by ſubſcription alſo (a poſthumous publication, completed by the Rev. Mr. *Meen* of *Emanuel College, Cambridge*) 8vo, 1780. He died
Auguſt 26, 1777.

   ‖ Reprinted in his Poems, 1761, 8vo. p. 3.

                                         " ſeveral

" several Arts and Sciences, by Mr. *Ferguson* *," 8vo; " An
" Essay

* *James Ferguson* was born in the year 1710, a few miles from the village of *Keith*
in *Bamffshire*, in the North of *Scotland*. At the earliest age his extraordinary genius
began to exert itself. He first learned to read by overhearing his father teach his elder
brother: and he had made this acquisition before any one suspected it. Between seven
and eight years old he drew his idea of mechanic powers from an accident, which
obliged his father to use a lever in supporting the roof of his little cottage. As soon
as his age would permit, he went to service, in which he met with hardships, which rendered his constitution feeble through life. He kept sheep for four years, and
next served with a farmer, whose name was *James Glashan*, whom he commemorates
for his kindness and indulgence. Before he went into this service he learnt the practice
of marking the position of the stars with a thread and bead; which he there was enabled to continue by the goodness of this honest man, who, observing these marks of
his ingenuity, procured him the countenance and assistance of his superiors. Mr. *John*
Gilchrist, minister of *Keith*, encouraged and assisted his growing genius; and when
his service was ended (for he would not leave it sooner, though a substitute
was offered) *Thomas Grant*, Esq; received him for instruction into his family, where
his butler *Alexander Cantley* (of whose extensive abilities and knowledge an extraordinary account is given by our philosopher) became his tutor. Of him he learnt
decimal arithmetic, algebra, and the elements of geometry; and from the description
of the sphere, aided with a map of the earth, made a terrestrial globe; though he had
never seen one before. He then went into two very hard services, one of them to a
miller, and had nearly perished by ill health and want of assistance, had it not been
for the medicines and care of his valuable friend *Cantley*. When he was still too weak
for labour, he made a wooden clock, and afterwards a watch, from the casual sight of one.
His ingenuity introduced him to Sir *James Dunbar*, when he learnt to draw, and began to take portraits, an employment by which he supported himself and family for
several years, both in *Scotland* and *England*, whilst he was pursuing more serious studies.
The Rev. Dr. *Keith* of *Edinburgh* encouraged his efforts, and recommended him to the
patronage of Lady *Jane Douglas*, of whose beauty and merit he speaks in the most
affecting language of native simplicity, which was always his language. He now began
to be the œconomist of a little stock which the good-will of his friends enabled him to
acquire. He next made some attempts in the medical line; but honestly laid them aside
soon, not venturing far in an employment to which experimental knowledge is no less
required than genius, and where the consequences of error are so fatal. In his twenty-
ninth year he married. And when he was thirty, with very scanty data, and hardly any
means from books or instruments to assist him, he invented that excellent machine for shewing
the new moons and eclipses, called his Astronomical Rotula, which acquired him the friendship of that admirable philosopher and good man, Mr. *M'Laurin*. By sight of an Orrery, though its machinery was concealed, he made a Tellurian for the motions of the
earth and moon; and gave his first Lecture on its use by the desire of his ' great and good
friend,' as he justly calls him. In 1743 he made another Orrery, soon after purchased by
Sir *Dudley Ryder*, so eminent for his professional and general abilities. After this he
came up to *London*, where he first published some curious astronomical tables and calculations, and afterwards gave public lectures in experimental philosophy, which he repeated
(by subscription) in most of the principal towns in *England*, with the highest marks of
general approbation. By a letter of recommendation from Mr. Baron *Edlin* of *Edin-*
burgh,

" Eſſay towards an Improvement in the Cure of thoſe Diſ-

burgh, he was made acquainted with the Honourable *Stephen Poyntz*, the friend of Lord *Lyttelton*, and of Virtue, whom he mentions with the warmeſt gratitude and merited veneration. A delineation of the complex line of the moon's motion recommended him to the notice of the Royal Society, and particularly of Mr. *Ellicot*, who had before made a ſimilar ſcheme, and ingenuouſly acknowledged Mr. *Ferguſon's* equal title to the invention. He was elected a Fellow of the Royal Society without paying for admiſſion, an honour ſcarcely ever conferred on a native. About 1752 he made his Aſtronomical Inſtrument for ſhewing the riſing and ſetting of the Sun, Moon, and Stars; having publiſhed his Diſſertation on the Phænomena of the Harveſt Moon about five years before (in 1747), and read his firſt Courſe of Lectures about the year 1748. He had from various reſpectable characters encouragement, which his modeſty thought more ample than it appeared to thoſe who could beſt judge of his merit; and had a penſion of fifty pounds a year from his preſent Majeſty at his acceſſion, who had heard lectures from him, and frequently ſent for and converſed with him on curious topics; and had alſo given him ſeveral preſents. Mr. *Ferguſon* poſſeſſed the cleareſt judgement, and the moſt unwearied application to ſtudy; was benevolent, meek and innocent in his manners as a child: humble, courteous and communicative. Philoſophy ſeemed to produce in him only diffidence and urbanity, a love for mankind and for his Maker. His whole life was an example of reſignation and chriſtian piety. In the year 1773, the 63d of his age, he publiſhed " Select Mecha-" nical Exerciſes," with an account of his life. His " Introduction to Electricity" had appeared in 1770, his " Introduction to Aſtronomy" in 1772. His great work, " Aſtro-" nomy explained on Sir *Iſaac Newton's* Principles," had gone through four editions in the year 1770. His " Lectures on Select Subjects in Mechanics, Hydroſtatics, Hy-" draulics, Pneumatics, and Optics," had deſervedly attained to a fifth edition in the year 1776. His laſt publiſhed work was a " Treatiſe on Perſpective," in the year 1775. After a long and uſeful life, unhappy in his family connections, and in a feeble and precarious ſtate of health, worn out with ſtudy, age, and infirmities, he died on the 16th of *November* 1776, having ſtruggled with a conſtitution naturally infirm longer than could have been reaſonably expected. His only daughter was loſt in a very ſingular manner about the age of eighteen. She was remarkable for the elegance of her perſon, the agreeableneſs and vivacity of her converſation, and in philoſophical genius and knowledge worthy of ſuch a father. He left no inconſiderable ſum of money to his ſon, Mr. *Murdoch Ferguſon*, now in the navy. Some manuſcript tables, diagrams, and a philoſophical correſpondence of this ſelf-taught philoſopher, are in the hands of the ingenious Mr. *Loft*; which were given by him to Mrs. *Loft* (then Miſs *Emblin*) before marriage: than whom he had no pupil whoſe genius and diſpoſition he more eſteemed. I copy the ſubſtance of this note from his own narrative; from his character as delineated by Dr. *Houlſton* of *Liverpool*; and from " *Eudoſia*, or a Poem on the Univerſe," by Mr. *Loft*, who, having paid an elegant compliment to the immortal *Newton*, proceeds,

> " Nor ſhall thy guidance not conduct our feet,
> " O honour'd SHEPHERD of our later days!
> " Whom from the flocks, while thy untutor'd ſoul,
> " Mature in childhood, trac'd the ſtarry courſe,
> " ASTRONOMY, enamour'd, gently led
> " Through all the ſplendid labyrinths of Heaven;
> " And taught thee her ſtupendous laws; and cloath'd
> " In all the light of fair ſimplicity,
> " Thy apt expreſſion."

" eaſes,

" eafes, which are the Caufe of Fevers, by *Thomas Kirk-*
" *land* *, Surgeon," 8vo ;   Dr. *Worthington's* † " Sermons

* Of *Afhby de la Zouch*, and now a phyfician of great eminence.   The little Tract
above-mentioned is well written, and deferves the attention of thofe whofe ftudies peculiarly
qualify them to judge of its merit.   Dr. *Kirkland* has obliged the medical world with
fome other valuable pieces.

† Dr. *William Worthington* was born in *Merionethfhire* in 1703, and educated at
Ofweftry-fchool, from wence he came to *Jefus College*, *Oxford*, where he made great
proficiency in learning.   From college he returned to *Ofweftry*, and became ufher in
that fchool.   He took the degree of M. A. at *Cambridge* in 1742 ; was afterwards
incorporated at *Jefus College*, *Oxford*, *July* 3, 1758 ; and proceeded B. and D. D.
July 10, in that year.   He was early taken notice of by that great encourager of learning Bp. *Hare*, then bifhop of *St. Afaph*, who prefented him firft to the vicarage of *Llany-
blodwell*, in the County of *Salop*, and afterwards removed him to *Llanrhayader* in *Den-
bighfhire*, where he lived much beloved, and died *Oct.* 6, 1778, much lamented.   As he
could never be prevailed upon to take two livings, Bifhop *Hare* gave him a ftall
at *St. Afaph*, and a finecure, " to enable him," he faid, " to fupport his charities ;" for
charitable he was in an eminent degree.   Afterwards Archbifhop *Drummond* (to whom
he had been chaplain for feveral years) prefented him to a ftall in the cathedral of *York*.
Thefe were all his preferments.   He was a ftudious man ; and wrote feveral books, of
which the principal are the following : 1. " An Effay on the Scheme and Conduct, Pro-
" cedure and Extent of Man's Redemption ; defigned for the Honour and Illuftra-
" tion of Chriftianity.   To which is annexed, a Differtation on the Defign and Argu-
" mentation of the Book of *Job*.   By *William Worthington*, M. A. Vicar of *Blodwel*
" in *Shropfhire*.   *London*, printed for *Edward Cave*, at St. *John's Gate*, 1743," 8vo.
2. " The Hiftorical Senfe of the *Mofaic* Account of the Fall proved and vindicated, 17 ,"
8vo ; 3. " Inftructions concerning Confirmation, 17 ," 8vo ; 4. " A Difquifition
" concerning the Lord's Supper, 17 ," 8vo ; 5. " The Ufe, Value, and Improvement
" of Various Readings fhewn and illuftrated, in a Sermon preached before the Univerfity
" of *Oxford*, at St. *Mary's*, on *Sunday*, *Oct.* 18, 1761, *Oxford*, 1764," 8vo ; 6. " A
" Sermon preached in the Parifh-Church of *Chrift-Church*, *London*, on *Thurfday*, *April*
" the 21ft, 1768 ; being the Time of the Yearly Meeting of the Children educated in
" the Charity-Schools in and about the Cities of *London* and *Weftminfter*, 1768," 4to ;
7. " The Evidences of Chriftianity, deduced from Facts, and the Teftimony of Senfe,
" throughout all Ages of the Church, to the prefent Time.   In a Series of Difcourfes,
" preached for the Lecture founded by the Hon. *Robert Boyle*, Efq. in the Parifh-church
" of St. *James*, *Weftminfter*, in the Years 1766, 1767, 1768 ; wherein is fhewn, that,
" upon the whole, this is not a decaying, but a growing Evidence, 1769," 2 vols. 8vo ;
8. " The Scripture Theory of the Earth, throughout all its Revolutions, and all the
" Periods of its Exiftence, from the Creation to the final Renovation of all things ;
" being a Sequel to the Effay on Redemption, and an Illuftration of the Principles on
" which it is written, 1773," 8vo ; 9. " *Irenicum* ; or, the Importance of Unity in the
" Church of Chrift confidered ; and applied towards the healing of our unhappy Dif-
" ferences and divifions, 1775," 8vo ; 10. " An impartial Enquiry into the Cafe of the
" Gofpel Demoniacks ; with an Appendix, confifting of an Effay on Scripture Demo-
" nology, 1777," 8vo.   This laft was a warm attack on the opinion held out by a refpectable Diffenting Divine, the Rev. *Hugh Farmer*, in his " Effay on the Demoniacks, 1775,"
8vo ; and, having produced a fpirited reply, 1778, Dr. *Worthington* prepared for the prefs
(what by the exprefs directions of his will was given to the publick after his death) " A
" further Enquiry into the Cafe of the Gofpel Demoniacks, occafioned by Mr. *Farmer's*
" Letters on the fubject, 1779," 8vo.

" at

" at *Boyle's* Lectures," 8vo ; and " Poems and Translations.
" by the Author * of the Progress of Physic," 8vo.

Early in 1768 Mr. *Bowyer* received from *New England*
the following polite acknowledgement † of his abilities and
his bounty :.

"S I R, *Cambridge, Dec.* 1767.

"The President and Fellows of *Harvard College* in *Cam-*
" *bridge* beg leave to return you their grateful acknow-
" ledgements for the valuable donation you have been
" pleased to make to their library, through the hands of their
" moft worthy friend and generous benefactor, *Thomas*
" *Hollis* ‡, Efq.

"We

---

* *Afhley Cowper*, Efq. barrifter at law, fecond fon of *Spencer Cowper*, Efq; (one of the
Judges of the Court of Common Pleas) and nephew to the firft Earl *Cowper*. This gentleman is now, and has been for many years, Clerk of the Parliaments. The " Progrefs
" of Phyfic," the principal poem in the above-mentioned volume (which was dedicated to his firft coufin, the Hon. and Rev. Dr. *Spencer Cowper*, Dean of *Durham)* was
firft publifhed in 1744. He was alfo editor of " The *Norfolk* Mifcellany, 1744," 2 vols.
8vo. In *Dodfley's* fourth volume are fome " Verfes written in his *Coke upon Littleton*,"
by his fifter, the truly ingenious Mrs. *Madan*.

† This Letter is alfo printed in the " Memoirs of Mr. *Hollis*," p. 805.

‡ *Thomas Hollis*, of *Corfcombe*, in the county of *Dorfet*, Efq; was born in *London*,
April 14 ‖, 1720. His great-grandfather *Thomas*, of *Rotherham*, in *Yorkfhire*, a whitefmith
by trade, and a Baptift by perfuafion, fettled in *London* during the civil wars, and died
there in 1718, aged 84, leaving three fons, *Thomas*, *Nathaniel*, and *John*. Of thefe the
eldeft, *Thomas*, a confiderable merchant, is chiefly memorable for his benefactions to
New-England, particularly to *Harvard College* in *Cambridge* (where he founded a pro-
fefforfhip, fcholarfhips, &c.) to the amount of near 5000l. in which his brothers were
joint contributors, without any reftriction in regard to religious fects. *Thomas*, the only
fon of *Nathaniel*, died in 1735 (three years before his father), leaving one fon, the fubject
of this note, and of courfe the heir to his father, and alfo to his great uncle, *Thomas*, who died in 1730. His mother was the daughter of Mr. *Scott*, of *Wolverhampton*,
in whofe family Mr. *Hollis* was nurtured in his infancy. The above account will rectify
a miftake which has prevailed, of his being a defcendant of *Denzil* Lord *Holles*, though
his grandfather ufed to fay, they were of one family, which feparated in the time of
Henry VIII. He was educated at the free-fchool of *Newport*, in *Shropfhire*, till he was
about eight or nine years of age (probably), by a Mr. or Dr. *Lee*, and afterwards at

‖ It is obfervable that Mr. *H.* was abfurd enough to obferve this nominal birth-day ever afterwards, without regard to the change of ftyle.

St.

" We have not been strangers to your character as a
" learned editor, a character by no means common in the
" present

St. *Alban's* by Mr. *Wood*. In his 13th or 14th year he was sent to *Amsterdam*, to learn
the *Dutch* and *French* languages, writing, accompts, &c. staid there about fifteen months,
and then returned to *London* to his father, with whom he continued till his death in
1735. After this he was some years in the house of his cousin *Timothy* * *Hollis*, Esq.
His guardian was Mr. *John Hollister*, then treasurer of *Guy's* Hospital, who, to give him
a liberal education suitable to the ample fortune he was to inherit, put him under the
tuition of Professor *Ward*, whose picture, to preserve his memory, Mr. *Hollis* presented to
The British Museum ; and, in honour of his father and guardian, he caused to be inscribed
round a valuable diamond ring, *Mnemosynon Patris Tutorisque*. From Dr. *Jeremiah Hunt*,
Dr. *Foster*, and other eminent persons, he imbibed that ardent love of liberty, and freedom of sentiment, which strongly marked his character. He professed himself a Dissen-
ter. In *February* 1739-40 he went to chambers in *Lincoln's-Inn*, being admitted as a
law-student ; but does not appear to have studied the law as a profession, though he resided there till *July* 19, 1748, when he set out on his travels for the first time, and
passed through *Holland*, *Austrian* and *French Flanders*, part of *France*, *Switzerland*,
Savoy, and part of *Italy*, and returned through *Provence*, *Brittany*, &c. to *Paris*. His
fellow traveller was *Thomas Brand*, Esq; of *The Hyde*, in *Essex*, his particular friend and
heir. His second tour, which commenced *July* 16, 1750, was through *Holland* to *Emb-
den*, *Bremen*, *Hamburgh*, the principal cities on the north and east side of *Germany*, the
rest of *Italy*, *Sicily* and *Malta*, *Lorrain*, &c. The journals of both his tours is preserved,
and would be a valuable acquisition to the publick. On his return home, finding he could not
obtain a seat in Parliament in the disinterested manner he wished, without the smallest
appearance of bribery, he began his collection of books and medals, " for the purpose
" of illustrating and upholding liberty, preserving the memory of its champions, to
" render tyranny and its abettors odious, to extend science and art, to keep alive the
" honour and estimation of their patrons and protectors, and to make the whole as
" useful as possible ; abhorring all monopoly ; and, if such should be the fitness of things,
" to propagate the same benevolent spirit to posterity." Among Mr. *Hollis's* noble
benefactions to foreign libraries, none is more remarkable than that of two large collections of valuable books to the public library of *Berne*, which were presented anonymously, as by " an *Englishman*, a lover of liberty, his country, and its excellent constitu-
" tion, as restored at the happy Revolution." *Switzerland*, *Geneva*, *Venice*, *Leyden*,
Sweden, *Russia*, &c. shared his favours. His benefactions to *Harvard College* commenced
in 1758, and were continued every succeeding year, to the amount in all of 1400l. Dr.
Jonathan Mayhew, pastor of the West-church in *Boston*, was his confidential friend and
correspondent, and partook largely of his esteem and beneficence. But his liberality to
individuals, as well as to public societies, cannot here be specified. Mr. *Hollis* purchased at Mr. *Charles Stanhope's* sale, *June* 3, 1760, an original of *Milton* when
a boy, painted by *Cornelius Jansen*. A fire happening at his lodgings in *Bedford-
street*, *January* 23, 1761, he calmly walked out, taking this picture only in his hand.
The fire, however, was happily got under without any loss. A new edition of
Toland's Life of *Milton* was published under his care and direction in 1761. He pre-

* The son, probably, of *John* above-mentioned.

sented,

" prefent age; and the very accurate editions of many
" learned authors, which have come abroad into the world
" under

fented, *October* 29, 1761, an original portrait of Sir *Ifaac Newton*, painted by *Zeeman*, 1726, to *Trinity-College*, *Cambridge*. All the tracts that were publifhed againft the Jefuits he collected in 1762, and fent to the public library of *Zurich*, having been flighted, as he thought, by the curators of *The Britifh Mufeum*. In *April*, 1763, Mr. *Hollis* gave the publick a new and accurate edition of *Algernon Sydney's* Difcourfes on Government, on which the pains and expence he beftowed are almoft incredible. His patronifing this edition, and other works of the fame kind, procured him, and no wonder, the name and reputation of a republican. " *Roma Antica*," by the Abbate *Venuti*, though a pofthumous work, owed its birth to Mr. *Hollis*. In 1763 his friend Count *Algarotti* publifhed his " *Saggio fopra l'Academia de Francia che è in Roma*," with a dedication to Mr. *Hollis*, to his great furprife, as, when he could, he always declined fuch compliments. The noble library, philofophical apparatus, &c. of *Harvard College* being confumed by fire *Jan.* 24, 1764, Mr. *Hollis* immediately fubfcribed 200l. towards repairing the lofs. In this year Mr. *Locke's* two Treatifes on Government, and in the next his Letters on Toleration, were publifhed feparately under the aufpices of Mr. *Hollis*. In *June* he prefented fome *Egyptian* antiquities, anonymoufly, to Count *Caylus* at *Paris*. Dr. *Wallis's* Latin Grammar of the *Englifh* Tongue was reprinted at Mr. *Hollis's* defire, to promote the knowledge of our language among foreigners. The elegant preface prefixed was written, as has been already faid, p. 361, by Mr. *Bowyer*, who was ever defirous of forwarding Mr. *Hollis's* public-fpirited intentions. A fine collection of books, intended by Mr. *Hollis* for *Harvard College*, being burnt, with his bookbinder's houfe, *June* 6, he immediately began collecting " a finer parcel." One of his prefents this year being configned to the public library, " if any," at *Bermuda*; on Dr. *Mayhew's* replying that he believed there was none, the biographers of Mr. *Hollis* add, " Though Bp. *Berkeley's* pro-" ject of eftablifhing and endowing a college at *Bermuda* mifcarried, yet, one would think, " he did not bring back the collection of books he intended for that foundation." He certainly did not; but it does not appear that he ever was at *Bermuda*, or got nearer to it than *Newport* in *Rhode-Ifland*. There he refided, and there he left his books. A fecond magnificent prefent of books was fent by our patriot to *Berne* this year. His expences in books, virtù, prefents, charity, &c. amounted in 1764 to above 800l. and were feldom much lefs. In this year he fent to *Sidney College*, *Cambridge*, where *Cromwell* was educated, an original portrait of him by *Cooper* *. Dr. *Mayhew* died of a nervous fever, *July* 9, aged 49, " overplied," as Mr. *Hollis* expreffes it, in *Miltonic* phrafe, " by public energies." For a drawing of him, by *Cipriani*, from a picture at *Bofton*, Mr. *Hollis* paid 30 guineas. Dr. *Andrew Elliot* fucceeded to his correfpondence. In 1767 Mr. *Hollis's* projected republications of *Andrew Marvell's* works, and of *Milton's* profe works, both proved abortive. For a frontifpiece to the latter, *Cipriani* had drawn and etched *Milton* victorious over *Salmafius*. In *Auguft* 1770, Mr. *Hollis* carried into execution a plan which he had formed five years before, of retiring into *Dorfetfhire*, and of his fituation there he gives the following account from *Corfcombe*, *Sept.* 24: Retreat " is now become more and more acceptable to me. Where I fhall dwell afterwards pre-" cifely, I do not know at prefent; but as near to this place as may be. It is called

* Since etched by *P. S. Lambourne* and *J. Bretherton*.

" Urles,

" under your infpection, affure us of your great merit in
" that refpect.

" It is a particular pleafure to us to mention your very
" curious edition of the *Greek* Teftament, in two volumes,

" *Urles*, or *Urles-farm*; and is a moft healthy, and, I think, beautiful fpot; the very earth
" itfelf is fweet beyond a nofegay; but the houfe is a bad and very old farm-houfe.
" I thank God, I am well; but I feel, in feveral ways, the effects of my late long moft
" rigid plan: I rife from fix to feven, and to bed from eleven to twelve; and the
" whole day, each to the other, paffes into fuch a variety of tranfactions, fome not per-
" fonal and of fcope, that I am often furprifed at the recollection of them. That of
" which I am moft chary, is my time; and people knowing the ftreightnefs of my apart-
" ment, and that I mean well under certain fingularities, are cautious enough, in general,
" not to break in upon and confume it. The idea of fingularity, by way of fhield, I try
" by all means to hold out." Early in the afternoon of New Year's-day, 1774, Mr.
Hollis was in a field at fome diftance from his place of refidence at *Corfcombe*, attended
by only one workman, who was receiving his directions concerning a tree which had been
lately felled. On a fudden, he put one of his fingers to his forehead, faying, " *Richard*,
" I believe the weather is going to change; I am extremely giddy." Thefe words were
fcarce off his lips, when he fell on his left fide, The man fprung to his affiftance, and,
raifing him up, adminiftered what little relief he could. He was ftill fufficiently himfelf
to fay, " Lord have mercy upon me; Lord, have mercy upon me; receive my foul;"
which were the laft words he was able to pronounce. His lips moved afterwards, but
no found was formed, and he expired prefently after. The following quaint character of this extraordinary man appeared in one of the public prints fome years
before his death, viz. *July* 5, 1770: " *Thomas Hollis* is a man poffeffed of a large
" fortune; above the half of which he devotes to charities, to the encouragement of
" genius, and to the fupport and defence of liberty. His ftudious hours are devoted to
" the fearch of noble authors, hidden by the ruft of time; and to do their virtues juf-
" tice by brightening their actions for the review of the public. Wherever he meets
" the man of letters, he is fure to affift him; and were I to defcribe in paint this illuf-
" trious citizen of the world, I would depict him leading by the hands Genius and dif-
" treffed Virtue to the temple of Reward." Mr. *Hollis*, in order to preferve the
memory of thofe heroes and patriots for whom he had a veneration, called many of
the farms and fields in his eftate at *Corfcombe* by their names; and by thefe names
they are ftill diftinguifhed. In the middle of one of thefe fields, not far from his
houfe, he ordered his corpfe to be depofited in a grave ten feet deep, and that the field
fhould be immediately plowed over, that no trace of his burial-place might remain.
In the teftamentary difpofition of his fortune he fhewed himfelf as much fuperior to common connections as he affected to be through life; for, without the leaft regard to his
natural relations, he bequeathed all his real and the refidue of his perfonal eftate to his
dear friend and fellow-traveller, *Thomas Brand*, Efq; of *The Hide*, in *Effex*, who has taken
the name and arms of *Hollis*, and whofe firft application of his liberality was to folicit a
place in parliament. To the books which Mr. *Hollis* publifhed, or procured to be publifhed, before-mentioned, we may add the following: " *Nedham's* Excellence of a Free
" State;" " *Neville's* Plato Redivivus" (a republication of Mr. *Spence's* edition); " *Neville's*
" Parliament of Ladies," and " Ifle of Pines;" and " *Staveley's Romifh* Horfeleech *."

* This laft is claimed by the biographers of Mr. *Hollis*. But the merit of the republication is
due to Mr. *Thomas Davies*, who alfo republifhed Mr. *Staveley's* Hiftory of Churches; and in both
I ad fome affiftance from Dr. *Ducarel*.

" with

" with critical notes, and many happy conjectures, especially
" as to punctuation, an affair of the utmost importance as
" to ascertaining the sense. This work, though small in
" bulk, we esteem as a rich treasure of sacred learning, and
" of more intrinsic value than many huge volumes of the
" commentators.

" We are greatly obliged to you for the favourable sen-
" timents you have been pleased so elegantly * to express of

---

* I should have been glad to have annexed the inscription, if a copy of it had been
preserved. Mr. *Bowyer* had a happy turn for that species of writing. One specimen
has been given in p. 356-7.—A second I recollect, which was prefixed to another book
presented to *Harvard College*:

HAS ERASMI EPISTOLAS,
CAETERORVMQVE LITERATVRAE PER EVROPAM INSTAVRATORVM,
COLLEGIO HARVARDENSI,
FELICIBVS AVSPICIIS NASCENTI,
DONAT GVLIELMVS BOWYER,
TYPOGRAPHVS LONDINENSIS.

I shall add a third, drawn up in 1770, as an introduction to a present of his friend Mr.
Clarke's book on Coins:

TO THE ROYAL SOCIETY,
WHOSE COMPREHENSIVE RESEARCHES PENETRATE
INTO VNIVERSAL NATVRE, SCIENCE, AND ART,
THIS HISTORY
OF THE MINVTE FRAGMENTS OF TIME,
THE FVTVRE RIVALS OF IT,
FABRICATED IN BRASS, SILVER, GOLD,
AMONG THE ROMANS, SAXONS, AND ENGLISH;
THE FIRST OF WHOM SOVGHT THE ADVANTAGE
OF GERMAN ALLIANCES,
THE SECOND OF THEIR LAWS,
AND TO WHOM THE THIRD NOW OWE
THEIR BEST OF KINGS;
IS PRESENTED,
AS A MONVMENT OF HIS DVTY AND GRATITVDE,
BY THEIR MOST OBLIGED AND OBEDIENT SERVANT,
W. BOWYER.

This last inscription Mr. *Bowyer* had intended to accompany with a motto; which he
omitted in consequence of the following hint: " The most proper motto I should think
" for many reasons to be *none at all*. These researches into Nature have nothing to do
" with the subject of the Book. *Virgil's* ' Tibi res antiquæ laudis, et artis,' has some
" relation to them, but more to the Antiquarian Society." *MS. Letter from Mr.
Markland.*

" our

"our Seminary, in the blank leaf of the New Teſtament;
" and we hope it will prove a powerful ſtimulus to our
" youth, more and more to deſerve ſo good a character.

" This Society is as yet but in its infant-ſtate; but we
" truſt, that, by the generoſity of the benefactors whom the
" Divine Providence is raiſing up to us, and by the ſmiles
" of Heaven upon our endeavours to form the youth here
" to knowledge and virtue, it will every day more effectu-
" ally anſwer the important ends of its foundation. We
" are, with great reſpect, your moſt obliged, and humble
" ſervants, (at the direction and deſire of the Corporation
" of *Harvard College,)*   EDW. HOLYOKE, Preſident.

" Sir, incloſed you have our vote of thanks for your
" valuable preſent.

" At a meeting of the Preſident and Fellows of *Harvard
College, Dec.* 10, 1767.

" VOTE IV. That the thanks of this Corporation be given
" to Mr. *William Bowyer* of *London,* for ſeveral valuable
" books ſent to *Harvard College*; particularly his late
" curious Edition of the *Greek* Teſtament, with learned
" Notes.

" A true Copy, extr. de Lib. vii. p. 175.

" Per EDW. HOLYOKE, Preſident.

" Preſent,
" THE PRESIDENT.
" MR. APPELTON.
" MR. WINTHROP.
" MR. ELLIOT.
" MR. COOPER.
" MR. DANFORTH.
" MR. TREASURER."

3

In

In 1768, Mr. *Bowyer* printed Mr. *Holdfworth's* * Remarks on *Virgil*, 4to; "*Ferney*, a Poem," by Mr. *Keate*, 4to; " Labour and Genius, a Poem," by Mr. *Jago*, 4to; the fecond edition of *Moſheim's* " Eccleſiaſtical Hiſtory," 5 vols. 8vo; " Thoughts on Popery," by Archdeacon *Blackburne*, 8vo; the firſt volume of the " Medical Tranſactions, publiſhed by

" the

---

* Mr. *Edward Holdſworth* (author of the " Muſcipula," a poem which is eſteemed a maſter-piece in its kind, written with the purity of *Virgil*, whom the author ſo perfectly underſtood, and with the pleaſantry of *Lucian*) after having imbibed his truly claſſical taſte at *Wincheſter-ſchool* †, was elected demy of *Magdalen College, Oxford*, in *July*, 1705; took his degree of M. A. *April* 18, 1711; became a college-tutor, and had a conſiderable number of pupils. In *January* 1715, when, according to the order of ſucceſſion at that time obſerved, he was the next to be choſen into a fellowſhip, he reſigned his demyſhip, and left the college, being determined againſt taking the oaths to the new government. From that period he was employed to the time of his death in travelling with young noblemen as tutor. In 1741 he was at *Rome* with Mr. *Pitt* ‡; and again in 1744 with Mr. *Drake* and Mr. *Townſon* §. He died of a fever at Lord *Digby's* houſe at *Coleſhill*, in *Warwickſhire*, *Dec.* 30, 1747. Of him Mr. *Spence* ſpeaks in *Polymetis*, p. 174, as one who underſtood *Virgil* in a more maſterly manner than any perſon he ever knew. See alſo pp. 232 and 276. He was the author of a diſſertation intituled " *Pharſalia* and *Philippi*, or the two *Philippi* in *Virgil's* Georgics attempted to be ex- " plained and reconciled to hiſtory, 1741," 4to. and of the above-mentioned quarto vo- lume of " Remarks and Diſſertations on *Virgil*; with ſome other claſſical obſervations, " publiſhed with ſeveral notes and additional remarks by Mr. *Spence*, 1768." 4to. In the fifth volume of *Dodſley's* Miſcellanies is a very good tranſlation of the " Muſcipula," 1737, by Dr. *John Hoadly*; and among the Poems of Dr. *Cobden*, 1757, 4to. is another tranſlation of it, made ſo early as 1718, introduced by a Poetical Epiſtle from Dr. *Cobden*, exhibiting much friendſhip at leaſt, if not good poetry; and in a note upon his " Strena " ad Reverendum virum Doctorem *Lavington* Epiſcopum nominatum," the good Arch- deacon thus laments the death of Mr. *Holdſworth:* " How frail are the hopes! how " confuſed and uncertain the lots of mankind! Whilſt I am writing this, and congra- " tulating the fortune and dignity of one old ſchool-fellow and friend, bad news, alas! " has been brought me, which afflicts me with the greateſt ſorrow; that Mr. *Holdſ-* " *worth*, my other *quondam* ſchool-fellow, and moſt delightful friend throughout his " whole life, is lately dead;

 " Qualem neque candidiorem
 " Terra tulit, neque cui me ſit devinctior alter.
" For we were play-fellows, when boys; and likewiſe mutually intermixed our joys and " ſorrows, being chamber-fellows for ſix years together. He was of a natural diſpo- " ſition ſo ingenuous, that if ever any other perſon was, he ſeemed to be born without " vices. A pleaſant companion, and a man of probity, becauſe he could ſcarcely be

† " O once with me by *Wickham's* bounty fed,
 " Lodg'd in one chamber, with one manchet fed !"
    Dr. Cobden's Epiſtle, p. 186.
‡ See " Letters from a Young Painter," vol. I. p. 58.
§ Ibid. p. 140.
7

" otherwiſe.

" the College of Phyſicians in *London*," 8vo ; Mr. *Markland's* excellent edition of the "Iphigeniæ" of *Euripides*, 8vo ; " A Letter to *David Garrick*, Eſq; by *Richard Warner* *, Eſq;" 8vo; and the State of " *Holton-ſchool*," in *Suffolk*, for the benevolent Mr. *Stephen White* †, its founder, 8vo.

In 1769 Mr. *Bowyer* printed "Antiquities, Hiſtorical, " and Monumental, of the County of *Cornwall*; conſiſting " of ſeveral Eſſays on the firſt Inhabitants, Druid-Super- " ſtition, Cuſtoms, and Remains of the moſt remote Anti-

" otherwiſe. It is indeed to be lamented, that he fell into *one error* ‡, by which he " became loſt to his country long before he died. As his life incited all to the practice " of virtue and piety; ſo his death more admoniſhes us veteran fellow-ſoldiers, now re- " duced to a ſmall number, to embrace one another the more cloſely; for the more " contracted the rays are, ſo much the more they ought to warm."

* This worthy man was the younger ſon of a banker, who is ſomewhere mentioned by *Addiſon* or *Steele* as having always worn black leather garters buckled under the knee, a cuſtom moſt religiouſly obſerved by our author, who in no other inſtance affected ſingu- larity. He was bred to the law, and had chambers in *Lincoln's-Inn* ; but, being poſ- ſeſſed of a genteel fortune, reſided chiefly at a good old houſe, with an extenſive garden belonging to it, on *Woodford Green* in *Eſſex*. That he was a botaniſt of no common ſkill and experience, appears by his little tract, intituled, " Plantæ *Woodfordienſes*, " 1771," 8vo; and his taſte for polite literature appears in the above-mentioned " Let- " ter to *David Garrick*, Eſq; concerning a Gloſſary to the Plays of *Shakeſpeare*, &c." Indeed he had been long making collections for a new edition of that author; but on Mr. *Steevens's* advertiſement of his deſign to engage in the ſame taſk on a different plan, he deſiſted from the purſuit of his own; and was afterwards the tranſlator of all ſuch comedies of *Plautus* as the late Mr. *Thornton* did not live to finiſh. In his youth he had been remarkably fond of dancing; nor till his rage for that diverſion ſubſided, did he convert the largeſt room in his houſe into a library. To the laſt hour of his life, however, he was employed on the Gloſſary already mentioned, which, ſince the appear- ance of our great dramatic writer's plays in ten volumes, 8vo. 1778, with an accompa- nying Supplement of two more volumes, may be regarded as a work of ſupererо- gation. At his death, which happened on the 11th of *April*, 1775, he bequeathed all his valuable books to *Wadham College*, *Oxford*, where he received his education; and if we are not miſ-informed, he left to the ſame ſociety a ſmall annual ſtipend to maintain a botanical lecture.

† Of whom ſee above, p. 268.

‡ The *one* error (on which Dr. *Cobden* more particularly dwelt in the Poetical Epiſtle) was his declining to take the oaths. This error, however, did not render him entirely *loſt to his country*: ſince, in his capacity of travelling tutor, he cultivated the minds of ſeveral young gentlemen, not only with all polite literature, but formed their manners, by the ſtricteſt rules of morality, and in- cited them, by his own example as well as precepts, to the practice of virtue and piety.

G g g " quity

" quity in *Britain*, and the *British* Isles, exemplified and
" proved by monuments now extant in *Cornwall* and the
" *Scilly Islands*; with a Vocabulary of the *Cornu-British*
" Language, by *William Borlase* *, LL. D. F. R. S. Rector
" of

* Dr. *William Borlase* was born at *Pendeen*, in the parish of *St. Just*, *Cornwall*, on the 2d of *February*, 1695-6. He was entered of *Exeter College*, *Oxford*, March 1712-13; where, 1719, he took the degree of M. A. and the same year was admitted to Deacon's orders, and ordained Priest in 1720. In 1722, he was instituted, by Dr. *Weston*, Bishop of *Exeter*, to the rectory of *Ludgvan* in *Cornwall*, to which he had been presented by, *Charles* Duke of *Bolton*. In 1724 he married *Anne*, eldest surviving daughter and co-heir of *William Smith*, M. A. rector of the parishes of *Camborn* and *Illuggan*. In 1732, the Lord Chancellor *King*, by the recommendation of Sir *William Morice*, bart. presented Mr. *Borlase* to the vicarage of *St. Just*, his native parish, and where his father had a considerable property. This vicarage and the rectory of *Ludgvan* were the only ecclesiastical preferments he ever received. But he held afterwards the respectable office of vice-warden of the Stannaries. When Mr. *Borlase* was fixed at *Ludgvan*, which was a retired, but delightful situation, he was esteemed and respected by the principal gentry of *Cornwall*. In the pursuit of general knowledge he was active and vigorous; and his mind being of an inquisitive turn, he could not survey with inattention or indifference the peculiar objects which his situation pointed to his view. There were in the parish of *Ludgvan* rich copper works belonging to the late Earl of *Godolphin*. These abounded with mineral and metallic fossils, which Mr. *Borlase* collected from time to time; and his collection increasing by degrees, he was encouraged to study at large the natural history of his native county. While he was engaged in this design, he could not avoid being struck with the numerous monuments of remote antiquity that are to be met with in several parts of *Cornwall*; and which had hitherto been passed over with far less examination than they deserved. Enlarging, therefore, his plan, he determined to gain as accurate an acquaintance as possible with the Druid learning, and with the religion and customs of the ancient *Britons* before their conversion to Christianity. To this under-taking he was encouraged by several gentlemen of his neighbourhood, who were men of literature and lovers of *British* antiquities; and particularly by Sir *John St. Aubyn*, grandfather of the present baronet of that family, and the late Rev. *Edward Collins*, vicar of *St. Erth*, Dr. *Charles Lyttelton*, late Bishop of *Carlisle*, and Dr. *Milles*, the present Dean of *Exeter*. In 1750, being at *London*, he was admitted a Fellow of the Royal Society, after having shewn how well he deserved that honour, by communicating an ingenious and curious essay on the *Cornish* crystals. Mr. *Borlase* having completed, in 1753, his manuscript of the antiquities of *Cornwall*, carried it to *Oxford*, where he finished the whole impression, in folio, in the *February* following. A second edition of it, in the same form, was published at *London*, in 1769. His next publication was, " Observations on the ancient and present State of the Islands of *Scilly*, and their Im-" portance to the Trade of *Great Britain*, in a letter to the Rev. *Charles Lyttelton*, " LL. D. Dean of *Exeter*, and F. R. S." This work, which was printed likewise at *Oxford*, and appeared in 1756, in quarto, was an extension of a paper that had been read before the Royal Society, on the 8th of *February*, 1753. At the request of Dr.

Lyttelton

" of *Ludgvan, Cornwall.* The Second Edition revifed, with
" feveral

Lyttelton this account was enlarged into a diftinct treatife, intituled, " An Account of
" the great alterations which the Iflands of *Scilly* have undergone, fince the time of
" the ancients, who mention them, as to their number, extent, and pofition." In
1757, Mr. *Borlafe* again employed the *Oxford* prefs, in printing his " Natural
Hiftory of *Cornwall*," for which he had been many years making collections, and which
was publifhed in 1758. He fent a variety of foffils, and remains of antiquity, which he
had defcribed in his works, to the *Afhmolean* Mufeum, to which repofitory he continued
to fend every thing curious of the like kind which fell into his hands. For his benefactions in this refpect that learned body conferred on him the degree of Doctor of
Laws. Though Dr. *Borlafe*, by the time he had completed his three principal works,
had exceeded his fixtieth year, he continued to exert his ufual diligence and vigour.
The chief objects of his attention were his paftoral duty, and the ftudy of the fcriptures.
In the courfe of this ftudy, he drew up paraphrafes on the book of *Job* and the books
of *Solomon*, and wrote fome other pieces of a religious kind; all which, however, he
feems to have compofed rather for his private improvement, than with a view to publication. The correction and enlargement of his Antiquities of *Cornwall* for a fecond
edition engaged fome part of his time; and when this bufinefs was completed, he applied his attention to a minute revifion of his Natural Hiftory, and to interfperfe
the additional difcoveries which had occurred to him. As this work is already become fcarce, a new edition of it, with the author's improvements, would probably
be very acceptable to the publick. After he had revifed his Natural Hiftory, he
alfo prepared for the prefs a Treatife he had compofed fome years before, concerning the
Creation and Deluge. This curious work was actually put into my hands, and two
pages of it printed in octavo as a fpecimen; when a violent illnefs, in *January* 1771,
and the apprehenfions of entangling himfelf in fo long and clofe an attention as the correcting of the fheets folely, and at fuch a diftance from *London*, would require, induced
him to drop his defign, and to recall the manufcript from Mr. *B. White*, his bookfeller.
From the time of his illnefs, he began fenfibly to decline; the infirmities of old age came
faft upon him; and it was vifible to all his friends that his diffolution was approaching.
This expected event happened on the 31ft of *Auguft*, 1772, in the 77th year of his age.
He was lamented in the feveral relations of a kind father, an affectionate brother,
a fincere friend, an inftructive paftor, a man of erudition, and a good citizen. He was
buried within the communion rails in *Ludgvan* church, by the fide of Mrs. *Borlafe*, who
had been dead above three years, and over whofe grave he had caufed to be inferibed the
following elegant teftimony of the mutual harmony and affection in which they had lived:

Annæ fuæ,
Per annos propemodum quadraginta et quinque
Uxori peramatæ, amanti, amabili,
Extremum hoc qualecunque
Grati animi pignus,

Pofuit
Gulielmus Borlafe.
Deceffit in Chrifto multum defiderata
Aprilis xxi^mo die. MDCCLXIX.
Ætat. LXIV.

The epitaph placed over Dr. *Borlafe* by his executor is as follows:

Hic etiam funt repofitæ
Reliquiæ *Annæ* mariti
Gul. Borlafe, LL. D. R. S. S.
Perurbani, perhumani, perquam pii,
Hujufce parochiæ per annos LII

Rectoris defideratiffimi,
In republica necnon literaria verfatiffimi.
Loquuntur fcripta,
Teftantur pofteri.
Ob. xxxi *Aug.* A. D. MDCCLXXII.

The

" feveral Additions by the Author*," folio; Dr. *Taylor's* " Elements of Civil Law," 4to ; " Fables for Grown Gentlemen," by Mr. *Hall*, 4to ; " The Prefent State of the Nation," and " Sentiments

The Doctor had by his lady fix fons †, two of whom alone furvived him, the Rev. Mr. *John Borlafe* (now living in *Cornwall*), and the Rev. Mr. *George Borlafe* (late Fellow of *All Souls College* in *Oxford*), fince deceafed. Befides Dr. *Borlafe's* literary connections with Dr. *Lyttelton* and Dr. *Milles*, before mentioned, he correfponded with moft of the ingenious men of his time ‡. He had a particular intercourfe of this kind with Mr. *Pope* ; and there is ftill exifting a large collection of letters written by that celebrated poet to our author. He furnifhed Mr. *Pope* with the greateft part of the materials for forming his grotto at *Twickenham*, confifting of fuch curious foffils as the county of *Cornwall* abounds with : and there may ftill be feen Dr. *Borlafe's* name in capitals, compofed of cryftals. On this occafion a very handfome letter was written to the Doctor by Mr. *Pope*, in which he fays, " I am much obliged to you for your valuable collection of " *Cornifh* diamonds. I have placed them where they may beft reprefent yourfelf, *in a* " *fhade, but fhining* ;" alluding to the obfcurity of Dr. *Borlafe's* fituation, and the brilliancy of his talents. A lift of his valuable communications to the Royal Society, nineteen in number, is printed in the Biographia Britannica, 1780, vol. II. p. 425.

* " Some of the miftakes and errors I muft take wholly upon myfelf. The literal " errors of the prefs, the Printer and I muft take betwixt us." *Author's Preface.*—" I " cannot take leave of my printers without expreffing my very great fatisfaction at the " pains they have taken to fave me trouble in correcting the proof-fheets, and for their " fingular attention to the beauty and perfection of the book." *MS. Letter.*

† For one of his fons, who died young in the naval fervice, there is the following infcription on a fmall plate in *Ludgvan* church, written by the Doctor :

By the fmallnefs of this table,
Judge not, reader, of that lofs
Which it deplores.
Cbr. Borlafe, a youth of fweet and amiable difpofition,
Choofing the life of a failor,
And making quick advances to deferve
The honours of his profeffion,
Died, neither by the fury of war,
(In which he was engaged about four years)
Nor by the dangerous element
On which he ferved his country,
But by a fever.

Like a fair flower that had furvived
The winter's hail and ftorms,
Referved to be gathered, not torn off,
In time of peace,
He was taken by God to himfelf,
On the coaft of *Guinea*, *Feb.* 21, 1749.
His affectionate parents, deprived of a moft hopeful fon,
And unable to pay him the proper funeral duties,
Engrave their remembrance of him
In this plate :
Contented, becaufe fuch was the will of God.

‡ I have accidentally two valuable letters from Dr. *Borlafe* to Dr. *Parfons*, which my readers will not be difpleafed to fee in print : 1. " Dear Sir, I have many obligations to Dr. *Parfons* ; but that you " have not only given my two poor Effays your reading, but, like a real friend, pointed out to me " what is to be reconfidered, is the greateft of all : I will keep your ftrictures conftantly in view, " and if ever thofe pieces are worth revifing for the prefs, your arguments will have great weight " with me. It was far from my intention, when I was fearching after fecond caufes, to depreciate " the firft. Nothing in your excellent letter pleafes me more, than the conftant reverence which " you exprefs for the Author of Nature. Your juft application of Natural Knowledge to the fup- " port of Religion is evident in all your writings, and I am the lefs furprifed to find fo much " allowed to the *fupernatural Fiat of God*. 'Tis a proper exercife of the human faculties to enquire " into fecondary caufes, but to decide peremptorily, and not ultimately refer to the wifdom and " goodnefs of God, is very wrong. After confidering the great cataftrophe of the Deluge as much " as I could, I really found the account of *Mofes* the beft I could follow : I am no *Hutchinfonian*, " as you muft have obferved in feveral paragraphs ; but my Theory, I found, could not be con- " fermable to Scripture, becaufe every principal circumftance which the nature of things fuggefted
" throughout

" Sentiments of an *Englifh* Freeholder," two popular pamphlets by Mr. *Burke*, 4to ; " The " Microfcope made Eafy,"
by Mr. *Henry Baker* *, 8vo ; Dr. *Owen's* " Enquiry into
" the

* This ingenious and diligent Naturalift was born in *Fleet-Street, London*, either
near the end of the laft, or very early in the beginning of the prefent century. His

" throughout the whole procefs, is to be found, one where or other (at leaft aecording to my appre-
" henfion) in Holy Writ. When I fuppofe that the bed of the Ocean was raifed, and conclude
" that effect not to be fo great and ftupendous as it may at firft appear, when the fmall depth of
" the Sea in proportion to the extent of the Globe is laid into the fame eftimate, I would not be
" underftood but that the fupernatural power of God attended as well as caufed this Elevation
" throughout, regulated and conducted it to a certain height, and with the fame care (if I may fo
" fay) adjufted it's fubfidence, fo that far it was from my thoughts to exclude the preternatural
" interpofition of God ; I only fuggeft the probable materials with which this effect might have
" been produced, which no one knows better than yourfelf that former Theorifts have been fo
" much diftreffed about, that they have fallen into the moft abfurd fuppofitions, have torn the Earth
" to pieces, moved the Sun from its place, called down the Comets, had recourfe to a new Creation,
" in fhort, reverfed the World, and thrown imputations of defect on the Mofaical writings, which
" I think they do not at all deferve.—In oppofition only to fuch chimeras, I endeavour to fhew
" that the earth is ftored (and ought to be fo, when we confider the wifdom and knowledge of God)
" with a fufficiency of the requifite materials, and by its frame adapted to, and capable of producing,
" the effect ; but the marfhalling, difpofing, and exciting thefe materials, I hope I have referred
" only to God's almighty power. I am fure it is my opinion. As to the caufe of Earthquakes, I
" do not enter into the difpute, neither do I at all deny that electrical fhocks may be attended with
" like effects ; I fhould be extremely obliged to you, however, if you would inform me whether
" ignition or explofion in the bowels of the earth, affecting whole regions at once, will not prefup-
" pofe that cavernous texture which I have attributed to the earth as the natural confequence of its
" firft fettlement. I writ the two theories as an introduction to the obfervations I am making on
" the Natural Hiftory of *Cornwall*, and am glad you think them fit for a Propylæum. Your opi-
" nion of the formation of Corals is very agreeable to what I take to be truth ; the *French* Philo-
" fopher has proved the inhabitancy of the Polypi, but no more ; and I can as eafily believe that
" man formed the earth, becaufe he builds upon and dwells in it, as that the femi-animal Polypi
" could form the branchy, and to all appearance, vegetable Coral. I could almoft wifh that your
" regard for me had been lefs, becaufe I am afraid it has made you think more favourably of the
" theory and antiquities than they deferve. I remain, Sir, your moft obliged and obedient humble
" fervant. WILLIAM BORLASE. *Ludgvan, June* 15, 1754."
   2. " SIR, The fubjects of yefterday's converfation were fo very entertaining, that it was
" impoffible to prevent my recollecting and reviewing what had made fo agreeable an impreffion
" upon me. As to the ring, upon fecond thoughts, I believe I was guilty of a miftake, and
" therefore I take the firft opportunity of acknowledging it : I thought that ΔIAΒIΩV might
" be two words, and the verb for *tranfigas*, or fome fuch word might be underftood, as is ufual
" in the concife Infcriptions of the *Greeks*: but I am apprehenfive, for I have neither Grammar
" nor Lexicon to make me certain, that *ĩa*, when it fignifies *per*, will govern an accufative
" cafe ; and therefore, if it had been uncompounded, that line would have been *ĩa ƨov*, or *ĩa tov βiov* :
" I therefore willingly retract, and think that ΔIAΒIΩV is one word, a verb of the Imperative
" Mood, which in our language, literally, muft be tranflated, *Live thou* ; but the *Greek* is much
" more expreffive, and, by the happy idiom of that language which gives fpirit to their verbs
" by annexing prepofitions, fignifies in one word all that we can fay in *Live thou all thy life long—*
" *happily*. It has alfo occurred to me fince I faw you, that the SECVRITAS of the ancients
" is frequently reprefented on medals, as reclining on a low pillar, or rather tall pedeftal, to
" exprefs, if I am not miftaken, the ftability of the empire ; and I refer to your better judgment,
" whether *Cupid's* ftanding on fuch a pillar may not intend the Conftancy of Love. This An-
" tique, by the engraving on one fide, and the Legend on the other, feems to me to have been
" defigned as a Love-amulet or charm, which the ancients perfuaded themfelves that as long as
" they carried about with them, they fhould not be unhappy ....If thefe amulets were ever fo
" powerful, you are fo happy in domeftic life, as to have no occafion for them. I remain, Sir, your
" moft obedient fervant, WILLIAM BORLASE. *Norfolk-ftreet, Monday nine o'clock*."

father's

" the prefent State of the Septuagint Verfion," 8vo;
Pope's

father's profeffion is not known ; but his mother was, in her time, a Midwife of great practice. He was brought up, under an eminent bookfeller who preceded the elder *Dod-fley*, to the bufinefs of a Bookfeller, in which, however, he appears not to have engaged at all after his apprenticefhip ; or, if he did, it was foon relinquifhed by him : for though it was in his power to have drawn away all his mafter's beft cuftomers, he would not fet up againft him. Mr. *Baker* being of a philofophical turn of mind, and having diligently attended to the methods which might be practicable and ufeful in the cure of ftammering, and efpecially in teaching deaf and dumb perfons to fpeak, he made this the employment of his life. This idea was fuggefted to him by a vifit to the late Mr. Serjeant *Forfter*, at *Enfield*, who had two fifters both deaf and dumb. In the profecution of fo valuable and difficult an undertaking, he was very fuccefsful ; and feveral of his pupils, who are ftill living, bear teftimony to the ability and good effect of his inftructions. He married *Sophia*, youngeft daughter of the famous *Daniel Defoe*, who brought him two fons, both of whom he furvived. On the 29th of *January*, 1740, Mr. *Baker* was elected a fellow of the Society of Antiquaries ; and, on the 12th of *March* following, the fame honour was conferred upon him by the Royal Society. In 1744, Sir *Godfrey Copley's* gold medal was beftowed upon him, for having, by his microfcopical experiments on the cryftallizations and configurations of faline particles, produced the moft extraordinary difcovery during that year. This medal was prefented to him by Sir *Hans Sloane*, late Prefident of the Royal Society, and only furviving truftee of Sir *Godfrey Copley's* donation, at the recommendation of Sir *Hans's* worthy fucceffor, *Martin Folkes*, Efq; and of the Council of the faid Society. Having led a very ufeful and honourable life, he died, at his apartments in *The Strand*, on the 25th of *November*, 1774, being then above feventy years of age. His wife had been dead fome time before ; and he only left one grandfon, *William Baker*, who was born *Feb.* 17, 1763, and to whom, on his living to the age of twenty-one, he bequeathed the bulk of his fortune, which he had acquired by his profeffion of teaching deaf and dumb perfons to fpeak. It is much to be regretted, that Mr. *Baker* fhould fuffer his art to die with him, which we are affured was the cafe, and all his patients were enjoined to fecrecy *:. He gave alfo, by his will, a hundred pounds to the Royal Society, the intereft of which was to be applied in paying for an annual Oration on Natural Hiftory or Experimental Philofophy. He gave to each of his two executors one hundred pounds † ; and his wife's gold watch and trinkets in truft to his daughter in-law *Mary Baker* for her life, and to be afterwards given to the future wife of his grandfon. To Mrs. *Baker* he gave alfo an annuity of fifty pounds. His furniture, printed books (but not Mff.), curiofities, and collections of every fort, he directed fhould be fold, which was accordingly done. His fine collection of native and foreign foffils, petrefactions, fhells, corals, vegetables, ores, &c. with fome antiquities and other curiofities, were fold by auction, *March* 13, 1775, and the nine following days. He was buried, as he defired, in an unexpenfive manner, in the church-yard of *St. Mary-le-Strand*; within which church, on the South-wall, he ordered a fmall tablet to be erected to his memory. " An infcription for it," he faid,

* At the end of his inftruction he took a bond for 100*l*. of each fcholar not to divulge his method ; and he is faid to have ftood a fuit for it with a fon of the late Earl *Buchan*.

† In cafe the grandfon fhould not attain the age of twenty-one, Mr. *Baker* gave to each of his executors 500*l*. ; to Mrs. *Baker* 100*l*. a year ; to the Royal Society 500*l*. ; to the Society of Antiquaries, 300*l*. ; to Mrs. *Rofa Dupleffis*, 200*l*. ; to Mr. *Boddington* 100*l*. ; to Dr. *Parfons* (and, in cafe he fhould be dead, to his fifter-in-law Mifs *Reynolds*) 100*l*. ; and fome other legacies.

" would

Pope's " Letters to a Lady," 8vo, then printed for the firſt time ;

" would probably be found among his papers ; if not, he hoped ſome learned friend " would write one agreeably to truth." This friendly office, however, remains as yet to be performed. Mr. *Baker* was a conſtant and uſeful attendant at the meetings of the Royal and Antiquarian Societies, and in both was frequently choſen one of the Council. Mr. *Baker* was peculiarly attentive to all the new improvements which were made in Natural Science, and very ſolicitous for the proſecution of them. Though he was ſo reſpectable a member of the Royal Society, he did not eſcape the ſtrictures of Dr. *Hill,* in the Doctor's review of the works of that illuſtrious body. Several of his communications are printed in the Philoſophical Tranſactions * ; and, beſides the papers written by himſelf, he was the means, by his extenſive correſpondence, of conveying to the Society the intelligence and obſervations of other inquiſitive and philoſophical men. His correſpondence was not confined to his own country. To him we are obliged for a true hiſtory of the *Coccus Polonicus,* tranſmitted by Dr. *Wolfe.* It is to Mr. *Baker's* communications that we owe the larger *Alpine Strawberry,* of late ſo much cultivated, and approved of, in *England.* The ſeeds of it were ſent in a letter from Profeſſor *Bruns* of *Turin,* to our Philoſopher, who gave them to ſeveral of his friends, by whoſe care they furniſhed an abundant increaſe. The ſeeds, likewiſe, of the true Rhubarb, or *Rheum Palmatum,* now to be met with in almoſt every garden in this country, were firſt tranſmitted to Mr. *Baker* by Dr. *Mounſey,* Phyſician to the Empreſs of *Ruſſia.* Theſe, like the former, were diſtributed to his various acquaintance, and ſome of the ſeeds vegetated very kindly. It is apprehended that all the plants of the Rhubarb now in *Great Britain* were propagated from this ſource. Two or three of Mr. *Baker's* papers, which relate to Antiquities, may be found in the Philoſophical Tranſactions †. The Society for the Encouragement of Arts, Manufactures, and Commerce, is under ſingular obligations to our worthy Naturaliſt. As he was one of the earlieſt members of it, ſo he contributed in no ſmall degree to its riſe and eſtabliſhment. At its firſt inſtitution, he officiated for ſome time, *gratis,* as ſecretary. He was many years chairman of the Committee of Accounts : and he took an active part in the general deliberations of the Society. In his attendance he was almoſt unfailing, and there were few queſtions of any moment upon which he did not deliver his opinion. Though, from the lowneſs of his voice, his manner of ſpeaking was not powerful, it was clear, ſenſible, and convincing ; what he ſaid, being uſually much to the purpoſe, and always proceeding from the beſt intentions, had often the good effect of contributing to bring the ſociety to rational determinations, when many of the members ſeemed to have loſt themſelves in the intricacies of debate. He drew up a ſhort account of the original of this ſociety, and of the concern he himſelf had in forming it ; which was read before the Society of Antiquaries, and would be a pleaſing preſent to the publick. Mr. *Baker* was a poetical writer in the early part of his life. His " Invocation of Health" got abroad without his knowledge ; but was reprinted by himſelf in his " Original Poems, ſerious and humourous," Part the firſt, 8vo. 1725. The ſecond part came out in 1726. Among theſe Poems are ſome Tales as witty and as looſe as *Prior's.* He was the author, likewiſe, of " The Univerſe,

* Phil. Tranſ. Nº 457. p. 441. 448. Nº 458. p. 503. Nº 459. p. 655. Nº 471. p. 616. Nº 472. p. 35. 77. Nº 477. p. 520. Nº 482. p. 432. Nº 483. p. 557. Nº 484. p. 576. Nº 486. p. 174. 270. Nº 491. p. 37. Nº 494. p. 334. Nº 497. p. 601. 617. To which ſome other references might, it is believed, be added.

† Phil. Tranſ. Nº 477. p. 520. Nº 483. p. 557.

" a

time; and Mr. *Nevile's* * " Imitations of *Juvenal* and *Per-*
" *fius*," 8vo.

In the fame year (1769) he printed, for Mr. *Wood* †, " An
" Effay on the Original Genius of *Homer*," 4to. Of this
literary

" a Poem, intended to reftrain the Pride of Man," which has been feveral times reprinted.
His account of the Water Polype, which was originally publifhed in the Philofophical
Tranfactions, was afterwards enlarged into a feparate treatife, and hath gone through
feveral editions. But his principal publications are, " The Microfcope made Eafy,"
and " Employment for the Microfcope." The firft of thefe, which was originally publifhed in 1742, or 1743, hath gone through fix editions. The fecond edition of the other,
which, to fay the leaft of it, is equally pleafing and inftructive, appeared in 1764.
Thefe Treatifes, and efpecially the latter, contain the moft curious and important of
the Obfervations and Experiments which Mr. *Baker* either laid before the Royal Society,
or publifhed feparately. It has been faid of Mr. *Baker*, that " he was a philofopher in
" little things." If it was intended by this language to leffen his reputation, there is no
propriety in the ftricture. He was an intelligent, upright, and benevolent man, much
refpected by thofe who knew him beft. His friends were the friends of fcience and virtue: and it will always be remembered by his contemporaries, that no one was more
ready than himfelf to affift thofe with whom he was converfant in their various refearches
and endeavours for the advancement of knowledge and the benefit of fociety. This
tranquil good man was unhappy in his children. His eldeft fon, *David Erfkine*
Baker, was a young man of genius and learning. Having been adopted by an uncle,
who was a filk-throwfter in *Spital-fields*, he fucceeded him in the bufinefs; but wanted
the prudence and attention which are neceffary to fecure profperity in trade. He married the daughter of Mr. *Clendon*, a reverend empiric. Like his father, he was both a
philofopher and a poet; and wrote feveral occafional poems in the periodical collections;
fome of which were much admired at the time, but fo violent was his turn for dramatic
performance that he repeatedly engaged with the loweft ftrolling companies, in fpite of
every effort of his father to reclaim him. The publick was indebted to him for " The
" Companion to the Play-houfe," in two volumes, 1764, 12mo; a work which, though
imperfect, had confiderable merit, and fhewed that he poffeffed a very extenfive knowledge of our dramatic authors; and which has fince been confiderably improved by the
attention of a gentleman in every refpect well qualified for the undertaking. Mr. *Baker's*
other fon *Henry* followed the profeffion of a lawyer, but in no creditable line; and left
one fon, *William*, who has been already mentioned as the grandfather's heir.

* I have already had occafion (in p. 279) to mention this amiable poet; and have
fince reafon to lament his death, which happened *September* 17, 1781.

† *Robert Wood*, Efq; under-fecretary of ftate; who, in the earlier part of life, had
vifited the fcenes which *Homer* has fo beautifully defcribed; where it is not furprifing
that he caught what he calls " the fpecies of enthufiafm which belongs to fuch a journey,
" performed in fuch fociety, where *Homer* being my guide, and *Bouverie* and *Daw-*
" *kins* my fellow travellers, the beauties of the firft of Poets were enjoyed in the company
" of the beft of friends. Had I been fo fortunate," he adds, " as to have enjoyed their
" affiftance, in arranging and preparing for the publick the fubftance of our many friend-
" ly converfations on this fubject, I fhould be lefs anxious about the fate of the follow-

I

" ing

literary curiofity no more than SEVEN copies were taken off; one of which having by the Author's pemiffion been retained by Mr. *Bowyer*, he fhewed it to Mr. *Clarke*; which

" ing work: But whatever my fuccefs may be in an attempt to contribute to the amufe-
" ment of a vacant hour, I am happy to think, that though I fhould fail to anfwer the
" expectations of public curiofity, I am fure to fatisfy the demands of private friend-
" fhip; and that, acting as the only furvivor and truftee for the literary concerns of my
" late fellow-travellers, I am, to the beft of my judgement, carrying into execution the
" purpofe of men for whofe memory I fhall ever retain the greateft veneration; and
" though I may do injuftice to thofe honeft feelings which urge me to this pious tafk,
" by mixing an air of compliment in an act of duty, yet I muft not difown a private,
" perhaps an idle confolation, which, if it be vanity to indulge, it would be ingratitude
" to fupprefs, *viz.* that as long as my imperfect defcriptions fhall preferve from oblivion
" the prefent ftate of the *Troade*, and the remains of *Balbeck* and *Palmyra*, fo long will
" it be known that *Dawkins* and *Bouverie* were my friends." Mr. *Wood* had drawn up
a great part of this effay in the life-time of Mr. *Dawkins*, who wifhed it to be made
public. " But," fays Mr. *Wood*, " while I was preparing it for the prefs, I had the
" honour of being called to a ftation, which for fome years fixed my whole attention
" upon objects of fo very different a nature, that it became neceffary to lay *Homer* afide,
" and to referve the further confideration of my fubject for a time of more leifure.
" However, in the courfe of that active period, the duties of my fituation engaged me in
" an occafional attendance upon a Nobleman [the late Earl *Granville*], who, though he
" prefided at his Majefty's councils, referved fome moments for literary amufement.
" His Lordfhip was fo partial to this fubject, that I feldom had the honour of receiving
" his commands on bufinefs, that he did not lead the converfation to *Greece* and *Homer*.
" Being directed to wait upon his Lordfhip a few days before he died, with the Preli-
" minary Articles of the Treaty of *Paris*, I found him fo languid, that I propofed poft-
" poning my bufinefs for another time; but he infifted that I fhould ftay, faying, ' it could
" not prolong his life, to neglect his duty;' and, repeating a paffage out of *Sarpedon's*
" fpeech, dwelt with particular emphafis on a line which recalled to his mind the diftin-
" guifhing part he had taken in public affairs:

Ὦ πέπον, εἰ μὲν γὰρ πόλεμον περὶ τόνδε φυγόντες,
Ἀιεὶ δὴ μέλλοιμεν ἀγήρω τ' ἀθανάτω τε
Ἔσσεσθ', ΟΥΤΕ ΚΕΝ ΑΥΤΟΣ ΕΝΙ ΠΡΩΤΟΙΣΙ
    ΜΑΧΟΙΜΗΝ,
Οὔτε κέ σε ςέλλοιμι μάχην ἐς κυδιάνειραν·
Νῦν δ', ἔμπης γὰρ κῆρες ἐφεςᾶσιν θανάτοιο
Μυρίαι, ἃς οὐκ ἔςι φυγεῖν βροτὸν, οὐδ' ὑπαλύξαι,
Ἴομεν.   Il. M. 322.

Could all our care elude the gloomy grave,
Which claims no lefs the fearful than the brave,
For luft of fame, I fhould not vainly dare
In fighting fields, nor urge thy foul to war.
But fince, alas! ignoble age muft come,
Difeafe, and death's inexorable doom;
The life which others pay let us beftow,
And give to Fame what we to Nature owe.
                        Pope's Hom. Il. xii. 387.

" His Lordfhip then repeated the laft word feveral times with a calm and determined re-
" fignation; and, after a ferious paufe of fome minutes, he defired to hear the Treaty
" read; to which he liftened with great attention; and recovered fpirits enough to de-
" clare the approbation of a dying Statefman (I ufe his own words) on the moft glo-
" rious war, and moft honourable peace, this country ever faw."

H h h   produced

produced the two Letters printed below*. I have now by me the copy which Mr. *Bowyer* kept, with a few of his

* 1. Mr. CLARKE to Mr. BOWYER.

" DEAR SIR,

" I thank you for the fight of this curiofity. It is like an Oriental Novel, wild and
" entertaining. The author is certainly a man of genius and diligence, and is poffeffed
" of a fpirit of enthufiafm, very proper for his fubject, and agreeable to his readers.
" But then fuch a paffion for Paradoxes, as does not agree fo well with us old folks; it
" cools our appetites rather too much, who are willing to read not only for amufement,
" but ufe. What fignifies tilting againft fome of the beft eftablifhed parts of ancient
" Hiftory, unlefs you were armed for the purpofe, with confiderable evidence to fupport
" it? The Introduction of Letters among the *Greeks* is a fact well-attefted: and he who
" can believe that all *Homer* was preferved only by memory, muft believe that the me-
" mory of fo remarkable a fact was eafily tranfmitted by the fame conveyance. Nor
" do I fee any thing proved in this whole differtation, but that *Homer* was an *Afiatic*.
" The verfe you quote from the Iliad is a ftrong prefumption that *Homer* was no ftranger
" to alphabetical writing. It does not appear to me that *Syria*, the ifland *Homer* men-
" tions, was the *Syros* near *Delos*, but perhaps fome unknown ifland, far enough from
" *Delos*, Ὀρ͡υγίας καθύπερθεν; from whence the Sun in the Winter Solftice was returning.
" There is no making any fenfe of the τροπαὶ ἠελίοιο any other way: nor can καθύπερθεν
" fignify *juft by Delos*. Remarks upon Mr. *Pope's* Tranflation was a matter of no great
" moment. He does not alter the fituation; but decorates the places with more ver-
" dure, perhaps, or beauty, than they deferved. If he places the fall of the *Scamander*
" into the *Ægean* fea, inftead of the *Hellefpont*; it is no more than, I think, all the old
" maps had done before him. Is it certain that *Homer's* is what falls into the *Hellef-*
" *pont?* As to the defence of *Homer's Pharos*, I leave that to Mr. *Bryant*. To think
" that all the *Delta* was an acquifition to the *Egyptian* coaft between *Homer's* time and
" *Alexander's*, is beyond my imagination. Was nothing of that kind done before the
" *Ifraelites* were in *Egypt*, and after that, before *Homer* was born? His comparifon
" between the Patriarchal, Heroic, and Bedouin manners is far from being exact. There
" was no unnatural feparation between the fexes in the Patriarchal times. The Patri-
" archs travelled from *Euphrates* through all *Palestine* down to *Egypt*, without meet-
" ing any difficulties in their way, and had a focial intercourfe with many of the in-
" habitants. There were many cities formerly upon the Weftern fide of *Arabia Deferta*.
" The ruins of one of them, called *Maccacee*, are (if we believe the *Arabs*, whofe ve-
" racity Mr. *Wood* does not queftion) greater than thofe at *Palmyra*, and were not yet
" vifited by any *European*. But enough of this, efpecially by candle-light. I have
" fcarce had a leifure hour fince I received this favour, and fo was forced to run it over
" very curforily. That *Troas* and *Phrygia* were, in *Homer's* time, different kingdoms,
" may be eafily believed, fince he places no lefs than eight Principalities in *Theffaly* only.
" I am, Sir, your much obliged, and affectionate, &c."

2. Mr. WOOD to Mr. BOWYER.

" DEAR SIR, *Stanhope-Street, Thurfday Night.*

" I find your obliging letter on my table returning from office; I fhall call on you
" fome day to thank you for it: in the mean time accept my acknowledgements for
" yourfelf

his own notes*; and, what is more curious, the margin contains every addition and variation made afterwards by Mr. *Wood* when he gave his improved thoughts to the publick.

In 1770 he printed, among many other articles, the " Miscellanea Sacra" of the late Lord Viscount *Barrington* †, revised

" yourself and your friend ‡. I like his manly freedom, especially as I see he speaks as
" he thinks. If my little farrago of Classical Conjectures sees the light, I shall profit
" of his animadversions. Upon the whole, I think he is very fair; and if he is not
" more attached to his old opinions than I am to my new ones, we shall meet in a
" point; nay, I shall go more than half-way towards him, if it is Mr. *Markland*; for,
" however disposed I may be to think for myself, I am not deaf to respectable authority.
" I am, in great haste, but with no less truth, your humble servant."

* One of these is worth inserting here: " *Homer*," says Mr. *Wood*, " has been highly
" extolled for his knowledge of Medicine and Anatomy, particularly the latter; and his
" insight into the structure of the human body has been considered so nice, that he has
" been imagined by some to have wounded his hearers with too much science." On this
passage Mr. *Bowyer's* note stands thus: " Mr. *Pope*, as he read over every book he could
" think of that could give him any light into the life of *Homer*, had gotten an old
" *Latin* edition of *Diodorus Siculus*, wherein he found *Homer* was said to be *medicus*.
" At which he was overjoyed, and thought he should communicate a great discovery.
" But, behold, when he consulted another edition, he found the true reading was *mendicus*.
" This I had from his own mouth, at *Twickenham*."

† *John Shute*, Lord Viscount *Barrington*, a nobleman of considerable learning, and author of several books, was the youngest son of *Benjamin Shute*, merchant, youngest son of *Francis Shute*, of *Upton*, in the county of *Leicester*, Esquire. He was born at *Theobald's*, in *Hertfordshire*, in the year 1678 §; and received part of his education at *Utrecht*, as appears from a *Latin* oration which he delivered at that university, and which he published there in 1698, in 4to. under the following title: " Oratio de stu-
" dio Philosophiæ conjungendo cum studio Juris *Romani*; habita in inclyta Academia
" *Trajectina* Kalendis *Junii*, 1698, a *Johanne Shute, Anglo*, Ph. D. & L. A. M." After his return to *England*, he applied himself to the study of the law in *The Inner Temple*. In 1701, he published, but without his name, " An Essay ‖ upon the Interest of *England*,
" in respect to Protestants dissenting from the established Church," 4to. This was reprinted two years after, with considerable alterations and enlargements. Some time after this he published another piece in 4to. intituled, " The Rights of Protestant Dis-
" senters, in two parts." During the prosecution of his studies in the law, he was applied to by Queen *Anne's* Whig Ministry, at the instigation of Lord *Somers*, to engage the Presbyterians in *Scotland* to favour the important measure, then in agitation, of an union of the two kingdoms. Flattered, at the age of twenty-four, by an application, which

‡ Whose name Mr. *Bowyer* had not *then* communicated.
§ His mother was a daughter of the famous Mr. *Caryl*, author of the Commentary on *Job*.
‖ This Essay is mentioned by Dr. *Watts*, in a copy of verses addressed to the Author, and printed in the " *English* Poets," vol. XLVI. p. 169.

shewed

revised for the press by his son the learned and worthy
Bishop

shewed the opinion entertained of his abilities and influence by the greatest Lawyer and
Statesman of the age, he readily sacrificed the opening prospects of his profession, and
undertook the arduous employment. The happy execution of it was rewarded in 1708
by the place of Commissioner of the Customs; from which he was removed by the Tory
Administration in 1711, for his avowed opposition to their principles and conduct.
How high Mr. *Shute's* character stood in the estimation even of those who differed most
widely from him in religious and political sentiments, appears from the testimony borne
to it by Dr. *Swift**. In the reign of Queen *Anne*, *John Wildman*, of *Becket*, in the
county of *Berks*, Esq; adopted him for his son, after the *Roman* custom, and settled his
large estate upon him, though he was no relation, and is said to have been but slightly
acquainted with him. Some years after, he had another considerable estate left him by
Francis Barrington, of *Tofts*, Esq; who had married his first cousin, and died without
issue. This occasioned him to procure an act of parliament, pursuant to the deed of
settlement, to assume the name, and bear the arms of *Barrington*. On the accession of
King *George* I. he was chosen member of parliament for the town of *Berwick upon
Tweed*. On the 5th of *July*, 1717, he had a reversionary grant of the office of Master
of the Rolls in *Ireland*, which he surrendered the 10th of *December*, 1731. King *George*
I. was also pleased, by privy seal, dated at *St. James's* the 10th of *June*, and by patent
at *Dublin*, *July* 1, 1720, to create him Baron *Barrington* of *Newcastle*, and Viscount
Barrington of *Ardglass*. In 1722, he was again returned to parliament as member for
the town of *Berwick*; but in 1723, the house of commons taking into consideration the
affair of the *Harburgh* lottery, a very severe and unmerited censure of expulsion was
passed upon his Lordship †, as sub-governor of the *Harburgh* Company, under the Prince
of *Wales*. In 1725 he published, in two volumes, 8vo, his " Miscellanea Sacra; or a
" new Method of considering so much of the History of the Apostles, as is contained
" in Scripture; in an abstract of their History, an Abstract of that Abstract, and four
" critical Essays." In this work the noble author has traced, with great care and judgement, the methods taken by the apostles, and first preachers of the Gospel, for propagating Christianity; and explained with great distinctness the several gifts of the spirit, by which they were enabled to discharge that office. These he improved into an
argument for the truth of the Christian religion; which is said to have staggered the
infidelity of Mr. *Anthony Collins*. In 1725, he published, in 8vo, " An Essay on the several
" Dispensations of God to Mankind, in the order in which they lie in the Bible; or, a
" short System of the Religion of Nature and Scripture," &c. He was also author of
several other tracts, which will be mentioned below ‡. He sometimes spoke in parliament,

---

* Dr. *Swift* writes thus to Archbishop *King*, in a letter dated *London*, *Nov.* 30, 1708. " One
" Mr *Shute* is named for secretary to Lord *Wharton*. He is a young man, but reckoned the shrewdest
" head in *England*; and the person in whom the Presbyterians chiefly confide; and if money be
" necessary towards the good work, it is reckoned he can command as far as 100,000l. from the
" body of the Dissenters here. As to his principles, he is a moderate man, frequenting the church
" and the meeting indifferently."
† A vindication of Lord *Barrington* was published at the time, in a pamphlet which had the appearance of being written by him, or at least of being published under his directions.
‡ 1. " A Dissuasive from Jacobitism; shewing in general what the nation is to expect from a Po-
" pish King; and, in particular, from the Pretender." The fourth edition of this was printed in 8vo,
in 1713.—2. " A Letter from a Layman, in communion with the Church of *England*, though dis-
" senting from her in some points, to the Right Rev. the Lord Bishop of ———. With a Post-
" script,
4

Bishop of *Landaff*, in 3 volumes, 8vo; a volume of
Sermons

ment, but appears not to have been a frequent speaker. He died at his seat at *Becket* in *Berkshire*, after a short illness, on the 14th of *December*, 1734, in the sixty-sixth year of his age. He generally attended divine worship among the Dissenters, and, for many years, received the sacrament at *Pinner's-Hall*, when Dr. *Jeremiah Hunt*, an eminent and learned Nonconformist divine, was pastor of the congregation that assembled there. He had formerly been an attendant on Mr. *Thomas Bradbury*, but quitted that gentleman on account of his bigoted zeal for imposing unscriptural terms upon the article of the Trinity. His Lordship was a disciple and friend of Mr. *Locke*, had a high value for the sacred writings, and was eminently skilled in them. As a writer in theology, he had great merit; and contributed much to the diffusing of that spirit of free scriptural criticism, which has since obtained among all denominations of Christians. As his attention was much turned to the study of divinity, he had a strong sense of the importance of free enquiry in matters of religion. In his writings, whenever he thought what he advanced was doubtful, or that his arguments were not strictly conclusive, though they might have great weight, he expressed himself with a becoming diffidence. He was remarkable for the politeness of his manners, and the gracefulness of his address, as we are assured by those who personally knew him. He married *Anne*, eldest daughter of Sir *William Daines*, by whom he left six sons and three daughters. *William*, his eldest son, succeeded to his father's honours; was elected, soon after he came of age, member for the town of *Berwick*, and afterwards for *Plymouth*; and, in the late and present reigns, has passed through the successive offices of Lord of the Admiralty, Master of the Wardrobe, Chancellor of the Exchequer, Treasurer of the Navy, and Secretary at War. *Francis*, the second, died young. *John*, the third, was a Major-General in the army, commanded the land forces at the reduction of the Island of *Guadeloupe* in 1758, and died in 1764. *Daines**, the fourth, King's Counsel, and one of the Justices of the grand session for the counties of *Chester*, &c. is author of 1. " *Observations upon* " the Ancient Statutes, 1766;" a work reprinted in the same year, and again in 1769 and 1775; 2. "The Naturalist's Journal, 1767," 4to; 3. "Directions for collecting Specimens " of Natural History, 1772," 4to; 4. "The *Anglo-Saxon* Version of *Orosius*, with an " *English* Translation and Notes, 1773," 8vo; 5. Several tracts relative to the proba-

" script, shewing how far the Bill to prevent the growth of schism is inconsistent with the Act of " toleration, and the other laws of this realm." The second edition of this was printed in 1714, 4to.—3. "The Layman's Letter to the Bishop of *Bangor*." The second edition of this was published in 1716, 4to.—4. "An Account of the late proceedings of the Dissenting-ministers at " *Salters-Hall*; occasioned by the differences amongst their brethren in the country: with some " thoughts concerning imposition of human forms for articles of faith. In a letter to the Rev. Dr. " *Gale*, 1719." 8vo.—5. "A Discourse of Natural and Revealed Religion, and the relation they bear " to each other, 1732." 8vo.—6. "Reflections on the 12th Query, contained in a paper, intituled, " Reasons offered against pushing for the Repeal of the Corporation and Test-Acts, and on the ani- " madversions on the answer to it, 8vo, 1733."

* The worthy Judge has already been mentioned (p. 10.) as the friend and patron of Mr. *Bowyer*; and I cannot pass by this fair opportunity of expressing my own obligations both to him and to his brother the Bishop. To the Admiral I am also indebted for his friendship to a near relation, who shared with him in the perils and the laurels of the war of 1747 †, which he did not long survive; had his life been spared, the writer of this note would probably have been engaged, under the banners of the gallant Admiral, in the naval service of his country.

† Mr. *Thomas Wilmot*, who was a lieutenant of *The Bellona*, under Captain *Barrington*, when in *August* 1747 he captured *The Duke of Chartres East India-man*.

bility

Sermons on several occasions, by Dr. *Ashton* *, 8vo; and a Translation from the *German* by *John Reinhold Forster*, of

Peter

bility of reaching the *North Pole*, 4to. 1775, &c. which are collected and enlarged in a volume of " Miscellanies, 1781," 4to ; 6. " Proposed Forms of Registers for Baptisms " and Burials, 1781," 4to. He is also author of many curious papers in the Philosophical Transactions and Archæologia ; some of which are likewise incorporated in the volume of " Miscellanies." *Samuel*, the fifth, is Vice-Admiral of the White, and greatly distinguished himself in the wars of 1747 and 1756, as well as in the present. *Shute*, the sixth, had his education at *Eton-school*, and the university of *Oxford* ; took orders in 1756, the degree of LL. D. in 1762, and was promoted to the Bishoprick of *Landaff* in 1769.

* Dr. *Thomas Ashton* was educated at *Eton* ; and was elected from thence to *King's College, Cambridge*, in 1733. He was probably the person to whom Mr. *Horace Walpole* addressed his Epistle from *Florence*, in 1740, under the title of " *Thomas Ashton*, Esq; " tutor to the Earl of *Plymouth* †." He was presented to the rectory of *Aldingham* in *Lancashire* in 17...; which he resigned ‡ in *March* 1749 ; and on the 3d of *May* following was presented by the provost and fellows of *Eton* to the rectory of *Sturminster Marshall* in *Dorsetshire*. He was then M. A. and had been chosen a fellow of *Eton* in *December* 1745. In 1752 he was collated to the rectory of *St. Botolph, Bishopsgate* ; in 1759 took the degree of D. D. ; on the 10th of *December*, 1760, he married Miss *Amyand* ; and in *May* 1762 was elected preacher at *Lincoln's-Inn*, which he resigned in 1764. Dr. *Ashton* died *March* 1, 1775, at the age of fifty-nine, after having for some years survived a severe attack of the palsey. His Discourses, admirable as they are in themselves, were rendered still more so by the excellence of his delivery. Hence he was frequently prevailed on to preach on public and popular occasions. He printed a Sermon on the Rebellion in 1745, 4to ; and a Thanksgiving Sermon on the close of it in 1746, 4to. In 1756 he preached before the Governors of the *Middlesex Hospital*, at *St. Anne's, Westminster* ; a Commencement Sermon at *Cambridge* in 1759 ; a Sermon at the annual meeting of the Charity Schools in 1760 ; one before the House of Commons, on the 30th of *January*, 1762 ; and a Spital Sermon at *St. Bride's* on the *Easter Wednesday* in that year. All these, with several others preached at *Eton*, *Lincoln's Inn*, *Bishopsgate*, &c. were collected by himself in the volume above-mentioned, which is closed by a " Concio ad Clerum habita *Cantabrigiæ* in Templo *Beatæ Mariæ*, 1759, pro gradu Doc-" toratûs in Sacrâ Theologiâ." His other publications were, 1. " A Dissertation on " 2 *Peter* i. 19. 1750." 8vo. 2. In 1754 the famous Methodist *Jones* preached a Sermon at *Bishopsgate Church* ; which being offensive to Dr. *Ashton*, he preached against it ; and some altercation happening between the two Divines, some pamphlets were published on the occasion ; and one intituled " A Letter to the Rev. Mr. *Thomas Jones*, " intended as a rational and candid answer to his Sermon preached at *St. Botolph*, " *Bishopsgate*," 4to, was probably by Dr. *Ashton*.—3. " An Extract from the Case of the " obligation of the Electors of *Eton College* to supply all vacancies in that Society with " those who are or have been Fellows of *King's College, Cambridge*, so long as persons " properly qualified are to be had within that description. *London*, 1771," 4to, proving, that Aliens have no right at all to *Eton* Fellowships, either by the foundation, statutes,

† See *Dodsley's* Poems, vol. III. p. 75.

‡ He was succeeded at *Aldingham* by *John Ashton*, M. A. fellow of *Trinity College, Cambridge*.

Peter Osbeck's * " Voyage to *China* and *The East-Indies*," 2 vols. 8vo.

On the 14th of *January*, 1771, Mr. *Bowyer* became a second time a widower, by the death of his wife at the age of 70. Mr. *Clarke*, who had endeavoured to administer confolation to him on a similar occasion near forty years before, again addressed him with tenderness on this event:

"DEAR SIR, *Jan.* 18, 1771.

" I find, by the last papers, that you have lost poor Mrs.
" *Bowyer*. It is very happy for her that she was relieved
" from the severe trial she had undergone so long. In
" that weak and painful state, none of her friends could
" wish her to continue any longer. And I hope, as you
" must have expected this event, that you will receive this
" parting summons with due submission. Losing a com-
" panion that we have been long used to, must, at our
" time of life, be a mournful circumstance. But as you
" must part at last, your connexions with the world are
" much lessened by her going first. You have nothing
" now to do but to make a provision for your son; and
" keep as much in business only as serves to amuse you,
" throwing off the great weight of it into other hands.
" It is a very desirable thing to have the world sit easy
" upon us when we are going to leave it."

or archbishop *Laud's* determination in 1636. This is further proved in, 4. " A Letter to the
" Rev. Dr. *M.* [*Morell*] on the question of electing Aliens into the vacant places in
" *Eton College*. By the author of the Extract, 1771." 4to. 5. " A Second Letter to
" Dr. *M.*"—The three last were soon after republished, under the title of, " The Election
" of Aliens into the vacancies in *Eton College* an unwarrantable practice. To which
" are now added, Two Letters to the Rev. Dr. *Morell*; in which the cavils of a writer in
" the General Evening Post, and others, are considered and refuted. Part I. By a late
" Fellow of *King's College, Cambridge. London*, 1771." 4to. Part II. was never published.
 * A *Swede*, Rector of *Hasloef* and *Woxtorp*, member of the academy of *Stockholm*,
and of the Society of *Upsal*; and chaplain to a *Swedish East-Indiaman*.

Very

Very foon after this event he printed a fpecimen of
" *Apollonii* Sophiftæ Lexicon *Homericum*," for M. de *Villoifon*
of *Paris*, on a plan which was not put in execution in
this country (though the Lexicon appeared afterwards at
Paris, in 2 vols. 8vo, 1773.) I fhall preferve below the fubftance of a letter * which accompanied the MS. It was

* " Vigilantiffimo rei typographicæ præfecto falutem plurimam dicit *d'Anffe de Villoifon*.
" Antequam, doctiffime typographe, ad hoc opus te accingas, paucis te monitum volo,
" quibus inftructus faciliori fimul et rapidiori proveharis curfu. Primum, te fupplex
" oro atque obteftor, ut quantum poteris, adhibeas celeritatem, præfertim in hâc primâ
" parte; nec prius intermittas opus, quam totum ad finem perductum omnibusque
" numeris abfolutum fuerit. Accuratam enim induftriam et perfpicacem folertiam tibi
" non commendo, ex eâ fcilicet gente oriundo, quæ in literis *Græcis*, ut in aliis omni-
" bus, non habitat, fed regnat. Non enim obtufa adeo gerimus pectora, ut *Oxonii* et
" Theatri *Sheldoniani* famam non audiverimus. Nam, ut ait poeta, ' Quæ regio in terris
" *veftri* non plena laboris ?' Ne te, quæfo, terreant mearum litterarum ductus qui for-
" taffe primâ facie intricatiores videri poffint, fed funt facillimi, cum ubique femper
" iidem, eodemque prorfus modo depicti appareant, ut qui unius duntaxat paginæ lec-
" tionem calluerit, is omnes alias fine morâ et inoffenfo pede percurrat. Spondeo reli-
" quas partes quæ fubfequentur multò nitidius et fcitius exaratum iri: interim hanc pro
" tuâ humanitate excufatam habeas. Nota diligenter, quidquid in verfione Latinâ
" lineolâ inferius fuppofitâ diftinguitur, id locum effe verfum *Homericum*; ac proinde
" ita typis edendum, ut extet feparatum, a filo orationis abruptum, novumque inchoet
" verfum, qui haud fcio annon variis varioque modo efformatis typis, feu etiam literis
" quas vocant *Italicis* imprimendus fit: quod ultimum tuæ permitto elegantiæ, et huic
" quâ polles fagacitati ac peritiæ.... Cum folam verfus finem afferat *Apollonius* noftri
" Lexici author, huic verfui lineolam præpofui, quæ in editione quoque retinenda eft....
" Cum ad me emendanda mittentur quæ prima ex prælis gementibus exibunt fpeci-
" mina, fimul et fequatur meum, quod habeo unicum apographum ad cujus nor-
" mam ea exigere poffim. Alterum quoque eorumdem fpeciminum exemplar apud
" vos remaneat, ne forte ventis et mari infido ludibria debeat pars mei operis.
" Ultima emendabo fpecimina: in prioribus omnem diligentiam adhibebit, cui hæc
" cura incumbit, quem oro atque imploro ut omnem nævum excutiat, imo etfi
" quæ fortè tranfvolans calamus omifit, aut præ celeritate aberrans malè dedit
" puncta accentufque, ea reftituat pro fuâ eruditione. Quælibet pagina non pluribus
" quam fex et viginti conftet verfibus. Titulum operis et præfationem ultimo loco
" mittam. Iis literarum typis utendum eft qui in luculentiffimo *Robinfoni Hefiodo*
" adhibiti funt: idem infpiciatur cultus externus editionis et nitor. Hæc habui, doctif-
" fime typographe, de quibus te certiorem facerem: nihil aliud mihi reftat, nifi ut tuam
" opem implorem in celeritate præftandâ, finceroque obtefter animo quam lætus fim
" quod tam doctorum typographorum curis fuperbiat hæc, quantulacumque fit, noftra
" opella, cui paulo immutatum accommodabo *Ovidii* verfum: Parve, *quod* invideo, fine
" me liber ibis in urbem; in urbem fcilicet, quæ orbis eruditi compendium reipublicæ
" literariæ caput merito dici poteft. Vale, et mihi meifque laboribus fave. Dabam
" *Lutetiæ Parifiorum*, fexto *Februarii* die, anno reparatæ falutis 1771."

not

not *intended* for Mr. *Bowyer*; though, not being directed to any particular person, it was delivered to him on the *Oxford* printer's declining the work.

In 1771 he finished the last volume of Lord *Lyttelton's*[*] valuable " History of the Life and Reign of King *Henry*
" the

* *George Lyttelton*, the eldest son of Sir *Thomas Lyttelton* of *Hagley* in *Worcestershire*, Bart. was born in 1709. He was educated at *Eton*, where he was so much distinguished, that his exercises were recommended as models to his school-fellows. From *Eton* he went to *Christchurch*, where he retained the same reputation of superiority, and displayed his abilities to the publick in a poem on *Blenheim*. He was a very early writer, both in verse and prose. His " Progress of Love," and his " *Persian* Letters," were both written when he was very young. He staid not long at *Oxford*; for in 1728 he began his travels, and visited *France* and *Italy*. When he returned, he obtained a seat in parliament, and soon distinguished himself among the most eager opponents of Sir *Robert Walpole*, though his father, who was one of the lords of the Admiralty, always voted with the Court. For many years the name of *George Lyttelton* was seen in every account of every debate in the House of Commons. He opposed the standing army; he opposed the excise; he supported the motion for petitioning the King to remove *Walpole*. The Prince of *Wales*, being (1737) driven from *St. James's*, kept a separate court, and opened his arms to the opponents of the ministry. Mr. *Lyttelton* was made his secretary, and was supposed to have great influence in the direction of his conduct. He persuaded his master, whose business it was now to be popular, that he would advance his character by patronage. *Mallet* was made under-secretary, and *Thomson* had a pension. For *Thomson* he always retained his kindness, and was able at last to place him at ease. *Moore* courted his favour by an apologetical poem, called " The Trial of *Selim*," for which he was paid with kind words, which, as is common, raised great hopes, that at last were disappointed. He now stood in the first rank of opposition; and *Pope*, who was incited, it is not easy to say how, to increase the clamour against the ministry, commended him among the other patriots. This drew upon him the reproaches of Mr. *Fox*, who, in the house, imputed to him as a crime his intimacy with a lampooner so unjust and licentious. *Lyttelton* supported his friend, and replied, that he thought it an honour to be received into the familiarity of so great a poet. While he was thus conspicuous, he married (1741) Miss *Lucy Fortescue*, sister to Lord *Fortescue*, of *Devonshire*, by whom he had a son, the late Lord *Lyttelton*, and two daughters, and with whom he appears to have lived in the highest degree of connubial felicity: but human pleasures are short; she died in childbed about six years afterwards (1747), and he solaced his grief by writing a Monody to her memory; without however condemning himself to perpetual solitude and sorrow; for soon after he sought to find the same happiness again in a second marriage with the daughter of Sir *Robert Rich* (1749); but the experiment was unsuccessful. At length, after a long struggle, *Walpole* gave way, and honour and profit were distributed among his conquerors. *Lyttelton* was made (1744) one of the Lords of the Treasury; and from that time was engaged in supporting the schemes of the ministry. Politicks did not, however, so much engage him as to withhold his thoughts from things of more importance. He had, in the pride of juvenile confidence, with the help of corrupt conversation, entertained doubts of the truth of Christianity; but he thought the time now

come

" the Second," 4to, (fee p. 348). The other principal books of that year were, Mr. *Whitaker's* " History of *Man-* " *chester*," 4to; " Critical Obſervations on the Buildings in " *London* and *Weſtminſter*," 4to and 8vo; a new edition of

Dr.

come when it was no longer fit to doubt or believe by chance, and applied himſelf feri-ouſly to the great queſtion His ſtudies, being honeſt, ended in conviction. He found that Religion was true, and what he had learned he endeavoured to teach (1747), by " Obſervations on the Converſion and Apoſtleſhip of St. *Paul*;" a treatiſe to which In-fidelity has never been able to fabricate a ſpecious anſwer. This book his father had the happineſs of ſeeing, and expreſſed his pleaſure in a letter which deſerves to be inſerted, and muſt have given to ſuch a ſon a pleaſure more eaſily conceived than deſcribed : " I " have read your religious treatiſe with infinite pleaſure and ſatisfaction. The ſtyle is " fine and clear, the arguments cloſe, cogent, and irreſiſtible. May the King of kings, " whoſe glorious cauſe you have ſo well defended, reward your pious labours, and grant " that I may be found worthy, through the merits of *Jeſus Chriſt*, to be an eye-witneſs " of that happineſs which I don't doubt He will bountifully beſtow upon you ! In the " mean time, I ſhall never ceaſe glorifying God, for having endowed you with ſuch uſeful " talents, and given me ſo good a ſon. Your affectionate father, Thomas Lyttelton." A few years afterwards (1751), by the death of his father, he inherited a baronet's title with a large eſtate, which, though perhaps he did not augment, he was careful to adorn, by a houſe of great elegance and expence, and by great attention to the decoration of his park. As he continued his exertions in parliament, he was gradually advancing his claim to profit and preferment ; and accordingly was made in 1754 cofferer and privy-counſellor. This place he exchanged next year for the great office of chancellor of the Exchequer ; an office, however, that required ſome qualifications which he ſoon per-ceived himſelf to want. The year after, his curioſity led him into *Wales*; of which he has given an account, perhaps rather with too much affectation of delight, to *Archibald Bower*, a man of whom he had conceived an opinion more favourable than he ſeems to have deſerved, and whom, having once eſpouſed his intereſt and fame, he never was per-ſuaded to diſown. About this time he publiſhed his " Dialogues of the Dead," which were very eagerly read, though the production rather, as it ſeems, of leiſure than of ſtudy, rather effuſions than compoſitions. When, in the latter part of the laſt reign, the inauſpicious commencement of the war made the diſſolution of the mi-niſtry unavoidable, Sir *George Lyttelton*, loſing his employment with the reſt, was recompenſed with a peerage (1757); and reſted from political turbulence in the Houſe of Lords. His laſt literary production was " The Hiſtory of *Henry* the Second, 1764," elabo-rated by the reſearches and deliberations of twenty years, and publiſhed with the greateſt anxiety [*]. The ſtory of this publication is remarkable. The whole work was printed twice over, a great part of it three times, and many ſheets four

---

[*] Why this " anxiety" ſhould be attributed to " vanity," when good motives were avowed by the author and known to his friends, ſuch as his deſire to correct miſtakes, his fear of having been too harſh on *Becket*, &c. we do not ſee; but ſincerely wiſh that in this and ſome other paſſages Dr. *Johnſon* (for it is from his Biographical Prefaces the greater part of this note is taken) had obſerved his own humane maxim (in the Life of *Addiſon*) of not giving " a pang to a daughter, " a brother, or a friend."

or

Dr. *Hurd's* " Dialogues," 3 vols. 8vo; Dr. *Jortin's* " Ser-
" mons,"

or five times *. The bookfellers paid for the first impreffion †; but the charges and repeated operations of the prefs were at the expence of the author, whofe ambitious accuracy is known to have coft him at leaft a thoufand pounds. He began to print in 1755.
Three volumes appeared in 1764, a fecond edition of them in 1767, a third edition in 1768,
and the conclufion in 1771. *Andrew Reid*, a man not without confiderable abilities, and
not unacquainted with letters or with life, undertook to perfuade the noble author, as
he had perfuaded himfelf, that he was mafter of the fecret of punctuation; and, as fear
begets credulity, he was employed, I know not at what price, to point the pages of
" *Henry* the Second." The book was at laft pointed and printed, and fent into the
world. His Lordfhip took money for his copy, of which, when he had paid the pointer,
he probably gave the reft away; for he was very liberal to the indigent. When time
brought the Hiftory to a third edition, *Reid* was either dead or difcarded: and the fuper-
intendence of typography and punctuation was committed to a man originally a comb-
maker, but then known by the ftyle of Dr. *Saunders* [a *Scotch* LL. D.]. Something uncommon was probably expected, and fomething uncommon was at laft done; for to the
edition of Dr. *Saunders* is appended, what the world had hardly feen before, a lift of
errors of nineteen pages. But to politicks and literature there muft be an end. Lord
Lyttelton had never the appearance of a ftrong or of a healthy man; he had a flender
uncompacted frame, and a meagre face ‡: he lafted, however, above fixty years, and
then was feized with his laft illnefs. Of his death a very affecting and inftructive account has been given by his phyfician §, Dr. *Johnfon* of *Kidderminfter*. His Lordfhip was
buried at *Hagley*; and the following infcription is cut on the fide of his Lady's monument:

" This unadorned ftone was placed here
" By the particular defire and exprefs directions
" Of the late Right Honourable GEORGE Lord LYTTELTON,
" Who died *Auguft* 22, 1773, aged 64."

* The copy was all tranfcribed by his Lordfhip's own hand, and that not a very legible one, as
he acknowledges: " Pray take care of the manufcript, as I have no other copy, and look yourfelf
" to the printing, after I have made my corrections in the firft and fecond revifals, which I would
" have fent me as faft as the prefs can afford them. I fear you will have fome difficulty in reading
" my copy, as it is not very fair; but, being ufed to my hand, you will make it out. I am moft
" afraid of faults in the laft impreffions, becaufe they can't be corrected without cancelling fheets.
" Be particularly careful of the references in the margin. I wifh you health and happinefs till I
" fee you again, and am, with fincere regard and efteem, Sir, your moft obedient humble fervant."
        MS. Letter to Mr. Bowyer.

† This fact is undoubtedly true. I fhall not fcruple, however, to add to it a trifling circumftance,
which fhews that the excellent Peer (whofe finances were not in the moft flourifhing fituation)
could bear with great fortitude what by many would have been deemed an infult. The bookfellers, at
a ftated period, had paid the ftationer for as much paper as they had agreed to purchafe. His Lordfhip
then became the paymafter; in which ftate the work went on for fome years, till the ftationer,
having been difappointed of an expected fum, refufed to furnifh any more paper. With great reluctance Mr. *Bowyer* was prevailed on to carry this report to his Lordfhip; and began the tale with
much hefitation.—" Oh! I underftand you," fays his Lordfhip very calmly, " the man is afraid to
" truft me! I acknowledge I am poor, but let me requeft you to be my fecurity." It is needlefs
to add, that Mr. *Bowyer* obliged his Lordfhip, and had no reafon to repent of the civility.

‡ In a political caricature print levelled againft Sir *Robert Walpole* he is thus defcribed:
        " But who be dat fo lank, fo lean, fo bony?
        " O dat be de great orator, *Lytteltony*."

§ " On *Sunday* evening the fymptoms of his Lordfhip's diforder, which for a week paft had
" alarmed us, put on a fatal appearance, and his Lordfhip believed himfelf to be a dying man.

" From

" mons," 4 vols. 8vo; " The Duty, Circumftances, and
" Benefits of Baptifm," by *Thomas Barker**, Efq; 8vo; " A
" Difquifition on Medicines that diffolve the Stone; in which
" Dr. *Chittick's* Secret is confidered and difcovered; in two
" parts; the fecond part now firft publifhed, and the
" firft † confiderably improved; by *Alexander Blackrie* ‡,"

* Thomas Barker*, Efq; of *Lyndon* in *Rutland*, well known by his accurate meteoro-
logical obfervations in the Philofophical Tranfactions; and by his " Difcoveries con-
" cerning Comets, 1757," 4to. Mr. *Barker* has alfo lately publifhed " The Meffiah;
" being the Prophecies concerning him methodifed, with their Accomplifhments, 1780,"
8vo. This gentleman's father, *Samuel Barker*, Efq; was author of a letter in the
" Bibliotheca Literaria," N° X. referred to by Mr. *Chifhull*, Antiq. Afiat. p. 38; and
of a learned tract publifhed in 1761, 4to, under the title of " Poefis *Hebraica* refti-
" tuta." His mother was daughter to Mr. *William Whifton*, the celebrated Mathematician and Divine.
  † Originally publifhed in 1766.
  ‡ Apothecary at *Bromley* in *Kent*. He died *May* 29, 1772.

" From this time he fuffered by reftleffnefs rather than pain; and though his nerves were appa-
" rently much fluttered, his mental faculties never feemed ftronger, when he was thoroughly awake.
" His Lordfhip's bilious and hepatic complaints feemed alone not equal to the expected mournful
" event; his long want of fleep, whether the confequence of the irritation in the bowels, or, which
" is more probable, of caufes of a different kind, accounts for his lofs of ftrength, and for his death,
" very fufficiently. Though his Lordfhip wifhed his approaching diffolution not to be lingering,
" he waited for it with refignation. He faid, ' It is a folly, a keeping me in mifery, now to at-
" tempt to prolong life;' yet he was eafily perfuaded, for the fatisfaction of others, to do or take
" any thing thought proper for him. On *Saturday* he had been remarkably better, and we were
" not without fome hopes of his recovery. On *Sunday*, about eleven in the forenoon, his Lordfhip
" fent for me, and faid he felt a great hurry, and wifhed to have a little converfation with me in
" order to divert it. He then proceeded to open the fountain of that heart, from whence goodnefs
" had fo long flowed as from a copious fpring. ' Doctor,' faid he, ' you fhall be my confeffor:
" when I firft fet out in the world, I had friends who endeavoured to fhake my belief in the Chrif-
" tian religion. I faw difficulties which ftaggered me; but I kept my mind open to conviction.
" The evidences and doctrines of Chriftianity, ftudied with attention, made me a moft firm and
" perfuaded believer of the Chriftian religion. I have made it the rule of my life, and it is the
" ground of my future hopes. I have erred and finned; but have repented, and never indulged
" any vicious habit. In politicks, and public life, I have made the public good the rule of my con-
" duct. I never gave counfels which I did not at the time think the beft. I have feen that I was
" fometimes in the wrong, but I did not err defignedly. I have endeavoured, in private life, to do
" all the good in my power, and never for a moment could indulge malicious or unjuft defigns upon
" any perfon whatfoever.' At another time he faid, ' I muft leave my foul in the fame ftate it
" was in before this illnefs; I find this a very inconvenient time for folicitude about any thing."
" On the evening, when the fymptoms of death came on, he faid, ' I fhall die; but it will not be
" your fault.' When Lord and Lady *Valentia* came to fee his Lordfhip, he gave them his folemn
" benediction, and faid, ' Be good, be virtuous, my Lord. You muft come to this §.' Thus he
" continued giving his dying benediction to all around him. On *Monday* morning a lucid interval
" gave fome fmall hopes, but thefe vanifhed in the evening; and he continued dying, but with
" very little uneafinefs, till *Tuefday* morning, *Auguft* 22, when between feven and eight o'clock he
" expired, almoft without a groan."

  § Very fimilar to what *Addifon* faid to Lord *Warwick*.

I

" 8vo;

8vo; a new edition of *Mounteney's* * " *Demosthenes*," 8vo;
a new edition of the " Clavis *Homerica*," with the Corrections of Dr. *Samuel Patrick* †; and the fourth edition,
corrected, of Bishop *Pearce's* ‡ " *Cicero* de Oratore," 8vo.

* Of whom, see p. 204. His intimacy with Sir *Edward Walpole* at college, and his
excellent dedication of these Orations to Sir *Robert*, together with his strict honour and
great abilities, raised him in 1741 to the honourable office of baron of the Exchequer in
Ireland; which he filled with much reputation. Some elegant verses addressed to him
on his poetical talents are printed in Gent. Mag. 1781, p. 384.

† Already mentioned, in p. 109, as editor of an improved edition of *Ainsworth's*
Dictionary.

‡ Dr. *Zachary Pearce*, born in 1690, was the son of a Distiller in *High-Holborn*. He
married Miss *Adams*, the daughter of another Distiller in the same neighbourhood, with
a considerable fortune, who lived with him fifty-two years in the highest degree of connubial happiness §. He had his education in *Westminster-school*, where he was distinguished by his merit, and elected one of the King's Scholars. In 1710, when he was
twenty years old, he was elected to *Trinity College, Cambridge*. In 1716 he published
the first edition of his " *Cicero* de Oratore," and, at the desire of a friend, luckily
dedicated it to Lord Chief Justice *Parker*, (afterwards Earl of *Macclesfield*,) to whom
he was a stranger. This incident laid the foundation of his future fortune: for Lord
Parker soon after recommended him to Dr. *Bentley*, Master of *Trinity*, to be made one
of the Fellows; and the Doctor consented to it on this condition, that his Lordship
would promise to unmake him again as soon as it lay in his power to give him a living.
In 1717, Mr. *Pearce*, being then M. A. was ordained at the age of twenty-seven; having
taken time enough, as he thought, to attain a sufficient knowledge of the sacred office.
In 1718 Lord *Parker* was appointed Chancellor, and invited Mr. *Pearce* to live with him
in his house, as chaplain. In 1719 he was instituted to the rectory of *Stapleford Abbots*,
in *Essex*; and in 1720 to that of St. *Bartholomew* behind the *Royal Exchange*, worth
400l. *per annum*. In 1723 the Lord Chancellor presented him to St. *Martin's in the
Fields*. His Majesty, who was then at *Hanover*, was applied to in favour of Dr.
Claget, who was there along with him; and the Doctor actually kissed hands upon
the occasion; but the Chancellor, upon the King's return, disputed the point, and
carried it in favour of Mr. *Pearce*. In 1724 the degree of Doctor in Divinity was
conferred on him by Archbishop *Wake*. The same year he dedicated to his patron,
the Earl of *Macclesfield*, (who the next year resigned the Great Seal) his edition of
" *Longinus* de Sublimitate," with a new *Latin* version and notes ‖, which has passed
through

§ The fiftieth year of their union they celebrated as a year of jubilee, on which occasion they
invited all their friends, and were complimented by a friend in the following stanzas:

No more let Calumny complain
That *Hymen* binds in cruel chain,
  And makes his subjects slaves:
Supported by the Good and Wise,
Her keenest slander he defies,
  Her utmost malice braves.

To-day—he triumphs o'er his foes,
And to the world a pair he shows,
  Tho' long his subjects—free:
Who happy in his bands appear,
And joyful call the Fiftieth Year
  A Year of Jubilee.

‖ The Bishop's other works are, 1. Two papers in " The Spectator," No 572, on Quacks; and
No 633, on Eloquence.—2. The letter signed *Ned Mum* in " The Guardian," No 121.—3. No 114.
in

In 1772, appeared a new edition, confiderably enlarged,
of the " Conjectures on the New Teftament." At the conclufion of the Preface, Mr. *Bowyer* thus pathetically defcribes
the diforders which had been fome years undermining his
conftitution : " It is time for me to withdraw my difabled
" hand,

through four editions. Dr. *Pearce* was alfo fortunate in the good graces of Lady *Sunden* ;
upon whofe recommendation of him to the Queen, he was defigned for a Deanry,
and was frequently honoured with her Majefty's converfation in the drawing-room.
After feveral difappointments, the Deanry of *Winchefter* becoming vacant, Dr. *Pearce*
was appointed Dean in 1739 *. His friends now began to think of him for the epifcopal dignity, but the Dean's language rather declined it. However, after feveral difficulties had been ftarted and removed, he confented to accept the Bifhoprick of *Bangor*,
and promifed Lord *Hardwicke* to " do it with a good grace." He accordingly made
proper acknowledgements of the Royal Goodnefs, and was confecrated, *February* 21,
1748. Upon the declining ftate of health of Dr. *Wilcocks*, Bifhop of *Rochefter*, the
Bifhop of *Bangor* was feveral times applied to by Archbifhop *Herring* to accept
of *Rochefter*, and the Deanry of *Weftminfter*, in exchange for *Bangor*, but the Bifhop then
fignified his defire to obtain leave to refign, and retire to a private life. His Lordfhip,
however, upon being preffed, fuffered himfelf to be prevailed upon :— " My Lord, (faid
" he to the Duke of *Newcaftle)* your Grace offers thefe dignities to me in fo generous and
" friendly a manner, that I promife you to accept them." Upon the death of Bifhop
Wilcocks, he was accordingly promoted to the See of *Rochefter*, and Deanry of *Weftminfter*, in 1756. Bifhop *Sherlock* died in 1761, and Lord *Bath* offered his intereft for
getting the Bifhop of *Rochefter* appointed to fucceed him in the Diocefe of *London* ; but

in " The Free-Thinker."—4. " An Account of *Trinity College, Cambridge*, 1721."—5. " Epiftolæ
" duæ, ad *F. V.* profefforem *Amftelodamenfem* de editione Novi Teftamenti a *Bentleio*, 1721," 4to.
(reprinted with the " Commentary," in 1777).—6. " A Letter to the Clergy of the Church of
" *England*, on occafion of the Bifhop of *Rochefter's* Commitment to *The Tower*, 1722," of which two
editions were printed, and a tranflation into *French.*—7. " The Miracles of *Jefus* vindicated,"
1727 and 1728 —8. " A Review of the Text of *Milton*, 1733."—9. *Cicero* de Officiis, 1745,"
which has been twice reprinted.—10. " Two Letters againft Dr. *Middleton*," third edition, 1752.
—11. " A Letter to the Rev. Dr. *Hunt*, *Hebrew* Profeffor at *Oxford*," containing a curious
account relative to the publifhing of Sir *Ifaac Newton's* Chronology, 1754.—12. " Nine Sermons
" upon public occafions, one on Self-murder, and a Concio ad Clerum."—13. " A Commentary,
" with Notes, on the Four Evangelifts, and the Acts of the Apoftles ; together with a new Tran-
" flation of St. *Paul's* Firft Epiftle to the *Corinthians*, with a Paraphrafe and Notes," 2 vols. 4to.
publifhed (1777) after his death, by his chaplain, Mr. *Darby.*

* As foon as it was known that the Doctor was to be Dean of *Winchefter*, his friend Mr. *Pulteney*
came to congratulate him on the occafion, and among other things which he then faid, one was,
" Dr. *Pearce*, though you may think that others, befides Sir *Robert*, have contributed to get you
" this dignity, yet you may depend upon it that he is all in all, and that you owe it entirely to his
" good will towards you : and therefore, as I am now fo engaged in oppofition to him, it may hap-
" pen that fome who are of our party may, if there fhould be any oppofition for Members of Par-
" liament at *Winchefter*, prevail upon me to defire you to act there in affiftance of fome friend of
" ours, and Sir *Robert*, at the fame time, may afk your affiftance in the election, for a friend of his
" own againft one whom we recommend : I tell you, therefore, before-hand, that if you comply
" with my requeft, rather than Sir *Robert's*, to whom you are fo very much obliged, I fhall have the
" worfe opinion of you."

he

" hand, and to afk pardon of thofe learned friends whofe
" collections I have purloined. That is the leaft injury I
" have done them : I have fo unconfcionably ufed the
" liberty indulged me by one * of them, that to him I
" can make no apology ; except that I need one to my
" readers, for not making greater ufe of that indulgence.
" My imperfections they will impute to age, and the con-
" fequent infirmities of it. Torpid with the palfy, and
" only quickened by a painful viciffitude of the ftone †, I

He had determined never to be Bifhop of *London*, or Archbifhop of *Canterbury*. In the
year 1763, being feventy-three years old, and finding himfelf lefs fit for the bufinefs
of his ftations as Bifhop and Dean, he informed his friend Lord *Bath* of his intention
to refign *both*, and live in a retired manner upon his private fortune. His Lordfhip undertook to acquaint his Majefty, who named a day and hour, when the Bifhop was
admitted alone into the clofet. He told the King, that he wifhed to have fome interval
between the fatigues of bufinefs and eternity, and defired his Majefty to confult proper
perfons about the propriety and legality of his refignation. In about two months the
King informed him, that Lord *Mansfield* faw no objection, and that Lord *Northington*, who
had entertained fome doubts, on farther confideration, thought that the requeft might
be complied with. Unfortunately for the Bifhop, Lord *Bath* applied for Bifhop *Newton* to
fucceed. This alarmed the Miniftry, who thought that no dignities fhould be obtained
but through their hands. They, therefore, oppofed the refignation, and his Majefty
was informed that the Bifhops difliked the defign. The King fent to him again, and
at a third audience told him, that he muft think no more of refigning. The Bifhop replied, " Sir, I am all duty and fubmiffion;" and then retired. In 1768 he obtained leave
(for different reafons, probably, from thofe above-mentioned) to refign the Deanry; in
1773 he loft his Lady, and after fome months of lingering decay, he died at *Little Ealing*,
June 29, 1774. Being afked one day how he could live with fo little nutriment?
" I live," faid he, " upon the recollection of an innocent and well-fpent life, which is
" my only fuftenance." His charitable addition to the penfions of the poor widows in
Bromley-College will long be remembered to his honour.

* Mr. *Markland*, whofe notes (by his own direction) were diftinguifhed by the letter *R*.
To Mr. *Clarke*, Dr. *Owen*, and many other refpectable names, he acknowledges his obligations in that ufeful collection; of which a *third* edition, ftill much more confiderably
improved, is preparing for the publick, by the Editor of thefe Anecdotes, under the infpection of Dr. *Owen*.

† A fhort extract from a friendly letter received by Mr. *B.* on this occafion may not
be unacceptable : " Mr. *N.* has tranfmitted to me your *Conjectures* on the New Tefta-
" ment; for which very obliging and acceptable proof of your regard, I beg leave to
" offer you my fincereft thanks. I fhould have been happy not to have had the me-
" lancholy defcriptions which you give of your health in your Preface, fo frequently
" confirmed by the accounts I have received in *Red Lion Paffage*. I hope you will ex-
" cufe my prefuming to wound your *cruditas aures* with barbarous *Latin* ; and permit
" me to apply to you what was faid of (I think) Bp. *Hall*:—*Cui nihil ineft acre neque
" acerbum, præter ftranguriæ calculique cruciatus.*"

3.   " feell

" feel the worſt ſide of humanity : they will have the
" pleaſure of exerciſing the better ſide, even of forgiving,
" which approaches neareſt to Divinity."

With a copy of this book the following conciliatory
letter was ſent to Biſhop *Warburton* *, who had cenſured a
paſſage in the former edition :

" MY

* This learned Prelate was born at *Newark upon-Trent*, in the county of *Nottingham*
Dec. 24, 1698. His father was *George Warburton*, an attorney, and town-clerk of the place,
in which this his eldeſt ſon received his birth and education. His mother was *Elizabeth*,
the daughter of *William Hobman*, an alderman of the ſame town, and his parents were
married about the year 1696. The family of Dr. *Warburton* came originally from the
county of *Cheſter*, where his great grand-father reſided. His grand-father, *William
Warburton*, was the firſt who ſettled at *Newark*; where he practiſed the law, and was
Coroner of the county of *Nottingham*. *George Warburton*, the father, died about the
year 1706, leaving his widow with four chi'dren, two ſons and two daughters, of which
the ſecond ſon *George* died young ; but of the daughters one ſtill ſurvives her brother.
The Biſhop received the early part of his education under Mr. *Weſton*, then maſter of
Okeham ſchool in *Rutlandſhire*, and afterwards vicar of *Campden* in *Glouceſterſhire*;
where he ſhewed no indication of ſuperior genius. His original deſignation was to
the ſame profeſſion as that of his father and grand-father ; and he was aceordingly
placed clerk to an attorney, with whom he remained until he was qualified to engage
in buſineſs upon his own account. He was then admitted to one of the courts at
Weſtminſter, and for ſome years continued the employment of an attorney and ſoli-
citor at the place of his birth. The ſucceſs he met with as a man of buſineſs was
probably not great. It was certainly inſufficient to induce him to devote the reſt of
his life to it : and it is probable, that his want of encouragement might tempt him
to turn his thoughts towards a profeſſion in which his literary acquiſitions would
be more valuable, and in which he might more eaſily purſue the bent of his inclination.
He appears to have brought from ſchool more learning than was requiſite for a
practiſing lawyer. This might rather impede than forward his progreſs, as it has been
generally obſerved, that an attention to literary concerns, and the buſtle of an attorney's
office, with only a moderate ſhare of buſineſs, are wholly incompatible. It is therefore
no wonder that he preferred retirement to noiſe, and relinquiſhed what advantages
he might expect from continuing to follow the law. It has been ſuggeſted by an
ingenious writer, that he was for ſome time uſher to a ſchool. In the year 1724, his
firſt work, conſiſting of tranſlations from *Cæſar*, *Pliny*, *Claudian*, and others, appeared,
under the title of " Miſcellaneous Tranſlations in Proſe and Verſe, from *Roman* Poets,
" Orators, and Hiſtorians," 12mo. It is dedicated to his early patron, Sir *Robert Sutton*,
and ſeems to have laid the foundation of his firſt eccleſiaſtical preferment. At this period it is probable he had not abandoned his profeſſion, though it is certain he did not
attend to it much longer. About *Chriſtmas*, 1726, he came to *London*, and while
there, was introduced to *Theobald*, *Concanen*, and others of Mr. *Pope's* enemies, with
whoſe converſation he was extremely pleaſed. It was at this time that he wrote a

letter

" MY LORD, *February,* 1772.

" I beg your acceptance of thefe *Conjectures* on the N. T.
" drawn up under all the imperfections of nature; which
" your

letter * to *Concanen,* dated *Jan.* 2, 1726, which, by accident, falling into the hands of the late Dr. *Akenfide,* was produced to moft of that gentleman's friends, and by that means became the fubject of much fpeculation. About this time he alfo communicated to *Theobald* fome notes on *Shakfpeare,* which afterwards appeared in that critic's edition of our great dramatic poet. In 1727, his fecond work, intituled, " A Critical and Phi-
" lofophical Enquiry into the Caufes of Prodigies and Miracles, as related by Hifto-
" rians," &c. was publifhed in 12mo. and was alfo dedicated to Sir *Robert Sutton.* He was at this time in orders, and on the 25th of *April,* 1728, had the honour to be in the King's Lift of Mafters of Arts, created at *Cambridge,* on his Majefty's vifit to that univerfity †. In *June,* the fame year, he was prefented by Sir *Robert Sutton* to the rectory of *Burnt Broughton,* in the county of *Lincoln* ‡; a living which he retained till his death, at which he fpent a confiderable part of his middle-life in a ftudious retirement, devoted entirely to letters, and there planned, and in part executed, fome of his moft important works. Several years elapfed, after obtaining this preferment, before Mr. *Warburton* appeared again in the world § as a writer. In 1736 he exhibited a plan of a new edition of *Velleius Paterculus,* which he printed in the " Bibliotheque *Britan-*
" *nique,* ou Hiftoire des Ouvrages des Savans de la *Grande Bretagne,* pour les Mois
" *Juillet, Aout,* & *Sept.* 1736. *A la Haye.'* The defign never was compleated. Dr. *Middleton,* in a letter to him, dated *April* 9, 1737 ‖, returns him thanks for his letters, as well as the Journal, which, fays he, " came to my hands foon after the date of my
" laft. I had before feen the force of your critical genius very fuccefsfully employed on
" *Shakfpeare,* but did not know you had ever tried it on the *Latin* authors. I am pleafed
" with feveral of your emendations, and tranfcribed them into the margin of my edi-
" tions, though not equally with them all. It is a laudable and liberal amufement, to
" try now and then in our reading the fuccefs of a conjecture; but in the prefent ftate
" of the generality of the old writers, it can hardly be thought a ftudy fit to employ a
" life upon, at leaft not worthy, I am fure, of your talents and induftry, which, inftead
" of trifling on words, feem calculated rather to correct the opinions and manners of
" the world." Thefe fentiments of his friend appear to have had their due weight; for, from that time, the intended edition was laid afide, and never afterwards refumed. It was in this year, 1736, that he may be faid to have emerged from the obfcurity of a

* This letter, which, Dr. *Akenfide* fays, will probably be remembered as long as any of the Bifhop's writings, has been lately given to the world by Mr. *Malone,* in the " Supplement to *Shakfpeare.*"

† Monthly Chronicle. ‡ Political State, vol. XXXV. p. 602.

§ At leaft, there was nothing publifhed which can be with certainty afcribed to him. In the year 1732, his patron, Sir *Robert Sutton,* having been a member of the Charitable Corporation, fell under the cenfure of the Houfe of Commons, on account of that iniquitous bufinefs. He was expelled the houfe, and his fortune for fome time feemed to be held but on a precarious tenure. On this occafion a pamphlet appeared, intituled, " An Apology for Sir *Robert Sutton.*" It can only be conjectured, that Dr. *Warburton* had fome concern in this production; but when the connexion between him and Sir *Robert,* and the recent obligation received from that gentleman, are confidered, it will not be thought unlikely that he might, on this occafion, afford his patron fome affiftance by his pen.

‖ *Middleton's* Works, Vol. II. p. 470.

" your Lordſhip will perceive by the incorrectneſs. Theſe
" both you and I muſt overlook, as being the will of the

private life into the notice of the world. The firſt publication which rendered him
afterwards famous now appeared, under the title of " The * Alliance between Church
" and State ; or, the Neceſſity and Equity of an eſtabliſhed Religion and a Teſt-law,
" demonſtrated from the Eſſence and End of Civil Society, upon the fundamental Prin-
" ciples of the Law of Nature and Nations." In three parts : the firſt, treating of a
civil and religious ſociety; the ſecond, of an eſtabliſhed church; and the third, of a
teſt law, 8vo. At the end was announced the ſcheme of " The Divine Legation of
" Moſes," in which he had at this time made a conſiderable progreſs. The firſt volume
of this work was publiſhed in January 1737-8, under the title of " The Divine Legation
" of Moſes demonſtrated on the Principles of a religious Deiſt, from the omiſſion of the
" doctrine of a future ſtate of rewards and puniſhments in the Jewiſh diſpenſation. In
" ſix Books. By William Warburton, M.A. Author of The Alliance between Church
" and State ;" and met with a reception which neither the ſubject, nor the manner in
which it was treated, ſeemed to authoriſe. It was, as the author afterwards obſerved,
fallen upon in ſo outrageous and brutal a manner, as had been ſcarce pardonable, had it
been " The Divine Legation of Mahomet."—It produced ſeveral anſwers, and ſo much
abuſe from the authors of " The Weekly Miſcellany," that in leſs than two months he was
conſtrained to defend himſelf, in " A Vindication of the Author of the Divine Legation
" of Moſes, from the Aſperſions of the Country Clergyman's Letter in the Weekly Miſ-
" cellany of February 24, 1737-8," 8vo. Mr. Warburton's extraordinary merit had now
attracted the notice of the Heir-apparent to the Crown, in whoſe immediate ſervice we
find him, in June 1738, when he publiſhed " Faith working by Charity to Chriſtian
" Edification ; a ſermon preached at the laſt epiſcopal viſitation for confirmation in the
" dioceſe of Lincoln ; with a preface, ſhewing the reaſons of its publication, and a poſt-
" ſcript, occaſioned by ſome letters lately publiſhed in the Weekly Miſcellany. By
" William Warburton, M.A. Chaplain to his Royal Highneſs the Prince of Wales."
A ſecond edition of " The Divine Legation" alſo appeared in November, 1738. In
March, 1739, the world was in danger of being deprived of this extraordinary Genius
by an intermitting fever, which with ſome difficulty was relieved by a plentiful uſe of the
bark. The " Eſſay on Man" had been now publiſhed ſome years ; and it is univerſally ſuppoſed that the author had, in the compoſition of it, adopted the philoſophy of Lord
Bolingbroke, whom on this occaſion he had followed as his guide, without underſtanding
the tendency of his principles. In 1738, M. de Crouſaz wrote ſome remarks on it,
accuſing the author of Spinoſiſm and Naturaliſm ; which falling into Mr. Warburton's
hands, he publiſhed a defence of the firſt epiſtle, and ſoon after of the remaining three,

* This volume, which was publiſhed anonymouſly, was pronounced, in " The Preſent State of the
Republic of Letters," Vol. XVII. p. 471. to be " the work of a gentleman, whoſe capacity, judge-
" ment, and learning, deſerve ſome eminent dignity in the church, of which he is now an inferior
" miniſter." Four editions of this work were printed in the author's life-time, and each with conſiderable variations. Mr. Edwards, in his " Canons of Criticiſm," p. 261. Ed. 1758, ſarcaſtically ſays,
" The firſt edition of The Alliance came out without a dedication, but was preſented to the
" Biſhops; and, when nothing came of that, the ſecond was addreſſed to both the Univerſities ;
" and when nothing came of that, the third was dedicated to a noble Earl (Lord Cheſterfield) and
" nothing has yet (i. e. 1748) come of that." It muſt be confeſſed, all this is very ſeverely ſaid ;
but the long neglect and late advancement of a perſon of Biſhop Warburton's talents will, now perſonal rancour has ſubſided, and the ſtill voice of reaſon may be heard, reflect diſgrace only on thoſe
who ought to have noticed him ſooner.

5   in

" Supreme Being. But may I hope you will acquit me for
" differing from you in some points wherein I fell under
" your

in seven letters, of which six were printed in 1739, and the seventh in *June* 1740, under
the title of " A Vindication of Mr. *Pope's* Essay on Man, by the Author of the Divine
" Legation." The opinion which Mr. *Pope* conceived of these defences, as well as of their
author, will be best seen in his letters. In consequence, a firm friendship was established
between them, which continued with undiminished fervour until the death of Mr. *Pope*,
who, during the remainder of his life, paid a deference and respect to his friend's judgement
and abilities, which will be considered by many as almost bordering on servility *. In
1741, the second volume of " The Divine Legation," in two parts †, containing books
IV. V. VI. was published; as was also a second edition of the " Alliance between
" Church and State." In the summer of that year, Mr. *Pope* and Mr. *Warburton*, in
a country ramble, took *Oxford* in their way, where they parted; Mr. *Pope*, after one
day's stay, going westward; and Mr. *Warburton*, who stayed a day after him to visit Dr.
Coneybeare, then Dean of *Christ Church*, returning to *London*. On that day the Vice
Chancellor, Dr. *Leigh*, sent a message to his lodgings, with the usual compliment, to
know if a Doctor's degree in divinity would be acceptable to him; to which such an
answer was returned as so civil a message deserved. About the same time, Mr. *Pope* had
the like offer made him of a Doctor's degree in law, which he seemed disposed to accept,
until he learnt that some impediment had been thrown in the way of his friend's receiving the compliment intended for him by the Vice-Chancellor. He then absolutely
refused that proposed to himself. Both the degrees were therefore laid aside; and the
university of *Oxford* lost some reputation by the conduct of this business, being thus
deprived of the honour of two names, which certainly would have reflected credit on
the society in which they were to have been enrolled. Mr. *Pope's* affection for Mr.
Warburton was of service to him in more respects than merely increasing his fame.
He introduced and warmly recommended him to most of his friends ‡, and amongst the
rest to *Ralph Allen*, Esq. of *Prior-Park*, whose niece he some years afterwards married,
and whose great fortune at length came to his only son. In consequence of this introduction, we find Mr. *Warburton* at *Bath* in 1742. There he printed a Sermon which
had been preached at the *Abbey-Church*, on the 24th of *October*, for the benefit of Mr.
Allen's favourite charity, the *General Hospital*, or *Infirmary*. To this Sermon, which
was published at the request of the governors, was added, " A Short Account of the
" Nature, Rise, and Progress, of the *General Infirmary* at *Bath*." In this year also he
printed a Dissertation ‖ on the Origin of Books of Chivalry, at the end of *Jarvis's* Preface to
a Translation of *Don Quixote*, which, Mr. *Pope* tells him, he had not got over two paragraphs of, before he cried out, *Aut Erasmus, aut Diabolus*. " I knew you (adds he)
" as certainly as the Ancients did the Gods, by the first pace and the very gait. I
" have not a moment to express myself in, but could not omit this, which delighted

* See Mr. *Pope's* Letters, passim.

† At the end of Part II. was added, " An Appendix; containing some remarks on a late book,
" intituled, Future Rewards and Punishments believed by the Ancients, particularly the Philoso-
" phers, wherein some Objections of the Reverend Mr. *Warburton*, in the Divine Legation of
" *Moses*, are considered."

‡ We find Mr. *Pope* very solicitous to bring Lord *Bolingbroke* and Mr. *Warburton* together, as
persons who would be pleased to meet each other. (See Letters 95 and 96, to Mr. *Allen*). This
wished-for meeting seems never to have taken place.

‖ Taken to pieces and completely demolished by Mr. *Tyrwhitt*. See Mr. *Malone's Supplement to
Shakspeare*. T. F.

" me

" your cenfure ? If I may be allowed to offer my reafons

" with

" me fo much *." Mr. *Pope's* attention to his intereft did not reft in matters which were in his own power;—he recommended him to fome who were more able to affift him : in particular, he obtained a promife from Lord *Granville*, which probably, however, ended in nothing †. In 1742, Mr. *Warburton* publifhed " A Critical and Philofo-
" phical Commentary on Mr. *Pope's* Effay on Man. In which is contained a Vindication
" of the faid Effay from the Mifrepefentations of Mr. *de Refnel*, the *French* Tranflator,
" and of Mr. *de Croufaz*, Profeffor of Philofophy and Mathematics, in the Academy of
" *Laufanne*, the Commentator." It was at this period, when Mr. *Warburton* had the entire confidence of Mr. *Pope*, that he advifed him to complete the *Dunciad*, by changing the Hero, and adding to it a fourth Book. This was accordingly executed in 1742, and publifhed early in 1743, 4to. with notes by our author, who, in confequence of it, received his fhare of the fatire which Mr. *Cibber* liberally beftowed on both Mr. *Pope* and his Annotator ‡. In the latter end of the fame year, he publifhed complete editions of " The Effay on Man," and " The Effay on Criticifm ;" and, from the fpecimen which he there exhibited of his abilities, it may be prefumed, Mr. *Pope* determined to commit the publication of thofe works, which he fhould leave, to Mr. *Warburton's* care. At Mr. *Pope's* defire, he about this time revifed and corrected the " Effay on *Homer*," as it now ftands in the laft edition of that tranflation §. The publication of " The Dunciad" was the laft fervice which our author rendered Mr. *Pope* in his life-time. After a lingering and tedious illnefs, the event of which had been long forefeen, this great poet died on the 30th of *May*, 1744; and by his will, dated the 12th of the preceding *December*, bequeathed to Mr. *Warburton* one half of his library, and the property of all fuch of his works already printed as he had not otherwife difpofed of or alienated, and all the profits which fhould arife from any edition to be printed after his death ; but at the fame time directed, that they fhould be publifhed without any future alterations. In 1744, his affiftance to Dr. Z. *Grey* was handfomely acknowledged in the Preface to *Hudibras* ‖. " The Divine Legation of *Mofes*" had now been publifhed fome time, and various anfwers and objections to it had ftarted up from different quarters. In this year, 1744, Mr. *Warburton* turned his attention to thefe attacks on his favourite work ; and defended himfelf in a manner which, if it did not prove him to be poffeffed of much humility or diffidence, at leaft demonftrated that he knew how to wield the weapons of controverfy with the hand of a mafter. His firft defence now appeared under the title of " Remarks on feveral Occafional Reflections ; in An-
" fwer to the Rev. Dr. *Middleton*, Dr. *Pococke* **, the Mafter of the *Charter-Houfe* ††,
" Dr. *Richard Grey*, and others ; ferving to explain and juftify divers Paffages in The
" Divine Legation, objected to by thofe learned Writers. To which is added, A General
" Review of the Argument of The Divine Legation, as far as it is yet advanced :
" wherein is confidered the Relation the feveral Parts bear to each other, and the

---

* Letter 113, to Mr. *Warburton*. See *Pope's* Works.
† Letter 114, to the fame.
‡ See " Another Occafional Letter from Mr. *Cibber* to Mr. *Pope*," 1744, 8vo.
§ Letter 117, to Mr. *Warburton*.
‖ On this head, fee above, pp. 352. 354.
** The learned Bifhop of *Meath* ; whofe account of hieroglyphics, and the relation they had to language, given in his Obfervations on *Egypt*, differed from what is advanced on that fubject in " The Divine Legation."
†† *Nicholas Mann*, Efq; author of feveral valuable works.

" Whole

" with decency and good-manners, I will take care to of-
" fend

" Whole. Together with an Appendix, in Answer to a late Pamphlet, intituled, An
" Examination of Mr. *W*————'s Second Proposition," 8vo. And this was followed
next year by " Remarks on several Occasional Reflections ; in Answer to the Rev. Doc-
" tors *Stebbing* and *Sykes*; serving to explain and justify the Two Dissertations in The
" Divine Legation, concerning the command to *Abraham* to offer up his Son, and the
" Nature of the *Jewish* Theocracy, objected to by those learned writers. Part II. and
" last ;" 8vo. Both these answers are couched in those high terms of confident superiority, which marked almost every performance that fell from his pen during the remainder of his life. On the 5th of *September*, 1745, the friendship between him and Mr.
Allen was more closely cemented by his marriage with Miss *Tucker*, who survived him, and
is now (1781) the wife of the Rev. Mr. *Smith*. At this juncture the kingdom was under a
great alarm, occasioned by the rebellion breaking out in *Scotland*. Those who wished well to
the then established Government found it necessary to exert every effort which could be used
against the invading enemy. The Clergy were not wanting on their part ; and no one did
more service than Mr. *Warburton*, who printed three very excellent and seasonable Sermons *,
at this important crisis. I. " A faithful Portrait of Popery, by which it is seen to be the
" reverse of Christianity, as it is the Destruction of Morality, Piety, and Civil Liberty. A Ser-
" mon preached at St. *James's Church, Westminster*, Oct. 1745." 8vo. II. " A Ser-
" mon occasioned by the present unnatural Rebellion, &c. preached in Mr. *Allen's* Cha-
" pel, at *Prior-Park*, near *Bath*, Nov. 1745, and published at his Request." 8vo. III.
" The Nature of National Offences truly stated. A Sermon preached on the General
" Fast-Day, Dec. 18, 1745." 8vo. 1746. On account of the last of these Sermons, he
was again involved in a controversy with his former antagonist, Dr. *Stebbing*; which
occasioned " An Apologetical Dedication to the Rev. Dr. *Henry Stebbing*, in Answer to
" his Censure and Misrepresentations of the Sermon preached on the General Fast-Day
" to be observed Dec. 18, 1745." 8vo. 1746. Notwithstanding his great connections,
his acknowledged abilities, and his established reputation ; a reputation founded on the
durable basis of learning, and upheld by the decent and attentive performance of every
duty incident to his station ; yet we do not find that he received any addition to the
preferment given him in 1728 by Sir *Robert Sutton* (except the chaplainship to the
Prince of *Wales*), until *April*, 1746, when he was unanimously called by the Society of
Lincoln's-Inn to be their preacher. In *November* he published " A Sermon preached
" on the Thanksgiving appointed to be observed the 9th of Oct. for the Suppression of
" the late unnatural Rebellion." 8vo. 1746. In 1747, appeared his edition of *Shakspeare*,
and his Preface to *Clarissa*; and in the same year he published, I. " A Letter from an
" Author to a Member of Parliament, concerning Literary Property." 8vo. II. " Pre-
" face to Mrs. *Cockburn's* Remarks upon the Principles and Reasonings of Dr. *Ruther-
" forth's* Essay on the Nature and Obligations of Virtue," &c. 8vo. III. " Preface to
" a Critical Enquiry into the Opinions and Practice of the Ancient Philosophers, con-
" cerning the Nature of a Future State, and their Method of teaching by double Doc-
" trine," [by Mr. *Towne*] 8vo. 1747, 2d edition. In 1748, a third edition of " The Alli-
" ance between Church and State : corrected and enlarged." In 1749, a very extraordinary attack was made on the moral character of Mr. *Pope*, from a quarter where it
could be the least expected. His " Guide, Philosopher, and Friend," Lord *Bolingbroke*,

* Afterwards reprinted in his three volumes of Sermons.

published

" fend no more with the *liberty of prophesying* *; and am,

" my

published a book which he had formerly lent Mr. *Pope* in MS. The Preface to this work, written by Mr. *Mallet*, contained an accusation of Mr. *Pope's* having clandestinely printed an edition of his Lordship's performance without his leave or knowledge. A defence of the poet soon after made its appearance, which was universally ascribed to Mr. *Warburton*, and was afterwards owned by him. It was called, " A Letter to the Editor of " the Letters on the Spirit of Patriotism, the Idea of a Patriot King, and the State " of Parties, &c. occasioned by the Editor's Advertisement," &c. which soon afterwards produced an abusive pamphlet, under the title of " A Familiar Epistle to the " most impudent Man living," 8vo. a performance, as hath been truly observed, couched in language bad enough to disgrace even gaols and garrets. About this time the publication of Dr. *Middleton's* Enquiry concerning the Miraculous Powers gave rise to a controversy, which was managed with great warmth and asperity on both sides, and not much to the credit of either party. On this occasion Mr. *Warburton* published an excellent performance, written with a degree of candour and temper, which, it is to be lamented, he did not always exercise. The title of it was, " *Julian*; or, A Discourse " concerning the Earthquake and Fiery Eruption which defeated that Emperor's at- " tempt to rebuild the Temple at *Jerusalem*," 8vo. 1750. A second edition of this Discourse, " with additions," appeared in 1751; in which year he gave the publick his edition of Mr. *Pope's* Works, with notes, in nine volumes, 8vo. and in the same year printed " An Answer to a Letter to Dr. *Middleton*, inserted in a pamphlet intituled, " The Argument of the Divine Legation fairly stated," &c. 8vo. and " An Account of " the Prophecies of *Arise Evans*, the *Welch* Prophet, in the last century †," the latter of which pieces afterwards subjected him to much ridicule. In 1753, Mr. *Warburton* published the first volume of a Course of Sermons preached at *Lincoln's-Inn*, intituled, " The " Principles of Natural and Revealed Religion occasionally opened and explained;" and this, in the subsequent year, was followed by a second. After the publick had been some time promised, it may, from the alarm which was taken, be almost said threatened with, the appearance of Lord *Bolingbroke's* Works, they were about this time printed. The known abilities and infidelity of this nobleman had created apprehensions, in the minds of many people, of the pernicious effects of his doctrines: and nothing but the appearance of his whole force could have convinced his friends, how little there was to be dreaded from arguments against religion so weakly supported. The personal enmity which had been excited many years before between the peer and our author, had occasioned the former to direct much of his reasoning against two works ‡ of the latter. Many answers were soon published, but none with more acuteness, solidity, and sprightliness, than " A View of Lord *Bolingbroke's* Philosophy, in two Letters to a Friend, 1754;" the Third and Fourth Letters were published in 1753, with another edition of the two former; and in the same year a smaller edition of the whole; which, though it came into the world without a name, was universally ascribed to Mr. *Warburton*, and afterwards

publicly

---

* See Div. Leg. b. vi. § 6. vol. V. p. 304. ed. 1765.

† This account is annexed to the first volume of Dr. *Jortin's* " Remarks on Ecclesiastical History." In 1772, a pamphlet was published, called " Confusion worse confounded; Rout on Rout; " or the Bishop of G———r's Commentary upon *Rice* or *Arise Evans'* Echo from Heaven Examined and Exposed by *Indignatio*."

‡ " The Divine Legation" and " The Alliance."

" my Lord, your Lordſhip's moſt dutiful and obliged
" humble ſervant, WILLIAM BOWYER."
The

publicly owned by him. To ſome copies of this is prefixed an excellent complimentary
epiſtle from the Preſident *Monteſquieu*, dated *May* 26, 1754. At this advanced period
of his life, that preferment which his abilities might have claimed, and which had hitherto been withheld, ſeemed to be approaching towards him. In *September*, 1754, he
was appointed one of his Majeſty's Chaplains in ordinary, and in the next year was
preſented to a prebend * in the cathedral of *Durham*, on the death of Dr. *Mangey*. About
the ſame time the degree of Doctor of Divinity was conferred on him by Dr. *Herring*, then
archbiſhop of *Canterbury*; and a new impreſſion of " The Divine Legation" having been
called for, he printed a fourth edition of the firſt part of it, corrected and enlarged, divided into two volumes, with a dedication to the Earl of *Hardwicke*. The ſame year appeared " A Sermon preached before his Grace *Charles* Duke of *Marlborough*, Preſident,
" and the Governors of the Hoſpital for the Small-pox and for Inoculation, at the
" Pariſh Church of St. *Andrew*, *Holborn*, on *Thurſday*, *April* the 24th, 1755," 4to.
And in 1756, " Natural and Civil Events the Inſtruments of God's Moral Government,
" A Sermon preached on the laſt public Faſt-Day, at *Linco'n's-Inn* Chapel," 4to. In 1757;
a pamphlet was publiſhed called " Remarks on Mr. *David Hume's* Eſſay on the Na-
" tural Hiſtory of Religion;" which is ſaid to have been compoſed of marginal obſervations made by Dr. *Warburton*, on reading Mr. *Hume's* book; and which gave ſo much
offence to the author animadverted upon, that he thought it of importance enough to
deſerve particular mention in the ſhort account of his life. On the 11th of *October*,
in this year, our author was advanced to the deanry of *Briſtol*; and in 1758 republiſhed the Second Part of " The Divine Legation," divided into Two Parts, with a dedication to the preſent Earl of *Mansfield*, which deſerves to be read by every perſon who
eſteems the well-being of ſociety as a concern of any importance. In one of theſe volumes Dr. *Taylor* is treated with much ſeverity, in conſequence, of a private pique. At
the latter end of the next year, Dr. *Warburton* received the honour, ſo juſtly due to his
merit, of being (on the 22d of *December)* dignified with the Mitre, and promoted to
the vacant See of *Gloucefter*. He was conſecrated on the 20th of *January*, 1760; and on
the 30th of the ſame month preached before the Houſe of Lords. In the next year he
printed " A Rational Account of the Nature and End of the Sacrament of the Lord's
" Supper," 12mo. In 1762, he publiſhed " The Doctrine of Grace: or, the Office
" and Operations of the Holy Spirit vindicated from the Inſults of Infidelity and the
" Abuſes of Fanaticiſm," 2 volumes, 12mo. and in the ſucceeding year drew upon
himſelf much illiberal abuſe from ſome writers † of the popular party, on occaſion of
his complaint in the Houſe of Lords, on the 15th of *November*, 1763, againſt Mr. *Wilkes*,
for putting his name to certain notes on the infamous " Eſſay on Woman." In 1765,
another edition of the Second Part of " The Divine Legation" was publiſhed as volumes
III. IV. and V.; the two parts printed in 1755 being conſidered as volumes I. and II.

* Soon after he attained this preferment, he wrote the Remarks on *Neale's* Hiſtory, which have
been already mentioned in p. 356.

† See *Churchill's* Ducelliſt, the Dedication of his Sermons, and other pieces. In making his complaint, the Biſhop, after ſolemnly diſavowing both the Poem and the Notes, averred, that the former
was worthy of the Devil; then, after a ſhort pauſe, added, " No, I beg the Devil's pardon, for he
" is incapable of writing it."

It

The other principal books of 1772 were, a beautiful edition of Dr. *Akenside's* " Poems" in 4to; " *Fitz-Stephen's* " Description of the City of *London*, newly translated from " the *Latin* Original, with a necessary Commentary, &c.

It was this edition which produced the well-known controversy between him and Dr. *Lowth*. On this occasion was published, " The Second Part of an Epistolary Corre- " spondence between the Bishop of *Gloucester* and the late Professor of *Oxford*, without " an *Imprimatur*; i. e. without a cover to the violated laws of honour and society, 1766." 8vo. In 1776, he gave a new edition of " The Alliance between Church and State," and a " Sermon preached before the incorporated Society for the Propagation of the " Gospel in Foreign Parts; at the Anniversary Meeting in the Parish Church of St. " *Mary-le-bow*, on *Friday*, *Feb.* 21," 8vo. The next year produced a third volume of his Sermons, dedicated to Lady *Mansfield*; and with this, and a single " Sermon " preached at St. *Lawrence Jewry*, on *Thursday*, *April* 30, 1767, before his Royal High- " ness *Edward* Duke of *York*, President, and the governors of the *London* Hospital, &c. " 4to." he closed his literary labours. His faculties continued unimpaired for some time after this period; and in 1769 he gave considerable assistance to Mr. *Ruffhead*, in his life of Mr. *Pope*. He also transferred 500l. to Lord *Mansfield*, Judge *Wilmot*, and Mr. *Charles Yorke*, upon trust, to found a Lecture in the form of a course of Sermons; to prove the truth of Revealed Religion in general, and of the Christian in particular, from the completion of the prophecies in the Old and New Testament, which relate to the Christian Church, especially to the apostacy of Papal *Rome*. To this found- ation we owe the admirable Introductory Lectures of Bishop *Hurd*; and the well- adapted continuation of Bishop *Halifax* and Dean *Bagot*. It is a melancholy reflection, that a life spent in the constant pursuit of knowledge frequently terminates in the loss of those powers, the cultivation and improvement of which are attended to with too strict and unabated a degree of ardour. This was in some degree the misfortune of Dr. *War- burton*. Like *Swift* and the great Duke of *Marlborough*, he gradually sunk into a situ- ation in which it was a fatigue to him to enter into general conversation. There were, however, a few old and valuable friends in whose company, even to the last, his mental faculties were exerted in their wonted force; and at such times he would appear chear- ful for several hours, and on the departure of his friends retreat as it were within himself. This melancholy habit was aggravated by the loss of his only son, a very promising young gentleman, who died of a consumption but a short time before the Bishop himself resigned to fate, in the 81st year of his age. A neat marble monument has been lately erected in the cathedral of *Gloucester*, with this inscription:

" To the Memory of
WILLIAM WARBURTON, D.D.
For more than xix Years Bishop of this See.
A Prelate
Of the most sublime Genius, and exquisite Learning.
Both which Talents
He employed through a long Life,
In the Support
Of what he firmly believed,
The CHRISTIAN RELIGION;

And
Of what he esteemed the best Establishment of it,
The CHURCH of ENGLAND.
He was born at *Newark upon Trent*, Dec. 24, 1698.
Was consecrated BISHOP of *Gloucester*, Jan. 20, 1760.
Died at his Palace, in this City, June 7, 1779,
And was buried near this place."

Beneath the entablature is his head in a medallion.

" By

" By an Antiquary *," 4to ; *Evelyn's* " Fumifugium," 4to ;
" Miscellaneous Poems, consisting of Originals and Tran-
" slations by *Vincent Bourne* †, M. A. formerly fellow of *Tri-*
" *nity-College, Cambridge,* and usher of *Westminster* school,"
4to ; " De Ratione & Usu Interpungendi ; an Essay on
" Punctuation, by *James Burrow*‡, Esq; F. R. S. and
F. S. A. 4to ; two editions of Dr. *Hurd's* " Lectures at
Lincoln's-Inn," (a third in 1773, and a fourth in 1776)
8vo ; two editions of " The Select Works of *Cowley,"*
with Notes by Dr. *Hurd,* 8vo ; three more volumes of
" Dr. *Jortin's* Sermons," 8vo ; " The Principles of Penal

---

* It is now no secret, that this learned Antiquary is the Rev. *Samuel Pegge,* M. A.
rector of *Whittington,* near *Chesterfield, Derbyshire* ; to whose literary labours the learned
world has very frequently been obliged ; and to whose unvaried friendship to Mr. *Bowyer*
the Author of these Anecdotes (who has himself also many obligations to Mr. *Pegge)* is
happy to inscribe this note.

† This amiable writer's classical taste was equalled by the goodness of his heart.
From conscientious motives he was induced to refuse a very valuable ecclesiastical
preferment offered him in the most liberal manner by a noble duke. In a letter to his
wife, written not long before his death, he says, " There is one thing which I have
" often heard myself charged with ; and that is my neglect of entering into holy
" orders, and a due preparation for that sacred office. Though I think myself in
" strictness answerable to none but God and my own conscience ; yet, for the satis-
" faction of the person that is dearest to me, I own and declare, that the importance
" of so great a charge, joined with a mistrust of my own sufficiency, made me fearful
" of undertaking it : if I have not in that capacity assisted in the salvation of souls, I
" have not been the means of losing any : if I have not brought reputation to the
" function by any merit of mine, I have the comfort of this reflection, I have given
" no scandal to it by my meanness and unworthiness. It has been my sincere desire,
" though not my happiness, to be as useful in my little sphere of life as possible : my
" own inclinations would have led me to a more likely way of being serviceable, if I
" might have pursued them ; however, as the method of education I have been brought
" up in was, I am satisfied, very kindly intended, I have nothing to find fault with, but
" a wrong choice, and the not knowing these disabilities I have since been truly con-
" scious of : those difficulties I have endeavoured to get over ; but found them insuper-
" able. It has been the knowledge of those discouragements, that has given me the
" greatest uneasiness I have ever met with : that has been the chief subject of my sleep-
" ing as well as my waking thoughts, a fear of reproach and contempt."

‡ Now Sir *James Burrow,* Master of the Crown-Office ; a very worthy friend
both to Mr. *Bowyer* and to the Writer of this Note.

" Law,"

" Law," by Mr. *Eden**, 8vo; Sir *William Hamilton's*
" Letters on Volcanos," 8vo. (reprinted in 1773); the
" second volume of the " Medical Transactions," 8vo ;
" The Tragedy of King *Lear* as lately published vindi-
" cated from the abuse of the Critical Reviewers, and
" the wonderful Genius and Abilities of those Gen-
" tlemen for Criticism set forth, celebrated and ex-
" tolled. By the Editor † of King *Lear*," 8vo ; Mr. *Whitaker's*

* *William Eden*, Esq; a younger brother of Sir *John Eden*, bart. afterwards Under-
Secretary of State, a Lord of Trade and Plantations, Auditor of *Greenwich Hospital*,
and one of the Commissioners for restoring Peace with *America*, 1778 ; and now member
of parliament for *Woodstock*, Chancellor of *Richmond* in the diocese of *York*, Principal
Secretary to the Lord Lieutenant of *Ireland*, &c. Mr. *Eden* also published " Four
" Letters to the Earl of *Carlisle*," &c. in 1780.

† *Charles Jennens*, Esq; a Nonconformist gentleman of considerable fortune at *Gopsal*,
in *Leicestershire*. In his youth he was so remarkable for the number of his servants,
the splendor of his equipages, and the profusion of his table, that from this excess
of pomp he acquired the title of *Solyman the Magnificent*. He is said to have composed the words for some of *Handel's* Oratorios, and particularly those for " The
" *Messiah*," an easy task, as it is only a selection from scripture verses. Not long
before his death he imprudently thrust his head into a nest of hornets, by an edition of
Shakspeare, which he began, by publishing " King *Lear*," in 8vo. For this gentleman
Mr. *Bowyer* printed afterwards, on the model of his *Lear*, the tragedies of " *Hamlet*,"
1772 ; " *Othello*" and " *Macbeth*," 1773. He would have proceeded further, but death
prevented him. The tragedy of " *Julius Cæsar*," which was in his life-time put to the
press, was published in 1774. He had a numerous library, and a large collection of
pictures, both in *Great Ormond Street* ‡ and at *Gopsal*.—I have the less occasion to
enlarge on his character, as it has been very faithfully delineated for me by a gentleman who knew him well : " The chief error of Mr. *Jennens's* life consisted in his per-
" petual association with a set of men every way inferior to himself. By these means he
" lost all opportunities of improvement, but gained what he preferred to the highest
" gratifications of wisdom—flattery in excess. He generally took care to patronise such
" tradesmen and such artists as few other persons would employ. Hence his shelves
" were crowded with the lumber of *Russel's* needy shop, and his walls discoloured by
" the refuse of *Hayman's* miserable pencil. He wrote, or caused to be written by some
" of his numerous parasites, a pamphlet against Dr. *Johnson* and Mr. *Steevens*, the edi-
" tors of *Shakspeare*, whom he suspected (perhaps justly enough) of having turned his
" commentatorial talents into ridicule. This doughty performance he is said to have had
" read aloud to him every day for at least a month after its publication, while he himself
" kept a constant eye on the news-papers, that he might receive the earliest intelligence

‡ Dispersed by public auction soon after his death. See a Catalogue of them in " The Con-
" noisseur," 8vo.

" of

ker's " Genuine History of the *Britons* afferted," 8vo; " A
" free Inquiry into the Origin, Progrefs, and prefent
" State of Pluralities," by Mr. *W. Pennington,* 8vo; " The
" Chriftian

" of the moment at which thefe gentlemen fhould have hanged or drowned themfelves
" in confequence of his attack on their abilities and characters. But, alas! while they
" were only laughing, he, poor man, was fo much hurt by the playful feverity they had
" exerted, that he rarely met with a forlorn object in the ftreet, but he was ready to afk
" what unfuccefsful work of literature had reduced him to fuch wretchednefs, being
" unwilling to admit that any thing

   " ———— could have fubdued nature
  " To fuch a lownefs, but his unkind *critics.*

" In fhort, his companions having continually intercepted every approach of unwelcome
" truth to his ears, he was confounded when it reached him through the pen of an op-
" ponent; and he faw himfelf publicly reprefented as the only editor to whom the fcenes
" of *Shakfpeare* had not even the moft inconfiderable obligation. He might indeed
" with equal prudence have enlifted his age under the banners of *Venus,* where it would
" have appeared to as much advantage as in the fervice of literature.——That the two
" critics already mentioned may efcape the accufation of having difturbed an unoffend-
" ing old man in his harmlefs amufement, it is neceffary we fhould add, that hoftilities
" were commenced by himfelf, he having, in his Preface and Notes to King *Lear,*
" charged all his predeceffors, by implication at leaft, with negligence and infidelity.——
" A pleafant circumftance, however, relative to his mode of collation, ought not to be
" forgotten. An eminent furgeon called at his houfe one evening, and found him be-
" fore a long table, on which all the various editions of his author were kept open by
" the weight of wooden bars. He himfelf was hobbling from one book to another
" with as much labour as *Gulliver* moved to and fro before the keys of the *Brobdingna-*
" *gian* harpfichord fixty feet in length. The obftinacy of Mr. *Jennens* was equal to his
" vanity. What he had once afferted, though manifeftly falfe, he would always main-
" tain. Being in poffeffion of a portrait by *Cornelius Janfen,* he advertifed it as the
" head of *Shakfpeare*; and though it was found to be dated in 1610, before *Janfen* was
" in *England,* our critic not only difdained to retract his firft pofition, but wrote letters
" in the news-papers to compliment himfelf on the ownerfhip of fuch an undoubted
" original of his favourite bard. So enamoured (as has been before obferved) was our
" Magnifico of pomp, that if his tranfit were only from *Great Ormond Street, Blooms-*
" *bury,* where he refided, to Mr. *Bowyer's* in *Red Lion Paffage, Fleet Street,* he always
" travelled with four horfes, and fometimes with as many fervants behind his carriage.
" In his progrefs up the paved-court, a footman ufually preceded him, to kick oyfter-
" fhells and other impediments out of his way. He changed his publifhers more than
" once, having perfuaded himfelf that the ill-fuccefs of his projected edition of our
" great dramatic poet was in fome meafure owing to their machinations, in conjunc-
" tion with thofe of the bookfellers. The important finecure of vending his works he
" at laft conferred on the truly honeft Mafter *Owen* of the Mineral Water Warehoufe
" at *Temple Bar,* who deferved a more creditable occupation than that of expofing to
" fale what no man would purchafe. To his firft printer, Mr. *Richardfon,* as often as
" he difappointed him of a proof, he would difplay all the infolence of confcious wealth;

" Chriſtian Whig," 8vo; and a new edition of *Dawſon's*
" Lexicon Novi Teſtamenti," 8vo.

A very ingenious " Inquiry into the Value of the An-
" cient *Greek* and *Roman* Money, by *Matthew Raper*, Eſq.
" F. R. S." was printed in the Philoſophical Tranſactions
for 1771. This reſpectable gentleman's opinion on theſe
ſubjects not coinciding with that of Mr. *Bowyer*, he printed
a little pamphlet, under the title of " Remarks occaſioned
" by a late Diſſertation on the *Greek* and *Roman* Money,
" 1772, 4to;" which was intended as an Appendix to
Mr. *Clarke's* book on Coins*. The opinions of many excellent

" and on his domeſtics he occaſionally poured out a turbulence of rage that was not
" over-delicate in its choice of expreſſions. The fate of his critical undertakings may
" convey a uſeful leſſon to thoſe who commence authors in their dotage. It may likewiſe
" teach the ' golden fool,' (as *Shakſpeare* calls the man of greater opulence than learn-
" ing) that though the praiſe of a few ſycophants is an eaſy purchaſe, the world at
" large will never ſell its approbation, were there, as *Jugurtha* ſaid, any merchant rich
" enough to buy it. Let us, however, do juſtice to Mr. *Jennens's* merits where we are lucky
" enough to find them. He was profuſely liberal to thoſe who in his opinion deſerved
" liberality. The indigent Nonjuror and Nonconformiſt never ſolicited relief in vain.
" At his country ſeat, as well as at his houſe in town, he chiefly lived in intimacy with
" theſe diſcontented members of the commonwealth, and to a lower order of the ſame
" beings his munificence was in general confined. The Reviewers indeed might have
" made their fortunes out of his purſe, could they have been bribed to applaud his
" editorial abilities, prefer *Hayman* to *Raffaelle*, and ſupport his aſſertion relative to
" *Cornelius Janſen*, by ſetting both chronology and probability at defiance." Mr. *Jennens* died on the 20th of *November*, 1773.

* Before the publication of theſe " Remarks," Mr. *Bowyer* addreſſed the following
letter to the worthy gentleman whoſe opinions he had ventured to examine:

" SIR,
" Having an opportunity of ſending to the King of *France's* Library a copy of Mr.
" *Clarke's* Book on Coins, as he in his life-time adviſed me to do, I took occaſion to en-
" cloſe to Monſ. *Capperonier*, the Library-Keeper, and Member of the Academy of
" Inſcriptions, the ſmall Memoir I had drawn up on the difficult paſſage of *Pliny*, Nat.
" Hiſt. l. xxxiii. I hope this Appeal to a Nation, no leſs famous for its humanity than
" literature, will give no more offence to you, equally remarkable for both, than it will to
" them for differing from Pere *Harduin, Crevier, La Barré*, and others. The cauſe of
" Learning is the cauſe of All; and I beg your acceptance of Mr. *Clarke's* Book, which,
" at leaſt I may ſay, is written very entertainingly. I ſhall deliver out in *England* no
" more

cellent writers in *Germany* and *France* having been ably controverted in that volume, Mr. *Bowyer* tranfmitted a copy of it to the *French* King's Library, and infcribed his little Appendix,

"REGI CHRISTIANISSIMO

" GUILIELMUS BOWYER, TYPOGRAPHUS ANGLICANUS.

" Judicium ut fubeat magis æquum, candidiufve,

" Quî poni potuit commodiore loco ?"

It was very much his wifh, that the work fhould have been tranflated and reprinted in *France* ; and he took fome pains to have it performed* ; but without effect.

In

" more of the Memoir than what I inclofe to you, without your exprefs permiffion : " intending chiefly to raife fome friendly debates among the *French* criticks, who have " ftudied this branch of Learning more than we have, though I think with lefs fuccefs " than this our valuable Countryman ; and hope I fhall ftill continue in your efteem and " favour ; and remain, Sir, your obedient and moft humble fervant, W. BOWYER."
[Mr. *Raper* returned a very polite anfwer to this letter, and full permiffion to publifh the Memoir.]

* It was his firft wifh that the tranflation fhould have been made by the friend who declined the tafk in the following terms :

" DEAR SIR, *September* 9, 1773.
" After confidering the inclofed, with as much attention as other unavoidable and " urgent affairs would permit, the beft I can do is, to make what hafte I can to fend it " back ; and acquaint you, that it is utterly impoffible for me, either to undertake a " tranflation of the fame at prefent, or even forefee a time when I might be better able " to undertake it. I hope this forced refufal will not be taken amifs, from one who " (within the too fmall compafs of his power) is moft well-wifhingly your humble fer- " vant, CÆSAR DE MISSY.
" P. S. Nor will you, I hope, take it as a piece of unkindnefs if I amicably tell you, " that I fear the *Latin* infcription *Regi Chriftianiffimo*, &c. will hardly have a good " effect ; becaufe it looks as though you wifhed to obtain from His Moft Chriftian Ma- " jefty the decifion of a controverfy, concerning which (were it indeed to come before " him) he might be ready to fay fome thing equivalent to the *Greek*, Τίς με κατέςησε δι- " καςὴν ἐφ' ὑμᾶς."
Mr. *Bowyer* next applied to another gentleman, who undertook to get the work tran- flated at *Paris*. Two copies of it were accordingly fent ; and the receipt of them was thus acknowledged :

" SIR, *Ipres, May* 17, 1774.
" Some unforefeen accidents obliged me to put off my journey to *France* much longer " than I intended. I returned from *Paris* but five days ago, and could not have the
" pleafure

In 1773, he publifhed three little tracts, under the title of " Select Difcourfes : 1. Of the Correfpondence of the " *Hebrew* Months with the *Julian*, from the *Latin* of Pro- " feffor *Michaelis*. 2. Of the Sabbatical Years, from the " fame. 3. Of the Years of Jubilee ; from an Anonymous " Writer, in *Maffon's* Hiftoire Critique de la Republique " des Lettres."

The other principal books of that year were " The Anti- " quities of *Herculaneum*," by Meffrs. *Lettice* and *Martyn*, BB.D. and Fellows of *Sidney-College*, *Cambridge*, the latter Profeffor of Botany, 4to; " *Ben Mordecai's* Letters," 4to ; Mr. *Combe's* " Index Nummorum omnium, Imperatorum, " *Auguftarum*, et *Cæfarum*, a *Julio Cæfare* ufque ad *Poftumum*, " qui tam in *Roma* & Coloniis, quam in *Græcia*, *Ægypto*, & " aliis locis, ex aere magni moduli fignabantur," 4to ; Mr. *Keate's* " Monument in *Arcadia*," 4to ; " *Joannis Davidis Mi-*

" pleafure of acquainting you fooner, how I difpofed of the two copies you gave me of " Mr. *Clarke's* Connexion of Ancient Coins. One copy is to be placed in the King's " Library, and another to be given to Monfieur *Le Seur* to be tranflated into *French*. " He is an elegant writer ; and his Tranflations of Dr. *Robertfon's* Hiftory of *Charles* V. " and of the Voyages publifhed by Dr. *Hawkefworth*, fufficiently fhew that he is quali- " fied to do juftice to Mr. *Clarke's* performance. Monf. *Capperonier* defires that " the plates may be fent by the way of *Calais*, addreffed to Monf. *Piffot*, *Libraire*, *Quai* " *de Conti à Paris* ; and promifes they fhall be returned when the Tranflation is finifhed. " I am forry it was not in my power to convince you fooner that I have not neglected " what you recommended to me. I am, Sir, your moft obedient humble fervant,

" ALEXANDER MAC AULAY."

The plates were next fent to Monfieur *Capperonier*, who not long after returned them with this anfwer :

" J'ai reçu, Monfieur, les planches de l'ouvrage de M *Clarke*, dont je fuis très faché " d'apprendre la mort par la lettre que vous m'avez fait l'honneur de m'écrire, et la- " quelle mes occupations m'ont empeché de repondre jufqu'a ce moment. J'avois " trop prefumé de la bonne volonté de nos Libraires pour les monnoyes *Saxonnes*. De- " puis qu'ils ont vû l'ouvrage, ils ne le croyent plus fufceptible d'un certain debit en " *France*, et ils ont renoncé le projet de le traduire. C'eft pourquoi j'aurai l'honneur " de vous en renvoyer les planches à la premiere occafion. Je vous offre d'ailleurs mes " fervices pour notre pays ; et je fuis trés parfaitement, Monfieur, votre très humble et très " obeifant ferviteur, CAPPERONNIER, Garde de la Bibliotheque du Roi. *Sept.* 10, 1774."

" chaelis,

" chaelis, Prof. Ordin. Philof. & Soc. Reg. Scient. Goettingenfis
" Collegæ, Epiftolæ * de LXX Hebdomadibus Danielis ad
" D. Joannem Pringle, Baronettum : primò privatim
" miffæ, nunc verò utriufque confenfu publicè editæ,"
8vo; " The Canterbury Tales of Chaucer, to which are
" added, an Effay upon his Language and Verfification, an
" Introductory Difcourfe, and Notes †," by Thomas Tyrwhitt,
Efq; 4 vols. 8vo; " Fragmenta duo Plutarchi ‡," publifhed
by the fame learned editor, a fingle fheet, 8vo; Mr. Barrington's edition of " Orofius," 8vo; a third edition of Dr.
Hurd's Lectures at Lincoln's Inn, 8vo; Dr. Owen's " Ser-
" mons at Boyle's Lectures," 8vo; Dr. Percy's " Key to
" the New Teftament," 8vo; a new edition § of Hutchin-
" fon's " ΚΥΡΟΥ ΠΑΙΔΕΙΑ," 8vo; Mr. Whitaker's " Hiftory
" of Manchefter," 2 vols. 8vo; " A Brief State of the
" Principles of Church Authority," 8vo; the firft volume
of Mr. [now Dr.] Carr's very happy tranflation of " Lucian,"
8vo; Mr. Jennens's editions of " Othello" and of " Macbeth,"
8vo; and " The Spiritual Quixote, or Summer's Ramble of
" Mr. Geoffrey Wildgoofe," 3 vols. 12mo. by Mr. Graves ‖.

In

* Thefe Letters were revifed through the prefs by Sir John Pringle, then Prefident
of the Royal Society.

† A fifth volume, containing a Gloffary, &c. was added in 1778.

‡ " Fragmenta hæc Plutarchi huc ufque, ut opinor, inedita, ex Codice manufcripto,
" qui inter Harleianos in Mufeo Britannico affervatur N. 5612. vifum eft typis defcribere,
" non quod ipfe de illis magnifice nimis fentirem, fed ut, propofito hujus ἐρμαιε exemplo,
" homines otiofos, & eos præfertim quibus Bibliothecarum cura demandata eft, ad codices
" manufcriptos diligentius excutiendos ftimularem." Editor's Advertifement.

§ In the courfe of printing this volume, Mr. Bowyer made an accurate " Index to
" the places of the N. T." which is inferted in a later edition of the volume, 1781.

‖ Richard Graves, M. A. fecond fon of Richard Graves, Efq; born at Mickleton, in
the county of Gloucefter, May 4, 1715, was educated at Abingdon fchool, in Berks;
elected from thence, Nov. 4, 1732, a fcholar of Pembroke College, Oxford, and chofen
fellow of All-Souls College, 1736; M. A. 1740. He is now, 1781, rector of Claverton,
and vicar of Kilmerfden, in the county of Somerfet. He contracted an intimacy with
Mr.

In 1773 was publifhed the then lately .difcovered Fragment of *Livy* ; which Mr. *Markland* defired Mr. *Bowyer* to
fend him *, with a remark, that " many, he fancied,
" would buy the Fragment, who never read a line in the
" Author †."

In *December* that year died Dr. *Knowler* ‡, an old and valuable friend of Mr. *Bowyer* ; who received foon after a polite
letter from Mrs. *Knowler*, with an intimation that a legacy
of twenty pounds was ready for his acceptance. I wifh I
had a copy of this letter and of his anfwer, which I remember to have feen ; the purport of the letter, however,
was a proper acknowledgement of the lady's civility, a very

Mr. *Shenftone* at *Pembroke College*, and has publifhed, befides feveral poems in *Dodfley's*
Colleltion, the following ingenious pieces : 1. " The Feftoon, or a Collection of Epi-
" grams, 1767." 2. " The Spiritual Quixote ||," above-mentioned. 3. " *Il Galateo*,
" or a Treatife on Politenefs, from the *Italian* of *De la Cafa*." 4. " *Euphrofyne*, a
" Collection of Poems, 1776," 2 vols. 5. A Novel, intituled, " *Columella*, or the
" Diftreffed Anchoret, 1778 ;" in which he is thought to glance at his friend Mr. *Shen-
ftone*.

* After having perufed it, Mr. *Markland* fays, " The Editor of the Fragment, who,
" I find, is an honorary Doctor of Laws § of the laft brood at *Oxon*, feems to be pleafed
" at having found an old fhoe-buckle of a thoufand years age, of no ufe to any man living,
" The *Greek* man's ἕυρημα ** is of the fame value : but the *finders* I believe to be of very
" *different* worth. I thank you for the Bifhop of *Clogher*, who I think was a great man."

† This remark is very pretty, but rather too ftrong : " who never have read, or
" never will read the whole," would have been fufficient. One may well wonder why
fuch people fhould act fo ; but three good reafons may be given : 1. The little trouble
and time beftowed on two or three pages, in comparifon of five or fix large quartos.
2. It affording fafhionable talk. 3. The chance of fome new fact turning up. *T. F.*

‡ *William Knowler*, LL. D. baptifed *May* 9, 1699, was the third fon of *Gilbert
Knowler*, gent. of *Herne* in *Kent*, and uncle to the prefent *Gilbert Knowler*, Efq; the
laft of a family which *Philipott* mentions as being fettled in that parifh in the reign of
Queen *Elizabeth*. Dr. *Knowler* was educated at *St. John's College, Cambridge*, where
probably his friendfhip commenced with Mr. *Bowyer*. He was chaplain to the firft
Marquis of *Rockingham*, who prefented him firft to the rectory of *Irthlingborow*, and
afterwards to the more valuable one of *Boddington*, both in *Northamptonfhire*. He was
editor of " The Earl of *Strafforde's* Letters and Difpatches, 1739," folio. (See p. 149.)
He left only three daughters.

|| Some entertaining anecdotes relative to this work are fcattered throughout Mr. *Graves's* cor-
refpondence with Mr. *Shenftone*.
§ Dr. *Bruns*. ** See the preceding page.

fuitable

fuitable condolance on her lofs, and a requeft, that, to fave trouble, fhe would keep the twenty pounds intended for him, which otherwife fhe would have to receive back from his executors at a period which he had reafon to think would not be far diftant.

In 1774, Mr. *Bowyer* corrected a new edition of *Schrevelius's* Lexicon, and added a confiderable number of words collected in the courfe of his own ftudies *: thefe are diftinguifhed by an afterifk. The Lexicons of *Hederic* and of *Buxtorf*, the *Latin* ones of *Faber* † and *Littleton*, and the *Englifh* Dictionary of *Bailey*, were all confiderably enlarged by him: thefe additions are ftill in MS. His *Greek* and *Latin* Grammars in general, and particularly fuch of them as he had in common ufe when at fchool and at college, are filled with fuch curious explanatory notes as bear the moft convincing marks of confummate critical knowledge in thofe languages. And that knowledge he applied in a fpecial manner to the advancement of facred learning. It was his conftant cuftom, in the courfe of his reading, to note down every thing which he thought might contribute to illuftrate any paffage of Scripture, efpecially of the *Greek* Teftament. In purfuance of this method, it is hardly to be conceived what a number of ufeful and curious remarks ftand inferted in the margin ‡ of his Theological Books, which may greatly contribute

* Reprinted in 1781 from his corrected copy.

† Mr. *Bowyer* had an intention of republifhing this valuable Lexicon in a more commodious manner, by changing its prefent radical form into an alphabetical one.

‡ He left feveral MS. Notes on *Middleton's* Life of *Cicero* ‖ ; on *Bladen's* and *Duncan's* *Cæfar* ‖ ; on *Theocritus*; on *Baxter's Horace*; on the Old and New Teftaments; on *Fleetwood's* Chronicon Pretiofum; on *Whifton's Jofephus*; on *Xenophon*; on *Stephens's* Thefaurus; on *Hefychii* § Lexicon, 1514; and many other books.

‖ The Notes on *Cicero* and *Cæfar* are printed in his "Mifcellaneous Tracts."

§ "The Dictionary of *Hefychius* is a collection of all the difficult, fcarce, fingular, and irregular "words which a ftudious man has remarked in all the ancient *Greek* authors, explained and placed

tribute to improve future editions. On two books in particular he beftowed much pains; viz. *Leigh's* * " Critica Sacra,
" 1662," and *Du-Gard's* " Lexicon *Græci* Teftamenti Alpha-
" beticum, 1660 †," both which he has left accurately
corrected and much enlarged. Thefe he often wifhed,
in his latter days, he had been able to publifh, for the ufe of
Schools, and the benefit of young Students in Divinity. The
firft of them, full of critical notes, is now in the poffeffion of
Dr. *Owen*; and the latter in the hands of his fucceffor in
bufinefs.

In 1774 was alfo publifhed, " The Origin of Printing,
" in Two Effays. 1. The Subftance of Dr. *Middleton's* Dif-
" fertation on the Origin of Printing in *England*. 2. Mr.
" *Meerman's* Account of the Invention of the Art at *Harleim*,
" and its Progrefs to *Mentz*, with occafional Remarks; and
" an Appendix." The original idea ‡ of this little pamphlet
was

---

* *Edward Leigh*, Efq; born at *Shawell*, in *Leicefterfhire*, and educated at *Magdalen Hall, Oxford*. He was a member of the Long Parliament, and one of the members of the Houfe of Commons who were appointed to fit in the Affembly of Divines.
He was afterwards colonel of a regiment for the Parliament; but in 1648 was numbered
among the Prefbyterian members who were turned out; and in *December* he was impri-
foned. From this period to the Reftoration he employed himfelf in writing a confiderable number of learned and valuable books (as may be feen in *Wood*, Ath. Oxon. II. 483).
He died *June* 2, 1671; and was buried at *Rufhall*, in *Staffordfhire*.

† Mr. *William Du-Gard* was at that time mafter of *Merchant-Taylors School*.

‡ This idea was in part taken up immediately after the publication of Dr. *Middleton's*
tract in 1735; which received the following animadverfions from Mr. *Bowyer*, in *The
Grub-ftreet Journal, March* 20, 1735; the fubftance of which is preferved in the Notes
to " The Origin of Printing:"

" in an alphabetical order. Few words of that fort are to be met with in thofe authors but what
" are here interpreted. We may hereby form a judgement of the ufefulnefs of this work, but we
" fee, at the fame time, the difficulty of it; how liable it was to the errors of tranfcribers and the
" licentioufnefs of grammarians, and that it can be ufeful only to thofe who are thoroughly verfed
" in *Greek* literature. Formerly, a man who had not corrected five or fix paffages in *Hefychius*, was
" not thought a good critic. The *Dutch* Edition has, without doubt, cleared it from many faults,
" but not from all, and it may be queftioned whether in fome places it has not added new ones."
HUETIANA, Art. XLVI.

6

" To

was Mr. *Bowyer's*; the completion of it his Partner's. The
two

" To Mr. *Bavius*, Secretary to the Society of *Grub-street*.

" Sir,

" As the numerous writers of your Society are the chief support and ornament of
" Printing; you muſt be nearly intereſted in every circumſtance that contributes to the
" honour of it. I congratulate you therefore upon the advantageous figure which *Cax-*
" *ton*, our country-man and fellow-citizen, makes in Dr. *Middleton's* Diſſertation con-
" cerning the origin of this art in *England*. But, good Mr. *Bavius*, is not the old
" man's authority placed a little too high, when moſt, if not all, our *Engliſh* Chronicles
" are made to ſubmit to his; and a new æra is preſcribed to one of our kings by it?
" Dr. *Middleton* maintains from him, p. 3, that *Edward* IV. was proclaimed in *London*
" at the end of 1459, according to our computation, on the 4th of *March*, and crowned
" about the *Midſummer* following (*i. e.* 1460.) Is not *Caxton*, you'll ſay, a good evi-
" dence of a fact that happened in his own time? May be ſo: but the good Doctor's
" Diſſertation is even built upon the ſuppoſition that the preſs was not infallible in
" thoſe days; and might not M CCCC LIX, by an eaſy transpoſition, eſcape inſtead of
" M CCCC LXI? I need not appeal to other contemporary hiſtorians, where we are capa-
" ble of producing demonſtration. The firſt inſtrument in *Rymer*, under *Edward* IV,
" begins thus: ' *Memorandum quod die Martis, decimo die Martii, anno regni regis*
" *Edwardi* primo, &c.' Now in the year 1460-1, the tenth of *March* fell on a *Tueſday*;
" but in 1459-60, on a *Monday*. I will venture therefore to vindicate the true reading
" of our old almanacks, and to exterminate a falſe one from *Caxton's Chronicle.*

" But the Doctor raiſes a triumph upon his great diſcovery; and poor *Echard* is
" ſingled out to be laſhed for not reading this *Chronicle*, or not making the ſame uſe of
" it with the Doctor. ' Mr. *Echard* (ſays he, p. 21.) at the end of *Edward* IV's
" reign, among the Learned of that age, mentions *William Caxton* as a writer of *Engliſh*
" hiſtory; but *ſeems* to doubt whether he was the ſame with the printer of that name.
" Had he ever looked into *Caxton's* books, the doubts had been cleared; or had he con-
" ſulted his *Chronicle of England*, (which it is ſtrange that an *Engliſh* hiſtorian could
" neglect!) he would have learned at leaſt to fix the beginning of that reign with more
" exactneſs, as it is noted above juſt *two* years earlier than he has placed it.' Juſt *one*
" year, the Doctor ſhould have ſaid: *Echard* fixing it, very right, *March* 4, 1461, ac-
" cording to the computation in thoſe days (*i. e.* 1460-1); the Doctor 1459 according to
" our computation (*i. e.* 1459-60).—But this gentleman ſeems reſolved to be at vari-
" ance with that hiſtorian as far as poſſible. He gives us his doubts, but ſo much the
" worſt ſide of them, that it is but juſt to let the hiſtorian ſpeak for himſelf: ' In this
" reign flouriſhed *John Harding* and *William Caxton*, both writers of the *Engliſh*
" hiſtory. And that which now began to give new encouragement to learning, was the
" famous art of printing, which was firſt found out in *Germany* by *John Guttenberghen*
" about 1440, or ſomewhat later, and was brought into *England* by *William Caxton*, a
" mercer of *London*, and *probably* the ſame with the hiſtorian, who firſt practiſed the
" ſame in the Abbey of *Weſtminſter*, 1471, and the eleventh of this reign.' The hiſto-
" rian writes ſo agreeably to the Doctor's hypotheſis, that one would think he need not
" be ſo much aſhamed of his company.

" As we are now upon chronology, I will give you another inſtance of the Doctor's
" fondneſs of ſingularity in it. Pag. 11. he cites, from Mr. *Maittaire*, *Auſonius's* Epi-
" grams, printed at *Venice*, 1472, with this deſignation of the year at the end, *A nati-*

" *vitate*

two learned friends, whose assistance is acknowledged in their preface, were the Rev. Dr. *Henry Owen* * and the late

" *vitate Christi ducentesimæ nonagesimæ quintæ Olympiadis anno* II. Where, by the " way, to make the designation of the year at the end correspond to the figures at the " beginning, 1472, it should be read *nonagesimæ quartæ.* Whether this is an error of " the press in the *Venice* edition, or only in Mr. *Maittaire's* account of it, I know not. " But the point I am coming to, Mr. *Bavius,* is the Doctor's pompous remark. 'The " printer, says he, follows the *common* mistake, both of the *ancients* and *moderns,* of " taking the Olympiad for a term of five years complete: whereas it included but " four, and was celebrated every fifth; as the *Lustrum* likewise of the *Romans.*' I " have consulted upon this occasion various modern writers of chronology, from *Joseph* " *Scaliger,* down to *Adam Littleton;* and all I have yet met with make an Olympiad to " consist, as the Doctor does, of no more than *four* years complete. There are some " passages indeed among the *Roman* poets to the contrary; who, out of poetical liberty, " have extended the Olympiad to five years, the usual term of their own *Lustrum.* " But they have not been supposed to speak with chronological exactness, since there " are more express authorities against them: so that the Doctor's opinion here, and I " like it never the worse, is the *common* one. But that the *Roman Lustrum* included " only *four* years, is too singular, I dare say, for him to stand by. It was ordinarily " *celebrated,* as he says, *every fifth year;* that is, the 5th, the 10th, 15th, 20th, &c. but " not in the same manner as he himself understands the Olympiad, the 1st, 5th, 9th, " 13th, 17th, 21st, &c. the latter being a period of four years, the former of five."

Mr. *Clarke,* a few days after its appearance, says, " I thank you for your packet. I " set out next morning to our city of *Uckfield,* to enquire after your corrections of Dr. " *Middleton.* The whole is extremely well; you have used more decency than he de- " serves. I am only sorry that you contracted your Remarks into such a narrow com- " pass. Was it not possible to enlarge to a six-penny pamphlet? He will naturally " overlook a letter in such a Journal, and pretend that he has never heard of it. I have " never seen Dr. *M's* pamphlet; but sure it was a monstrous thing, to advance so re- " markable an alteration as the æra of a King's Reign upon so precarious an authority " as the A. D. of a title-page. Perhaps he had some other vouchers: but, whatever " they were, you have taught him a secret in Chronology, that, when there are sufficient " materials, it is very dangerous indulging conjecture, and neglecting demonstration. " That article of King *Edward* is only silly and singular; the next is scandalous. I " am no admirer of *Echard,* but a great friend to justice. To raise such unreasonable " doubts from a modest way of saying the same thing with himself, and from thence to " draw such groundless consequences to an author's prejudice, is a sort of *pettyfogging* " in writing, that deserves great contempt."

* Rector of *St. Olave's, Hart-Street,* and vicar of *Edmonton* in *Middlesex.* The " Collation of the Account of the Dedication of the Temple" was given by this judicious and friendly Divine; and was followed by a learned treatise under the title of " Critica " Sacra, or a short Introduction to *Hebrew* Criticism, 1774," 8vo; and this by a " Sup- " plement, 1775," in answer to some remarks on it by Mr. *Raphael Baruh,* a learned *Jew.* To Dr. *Owen* the world is also indebted for " Harmonia Trigonometrica, or a short " Treatise on Trigonometry, &c. 1748," 8vo; some excellent " Observations on the Four " Gospels, 1764," 8vo; " Directions to young Students in Divinity, 1766," 8vo; " An " Enquiry into the Septuagint Version, 1769," 8vo; a series of " Sermons at *Boyle's* " Lectures, 1773," 8vo; an accurate edition of *Grabe's* Collation of the celebrated *Cottonian* MS. of *Genesis* with the printed *Vatican,* 1778; and for many very valuable annotations in Mr. *Bowyer's* " Conjectures on the New Testament," more particularly in the quarto edition of that useful volume.

Mr.

Mr. *Cæsar De-Miſſy* *. Though publiſhed anonymouſly, it was immediately pronounced to be Mr. *Bowyer's* ; and on

* Many of Mr. *De-Miſſy's* valuable remarks are ſcattered throughout the Appendix, and his ingenious Letter on the variations in the copies of Biſhop *Walton's* Polyglott deſerves particular attention : The following ſtriking particulars of this gentleman's character are tranſlated from an advertiſement to " The Origin of Printing," (the amiable effuſions of friendſhip enlivened by conjugal veneration) prefixed in 1776 to the third edition † of his " Paraboles ou Fables ‡ et aûtres petites Narratious d'un Citoyen " de la Republique Chrétienne du dix-huitième ſiècle," which the author had reviſed and corrected for the preſs, but did not live to publiſh : " In the midſt of his ſtudies he was " ſtopped, not ſurpriſed, by Death. For ſeveral years he had accuſtomed himſelf to " conſider every new day as another day added by the Divine Goodneſs to a life which " had already attained the uſual boundaries ; this, without the evenneſs of his temper, " or his natural chearfulneſs, being in the leaſt abated, ſupported him in the troubles " and embarraſſments which he found in his journey, by a rational conviction of the " great truths which he preached to the laſt, with a zeal which aroſe from that con-" viction, he had, properly ſpeaking, no other deſire, no other object, in all his actions, " even in his amuſements, than the propagation of thoſe truths. Filled with the ſin-" cereſt benevolence, the moſt cordial charity for mankind, he ſaw that nothing but " Chriſtianity well underſtood could make mankind happy, and his own happineſs con-" ſiſted in diffuſing the knowledge of it. *Go, and do thou likewiſe.*" Mr. *De-Miſſy* was many years miniſter of the *French* Chapel at St. *James's Palace* ; and the publick have lately been favoured with three volumes of " Sermons ſur divers Textes de l'Ecri-" ture Sainte ; par feu Monſieur *Céſar de-Miſſy*, un des Chapelains *François* de ſa " Majeſté *Britannique*, 1780," 8vo. His Letter to Mr. *Bowyer* on the opinions of Father *Harduin* has been already mentioned in p. 368. He died *Aug.* 10, 1775, aged 72 years, and 10 weeks. His valuable library was ſold by auction, by Meſſrs *Baker* and *Leigh, March* 18—26, 1778 ; among which the following books were enriched with his MS. notes : *Cicero's* Academics, in *French,* by *Durand,* 1740 ; *Stephens's* Theſaurus Linguæ *Græcæ* ; Poetæ Minores *Græci, Cant* 1677 ; Bibliotheque de *Du Verdier,* 1585 ; *Aldus's Lucian,* 1532 ; *Barnes's Homer* ; *Pauw's Horapollo* ; *Montfaucon's* Palæographia *Græca* ; beſides ſeveral valuable MSS. of the Old and New Teſtament ; Lectionaria ; Pſalters ; the Fathers ; *Plutarch, Heſiod, Sophocles,* and *Euripides.* Many of his Biblical collations are now in *The Britiſh Muſeum* ; ſeveral cf the moſt curious printed books were purchaſed for his Majeſty's Library, and others by Dr. *Hunter.* Among Dr. *Birch's* MSS. is a letter, in *French,* from Mr. *De-Miſſy,* in 1736, recommending his brother to ſome employment in one of the *Mediterranean* Iſlands.

† In the title-page of this volume is a moſt ſtriking portrait of Mr. *De-Miſſy,* engraved by C. *Powle,* in 1773, and inſcribed VOLENTIBUS AMICIS. And to this edition were annexed, " Vers " de Monſieur *De-Miſſy,* pour le Tableau de la nouvelle Egliſe de *St. Jean,* mis en vüe dans la " Chambre Conſiſtoriale de la dite Egliſe. Aux quels on a joint une petite Epître du même, qu'on " a intitulée Envoi des Vers précédens à Monſ. *Beuzeville,* Paſteur de la ſus-dite Egliſe."

‡ " Three of Mr. *De-Miſſy's French* Fables freely tranſlated by himſelf, *in uſum Amicorum,*" were printed in 1772, 8vo ; the ſhorteſt of which is here ſubjoined as a ſpecimen :

FORTUNE, DEATH, and TIM, (from N° 9, of the *Frensh*) :

Tim after *Fortune* ran full-hardy,
  While *Death* was running after *Tim* :
But he for *Fortune* prov'd too tardy,
  And *Death,* alas ! too ſwift for him.

Thus Fools fall victims to a fate
  Which eaſily the Wiſe will ſhun.
For *Death* and *Fortune* let us *wait* !
  'Tis mad for either's ſake to *run.*

that

that fuppofition met, perhaps, with a better fate in the world of letters than it might otherwife have been honoured with. The periodical publications of the continent joined thofe of *England* in its commendation. Of thefe let one extract ferve as a fample: " Of the many treatifes con-
" cerning the Origin of Printing, there are few, if any,
" which will be found more fatisfactory than the prefent;
" and there is no one that contains fo much information in
" the fame compafs. The Author profeffes only to give
" the fubftance of two books; but he goes much further.
" He has interfperfed, through the whole piece, a number of
" valuable notes, which will greatly increafe the general ftock
" of knowledge upon the fubject, and correct the miftakes
" of the works he has abridged; this is remarkably the
" cafe with Dr. *Middleton's* Differtation. Without pretend-
" ing to exhibit a complete hiftory of the origin of the art,
" our author ventures to affert, that he has here given a
" clearer account of it than is to be met with in any book
" hitherto publifhed in *England*; and we are fully fatisfied
" of the truth of his affertion. We apprehend, that the
" publick is indebted, for this valuable account of the origin
" and progrefs of the art of printing, to one of the laft of
" our learned Printers; a race of men whom we have ob-
" ferved, with concern, to be almoft extinct in *Europe*, or
" at leaft in our own country *." A fecond edition of this tract, with many improvements, appeared in 1776; and a " Supplement" to it in 1781.

* Monthly Review for *January* 1775. This critique (which, as appears by the article Bowyer in the " Biographia," was written by Dr. *Kippis*) was literally tranflated in the " Journal des Sçavans," for *April* 1775.

The

The moſt material books of 1774 were, " The Hiſtory " and Antiquities of the County of *Dorſet*, by Mr. *Hutchins* *," 2 vols. folio; " Miſcellanies, by *George* (late) Lord *Lyttelton*," publiſhed by his nephew Captain *Ayſcough* †, 4to, two editions;.

* Of whom ſee above, p. 150. The number of beautiful plates in this hiſtory, of which only 600 copies were printed (a number not quite ſufficient for the ſubſcribers). raiſed the value of it, immediately after publication, to twice the original price, which. was only a guinea a volume. Nothing but the ſtricteſt adherence to juſtice induced the author and his friends to relinquiſh, if we may ſay it, ſo advantageous a publication. Bluſh, ye compilers of county hiſtories, who ſcruple not to encroach on the liberality of. the publick, by taking the whole ſubſcription-money on the delivery only of the firſt vo- lume. Bluſh with the deepeſt tinge, when you compare your plates with thoſe which decorate the Hiſtory of *Dorſet*.

† *George-Edward* ‡ *Ayſcough*, Eſq; a lieutenant in the firſt regiment of foot-guards, only ſon of the Rev. Dr. *Francis Ayſcough* (who was tutor to Lord *Lyttelton* at *Oxford*, and at length Dean of *Briſtol*) by *Anne* fifth ſiſter to his Lordſhip, who addreſſed a Poem to the Doctor from *Paris*, in 1728, printed in *Dodſley's* ſecond volume. The above- mentioned publication was dedicated by the Editor to his couſin the laſt Lord *Lyttelton*, who has artfully developed his noble father's motives in this appointment in his " Let- " ters, 1780," Letter 25 : " The dedication to myſelf is a wretched buſineſs, and diſ- " graces the volume to which it is prefixed. You wonder I did not write a better for him " myſelf; and I would moſt ſurely have done it, but, among many excellent qualities " which this dedicator poſſeſſes, he is a blab of the firſt delivery, and I dared not venture " to truſt him. The teſtamentary arrangement which appointed him to the honourable " labours of an editor, took its riſe from three motives : 1. To mark a degree of parental " reſentment againſt an ungracious ſon; 2. From an opinion that a gracious nephew's " well-timed flattery had created of his own underſtanding; and, 3. From a deſign of " beſtowing upon this ſame gracious nephew, a legacy of honour from the publication, " and profit from the ſale of the volume. He is as proud of the buſineſs as a new-made " knight of his title," &c. In his laſt letter the young Lord § regrets (with great reaſon) the loſs of " ſome biographical ſketches" by his father. And there are ſome verſes to Capt. *Ayſcough* in this young Nobleman's " Poems, 1780." He figures in " The Diabo- " liad," as does his noble kinſman, " Part I." [See Gent. Mag. for 1777, p. 87.] Capt. *Ayſcough* was alſo author of " *Semiramis*, a Tragedy," 1777.—It is painful to reflect on the miſcarriages of families, or the profligacy of individuals; yet truth obliges me to obſerve, that the honour of the reſpectable houſe of *Lyttelton* derives little advantage from the conduct of this unhappy member of it. Though a military man, he ſubmitted to be inſulted by a gentleman ‖ who repeatedly treated him as a poltroon; and though in no affluent circumſtances, he gave up his commiſſion, to avoid doing his duty, when called upon by his Sovereign to fight in *America*. At length his debaucheries affected his con- ſtitution; and in *September*, 1777, he went to the continent for the recovery of his health.

† His preſent Majeſty and the late Duke of *York* were his god-fathers.
§ Or rather the fabricator of the " Letters," which have ſince been declared by the family to be ſpu- rious. They contain, however, ſeveral lively ſtrokes of wit and fancy, and even of good ſenſe and thinking; and do his Lordſhip much more credit than his (pretended) Poems.
‖ Mr. *Swift*, author of an ingenious poem called " The Gamblers."

While

" The Hiſtory of *Jamaica*, or general Survey of the an-
" tient and modern State of that Iſland * ," 3 vols. 4to ;
" A Voyage towards the North Pole," by the Hon. Captain
Phipps (now Lord *Mulgrave*), 4to ; Sir *Joſeph Ayloffe's* †
" Hiſtorical

While on his travels, he wrote an account of his journey, which on his return, he publiſhed under the title of " Letters from an Officer in the Guards to his Friend in *Eng-
" land* ; containing ſome Accounts of *France* and *Italy*," 1778, 8vo. He received however but a temporary relief from the air of the continent. After lingering for a ſhort
time, he died *October* 14, 1779 ; and, what is remarkable, a few weeks only before his
couſin the ſecond Lord *Lyttelton. Par nobile conſobrinorum!* He left behind him a
monument of his unexampled diſregard of every principle of virtue and decency in a
journal of the moſt ſecret tranſactions of his life ; in which, from the moſt authentic information, I am aſſured that he in the groſſeſt terms has recorded facts which *Aretine*
himſelf would be aſhamed to paint, and the moſt abandoned haunter of the ſtews would
bluſh to read.

* By *Edward Long*, Eſq; whoſe high ſtation in the Iſland of *Jamaica* (where he is
Judge of the Admiralty Court) gave every opportunity of procuring authentic materials,
which have been digeſted with great ingenuity and candour. To this gentleman the
publick are indebted for, 1. a humourous pamphlet, intituled, " The Trial of Farmer
" *Carter's* Dog *Porter*, for Murder, 1771," 8vo ; 2. Some excellent " Reflections on the
" Negro Cauſe, 1772," 8vo ; 3. " Letters on the Colonies, 1775," 8vo ; and 4. " *Engliſh*
" Humanity no Parodox, 1778," 8vo.

† Sir *Joſeph Ayloffe*, bart. V. P. A, S. and F. R. S. of *Francfield* in *Suſſex*, was deſcended from a *Saxon* family, anciently ſeated at *Bocton Alof* near *Wye*, in the county of
Kent, in the reign of *Henry* III. who removed to *Hornchurch*, in the county of *Eſſex*, in
that of *Henry* IV. and to *Sudbury* in that of *Edward* IV. Sir *William Ayloffe* ‡ of *Great
Braxtead*, in the county of *Eſſex*, was knighted by *James* I. *May* 1, 1603 ; and created a
baronet *Nov.* 25, 1612 ; and from his eldeſt ſon by his third wife, the late baronet was
the fourth in deſcent and fifth in title. His father ‖ and grandfather were both of *Gray's
Inn*. He was born about the year 1708 ; received the early part of his education at *Weſt-
minſter-ſchool* ; admitted of *Lincoln's Inn* 1724, and in the ſame year was entered a gentleman-commoner at *St. John's College, Oxford*, which college he quitted about 1728 ;
elected F. A. S. *February* 10, 1731, one of the firſt council under their charter 1751, vice
preſident 17 .. ; and F. R. S. 1734. He prevailed on Mr. *Kirby*, painter in *Ipſwich*, to
make drawings of a great number of monuments and buildings in *Suffolk*, of which 12
were engraved, with a deſcription, 1748 ; and others remain unpubliſhed. He had
at that time an intention to write a hiſtory of the county ; and had drawn up Propoſals
for that purpoſe ; but, being diſappointed of the materials which he had reaſon to expect
for ſo laborious a work, they were never publiſhed. On the building of *Weſtminſter-
Bridge*, he was appointed ſecretary to the commiſſioners 1736-7 ; and on the eſtabliſhment of the Paper-office on the reſpectable footing it at preſent is, by the removal of the

‡ Of whom, and of his family and eſtate, ſee more particulars in *Morant's Eſſex*, vol. II. p. 139.
‖ *Joſeph*, a barriſter of *Gray's Inn*. He married a daughter of *Bryan Ayliffe*, an eminent merchant
of *London*, (*Morant* I. 69.) ; and died in 1727.

ſtate-

" Hiſtorical Deſcription of the Interview between *Henry*
" VIII. and *Francis* I." &c. and alſo his account of ſome
pictures of the ſame age at *Cowdray*, 4to; a Tranſlation of
Job into *Latin* Verſe, by the late Sir *William Browne* ✻, Knt.
well

ſtate-papers from the old gate at *Whitehall* † to new apartments at the Treaſury, he was
nominated the firſt in the commiſſion for the care and preſervation of them. In 1772 he
publiſhed in 4to, " Calendars of the Ancient Charters, &c. and of the *Welch* and
" *Scottiſh* Rolls now remaining in the Tower of *London*, &c." (which had begun to be
printed by the late reverend Mr. *Morant)*, and in the introduction gives a moſt judicious and exact account of our Public Records. He drew up the account of the chapel on *London-Bridge*, of which an engraving was publiſhed by *Vertue* 1748, and again
by the Society of Antiquaries 1777. His hiſtorical deſcription of the interview between
Henry VIII. and *Francis* I. on the Champ de Drap d'Or, from an original painting at
Windſor, and his account of the paintings of the ſame age at *Cowdray*, were inſerted
in the Archæologia, vol. III. 1775, and printed ſeparately, as above mentioned, to
accompany engravings of two of theſe pictures by the Society of Antiquaries. His account of the body of *Edward* I. as it appeared on opening his tomb, 1774, was printed
in the ſame volume, p. 376. Having been educated, as has been obſerved, at *Weſtminſter*, he acquired an early affection for that venerable cathedral ; and his intimate
acquaintance with every part of it diſplayed itſelf in his accurate deſcription of five
monuments in the choir, engraved in 1779 by the ſame Society, who muſt reckon,
among the many obligations which they owe to his zeal and attention to their intereſts,
the laſt exertions of his life to put their affairs on the moſt reſpectable and advantageous
footing, on their removal to their new apartments in *Somerſet-Place*. He ſuperintended
the new edition of *Leland's* Collectanea, in 9 vols. 8vo. 1770, and alſo of the Liber Niger
Scaccarii, in 2 vols. 8vo. 1771 ; to each of which he added a valuable appendix ; to the
latter the charters of *Kingſton on Thames*, of which his father was recorder. He alſo
reviſed through the preſs, a new edition of *Hearne's* " Curious Diſcourſes, 1771," 2 vols.
8vo ; and likewiſe the " Regiſtrum *Roffenſe*," publiſhed by Mr. *Thorpe*, in 1769, folio.
In *January*, 1734, he married Mrs. *Margaret Railton*, (a native of *Carliſle*, and
relict of *Thomas Railton*, Eſq; who died in the commiſſion of the peace for the city of
Weſtminſter, *September* 4, 1732); and by this lady, he had one ſon of his own name, who
died of the ſmall-pox, at *Trinity-Hall*, *Cambridge*, at the age of 21, *December* 19, 1756.
Sir *Joſeph* died at his houſe at *Kenington-Lane*, *Lambeth*, *April* 19, 1781, aged 72 ; and
was buried in a vault in *Hendon* church with his father and his only ſon. His extenſive knowledge of our national antiquities and municipal rights, and the agreeable
manner in which he communicated it to his friends and the publick, muſt make him
ſincerely regretted by all who had the pleaſure of his acquaintance.

* This was the laſt production of a Muſe of more than fourſcore. The good old
Knight originally ſettled as a phyſician at *Lynn* in *Norfolk* ; where he publiſhed " Dr.
" *Gregory's* Elements of Catoptrics and Dioptrics. Tranſlated from the *Latin* Original, by
" *William Browne*, M. D. at *Lynn Regis* in *Norfolk*. By whom is added, 1. A Method
" for finding the Foci of all Specula, as well as Lens's univerſally ; as alſo magnifying or
" leſſening a given Object by a given Speculum, or Lens, in any aſſigned Proportion.'

† Engraved by the Society of Antiquaries, in their " Vetuſta Monumenta."

well known as Prefident of the College of Phyficians, 4to;
" Difcord,

" 2. A Solution of thofe Problems which Dr. *Gregory* has left undemonftrated. 3. A
" particular Account of Microfcopes and Telefcopes, from Mr. *Huygens*; with the Dif-
" coveries made by Catoptrics and Dioptrics. The fecond edition *. Illuftrated with
" ufeful cuts, curioufly and correctly engraven by Mr. *Senex*, 8vo. Price 5s." By the
epigram tranfcribed below †, he appears to have been the champion of the fair fex at
Lynn in 1748. Having acquired a competency by his profeffion, he removed to *Queen's
Square, Ormond Street, London*, where he refided till his death, which happened *March*
10, 1774, at the age of 82. It has been already mentioned, p. 178, that by his daughter,
who was married to Mr. *William Folkes*, Sir *William* was grand-father to the prefent Sir
Martin Browne Folkes, bart. By his will he left two prize-medals to be annually contended for by the *Cambridge* poets. A great number of lively effays, both in profe and
verfe, the production of his pen, were printed and circulated among his friends. Among
thefe, there iffued from Mr. *Bowyer's* prefs, 1. " Ode in Imitation of *Horace*, Ode
" III. L. III. addreffed to the Right Honourable Sir *Robert Walpole* ‡, on ceafing
" to be Minifter, *Feb.* 6, 1741; defigned as a juft Panegyric, on a great Minifter, the
" glorious Revolution, Proteftant Succeffion, and Principles of Liberty. To which is
" added, the Original Ode, defended, *in Commentariolo*, by Sir *William Browne*, M. D.
" 1765," 4to; 2. " Opufcula varia § utriufque Linguæ, Medicinam; Medicorum
" Collegium; Literas, utrafque Academias; Empiricos, eorum Cultores; Solicita-
" torem, Praeftigiatorem; Poeticen, Criticen; Patronum, Patriam; Religionem,
" Libertatem, fpectantia. Cum Præfatione eorum editionem defendente. Auctore
" D. *Gulielmo Browne*, Equite Aurato, M. D. utriufque et Medicorum et Phy-
" ficorum S. R. S. 1765," 4to; 3. " Appendix Altera ad Opufcula; Oratiuncula ‖,
" Collegii

---

* To this edition was prefixed a recommendatory introduction by Dr. *Defaguliers.*

† Domino *Wilhelmo Browne* Militi.

Sic, miles, terror, caftigatorque Gigantis,
Victima cui Virgo nocte dieque cadit.
Herculeo monftris purgata eft *Lerna* labore,
Monftris purgetur *Lenna* labore tuo.

In *English.*

Be thou, O Knight, the Giant's fcourge and dread,
Who night and day preys on the victim-maid.
Herculean labour *Lerna's* monfters flew;
Oh, may thy labour thofe of *Lynn* fubdue!

‡ This edition of the Ode was infcribed to *George* Earl of *Orford*, as an acknowledgement of
favours conferred by his Lordfhip, as well as by his father and grandfather. On the firft inftitution
of the Militia, Sir *William Browne* had the honour of being appointed one of the Earl's deputy lieu-
tenants, and was named in his Lordfhip's firft commiffion of the peace.

§ This little volume (which was dated " ex areâ dicta reginali, MDCCLXV, III nonas *Januarias*,
" ipfo *Ciceronis* et auctoris natali) contained, 1. " Oratio *Harveiana*, in Theatro Collegii Medicorum
" *Londinenfis* habita, 1751." 2. " A Vindication of the College of Phyficians, in reply to Solicitor Ge-
" neral *Murray*, 1753." 3. " Ode, in Imitation of *Horace*, Ode I. addreffed to the Duke of *Montagu*.
" With a new Interpretation, *in Commentariolo*, 1765." 4. The Ode, above-mentioned, to Sir
Robert Walpole. [This Ode is alfo preferved in the " Select Collection of Mifcellany Poems, 1780,"
vol. VI. p. 205.]—Some time before, Sir *William* had publifhed " Odes in Imitation of *Horace*;
" addreffed to Sir *John Dolben*; to Sir *John Turner*; to Doctor *Afkew*; and to Robert Lord *Walpole*."

‖ This farewell Oration contains fo many curious particulars of Sir *William's* life, that the reader
will not be difpleafed to fee fome extracts from it : " The manly age and inclination, with con-
" formable ftudies, I diligently applied to the practice of phyfic in the country : where, as that age
" advifeth, I fought riches and friendfhips. But afterward, being fatiated with friends, whom
" truth, not flattery, had procured, fatiated with riches, which *Galen*, not Fortune, had prefented, I
" reforted immediately to this College : where, in farther obedience to the fame advifer, I might
" totally addict myfelf to the fervice of honour. Conducted by your favour, inftead of my own
" merit, I have been advanced, through various degrees of honour, a moft delightful climax in-
" deed,

" Difcord, a Poem," 4to ; the very remarkable State of the

" Collegii Medicorum *Londinenfis* Cathedræ valedicens. In comitiis, poftridie Divi
" *Michaelis*, MDCCLXXVII, ad Collegii adminiftrationem renovandam defignatis ; Machi-
" naque Incendiis extinguendis apta contra Permiffos Rebelles munitis * ; habita à D.
" *Gulielmo Browne*, Equite Aurato, Præfide, 1768," 4to ; 4. " A Farewell Oration, &c.
a tranflation of the preceding article, 1768, 4to ; 5. " Fragmentum *Ifaaci Hawkins*

" deed, even to the very higheft of all, which the whole profeffion of Phyfic hath to confer. In
" this Chair therefore, twice received from the Elects, fhewing their favour to himfelf, he con-
" feffeth, much more than to the College, your Praefident

 " Acknowledges, that he has happy been,
 " And, now, content with acting this fweet fcene,
 " Chufes to make his *exit*, like a gueft
 " Retiring pamper'd from a plenteous feaft :
" in order to attach himfelf and the remainder of his life, no longer, as before, folely to the College;
" but, by turns, alfo to the medicinal fprings of his own country, although, as a Phyfician, never
" unmindful of his duty, yet after his own manner, with hilarity rather than gravity : to enjoy
" liberty more valuable than filver and gold, as in his own right, becaufe that of mankind, not with-
" out pride, which ever ought to be its infeparable companion.
 " Now the free foot fhall dance its fav'rite round.
" Behold an inftance of human ambition ! not to be fatiated, but by the conqueft of three, as it were,
" medical worlds ; lucre in the country, honour in the College, pleafure at medicinal fprings ! I
" would, if it were poffible, be delightful and ufeful to all : to my felf even totally, and aequal ; to
" old age, though old, diametrically oppofite, not a cenfor and chaftifer, but a commender and en-
" courager, of youth. I would have mine fuch as, in the Satire,
 " *Crifpus's* hoary entertaining age,
 " Whofe wit and manners mild alike engage.
" The age of praefiding, by the cuftom of our praedeceffors, was generally a *luftrum*, five years ;
" although our *Sloane*, now happy, like another *Neftor*, lived to fee three ages, both as Praefident,
" and as man. But two years more than fatisfy me : for, that each of the Elects may in his turn
" hold the fceptre of prudence, far more defirable than power, given by *Caius*, which the law of
" juftice and aequity recommends,
 " No tenure pleafes longer than a year.
" But in truth, among fuch endearing friendfhips with you, fuch delightful converfations, fuch ufe-
" ful communications, with which this amiable fituation hath bleffed me, one or two things, as is
" ufual, have happened not at all to my fatisfaction. One, that, while moft ftudious of peace my-
" felf, I hoped to have praeferved the peace of the College fecure and intire, I too foon found, that
" it was not otherwife to be fought for than by war : but even after our firft adverfary, becaufe in-
" confiderable, was inftantly overthrown, and his head completely cut off by the hand of the Law,
" yet from the fame neck, as if *Hydra* had been our enemy, fo many other heads broke out, yea
" and, with inhuman violence, broke into this very fenate, like monfters fwimming in our medical
" fea, whom I beheld with unwilling indeed, but with dry or rather fixed eyes, becaufe not fufpect-
" ing the leaft mifchief from thence to the College, and therefore laughing, fo far from fearing.
" The other, in reality, never enough to be lamented, that, while I flattered myfelf with having,
" by my whole power of perfuafion, in the room of *Orphaean* mufic, raifed the *Croonian* medical
" lecture as it were from the fhades into day, if there could be any faith in folemn promifes ; that
" faith being, to my very great wonder, violated, this lecture, like another *Eurydice*, perhaps looked
" after by me too haftily, beloved by me too defperately, inftantly flipped back again, and fled in-
" dignant to the fhades below." He ufed to fay he refigned the prefidentfhip becaufe he would not
ftay to be beat :—alluding to the attack of the Licentiates.
 * The active part taken by Sir *William Browne*, in the conteft with the Licentiates, occafioned his
being introduced by Mr. *Foote* in his " Devil upon Two Sticks." Upon *Foote's* exact reprefentation
of him with his identical wig and coat, tall figure, and glafs ftiffly applied to his eye, he fent him a
card complimenting him on having fo happily reprefented him ; but, as he had forgot his muff, he
had fent him his own. This good-natured method of refenting difarmed *Foote*.

   " *Browne*,

the Cafe between Mr. *Whitaker* and Mr. *Hughes*, relative

" *Browne*, Arm. five *Anti-Bolingbrokius*, Liber primus *. Tranflated for a Second *Re-*
" *ligio Medici*. By Sir *William Browne*, late Prefident, now Father, of the College of
" Phyficians; and Fellow of the Royal Society, 1768," 4to; " Fragmentûm *Ifaaci*
" *Hawkins Browne* completum, 1769," 4to; 7. " Appendix ad Opufcula; Six Odes †,
" 1770," 4to; 8. Three more " Odes, 1771," 4to; 9. A Propofal on our Coin ‡; to
" remedy

* The author modeftly calls this " a very hafty performance;" and fays, " In my journey from
" *Oxford* to *Bath*, meeting with continued rain, which kept me three days on the road, in com-
" paffion to my fervants and horfes; and having my friend a pocket-companion, I found it the beft
" entertainment my tedious baiting could afford to begin and finifh this tranflation." This was
dated *Oct.* 24, 1768; and his fecond part was completed on the 20th of the following month: " My
" undertaking." he fays, " to complete, as well as I could, the Fragment of my friend, hath ap-
" peared to me fo very entertaining a work, even amongft the moft charming delights, and moft
" chearful converfations at *Bath*; that I have ufed more expedition, if the very many avocations
" there be confidered, in performing this, than in that former tranflation;" and to this part was prefixed a congratulatory poem, " to *Ifaac Hawkins Browne*, Efq; fon of his deceafed friend, on his
" coming of age, *Dec.* 7, 1766."—The good old Knight's " Opufcula" were continually on the increafe. The very worthy mafter of a College at *Cambridge*, now living, relates a ftory of him, that,
waiting for Sir *William* in fome room at the College where he was come to place a near relation, he
found him totally abforbed in thought over a fine quarto volume of thefe " Opufcula," which he conftantly, he faid, carried about with him, that they might be benefited by frequent revifals.—Once
making a vifit to the late Bifhop of *Gloucefter* at *Prior-Park*, while he waited, he amufed himfelf
with reading *Horace*, which he had in his pocket. After the firft compliments were paft, he took an
opportunity to afk his Lordfhip's fenfe of a paffage, adding, that he himfelf underftood it fo. The
Bifhop replied, he doubted not his idea was right; and afked him to walk in the garden; at the fame
time he winked to the fervant to keep him there a good while, and then to let him out at a back door,
which was done.—On a controverfy for a raker in the parifh where he lived in *London*, carried on
fo warmly as to open taverns for men, and coffee-houfe breakfafts for ladies, he exerted himfelf
greatly; wondering a man bred at two univerfities fhould be fo little regarded. (He had been expelled one, and therefore taken degrees at another.) A parifhioner anfwered, " he had a calf that
" fucked two cows, and a prodigious great one it was."—He ufed to frequent the annual ball at the
ladies boarding fchool, *Queen's Square*, merely as a neighbour, a good-natured man, and fond of the
company of fprightly young folks. A Dignitary of the church being there one day to fee his
daughter dance, and finding this upright figure ftationed there, told him he believed he was *Her-*
mippus redivivus, who lived *anhelitu puellarum*.—When he lived at *Lynn*, a pamphlet was written
againft him: he nailed it up againft his houfe-door.—At the age of 80, on St. *Luke's* day, 1771, he
came to *Batfon's* coffee-houfe in his laced coat and band, and fringed white gloves, to fhew himfelf
to Mr. *Crofby*, then Lord-Mayor. A gentleman prefent obferving that he looked very well, he
replied, " he had neither wife nor debts."

† 1. " De Senectute. Ad amicum D. *Rogerum Long*, apud *Cantabrigienfes*, Aulæ Cuftodem
" *Pembrokianae*, Theologum, Aftronomum, doctiffimum, jucundiffimum, annum nonagefimum agen-
" tem, fcripta. Adjecta Verfione *Anglicâ*. Ab Amico D. *Gulielmo Browne*, annum agente ferè
" octogefimum." 2. " De Choreis, et Feftivitate. Ad Nobiliffimum Ducem *Leodenfem*, diem
" *Walliæ* Principis natalem Acidulis *Tunbrigienfibus* celebrantem, fcripta. A Theologo feftivo,
" D. *Georgio Lewis* §. Adjecta Verfione *Anglicâ* ab Amico, D. *Gulielmo Browne*." 3. " De Ingenio,
" et Jucunditate. Ad *Lodoicum* § Amicum, Sacerdotem *Cantianum*, ingeniofiffimum, jucundiffimum,
" fcripta. Adjecta Verfione *Anglicâ*. A D. *Gulielmo Browne*, E. A. O. M. L. P. S. R. S." 4.
" De *Wilkefio*, et Libertate. Ad Doctorem *Thomam Wilfon*, Theologum doctiffimum, liberrimum,
" tam mutui Amici, *Wilkefii*, Amicum, quam fuum, fcripta." 5. " De Otio Medentibus debito.
" Ad *Moyfaeum* ‖ Amicum, Medicum *Bathoniae* doctiffimum, humaniffimum, fcripta." 6. " De
" potiore Metallis Libertate: et omnia vincente Fortitudine. Ad eorum utriufque Patronum, *Guli-*
" *elmum* illum *Pittium*, omni et titulo et laude majorem, fcripta."

‡ " To the moft revered memory of the Right Honourable *Arthur Onflow*, Speaker of the Houfe of
" Commons during XXXIII years; for ability, judgement, eloquence, integrity, impartiality;

§ Vicar of *Wefterham* in *Kent*, famous for his performance of *Ignoramus* when a *Wefminfter* fcholar.
‖ Dr. *Moyfy*.

" never

" tive to the Morning-Preacherſhip of *Berkeley Chapel*," 4to ;

" remedy all praeſent, and prevent all future Diſorders. To which are praefixed, prae-
" ceding Propoſals of Sir *John Barnard*, and of *William Shirley*, Eſq; on the ſame ſub-
" ject. With Remarks, 1774," 4to ; 10. " A New Year's Gift. A Problem and De-
" monſtration on the XXXIX Articles *, 1772," 4to ; 11. " The Pill Plot. To Doctor
" *Ward*, a Quack of Merry Memory, written at *Lynn, Nov.* 30, 1734, 1772," 4to ; 12.
" Corrections in Verſe †, from the Father of the College, on Son *Cadogan*'s Gout Diſ-

" never to be forgotten, or excelled : who ſitting in the Gallery, on a Committee of the Houſe, the
" day of publiſhing this Propoſal, and ſeeing the Author there, ſent to ſpeak with him, by the
" Chaplain ; and, after applauding his performance, deſired a frequent correſpondence, and honoured
" him with particular reſpect, all the reſt of his life ; this was, with moſt profound veneration, in-
" ſcribed."
    * " This Problem, and Demonſtration, though now firſt publiſhed, on account of the praeſent
" controverſy concerning theſe Articles, owe their birth to my being called upon to ſubſcribe them,
" at an early period of life. For in my *Soph's* year, 1711, being a Student at *Peter-houſe*, in the
" univerſity of *Cambridge*, juſt nineteen years of age, and having performed all my exerciſes in the
" ſchools, (and alſo a Firſt Opponency extraordinary to an ingenious pupil of his, (afterwards Dr.
" *Barnard*, Prebendary of *Norwich*), on Mathematical Quaeſtions, at the particular requeſt of Mr.
" Proctor *Laughton*, of *Clare-hall*, who drew me into it by a promiſe of the *Senior Optime* of the
" year), I was then firſt informed, that ſubſcribing theſe Articles was a neceſſary ſtep to taking my
" degree of B. A. as well as all other degrees. I had conſidered long before at ſchool, and on my
" admiſſion in 1707, that the univerſal profeſſion of religion muſt much more concern me through
" life, to provide for my happineſs hereafter ; than the particular profeſſion of phyſic, which I
" propoſed to perſue, to provide for my more convenient exiſtence here : and therefore had ſelected
" out of the library left by my father, (who had himſelf been a regular phyſician, educated under
" the tuition of Sir *John Ellis*, M. D. afterwards Maſter of *Caius* College,) *Chillingworth's Religion*.
" of a Proteſtant ; the whole famous Proteſtant and Popiſh Controverſy ; Commentaries on Scrip-
" ture ; and ſuch other books as ſuited my purpoſe. I particularly pitched upon three for perpetual
" pocket-companions, *Bleau's* Greek Teſtament, *Hippocratis Aphoriſtica*, and *Elzivir Horace* ; ex-
" pecting from the firſt to draw Divinity, from the ſecond Phyſick, and from the laſt Good Senſe
" and Vivacity. Here I cannot forbear recollecting my partiality for St. *Luke*, becauſe he was a
" Phyſician ; by the particular pleaſure I took in perceiving the ſuperior purity of his *Greek*, over
" that of the other Evangeliſts. But I did not then know, what I was afterwards taught, by Dr.
" *Freind's* learned Hiſtory of Phyſick, that this purity was owing to his being a Phyſician, and con-
" ſequently converſant with our *Greek* Fathers of Phyſick. Being thus fortified, I thought myſelf
" as well praepared for an encounter with theſe Articles, as ſo young a perſon could reaſonably be
" expected. I therefore determined to read them over as carefully and critically as I could : and
" upon this, met with ſo many difficulties, utterly irreconcileable by me to the Divine Original,
" that I almoſt deſpaired of ever being able to ſubſcribe them. But, not to be totally diſcouraged,
" I reſolved to reconſider them with redoubled diligence ; and then at laſt had the pleaſure to diſ-
" cover, in Article VI, and XX, what appeared to my beſt private judgment and underſtanding a
" clear ſolution of all the difficulties, and an abſolute defeazance of that exceptionable authority,
" which inconſiſtently with Scripture they ſeem to aſſume. I ſubſcribe my name to whatever I
" offer to the public, that I may be anſwerable for its being my ſincere ſentiment : ever open how-
" ever to conviction, by ſuperior Reaſon and Argument.   WILLIAM BROWNE."
    † Although the corrections are jocular, it is not intended, that they ſhould be leſs, but more
ſenſibly felt, for that very reaſon : according to the rule of *Horace*
        " ———— Ridiculum acri
    " Fortius et melius magnas plerumque ſecat res.
            A D   F I L I V M.
    " Vapulans lauda Baculum Paternum,
    " Invidum, FILI, fuge ſuſpicari,
    " Cujus ℔-denum trepidavit aetas
            " Claudere Luſtrum."
The author repeating theſe verſes to Dr. *Cadogan* himſelf, who cenſured their want of rhyme ; he
anſwered, that " the gout had a fourth cauſe, ſtudy, which was never his caſe : if he did not
" underſtand law and gavelkind, he would not talk to him ; for there were two ſorts of gout, free-
" hold and copyhold : the firſt where it was hereditary, the other where a perſon by debauchery
" took it up."

                                                                " ſertation :

4to *; The Natural Hiſtory of the Coffee-Tree," by *John Ellis*†, Eſq; 4to; the ſecond number of " Select Papers," " chiefly relating to *Engliſh* Antiquities; publiſhed from " the

" ſertation: containing Falſe Phyſic, Falſe Logic, Falſe Philoſophy, 1772," 4to; 13. " Speech to the Royal Society, 1772," 4to; 14. " Elogy and Addreſs, 1773," 4to; 15. " The *Latin* Verſion of *Job*," mentioned above, 4to.—I ſhall ſubjoin a well-known Epigram ‡, by Sir *William Browne*, which the Critics have pronounced to be a good one * :

" The King to *Oxford* ſent a troop of horſe,
" For Tories own no argument but force;
" With equal ſkill to *Cambridge* books he ſent,
" For Whigs admit no force but argument,"

The following Verſes were ſent to Sir *William Browne*, by unknown initials, *D. G.* (or rather written by himſelf) vindicating him againſt the abuſe, and anger, of *Scots* Rebel Licentiates.

AD FVSCVM EQVITEM, PRAESIDEM,
Horace, Ode XXII. B. I.
Integer vitae, ſceleriſque purus
Non timet Scoti obloquium, neque iram,
Nec venenatis gravidam ſagittis,
    FVSCE, pharetram.
Pone Te *Scotis* ubi nulla campis
Arbor aeſtiva recreatur aura;
Dulce ridentem comites Te habebunt,
    Dulce loquentem.

TO BROWNE, KNIGHT, PRAESIDENT.
He, whoſe juſt life due honour bears,
Nor *Scot's* abuſe, nor anger fears,
    Nor his full loaded quiver:
BROWNE, let him try his treach'rous arts,
To wound Thee with his poiſon'd darts,
    Thou ſhalt retort them ever.
Place Thee in *Edin's* fouleſt air,
Which neither tree, nor noſe can bear,
    Nor lungs with pleaſure take in ;
Ev'n there, ſuch Spirits ſlow in Thee,
Thee ſweetly laughing all ſhall ſee,
    All hear Thee ſweetly ſpeaking.
Sept. 10, 1767.

* Mr. *Whitaker*, who had been appointed morning-preacher of *Berkeley-Chapel* by Mr. *Hughes*, entered on that office, *Nov.* 7, 1773; from which he was removed on the 30th of *December* following. The Hiſtorian of *Mancheſter*, in the above-mentioned " Caſe," relates the whole progreſs of the buſineſs in his uſual animated language; and declares himſelf " unalterably determined to carry the matter into *Weſtminſter-Hall.*" This he did; but, in the ardour of reſentment, expreſſed himſelf ſo unguardedly, that his " Caſe" was conſidered as a libel by the Court of King's Bench.

† *John Ellis*, Eſq; F. R. S. agent for the province of *Weſt Florida*, and a Naturaliſt of uncommon abilities. He was a real friend to his country, and indefatigable in promoting its true intereſts. His " Eſſay on Corals and Corallines" is a work of the firſt rank in that department of literature. To this gentleman we owe the accurate diſtinctions that are now made between the animal and vegetable productions of the Ocean. A capital room in " *The Britiſh Muſeum*" is ornamented with his ſkilful labours. In 1770 he publiſhed, " Directions for bringing over Seeds and Plants from the *Eaſt Indies* " and other diſtant Countries in a State of Vegetation, together with a Catalogue of ſuch " Foreign Plants as are worthy of being encouraged in our *American* Colonies, for the " purpoſes of Medicine, Agriculture, and Commerce. To which is added, The " Figure and Botanical Deſcription of a New Senſitive Plant, called *Dionæa Muſcipula*,

‡ The following by an *Oxonian*, which gave riſe to that by Sir *William*, is at leaſt as good :
    " The King, obſerving with judicious eyes,
    " The ſtate of both his univerſities,
    " To *Oxford* ſent a troop of horſe; and why ?
    " That learned body wanted loyalty :
    " To *Cambridge* books, as very well diſcerning,
    " How much that loyal body wanted learning."

4

" or,

"the originals in the poſſeſſion of *John Ives* *, F. R. and
" A. S. S. 4to; " The Plays and Poems of *William*
" *Whitehead*, Eſq;" Poet Laureat, 2 vols. 8vo; " *Heylin's*
" Help

" or, *Venus's* Fly Trap." 4to.—" Some Additional Obſervations, on the method of pre-
" ſerving Seeds from Foreign Parts, for the Benefit of our *American* Colonies; with an
" Account of the Garden at *St. Vincent*, under the care of Dr. *George Young*," in
1773; and in the Philoſophical Tranſactions are a great number of curious papers by
Mr. *Ellis*, who died *Oct.* 5, 1776.

* *John Ives*, Eſq; was the only ſon of a gentleman now living, who has for a conſiderable
time been one of the moſt eminent merchants at *Yarmouth*. He was entered a member
of *Caius College, Cambridge*, where he did not long reſide; but, returning to *Yarmouth*,
became acquainted with that celebrated Antiquary *Thomas Martin* of *Palgrave*, and
caught from him the taſte for antiquities, which he purſued during the ſhort period of
his life. He was elected fellow of the Society of Antiquaries 1771, and of the Royal
Society 1772; and, by favour of the Earl of *Suffolk*, in him the honour of *Suffolk* Herald
Extraordinary was revived; an office attended with no profit, but valuable to him by the
acceſs it gave to the MSS. muniments, &c. of the Heralds College, of which he thereby
became an honorary member. His firſt attempt at antiquarian publication was by Propoſals (without his name), in 1771, for printing an account of *Lothingland* hundred in
Suffolk; for which he had engraved ſeveral ſmall plates of arms and monuments in the
churches of *Friſton, Gorleſton, Lound, Loweſtoffe*, and *Somerliton*, from his own drawings.
His next eſſay was the ſhort preface to Mr. *Swinden's* " Hiſtory and Antiquities of *Great*
" *Yarmouth* in the county of *Norfolk*," 1772, 4to. Mr. *Swinden*, who was a ſchool-
maſter in *Great Yarmouth*, was a moſt intimate friend of Mr. *Ives*, who not only aſſiſted
him with his purſe, and warmly patronized him, while living, but ſuperintended the
book for the emolument of the author's widow, and delivered it to the ſubſcribers †. In
1772 he cauſed to be cut nine wooden plates of old *Norfolk* Seals, intituled, " Sigilla
" antiqua *Norfolcienſia*. Impreſſit *Johannes Ives*, S. A. S." and a copper-plate portrait
of Mr. *Martin* ‡ holding an urn. On the 16th of *Auguſt*, 1773, by a ſpecial licence
from the archbiſhop of *Canterbury*, he was married, at *Lambeth* Church, to Miſs *Kett*
(of an ancient family in *Norfolk*). This marriage, no otherwiſe imprudent than from
a deficiency of fortune, was contrary to the father's wiſhes, who had ſome other
lady in view; but he was in a very ſhort time reconciled; and fitted up a houſe at *Yarmouth* in an elegant ſtyle for their reception. In imitation of Mr. *Walpole* (to whom the

† " The author," ſays Mr. *Ives*, " cloſed his life and his work together. The laſt ſheet was in
" the preſs at the time of his deceaſe. To me he committed the publication of it. A ſhort, but un-
" interrupted, friendſhip ſubſiſted between us. His aſſiduity, induſtry, and application, will appear
" in the courſe of the work." Mr. *Swinden* was buried in the church of *St. Nicholas* at *Yarmouth*,
in the North-aiſle, where a handſome mural monument is erected to his memory, with this inſcription:

<table>
<tr><td>" Near
This place are
Depoſited the Remains of
HENRY SWINDEN,
Author of the Hiſtory and Antiquities of
Great Yarmouth.</td><td>Who died *June* 14, 1772,
Aged 55.
To whoſe memory
This marble is erected
by
John Ives, F. S. A."</td></tr>
</table>

‡ Since prefixed to Mr. *Martin's* " Hiſtory of *Thetford*."

" Help to *Englifh* Hiftory," improved by the Rev. *Paul Wright**, B. D. F. S. A. (now D. D.) 8vo.

Thofe of 1775 were, a fecond edition of " Sir *Dudley* " *Carleton's* Letters," 4to. publifhed by the prefent Earl of

firft number was infcribed) he began in 1773 to publifh " Select Papers †," from his own collection; of which the fecond number (as above-mentioned) was printed in 1774, and a third in 1775. In 1774 he publifhed, in 12mo, " Remarks upon the *Garianonum* of " the *Romans*: the fite and remains fixed and defcribed;" with the ichnography of *Garianonum*, two plates, by *B. T. Pouncey*; fouth view of it, *Roman* antiquities found there, map of the river *Yare*, from the original in the corporation cheft at *Yarmouth*, and an infcription on the mantletree of a farm-houfe. He died of a deep confumption, when he had juft entered his 25th year, *June* 9, 1776. Confidered as an Antiquary, much merit is due to Mr. *Ives*, whofe valuable collection was formed in lefs than five years. His library was fold by auction, by Meffrs. *Baker* and *Leigh*, *March* 3—6, 1777, including fome curious MSS. (chiefly relating to *Suffolk* and *Norfolk*) belonging to *Peter Le Neve*, *T. Martin* ‡, and *Francis Blomefield*, of which fee more in Brit. Top. I. 192. II. 32, 33. The fine copy of *Norfolk* Domefday, mentioned there, p. 1, has on the back in capitals, *BIBLIO-THECÆ IVESIANÆ*. His coins, medals, ancient paintings, and antiquities, were fold by auction by Mr. *Langford*, *February* 13 and 14, 1777. A fmall portrait of him, extremely like, in a round, infcribed " J. I. F. R. S. and F. A. S." was engraved in 1774. We cannot conclude our account of this extraordinary man, without inferting the following note, tranfcribed from the original in his own hand in one of his printed books : " I leave this ftudy with the greateft reluctance, becaufe in it is contained fo great a fund " of curious and ufeful knowledge. I fincerely wifh the Poffeffor all the happinefs that " he fo truly doth deferve. My heart overflows with grateful acknowledgements for his " kind communications to me as an Antiquary, and for the polite reception I met with, " both from him and his amiable fpoufe, as a vifitor. JOSEPH STRUTT.—This note I " found in my ftudy the day after Mr. *Strutt* left me ; he came upon a vifit, in order to " take fome drawings, &c. *Oct.* 1, 1774, and went to *Norwich* the 7th following. *J. I.*"

* Dr. *Wright* was educated at *Pembroke Hall, Cambridge*; and was prefented, by the Governors of *Bridewell, St. Thomas's*, and the other city hofpitals, to the vicarage of *Oakley* with the parochial chapel of *Burden*, in *Effex*, and alfo to the rectory of *Snoreham* in the fame county, 1739. In 1773 he publifhed Propofals for printing by fubfcription, in one vol. 4to, price One Guinea, Sir *Henry Chauncey's* Hiftory of *St. Albans* and its archdeaconry continued to the prefent time, with the Antiquities of *Verulam*, including, among other MS. collections, thofe of Mr. *Webfter*, many years furgeon there, whofe drawings of various antiquities in that neighbourhood were to be engraved. In *May*, 1775, the work was promifed to be put to prefs as foon as the editor met with fufficient encouragement. Failing of this, he has this year [1781] prefixed his name to " The Complete *Britifh* Family Bible," in 80 folio numbers.

† Among thefe are, " Remarks upon our *Englifh* Coins, from the *Norman* Invafion down to the " end of the Reign of Queen *Elizabeth*," by Archbifhop *Sharp*; Sir *W. Dugdale's* " Directions for " the Search of Records, and making ufe of them, in order to an Hiftorical Difcourfe of the Antiquities of *Staffordfhire*;" with " Annals of *Gonvile* and *Caius College, Cambridge*;" the " Coronation of *Henry* VII. and of Queen *Elizabeth*," &c. &c.

‡ Many of thefe MSS. had been purchafed by Mr. *Ives* in the life-time of Mr. *Martin*.

Hardwicke

Hardwicke (of which no more than 50 copies were printed); Mr. *Barrington's* " Tracts on the Probability of " reaching the North Pole," 4to; " An Essay towards " establishing the Melody and Measure of Speech, to be " expressed and perpetuated by peculiar Symbols *," by *Joshua Steele*, Esq; 4to; " The Will † of King *Henry* VII. " with a Preface and Notes, by *Thomas Astle*, Esq;" 4to; Serjeant *Glanville's* " Reports of Determinations on Con- " tested Elections," published by the late Mr. *Blyke* ‡, in conjunction with my worthy and ingenious friend *John Topham*, Esq; F. R. and A. S. S. 8vo; " A Moral Demon- " stration of the Truth of the Christian Religion," 8vo; the ingenious Mr. *Tassie's* " Catalogue of Gems," 8vo; an edition of " *Rochefoucault's* Maxims," much improved by Mr. *L. Davis*, 8vo; the seventeenth volume of " *Swift's* §

" Works,"

---

* For which a variety of characteristic types were formed, as has been observed in p. 319. A second edition appeared in 1780 under the title of " Prosodia Rationalis."

† This curious publication suggested to the Writer of these Anecdotes the idea of publishing in 1780 a volume under the title of " A Collection of all the Wills, now " known to be extant, of the Kings and Queens of *England*, Princes and Princesses of " *Wales*, and every Branch of the Blood Royal, from the Reign of *William* the Conqueror " to that of *Henry* the Seventh exclusive. With explanatory Notes, and a Glossary," 4to.

‡ Of this gentleman some account will be given in the Appendix. *605*

§ Whilst the above-mentioned volume was in the press, the Editor applied to Mr. *Faulkner* for assistance, and received from that worthy-hearted printer an answer, dated *October* 22, 1774, which is here subjoined: " Dear Sir, Had I any original works " whatever of Dr. *Swift's*, worth publication, that could be of honour to his memory, " and any profit to you, I should be glad to send them; but I have not, although I " know many people have laid themselves out to collect the most *Grub-street* trash that " would disgrace the poorest and meanest of presses: however, should it happen in my " life that I meet with any to his credit and your benefit, as I always did to my most " worthy master, friend, and benefactor, Mr. *Bowyer*, whose politeness and civility to " me in the early part of my life I shall never forget ‖; for, when I was a journeyman to " him, who was then the most distinguished master-printer in *London* for his knowledge " and integrity, his father and he both treated me with the highest respect and fami- " liarity, doing me the favour to have me at their table to dine, drink tea, and sup

‖ Mr. *Faulkner*, who died *August* 28, 1775, left Mr. *Bowyer* ten guineas for a mourning ring. Another letter from Mr. *Faulkner* to Mr. *Bowyer* is printed in the " Supplement to *Swift*."

O o o

" with

" Works," publifhed by *J. Nichols*, 8vo; and part of an edition of Bifhop *Sherlock's* * " Sermons," in three vols. 12mo; to
which

" with them, which was not cuftomary, in the year 1726, and often afterwards. I have
" not one original paragraph of *Swift* that has not appeared in your *Englifh* edition;
" and fhall be obliged to you, on your kind offer, to fend me the fheets of the edition
" you are now printing. Had my health permitted me, I fhould have gone to *London*
" this year, to have paid my laft refpects to Mr. *Bowyer*, to you, and other friends; but
" being very old (72 years) and infirm, I could not travel with any pleafure; but, with
" all my complaints, I fincerely wifh to take a final adieu of all my friends in *England*
" next year; and, if health will permit, to go to the Continent, having no wife or chil-
" dren, and but few relations. I fincerely congratulate with Mr. *Bowyer* on his having
" the gout, which I frequently have; and inftead of ftrong mundungus port, I quaff good
" claret, being lighter, cooler, and eafier of digeftion. I fincerely wifh you and Mr.
" *Bowyer* every happinefs in this and the next world; and am, with the greateft refpect and
" efteem, both his and your very much obliged and humble fervant, GEORGE FAULKNER."
I truft I fhall be excufed if I here tranfcribe an extract from an earlier letter from Mr.
Faulkner, to Mr. *Bowyer*, dated *November* 5, 1767: " My deareft and worthy Sir, Very
" few opportunities happen to me to return your many kind favours to me, and parti-
" cularly your laft. By this poft you will receive in franks a Lift of the Abfentees of
" *Ireland*, which, I think, may anfwer with you. I fhould have fent it fooner had it
" been in my power, which it was not, the author having employed five different print-
" ing-offices to print it: and, as he hath given the property to me, I transfer it to you.
" I wifh what you receive may be the firft, as I cannot anfwer for my *Englifh* journey-
" men and fhopkeepers, who may have their friends in *London*. Many people of *Ire-
" land*, as well as of *England*, may have a curiofity to fee this lift, and therefore, I
" hope, it will at leaft quit your coft, and, I fincerely wifh, afford fome profit, which, if
" in my power, I would heap on you, fuperior to the Duke of *Northumberland's*. Your
" partner is a moft worthy man, whofe correfpondence I fhould be very proud of, and
" hope he will favour me with it. I fhall be very glad to hear that Mrs. *Bowyer* is not
" under the care of phyficians or apothecaries, thofe job-making gentry. My apothe-
" cary's bill doth not amount to five fhillings a year for all my family, two-pence of
" which is not my fhare. Claret is the univerfal medicine here, and mundungus port
" the bane and ftupefaction of all fociety. We celebrate the 5th of *November* here as
" you do in *London*, upon which occafion I had the honour of dining with our Viceroy
" Lord *Townfhend* at our Mayoralty-houfe, with Lord-Mayor, &c. where we drank many
" loyal toafts, not forgetting *Old England*. I fhall foon publifh a defcription of the fa-
" mous Lake of *Killarney*, which you fhall have by poft before publication, which, I
" believe, will not quit expence in a pamphlet; but, if you are a proprietor in a ma-
" gazine or news-paper, it may not be difagreeable. Pray excufe all blunders in this
" letter, being juft returned from a feaft of all delicacies of viands, grapes, melons,
" pine-apples, and all the catalogue of the moft delicious fruits. I am, Sir, your very
" much obliged, moft faithful, obedient, and humble fervant, GEORGE FAULKNER."
  * Dr. *Thomas Sherlock*, fon of Dr. *William Sherlock*, Dean of *St. Paul's*, was born in
London in 1678. He was educated at *Eton School*; and though it has been faid that his
great genius and talents did not fhew themfelves till he was more advanced in life, it appears, from the teftimony of thofe who knew him in his early youth, that in this, as in
all

which was prefixed, by the ingenious but anonymous
editor,

all other parts of life, he stood on the highest ground; that, in the course of his education, he was always at the head of his class, and never failed to lead his equals and companions, even in the puerile sports and amusements. From *Eton*, he removed to *Catharine Hall, Cambridge*. *Hoadly* and he were both exact contemporaries at this very small
college; and it should seem that the seeds of rivalry between those two very great men
were sown at that time. One day, as they came away from their tutor's lecture on
" *Tully's* Offices," *Hoadly* said, " Well, *Sherlock*, you figured away finely to-day by
" help of *Cockman's* Translation:"—" No, really," says *Sherlock*, " I did not; for I
" tried all I could to get one; and could hear of only one copy, and that you had
" secured." If we consider that probably there were not half a dozen more under-gra-
duates in the whole society, how extraordinary must we think it, that these two should
both arrive, by their own abilities, at the highest point of ecclesiastical rewards, and
that by the most opposite route of politics. *Sherlock* afterwards became Master; and
was a kind benefactor to his college, gave them a large quantity of iron railing, fitted up
a room for a library, and furnished it with great part of his own library: left twenty
pounds a year for an under-graduate librarian, appointed the King's professors of divinity, &c. to be trustees, and has bestowed many lines in his will in direction of their
choice. He probably did not consider that the sum was neither considerable enough
to occasion much competition; and that in so small a society they might think themselves well off if a decent person could be found to accept it, especially if a close attendance is required. In 1714 he was elected vice-chancellor of the university; and
while he held this office, he searched into the public archives, where papers and public
instruments of great value had lain for many years in a most confused and useless state.
These he carefully examined, and reduced into proper order; and, from their help,
obtained such a knowledge of the constitution of the university, and of the different
sources from whence it derived its power and immunities, that, in the subsequent parts
of his life, he was appealed to as a kind of oracle, in doubts and difficulties that occasionally arose in regard to its jurisdiction and government. At the age of twenty-six
(Nov. 28, 1704) he was appointed master of *The Temple*, upon the resignation of his father.
This office he held near fifty years, constantly preaching at their church in term-time, and
universally beloved, esteemed, and honoured among them. He was made dean of *Chichester*
in *November* 1715. Excepting " Eight Sermons preached on public occasions," his first appearance as an author was in the famous *Bangorian* controversy; and he was by far the
most powerful antagonist Bishop *Hoadly* had. He published a great number of pamphlets
upon this occasion; the principal of which is intituled, " A Vindication of the Corpo-
" ration and Test Acts, in answer to the Bishop of *Bangor's* Reasons for the Repeal of
" them, 1718." To this Bishop *Hoadly* replied; yet, while he opposed strenuously the
principles of his Adversary, he gave the strongest testimony to his abilities. In the course
of this controversy the part he took in it gave offence at Court; and on *Nov.* 5, 1717,
he and Dr. *Snape* were removed from the post of King's Chaplains. It has been said,
Bishop *Sherlock* afterwards disapproved the part he took in this dispute, and would
never suffer his pamphlets to be reprinted. About this time some bold attacks were
made upon Christianity, and particularly by *Collins*, in his " Discourse on the Grounds
" and Reasons of the Christian Religion." This work occasioned a great number of
pieces to be written on the subject of prophecy; and, though Dr. *Sherlock* did not enter-

directly

editor, a good Life of that learned Prelate, which has furnished me with materials for the note below.

It

directly into the controversy, yet he took occasion to communicate his sentiments in " Six Discourses delivered at *The Temple Church*," in *April* and *May* 1724, which he printed the following year, under this title, " The Use and Intent of Prophecy in the " several Ages of the World." It was an obvious remark upon this subject, that (besides the argument from prophecy) the Miracles of our Saviour were illustrious attestations given to him from Heaven, and evident proofs of his divine mission. Then arose Mr. *Woolston*, who, under pretence of acting the part of a moderator in this controversy, endeavoured to allegorise away the miracles, as Mr. *Collins* had done the prophecies. And here again Bishop *Sherlock* took up the cause. Mr. *Woolston* having bent his efforts with particular virulence against our Saviour's Resurrection, this subject was fully and distinctly considered in a pamphlet written by his Lordship, intituled, " The Trial " of the Witnesses of the Resurrection of *Jesus*, 1729." This pamphlet, in which the evidences of the resurrection are examined in the form of a judicial proceeding, went through fourteen editions; and has been universally admired for the polite and uncommon turn, as well as the judicious way of treating the subject. On the 4th of *February*, 1727, he was appointed Bishop of *Bangor*, in the room of Dr. *William Baker*, who was translated to *Norwich*; and, upon the promotion of Dr. *Hoadly* to the See of *Winchester*, Dr. *Sherlock* succeeded him in the Bishoprick of *Salisbury*, November 8, 1734. He now entered upon a new scene of life, in which his great abilities, the deep knowledge he had acquired of the laws and constitution of his country, his eloquence, his learning, gave him great weight and dignity, both as a governor of the church, and as a lord of parliament. When he assisted at the deliberations of that great assembly, he was not content to bear a silent testimony, but often took upon himself an active part; and though his profession and manner of life had hitherto afforded him no opportunity of exercising his talent for extemporaneous speaking, he delivered himself in his first attempts, before the most august assembly in the world, with the same ease, elegance, and force, as if oratory had been the study and practice of his life, or as if it had been a gift of Nature, and not an art to be attained by time and trial. But he was sensible of the reserve that became his order and profession in that place, and seldom rose up to declare his opinion, except on points in which the Ecclesiastical or Civil Constitution were essentially concerned, or by which the authority of the crown, or the liberties of the subject, were materially affected. In cases of Ecclesiastical Law, which were brought before the Lords as a Court of Judicature, he had sometimes the honour of leading their judgements, in opposition to some of the greatest lights of the law, who had first declared themselves of a different opinion; particularly in an appeal to the house upon an ecclesiastical case in *Ireland*. Several of his speeches are preserved in the printed collection of parliamentary debates; which do honour to his genius, his disinterestedness, his independence, and his virtue. The splendor of his character now became so great, that, upon the death of Archbishop *Potter*, in 1747, he was offered to be placed at the head of the church, in the Archbishoprick of *Canterbury*; which, however, he thought proper to decline, on account of the ill state of his health at that juncture. But soon after, recovering his usual strength, he accepted a translation to the see of *London*, in 1748, void by the death of Doctor *Edmund Gibson*. Upon this promotion he had some difference with Archbishop *Herring*, about his Grace's right to an option. The Archbishop

It would be unjuft, if, among many far fuperior obligations, the Collector of thefe Anecdotes did not acknowledge
the affiftance he received from Mr. *Bowyer*, in revifing the
" Original Works of Dr. *King* of the Commons," publifhed
by

bifhop had made his option of *St. George's, Hanover Square* ; but the matter was com-
promifed by his Grace's acceptance of *St. Anne's, Soho* *. In the following year, when
thefe cities were put into the moft dreadful confternation by two violent fhocks of an
earthquake, Bifhop *Sherlock* wrote " A Paftoral Letter to the Clergy and Inhabitants of
" *London* and *Weftminfter*, on occafion of the late Earthquakes ;" which was fo greedily
bought up by all ranks of people, that it is computed upwards of a hundred thoufand
copies were fold within one month. With all his dignities, he continued to hold the
mafterfhip of *The Temple* till the year 1753 ; when, his growing infirmities rendering
him unable to perform the duties of it, he wrote the letter of acknowledgement which
is printed below †. From this time his infirmities conftantly increafed upon him, but
the powers of his underftanding all along remained in their full vigour ; and he continued to difpatch the variety of bufinefs that came before him, with eafe to himfelf, and
fatisfaction to thofe who had occafion to apply to him. It was under this weak ftate of
body he revifed and corrected his Sermons, which he publifhed in 1755 and 1756, in four
volumes 8vo, [to which a fifth was added in 1776.] When he firft appeared in the character of a public preacher, he furpaffed the moft eminent preachers of thofe times, in
folidity of matter, in ftrength of reafoning, and true pulpit-eloquence. There are few
now living who are able to remember thofe times ; but, if general report did not confirm this obfervation, we might appeal to the teftimony of his own printed Sermons ;
which, with very few exceptions, were all the product of his younger years. The re-

* Bifhop *Sherlock*, however, in 1755, printed his thoughts on this fubject, in a folio pamphlet,
intituled, " The Option ; or an Enquiry into the Grounds of the Claim," &c. which was never
made public, but 50 copies only of it given to thofe whom it interefted. A friend, to whom this
pamphlet was once fhewn, tells me, " he had only time to obferve a miftake which one fhould not
" have expected in Bifhop *Sherlock*. Affigning a very early origin to the Archbifhop's claim, he
" foon after laments the hard fate of the clergy's wives and children ; forgetting probably that in
" thefe times no fuch relations exifted."—Archbifhop *Herring*, it is believed, caufed it to be reprinted in 4to, which he gave to a few friends, with a fhort anfwer in one page.
† " To the Treafurers, &c. of the Two Societies of *The Temple*.
" GENTLEMEN, *Fulham, Nov.* 5, 1753.
" His Majefty having been gracioufly pleafed (in confideration of my age and infirmities) to ac-
" cept of my refignation of the Mafterfhip of *The Temple* ; permit me to take the opportunity of
" your meeting, after the recefs of the vacation, to return you my thanks for your great goodnefs
" to me, during the continuance of the long courfe of my miniftry among you. It would be a fatis-
" faction and pleafure to me to acknowledge thefe obligations, and to exprefs the fenfe I have of
" them, in perfon. But, as I cannot promife myfelf, in the uncertain ftate of my health, that I fhall
" be able to do it in proper time, I fhall beg leave to do it by writing ; and to affure you, that I
" fhall always remember the many inftances of your favour to me, fome of which were fo diftin-
" guifhing marks of your approbation of my fervices, as I muft never—I can never forget ; and
" yet, to mention them particularly, might be conftrued as an effect rather of vanity than of grati-
" tude. I efteem my relation to the Two Societies to have been the great happinefs of my life, as
" it introduced me to the acquaintance of fome of the greateft men of the age, and afforded me the
" opportunities of improvement, by living and converfing with gentlemen of a liberal education,
" and of great learning and experience. I am, Gentlemen, your moft obedient, and moft humble
" fervant, " THOMAS LONDON."

ception

by *J. Nichols* in 1776, in three volumes, 8vo. Many useful hints were suggested, and illustrations added, by Mr. *Bowyer*, as the sheets passed through the press. The same friendly and judicious assistance was experienced in the "Supple-

ception they have met with is a full proof of their merit; and it is but declaring the judgement of the publick to say, that, for variety and choice of matter, and the judicious arrangement of it; for strength and solidity of reasoning; for force and elegance of language, and for a natural flow of manly eloquence, they stand in the first rank of reputation of any theological discourses in the *English* or any other language *. In the year 1759 he printed and distributed in his Diocese " A Charge to his Clergy;" wherein a masterly knowlege of the law, both of church and state, is applied, with a paternal affection, to their use and service. And, within a very few months of his death, upon the accession of his present Majesty to the throne, he is said to have written a letter of condolence and congratulation to the King †. He died without issue, *July* 18, in the year 1761, and in the 84th year of his age; during the last eight years of which he had been almost entirely deprived of the use of his limbs and of his speech, insomuch that he could be understood only by those who were constantly about him. Under this uncommon state of weakness and decline, nothing was more worthy admiration than the extraordinary composure of his mind. Though Bishop *Sherlock* had naturally a quickness and sensibility of temper, age and sickness were so far from stimulating, that they served rather to smooth and soften it; as infirmities increased upon him, he became more quiet and composed; and, though in the common course of business, and his general intercourse with the world, as well as the interior œconomy of his own family, incidents must have arisen frequently that were displeasing to him, yet nothing could ever ruffle that constancy of mind, and that uniform tranquillity and composure, that happily possessed him. And he added to his other public and private virtues, a constant

---

* When Dr. *Nichols* waited upon Lord Chancellor *Hardwicke* with the first volume of these Sermons (which was published singly in 1755) his Lordship asked him whether there was not a Sermon on *John* xx. 30, 31' and on his replying in the affirmative, desired him to turn to the conclusion, and repeated *verbatim* the animated contrast between the Mahometan and Christian religions, beginning " Go to your Natural Religion," (Discourse IX.) to the end. Such was the impression which this great and good man had retained of it for thirty years.

† " SIRE, *Nov.* 1, 1760.
" Amidst the congratulations that surround the Throne, permit me to lay before your Majesty a
" heart, which, though oppressed with age and infirmity, is no stranger to the joys of my country.
" When the melancholy news of the late King's demise reached us, it naturally led us to consider
" the loss we had sustained, and upon what our hopes of futurity depended. The first part excited
" grief, and put all the tender passions into motion; but the second brought life and spirit with it,
" and wiped away the tears from every face. Oh! how graciously did the Providence of God pro-
" vide a Successor, able to bear the weight of government in that unexpected event! You, Sir, are
" the Person whom the people ardently desire: which affection of theirs is happily returned by
" your Majesty's declared concern for their prosperity; and let nothing disturb this mutual consent.
" Let there be but one contest between them, whether the King loves the People the best, or the
" People Him: and may it be a long, a very long contest! may it never be decided, but let it re-
" main doubtful! and may the paternal affection on the one side, and the filial obedience on the
" other, be had in perpetual remembrance. This will probably be the last time I shall ever trouble
" your Majesty. I beg leave to express my warmest wishes and prayers on your behalf. May the
" God of Heaven and Earth have you always under his protection, and direct you to seek his ho-
" nour and glory in all you do; and may you reap the benefit of it, by an increase of happiness in
" this world and in the next!"

and

" ment* to the Works of Dr. *Swift*."——In both thofe publications the Editor was moft materially indebted to the
judicious remarks of Mr. *Reed* of *Staple Inn*, whofe friendly
affiftance has alfo in many inftances contributed to render
thefe Anecdotes completer than they otherwife could poffibly have been.

The other books of 1776 were, " A Defcription of
" feveral of Mr. *Vertue's* Prints," for the Society of Antiquaries, folio; " Extract from the Statutes of the Houfe,
" and Orders of the Governers; refpecting the Penfioners
" or poor Brethren," [of *The Charter-houfe*,] a large

and exemplary piety, a warm and fervent zeal in preaching the duties, and maintaining
the doctrines of Chriftianity, and a large and diffufive munificence and charity. He was
interred in the church-yard at *Fulham*; where a monument, with the following infcription, drawn up by Dr. *Nichols*, is erected to his memory:

" In this vault is depofited
The body of
The Right Reverend Father in God
Dr. THOMAS SHERLOCK,
Late Bifhop of this Diocefe,
Formerly Mafter of *The Temple*,
Dean of *Chichefter*,
And Bifhop of *Bangor* and *Salisbury*.
Whofe beneficent and worthy conduct
In the feveral high ftations which he filled,
Entitled him to the gratitude of multitudes,
And the veneration of all.
His fuperior genius,
His extenfive and well-applied learning,
His admirable faculty and unequalled power
Of reafoning,
As exerted in the explanation of Scripture,
In exhortations to that piety and virtue
Of which he was himfelf a great example,
And in defence efpecially of revealed religion,
Need no encomium here.

They do honour to the age wherein he lived; and
will be known to pofterity, without the help
Of this perifhable monument of ftone."

Underneath, on another Tablet, is,
" He died the 18th day of *July*, in the year
Of our Lord 1761, and the 84th of his age.
The Powers of his Mind continuing unimpaired
Throughout a tedious courfe of
bodily infirmities,
Which he fuftained to the laft with amoft chearful
And edifying refignation to the will of God."

On the fide of a monument, to the memory of
his Lady, placed on the top of the above-
mentioned Tablet, are thefe words,
" JUDITH FOUNTAINE
Was married to Dr. THOMAS SHERLOCK,
Mafter of *The Temple*, *Aug.* 8, 1707.
Died *July* 23, 1764;
aged 77."

* The firft volume of this Supplement in 8vo. (which forms volume XXIV. of
Swift's Works) was publifhed in 1776; the fecond (vol. XXV.) in 1779.—The whole
has been reprinted in one volume, 4to. (the XIVth in that fize) 1779; and at the fame
time in three volumes of fmall 8vo. and XVIII°, (vols. XXV. XXVI. XXVII.)

single

single sheet in folio by Dr. *Salter**; the first volume

* Eldest son of *Samuel Salter* †, D. D. prebendary of *Norwich* and archdeacon of *Nor-folk*, by *Anne-Penelope*, the daughter of Dr. *John Jeffery*, archdeacon of *Norwich*. He was educated for some time in the free-school of that city, from whence he removed to that of *The Charter House*. After having laid a good foundation in the learned languages, he was admitted of *Bene't College, Cambridge, June* 30, 1730, and soon after his taking the degree of B. A. was chosen into a fellowship. His natural and acquired abilities recom-mended him to Sir *Philip Yorke*, then Lord Chief Justice of the King's Bench, and after-wards Earl of *Hardwicke*, for the instruction of his eldest son the present Earl, who, 1737—40, with three of his brothers, in compliment to archbishop *Herring*, were edu-cated at that college. As soon as that eminent lawyer was made Lord Chancellor, he ap-pointed Mr. *Salter* his domestic chaplain, and gave him a prebend in the church of *Glou-cester*, which he afterwards exchanged for one in that of *Norwich*. To this he added the rectory of *Barton Coggles*, in the county of *Lincoln*, in 1740; where he went to reside soon after, and marrying Miss *Secker*, a relation of the then bishop of *Oxford*, continued there till 1750, when he was nominated minister of *Great Yarmouth* by the dean and chapter of *Norwich*; where he performed the duties of that large parish with great di-ligence, till his promotion to the preachership at *The Charter House* in *January*, 1754; some time before which (in *July*, 1751) Archbishop *Herring* had honoured him with the degree of D. D. at *Lambeth*. In 1756 he was presented by the Lord Chancellor to the rectory of *St. Bartholomew* near the *Royal Exchange*, which was the last ecclesiastical pre-ferment he obtained. But in *Nov.* 1761, he succeeded Dr. *Bearcroft* as Master of *The Charter House*, whom he had before succeeded in the preachership. While he was a member of *Bene't College*, he printed *Greek Pindaric* Odes on the nuptials of the Princes of *Orange* and *Wales*, and a copy of *Latin* Verses on the Death of Queen *Caroline*. It was his custom to preach *extempore*, of which there are several remark-able anecdotes. Besides a Sermon preached on occasion of a Music-meeting at *Glou-cester*, another before the Lord Mayor, *September* 2, 1740, on the anniversary of the fire of *London*, and a third before the Sons of the Clergy, 176 , which was much noticed at the time, and underwent several alterations before it was printed. He pub-lished " A complete Collection of Sermons and Tracts" of his grandfather Dr. *Jeffery*, in 2 volumes, 8vo, 1751, with his Life prefixed ‡; and a new edition of " Moral and
" Religious

† Of whom there is a good portrait, not very common, without any engraver's name, and marked only with the letters " *S. S. D. D.*"

‡ " In *August*, 1750, an advertisement was inserted in the public papers, giving notice, that " a Complete Collection, in one volume 8vo, of the Sermons and Tracts written by *John Jeffery*, " D. D. Archdeacon of *Norwich*, was in the press, and would be speedily published; and repeated " inquiries after the descendants of Dr. *Jeffery* having been made without success, of this Collection " I myself undertook to be the Editor." Mr. *J. Payne*, [then bookseller in *Pater-Noster-Row*, and now Accomptant of the *Bank*] *in a Case, published in* 1761, 8vo.—In consequence of the advertisement, Mr. *Payne* received, *Sept.* 13, a letter from the Rev. *Samuel Salter*, who was then at *Norwich*, in-forming him " that he was a prebendary of that cathedral, the grandson of Dr. *Jeffery*, the sole " possessor of his MSS. and the only person who could either give or refuse leave to print the Col-" lection that had been advertised; that he had objections to many parts of this Collection; that he " would, however, concur in and assist any scheme towards benefiting the world, without disho-" nouring the memory of his highly esteemed grandfather; and to give weight to what he had said, " and procure respect for his character, that he had had the honour and happiness to be tutor to

6
" Lord

lume of " Sermons preached at *Lincoln's* " *Inn*," by Dr. *Hurd*, who, whilft that volume * was in the prefs, to the great fatisfaction of every admirer of virtue and of learning, was promoted to the Bifhoprick of *Litchfield and Coventry*, and obtained the important office of Preceptor to

" Religious Aphorifms," by Dr. *Whichcote* †, with large additions and a biographical preface, 8vo, 1751. To thefe may be added, " Some Queries relative to the *Jews*," occafioned by a late Sermon, with fome other papers occafioned by the Queries, publifhed the fame year. In 1773 and 1774 he revifed through the prefs Seven of the celebrated " Letters ‡ of *Ben Mordecai*;" in 1776 he printed, for private ufe, " The firft 106 Lines of the Firft Book of the Iliad ‖; nearly as written in *Homer's* Time and Country;" in 1777 he corrected the proof-fheets of *Bentley's* Differtation on *Phalaris* (of which hereafter) ; and not long before his death, which happened *May* 2, 1778, he printed alfo this infcription to the memory of his parents :

" M. S.
Quorum, hofpes, offa hic mixta calcas pulvere ;
Si curiofus, quale par fuerit, rogas ;
Hinc difce : doctus & tibi ipfe profpice.

Vixêre quondam hi, vota ni fuperftites
Spes lactat, atque illudit error devius ;
(Amantiores nempe jufto ut adfolet :)
Chari Deo iidem, iidémque dilecti Hominibus :
Suis & occidêre cunctis flebiles.

Hoc vera Pietas, fancta Probitas hoc dedit ;
Gravitáfque morum & fumma temperantia,
Sibi fevera, nulli acerba aut afpera ;
At, comitati juncta, veniens gratior.
Nunc hocce mundo, mundi & hifce frivolis
Valere juffis, unico vivunt Deo.

Tu, chare lector, quantulum quantum his boni
Cúnque inerat, æmulare ; quoad potes, ac decet :
Si fortè quid perversè adhærebat mali,
(Ut funt fere imperfecta quæ mortalia ;
Fuge cautus : at cenfura, fi fapis, tua
Sit parca in Alios ; Tete in unum libera :
Hos perparum, Hunc nôfti unus omnium optume.
Aeternitatem porro cogita ; & Vale.

SAMUELI SALTER, S. T. P. &
ANNAE-PENELOPAE JEFFERY,
Parentibus optimis ; Filius unicus fuperftes,
L. M. H. T. I. J."

Dr. *Salter* was buried, by his own exprefs direction, in the moft private manner, in the common burial-ground belonging to the Brethren of *The Charter-Houfe*.

* Two more volumes have been fince publifhed in 1780.

" Lord Chancellor's fon, and chaplain to himfelf." Dr. *Salter's* affiftance was accepted ; and the collection. extended to two volumes. An intimacy alfo was formed, which led to the loan of 100l. from Dr. *Salter*, 100l. from his father the Archdeacon of *Norwich*, and 100l. from Dr. *Plumptre* ; the re-payment of which fums (having been demanded fomewhat abruptly) occafioned the publication of the above-mentioned very extraordinary Cafe, of which only a fmall number was printed, with *blanks* for every name which could poffibly give a ftranger the leaft idea of the parties. The prefent note is taken from a copy in the poffeffion of Mr. *Reed*, in which all the blanks are filled up in MS.

† This volume was likewife undertaken by Mr. *J. Payne*, in conjunction with Dr. *Salter*.

‡ By the Rev. Mr. *H. Taylor*, of *Crawley*, *Hants* ; author of feveral other very valuable publications.

‖ Thefe (with Dr. *Salter's* fentiments on the *Digamma*) have been fince copied in an improved edition of " *Dawes's* Mifcellanea Critica, *Oxford*, 1781," 8vo, p. 434—439. For the fake of the learned reader, I will tranfcribe a note from the *Oxford* Editor : " Huic fpecimini, (cujus, typis " impreffi fed non antehac editi, notitiam amico cuidam meo, et *Salteri* familiari debeo,) novam et " minufculam Digamma formam Ϝ pro vetufta illa F feci curavit *Salterus*, quæ cæteris literis con- " veniret æque ac ꟷ, θ, ξ, &c. Recordari quoque potuit notiffimum *Popii* locum, ubi Satyricus ille, " in verfibus quidem facetis et admodum ridiculis, *Bentleium*, et Digamma *fuum* fcilicet, in ludi- " brium vertit §, ingeniofior fane quam doctior poeta. De loco illo, cujus fales nonnihil defipuit " *Salteri* inventum, vide quoque *Fofterum*, p. 133."

§ " While tow'ring o'er your Alphabet, like *Saul*,
" Stands our *Digamma*, and o'ertops them all." *Dunciad*, iv. 217.

the Heir Apparent to the Crown *. At the same time Mr. *Bowyer* printed a new edition of this learned Prelate's " Commentary on *Horace*," 3 vols. 8vo; and a fourth edition of his " Lectures at *Lincoln's Inn*," 2 vols. small 8vo; a volume of " Sermons" by his old and esteemed friend Dr. *Powell* †, 8vo; a fourth edition, corrected, of Lord *Lyttelton's*

* His Lordship's eminent services on this occasion have been lately (1781) rewarded by a translation to the See of *Worcester*, and the respectable office of Clerk of the Closet to the King.

† Of this very valuable volume and its excellent author, I cannot give a better account than in the words of the advertisement prefixed to it by Dr. *Balguy*, who superintended the publication : " The following Discourses ‡ are not published for the credit " of the Writer, but for the benefit of his Readers : especially that class of Readers, for " whom they were chiefly intended, the younger Students in Divinity. The Author's " reputation stands on a much wider bottom : a whole life uniformly devoted to the " interests of sound Philosophy and true Religion. The means he employed, for the " service of both, at different times and in different stations, may best be reported by " those who were the immediate objects of his care. Nothing shall be added here, but " some facts and dates, for the satisfaction of his friends. *William Samuel Powell* was " born at *Colchester*, *Sept.* 27, O. S. 1717. He was admitted at *St. John's College*, *Cambridge*, in 1734; began to reside there the year following; took the degree of B. A. " in 1738-9; and was admitted Fellow *March* 25, 1740. In the year 1741, he was " taken into the family of the late Lord Viscount *Townshend*, as private tutor to his se- " cond son, *Charles Townsend*, afterwards Chancellor of the Exchequer. Towards the " end of the year, he was ordained Deacon and Priest by Dr. *Gooch*, then Bishop of *Nor- " wich*; and instituted by him to the rectory of *Colkirk* in *Norfolk*, on Lord *Townshend's* " presentation. He returned to college the year after · took the degree of M. A. and " began to read Lectures, as assistant to Mr. *Wrigley* and Mr. *Tunstall*. In the year

‡ These are, I. Three Discourses preached before the University : 1. " Of the Vices incident " to an Academical Life," 1756; 2. " Of the Subscriptions required in the Church of *England*," 1757; 3. " On the Anniversary of the Martyrdom of *Charles I.*" 1766; II. Thirteen Discourses preached in the College Chapel : 4. " The Authenticity of the Books of the New Testament," 1765; 5. " The Credit due to the Sacred Historians ;" 6. " The Insufficiency of Mr. *Hume's* " Objection to the Credibility of Miracles ;" 7. " On the Use of Miracles in proving the Divine " Mission of our Saviour and his Apostles ;" 8. and 9. " Of the Evidence arising from the Pro- " phecies of the Old Testament;" 10. " Of the Argument drawn from the swift Propagation of " the Gospel ;" 11. " Of the Character given by Heathen Writers of the First Christians ;" 12. " Recapitulation of the Arguments brought in Support of Christianity ;" 13. " Intemperance in " the Gratification of our Appetites, not consistent with Spiritual Improvements," 1765; 14. " The Prodigal Son ;" 15. " The Nature and Extent of Inspiration, illustrated from the Writings " of *St. Paul*," 1770; 16. " The Diversity of Character belonging to different Periods of Life ;" III. A Discourse " on Public Virtue, preached before the University, *November* 5, 1775." This Discourse was added (though out of place, and, perhaps, out of season) in compliance with the de- sire of some of the Author's friends; IV. Three Charges delivered to the Clergy of the Arch- deaconry of *Colchester* : 1. " On Religious Controversies ;" 2. " On the Connexion between Merit " and the Reward of Merit in the Profession of a Clergyman ;" 3. " On the Use and Abuse of " Philosophy in the Study of Religion ;" V. Disputatio habita in Scholis Publicis, anno 1756, " Pro gradu Doctoratûs in Sacrâ Theologiâ."

4 " 1774,

telton's * " Hiftory of the Life and Reign of King *Henry* the
" Second," 8vo, with a third edition of his Lordfhip's
" Mifcellanies," 3 vols. 8vo; Mr. *Da Cofta's* " Elements of
" Conchology," 8vo; " The Rudiments of War," 8vo;
" Differtatio de *Babrio,* Fabularum *Æfopearum* Scriptore,"
publifhed by Mr. *Tyrwhitt,* 8vo; and " Differtatio de Byffo
" *Ægyptiorum,*" by Dr. *John Reinhold Forfter,* 8vo.

Thofe of 1777 were, Dr. *Hampe's* † " Experiments
" on Metallurgy," folio; the LXVIIth volume of the " Phi-
" lofophical Tranfactions," 4to; which he had continued to

" 1744, he became principal tutor: and in 1749 took the degree of B. D. In the year
" 1753, he refigned the rectory of *Colkirk,* that it might be confolidated with *Stibbard,*
" another of Lord *Townfend's* livings: and was again inftituted the next day. He was ad-
" mitted to the degree of D. D. in 1756; and created at the following Commencement
" 1757. In 1759, he came into poffeffion of an eftate in *Effex;* which was devifed to him by
" Mr. *Reynolds,* a relation of his mother's ‡. In 1761, he left college, and took a
" houfe in *London;* but did not refign his fellowfhip till 1763. In 1765, he was elected
" Mafter: foon after, he went to refide in college; and was chofen Vice-Chancellor of
" the Univerfity in the *November* following. The year after, he obtained the arch-
" deaconry of *Colchefter,* which was in his Majefty's gift, for that turn, on the promo-
" tion of Dr. *Mofs* to the bifhoprick of *St. David's:* and in 1768, he was inftituted
" to the rectory of *Frefhwater* in the *Ifle of Wight,* [on the prefentation of this
" College.] He died *Jan.* 19, 1775. It is fcarce needful to mention, that the
" ' Sermon on Subfcription' and the Third Charge were publifhed in the Author's life-
" time."—To thefe fatisfactory particulars, it may be fufficient to add, that Dr. *Powell's*
Sermon on Subfcription was animadverted upon with much feverity in a Letter
addreffed to him, and alfo in a pamphlet, probably by the Author of " The Con-
" feffional," intituled, " Remarks on the Rev. Dr. *Powell's* Sermon in defence of
" Subfcriptions, preached before the Univerfity of *Cambridge* on the Commencement
" *Sunday,* 1757, wherein the latitude faid to be allowed to Subfcribers to the Liturgy
" and Articles of the Church of *England* is particularly confidered. With a Dedication
" to the younger Students in both our Univerfities who are defigned for the Miniftry of
" the Church, 1758," 8vo; and that he is mentioned in thefe pages not merely as an
Author, but as an early and particular friend of Mr. *Bowyer,* who was for many years
the Doctor's banker in *London.* His Obfervations on " Mifcellanea Analytica, 1760,"
have been mentioned in p. 300; a fhort " Defence" of this pamphlet was alfo printed
for him in that year,—Dr. *Powell's* Will was remarkably precife, neat, and elegant, which
was the characteriftic of all his performances. He left twenty friends, moft, if not all,
of the college, one hundred pounds apiece.

* See above, p. 425.

† Of whom, fee more in the Appendix.

‡ This lady had two other children, who furvived her: the Rev. Mr. *Jolland* by her firft hufband, and Mrs. *Sufanna Powell* (Matron of *Chelfea Hofpital*) by her fecond.

print from the LIId inclufive; the fourth volume of the
" Archæologia," for the Society of Antiquaries, 4to; (he had
printed the three preceding volumes in 1770, 1773, and
1775); " Poems, confifting chiefly of Tranflations from the
" Afiatick Languages," by the matchlefs Orientalift *William*
Jones *, Efq; 8vo; two editions of the celebrated " Poems'
afcribed to *Rowley*, 8vo; " A Lift † of various Editions of
" the Bible, and parts thereof, in *Englifh*, from the year 1526
" to 1776," a fingle fheet, 8vo; " The Repofitory, a Select
" Collection of Fugitive Pieces of Wit and Humour, in
" Profe and Verfe, by the moft eminent Writers," 2 vols.
8vo; " La Vie ‡ de *Jean Frederic Oftervald*, Pafteur de *Neuf-*
" *châtel* en *Suiffe*, par M. *David Durand* §, Miniftre de la
" Chapelle *Françoife* de la *Savoye*, & Membre de la Societé
" Royale," 8vo; and " The Excurfion," by Mrs. *Brooke*,
2 vols. 12mo.

Our eminent Printer now drew to the end of his literary
career; but he had firft the fatisfaction of completing in
in this " The Rolls of Parliament ||," in fix volumes,

---

* " The publick," fays Mr. *Gibbon*, " muft lament that Mr. *Jones* has fufpended
" the purfuit of Oriental learning."

† Of this Lift an improved edition was printed in 1778, at the expence of his Grace
the Lord Archbifhop of *Canterbury*. This little volume owed its rife to a manufcript
lift of *Englifh* Bibles, copied from one compiled by the late Mr. *Jofeph Ames*, and prefented by Dr. *Gifford* to the *Lambeth* Library. It was completed by Dr. *Ducarel*, from
his own obfervations and the later difcoveries of his learned friends.

‡ This volume, having been publifhed late in 1777, is dated (according to the cuftom
of printers) in 1778. And the fame circumftance (to mention it once for all) will be
found to have happened in fome other of the dates which occur in thefe " Anecdotes."
The rule in general obferved among printers is, that when a book happens not to be
ready for publication before *November*, the date of the enfuing year is ufed.

§ Of whom fome particulars will be given in the Appendix.

|| Thefe volumes were revifed through the prefs by the Rev. Dr. *Strachey* (now arch-
deacon of *Norwich)* from a copy prepared for that purpofe by *Richard Blyke*, Efq; the
Rev. Mr. *Morant*, *Thomas Aftle*, Efq; and *John Topham*, Efq. To each of thefe gentlemen the Printers were greatly indebted for their kind attention to facilitate and expedite the bufinefs.

folio;

folió; and thirty-one volumes of " The Journals of the
" House of Lords *."

The laſt publication in which Mr. *Bowyer* aſſumed the
office of an editor, was a new impreſſion of the " Diſſertation
" on the Epiſtles of " *Phalaris.*" Dr. *Bentley* † was a writer
whom he had always held in the higheſt eſtimation. In
the

* Which were wholly ſuperintended by *George Roſe*, Eſq; whoſe great abilities (to
ſay nothing of his uncommon diligence through the progreſs of ſo large and important
an undertaking) are too well known to require the encomium of one who is proud to
acknowledge the various inſtances of friendſhip he has received from him.

† Dr. *Bentley's* Diſſertation was become ſcarce; and therefore this re-publication
could not fail of being acceptable to the learned; eſpecially as it was improved by
ſeveral uſeful remarks ‡. It gave riſe, however, to ſome animadverſions in " The Critical
" Review," which were written, I have been informed, by the Reverend and ingenious
Mr. *Robertſon,* and which the reader will not be diſpleaſed to ſee preſerved ‖. The peculiarities

‡ " This Diſſertation, commonly known by the name of ' *Bentley* againſt *Boyle*,' having long been
out of print, the learned world are obliged to theſe *Engliſh Stephani* §, who can read and taſte, as
well as print and publiſh, for its re-publication. The ſubject of this controverſy is ſo well known,
and its merits now ſo well underſtood, that it is ſcarce neceſſary to add, that wit and judgement, as
it often happens, were here at variance, each of them occaſionally aſſiſted by learning, and that the
bees of the *Chriſt-Church* hive, *Aldrich, Atterbury, Smallridge,* &c. combined their forces to teaſe,
though they could not wound, this *Cambridge Goliath.* That Mr. *Boyle* was thus aſſiſted, ſeems allowed by *Swift,* when in the " Battle of the Books" he introduces him " clad in a ſuit of armour,
" which had been given him by all the gods;" which, however, his ſon (the late Lord *Corke*), in
his remarks on this paſſage, does not diſpute, but well obſerves, " that the gods never beſtowed ce-
" leſtial armour except upon heroes, whoſe courage and ſuperior ſtrength diſtinguiſhed them from
" the reſt of mankind." This edition is rendered more valuable by the marginal remarks of the
editor (Mr. *Bowyer*), ſelected from the writings and perſonal communication of Biſhops *Warburton*
and *Lowth,* Mr. *Upton,* Mr. *W. Clarke,* Mr. *Markland,* Dr. *Salter,* Dr. *Owen,* and Mr. *Toup*." Gent.
Mag. 1777, p. 35.

‖ *viz.* " There are ſome peculiarities in this impreſſion, which we can by no means admire. The
editor has given an air of ſtiffneſs and formality to *Bentley's* language by his method of pointing; partly
by the uſe of the ſemicolon, inſtead of the comma. For example: " It is evident then; that, if *Atoſſa*
" was the firſt inventreſs of epiſtles; theſe, that carry the name of *Phalaris,* who was ſo much older
" than her, muſt needs be an impoſture.—But, if it be otherwiſe; that he does not deſcribe me
" under thoſe general reproaches: a ſmall ſatisfaction ſhall content you; which I leave you to be
" judge of . . . Pray, let me hear from you; as ſoon as you can "—This punctuation ſeems to be
calculated for ſhort-winded readers. The editor has likewiſe adopted a mode of ſpelling, which has
the appearance of an affected ſingularity. For inſtance: *ſuſtein, diſdein, nibble'd, hear'd, rea'd,* &c.
Theſe words are indeed in the notes; where, it may be ſaid, the author is at liberty to purſue his
own opinion. But what ſhall we ſay to his introducing theſe, and the like, innovations into *Bentley's*
text?—buis'neſs, elechter, retein, reproch, tun'able, ſaught. If *ſaught* be admitted, muſt we not by
analogy write, *baught,* inſtead of *bought,* and *thaught,* inſtead of *thought?* It may be obſerved, that
theſe words, in the *Saxon,* are pohre, bohre, ðohre. The editor's alteration therefore ſeems to
be indefenſible. But what is more remarkable, from page 157, to the end of the volume, theſe and
the like abbreviations are introduced: " *Phalaris'* letters, *Polybius'* author, *Suidas'* words, *Timæus'*
" time, *Æſchylus'* plays, the law about the rope was *Zaleucus',* the oration may well enough be *Ly-*

§ The Reviewer's illuſtration I muſt neceſſarily ſuppreſs.

" *ſias',*

the re-publication of this great Critic's Differtation, Mr. *Bowyer* inferted the remarks which had occurred to him,

in

culiarities of orthography and punctuation (which I cannot vindicate) are not, however, to be afcribed to Mr. *Bowyer*, but to his friend Dr. *Salter*, who revifed alfo, and in the fame whimfical mode, the celebrated " Letters of *Ben Mordecai*." His " Sermon before " the Sons of the Clergy" was printed and fpelt in the fame manner.

" *fias*', the bull in *Agrigentum* was fhewn for *Phalaris*." As this is a circumftance of fome importance in the formation of our language, it may not be improper to enquire, upon what principle it is founded. Dr. *Wallis* fays, that, when a proper name ends in *s*, the *s*, which forms the poffeffive cafe, is often omitted : as, " *Priamus* daughter, for *Priamus's* daughter, *Venus* temple, for *Venus's* temple." But here it muft be obferved, that he does not pretend to juftify this mode of writing; but only fays, " fieri non raro folet", ' the *s* is often omitted:' very probably by poets, for the fake of their meafure. He adds : " Sed et plena fcriptio retinetur, et quidem nunc dierum frequentius quam olim;" that is, " the word itfelf, and the additional fign of the poffeffive cafe, are likewife expreffed at full " length : and this way of writing is indeed more frequently adopted at prefent, than it was for- " merly : as King *Charles's* Court, *St. James's* Park." *Wallifii* Gram. p. 91. ed. 1765. If this laft be the *plena fcriptio*, the genitive cafe at full length, it muft be allowed, that the former is only a contraction, and fhould not be admitted, except in poetry. For it can never be neceffary in profe. If the pronunciation be difficult, we can at once make it eafy, by the help of the prepofition *of*. If we do not choofe to fay, " *Ulyffes's* fon," we may alter the phrafe, and fay, " the fon of *Ulyffes*." In this circumftance the *Englifh* has the advantage of the *French*, the *Italian*, and other modern languages, which have only the figns, *du, de* ; *di, del, dello, della*, &c. If we go back to the fource of the *Englifh* language, the *Saxon*, as it ftands in the *Anglo-Saxon* verfion of *Orofius*, faid to have been written by king *Ælfred*, in the latter part of the ninth century, we find, that proper names ending in *s*, form the genitive and poffeffive cafe by the addition of *es* : as, Nom. Tituſ, Gen. Tituſeſ, Titus, Tituſes ; Tibeniuſ, Tibeniuſeſ, Tiberius, Tiberiuſes ; Cinuſ, Cinuſeſ, Cirus, Ciruſes ; Ninuſ, Ninuſeſ, Ninus, Ninuſes ; Philippuſ, Philippuſeſ, Philippus, Philippuſes ; Iuliuſ, Iuliuſeſ, Julius, Juliuſes ; Pinnuſ, Pinnuſeſ, Pirrus [Pyrrhus] Pirruſes, &c. and that *s* or *es* makes the fign of the genitive cafe in a multitude of other words : as, þannibal, þannibaleſ, Hannibal, Hannibales ; Alexanden, Alexandneſ, Alexander, Alexandres ; Careſe, Careſeſ, Cafere [Cæfar] Caſeres ; Ioſeph, Ioſepeſ, Joſeph, Joſephes ; Amilcon, Amilconeſ, Amilcor, Amilcores ; Cob, Cobeſ, God, Godes ; Cniſt, Cniſteſ, Chrift, Chriftes, &c. In this language there are fix, or, according to fome grammarians, feven declenfions ; and three of them form the genitive fingular by taking *es* : as, ſmið a ſmith, ſmiðeſ of a ſmith; andᵹit fenfe, andᵹiteſ of fenfe ; ponð a word, ponðeſ of a word : but not one by taking *is*. On the firft Dr. *Hickes* makes the following remark : " Inde in noftrati-fermone nominum fubftantivorum genitivus fingu- " laris et nominativus pluralis exeunt regulariter in *s* vel *es*, ut in *ftones*, quod lapidis et lapides fig- " nificat." *Inft. Gram. Anglo-Sax.* p. 10. " Hence, fays he, in our language the genitive fingular " and the nominative plural of noun fubftantives regularly end in *s* or *es* : as, *ftones*, which may " either fignify *of a ftone*, or *ftones*." This learned author thus defcribes the affinity between the *Saxon* and the *Englifh* language : " Lingua *Anglorum* hodierna avitæ *Saxonicæ* formam in plerifque " orationis partibus etiamnum retinet. Nam quoad particulas cafuales, quorundam cafuum termi- " nationes, conjugationes verborum, verbum fubftantivum, formam paffivæ vocis, pronomina, par- " ticipia, conjunctiones, & præpofitiones omnes denique, quoad idiomata, phrafiumque maximam " partem, etiam nunc *Saxonicus eft Anglorum Sermo*." *Hickefii* Thefaur. Ling. Sept. præf. p. vi. Nothing indeed can be more obvious, than the affinity of thefe two languages in the cafe we have been confidering. The only difference is this : inftead of writing Cobeſ ponð, manner ſirðom, ſmiðeſ heonð, Cniſteſ moðon, Tituſeſ bnoðon, Cinuſeſ ſunu, we write God's word; man's wifdom, fmith's hearth or forge, *Chrift's* mother, *Titus's* brother, *Cyrus's* fon, &c. with an apoftrophe, denoting the omiffion of the *e*. We find the *e* frequently retained by fome of our ancient writers. Thus, in the verfes on *Seint Vinefrede*, which, according to Bifhop *Fleetwood*, are near five hundred years old, or perhaps much older, the author writes, *kinges fone*, and *Goddes grace*. *Gower*, who lived in the fourteenth century, fays Goddes folke, Goddes fande [a *Saxon* word fignifying

in the courfe of many years attention to the fubjects there treated of; and he hath afcribed them to the refpective authors from whofe books or perfonal communication they were felected.

The only books in which he much interefted himfelf, after the publication of this volume, were an edition of the

fying *miſſion* or *being ſent*] worldes welth, mennes helth. *Chaucer*, who wrote about the fame time, has Goddes fonne, *Chriſtes* fake, worldes tranſmutacion, kynges lawe, ladyes name, knyghtes tale, mannes voice, childes play, *Agenores* doughter, *Philippes*-fonne, *Cupides* bowe, &c. [Edit. 1542.] Our old *Engliſh* writers were however extremely inaccurate in the termination of the genitive cafe. The poets followed no rule in this refpect; but fometimes inferted the *e*, and fometimes left it out; fometimes cut off, and fometimes added a fyllable, for the fake of the meafure. Bifhop *Lowth* obſerves, that ‘ *God's grace* was formerly written-*Godis grace* ;' and Dr. *Johnſon* remarks, ‘ that *knitis* is uſed for *knight's*, in *Chaucer*.' But this, we apprehend, is an irregular mode of fpelling, not fupported by analogy, or agreeable to the original formation of the genitive cafe. Several eminent writers, to avoid a harfhnefs in the pronunciation of fome genitives, have fubjoined to the fubftantive the pronoun *his*: as, “ Afa *his* heart.” 1 Kings xv. 15. “ Chrift *his* fake.” Liturgy. “ The firft book of Statius *his* Thebais.” *Pope's* tranflation of *Statius*. “ Socrates *his* fetters were ftruck off.” Spect. N° 183. “ Ulyffes *his* bow.” Guard. N° 98. Mr. *Addiſon* tells us, ‘ that the *s* reprefents the *his* and *her* of our forefathers.' Spect. N° 135. But analogy eafily overturns this fuppofition : for, ‘ the queen *his* palace,' ‘ the children *his* bread,' would be abfurd. We therefore conclude, that the termination of our genitive cafe in *'s* is regularly derived from the *Saxon*; and that the apoſtrophe implies the omiffion of the letter *e*, as we have already obferved. Bifhop *Lowth* remarks, ‘ that in poetry, the fign of the poffeffive cafe is frequently omitted after proper names ending in *s*, or in *x*; as, ‘ the wrath of *Peleus'* fon,' ‘ *Ajax'* fev'n-fold fhield.' *Pope*. But this, he adds, ‘ feems not fo allowable in profe:' and we are entirely of his opinion. If the editor of *Bentley's* Differ-tations, when he omitted the fecond *s*, in the poffeffive cafe of words ending with that letter, en-deavoured to prevent that hiffing, which, Mr. *Addiſon* in the Spectator fays, is taken notice of by foreigners, he has attempted to obviate a fault, which is entirely imaginary. Mr. *Addiſon's* objec-tion may with much greater reafon be urged againft the *Latin* language. For it is impoffible to produce a fentence from an *Engliſh* writer, in which there is more fibilation, than in the following : “ Dicitur *Sulpicius* pretiofas habuiffe poffeffiones in *Siciiiâ*.”—“ Receptos ad fe focios fibi adfcif-cunt.” *Cæſar de Bell. Gall.* i. 4.—“ Cùm fevis ætheriis delapfus fomnus ab aftris.” *Virg. Æn.* v. 838. In the cafe before us we will venture to affirm, that, to almoft nineteen ears in twenty, the ufual pronunciation of the *s's* in *Phalaris's* letters, *Polybius's* author, *Suidas's* words, *Timæus's* time, and *Æſchylus's* plays, founds more agreeably than *Phalaris'* letters, *Polybius'* author, *Suidas'* words, *Timæus'* time, and *Æſchylus'* plays. The reader, we will allow, perceives, by the apoftrophe, that *Phalaris'*, *Polybius'*, &c. are in the genitive or poffeffive cafe. But how would an unlearned hearer underftand the following fentence ? “ The bull in *Agrigentum* was fhewn for *Phalaris*.” Would he not fuppofe, that the people of *Agrigentum* impofed upon ftrangers, by fhewing them the Bull for the Tyrant ? If Dr. *Bentley* has treated his antagonift with contempt, for having ufed the word cotem-porary, inftead of contemporary, what would he fay to fome of the innovations we have mentioned ? Would he thank his editor for the improvement ? or rather, would he not look upon fome of the foregoing corrections and defalcations with indignation ? There is a deference due to the character of one of the moft illuftrious critics, that has ever appeared in this nation. Not a phrafe, not a let-ter of his, fhould be altered, upon a mere hypothefis. In points of orthography, the learned, both in our own country and in others, nay even the literati of future ages, may be curious to know the fentiments and practice of Dr. *Bentley*. It is therefore a piece of juftice we owe to the republic of letters, to exhibit a faithful copy of a work, which will be tranfmitted with applaufe to the lateft pofterity.” *Critical Review*, vol. XLIII. p. 8—12.—In addition to this critique, it may not be improper to refer to Mr. *Tyrwhitt's* Gloffary to *Chaucer*, p. 269 ; and to a fenfible correfpondent in Gent. Mag. 1781 p. 12.

valuable

valuable and curious record called " Doomfday Book *," in
2 vols. folio ; the Defcription of " A Collection of Prints
" in Imitation of Drawings ; to which are annexed, Lives
" of their Authors, with Explanatory and Critical Notes,
" by *Charles Rogers*, Efq; F. R. S. and S. A." 2 volumes, folio ;
" Lord *Chefterfield's* Mifcellaneous Works, with Memoirs of
" his Lordfhip's Life by Dr. *Maty* †," 2 vols. 4to ; Mr. *Gough's*
" *Britifh* Topography," 2 vols. 4to.; and his old friend *Tom
Martin's* " Hiftory of *Thetford*," 4to. All thefe were far
advanced in the prefs at the time of his death ; but he
lived not to fee any of them completed.

Mr. *Bowyer* had always been fubject to a bilious colic,
and during the laft ten years of his life was afflicted
with the palfy and the ftone : but, notwithftanding thefe
infirmities, he preferved, in general, a remarkable chearful-
nefs of difpofition ; and received great fatisfaction from the
converfation of a few literary friends, by whom he continued to be vifited. The faculties of his mind, though
fomewhat impaired, were ftrong enough to fupport the
labour of almoft inceffant reading, which had ever been
his principal amufement ; and he regularly corrected the
learned works, and efpecially the *Greek* books, which came
from his prefs. This he did till within a very few weeks
of his death ; which happened on the 18th of *November*,
1777, when he had nearly completed his 78th year.

* Tranfcribed from the original, and moft accurately revifed through the prefs, by
Abraham Farley, Efq; whofe long and intimate acquaintance with the original record
rendered him of all men the propereft perfon for fo important a truft ; and whofe friendfhip I am glad to have this opportunity of acknowledging.

† Of this worthy and learned Phyfician, whom I am happy to fay was my good friend,
fome memoirs fhall be given in the Appendix.

The

The publications of Mr. *Bowyer* are an incontrovertible evidence of his abilities and learning; to which may be added, that he was honoured with the friendſhip and patronage of many of the moſt diſtinguiſhed perſonages of his age. I have already had occaſion to mention ſo many reſpectable Scholars and Antiquaries of the preſent century, that to enumerate them here would be ſuperfluous. His intimacy with Mr. *Markland* and Mr. *Clarke* appears by the various extracts which have been given from their epiſtolary correſpondence; and his connexion with Dr. *Owen* and Dr. *Heberden*, thoſe ornaments of their reſpective profeſſions, and with *Richard Gough*, Eſq; ſo well known by his eminent acquaintance with *Britiſh* Topography and Antiquities, is apparent from his laſt will; where his obligations to Dr. *Jenkin*, Dean *Stanhope*, and Mr. *Nelſon*, are alſo acknowledged.

For more than half a century he ſtood unrivalled as a learned printer; and ſome of the moſt maſterly productions of this kingdom have been deſcribed as appearing from his preſs. Nor was his pen unknown to the world of letters. The work which ſtamps an immortal honour on his name is his truly ingenious " Conjectures on the New Teſtament," a book in which the profoundeſt erudition and the moſt candid criticiſm are happily united. And of the ſacred text, there is not an edition which ever paſſed through his correction, but what has its peculiar value *.

To his literary and profeſſional abilities he added an excellent moral character. His regard to religion was diſplayed in his publications, and in the courſe of his life

* See the ingenious Mr. *Knox's* " Eſſays," vol. I. p. 361.

Q q q   and

and studies; and he was particularly distinguished by his
inflexible probity, and an uncommon alacrity in assisting
the necessitous. His liberality in relieving every species
of distress, and his endeavours to conceal his benefactions,
reflect great honour on his memory. Though he was
naturally fond of retirement, and seldom entered into
company, excepting with men of letters, he was, perhaps, excelled by few in the talent of justly discrimi-
nating the real characters of mankind. He judged of
the persons he saw by a sort of intuition; and his
judgements were generally right. From a consciousness
of literary superiority, he did not always pay that attention to the booksellers which was expedient in the way of
his business. Being too proud to solicit the favours in
that way which he believed to be his due, he was often
disappointed in his expectations. On the other hand, he
frequently experienced friendships in cases where he had
much less reason to have hoped for them; so that, agreeably to an expression of his own, " in what he had received,
" and what he had been denied, he thankfully acknow-
" ledged the will of Heaven." The two great objects
he had in view, in the decline of life, were to repay the
benefactions his father had received, and to be himself a benefactor to the meritorious of his own profession. These
purposes are fully displayed in his last will, for which reason,
and because it illustrates the turn of his mind in other respects, it is inserted below at large *.

Mr.

* I *WILLIAM BOWYER*, Printer, Citizen and Stationer of *London*, being
mercifully warned by the Decays of Age, and by the Loss of almost all my Friends, am
fully sensible that I have not long an Abiding here: And therefore make this my last
Will and Testament; and dispose of those Worldly Goods with which it has pleased
God

Mr. *Bowyer*, agreeably to his own direction, was buried with

God to intruſt me, in the following Manner. My Farms in *Yorkſhire* *, which were entailed on my only Son *Thomas*, will, at my Deceaſe, fall-in to him; and that at *Naveſtock*

* The farms both in *Yorkſhire* and *Eſſex* were acquired by Mr. *Bowyer* when he married his firſt
wife, who was niece to his mother, and was left under the guardianſhip of the elder *Bowyer*
by her father's will; of which a copy is here ſubjoined: " In the name of God, Amen. I
" *Thomas Prudom*, Citizen and Fiſhmonger of *London*, being ſomething indiſpoſed in body, but of
" ſound and perfect mind and memory, praiſed be Almighty God, and conſidering the certainty of
" death, and uncertainty of the time thereof, do therefore make and declare my laſt Will and Teſ-
" tament in manner and form following; (that is to ſay,) Firſt and principally, I commend my
" ſoul into the hands of Almighty God my Creator, hoping and aſſuredly believing, by and through
" the merits, death, and paſſion of my only Saviour and Redeemer *Jeſus Chriſt*, to obtain full par-
" don and free remiſſion of all my ſins, and to inherit eternal life. My body I commit to the
" earth, in hopes of a joyful reſurrection, to be decently buried according to the direction of my
" Executors herein after named. And as touching ſuch temporal eſtate as God of his infinite mercy
" hath been pleaſed to bleſs me with, I give, deviſe, bequeath and diſpoſe thereof, in manner fol-
" lowing, *viz.* IMPRIMIS, I will, order, direct, and appoint, that all ſuch juſt debts as I ſhall
" owe at the time of my deceaſe, together with my funeral charges, ſhall be fully paid and ſatisfied.
" *Item*, I give to my mother-in-law *Elizabeth Prudom* the ſum of Five Pounds. *Item*, I give to my
" ſon-in-law Mr. *James Greenwell* Twenty Pounds for mourning; and I give more to him the
" Furniture of the Room, two pair of ſtairs forwards, in his dwelling-houſe. *Item*, I give to my
" ſiſter *Dorothy Bowyer*, Ten Pounds for mourning. *Item*, I give to all my own ſiſters, and to all
" the reſt of the ſiſters of my late wife *Dorcas Prudom* deceaſed, that ſhall be living at the time of
" my deceaſe, Five Pounds apiece. *Item*, I give to my uncle *Nathaniel Prudom* Five Pounds.
" *Item*, I give to my couſin *Ann Bradford* Five Pounds. *Item*, I give to my brothers, *John Prudom*
" and *William Bowyer*, Twenty Pounds apiece. *Item*, I give to my Nephew *William Cutbert* Five
" Pounds. *Item*, I give to my friend *Henry Bedell*, Scrivener, Ten Pounds. *Item*, I give to the
" Poor of *Danby-Dale*, in the County of *York*, Two Pounds, to be diſtributed amongſt them, as the
" Miniſter and Churchwardens of the ſaid Pariſh ſhall think fit. *Item*, I give my Freehold Eſtates
" in *Danby-Dale* and *Broughton* in the ſaid County of *York*, and my Freehold Eſtate in the Pariſh of
" *Naveſtock* in the County of *Eſſex*, now in the occupation of *John Fellows*, or his under-tenants,
" that I lately purchaſed of Captain *Gilbert Lacy*, and all other my Eſtates of Inheritance whatſoever
" or whereſoever, unto my loving daughter *Ann Prudom*, and the Heirs of her body lawfully to be
" begotten; and for want of ſuch iſſue †, then I give the ſaid Eſtates to my brother *John Prudom*,
" and to my ſiſters, *Ann Audas*, *Eleanor Talboyes*, *Mariel Cutbert*, *Alice Dawſon*, and *Margaret Audas*,
" equally, and to their Heirs and Aſſigns for ever, equally, part and ſhare alike, to hold as Tenants
" in common, and not as Joint-tenants, chargeable, neverthelelſs, with the payment of the ſum of
" Fifty Pounds to my ſiſter *Elizabeth Mewborne*, within ſix months next after the deceaſe of my
" ſaid daughter without iſſue of her body lawfully to be begotten. The reſt, reſidue, and re-
" mainder of my Eſtate, conſiſting of Ready Money, Plate, Jewels, Houſehold Goods, or in Leaſes,
" or in Monies due to me from the Government, or upon Statute, Judgement, Mortgage, Bond,

† On this contingency, the ſurviving repreſentatives of *Eleanor Talboyes*, *Mariel Cutbert*, and *Margaret Audas*,
(ſiſters and coheireſſes of the Teſtator *Thomas Prudom*) put in their plea, in *Eoſter* Term, 19 *George* III. to obtain
poſſeſſion of the Eſtates, on the frivolous pretence that the late Mr. *Bowyer* was dead without legitimate iſſue.
A pretence ſo groundleſs met of courſe with the fate it deſerved. It occaſioned, however, no little trouble and
expence to Mr. *Thomas Bowyer*, who was under the neceſſity of obtaining regular certificates of his father's marriage at *St. Clement's Danes*; his mother's and his own baptiſms at the ſame church; and his mother's and brother's burial at *Low-Leyton*. Theſe were all printed on the occaſion; with a copy of Mr. *Prudom's* Will; the
" Plaintiff's plea, in order to get the Eſtates belonging to Mr. *Thomas Bowyer*;" and the following Extract of
a Letter, dated *Nov.* 28, 1778, from Mr. *James Emonſon*: " In anſwer to your enquiry, I ſend this to inform
" you, that I lived with your Grandfather and Father at the time of your birth. I farther remember, that
" when your mother was in labour, I was ſent for, and fetched the Midwife, whoſe name was *Baker*, and who
" lodged at Mr. *Parſons's*, the Corner of *White-Fryers Gateway*, *Fleet-Street*: I cannot at preſent recollect any
" other Perſon alive, who lived with your Grandfather and Father at that period; but if any one ſhould occur
" to me hereafter, I will inform you of it. The above I am ready to atteſt. I am, &c. *James Emonſon*."

" Bill,

with his friends, in the church-yard of *Low-Leyton*, in
Essex;

stock in *Essex*, which he has given to me by paffing a Fine and Recovery, I hereby return, give, and devife, to him, his Heirs, and Affigns, for ever, together with the Land fince added to it by Lord *Waldegrave*'s Donation in Lieu of my Right of Commonage. I GIVE AND BEQUEATH to my faid Son * Twenty Pounds *per Annum* in the Bank Long Annuities, which now ftand in our joint names. I GIVE AND BEQUEATH the Sum of Six Thoufand Pounds Four † *per Cent.* Confolidated Bank Annuities, to be placed in the joint Names of him my Son and my Executors hereafter named, *in Truft,* that my faid Son may receive the Dividends thereof for his Life, for his fole Ufe; with this exprefs Provifo, that my faid Executors fhall not confent to the felling or alienating any Part thereof, or of the faid Dividends thereof, during my faid Son's Life; but that he may, by his Will, difpofe of it to whom he pleafes; or, in cafe he marries with the Confent of my Executors in Writing, that he may make fuch Settlement of it, for the Benefit of himfelf, his Wife, and Children, as he fhall think proper: AND, IN CASE he marries with fuch Confent, I give and bequeath to him the further Sum of Three Thoufand Pounds Four *per Cent.* Confolidated Bank Annuities. *I alfo give* to my faid Son all my Houfehold Goods, Furniture, and Utenfils not in Partnerfhip, except my Old Bureau in the little Back Room, which I give to Mr. *John Nichols,* my prefent Partner in Bufinefs, to furvey and preferve my Papers in. *I likewife give* to my Son all my Plate; except the fmall Silver Cup which was given to my Father (after his Lofs by Fire) by Mrs.

" Bill, Book, Specialty or Account, or in Shipping, or in any other thing whatfoever or wherefoever,
" I give, devife, and bequeath unto my faid loving daughter *Ann Prudom,* and her Affigns; and I
" make, name, and appoint my faid brothers, *John Prudom* and *William Bowyer,* my joint Executors
" of this my Will, and Guardians to my faid daughter *Ann Prudom* during her minority; and I
" direct and order them my faid Executors, and the furvivor of them, during the minority of my
" faid daughter *Ann Prudom,* to make the beft improvement that they can of the Rents of the feveral
" Eftates given to her aforefaid; as alfo the Refiduary Part of my Eftate given to her, by placing
" the fame out to Intereft, or otherwife laying out the fame, as they my faid Executors, or the Sur-
" vivors or Survivor of them fhall think fit; and fo much of the Intereft, or Improvement, that fhall
" be made of the fame as fhall be neceffary, I appoint and order fhall be applied and paid for the
" Maintenance, Education, and bringing up, of her my faid daughter; and the Refidue thereof,
" my Will and Mind is, fhall be added to her Fortune, and paid to her at her age of One and
" Twenty Years, or Day of Marriage (which fhall firft happen). And my Will and Mind is,
" that neither of them my faid Executors fhall be accountable with or for the act of the other, nor
" for no more of my Eftate than fhall come to their refpective hands, nor for any lofs that may
" happen by their or either of their placing or laying out any Monies purfuant to this my Will,
" unlefs fuch lofs fhall happen by any wilful defign or neglect of theirs; my Will and Intent being,
" that if any fuch lofs fhall happen without any fuch wilful defign or neglect, that fuch lofs fhall
" be borne by her my faid Daughter, and not by the faid Executors, or either of them. And
" laftly, I do hereby revoke, difannul, and make void, all former Wills, Bequefts, and Legacies by
" me at any time heretofore made, bequeathed, or given, and declare this only to be my laft Will
" and Teftament. IN WITNESS whereof, I, the faid *Thomas Prudom,* the Teftator, have to each
" fheet of two parts of this my Will, both of the fame tenor and date, fet my hand, and to the laft
" fheet of each part, and to the top, where the fheets of each part are faftened together, have fet my
" feal, the Thirtieth Day of *April,* Anno Domini 1719, *Annoque Regni Georgii Regis Magnæ Britan-*
" *niæ, &c. Quinto,* THOMAS PRUDOM."

* Of whom fee p. 55. The teftamentary arrangement of his father having fecured to him a comfortable maintenance; and having been a witnefs to the troubles and inconveniencies attending the purfuit of bufinefs; the fon of Mr. *Bowyer* preferred the retirement of a country life, to which he had long been accuftomed.

† Which, at *Chriftmas* 1780, were reduced to Three *per Cent.*

James,

Effex; near the South Weft corner of the church, where
the

James *, and which *I give* to the Company of Stationers in *London,* hoping they will
preferve it as a Memorial. I GIVE AND BEQUEATH to Mr. *John Henry Browne* and
Mr. *Nathaniel Conant,* Two of my Executors hereinafter-mentioned, Five Hundred
Pounds each. IF I DIE WITHIN Five Miles of *London,* I defire to be buried at *Low
Leyton* in *Effex,* where the reft of my Friends are laid, in as private a Manner as poffible,
with a Hearfe, and a Coach and Four; attended only by the above-named Mr. *John
Nichols,* and my Neighbour Mr. *Nevil Fether,* to whom I give Twenty Pounds. And
now, having committed my Body to the Earth, I would teftify my Duty and Gratitude
to my few Relations, and numerous Benefactors after my Father's Lofs by Fire. I GIVE
AND BEQUEATH to my Coufin *Scott* † lately of *Weftminfter* Brewer, and to his Sifter, Fifty
Pounds each. I GIVE AND BEQUEATH to my Relations Mr. *Thomas Linley* and his Wife
One Thoufand Pounds Four *per Cent.* Confolidated Annuities, to be transferred to them,
or to the Survivor of them; and which I hope they will take Care to fettle, at their
Deaths, for the Benefit of their Son and Daughter. *Another Relation* ‡ I have, whom, as
he

---

* On this cup is infcribed, " The Gift of Mrs. *Elianor James* § to *W. Bowyer,* after his lofs by
" fire, *Jan.* 30, 1712."—It is now depofited among the Company's plate, and ufed by them on days
of public feftivity. Under the original infcription is placed the following : " Bequeathed, in 1777,
" by *William Bowyer,* to the Company of Stationers, as a Memorial of their Munificence to his
" Father after his lofs by fire, *Jan.* 30, 1712-13."

† This name occurs among the benefactors to his father.

‡ Who has been already mentioned in p. 239. The degree of confanguinity will appear by the
following table, drawn out by Mr. *Emonfon* not long before his death :
" *William King,* Citizen and Vintner of *London.* He kept the *King's-Head* Tavern in *The Poultry;*
and had one fon and one daughter, *viz.*

William King, who fucceeded his father in bufi-nefs ‖. He had feveral children; but only one daughter furvived him, *viz.*	*Mary King.* She married with *John Bowyer,* Grocer. He not fucceeding in bufinefs, and dying foon after, the widow was taken home by her brother, with her only fon,
Rebecca King, married to *Thomas Davie,* who ferved his time with and fucceeded her father in bufinefs. She had feveral children, who all died without iffue, except	*William Bowyer,* who was born in *July,* 1663. He was twice married. By his firft wife he had no iffue; by his fecond he had two children;
Mary Davie, married to *Samuel Emonfon.* They had feveral children, three of whom furvived them, *viz.*	1. *William,* married *Oct.* 9, 1728, to *Ann Pru-dom,* by whom he had 2. *Dorothy.* She mar-ried with *Peter Wallis,* Jeweller, in *Fleet-ftr.* They had two or three children, who all died infants; and Mr. *Wallis* died foon after them. Mrs. *Wallis* died *April* 14, 1731, aged 23.
James Emonfon, died 1780. *Sarah* deceafed. *Mary* living 1778.	1. *William,* buried at *Low Leyton,* February 6, 1729-30. 2. *Thomas,* living 1782. 3. Of a third, Mrs. *Bow-yer* died in child-birth.

§ Mr. *James* was the widow of a printer, and carried on that bufinefs after the death of her hufband. She
was a benefactrefs to the church of *St. Bennet, Paul's Wharf,* where fhe gave fome communion plate.

‖ On the day of King *Charles's* Reftoration, the wife of this Mr. *King* happened to be in labour, and longed to
fee the returning Monarch. *Charles,* in paffing through *The Poultry,* was told of her inclination, and ftopt at the
tavern to falute her.

" My

the following infcription is placed to the memory of him-felf and feveral of his relations :

ICHABOD

he wants not my Affiftance, I draw a Veil over. I GIVE to the two Sons and one Daughter * of the late Reverend Mr. *Maurice* of *Gothenburg* in *Sweden*, who married the only Daughter of Mr. *Richard Williamfon* † Bookfeller (in Return for her Father's Friendfhip to mine), One Thoufand Pounds Four *per Cent.* Confolidated Annuities, to be divided equally between them, and to be transferred (after deducting what I have already advanced, or fhall advance, on their Account, in my Life-time, fuch Accompt to be afcertained by my Books of Accompt) to whom they fhall order for that Purpofe. I GIVE AND BEQUEATH to Mrs. *Catharine Markland*, Sifter to my late worthy friend Mr. *Jeremiah Markland* ‡, Three Hundred and Fifty-one Pounds, deducting from that Sum whatever I fhall from this Time advance to her in my Life-time, fuch Accompt to be afcertained by my Books of Accompt. I GIVE AND BEQUEATH to Dr. *Henry Owen*, of *St. Olave's, Hart-Street*, One Hundred Pounds ; to Mr. *Lockyer Davis*, One Hundred Pounds ; to Mr. *James Dodfley*, One Hundred Pounds ; to Mr. *Nathaniel Thomas* of *White Fryars*, Fifty Pounds ; *and* to Mr. *Matthews*, Attorney, of *Stokefley* in *Yorkfhire*, to Mr. *William Redknapp* Clerk to the *Hudfon's Bay* Company, to Mr. *Edmond Stal-lard*, and to Mr. *Anthony Wyllan* fometime Servant to the Right Honourable *Arthur Onflow*, Thirty Pounds each ; to Mr. *John Farmer*, Senior, who has wrought long with me, Twenty Pounds ; *and* to my Maid *Martha Chadley*, if fhe be living with me at my Deceafe, Six Hundred Pounds.—*Among* my Father's numerous Benefactors, there is not, that I can hear of, one alive : To feveral of them I made an Acknowledgement. But one refpectable Body I am ftill indebted to, the Univerfity of *Cambridge* ; to whom I give, or rather reftore, the Sum of Fifty Pounds, in Return for the Donation of Forty Pounds made to my Father at the Motion of the learned and pious Mafter of *Saint John's College*, Dr. *Robert Jenkin :* to a Nephew of his I have already given another Fifty

---

" My fifter *Sarah* married twice : firft, *Thomas Whatley*, by whom he had two daughters, living
" 1778. 1. *Selina*, married to *Richard Stokes*, a Glazier. They had no children ; and fhe has
" had the ufe of one fide taken from her by a palfy ftroke, and probably will ever cont'ue helplefs.
" —2. *Mercy*, fecond daughter, a year or two younger than her fifter, unmarried. She lives with
" her aunt *Mary*. By my fifter *Sarah's* fecond hufband, *Peter Davis*, fhe had one only daughter,
" named *Sarah*, now about 40 years of age. She married to *Charles Elton*, Surgeon and Apothe-
" cary ; who, dying fome years fince, left her and her fon unprovided for. She now lives with me,
" and behaves very well. I have her fon *Charles* apprentice. He has ferved about half his
" time, and is between 17 and 18 years of age. He has a good capacity, has had a pretty good
" fchool education in *Latin, &c.* and I hope will turn out well, as he is the laft of my branch.
" My fifter *Mary*, now living, is near 68 years. She kept herfelf fingle, to bring up the above
" three children of her fifter *Sarah*. She now begins to grow infirm. I have affifted, and fhall
" always continue to affift her. She has much merit, and I fhould be glad to affift her further
" than I do. *Letter from Mr. James Emonfon to Mr. Thomas Bowyer, Nov. 28, 1778.*

* *Peter* the eldeft, a cadet in the *Swedifh Eaft India* Company's fervice, was born in *London*, 1751 ; *Jacob* the fecond in *Gothenburg*, 1760 ; and *Catherine* the youngeft in *September*, 1761.

† Who died *Jan.* 7, 1736-7, aged 51. He was fucceffor to Mr. *Sare*, deputy receiver general of the Poft-Office revenue, and clerk of the mis-fent and mis-directed letters.

‡ He had before advanced 149*l* ; making in the whole 500*l* ; and had given Mrs. *Markland* per-miffion to draw upon him for the whole fum if fhe thought proper. He had fome years before made the fame offer to her brother ; fee p. 26.

Pounds,

{ICHABOD DAWKS, died *February* 27, 1730, aged 70.}
{SARAH, his Wife, died *June* 6, 1737, aged 80.}

{WILLIAM BOWYER, Sen. died *Decem.* 27, 1737, aged 80.
{DOROTHY, his Wife, Sifter to I. DAWKS, died *December*
20, 1727, aged 63.

{WILLIAM BOWYER, Jun. died *Novem.* 18, 1777, aged 77.
{ANNE, his firft Wife, died *October* 17, 1731, aged 26.
{ELIZABETH, his fecond Wife, died *Jan.* 14, 1771, aged 70.

In

Pounds *, as appears by his Receipt of the Thirty-firft of *May*, One Thoufand Seven Hundred and Seventy. *The Benefactions*, which my Father received from *Oxford*, I can only repay with Gratitude; as he received them, not from the Univerfity as a Body, but from particular Members. I GIVE Thirty Pounds to the Dean and Chapter of *Canterbury*†, in Gratitude for the Kindnefs of the worthy Doctor *Stanhope* (fometime Dean of *Canterbury*) to my Father; the Remembrance of which amongft the Proprietors of his Works I have long out-lived, as I have experienced by not being employed to print

---

* Previous to this donation, he wrote the following anonymous letter, which was conveyed to Mr. *Jenkin* through the hands of the writer of this note:
" REV. SIR,
" As you are the Grandfon ‡, I underftand, of Dr. *Jenkin*, the late worthy mafter of *St. John's*
" *College, Cambridge*, who by his intereft obtained a donation of Forty Pounds from that Univerfity
" to my father, after his lofs by fire, in *Jan.* 1713; I beg your acceptance of Fifty Pounds in return;
" which I fhall fend you in a bank note the next poft after I hear this letter fafely reaches you,
" defiring you will not mention it during my life at leaft. I fhall further beg you will fend me a
" receipt of it, as I have mentioned it in my will; but, thinking it will be more acceptable now, I
" beg leave, in this inftance, to be my own executor. I am, Sir, your fincere friend and humble
" fervant."
The anfwer was fhort, but fignificant:
" SIR, May 27, 1770.
" Your propofal expreffes your gratitude in the moft eminent manner; and I wifh I knew your
" name, to fet forth your praife. I am, Sir, your greatly obliged and humble fervant."
The money was immediately fent; which produced the following acknowledgement:
" SIR, May 31, 1770.
" I return you my earlieft and moft hearty thanks for your genteel and valuable prefent, which is
" ftill enhanced by the occafion of it; that points out in the moft friendly manner the value your
" father fet upon an intereft in Dr. *Jenkin*, and the honour and fervice you have done me in my
" relation to him. Gratitude, Sir, is a virtue that will fhine with great brightnefs in that pious and
" learned man; and I can't but wifh, if not hope for, the honour of a future knowledge of you
" my benefactor, who eminently refembles him in that capital ornament of a Chriftian. I am, Sir,
" your moft obliged and moft obedient humble fervant to command, ROBERT JENKIN.
" Received *May* 31, 1770, of *A. B. C.* by the Hands of Mr. *John Nichols*, Fifty Pounds as a
" free gift in return for a donation made him by the intereft of the Rev. Dr. *Jenkin*,
" mafter fome time of *St. John's College, Cambridge*. *Per* ROBERT JENKIN."
† This fum the refpectable gentlemen who received it have handfomely appropriated to the purchafe of valuable books, as the moft honourable mode of perpetuating the teftator's gratitude.

‡ The gentleman (it afterwards appeared) was *nephew* to Dr. *Jenkin*. He died *Oct.* 8, 1778. See p. 17.

them:

In the Church also there is a neat marble monument
erected

them [*]: The like I might fay of the Works of Mr. *Nelfon*, another refpectable Friend and Patron of my Father's; and of many others. I GIVE to Doctor *William Heberden* my little Cabinet of Coins, with *Hickes's Thefaurus, Triftan* and the odd Volume, *Spanheim's Numifmata, Harduin's Opera Selecta* in Folio, *Nummi Populorum et Urbium* in Quarto, and any other of my Books he chufes to accept: To the Reverend Doctor *Henry Owen*, fuch of my *Hebrew* Books, and Critical Books on the New Teftament, as he pleafes to take: To *Richard Gough*, Efquire, in like Manner, my Books on Topographical Subjects: To the before named Mr. *John Nichols*, all Books that relate to *Cicero, Livy*, and the *Roman* Hiftory, particularly the *Cenotaphia* of *Noris* and *Pighius*, my Grammars and Dictionaries, with *Swift's* and *Pope's* Works: To my Son, whatever Books (not defcribed above) he thinks proper to take.—*And now I hope* I may be allowed to leave fomewhat for the Benefit of Printing. To this End, I give to the Mafter and Keepers or Wardens and Commonalty of the Myftery or Art of a Stationer of the City of *London*, fuch a Sum of Money as will purchafe Two Thoufand Pounds Three *per Cent.* Reduced Bank Annuities, *upon Truft*, to pay the Dividends and Yearly Produce thereof, to be divided for ever equally amongft Three Printers, Compofitors or Preffmen, to be elected from Time to Time by the Mafter, Wardens, and Affiftants, of the faid Company, and who at the Time of fuch Election fhall be Sixty-three Years old or upwards, for their refpective Lives, to be paid Half-yearly; hoping that fuch as fhall be moft deferving will be preferred. AND WHEREAS I have herein before given to my Son the Sum of Three Thoufand Pounds Four *per Cent.* Confolidated Annuities, in cafe he marries with the Confent of my Executors: Now, I do hereby give and bequeath the Dividends and Intereft of that Sum, till fuch Marriage takes Place, to the faid Company of Stationers, to be divided equally between Six other Printers, Compofitors or Preffmen, as aforefaid, in Manner as aforefaid; and, if my faid Son fhall die unmarried, or married

---

[*] The following Letter was not fent, but read, to an eminent Bookfeller, in *March*, 1764:

"SIR, The Advertifement which I fee in the papers, of a new edition of Dean *Stanhope's* 'Comment on the Epiftles and Gofpels,' recalls to my mind thofe paft and valuable friendfhips, which I cover in my breaft, that I may there more tenderly cherifh them. The inclofed † will teftify that of the Dean's to my Father, written, as it came from the heart, on a moft affecting occafion. I leave you to judge what fentiments I muft feel, when I reflect on having enjoyed the living patronage of that pious writer, and being excluded after his death from printing a fingle fheet of his works. On the other hand, when I compare the afflicting difpenfation of Providence at that time with my prefent circumftances in the World, I have great reafon to be abundantly thankful, and to fay within myfelf, *Shall I receive good at the hand of man in my youth*, and *repine at his neglect of me in old age?* No, *it is mine own infirmity*, it is the natural confequence of the decays of nature; and I will not blame *her* great Author and Director. I fend you the good Dean's Letter, that it may find a place perhaps in fome future edition of his Works, provided only you fubjoin to it the following Memorandum: 'Communicated by the Son of the above Mr. *Bowyer*, who was defirous of perpetuating this page among the valuable Writings of the Author, when denied the privilege of printing any part of them.' I am, Sir, &c. WILLIAM BOWYER.

"N. B. The 'Comment on the Epiftles and Gofpels' was only, it feems, advertifed afrefh on this occafion, but not reprinted. However, the Letter was not without a proper foundation. Of the very laft edition, I had the favour of printing One Volume only, who had printed heretofore the whole Four. And of the other Works of the Dean, had not a fingle fheet given me; as his *Thomas à Kempis*, St. *Auftin's* Meditations, and others. The fame I might obferve of Mr. *Nelfon's* Feafts and Fafts, of which I have lived to fee Two or Three Editions printed, and myfelf thrown out. W. B."

† The letter which is already printed in p. 8.

without

erected to his father's memory and his own, with the following

without such Consent as aforesaid, then I give and bequeath the said Capital Sum of
Three Thousand Pounds to the said Company of Stationers, the Dividends and Yearly
Produce thereof to be divided for ever equally amongst Six other such old Printers,
Compositors or Pressmen, for their respective Lives, to be qualified, chosen, and paid,
in Manner as aforesaid.—It has long been to me Matter of Concern, that such Numbers
are put Apprentices as Compositors * without any Share of School-learning, who ought
to have the greatest: In hopes of remedying this, I give and bequeath to the said Company of Stationers such a Sum of Money as will purchase One Thousand Pounds Three
per Cent. Reduced Bank Annuities, for the Use of One Journeyman Compositor, such
as shall hereafter be described; with this special Trust, that the Master, Wardens, and
Assistants, shall pay the Dividends and Produce thereof Half-yearly to such Compositor †:
The said Master, Wardens, and Assistants, of the said Company, shall nominate for this
Purpose a Compositor who is a Man of good Life and Conversation, who shall usually
frequent some Place of Public Worship every *Sunday* unless prevented by Sickness, and
shall not have worked on a Newspaper or Magazine for Four Years at least before such
Nomination, nor shall ever afterwards whilst he holds this Annuity, which may be for
Life if he continues a Journeyman: He shall be able to read and construe *Latin*, and
at least to read *Greek* fluently with Accents; of which he shall bring a Testimonial from
the Rector of *St. Martin's Ludgate* for the Time being: I could wish that he shall have
been brought up piously and virtuously, if it be possible, at *Merchant Taylors*, or some
other public school, from Seven Years of Age till he is full Seventeen, and then to serve
Seven Years faithfully as a Compositor, and work Seven Years more as a Journeyman, as
I would not have this Annuity bestowed on any one under Thirty-one years of Age: If
after he is chosen he should behave ill, let him be turned out, and another be chosen in
his stead. AND WHEREAS it may be many Years before a Compositor may be found that
shall exactly answer the above Description, and it may at some Times happen that such
a one cannot be found; I would have the Dividends in the mean Time applied to such
Person as the Master, Wardens, and Assistants, shall think approaches nearest to what I

---

* That this was not a new idea with him, will appear from the following advertisement, which
he many years ago inserted in a public paper : " Wanted, an apprentice, with some share of Learn-
" ing, the more the better, to a Freeman of *London*; Fifty Pounds to be paid down, Thirty of
" which shall be returned at the end of seven years, if the person behaves well during that term,
" which shall be left to the judgement of two or three indifferent arbitrators. The master, on the
" other hand, to be at liberty to return him to his friends, any time after the first year, and before
" the last, if he behaves ill. Any reasonable complaint against the master shall be redressed, at any
" time; or the indentures dissolved on such terms as the arbitrators shall determine. Direct for
" Z. Z. expressing the name, circumstances, and place of abode, of the person proposed : an answer
" will be returned within ten days."—When I was bound to him, my Father received from Mr.
Bowyer a promissory note to *return* half the apprentice-fee, at the expiration of the seven years, *on
condition that I behaved suitable to his expectation.* This sum he very honourably paid me. *J. N.*

† It may not be improper to observe, that this annuity was bestowed, by the Company of Stationers, on Mr. *Jacob Wragg*, a compositor in every respect deserving of it. It has been remarked,
however, as a somewhat strange circumstance, that in an occupation so nearly allied to literature as
that of Printing, a single candidate only should have offered himself as qualified to enjoy so comfortable a stipend. Mr. *Wragg* died at *Bury*, in *Feb.* 1781; and after his death there were several
candidates, when Mr. *Fletcher* (formerly printer of a news-paper at *Cambridge*) was elected.—The
other annuities were judiciously given to *nine* deserving and necessitous old printers ‡; and from the
circumstance of none being admitted under the age of 63, there have already been several vacancies.

‡ The making of a Will has been very properly called " the last great act of a wife's man's life." That of
Mr. *Bowyer* was framed from the result of long deliberation. In his latter years some improvement perpetually occurred to him in the form of his charitable bequests. Whenever a new Will was made, he of course
cancelled those which had preceded, which were preserved, however, in a paper thus endorsed, " WILLS, all of
" which are cancelled and revoked by me *W. Bowyer*; who fears not to leave these testimonies of his mind at
" different periods, that those whom it may concern may see how uniform it has been, or how variable."

R r r
have

lowing infcription*, written by himfelf many years before his death :

have defcribed. AND WHEREAS the above Trufts will occafion fome Trouble ; I give to the faid Company, in cafe they think proper to accept the Trufts, Two Hundred and Fifty Pounds †.—I GIVE AND BEQUEATH all the Reft and Refidue of my Perfonal Eftate, not herein before difpofed of, unto the faid Mr. *John Nichols*, for his own Ufe and Benefit. And I nominate and appoint the faid *John Nichols*, *John Henry Browne*, and *Nathaniel Conant*, (all of them being Liverymen of the Company of Stationers,) Executors of this my Will; hereby declaring, that neither of them fhall be anfwerable for the Acts, Deeds, or Receipts, of the others or other of them.

In Witnefs whereof, I have hereunto fet my Hand and Seal, this Thirtieth Day of *July*, in the Year of our LORD One Thoufand Seven Hundred and Seventy-feven.

Signed, fealed, publifhed, and declared, by the faid *William Bowyer* the Teftator, as and for his Laft Will and Teftament, &c. &c.   *W. BOWYER.*

* Another epitaph propofed for Mr. *Bowyer*, and drawn up by his ingenious friend Mr. *Edward Clarke*, is here copied from the Gentleman's Magazine :

" Memoriæ Sacrum
WILHELMI BOWYER,
Typographorum poft *Stephanos* & *Commelinos*
Longè doctiffimi :
Linguarum *Latinæ, Græcæ*, et *Hebraicæ*
peritiffimi :
Adeo ut cognoviffe videatur
Naturæ atque orbis alphabetum.
Quot et quanta Opera
ab illius Prelo
Splendidè, nitidè, et, quod majus eft,
Fide et integritate fummâ
Tanquam ex equo *Trojano*
Meri principes exierint ;
Annales Typographici et nunc et olim
teftati funt :
Et præcipuè quod acta diurna

Superioris Cameræ
Britannici Parliamenti
Suo Prelo, fuæ fidei
Honorificè commiffa.fuerant.
Hæc Typogapho debentur :
Sed quod fe femper geffit,
Ut virum decuit honeftiffimum,
Amiciffimum et pium,
In fui ipfius et familiæ decus,
Majorem laudem cedet.
Tanti Typographi et Hominis Memoriæ
Mœrens infcripfit Saxum
olim Familiaris,
et nunc Amicus.
Obiit 18 die *Novembris*,
Annum agens feptuagefimum octavum,
Æræ Chriftianæ 1777."

† Befides Mr. *Bowyer's* legacies, the company pay above 200*l.* a year in penfions and other charities. See *Chambers*, art. COMPANY. The names of their benefactors are here copied from four tables which hang in the Hall :

Mr. *William Lamb*	Mr. *Chriftopher Meredith*	Mr. *John Martin*	*James Brooke*, Efq;
Mr. *William Norton*	Mr. *John Haviland*	Mr. *Thomas Newcombe*	*Nathaniel Cole*, Efq;
Mr. *Robert Dexter*	Mr. *Robert Mead*	Mr. *Evan Tyler*	*Richard Manby*, Efq;
Mr. *Henry Billage*	Mr. *John Sweeting*	Mrs. *Sufanna Latham*	*Daniel Midwinter* †, Efq;
Mr. *Cutbbert Burbies*	Mr. *Thomas Cowley*	Mrs. *Anne Mearne*	*Richard Brooke*, Efq;
Mrs. *Mary Bifhop*	Mr. *Thomas Triplett*	Mr. *Henry Herringman*	Mrs. *Hannah Knaplock*
Mr. *John Norton*	Mr. *Crofts*	Mr. *William Rawlins*	Sir*Steph.Theodore Janffen* ‡,
Mr. *Humphry Lownes*	Mr. *Miles Flefher*	*Thomas Guy*, Efq;	Bart.
Mr. *Peter Short*	Mr. *Humphry Robinfon*	*John Lilly*, Efq;	Mr. *William Bowyer*
Mrs. *Lucretia Eofte*	Mrs. *Mary Brooke*	Mr. *Theophilus Cater*	Mr. *John Boydell* ‖
Mr. *Lock*	Mrs. *Anne Man*	Mr. *Richard Mount* *	
Mr. *Robert Allott*	Mr. *Thomas Vere*	Mr. *John Ofborn* *	
Mr. *Anthony Uphill*	Mr. *Thomas Roycroft*	Mr. *William Mount*	
Mr. *Edmund Brewfter*	Mr. *Richard Royfton*	Mr. *Arthur Bettefworth*	

* Mr. *Mount* and Mr. *Ofborn* gave in 1734 the brafs chandeliers.

† Formerly an eminent bookfeller in *St. Paul's Church Yard*. He died *Jan.* 19, 1757, and left 1000*l.* to the Company ; the intereft of which is to put out apprentice a boy yearly from the Parifh of *Hornfey*, and one from *St. Faith's, London*, at 14*l.* each.

‡ Lord Mayor in 1754; when the arms now in the Hall were painted ; Mr. *Samuel Richardfon* being then Mafter ; *John March* and *Thomas Wotton* Wardens.

‖ Who gave the beautiful hiftorical painting (King *Alfred* beftowing a fmall loaf on a Beggar) which ornaments the Court-room.

4   HUIC

HUIC MURO AB EXTRA
VICINUS JACET
GULIELMUS BOWYER,
TYPOGRAPHUS LONDINENSIS,
DE CHRISTIANO ET LITERATO ORBE
BENE MERITUS;
AB UTROQUE VICISSIM REMUNERATUS:
QUIPPE CUNCTIS BONIS ET FORTUNIS SUIS
SUBITO INCENDIO PENITUS DELETIS,
MUNIFICENTIA SODALIUM STATIONARIORUM,
ET OMNIUM BONORUM FAVOR,
ABREPTAS FACULTATES CERTATIM RESTAURAVERE*:
TANTI HOMINEM VITÆ INTEGRUM,
SCELERISQUE PURUM, ÆSTIMANTES,
UT INGENII PRÆMIO EXUTUM
REDONARENT MERCEDE VIRTUTIS:
VIRIDEM DEPOSUIT SENECTAM, DEC. 27,
ANNO $\begin{cases} \text{ÆTATIS 74.} \\ \text{SALUTIS 1737.} \end{cases}$
PATRI, PATRONIS, POSTERISQUE EORUM,
IN PII ET GRATI ANIMI MONUMENTUM
PONI CURAVIT FILIUS,
MORIENS NOV. 18, 1777;
ANNUM AGENS SEPTUAGESIMUM OCTAVUM.

---

* In grateful remembrance of this event, the elder Mr. *Bowyer* had several metal cuts engraved, reprefenting a phœnix rifing from the flames, with fuitable mottoes; which were ufed by him, and by his fon, as ornaments in fome of the moft capital books they printed.

A buft

A buſt * of him is placed in Stationers Hall; with a good portrait of his Father *, and another of his Patron, Mr. Nelſon *. A braſs plate under the buſt is thus inſcribed in his own words, in conformity to a wiſh he had many years before communicated to his Partner:

" To the united muniſicence of
THE COMPANY OF STATIONERS,
And other numerous Benefactors:
Who,
When a calamitous Fire, *Jan.* 30, $17\frac{12}{13}$,
Had in one night deſtroyed the effects
Of WILLIAM BOWYER, Printer,
Repaired the loſs with unparalleled humanity:
WILLIAM, his only ſurviving Son,
Being continued Printer of the Votes of the Houſe of Commons,
By his father's merits,
And the indulgence of three Honourable Speakers;
And appointed to print the Journals of the Houſe of Lords,
At near LXX years of age,
By the patronage of a noble Peer;
Struggling with a debt of gratitude which could not be repaid †,
Left this Tablet to ſuggeſt
What worn-out Nature could not expreſs.

EX VOTO PATRONI OPTIMI AMICISSIMI
PONI LUBENTER CURAVIT CLIENS DEVINCTUS
J. NICHOLS, MDCCLXXVIII.

---

* Theſe were preſented to the Company of Stationers by *J. Nichols.*
† After this line, Mr. *Bowyer* had originally written as follows:
  " With an attachment to Literature which could not be indulged;
  " With deluſive hopes from a College intereſt or reputation;
" Experienced the conflicts of two oppoſite paſſions, Reſignation and Ambition.

A P-

A P P E N D I X.

P. 1. A ſon of *Ichabod Dawks* (who died *Feb.* 27, 1730, aged 70; and of whom ſee *Tatler*, N° 178.) is introduced by the author of " *Phædra* and *Hippolitus*," in his excellent poem, intituled, " *Charlettus Percivallo ſuo*,"

" Scribe ſecurus, quid agit Senatus,
" Quid caput ſtertit grave *Lambethanum* *,
" Quid Comes *Guilford*, quid habent novorum
                                    Dawksque Dyerque."

The intelligence of *Dawks* and *Dyer* † was conveyed throughout the kingdom, not by *printed* news-papers, but *in writing*, as the parliamentary minutes are now circulated ‡. The *Gallo-Belgicus* was the firſt news-paper publiſhed in *England*. *Cleiveland*, in his *Character of a London Diurnal*, ſays, " The original ſinner of this kind was *Dutch* ; *Gallo-Belgicus* the *Protoplaſt*, and the *modern Mercuries* but *Hans en Kelders*." The
                                                                                exact

* *Teniſon*.

† *Robert Dyer*, Eſq; ſon of this writer, died in *Gray's-Inn*, *September* 4, 1748; and left 20,000*l.* to *Chriſt's Hoſpital*.

‡ Yet it appears, by a periodical paper of 1709, that there were then actually publiſhed every week fifty-five regular papers ; " beſides a vaſt number of poſtſcripts, and other ſcandalous and ſe-
" ditious papers and pamphlets, that were hawked about the ſtreets." Many of theſe being at pre-
ſent totally forgotten, it may be a curioſity to point out their names :

The Daily Courant, (as its Title ſhews) 6 times a week,		6
The Supplement,		
The General Remark,	Monday, Wedneſday,	
The Female Tatler,	and Friday,	12
The General Poſtſcript,		
The *Britiſh* Apollo, *Monday* and *Friday*,		2
The *London* Gazette,		
The Poſtman,	Tueſday, Thurſday,	
The Poſtboy,	and Saturday,	12
The Flying Poſt,		

The Review,		
The Tatler,		
The Rehearſal Revived,	Tueſday, Thurſ-	
The Evening Poſt,	day, and Satur-	
The Whiſperer,	day,	21
The Poſtboy Junior,		
The City Intelligencer,		
The Obſervator, *Wedneſday* and *Saturday*,		2

55

See a ſhort character of each, in " The General Poſtſcript, *Oct.* 24, 1709."
   Between the years 1640 and 1660 appeared " The Parliament's Scout," " The Faithful Scout," " The *Scotch* Dove," " A Diary or an exact Journal of Parliaments," " The Diurnal, 1641— " 1659," " Perfect Occurrences," " The Moderate Intelligencer," " The Moderate Impartial " Intelligencer," " The Parliamentary Intelligencer," " The Kingdom's Intelligencer," &c. Theſe were ſucceeded by " The Gazette," " The Gazettes of *London* in *French*," *Engliſh* Gazettes, " 1680," " *Paris* Gazette," " *Weſtminſter* Gazette," " *Harlem's* Courant," " *L'Eſtrange's* Obſer-
" vators, 81, 82, 83," " *Mercurius Reformatus*, 89, 90, 91, 92," " *Heraclitus* ridens, 1681," " *Democritus* ridens by *Smith*," " *Momus* ridens, 90, 91," " *London* Mercury, 82, by *Croome*," " The *Orange* Intelligencer," " *London* Mercury," " News Domeſtick and Foreign by *T. Violett*," " Loyal, Impartial Mercury, by *E. Brooks*, 1682," " The True Proteſtant Mercury, 80, 81, 82, by " *Janeway*," " City Mercury concerning Trade, by *Everingham*," " *Mercurius Civicus*, 1669," " *Mercurius Anglicus*, 80, 81," " *Mercurius Publicus*, 80," *Veridicus* communicating the beſt " News, 81," " *Bifrons*, or, the *Engliſh Janus*, containing Domeſtick and Foreign News, 81," " *Urbanicus* § and *Ruſticus*, or the City and Country Mercury," " Infernus, or, News from the

§ An anceſtor of *Sylvanus Urban*, Gent.

                                                                " other

exact time when they were first printed I am unable to difcover ; but the intelligent editor of *Dodfley's* Old Plays, to whom I owe this information, has proved, vol. VIII. p. 112, that they were as early as the reign of Queen *Elizabeth*. In 1663 Sir *Roger L'Eftrange* (after more than twenty years fpent in ferving the royal caufe, near fix of them in jails, and almoft four under fentence of death in *Newgate)* fet up a news-paper, called, " The Public Intelligencer, and the News ;" the firft of which came out the 1ft of *Auguft*, and the fecond on *Thurfday, September* 3, and continued to be publifhed twice a week, *Mondays* and *Thurfdays*, till *Friday* the 19th of *January*, 1665, when he laid it down, on the defign then concerted of publifhing the *London* Gazette *, the firft of which papers made its appearance on *Saturday* the 4th of *February*. This paper fucceeded " The Parliamentary Intelligencer and Mercurius Pub-" licus," publifhed in defence of the Government, againft the " Mercurius Politicus." *L'Eftrange* defifted, becaufe, in *November* preceding, the *Oxford* Gazette began to be publifhed twice a week, in a folio half-fheet, the firft of which came out *November* 7, 1665, the king and queen, with the court, being then at *Oxford*; but, upon the removal of the court to *London*, they were called " The *London* Gazette," the firft of which was publifhed in *February* following, on a *Saturday*, the *Oxford* one having been publifhed on a *Tuefday* ; and thefe have been the days of publifhing that paper ever fince.

P. 3. The following authentic papers confirm what has been advanced in the text ; and are at the fame time an abundant proof of the benevolence of that age, and of the good opinion entertained of Mr. *Bowyer* by his contemporaries.

" *William Bowyer*, of the Precinct of *White Fryars*, within the City of *London*, Prin-
" ter, maketh oath, That, on the 30th day of *January*, in the year of our Lord 1712,
" there happened, between the hours of three and four, a fudden fire to break out, by
" accident unknown, in the working-rooms of him the faid *William Bowyer* ; which
" being directly over his lodging chambers, and burning with great violence, forced
" him, with his wife and children, to fave their lives by flight from their beds, with
" only fuch a fmall part of their common wearing-apparel as could on the fudden be
" taken with them, though not fufficient to cover them, leaving behind them a gentle-
" man of their family, who perifhed in the flames and was burnt to afhes. And the
" faid fire, in a very fhort time, not only burnt down to the ground the dwelling-houfe
" of the faid *William Bowyer*, and demolifhed and damaged others next the fame, to
" the value of eight hundred and two pounds fifteen fhillings and upwards, as the faid
" lofs and damages done to the deponent's faid houfe and thofe next the fame hath been
" computed by *George Quick*, Bricklayer, and *Edward Bayley*, Joiner ; but alfo totally
" confumed all the houfehold goods, apparel, books of accompts, wares, ftock in trade,
" printing preffes, types, and other the utenfils of his profeffion, together with feveral
" hundred reams of paper bought and prepared for printing, and great numbers of
" divers and fundry books, and parts of books, printing and printed, to the value of four
" thoufand three hundred forty-four pounds two fhillings and five-pence, to the utter
" impoverifhment of this deponent and his family. And this deponent does verily be-
" lieve this to be fo moderate a computation, that it is rather much lefs than the true
" value of the whole lofs, than in any wife to exceed the fame. WILLIAM BOWYER.
" *Jurat.* 6to *Martii*, 1713, *coram me*, JAMES MEDLYCOTT."

" other World, by *Thomas Marlow*," " *Englifh* Intelligencer, by *Thomas Burrell*," " *London* Intelli-
" gencer, by *John Wallis*, 88, 89," " Moderate Intelligencer, by *Robinfon*," " Univerfal Intelli-
" gencer, *J. Wallis*, 88, 89," " Friendly Intelligencer, 79," " Domeftick Intelligencer, *Harris*, 79,
" 80, 81," " Intelligencer for promoting Trade, by *Harris*, 83," " True Domeftick Intelligencer
" both from City and Country, 79, 80," " Loyal Proteftant and True Domeftick Intelligencer,"
" The Proteftant *Oxford* Intelligencer, 71, by *T. Benfkin*," " Poor *Robin's* Intelligence, 76,"
" *Englifh* Courants, 80," " Proteftant Courant, 82," and " *London* Courant, 88."
* So called from its being fold for a piece of money called a gazet. See *Dodfley's* Plays, X. 64.
" To

" To the Right Honourable Sir *Samuel Stannier*, Knt. Lord Mayor of the City of *Lon-*
" *don*, and to the Worſhipful the Court of Aldermen of the ſaid City ;
" The humble Petition of *William Bowyer*, of the Precinct of *White-Fryars*, within the
" City of *London*, Printer,

" MOST HUMBLY SHEWETH,

" That on the 30th of *January*, 1712, there happened a dreadful and ſudden fire in
" the night-time, which not only burnt down to the ground the dwelling-houſe of your
" Petitioner, and demoliſhed and damaged others adjoining to the ſame, but alſo con-
" ſumed all the houſehold goods, apparel, books of accompts, wares, ſtock in trade,
" printing preſſes, and other utenſils of his profeſſion, together with ſeveral hundred
" reams of paper bought and prepared for printing, and great numbers of divers and
" ſundry books, and parts of books printing and printed, as appears by the oath of your
" Petitioner and others. That the whole loſs, upon a moderate computation, amounts
" unto the ſum of five thouſand one hundred and forty-ſix pounds and upwards,

" That your Petitioner and family (who before this ſaid accident happened lived in a
" reputable manner, and had acquired a conſiderable ſubſtance, and were helpful to
" others) are now reduced to extreme want and poverty, and not able to ſupport him-
" ſelf and family without the charity of her Majeſty's loving ſubjects.

" Your Petitioner therefore humbly prays your Lordſhip and the Worſhipful the
" Court of Aldermen of this City to take his deplorable condition into conſi-
" deration ; and to certify the premiſſes to the Right Honourable the Lord High
" Chancellor of *Great Britain*, to the end that your Petitioner may obtain her
" Majeſty's moſt gracious Letters Patent, by way of Brief, for a collection of
" the charity of her Majeſty's loving ſubjects for the relief of your Petitioner
" and his family in this their great diſtreſs. And your Petitioner, as in duty
" bound, ſhall ever pray, &c."

" * To the Right Honourable SIMON Lord HARCOURT, Baron of STANTON HARCOURT,
" Lord High Chancellor of *Great Britain*.

" MAY IT PLEASE YOUR LORDSHIP,

" We whoſe names are hereunto ſubſcribed, being the Mayor, Aldermen, and Juſtices
" of the Peace, of the City of *London*, and other inhabitants of the ſaid City, do hum-
" bly certify your Lordſhip, That it hath been made appear to us, upon the humble
" Petition of *William Bowyer*, of the Precinct of *White Fryars*, within the ſaid City of
" *London*, Printer, That, on the 30th day of *January*, in the year of our Lord 1712,
" there happened a dreadful and ſudden fire in the night-time, by accident unknown,
" which, by reaſon of the ſuddenneſs and violence thereof, forced the ſaid *William*
" *Bowyer*, with his wife and children, to fly for their lives out of their beds with only
" ſuch a ſmall part of their common wearing apparel as could on the ſudden be taken
" with them, though not ſufficient to cover them, leaving a gentleman of their family
" behind, who periſhed in the flames, and was burnt to aſhes ; and in a very ſhort time
" the ſaid fire not only burnt down to the ground the dwelling houſe of the ſaid *William*
" *Bowyer*, and demoliſhed and damaged others next the ſame, amounting to the value
" of eight hundred and two pounds fifteen ſhillings and ſeven-pence, as appears by the
" oaths of *George Quick* and *Edward Bayley*, creditable and ſubſtantial workmen, but
" alſo totally conſumed all the houſehold goods, apparel, books of accompts, wares,
" ſtock in trade, printing preſſes, types, and other the utenſils of his profeſſion, together
" with ſeveral hundred reams of paper bought and prepared for printing, and great

* The form of this petition was taken from an earlier one (of which I have a copy in MS.) to Lord Chancellor *Cowper*, by which it appears, that on the 9th of *February*, 1707-8, there was ſo dreadful a fire in the pariſhes of *St. Clement Danes* and *St. Martin in the Fields*, as to burn down 36 houſes and demoliſh 14 others, to the impoveriſhment of 100 families, who loſt 17,880*l.* 5*s.* 6*d.*

" numbers

" numbers of divers and sundry books and parts of books, printing and printed, to the
" value of four thousand three hundred and forty-four pounds two shillings and five-
" pence, or thereabouts, as appears upon the oath of the said sufferer, so that the whole
" loss, upon a moderate computation, amounts to the sum of five thousand one hundred
" and forty six pounds eighteen shillings: that the said poor sufferer, before this sad
" calamity, had acquired considerable substance, and lived in a creditable manner, but
" is now reduced to extreme want and poverty, and not able to support himself and
" family without the relief of her Majesty's loving subjects. We therefore recommend
" the premisses to your Lordship's charitable consideration, to the end your Lordship
" will be pleased to grant unto the said poor sufferer Her Majesty's most gracious Letters
" Patent, Licence, and Protection, under the great seal of *Great Britain*, for a collection
" of charity for the relief of the said poor sufferer and his family, as to your Lordship
" shall seem meet. Given under our hands this 6th Day of *March*, 1713."

A brief was accordingly granted; of which the clear amount was 1514*l.* 13*s.* 4¾*d*; from which Mr. *Bowyer* received 1377*l.* 9*s.* 4*d.* being a dividend of 5*s.* 4¼*d.* in the pound on his whole loss. The remainder (viz. 136*l.* 14*s.* 0¾*d.*) was paid to other sufferers. In the mean time the following paper was circulating among his private friends:

" WHEREAS, by the Providence of Almighty God, Mr. *William Bowyer*, Printer,
" hath lately had his dwelling house, his goods, his founts of letters, presses, and other
" utensils, all suddenly destroyed by a sad and lamentable fire; inasmuch that he was
" not able to save either his own, or his family's wearing cloaths, and very little else
" of any thing, the whole loss amounting to several thousands of pounds, to the ruin of
" himself and family, not to mention others that have suffered together with him:
" We whose names are hereunto subscribed, not knowing how soon it may be our own
" case, do, out of compassion to him, give and contribute the sums following; viz.

John Baskett, five guineas	*Thomas Simpson*, three guineas	*J. Osborn*, one guinea
Timothy Goodwin, ten guineas	*R.* and *J. Bonwicke**, two guineas	*James Round*, one guinea
John Walthoe, five guineas	*Richard Wilkin*, two guineas	*Thomas Caldecott*, one guinea
Benjamin Tooke, five guineas	*Andrew Bell*, two guineas	*Thomas Medcalfe*, two guineas
Robert Vincent, five guineas	*Edmund Parker*, one guinea	*Elizabeth Pawlett*, one guinea
Christopher Bateman, five guineas	*Eben. Tracey*, one guinea	*Arthur Bettesworth*, one guinea
Samuel Manship, five guineas	*Thomas Norris*, one guinea	*Thomas Brewer*, three guineas
Nicholas Bodington, five guineas	*Ralph Smith* †, two guineas	*Edmund Curll*, one guinea
John Nicholson, five guineas	*George Strahan* ‡, two guineas	*Philip Overton*, one guinea
Samuel Hoole, ten guineas	Mr. *Mount*, two guineas	*Nathaniel Dodd*, one guinea
Jacob Tonson, five guineas	Mr. *Chiswell*, two guineas	*Owen Lloyd*, one guinea
William Freeman, five guineas	*Richard Parker*, one guinea	*Isaac Cleave*, one guinea
Charles Harper, five guineas	*Richard Mount*, two guineas	*Robert Podmore*, one guinea
Daniel Midwinter, five guineas	*John Sprint*, three guineas	*John Taylor*, two guineas
William Taylor, five guineas	*Daniel Browne* §, two guineas	*R. Robinson*, three guineas
S. Sheafe, five guineas	*S. Butler*, one guinea	*Thomas Bever*, one guinea
Jacob Tonson, [jun.] five guineas	*George Conyers*, one guinea	*Thomas Clark*, two guineas
Edward Farell, five guineas	*James Knapton*, three guineas	Widow *Jones*, one guinea
Thomas Guy, five guineas	*Emanuel Matthews*, one guinea	Madam *Phillips*, three guineas
Bernard Lintott, five guineas	*John Baker*, one guinea	Madam *Geary*, one guinea
William Innys, five guineas	*Henry Overton*, one guinea	Mr. *Eston*, one guinea
H. Clements, five guineas	*A. Baldwin*, two guineas	Mr. *Poulett*, one guinea
Francis Horton, five guineas	*Jonah Bowyer*, two guineas	Mr. *Harding*, ten shillings
Henry Rhodes, five guineas	*Matthew Wotton*, one guinea	Mr. *Bowles*, ten shillings
Mr. *Donall*, five guineas	*Edward Castle*, two guineas	Mr. *Browne*, ten shillings
John Morphew, one guinea	*John Pemberton*, one guinea	Mr. *Bright*, ten shillings
Robert Whitledge, one guinea	*Samuel Keble* ‖, two guineas	Madam *Isted*, ten shillings

* " Lost by *Bonwicke* 4*l.* 8*s.* 5¼*d.*" *W. B.*

† " Lost by Mr. *Smith's* widow for printing *Bull's Latin* Works, not paid for, 100*l.* for which
" my father had some books assigned over to him, which did not bring a quarter of the money." *W. B.*

‡ " Lost by him *l.*" *W. B.*   § " Lost by the son's death . . . . . ." *W. B.*

‖ " Given to Mr. *Keble's* son two guineas, *Dec.* 25, 1766." *W. B.*

These

These names have been particularly specified, not only as it shews who were then the principal persons in the profession of bookselling, but because it happens that the original subscription-papers signed by each of them is now before me. The contributions of the Printers were as follows:

Mr. *Baskett**, and others her Majesty's Printers, ten guineas

Mr. *Andrews*,
Mr. *Barker*,
Mr. *Nutt*,
Mr. *James*, } five guineas each

Mr. *Rawlins*,
Mr. *Heptinstall*, } four guineas each
Mr. *Wilde*,

Mr. *Williams*,
Mr. *Darby*,
Mr. *Matthews*, } three guineas each
Mr. *Wilmer*,
Mr. *Leach*,

Mr. *Hodgkin*,
Mr. *Downing*,
Mr. *Roberts*,
Mr. *Browne*, } two guineas each
Mr. *Buckley*,
Mr. *Grover*,

Mr. *Meers*,
Mr. *Watts*, } two guineas each

Mr. *Humfreys*,
Mr. *Gwillim*,
Mr. *Tookey*,
Mr. *Clarke*,
Mr. *Beardwell*,
Mr. *Sowle*,
Mr. *Wilde*,
Mr. *Mayo*,
Mr. *Howlett*, } one guinea each
Mr. *Gardyner*,
Mr. *Downing*,
Mr. *Holt*,
Mr. *Leake*,
Mr. *Pearson*,
Mr. *Botham*,
Mr. *Jenour*,
Mr. *Motte*,

Mrs. *James*, a silver cup. (See p. 485.)

The collection among the Printers was 96*l.* 15*s* †. Thus far the names have been given of his own fraternity only; but from other friends Mr. *Bowyer* received large sums. Mr. *Nelson* obtained for him, from the Earl and Countess of *Thanet*, 25*l.*; from Lord *Weymouth* 20*l.*; from Lord *Guilford* 10*l.*; and from others of his friends 412*l.* 7*s.*; Mr. *Sare* collected 66*l.* 3*s.* 3*d.*; Mr. *Sherlock* 48*l.* 17*s.* 6*d.*; the University of *Cambridge* gave 40*l.*; the Dean and Chapter of *Canterbury* 30*l.*; and his " Cousin *Scott*" ten guineas.

The whole of the contributions thus raised amounted to   —   £.1162 5 10
His dividend on the brief   —   —   —   1377 9 4

Total sum received by Mr. *Bowyer*   —   —   —   2539 15 2

P. 3. l. 28. The library of Sir *Berkeley Lucy*, including that of Mr. *Nelson*, was sold by auction, not in 1759, but in 1760: the sale lasted 33 days, and there were 4886 articles, besides some others not then come to hand, but which were sold the following year in an anonymous auction.

P. 6. To the letters of Mr. *Nelson* already printed, I shall add another ‡; which is more particularly applicable to the subject of the present volume:

" Mr. WANLEY,   *May* 19, 1713.

" Pray do me the favour to write out the *Saxon* characters for Mr. *Bowyer*, as you " have kindly promised; dispatch in this affair is of great consequence, because my " Lord Chief Justice *Parker* does intend to assist towards repairing his misfortunes by " giving him a set of press letters, and is very uneasy that he is not ready to begin his " friend's book, which requires those characters to perfect it. You will oblige me very " much by your kindness to Mr. *Bowyer*, and I shall be ready to make you any acknow-

* " Given to Mr. *Baskett*, after his loss by fire, by *W. Bowyer* the son, a press complete out of " his own house, and the iron-work of another." *W. B.*
† A guinea then passed in circulation for 1*l.* 1*s.* 6*d.*
‡ I have copies of two excellent letters of advice from Mr. *Nelson* to his young cousins *George* and *Gabriel Hanger*, on their going to settle in *Turkey*; which are too long for a place in this volume, but are at the service of any future Biographer of Mr. *Nelson*.

" ledgement.

" ledgement. I have been confined near a month by the gout, but am now upon re-
" covery. I am, Sir, your affectionate fervant, ROBERT NELSON."

" I did do what is required underneath," fays Mr. *Wanley*, at the top of Mr. *Nelfon's*
letter, " in the moft exact and able manner that I could in all refpects. But it fignified
" little; for when the alphabet came into the hands of the workman (who was but a
" blunderer) he could not imitate the fine and regular ftroke of the pen; fo that the
" letters are not only clumfy, but unlike thofe that I drew. This appears by Mrs. *El-*
" *ftob's Saxon* Grammar, being the book mentioned by Mr. *Nelfon*."

P. 7. In addition to what has been faid of Dr. *Stanhope*, in pp. 7 and 30, it may be
added, that he was born *March* 5, 1659-60. His grandfather *George Stanhope*, D. D.
was chaplain to *James* I. and *Charles* I.; had the chancellorfhip of *York*, where he was
alfo a canon-refidentiary, held a prebend, and was rector of *Wheldrake* in that county.
He was, for his loyalty, " driven to doors with eleven children," and died in 1644. See
Walker's " Sufferings of the Clergy," Part II. p. 83. The Dean was twice married;
1. to *Olivia Cotton* (whofe epitaph is tranfcribed below *), by whom he had one fon
and four daughters. His fecond lady, who was fifter to Sir *Charles Wager*, furvived
him, dying *October* 1, 1730, aged about 54. One of the Dean's daughters was married
to a fon of Bifhop *Burnet*. Bifhop *Moore*, of *Ely*, died the day before Queen *Anne*;
who, it has been faid, defigned our Dean for that See, when it fhould fo have become
vacant. However, fee *Mafters's* " Hiftory of C. C. C." p. 348. Within the rails of
the communion-table at *Lewifham*, on a grave-ftone, is this memorial:

" Depofitum GEORGII STANHOPE,
S. T. P. Dec. *Cant.* et
Ecclefiæ hujus Vicarii, 1728."

And another monument, erected to him by his widow, is thus infcribed:

" In memory
Of the very Rev. GEORGE STANHOPE, D. D.
38 Years Vicar of this Place, and 26 of
the neighbouring Church at DEPTFORD;
Conftituted Dean of CANTERBURY,
A. D. 1703;
and thrice PROLOCUTOR of the Lower
Houfe of Convocation.
Whofe Piety was real and rational,
his Charity great and univerfal,
fruitful in Acts of Mercy,
and in all good Works:
His Learning was elegant and comprehenfive,
His Converfation polite and delicate,
Graceful without Precifenefs,
Facetious without Levity:
The good Chriftian,
the folid Divine,
and the fine Gentleman,
in him were happily united;

Who, though amply qualified for the higheft
Honours of his Sacred Function,
Yet was content with only deferving them,
In his Paftoral Office a Pattern to his People,
And to all who fhall fucceed him
in the Care of them.
His Difcourfes from the PULPIT
were equally pleafing and profitable;
a beautiful intermixture of the cleareft
Reafoning with the pureft Diction,
attended with all the Graces
of a juft ELOCUTION;
as his Works from the PRESS have fpoken
the Praifes of his happy Genius,
his Love of God and Men;
for which Generations to come
will blefs his Memory.
He was born *March* the 5th.
He died *March* the 18th, 1727-8,
aged 68 Years."

In the publications enumerated in p. 7, read " *Epictetus's* Morals, with *Simplicius's*
" Comment; and the Life of *Epictetus*, 1700," 8vo; and " The Truth and Excellence
" of the Chriftian Religion afferted againft *Jews*, *Infidels* and *Hereticks*; in Sixteen Ser-

* On a mural monument of white marble in *Lewifham* church: " In memory of *Olivia*, daughter
" of *Charles Cotton*, late of *Beresford*, in the county of *Stafford*, Efq; and wife of *George Stanhope*, D. D.
" Dean of *Canterbury*, and Vicar of this parifh church. By him fhe had iffue *Catharine* (deceafed),
" *Mary*, *Jane*, *George*, *Elizabeth*, and *Charlotte*. She departed this life *June* the 1ft, A. D. 1707."

" mons.

" mons, 1701, 1702, at *Boyle's* Lecture, 1706," 4to ; and add to the list twenty Sermons
published singly between the years 1692 and 1724, which are all particularised in *Let-
fame's* " Historical Register," p. 184. Add also, " The Grounds and Principles of the
" Christian Religion explained in a Catechetical Discourse for the Instruction of young
" People, written in *French*, by *J. F. Ostervald*. Rendered into *English* by Mr. *Humphrey Wanley*, and revised by *George Stanhope*, D.D. 5th edition, 1734, 7th edition,
" 1765 ;" and " Private Prayers for every Day in the Week, and for the several Parts
" of each Day * ; translated from the *Greek* Devotions of Bishop *Andrews*, with Addi-
" tions, 1730." In Dr. *Birch's* MSS. is a letter of Dean *Stanhope*, with some inscriptions relative to the *Boyle* family. There is a fine mezzotinto of him by *Faber*, from a
painting by *Ellis*.

P. 9. I shall transcribe below † one more of the consolatory letters received by Mr.
Bowyer.

* Of this posthumous volume the editor was Mr. *James Hutton*; who observes, that " Dean
" *Stanhope's* personal qualifications, prudence, and public spirit, bore a considerable resemblance to
" those of Bishop *Andrews*. His life was a constant, uniform pattern of chearful, undisguised, and
" unaffected piety. His uncommon diligence and industry, assisted by his excellent parts, had en-
" riched him with a large stock of polite, solid, and most useful learning. He had not indeed ac-
" quired the knowledge of so many languages as Bishop *Andrews*; but yet, besides his mother
" tongue, in which he had so great a command, he was a master of the *Latin, Greek, Hebrew*, and
" *French*. These he put to their proper use, not for any vain ostentation, but as instruments of pro-
" curing the knowledge of all those things which have rendered him an accomplished gentleman, a
" worthy man, and a substantial divine. His well-digested learning, accurate judgement, candour,
" and good-nature, shone very brightly in his conversation, as well as in his preaching and his writ-
" ings, all consecrated to the honour of God, and the promoting of virtue and religion : indeed
" some who have conversed most intimately with him have assured me, they never knew any that
" so continually spoke and acted with a regard to these ends. His preaching was really admirable
" and edifying; his style clear and plain, but noble; his reasonings easy and strong; his persua-
" sions powerfully moving; his action, and way of speaking, graceful, just, and affecting; his sub-
" jects well chosen and suited to his auditory. The greatest and best of his hearers (and he often
" had the greatest in this nation) might learn what was profitable from him ; which if they neg-
" lected to do, his Discourses will rise in judgement against them, and in the mean time demonstrate,
" that he omitted nothing necessary to deliver his own soul. His writings are, or may be, in every
" body's hand, and every body will judge of them as they please ; I shall therefore leave them to do
" so, and only affirm what I know from more than a single experience, that they are an inestimable
" treasure for the devout people of this nation. Were I to speak particularly of all his private and
" public virtues, of his constant preaching, and prudent and faithful discharge of all the parts of his
" ministry, the many charities and good works he did in the course of his life, and the liberal pro-
" vision (in proportion to his substance) which he made for them in his last will and testament, I
" should far exceed the brevity I propose. I hope some abler hand will give his life and character
" at large, and do justice to his memory; and so convince the world, that (though he was thereby
" eased of a great burden, yet) it was no small unhappiness to the church, that he was not raised
" to the highest order in it. In his translations, it is well known, Dr. *Stanhope* did not confine
" himself to a strict and literal version; but took the liberty of paraphrasing, explaining, and im-
" proving upon his author; as will evidently appear (not to mention any other work) by the
" slightest perusal of St *Augustine's* Meditations and the Devotions of Bishop *Andrews*."

† " Dear Sir, I cannot express how sorry I am for your loss. I do assure you, I am mightily con-
" cerned for you and Mrs. *Bowyer*, and do sympathize with you as with my own brother and sister. I
" heard that your loss happened on King *Charles* the Martyr's Day, and therefore I hope you will bear
" it with some Christian fortitude and magnanimity, as He did his great losses. In him you see that
" the greatest of kings and best of men are not exempted from worldly loss and crosses. *Job* was a
" very good man; for he had that character from Him who is the best Judge of men, ' That there
" was none like him in all the earth, a perfect and an upright man; one that feared God, and es-
" chewed evil.' Yet, you know, he lost not only all his great riches, but all his children too by
" violent deaths (which, blessed be God, you now enjoy safe!) He lost his health also, being afflicted
" with a most loathsome disease; and one of his greatest trials was, that his friends endeavoured to
" rob him of his integrity and innocence, and fix the odious character of hypocrite upon him.

" Now

P. 10. Mr. *Ballard*, born at *Campden* in *Gloucestershire*, was of a weak and sickly constitution, which determined his parents to put him to a habit-maker, as an easy business not requiring much bodily strength. The time he took up in learning the *Saxon* language was stolen from sleep, after his day's labour was over. The communicator of this article celebrated with him a festival, which he held for his friends, on having completed a transcript of a *Saxon* Dictionary, which he borrowed of Mr. *Browne Willis*, being not able to purchase it, and which he had improved with the addition of near a

" Now pray observe his deportment under all these great losses, crosses, and trials : ' Naked came
" I out of my mother's womb, said he, and naked shall I return thither. The Lord gave, and
" the Lord hath taken away, and blessed be the name of the Lord !' What a wonderful pattern is
" this of resignation of our wills to God's will, under the greatest losses that can befall us in this
" world ! And you know how God rewarded his patient suffering even in this life, for he made him
" twice as rich as ever he was before ; which I hope in God that he will so bless you, as he did many
" who lost all in the great fire of *London*. I verily believe that your friends will readily send you
" what money you have occasion for. For my own part, if I had money, I would as freely send it
" you as any man in *London* ; I am so well satisfied of your integrity and honesty of your principles,
" your diligence and faithfulness in your employment ; and I do assure you, that when God blesses
" me with money, neither you nor yours shall ever want as long as I have. I cannot comprise the
" half I have to say to you in a letter, but will come and see you next week. In the mean time I
" beg and pray you not to be dejected under your sufferings, but to stir up and exercise all your
" graces of faith, hope, patience, meekness, self-denial, and resignation, &c. according to examples
" of the Prophet *Habbakuk*, chap. iii. ver. 17. ' Although the fig-tree shall not blossom, &c. yet
" will I rejoice in the Lord, and joy in the God of my salvation.' But, above all, I recommend
" to your imitation the example of our blessed Lord and Saviour, and his Apostles, and the primi-
" tive Christians and Martyrs, and those Saints recorded in the eleventh chapter to the *Hebrews*, ' of
" whom the world was not worthy ;' yet, ' they wandered about in sheep-skins and goat-skins, being
" destitute, afflicted, and tormented ; wherefore, seeing we are encompassed with so great a cloud
" of witnesses, let us run with patience the road that is set before us ;' and so to the end of the twelfth
" chapter ; and pray make a collection of God's promises recorded in Scripture, and meditate often
" on them ; they will support and comfort you wonderfully ; as that *Rom.* viii. 28. that ' All things
" shall work together for good to them that love God.' This is infallibly certain, and never fails ;
" and so of the rest. In the great Dean of *Worcester's*[*] excellent Devotions, there is an admirable
" prayer for the assistance of the Holy Spirit to support us under all trials and sufferings, which I
" pray you both to make use of frequently, and get it by heart ; and pray visit that great and good
" man often, whom God preserve long a great ornament and blessing to the Church of *England* !
" I am sure you will reap great comfort and benefit by his conversation. Now, dear Sir, my
" prayers shall be as frequent for you both as for myself, that God would support you under your
" great trial, and grant you a happy issue out of all your sufferings, and prosper you with all hap-
" piness, which shall be the daily prayer of, dear Sir, your affectionate and sympathising friend,

" R. MONTGOMERY."

[*] Dr. *George Hickes* (who has been already mentioned in p. 6, as the biographer of Dr. *Grabe*) was born *June* 20, 1642 ; and entered of *St. John's College, Oxford*, in 1659. After the Restoration, he removed to *Magdalen-College*, and thence to *Magdalen Hall* ; and at length, in 1664, was chosen fellow of *Lincoln College*. He was made chaplain to the duke of *Lauderdale* in 1676 ; who took him next year into *Scotland*, where he received the degree of D. D. in a manner particularly honourable to him. He was promoted to a prebend of *Worcester* in *March*, 1679-80 ; made chaplain to the King in 1681 ; and dean of *Worcester* in *August* 1683. At the Revolution, refusing with many others to take the oaths, he fell under suspension in *August* 1689, and was deprived in *February* following. He continued in possession, however, till *May* ; when, reading in the *Gazette* that his deanry was granted to Mr. *William Talbot* (afterward successively bishop of *Oxford, Salisbury*, and *Durham*). he immediately drew up, in his own hand-writing, a claim of right to it, directed to all the members of that church, and in 169 t. affixed it over the entrance into the choir. The earl of *Nottingham*, then secretary of state, called this " Dr. " *Hickes's* Manifesto against Government." From this time he was under the necessity of absconding till *May* 18, 1699, when Lord *Somers* obtained an act of council for a *Noli prosequi*. He was in the mean time consecrated, *Feb.* 4, 1693-4, among the Nonjurors, suffragan bishop of *Thetford*. Some years before he died, he was grievously tormented with the stone ; and at length his constitution, though naturally very strong, gave way to that distemper, *Dec.* 15, 1715.—He was a man of universal learning, and particularly skilful in the old Northern languages and antiquities ; and has given us some writings in this way, which will be valued when all his other works (consisting principally of controversial pieces on politicks and religion) are forgotten. He was also deeply read in the primitive Fathers of the Church, whom he considered as the best expositors of Scripture.

thousand.

thousand words, collected from his own reading. Lord *Chedworth* and the gentlemen of his hunt, who were used to spend annually in the hunting season about a month at *Campden*, hearing of his fame, generously allowed him an annuity of sixty pounds * for life, upon which he retired to *Oxford*, for the benefit of the *Bodleian* Library. Dr. *Jenner*, President, made him one of the eight clerks of *Magdalen College*; and he was afterwards one of the university beadles. He died rather young, owing, it was thought, to intense application to his studies. He left large collections behind him, but published only the "Memoirs of illustrious Ladies," of which Mr. *Gough* has the original MS. He drew up an account of *Campden* church in 1731, which was read by Dr. *Morell* at the Society of Antiquaries, *Nov.* 21, 1771. Among the benefactors to the church and poor of *Campden*, is Mr. *John Ballard*, physician of *Western-sub-edge* (as by the inscription on his tomb 1678); who was elder brother to *George Ballard's* grandfather *Thomas*. Mr. *Mores*, who mentions a curious MS. transcribed by Mr. *Ballard*, calls him "a mantua-maker +, a person studious in *English* antiquities, laborious in his "pursuits, a *Saxonist*, and after quitting external ornaments of the sex, a contemplator "of their internal qualifications." He died in the latter end of *June*, 1755.—I shall insert below an extract of an unpublished letter from Mr. *Ballard* ‡ to Dr. *Rawlinson*, which has been obligingly communicated by the Rev. Mr. *Price*, from the original in the *Bodleian* Library.

* They offered him an annuity of 100l.; but he modestly told them that 60l. were fully sufficient to satisfy both his wants and wishes.

+ "I know not what additions Mr. *George Ballard* can make to Mr. *Stowe's* Life. This I "know, that being a taylor himself, he is a great admirer of that plain honest Antiquary." *Letter from Mr. Thomas Hearne to Mr. Baker, Oxford, July 3, 1733.*

‡ "HONOURED SIR,
"Having been informed by my friend Mr. *Rawlinson* of *Pophills* of your noble design of conti-
"nuing Mr. *Wood's* 'Athenæ,' and that any notices which would be serviceable toward such an
"undertaking would be kindly received, I drew up a short account of the life of my late learned
"and ingenious friend Mr. *Graves*. I am truly sensible how unfit I am to attempt any thing of
"this kind, and especially of so worthy a person; but the great veneration I have for the memory
"of so dear a friend, and imagining but few of his other more learned correspondents had an oppor-
"tunity of having a more perfect knowledge of him, I have therefore ventured to inform you that
"*Richard Graves* ||, Esq; was born at *Mickleton*, in *Gloucestershire*, anno 1676, and was the son of
"*Samuel Graves*, Esq; who was the son of *Richard Graves* §, (who was Lord of the Royalty of the
"Hundred of *Kiftesgate*, and of the manors of *Mickleton*, *Aston*, and *Weston*, in this county; for
"many years one of the benchers, and at length reader of *Lincoln's Inn*) who was the son of *Ri-*
"*chard Graves*, who was the son of *John Graves* §, of *Beamsly* in *Yorkshire*, Gent. of the family of
"*Graves* of *Heyton* in that county. He was educated in grammar learning partly at *Campden*, and
"partly at *Stratford upon Avon* in *Warwickshire*, but chiefly at the former place, under the tuition
"of Mr. *Robert Morse*. From thence he was sent to *Oxford* about the year 1693; was fixed in
"*Pembroke College*; how long he continued there, or what degrees he took, as yet I am ignorant.
"But being delighted with a private life, he retired to his manor-house at *Mickleton*; where he was
"an indefatigable student in antiquities. He was a very obliging communicative gentleman, and
"of such a sweet deportment, as gained him the love and esteem of all those that had the honour
"and happiness of his conversation. To be short, he was a gentleman endowed with all those ex-
"cellent qualifications which might justly intitle him Great and Good; he was a complete master
"of the *Greek*, *Latin*, and *Saxon* tongues; was admirably well read and skilled in the *Roman* and
"*British* antiquities; and was a most curious Historian, Antiquary, and Medalist. Besides curious
"letters, pedigrees, &c. that are made public in the performances of several learned men; he has
"drawn up (in middle-sized octavo) an Historical Pedigree of his own family, most elaborately
"done; and had likewise made vast collections towards the history and antiquities of *Kiftesgate*

|| Whose portrait, engraved by *Vertue*, is preserved in Dr. *Nash's* "History of *Worcestershire*," vol. I. p. 298; where there is a pedigree at large of this family, so "eminent for producing many learned and valuable men." Of his son, *Morgan Graves*, Esq; there is a portrait in mezzotinto by *Valentine Green*.

§ Portraits of both these gentlemen, by *Vertue*, are likewise preserved by Dr. *Nash*.

"Hundred,

P. 11. *Effay on the great affinity, &c.*] " Mr. *Pegge* wrote to me, *November* 1775, that
" this was fo fcarce and unknown, that Mr. *Philip Carteret Webbe* infifted upon it that
" there was no fuch work. He defired my advice; and I fent him an abftract or view of
" it from the prefent-book to Mr. *Baker*, I think, which ftands in *St. John's College* Li-
" brary, *Cambridge*. 'Tis a thin 8vo." *T. F.* Mr. *Gough* has a copy, and it is not
very fcarce.

P. 12. To the books here enumerated add, " *Hickes's* Thefaurus, 1711," 3 vols. folio;
" Oratio in publicis Academiæ *Oxonienfis* Scholis, in laudem clariffimi doctiffimique viri
" *Thomæ Bodleii*, Equitis Aurati, Publicæ ibidem Bibliothecæ Fundatoris habita ab infig-
" niffimo viro, tam ingenio quàm doctrinâ excellenti, *Edmundo Smith*, A. M. ædis Chrifti
" alumno, 1711," 4to; *Ecton's* " Liber Valorum, 1711," 8vo; " The Corruptions of
" the Church of *Rome*, in relation to Ecclefiaftical Government, the Rule of Faith, and
" Form of Divine Worfhip. In anfwer to the Bifhop of *Meaux's* Queries. By the
" Right Reverend Dr. *Bull*, late Lord Bifhop of *St. David's*. With an Introductory
" Letter from the Bifhop of *Meaux* to Mr. *Nelfon*. The fourth edition. *London*,
" printed by *W. B.* for *Richard Sare*, 1714," 8vo. " *C. Plinii* Panegyricus, &c. in ufum
" Delphini, 1716," 8vo; *Rowe's* " Tranflation of *Salluft*, 1716," 12mo; a moft beau-
tiful edition of " *Schrevelius's* Lexicon, 1717," 8vo; the fubfcription edition of *Pope's*
Homer, and feveral fubfequent editions in folio and 12mo. It may be worth obferving, that fcarcely a fingle circumftance relative to this publication is forgotten. By Mr.
Bowyer's accompt-books it appears, that no more than 660 were printed in 4to. Befides that number, Mr. *Lintot* printed of vol. I. in folio *for fale*, 250 on *large paper*, and

" Hundred, and the feveral places where his eftate lay, which he had collected with very great
" pains and expence from the Domefday Book, from MSS. and records in the *Tower*, *Cottonian*
" and *Bodleian* libraries, and many other ways; which he defigned by way of annals, in imitation
" of *Kennet's* Parochial Antiquities. And a little before his death had defigned to have metho-
" difed and compiled it in 3 volumes, folio. He was mafter of many much efteemed MSS. the
" greater part of which were purchafed after his death by *J. Weft*, Efq; a gentleman of very extra-
" ordinary accomplifhments. His collection of medals (which were about 500, among which were
" many very valuable pieces) confifted chiefly of *Greek* and *Roman* coins, a great part of which I
" collected for him, from *Worcefter*, *Gloucefter*, *Marlborough*, *Devizes*, and feveral other places; all
" which coins were purchafed after his death by *Roger Gale*, Efq; an intimate acquaintance of Mr.
" *Graves*, who is a great mafter of thofe ftudies, and many other ufeful parts of learning. He died
" (to the great grief of all true lovers of antiquity, as well as of all thofe who knew him) upon
" *Wednefday* about feven o'clock in the morning, being the 17th day of *September*, 1729, in the 53d
" year of his age, and is buried in a vault in the North Ifle of *Mickleton* Church, near to which is
" a very neat marble monument fixed in the wall, with the following infcription, compofed by
" *James Weft*, Efq;

" Subtus requiefcit
Ricardus Graves armiger, hujufce maneriidominus;
Vir fi quis alius defideratiffimus;
Qui eximias animi dotes mira indolis fuavitate
temperans,
Tam charus omnibus vixit quam effufa erat erga
omnes benevolentia:
Liberos tenerrimo affectu,
Amicos inconcuffâ fide, femper profecutus.
Inter hæc otii literati ftudiis effiorefcens,
Ruris feceffum hiftoriarum varietate eleganter
defluxit.
Nec vero ut doctis fæpe contingit,
nullibi nifi in patria fua peregrinus,
Cum res *Græcas Romanafque* penitus perfpectas
haberet,
Noftras faftidiofe prætermifit.
His profecto unice deditus inveftigandis

Acerrimam operam navavit;
Dilucidandis omnem adhibuit diligentiam.
Antiquitates demum loci vicinitate commendatas
Propriis illuftrare fcriptis occeperat;
Incheati operis gloriam adeptus,
Confummati fama mortis interventu privatus.
Uxorem duxit *Elizabetham* filiam et cohæredem
Thomæ Morgan armigeri,
Ex qua
Quatuor filios duafque filias fuperftites reliquit.
Quarum una (pro dolor) fubtus paterno fateri
adhæret.
Obiit Ille decimo feptimo *Septembris*,
Anno Domini 1729, æt. 53.
Ne tantas patris virtutes nefcirent pofteri,
Hoc monumentum pofuit
Morgan Graves, arm.
Filius natu maximus."

1750

1750 on *small paper*. Of the following volumes the same number of large copies, but only 1000 of small. Of the first 12mo edition 2500 copies were printed, which were soon sold, and another edition of 5000 immediately printed *.

P. 12. l. 1. *Add this note* †, " Agreement *Aug*. 16, 1715, between *William Brome* exe-
" cutor to Mr. *Urry*, the Dean and Chapter of *Christ Church, Oxon*, and *Bernard Lintot*,
" bookseller ; reciting the Queen's licence to *Urry*, to print *Chaucer* for 14 years, from
" *July* 25, 1714, assigned over by him to *Lintot*, *December* 17 following. *Urry* dying
" soon after left *Brome* executor. The agreement recites *Urry's* intention to apply part
" of the profits towards building *Peckwater* Quadrangle. *Brome* assigns his right to
" the Glossary and licence to *Lintot* for remainder of the term ; the Dean and Chapter
" and Mr. *Brome* to deliver to *Lintot* a complete copy of *Chaucer* and Glossary, and to
" correct it, or get it corrected. *Lintot* to print 1250 copies, 250 on royal paper, and
" 1000 on demy, at his own charge, and to furnish a number of copies not exceeding 1500,
" and have one third of the profit. If the subscribers did not amount to 1250, then the
" remainder to be sold, and the profits equally divided ; the Dean and Chapter's share
" to be applied to finish *Peckwater* Quadrangle.

" 1000 copies small paper, at 30s.   — — —   £.1500
" 250 large, at 50s.   — — — —   625

                     £.2125

" *Lintot* one third   — — —   £.708 6s. 8d.
" Remainder for Dean and Chapter and Mr. *Brome*   £.1416 13s. 4d.
   L. 5. read 5 volumes, 8vo.

L. 7. The *Greek* " Spicilegium in usum scholæ *Felstediensis* sub *S. Lydiat* gymnasi-
" archo," was printed 1698, 12mo, for *H. Bonwicke* ‡, at the *Red Lion, St. Paul's Church
Yard* ; and the edition of 1738, for *J.* and *J. Bonwicke*, at the same place and sign.

* " The greatness of the design, the popularity of the author, and the attention of the literary world, naturally raised such expectations of the future sale, that the booksellers made their offers with great eagerness ; but the highest bidder was *Bernard Lintot*, who became proprietor on condition of supplying, at his own expence, all the copies which were to be delivered to subscribers, or presented to friends, and paying two hundred pounds for every volume. The encouragement given to this translation, though report seems to have over-rated it, was such as the world had not often seen. The subscribers were five hundred and seventy-five. The copies, for which subscriptions were given, were six hundred and fifty-four. For those copies *Pope* had nothing to pay; he therefore received, including the two hundred pounds a volume, five thousand three hundred and twenty pounds four shillings without deduction, as the books were supplied by *Lintot*. Of the Quartos it was, I believe, stipulated that none should be printed but for the author, that the subscription might not be depreciated ; but *Lintot* impressed the same pages upon a small folio, and paper perhaps a little thinner ; and sold exactly at half the price, for half a guinea each volume, books so little inferior to the quartos, that, by a fraud of trade, those folios, being afterwards shortened by cutting away the top and bottom, were sold as copies printed for the subscribers. *Lintot* printed some on royal paper in folio for two guineas a volume ; but of this experiment he repented, and his son sold copies of the first volume with all their extent of margin for two shillings. It is unpleasant to relate that the bookseller, after all his hopes and all his liberality, was, by a very unjust and illegal action, defrauded of his profit. An edition of the *English Iliad* was printed in *Holland* in duodecimo, and imported clandestinely for the gratification of those who were impatient to read what they could not yet afford to buy. This fraud could only be counteracted by an edition equally cheap and more commodious ; and *Lintot* was compelled to contract his folio at once into a duodecimo, and lose the advantage of an intermediate gradation. The notes, which in the *Dutch* copies were placed at the end of each book, as they had been in the large volumes, were now subjoined to the text in the same page, and are therefore more easily consulted. Of this edition the sale was doubtless very numerous ; but indeed great numbers were necessary to produce considerable profit." Dr. *Johnson*.

† See Gent. Mag. 1779, p. 438.
‡ Brother to the schoolmaster.

P. 13.

P. 13. *note*, l. 2. Read, Mrs. *Bowyer's* daughter by Mr. *Alport*, her former husband. She had been married but a few weeks before the fire happened; and died *Dec.* 8, 1716, aged 30. Mr. *Bettenham* had a second wife, who died *July* 9, 1735, aged 39. His own death has been already mentioned to have happened in 1774, eight years after he had retired from business, which he had carried on to a great extent for more than fifty years. It may furnish, however, an additional instance of the uncertainty of human affairs, to observe that he died worth less than 400*l*.

P. 14. *Expunge the note on* Wanley, *and reform the whole thus:* Mr. *Humphrey Wanley*, son of *Nathaniel Wanley*[*], was born *March* 21, 1671-2. What time he could spare from the handicraft trade, to which his father put him, he employed in turning over old MSS. and copying the various hands, by which he acquired an uncommon faculty of distinguishing their dates. Dr. *Lloyd*, his diocesan, sent him to *St. Edmund's Hall, Oxford*, of which Dr. *Mill* was then principal, whom he greatly assisted in his collations of the New Testament; but he afterwards removed, by Dr. *Charlet's* advice, to *University College*. Mr. *Nelson*, who had endeavoured to procure for Mr. *Wanley* the office of librarian to the *Cottonian* library, introduced him to the office of Secretary [†] to the Society for propagating Christian Knowledge. He was soon after employed in arranging the valuable collections of *Robert* Earl of *Oxford*, with the appointment of librarian to his Lordship. In this employ he gave such particular satisfaction, that he was allowed a handsome pension by Lord *Harley*, the earl's eldest son and successor in the title, who retained him as librarian till his death. In Mr. *Wanley's Harleian* journal, preserved in the Earl of *Shelburne's* library, are several remarkable entries, as will appear by the specimens transcribed below. The journal, which begins in *March*, 1714-15, and is regularly continued till within a fortnight of his death, is kept with all the dignity as well as the exactness of the minutes of a public body. For instance, " *March* 2, 1714-15, Present my Lord *Harley* and myself. The Secre-
" tary related, that the Rev. and learned Mr. *Elstob* deceased some time since; and that
" he having seen Mrs. *Elstob* his sister, and making mention of the two MSS. which
" Mr. *Elstob* had borrowed from the Library (being 34. A. 16. and 42. A. 12.) she said
" she would take all due care to see them restored.—My Lord *Harley* expressing some
" compassion upon the unexpected decease of Mr. *Urry* of *Christ Church*; the Secre-
" tary shewed that two MSS. borrowed for his use by the present Bishop of *Rochester* [‡],
" while Dean of *Christ Church*, are not yet restored; and that he had a note under the
" Bishop's hand for the same. My Lord undertook to manage this matter."—" *July*
" 21, 1722, This day it pleased the most illustrious and high born lady, the Lady *Hen-*
" *rietta Cavendish Holles Harley* [§], to add to her former bounties to me, particularly
" to a large silver tea-pot formerly given to me by her noble Ladyship; by sending
" hither (to this library) her silversmith with a fine and large silver tea-kettle, lamp
" and plate, and a neat wooden stand, all of her Ladyship's free gift; for which great
" honour, as in all duty and gratitude bound, I shall never cease from praying Al-
" mighty God to bless her and all this noble family with all blessings temporal and eter-
" nal."—" *Sept.* 1, 1722, Mr. *Bowyer* [*Jonah* the bookseller] gave a small number of
" original and other papers."—" *August* 4, 1725, Mr. *Pope* came, and I shewed him but

* Of *Trinity College, Oxford*, B. A. 1653; M. A. 1657; vicar of *Trinity Church, Coventry*; and author of " The Wonders of the Little World." Brit. Top. I. pp. 158. 668.

† Several of their Letters on this occasion are preserved among the *Harleian* MSS. where are also a great number from Mr. *Bagford* and Mr. *Baker*, addressed to Mr. *Wanley* at the Coach-office in *Surrey Street*.

‡ Dr. *Atterbury*.   § Now Dutchess Dowager of *Portland*.

" few things, it being late."—" *Sept.* 11, 1725, The laft night, being in company with
" Mr. *Mofes Williams*, he told me, that he had that day feen, in the hands of young Mr.
" *Bowyer*, a fmall parcel of MSS. which were to be fold. Hereupon I went to Mr. *Bow-*
" *yer* this day, and bought them for my Lord in his abfence : they will be all marked with
" the date of this day. Thefe books [7 in number *] formerly belonged to the Rev. and
" learned Mr. *Ambrofe Bonwicke*, deceafed, who was formerly head-mafter of *The Mer-*
" *chant Taylors* fchool in *London*."—" *Jan.* 31, 1725-6, Young Mr. *Lintot* the bookfeller
" came enquiring after arms, as belonging to his father, mother, and other relations, who
" now, it feems, want to turn gentlefolks. I could find none of their names."—" *Feb.* 9,
" 1725-6, Went to Mr. *Bridges's* Chambers, but could not fee the three fine MSS. again, the
" Doctor his brother having locked them up. He openly bid for his own books, merely
" to enhance their price ; and the auction proves to be, what I thought it would be-
" come, very knavifh."—" *Feb.* 11, 1725-6, Yefterday at five I met Mr. *Noel*, and
" tarried long with him. We fettled then the whole affair touching his bidding for my
" Lord at the roguifh auction of Mr. *Bridges's* books. The Rev. Doctor, one of the
" brothers, hath already difplayed himfelf fo remarkably, as to be both hated and de-
" fpifed : and a combination among the bookfellers will foon be againft him and his
" brother-in-law, a lawyer. Thefe are men of the keeneft avarice ; and their very
" looks (according to what I am told) dart out harping-irons. I have ordered Mr. *Noel*
" to drop every article in my Lord's commiffion when they fhall be hoifted up to too
" high a price. Yet I defired that my Lord may have the *Ruffian* Bible, which I know
" full well to be a very rare and a very good book, &c."—" *March* 25, 1725-6, Young
" Mr. *Bowyer* the printer came, and faw many fine things here." Mr. *Wanley* died
July 6, 1726 †. There is an original picture of him in the *Bodleian* library : another
half-length fitting, in the room of the Society of Antiquaries. A mezzotinto print of
him was fcraped by *Smith* in 1718 from a painting by *Hill*. When admitted to the *Bod-*
leian Library, he made large extracts from the MSS. and promifed a fupplement to *Hyde's*
Catalogue of the printed books, which *Hearne* ‡ completed (and which was publifhed by
Robert Fyfher, B. M. in 1738.) He intended a treatife on the various characters of
MSS. with fpecimens, *Mabillon's* work on that fubject being corrupted by the conceits of
the engravers, who inferted characters that never were nor could be ufed. Upon leaving
Oxford, he travelled over the kingdom in fearch of *Anglo-Saxon* MSS. at Dr.
Hickes's defire, and drew up the catalogue of them in his Thefaurus. Mr. *Bagford* ‖
mentions fome defign of his relating to a *Saxon* Bible.

* For which Lord *Oxford* paid feven guineas.
† " Infcription on Mr. *Wanley's* tomb-ftone in the parifh-church of *St. Mary-le-bowe* :

" Here lyes
Mr. *Humphry Wanley*,
Library-Keeper to the Right Honourable

ROBERT and EDWARD Earls of OXFORD, &c.
Who died the 6th day of *July*, MDCCXXVI.
In the 55th year of his age."

" N. B. This ftone lyes crofs the paffage from the North door, at the diftance of 6 feet 9 inches
" from it ; and on the other fide is within 6 inches of the communion rails." *Hearne*, Preface to
Chron. five Ann. de *Dunftaple*, p. vii.
‡ Ibid. p. xii. See alfo *Fyfher's* Preface to " Catalogus Imprefforum Librorum Bibliothecæ *Bod-*
" *leianæ*, 1738," where (ftrange to tell !) no mention is made at all of *Hearne's* labours on that fcore.
‖ *John Bagford*, the antiquary and great collector of old *Englifh* books, prints, &c. was born in
London. He had been in his younger days a fhoe-maker, afterwards a bookfeller ; and laftly, for the
many curiofities wherewith he enriched the famous library of Dr. *John Moore*, bifhop of *Ely*, his
Lordfhip got him admitted into *The Charter-Houfe*. He was feveral times in *Holland*, and in other
foreign parts, where he procured many valuable old books, prints, &c. fome of which he difpofed
of to the late Earl of *Oxford*, who, after his death, purchafed all his collections, papers, &c. for his
library. In 1707, were publifhed, in the Philofophical Tranfactions, his propofals for a General
Hiftory of Printing. He died at *Iflington*, a little before fix in the morning, *May* 15, 1716, aged 65

P. 14. *note*, l. 6, Read " petitioned the Merchant Taylors Company," &c.—A *Latin* copy of verſes by " *Ambroſe Bonwicke*, S. T. B. Coll. Div. *Jo. Bapt.* Soc." is in the *Oxford* Collection on the Death of King *Charles* II. 1685.

P. 15. To the ſhort note on Mr. *Sare* may be added the title of a pamphlet, pointed out to me by Mr. *Reed*, which is now become curious from its ſcarcity : " A Narrative " of the Proſecution of Mr. *Sare* and his ſervant *, for ſelling the ' Rights of the " Chriſtian Church,' in anſwer to what relates to that proſecution in the ſecond Part of " the Defence of the book, by *Samuel Hilliard*, M. A. Prebendary of *Lincoln*, 1709," 8vo. Mr. *Sare's* conduct in this tranſaction appears to have been uniform with his ge- neral good character through life. He was not the original publiſher of the book in queſtion; but a copy of it was ſold by his ſervant in the ordinary courſe of his trade. He had given offence, however, to ſome violent partymen, by having publiſhed ſome trea- tiſes of his friend Dean *Hickes*; and Mr. *Hilliard* took the opportunity of the above- mentioned obnoxious treatiſe to harraſs Mr. *Sare* with a proſecution, which ended in expoſing the malevolence of his accuſer, and an acknowledgement of Mr. *Sare's* " inte- " grity and good affection to the church and eſtabliſhment." Dean *Kennet*, who had countenanced Mr. *Hilliard* in preſenting the " Rights of the Chriſtian Church," became diſguſted at the attempt to proſecute a reputable bookſeller for a ſervant's ſelling a book in his abſence ; and in conſequence received his ſhare of abuſe in the pamphlet, from which he is properly vindicated in the " Life," publiſhed in 1730, 8vo. p. 107.

P. 15. *Humphrey Gower*, D. D. fellow of *St. John's College*, was one of the univerſity taxers in 1667 ; in which year he became rector of *Pagleſham* in *Eſſex* ; but reſigned that living, on being collated, by Biſhop *Gunning*, *Nov.* 20, 1675, to the rectory of *Newton* in the Iſle of *Ely* ; the ſame patron alſo conferred on him *Fen-Ditton* in *Cambridgeſhire*, *July* 4, 1677, being then D. D. and two years after made him maſter of *Jeſus College*, *July* 7 ; and prebendary of *Ely*, *Oct.* 25, 1679 : on *December* 3 following, he was elected maſter of *St. John's College* ; vice-chancellor of the Univerſity in 1680 ; and Lady *Margaret's* Profeſſor of Divinity in 1688. He was accounted a very learned man, and an excellent Governor of his college, to which he left 500*l.* towards purchaſing livings, and an eſtate at *Triplow*, worth nearly 100*l.* a year, to be annexed to the headſhip for ever. He died *March* 27, 1711, and was buried in *St. John's College* Chapel, with the follow- ing inſcription : " M. S. Depoſitum viri admodùm reverendi *Humphredi Gower*, S. T. P. " Coll. Divi *Johannis* Præfecti ; S. Theolog. pro D'na *Margareta* Profeſſoris ; Eccl. " *Elienſis* Canonici ; qui Collegium hoc per annos triginta & amplius ſtrenue & feliciter " rexerat. Obiit 27 *Martii*, A. D. 1711, ætatis ſuæ 74." He was probably, as bene- ficed in *Eſſex*, a benefactor to the re-building of *Harlow* church, which had been burnt 1708, his arms being among thoſe of other benefactors in the windows of the nave.

Ibid. *Francis Roper*, B. D. *Dunclmenſis*, fellow of *St. John's*, *Cambridge*, *Apr.* 2, 1666 (deceſſit † 1688) and vicar of *Waterbeach* in *Cambridgeſhire*, was collated to a

years ; and was buried the *Monday* following in the church-yard belonging to *The Charter-Houſe*. In 1728 a print was engraved of him, from a painting of Mr. *Howard*, by *George Vertue*. See an account of his entries, which was deſigned for a General Hiſtory of Printing, in the Catalogue of the *Harleian* Collection of MSS. vol. II. fol. *London*, 1759, from Nº 5892 to Nº 5910. His MSS. may be of uſe to ſuch as will take pains to extract good matter from a bad hand and worſe ortho- graphy. This may be eaſily forgiven to his education, far from learned, and all his improvements owing to the ſtrength of genius, ſeconded by unuſual diligence and induſtry. A number of his letters to *Humphry Wanley* may be ſeen in *The Britiſh Muſeum* ; and a large part of his collections is in the Public Library at *Cambridge*.

* Mr. *William Williamſon*, who ſucceeded his maſter in buſineſs. See p. 486.
† *Deceſſit* in College regiſters means, left the college, and cut his name out. A *bene deceſſit* granted to a member permits him to transfer himſelf to another college.

prebend

prebend in the church of *Ely* on the day his predeceſſor, Biſhop *Womack*, died, *March* 12, 1685-6; and was inſtalled *April* 1. He reſigned *Waterbeach* about *Michaelmas* following, and became rector of *Northwold* in *Norfolk*, *June* 7, 1687, which he reſigned ſoon after the acceſſion of King *William* III. He was deprived in 1690, for refuſing to take the oaths appointed by act of parliament; and dying *April* 13, 1719, was buried in *St. John's College* Chapel, without any memorial. *Bentham's Ely*, 258.

Ibid. Dr. *Jenkin*, whoſe mother's name was *Mary*, was baptized *Jan.* 31, 1656; *deceſſit* 1691; and became maſter *April* 11, 1711, ſucceeding Dr. *Gower*.

P. 16. l. 25. Read " *Phereponi* in ejus Opera Animadverſiones."

L. penult. *the youngeſt*] Fellow of *St. John's College*, *Cambridge*, now rector of *Ufford* (a college living) between *Peterborough* and *Stamford*.

P. 16. *refuſal of the abjuration oath*] " Mr. *Baker*, who died in 1740, was probably " the ſurvivor of all theſe. Theſe principles of the members of this ſociety made it " little agreeable at court, where however they had always one good friend (though he " by no means agreed with them in their ſentiments) Commiſſary Dr. *Rowland Hill*, " Paymaſter to the army in *Flanders* under King *William*. See Baronetage V. 215. One " day, upon ſome bad reports there from *Cambridge*, the then Lord *Carteret* ſaid, " ' Well, Mr. Commiſſary, what have you to ſay for your college now ?' ' Why, to be " ſure, I muſt own that circumſtances are rather againſt us, but though I hardly ſhall, " who am an old man, yet I dare ſay your Lordſhip will live to ſee that college as obſe- " quious as any other.' This prediction was completely fulfilled, when his Lord- " ſhip nobly promoted Dr. *Taylor*, who was the laſt that retained in ſecret the ſlighteſt " principles of this party. *From Dr. Taylor himſelf to me, all but the concluſion*." T. F.

P. 17. The MSS. of Mr. *Baker* ſupply the following dates:

" *Chriſtophorus Anſtey, Bercerienſis*, electus Socius *Apr.* 9, 1710,; *Brinkley* 1730— " 1733.

" *Johannes Newcome, Lincolnienſis*, Socius *Mart.* 31, 1707. Electus Magiſter *Feb.* " 6, 1734." Dr. *Newcome*, who was alſo rector of *Morton* in *Eſſex*, publiſhed a Sermon " On the ſure word of Prophecy, 1724," 8vo. Some verſes of his to Mr. *Prior* are in the Poſthumous Works of that Author.—Mrs. *Newcome* died ſome time before her huſband.

Ibid. Add to the books, *Motte's* and *Lowthorpe's* " Abridgements of the Philoſophical " Tranſactions," 4to; and " Pharmacopœia Collegii Regalis Medicorum *Londinenſis*, " *Londini*, Typis *G. Bowyer*, 1721," folio; with a View of the College Gate for a frontiſpiece.

P. 17. In a copy of the firſt edition of theſe Anecdotes, ſent to *St. John's College* library, ſome gentleman has entered this note: " It appears from the College books that " Mr. *Bowyer* never took the degree of B. A. and therefore never could be a candidate " for a fellowſhip."

Ibid. note †. " *Harbin* wrote a remarkable epitaph on Sir *Iſaac Newton*, and was har- " boured by Lord *Weymouth*, who, not knowing that he was author of the book on He- " reditary Right, gave him 100*l.* to carry to Mr. *Bedford*, who pocketed it without " ceremony." T. F.

P. 18. *Note. defuncti amici*] Young *Bonwicke* was here meant; and Mr. *Roper* was the *patronus* in p. 19.

P. 20. note, l. 3. " Mr. *Markland* had a right to read, or not to read, what book he " pleaſed: but would he have thought himſelf civilly uſed, had *Bentley* wrote ſo in the " ' Epiſtola Critica,' he that, when young, could reſent ſo warmly a meſſage intended " to ſet him right from a veteran of the firſt claſs ?" See p. 22. T. F.—The ſmart

pamphlet

pamphlet against Mr. *Markland*'s Remarks was written by the present Bishop of *Exeter*, just before he was chosen fellow, who also published an excellent edition of *Cicero's* " Epistolæ ad Familiares, *Cant.* 1749," 2 vols. 8vo.

P. 21. Having had occasion to consult Mrs. *Markland* on the subject of these Memoirs, she kindly told me, " I wish it was in my power to furnish you with any materials con- " cerning my poor brother's life, that would be useful to your designs. He was sent " early in life to a distant school, that I had not the least knowledge of him ; and it so " happened, that I was 30 years old before I saw him. He was son to the Rev. Mr. " *Markland*, vicar of *Childwall*, *Lancashire*. His father's life was strictly conformable " to the doctrine he preached to his flock, and was by all that knew him esteemed as an " ornament to the church, and a dignity to human nature."

Mr. *Abraham Markland* * of *Oxford* (very possibly a relation) published " Poems " on his Majestie's Birth and Restauration, his Highness Prince *Rupert*'s and his Grace " the Duke of *Albemarle*'s Naval Victories ; the late Great Pestilence and Fire of *London*. " *London*, 1667," 4to. The licence from *Lambeth* is granted " ingeniosissimo *Abrahamo* " *Marklando, Oxoniensi*."

P. 21. l. 9. read " *Euripidis Hippolytus* ex MS. Bibliothecæ Regiæ *Parisiensis* emen- " datus. Variis Lectionibus & Notis Editoris accessere Viri Clarissimi *Jeremiæ Mark-* " *land* Emendationes, *Oxon.* 1756," 4to.

Ibid. *Augustin Bryan* published a Sermon on the election of the Lord Mayor, 1718, 8vo.

P. 22. *Venusinæ*] See *Horace*, Od. III. iv. 9. and Sat. II. 1. 35. The " Quæstiones," I am happy to say, were finished, and have not been destroyed.—Mr. *Markland* found the Silvæ of *Statius* very corrupt, and much in need of the Critic's se- verest art. To say the truth, he must have had a great deal of courage to undertake the restoring a work so obscure in itself, and so mangled by others. The degree in which he has succeeded has been long since determined by the Learned. He himself seemed very con- fident that of 500 places which were before unintelligible, he had not left 40 unamended ; and the greater praise is due to him, as the corrections he made were chiefly *ex ingenio* & *conjectura*, there being no MS. copies of this book in *England*, and indeed very few any where. However, he owned himself much indebted to two old and valuable editions, which the commentators before him do not seem to have seen, or even heard of. The one was printed at *Venice*, A. 1472, and seen by him in the Duke of *Devonshire*'s library ; the other was printed at *Parma*, A. 1473, and belonged to the Earl of *Sunderland*; both of them in folio. Mr. *Markland* also occasionally corrected several passages in *Virgil*, *Horace*, *Ovid*, and the other *Latin* Poets. In the course of his remarks on *Virgil*, Mr. *Markland* took occasion to declare, " that there are a great many verses in the *Æneid*, " which he, though a very bad poet, would not have suffered to appear in any compo- " sition of his own, and that he had a pretty large collection of them by him." It is a pity he did not publish them : they would have entertained the curious, and perhaps have undeceived the prejudiced. The " *Statius*" as well as the " Epistola Critica" were addressed to his learned friend Bishop *Hare*, and Mr. *Markland* at that time was pre- paring an edition of *Propertius* with short Notes, and promised to oblige the world with

---

* Son of *Michael Markland* of *London*; elected from *Merchant Taylors* school a scholar of *St. John's College, Oxford*, in 1662, at the age of 17 ; B. A. *May* 8, 1666; M. A. *Feb.* 11, 1668-9. He was Senior of the great Act celebrated *July* 14, 1669. Afterwards he retired into *Hampshire*, and cultivated his talents for poetry and the *belles lettres*. Entering into holy orders, he was en- stalled in a prebend of *Worcester*, *July* 4, 1679; was afterwards beneficed near that place ; admitted D. D. *July* 5, 1692; and became master of *St. Cross* in *August* 1694. He published, in 1682, a Sermon preached before the Court of Aldermen of *London*; and two volumes of his Sermons, preached in the Cathedral of *Winchester*, were printed in 1729, 8vo.

4   the

the other poems of *Statius*; for which purposes he requested the communications of the Learned.

L. 14. *The Paralytic*] Q. Dr. *S. Clarke?*

P. 22. sub-note, l. 14. read, " I shall *not* change," &c.

P. 23. sub-note, l. 1. read, " his private tuition."

P. 24. note, l. 9. The old acquaintance was Bishop *Keene.* Mr. *Hall*, in the sub-note was *William Hall*, Esq; of *The Temple*.

P. 27. twice declined the *Greek* professorship] " The election is in the vice-chancellor, " master of *Trinity*, and two senior fellows of the same. There is another elector or " two: but *Trinity* usually makes a majority within itself, and always names a fellow " of their own society. From 1572, *i. e.* for above 200 years, there have been only " three exceptions, viz. *Andrew Downes* of St. *John's*, *Ralph Widdington* of *Christ*, " and *Joshua Barnes* of *Emanuel*; nor do I expect to see another instance *. In vain did " Dr. *Barford* try to break through the routine on *Fraigneau's* death. The *Hebrew* " Professorship is disposed of in the same way; so that, unless it could be proved that a " majority of the electors offered *Markland* their votes, he can by no means be said to " have declined the *Greek* Professorship. He rather declined to stand, or offer himself " a candidate for it; and no wonder, as I dare say he would never have got it, without " as much influence being employed by the Duke of *Newcastle* with the electors as " would have got it for a dunce.—Mr. *M.* received from 70 to 100*l.* from his fellow- " ship; which astonished us residents, who received only 20*l.* then. His expences must " have been contracted." *T. F.*

Ibid. In the sub-note, read *Walter Taylor*, M. A.

P. 28. Mr. *Clarke* took the degree of B. A. 1731; M. A. 1735; decessit 1736.—In l. 5. read, prebendary and residentiary † of *Chichester* in *September*, 1738; and chancellor of that church in *June*, 1770. He resigned *Buxted*, *November* 4, 1768, after having held that living more than 34 years. He had originally obtained it in the most respectable manner by the favour of Bishop *Hare*, assisted by the Duke of *Newcastle*. The Duke, I am assured, was some years afterwards so angry with him for offering to vote for Mr. *Mellish*, the Squire of the parish, as to abuse him grossly and forbid him his house. In 1767, however, Mr. *Clarke* repaid the original service by the excellent Dedication prefixed to his " Connexion of Coins;" where he takes a public opportunity not only of thanking his Grace for the obligations he had received, but also of acknowledging that they were not the effects of importunity, but owing to that disposition of doing good to others, that spirit of beneficence, by which his Grace was so remarkably distinguished. The excellent " Discourse on the Commerce of the *Romans*," so highly extolled by Dr. *Taylor* in his " Elements of the Civil Law," was written either by Mr. *Clarke* or Mr. *Bowyer*, and is reprinted in the " Miscellaneous Tracts." Mr. *Clarke* took a copy of the famous *Chichester* inscription mentioned in British Topography II. 287. which he caused to be engraved, and gave the plate to Mr. *Burrell*, with many curious papers relative to this county, and a drawing of a piece of *Roman* pavement found in the bishop's garden at *Chichester*, which he supposed, by the proportions, covered a room 30 feet square, and of which the Duke of *Richmond* gave the Society of Antiquaries a drawing, 1749.—I shall add to this article an extract from an unpublished letter of Mr. *Maurice Johnson* to Mr. *R. Gale*, dated *March* 17, 1743-4: " We had last *Tuesday* a letter from " Mr. *W. Bowyer*, the printer, a member, who wrote, that his friend, Mr. *Clarke*, a

---

* This was written in 1780. There is another since; the present *Greek* Professor, Mr. *Cooke*, being of *King's*.

† To this preferment Dr. *Taylor* alludes, in the friendly letter prefixed to his " Lectiones Lysiacæ."

" prebendary

" prebendary of *Chichester* (likewise a most learned and worthy member) had acquainted
" him, there had lately been found in that city a *Roman* coin, representing *Nero* and
" *Drusus*, sons of *Germanicus*, on horseback, and on the reverse, C. CAES. DIVI. AUG.
" PRON. AVG. P. M. TR. P. III. P. P.   In the middle S. C. (which I find in
" *Occo's* Caligula A. U. C. 791, A. D. 40. p. 69) which, says he, though the very same
" which *Patin* on *Suetonius*, *Mediobarbus*, &c. have given us before ; yet brings one ad-
" vantage to the place where it was found, as it is a confirmation of the antiquity of the
" *Chichester* inscription, which, you know, is a little contested in *Horseley*, and proves
" the early intercourse of the *Romans* with the *Regni*, contrary to the opinion which
" bishop *Stillingfleet* conceived for want of such remains.   That ingenious gentleman,
" Mr. *Bowyer*, in a postscript to his letter, informs us, he is printing Mr. *Folkes's* Tables
" of our Silver Coins from the Conquest, about five sheets, I presume, at the expence
" of the Society of Antiquaries ; and believe it will be the most accurate account extant."
Some Letters of Mr. *Boyle*, in possession of the Rev. *Henry Miles* of *Tooting*, F. R. S.
increased by a part of the collection which had been communicated to Dr. *Wotton* by
Mr. *Boyle*, were presented by his son-in-law Mr. *Clarke* to Dr. *Birch*, through the hands
of Mr. *Bowyer*.

P. 28. sub-note, read *Chappelow* (afterwards *Arabic* professor) ; and for *Rowtell*
read *Bowtell*.   The examination for fellowships is in the week following *Midlent Sunday*,
and the election the *Monday* after that.   This extraordinary election is accounted for
in p. 16.

P. 29. *Vere Foster*, B. A. 1718 ; M. A. 1722 ; and B. D. . . . . .   He was a man of wit
and humour, as appears not only from the letters mentioned in p. 29, but from the following whimsical anecdote: " In his time *St. John's* was reckoned a Tory college * ; and
" a young fellow, who was looked upon as a Whig, was appointed to speak in the col-
" lege-hall an oration on the fifth of *November*.   After having dwelt for some time upon
" the double deliverance of that day, in his per-oration he passed from King *William* to
" King *George*, on whom he bestowed great encomium.   When the speech was over, Mr.
" *Foster* and the young orator being at table together, says the former to the latter, ' I
" did not imagine, sir, that you would decline King *George* in your speech.'—' Decline !
" what do you mean? I spoke very largely and handsomely of him.'—' That's what I
" mean too, sir, for you had him in every case and termination: *Georgius—gii—gio—*
" *gium.   O Georgi !*" This flash of merriment set the whole table in a roar." *W. S.*

Ibid. At *Barrow upon Soar* the best lime in *England* is got from a very hard blue stone.

P. 31. *note on Madox*, l. 3. read " Baronia Anglica, 1736."   His collections were bequeathed to *The Museum* by his widow, as an addition to the *Cotton* Library.   See more
of him in p. 93.

Ibid. The following description of Dr. *Thirlby* and some of his pupils is taken from a
worthless poem, published in folio, without a date, called " The Session of the Criticks."

" An embryo *Claudian* † was *Jortin's* pretence,
" Which was render'd abortive for want of the pence.
" The Censor view'd *Toby* with a smile of applause,
" And was almost inclin'd to have granted his cause,
" And bade him retire to his snarling vocation,
" He'd ensure him the nettle for the next dedication ;

---

* In proof of this, about the same time a gentleman walking through that college with Dr. *Sykes*,
and observing the inscription on the dial in one of the courts, *Vergo ad occasum*, the Doctor styled it
" a good motto for a nest of Tories."

‡ From this passage it seems as if Dr. *Jortin* had once intended to publish an edition of *Claudian*.

" But

" But as for friend *Jortin*, he only was fit
" To coax his Præceptor, and cry up his wit ;
" And since *C——b* to publish was not very forward,
" Let him drink his subscriptions with *R—s—t* and *N——d.*
" From his garret, where long he had rusted, came down
" *Toby Thirlby*, cock-sure that the prize was his own,
" Crying, ' Z—ds ! where's this *Bentley ?* I'll give him no quarter !'
"" And haul'd out the Preface to his fam'd *Justin Martyr.*
" His disciples came next ; *C——b* scar'd at the sight,
" As he thought of *Tom Tristram*, ran away in a fright."

P. 32. " There are many pretty places in the Custom-house that a scholar might be
" glad to accept. Queen *Elizabeth* made *Roger Ascham* bear-keeper." *T. F.*

P. 32, 33. I shall make no apology for enlarging the article of the GALES; though
some particulars have been already added in p. 96.—The Dean, who was born at *Scruton*
in 1636, was sent, at a proper age, to *Westminster* school ; and being admitted king's-scho-
lar there, was elected in his turn to *Trinity College* in *Cambridge*, and became fellow of
that society. Having taken his first degree in arts in 1656, he commenced M. A. in 1662.
In the prosecution of his studies he applied himself to classical and polite literature ;
his extraordinary knowledge in the *Greek* tongue recommended him, 1666, to the Regius
Professorship of that language in the university ; and the choice was approved,
by the accurate edition which he gave of the ancient Mythologic writers, as well phy-
sical as moral, in *Greek* and *Latin*, published at *Cambridge* in 1671, 8vo. This brought
his merit into public view, and, upon the death of Mr. *Samuel Cromleholme*, the following year, he was appointed to succeed him as head-master of *St. Paul's School* in *London* ;
soon after which, by his Majesty's direction, he drew up those inscriptions which are to
be seen upon *The Monument*, in memory of the dreadful conflagration of the metropolis
in 1666, the elegance of which will be a perpetual monument of his literary merit, for
which he was also honoured with a public testimony in a present of plate made to him
by the city. His excellent conduct and commendable industry in the school abundantly
appear from the great number of persons eminently learned who were educated by him.
He accumulated the degrees of Bachelor and Doctor of Divinity in 1675 ; and *June* 7,
1676, he was collated to the prebend *Consumpt. per mare* in the cathedral of *St. Paul.*
He was also elected into the Royal Society in 1677, of which he became a very constant and
useful member, was frequently of the council, and presented them with many curiosities,
particularly a *Roman* urn with the ashes, found near *Peckham* in *Surrey*. Part of these burnt
bones he gave to Mr. *Thoresby* ; and on *St. Andrew's-Day*, 1685, the society having resolved to have honorary secretaries, who would act without any view of reward, Dr. *Gale*
was chosen with Sir *John Hoskins* into that office, when they appointed the celebrated
Mr. (afterwards Dr.) *Halley* for the clerk-assistant, or under-secretary, who had been a
distinguished scholar of our author's at *St. Paul's School*; at the head of which Dr. *Gale*
continued with the greatest reputation for the space of twenty-five years, till 1697, when
he was promoted to the deanry of *York* ; and being installed into that dignity *September*
16, that year, he removed thither. This preferment was no more than a just reward of
his merit, but he did not live to enjoy it many years. On his admission, finding the
dean's right to be a canon-residentiary called in question, he was at the expence of
procuring letters patent in 1699, to annex it to the deanry, which put the matter out
of all dispute. On his removal from *London*, he presented to the new library, then
lately finished, at his College in *Cambridge*, a curious collection of *Arabic* manuscripts.
During the remainder of his life, which was spent at *York*, he preserved an hospitality

suitable

fuitable to his ftation; and his good government of that church is mentioned with honour *. Having poffeffed this dignity little more than four years and a half, he was taken from thence, and from the world, *April* 8, 1702, in the 67th year of his age. He died in the deanry-houfe, and was interred in the middle of the choir of the cathedral. Over his grave is a black marble with the following infcription :

" Æ. M. S.
THOMÆ GALE, S. T. P. Decani *Ebor.*
Viri, fi quis alius,
Ob multifariam eruditionem,
Apud fuos exterofque celeberrimi.
Quale nomen & fui defiderium pofteris reliquit,
Apud *Cantabrigienfes*,
Collegium S. S. *Trinitatis* et
Græcæ linguæ Profefforis Regii cathedra ;
Apud *Londinates*,
Viri literatiffimi in Rempublicam
Et Patriæ commodum,
Ex Gymnafio *Paulino* emiffi ;

Apud *Eboracenfes*,
Hujus res Ecclefiæ
Heu ! vix quinquennio,
At dum per mortem licuit,
Sedulò et fideliter adminiftrata ;
Et ubicunque agebat donata luce
Veneranda linguæ *Græca*
Et Hiftoriæ *Anglicana*
Monumenta, Marmore loquaciora,
Perenniora,
Teftantur.
Obiit *Apr.* viii. A. S. H. MDCCII.
Ætat. fuæ LXVII."

Dr. *Gale* married *Barbara* daughter of *Thomas Pepys*, Efq; of *Impington*, in the county of *Cambridge*, who died 1689, and by whom he had three fons and a daughter, of whom in their order. To his eldeft fon he left his noble library of choice and valuable books, befides a curious collection of many efteemed manufcripts, a catalogue of which is printed in the Catalogus MSStorum *Angliæ* & *Hiberniæ* III. p. 185.

Roger Gale, Efq; F. R. and A. SS. eldeft fon of the Dean, was educated under his father at *St. Paul's School* ; admitted at *Trinity College, Cambridge*, 1691, made fcholar of that houfe 1693, and afterwards fellow (being then B. A.) in 1697. He was poffeffed or a confiderable eftate at *Scruton, Yorkfhire*, now in the poffeffion of his grandfon *Henry Gale*, Efq; and reprefented *North Allerton*, in that county, in the firft, fecond, and third Parliaments of *Great Britain*, at the end of which laft he was appointed a Commiffioner of Excife. He was the firft Vice-Prefident of the Society of Antiquaries, and Treafurer to the Royal Society. He died at *Scruton, June* 25, 1744, in his 72d year, univerfally efteemed, and much lamented by all his acquaintance; and left all his MSS. by will to *Trinity College*, and his cabinet of *Roman* coins to the public library there, with a complete catalogue of them drawn up by himfelf. The Rev. Mr. *Cole* of *Milton* has feveral of his letters to Mr. *Browne Willis*, concerning various matters of Antiquity. He married *Henrietta*, daughter of *Henry Raper*, Efq; of *Cowling*, who died 1720, by whom he had *Roger-Henry*, born 1710, admitted fellow-commoner of *Sidney College*, who married *Catharine* daughter of *Chriftopher Crowe*, Efq; of *Kipling*, and had iffue, *Catharine*, born 1741, died 1744; *Roger*, born 1743, died 1751; *Henry*, born 1744, now living at *Scruton*; *Harriet*, born 1745; *Samuel*, born 1746, admitted at *Trinity College*, 1769, fellow-commoner of *Bene't* 1770, prefented to the rectory of *Everingham*, in the Eaft Riding of the county of *York*, 1774; *Catharine*, born 1752; *Chriftopher*, born 1756.

Charles Gale, the Dean's fecond fon, was admitted penfioner of *Trinity College*, 1695, and fcholar of the Houfe *April* 23, 1697. He was afterwards rector of *Scruton*, and died in 1738, having married *Cordelia*, daughter of Mr. *Thomas Thwaits* of *Burrel*, who died 1721, leaving four fons, of whom the eldeft, *Thomas Gale*, M. A. fucceeded to his father's rectory in 1738, and to that of *Weft Rumton*, in the fame county, in *April* 1742, and died *July* 7, 1746.

* See *Drake's Eboracum*, pp. 480. 527. 572.

Samuel,

Samuel, the youngest of the Dean's sons, was born in 1682; but of this learned gentleman I have little to add to what has been said in p. 33. The reader who wishes to see a complete account of the whole family, and their various learned publications, will receive ample satisfaction by consulting the "Reliquiæ *Galeanæ*," which form the second number of the "Bibliotheca Topographica *Britannica*."—The following pictures, belonging to this family, are still remaining at *Scruton*: Dean *Gale*, by Sir *Godfrey Kneller*, in 1689; *Roger Gale*, by *Vanderbank*, in 1722; and *Samuel Gale*, by *Whood*.

P. 34. Mr. *Joseph Sparke*, registrar of *Peterborough* cathedral, published in folio, 1723, a good edition of "Historiæ *Anglicanæ* Scriptores varii;" viz. "Vita S. *Thomæ Cantua-* "*riens.* à *W. Stephanide* conscripta; Chronicon *Johannis* Abbatis S. *Petri* de *Burgo*; "Chronicon *Angliæ* per *Robertum* de *Boston*:" "Historiæ Cœnobii *Burgensis* Scrip- "tores varii;" viz. "*Hugonis Candidi* Cœnobii *Burgensis* Historia; *Roberti Swaphami* "Cœnobii *Burgensis* Historia; *Walteri* de *Whittlescye* Cœnobii *Burgensis* Historia; "Historiæ Cœnobii *Burgensis* Continuatio per Anonymum; Historia Cœnobii *Burgensis* "Versibus *Gallicanis*." He intended a second volume, to contain *Whittlesey's* Life of *Hereward* abbot of *Peterborough*, and had actually engraved the arms of the knights whose fiefs were instituted by abbot *Thorold*; but died 1740. His dedication of the first part of the work to Dr. *Mead* is dated from the library of *John Bridges*, Esq; who died the year after him. The Society of Antiquaries engraved, 1720, a seal of *Peterborough* minster in the possession of Mr. *Sparke*, who will be mentioned again in p. 524.

Ibid. The following very curious memorandum from the MSS. of the Rev. Dr. *Richard Bowes*, rector of *Eastling*, and vicar of *New Romney* in *Kent*, was communicated by his grandson the Rev. Mr. *Wheler Bunce*, vicar of St. *Clement's*, *Sandwich*: "Nov. 17, "1741, departed this life the Rev. Mr. *John Blackbourne*, M. A. of *Trinity College, Cam-* "*bridge*. Soon after the Revolution, he became one of those few truly conscientious, who "refused the new oaths. From that time he lived a very exemplary, good life, and studied "hard; endeavouring to be useful to mankind, both as a scholar and divine. To keep "himself independent, he became corrector of the press to Mr. *Bowyer*, Printer; and was, "indeed, one of the most accurate of any that ever took upon him that laborious em- "ploy. He has given us a curious edition of Lord *Bacon's* Works. As I had the "happiness of being long known to my most valuable friend, and receiving him twice "at *Eastling*, he was so kind to communicate the following particulars. That *Oppro-* "*brium Historiæ*, *Burnet's* Memoirs *, were first put into his hands to be corrected for "*Bowyer's* press. But the honest sons of the Bishop made shamefully free with their "Father's manuscript. Mr. *Blackbourne* shewed some pages left out relating to the "Prince of *Orange*, where his character was more at large, and better drawn, more to "truth and life. Several sheets, concerning the *Scotch* especially, left out. I remember "Lord *Stair* and family made a much worse figure than we see now. As he was him- "self too honest to deal with such as have had no honesty, he advised *Bowyer* to be "concerned no farther in the impression, so it was taken out of his hands. This good "man, for several years past, has been a Nonjuring bishop, equal to most of our bench. "I waited on him often in *Little-Britain*, where he lived almost lost to the world, and hid

---

* "His characters †," says *Swift*, "are miserably wrought, in many things mistaken, and all "of them distracting, except of those who were friends to the Presbyterians."

† Many of which were struck through with his own hand, but left legible in the MS. which he ordered, in his last will, "his executor to print faithfully, as he left it, without adding, suppressing, or altering it in any "particular." In the second volume, Judge *Burnet*, the Bishop's son and executor, promises that "the original "manuscript of both volumes shall be deposited in the *Cotton* Library." But this promise does not appear to have been fulfilled; at least it certainly was not in 1736, when Two Letters were printed, addressed to *Thomas Burnet*, Esq. In p. 8, of the second letter, the writer asserted, that he had in his own possession "an authentic "and compleat collection of castrated passages." Mr. *Bowyer's* copy of the History (mentioned in p. 34) went no further than the first volume; and was given by him to Mr. *Gough*. The Earl of *Shelburne* has a copy of *Burnet's* History with marginal remarks by *Swift*.

"amongst

" amongst old books. One day, before dinner, upon his enquiring after my ever-honoured
" Patron Lord ***** [*Winchelsea*], he went to his bureau, and took out a paper to shew
" me. It was a copy of the testimonial sent to King *J.* (as he called him) signed by
" his Lordship and two more (I think) in his behalf. He afterwards shewed me the
" commission for his consecration. Upon this I begged his blessing, which he gave me
" with the fervent zeal and devotion of a primitive Bishop *. I asked him if I was so
" happy to belong to his diocese ? His answer was (I thought) very remarkable : Dear
" Friend (said he) we leave the sees open, that the gentlemen, who now unjustly possess
" them, upon the restoration, may, if they please, return to their duty and be conti-
" nued. We content ourselves with full episcopal power, as suffragans."

Mr. *Blackbourne* was the editor of *Bale's* " Chronycle concernynge Syr *Johan Olde-*
" *castell*," with an Appendix, *Lond.* 1729, 8vo. *Hearne* had mentioned the first edition
of it " as wonderful rare," in p. 645 of his Glossary to " *Peter Langtoft's* Chronicle,"
in 1725 ; which might occasion *Blackbourne's* republication of it ; though it was only
valuable from being scarce, as appears from p. 441 of " Hist. *Ricardi* II." &c. published
by *Hearne* in 1729. The edition of *Bacon*, 1740, 4 vols. folio, was by Mr. *Blackbourne* ;
to whom a very handsome compliment is paid in *Maittaire's* Lives of the *Paris* Printers,
1717 ; and again in his " Miscellanea aliquot Scriptorum Carmina, 1722." Mr. *Black-*
bourne died *Nov.* 17, 1741 ; and his library was sold by auction in *February* 1742. He
was buried in *Islington* church-yard ; where, when a school-boy, I have gazed with astonishment at the following epitaph, the meaning of which I was unable to comprehend :

" Hic situm est quod mortale fuit
Viri verè reverendi
JOHANNIS BLACKBOURNE, A. M.
Ecclesiæ *Anglicanæ* Presbyteri,
Pontificiorum æque ac Novatorum mallei,
Docti, clari, strenui, prompti :
Qui (uti verbo dicam, cætera enim quis nescit?)
Cum eo non dignus erat,
Usque adeò degener, mundus,
Ad Beatorum sedes
Translatus est, 17° die *Novembris*,
A. D. MDCCXLI, ætat. suæ LVIII.

Cui tandem hic restituta est
PHILADELPHIA, olim ejus Relicta,
Postea vero Conjux
RIC. HEYBORNE, Civis *Londini*,
Quæ obiit 10° die *Januarii*,
A. D. MDCCL. ætat. suæ 70."

On the Foot Stone :
" *Christo* qui vivit, morte perire nequit.
Resurgam. *J. B.*
Nunc, amice Lector, quisquis sis,
Ex hinc disce, qui es, & quid eris."

P. 37. l. 2. On this passage a friend remarks, that " it was by no means at all inte-
" resting to the professors, but a mere literary question. *J. J. Rousseau* has observed,
" that physicians of all men least like your sporting with them. Perhaps churchmen
" have been laughed at so long that they are grown callous. The question by no
" means was, whether they were vile and despicable, but whether they were slaves :
" and that the fact was so, I suppose nobody doubts now. *Epictetus*, though a slave,
" was no more vile and despicable, than the truly great *Marcus Antoninus. Mead* and
" his friends might be mistaken ; yet *Middleton* must, if he spoke of him at all, allow
" that he was a famous practitioner, a princely *Mæcenas* to all the Learned that wanted
" his services, and a great importer of Virtù." *T. F.*

P. 38. *note*, " The hand fortified with a tremendous cæstus, and accompanied with
" a palm-branch, looks more as if designed for prize-fighting boxers than physicians ;
" like the *Roman* contorniates for charioteers." *T. F.*

P. 39. " I have no doubt that Mr. *Chishull* is wrong in every word he says about the
" coin which has CKШПI on it : though I am not as yet equally sure what the right
" meaning is." *T. F.*—See his letter on it to *Haym* at the end of his " Antiquitates
" Asiaticæ."

* Dr. *Bowes* also received Bishop *Atterbury's* blessing in *The Tower* just before he went into banishment. And he was one of Dr. *Sacheverell's* bail.

P. 40.

P. 40. " The honours of the *Greek* phyficians are nothing to Dr. *Middleton's* inquiry. *Hawkins* and *Pennel* would not allow that furgery was not a liberal fcience. It was " not very liberal in *Pythagoras* to keep his writings on botany fecret." *T. F.*

P. 45. The Index to *Aretæus*, comprifed in fourteen fheets folio, is annexed to the fplendid edition of Dr. *Wigan*, which was printed at the *Clarendon* prefs in 1723; and is by much the moft difficult, and not the leaft handfome, part of that elegant volume. This Index was compiled at the requeft, and printed at the expence, of Dr. *John Freind*, by Mr. *Maittaire*, who has introduced it with a fhort *Latin* Preface.

L. 5. read " Mr. *James Bonwicke*, a fon of Mr. *Bowyer's* worthy fchoolmafter," &c.— As the circumftances attending this executorfhip are curious, I fhall annex, from Mr. *Bowyer's* hand-writing, a copy of the Will: " In the Name of the Father, and of " the Son, and of the Holy Ghoft, one God Bleffed for ever. I *James Bonwicke*, being " now, by the bleffing of God, in good health, do, by this my laft Will and Teftament, " difpofe of that temporal eftate He hath been pleafed in much mercy to blefs me withal. " I have been a miferable finner, God he knows, and unworthy of the leaft of thofe " many mercies he has vouchfafed me all my life long; yet humbly hope for the greateft " of all, even the falvation of my poor foul, through the merits of our Bleffed Redeemer " *Jefus Chrift*. I give and bequeath to my fifters *Thea* and *Winny*, to each of them " the fum of Sixty Pounds, to be paid them immediately upon my deceafe; to my fifter " *Molly* the like fum, to be difpofed to her own private advantage in a fmall fettle-" ment; to my fifter *Betty* the fum of Twenty Pounds at my death, and Forty more at " the birth of her firft child; to my fifters *Henny* the like fum, to be paid, one moiety " at my deceafe, and the other at the day of marriage, if they marry with confent of " my uncle *James Bonwicke*, Efquire; to my brother *John* Forty Pounds, to be paid " when he fhall have been fettled one whole year in fome bufinefs with the approbation " of my uncle; to my grandmother *Stubbs*, and uncle Mr. *Samuel Stubbs*, and my god-" fon *James Jones*, to each of them Twenty Pounds; and to Mrs. *Sarah Norton* Ten " Pounds, to be laid out for her private ufe; I defire alfo that Twenty Pounds may be " laid out in the building of a monument for my dear *F.* and *M.*; I defire that One " Hundred Pounds may be difpofed of to augment two poor livings, particularly where " my friends Mr. *B. C.* Mr. *G. H.* Mr. *R. M.* or Mr. *M. B.* may be incumbents; " and One other Hundred Pounds, whofe annual product for eight years may be given " to two poor children born in the year of my deceafe in the parifhes of *Mickleham* " or *Headley*, and to be nominated by the vicar of *Leatherhead* and the rectors of " *Mickleham* and *Headley*; I leave my cabinet of medals to my dear friend Mr. *Wil-" liam Bowyer*, Junior, to whom I bequeath all my other goods and chattels what-" foever; I appoint him likewife executor of this my laft Will and Teftament."

On this Will were grounded the following Cafes, drawn up by Mr. *Bowyer*; and anfwered by two Lawyers of great eminence.

CASE I.

" *J. B.* dying, bequeaths above 600*l.* in legacies, and among the reft 200*l.* for " charitable ufes, by a Will of his own hand-writing before his ficknefs, though " neither dated, figned, nor fealed, but which he delivered before his death to one " of the legatees mentioned in the faid Will, declaring it to be his laft Will and Tefta-" ment. Upon a view of the effects of the faid Teftator, it appears there are not affets " near fufficient to pay the faid legacies, unlefs an eftate be fold for that purpofe, " which the Teftator received the profits of when living, but which was bought in the " name of another perfon, and by that perfon held in truft for the faid Teftator, of " which eftate no mention is made in the faid Will.

" Query: Shall the faid eftate go to the heir at law, in prejudice to the faid legacies " and charities, or to the executor, to enable him to perform the faid Will of the " Teftator?"

ANSWER.

Answer. " I conceive very clearly, that, in this cafe, the truft of the real eftate will
" defcend to the Teftator's heir at law, and that the Will is perfectly void as to lands, it
" not being executed according to the folemnities directed by the ftatute. But as to
" the perfonal eftate, the Will, being all of the Teftator's own hand-writing, is good for
" that, and may, and ought to be proved by the executor, who is entitled to retain
" the legacy fpecifically devifed. Edmund Sawyer, *March* 8, 1724."

CASE II.

" I give and bequeath to my fifter *Betty* the fum of 20l. at my death, and Forty
" more at the birth of her firft child. To my fifters *Henny* the like fum, to be paid
" one moiety at my deceafe, and the other at the day of marriage, if *they* marry with
" confent of my uncle *James Bonwicke*, Efq.

" I. Query, what fum is implied in the *like* fum, to be paid, &c.? whether the 40l.
" juft before mentioned, or the 20l. and 40l. added together, as the legacies to the
" other fifters are all 60l. each * ?

* The whole progrefs of this bufinefs reflects honour on the integrity of Mr. *Bowyer*; but his conduct to the *unprovided* fifter deferves to be particularly known. I have now before me an exact debtor and creditor account † of the whole of his executorfhip, by which it appears that he not only paid to *Margaret Bonwicke* 21l. 8s. the whole furplus which remained after all the other legacies were paid, and added 10l. to it as a free gift, but, at the diftance of thirty years, made up the fum which her brother had moft probably intended for her. This circumftance is confirmed by the following remarkable receipt: " Whereas a legacy of Sixty Pounds was probably intended to have
" been left to my wife *Margaret*, when a maiden, by her brother Mr. *James Bonwicke*, who died
" *January* 1724-5; but her name being omitted in his Will, and there not being affets fufficient
" to pay the whole of the faid intended legacy, fhe gave a difcharge in full to his executor Mr.
" *William Bowyer*, May 23, 1729, on receiving Twenty-one Pounds Eight Shillings, being the
" whole furplus which remained after the other legacies were paid: And whereas the faid *William*
" *Bowyer* did, out of his own good will, pay at the fame time, and at his own expence, Ten Pounds
" more in aid of the faid intended legacy; and afterwards, on or about *July* 16, 1747, did give to
" my faid wife *Margaret* Four Pounds Five Shillings more out of the fecond dividend made to him
" on account of Mr. *Edward Jones's* bond of a Hundred Pounds; which fums made in all Thirty-
" five Pounds, Thirteen Shillings: And whereas Mr. *Samuel Stubbs*, dying on or about *December*
" 12, 1756, left the following claufe in his Will: ' I give and bequeath unto Mr. *William Bowyer*,
" of *Hatton Garden, London*, Printer, the fum of Thirty-one Pounds Ten Shillings (willing him to
" take it as part of my late nephew *James Bonwicke's* eftate) and to difpofe of it as he fhall think
" proper:' by which claufe the faid Mr. *William Bowyer*, having received Thirty-one Pounds Ten
" Shillings, hath thought proper to difpofe of Twenty-four Pounds Seven Shillings to me: I hereby
" acknowledge to have received the faid Twenty-four Pounds Seven Shillings; which, with the
" fums before received by my wife and myfelf, amounting to Sixty Pounds, is in full of the in-
" tended legacy of Mr. *James Bonwicke* to my wife, and of the utmoft intention of the late Mr.
" *Samuel Stubbs*. Witnefs our hands,   " Edward Andrews,
                                                      " Margarett Andrews."

" Received of Mr. *William Bowyer*, each of us refpectively, Two Pounds Eight Shillings, the
" fum which he hath thought proper to difpofe of in purfuance of the before-mentioned claufe in
" the late Mr. *Samuel Stubbs's* Will.   " Mary Jones,
                                                      " Dorothy Wildman,
                                                      " Winefrid Cooke."

† I tranfcribe a few *Items* from this account, as a curiofity:

EXECUTORSHIP	Debtor.				Creditor.		
Found in a box dedicated to the poor	£6	9	1	Paid for my journey to *London* upon Mr. B's horfe, waterage to and from *Vauxhall*, and putting up the horfe at *The Vine*;	0	2	9
Sold 3 fheets of paper	0	0	1				
Sold Mifs *Henny* a book called *Hygiafticon*	0	0	4				
Sold Mrs. *Winny* a pair of black buttons	0	0	2	Paid neighbour *Martyr's* fcore	1	11	3½
Received of the Adminiftrators of Mr. A. B. and E. B. an 8th fhare of odd things, which were not divided in their brother's life-time	0	2	5½	Paid Goody *Hubbard*, for her trouble in attending Mr. *J. B.* during his laft ficknefs	0	10	6
——— for houfhold goods	146	0	0	Spent at a coffee-houfe waiting for Mr. *Stubbs*	0	0	1
——— for eatables and drinkables	4	15	0	Paid counfel for refolving three cafes	3	3	0
——— of Mr. *Woodward* for books	102	2	0	Paid the pocket expences of Mrs. *Elizabeth, Dorothea, Winefrid, Henrietta*, and *Margaret Bonwicke*, when they went to *London*, to give teftimony to their Brother's Will,	0	11	6
——— of Mr. *Bonwicke*, Bookfeller;	185	0	0				
——— for 7 MSS. of Lord *Oxford*	7	7	0				
——— of Mr. *May* for MS. Sermons	12	0	0				

" II.

" II. The Teſtator here bequeaths to one brother and five ſiſters legacies, and a ſixth
" ſiſter is omitted. When no cauſe can be alledged from any diſtaſte the Teſtator had
" againſt that ſiſter in his life-time, why ſhe was omitted, is not that ſiſter ſufficiently
" implied in the word ſiſters *Henny*, and afterwards by the Teſtator's referring to more
" than one in the ſame clauſe, and ſaying, if *they* marry, &c. ? and is not this ſixth ſiſter
" entitled to her legacy, or the proportion thereof, if there are not aſſets to pay the
" whole ?"

ANSWER. " 1. I conceive that *Henny* will be entitled to 60*l.* under this Will, in caſe ſhe
" perform the condition annexed to the deviſe, the ſum bequeathed to her other ſiſter
" *Betty* being ſo much, though made payable at different times; and therefore I con-
" ceive the *like* ſum will be conſtrued to extend to the whole ſum bequeathed to the
" other ſiſter, and not to the 40*l.* only; which conſtruction is fortified by the ſame
" legacies being bequeathed to the other ſiſters.

" 2. " The other ſixth ſiſter not being mentioned in the Will, I conceive there is not a
" ſufficient deſcription in the words referred to in the query to entitle her to the ſame
" legacy with her other ſiſters: though there was no diſtaſte in the Teſtator to her, and
" it might poſſibly be the Teſtator's intention to give her the ſame legacy with the reſt;
" yet here being only one ſiſter named, and one ſum bequeathed, I conceive it is *caſus*
" *omiſſus*, and conſequently ſhe will not be entitled."

" Item, To my brother *John* 40*l.* to be paid when he ſhall have been ſettled one
" whole year in buſineſs, with the approbation of my uncle.

" Query, May not that man be ſaid to be ſettled in buſineſs, who, having ſerved a
" clerkſhip to an attorney, is ready to practiſe that profeſſion whenever any one offers
" him any buſineſs; and if he make but a bond once or twice a year, or exerciſes any
" other ſmall part of his profeſſion, may he not be called a practitioner of the law ?
" If ſo, will it not be determined, that the uncle's refuſing to give his approbation of
" his being ſettled in buſineſs, ſhall be no bar to the legatee's demanding his legacy ?
" Or, in caſe the uncle dies, is not the legatee entitled to his legacy, ſince it is then out
" of the uncle's power either to give or refuſe his approbation ?"

ANSWER. " I conceive that *John* is entitled to the legacy in caſe he has been one year
" out of his clerkſhip, and purſues the buſineſs of an attorney when required by his clients.
" The condition annexed to the legacy, of ' being ſettled in buſineſs one whole year with
" the approbation of his uncle,' can, as I conceive, extend no further than that the
" legatee be diligent and induſtrious in the profeſſion he was bred up in (to which 'tis
" probable he was placed by his uncle's or father's directions), and not that the uncle can
" put the legatee to any new buſineſs. Nor will the uncle's refuſal of his approbation
" prevent the legatee's being entitled to this legacy, if he is willing and ready to prac-
" tiſe in his profeſſion when called upon to it by his clients. Upon the death of his
" uncle, the legacy becomes abſolute."

" I deſire alſo that 20*l.* may be laid out in a monument for my dear *F.* and *M.*

" Query, whether the letters *F.* and *M.* ſufficiently imply Father and Mother, ſo as
" to oblige the executor to appropriate 20*l.* for the ſaid monument, or the proportion
" of that legacy, if there are not aſſets to pay the ſeveral legacies mentioned in the
" Will ?"

ANSWER. " I conceive theſe initial letters are not ſo ſufficient an evidence of the Teſtator's
" intention as to oblige the executor to lay out 20*l.* in a monument for the Teſtator's
" Father and Mother, nor can I adviſe the executor ſo to do without the direction of
" the Court to indemnify him."

" I

" I defire that 100l. may be difpofed of to augment two poor livings, particularly
" where my friends Mr. *B. C.* Mr. *G. H.* Mr. *R. N.* or Mr. *M. B.* may be incumbents.
" Query, Is this legacy perfectly void ? or is it valid with refpect to fome two poor
" livings or other being entitled to the 100l. ? Though no perfons fuppofed to be meant
" by Mr. *B. C.* &c. can lay claim to it, nor any other particular livings, yet may not
" the Attorney-General, or fome other commiffioner who is to look after the augmen-
" tation of poor livings ?"

ANSWER. " The intention of the Teftator being to augment two poor livings, and that
" not in general, but for a particular purpofe, *viz.* where his friends Mr. *B. C.* Mr. *G. H.*
" &c. may be incumbents, and the Will being manifeftly void as to them ; I conceive that
" the bequeft is likewife void, and that a Court of Equity (upon an information brought
" in the Attorney-General's name) will not eftablifh the Will in part, when the perfons
" for whom this augmentation was intended cannot have the benefit of it.

" *April* 10, 1725. EDMUND SAWYER."

CASE III.

" *A. B.* by his laft Will and Teftament in writing, gives and devifes unto his five
" daughters the fum of 400l. apiece, and unto his wife and two fons *John* and *James*
" doth *(inter al.)* give and bequeath as follows ; *viz.* ' I give and bequeath to my
" dear Wife all that my Meffuage, or Tenement and Farm, of all thofe Lands, Tene-
" ments, and Hereditaments, with all the appurtenances thereunto belonging, or there-
" with ufed, occupied or enjoyed, as part, parcel, or member thereof, commonly called
" or known by the name or names of *Burford* and *Boxland*, fituate, lying, and being in
" the parifh of *Mickleham* aforefaid, and all other my Freehold Meffuages, Lands, Te-
" nements, and Hereditaments whatfoever, within the faid parifh of *Mickleham*, with
" the appurtenances, to have and to hold during her natural life, if fhe continues a
" widow fo long ; and upon her deceafe or marriage, to my fon *James* and his heirs, he
" paying within fix months after he comes to the poffeffion of the faid eftate 200l. to
" his brother my fon *John*.'

" *A. B.* died *Oct.* 20, 1722 ; and on *Dec.* 3 following, his widow and relict alfo died.
" Whereupon *James*, the faid Teftator's younger fon, being then of the age of 18 years,
" received the rents and profits of the faid eftate from *J. B.* Efq; the Teftator's brother,
" in whofe name the faid eftate was purchafed in truft for the faid Teftator, and in whom
" the legal right was to the day of *James's* death, he having never made any convey-
" ance thereof to the Teftator's widow, or the faid *James* the fon.

" That the faid *James*, about two years after his mother's deceafe, at the age of 21,
" died likewife, without having paid to his elder brother *John* the 200l. or any part
" thereof, mentioned in the faid Will to be paid to him by the faid *James* within fix
" months after he fhould come to the poffeffion of the faid eftate.

" That the faid *James*, by his Will, neither dated, figned, nor fealed, but all of his
" own hand-writing, (and for the validity whereof fentence has been given in *Doctors
" Commons)* bequeaths feveral legacies, and among the reft 200l. to charitable ufes, no
" mention being made therein of the eftate given him by his Father's Will, but only in
" general words leaves his cabinet of medals to his dear friend Mr. *W. B.* junior, to
" whom he bequeaths all his other goods and chattels whatfoever, and appoints him
" likewife Executor of his laft Will and Teftament.

" That, without the faid eftate, there will not be affets fufficient to difcharge his lega-
" cies ; notwithftanding which, the faid *John* the brother not only claims the faid
" eftate, but alfo the 200l. with intereft for the fame, and 40l. being a legacy left him
" by his faid brother *James's* Will.

" I. Query,

" I. Query, Is *James's* Will fufficient to convey to his Executor the faid Eftate held " in truft, to enable him to fulfil the faid Will; or muft it go to the brother *John* as " heir at law, in prejudice to the faid charities and legacies ?"

Answer. " This Will is not fufficient to pafs Lands of freehold or inheritance, not " being figned or executed according to the ftatute, and therefore it defcends to the " heir at law *John*, and not affected with the charities or other legacies."

" II. If the truft of the eftate defcends to *John*, the heir at law, is it not fufficiently " implied in the father's Will that the 200*l.* legacy, he bequeaths to the faid *John*, fhould " be an incumbrance on the eftate bequeathed to *James*? Can *John* therefore claim " the faid 200*l.* as a debt of *James's* executor, when he poffeffes that eftate which feems " to be charged with the very incumbrance he claims ?

" Or, farther, may not *James's* neglect to pay the faid 200*l.* (that is, to perform the " conditions by which he was to hold the faid eftate) be interpreted as a refufal to ac- " cept of that eftate, to which his father had annexed fuch conditions? Or fhall his " receiving the rents and profits of the eftate during his minority be looked upon as an " acceptance of that eftate, which was never made over to him, and the profits whereof " he never received after he came of age ?"

Answer. " I think, the land devifed to *James* being charged with the 200*l.* and the " land fo charged defcending to *John* (to whom the 200*l.* was alfo payable) it amounts " to an extinguifhment or fatisfaction of the 200*l.* and all intereft due on that account; " and cannot be claimed by *John* of the executor of *James*."

" III. If the 200*l.* is likewife due to *John* as a debt from *James*, is *James's* executor " obliged to pay intereft for the faid 200*l.* to the claimant *John* any longer than to the " time of the faid *James's* death, provided the executor has made no intereft of the faid " money ; and efpecially confidering that the claimant *John*, by litigating his brother's " Will for near half a year, hindered the executor from paying either intereft or prin- " cipal ?"

Answer. " I think *James's* executor is liable to pay neither principal nor intereft."

" IV. When was *James*, according to the words of his father's Will, poffeffed of the " eftate? Was it from the time he received the rents and profits of the faid eftate, " which was from the *Michaelmas* before his father, who gave it him, died, his father " and mother both dying between *Michaelmas* and *Chriftmas*? Or was he not rather " then only poffeffed of it, when his mother, who during her life was the obftacle to his " poffeffing it, was dead? Or, laftly, was he, or could he be poffeffed of it, before he was " of the age of 21? Confequently, muft the intereft the elder brother *John* claims " with the 200*l.* commence from fix months after the *Michaelmas* which preceded the " father's death, or from fix months after the younger brother *James* came of age ?"

Answer. " *James* was poffeffed of the eftate within the meaning of the Will when " the mother died, and the devife to him took place ; and whether he was 21 or not, " as long as he was entitled to the rents and profits, it was fufficient ; and if *James* " had lived, *John* might have demanded intereft from fix months after his mother's " death ; but he dying, and the eftate out of which both principal and intereft was " to be paid coming to *John*, the demand, I think, is extinguifhed.

" Thomas Lutwyche, *April* 25, 1726."

P. 45. *Fourth note.* Such a tranflation of *Pliny* the *French* have lately got in feveral volumes, 4to. by M. *Poinfinet*, and other learned hands, 1772, &c.

P. 47. l. 7. The office of reader at *The Temple* was held at a great charge to the per- fon who executed it. See a curious note on this fubject in *Dodfley's* Old Plays, IX. 364.—*Granger* mentions feven different prints of Mr. *Selden*. There is a medal of him,

struck

struck in the prefent century, by one of the *Daffiers*; I know not which, for it has not the artift's name; it was left without a reverfe, and that of the medal of *Wolfius* added to it. This laft has the initials of *Daffier* the father.—*Selden* had fent his library to *Oxford* in his life-time: but hearing that they had lent out a book without a fufficient caution, he fent for it back again. After his death, it continued fome time at *The Temple*, where it fuffered fome diminution: at laft, the executors thinking that they were executors of his will rather than his paffions, generoufly and nobly fent the whole to *Oxford*.

P. 47. l. 11. For *James* read *Charles*.

P. 48. Of Dr. *Wilkins*, fee more in p. 91.—The learned *Henry Wharton*, librarian at *Lambeth* under archbifhop *Sancroft*, is faid to have drawn up an accurate catalogue of the MSS. there, with tranfcripts of all the unprinted tracts, and an exact collation of all the printed ones; but into whofe hands that catalogue has fallen is now unknown. His own MSS. were purchafed by archbifhop *Tenifon*, and depofited in this library. The original catalogue of thefe, in his own hand-writing, is in the library of *John Loveday*, Efq. A lift of them is incorporated in the firft volume of the catalogue of the *Lambeth* MSS. drawn up by Dr. *Wilkins*, 1718. Many MSS. having fince been added to that valuable library, a fecond volume of the catalogue has been drawn up by Dr. *Ducarel*. A life of Mr. *Wharton* is prefixed to two volumes of his Sermons; and a fmall monument is erected to his memory in *Westminster Abbey* with this infcription:

"H. S. E.
HENRICUS WHARTON, A. M.
Ecclefiæ *Anglicanæ* Prefbyter,
Rector Ecclefiæ de *Chartham*,
Necnon Vicarius Ecclefiæ de *Minfter*
In Infula *Thanato*, in Diœcefi *Cantuarienfi*:
Reverendiffimo ac fanctiffimo Præfuli
Wilhelmo Archiepifcopo *Cantuarienfi*

A Sacris Domefticis,
Qui multa ad augendam & illuftrandam
Rem literariam,
Multa pro Ecclefia *Chrifti*
Confcripfit,
Plura moliebatur.
Obiit 3° Non. *Mart.* A. D. MDCXCIV,
Ætatis fuæ XXXI."

P. 48. *Note. hazard of Mr. Harley's perfon*] By *Guifcard's* ftab. See the particulars in the "Supplement to *Swift*."

P. 49. l. 3. *read* memoranda.

Ibid. fub-note. Mr. *Thwaites* publifhed an edition of "*Ephraim Syrus*, Oxon. 1709."

P. 50. Mr. *Baxter*, late in life, married a woman without a fortune, but of a very good character, named *Sarah Carturit*, by whom he had two fons and three daughters. He died *May* 31, 1723, and was buried *June* 4, at *Iflington*. Prefixed to his "Gloffarium "Antiquitatum *Britannicarum* * 1719," 8vo. is a fine head of him by *Vertue*, from a picture by *Highmore* †, when *Baxter* was in the 69th year of his age; in fome of the earlieft impreffions of which the painter's name is fpelt *Hymore*. His edition of *Horace* has con-

---

* "Mr. *Gough*, fpeaking of this work (*Brit.* Top. I. 9) obferves, that Mr. *Baxter*, from his fkill in the old *Britifh* language, attempted to determine the geography by etymology. It is juftly added, by Mr. *Gough*, that this is a method the moft uncertain, and which too often mifled *Camden* before, and others fince. In the firft volume of the Archæologia of the Society of Antiquaries, are four *Latin* letters, written by Mr. *Baxter* to the late Dr. *Geekie*, [who had been his fcholar,] when firft entered at *Cambridge*. In thefe letters, the learned critic fhews how entirely his attention was devoted to etymological and philological inquiries. From the fourth letter it appears, that Mr. *Baxter* was folicited to give a new edition of the writers *De Re Ruftica*; but that he declined it, on account of his age, and the difficulty of the undertaking. Dr. *Harwood*, in his View of the Claffics, calls Mr. *Baxter's Anacreon* an excellent edition; and with regard to his *Horace* expreffes himfelf in the following ftrong terms: "This fecond edition of *Horace*, in 1725, is by far the beft edition of *Horace* ever publifhed. "I have read it many times through, and know its fingular worth. *England* has not produced a "more elegant and judicious critic than Mr. *Baxter*." Biographia *Britannica*, vol. II. p. 24.

† This picture was painted for a club-room, where Mr. *Baxter* prefided, in *The Old Jewry*; but the landlord removing, took it away with him, and it has never been heard of fince. Mr. *Highmore* enquired after it a few years ago in vain.

5

tinued

tinued in such esteem abroad, that the learned *Gesner* gave a new edition of it in 1752 at *Leipsick*, with additional notes ; and it has been again printed in the same place in 1772 and 1778. *Baxter* wrote his own life, a transcript of which is in the library of Mr. *Tutet*, under this title, " Vitæ D. *Gulielmi Baxteri*, sive *Popidii*, a se ipso conscrip- " tæ Fragmentum ; ex ipsius schedis manu propria exaratis erutum, *Dec.* 26º, 1721, " *W. T.*" *W. T.* means *William Thomas*, Esq; who wrote an *English* draught of (1) a dedication to Dr. *Mead* of the " Glossarium Antiquitatum *Britannicarum*," which he then (2) translated into *Latin* ; afterwards (3) a different one, which was turned into (4) *Latin* by Mr. *Timothy Thomas*; and this last, after many corrections, was put into Dr. *Mead's* hands, who, with Mr. *Maittaire*, altered it to what it appears in print, ex- cept some few passages corrected by Mr. *William Thomas* and the Rev. Mr. *Moses Wil- liams*. The papers marked 1, 2, 3, and 4, Mr. *Tutet* possesses ; and the remainder of the information is in a note written by Mr. *William Thomas*, who also wrote the printed preface to *Llhuyd's* " Adversaria Posthuma," subjoined to the " Glossarium Antiquita- " tum *Britannicarum*," but Mr. *Tutet* has a different one in his own hand-writing. Mr. *Thomas* revised the whole work before it went to the press.

P. 51. Of Dr. *Wotton*, see more in p. 73. In Mr. *Baker's* valuable MSS. occurs this entry : " *Gulielmus Wotton, Suffolciensis*, electus Socius sub Magistro *Berisford, April* " 8, 1685, decessit 1694. *Thomas Baker* * eodem die immediate junior." I have two little tracts, each of them only a half-sheet in folio, one intituled, 1. A Letter sent to Mr. " *William Wotton*, B. D. Chaplain to the Right Honourable the Earl of *Nottingham*, " concerning ' Some late Remarks,' &c. written by *John Harris*, M. A." signed *Tancred Robinson*, who acknowledges himself to be the author of the " Introduction to Sir *John* " *Narborough's* Voyage," the " Epistle Dedicatory before the *English* Translation of " Father *Le Compte's China*," and of " all the Extracts of the *Hortus Malabaricus*" in " the Philosophical Transactions." The other tract is, " A Letter to Dr. *Tancred Ro- " binson*, in answer to some Passages in his to Mr. *Wotton*, and is signed by *J. Harris*."

Ibid. " *Bartlemy Fair*," &c. on the authority of a presentation-copy of the second edition of it, 1722, now in the library of *James Bindley*, Esq; may be ascribed to the celebrated Mrs. *Astell* †, of whom there is a life in the " Biographia."

P. 52. Mr. *Lindsay* for many years officiated as minister of the Nonjuring society in *Trinity Chapel, Aldersgate-street*; and is said to have been their last minister. I have several of his letters to Dr. *Zachary Grey* ; of which a few extracts shall be given below ‡.

He

---

* Of whom some memoirs shall be given in this Appendix.

† It is remarkable that Mr. *Ballard*, who in his " Memoirs of Learned Ladies," has given a parti- cular account of Mrs. *Astell* and her writings, takes no notice of this tract. But it can hardly be doubted that it was written by her, as in the copy above-mentioned, which is directed " To the " Lady *Blount, Dec.* 17, 1724," that Lady has written, " Given me by Mrs. *Astell*, the author of this " and several Books, Pamphlets, and Papers, which I have also." In the second edition the words *Bartlemy Fair* were left out of the title-page.

‡ " You give me great satisfaction by telling me that my poor endeavours § are favourably cen- " sured by yourself and other friends at *Cambridge* ; but I shall not grow proud on that account, " because I know how much more is due to your candour than to my own abilities. Your pro- " moting its sale will be a great obligation to me ; for you know the booksellers will not promote " any thing which is not their own property ; and this is a very weighty burthen for my weak " shoulders. I heartily thank you for your kind invitation to *Houghton* ; which I please myself " with the hopes of an opportunity of accepting ; for I am now, by the Doctor's direction, to ride " moderately and frequently ; in pursuance of which, I am looking out for a horse able to carry my " weight easy journeys. Whether I can disengage myself from the good old Lady *Fanshaw*, with- " out getting a curate, I cannot tell. I am every day at her Ladyship's house in *Little Ormond* " *Street. May* 23, 1728."—" It would very much grieve me, if I thought you would suspect me " of negligence in any affair you think fit to intrust me. The truth is, that after divers meetings

§ His translation of *Mason's* " Vindication of the Church of *England*."

X x x

" and

He died in 1768, and was buried in *Iſlington* church-yard, where the following epitaphs remain to his and his wife's memory :

On a flat ſtone :
" Hic requieſcit in Domino
M A R I A uxor J O H A N N I S L I N D S A Y,
Ecclefiæ *Anglicanæ* Preſbyteri,
De quâ
Nil dicere non fas eſt, ſatis non tutum.
Vin' verbo dicam ?
In illa omnis enituit
Quæ fœminam optimam ornaret
Virtus,
Cujus ad exemplum ſi vixeris,
Amice Lector,
Mori non eſt quod timeas.
Vale.
Obiit in Feſto Omnium Animarum,
A. D. MDCCXXVII,
Ætat. ſuæ 43."

On an upright ſtone adjoining :
" Hic etiam reſtant Exuviæ
Reverendi J. LINDSAY, *Aulæ Mariæ*
Apud *Oxonienſes* olim Alumni,
Qui, Ecclefiæ *Anglicanæ* exinde Miniſter,
(Beneficiis cujus, OPULENTIS licet,
Interiori ſtimulo, Aditûs cauſa, RECUSATIS).
Animo in adverſis æquo magnoque,
Sincerâ fide, nudâque veritate,
Honos Poſteris effulſit.
Eruditione inſuper eximius,
Vitæ integer, propoſitique tenax,
Spectatâ pietate inſignis,
Moreſque præcipue ingenuus, vixit.
Curſu tandem bene peracto,
Fortiter diuque pro fide certando emeritus,
Obdormientis more, benedicens, obiit
Jun. 21, A. D. 1768, ætat. 82.
En VIRTUS ! En PRISCA FIDES !"

Mr. *Lindſay* publiſhed " The Short Hiſtory of the Regal Succeſſion, &c. with Remarks " on *Whiſton's* Scripture Politicks," &c. *Lond.* 1720, 8vo ; which occurs in the *Bodleian* Catalogue. His valuable Tranſlation of " *Maſon's* Vindication" has a large and elaborate Preface, containing " A full and particular Series of the Succeſſion of our Biſhops, " through the ſeveral Reigns ſince the Reformation," &c. He dates it from " *Iſlington*, " 13 *Dec.* 1727." In 1747, he publiſhed in the ſame ſize " Two Sermons preached at " Court in 1620, by *Francis Maſon* ;" which he recommends " as well for their own " intrinſick value, as to make up a complete Collection of that learned Author's Works." He had a nephew, who died curate of *Waltham Abbey, Sept.* 17, 1779.

" and advances made towards the publication of your preſent work *, when I had reaſon to think " there was nothing more to do but to report to you the concluſion of a contract, no ſooner did we come " to the point, but I found, the taſte of the times is ſuch, that the three former parts of the ſame " work did not anſwer in trade; and therefore I have no hopes of dealing for it, unleſs you will " print it at your own hazard. I wiſh I could have anſwered you more effectually. But this mo- " ment I received the anſwer I have given you. As to the pamphlets, The Caſe of Allegiance to " a King in poſſeſſion (as well as a Defence of it), were Mr. *T. Browne's*, formerly of your *St.* " *John's*, B. D. The Anſwer to Obedience and Submiſſion (as well as to *Sherlock's* Vindication on " the ſame ſubject) were written by Mr. *Wagſtaffe*. The Examination of the Arguments from " Scripture and Reaſon, by Mr. *Theophilus Downes*. Dr. *Sherlock's* Caſe of Allegiance conſidered, " by Mr. *Jeremiah Collier. July* 20, 1738."—" Dear Sir, I am very glad you approve of the " ſcheme propoſed for the Animadverter. As to the objection againſt the way of dialogue, I would " be very ſorry to differ in opinion, and much rather give up my own to that of better judges : but " I humbly preſume, when they conſider my caſe, and the frequent occaſions which will occur to " make a breach in the thread of diſcourſe, they will be convinced that I could not acquit myſelf " well in the other way. This was found by experience of ſome who trod the ſame path before ; " and particularly by *Tutchin*, who began (as I remember) in a ſeries of obſervations, but was " ſoon forced to fall into the way of dialogue, as *L'Eſtrange* did before, and *Leſlie* after him. I " hope therefore the objection will be dropped. And whenever I find myſelf enabled to begin, I " muſt find out ſome freſh topick to ſet out with, which may tempt the reader to peruſe it. The " Caſe of the Diſſenters (juſt now publiſhed) ſeems a very proper one, and would afford matter " enough for animadverſion : but I fear it will be expoſed to death, before I can be ready to caſt a " ſtone at it. I ſhall not ſay any thing of it here, becauſe you probably have or will ſoon ſee it. " But I hear one curious piece of *fineſſe* relating to it, that ſome people will have it, that the repeal " of the Teſt, &c. is to be brought in by the Tories, and rejected by the Miniſtry. But I rather

* The fourth part of the " Examination of *Neal*." See p. 356.

" think

P. 52. Add to the books of 1726, " *Xenophontis Ephesii Ephesiacorum* Libri V. de " *Amoribus Anthiæ* & *Abrocomæ* *. Nunc primum prodeunt e vetusto codice Biblio- " thecæ Monachorum *Caffinenfium Florentiæ*, cum *Latinâ* Interpretatione *Antonii Coc- " chii* ╪," 4to ; and " *Dionyfii* Geographia emendata & locupletata, additione fcil. Geo- " graphiæ Hodiernæ *Græco* carmine pariter donatæ. Cum xvi Tabulis Geographicis. " Ab *Andrea Wells*, M. A. Ædis *Chrifti* Alumno. Editio quinta ╪," 8vo.

P. 53. On a mourning ring, for his mother, Mr. *Bowyer* caufed to be infcribed, " MATERTERA VICE MATRIS ;" and on another, on the fame occafion, " ΩΣ ΑΠΟ- " ΓΕΓΑΛΑΚΤΙΣΜΕΝΟΝ."—The following paper was found in the hand-writing of this affectionate parent : " The laft requeft of *Dorothy Bowyer* to her loving hufband *Wil- " liam Bowyer* : if he will be fo kind as to grant it, then my relations cannot but fay, " but that he has been a very good friend to them in my life-time, and alfo at my death. " So foon after my death as he can conveniently fpare fo much money, my defire is, " that he will give to my brother *Ichabod Dawks* ten pounds ; to my fifter *Ann Tracey* " ten pounds ; to my fifter *Jemima Pemmel* ten pounds ; to *Dorothy Lingly* five pounds ; " to *John Bifhop* five pounds ; and to *Ann Prudom* five pounds §."

P. 54. Add to the folio books, Mr. *Chifhull's* " Antiquitates Afiaticæ."

" think it will be brought in by the Craftfmen ; who (if they have any principles) may probably " wifh to fee *Jack Presbyter* once again with jack-boots on ; and the Miniftry then perhaps may " throw it out, in oppofition to them who take the patronage of it. I flatter myfelf with the hopes " of fuch a number of fubfcribers as will anfwer the expence at leaft, and then I fhall be lefs foli- " citous about the profit : but if fome of my friends here are not out in their calculations, it might " (with a little pains, feconded by the intereft of our friends) become confiderable in that refpect " alfo. I doubt not, Sir, of your friendfhip in it fo far as may be proper for you to appear in its " favour : but if fome of the young gentlemen would ftir in it, it would probably much increafe the " numbers. *Dec.* 13, 1738."—" This Catalogue is this moment come to my hand. The books " were Mr. *Blackbourne's*. I fhall attend the auction conftantly ; and if you have any commands, " they fhall be duly executed. *Brick-Court, Temple, Feb.* 26, 1742."—" As I gladly embrace all " opportunities of paying my refpects to you, the inclofed letter from my brother (fent by one of " his fons lately come to *London*) prefents me this occafion to acquaint you, that I removed laft " *Chriftmas* from *The Temple*, and took a fmall houfe in *Peartree-ftreet*, near *St. Luke's, Old-ftreet*, " where I fpend my time chiefly among books, or in my garden. That I am ftill a dealer in the " former, you may perceive by thefe propofals. You know I publifhed the greateft part of *Mafon's* " Works feveral years ago ; but had not then the whole. Now, having luckily procured the laft " Sermons, which I had been fo long in queft of, I have printed them on the fame paper and letter " with the reft, which makes the collection complete. There are a good many copies of the for- " mer ftill on my hands ; which I hope may go off now. Thofe who have the reft already, may " have thefe Sermons by themfelves. I prefume, Sir, upon the favour of your intereft to promote " this method of diftributing them. All I need to obferve to you is, that they will coft no more " than five farthings *per* fheet. I fhall begin to publifh the firft week in *June*. Whatever encou- " ragement you procure me, fhall be placed to the long account of former obligations. *May* 11, 1747."

* *Suidas* mentions this work of *Xenophon* of *Ephefus* ; which is alfo taken notice of by *Politian* and *Montfaucon*. The publick were indebted for the abovementioned impreffion of it to *Henry Dave- nant*, Efq; who lent a copy of the MS. to Dr. *Cocchi*, by whom it was tranflated into *Latin*. It was alfo tranflated into *Italian* by *Salvini*.

† The Earl of *Corke* gives the following character of this learned Phyfician in his tenth letter from *Italy* to Mr. *Duncombe*, dated " *Florence, Nov.* 29, 1754. Mr. [now Sir *Horace*] *Mann* is fortunate " in the friendfhip, fkill, and care of his phyfician, Dr. *Cocchi*, who has formerly been in *England* " with the late Lord *Huntingdon*. The Doctor is much prejudiced in favour of the *Englifh*, though " he refided fome years among us. He is a man of moft extenfive learning, underftands, reads, and " fpeaks all the *European* languages, is ftudious, polite, modeft, humane, and inftructive. He will " always be admired and beloved by all who know him. Could I live with thefe two gentlemen " only, and converfe with few or none others, I fhould fcarce defire to return to *England* for many " years." And in a note it is faid, " Dr. *Cocchi* is now (1773) no more. His fon is one of the " prefent *literati* of *Florence*."

‡ This he again reprinted in 1733.

§ That the requeft was complied with, appears by their five receipts, dated *May* 23, 1728, now in the hands of Mr. *Thomas Bowyer*.

P. 54. *In the article* Kennet, *read,* M. A. *Jan.* 22, 1684; B. D. *May* 5, 1694; D. D. *July* 19, 1700. His numerous and valuable MS. collections, which were once in the collection of Mr. *West*, were purchased by the Earl of *Shelburne*; among these are two volumes in a large Atlas folio, which were intended for publication under the following comprehensive title:

" DIPTYCHA ECCLESIÆ ANGLICANÆ:	Priores,
five	Decani,
TABULÆ SACRÆ; in quibus facili ordine	Thesaurarii,
recensentur	Præcentores,
ARCHIEPISCOPI,	Cancellarii,
EPISCOPI, eorumque	Archidiaconi,
SUFFRAGANEI,	et melioris notæ Canonici,
VICARII GENERALES,	continua serie deducti
et CANCELLARII;	a GULIELMI I. Conquestu,
Ecclesiarum insuper Cathedralium	ad auspicata GUL. III. tempora."

Among the numerous publications of Bishop *Kennet*, occurs a tract printed in 4to, 1713, under the title of " Bibliothecæ *Americanæ* Primordia; an Attempt towards lay-" ing the Foundation of an *American* Library, in several Books, Papers, and Writings, " humbly given to the Society for Propagation of the Gospel in Foreign Parts;" in the Preface to which, he mentions a design of " gathering together an Antiquarian and " Historical Library for the use of a Cathedral Church; wherein some progress was " then made, and he hoped in a few years to finish it, and settle it for ever *." In a late publication, called " Collectanea Curiosa," Vol. II. p. 433, is a copy of a letter written by Mr. *White Kennet* about the year 1698, and sent without a name to Bishop *Stilling-fleet*, at whose disposal it was then said Sir *Thomas Winford Cook's* 10,000l. was left.

* " Dr. *Kennet*, with strict enquiries, and considerable expences, had been long gathering up the scattered remains of our *English* writers, or any other authors upon the subject of our *English* affairs, from the very beginning of *English* printing, to the latter end of Queen *Elizabeth*, which, when put in order of time, would make up such a series and connexion of the Antiquities and History of this Church and Nation, as would be of great light and service to the world; and would be an ornament of public use in any cathedral or collegiate church, of the most easy access to men of letters, engaged in satisfying their own curiosity, or rather in serving posterity. This collection, amounting to about fifteen hundred volumes and small tracts, was placed in a private room at *Peterborough*, in order to be daily supplied and augmented, under the care of the Rev. Mr. *Joseph Sparke*†, a member of that church, of very good literature, and very able to assist in that good design. There is a large written Catalogue of them, thus inscribed:

" Index Librorum
" Aliquot Vetustis
" Quos in commune bonum congessit
" W. K. Decan. Petriburg. MDCCXII."

In this collection, there are most of the printed Legends of Saints; the oldest Rituals and Liturgies; the first printed Statutes and Laws, the most ancient Homilies and Sermons, the first editions of the *English* Schoolmen, Postillers, Expounders, &c. with a great many fragments of our ancient Language, Usage, Customs, Rights, Tenures, and such other things as tend to illustrate the Antiquities and History of *Great Britain* and *Ireland*, and the successive state of Civil Government, Religion and Learning in them ‡. Besides this, the Dean enriched the Common Library of the Church with some very useful books; and added to their stock of monuments and records, an abstract of the Collections made by Dr. *John Cosens*, one of his worthy predecessors." *Life of Bp.* Kennet, by the Rev. Mr. *William Newton*, 1730, p. 149.

† Afterwards, in conjunction with the Rev. *Timothy New*, founder of the Gentlemen's Society at *Peterborough*. See the " Reliquiæ Galeanæ," p. 98.—*Charles Balguy*, M. D. and Dr. *Thomas Robinson* prebendary of that church, were members of the Society.

‡ In a letter from the Dean to a friend, dated, *Pet. July* 27, 1717, he has these words: " I have improved " the Collection I have been long making for an Historical Antiquarian Library, consisting of the oldest books " relating to *English* writers and affairs. I have considerably increased my Catalogue of the Lives of eminent " Men."—Such a work from so able a writer would have been a great acquisition to Biography.

" I am

I am happy to add to this article a letter, which I have in the Bishop's hand-writing, addressed to " The Reverend Mr. *Thomas Baker*, B. D. at *St. John's College* in *Cambridge*;" and endorsed by that learned and conscientious Divine " The last letter I " had from my honoured Friend the Bishop of *Peterborough*."

" Reverend Sir, *Westminster, June* 13, 1728.
" I have taken an opportunity by my curate Mr. *Land*, of *Clare-Hall*, to send down
" a tedious heavy book for your acceptance of it; not a present so much as a debt in
" all justice due to you for lending me so many good materials, that your own hand
" could have put into better order and more correctness. The volume too large brings
" me no profit, and, I dare say, no credit. In good truth, the scheme was laid for con-
" science sake, to restore a good old principle, that History should be purely matter of
" fact; and when such matters are delivered upon professed authorities for them, every
" reader by examining and comparing may make out a History upon his own judgement.
" I have collections transcribed for another volume, if the bookseller will run the ha-
" zard of printing, which will reach to 1670. If within that compass you have any
" notes of like nature, I desire you to be of the same communicative mind; and if you
" ever submit to the dull work of running over this first volume, nothing can oblige
" me more than to be told of my faults of commission or omission, that in a second vo-
" lume the world may be honestly informed of them. You will see I have been in too
" much hurry for a writer; and without any ill meaning, I could envy your recess in a
" college-life, where I am sure you are doing true service to posterity, and (what is
" greater) can there despise the present world. I have delivered to our good friend Dr.
" *Knight* your second volume of Dr. *Calamy's* Abridgement, with your exact notes upon
" it; and thank you for the use of that and many like favours. I pray God give a
" blessing to your life and studies. I am your very much obliged friend and brother,
" WH. PETERBOR."

P. 55. There is a portrait of Mr. *Spinckes*, engraved by *Vertue*, from a painting of
J. Wollaston, with this inscription: " The Reverend Mr. *Spinckes*. This very eminent
" Divine was venerable of aspect, orthodox in faith; his adversaries being judges. He
" had uncommon learning and superior judgement. His patience was great, his self-
" denial greater, his charity still greater. His temper sweet and unmoveable beyond
" comparison. His exemplary life was concluded with an happy death *July* 21, 1727,
" in his 74th year."

P. 58. l. 5, 6. read, " The Tragedies of *Sophocles*, translated from the *Greek*, with
" notes historical, moral, and critical, wherein several mistakes of editors and the old
" scholiasts are corrected, and the true sense of the author cleared. By *George Adams*,
" A. B. late of *St. John's College*, in *Cambridge*," 2 vols. 8vo.

Ibid. Mr. *Bonwicke's* letter to his wife is here preserved;

" My Dearest, [*Undated.*]
" You were thinking, quickly after dear *Ambrose's* [*] death, that an account of his life
" might be of some benefit to the world. I have here drawn it up as well as I could:
" if any thing material be omitted, dear *Jemmy* [+], by your direction, will be able to sup-
" ply it. He, therefore, must be let into the secret; and I depend upon you two, that
" it shall for ever be a secret to all the world beside, who was the author. He must
" therefore take the trouble of transcribing it as soon as he comes hither after my
" death, for which I bequeath him the two inclosed guineas: and if my dear friend
" Mr. *Roper* be living, I would have that copy be shewed him by *Jemmy* as of his own
" motion, and wholly submitted to his judgment, to be altered as he shall think fit. I
" would have my good friend Mr. *Browne's* consent likewise procured (if it may be)
" for the publishing his letter in this account. And if Mr. *Jackson* [‡] and Mr. *Newton* [§],

[*] See pp. 18. 45. [+] Another son, to whom Mr. *Bowyer* was executor. See p. 45.
[‡] Of Mr. *Jackson* see above, p. 59. [§] Printed in this volume, p. 60.

" are

" are willing to make any alterations in their verses, pray let it be done before they are
" published. I hope, my dearest, you will be at the charge of printing it handsomely;
" and if your bookseller be faithful, it is possible that charge may be made up to you
" again in a little time. You will, I know, think it proper that the Master of the Col-
" lege, Mr. *Roper*, Mr. *Baker*, and Mr. *Verdon*, dear *Ambrose's* special benefactors,
" should be presented with these better bound than ordinary; and that *Jemmy* should
" give his tutor one handsomely bound, and distribute about a score among the lads
" where he thinks they may do most good. I am sorry I must bequeath you both this
" trouble; but if by this means one soul be gained, your reward will be great. How-
" ever, I hope our good God will graciously accept the honest intention of us all,
" through the merits of our blessed Saviour *Jesus Christ*. Amen."

P. 61. The List of Printers was gathered up by one *Samuel Negus*, about the year
1724, who took upon him to distinguish them by their political principles; and was rewarded by a letter-carrier's place in the Post-Office. *(Oldys* in Brit. Top. I. 82.) His
letter *, with the list which accompanied it, is copied at large below.

* " To the Right Honourable Lord Viscount TOWNSHEND, One of his Majesty's Principal
" Secretaries of State.

" MY GOOD LORD,

" I was persuaded by some friends, who have the honour to be known to your Lordship, (which
" is a happiness I have not yet arrived at) to offer this List to your Lordship's perusal. I have the
" misfortune of being brought up to this business, and was set up of my trade by the goodness and
" generosity of my ever-honoured uncle, Captain *Samuel Brown* of *Norwich* (through the persua-
" sions of my two excellent friends Mr. *John Gurney* and Mr. *John Eccleston*). Your Lordship
" may not be altogether insensible of the hardships and the temptations a young beginner in Printing
" may meet with from the disaffected; and how hard it is for such men to subsist, whose natural
" inclinations are to be truly loyal and truly honest, and at the same time want employ; while the
" disaffected printers flourish, and have more than they can dispatch. I have been a printer about
" 23 years, but have not been for myself above two years; in which time I have suffered very
" much for want of employ. On this account I have implored Counsellor *Britiff*, Mr. *Bacon*, Mr.
" *Gurney*, Colonel *Francis Negus*, Mr. *Churchill*, and some other gentlemen, that they would please
" to move your Lordship on my behalf, that you would please to get me admitted as an Extraordi-
" nary Messenger, in which station I should not doubt of pleasing your Lordship.

" When your Lordship is pleased to cast an eye on the number of Printing-houses there are in
" and about the Cities of *London* and *Westminster*, your Lordship will not be so much surprized
" at the present ingratitude and disaffection of a rebellious set of men. They have no way to
" vend their poison, but by the help of the press; thus printing-houses are daily set up, and
" supported by unknown hands. The country printers in general copy from the rankest pa-
" pers in *London*; and thus the poison is transmitted from one hand to another through all his
" Majesty's dominions: how far this may tend to the corrupting the minds of his Majesty's
" subjects, and how detrimental it may prove to the State, your Lordship is a competent judge.
" It was thought fit by an order of Council, in the Reign of Queen *Elizabeth* †, That there
" should be no more than 30 Printing-houses in the Cities of *London* and *Westminster*, one
" at the University at *Oxford*, and one at the University at *Cambridge*; so that by this
" means the State had them always under its eye, and knew presently where to find, those
" printers who any way disturbed or offended her. It was said by a judicious gentleman,
" that it might not be an improper question, ' Whether the ill use made of the liberty given
" to the press, was not the principal occasion of the late rebellions and disturbances?' It
" is impossible, my good Lord, to reduce the number of printers to what once they were;
" yet I would humbly inform your Lordship, that there are many of them who give great
" offence and disturbance to the state, and who never have been brought up to that busi-
" ness, and ought to be put down. If the hints here offered may be of service, and not
" displease your Lordship, they will answer their desired end."

† In p. 493 the reader has seen the names of all the news-papers in the reign of Queen *Anne*. They are given
above in that of *George* the First. Innumerable are those of the present day. Besides *The Gazette*, *London* alone
produces ten daily papers (*Daily Advertiser*, *Gazetteer*, *Public Advertiser*, *Morning Chronicle*, *Morning Post*, *London
Courant*, *Morning Herald*, *General Advertiser*, and *Noon Gazette*); and nine which appear each three evenings in a
week (*St. James's Chronicle*, *General Evening Post*, *Whitehall Evening Post*, *London Chronicle*, *Lloyd's Evening Post*,
London Evening Post, *English Chronicle*, *Middlesex Journal*, and *London Packet*). A Sunday's paper and a great variety of Weekly Miscellanies may be added to the list. The country news-papers are also very numerous.

A compleat and private Lift of all the Printing-houfes in and about the Cities of *London* and *Weftminfter*, together with the Printers Names, what News-papers they print, and where they are to be found : alfo an account of the Printing-houfes in the feveral Corporation Towns in *England*. Moft humbly laid before the Right Honourable the Lord Vifcount *Townfhend*.

Known to be well-affected to His Majefty King *George*.

Bafket, *Black-Fryers*, and Printer to the King's moft excellent Majefty

Buckley, *Amen-Corner*, the worthy Printer of the Gazette

Botham, *Jewin-ftreet*

Bridge, *Little Moor-fields*

Burton, *St. Jones's-lane*

Darby, *Bartholomew-clofe*

Downing, *Eodem*

Downing, *St. Jones's-lane*

Hunter, *Jewin-ftreet*

Humpheries, *Bartholomew-lane*

Holt, *St. Jones's-lane*

Jenour, *Giltfpur-ftreet*, and Printer of the Flying-Poft

Janeway, *White Fryers*

Leach, *Old-Baily*, and Printer of the Poft-Man

Larkin, *Bifhopfgate-ftreet*

Mount, late of *Tower-Hill*

Norton, *Little-Britain*, Printer of Latin, Greek, and Hebrew to his Majefty

Negus, *Silver-ftreet*, near *Wood-ftreet*

Pearfon, *Alderfgate-ftreet*

Parker, *Gofwell-ftreet*

Parker, Sen. *Salifbury-ftreet*, and Printer of a Half-penny Poft

Pickard, *Salifbury-Court*

Palmer, *Great Swan-Alley, Gofwell-ftreet*

Roberts, *Warwick-lane*

Read, *White-Fryers, Fleet-ftreet*, and Printer of a Half-penny Poft, and a Weekly-Journal

Raylton, *George-Yard, Lombard-ftreet*

Sam. Aris, *Creed-Lane*

Staples, *St. Jones's-Lane*

Tonfon and Watts, *Cov. Garden*.

Tookey, behind the *Royal-Exchange*

Wilkins, *Little-Britain*, and Printer of the White-hall Evening-Poft, the White-hall and London Journal

Wood, *Eodem*

Woodfall, Without *Temple-Bar*

Wilmot, *Fenchurch-ftreet*

Nonjurors.

Bettenham, *St. Jones's-Lane*

Dalton, *St. Jones's-Lane*

Bowyer, *White-Fryers, Fleet-ftreet*

Said to be High-Flyers.

Applebey, *Fleet-Ditch*, Printer of the Daily Journal, and of a Weekly Journal bearing his own Name

Barber, *Lambeth-Hill*, (one of the Aldermen of *London*)

Badham, *Fleet-ftreet*

Bruges, *Jewin-ftreet*

Clark, *Thames-ftreet*

Collins, *Old-Baily*

Cluer, *Bow Church Yard*

Edlin, near the *Savoy*

Gilbert *and* Phillips, *Smithfield*

Gent, *Pye Corner*

Grantham, *Pater-Nofter-Row*

Heathcot, *Baldwin's Gardens*, Printer of a Half-penny-Poft bearing his own Name

Hind, *Old-Baily*

Humpheries, Printer to the Parifh-Clerks, *Silver-ftreet*, in the City

James, *Little-Britain*, Author and Printer of the Poft-Boy

Ilive, *Alderfgate-ftreet*

Lee, *St. John's-Lane*

Lightbody, *Old-Baily*

Meere, *Old-Baily*, and Printer of the Daily-Poft and *Britifh* Journal

Midwinter, *Pye-Corner*

Mift, *Great Carter-ftreet*, and Printer of a fcandalous Weekly Journal bearing his own Name

Motte, *Alderfgate-ftreet*

Moor, *Southwark*

Norris, *Little-Britain*

Nut, in the *Savoy*

Powell, *Alderfgate-ftreet*

Redmayne, *Jewin-ftreet*

Richardfon, *Salifbury-Court*

Says, *Alderfgate-ftreet*

Sharp, *Ivy-Lane*, Printer of the Freeholder's Journal

Says, *Bifhopfgate-ftreet*

Took, *Old-Baily*

Todd, *Fleet-ftreet*

Wild, *Alderfgate-ftreet*

Roman Catholicks.

Berrington, *Silver-ftreet* in *Bloomsbury*, Printer of the Evening-Poft

Howlett, *Eodem*

Gardiner, *Lincoln's-Inn-Fields*

Clifton, *Old-Baily*

A Lift of the feveral News-Papers publifhed in *London*, with the Printers Names, and where they may be found.

Daily Papers.

Daily Courant, printed by the worthy Mr. Buckley, *Amen-Corner*

Daily Poft, Meere, *Old-Baily*

Daily Journal, Applebey, near *Fleet-Ditch*

Weekly Journals.

Mift's Journal, *Gr. Carter-Lane*

Freeholder's Journal, Sharp, *Ivy-Lane*

Applebey's Journal, near *Fleet-Ditch*

Read's Journal, *White-Fryers* in *Fleet-ftreet*

London Journal, *Wilkins*, in *Little-Britain*

White-Hall Journal, *Wilkins*, in *Little-Britain*

Papers publifhed three Times every Week.

Poft-Man, Leach, *Old-Baily*

Poft-Boy, James, *Little-Britain*

Fly-Poft, Jenour, *Giltfpur-ftreet*

White-Hall Evening Poft, Wilkins, in *Little-Britain*

St. *James's* Poft, Grantham, in *Pater-Nofter-Row*

Berrington's Evening Poft, *Silver-ftreet, Bloomsbury*

The *Englifhman*, Wilkins, in *Little-Britain*

Half-penny Pofts, publifhed three times every Week.

Heathcot's, *Baldwin's Gardens*

Parker's, *Salifbury-Court*

Read's, *White-Fryers, Fleet-ftreet*

Printing Houfes in the Country.

Norwich	2	*Canterbury*	2
Stamford	1	*Briftol*	2
Northampton	1	*Bury St. Edmonds*	1
Gloucefter	1		
Nottingham	2	*Shrewsbury*	2
Derby	1	*Salifbury*	1
Gofport	1	*Winchefter*	1
Weftchefter	2	*Ipfwich*	1
Chichefter	1	*Coventry*	1
Leicefter	1	*Doncafter*	1
Newcaftle	1	*York*	2

P. 64. note, l. 1. The *third* volume was published nine years before the *second.*

P. 65. Some other Poems by Dr. *Taylor* are preserved in the " Select Collection, 1782," vol. VII.

Ibid. First sub-note, for *Durham* read *London.*

Ibid. Second sub-note. " If there is any doubt of the merit of the *Cambridge* prefs, " look at *Virgil, Terence,* &c. 4 volumes in 4to ; *Bentley's Horace;* Pieces of *Tully* by " *Davies; Cæsar* by the same ; *Bentham's Ely,* &c." *T. F.*

P. 66. *Jurin* was master of the Free-school at *Newcastle* in the former part of his life, till he had got money enough to follow his favourite profession. He acquired by it a fortune at *Hackney;* and as he did not begin very early, he could not be young at his death.

P. 67. l. 31. *badness of his furniture*] " At *St. John's,* and, I believe, most colleges, the " under-graduate that first had a set of mahogany chairs is still well remembered." *T. F.*

P. 68. " If Dr. *Taylor* could have attained to the gout, he probably would have had " no need of the surgeon's knife." Mr. *Markland* to Mr. *Bowyer, Mar.* 24, 1766.— " What Mr. *Clarke* told me, that Dr. *Taylor* died worth 14 or 1500*l.* surprizes me, in so " learned and generous a man." Ibid. *April* 13.

P. 75. Last note, after 1755, add, as a *sixth* had been in 1735.

P. 77. In a letter which will be printed in the Appendix to p. 168, Mr. *Maittaire* tells Lord *Oxford* that " he repents of having printed so many copies as 300, when 200 " might have sufficed."

P. 81. Mr. *Bowyer* printed Mr. *Jebb's* translation of *Martin's* " Answer to *Emlyn,"* in 1718; and a new edition of it in 1719. The worthy Dean of *Cashell,* who is now near fourscore, very happily possesses the health and activity of forty.

Ibid. An Act of Parliament was passed " for granting to *Samuel Buckley,* Citizen and " Stationer of *London,* the sole liberty of printing and reprinting the Histories of *Thu-* " *anus,* with additions and improvements, during the term therein limited." Whilst the Bill was depending in Parliament, Mr. *Buckley* published " A short State of the " publick Encouragement given to Printing and Bookselling in *France, Holland, Ger-* " *many,* and at *London.* With Reasons humbly offered to the Lords Spiritual and Tem- " poral in Parliament assembled, for granting to S. *Buckley* such Privilege for *Thuanus* " in *Latin,* as is already granted to every *British* Subject who is possessed of the Copy " of any Book in *English."*

Ibid. The remains of Mr. *Mompesson* were brought to *England,* and interred in the family-vault in the church-yard of *Sundrich,* in *Kent,* where the following inscription was placed to his memory by his elder brother, *Thomas Mompesson,* Esq; a bencher of *The Middle Temple* (who died *May* 11, 1767) :

" M. S.
HENRICI MOMPESSON,
Thomæ Mompesson de *Durnfold,*
in agro *Dorsetensi,* Arm.
Filii natu minoris :
Qui tabe pulmonari graviter affectus,
ad leniores *Galliæ Narbonensis* auras
ut unicum quod restabat remedium,
perfugere hortatus,
Dum istuc iter faceret,
Septimo à *Portu Iccio* lapide
truculenti sex latrones imparatum adorti.

direptis pecuniis juguloque fœdissimè discisso,
pro mortuo reliquerent.
Hoc vulnere,
Cum per 48 horas elanguisset,
Spiritum Deo piè reddidit,
Anno Salutis 1723,
Ætatis suæ 26.
Carissimi (dum vixerit) reliquias,
Ex *Gallia* deportatas,
Hoc tumulo condi curavit
Mœrens frater unicus
T. M."

P. 82. l. 5. read, a single sheet in folio. See p. 95.

P. 82. Add to the books of 1733 " Bishop *Hare's Hebrew* Psalter," 8vo. The celebrated *Psalmanazar* * had some years before prepared an edition of the Psalms with *Leusden's Latin* Version in the opposite column, and critical Notes ; intending it should be printed by Mr. *Palmer*, who declined undertaking it, being in treaty with Dr. *Washburn* to print the edition of Bishop *Hare*, which passed afterwards through the press of Mr. *Bowyer* †.

P. 83.

* Author of the fabulous " History of *Formosa* ;" and of a very considerable part of " The Universal History." *Psalmanazar's* portion of that useful and laborious work is particularly pointed out in his own Memoirs of himself, published the year after his decease, which happened *May* 3, 1763, at the age of 83.

† " This performance did not appear in print till seven or eight years after ‡ ; and then to my great surprise, for Mr. *Palmer* had amused me with the belief that the design was set aside, either on account of its being found impracticable, or at least too difficult and dangerous. It appeared, however, that Mr. *Palmer* imposed upon me, and that he knew that the design was carried on in another printing-house, though with such privacy, that I never heard or dreamed of it, though I had been long acquainted with Mr. *Bowyer*, who was employed in the printing of it. So far from it was I, that I began to think Mr. *Palmer* had only invented that story to divert me from printing my proposed edition, in order to set me upon another work, in which he was more immediately concerned, and expected greater credit, as well as present profit from. This was his History of Printing, which he had long promised to the world, but for which he was not at all qualified. However, he designed

‡ The cause of this delay is thus related by *Psalmanazar*. " His Lordship had excepted against Mr. *Palmer's Hebrew* types, which were of *Athias's* font, and a little battered, and insisted upon his having a new set from Mr. *Caslon*, which greatly exceeded them in beauty. But Mr. *Palmer* was so deep in debt to him, that he knew not how to procure it from him without ready money, which he was not able to spare. The Bishop likewise insisted upon having some *Roman* and *Italic* types cast with some distinguishing mark, to direct his readers to the *Hebrew* letters they were designed to answer, and these required a new set of punches and matrices before they could be cast, and that would have delayed the work, which Mr. *Palmer* was in haste to go about, that he might the sooner finger some of his Lordship's money. This put him upon such an unfair stratagem, as, when discovered, quite disgusted his Lordship against him, viz. representing Mr. *Caslon* as an idle, dilatory workman, who would in all probability make them wait several years for those few types, if ever he finished them. That he was indeed the only artist that could supply him with those types, but that he hated work, and was not to be depended upon, and therefore advised his Lordship to make shift with some sort which he could substitute, and would answer the same purpose, rather than run the risk of staying so long, and being perhaps disappointed. The Bishop, however, being resolved, if possible, to have the desired types, sent for Mr. *Bowyer*, and asked him whether he knew a letter-founder that could cast him such a set out of hand, who immediately recommended Mr. *Caslon* ; and, being told what a sad and disadvantageous character he had heard of him, Mr. *Bowyer* not only assured his Lordship that it was a very false and unjust one, but engaged to get the above-mentioned types cast by him, and a new font of his *Hebrew* ones, in as short a time as the thing could possibly be done. Mr. *Caslon* was accordingly sent for by his Lordship, and having made him sensible of the time the new ones would require to be made ready for use, did produce them according to his promise, and the book was soon after put to the press. As soon as I had finished what I, and some of my friends as well as I, thought a sufficient confutation of the Bishop's performance, and in the same language, though not so florid and elegant *Latin*, I sent to desire one of my booksellers to enquire of Mr. *Bowyer*, whether the new types cast for his Lordship were still in his possession ? and whether I might be permitted the use of them, in the answer I had prepared for the press ? I was answered in the affirmative ; but one bookseller took it into his head to ask at the same time, what number of copies his Lordship had caused to be printed of his Psalter ? and was answered only five hundred ; one half of which had been presented by his Lordship to his learned friends, both in and out of *England*, and most of the rest were still unsold, there being but few among the learned, that were curious in such matters ; the performance having been disapproved by all that had seen it. This news so cooled the booksellers eagerness after my answer, that, upon my coming to town, and their acquainting me with the state of the case, I was quite discouraged from printing it. For they concluded, from what Mr. *Bowyer* had said, that it would be dangerous to print above three hundred of mine, the charge of which being deducted, the profit, upon a supposition that they were all sold, would be so small, that they could not afford me above two or three guineas for my copy (which would have made about seven or eight sheets of a middling octavo) without being losers. This was their way of computing the matter, against which having nothing to object, I locked up the papers in my cabinet, where they have lain ever since. They did indeed offer me better terms, and to print a greater number of copies, if I would be at the trouble of printing it in *English*, which they thought would be more universally read, out of dislike to the Bishop ; but, besides that I cared not to be at the pains of *Englishing* it, I thought it beneath the subject to print it in any other language but that in which his was wrote, and so wholly declined it."

Y y y

to

P. 83. Dr. *Madden* ("a name," says Dr. *Johnson*, "which *Ireland* ought to honour,") received his education at *Dublin*. He appears however to have been in *England* in 1729; and having written a tragedy, was, as he himself says, tempted to let it come out by the offer of a noble study of books from the profits of it. In 1732, he published his

to have added a second part, relating to the practical part, which was more suited to his genius, and in which he designed to have given a full account of all that relates to that branch, from the letter-founding, to the most elegant way of printing, imposing, binding, &c. in which he had made considerable improvements of his own, besides those he had taken from foreign authors; but this second part, though but then as it were in embryo, met with such early and strenuous opposition from the respective bodies of letter-founders, printers, and book-binders, under an ill-grounded apprehension, that the discovery of the mystery of those arts, especially the two first, would render them cheap and contemptible (whereas the very reverse would have been the case, they appearing indeed the more curious and worthy our admiration, the better they are known) that he was forced to set it aside. But as to the first part, *viz.* the History of Printing, he met with the greatest encouragement, not only from them, but from a very great number of the Learned, who all engaged to subscribe largely to it, particularly the late Earls of *Pembroke* and *Oxford*, and the famous Doctor *Mead*, whose libraries were to furnish him with the noblest materials for the compiling of it, and did so accordingly. The misfortune was, that Mr. *Palmer*, knowing himself unequal to the task, had turned it over to one *Papiat*, a broken *Irish* bookseller then in *London*, of whom he had a great opinion, though still more unqualified for it than he, and only aimed at getting money from him, without ever doing any thing towards it, except amusing him with fair promises for near three quarters of a year. He had so long dallied with him, that they were come within three months of the time in which Mr. *Palmer* had engaged to produce a complete plan, and a number or two of the first part, by way of specimen of the work, *viz.* the invention and improvement of it by *John Faust* at *Mentz*; and these were to be shewn at a grand meeting of learned men, of which Dr. *Mead* was president that year, and, being his singular friend and patron, was to have promoted a large subscription and payment, which Mr. *Palmer* stood in great need of at that time; whereas *Papiat* had got nothing ready but a few loose and imperfect extracts out of *Chevallier*, *Le Caille*, and some other *French* authors on the subject, but which could be of little or no use, because he frequently mistook them, and left blanks for the words he did not understand. These, however, such as they were, Mr. *Palmer* brought to me, and earnestly pressed me that I would set aside all other things I might be then about, and try to produce the expected plan and specimen by the time promised, since he must be ruined both in credit and pocket, if he disappointed his friends of it. It was well for him and me, that the subject lay within so small a compass as the consulting of about twelve or fourteen principal authors; so that I easily fell upon a proper plan of the work, which I divided into three parts, the first of which was, to give an account of the invention of the art, and its first essays by *Faust* at *Mentz*, and of its improvement by fusile or metal types, varnish, ink, &c. by his son-in-law *Peter Schoeffer*. The second to contain its propagation and further improvement, through most parts of *Europe*, under the most celebrated printers; and the third an account of its introduction and progress into *England*. This, together with above one half of the first part, were happily finished, and produced by the time appointed, and met with more approbation and encouragement from his friends than I feared it would, being conscious how much better it might have turned out, would time have permitted it. And this I chiefly mention, not so much to excuse the defects of such a horrid performance, as because it hath given me since frequent occasion to observe how many much more considerable works have been spoiled, both at home and abroad, through the impatience of the subscribers; though this is far enough from being the only, or even the greatest inconvenience that attends most of those kinds of subscriptions. As to Mr. *Palmer*, his circumstances were by this time so unaccountably low and unfortunate, considering the largeness and success of his business, and that he was himself a sober industrious man, and free from all extravagance, that he could not extricate himself by any other way, but by a statute of bankruptcy, which caused his history to go sluggishly on; so that notwithstanding all the care and kind assistance of his good friend Dr. *Mead*, a stubborn distemper, which his misfortunes brought upon him, carried him off before the third part of it was finished. This defect, however, was happily supplied by the late noble Earl of *Pembroke*, who being informed by Mr. *Pain* the engraver, Mr. *Palmer*'s brother-in-law, what condition the remainder was left in, and that I was the person who had wrote the former parts, sent for me, and, with his usual generosity, enjoined me to complete the work, according to the plan; and not only defrayed all the charges of it, even of the paper and printing, but furnished me with all necessary materials out of his own library; and, when the work was finished, his Lordship reserved only some few copies to himself, and gave the remainder of the impression to Mr. *Palmer*'s widow, not without some farther tokens of his liberality."

5.

" Memoirs

" Memoirs of the Twentieth Century *." In 1740, we find him in his native country, and in that year setting apart the sum of one hundred pounds to be distributed in premiums for the encouragement of arts, manufactures, and science ; and the same sum he continued to bestow every year while he lived. The good effects of these well-applied benefactions have not only been felt to advantage in the kingdom where they were given, but have even extended their influence to its sister country, having given rise to the society for the encouragement of arts and sciences in *London*. In an oration spoken at *Dublin*, *Dec.* 6, 1757, by Mr. *Sheridan*, that gentleman took occasion to mention Dr. *Madden*'s bounty, and intended to have proceeded in the following manner, but was prevented by observing the Doctor to be then present. Speaking of the admirable institutions of premiums, he went on, " Whose author, had he never contributed any thing farther to the " good of his country, would have deserved immortal honour, and must have been held " in reverence by latest posterity. But the unwearied and disinterested endeavours, dur- " ing a long course of years, of this truly good man, in a variety of branches to pro- " mote industry, and consequently the welfare of this kingdom ; and the mighty bene- " fits which have thence resulted to the community ; have made many of the good " people of *Ireland* sorry, that a long-talked-of scheme has not hitherto been put in " execution : that we might not appear inferior in point of gratitude to the citizens of " *London*, with respect to a fellow citizen † (surely not with more reason), and that like " them we might be able to address our patriot, *Præsenti tibi maturos largimur honores*." Dr. *Madden* had some good church preferment in *Ireland*, where he died *Dec*. 30, 1765. It is on his authority that Dr. *Johnson* has authenticated the marriage of *Swift* and *Stella*. Six very striking lines from his poem called " *Boulter's* Monument" are quoted in *Johnson's* Dictionary, art. SPORT. There is a fine mezzotinto of him, a whole length, by *J. Brooks*, with this inscription:

" SAMUEL MADDEN, D.D.
" Quique sui memores alios fecere merendo,
" Omnibus his niveâ cinguntur tempora vittâ." VIRG. Æn. vi. 664.

P. 83. Dr. *Webster*, who was born in *December* 1689, was grandson to Dr. *Sparrow*, (" a Bishop of great learning and piety, whose family were gentlemen generations before " he was a Lord ‡") and a member of the university of *Cambridge*. In 1715 he was made curate of *St. Dunstan in the West* ; and had taken the degree of M. A. in 1723, when Mr. *Bowyer* printed for him " The Life of General *Monk*, late Duke of *Albermarle* ; " from an original Manuscript of *Thomas Skinner*, M. D. Author of ' Motus Compositi' ; " in which is a particular Account of that most memorable March from *Coldstream* to " *London*, the Preparations for it in *Scotland*, and of the happy Consequences of it in " *England*. To which is added a Preface, giving an Account of the Manuscript, and " some Observations in Vindication of General *Monk's* Conduct," 8vo. This volume he dedicated to the Countess *Granville* and to *John* Lord *Gower*, who were descended from the *Monks*. His next production was, " The Clergy's Right of Maintenance vindicated," 8vo ; which is also inscribed to Lord *Gower*, who was afterwards his patron. In 1729 he published " Two Discourses ; the first concerning the nature of Error in Doctrines merely specu- " lative, shewing that the Belief of such Doctrines may be required of us as necessary " Terms of Salvation ; wherein also the Case of positive Institutions is considered. The " second, shewing that the Doctrine of the Trinity is not merely speculative. In An- " swer to the Arguments of Mr. *Sykes* and Mr. *Chubb*. With a Preface, containing some

* The great scarcity of this book has been already mentioned. A second copy of it (marked only at 10s. 6d.) appeared in the Catalogue of *H. Chapman*, in *January* 1782.
† Sir *John Barnard*.
‡ Dr. *Webster's* words are here used.

" Remarks

" Remarks on the prefent Times, particularly in relation to the Clergy." In 1730,
" The New Teftament of our Saviour *Jefus Chrift*, according to the ancient *Latin* Edi-
" tion, with Critical Remarks upon the Literal Meaning in different Places. From the
" *French* of Father *Simon*," 2 vols. 4to; and in the fame year, " The Duty of keeping
" the whole Law; a Difcourfe on St. *James*, **x. 11.** wherein are fome feafonable Re-
" marks upon the Deifts," 8vo. In 1731 he was removed from his curacy at *St. Dunftan's*; and publifhed in that year " The Fitnefs of the Witneffes of the Refurrection of
" *Chrift* confidered; in Anfwer to the principal Objections againft them," 8vo; and alfo
" two fhilling-pamphlets and a letter in a news-paper" in defence of Bifhop *Hare*, who
had been attacked by Mr. *Gordon*, the tranflator of *Tacitus*, on fome paffages in a 30th of
January Sermon; for which he received the thanks of Bp. *Hare*, but " no preferment, nor
" one farthing of reward." He was after this period a year and a half out of employment,
and living all the while upon credit, or (to ufe an expreffion of his own) he " muft have died
" in obfcurity like a poifoned rat in a hole." In this fituation his eldeft brother was at the
expence of obtaining for him in 1732 his Doctor's degree in divinity; foon after which, he
was kindly noticed by Bifhop *Gooch*, who gave him in *Auguft* that year the curacy of *St.
Clement Eaft Cheap*, with a falary of 70l.; and in *February*, 1732-3, he was prefented by a
relation to the rectory of *Deptden* in *Suffolk*, worth 102l. a year. In 1733 Mr. *Bowyer*
printed for him " A Vindication of *Euftace Budgell*," and " Propofals for printing
" F. *Simon's* Critical Hiftory * ;" and in that year he began " The Weekly Mifcellany,"
under the fictitious name of " *Richard Hooker*, Efq; of *The Inner Temple*." This undertaking, which, he fays, "was more approved of than fupported, procured him no-
" thing but great trouble, much ill-will, and abufe of all forts, great expence, and much
"† difficulties." From being crowded with religious effays, the news-paper foon acquired the quaint appellation of " Old Mother *Hooker's* Journal." In 1734, if his own
account may be credited, he rejected an offer of 300l. a year, befides preferment, offered
him by Lord *Palmerfton*, if he would have turned the Mifcellany into a minifterial paper.
In 1737 he publifhed a Sermon under the title of " The Sin of being afhamed of our
" Religion;" and in 1738, " A Sermon preached at *St. Edmond's Bury, March* 21."
On the tranflation of Bifhop *Sherlock* to the fee of *Salifbury* (1738), Dr. *Webfter* † flattered himfelf with the hopes of obtaining a prebend in that church, which happened to
be vacant; but was mortified with a pofitive denial. In 1740 he was editor of a pamphlet ‡
concerning the Woollen Manufactures, intituled, " The Confequences of Trade to the
" Wealth and Strength of the Nation. By a Draper of *London*, 1740." Mr. *Webber*,
who had carried on a confiderable trade in that article in the country, and who had been
ruined by his endeavours to prevent the running of that valuable commodity, furnifhed

---

* The fmall debt incurred for thefe articles remaining undifcharged at the end of feven years,
Mr. *Bowyer* reminded Dr. *Webfter* of it by a letter; and received this laconic anfwer, dated *Auguft*
7, 1740 : " I moft heartily afk your pardon for being fo long in your debt; and give you my word,
" that, as foon as poffible, I fhall with great pleafure pay you without giving you the trouble of
" DUNNING."

† On his firft coming to *St. Dunftan's*, he had the honour of an intimacy with Dr. *Sherlock*,
for whom he frequently preached at *The Temple*; " and this kind intercourfe," he fays, " con-
" tinued till the Dean of *Chichefter* was made Bifhop of *Bangor*, when his Lordfhip made me great
" profeffions of friendfhip;" which no occafion offered of putting in practice. When the Bifhop
was afterwards removed to *London*, his old acquaintance applied to him at *Fulham* for charity; and
received " a reprimand for going about the country in that manner, without being afked to drink,
" though he had walked all the way from *London*."

‡ " I publifhed a pamphlet, and fpent a great deal of money, in the purfuit of a fcheme to prevent
" the exportation of unmanufactured Wool. This pamphlet was in fuch great reputation all over the
" kingdom, that, without knowing who was the author of it, it was faid that he deferved to have his
" ftatue fet up in every trading town in *England*." Dr. WEBSTER.

the

the materials, which were methodized by the Doctor. The copy, which made a fix-penny pamphlet, was given to Mr. *Henry Woodfall* of *Little-Britain*, who printed it at his own hazard, and fold 8000 or upwards. When the demand for it began to fubfide, the Doctor, who was not unacquainted with the arts of trade, wrote an anfwer to it, under the title of " The Draper's Reply, 1741," which went through two or three edi-tions. In 1741 he refigned his rectory and curacy, on being prefented by Abp. *Potter* to the vicarages of *Ware* and *Thundridge*. In 1742 he publifhed " A Sermon before the " Houfe of Commons ;" in the fame year, " A Sermon on the Faft at *Ware* ;" in 1745, " Two Sermons preached at *Ware* ;" a volume of " Tracts, Sermons, Difcourfes, " and Letters," 8vo ; and a fecond edition enlarged of " An Appeal to the Laity on " Tithes." He was in this year (1745) recommended by Earl *Gower* (to whom he had twenty years before dedicated two of his earlieft productions) to the Earl of *Chefterfield*, then lord-lieutenant of *Ireland* ; to which kingdom he was about to depart, when the noble Earl's recall, to take upon him the office of fecretary of ftate, put an end to that fcheme, but not to the expectations of Dr. *Webfter*, who was called upon to defend Earl *Gower* againft the Jacobites, and vifited *Trentham* to obtain materials, which were after-wards digefted, but never appeared in print, and for which he complains that he was not rewarded. He afterwards wrote a political pamphlet, of which the proof-fheets were corrected by Earl *Gower*, and which received the royal approbation ; his Majefty doing him the honour to fay, " it was a very good effay." In 1746, he publifhed " A " Sermon preached at *Ware* on the Rebellion ;" in 1748, " Two Sermons ; 1. on the " Duty of living peaceably ; 2. of Self-love and Benevolence ;" in 1750, " An Effay " on Anger and Forgivenefs *," 12mo ; in 1751, " Two Sermons on the Sabbath ;" in 1753, " Two Difcourfes on Prayer † ; wherein are feveral things with great Impar-" tiality recommended particularly to the Papifts and Diffenters of all Denominations ; " with a becoming Freedom to the Infidels ; with the moft affectionate Efteem to the " Clergy ; with the higheft Deference to the Nobility and Gentry. 2. On the Obferva-" tion of the Sabbath. 3. On the Importance of Public Worfhip," 8vo ; in 1754, " The " new Art of Contentment, contained in an Effay upon *Phil.* iv. 2." 8vo ; in 1757, " A " Treatife on Places and Preferments, efpecially Church Preferments," &c. 8vo. In this year he was under the neceffity of petitioning the Archbifhops and Bifhops for charity ; to whom he reprefented, " that he had been upwards of 43 years employed in pa-" rochial duties in the diocefe of *London*, and 35 years a public writer; that he was a year " and a half out of all bufinefs, which involved him in debt ; and his diftreffes had been " much increafed by a fit of the palfy ; and that the addition of 40*l.* or 50*l.* a year to his " income would fave him from great diftrefs." That the petition was of little effect, ap-pears by " A plain Narrative of Facts, or, the Author's Cafe ‡ fairly and candidly

" ftated,

---

* Mr. *Smart* addreffed an Ode to him on this work.

† His book " on Prayer and on the Sacrament" was infcribed to Archbifhop *Herring*, who ho-noured him with his patronage and correfpondence. On this publication he received the following fhort billet from the excellent Author of the Night Thoughts : " Dear Sir, I have read over your " difcourfes with appetite ; and I find in them much piety, perfpicuity, eloquence, and ufefulnefs. " God grant them all the fuccefs they deferve, you wifh, and the world wants. Moft affuredly, " Devotion is the balm of life ; and no man can go unwounded to the grave. I am yours af-" fectionately, ED. YOUNG."

‡ In this Narrative he acknowledges his great obligations to the Earl of *Hardwicke*, for a hand-fome prefent ; to Mr. *Plummer*, knight of the fhire and his parifhioner, for 50*l.* given at a time when he muft have gone to prifon ; and to " another perfon, not lefs honourable for not being a gentleman, " who is abfolutely the greateft genius, the beft, and the moft amiable man that I know in the " world ; I mean, Mr. *Richardfon* the printer. When I came to *Ware*, I was 90*l.* in his debt,

" though

" stated, by way of Appeal to the Publick, 1758," 8vo; the publication of which he survived but a few months, as he died *Dec.* 4, 1758. Some further particulars of him may be gathered from the extracts printed below from his letters to Dr. *Zachary Grey* *. It is not at all surprising that a writer who employed himself so indiscriminately on all topics should have been honoured with a niche in *The Dunciad*; where we find him coupled with the celebrated Arch-methodist:

" Or such as bellow from the deep Divine;
" There, *Webster!* peal'd thy voice, and *Whitefield!* thine.

On which the learned Commentator remarks, " The one the writer of a News-paper " called the Weekly Miscellany, the other a Field-preacher. This thought the only " means of advancing Religion was by the New-birth of spiritual madness: That by " the old death of fire and faggot: And therefore they agreed in this, though in no " other earthly thing, to abuse all the sober Clergy. From the small success of these " two extraordinary persons, we may learn how little hurtful Bigotry and Enthusiasm are, " while the Civil Magistrate forbears to lend his power to the one, in order to the em- " ploying it against the other."—In the Preface to " The Divine Legation, 1740," Dr.

Webster

" though I had cleared off regularly, by quarterly payments, 50l. and never could save any thing " out of my income, ever since the change of my livings, towards getting out of debt. As soon as " I was possessed of *Ware*, or, rather, as soon as *Ware* was possessed of *me*, he sent me a kind letter; " told me, that any sum of money that I wanted was at my service; and when he saw that I lived " as frugally as possible, he forgave me the whole debt. I forbear to enlarge upon his character, " because I know not how to do it justice."—In the close of life, he represents himself as " inca- " pable of doing his duty, and incapable of hiring people to assist him;" and " his parishioners at " *Ware* (some good people excepted) as more ready to defraud him of his right, than to bestow " favours; to make his life as uneasy as possible, instead of rendering it comfortable." A great part of his living depended on voluntary contributions; " and for several years Trade and Religion " had declined together. The people had less money, and less inclination to part with it."
* " I sent a pamphlet to your bookseller, and hope it came safe. I have not yet heard from Mr. " *Clarke*, your curate. I think myself much obliged to him for his assistance in disposing of so " many books; but if he could conveniently have remitted the money sooner, the obligation had " been greater, because curates have but little credit with stationers and printers. It is now above " a year since the book was published, and I have not sold enough to pay charges, which is hard " upon me, since a great part of my maintenance depends upon the success of such undertakings. " I am now without any settled business, the vicar of *St. Dunstan's* [Dr. *Grant*] having put another curate " over my head in such a manner that I should have had only some of the lowest offices, at the rate " of 20l. a year, after sixteen years servitude † in the parish, and with such a character from the Bishop " as ought to recommend me to other treatment. *Aug.* 19, 1731."—" I must desire you to send me a " parcel of your own MS. sermons for the supply of my new cure [*East-Cheap*], where I preach two ser- " mons in a week in the same church. I have been so much employed upon other things, I am but ill- " stocked with sermons, and my last undertaking will take up almost all my time. *Sept.* 7, 1732."
—" Having but little time, I can afford none for ceremony, so to the point. *Saturday* the Miscel- " lany comes out, and I shall send 30 to Dr. *Waterland*, to whom you may apply for one. I have " received my Bookseller's proposals to Mrs. *Moss*, which I think are fair, and better than you will " get from any of those with whom you are in treaty. For one impression of 1000 he offers, for " 2 volumes of Sermons, 40 guineas; and if you think of publishing the MS. ‡ against the Rights " of the Christian Church, with the Quakers Bill, he will give 10 guineas for that, in all 50; and " would willingly treat further with you for the future impressions of the whole. If Mrs. *Moss* ac- " cepts this offer, it will be proper to come out while the Parliament is sitting; and I believe you " would think it most proper to have them printed in *London*, where they are much more expe- " ditious than the *Cambridge* presses. *December* 14, 1732."—" *Neal* is like the rest of his tribe, " a writer never to be trusted. May you live long, and continue to be what you ever was; " useful to the world, kind to your friends, and agreeable to all that know you! *Sept.* 22,

† His parishioners at *St. Dunstan's* (the Dissenters not excepted) were very kind to him, and subscribed 25 guineas a year toward the daily prayers. He was at that time particularly noticed by Judge *Price* and Lord *Palmerston.*
‡ A Letter on this subject will appear in the Correspondence of Bishop *Atterbury.*

" 1733."—

Webſter is alſo thus pointedly noticed: " The attack was opened by one who bore the
" reſpectable name of a *Country Clergyman*, but was in reality a Town-writer of a Weekly
" News-

" 1733."—" You may well wonder that you have not heard from me ſo long; and that,
" after ſo long a ſilence, I ſhould have the aſſurance to aſk any thing of you. Variety and hurry
" of buſineſs muſt be my only excuſe for the firſt, and neceſſity for the ſecond. Through the
" indefatigable induſtry of Infidels, Hereticks, and Diſſenters, and the indolence and inactivity of
" our friends, the proprietors of the Miſcellany are quite diſcouraged, and laſt week reſigned their
" ſhares; ſo that I am not able to ſupport the paper, unleſs I can get 3 or 400 fixed cuſtomers. I
" have therefore opened a ſubſcription, and have met with encouragement; ſeveral ſubſcribing for
" ſix papers every week. As I know you wiſh as well as any man to the cauſe of Chriſtianity and
" the Church of *England*, I have taken the liberty to deſire you to do ſomething in this way, and to
" propoſe your example to your friends. It would be great glee to the enemies, if a deſign of this
" kind ſhould not have friends enough in the kingdom to ſupport it. Some have all their papers
" ſent them, and ſome leave me to give them away at public-houſes. *Sept.* 18, 1735."—" I received
" the favour of your kind compliment, and will read it as ſoon as my buſineſs will permit. I make
" no doubt but it is ſubſtantially done, and I ſhall take the firſt opportunity to let you know in the
" Miſcellany what I think of it. Have you communicated my letters to the 'ſquires? I aſk no
" more of you than barely to ſhew the letters, which you may do without injuring your friends.
" Deſire Mr. *Burrough* to give me a letter as ſoon as he knows what to ſay to me; and ſuch a letter
" as I may ſhew to his Grace of *Canterbury*. I was with him *Sunday* night, and he aſked me
" whether I had heard any thing from College. *March* 22, 1736."—" When I received the
" favour of your kind letter, I could not anſwer it becauſe I was going into the country, and
" had no opportunity of waiting on the Biſhop of *London*; but yeſterday I was with his Lord-
" ſhip, and acquainted him with your generous offer, which is accepted with great thankfulneſs.
" My Lord and Dr. *Maddox* * are truly ſenſible how much your accurate remarks contributed to-
" wards the perfection and credit of his reply; and unleſs you ſuffer the ſecond volume to have the
" ſame advantage, I am ſure it will not have the ſame ſucceſs, and do the ſame good ſervice to the
" Church of *England*. My good friend, though I mention the intereſt of our common cauſe as
" what will weigh moſt with a perſon ſo well affected to it as you are, yet it is not with any intention
" to diſcharge myſelf from the obligation which you have laid me under by the particular kindneſs
" intended me. I think myſelf ſingularly obliged to you for ſo great an inſtance of your reſpect
" and affection for me, and return you my moſt hearty thanks; but as the undertaking is in the
" hand of a gentleman who has performed ſo well in it, 'twould be both a piece of impertinence
" and vanity in me to offer to interfere with him: wherefore I hope you will direct your farther
" obſervations to me with leave to convey them to Dr. *Maddox.*" *No date.*—" I have not ſent your
" MS. to *Maddox*. A parcel of ſcrubs! Why ſhould we help them to credit when they will
" neither return the civility, nor own it? They did not ſo much as acknowledge your aſſiſtance.
" Your MS. with a Preface, will make a volume; and as you intended me a kindneſs, what think
" you of my publiſhing them without a name?" *No date.*—" My friendſhip and obligations, my
" approbation of your undertaking and regard for the cauſe, all conſpire to diſpoſe me to do every
" thing in my power; but your equity and candour, in judging of my capacity, will make proper
" allowances for the neceſſity I am under of recommending my own books. I will talk with our
" Bookſellers about it, and let you know what they ſay. I wiſh you had told me what my friends
" think of my laſt letter upon *Warburton*, and what you hear of him. *July* 15, 1738."—" I am very
" ſorry for your conſtant reſidence in *Bedfordſhire*, becauſe it deprives me of the pleaſure of ſeeing you
" in my viſits to *Cambridge*, which is now an eaſy day's journey for me. I preſume you have ſeen it
" in the papers, that his Grace of *Canterbury* [Dr. *Potter*] has given me the vicarages of *Ware* and
" *Thundridge*, adjoining to it, which I was obliged in prudence to accept, though they add but little
" to my income, and put me to conſiderable expences †. His Grace is not willing that I ſhould drop

---

* Then Dean of *Wells*; Biſhop of *St. Aſaph* 1736, and of *Worceſter* 1743.

† " I was forced, in a little time, to lay out 70l. upon two old houſes, and had no more than 20l. allowed me
" for dilapidations. The houſe at *Ware* is very large, ſix rooms on a floor, two coach-houſes and a ſtable that I
" can make little uſe of; about three hundred feet of paling, between five and ſix thouſand feet of tiling, and a
" large expenſive garden, to be kept in conſtant repair, not an acre of glebe land, and I myſelf in a more expen-
" ſive ſituation than when I was a curate in *London*.—After ſome time, I recovered the arrears of an augmenta-
" tion, payable to the ſmall living of *Thundridge*; but, then, my former living being a rectory, and I quitting it
" juſt before harveſt, the loſs of all the corn, and the dilapidations which I paid my ſucceſſor, balanced that
" account." Dr. WEBSTER.

" the

" News paper; and with such excess of insolence and malice as the publick had yet never
" seen on any occasion whatsoever."

P. 83. *Bellus Homo* was personated by Mr. *Thomas Draper Baber*; and *Academicus*
by Mr. *George Lewis Langton.*

P. 84. Note, l. 1. read, on the 28th of *August*, 1727.—As it is something uncommon for
a *Roman* Catholic clergyman to be admitted to degrees in divinity by Protestant universities, the curious may be gratified with a sight of the diploma, by referring to " The
" Present State of the Republick of Letters for *June*, 1728," p. 485; where they will
also find (p. 487) the Doctor's answer, which is written with moderation, charity, and
temper. Mr. *Markland*, in a letter to Mr. *Bowyer*, Sept. 29, 1746, says, " Mr. *Clarke*
" has given me F. *Courayer's* Translation of the History of the Council of *Trent* *; with
" whose Preface I am so greatly pleased (having just now read it) that if he be no
" more a Papist in other tenets than he is in those he mentions (which are many, and
" of the most distinguished class) I dare say there are very few considerate Protestants
" who are not as good Catholics as he is. If you have not read it, you have a great
" pleasure to come." In the South Cloister of *Westminster-Abbey*, directly over the
effigies of abbot *Vitalis*, is an inscription to his memory, the production of an ingenious
Fellow of *Brazen-Nose* college, by whose friendship a more accurate copy of it than
that upon the monument (which was put up too hastily before the author's last revisal)
is now presented to the publick:

" the Miscellany; and in order to carry it on, I am forced to get more help than otherwise I should
" want at my livings, if I could be constantly there to do all the parochial duties; I must keep a
" lodging in town, and a horse always in the stable; besides unavoidable expences in going back-
" ward and forward every week. All together the Miscellany will cost me at least 40l. a year;
" which is a charge that I can't possibly support till I can get some addition to my income. You
" know, before the paper could be established, it brought me in debt to my printer † 140l. ninety of
" which is still unpaid. To encourage my present printer to undertake and propagate it with in-
" dustry, I insured to him all the profits that he could make it bring in, preserving to myself nothing
" but the power of conducting all the labour of supporting the design. To drop so good a design,
" and give the enemy such an occasion of triumph, I can't bear the thoughts of; and therefore I
" am soliciting amongst the friends of the paper, a half-yearly subscription, the first payment to be
" made at the time of subscribing. You, my good friend, are quite out of this question, because
" you do handsomely already, and as much as can reasonably be expected; but if you would repre-
" sent the case to some others, I should thank you. If I give up so much of my time and pains,
" which I could employ more profitably to myself, though not so usefully to the publick, those who
" are in better circumstances can't think much of joining to support the expences it puts me to.
" There is a worthy Lord *(Trevor)* in your neighbourhood, who, if the case were justly represented
" to him, would readily do something. He has the Miscellany every week, and is a hearty friend
" to it. Now, the Archbishop having given a sanction to my character, I shall get something else;
" and as soon as I am made a little easier, as to my circumstances, I shall no longer desire any help,
" but at present I am terribly embarrassed; and the more by the great expence of coming into these
" livings." *No date.*—" I suppose you saw my dying speech in the Miscellany, and are convinced,
" without a coroner's inquest, that I did not lay violent hands upon myself, though I died an un-
" timely death. I am coming out with a pamphlet, but can't afford to make presents. I never was
" so distrest as now. My last preferment has absolutely ruined me." *No date.* [1741.]

* Notwithstanding the excellence of F. *Courayer's French* translation of Father *Paul*, the
Literati have reason to regret that an *English* ‡ translation (which was begun in 1738, and some
sheets of it actually printed off) was not proceeded with. This assertion will be readily credited,
when I add that it was undertaken by Dr. SAMUEL JOHNSON. The part that was printed has long
since been converted into waste paper, and (unfortunately) not a single copy of it is known to have
been preserved.

† Mr. *Richardson.* See above, p. 541.
‡ There had been an earlier *English* translation of it published by Sir *Nathaniel Brett* in the latter end of the
last century.

" H. S. E.

" H. S. E.
Annis morumque integritate juxtà reverendus
PETRUS FRANCISCUS COURAYER,
Cœnobii de Sanctâ Genovevâ dicti
Apud urbem Lutetiam Parisiorum
Regularis olim Canonicus.
Vir, si quis alius,
De Ecclesiâ atque Politiâ Anglicanâ
Animo pariter ac scriptis,
Optimè meritus.
Quippe qui Episcopalium jus administrationum
Jamdiù à Pontificiis acerrimè impugnatum
Huic eidem Ecclesiæ
Et Gallus ipse, et Pontificius
Invictâ argumentorum vi asseruit et vindicavit:
Quique adeò, ob id vindicandum,

Pulsus jam patriâ, profugus,
Omnibusque demum exutus fortunis,
Hâc in urbe quærebat asylum, et inveniebat;
Ibique per annos propè quinquaginta
Honestæ mentis otio egregius fruebatur exul,
Bonorum omnium deliciæ vivus,
moriens commune desiderium.
Obiit quintadecimâ die Octobris
Anno post natum Christum MDCCLXXVI;
Post se natum XCV.

Huic tali tantoque Viro
Marmor hoc, amoris sui monimentum,
posuêre Amici,
Cui famam marmore perenniorem peperit
Defensa veritas, refutatus error."

There is a small oval portrait of him by *Elizabeth Gulston*, from a painting of *Hamilton*, with this inscription: " *Pierre Francis Courayer*, who was banished *France* for " writing in defence of the *English* ordination. He was born at *Rouen, Nov.* 17, 1681, " and is still living. Published *June* 1, 1774."

P. 85. Add to the books of 1734, " Letters and Remains of the Lord Chancellor " *Bacon*; collected by *Robert Stephens* *, Esq; late Historiographer Royal," 4to.

Ibid. Note, l. 1. read, the former of them the celebrated painter, " now better " known by his books than by his pictures;" the latter a connoisseur.

Ibid. Sub-note. The " Journey to *Paris*" was written by the Rev. *W. Jones*, B. A. then rector of *Pluckley* in *Kent*, and now of *Paston* in *Northamptonshire*, author of " Physiological Disquisitions, &c. 1781," and other learned works.

---

* Fourth son of *Richard Stephens*, Esq; of the elder house of that name at *Eastington* in *Gloucestershire*, by *Anne* the eldest daughter of Sir *Hugh Cholmeley*, of *Whitby*, in *Yorkshire*, baronet. His first education was at *Wotton* school, whence he removed to *Lincoln* college, *Oxford, May* 19, 1681. He was entered very young in *The Middle Temple*, applied himself to the study of the common-law, and was called to the bar. As he was master of a sufficient fortune, it may be presumed that the temper of his mind, which was naturally modest, detained him from the public exercise of his profession, and led him to the politer studies, and an acquaintance with the best authors, ancient and modern: yet he was esteemed by all who knew him to have made a great proficience in the Law, though History and Antiquities seem to have been his favourite study. When he was about twenty years old, being at a relation's house, he accidentally met with some original letters of the Lord Chancellor *Bacon*; and finding that they would greatly improve the collections then extant relating to King *James's* reign, he immediately set himself to search for whatever might elucidate the obscure passages, and published a complete edition of them in 1702, with useful notes, and an excellent historical introduction. He intended to have presented his work to King *William*; but that monarch dying before it was published, the dedication was omitted. In the preface he requested the communication of unpublished pieces of his noble author, to make his collection more complete; and obtained in consequence as many letters as formed the second collection published in 1734, two years after his death. Being a relation of *Robert Harley* Earl of *Oxford* (whose mother was a *Stephens*) he was preferred by him to be chief solicitor of the customs, in which employment he continued with undiminished reputation till 1726, when he declined that troublesome office, and was appointed to succeed Mr. *Madox* in the place of historiographer royal. He then formed a design of writing a History of King *James* the First, a reign which he thought to be more misrepresented than almost any other since the Conquest: and, if we may judge by the good impression which he seems to have had of these times, his exactness and care never to advance any thing but from unquestionable authorities, besides his great candour and integrity, it could not but have been a judicious and valuable performance. He married *Mary* the daughter of Sir *Hugh Cholmeley*, a lady of great worth; died at *Gravesend*, near *Thornbury*, in *Gloucestershire, Nov.* 9, 1732; and was buried at *Eastington*, the seat of his ancestors.

P. 87. l. *antep.* read, " the hand that is now writing," &c.—This note was revised by the incomparable author in 1781.

P. 88. There is a good portrait of Mr. *Cave*, engraved by *Grignion*, with emblematical devices, and this inscription :

" *Edward Cave*, ob. 10 *Jan.* 1754, ætat. 62.

" The first Projector of the Monthly Magazines.

" Th' Invention all admir'd, and each how he

" To be th' Inventor mifs'd."

The following inscription is on a stone erected in *St. James's* church, *Clerkenwell*, to the memory of the late Mr. *Richard Cave* *, of *St. John's Gate*, and his Wife :

" Reader, if native worth may claim a tear,

" Or the sad tale of death affect thy ear,

" Heave from thy breast one sympathising sigh,

" Since here such fair examples mouldering lie.

" Here lies a pair, whom Honesty approv'd,

" In death lamented, and in life belov'd;

" Who never meant a neighbour to offend ;

" Who never made a foe, nor lost a friend ;

" Whose only strife was, who should ACT the best ;

" Whose only hope, to rise among the blest."

P. 90. col. 2. " Blest sons,"&c.] These lines are part of a poem printed more at length in p. 160.

P. 91. l. 1. read " Differtationes in librum *Jobi*, auctore *Samuele Wesley*, rectore de " *Epworth*, in diœcesi *Lincolniensi*."

P. 94. l. 6. read, " Antiquæ Inscriptiones Duæ, *Græca* altera, altera *Latina*; cum " brevi Notarum & Conjecturarum Specimine," folio.

Ibid. There is now a probability that the " *Eboracum*" of Mr. *Drake* will be published with new plates.

P. 97. The epitaph on Mr. *Petyt* (which is in the west part of *The Temple* church) is printed incomplete. Instead of the last line, read, " In *Storithes* propè Abbatiam " de *Bolton* non ita longè a vico de *Skipton in Craven* in comitatu *Eborum* natus fuit. " Ad plures abiit apud *Chelseam* in agro *Middlesexiæ* 3^{tio} die *Octobris* anno Domini " MDCCVII, ætatis suæ LXXI. Neque dum vixit ipsius *Chelseæ* immemor erat, sed eri- " gebat ibi ædificium quod eidem Parochiæ alacri & liberâ manu dedit; in se com- " plectens (quod dicitur) vestiarium in usum parochianorum, gymnasium ad pueros " erudiendos, & cameras præceptori satis commodas.

" Monumentum hoc *Sylvester Petyt* de Hospitio *Barnardiensi* generosus, & ejusdem " olim Principalis, in memoriam charissimi sui Fratris posuit."

On a grave-stone on the floor :

" The Body of

" *William Petyt*, Esquire,

" Buried here the IXth

" Day of *October*,

" MDCCVII."

Ibid. An original portrait of Mr. *Pepys* is preserved at the Royal Society.

---

* Nephew to the original projector of the Magazine, and for some years printer of it in conjunction with my friend Mr. *David Henry*, who wrote the epitaph printed above, and whose laudable exertions have long supported and increased the original credit of " one of the most chaste and " instructive Miscellanies of the age." (See Annual Register, 1780, p. 184.)

P. 98. note, l. 1. who was bred at *Eton*, and was clerk under his father; but died, aged 25, many years before his father.

Ibid. Dr. *Knight* drew up a Life of Bishop *Patrick*, which he lent Mr. *Whiston* in MS. See *Whiston's* Memoirs, vol. I. p. 2.—In a Letter printed in the Reliquiæ *Galeanæ*, p. 168, he mentions Mr. *Strype's* having recommended it to him to write a Life of Archbishop *Bancroft*. I have several of his original letters to Dr. *Zachary Grey*.—Dr. *Knight's* son now (1782) lives in the parish of *Milton*, near *Cambridge*, being lord of the manor and rector of the church, as also rector of *Stanwick* in *Northamptonshire*, and of the sinecure of *Fulham* near *London*.

P. 99. add, The Life of Mr. *Anthony a Wood*, historiographer of the most famous university of *Oxford*, with an account of his nativity, education, works, &c. [collected and composed from MSS. by *Richard Rawlinson*, gent. commoner of *St. John's College, Oxon.*] *London*, 1711. A copy of this life, with MS. additions by the author, is in the *Bodleian* library. Historical passages collected by him from *Wood* were printed as a Supplement to *Wood's* Life, *Oxford*, 1772, vol. II. p. 249.

P. 100. sub-note, read, *Hearne's* Diaries and his other MSS.

P. 101. Of Mr. *Bell* some further particulars will be given in the 'Reliquiæ Galeanæ,' where several of his letters are printed.

Ibid. sub-note, *Thomas Papillon* was son of *David Papillon*, Esq; in the county of *Leicester*. *Thomas* was apprenticed *Nov.* 2, 1638; admitted to the freedom of the Mercers Company *Sept.* 4, 1646; and elected master *Sept.* 5, 1698. His portrait still adorns their hall; and he bequeathed one thousand pounds to the company, to relieve any of his family that might in future come to want.

P. 103. Note on *Tanner*, l. 5, read, Fellow of the same, 1697; l. 7. *Norfolk*.

P. 104. There is a mezzotinto portrait of Mr. *Warburton* by *Miller*, from a painting by *Vandergucht*, with this inscription: " *John Warburton*, Esq; *Somerset* Herald at " Arms, fellow of the Royal Society, and of the Antiquarian Society of *London*, 1746. " Author of the Maps by actual survey of *Middlesex*, *Essex*, *Hertfordshire*, *York-* " *shire*, *Northumberland*."

P. 105. l. 4. In a copy of this book bought for 1*l*. 2*s*. (at the sale of *G. Scott*, Esq; of *Woolston Hall*) by *George Harrison*, Esq; *Windsor* Herald, were many MS. letters of Mr. *Anstis* to Dr. *Derham*. In *Gutch's* " Collectanea Curiosa," vol. II. p. 186, is a very curious History of Visitation Books, under the title of " Nomenclator Fecialium, " qui *Angliæ* & *Walliæ* comitatus visitârunt, quo anno & ubi autographa seu apographa " reperiuntur, per *Johannem Anstis* Garter. Principal. Regem Armorum *Anglicano-* " rum," from a MS. in the library of *All Souls College*.

L. 12. *After* papers, *add*, particularly a good collection of epitaphs and other inscriptions in *England*, and many in *Wales*, all fine fac similes.

P. 106. The following eloge was written by the late Mr. *Collinson* immediately after the death of Mr. *Lethieullier*: " He was descended from an ancient family from *France* in time " of persecution, and a gentleman every way eminent for his excellent endowments. His " desire to improve in the civil and natural history of his country, led him to visit all " parts of it; the itineraries in his library, and the discoveries he made relating to its " antiquities, with drawings of every thing remarkable, are evidences of his great appli- " cation to rescue so many ancient remains from mouldering into oblivion. His happy " turn of mind was not confined solely to antiquities, but in these journeys he was in- " defatigable in collecting all the variety of *English* fossils, with a view to investigate " their origin: this great collection, which excells most others, is deposited in two large

" cabinets

" cabinets, difpofed under their proper claffes. The moft rare are elegantly drawn,
" and defcribed in a folio book, with his obfervations on them. As the variety of ancient
" marbles had engaged his attention, and he found fo little faid on them with refpect
" to their natural hiftory, it was one of his motives in vifiting *Italy*, to furnifh himfelf
" with fuch materials as he was able to procure from books, and learned men, relating
" to them. He collected fpecimens of the moft curious, and had drawings, finely painted,
" of the moft remarkable monuments of the ancient marbles ; thefe are bound up in a
" folio volume, with all the obfervations he could gather relating to their natural hiftory
" and antiquity. His cabinet of medals, his collection of antiquities of various kinds,
" and moft elegant books of the fineft engravings, are inftances of the fine tafte with
" which he has enriched his library and cabinet, with the fpoils of *Italy*. This fhort,
" but imperfect memoir, is candidly offered as a tribute due to a long friendfhip. It is
" wifhed it may excite an abler pen, to do more juftice to the memory of this great
" and good man. But it is humbly hoped that thefe hints will be accepted not only as
" a teftimony of refpect, but may alfo inform an inquifitive genius in thefe branches of
" fcience where he may be affifted with fuch valuable materials for the profecution of
" his future ftudies. *P. C.*"

L. 27. A committee of the truftees waited on the Colonel's executors, *Feb.* 23, 1756,
to return thanks for the valuable legacy of a fine mummy, and a curious collection of
Englifh antiquities. On this occafion *Pitt Lethieullier*, Efq; nephew to the colonel,
prefented them with feveral antiquities, which he himfelf had collected during his refidence at *Grand Cairo*.

L. 39. *After* 1713, *add*, and in the " Mufæ *Anglicanæ*," vol. III. p. 303, under the
title of " Mufarum Oblatio ad Reginam."

Ibid. fub-note, read, eldeft fon of Sir *Richard*, fon of Sir *Edward Hulfe*.

P. 107. l. 5. *Litteraria*.] A fociety whofe bufinefs it was to correct, increafe, and
beautify the *Italian* poetry, as that of the *Crufca* was to purify, illuftrate, and fix their
language. Some curious particulars of both are given by *Baretti*, in his " Account of
" *Italy*," vol. II. p. 246. 243.

L. 13. The pictures, marble tables, urns, vafes, and other antiquities, were fold
for 904*l*. 13*s*. 6*d*.

P. 109. fub-note, l. 2. read Mr. *Kemp* died, &c.

P. 110. l. 18. Due famofi.

P. 111. fub-note, l. 41. read, Triumvir.

Ibid. *Montfaucon*, in the Preface to " L'Antiquité Expliquée," calls Sir *Andrew Fountaine* an able antiquary, and fays, that Gentleman during his ftay at *Paris* furnifhed
him with every piece of antiquity that he had collected, and which could be of ufe to
his work; feveral were accordingly engraven and defcribed, as appears by Sir *Andrew's*
name on the plates. Sir *Andrew* is faid to have fhewed his craft abroad, as well as his
fkill, and to have been too hard even for the *Italians*; one of whom bringing him fome
medals, he felected a few that he faid were of no value, and managed fo as to get them
for a trifle.

P. 113. " *Welwyn Spaw*," a kind of plaintive Ode by Mr. *North*, in which he laments
the cold difdain of fome apparently real *Celia*, appeared in the Literary Magazine for
1756, p. 209.

P. 115.

P. 115. The following epitaph is tranfcribed from the hand-writing of Dr. *Birch:*

" H. S. E.   Miferefcat quicunque in conjugio felix
HANNAH BIRCH,   Infelicis Mariti,
Candore morum ac fuavitate,   Cui fato tam immaturo abrepta
Ingenio fupra fexum, fupra ætatem,   In lætis confors,
Politioribus literis exculto,   In adverfis folamen,
Infignis.   Et quicquid in vitâ fuerat amœnius,
Quæ cum longioris in conjugio felicitatis   Præter memoriam femper amabilem.
Spem faceret,   Vale, anima candidiffima et optima;
Et tabe & puerperio fimul correpta   Te exemplo in terris præeuntem,
Occidit.   Te fede jam ex fublimiori vocantem,
Ploret Lector elegans et humanus   Tuo ufque fuftentatus amore,
Talem tam citò interiiffe fœminam,   Quam citiffimè Deo vifum fuerit,
Egregium fui fexûs exemplar.   Lætus lubenfque fequar."

P. 116. add, " Lord *Hardwicke* did not prefent Dr. *Birch* to *Depden* near *Newport*
" in *Effex*, but allowed him to make an exchange with my firft coufin, *John Cock*, D. D.
" then patron and rector of *Depden*, who taking a difguft on being rifled and gagged
" by a gang of fmugglers, who haunted that neighbourhood, fought for an exchange;
" and this accommodating Dr. *Birch* for diftance wth other preferments [in *London*],
" Lord *Hardwicke* was pleafed to allow him to quit the valuable rectory of *Great*
" *Horkefley* near *Colchefter*, to which he had lately preferred him *, for that of *Depden*,
" nearly of equal value.; fo. that, upon Dr. *Birch's* unfortunate death, my coufin Dr.
" *Cock* came, of courfe, into his own living again, and is now poffeffed of both; and to
" repay Lord *Hardwicke*, in fome degree, for keeping poffeffion of *Horkefley*, has ex-
" pended, on the parfonage and offices, I fuppofe at leaft 4 or 5000l." *I am obliged to*
the Rev. Mr. Cole of Milton for this additional information.

Ibid. fub-note, l. penult. read, " in the Tranfactions of the Earl of *Glamorgan.*"

P. 120. Since the note on Mr. *Nickolls* was printed, the Friend to whom I was obliged
for the greater part of the information it contains is loft to the learned world. I fhall
forbear, however, in this place to add any memoirs of Dr. *Fothergill*, being unwilling
to anticipate the pleafure to be expected from a Life of him by his intelligent and excellent friend Dr *Letfome*. The curious may in the mean time be gratified by the particulars recorded in the Gentleman's Magazine, 1781, p. 165.

Ibid. Mr. *Granger*, in his Preface, had faid Mr. *Weft* bought the 10 volumes of Mr.
Nickolls's Collection of portraits; but, on the better information of Dr. *Ducarel*, corrected himfelf in his Supplement, p. 2. It was formed from *Moorfields* and ftalls, confequently was not firft-rate. Prince *Eugene* may be efteemed the firft collector of portraits in *Europe* †, which on his death were difperfed. He collected in almoft every other
branch. The Earl of *Oxford* began the firft collection in *England*, which afterwards

---

* But of which Dr. *Birch* (from its being out of diftance probably) appears never to have taken
poffeffion. Dr. *Browne* held *Great Horkefley* from 1756 to 1761, when Dr. *Cock* took it and refigned
Depden to Dr. *Birch*, " The opening of Dr. ——'s letter," fays Mr. *Morant*, in an unpublifhed
letter to Dr. *Birch*, dated *July* 23, 1760, " gave me infinite pleafure, thinking that I was going to
" have you for a near neighbour. In reading further, I was foon difappointed. However, I rejoice
" at your happinefs, wherever the object of it may happen to be." In a letter written the fame day
to another friend, Mr. *Morant* fays, " *Great Horkefley* I perfectly know. It is a fine parifh, well
" fituated, four miles North of *Colchefter*; a good parfonage-houfe near the church, 40 acres of
" glebe, &c. We reckon it a good 270l. a year; which may produce 200l. clear, as the premifes
" are in good repair. But, by way of exchange, the Doctor can hardly expect to meet one equal to
" it in all refpects; little more than 200 or 240l. *per annum* perhaps, as people are naturally fond
" of being rather near *London*. The tithe and glebe of *Fordham* rectory, exclufive of the houfe,
" were let for 197l. in 1750."

† Mr. *Afhby* furnifhed *Granger* with fome accounts of collections earlier than Prince *Eugene*, from
Lifter's " Journey to Paris," *Vigneul Marville*, &c. which he does not appear to have made ufe of.

cam.

came in part to Mr. *West*, and on his death was difperfed by the rude hand of the Auctioneer.

P. 121. It might have been obferved, that the nobility and gentry frequently honoured Mr. *Edwards* with their friendfhip and generous fupport. He mentions with peculiar pleafure being patronized by the late Duke of *Richmond*, Sir *Hans Sloane*, Dr. *Mead*, and Mr. *Folkes*; and his character of thofe four very eminent perfonages fhall be exhibited below *.

P. 122.

* " The DUKE, noble in his lineage, and defcent from the royal houfe of thefe kingdoms; but
" ftill more noble and great from the innate magnificence, generofity, and goodnefs of his foul.
" Though by his high offices his time was taken up by the important affairs of the publick, yet his
" doors were always open to men of learning, fcience, and ingenuity.
" The fecond was the good Sir *Hans Sloane*, Bart. who employed me, for a great number of
" years, in drawing miniature figures of animals, &c. after nature, in water colours, to increafe his
" very great collection of fine drawings by other hands; which drawings are now all fixed in *The
" British Mufeum*, for the help and information of thofe in future generations, that may be curious
" or ftudious in natural hiftory. Sir *Hans*, in the decline of his life, left *London*, and retired to his
" manor-houfe at *Chelfea*, where he refided about fourteen years before he died. After his retire-
" ment to *Chelfea*, he requefted it as a favour to him (though I embraced his requeft as an honour
" done to myfelf), that I would vifit him every week, in order to divert him, for an hour or two,
" with the common news of the town, and with any thing particular that fhould happen amongft
" his acquaintance of the Royal Society, and other ingenious gentlemen, many of whom I was
" much converfant with; and I feldom miffed drinking coffee with him on a *Saturday* during the
" whole time of his retirement at *Chelfea*. He was fo infirm as to be wholly confined to his houfe,
" except fometimes, though rarely, taking a little air in his garden in a wheeled chair: and this
" confinement made him very defirous to fee any of his old acquaintance to amufe him. During
" this latter part of his life, he was frequently petitioned for charity by fome decayed branches of
" eminent men, late of his acquaintance, who were famous for their learned works, &c. which peti-
" tions he always received, and confidered with attention; and, provided they were not found
" fraudulent, they were always anfwered by his charitable donations. He has often defired that I
" would enquire into the merits of fuch petitioners; and, if found fatisfactory, he commiffioned me
" to convey his bounty to the diftreffed. The laft time I faw him, I was greatly furprifed and con-
" cerned to find fo good a man in the agonies of death; this was on the 10th day of *January*, 1753,
" at four o'clock in the afternoon: he died on the 11th, at four in the morning. I continued with
" him later than any one of his relations, but was obliged to retire, his laft agonies being beyond
" what I could bear; though, under his pain and weaknefs of body, he feemed to retain a great
" firmnefs of mind and refignation to the will of God.
" The third of my patrons was the Great *Richard Mead*, M. D. He was certainly magnanimous
" beyond the common meafure, and deferved the title of Great in as extenfive a fenfe as any man in
" his ftation could do. He, as well as Sir *Hans Sloane*, died in the higheft ftations of phyfic they
" could arrive at, *viz.* Phyficians in ordinary to the King. Dr. *Mead*, indeed, never was at the
" head of the College of Phyficians of *London*; but it was becaufe he always abfolutely declined it,
" for he had been elected into that honourable ftation, but never could be perfuaded to accept of
" it. His perfonal fervice, his ample fortune, his houfe, and every thing in his power, always con-
" tributed, in the moft extenfive manner, to the promotion of learning, fcience, arts, mechanics, and,
" in fhort, every thing that tended to the public benefit and honour of his country, or was of ufe to
" particular members of the community he lived in. In fhort, his generofity was fo diffufive, that
" he may be juftly deemed a benefactor to the whole community; whilft, inftead of hoarding up
" that great wealth his practice gained to raife a vaft eftate, as he might eafily have done, his public
" fpirit was unconfined, and he was contented to leave behind him a moderate fortune only. The
" worthy Dr. *Afkew*, from a laudable veneration for the memory and public character of fo great a
" patron of learning, &c. caufed a fine marble buft of him to be made by one of the moft eminent
" fculptors of the prefent age, which is placed in the College of Phyficians, *London* †. And, on this

† The following anecdote refpecting this buft has been communicated. *Roubilliac* agreed with Dr. *Afkew* for 50*l*.; the Doctor found it fo highly finifhed that he paid him 100*l*. The Statuary faid this was not enough, and brought in a bill of 108*l*. 2*s*. Dr. *Afkew* paid this demand even to the odd fhillings, and then inclofed the receipt to Mr. *Hogarth* to produce at the next meeting of Artifts.—*Sydenham's* buft in the College of Phyficians coft 100*l*. for its excellence.

5

" occafion,

P. 122. l. 5. Mr. *Edwards* was elected F. A. S. *Feb.* 13, 1752; it was some years after before he was F. R. S.—In *Gutch's* " Collectanea Curiosa," vol. II. p. 354, is " Dean " *Lyttelton's* Memoir concerning the authenticity of *his* [copy of] Magna Charta, from " the Minutes of the Antiquary Society, *June* 3, 1761 ;" and in p. 357, of the same work, is " Mr. *Blackstone's* Memoir in answer to the late Dean of *Exeter* [Dr. *Lyttelton*], " now Bishop of *Carlisle, May* 29, 1762."

P. 123. read, " uncle to the present Lord *Fairfax* of *Scotland* ;" and add, " and in " 1754 elected one of the knights of the shire for *Kent*."

P. 124. *Cromwell Mortimer*, M. D. was second son of *John Mortimer* *, F. R. S. He was many years secretary to the Royal Society, fellow of the College of Physicians, 1744, and a member and regular correspondent of the Gentlemens Society † at *Spalding*. The Doctor's eldest brother left him the family estate at *Topping-Hall*, in *Hatfield Peverel* parish, *Essex*, where he died *Jan.* 7, 1752, and has an epitaph. He left an only son, *Hans*, of *Lincoln's-Inn*, and of *Cawldthorp* near *Burton on Trent*. (See *Morant's Essex*, II. 133.) There is a curious letter of Dr. *Mortimer* in the " Reliquiæ Galeanæ." He drew up an Index to *Willoughby's* Plates of Fishes. And see his " Plan of Practice" in Gent. Mag. 1779, p. 541.

Ibid. Mr. *Frank* died *May* 22, 1762, aged 60.

Ibid. sub-note, read, received from his *Sicilian* Majesty, by the hands of the *Neapolitan* minister, in *November* 1760, a present of a diamond ring worth 300*l.*

P. 125. Mr. *Maitland*, whose relations resided at or about the town of *Montross*, was originally a hair-merchant, and went to *Sweden, Denmark, Hamburgh*, &c. in that employ : it is uncertain if he followed that branch of business in *Edinburgh* ; but latterly he applied entirely to the antiquities of his native country, for which he had a wonderful genius. His first publication was, " The History of *London*, from its foundation by the

" occasion, I cannot help informing succeeding generations, that they may see the real features of " Dr. *Mead* in this said bust ; for I, who was as well acquainted with his face as any one living, do " pronounce this bust of him to be so like, that, as often as I see it, my mind is filled with the " strongest idea of the original.

" *Martin Folkes*, Esq; the last of my deceased principal patrons, was a friend and intimate ac- " quaintance of the other three. He had made the grand tour of *Europe*, not in the younger part " of his life, but after his marriage. He travelled with part of his family and servants, at a proper " age to make just observations, and gather all the commendable parts of the learning, customs, and " manners of the countries through which he passed, in order to refine and polish those of his own. " He travelled not in haste, as is the general custom ; but proceeded slowly, and spent what time " was necessary to inform himself of all that was worth notice : and, indeed, he seemed to have " attained to universal knowledge ; for, in the many opportunities I have had of being in his com- " pany, almost every part of science has happened to be the subject of discourse, all of which he " handled as an adept in each. He was a man of great politeness in his manners, free from all " pedantry and pride, and, in every respect, the real unaffected fine gentleman.

" The loss of four personages, so truly noble, so good, so great, and every way so highly accom- " plished, in the small space of three or four years, was an event that greatly humbled me. I ima- " gined, that after such a loss to arts and sciences in general, and to myself in particular, all endea- " vours to excell in any branch of knowledge would be fruitless, and of little avail to its author, " for want of eminent men to inspire the rising generation ; and I thought of discontinuing any far- " ther progress in natural history : but the national spirit for the promotion of learning and arts, in " the establishment of that grand repository and immense fund of science, *The British Museum*, has " in some measure revived the passion for learning and useful knowledge ; and I hope these seeds, " sown by public authority, cherished and protected by a Prince distinguished for virtue and learn- " ing, will take root, spring up, and yield a plentiful harvest. *G. E.*"

* Author of the " Whole Art of Husbandry, 1708, 1765," 8vo. by experiments in which he almost ruined himself. His first wife was *Dorothy*, eldest daughter of the Protector *Richard Cromwell*.

† He was furnished by Mr. *Johnson*, the founder of this society, with a history of their origin, and many curious particulars of the Society of Antiquaries, which were intended for publication.

" *Romans*,

" *Romans*, to the prefent time; containing a faithful relation of the publick tranfactions
" of the citizens; accounts of the feveral parifhes; parallels between *London* and other
" great cities; its government, civil, ecclefiaftical, and military; commerce, ftate of
" learning, charitable foundations, &c. With the feveral accounts of *Weftminfter*,
" *Middlefex*, *Southwark*, and other parts within the bill of mortality. In nine books.
" The whole illuftrated with a variety of fine cuts. With a complete Index. By *Wil-*
" *liam Maitland*, F. R. S." folio *. This was followed by " The Hiftory of *Edinburgh*,
" from its foundation to the prefent time: containing a faithful relation of the public
" tranfactions of the citizens; accounts of the feveral parifhes; its governments, civil,
" ecclefiaftical, and military; incorporations of trade and manufactures; courts of juf-
" tice; ftate of learning; charitable foundations, &c. with the feveral accounts of the
" parifhes of the *Canongate*, *St Cuthbert*, and other diftricts within the fuburbs of *Edin-*
" *burgh*. Together with the ancient and prefent ftate of the town of *Leith*, and a
" perambulation of divers miles round the city. With an alphabetical index. In nine
" books. By *William Maitland*, F. R. S. author of the Hiftory of *London*. The whole
" illuftrated with a plan of the town, and a great variety of other fine cuts of the prin-
" cipal buildings within the city and fuburbs. *Edinb*. 1753." folio. About the year 1750
(in the autumn of which year, it appears, he was fix weeks at *Bath* for the recovery of his
health) he propofed to write a general defcription of *Scotland*, for which purpofe he printed
a large fet of queries, with a general letter, and tranfmitted both to every clergyman in
Scotland. The return fell fo very fhort of his expectation, that he laid afide his defign
in difguft, but feveral years after made a tour over the whole kingdom himfelf; the refult of which has appeared in the firft volume of his " Hiftory and Antiquities of *Scot-*
" *land*," written in a moft uncouth ftyle, and printed in two volumes, folio, at *London*,
1757, after his death. What few defcriptions came to his hands are mentioned by Mr.
Gough in his " *Britifh* Topography," under the refpective counties. Upon the whole,
it is very unfortunate that few or no copies of thefe defcriptions were kept by the collectors of them, and what ufe *Maitland* made of them is hard to get information: none
fuch appear amongft his papers now in the hands of his heirs. He was felf-conceited,
credulous, knew little, and wrote worfe.

Ibid. *Nicholas Tindal* (nephew to the celebrated author of the " Rights of the
" Chriftian Church," from whom he had expectations of being provided for, but, by
the artifices of *Euftace Budgell*, was tricked and defrauded) was of *Exeter College*, *Oxford*,
where he took the degree of M. A. *June* 5, 1713. He was prefented to the rectory of
Alverftoke in *Hampfhire* by the Bifhop of *Winchefter*, and to the vicarage of *Great Wal-*
tham, near *Chelmsford*, *Effex*, 1722, by *Trinity College*, *Oxford*, of which he had become
a fellow. He quitted this laft living 1740, and became chaplain to *Greenwich Hofpital*,
where he died, at a very advanced age, *June* 27, 1774. In 1727 he tranflated the text
printed with Mr. *Morant's* Tranflation of the Notes of Meff. de *Beaufobre* and *L'Enfant*
on *St. Matthew's* Gofpel, (fee p. 328).—On the difcovery of the impofition practifed on
his uncle, he entered into a controverfy with the perfon who had cheated him; and
publifhed, among other things, a pamphlet, intituled, " A Copy of the Will of Dr.
" *Matthew Tindal* †, with an Account of what paffed concerning the fame between Mrs.

---

* A fecond edition, 1765, folio, enlarged to two volumes, continued to the time of publication,
and illuftrated with plans of the city and wards, views of the former at different times, and of all the
churches and public buildings, and a map of the country ten miles round.

† By which 2000 guineas, and the MS. of a fecond volume of " Chriftianity as old as the Cre-
" ation," were bequeathed to Mr. *Budgell*; and only a fmall refidue to his nephew, whom, by a
regular will, he had not long before appointed his fole heir. The tranfaction, which occafioned fome
fufpicions of fraud, is thus alluded to by *Pope*:

" Let *Budgell* charge low *Grub-ftreet* on my quill,
" And write whate'er he pleafe, except my Will."

" *Lucy*

" *Lucy Price*, *Euftace Budgell*, Efq; and Mr. *Nicholas Tindal*, 1733," 8vo. He began a Hiftory of *Effex*, of which he publifhed a fmall part in two quarto numbers, propofing to include it in three quarto volumes at one guinea each, (Brit. Top. I. p. 345, n.) and left it in 1726 for the tranflation of *Rapin*'s Hiftory of *England* * ; in which work, as well as in the " Continuation" of it, he was moft materially affifted by Mr. *Morant* (fee p. 328) ; and the fale of both fo far exceeded the expectation of his bookfellers (*J.* and *P. Knapton*), that they complimented him with a prefent of 200*l.* In 1734 he publifhed a tranflation of " Prince *Cantemir*'s Hiftory of the *Othman* Empire," folio. He was alfo editor of " A Guide to Claffical Learning, or *Polymetis* abridged, for Schools ;" a publication of much ufe, and which has paffed through feveral editions.—Mr. *Tindal* died at the age of 74. A portrait of him is prefixed to the fecond volume of his tranflation of *Rapin*.

P. 125. Since the note on Dr. *Middleton* was printed, I have been favoured with the following titles of fome works he left behind him in MS. 1. " Brouillon of an Apology " for Dr. *Middleton*'s Writings, and how far it is allowable to conform to the Religion of " any Country." 2. " Dr. *Laughton*'s Account of finding Dr. *Middleton* at a Tavern. " [*July* 3, 1710.]" 3. " An Univerfity Grace for eftablifhing the Office of Library-Keeper." " 4. An Advertifement for the intended Publication of a ferious Apology for the Letter to " Dr. *Waterland*." 5. " Oratio *Woodwardiana*." 6. " Brouillon of a *Latin* Differ- " tation concerning the Power of Miracles to prove a Religion." 7. " A *Latin* Differ- " tation on the Gift of Tongues." 8. " Remarks on the Letters from *Agbarus* to *Jefus*." 9. " A *Latin* Speech intended to be fpoken before King *George* II. on his Vifit to *Cam-* " *bridge*." 10. " An Expoftulatory Letter to the Rev. Dr. *Waterland*." 11. " The " firft and fecond Books of *Cicero*'s Epiftles tranflated into *Englifh* ‡." 12. " Brouillon " concerning

---

* This tranflation, originally publifhed in 8vo, 1726, and dedicated to *Thomas* Lord *Howard* baron of *Effingham*, was reprinted in weekly numbers, in two volumes folio, 1732 and 1733 ; the firft of which was infcribed, in a manly dedication, to *Frederick* Prince of *Wales*, who rewarded Mr. *Tindal* with a gold medal, worth 40 guineas. The fecond volume of the 8vo edition had been infcribed to Sir *Charles Wager*, when the tranflator was chaplain on board *The Torbay* in the Bay of *Revel* in the Gulf of *Finland*. Vol. IV. is dedicated to the fame, from the fame place, 1727. Vol. VI. from *Great Waltham*, 1728, to the *Englifh* factors at *Lifbon*, where the tranflator officiated as chaplain five months in the abfence of Mr. *Sims*. The " Continuation" was likewife publifhed in weekly num- bers, which began in 1744, and were completed *March* 25, 1747, which is the date of the dedication to the late Duke of *Cumberland*. When the " Hiftory" was publifhed, Mr. *Tindal* was " Vicar of " *Great Waltham*." In the " Continuation" he is called " Rector of *Alverftoke*, and Chaplain to the " Royal Hofpital at *Greenwich*." This laft was printed in two volumes, but is accompanied with a recommendation to bind it in three ; vol. III. to contain the reign and medals of King *William* ; vol. IV. the reign of Queen *Anne* ; and vol. V. the reign of King *George* I. with the medals of Queen *Anne* and King *George* ; a fummary of the Hiftory of *England*, and the Index. A fecond edition of the " Continuation" appeared in 1751 ; and a new edition of the whole, in 21 volumes 8vo, 1757.

† The celebrated tutor of *Clare-Hall*, then fenior proctor, and warmly attached to Dr. *Bentley*. See *Middleton*'s " Remarks on the Cafe of Dr. *Bentley* further ftated," &c. in his Works, 4to, vol. III. p. 341.

‡ " The ftyle of *Middleton*," fays Dr. *Warton*, in his 'Effay on *Pope*,' vol. II. p. 324, " which " is commonly efteemed very pure, is blemifhed with many vulgar and cant terms. Such as *Pompey* " *had a month's mind*, &c. He has not been fuccefsful in the tranflations of thofe many epiftles of " *Tully* which he has inferted ; which, however curious, yet break the thread of the narration. " *Mongault* and *Melmoth* have far exceeded him in their excellent tranflations of thefe pieces, which " are, after all, fome of the moft precious remains of antiquity."—" The Life of *Tully*," the fame learned critic informs us, " procured Dr. *Middleton* a great reputation, and a great fum of money. It " is a pleafing and ufeful work, efpecially to younger readers, as it gives a comprehenfive view of a " moft interefting period in the *Roman* hiftory, and of the characters principally concerned in thofe " important events. It may be worth obferving, that he is much indebted, without acknowledging " it, to a curious book little known, intituled, ' *G. Bellendini*, *Scoti*, de *Tribus Luminibus Romanorum*, " Libri 16. *Parifiis* ; apud *Taffunum du Bray*, 1634,' folio ; dedicated to King *Charles*. It com- " prehends a hiftory of *Rome*, from the foundation of the city to the time of *Auguftus*, drawn up in " the very words of *Cicero*, without any alteration of any expreffion. In this book *Middleton* found

" every

" concerning the Characters of some Writers, and the State of the Church in the third
" and fourth Centuries." Several other works of Dr. *Middleton* were known to have
existed, particularly the two following, which were burnt by himself. 1. " The First
" Part of some Considerations in Defence of the Plain Account * of the Sacrament.'
2. " A *Latin* Dissertation on the Proofs of the Divinity and Truth of Religion."
Of the last mentioned article a copy had been taken by Lord *Bolingbroke*. There were
also found among his papers some materials for a life of *Demosthenes*, correspondent
to that of *Cicero*.—A friend once lamenting to Dr. *Middleton* that he had not been
made a bishop, " Then Sir," he replied, " as they have not thought fit to trust me, I am
at liberty to speak my mind †."—His death happening about the same period with that
of Mr. *Gordon* the translator of *Tacitus*, Lord *Bolingbroke* said to a most amiable Physician now living, " Then there is the best writer in *England* gone, and the worst."

P. 126. On Dr. *Middleton's* third marriage, Bishop *Gooch* making him a matrimonial
visit, before the Doctor appeared told Mrs. *Middleton* ‡ that " he was glad she did not dis-
" like the ancients so much as her husband did." She replied, " that she hoped his Lordship
" did not reckon Dr. *Middleton* among the ancients yet." The bishop answered, " You,
" Madam, are the best judge of that!"—Dr. *Middleton* had a niece, a brother's daughter,
who resided some time in his family, as did also a niece of his last wife, Miss *Hester Powell*,
afterwards married to the Rev. Dr. *Barnardiston*, late master of *Bene't College*, both
since dead, leaving one daughter of their name. Dr. *Middleton's* resignation of his
Woodwardian lectureship (to which he was presented by Colonel *King*, as Dr. *Woodward's* executor) was probably owing to his second marriage, it being tenable only by a
batchelor. The salary certainly was an object to him. The living in *Surrey*, which
towards the end of his life, he accepted from Sir *John Frederick*, was only 50*l.* a year.
It may be added, that Mrs. *Montagu*, nearly related to his first wife, was educated at the
feet of this *Gamaliel*. The present Lord *Montfort*, then Mr. *Bromley*, was also under his

" every part of *Cicero's* own history, in his own words, and his works arranged in chronological or-
" der, without farther trouble. The impression of this work being shipped for *England*, was lost
" in the vessel, which was cast away, and only a few copies remained, that had been left in *France*."
I have quoted this heavy charge of plagiarism, that some friend of Dr. *Middleton*, or admirer of his
writings, may stand forth in his vindication.—Mr. *Knox*, speaking of *Cicero's* Epistles, says, " They
" are thought not to appear to the best advantage in the specimens which Dr. *Middleton* has inserted
" in his Life of *Cicero*. No one was better able to do them justice than that great biographer; but
" it is said he committed the task of translation to some inferior writer." Essays, vol. II. p. 56.—
Some MS. Remarks by Mr. *Bowyer* on the Life of *Cicero* will be printed in his " Miscell. Tracts."

* Speaking of Bishop *Hoadly's* " Plain Account," in a letter to Lord *Harvey*, *July* 28, 1735, not
published in his Works, Dr. *Middleton* says, " I like both the design and the doctrine, as I do every
" design of reconciling religion with reason; or, where that cannot be, of bringing them as near to-
" gether as possible. His enemies will insult him with the charge of lessening Christian piety; but
" the candid will see, that he seeks only to destroy a superstitious doctrine, by establishing a rational
" one in its place. But as, by throwing down the shrines and altars of the church, he will raise no
" small stir from the men of craft, so I rejoice much with your Lordship, that he has secured the
" good Castle of *Farnham* for his retreat." And again, *Feb.* 8, 1736, " You would advise him to
" waste no more of his time in controversy; which, generally speaking, means no more at the best,
" than to make plausible to weak men, what is contemptible to men of sense."

† " These slumberers in stalls," he observes in another letter to Lord *Harvey*, *Sept.* 13, 1736,
" suspect me very unjustly of ill-designs against their peace; for though there are many things in the
" church that I wholly dislike, yet, whilst I am content to acquiesce in the ill, I should be glad to
" taste a little of the good, and to have some amends for that *ugly assent* and *consent*, which no man
" of sense can approve of. We read of some of the earliest disciples of *Christ*, who followed him,
" not for his works, but his loaves. These are certainly blameable, because they saw his miracles:
" but to us, who had not the happiness to see the *one*, it may be allowable to have some inclination
" to the *other*. Your Lordship knows a certain prelate, who, with a very low notion of the church's
" sacred bread, has a very high relish for, and a very large share of, the temporal. My appetite to
" each is equally moderate, and would be satisfied almost with any thing but mere emptiness. I
" have no pretensions to riot in the feast of the elect, but, with the sinner in the Gospel, to gather up
" the crumbs that fall from the table."   ‡ The relict of Mr. *Wilkins*, a *Bristol* merchant.

tuition; as was, from 1745 till his death, the late Mr. *Robartes*, nephew to the Earl of *Radnor*, who generously continued the annual allowance to Dr. *Middleton* after the young man was dead.

P. 127. Dr. *Chandler* studied at *Leyden*, where he was contemporary with Archbishop *Secker* and Bishop *Chandler*, and the late Lord *Bowes* chancellor of *Ireland*.

P. 128. Add, " The two Conferences held on *February* 7 and 13, 1734-5, at *The Bell* " *Tavern* in *Nicholas Lane*, between two *Romish* Priests, a Divine of the Church of *Eng-* " *land*, and Dr. *Hunt* and Mr. *Chandler*, Dissenting Divines, truly stated; with some Ad- " ditions and Supplemental Remarks on a late printed Account of the said Conferences. " By a Gentleman who was present at both Conferences," was published in 1735, 8vo.

Ibid. Dr. *Chandler's* Bible was to have been presented by his widow to one of our uni- versities. Some of the most eminent and learned dissenting ministers gave her 20 guineas for it, and offered it to an eminent bookseller to print, only desiring to be re-imbursed the purchase-money, and the surplus-money to be insured to the widow. He calculated the printing at 90*l.* his own profit at 25*l. per cent.* yet would give nothing to print it himself, and asked too great allowance as publisher. Dr. *Lardner* was for publishing it by subscription.

P. 129. Since the account of Mr. *Hardinge* was printed, his Son has obliged the learned world with a curious little volume of his father's " *Latin* Verses;" amongst which is a corrected copy of the Ode in the " Select Collection." It was written at *Knowle Hill* in 1739, and addressed " to *Stephen Poyntz*, Esq; Preceptor to the Duke of " *Cumberland* *." Mr. *Hardinge*, it is said, translated this Ode, and at the same time engaged Dr. *Davies* to make another translation. Both are preserved, and printed in a volume of *English* verses, which I have not had the pleasure of seeing. The *Latin* poems are of various dates; some of them school exercises at *Eton* in 1717, 1718; others at *Cambridge* 1719—1722; a poem on the death of his eldest son, 1746; an epitaph on his father *(George Hardinge*, M. A.) 1750; one small poem in 1754; and epistles to several of his friends between 1730 and 1750. I mention these so minutely, as the volume in which they are printed has been circulated only among a few friends.—In the note, for *Denhilliad*, read " *Den-hill* Iliad."

P. 130. " *Joseph Ames*, secretary to the Society of Antiquaries, was originally a ship- " chandler in *Wapping*. Late in his life he took to the study of antiquities; and besides " his quarto volume †, containing accounts of our earliest printers and their works, he " published a list in duodecimo ‡ of *English* heads, engraved and mezzotinto, and drew " up the ' Parentalia' from Mr. *Wren's* papers. He died [*Oct.* 7,] 1759 §." Mr. *Ames's* daughter, since dead, was married to Captain *Dampier*, late a captain of an *East-India* man, now an officer in the *East-India* house, and we believe descendant or relation of the voyager of that name.

Ibid. sub-note, *daughter*] This woman, whose name was *Esther*, was a stout athletic person, and as much noticed for the decency of her behaviour, as for her strength.

P. 135. It appears by Dr. *Birch's* MSS. that Mr. *Gordon's* salary as secretary to the society for the encouragement of learning was 50*l.* a year. On the 30th of *June*, 1739,

---

* To whom, in *December* 1732, Mr. *Hardinge* had been appointed law reader, with a salary of 100*l.*

† " Typographical Antiquities; being an Historical Account of Printing in *England*; with some " Memoirs of our ancient Printers, and a Register of the Books printed by them, from the year " MCCCCLXXI, to the year MDC. With an Appendix, concerning Printing in *Scotland* and *Ire-* " *land* to the present Time, 1749." Of this useful book, which has long been scarce, a new edition has been some time in the press, with large improvements by Mr. *Herbert*, from whom some copious memoirs of Mr. *Ames* may be expected, with his portrait.

‡ It is in octavo.

§ Mr. *Walpole's* Catalogue of Engravers, p. 2. note.—Mr. *Ames's* coins, medals, shells, fossils, ores, minerals, natural and artificial curiosities, inscriptions, and antiquities, were sold by *Langford*, *Feb.* 20 and 21, 1760; his library and prints by the same, *May* 5, &c. 1760.

Mr. *Alexander Blackwell**, " who had had a univerſity-education, underſtood ſome of " the modern languages, and had practiſed the printing-buſineſs for ſome years, was a " candidate to ſucceed Mr. *Gordon*." Mr. *Daniel Lyon* was afterwards ſecretary. Dr. *Birch's* accompts as treaſurer are preſerved among his MSS. Mr. *Stephen Le Bas*, who ſucceeded him in that office, received, *Feb.* 9, 1738, a balance of 59*l*. 3*s*. 9½*d*.—*Gordon* made trial of all the ways by which a man could get an honeſt livelihood. He ſet about the ſtudy of *Greek*, but is ſaid to have been ſo ill furniſhed with *Latin*, as to have tranſ-lated in one of his publications the concluding ſentence of *Herodotus'* firſt book, where horſes are ſaid to be ſacrificed to the ſun, as *deo perniciſſimo*, the moſt *pernicious* deity.

* Son of a dealer in knit hoſe at *Aberdeen*; where he received a liberal education. He afterwards ſtudied phyſic under *Boerhaave* at *Leyden*, took the degree of M. D. and acquired a proficiency in the modern languages. On his return home, happening to ſtay ſome time at *The Hague*, he contracted an intimacy with a *Swediſh* nobleman. Marrying a gentleman's daughter in the neighbourhood of *Aberdeen*, he propoſed practiſing his profeſſion in that part of the kingdom; but in two years finding his expectations diſappointed, he came to *London*, where he met with ſtill leſs-encouragement as a phyſician, and commenced corrector of the preſs for Mr. *Wilkins* a printer. After ſome years ſpent in this employment, he ſet up as a printer himſelf, and carried on ſeveral large works, till 1734, when he became bankrupt. In what manner he ſubſiſted from this event till the above-mentioned application we do not learn, unleſs it was by the ingenuity of his wife, who pub-liſhed " A curious Herbal, containing Five Hundred Cuts, of the moſt uſeful Plants, which are now " uſed in the Practice of Phyſick, engraved on folio Copper Plates, after Drawings taken from the " Life, by *Elizabeth Blackwell*. To which is added, a ſhort Deſcription of the Plants, and their " common Uſes in Phyſick, 1739 †," 2 vols. folio. In or about the year 1740 he went to *Sweden*, and, renewing his intimacy with the nobleman he knew at *The Hague*, again aſſumed the medical profeſſion, and was very well received in that capacity; till, turning projector, he laid a ſcheme be-fore his *Swediſh* Majeſty for draining the fens and marſhes, which was well received, and many thouſands employed in proſecuting it under the Doctor's direction, for which he had ſome ſmall al-lowance from the King. This ſcheme ſucceeding ſo well, he turned his thoughts to others of greater importance, which in the end proved fatal to him. He was ſuſpected of being concerned in a plot with Count *Teſſin*, and was tortured; which not producing a confeſſion, he was beheaded *Auguſt* 9, 1748 ‡; and ſoon after this event appeared " A genuine Copy of a Letter from a Merchant in " *Stockholm*, to his Correſpondent in *London*; containing an Impartial Account of Doctor *Alexander* " *Blackwell*, his Plot, Trial, Character, and Behaviour, both under Examination, and at the Place " of Execution; together with a Copy of a Paper delivered to a Friend upon the Scaffold §." He poſ-ſeſſed a good natural genius, but was ſomewhat flighty, and a little conceited. His converſation, however, was facetious and agreeable; and he might be conſidered on the whole as a well-bred ac-compliſhed gentleman.

† To the firſt volume is prefixed a recommendation from the diſtinguiſhed names of Dr. *Mead*, Dr. *Teiſſier*, Dr. *Stuart* Dr. *Douglas*, Dr. *Sherard*, Mr. *Cheſelden*, Mr. *Miller*, Mr. *Rand*, and Mr. *Nicholls*, dated *Oct.* 1, 1735; and another from the preſident and cenſors of the College of Phyſicians, dated *July* 1, 1737.

‡ The Britiſh ambaſſador was recalled from *Sweden* in 1748, among other reaſons, for the imputations thrown on his Britannic Majeſty in the trial of Dr. *Blackwell*.

§ Which may now perhaps be deemed a curioſity: " Gentlemen Spectators, I came into your country as a " ſtranger, in order to earn an honeſt livelihood in the way of my profeſſion as a phyſician. For ſome years " that I have reſided among you, I muſt acknowledge that I met with a reception and encouragement beyond " any poor merit I can boaſt of, which in gratitude has begot in me a real and ſincere affection for this country, " and its inhabitants. As I met with civility from all ranks, I could have no particular enmity at any perſon " in the kingdom. As my profeſſion was all I minded (except ſo far as I was happily inſtrumental in draining " the marſhes of this kingdom) I had no ambition or capacity for meddling in court-affairs, and conſequently " could have no plot of ſupplanting any of the miniſtry. As I had never ſuffered by the laws of *Sweden*, and " as the conſtitution nearly reſembles that form under which I have been educated, I could have no biaſs upon " me to ſeek a change in the conſtitution of this country; where, whatever form it might aſſume, I could enjoy " ſo greater liberty than I did before, nor could ever expect to be any thing elſe but a phyſician. Yet it has " been my misfortune to come under the ſuſpicion of acting a part inconſiſtent with my character, ability, or " even ſuch principles as ſhould direct me in the moſt trifling as well as the moſt important concerns of life, for " which I am now about to ſuffer; but, as I am a dying man, and in thoſe circumſtances where falſehood is of " the utmoſt bad conſequence, and can avail me in nothing, I declare I never intended, plotted, or contrived any " alteration or diſturbance of the *Swediſh* conſtitution, nor ever received any encouragement whatſoever on " that head from any power whatever, as has been falſely ſurmiſed. I die in charity with all mankind, and " forgive from the bottom of my heart all thoſe who have injured, oppreſſed, or calumniated me in any ſhape: " And in the ſame manner expect forgiveneſs from all ſuch whom I may any ways have injured, eſpecially of " all thoſe who may be any ways ſcandalized by the ignominious death which my folly has brought me to, and " that the reputation of the innocent may not ſuffer upon my account. ALEXANDER BLACKWELL."

His obfervations on Captain *Lethieullier's* and Dr. *Mead's* mummies were given him by Mr. *R. Gale* and Dr. *Mead.* Thefe two effays being defigned to explain three of the twenty-five plates delivered to the fubfcribers, " an explanation of the remaining prints was to have come forth with all convenient fpeed; firft, what belongs to the other ancient mummies exhibited in the faid plates ; next, what regards the reft of the monuments on ftone, wood, metal, &c. When this was finifhed according to the terms of the fubfcription, the author intended to offer to the publick another work, viz. the Hiftory of the *Ægyptians*, from the earlieft accounts given of them to the time of *Darius* contemporary with *Alexander* the Great ; which was not intended to be publifhed by fubfcription, and was then very near ready to put to prefs." Mr. *Gordon* went abroad in 1741 to *Carolina,* where he purchafed a fecretary's place, and died. On this occafion his place of fecretary to the Antiquarian Society became vacant, his holding which was urged, among other reafons, by Dr. *Rawlinfon,* for not leaving his papers to that learned body, becaufe their fecretary was a *Scotchman.*

P. 137. l. 9. For this treatife Dr. *Stuart* obtained a gold medal from the Royal Academy of Sciences, of which he was a member. He died *Sept.* 15, 1742.

Ibid. fub-note, *add,* Or poffibly from *Congeries.*

P. 138. *fcattered papers*] In one of thefe, endorfed " Cafh laid out, 1737-8, after the " death of my father, who left no will, but given by *W. B.* his fon, chiefly at his own " difcretion," it appears that Mr. *Bowyer* gave 100*l.* to Mr. *Wallis* *, who had married his only fifter †; and 20*l.* to Mr. *Bettenham,* who had married his half-fifter †. He alfo paid Mr. *Wallis* 20*l.* 4*s.* for mourning rings ; and the funeral expences were 37*l.* 10*s.*

P. 141. Of the largeft paper there were only *ten* copies of *Robinfon's Hefiod* printed ; which accounts for their great fcarcity, and the enormous price for which a copy has been fometimes fold.

P. 144. fub-note, read, " the King of *Scotland* to our King, for the earldom of *Cumberland,"* &c.

P. 145. On *Monday* the 16th of *March,* 1723-4, died *John Bridges,* Efq; at his chambers in *Lincoln's Inn Square.* He was one of the governors of *Bethlem Hofpital,* and F. R. S. In the year 1695 he was made folicitor of the cuftoms ; and in 1711 one of the commiffioners of the fame duties ; and in 1715 cafhier of the excife. POLITICAL STATE, 1724.—He was alfo F. S. A. and we believe firft collector for the Hiftory of *Northamptonfhire,* and father to the other *John Bridges,* who was alfo F. S. A. A portrait of him by *Kneller,* 1706, was engraved by *G. V.* 1726. He about 1665 purchafed the manor of *Barton Segrave,* near *Kettering.* Hiftory of *Northamptonfhire,* vol. II. p. 218. In the note to this page, the article of Mr. *Bridges's* will, dated 1723, belongs to this gentleman. His library was accordingly fold by auction by Mr. *Cock, February* the 7th, 1725, at his chambers, *Lincoln's Inn,* and produced 4000*l.*; and though the auction was from 11 to 2 in the morning, and from 5 to 8 in the evening, it took up 27 days. To the Catalogue was prefixed a print by *A. Motte,* of an oak felled, and this motto, Δρυος ɯιϭϭϭνϛ παϛ ανηρ ξυλευεται—an affecting memento to the collectors of great libraries, who cannot or do not leave them to fome public acceffible repofitory.

P. 147. Since the note on Bifhop *Atterbury* was printed off, I have met with a large and valuable collection of his MS. Letters, which fhall fpeedily be laid before the publick, with fome further particulars of this diftinguifhed Prelate's life.

P. 150. The Dictionary of Mr. *Chambers* is now re-publifhing in weekly numbers, with a fuccefs unexampled in the annals of modern literature. As this very ufeful and laborious author has hitherto been entirely neglected by his friends, and by the writers of biographical works, the following particulars are inferted at the defire of a friend who received fome of the information from the late *William Ayrey,* efq. deceafed. *Ephraim Chambers* was born at *Kendal,* in the county of *Weftmoreland,* of Quaker parents, who bred him up

* See the pedigree in p. 485.　　　† See above, pp. 2. and 13.

in the principles of the sect; which, however, as he advanced in life, he shewed no attachment to, if he even did not abandon them. He was put apprentice to Mr. *Senex* the globe-maker; and, during his connexion with that skilful mechanick, acquired the taste for learning, which continued his prevailing passion during the remainder of his days. His principal work, The " Cyclopædia," was the result of many years application. It was first published in two volumes folio, 1728, by a subscription of four guineas, and has a very respectable list of subscribers. The dedication to the King is dated *Gray's Inn*, *Oct.* 15, 1727. A second edition *, with corrections and additions, was printed in 1738 †; a third in 1739; a fourth in 1741; and a fifth in 1746. Mr. *Chambers*'s attention was not wholly devoted to this undertaking. He was elected a fellow of the Royal Society *Nov.* 6, 1729; and joined in a translation and abridgement of " The Philoso- " phical History and Memoirs of the Royal Academy of Sciences at *Paris*; or an " Abridgement of all the Papers relating to Natural Philosophy, which have been published " by the Members of that illustrious Society, 1742," 5 vols. 8vo. His share in this work has been much censured by his coadjutor and assistant Mr. *John Martyn*, F. R. S. and Professor of Botany at *Cambridge* ‡. He likewise was concerned in a periodical work, called " The " Literary Magazine," which was begun in 1735, and wrote many articles therein, particularly the Review of Dr. *Morgan's* Book. Mr. *Ayrey*, who was his amanuensis from the age of 12 in 1728 to 1733, said, that in that time he copied near 20 folio volumes, which, Mr. *Chambers* used to say, comprehended materials for more than 30 volumes of that size, though he at the same time added, they would neither be sold nor read if printed. He was represented as a man equally indefatigable, perspicacious, and attentive; yet never acquired much money by his labours; very chearful, but hasty and impetuous; free in his religious sentiments; kept little company, and had but few acquaintance. He was also very exact in money matters. He made a will shortly before his death (which was never proved) in which he declared he owed no debts, except to his taylor for a rocquelaure. He lived in chambers at *Gray's Inn*, but died at *Canonbury House* at *Islington*; and was buried at *Westminster*, where the following inscription, written by himself, is placed in the cloysters of the abbey:

" Multus pervulgatus,   Qui humani nihil à se alienum putavit.
    Paucis notus;   Vitâ simul, et laboribus functus,
Qui vitam, inter lucem et umbram,   Hic requiescere voluit,
    Nec eruditus nec idiota,   Ephraim Chambers, F. R. S.
Literis deditus, transegit; sed ut homo   Obiit xv *Mart.* mdccxl."

He had two brothers: *Nathaniel* the elder was an eminent solicitor in Chancery, and married the daughter of Mr. *Woolley*, secretary to the *East India* Company, and

* In an advertisement to the second edition, he obviates the complaints of such readers as might, from his paper of " Considerations" published some time before, have expected a new work instead of a new edition. A considerable part of the copy was prepared with that view, and more than twenty sheets were actually printed off, with design to have published a volume in the winter of 1737, and to have gone on publishing a volume yearly till the whole was completed; but the booksellers were alarmed by an act then agitating in parliament, which contained a clause obliging the publishers of all improved editions of books to print their improvements separately. The bill passed the commons, but failed in the house of lords.

† " While the second edition of *Chambers's* Cyclopædia, the pride of booksellers, and the honour " of the *English* nation, was in the press, I went to the author, and begged leave to add a single syl- " lable to his magnificent work; and that, for Cyclopædia, he would write *Encyclopædia*. To talk " to the writer of a Dictionary, is like talking to the writer of a Magazine; every thing adds to his " parcel: and, instead of contributing one syllable, I was the occasion of a considerable paragraph. " I told him that the addition of the preposition *en* made the meaning of the word more precise; " that Cyclopædia might denote the instruction of a circle, as Cyropædia is the instruction of *Cyrus*, " the *ou*, in composition, being twined in *o*; but that, if he wrote Encyclopædia, it determined it to " be from the dative of Cyclus, instruction in a circle. I urged, secondly, that *Vossius* had observed, " in his book de Vitiis Sermonis, that ' Cyclopædia was used by some authors, but Encyclopædia " by the best.' This deserved some regard, and he paid to it the best he could: he made an ar- " ticle of his title to justify it.   W. Bowyer."

‡ See Preface to his " Dissertation on *Virgil*, 1770," 12mo. p. 361.

widow

widow of —— *Newsham*, a captain of one of their ships, by whom he had a son who died young, and two daughters; the second, *Zachary*, was bred a writing-master, and became steward to Sir *Harry Gough's* grandfather and father, and afterwards deputy-surveyor of the crown lands for near 50 years, in which place his son-in-law officiated for him till a short time before the death of Mr. *Chambers*, who was dispossessed of it for his last year. He died *Dec.* 20, 1780, aged 86, at *Kensington*, leaving, by a second wife, a daughter who married (1765) to Sir *William Wolsley*, bart. by whom she has several children. Mr. *Zachary Chambers* married to his first wife another daughter of Mr. *Woolley* before-mentioned, widow of —— *Lomax*, Esq.

P. 151. Of Mr. *Haynes* I hope to obtain some anecdotes for a future page.

P. 154. Of Mr. *Benson* I shall add the following anecdote, which I lately received from a person well acquainted with him. Though a man who had spent the greater part of his life among books, yet a short time before his death he acquired an aversion to them which was unconquerable. He could not even bear the sight of any, and remained stedfast in his abhorrence of them as long as he lived. In the like manner, according to Dr. *Warton* *, *Cowley* latterly could not endure the company of women.— Besides Mr. *Benson's* " Conclusion to his Prefatory Discourse," &c. 1741, he published, in the same year, " A Supplement to it, in which is contained, a Comparison betwixt " *Johnston* and *Buchanan*." On both these some marginal notes by the Rev. Mr. *Samuel Say*, one of Dr. *Watts's* fellow-pupils, and as such mentioned with due encomiums by Dr. *Gibbons*, are preserved in the Gent. Mag. 1780, p. 607. No one had a better taste, or a more thorough acquaintance with the classics, than Mr. *Say*. It is no wonder therefore that he should prefer *Buchanan* to *Johnston*.

P. 156. Miss *Lintot* is now married to *Henry Fletcher*, Esq; one of the knights of the shire for *Cumberland*. He was created a Baronet april 24. 1782.

P. 164. note, l. 2. read, afterwards LL. and D. D.—Dr. *Taylor's* very elegant inscription to Dr. *Mangey*, prefixed to " *Lysiæ* Fragmenta," might here be noticed.

P. 169. Mr. *Maittaire*, it should be added, was *Latin* tutor to Lord *Chesterfield's* son. He had the honour of being patronized † by the first Earl of *Oxford*, both before and after

---

* Essay on *Pope*, vol. II. p. 109.

† Of this let some extracts from his own letters be a proof: " Honoured Sir, I beg your pardon " if I presume upon your late favour so far as to venture this trifle of mine, as I have done the rest. " I know your censure deserves nothing less to be employed about than the weighty concerns of a " whole nation; and therefore must stoop much below its own sphere to vouchsafe but a look to- " ward the little business of letters and words. But, Sir, your judgement is universal, and extends " itself to the least as well as highest things. Your great abilities and enlarged genius have joined " in you the philosopher and the statesman, and have fitted you as much for the helm of literature " as for that of the state. Among the rest of your eminent virtues shines your great humility, " which, from the high station where the united consent of King and People has placed you, can " condescend to encourage the meanest to sue for your patronage. If none indeed had right to it " but such who deserved it, your goodness would lose its best quality, of being diffusive. And there- " fore, Sir, I hope want of merit may not hinder my most humble claim to it. May I, while others " more deserving appear nearer, admire at an aweful distance your perfections; esteeming it too " much honour already, and more than I can ever pretend to deserve, to have been once known " and countenanced by you. Next, Sir, I must with all submission implore your candid and favour- " able judgement in behalf of my poor imperfect writings, which were only designed to pass my " melancholy hours away, and which I never intended should go out of my hands, and step beyond " the bound of my narrow study, and when they return thither, I shall think them to have been as " much honoured by having been exposed to your view, as if they had appeared in public to the " world. Nothing can now hearten me so much to go on, nothing satisfy me more in the end, as " to have your approbation in the beginning. I have made bold to send you the *Greek* oration which " the Archbishop of *Philippopoly* made at the university of *Cambridge*, when he was presented there " to a doctor's degree ‡. I hope, Sir, the worth of it may make amends for the imperfection of the

‡ Λόγος τῷ ἱερωτάτῳ κỳ σεβασμιωτάτῳ Νεοφύτῳ μητροπολίτῃ τῆς Φιλιππουπόλεως πρὸς Ἀκαδημίαν τῆς Κανταβριγίας, ιỿ Σεπτεμβρίου ὅτ' εἰς τὴν τάξιν τῶν ἐκεῖ ἱεροδιδασκάλων τῆς Θεολογίας ἐνεγράφθη. Oratio, &c. cum versione *Latinâ. Cantab.* 1701, 4to.

" manuscript

after that great man's elevation to the peerage, and continued a favourite with his fon the fecond Earl. In his earlieft letters he writes his name *Michell Mattaire*.

P. 171.

" manuſcript I have ſent with it. Now, Sir, knowing that to rob you of the leaſt minute of your " time, is to rob a whole nation, I ſhall conclude with my prayers and beſt wiſhes for your life, and " conſequently for the welfare of this kingdom; and beg leave to ſubſcribe myſelf, with the pro- " foundeſt reverence, moſt worthy Sir, your moſt humbly devoted and obliged ſervant. *Nov.* 6, " 1701."—" Your extreme kindneſs to me has made me ſo bold as to trouble you with this letter, " and therein to pay all the acknowledgement I am capable of for all your favours, and to promiſe " my utmoſt readineſs to ſerve you, if it lie in the power of one who is ſo much below you as I am. " I almoſt wiſh myſelf at my old ſchool-drudgery again, that I might expreſs my thankfulneſs in " attending your fon, whom you told me you had ſome thoughts of putting to *Weſtminſter*. How- " ever, I ſhall be at your command, and entirely willing to give him any manner of aſſiſtance in " any way as you may think fit. A friend of mine has invited me to *Acton* on *Saturday* for three or " four days, which made me willing not to put off my thanks till I return, leſt I ſhould find you " gone into the country. And ſo, wiſhing you a ſafe journey and return, and ſuch a ſucceſs there " and here as your merits moſt deſervedly claim, I beg leave to ſubſcribe myſelf, with all humility, " worthy Sir, your moſt obliged and reſpectful ſervant. *July* 15, 1702."—" I beg your pardon for " this interruption, of which I had rather be guilty, than of failing to pay you that reſpect you " deſerve from all in general, and ſo much from me in particular. I don't doubt but by this you " think on your journey to *London*, in order to attend the Parliament, where all lovers of their " country, as they expect and pray for it, ſo they fear not but your ſignal deſerts, ſo much tried and " ſo well approved in the moſt difficult buſineſſes now theſe two ſeſſions, will meet with a moſt ſuit- " able return. I am ſure all true Church-men, having found you ſo good a patron to that good " cauſe, ought to be, and will, one and all, in the intereſt of one on whom theirs ſo much depend. " As for news of the town, it would be impertinent for me to trouble you with, when you have better " intelligence than I can pretend to, who for the moſt part am confined to my ſtudy, where old dead " company is my melancholy entertainment and diverſion. I made a viſit laſt *Sunday* evening to your " fon, aſked him how he did, and what form he was in. He told me he liked all well, but was not " placed yet. I promiſed him now and then to come and ſpend an hour with him. As I was ſeal- " ing this letter, the proclamation was cried for proroguing the parliament. *Aug.* 12, 1702."—" I " chanced lately to mention to you in our diſcourſe ſomething concerning the famous *Whiſton's* im- " pudent letters to the biſhop of *London*, wherein he oppoſed our doxology: you will pardon me, my " Lord, if I trouble your Lordſhip with this little pamphlet, which my zeal in the cauſe of religion " moved me to write. Neither my ſtudies nor calling have been turned to Divinity farther than a " Chriſtian ought, who has ſome little knowledge of the original text of his Bible. I know your " Lordſhip to be no leſs quick-ſighted in thoſe things than in others, which are more particularly " the object of men in your high ſtation; what I now offer to your reading muſt needs diſcover " much of my imperfections and ignorance: but your goodneſs will, I hope, excuſe its faults for the " ſake of its honeſt meaning. I have my aim, if I can confirm ſtill the good opinion your Lordſhip " has entertained of my ſtedfaſt and immoveable adherence to the Orthodox Church of *England*, as " well as to the true loyal intereſt of a country, to which (after I was driven from my own) I owe " every thing which I enjoy in the world. *Aug.* 2, 1719."—" When I had the honour to wait on " your Lordſhip laſt, I promiſed you to give you a copy of thoſe verſes which Dr. *South* made upon " the *Weſtminſter* School about the time he had his firſt degree at *Oxford*. I have tranſcribed them " from the very manuſcript I had from himſelf, and ſend them herein incloſed *, being glad of " any opportunity of aſſuring your Lordſhip that I am, &c. (*Aug.* 4, 1719.)—" I take this " opportunity of wiſhing your Lordſhip a happy new year, and many of them; the ſame alſo " to your noble family. I can't ſufficiently thank you for your laſt; and in it for your ac- " cuſtomed favours to an old friend, in your procuring me thoſe two ſubſcriptions you mention. I " am ſorry the notice of them came too late to be inſerted in the printed liſt. I will take care to " obey your Lordſhip's orders concerning the ten copies to be laid by for you; as alſo to return the " two exemplars of *Prideaux's* edition, the uſe of which your Lordſhip was ſo kind as to allow me. " I ſuppoſe I need not to carry them to your houſe till you are in town. The completing this work, " which lay ſo heavy on my ſhoulders, hath given me ſome eaſe; eſpecially ſince Providence has " continued my life to ſee it finiſhed, that I might not die indebted to my generous benefactors; " whom I beg to add one kindneſs more to the former, to excuſe all the imperfections and faults in " a work, the nature of which required a much abler hand than mine. I am, &c. *Jan.* 20, 1731-2." —" My Lord, in obedience to your orders by yours of the 25th, I delivered at your houſe laſt

* It may be ſufficient to refer to theſe verſes, which are printed in *South's* " Opera Poſthuma *Latina, Lond.* " 1722," 8vo. p. 179.

7

" *Friday*

P. 171. Among the MS. treasures in *The British Museum* are several volumes (4811—4827) the gift of Bishop *Pococke*; *viz.* " Minutes and Registers of the Philosophical Soci-" ety at *Dublin* *, from 1683 to 1687, with a copy of the papers read before them ;" and " Register of the Philosophical Society of *Dublin*, from *Aug.* 14, 1707, with copies of " some of the papers read before them ;" also " Several Extracts taken out of the Records " of *Bermingham's* Tower;" " An Account of the *Franciscan* Abbeys, Houses, and " Frieries, in *Ireland*;" and many other curious articles of *Irish* History.—Of Mr. *Isaac Milles*, who was a fellow of St. *John's College, Cambridge*, there is a portrait by *Virtue.*

P. 176. In 1744 Mr. *Bowyer* presented a copy of the Laws of *Howel Dha* to the Gentlemen's Society of *Spalding*, and received from their President an acknowledgement printed in the " Reliquiæ Galeanæ," p. 96, whence an extract is transcribed below †.

" *Friday* a copy of the Marbles stitched up. I hope your Lordship and the learned company at *Wim-* " *ple* will find a more agreeable way of diversion in the country, than of examining this poor work " of mine, which will, I am afraid, discover too much my ignorance. However, I promise myself " excuse from candid judges (such as your Lordship) in consideration of the labour I have spent in " it. Dr. *Middleton* is a subscriber ; and, when he comes to town, or whenever he orders it, I will " send him his copy. Mr. *Harbin*, who has been assisting to me by communicating some papers, " shall not fail of my thanks and acknowledgement. I have (in the 596th page, last line but 8, of " my work) expressed my sentiments of the worth of that great and good man. I am, my Lord, infi-" nitely obliged to your Lordship for your help in getting off this book of mine, of which I repent " of having printed so many copies as 300, when 200 might have sufficed, and much fewer, had it " not been for your Lordship's charitable kindness in promoting the subscription ; for which kind-" ness, and all others received from your Lordship, no other return can be given but the ardent " wishes and hearty prayers of, &c. *Jan.* 30, 1731-2."—" I take the liberty to trouble you with " this, and acquaint you that I have received your Lordship's two lists inclosed in your two last " letters. This night is the seventh of the auction, and I am now going to attend your commissions, " as I will do all the rest. I will certainly take care of them all, and I believe *in propriâ personâ.* " If by chance I should be forced to be at any time absent, I will provide a sure friend to supply " my place. However, I promise your Lordship that I will not fail to be present at the twelfth day " for N° 1374. Your Lordship's name (as you desired) shall not be known. *Nov.* 24, 1732."—" I have not trusted the commissions to any one ; but both have attended, and will attend, every " night myself. I must go this afternoon early to look at the books and examine them, and make " up the account with *Ballard* the auctioneer. I was told by Dr. *Freind*, that we should keep our " every other-year *Westminster* meeting next *January* ; in order to which, *Eunuchus* was a week ago " acted for the first time by this new set of King's scholars : *Gnatho* was represented to admiration. " *Dec.* 7, 1732."

* This society was founded, on the plan of the Royal Society of *London*, in 1683, by Mr. *William Molyneux*, the friend and correspondent of Mr. *Locke*, under the encouragement of Sir *William Petty*, who was the first president, as Mr. *Molyneux* was the first secretary, in which post he was succeeded by Mr. *Saint George Ashe*, professor of mathematics in the university of *Dublin*. The society met at first weekly ; and their minutes were from time to time communicated to the Royal Society. In the confusion of 1688 they were dispersed, and never resumed their meetings. (Brit. Top. II. 776.)

† " Dear Sir, The copy of Dr. *Wotton's Welsh* Laws of *Howel Dha*, your donation to the public " library of our Society, I lately received, and carried it to those Gentlemen at their meeting, who " are much obliged to you for that useful and valuable present. Our friend the Reverend Mr. " Prebend *William Clarke* might have much enlarged his Preface, not improperly, if, as an intro-" duction to those, he had prefixed what I promised the Doctor ‡ in *London*, and sent Mr. *Clarke* " notice I had made my clerk transcribe, from my common-place book, a collection in *Latin* from " *Cæsar, Tacitus, Dio, Xiphilin*, &c. supplied from fragments picked up by *Scaliger, Camden, Selden*, " *Hales*, of all the " Leges & Conciones *Britannorum* & *Saxonum* transmarinorum," and have his " thanks for, in a letter dated from *Buxted, Jan.* 16, 1713 ; and were accordingly by me I find car-" ried up to *London* for him, but judged too ancient for his purpose. I was however a subscriber, " had the book when published, and still have it in Chart. Mag. and esteem it much. Some time " after the receipt of yours, I sent our friend Mr. *R. Gale* the account you sent me in it of the coin " of *Caligula* found at *Chichester* §, which you had from our said friend the learned Prebendary ; and " he, in answer, says, it is a confirmation of the antiquities of that city, and of the inscription there " found in *April*, 1723, of King *Cogidunus*, whereon his Dissertations are published in the Philoso-" phical Transactions ‖, and Dr. *Stukeley's* Itin. Curios. ** and the inscription itself by Mr. *Clarke* " in his Preface to the *Welsh* Laws."

‡ Dr. *William Wotton.*   § See above, p. 509.   ‖ N° 379.   ** I. 188.

P. 177.

P. 177. note, l. 5, 6. read, such a vaſt ſpirit of learning and curioſity in that country as probably will never be extinguiſhed.

L. 15. read, *coup d'œil vif & lumineux.*

Ibid. The account of Mr. *Folkes* has already been enlarged in p. 348.—But, ſince that page was printed, I have been favoured with the following very copious memoirs, as drawn up for publication by Mr. *Birch.* Though ſome of the particulars may appear a repetition, the whole is too curious to be abridged: " *Martin Folkes,* Eſq; was deſcended " of a good family, and eldeſt ſon of *Martin Folkes,* Eſq; counſellor at law, by his wife " *Dorothy,* one of the two daughters and coheirs of *William Hovell,* of *Hillington-Hall,* " near *Lynn,* in the county of *Norfolk,* Knight ; the other daughter being married to " Dr. *William Wake,* afterwards Archbiſhop of *Canterbury.* He was born in the pa- " riſh of *St. Giles's in the Fields,* in the City of *Weſtminſter,* on the 29th of *October,* " 1690; and at the age of nine years was intruſted to the learned Mr. *Cappel,* ſon of " the celebrated *Lewis Cappel,* and ſucceſſor to him in the profeſſorſhip of the *Hebrew* " language at *Saumur* in *France,* till the ſuppreſſion of that univerſity in *January,* 1694-5. " He continued ſeven years under the tuition of Mr. *Cappel,* by whom he is deſcribed, " in a letter to Monſieur *Le Clerc,* dated at *Hillington-Hall* in *February,* 1706-7, as a " choice youth of a penetrating genius, and a maſter of the beauties of the beſt *Roman* " and *Greek* writers. Soon after the date of that letter, he was ſent to the univerſity of " *Cambridge,* and was placed in *Clare-Hall,* under the care of Dr. *Laughton,* fellow of " that college, and one of the moſt able and diligent tutors of that time. The progreſs " which he made there, and after he left the univerſity, in all parts of learning, and " particularly mathematical and philoſophical, diſtinguiſhed him at ſo early an age, that " when he was but three and twenty years old, he was eſteemed worthy of a ſeat in the " Royal Society, into which having been propoſed as a candidate on the 13th of *De-* " *cember,* 1713, he was on the 29th of *July* following elected, and on the 11th of *No-* " *vember* admitted a fellow of it. He had not been much above two years a member, " when, on account of his known abilities and conſtant attendance at the meetings of " the ſociety, he was, at the anniverſary election *November* 30, 1716, choſen one of " the council. His firſt communication to the ſociety was on the 6th of the following " month, *December,* concerning the eclipſe of a fixed ſtar in *Gemini,* by the body of " *Jupiter.* This was followed in 1717 by an account of a remarkable Aurora Borealis, " ſeen at *London* on the 30th of *March* that year ; which account is printed in the Philo- " ſophical Tranſactions, vol. XXX. N° 352. p. 586. On the 6th of *October* of the ſame " year, 1717, he had the degree of maſter of arts conferred on him by the univerſity of " *Cambridge,* when that learned body had the honour of a viſit from the late King *George* " the firſt. He was choſen a ſecond time of the council of the Royal Society on the 1ſt " of *December* 1718, and continued to be re-choſen every year till 1727; and the 17th " of *January,* 1722-3, had the farther diſtinction of being appointed by their illuſtrious " preſident, Sir *Iſaac Newton,* one of his vice-preſidents. Mr. *Lecuwenhoeck* having by " his laſt will left his curious microſcopes to the ſociety, of which he had been above " forty years a member, Mr. *Folkes* drew up an account of them, which he gave in on the " 23d of *January,* 1723-4, to the ſociety, who deſired it might be made public, as it was " ſoon after in the Philoſophical Tranſactions, vol. XXXII. N° 380. p. 446. At the firſt " anniverſary election of the Royal Society after the death of Sir *Iſaac Newton,* in 1727, " Mr. *Folkes* was competitor with Sir *Hans Sloane,* Bart. for the office of preſident ; his " intereſt being ſupported by a great number of members, though the choice was deter- " mined in favour of Sir *Hans.* The XXXIVth volume of the Philoſophical Tranſac- " tions for the years 1726 and 1727 was addreſſed to Mr. *Folkes* by Dr. *Jurin,* ſecretary

5   " of

" of the Royal Society, in a dedication, the motive of which was, as that very learned
" phyfician obferved, the fame which induced the greateft man that ever lived to fingle
" out Mr. *Folkes* to fill the chair, and to prefide in the affemblies of that fociety, when
" the frequent returns of his indifpofition would no longer permit him to attend them
" with his ufual affiduity. ' This motive, added Dr. *Jurin*, we all know, was your un-
" common love to, and your fingular attainments, in thofe noble and manly fciences, to
" which the glory of Sir *Ifaac Newton*, and the reputation of the Royal Society, is folely
" and entirely owing.' And he concludes his dedication with the higheft compliment to
" Mr. *Folkes*, that, ' It is fufficient to fay of him, that he was Sir *Ifaac Newton's* friend.'
" He was chofen of the council of the fociety on the 1ft of *December*, 1729, and conti-
" nued in it, till he was advanced to the prefidentfhip, twelve years after, having been
" appointed on the 8th of *February*, 1732-3, one of the vice-prefidents by Sir *Hans*
" *Sloane*. He fet out with his whole family on a tour into *Italy* the 25th of *March*,
" 1733; and, paffing through *Germany*, reached *Venice* in September following; whence
" he proceeded to *Rome*, where he refided for a confiderable time, as he did afterwards
" fome months at *Florence*. He returned by fea from *Leghorn* to *England*, where he
" arrived on the 1ft of *September*, 1735, after having fpent two years and a half abroad
" with the higheft fatisfaction to himfelf, and the greateft marks of efteem and refpect
" from the principal perfons in all places which he vifited. The opportunities which
" he had of confulting the beft-furnifhed cabinets in *Italy*, enabled him to compofe there
" an excellent Differtation on the weights and values of ancient coins. This he read
" to the Society of Antiquaries, *London*, of which he was a member, at two of their
" meetings, on the 15th and 22d of *January*, 1735-6, and received their unanimous
" thanks for it, with a requeft, that a copy of it might be regiftered in their books,
" which he promifed to give them *, after he had revifed it and made fome additions to
" it. In the following month he read them a Differtation upon the meafures of *Trajan's*
" and *Antonine's* Pillars; and in *April*, 1736, another upon the brafs equeftrian ftatue
" at the capitol in *Rome*; and on the 14th of that month communicated to them ' A
" Table of *Englifh* Gold Coins, from the 18th of King *Edward* the Third, when gold
" was firft coined in *England*, to the prefent time, with their weights and intrinfic va-
" lues;' which, at their defire, on the 22d of that month, he confented to publifh; and
" it was accordingly printed the fame year in 4to. Two years after he likewife read to
" them a Differtation upon an ancient *Latin* Infcription at *Nifmes*. Nor was he lefs
" obliging to the Royal Society, whom he favoured with his ' Remarks on the Standard
" Meafure preferved in the Capitol of *Rome*;' which were read at their meeting of the
" 5th of *February*, 1735-6, and publifhed in the Philofophical Tranfactions, vol. XXXIX.
" N° 442, p. 262. He exhibited to that fociety on the 8th of *July* following a model
" of an ancient fphere, in the *Farnefe* palace at *Rome*, which model had been made in
" plaifter of *Paris*, under his directions, during his refidence in that city; the original
" fphere in ftone, fupported by an *Atlas*, being conjectured by him upon good grounds
" to have been made in the year of the Chriftian æra 112, towards the end of the em-
" peror *Trajan's* reign. A draught of this was communicated by him to Dr. *Bentley*,
" then preparing his long-promifed edition of *Manilius*, in which it was afterwards
" publifhed in the year 1739 in 4to. His next communication to the Royal Society was
" on the 4th of *November*, 1736, an account of fome Mock Suns, or Parhelia, feen
" by him on the 17th of *September* preceding. See the Philofophical Tranfactions,
" vol. XL. N° 445. p. 59. His ingenious friend, Dr. *Robert Smith*, then *Plumian*
" Profeffor of Mathematicks in *Cambridge*, and afterwards mafter of *Trinity College*

* " This was never done." Dr. WARD, MS.

" there-

" there, being engaged in compofing ' A Complete Syftem of Optics,' Mr. *Folkes*
" furnifhed him with feveral curious remarks on the fallacies of vifion, on the fun's
" apparent diftance, on the apparent figure of the fky, on the apparent curvity of
" the fides of long walks and ploughed lands, and on the changes of curvity by the ob-
" ferver's motions; for which he received the acknowledgements of the profeffor in the
" preface to that work, publifhed in 1738 in 4to. As he had not feen *France* in his tra-
" vels to *Italy*, he made a tour to *Paris* in *May* 1739, chiefly with a view of feeing the
" academies there, and converfing with the learned men, who do honour to that city
" and the republic of letters, and by whom he was received with all the teftimonies of
" reciprocal regard. Sir *Hans Sloane* having, on account of his advanced age and
" growing infirmities, refigned the prefidentfhip of the Royal Society, at the annual
" election in 1741; Mr. *Folkes* was unanimoufly chofen to fill that honourable poft,
" which he did with the higheft reputation to the fociety and himfelf. Soon after his
" election he prefented the fociety with 100*l*. The death of Dr. *Edmund Halley* in *Ja-*
" *nuary*, 1741-2, occafioning a vacancy in the Royal Academy of Sciences at *Paris*, the
" eyes of that illuftrious body were immediately fixed upon the new prefident of the
" Royal Society, whom they chofe to place in the room of that great philofopher and
" aftronomer. On the 11th of *November*, 1742, he communicated to the Royal Society
" an account of the proportions of the *Englifh* and *French* meafures and weights, from
" the ftandards of the fame kept at that fociety: which account was printed in the Phi-
" lofophical Tranfactions, vol. XLII. N° 465, p. 185. An account of the difcovery of
" that extraordinary infect called the frefh-water Polypus, by Monf. *Trembley*, then re-
" fiding at *The Hague*, was no fooner brought to *England* than Mr. *Folkes* began to
" make experiments upon it; the refult of which he communicated to the Royal Society
" in a paper read before them the 24th of *March*, 1742-3, and printed in the Philofo-
" phical Tranfactions, vol. XLII. N° 469, p. 422. His curiofity with relation to the
" geography of his country having led him to a particular examination of fome of the
" oldeft maps of it, thofe of Mr. *Chriftopher Saxton*, he gave in a paper concerning
" them to the Royal Society on the 12th of *May*, 1743. In this paper he fhewed, that
" thofe maps were the firft which were made from an actual furvey; and that from them
" moft part of the prefent maps, except *Ogilby's* Roads, are taken: That it appears,
" from a privilege granted for ten years to Mr. *Saxton* by Queen *Elizabeth*, dated
" *July* 22, 1577, that his work was carried on at the expence of *Thomas Seckford*, Efq;
" mafter of the requefts, afterwards knighted, and was then in hand, but not com-
" pleted; that the date of the earlieft map is 1574, and that of the general title
" 1579. The next paper of his which appears in the Philofophical Tranfactions, vol.
" XLII. N° 470, p. 541, was read on the 16th of *June*, 1743, being an account of the
" Comparifon, lately made by fome members of the Royal Society, of the ftandard of a
" yard, and the feveral weights lately made for their ufe; with the original ftandards of
" meafure and weight in *The Exchequer*, and fome others kept for public ufe at *Guild-*
" *hall*, *Founders Hall*, *The Tower*, and other places. His excellent work, intituled,
" ' A Table of *Englifh* Silver Coins, from the *Norman* Conqueft to the prefent time:
" with their weights, intrinfic values, and fome remarks upon the feveral pieces,' pub-
" lifhed at *London* in *May*, 1745, in 4to. is a valuable fpecimen of the accuracy and judge-
" ment with which he treated every fubject that he thought proper to difcufs; and as
" it greatly furpaffed whatever had been publifhed of that kind before, fo it has left
" little room for either addition or amendment *. He printed this treatife, together
" with a fecond edition of his Table of *Englifh* Gold Coins, at his own expence, both

* On this head fee above, p. 179.

" for

" for the benefit of the Society of Antiquaries, and as prefents to his numerous friends.
" He intended likewife to have illuftrated it by a fet of prints of the filver and gold coins
" of *England*, of which he had engraved forty-four plates, which came down to the
" Reftoration of King *Charles* II.; and fince his death have been purchafed by the faid
" fociety, who are preparing to publifh them, with a new edition of his book to which
" they relate *. Several experiments having been made in *Holland* upon the fragility
" of unnealed glafs veffels, he not only gave an account of them, but likewife exhibited
" fome of them to the Royal Society on the 31ft of *October*, 1745; his account of both
" being publifhed in the Philofophical Tranfactions. vol. XLIII, N° 477 p. 505. His
" remarks on fome bones incrufted with ftone, which he had feen at *Rome* in the
" *Villa Ludovifia*, furnifhed him with the fubject of another paper, read before the fociety
" on the 12th of *December* the fame year, and printed in the fame volume and number of
" the Philofophical Tranfactions, p. 557. The univerfity of *Oxford* being defirous of
" having a gentleman of his eminence in the learned world a member of their body, as
" he was of the univerfity of *Cambridge*, conferred on him in *July* 1746 the degree
" of Doctor of Laws; upon receiving which, he returned them a compliment in a *Latin*
" fpeech, admired for its propriety and elegance. He was afterwards admitted to the
" fame degree at *Cambridge*, when his Grace the Duke of *Newcaftle*, their chancellor,
" made a vifit to it. A paffage in *Pliny's* Natural Hiftory, l. ii. §. 74, as publifhed by
" Father *Hardouin* at *Paris*, in his folio edition of 1723, and a remark by the editor
" upon it, gave occafion to fome obfervations of Mr. *Folkes*, communicated to the Royal
" Society *Jan.* 22, 1746-7, and printed in the Philofophical Tranfactions, vol. XLV.
" N° 482, p. 365. The defign was to fhew how the text of *Pliny* had been altered by
" the editor from all the former printed editions; and that it was upon mere conjecture,
" and againft the truth of the fact contained in the paffage in queftion: for his alter-
" ation implies, that the equinoctial fhadow of the Gnomon being made fhorter at
" *Ancona* than at *Rome*, the latitude of *Ancona* muft confequently be made lefs than
" that of *Rome*; whereas it is known to be confiderably greater, *Ancona* ftanding on
" the *Adriatic* about two degrees to the north of that capital. Mr. *Folkes* therefore
" juftifies the common reading of this paffage of *Pliny*, and gives a clear explanation of
" the fenfe of it. The laft paper communicated by him to the Royal Society, which
" was on the 8th of *March*, 1749-50, contains an account of the fecond fhock of an
" earthquake felt that morning at *London* and in the parts adjacent. It is printed in
" the Philofophical Tranfactions, vol. XLVI. N° 497, p. 613. *Algernon*, Duke of So-
" merfet, who had been many years Prefident of the Society of Antiquaries of *London*,
" dying *Feb.* 9, 1749-50, Mr. *Folkes*, who was one of the vice-prefidents, was immedi-
" ately chofen to fucceed his Grace in that poft, in which he was continued by the
" charter of incorporation of that fociety *Nov.* 2, 1751. But he was foon difabled
" from prefiding in perfon either in that or the Royal Society, being feized on the 26th
" of *September* the fame year with a palfy, which deprived him of the ufe of his left
" fide. In this unhappy fituation, which occafioned him on the 30th of *November*,
" 1753, to refign the prefidentfhip of the Royal Society, he languifhed near three years,
" till a fecond ftroke of his diforder, which attacked his right fide on the 25th of *June*,
" 1754, put an end to his life on the 28th of that month at four in the morning. He
" had two daughters who furvived him; his only fon of his own name having died at
" *Caen* in *Normandy*, in *July*, 1740. His regard for the Royal Society appeared from
" the above-mentioned benefaction and a legacy left to it in his laft Will, made juft
" before his fatal indifpofition, of 200l. and an excellent portrait of the Lord Chancellor

* Hence it appears that Dr. *Birch* had written this memoir before the year 1763.

" Bacon,

" *Bacon*, and a feal, with the arms of the fociety engraved on it, to his fucceffors in the
" prefidentfhip. His library was large and well-chofen; and his cabinet enriched with
" a collection of *Englifh* coins, fuperior to moft, whether public or private ones. The
" manufcripts of his compofition, which were not a few, and upon points of great curi-
" ofity and importance, not having received from him that perfection which he was ca-
" pable of giving them, were exprefsly directed by him to be fuppreffed, an injunction
" which the public has great reafon to regret. His knowledge was very extenfive, his judge-
" ment exact and accurate, and the precifion of his ideas appeared from the perfpicuity
" and concifenefs of his expreffion in his difcourfes and writings, on abftrufe and difficult
" topics, and efpecially in his fpeeches at the anniverfary elections of the Royal Society
" on the delivery of the prize-medals, in which he always traced out the rife and pro-
" grefs of the feveral inventions for which they were affigned as a reward. He had
" turned his thoughts to the ftudy of antiquity and the polite arts with a philofophical
" fpirit, which he had contracted by the cultivation of the mathematical fciences from
" his earlieft youth. Too many of thofe who have engaged in the former branch of
" literature, have been too little exercifed in logic, and contented themfelves with heap-
" ing up paffages from a multitude of authors, without being able to connect them, or
" to draw the proper conclufions from them. But his greater fagacity and habit of rea-
" foning feparated or united fuch paffages agreeably to their refpective force, laid upon
" each its juft weight, and deduced their true confequences with the utmoft exactnefs.
" Thefe talents appeared eminently upon the fubjects of coins, weights and meafures,
" which had been extremely perplexed by other writers for want of a moderate fhare
" of arithmetick; in the profecution of which he produced many arguments and proofs,
" which were the refult of his own experiments and obfervations on common things, not
" fufficiently attended to, or feen with lefs diftinguifhing and penetrating eyes, by others.
" Mathematicks and antiquities were by him, as philofophy was by *Socrates*, rendered
" familiar and intelligible to an ordinary underftanding. His notions of them were
" reprefented in the moft obvious lights, and the knowledge of them by that means
" rendered eafy and entertaining. He had a ftriking refemblance to *Peirefkius*, the
" ornament of the laft age, and particularly in fome parts of his character reprefented
" by the elegant writer of that great man's life. The generofity of his temper was no
" lefs remarkable than the civility of his converfation. His love of a ftudious and con-
" templative life, amidft a circle of friends of the fame difpofition, difinclined him in a
" very high degree to the bufinefs and hurry of a public one; and his only ambition
" was to diftinguifh himfelf by his zeal and activity for the promotion of fciences and
" literature."

P. 180. A fmall treatife in MS. by Mr. *Folkes*, " on the Principles of Perfpective," was
fold by auction at Mr. *Leigh's Feb.* 26, 1782 —There is a portrait of him, " *Martinus*
" *Folkes*, Arm. Societatis Regiæ Socius. *J. Richardfon* pinx. 1718. *J. Smith* fec. 1719."
Mezzotinto.—The medal ftruck at *Rome* is infcribed, MARTINVS FOLKES. REV. SVA
SIDERA NORVNT; a pyramid with a fphinx, &c. Exergue, ROMAE, 1742, A. L.

P. 191. l. 10. read " no child."

Ibid. *Samuel Carte* was fon of *Thomas Carte*, clothier of *Coventry*, where he was born
Cct. 21, 1652, and was inftructed in grammar-learning in the free-fchool there; became a
member of *Magdalen College, Oxford*, in 1669; and was matriculated at the fame time
into the univerfity, where he took the degrees in arts, that of B. A. 1672; M. A. 1675.
In the *Oxford* Catalogue of graduates, his name is fpelt *Chart*, though in the matriculus
it is fpelt right. He received deacon's orders from the Bifhop of *Litchfield* and *Coventry*,
at *Ecclefhail, Sept.* 21, 1673; prieft's from the Bifhop of *London*, at *St. James's* chapel,
June 10, 1677; was collated by the Bifhop of *Litchfield* and *Coventry* to the prebend of
Tachbrook

Tachbrook in the cathedral church of *Litchfield*, into which he was installed *Sept.* 30, 1682; presented by Sir *John Bridgman*, of *Castle Bromwich*, to the vicarage of *Clifton upon Dunmore*, to which he was instituted *March* 26, 1684, and inducted *March* 28 where he lived till 1691; when, for the better education of his children, he became master of the free-school at *Coventry*; collated by the Bishop of *Litchfield* and *Coventry* to the vicarage of *Dunchurch*, in the county of *Warwick*, *July* 2, 1697, inducted *July* 30; presented by the Lord Chancellor to the rectory of *Eastwell*, in the county of *Leicester*, instituted *Jan.* 7, and inducted *Jan.* 21, 1698-9; and in the beginning of 1700 he was presented by the Lord Chancellor to the vicarage of *St. Martin's* in *Leicester*, which depending on voluntary contributions, he held it without institution till the year 1712, when a person surreptitiously obtained from the Lord Chancellor a presentation to it; but being deterred by the affections of the parishioners from prosecuting it, Mr. *Carte* was again presented to it, instituted *Nov.* 21, and inducted *Nov.* 28, 1712. The titles of his sermons are, 1. " A Dissuasive from Murmuring, *London*, 1694," 4to; 2. " The Cure " of Self-conceit, *London*, 1705," 4to. His " Tabula Chronologica, &c." was reprinted in *Somers's* Tracts, first collection, vol. IV. p. 344. In *Gutch's* " Collectanea Curiosa," vol. II. p. 76, is printed " An Introduction to the History and Antiquities of the ancient " County Palatine and Bishoprick of *Durham*, and other places in the Northern Parts," from a MS. in the *Bodleian* Library corrected throughout by Mr. *Carte*. This is mentioned in the Appendix to *Macpherson's* Papers.—Since the note in p. 191 was printed, I have been favoured with a copy of Mr. *Carte's* " Account of the Town of *Leicester*," which shall be inserted in the " Bibliotheca Topographica."

P. 191. l. 12. read " second volume of Abbeys."

P. 193. l. 12. read, It appears by the Report of the Committee of the House of Commons, that *Carte* succeeded *Kelly* as secretary to Bishop *Atterbury*; and that a riotous election at *Coventry* had been greatly animated by *Carte*. By a letter to Mr. *Williams* *, preserved below †, it appears that he was in *Ireland* in 1732, collecting materials for his

History

---

* A *Welsh* clergyman, who had the honour of being one of the intimate friends and correspondents of Bishop *Atterbury*.

† " DEAR SIR, *London, Nov.* 21, 1732.

" I was in *Ireland* when yours arrived here by Mr. *Walker*; he left it for me, and I saw him af- " terwards at *Dublin*, where I was detained four months in digesting three *Irish*-cair-loads of papers " that I found at the Castle of *Kilkenny*, and which contain all the first Duke of *Ormond's* letters, and " those of the great men his correspondents, from 1660 to 1685, and a vast quantity of papers re- " lating to the administration of the government and the affairs of that kingdom within that time. " I did not return thence till last *Wednesday*; and calling on *Friday* and *Saturday* at the place where " Mr. *Walker* had left my letter, I received yours; but not the medals, which were in the city at the " merchant's who had taken them out of the Custom-house. As soon as I receive them, I will ar- " range them with the others, and insert them in the catalogue of the cabinet. I have not seen our " friend *Wat* yet, but hope to do it soon, and that the purchaser he had in his view may now be dif- " posed to buy them. Your former, which you sent by a private hand, I wrote an answer to as soon " as I received it, and told you nakedly all my sentiments and conduct on that occasion. I hope " you have received it, and then you will see by it how wrongfully I was charged with encou- " raging those reflections and reports on the person at whose request it was wrote. I always " had a great regard for him, and never believed any of those surmises; and whenever they were " mentioned where I was, I always declared my disbelief of them, and was his advocate instead of " being his accuser; and this the most intimate of his friends can assure him of, when he shall be able " to see them. I hope you have had my letter, in which I was more full and particular. I had " heard of a certain gentleman's extraordinary step; but, I own, I am so faithless with regard to fly- " ing reports, having found so many false ones of late, that I could not tell what to think of it, till " yours assured me of the truth of it. If it proved so, I naturally imagined it would produce the " consequence you mention. The accounts in yours were very agreeable to me; I wish I could " send you any from hence that would be as satisfactory to you. But I can only tell you that I am

" now

History of the Duke of *Ormond*; which useful and valuable work has since been of singular service to Dr. *Leland*, in the third volume of his History of *Ireland*. Lord *Orrery*, in a letter to Mr. *Carte*, soon after that History was published, tells him, " Your " History is in great esteem here. All sides seem to like it. The Dean of St. *Patrick's* " honours you with his approbation. Any name after his could not add to your satis- " faction. But I may say, the worthy and the wise are with you to a man, and you " have me into the bargain. *Feb.* 10, 1736."

P. 195. Of Mr .*James Gibbs*, see p. 243.

P. 197. note, l. 36. read, " Old pamphlets and journals published during the civil wars between 1639 and 1660."

" now finishing the Index to my *Thuanus*, and that the whole work will be printed off and delivered " to subscribers by the end of *February* or beginning of *March* next. I shall then be master of my- " self and my time ; but by what I say in the beginning of this letter you may guess how both will " be employed. The work will be very pleasing to me, because my materials are so numerous and " so authentick. They are printing on copper-plates Mr. *Anderson's* collection of the Seals of the " Kings of *Scotland* : the price is great, being six guineas ; and Mr. *Forbes* is going to publish a " very curious collection of public-papers and letters relating to Queen *Mary* and the *Scotch* affairs, " from the first to the last of Queen *Elizabeth*, which he has taken out of our Paper-office, the *Cotton* " Library, and other repositories. It will expose the ill faith or gross ignorance of *Rapin de Thoyras* " in what he says upon that subject in his history. This collection will make three volumes in " folio. We have little else, besides Dr. *Mangey's* edition of *Philo-Judæus*, going forward in the " way of literature. As to the affairs of the kingdom, they seem preparing every where for a new " election ; and interest is making in all places. Disputes never ran so high as they are likely to " do when that time comes. At the election of a Mayor of *Chester* in the last month 18000*l.* was " spent, and Sir *Thomas Grosvenor* carried it by a great majority. People (for what reason I can't " conceive) imagine that this parliament will be dissolved after the next session ; I do not see what " foundation they have for it, because the ensuing will be but the sixth session ; but we may be able " to guess better when we see the lists of sheriffs appointed for next year. There is a great talk of " a shilling in the pound being taken off the land, and of a general excise being established, and a " paper-war is carrying-on on this account. For my part, I am apt to think that a general excise is " not aimed at, at least for the present ; yet it is not improbable to suppose there may be a design to " lay an inland duty upon wine, as they did some years ago on coffee, tea, and chocolate. The " duty on these never brought in above 100,000*l.* a year, till that regulation, and since it has pro- " duced 290,000*l.* a year. If the inland duty on wine should produce a proportionable increase of " the revenue, it would raise an immense sum ; and, except some harm should appear in the manner " of levying it, I see none in a duty which would prevent our being poisoned with the detestable " wine we meet with in the country here, and put every body upon improving their own manufac- " ture of malt-liquor, of which you can hardly get any good at present, the use of it being almost " laid aside in gentlemens houses. Our *South Sea* Company have left off their *Greenland* trade, and " are going to part with their right of sending a ship to *The Spanish West Indies*, in consideration of " some equivalent or other. Our trade in general is certainly at a low ebb, and some measures must " be taken to retrieve it, or we shall lose all that of our sugar plantations, which has been the only " one (except the *Portugal*) that we have got by of late years. I am sorry to tell you that Mr. " *John Robinson* of *Gwersytt* was buried the day I landed at *Holyhead*, the 8th of this month ; and " his brother Mr. *W. Robinson* of *Knebworth* is since dead. We could not lose two more worthy " gentlemen, or more useful. I suppose you knew them, so I mention what gives me pain to relate. " My best wishes wait upon you and all friends where you are ; and I am ever, dear Sir, yours, &c.

" T. CARTE."

* He had also property at *Cheshunt*, where in the windows of his house are these arms : Az. 5 escallops Or. Crest a falcon Or. imp. O. a cap of maintenance, Sable and Argent, (*Robinson*). Crest a stag's head, Sable and Ermine, horned Or.

2. O. three blackmoors heads Sable, banded about A. Crest a hand Gules issuing from a cloud Azure, holding a sword piercing a blackmoor's head as before.

3. Per chevron Azure and Gules, 3 cups O. Crest on a helmet, a hand and arm A, holding a cup O. Supporters 2 leopards Sable. Motto : *Sal sapit omnia.* Salters Company.

P. 198. *William Burton* *, Efq; the *Leicefterſhire* antiquary, eldeſt ſon of *Ralph Burton*, Efq; of *Lindley*, in that county, on the confines of *Warwickſhire*, was born *Auguſt* 24, 1575, educated at the grammar-ſchool of *Sutton-Coldfield*, admitted commoner or gentleman-commoner at *Brazen-noſe* † 1591, at *The Inner Temple May* 20, 1593, B. A. *June* 22, 1594, and afterwards a barriſter and reporter in the court of Common-pleas. But " his natural genius leading him to the ſtudies of heraldry, genealogies, and anti- " quities, he became excellent in thoſe obſcure and intricate matters ; and, look upon " him as a gentleman, was accounted by all that knew him to be the beſt of his time for " thoſe ſtudies, as may appear by his deſcription of *Leicefterſhire* ‡." In 1702 he cor- rected *Saxton's* map of that county with the addition of 80 towns. His weak conſtitution not permitting him to follow buſineſs, he retired into the country ; and his greateſt work §, " The Deſcription of *Leicefterſhire*," was publiſhed in folio, 1622. He was affiſted in this undertaking by his kinſmen *John Beaumont* of *Gracedieu*, Efq; and *Auguſtus Vin- cent* ‖, Rougecroix; but the church notes were taken by himſelf. He drew up the co- rollary

* Mr. *Peck* had collected materials for the life of Mr. *Burton*, and his younger brother *Robert*, which are probably among the papers of the late Sir *Thomas Cave*, bart. M. P. who bought the greater part of Mr. *Peck's* MSS. from his widow on the ſuggeſtion of Mr. *Aſhby*. Several printed copies of *Burton's Leicefterſhire*, with MS. notes by different perſons, have been already mentioned in p. 198, as part of Sir *Thomas Cave's* collection; to which may be added, that a copy of the ſame work, with MS. additions by Mr. *Carte*, was in *T. Oſborne's* catalogue, 1756, vol. I. marked at five guineas. The copy in the *Harleian* library has MS. additions by *Peter Le Neve*. And ſee more particulars in Brit. Top. vol. I. p. 509—513.

† He calls himſelf ſcholar there 1592, when queen *Elizabeth* came to *Oxford.—Leic.* p. 68.

‡ Ath. Ox. vol. II. p. 75.

§ He tells his patron, *George Villars*, Marquis of *Buckingham*, that he has " undertaken to remove " an eclipſe from the ſun without art or aſtronomical dimenſion, to give light to the county of *Leicefter*. " whoſe beauty hath long been ſhadowed and obſcured ;" and in his preface declares himſelf one of thoſe who hold that " Gloria totius res eſt vaniſſima mundi;" and that he was unfit and unfur- " niſhed for ſo great a buſineſs ; " unfit," to uſe his own words, " for that myſelf was bound for " another ſtudy, which is jealous, and will admit no partner, for that all time and parts of time, that " could poſſibly be employed therein, were not ſufficient to be diſpended thereon, by reaſon of the " difficulty of getting, and multiplicity of kinds of learning therein. Yet if a partner might be " affigned or admitted thereto, there is no ſtudy or learning ſo fit or neceſſary for a Lawyer, as the " ſtudy of Antiquities." In concluding the book, he adds, " If there be any thing worthily done, " which may give content or ſatisfaction to the reader, it is what I deſired : if any thing omitted, *Ber- " nardus* non videt omnia ; if any thing miſtaken, erroneous, or fault-worthy, I muſt crave pardon ; " my intention was, that truth might be diſcovered ; and that thoſe clouds of darkneſs and black " miſts, wherewith this county's luſtre hath long been ſhadowed, might at length be diſperſed, and " that her ſun's glorious rays, ſo long eclipſed, might *rilucer*, ſhine out to the view of every one ; " which now doth *rilumbre*, ſomewhat clear appear, and by ſome more happy genius and judicious " pen may hereafter be better illuſtrated. But where the ſun's bright beams could not pierce into, " I have to thoſe *oſcure grotte*, dark caves and vaults, brought candle-light, my own conceit and " conjecture, which (as they are) I ſubmit to the favourable cenſure of the more learned and judi- " cious. And now having gone about and over the whole continent of this county, it is my good " fortune to end at the hithermoſt angle [*Worthington*], next to mine own home, whither I muſt now " retire myſelf; and having ſpent all my viatical proviſion in this my laborious journey, muſt here " ſurceaſe, and with that ingenious *Macaronicall* poet, conclude :

" Nunc quia candela eſt uſque ad culamen aduſta,
" Etiam conſumpſit vacuata lucerna ſtopino,
" Multa per adeſſo ſcripſi, gia ſcribere ceſſo."

Merlino Coccaio Macaron. Phantaſ. lib. xxiv. fol. 240.

‖ Third ſon of *William Vincent* of *Wellingborough* and *Thingdon* in the county of *Northampton*, and firſt Rougecroix purſuivant extra, then Rougecroix purſuivant, *Windſor* herald by patent 5 *June* 2: *James* I. and 1 *Jan.* 19 *James* I. Sir *William Segar*, *William Camden*, *Clarencieux*, and Sir *Richard St. George*, *Norroy*, granted him a ſeparate new brizure in his arms for diſtinction. He publiſhed " A Diſcovery of the Errors in the Catalogue of the Nobility by *Ralph Brooke*, *York* Herald." He was

4 C

a clerk

rollary of *Leland*'s life, prefixed to the Collectanea, with his favourite device, the sun recovering from an eclipse, and motto *Rilucera*, dated *Faledi* 1612, from *Falde*, a pleasant village near *Tutbury*, *Staffordshire*, an ancient patrimony belonging to his family, and then to him *. He also caused part of *Leland*'s Itinerary to be transcribed 1631, and gave both the transcript and the seven original volumes to the *Bodleian* library 1632; as also *Talbot*'s notes †. To him his countryman *Thomas Purefoy*, Esq; of *Barwell*, bequeathed *Leland*'s Collectanea after his death 1612. *Wood* charges him with putting many needless additions and illustrations into these Collectanea; from which charge *Hearne* defends him. *Wood* adds, he made a useful index to them, which, *Hearne* says, was only of religious houses and some authors. He died at *Falde* ‡, after suffering much in the civil war, *April* 6, 1645, and was buried in the parish church thereto belonging, called *Hanbury*. He left several notes, collections of arms and monuments, genealogies, and other matters of antiquity, which he had gathered from divers churches and gentlemen's houses. *Derby* collections are mentioned in *Gascoigne*'s notes, p. 53, probably by himself. In *Osborne*'s Catalogue, 1757, was *Vincent* on *Brooke*, with MS. notes by *William Burton*, probably not more than those on *Cornwall*, which Dr. *Rawlinson* had. He was one of Sir *Robert Cotton*'s ‖ particular friends, and had the honour to instruct Sir *William Dugdale*. He was acquainted with *Somner*; and *Michael Drayton*, Esq; was his " near countryman and acquaintance," being descended from the *Draytons* of *Drayton*, or *Fenny Drayton*, near *Lindley*. He married, 1607, *Jane*, daughter of *Humphrey Adderley*, of *Widdington*, *Warwickshire*; by whom he had one son, *Cassibelan*, born 1609, heir of his virtues as well as his other fortunes, who, having a poetical turn, translated *Martial* into *English*, which was published 1658. He consumed the best part of his paternal estate, and died *Feb*. 28, 1681, having some years before given most, if not all, his father's collections to Mr. *Walter Chetwynd*, to be used by him in writing the antiquities of *Staffordshire*.—Mr. *Burton*'s younger brother *Robert* was born at *Lindley*, *Feb*. 8, 1576, educated at *Sutton Coldfield*, admitted commoner of *Brazen-nose* college 1593, and student of *Christ-church* 1599, under the tuition of Dr. *John Bancroft*, afterwards bishop of *Oxford*. In 1616 he had, from the dean and chapter of *Christ-church*, the vicarage of *St. Thomas* in *Oxford* (in

a clerk under Sir *John Borough*, Garter, who was keeper of the *Tower* records, and thence made a large collection of extracts, reposited in the library of the College of Arms, being the legacy of *Ralph Sheldon*, of *Beoly*, Esq. He married *Elizabeth* daughter of *Ebenezer Primecourt*, of *Canterbury*; died *Jan*. 11, 1625, and was buried at *St. Bennet*, *Paul*'s wharf. He had made some collections towards a history of his native county; of which see *Aubrey*'s *Surrey*, vol. V. p. 231, *Burton*'s *Leicestershire*, ep. to the reader, and the dedication of *Lee*'s Chronicon *Cestrense* in *King*'s Antiquities of *Cheshire*. *Aubrey* says, he died while thus employed, and left great materials for a history of *Northamptonshire*, which, with all his other collections, are lodged in the Heralds office. He intended the lives of all such as had been knights of the Garter. See Brit. Top. vol. II. p. 37, 38.

* The county history was dated from the same village, *October* 30, 1622.—*Burton*'s ancestor was esquire of the body to *Richard* I.; and *Lindley* came into the family by marriage of his great grandfather with the heiress of *John Hardwicke*, who conducted the Earl of *Richmond* to the battle of *Bosworth*.

† Lel. III. 144.

‡ In 1625 he resided at *Lindley*, where, among other works, he compiled a folio volume under the title of " Antiquitates de *Dadlington* manerio com. *Leic*. sive Exemplificatio Scriptorum, Cartarum " veterum, Inquisitionum, Rotulorum Curiarum, Recordorum, & Evidentium probantium Antiqui- " tates dicti manerii de *Dadlington*, & hæreditatem de *Burton* in dicto manerio de *Dadlington*, quæ " nunc sunt penes me *Will'mum Burton* de *Lindley* com. *Leic*. modernum dominum dicti manerii de " *Dadlington*. Labore & studio mei *Will'mi Burton* de *Lindley*, Apprenticii Legum *Angliæ*, & Socii " Interioris *Templi Londini*; nuper habitantis apud *Falde* com. *Staff*. nunc apud *Lindley*, 25 *Aug*. " 1625. æt. 50."—This MS. is now (1782) the property of *William Hurst*, Esq; of *Hinckley*, who (jointly with his son *Nicholas Hurst*, gent.) is lord of the manor of *Dadlington*.

‖ Who had considerable estates in *Burton*'s neighbourhood. See the " History of *Hinckley*."

which

which parish he always gave the sacrament in wafers), and from *George* Lord *Berkeley* the rectory of *Segrave* in *Leicestershire*; both which he held till he died at *Christ-church Jan. 27, 1639.* " He was such a curious calculator of nativities, that the time of his " death answering exactly to his own predictions, it was whispered," says *Wood*, " that, " rather than there should be any mistake in the calculation, he sent up his soul to heaven " through a slip about his neck." He was a general scholar and severe student, melancholy yet humourous, and figured in the pedantry of the times; but withal a man of great honesty, plain-dealing, and charity. He wrote " The Anatomy of Melancholy," which went through several editions in folio. On his monument in *Christ-Church* is his bust, in ruff, gown, hair, and beard, with his nativity, as in the following scheme;

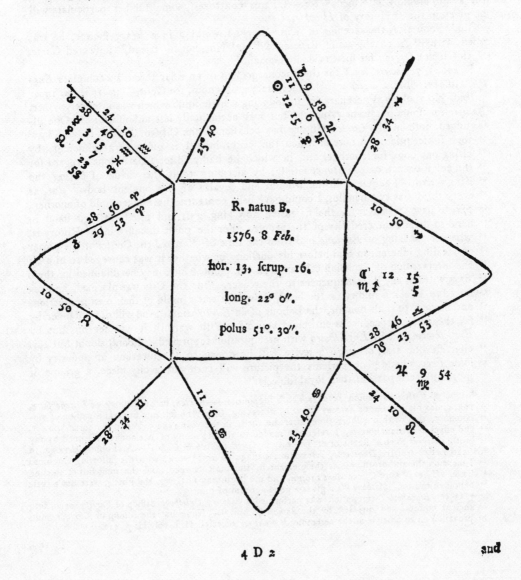

and

and on the middle of it this inscription by himself, put up by his brother.

" Paucis notus, paucioribus ignotus,
Hic jacet *Democritus* junior,
Cui vitam dedit & mortem *
Melancholia.
Obiit 8 Id. *Jan.* A.C. MDCXXXIX."

Arms: Az. on a bend O. between 3 dogs heads O. a crescent G.
He left a choice library, part of which he bequeathed to the *Bodleian*, and 100l. to buy five-pounds-worth of books yearly for *Christ-church* library.

P. 199. note, l. 19. read, " an attested copy of a grant," &c. This instrument, however, (as I am credibly informed)" &c.—Of this controversy some further particulars will be given in the " History of *Hinckley*."

Ibid. Soon after the accession of King *George* I. walking in a heavy shower, he was plied with " A coach, your Reverence?" " No, honest friend," answered *Carte*, " this is not a *reign* for me to ride in a coach."

P. 200. l. 7. *Society*, &c.] for the Encouragement of an Essay towards a complete *English* History. Mr. *Coxeter* was their secretary; of whom, see Gent. Mag. 1781, p. 174.

Ibid. No apology is necessary for introducing a little squib which was intended by Mr. *Bowyer* for some public news-paper, but was accidentally left unfinished : " One ill-
" judged note in Mr. *Carte's* History has occasioned the City of *London* to withdraw
" their subscription. A note in which the writer indeed is guilty of a misnomer, by
" citing one book for another, and in which he had paid too superstitious a regard for
" the eldest branch of the *Stuart* family, by ascribing to it the virtue of curing the
" King's-Evil. I acquiesce in the wisdom and loyalty of this opulent body. But, as
" every thing has two handles, I could have been content to have taken hold of another,
" *viz.* to have learned from the narration how king-craft and priest-craft go hand in
" hand to delude the credulity of the people. For the point discussed in the History is,
" whether the King of *England* had from the time of *Edward* the Confessor the power
" of Healing inherent in him before his unction, or whether it was conveyed to him by
" the intervention of Ecclesiastical hands †. A point which may be discussed in these
" days without any ill consequences to the reader. But the City was alarmed, and re-
" solved to knock a history on the head, though it was a child of their own production,
" and named, to their honour, the Labour of an *Englishman*. And will not a stander-by
" say the whole procedure is entirely *English?* With warmth it was set on foot by
" *Englishmen*, and by *Englishmen* with precipitation suppressed. I don't doubt but this
" characteristic trait of *English* levity will be drawn to the diversion of posterity by
" some *French* hand ; or perhaps the picture will turn out a city piece, a groupe of
" more aukward patrons than loyal subjects."

* Query, if this expression favours *Wood's* supposition?—*Burton*, in his History of *Leicestershire*, p. 105, closes his account of *Anthony Faunt* by observing, that " he fell into so great a passion of me-
" lancholy, that within a short time after he died, in the year 1588. What the force, power,
" and effect of melancholy is, I refer the reader to the Anatomy of Melancholy, penned by my
" brother *Robert Burton*, Bachelor of Divinity in *Christ-Church* in *Oxford*.—Archbishop *Herring*, in
his 42d Letter to Mr. *Duncombe*, refers to a passage in this work, with the following elogium :
" I mention the author to you as the pleasantest, the most learned, and the most full of sterling
" sense. The Wits of Queen *Anne's* reign, and the beginning of *George* the First's, were not a little
" beholden to him. *Anthony Wood* gives a good account of him."

† Queen *Elizabeth's* coronation was performed by *Owen Oglethorp* Bishop of *Carlisle*, according to ancient custom, and directed by the *Roman* Pontifical. None but the Bishop of *Carlisle* could be prevailed on to officiate at the ceremony." *Collyer's* Eccles. Hist. vol. II. p. 412.

P. 199. Extract from the Register of the Church of *Wadhurst* in *Sussex*, taken by Dr. *Ducarel*, *July* 28, 1749. "*January* 9, 1683, The King by proclamation declared, that
"the times of public touching for the King's-evil shall be from the Feast of *All Saints*,
"till a week before *Christmas*; and after *Christmas* till the first day of *March*, and then to
"cease till the Passion Week. Such as repair to the Court for this purpose must carry
"with them certificates under the hands and seals of the minister and church-wardens
"of the parish, that they have not at any time before been touched by His Majesty to
"the intent to be healed of that disease, and a register to be kept of all such certificates.
"The form of a Certificate.

"We, the minister and church-wardens of the parish of *Wadhurst*, in the county of
"*Sussex*, do hereby certify, that Mr. *Nicholas Barham* of this parish, aged about 24
"years, is afflicted (as we are credibly informed) with the disease commonly called the
"King's-evil; and (to the best of our knowledge) hath not heretofore been touched by
"His Majesty for the said disease. In testimony whereof, we have hereunto set our
"hands and seals this 23d day of *March*, 1684. JOHN SMITH, Vicar.

"ROBERT LONGLY, } Church-wardens.
"THOMAS YOUNGE, }

"Registered *per me*, JOHN SMITH."

N. B. Dr. *Ducarel* did not find in the register that any other person had any certificate for the King's-evil except *Nicholas Barham*. That branch of the family of the *Barhams* is lately extinct, though many of the same name remain now in the parish; and their estate is gone to the family of the *Eagles*. Memorandum: The proclamation mentioned above, concerning healing, is not to be found among "The *London* "Gazettes" of 1683; but in "The *London* Gazette," Nᵒ 1893, from *Monday*, *January* the 7th, to *Thursday January* the 10th, 1683, is the following advertisement, *viz.* "*Adenochoiradelogia*, or an Anatomick-Chyrurgical Treatise of Glandules and Strumaes, "or King's-Evil-Swellings. Together with the Royal Gift of Healing or Cure thereof, "by contact or imposition of Hands, performed for above 640 years by our Kings of "*England*, continued with their admirable Effects and miraculous Events; and concluded with many wonderful Examples of Cures by their Sacred Touch, all which are "succinctly described by *John Browne* *, one of his Majesty's Chyrurgeons in ordinary, "and

* To this volume is prefixed a head of the author, by *R. White*, not enumerated by Mr. *Granger*, on which is written, "*Johannes Browne*, Regis *Britannici*, nec non Nosocomii sui Chirurgus Ordi- "narius;" with a picturesque View of the Sovereign's performing the Ceremony †. By this publication it appears, that from *May*, 1660, to *April*, 1682, no less than 92,107 persons had been touched by the King.—The following ingenious remarks on Serjeant-Surgeon *Wiseman's* testimony concerning the efficacy of the Royal Touch in the King's-evil were written by a gentleman whose name would do honour to a work of much more consequence than the present volume pretends to be. "Though the superstitious notions respecting the cure of the King's-evil by the touch of our *English* "kings are probably at present entirely eradicated, it is still a curious and not uninstructive object "of enquiry, by what means they were so long supported, and by what kind of evidence they have "been able to gain credit even in the dawning of a more enlightened period. The testimony of "*Richard Wiseman*, Serjeant-Surgeon to King *Charles* I. has been alledged as one of the strongest "and most unexceptionable in favour of the touch. He was a man of the greatest eminence in his "profession, and his works ‡ bear all the marks of an honest and upright disposition in their author. "On the subject of the Royal Touch he delivers himself in the following strong and unequivocal "terms. ' I myself have been a frequent eye-witness of many hundreds of cures performed by his "Majesty's touch alone, without any assistance of chirurgery; and those many of them such as had

† Which is printed at length in Bishop *Kennet's* Register, p. 731.
‡ Collected in a folio volume, intituled, "Several Chirurgical Treatises, by *Richard Wiseman*, Serjeant-Chi- "rurgeon, 1676." The collection has since passed through several editions in 2 vols. 8vo.

"tired

" and Chyrurgeon of his Majefty's Hofpital; publifhed with His Majefty's Royal Ap-
" probation : Together with the Teftimony of many eminent Doctors and Chyrurgeons.
" Sold by *Samuel Lowndes* over againft *Exeter-Change* in the *Strand*." And in the
London Gazette, N° 2180, from *Thurfday, Oct.* 7, to *Monday, Oct.* 11, 1686, is the
following advertifement : " *Whitehall, Oct.* 8, His Majefty is gracioufly pleafed to ap-
" point to heal weekly for the *Evil* upon *Fridays*; and hath commanded his Phyficians
" and Chirurgeons to attend at the office appointed for that purpofe in *The Meufe*,
" upon *Thurfdays* in the afternoon, to give out tickets.   Hereof all minifters of parifhes
" are required to take notice, and to be careful to regifter the certificates they grant,
" in a book kept for that purpofe."

I fhall clofe this tedious note on a fubject now introduced merely as an hiftorical fact, by
Mr. *Carte's* vindication of himfelf, as printed in *The General Evening Poft* *, Feb. 23, 1747-8.
" When I publifhed my Hiftory, I did not doubt but a fhoal of little anonymous
" writers would be nibbling at fome particular paffages in it; and, in defect of fomething
" more material, would attack any fmall incident, even in the notes, though not in-
" ferted in the body of the work.   It is the duty of an hiftorian to give an account of
" every inftitution when it comes to take place in a kingdom; and I have difcharged
" that duty fo far as I have gone (I would fain hope) to the fatisfaction of the reader.
" This obliged me to make a fhort Difcourfe on the Unction of Kings, and to take no-
" tice of the extravagant effects afcribed to that unction.   The fanative Virtue of

" tired out the endeavours of able chirurgeons before they came thither.   It were endlefs to recite
" what I myfelf have feen, and what I have received acknowledgements of by letter, not only from
" the feveral parts of the nation, but alfo from *Ireland, Scotland, Jerfey,* and *Guernfey*.'   The quef-
" tion which will naturally arife upon this paffage is, did *Wifeman* really believe what he afferted, or
" was he knowingly promoting an impofture ?   Both fuppofitions have their difficulties, yet both
" are in fome degree probable.   His warm attachment to the royal family and early prejudices
" might in fome meafure make his faith preponderate againft his judgement; and, on the other
" hand, certain paffages in his treatife neceffarily fhow a confcioufnefs of collufion and fraudulent
" pretenfions.   It was his bufinefs as ferjeant-furgeon to felect fuch afflicted objects as were proper
" to be prefented for the royal touch.   In the hiftory of the difeafe, relating its various ftates and
" appearances, he fays, ' Thofe which we prefent to his Majefty are chiefly fuch as have this kind
" of tumour about the *mufculus maftoideus,* or neck, with whatever other circumftances they are
" accompanied; nor are we difficult in admitting the thick-chapped upper-lips, and eyes affected
" with a *lippitudo*; in other cafes we give our judgement more warily.'   Here is a felection of the
" flighteft cafes, and a manifeft doubt expreffed concerning the fuccefs in more inveterate ones.   A
" little below, obferving that the *ftruma* will often be fuppurated or refolved unexpectedly from ac-
" cidental ferments, he fays, ' In cafe of the King's touch the refolution doth often happen
" where our endeavours have fignified nothing; yea, the very *gummata,* infomuch that I am cau-
" tious of predicting concerning them (though they appear never fo bad), till 14 days be over.'
" From this we learn, that the touch was by no means infallible, and that the pretence of its fuc-
" ceeding was not given up till a fortnight had paffed without any change for the better.   Indeed
" it appears very plain that the worft kind of cafes were feldom or never offered the touch; for in
" no difeafe does *Wifeman* produce more obfervations from his practice of difficult and dangerous
" chirurgical treatment, and in not one of thefe did he call in the affiftance of the royal hand.   It
" was indeed propofed in a fingle inftance, but under fuch circumftances as furnifh a ftronger proof
" of impofture, than any thing hitherto related.   A young gentlewoman had an obftinate fcrophulous
" tumour in the right fide of the neck under the maxilla.   *Wifeman* applied a large cauftic to it,
" brought it to fuppuration, treated it with efcharotics, and cured it.   ' About a year after,' he fays,
" ' I faw her again in town, and felt a fmall gland of the bignefs of a lupin, lying lower on that
" fide of the neck.   I would have perfuaded her to admit of a refolvent emplafter, and to be
" touched; but fhe did not, as fhe faid, believe it to be the King's-evil.'   Here, after allowing his
" patient to undergo a courfe of very fevere furgery, he is willing to truft the relics of the difeafe to
" the royal touch, affifted by a refolving plafter; but the complaint was now too trifling to engage her
" attention.   Surely the greateft opponent of the touch will not place it in a more contemptible light !"

* See *Whifton's* Memoirs, vol. I. p. 363; where are likewife preferved two letters from *The General Evening Poft, Jan.* 7, and *Jan.* 16, which gave rife to the vindication.

" touching

" touching for the King's-evil being one of those effects, the relation of *Christopher Lo-*
" *vel* was inserted in a note, to shew it was erroneously ascribed to the unction. It was
" put there with no other view than to refute that notion, and without any design of
" publishing it; but the note (perhaps for want of a mark, directing it should not be
" copied, as I used in some other cases) being transcribed, together with the Discourse
" for the press, I did not, when the proof-sheet was sent me, strike it out, observing
" nothing in it that could reasonably give offence, were it not for the comments of male-
" volent people; for the person touching is not named, and what is said of him agrees to
" more than one person. I have not in that discourse delivered my own opinion on the
" subject, contenting myself with relating those mentioned by *W.* of *Malmesbury.* Se-
" veral curious and knowing persons have wrote upon it; particularly Dr. *Tooker,* a
" Divine, and Mr. *John Browne* Surgeon to King *Charles* II. the book of the former
" being published 1597 under the title of *Charisma;* that of the latter, 1684, under the
" title of *Charisma Basilicon.* I have not seen *Tucker's* or *Tooker's* book these thirty years;
" so long is it since the relation I quoted thence was copied. I have transcribed others,
" very remarkable, (particularly the cure of a *German,* who had been thirteen months his
" patient, by the royal touch), from *Clowes,* an experienced surgeon in Queen *Elizabeth's*
" time, who published, 1602, a treatise of the artificial cure of that distemper; though
" he owns throughout it, that the Queen's touch was the only infallible remedy. But
" though I have not these books by me, nor a thousand others from which I have ex-
" tracted passages, I think I may fairly make use of my own transcripts. The late
" learned Mr. *Anstis,* in the 26th page of a MS. discourse on Coronations, which he left
" at his death unfinished, hath these words, ' The miraculous gift in curing this dis-
" temper [the King's-evil] by the royal touch of our kings, as well as of the *French*
" kings, is undeniable;' and in p. 49, taking notice of his having convinced a surgeon
" of the antiquity of our king's touching by several citations from our records, he adds,
" ' That he [the surgeon] published these citations, and therefore I refer you [*i. e.* his
" son, the present Garter, to whom the discourse is addressed] to that pamphlet.' I passed
" some days with him at *Mortlake* about twenty-six years ago, when a pamphlet, wrote
" by a surgeon about the King's-evil, was advertised in the news-paper, and had a good
" deal of discourse with him on the subject; and by what was then said, I am persuaded
" that Mr. *Becket's* Enquiry into the Antiquity and Efficacy of Touching for the King's-
" evil, printed in octavo 1722 (according to the booksellers style, who begin their year
" even before *Christmas)* was the pamphlet in question: but I never saw it, and had
" entirely forgot the name of the surgeon; when having Mr. *Anstis's* discourse above-
" mentioned before me, and consulting a learned gentleman (who had studied and prac-
" tised physick above forty years, and transcribed my note for the press) about the
" name of the surgeon referred to by Mr. *Anstis,* it was either by his opinion, or my
" own inadvertence, that I put down *Tucker* for the name of that surgeon. I have en-
" deavoured to find out this pamphlet, but in vain; the present Mr. *Anstis* hath neither
" that nor any other treatise on the subject in his library. Whoever hath it, may ob-
" serve by the records cited in it (especially if the accounts of the houshold in 6th of
" *Edward* I. which there is scarce a man in *England,* besides the late Mr. *Anstis,* hath
" ever looked into, be cited for the cure of 182 persons of the King's-evil by that
" Prince) whether the author be the surgeon to whose book he refers. After all,
" whether the surgeon's name be *Tucker,* or *Becket,* or any other, is a matter of very
" little consequence *. *Dean's-Yard, Feb.* 13, 1747-8."

* See more on the subject in *Carte's* Hist. Book IV. Sect. 43. See also in *Plot's Oxfordsh.* c. 10,
§ 125. who, in Plate 16. N° 5, gives a drawing of the Touch-piece, supposed to be given by *Edward* the Confessor. The ribbon, Dr. *Plot* says, was white.

P. 201.

P. 201. I shall insert below " A proposal * of the Rev. Mr. *Thomas Carte*, M. A. for erecting a Library in the Mansion-House of the city of *London*, communicated by *Thomas Coxeter*, Esq; on *November* 9, 1643 [1743], to me R. R[awlinson.]"

P. 201.

* " There is not a great City in *Europe* so ill provided with Public Libraries as *London*. In *Paris* " there is not a day in the week but, both morning and afternoon, some Public Library, well fur- " nished with books of all kinds of learning, is, by the appointment of the Founder, open for the " convenience of learned men, who meet with no difficulty in finding any books they want to con- " sult in the course of their studies. In the same city they have noble hotels for the residence of " the Chancellor of the kingdom, and the First President of the Parliament, besides the town-house " for the *Prevôt'des Merchands* (who answers to our Lord-Mayor), and Libraries in these places, " which is the room of audience generally for particular friends and persons of distinction, though " the rooms of state serve for giving audience to the world in general, and for dispatching the or- " dinary business incident to those great offices. But I think *London*, the most opulent city upon " earth, should not be inferior to others in any respect, much less in a point of magnificence, which " is not barely pompous, but may be infinitely useful, by assembling together in one place a vast " collection of the materials of Learning, which are not perhaps to be found at all in any other: or " else, being dispersed in many different, remote, or unknown places, cannot be consulted by the " learned without a good deal of expence, without loss of time (which always sits heavy on a man " that knows how to use it), and without inconceivable inconveniencies to their private affairs. In " other countries, where arbitrary government prevails, or the truth of the established religion is " suspected, even by those who think to secure it by force and penalties, there are great restraints in " the way of learning, and an infinite number of books are prohibited. I have known [M. *Freret*] " one of the wisest and most learned men in *France*, and the best qualified by his knowledge of the " world, his deep searches into antiquity, his profound reflections on all historical events, his admir- " able judgement and unbiassed integrity to write the history of that Monarchy, clapped up in *The* " *Bastile* for several months together, only because he had set about that work, and it was thought " would execute it, with an inviolable regard to truth, and without flattery to that arbitrary Power, " which has now trampled on all the antient liberties of that nation; nor could he regain his li- " berty without a promise to desist from the enterprize. It is fit such a work should be undertaken " for *England*, whilst she yet retains her liberties: and a great city, the chief bulwark of the liber- " ties of our country, cannot exert her public spirit more properly than in procuring and preserving " for ever a library of the choicest materials for that purpose, and equally fit to clear up and vindi- " cate the just rights and privileges of a free people. There is now a magnificent structure almost " built for the habitation of future Lord-Mayors of this city; and it is still easy to contrive at the " top of it a gallery, or range of rooms, for a library. There is now likewise an opportunity of " buying a most valuable collection of books, *viz.* the late Earl of *Oxford's* Manuscripts. They contain " a noble treasure of *English* history and antiquities; and it will be an irreparable loss to learning, " and perhaps no inconsiderable one to liberty, if such a collection of rare manuscripts, singular in " their kind, and chiefly regarding the history of this nation, and the ancient rights and privileges " of *Englishmen*, comes to be sold by auction, and dissipated into a thousand hands *. To prevent " this loss, it were to be wished, that the twelve rich companies (out of which the Lord-Mayor is " usually chosen) would, out of their large revenues, give each 2000*l*. towards this purchase, and " repose it in the Mansion-house, where the most considerable members of those companies are in " their turns to reside, and to the furniture of which they can contribute nothing nobler than such " a library, the only thing wanting to complete its magnificence. It consists of about 10,000 ma- " nuscripts, which cost the late Right Honourable Proprietor prodigious sums of money; but as it " is in few people's ability to purchase, and the late Earl designed it for public use, the executors " may be willing to abate considerably of its value on those accounts, and I imagine it may be " bought for 20,000*l*. so the remaining 4000*l*. may serve for a fund to purchase printed books in all " languages, relating as well to trade, arts, and sciences, as to the history and antiquities of this " nation, or indeed of others in our neighbourhood, which in many cases help to illustrate our own; " as relations of voyages serve often to give light to several branches of commerce. 'Tis to these " subjects that the books to be purchased from time to time may be chiefly confined, and a fund of " this kind in the city may be most properly applied; and if a library was once founded, every " body would be naturally disposed to leave what is most curious in that way to it, as a safe and per-

* Happily those are preserved in that inestimable repository, *The British Museum*; which has totally superseded the necessity of adopting the plan so ingeniously suggested by Mr. *Carte*.

" petual

P. 201. *Letter to a Bystander*] Among Dr. *Birch's* MSS. is an advertisement, dated *Feb.* 2, 1742-3, assuring Mr. *Carte*, that he (Dr. *Birch*) had not the least hand in this " Letter," nor ever saw one line of it before it appeared in print.—There is also a tract, intituled, " A Second Letter to *Trotplaid*, Esq; Author of the Jacobite Journal, con-" cerning Mr. *Carte's* General History of *England*; plainly shewing, that the Letter in " The General Evening Post, *Feb.* 23, 1748, signed *Thomas Carte* *, could not have been " wrote by *Thomas Carte* the *Englishman*."

P. 203. l. 9. The consideration was fifty pounds.

Ibid. note, l. 2. Mr. *Jernegan* was a younger branch of the family of that name, settled at *Cossey*, in the county of *Norfolk*. He asked Lord *Hardwicke* 1500*l*. for Mr. *Carte's* papers. From these and from memory of what he read every day in the *Scots College* at *Paris*, Sir *John Dalrymple* compiled his Memoirs. The Jesuits intended to print the letters of *James* II. preserved in their college. Those from that King to *William* III. from his accession to within six weeks or a month of the Revolution, are signed, " yours " as you wish, as you desire, and as you deserve." An *English* nobleman now living saw the original letters of *William* III. to the Duke of *Marlborough* and others, which do the King great honour, and shew the duplicity of the other side.

P. 206. note. A beautiful Ode was addressed to Mr. *Edwards* by Miss *Mulso*, now Mrs. *Chapone*; to which he replied in as elegant a Sonnet.

P. 207. read, " Mr. *Lowth*."

Ibid. note, after " Dock-yard," add, " to which office (worth about 300*l*. a year) " he was appointed in *March*, 1745."

P. 210. note, l. 2. read, " *Kilncote* near *Lutterworth*;" and l. 3. " *Hinton* near *Brackley*."

Ibid. In a letter, dated 1733, Dr. *R. Grey* mentions his being far advanced in " a " Work upon the Downfall of Monarchy and Episcopacy. Something of this kind," he adds, " would be of service, to discourage thinking men, and all who have any regard for " Religion, from playing the same game over again." In 1740 he was soliciting sub-scriptions for " a work where the expence was to be extraordinary, and the readers " comparatively but few; yet he received much encouragement from his superiors. The " Master of *St. John's* [in *Oxford*] subscribed for 7 copies."

P. 211. l. 10. read, " Lord *Royston*, the present Earl of *Hardwicke*."

P. 212. l. 4. " Extracts from Mr. *Pope's* Translation, corresponding with the Beauties " of *Homer*, selected from the Iliad by *W. Holwell*, B. D. F. R. S. Chaplain in Ordinary " to His Majesty," were published in 2 vols. 8vo. 1776.

P. 213. See a fuller account of Mr. *Cheselden* and Mr. *Cotes* in pp. 341. 343. 589.

" petual repository, thereby to render it a complete magazine of every thing relating to trade, " history, and antiquity. Learning of this kind is of all others the most discouraged by a corrupt " administration, who would fain engross all the materials thereof to themselves, and care to see it " in no hands but those of their own creatures, who would prostitute it to their purposes. But when " all branches of learning whatever are neglected elsewhere, and discountenanced where they ought " most to be favoured, it would be exceedingly for the glory of the city to give it encouragement " there; and if it should meet with no other, it may still flourish under her protection. No body " of men have ever distinguished themselves more eminently in the cause of liberty than the city " has always done: the nation looks upon her as one of the chief bulwarks of her liberties, and " indeed the only body (when Parliaments by growing corrupt shall cease to be the guardians " thereof) capable, by its weight, to assert the rights and privileges of our country. She will take " a proper step to prevent these from being subverted, if she takes care to preserve so inestimable a " treasure of monuments of antiquity, which, if reposed in the library of the Mansion-house, will " remain to all future ages an irrefragable evidence of those rights and liberties which our ancestors " enjoyed, and, conveying down inviolate to our times, have entailed upon us the obligation of " transmitting them safe to posterity."

* See above, p. 574.   † See her Miscellanies.

P. 2*4. *Anthony Alsop* was educated at *Westminster* school, and from thence elected to *Christ-church, Oxford*, where he took the degrees of M. A. *March* 23, 1696, and of B. D. *December* 12, 1706. On his coming to the university, he was very soon distinguished by Dean *Aldrich*, and published " Fabularum *Æsopicarum* * Delectus, Oxon. 1698," 8vo. with a poetical dedication to Lord Viscount *Scudamore*, and a preface in which he took part against Dr. *Bentley* in the famous dispute with Mr. *Boyle*. He passed through the usual offices in his College to that of Censor, with considerable reputation; and for some years had the principal noblemen and gentlemen belonging to the society committed to his care. In this useful employment he continued till his merit recommended him to Sir *Jonathan Trelawney*, Bishop of *Winchester*, who appointed him his chaplain, and soon after gave him a prebend in his own cathedral, together with the rectory of *Brightwell*, in the county of *Berks*, which afforded him ample provision for a learned retirement, from which he could not be drawn by the repeated solicitations of those who thought him qualified for a more public character and a higher station. In the year 1717 an action was brought against him by Mrs. *Elizabeth Astrey* of *Oxford*, for a breach of a marriage contract; and a verdict obtained against him for 2000*l.* which probably occasioned him to leave the kingdom for some time. In an Ode to Dr. *Keill*, on that gentleman's marriage, of which the stanzas are somewhat deranged in " The Student †," he says,

" I, who, hard fate ! am forc'd to rove
" True to my nuptial vows,
" And leave my country out of love,
" An exile for my spouse:

" Fain would I hear the jests that pass,
" The mirth that's made on me;
" Fain would partake the circling glass,
" And vent my wit on thee.

" But I, by Heaven's decree, remain
" Blest on a foreign shore,
" And hourly such delights obtain,
" I need not wish for more.

" Me a kind wife's embraces chear,
" A lovely creature she;
" Nor can the sun find out a pair
" More hap'ly join'd than we."

How long this exile lasted is unknown; but his death happened *June* 10, 1726, and was occasioned by his falling into a ditch that led to his garden-door, the path being narrow, and part of it giving way. Besides the quarto volume of his Odes mentioned in p. 214, four *English* poems are in *Dodsley's* Collection, one in *Pearch's*, several in the early volumes of the Gentleman's Magazine ‡, and some in The Student. He seems to have been a pleasant and facetious companion, not rigidly bound by the trammels of his profession; and does not appear to have published any Sermons.—Mr. *Alsop* is respectfully mentioned by the facetious Dr. *King* of the Commons (vol. I. p. 236.), as having enriched the commonwealth of learning, by " Translations of Fables from *Greek, He-* " *brew*, and *Arabick*;" and most detractingly by Dr. *Bentley* §, under the name of " *Tony Alsop*, a late editor of the *Æsopean* Fables."

---

* " A book (says Dr. *Warton*, Essay on *Pope*, vol. II. p. 393.) not sufficiently known, and now " out of print."

† Vol. II. p. 30.

‡ Particularly in 1735, p. 384, an Ode (with a translation) to the Rev. Sir *John Dolben*, which declares his love for tobacco and a true poetical indolence; *Sappho* reproaching him as " a truant " bard, who had scarcely paid four offerings to the Muses in three years." In the same volume is a fine *Latin* Version of the " Te Deum." In 1737, p. 631, some compliments are paid to him in " Ode ab Amico || *Percivalli* conscripta, quâ nuperis *Alsopi* ineptiis respondetur."

§ " Who certainly had in the most sovereign contempt the classical (or rather critical) taste of *Christ-* *church*: and though the editions, which Dean *Aldrich* set on foot, were of some use and credit to the young editors, learned men considered them as rather disgraceful to literature; so *Burman* did *Mait-* *taire's*, yet *Maittaire* was far superior to the bulk of *Aldrich's* operators, one of the lowest and meanest of which was *Tony Alsop*, whom the *Westminster* men were so proud of, for the very reason Dr. *B.* gives p. lxix. of his Preface, ' If they can but make a tolerable copy of verses, with two or three " small faults in it, they must presently set up for authors, to bring the nation into contempt abroad,

|| *J U. M. A.* then fellow of *King's-College, Cambridge.*

" and

P. 215. note, l. 11. Thefe bones were found in a large urn, infcribed MARCVS ANTO-NINVS; and, according to the proportion of them, muſt have belonged to a perſon eight feet high *.—Ibid. l. 43. read, Mr. *Gambold* alſo publiſhed, in 1751, 8vo, " Max-" ims and Theological Ideas and Sentences, collected" &c.

P. 217. add, In 1750 Mr. *Bowyer* was appointed (with the preſent Sir *Thomas Frank-land*, bart. and others), one of the executors of the will of his old friend Captain *Lime-burner †*; and was requeſted, on this occaſion, to accept a cup which had been given to the Captain for ſome ſignally gallant ſervice. He politely refuſed the offered preſent ; but readily took on himſelf the whole active part of the truſt, which he faithfully exe-cuted till it was rendered unneceſſary by an only grand-daughter's coming of age to en-joy her fortune. He accepted, however, of the Captain's cane ; after having, through exceſs of delicacy, taken off the golden head, which he could by no means be pre-vailed on to keep.

Ibid. Mr. *Bladen's* ſiſter was married firſt to Colonel *Ruthven*, and afterwards to *Ed-ward Hawke*, Eſq; a barriſter of *Lincoln's Inn*, by whom ſhe had *Edward* (afterwards the firſt Lord *Hawke*) the brave admiral.

P. 225. note, l. 7. read, " if he had lived."

P. 226. ſub-note, l. 37. After " Life," add, " illuſtrated with proper figures."

Ibid. Two letters to the Earl of *Oxford*, inſerted below ‡, are copied from the originals.

P. 228. Mr. *Jackſon* was editor of " Novatiani Preſbyteri Opera, quæ extant omnia, " poſt *Jacobi Pamelii Brugenſis* recenſionem, ad antiquiores editiones caſtigata, & à " multis mendis expurgata, 1728," 8vo.

" and themſelves into it at home ‖.' I doubt he never wrote an anſwer to their examination of his *Æſop*; which indeed, he ſays, was little worth it; and I believe it : but, for all that, I wiſh he had; for, as he ſays of *Pearſon*, ' his very droſs was gold'." Dr. SALTER, in Gent. Mag. 1779, p. 547.—It is but candid, however, to acknowledge that Mr. *Alſop* and his friends were vindicated from this ſomewhat petulant attack in Gent. Mag. 1779, p. 640 ; and 1780, pp. 65. 221.

* " A large bone uſed to be ſhewed at *St. Alban's* for a giant's. Dr. *Rutherforth* told me, that " he clapt it to his own thigh, which was as long or longer. The bone above muſt have been two " feet long, and require a large urn. In *Shropſhire* towards *Wales*, a ſtone coffin of a giant is " ſhewn; a couſin of mine, about 6 feet one or two inches high, had the curioſity and ſpirit to lay " himſelf down in it, and he found it only juſt long enough for him." *T. F.*

† *Thomas Limeburner*, Eſq; a gentleman of approved bravery, and of long-ſtanding in the Royal Navy, was appointed Captain of *The Seahorſe* in *July*, 1740; and on the 29th of *March*, 1742, being then commander of *The Plymouth*, he took the *Galgo* privateer, of *St. Sebaſtian's*, of 12 guns, 12 patereros, and 140 men, which had then taken 21 *Engliſh* prizes. Soon after this event, he tranſ-mitted to Mr. *Bowyer* 4600l. to inveſt for him in the public funds. He was afterwards made Captain of *The Fubbs* yatch ; and died *Nov.* 5, 1750.

‡ " MY LORD, *Swaveſey, April* 9, 1716. " I have ſent the three *Hebrew* letters I promiſed. The firſt I received from Rabbi *Joſeph Aben-* " *danim* (the honeſt *Jew* I mentioned) in the year 1699. The other two were ſent me ſince I came " to this place by a rambling old fellow that travelled in ſeveral countries, and ſeemed to have " learned villainies of all. I am, &c. SIMON OCKLEY."

" MY LORD, *Swaveſey, October* 2, 1720. " It is a great concern to think that I muſt trouble your Lordſhip with ſo melancholy a ſubject ; " but, relying upon your Lordſhip's clemency, do humbly beg pardon for this attempt in laying " before you the deplorable ſtate of my affairs, which at preſent I labour under by the deceaſe of " the Profeſſor; his debts being beyond what his effects will amount to ; and the ſeverity of his " creditors is ſuch, that the executor is not allowed a reaſonable time to make the beſt of his aſſets, " but had yeſterday an intimation read in the church, with the allowance of but one week to come " in ; by which means I am deſtitute of neceſſaries, and alſo rendered incapable of aſſiſting my " children. This I offer to your Lordſhip's conſideration, humbly requeſting your charitable aſſiſt-" ance to the fatherleſs and widow. With humble duty and ſervice to my Lady, I remain in all " obedience your Lordſhip's moſt dutiful obedient ſervant, MARTHA OCKLEY."

‖ This reflection was made equally on Dr. *J. Freind*. See above, p. 330.

4 D 2

P. *231.

P. *231. fub-note. In a Collection of Poems, called "The Grove," is a Fable by Mr. *Theobald*, infcribed to *Barnham Goode*, Efq; with a Fable in Anfwer by Mr. *Goode*. There is alfo a facetious letter of Mr. *Goode* "To a Lady, who (after reading *Mani-* "*lius's* Aftronomy tranflated by Mr. *Creech*) was very defirous to know her Fortune," printed in *Curll's* edition of *Pope's* Letters, vol. II. p. 284.

P. *232. The fhort life of Dr. *Edward Littleton*, which does not appear in the 8vo edition, was added, by Dr. *Morell*, to. a third edition in 1749, 12mo; and, as it is not very commonly known, fhall be tranfcribed below †.

P. 238. To the epitaph already printed on Mr. *Vertue* (which was written by Dr. *Parfons*) the following lines have fince been added by *James Bindley*, Efq; F. A. S.

"*Margaret Vertue*, his faithful wife,
Who furvived him near twenty years,
Lies buried in the fame grave.
She died *March* 17, 1776, aged 76."

Mr. *Bindley* has a very fcarce portrait of *Vertue* (ornamented with his famous print of Sir *Hugh Middleton* after *Corn. Johnfon*) engraved by himfelf from a painting taken by

† "Mr. *Edward Littleton* was educated upon the royal foundation at *Eton* fchool, under the "care of that learned and excellent mafter, Dr. *Snape*; who never failed, by proper culture and en- "couragement, to give a genius like our author's fair play, and brighten it into all poffible per- "fection. And, from fome inftances pointed out to me of perfons, now eminent both in church "and ftate, who were formerly his clafs mates, I cannot but think he owed fomewhat to that emu- "lation, which in fuch great fchools is a conftant fpur to youth, and the peculiar advantage of pub- "lick education. Accordingly I am told that his fchool-exercifes were much admired; and, when "his turn came, he was tranfplanted to *King's College, Cambridge*, in the year 1716, with equal ap- "plaufe. A talent for poetry feldom refts unemployed; it will break out and fhew itfelf upon fome "occafion or other. Our author had not been long at the univerfity, before he diverted a fchool- "fellow, whom he had left at *Eton*, with an humourous poem, wherein he defcribes his change of "ftudies, and hints at the progrefs he had made in academical learning. This was followed by "that celebrated one on a Spider. And as both thefe poems have furreptitioufly crept into Mif- "cellanies, in a very imperfect condition; and, though undoubtedly (as the author was very "young when he wrote them) fome of the lines might have been improved, yet, on the contrary, "they have fuffered in the attempt, and names have been introduced altogether unknown to the "author: it was thought proper to give a genuine copy of them ‡, as tranfcribed by a gentleman "then at *Eton* fchool, from the author's own writing. To which is added, what remains I could "find of a Paftoral Elegy, written about the fame time by Mr. *Littleton*, on the death of *R. Banks*, "fcholar of the fame college; and I doubt not but with equal allowance for the age of the author, "they will be alike acceptable to the publick. Whether, as our author fays, his academical ftu- "dies checked his poetical flights, and he rejected thefe trifles for the more folid entertainment of "philofophy, I know not; but I could meet with nothing more of this kind. I have feen indeed "a poetical epiftle fent from fchool to *Penyfton Powney*, Efq; but as this was wrote occafionally, and "fcarce intelligible to any but thofe who were then at *Eton*, I have omitted it. In the year 1720, "Mr. *Littleton* was recalled to *Eton* as an affiftant in the fchool; in which office he was honoured "and beloved by all the young gentlemen that came under his direction, and fo efteemed by the "worthy provoft and fellows, that, upon the death of the Reverend Mr. *Malcher* in the year 1727, "they elected him into their fociety, and prefented him to the living of *Maple-Derham* in *Oxford-* "*fhire*. He then married *Frances*, one of the daughters of *Barnham Goode*, Efq; a lady endowed "with all the accomplifhments that can render the marriage ftate happy. On *June* the 9th, 1730, "he was appointed chaplain in ordinary to their majefties: and in the fame year took his doctor "of laws degree at *Cambridge*. But, though an admired preacher and an excellent fcholar, he "feems to have been as little ambitious of appearing in print, as the great Mr. *Hales*, formerly of "the fame college; not having printed any thing, that I know of, in his life-time; and I am apt "to think, from what I have heard, that, like him too, he never penned any thing, until he needs "muft. He died of a fever in the year 1734, and was buried in his own parifh-church of *Maple-* "*Derham*; leaving behind him a widow and three daughters; for whofe benefit, under the favour "and encouragement of her late majefty Queen *Caroline*, his Difcourfes were firft printed."

‡ Thefe verfes are inferted correctly in an edition of *Dodfley's* Poems enriched with notes, 1782.

1

Gibfon

Gibſon in 1715. Portraits alſo of Mr. and Mrs. *Vertue* have lately been etched by *W. Humphrey*, inſcribed, "*George Vertue* and *Margaret* his wife, in the very habits they "were married, *Feb.* 17th, anno Domini 1720. From the original drawing [by *Vertue* "himſelf] in the collection of the Right Honourable Lord *Cardiff*."

P. 240. Mr. *Cooke's* Medallic Hiſtory has ſince been publiſhed by Mr. *Dodſley*, 1781.

P. 241. Add to the books of Mr. *Burgh*, "The Art of Speaking: containing, 1. An "Eſſay, in which are given Rules for expreſſing properly the principal Paſſions and Hu- "mours, which occur in Reading, or public Speaking: And, 2. Leſſons taken from the "Ancients and Moderns (with Additions and Alterations, where thought uſeful) exhi- "biting a Variety of Matter for Practice; the emphatical Words printed in *Italics*; "with Notes of Direction referring to the Eſſay. To which are added, A Table of the "Leſſons, and an Index to the various Paſſions and Humours in the Eſſay and Leſſons;" of which a fifth edition appeared in 1781.

P. 242. l. 2. read "p. 239;" and l. 16, read, "*Gally's*."

P. 246. l. 20. *a ſquare marble ſtone*] "As Sir *Simon Benet's* monument was ſet up by "*Univerſity College* without the date of his death, I have at my own expence laid a ſmall "neat marble over his grave, and ſupplied that defect. My ſervice and thanks ever to "*Univerſity College*, for their generous regard to their benefactor. What they have "done looks very handſome, and all the country commend it much." Mr. *Browne Willis*, MS.—The following paragraph is extracted from a letter which he wrote very late in life, being dated *Nov.* 13, 1759: "Good Mr. *Owen*, this comes to thank you for your "favour at *Oxford* at St. *Frideſwide's* feſtival; and as your *Bodleian* viſitation is over, "I hope you are a little at liberty to come and ſee your friends; and as you was "pleaſed to mention you would once more make me happy with your good company, "I wiſh it might be next week, at our St. *Martin's* anniverſary at *Fenny Stratford*, "which is *Thurſday* ſe'nnight the 22d inſtant, when a Sermon will be preached by the "miniſter of *Buckingham*: the laſt I am ever like to attend, ſo very infirm as I am "now got; ſo that I ſtir little out of the houſe, and it will therefore be charity to "have friends come and viſit me." He died in leſs than three months after.

A portrait of Mr. *Willis* was etched in 1781 from a drawing taken by the late Mr. *Tyſon*, from an original painting by *Dahl*.—Mr. *Cole* of *Milton*, at whoſe requeſt the etching was made, thus ſpeaks of this portrait of his venerable friend: "The copy "pleaſes me infinitely; nothing can be more exact and like the copy I ſent, and which, "as well as I can recollect, is equally ſo to the original. To a perſon who only remem- "bers Mr. *Willis's* figure in his latter age, it will convey no reſemblance of him; and "few people are living, who remember him young. When I knew him firſt, about 35 "years ago, he had more the appearance of a mumping beggar than of a gentleman; "and the moſt like reſemblance of his figure that I can recollect among old prints, is "that of Old *Hobſon* the *Cambridge* carrier. He then, as always, was dreſſed in an old "ſlouched hat, more brown than black, a weather-beaten large wig, three or four old- "faſhioned coats, all tied round by a leathern belt, and over all an old blue cloak, "lined with black fuſtian, which he told me he had new made when he was elected "member for the town of *Buckingham* about 1707. I have ſtill by me, as relicks, this "cloak and belt, which I purchaſed of his ſervant. No wonder will it be, when the "print is given to any one who remembers this figure of Mr. *Willis*, that they immedi- "ately pronounce it unlike; and ſo it is in good truth; and if I had two pictures of "myſelf, one taken when I was in blooming youth, and the other in decrepid old age, "and was to give the world a print of one of them, would it be judicious to exhibit "myſelf in deformity, when it was in my power to ſhew away with equal truth as a "young man? Notwithſtanding the diſtance of time when *Dahl* drew his portrait,

and

" and that in which I knew him, and the ftrange metamorphofe that age and caprice
" had made in his figure, yet I could eafily trace fome lines and traits of what Mr. *Dahl*
" had given of him."

P. 247. In *Peck's Stanford*, the South Weft Profpect of Mr. *Brown's* Hofpital is infcribed, " To that curious and communicative Antiquary *Browne Willis*, Efq."

P. 250. l. 4. read, " Dr. *Gally's* Differtation againft pronouncing the *Greek* language
" according to accents."

Ibid. fub-note. Mr. *Sliford's* book was firft publifhed in 1733; again in 1741; and has
lately been continued to the year 1782 under the patronage of Sir *William Mufgrave*.

P. 251. note ‖, See fome particulars of " Old Dr. *Mead*," in Gent. Mag. 1781, p. 221.

P. 253. col. 2. l. 10. of the infcription (which was written by Dr. *Ward*) read DEGERAT.

P. 255. Dr. *Mead's* pictures were fold *March* 20, 21, 22, 1754; and produced (according to the Catalogue given to the Society of Antiquaries by Mr. *Theobald*) 3413*l.* 1*s.*

P. 256. This infcription was alfo written by Dr. *Ward*; and Q. whether the buft be
not dated 1739, though Dr. *Maty's* copy fays 1730?

L. 22. read, " an engraved portrait from the fame picture, by *Baron*, infcribed *Ri-*
" *cardus Mead*, Regis *Magnæ Britanniæ* Medicus Ordinarius, 1749."

Ibid. Mr. *Bowyer*, who was intimately acquainted with Dr. *Mead*, ufed to confult
him as a phyfician; nor would the Doctor accept from him a fee. And not unfrequently
having occafion for medical advice when Dr. *Mead* was unable to come to him, he generally received a friendly rebuke the next time he went to *Ormond-Street*: " If I was not
" able to come to you," the good Doctor would fay, " why could not you have fent
" for my fon *Wilmot*?"

P. 260. note, l. 5. read " the vicarage of *Eaftwell* (worth 120*l.* a year)."

Ibid. Mr. *Whifton*, in the Memoirs of his own Life, vol. I. p. 298. fays, " About the
" year 1736, and before queen *Caroline* died, Mr. *Jortin*, a great and learned friend of
" mine, and from whom I afterward received a remedy of Sir *Edward Hulfe's* for a great
" diforder I was then in, which, by God's bleffing, faved my life, told me, that the late
" duke of *Somerfet*, a great *Athanafian*, once forbad his chaplain to read the *Athanafian*
" creed (which I imagined was occafioned by a fuggeftion from the queen; to whom I
" had complained, that although fhe was queen, that creed was not yet laid afide):
" whereupon Mr. *Jortin* left off the fame creed for fome time. Mr. *Jortin* has alfo
" lately publifhed a very good book for the Chriftian Religion."

Ibid. fub-note. A worthy clergyman now living afked Dr. *Jortin* why he did not
publifh his Sermons. " They fhall fleep," he replied, " till I fleep." More inftances
of his laconic mode of fpeech might eafily have been produced.

P. 268. Mr. *White's* three letters were intituled, 1. " A Letter to a Gentleman dif-
" fenting from the Church of *England*, concerning the Lives of Churchmen and Dif-
" fenters," (four times printed). 2. " A fecond Letter to a Gentleman diffenting from
" the Church of *England*; wherein the great and popular Pleas of Diffenters againft
" Communion with the Church are refuted, and reflected back upon themfelves," (three
editions. 3. " The third and laft Letter; wherein the Defign of the fecond is farther
" purfued and completed. With an Appendix, containing fome Confiderations on the
" Lawfulnefs, Expediency, and Neceffity of requiring all who are to be admitted to
" the Miniftry, or to any Ecclefiaftical Preferment in the Church of *England*, or to be
" Preachers or Teachers in any Diffenting Congregations, to fubfcribe the Articles of
" Faith and Religion; and fetting forth the Inconfiftencies between the notorious
" Practices of Diffenters, and the avowed Principles of many of them touching that
" matter," (three editions).

P. 276. col. 2. l. 9. read, " profunt," l. 8. " Implentur, artes;"

P. 279. Some memoirs of Dr. *Stukeley* fhall appear in this Appendix.

P. 279.

P. 279. In *June* 1741 Dr. *Armstrong* solicited Dr. *Birch's* recommendation to Dr. *Mead*, that he might be appointed physician to the forces then going to *The West Indies*. —In 1753 Dr. *Theobald* addressed the two following Odes " Ad ingenuum Virum, tum " medicis, tum poeticis, facultatibus præstantem, *Johannem Armstrong*, M. D."

I. *Johanni Armstrong*, M. D.
 Fusis *Scotis*.
" Artifque *Coæ* O et Citharæ sciens,
Utroque mirè dexter *Apolline* !
 Quem Musa nascentem Deusque
 Arcitenens studiosiori
Finxere curâ ! Plectripotens modis
Festivioris carminis, agmine
 Clarum triumphato rebelli,
 Tolle Ducem, auspiciis paternis
Campos volantem per *Caledonios*,
(*Ales minister ceu *Jovis*) impetus
*Hydræ*que tundentem feroces
 Herculeo penitus vigore.
Io Triumphe ! Salva *Britannia*
Surgente dicat sole, cadenteque :
 Plausus pavimentum sacratum
 Donec ovans feriat polorum."

II. " Docte cui *Polyhymnia*
 Perblandum dederat tendere barbiton !
O multumque Poeticis
 Et multum Medicis splendide dotibus !
Nomen materia tuum
 Capta ecce ! egregia Musa avide insonat ;
Læte et per liquidum fuga
 Romani volitans aëra *Horatii*,
Ter sublime rapit, poli
 Et fugit rutilis purpurei choris :
Cous clarus ubi Senex
 Augustum radiis emicat aureis,
Vatum et nobilium plaga
 Cælestis resonat fervida plausibus.
Crescens laude nova, ætheri
 Tu jam sternis ovans sidereo viam ;
Jam jamque invidia caput
 Major cælicolum cœtibus inseris."

There is a mezzotinto portrait of him, from a painting by Sir *Joshua Reynolds*, inscribed, " *John Armstrong*, M. D.
" The suffrage of the wise, the praise that's worth competition,
 " Is attained by sense alone, and dignity of mind."

P. 283. Among other learned publications Mr. *Palairet* was author of " Thesaurus " Ellipsium *Latinarum*, five Vocum quæ in Sermone *Latino* suppressæ indicantur, & " ex præstantissimis Auctoribus illustrantur, cum Indicibus necessariis. Auctore *Elia* " *Palairet*, Reverendo in Deo Patri *Joanni Bangoræ* Episcopo à Sacris, & in Regiâ Æde " Vicario, 1760," 8vo.

P. 294. An additional circumstance of Mr. *Lyons* shall be given hereafter.

P. 295. note, for " archdeacon," read " præcentor" of *Litchfield*.

P. 297. " *Philip Carteret Webb*, Gent." occurs in 1725 among the subscribers to " Original Letters to the Tatler, &c."—He was admitted an attorney before Mr. Justice *Price*, *June* 20, 1729 ; and lived then in *The Old Jewry*.

P. 298. note, l. 22. read, " Pretender's eldest son's," &c. Of these " Remarks *," a second edition, corrected, was published the same year.

Ibid. sub-note. *Norton Court* has been lately rebuilt by *John Cockayne Sole*, Esq.

P. 299. *John Hodgson*, M. A. born in *Cumberland* or *Westmoreland*, was sent to *Queen's College*, *Oxford*, where He took his master's degree *July* 12, 1756. When a child, he accidentally fell into the fire, by which the fingers of his right hand were so miserably burnt, disfigured, and lamed, that he usually wore a glove to hide them ; and when he took up a pen, it was with his left hand, with which he stuck it into his right ; a stranger therefore would have thought he could not have written at all, but notwithstanding his misfortune he wrote a very good hand. At *Queen's College* he was much

---

* In the conclusion of the " Remarks," which are dated *November* 6, 1745, Mr. *Webb* apologises for such expressions as may at first sight seem too harsh. " The reader," he says, " will pro-" bably excuse them, when he reflects that where Truth and his Prince are abused and menaced in " the manner they are by the Declaration, it is very difficult, and possibly not expedient, to preserve " that moderation and decency of expression, which on all other occasions the author is sensible he " ought to prescribe to himself." And in the Postscript we learn that the " Declaration," and the " Commission and Declaration which were the subject of the former Remarks," were burnt at *The Royal Exchange*, by order of Parliament, *November* 12, 1745, with general acclamations.

esteemed

esteemed for his eminent parts, learning, candour and modest deportment, by Dr. *Smith*, the provost. About the year 1752 he was private tutor there to the present *Francis Lawson*, Esq; barrister at law, and in the following year he went to reside with *Philip Carteret Webb*, Esq; as tutor to his son ; in which employment he enjoyed great felicity : the well-furnished library and noble collection of ancient coins of Mr. *Webb* was a great resource to him, who was well versed in mathematicks, natural history and antiquities, and the civilities he received from Mr. *Webb* and all his family were very engaging to him. In 1756 he attended young Mr. *Webb* to *Bene't College, Cambridge*, where he was admitted *ad eundem*, and in vacation-time was frequently, with his pupil, at *Busbridge*, where in the intervals of giving instruction, for which he was eminently qualified, he attended very particularly to the study of antiquity. Thus he wrote to a friend from thence, *April* 17, 1756 : " Though I have an extreme regard for Madam *Flora*, and " have, in reality, paid my addresses to her with some warmth last summer, she has a " rival here that, for the present at least, engages my whole application ; 'tis no other " than the matron Antiquity, a personage of somewhat a forbidding aspect at first, but " whose features soften to a wonderful degree of beauty the longer you are acquainted " with her. This venerable lady, who holds one of her rural retreats in this place, " lays so many baits for me, that I can hardly steal out to an evening assignation with " the other." Whilst at *Busbridge*, Mr. *Hodgson* was employed in making a catalogue of Mr. *Webb's* library and of his medallions, and in studying the *Anglo-Saxon* language, of which he proposed to make himself fully master.—He had served two different curacies, and in 1757 that of *St. Antholin's, London*, where he began collecting what relates to the state of *English* poetry from the earliest times. In 1758 he was appointed one of the rectors of *Codrington College, Barbados*, for which island he embarked in *January* 1759, and arrived there the 9th of *April*. In the college he met with a worthy agreeable associate, and found the inhabitants of the island very kind and hospitable ; but the heat of the climate so disagreed with him, that, about the latter end of the year 1760, he left the island in a very bad state of health, and returning to *England* died on his passage. Thus was lost to the world this excellent young man, aged about 30. He was master not only of *Greek* and *Latin*, but of the *Hebrew*, and very well versed in *French* and *Spanish* ; had a turn to poetry, but never himself printed any thing. Some verses of his got abroad, and were printed in periodical publications of the time. One short poem the writer of this note remembers to have seen in a magazine, thought to be the *London*, which may be known by a typographical error, *Elian* for *Elean*. Another, an Epistle to a Friend, the writer has, but at present it is mislaid. The 27th of *May*, 1756, Mr. *Hodgson* was elected a member of the Society of Antiquaries, and in vol. II. p. 42, of the Archæologia, is a dissertation written by him on an ancient Cornelian, which with difficulty he was persuaded to suffer being read there ; such was the modesty of this valuable young man, this mild and unaffected scholar, to whose amiable character the author of this note laments that he cannot do greater justice, and will, therefore, conclude it with part of *Pope's* epitaph on *Gay*, the following lines being equally applicable to one as the other :

" Of manners gentle, of affections mild :
" In wit, a man ; simplicity, a child."

For the credit of Mr. *Hodgson* it should be observed, that the present Earl of *Massareene*, when he removed from *Oxford* to *Bene't College, Cambridge*, 1758, brought with him for tutor a very different kind of personage, one *Seth Pollard* of *Yorkshire*, who, after having taken the degree of M. A. at *University College, Oxford, June* 1, 1756, proceeded *ad eundem* at *Cambridge* in 1758, was curate of *Pudsey* near *Leedes*, and died 176 ; a man of an athletic constitution, whose *forte* was skill in rowing.

P. 300.

P. 300. To the note on Archbifhop *Potter* and his (eldeft) fon, might have been added, that the younger, the favourite *Jacob*, whom he thought more worthy of his eftate, was highly exceptionable in his moral character, however diftinguifhed by his abilities; and, in particular, his behaviour both before and after marriage to his firft lady (Mifs *Manningham*) whom his father obliged him to marry, is well known and remembered.

P. 304. fub-note, l. 3. read, " his party opinions."

Ibid. l. ult. read, " Son of the late" &c.

P. 312. fub-note, l. 1. read, "it was to make a work."

P. 314. The " Ordinale Quotidianum" began, " *Sufannæ Mores*," &c. The Hymn which accompanied it, " *Cœlos vidimus*," &c.—The printing materials belonging to Mr. *Mores* were fold by auction by Mr. *Paterfon*, *November* 20, 1781; and a catalogue of his large collection of matrices * (formed from the number of old founderies which were accumulated in that of Mr. *John James*, who died *June* 23, 1772,) is now *(March* 1782) preparing for the publick. There are two fmall portraits of Mr. *Mores*, each in a 1 oval.

P. 316. Mr. *Caflon's* firft refidence was in *Vine-Street* in *The Minories*, where one confiderable branch of his employment was to make tools for the book-binders and for the chafing of filver plate. Whilft he was engaged in this employment, the elder Mr. *Bowyer* accidentally faw in the fhop of Mr. *Daniel Browne*, bookfeller, near *Temple-Bar*, the lettering of a book uncommonly neat; and enquiring who the artift was by whom the letters were made, Mr. *Caflon* was introduced to his acquaintance, and was taken by him to Mr. *James's* foundery in *Bartholomew Clofe*. *Caflon* had never before that time feen any part of the bufinefs; and being afked by his friend if he thought he could undertake to cut types, he requefted a fingle day to confider the matter, and then replied he had no doubt but he could. From this anfwer, Mr. *Bowyer* lent him 200*l.* Mr. *Bettenham* lent the fame fum, and Mr. *Watts* 100*l.*; and by that affiftance our ingenious artift applied himfelf affiduoufly to his new purfuit, and was eminently fuccefsful. The three printers above-mentioned were of courfe his conftant cuftomers. It appears by *Ged's* † " Narrative of his Scheme for Block-printing," that fo early as 1730 " he had
" eclipfed

---

* The great attention of Mr. *Mores* to this refearch is evident from his " Differtation" on the fubject. The following fhort billet, dated *Leyton*, *July* 22, 1777, was the laft that Mr. *Bowyer* received from him: " Dear Sir, I am defirous of afcertaining the time at which the bodies received " their names, and I think I can do it pretty well. I fhall take as a great favour your opinion " why *Englifh* is called *Englifh*. An additional favour will be the *Italian* names of the bodies, or " a direction where to find them. Another additional, are the names given by other printing " nations befides the *German*, *French*, *Englifh*, and *Dutch*, to be found in books? I could go on " with additionals; but I muft not be further troublefome. I am, dear Sir, yours very fincerely, " EDWARD-ROWE MORES."

† An ingenious though unfuccefsful artift, who was a goldfmith in *Edinburgh*, and made this improvement in the art of printing in 1725. The invention was fimply this. From any types of *Greek* or *Roman*, or any other character, he formed a plate for every page, or fheet, of a book, from which he printed, inftead of ufing a type for every letter, as is done in the common way. This was firft practifed, but on blocks of wood, by the *Chinefe* and *Japonefe*, and purfued in the firft effays of *Cofter*, *Guttenberg*, and *Fauft*, the *European* inventors of the prefent art. " This im- " provement," fays *James Ged*, is principally confiderable in three moft important articles, viz. " expence, correctnefs, beauty, and uniformity." But thefe improvements are controverted by Mr. *Mores* and others. In *July* 1729, *William Ged* entered into partnerfhip with *William Fenner*, a *London* ftationer, who was to have half the profits, in confideration of his advancing all the money requifite. To fupply this, Mr. *John James*, then an architect at *Greenwich* (who built Sir *Gregory Page's* houfe, *Bloomfbury* church, &c.) was taken into the fcheme, and afterwards his brother ‡, Mr. *Thomas James*, a founder, and *James Ged*, the inventor's fon. In 1730 thefe partners applied to the univerfity of *Cambridge* for printing Bibles and Common Prayer Books by blocks

‡ *George James*, another brother, was printer to the City of *London*, and lived in *Little-Britain*.

4 E

inftead

" eclipſed his competitors in the art of letter-founding; but found more difficulty than " he apprehended in an attempt to make plates for block-printing." In the Univerſal Magazine for *June* 1750, is a good view of Mr. *Caſton's* work-ſhop in *Chiſwell-Street*, with portraits of ſix * of his workmen.—Mr. *Caſton* was three times married. The name of his ſecond wife was *Longman*; of the third *Waters*; and with each of theſe two ladies he had a good fortune. The abilities of *William Caſton*, jun. appeared to great advantage in a ſpecimen of types of the learned languages in 1748.

P. 324. Dr. *R. Freind* married the only daughter of *Samuel Del'angle*, D.D. and prebendary of *Weſtminſter*. In the Gentleman's Magazine for 1733, p. 152, are ſome verſes by *Stephen Duck* to Dr. *Freind*, on his quitting *Weſtminſter* ſchool; by which it appears that Lord *Carteret* (afterwards Earl of *Granville*), Lord *Hervey*, and the duke of *Newcaſtle*, were greatly indebted to him for part of their accompliſhments and future fame. And in 1737, p. 631, is an Ode to the Duke of *Newcaſtle* by Dr. *Freind* (who was that year made canon of *Chriſt-Church*) and the following elegant epigram:

" Reverendo doctiſſimoque
Roberto Freind, S.T.P.
Eccleſiæ Divi *Petri Weſtmonaſt*. Prebendario,
et *Ædis Chriſti Oxon*. Canonico.

De te, *Freinde*, duæ certant ſocialiter Ædes,
Hæc *Chriſti* inſignis nomine, et illa *Petri*,
Quæ potior charum titulis ornaret alumnum,
Jamque ſenem poſſet læta fovere ſinu.
Illuſtris fuerit Ducis hanc componere litem:
Utraque quem voluit mater utrique dedit.
R. L.

Dat. 14 Kal. *Julii*, A.S. 1737."

Thus indifferently tranſlated in 1738.
For you, moſt learned *Freind!* two churches ſtrove,
(For you, the darling object of their love;)
This *Chriſt Church* call'd, and that *St. Peter's* nam'd,
(Rare nurſing mothers, from paſt ages fam'd.)
Their friendly conteſt was, which church
    ſhould grace
Her foſter ſon with dignitary's place,
And cheer him, now grown old, with her
    moſt kind embrace.
A noble Duke, this conteſt to decide,
Each mother's cravings graciouſly ſupply'd,
And gave to each her darling ſon, right nobly
    dignified.

Dr. *R. Freind* wrote the epitaph on *Dodwell*, which is printed in *Aſhmole's Berkſhire*, vol. II. p. 492. He wrote alſo the beautiful epitaph on *George* Lord *Carteret's* younger

instead of ſingle types, and, in conſequence, a leaſe was ſealed to them *April* 23, 1731. In their attempt they ſunk a large ſum of money, and finiſhed only two Prayer Books, ſo that it was forced to be relinquiſhed, and the leaſe was given up in 1738. *Ged* imputed his diſappointment to the villainy of the preſs-men and the ill treatment of his partners (which he ſpecifies at large), particularly *Fenner*, whom *John James* and he were adviſed to proſecute, but declined it. He returned to *Scotland* in 1733, and had no redreſs. He there, however, ſet about *Salluſt*, which he printed at *Edinburgh* in 1736, 12mo. *Fenner* died inſolvent in or before the year 1735; and his widow married Mr. *Waugh*, an apothecary, who carried on the printing-buſineſs with her, and whom ſhe ſurvived. Her effects were ſold in 1768. *James Ged*, the ſon, wearied with diſappointments, engaged in the rebellion of 1745 as a captain in *Perth's* regiment, and being taken at *Carliſle*, was condemned, but, on his father's account, by Dr. *Smith's* intereſt with the duke of *Newcaſtle*, was pardoned, and releaſed in 1748. He afterwards worked for ſome time, as a journeyman, with Mr. *Bettenham*, and then commenced maſter; but, being unſucceſsful, he went privately to *Jamaica*, where his younger brother *William* was ſettled as a reputable printer. His tools, &c. he left to be ſhipped by a falſe friend, who moſt ungenerouſly detained them to try his ſkill himſelf. *James Ged* died the year after he left *England*; as did his brother in 1767. In the above purſuit Mr. *Thomas James*, who died in 1738, expended much of his fortune, and ſuffered in his proper buſineſs; " for the printers," ſays Mr. *Mores*, " would not employ him, becauſe the block-printing, had it ſucceeded, would have been prejudicial " to theirs." Mr. *William Ged* died, in very indifferent circumſtances, Oct. 19, 1749, after his utenſils were ſent for *Leith* to be ſhipped for *London*, to have joined with his ſon *James* as a printer there. Thus ended his life and project, which, ingenious as it ſeems, is not likely to be revived, if, as Mr. *Mores* ſuggeſts, " it muſt, had it at firſt ſucceeded, have ſoon ſunk under its own burthen," for reaſons needleſs here to recapitulate. " Biographical Memoirs of *William Ged*, including a par-" ticular Account of his Progreſs in the Art of Block-printing," were publiſhed by J. *Nichols* in 1781, 8vo.

* Of theſe the figure marked 3. is the portrait of *Jackſon* (ſee p. 318); and 4. is that of *Cottrell*.

ſon *Philip*, who died at that ſchool, 1710, in his 19th year *. His *Latin* poetry is much
ſuperior to his *Engliſh*. Two epigrams on this learned Divine and his epitaphs are preſerved in the Select Collection, vol. V. p. 310; and vol. VIII. p. 314.

P. 324. note, l. 1. read, " his father *William*."

P. 325. note, l. 4. read, " his ſon *William*."

Ibid. l. 9. read, " *Aug.* 9, 1754, aged 84."

P. 326. ſub-note, read, " miniſter of the donative or curacy of *Edgware*."

P. 329. read, "Concio ad Clerum in Synodo Provinciali *Cantuarienſis* Provinciæ, habita
" ad D. *Pauli* die 6º *Novembris* MDCCLXI. à *Gulielmo Freind*, S. T. P. Eccleſiæ
" Chriſti Metropoliticæ *Cantuarienſi* Decano; juſſu Reverendiſſimi & Commiſſariorum."
Dr. *William Freind* being made canon of *Chriſt Church* in 175.., and afterwards finding
that his patron was diſtreſſed (upon ſome political arrangement) for a canonry there,
generouſly reſigned it without making any conditions whatever; the conſequence of
which was, that upon the death of Dr. *Lynch* Dean of *Canterbury* (1760) he was without ſolicitation appointed to ſucceed him, and enjoyed that preferment till his death.
He had a moſt valuable collection of books, pictures, and prints, the latter of which,
after his death, were ſold by auction, by Mr. *Langford*, *Dec.* 14—18, 1767: and his
valuable library by Mr. *Baker*, *April* 28—*May* 6, 1767. An epitaph by Dr. *William
Freind*, on Dr. *Morres*, vicar of *Hinckley*, is printed in the Hiſtory of that town, p. 40.

P. 330. Dr. *J. Freind* was elected F. R. S. in 1711; and ſpoke the *Harveian* Oration
in 1720, which was afterwards printed in 4to. The monument in *Weſtminſter Abbey* of
Biſhop *Sprat* and his ſon the prebendary of *Rocheſter*, is inſcribed by Dr. *J. Freind*;
whoſe own memory is alſo perpetuated by the following epitaph:

" JOHANNES FREIND, M. D.
Archiater
Sereniſſimæ Reginæ *Carolinæ*;
Cujus perſpicaci judicio cum ſe approbâſſet,
Quantâ prius apud omnes Medicinæ famâ,
Tantâ apud regiam familiam gratiâ floruit.
Ingenio erat benevolo et admodum liberali,
Societatis et convictuum amans,
Amicitiarum
Etiam ſuo alicubi periculo
Tenaciſſimus.
Nemo beneficia
Aut in alios alacriùs contulit,
Aut in ſe collata libentiùs meminit.
Juvenis adhuc ſcriptis cœpit inclareſcere,
Et aſſiduo tum *Latini* tum Patrii ſermonis uſu
Orationem perpolivit;
Quam vero in umbraculis excoluerat facundiam,
Eam in ſolem atque aciem ſenator protulit.

Humanioribus literis
Domi peregréque operam dedit;
Omnes autem, ut decuit, nervos intendit
Suâ in arte ut eſſet verſatiſſimus:
Quo ſucceſſu, orbis *Britannici* cives et proceres,
Quam multiplici ſcienti
Viri omnium gentium eruditi,
Quam indefeſſo ſtudio et induſtriâ,
Id quidem, non ſine lachrymis, amici
Loquentur.
Miri quiddam fuit,
Quod in tam continuâ occupatione,
Inter tot circuitiones,
Scribendo etiam vacare poſſet:
Quod tanto oneri diutiùs ſuſtinendo impar eſſet,
Nihil miri;
Obiit ſiquidem, vigente adhuc ætate,
Annum agens quinquageſimum ſecundum,
Ær. Chriſti 1728, *Jul.* 6."

* Held out on a very large marble ſcroll by a figure of Time on his monument in the North-aiſle
of *Weſtminſter-Abbey*. The reader will not be diſpleaſed to ſee it here, and may compare the annexed
tranſlation of it with that by *Samuel Cobb* in the Antiquities of *Weſtminſter Abbey*, 1722, 8vo, vol. II.
p. 101.

Quid breves te delicias tuorum
Næniis *Phœbi* chorus omnis luget,
Et meæ falcis ſubito reciſum
Vulnere plangit?
En, puer, vitæ pretium caducæ!
Hic tuam cuſtos vigil ad favillam
Semper adſtabo, & memori tuebor
Marmore famam.
Audies claræ pietate, morum
Integer, multæ ſtudioſus artis:
Hæc frequens olim leget, hæc ſequetur
Emula pubes.

Short-lived delight of every friend,
Why do the tuneful Nine attend
To mourn my ſickle's ſtroke!
Behold, dear youth, what meed awaits,
Thy life thus ſhortened by the fates,
My ſentence to revoke.
Watchful I guard thy aſhes here:
In marble guard thy memory dear,
Thy piety and truth,
Thy ſpotleſs life, thy ſtudious pain,
Eternal monuments remain
T' inſtruct each rival youth.

There

There is also a medal of Dr. *John Freind*, finely executed, by *St. Urbain* a *Lorrainer*; on the reverse is the Doctor's bust, inscribed ioannes. freind. coll. med. lond. et. reg. s. s. and on the neck the initial letters of the artist's name, s. v. Reverse, an ancient and modern physician joining hands. medicina. vetvs. et nova. Exergue. vnam facimvs vtramqve. His valuable library was sold by auction by Mr. *Cock*, *Jan.* 2—14, 17... There is no date to the catalogue.—The following epigram by Mr. *S. Wesley* will perhaps be thought worth preserving;

" When *Radcliffe* fell, afflicted Physick cried,
" How vain my power! and languish'd at his side.
" When *Freind* expir'd, deep-struck, her hair she tore,
" And speechless fainted, and reviv'd no more.
" Her flowing grief no farther could extend;
" She mourns with *Radcliffe*, but she dies with *Freind*."

P. 331. " There is a traditional story that one of the name of *Freind* (I think it must be Mrs. *Pilkington's* hero) dreamt that two numbers in a lottery of Queen *Anne* would be the *two* greatest prizes; that he went and bought them, and they came up so; that he went backwards and forwards to his bureau to look at them, till he was almost mad; that he spent all, and died a beggar (I believe) in gaol. This story I had from Mr. *Holmes* the curate, and afterwards vicar, of *Wellingborough*, a gentleman of uncommon good sense, who died about eight years ago, and who was sent for to the inn by *Freind* to drink a bottle when he was in his meridian; and (as I recollect) had the story of the tickets from himself. If he would tell it on such an occasion, he must have told it to many: and one should like to know what one could about so extraordinary a tale. Dr. *Johnson* says truly, " One must not be too positive in disbelieving, as the story may be " true; nor too credulous, as it may be false." Mrs. *Pilkington* calls him " a clergyman; " and mentions the grandeur he had lived in." This is not the description of a common clergyman, however well provided, and you mention no preferment; so I think he must be the man, though I do not remember that my informant called him a clergyman; but I always thought he was a son or a younger brother of the master of *Westminster* school, though I could never make him out before. Yet surely Mrs. *Pilkington* would have heard this story from him if he ever told it to a stranger; and if so, she would surely have been glad to have swelled her Memoirs with it." *T. F.*

P. 332. Dr. *Warton*, in his " Essay on *Pope*," vol. II. p. 301. styles *Spence's* judicious Essay on the Odyssey " a work of the truest taste;" and adds, that " *Pope* was so far " from taking it amiss, that it was the origin of a lasting friendship betwixt them. I " have seen," says Dr. *Warton*, " a copy of this work, with marginal observations " written in *Pope's* own hand, and generally acknowledging the justness of *Spence's* ob- " servations, and in a few instances pleading, humourously enough, that some favourite " lines might be spared. I am indebted to this learned and amiable man, on whose " friendship I set the greatest value, for most of the anecdotes relating to *Pope*, men- " tioned in this work, which he gave me, when I was making him a visit at *Byfleet*, " in the year 1754."

P. 335. In a preface to the " Select Epigrams of *Martial*, translated and imitated by " *William Hay*, Esq; with an Appendix of some by *Cowley* and other hands, 1755," 12mo, the modest author says, " I can with truth and sincerity declare, that I never " once had a particular person in my eye. Were I to censure others, my own foibles " would reprove me. And it would ill become me to ridicule my neighbour, who lie " so open to ridicule myself. Nor have I the least provocation; for, I thank God, I " have no enemy. I know of none; and should be sorry to make any, and to offend " where I intended to divert."

P. 336. Sir *John Hill* died in *November* 1775.

P. 340.

P. 340. l. 1. read, " Odes defcriptive and allegorical."

Ibid. fub-note. To the publications of Mr. *Stackhoufe*, add, " The Nature and Property " of Language, 1731," 8vo. ; " An Abridgement of *Burnet's* Hiftory of his own Times," 8vo. ; a " *Greek* Grammar," 8vo. ; and " A Syftem of Practical Duties," 8vo. He was many years curate of *Finchley*, where he began his " Hiftory of the Bible." The portrait of him was engraved by *Vertue*, from a painting of *J. Woolafton*. He was then in the 63d year of his age, and we believe died and was buried at *Benham*.

P. 341. There is a portrait of Mr. *Chefelden* in mezzotinto ; " *William Chefelden*, Efq; " Surgeon to her late Majefty Queen *Caroline*, &c. *J. Faber fecit*, 1733."

P. 343. *Charles Cotes*, M. D. fellow of *All-Soul's College, Oxford*, who married Mifs *Chefelden*, and died without iffue, was a fon of *John Cotes*, of *Woodcote*, by Lady *Dorothy Shirley*. This *John* had feven fons ; *viz.* (1.) *John*, who married Lady Dowager *Delves* ; (2.) *Charles* ; (3.) *James*, the lieutenant-colonel ; (4.) *Thomas*, the vice-admiral ; (5.) *Shirley* ; (6.) *Washington* ; (7.) *Humphrey*. *Digby Cotes*, the public orator, was a younger brother of *John* the father of thefe feven fons. This account, received from a private hand, I am affured, may be depended upon.

Ibid. note, l. 8. read, " was elected furgeon."

P. 344. note, l. 3. for " *Dunciad*," read " Effay on Man," which was anonymous. The Dunciad was well known to be *Pope's*.—One more couplet, expreffive of that great Poet's opinion of our Anatomift, fhall here be added :

" I'll do what *Mead* and *Chefelden* advife,
" To keep thefe limbs, and to preferve thefe eyes."

Imitations of *Horace*, Ep. I. 51.

P. 345. Dr. *Harwood*, fpeaking of Mr. *Bowyer's* Teftament, fays, " This is a valu- " able *Greek* Teftament, and now fcarce. A copy of it fold at Dr. *Afkew's* fale for " 10s. 6d*. Mr. *Bowyer* is an excellent *Greek* fcholar, and it is to be feared will be " the laft learned printer in *England* †."

P. 347. Dr. *Pettingal*, who was prebendary of *Sneating* in the church of St. *Paul*, died in *July*, 1781. He had publifhed in 1769, 4to. " An Enquiry into the Ufe and " Practice of Juries among the *Greeks* and *Romans* ; from whence the Origin of the " *English* Jury may poffibly be deduced ; in three Parts, 1769," 4to. His " Dif- " fertation on the Courts of Pypowder" is printed in the Archæologia, vol. I. p. 190.

P. 348. note, Mr. *W.* was " vicar," not " rector," of *Hollingbourne*.

P. 349. Father *Bofcovich* is now profeffor of aftronomy at *Milan*.

P. 351. fub-note §, read, " informed a friend who repeated it to me."

P. 353. Of Mr. *Coftard*, who died in *January* 1782, fome particulars fhall be given in a future page.

P. 354. To the books of 1764, add, *Browne's* ‡ " *Sunday* Thoughts," 2d edit. 12mo.

P. 355. *Oldmixon* publifhed " A Review of Dr. *Grey's* Defence of our ancient and " modern Hiftorians."

P. 356.

* At Mr. *Beauclerk's* fale a copy of it (art. 615) was fold for more than double the original price, which was only 6s. I may add, that neither of thefe copies was rendered of additional value by the modern luxury of fplendid bindings, which often fwells the price of worthlefs books.

† " View of the various Editions of the *Greek* and *Roman* Claffics, with Remarks, 1775," p. 121.

‡ Mr. *Mofes Browne*, originally a pen-cutter, afterwards went into orders, and obtained the vica- rage of *Olney* in *Bucks*, and the chaplainfhip to *Morden* college. Befides the " *Sunday* Thoughts," and " An Effay on the Univerfe," he was author of " Poems on feveral occafions, with Pifcatory " Eclogues, 1739," 8vo; and of feveral poems in the early volumes of " The Gentleman's Maga- " zine," fome of which are poffeffed of confiderable merit. In his youth, for he was born in the year 1703, he wrote two pieces, which were both reprefented together, and have pretty nearly an equal degree of merit. They are entitled, 1. " *Polidus*, a Tragedy, 8vo, 1723;" 2. " An " bedevilled,

P. 356. note †, read, " Dr. *Maddox*, who was soon after made a bishop.". See p. 543.

P. 357. *Francis Peck*, born at *Stamford* in *Lincolnshire*, *May* 4, 1692, was educated at *Cambridge*, where he took the degrees of B. and M. A. The first work discovered of his writing is a poem, intituled, " Sighs on the Death of Queen *Anne*," printed probably about the time of her death in 1714. Two years afterwards he printed " ΤΟ ΥΨΟΣ " "ΑΓΙΟΝ ; or an Exercise on the Creation, and an Hymn to the Creator of the World ; " written in the express Words of the Sacred Text, as an Attempt to shew the Beauty " and Sublimity of the Holy Scriptures, 1716," 8vo' In 1721, being then curate of *King's Clifton* in *Northamptonshire*, he offered to the world proposals for printing the History and Antiquities of his native town, which work he produced in 1727, in folio, under the title of " *Academia tertia Anglicana* ; or the Antiquarian Annals of *Stanford* " in *Lincoln*, *Rutland*, and *Northampton* shires ; containing the History of the University, " Monasteries, Gilds, Churches, Chapels, Hospitals, and Schools there," &c. inscribed to *John* Duke of *Rutland* *. This publication was hastened by " An Essay on the ancient " and present State of *Stamford*, 1726," 4to, by *Francis Hargrave*, who, in the Preface to his pamphlet, mentions the difference which had arisen between him and Mr. *Peck*, on account of the former's publication unfairly forestalling that intended by the latter. Mr. *Peck* is also therein very roughly treated on account of a small work he had formerly printed, intituled, " The History of the *Stamford* Bull-running." He had before this time obtained the rectory of *Godeby*, near *Melton*, in *Leicestershire*, the only preferment he ever enjoyed. In 1729, he printed a single sheet, " Queries concerning the Natural History " and Antiquities of *Leicestershire* and *Rutland*," which were afterwards reprinted in 1740; but although the progress he had made in the work was very considerable, yet it never made its appearance, and as much as he had executed of it is supposed to have been, with other materials for the history of those counties, in the hands of the late Sir *Thomas Cave* †, bart. In 1732 he published the first volume of " *Desiderata Curiosa* ; " or,

" bedevilled, a Farce." The second was acted by way of an entertainment added to the first. Neither of them however were performed at a theatre-royal, or even by regular actors, but only by some gentlemen of the author's acquaintance, for their own diversion and the gratification of his vanity, at a place which in the title-page is called " The private Theatre in *St. Alban's* " *Street*," but this is imagined to have been nothing more than some school or assembly-room fitted up for the immediate occasion of this play, and other representations of that kind. In 1759 he published an edition of *Walton* and *Cotton's* " Complete Angler," which in 1760 drew on a most violent controversy between him and Sir *John Hawkins*, on the latter then publishing an improved edition of the same work. A third edition of the " *Sunday* Thoughts" appeared in 1781.

* Whose family name of *Manners*, Mr. *Peck* observes, is derived from Dominus de *Maneriis* ; no less than 24 manors belonging to the Duke being to be seen from *Belvoir-Castle* ; with *Croxton Park-house*, a seat built by the Duke ; and two other seats and four manors which his Grace acquired by marriage.

† The greater part of Mr. *Peck's* MSS. (as has been already said) became the property of this worthy Baronet. Among others, he purchased five volumes in quarto, fairly transcribed for the press in Mr. *Peck's* own neat hand, under the title of " Monasticon *Anglicanum*, Supplementis novis ad- " auctum : quo comprehenditur Arboris *Præmonstratensis* Ramus *Anglicanus*, per omnia triginta & " unum *Angliæ Walhæque* ejusdem Ordinis Cœnobia; e Chronicis, Registris, Cartis, aliisque " Testimoniis antiquis MSS. & autenticis, ad ipsa Monasteria olim pertinentibus, & hactenus " ineditis, sive imperfecte & mendose perquam editis, abunde illustratus. Cujus pars I. Generalia ; " II. Specialia ; III. Cœnobii *Croxtoniensis* Librum de Domesday continet ; omnia *Latina*, *Gallica*, " *Anglica*, ad eorum Exemplaria literatim expressa. Opera & Studio *F. P. A. M.* Ære incisa ad- " duntur aliquot Insignia, Sigilla, Monumenta, & Ædificiorum Reliquiæ." These volumes were on the 14th of *May*, 1779, presented to *The British Museum*, by the last Sir *Thomas Cave*, after the death of his father, who 10 years before had it in contemplation to bestow them on that excellent repository. They are a most valuable and almost inestimable collection. If the gentlemen at *Rome*, who have been some years composing the History of the *Præmonstratenses*, knew of them, doubtless they would consult and insert them, having made great enquiries after them many years ago. It is hoped some

5

J' industrious

" or, a Collection of divers scarce and curious Pieces relating chiefly to Matters of *Eng-*
" *lish* History; consisting of choice Tracts, Memoirs, Letters, Wills, Epitaphs, &c.
" Transcribed, many of them, from the Originals themselves, and the rest from divers
" ancient MS. Copies, or the MS. Collations of sundry famous Antiquaries and other
" eminent Persons, both of the last and present age: The whole, as nearly as possible,
" digested into Order of Time, and illustrated with ample Notes, Contents, Addi-
" tional Discourses, and a complete Index." This volume was dedicated to Lord *Wil-*
liam Manners; and was followed in 1735 by a second volume, dedicated to Dr. *Reynolds*
Bishop of *Lincoln*. Being grown scarce and high-priced, both volumes were re-printed
in one volume 4to, by subscription, by *Thomas Evans*, bookseller, 1779. In 1735 Mr.
Peck printed, in a 4to pamphlet, " A complete Catalogue of all the Discourses
" written both for and against Popery, in the time of King *James* the second;
" containing in the whole an account of four hundred and fifty-seven Books and
" Pamphlets, a great number of them not mentioned in the three former Cata-
" logues; with references after each Title, for the more speedy finding a further
" Account of the said Discourses and their Authors in sundry Writers, and an Alpha-
" betical List of the Writers on each side." In 1739 he was the Editor of " Nineteen
" Letters of the truly reverend and learned *Henry Hammond*, D. D. (Author of the
" Annotations on the New Testament, &c.) written to Mr. *Peter Stainnough* and Dr.
" *Nathaniel Angelo*, many of them on curious subjects, &c." These were printed from
the originals, communicated by Mr. *Robert Marsden*, archdeacon of *Nottingham*, and
Mr. *John Worthington*. The next year, 1740, produced two volumes in 4to, one of
them intituled, " Memoirs of the Life and Actions of *Oliver Cromwell*, as delivered in
" three Panegyrics of him written in *Latin*; the first, as said by Don *Juan Roderiguez*
" *de Saa Meneses, Conde de Penguiao*, the *Portugal* Ambassador; the second, as af-
" firmed by a certain Jesuit, the Lord Ambassador's Chaplain; yet both, it is thought,
" composed by Mr. *John Milton* (*Latin* secretary to *Cromwell*), as was the third: with
" an *English* Version of each. The whole illustrated with a large Historical Preface;
" many similar Passages from the Paradise Lost, and other Works of Mr. *John Milton*,
" and Notes from the best Historians. To all which is added, a Collection of divers cu-
" rious historical Pieces relating to *Cromwell*, and a great number of other remarkable
" Persons (after the Manner of *Desiderata Curiosa*, Vol. I. and II.)" The other, " New
" Memoirs of the Life and Poetical Works of Mr. *John Milton*; with, first, An Exa-
" mination of *Milton's* Style; and secondly, Explanatory and Critical Notes on divers
" Passages in *Milton* and *Shakespeare*, by the Editor. Thirdly, *Baptistes*; a sacred
" dramatic Poem in defence of Liberty, as written in *Latin* by Mr. *George Buchanan*,

industrious Antiquary will get permission to transcribe and print them. One small memorandum,
from the beginning of the fifth volume, I will present to my readers as a literary anecdote: After
an extract from " The History of the Church of *Ripon* by Sir *Thomas Herbert*," penes *Roger Gale*,
Esq; 1732, p. ult. (which I shall not repeat, as it has since been printed in *Drake's Eboracum*, Append.
p. xci). Mr. *Peck* has added, " In the same page it is said, the same Sir *Thomas Herbert* did also write
" the History of three other Cathedrals, *viz. York, Beverley*, and *Southwell*.—Upon reading which, and
" comparing Sir *Thomas Herbert's* MS. History of *Ripon* with Sir *William Dugdale's* printed History
" of that Church, as also a MS. account of *Beverley* Church, (lent me, with the former, by *Roger*
" *Gale*, Esq;) I could not forbear writing in my printed copy of Sir *William Dugdale's* History of the
" Northern Cathedrals, *London*, 1716, this note :—The following History of the Cathedral Church
" of *York*, and of the Collegiate Churches of *Ripon, Southwell*, and *Beverley*, were chiefly wrote by
" Sir *Thomas Herbert*, as I find by a MS. now in the hands of *Roger Gale*, Esq; And for this reason
" I question whether the said Sir *William* wrote even the following accounts of *Durham* and *Carlisle*.
" For he, who could defraud Sir *Thomas Herbert* of his due honour for writing the first four, might,
" for aught I know, as well rob somebody else of the credit of the other two.
" FRANCIS PECK, *Stanfordiensis*, 16 *Nov.* 1732."

" translated

" tranflated into *Englifh* by Mr. *John Milton*, and firft publifhed in 1641, by order of
" the Houfe of Commons. Fourthly, The Parallel, or Archbifhop *Laud* and Cardinal
" *Wolfey* compared, a Vifion, by *Milton*. Fifthly, The Legend of Sir *Nicholas Throck-*
" *morton*, knt. Chief Butler of *England*, who died of Poifon, anno 1570, an hiftorical
" Poem, by his Nephew Sir *Thomas Throckmorton*, knt. Sixth, *Herod* the Great, by
" the Editor. Seventh, The Refurrection, a Poem, in imitation of *Milton*, by a Friend.
" And eighth, A Difcourfe on the Harmony of the Spheres, by *Milton*; with Prefaces,
" and Notes." Thefe were the laft publications which he gave the world. When
thefe appeared, he had in contemplation no lefs than nine different works * ; but
whether he had not met with encouragement for thofe which he had already produced,
or whether he was rendered incapable of executing them by reafon of his declining
health, is uncertain : none of them, however, ever were made public. He concluded a
laborious, and, it may be affirmed, an ufeful life, wholly devoted to antiquarian purfuits,
Auguft 13, 1743, at the age of 61 years. There is a portrait of him prefixed to the
fecond edition of his " *Defiderata Curiofa*," infcribed, " *Francis Peck*, A. M. natus
" *Stanfordiæ*, 4 *Maii*, MDCXCII."

P. 357. line laft of note ‡, for the fecond " 1772," read " 1773."

P. 363. note, Place the reference ‡ at " to print other works," in l. 18.

P. 364. The Earl of *Macclesfield* was removed from the office of lord high chancellor
Jan. 4, 1724-5.

P. 379. One article of the charge on the tutor's bills is for *Income*; which, I now
find, is a fum of money allowed for college chambers to the former occupier, in confideration of repairs or fitting up, and is frequently transferred from one tenant to another in fucceffion, a tenant being anfwerable to a perfon fo repairing or fitting up at
two or three removes.

P. 382. Mr. *Bowyer's* zeal for his friend drew from him, in *The St. James's Chronicle*,
a fort of challenge to the Reviewers, dated *Oct.* 8, 1767 ; and as it contains at the
fame time a defence of another refpectable author, the reader will excufe my inferting
it at large in a note †.

P. 385.

* As the materials for the feveral volumes whofe publication he meditated may be ftill exifting,
and fome of them not unworthy the public attention, the following lift of them is given from an
advertifement at the end of the Memoirs of *Cromwell*. 1. " *Defiderata Curiofa*," vol. III. 2.
" The Annals of *Stanford* continued," vol. IV. 3. " The Hiftory and Antiquities of the Town and
" Soke of *Grantham*, in *Lincolnfhire*." 4. " The Natural Hiftory and Antiquities of *Rutland*." 5.
" The Natural Hiftory and Antiquities of *Leicefterfhire*." 6. " The Life of Mr. *Nicholas Ferrar*,
" of *Little Gidding*, in the county of *Huntingdon*, Gent. commonly called the Proteftant *St. Ni-*
" *cholas*, and the pious Mr. *George Herbert's* Spiritual Brother, done from original MSS." 7.
" The Lives of *William Burton*, Efq; Author of the Antiquities of *Leicefterfhire*, and his Brother
" *Robert Burton*, B. D. Student of *Chrift* Church, and Rector of *Segrave* in *Leicefterfhire*, better
" known by the name of *Democritus* Jun." 8. *Monafticon Anglicanum, Volumen Quartum*, all from
" Originals never yet publifhed." [This is part of the work mentioned above as preferved in *The
Britifh Mufeum*.] 9. " New Memoirs of the Reftoration of King *Charles* the Second (which may
" be alfo confidered as an Appendix to Secretary *Thurloe's* Papers) containing the Copies of Two
" Hundred and Forty-fix Original Letters and Papers, all written *annis* 1658, 1659, and 1660,
" (none of them ever yet printed). The whole communicated by *William Cowper*, Efq; Clerk of
" the Parliament."

† " I have often been amazed at the fuperiority the Critical Reviewers affume over the works
" of the Learned, often when they mifunderftand them, always when they mifunderftand themfelves.
" We have an inftance of this in their account of Mr. *Bryant's* Obfervations, &c. for the month of
" *July*. That very refpectable author has demonftrably fhewn that the *Malta* where *St. Paul* was
" fhipwrecked was not the *Malta* in the *Mediterranean Sea* againft *Africa*, but the *Malta* in the
" *Illyrian Gulf*; 1, becaufe, *Acts* xxvii. 27, it is faid to have been in the *Adria*. Now the name of
" the

P. 387. note †, read, " In *May* 1740."

P. 388. Dr. *Parsons* gave an Account of the Earthquakes in 1750, Phil. Tranf. Nº 497. p. 631.

P. 389. note ‡, " Some Account of the Animal, &c. in *The Tower*," &c. vol. LI. p. 648.

Ibid. note **, read, " Remarks upon a petrified Echinus of a fingular kind, fhewn to " the Royal Society, *April* 24, 1755, by the Reverend *Richard Pococke*, LL. D. archdeacon " of *Dublin*, and F. R. S. found on *Bunnan's* Land, in the Parifh of *Bovingdon*, in *Hert-* " *fordfhire*, which is a clay, and fuppofed to have been brought with the chalk dug out " of a pit in the Field. Phil. Tranf. vol. XLIX. part I. p. 155."

P. 393. Dr. *King* *, late principal of *St. Mary Hall* in *Oxford*, informed Dr. *Warton*,
" that

" the *Adriatic Sea* was not attributed to the fea fo low as the *The Mediterranean*, but was appropri-" ated to that fea within the *Illyrian Gulf*. This is fufficient to decide the controverfy : But, 2, " The inhabitants of this ifland are called *Barbari*, a character that ill-fuited thofe of *Melita Afri-* " *cana*, who, as *Thucydides* obferves, were of *Phœnician* original, and were famous for all forts of " artificers and linen manufacture ; but it every way correfponded with the *Illyrian Melitæans*, who, " by *Diodorus Siculus*, are exprefsly defcribed under that title. 3. *St. Paul* fays, they were to be " fhipwrecked on an ifland out of their deftined courfe, but the *African Malta* was directly in their " way. 4. Mr. *Bryant* obferves, modern travellers report of the *African Malta*, that it harbours no " ferpents ; a bleffing, we are told, bequeathed to the ifland by *St. Paul* at his departure. If this be " true, fays he, what they bring as a teft of the Apoftle having been on this ifland, is a proof that " he never was there. As there are no ferpents now in it, my conclufion is, that there never were " any ; it being owing not to *St. Paul's* grace, but to the nature of the ifland, which cannot give " them fhelter ; for it confifts of a foft white rock, with very little earth. What *If. Voffius* fays of " *Galata*, is true of the *African Malta* ; the fame caufe producing the fame effects. This is clear ; " but Mr. Reviewer ' thinks the inference is not quite conclufive. *Great Britain* was once over-" run with wolves, and part of it with wild-boars ; and he believes it would be as impoffible at this " time to produce a *Britifh* wolf, or wild-boar, as a *Maltefe* viper :' Perhaps fo ; from artificial " caufes thofe animals have been exterminated out of *Britain* : will Mr. Reviewer therefore con-" clude, they could not live here from natural caufes, upon which Mr. *Bryant's* argument is " founded ? But the Reviewer proceeds, ' Setting afide all confideration of the fact, whether [the " *African*] *Malta* does or does not produce ferpents, we are ftrongly of opinion, that Mr. *Bryant's* " fuppofition, that it did never produce them, is exprefsly confuted by the words of the apoftle's " own narrative, fuppofing [the *Illyrian*] *Malta* to be the place where he landed. Nay, it appears " as if vipers had been very frequent among thofe barbarians [the *African Maltefe*]. Had it been " otherwife, how did they know that the animal which faftened upon *St. Paul's* hand was a ferpent ? " How were they fenfible that the effect of a ferpent's bite was to make the party fwell, and fall " down fuddenly ? And why were they furprized that the apoftle received no harm ?' Snap, fays " the argument. The Reviewer has here put the circumftance of the cheat upon himfelf, and his " readers of the fame fize. He has transferred the circumftance of the ifland's not producing fer-" pents from the *African Malta*, where, for that reafon, Mr. *Bryant* contends *St. Paul* did not land, " to the *Illyrian Malta*, where, for that reafon, he fuppofes he did land. Thus the abfurdity is all " the Reviewer's own. I know not perfonally Mr. *Bryant*, or the Reviewer † ; but thought it a piece " of juftice to vindicate fo mafterly a writer from the mif-reprefentations of thofe who with fo ill a " grace hold the balance of literature. I fear for another learned work [Mr. *Clarke's*], which, " though publifhed, I think, this half-year, the Reviewers have not touched yet ; for prudential " reafons, no doubt !''

* Dr. *William King*, fon of the Rev. *Peregrine King*, was born at *Stepney* in *Middlefex* in 1685 ; and, after a fchool education at *Salifbury*, was entered of *Baliol College*, *Oxford*, *July* 9, 1701. Proceeding on the law line, he took his doctor's degree in 1715 ; was fecretary to the Duke of *Ormond* and the Earl of *Arran*, when chancellors of the univerfity ; and was made principal of *St. Mary Hall* in 1718. When he was candidate for the univerfity, in 1722, he refigned his office of fecretary ; but his other preferment he enjoyed (and it was all he did enjoy) to the time of his death. Dr. *Clarke*, who oppofed him, carried his election ; and after this difappointment, in the

† Who, I am well informed, was the late Mr. *Guthrie*.

year

that *Hooke's* Translation of the Travels of *Cyrus* was made at Dr. *Cheyne's* house at *Bath*, and that he himself had often been *Hooke's* amanuensis on the occasion, who dictated his translation to him with uncommon facility and rapidity. The Dutchess of *Marlborough* rewarded *Hooke* with 5000*l.* for his trouble in writing her " Account ;" but quarrelled with him afterwards, because, as she affirmed, he attempted to convert her to Popery. *Hooke* was a Myſtic, and a Quietiſt, and a warm diſciple of *Fenelon.* It was he who

year 1727, he went over to *Ireland,* where he wrote " The Toaſt," a celebrated political ſatire, which was printed and given to his friends *. On the dedication of the *Radcliffe* Library, 1749, he ſpoke a *Latin* oration in the theatre, which was received with the higheſt acclamations, and for which Mr. *Warton* pays him an elegant compliment in " The Triumphs of *Iſis.*" In 1755, when the memorable conteſt happened in *Oxfordſhire,* his attachment to the old intereſt drew on him the reſentment of the new. He was libelled in news-papers and pamphlets, and charged with the following particulars, *viz.* That he was an *Iriſhman*; that he had received ſubſcriptions for books never publiſhed to the amount of fifteen hundred pounds, of which ſum he had defrauded his ſubſcribers; that he had offered himſelf to ſale both in *England* and *Ireland,* and was not found worth the purchaſe; that he was the writer of *The London Evening Poſt* ; the author of a book in queen *Anne's* reign, intituled, " Political Conſiderations, 1710," in which there was falſe *Engliſh*; and of a book then juſt publiſhed, called, " The Dreamer, 1754." At this time he publiſhed his apology in quarto. and very clearly vindicated himſelf from the ſeveral matters charged on him, except only the laſt article, of his being author of " The Dreamer ;" and warmly retaliated on his adverſaries.—Mr. *Cole* had often ſeen him at *St. Mary's* church, *Cambridge,* when he uſed to be on a viſit to Mr. *Mackenzie,* who married Mr. *Chambers* the town-clerk's daughter. He was a tall, lean, well-looking man. Beſides ſeveral curious works of his own †, he publiſhed the five laſt volumes of Dr. *South's* Sermons.—He was known and eſteemed by the firſt men of his time for wit and learning; and muſt be allowed to have been a polite ſcholar, an excellent orator, and an elegant and eaſy writer both in *Latin* and *Engliſh.* Mr. *Cole* was informed that he lies buried in *Ealing* church, as lord of the manor, or leſſee of the great tithes. There is no monument or epitaph for him; but the Doctor himſelf, not long before his death, which happened *Dec.* 30, 1763, drew up the following very curious one in order to be engraved on a ſilver caſe, in which he directed his heart ſhould be preſerved, in ſome convenient part of *St. Mary Hall*:

Epitaphium GUILIELMI KING,
*A ſeipſo ſcriptum pridie nonas Junii,
Die natali Georgii* III. MDCCLXII.
" Fui
GUILIELMUS KING, LL. D.
Ab anno MDCCXIX. ad annum MDCC—.
Hujus Aulæ Præfectus.
Literis humanioribus à puero deditus.
Eas uſque ad ſupremum vitæ diem colui.
Neque vitiis carui, neque virtutibus;
Imprudens et improvidus, comis et benevolus ;
Sæpe æquo iracundior,
Haud unquam ut eſſem implacabilis.
A luxuriâ pariter ac avaritiâ
(Quam non tam vitium
Quàm mentis inſanitatem eſſe duxi)
Prorſus abhorrens.
Cives, hoſpites, peregrinos
Omnino liberaliter accepi
Ipſe et cibi parcus, et vini parciſſimus.

Cum magnis vixi, cum plebeiis, cum omnibus,
Ut homines noſcerem, ut me ipſum inprimis :
Neque, eheu, novi !
Permultos habui amicos,
At veros, ſtabiles, gratos,
(Quæ fortaſſe eſt gentis culpa)
Perpauciſſimos.
Plures habui inimicos ;
Sed invidos, ſed improbos, ſed inhumanos.
Quorum nullis tamen injuriis
Perinde commotus fui
Quàm deliquiis meis.
Summam, quam adeptus ſum, ſenectutem
Neque optavi, neque accuſavi.
Vitæ incommoda neque immoderatè ferens,
Neque commodis nimium contentus.
Mortem neque contempſi neque metui.
Deus optime,
Qui hunc orbem et humanas res curas,
Miſerere animæ noſtræ !"

There is a ſtriking likeneſs of Dr. *King* in *Worlidge's* View of the Inſtallation of Lord *Weſtmoreland* as Chancellor of *Oxford* in 1761.

* It now ſells for an extravagant price; and has been re-printed, but without (one of its principal beauties) the notes and obſervations, in *Wilkes's* " New Foundling Hoſpital of Wit."
† Among theſe are, 1. *Miltoni* Epiſtola ad *Pollionem* (Lord *Polwarth*); 2. Sermo Pedeſtris; 3. Scamnum, Ecloga; 4. Templum Libertatis, in three Books; 5. Tres Oratiunculæ; 6. Epiſtola Objurgatoria; 7. *Antonietti* Ducis *Corſcorum* Epiſtola ad *Corſcos* de rege eligendo; 8. Eulogium *Jacci Etonenſis*; 9. *Aviti* Epiſtola ad *Perillam,* virginem *Scotam,* &c. 9. " Oratiuncula habita in domo Convocationis *Oxon,* cum Epiſtola dedicatoria, 1757." He alſo was the author of " Epitaphium *Richardi Noſh.*"

brought

brought a catholic prieſt to take *Pope's* confeſſion on his death-bed. The prieſt had ſcarcely departed, when *Bolingbroke*, coming over from *Batterſea*, flew into a great fit of paſſion and indignation on the occaſion. Eſſay on *Pope*, vol. II. p. 201, 202. See another circumſtance of Mr. *Hooke* in the ſub-note, p. 599.

P. 397. I have alſo an " Apology for ſome of Mr. *Hooke's* Obſervations, &c. concern-" ing the *Roman* Senate, &c. in anſwer to a Short Review, &c." by Mr. *Bowyer*, which ſhall be printed among his " Tracts."

P. 398. Mr. *Julius Bate* was an intimate friend of the celebrated *Hutchinſon* (as we learn from Mr. *Spearman's* Life of that remarkable author) ; by whoſe recommendation he obtained from *Charles* duke of *Somerſet* a preſentation to the living of *Sutton* in *Suſſex*, near his Grace's ſeat at *Petworth*. His publications were, 1. " An " Eſſay towards explaining the Firſt Chapter of *Geneſis*, in Anſwer to Mr. *War-*" *burton ⁎*, 1741," 8vo. 2. " The Philoſophical Principles of *Moſes* aſſerted and " defended againſt the Miſrepreſentations of Mr. *David Jennings*, 1744," 8vo. 3. " Remarks upon Mr. *Warburton's* Remarks, ſhewing, that the Ancients knew " there was a Future State, and that the *Jews* were not under an equal Pro-" vidence, 1745;" 8vo. 4. " The Faith of the Ancient *Jews* in the Law of *Moſes* " and the Evidence of the Types, vindicated in a Letter to Dr. *Stebbing*, 1747." 8vo. 5. " *Micah* v. 2. and *Matthew* ii. 6. reconciled, 1749," 8vo. 6. " An " *Hebrew* Grammar, formed on the Uſage of the Words by the Inſpired Writers, 1750," 8vo. 7. " The Uſe and Intent of Prophecy and Hiſtory of the Fall cleared, 1750," 8vo. This was occaſioned by *Middleton's* Examination of *Sherlock*. 8. " The Bleſſing " of *Judah* and *Jacob* conſidered ; and the Æra of *Daniel's* Weeks aſcertained, in two " Diſſertations, 1753," 8vo. 9. " The Integrity of the *Hebrew* Text and many Paſ-" ſages of Scripture vindicated from the Objections and Miſconſtructions of Mr. *Ken-*" *nicott*, 1755," 8vo. 10. " A Reply to Dr. *Sharp's* Review and Defence of his Diſſer-" tations on the Scripture meaning of *Eloim* and *Berith*, 1755," 8vo. 11. " A Reply " to Dr. *Sharp's* Review and Defence of his Diſſertation on the Scripture-meaning of " *Berith*. With an Appendix in Anſwer to the Doctor's Diſcourſe on *Cherubim*, Part II. " 1755," 8vo. 12. " Remarks upon Dr. *Benſon's* Sermon on the Goſpel Method of " Juſtification, 1755," 8vo. 13. " *Critica Hebræa*, or a *Hebrew-Engliſh* Dictionary " without Points, &c. (as in p. 398), 1767," 4to. 14. " A new and literal Tranſlation " from the original *Hebrew* of the Pentateuch of *Moſes*, and of the Hiſtorical Books " of the Old Teſtament, to the End of the Second Book of *Kings* ; with Notes Critical " and Explanatory, 1773," 4to.—Mr. *Bate* attended *Hutchinſon* in his laſt illneſs (1737), and was by him in a moſt ſtriking manner recommended to the protection of an intimate friend, " with a ſtrict charge not to ſuffer his labours to become uſeleſs by " neglect." It having been reported that *Hutchinſon* had recanted the publication of his writings to Dr. *Mead* a little before his death; that circumſtance was flatly contradicted by a letter from Mr. *Bate* †, dated *Arundel*, *Jan.* 20, 1759. This learned writer died *April* 7, 1771.

P. 400.

⁎ In the Preface to the Divine Legation, 1740, " one *Julius Bate*" is accuſed, " in conjunction " with one *Romaine*, of betraying converſation, and writing fictitious letters."

† Printed in *Spearman's* Life of *Hutchinſon*, p. xiii.—One ſhort paſſage from it I am tempted to tranſcribe : " I was with Mr. *Hutchinſon* all the illneſs that robbed us of that invaluable life, and " am poſitive Dr. *Mead* was never with him but when I was by, and it was but a few hours day " or night that I was from him. Mr. *Hutchinſon* had not been long ill, when he took a diſguſt to " Dr. *Mead*, and forbad his farther attendance ; which the Doctor much wondered at, and ſeemed " greatly to reſent. *Lucas*, myſelf, and ſomebody elſe, I forget who, were ſtanding by the bed-ſide

P. 400. There is a good portrait of Mr. *Ferguson*, from a painting by *J. Townshend*, inscribed, " *James Ferguson*, F. R. S. Published *Dec.*7, 1776." His son was a surgeon, and attempted to settle at *Bury*, stayed but a little while, went to sea, was cast away, and lost his all a little before the father's death, but finds himself in no bad plight since.

P. 405. The " Memoirs of Mr. *Hollis*" were printed in two splendid volumes, in 4to, 1780, with a considerable number of capital plates by *Bartolozzi, Basire*, and other engravers of eminence. In the frontispiece is introduced an admirable profile of Mr. *Hollis*.

P. 408. note, l. 9, 10. read, " young noblemen and gentlemen."

P. 409. note, l. 7. Since this page was printed, I have been referred to *The Tatler*, N° 155, where an upholsterer (the original of *Murphy's Quidnunc*) is thus described. It may also be observed, that the portrait of Mr. *Adam Drummond* the banker is represented with the same peculiarity.—" A leather garter is called a decent ornament in " the Spectator, N° 596. I have lately read the Tatler and Spectator over carefully ; and " the variations in dress then and now are remarkable. In this instance, one can hardly " help smiling to hear the Spectator gravely mentioning a mode *as decent*, which now " would be thought below the notice of any body a degree above a drill-serjeant." *T. F.*

P. 411. No greater proof of Dr. *Borlase's* merit need be given, than that he lived to see a second edition of his *Cornish* Antiquities, and almost of his Natural History. Few ever treated both subjects so well, and so much at large ; none was so favourably received.

P. 412. note ‡, l. penult. read, " could not but be," &c.

P. 414. Mr. *H. Baker* was early introduced into the family of Mr. *Foster*, an eminent attorney (father of the late Serjeant *Foster*), who had two daughters and a younger son born deaf and dumb. Mr. *Baker's* happy method of instruction (for which, if we are not mis-informed, he received 100l. a year), succeeded so well, that the young ladies were qualified in all the parts of female education ; and, besides the advantage of good persons, possessed understandings as improved as could possibly be under the want of two such essential faculties, and the talent of elegant letter-writing, and every domestic accomplishment. Mr. *Baker* taught them also astronomy and geography ; and they were so capable of the politer instructions, that they appeared with advantage in public assemblies. They are still, we believe, living at *Peterborough*. Whether their younger brother came under Mr. *Baker's* tuition, does not appear. Their elder brother was bred to the church. The serjeant died, leaving, by a daughter of the late Sir *John Strange*, master of the rolls, one daughter, who survives him.

P. 416. Mr. *H. Baker*, by his method of taking off impressions of medals in paper, cards, wax, &c. by a hand-press, preserved a beautiful gold medallion, having on one side the head of *J. Cæsar*, laureate, with the lituus behind and before DIVI IVLI ; and on the reverse the head of *Agrippa* with a naval crown, M. AGRIPPA. L. F. COS. III. worth full 12 guineas, its relief high and noble. It belonged to Sir *John Wolstenholme*, from whom it came to his sister Mrs. *Wolstenholme* of *Enfield*, who lent it to Mr. *Baker*, who had no doubt of its genuineness. His impression of it is in a volume of Tracts (N° 1. [II.]) in the Library of the Society of Antiquaries.

Ibid. l. 21. See verses " to the Rev. Mr. *Clendon*, of *Sutton*, near *Maidstone*, on his " advertizing to cure Deafness and the King's-Evil." Gent. Mag. 1754. pp. 562. 614.

" one day, when Dr. *Mead* came in, and I believe it was the last time he was up stairs. ' Mr. *Hut-* " *chinson*,' says the Doctor, among other things, ' I cannot help looking upon you as one of the old " Prophets, with his Disciples standing about him with concern and attention in their faces, catch- " ing up the golden words as they drop,' or to that effect.—' Doctor,' says Mr. *Hutchinson*, ' if I am " a Prophet, what are you ? I have given you such evidence ;—look to it before it is too late.'"

P. 417.

P. 417. note, l. 32. read, " MAXOIMHN.

P. 419. Among the books of 1770 add, " Confpectus novæ editionis Hiſtoricorum
" veterum *Latinorum* qui extant omnium, ita diſponendæ, ut, pro ordine temporum,
" & rerum ſerie, integrum corpus componat Hiſtoriæ Sacræ & Orientalis, Fabuloſæ &
" Heroicæ, *Græcæ* & *Romanæ*, ab. orbe condito, ad excidium Imperii Occidentalis et
" initia Regni *Italici*. Cum ſingulorum Scriptorum Hiſtoria literaria, & Annotationibus
" Philologicis *Anglicè* conſcriptis; adjectis Nummis, Tabuliſque Chronologicis & Geo-
" graphicis," 4to. This comprehenſive plan, in which, from its magnitude, no bookſeller dared venture to engage, was projected by the very learned Dr. *Apthorp*, rector of
Bow, and vicar of *Croydon*, whoſe name may now be added to the reſpectable liſt of
preachers in p. 440.

. P. 422. note, l. 2. read, " 1781."

Ibid. note, A fine mezzotinto portrait of Dr. *Aſhton*, ſcraped by *Spilſbury* from a
painting by Sir *Joſhua Reynolds*, is prefixed to his Sermons, with this motto, " Inſto
" præpoſitis, oblitus præteritorum."—His ſon, *Thomas Aſhton*, Eſq; of *The Middle Temple*, died at *Briſtol, Dec.* 8, 1781, aged 19.

P. 425. " Mr. *H. Fox's* character may be given in few words : He ſet out in life an
" ambitious man ; he ended a moſt avaricious one." *T. F.*

P. 426. l. 3, 4. read, " on the Buildings and Improvements of *London*," with a caricature print of the Duke of *Cumberland's* ſtatue in *Cavendiſh-Square*.

P. 427. " A lady told me, that ſhe ſaw *Hagley-Houſe* laſt ſummer [1781], and was ſur-
" prized, after paſſing through many fine rooms, to find herſelf in a very ordinary bed-
" chamber ; and more ſo to hear the maid tell her, with tears in her eyes, that in
" that room, his conſtant one, his Lordſhip died." *T. F.*

P. 428. note, The very learned Biſhop *Lowth*, after conſidering the queſtion with
attention, has pronounced the poetry of the *Hebrews* to be perfectly irrecoverable.

P. 429. " It is a melancholy conſideration, that a young man from the foundation of
" *Weſtminſter*, who could publiſh *Tully's* Offices, muſt have a patron, to aſk the Maſter of
" *Trinity* (himſelf the firſt of ſcholars in the ſame line) that he may be a Fellow. Dr.
" *Pearce* was remarkably lucky in the choice of the two Authors he publiſhed, as their
" elegance and merit contributed greatly to the fame of their Editor." *T. F.*

P. 430. Four volumes of Biſhop *Pearce's* Sermons have been alſo publiſhed ſince
his death, 1778, 8vo, by his executor Mr. *Derby* *, who had married the Biſhop's niece.—
There is a mezzotinto portrait of him, when Biſhop of *Bangor*, " *J. Hudſon pinx*. 1754.
" *J. Faber fecit*;" an engraving of him is prefixed to his works ; and a fine buſt in
white marble, eſteemed a ſtriking likeneſs, is placed on his monument in *Weſtminſter-
Abbey*, which is thus inſcribed :

" M. S.	Teſtabuntur et mox edenda.
Viri admodum Reverendi	Seceſſûs, tandem, ac otii impensè cupidus,
ZACHARIÆ PEARCE, S. T. P.	Quò ſacris literis elucidandis vacaret,
Epiſcopi *Roffenſis*,	Decanatum hunc abdicavit,
Hujuſque Eccleſiæ Collegiatæ	Epiſcopatum, inſuper, modò licuiſſet, .
Necnon Honoratiſſimi Ordinis de Balneo Decani ;	Abdicaturus,
Pueritiâ in Scholâ *Weſtmonaſterienſi* bene acta,	Abſoluto, demùm, quod præcipuè in votis erat,
Uberiorem ſcientiæ fructum	In Sacroſancta Evangelia, et Acta Apoſtolorum,
Apud *Cantabrigienſes* collegit.	Limatiſſimo Commentario,
Quantus indè et Criticus prodiit, et Theologus,	A laboribus requievit
Teſtantur ſcripta ipſius jamdudum edita,	XXIX *Junii*, A. D. MDCCLXXIV. ætat. LXXXIV."

* *John Derby*, M. A. rector of *Southſleet* and *Longfield* in *Kent*; and one of the ſix preachers in
Canterbury Cathedral. He died *Oct.* 6, 1778 ; only five days after the date of his dedication to the
Biſhop's Sermons.

3

Bishop *Pearce* spent the part of the year, he did not reside at *Bromley*, in his paternal house at *Ealing*, where he was well respected. On the east-wall of the north aisle at *Ealing*, on a neat mural monument of white marble, is this inscription to the memory of his Lordship's father, who was in the distilling-business:

" To the memory of
THOMAS PEARCE,
of *Little Ealing*, Esq;
who lieth buried in the middle aisle of this
Church.
During forty years he was a constant

Inhabitant of this parish,
to which he retired from business.
He died on *August* 14, 1752,
aged 85 years,
having the character (which he well deserved) of
an honest man and a sincere Christian."

And at bottom Erm. in Chief, 3 Bees, a Lion rampant, Gules.

Mrs. *Pearce* died at *Bromley October* 23, 1773. Soon after her death the bishop gave 5000*l.* to *Bromley* college, to augment the stipend of the widows. He died at *Ealing*, and left legacies to the amount of 15,000*l.* to *Westminster Hospital*, Society for propagating the Gospel, Poor of *Ealing*, *Rochester*, and *Bangor*; 20*l. per annum* to each servant living with him at his death; and his valuable library to the College at *Westminster*.—" It was singular enough in Bishop *Pearce*, because the bishoprick was trouble-
" some and interrupted his studies, to resign the deanry, which did neither. He
" would have done more to the purpose, when he tried to get rid of this hindrance, if he
" could have got rid of old age, which was the most troublesome obstacle. The Bishop
" had probably in his life-time the full quantity of fame that he deserved as a writer.
" Dr. *Berkeley*, Bishop of *Cloyne*, pressed much for leave to resign; but I always under-
" stood that the difficulty was how to dispose of his right of acting as a Lord of Parlia-
" ment. But it seems that in this case Lord *Mansfield*, and even Lord *Northington*,
" saw no difficulty, or got over it. Among the Papists there is no difficulty; their
" bishops are not Lords of Parliament; and when they have a mind to resign, the
" Pope translates them to a bishoprick *in partibus infidelium*, which serves to preserve
" title and rank. Whether this was done in the case of Bishop *Huet* I do not stay to
" examine; I think he always writes himself *Ancien Eveque d'Avranches*. We have had
" several resignations of bishopricks in *Ireland* and *England*. Whether any of them since
" Popery was abolished, I cannot say *; but the question deserves disquisition." *T. F.*

P. 432. Mr. *Weston* was succeeded in the vicarage of *Campden* by his son, the now vicar; both from the gift of the Earl of *Gainsborough*.

P. 441. note, l. 11. The Lecture on Prophecy (as has been mentioned in p. 597), is resumed by Dr. *Apthorp*; and another of the learned Lecturers has been deservedly honoured with a mitre †.—A translation of the " Divine Legation" was published at *Amsterdam*, in 1771, by *Abr. Ar. Vander Meersch*, whose dedication to Bishop *Warburton* is printed in Gent. Mag. 1772, p. 266.—It may hardly be worth mentioning, that the learned *Blackwell*, in his Mythology, speaks of Dr. *Warburton* as a mere Antiquary; but Dr. *Johnson's* character of this literary *Colossus* is too remarkable to be omitted ‡.—The following

* *Miles Coverdale*, Bishop of *Exeter*, was deprived of his bishoprick by Queen *Mary*; and after her death refused to accept it again, but lived privately to the age of 81.

† Dr. *Bagot*, Dean of *Christ Church*, was recommended by the King to the See of *Bristol*, Feb. 23, 1782; and elected Bishop in *March*.

‡ " About this time [1738] *Warburton* began to make his appearance in the first ranks of learn-
" ing. He was a man of vigorous faculties, a mind fervid and vehement, supplied by incessant and
" unlimited enquiry, with wonderful extent and variety of knowledge, which yet had not oppressed
" his imagination, nor clouded his perspicacity. To every work he brought a memory full fraught,
" with a fancy fertile of original combinations; and at once exerted the powers of the scholar, the
" reasoner, and the wit. But his knowledge was too multifarious to be always exact, and his pur-
" suits were too eager to be always cautious. His abilities gave him an haughty confidence, which
" he disdained to conceal or mollify; and his impatience of opposition disposed him to treat his ad-
" versa

following **extract** from an unpublished letter of Bishop *Warburton* to Dr. *Birch* is equally an honour to them both: "I am very glad you intend to write *Milton's* Life. "Almost all the life-writers we have before *Toland* and *Desmaizeaux* are indeed strange "insipid creatures; and yet I had rather read the worst of them than be obliged to go "through with this of *Milton's*, or the other's Life of *Boileau*, where there is such a "dull, heavy succession of long quotations of uninteresting passages, that it makes their "method quite nauseous. But the verbose, tasteless *Frenchman* seems to lay it down as "a principle, that every life must be a book; for what do we know of *Boileau* after all "this tedious stuff? You are the only one, and I speak it without a compliment, that "by the vigour of your style and sentiments, and the real importance of your materials, "have the art, which one would imagine no one could have missed, of adding *agré-* "*mens* to the most agreeable subject in the world, which is, literary history." It gives me pleasure to close this article by announcing, that a complete and elegant edition of this learned Prelate's writings is intended for the publick by his all-accomplished friend the Bishop of *Worcester*.

P. 442. **To the books of** 1772, add, a beautiful edition of "Poems by *Michael Wod-* "*hull* *, Esq;" 8vo. of which only 150 copies were printed.

P. 447. Since this page was printed, the literary world has lost a valuable member by the death of my good friend Sir *John Pringle*. This excellent physician and philosopher was a younger son of Sir *John Pringle* of *Stitchel*, in the shire of *Roxburgh*, baronet; took the degree of M. D. at *Leyden*, 1730; and published there "Dissertatio Inaugu- "ralis de Marcore Senili," 4to. After having been some years professor of moral phi- losophy at *Edinburgh*, he was in *June* 1745 appointed physician to the duke of *Cumber-* *land*, and physician-general to the hospital of the forces in *Flanders*, where the Earl of

"versaries with such contemptuous superiority as made his readers commonly his enemies, and ex- "cited against him the wishes of some who favoured his cause. He seems to have adopted the *Ro-* "*man* Emperor's determination, *oderint dum metuant*; he used no allurements of gentle language, "but wished to compel rather than persuade. His style is copious without selection, and forcible "without neatness; he took the words that presented themselves: his diction is coarse and impure, "and his sentences are unmeasured. He had, in the early part of his life, pleased himself with the "notice of inferior wits, and corresponded with the enemies of *Pope*. A letter was produced, when "he had perhaps himself forgotten it, in which he tells *Concanen* 'that *Milton* borrowed by affecta- "tion, *Dryden* by idleness, and *Pope* by necessity.' And when *Theobald* published *Shakspeare*, in "opposition to *Pope*, the best notes were supplied by *Warburton*. But the time was now come when "*Warburton* was to change his opinion, and *Pope* was to find a defender in him who had contributed "so much to the exaltation of his rival †. From this time *Pope* lived in the closest intimacy with "his commentator, and amply rewarded his kindness and his zeal; for he introduced him to Mr. "*Murray* (now Earl *Mansfield*), by whose interest he became preacher at *Lincoln's-Inn*, and to Mr. "*Allen*, who gave him his niece and his estate, and by consequence a bishoprick; when he died, he "left him the property of his works; a legacy which may be reasonably estimated at four thousand "pounds."

* Notwithstanding the excellence of Mr. *Potter's* translation of *Euripides*, I may venture to promise much pleasure to the learned world, by mentioning that a complete poetical version of that excellent Tragedian, with critical notes, by Mr. *Wodhull*, in four volumes, 8vo, is in forwardness at the press.

† "Rescuing him," as Dr. *Johnson* expresses it, "from the talons of *Crousaz*.—By a fond and eager accep- "tance of an exculpatory comment, *Pope* testified that, whatever might be the seeming or real import of the "principles which he had received from *Bolingbroke*, he had not intentionally attacked religion; and *Bolingbroke*, "if he meant to make him without his own consent an instrument of mischief, found him now engaged with "his eyes open, on the side of truth. It is known that *Bolingbroke* concealed from *Pope* his real opinions. He "once discovered them to Mr. *Hooke*, who related them again to *Pope*, and was told by him that he must have "mistaken the meaning of what he heard; and *Bolingbroke*, when *Pope's* uneasiness incited him to desire an "explanation, declared that *Hooke* had misunderstood him. *Bolingbroke* hated *Warburton*, who had drawn his "pupil from him; and a little before *Pope's* death they had a dispute, from which they parted with mutual "aversion."—"His Philosopher and Guide," says an amiable living Prelate, "stuck close to him, till another "and higher star had got the ascendant."

Stair

Stair appears to have been his patron. In *February*, 1746, Dr. *Pringle*, Dr. *Armstrong*, and Dr. *Barker*, were nominated physicians to the hospital for lame, maimed, and sick soldiers, behind *Buckingham-house*; and in *April*, 1749, Dr. *Pringle* was appointed physician in ordinary to the King. In 1750 he published " Observations on the Na-
" ture and Cure of Hospital and Gaol Fevers, in a Letter to Dr. *Mead*," 8vo (reprinted in 1755); and in 1752 he favoured the publick with the result of his long experience in an admirable treatise under the title of " Observations on the Disorders of the
" Army in Camp and Garrison *," 8vo. On the 14th of *April*, 1752, he married *Charlotte* second daughter of Dr. *Oliver*, an eminent physician at *Bath*. In 1756 he was appointed jointly with Dr. *Wintringham* (now Sir *Clifton Wintringham*, bart.) physician to the hospital for the service of the forces of *Great-Britain*. After the accession of his present Majesty, Dr. *Pringle* was appointed physician to the queen's houshold, 1761; physician in ordinary to the queen in 1763, in which year he was admitted of the College of Physicians in *London*; and on the 5th of *June*, 1766, he was advanced to the dignity of a baronet of *Great-Britain*. In 1772 he was elected president of the Royal Society, where his speeches for five successive years, on delivering the prize-medal of Sir *Godfrey Copley*, gave the greatest satisfaction †. Sir *John Pringle* in 177 was appointed physician extraordinary to the King. He was also a fellow of the College of Physicians at *Edinburgh*; of the Royal Medical Society at *Paris*, and member of the Royal Academies at *Paris*, *Stockholm*, *Goettingen*, and of the Philosophical Societies at *Edinburgh* and *Harleim*; and continued president of the Royal Society till *November*, 1778; after which period he gradually withdrew from the world, and in 1781 quitted his elegant house in *Pall Mall* (where he had long distinguished himself as the warm friend and patron of literary men of every nation and profession), and made an excursion to his native country. He returned to *London* in the latter end of that year; died greatly beloved and respected *Jan.* 18, 1782; and having no children, was succeeded in estate and also (agreeably to the limitation of the patent) in title, by his nephew, now Sir *James Pringle*, bart. Among this worthy physician's communications to the Royal Society, the following articles have occurred to my researches: 1. " Some Experiments on Substances resisting
" Putrefaction," Phil. Transf. N° 495, p. 580; and N° 496, pp. 525. 550; reprinted, with additions, in *Martin*'s Abridgement, vol. XI. p. 1365. 2. " Account of some Persons
" seized with the Gaol Fever by working in *Newgate*; and of the manner by which the
" Infection was communicated to one entire family," vol. XLVIII. p. 42. At the request of Dr. *Hales*, a copy of this useful paper was inserted in the Gentleman's Magazine, 1753, p. 71, before its appearance in the Transactions. 3. " A remarkable Case of Fra-
" gility, Flexibility, and Dissolution of the Bones," Ib. p. 297. 4. " Account of the Earth-
" quakes felt at *Brussels*," vol. XLIX. p. 546. 5. " Account of sinking of a River near
" *Pontypool*, in *Monmouthshire*," Ib. p. 547. 6. " Account of an Earthquake felt *Feb.*
" 18, 1756, along the Coast of *England*, between *Margate* and *Dover*," Ib. p. 579.
7. " Account of the Earthquake felt at *Glasgow* and *Dumbarton*; also of a Shower
" of Dust falling on a Ship between *Shetland* and *Iceland*," Ib. p. 509. 8. " Se-
" veral Accounts of the Fiery Meteor which appeared on *Sunday*, *Nov.* 26, 1758, be-

---

* These excellent observations have been frequently re-printed in 8vo and 4to. A seventh edition appeared in 1775, 8vo; and an *Italian* translation of them at *Naples*, 1757, 4to.

† The writer of these Anecdotes recollects with pleasure the honour conferred on him by the worthy Baronet, in condescending to submit these speeches to his perusal before they were addressed to the Royal Society. Their titles are, 1. " Discourse on the different Kinds of Air, 1773," 4to; 2. " Discourse on the Torpedo, 1774," 4to. 3. " Discourse on the Attraction of Mountains, 1775," 4to; 4. " Discourse on the Improvements of the Means of the preserving the Health of Mariners, " 1776," 4to. 5. " Discourse on the Theory of Gunnery, 1777," 4to.

" tween

" tween eight and nine at Night," vol. L. p. 218. 9. "Account of the Virtues of " Soap in diffolving the Stone, in the Cafe of the Rev. Mr. *Matthew Simfon*," Ib. p. 221. 10. "Account of the Effects of Electricity in Paralytic Cafes," Ib. p. 481. And fee a letter to him on that fubject from Profeffor *Winthorp.*—"Some Account of the Succefs " of the Vitrum Ceratum Antimonii" was printed in the "*Edinburgh* Medical Effays," vol. V.—In 1773 he took great pains, and was at fome expence, to communicate to the publick a famous tract of *Michaelis*, the learned Profeffor at *Goettingen*, which has been mentioned in p. 447.—Dr. *Theobald*, from whom I have already tranfcribed two elegant Odes, addreffed, in 1753, " Ode, Viro ingenuo pariter, ac docto, *Joanni Pringle*, M. D. " & S. R. S. facra:

" Diva, *Romano* cata temperare	Inclytis nulli viget is fecundus
Barbiton Cantu, O habilis modorum	Laudibus, tu five animum benignum
Artifex, feftis mihi nuper horis	Refpicis, feu quo Medicum refulget
Sæpe vocata !	Clarus Honorem.
Fida *Pringelli* modulos corufco	Concini dignus meliore plectro,
Ede facratos merito, colendi	Fac, ut haud furda hoc bibat aure carmen,
Semper et culti, celebri revincti	Conditum parva licet arte, grato at
Tempore ferto.	Pectore textum."

P. 448. Mr. *Richard Graves* is fon of that eminent antiquary *Richard Graves*[*], Efq; of *Mickleton*, and great-nephew to Profeffor *Graves* of *Oxford*, and to Sir *Edward Graves*, bart. phyfician to *Charles* II. See the pedigree of this family in Dr. *Nafh's Worcefterfhire* Collections, Vol. I. p. 198, where this gentleman's name is omitted.

Ibid. In 1766 Dr. *Knowler* had prepared for the prefs an *Englifh* tranflation [†] of *Chryfoftom's* " Comment on *St. Paul's* Epiftle to the *Galatians*."

P. 453. Since the article of Mr. *De-Miffy* was printed off, I have not only been favoured with feveral corrections [‡], but alfo with an account of that worthy Divine, which, as it almoft wholly fuperfedes what has been already faid, there needs no apology for printing here at full length: it is principally taken from " La Gazette Littéraire de " *Berlin*," for the 19th and 26th of *January*, 1778.

Cæfar De-Miffy, born at *Berlin*, *June* 2, 1703, was eldeft fon of *Charles De-Miffy*, merchant at *Berlin*, native of the province of *Saintonge*, by his wife *Sufanna Godeffroy*, grand-daughter of *John Godeffroy*, Efq; Lord of *Richal*, who was mayor and captain general of the government of *Rochelle*, when befieged by *Lewis* XIII. He ftudied firft

---

[*] Whofe epitaph has been given in p. 502.

[†] I have now before me a preface intended to have been prefixed to this tranflation; in which Dr. *Knowler* introduces this judicious obfervation on the FATHERS : " Some have thought nothing " too much to be faid in their praife ; others have denied them a fhare of common fenfe. The " prefent cry is againft them; and if it continue a few years, they muft be a prey to moths and " worms, to the great detriment of young ftudents in divinity, not to fay to the publick in general. " I think they have not had a fair trial. Their works are locked up in the learned languages; " many pieces have been afcribed to them, which, were they alive, they would difown and be " afhamed of. Hence they are fwoln to an enormous bulk. Then comes an enemy, and culls out " of thefe fpurious pieces exceptionable paffages, produces them before a packed jury; the laugh " goes round, and they are condemned in the lump." The tranflation he reprefents to be " a plain " and literal one ;" and acknowledges that the beauty of *Chryfoftom's* original " muft fuffer greatly " in the garb a country divine has given him, who has refided fix-and-twenty years on his cure, " and feldom been abfent from his parifh." He then proceeds to give a good account of his author; and alfo of *Jerom*, who was contemporary with *Chryfoftom.*

[‡] In the note, l. 4, read, " are tranflated from an advertifement, the amiable effufions," &c.— l. 11, r. " boundaries, without" &c.—l. 12. r. " abated. Supported in," &c.—l. 14. r. " to the " laft with a zeal," &c.—l. 19. Go, and do thou likewife fhould be omitted.—l. 26. r. " the follow- " ing books, and feveral others,"—l. 30. for " befides" r. " There were alfo."—l. 31. The only collation of Mr. *De-Miffy* in *The Britifh Mufeum* is that of the fine old MS. purchafed for *The Mufeum*; which collation is in the margin of *Kufter's* edition of *Mill's Greek* New Teftament.— l. 35. r. " and others by Dr. *Hunter*, who alfo purchafed feveral valuable MSS."

at

at the *French* college at *Berlin*, and from thence removed to the univerſity of *Francfort on the Oder*. He was examined for the degree of candidate * at *Berlin*, and his letters of reception were dated 1725: but, by a kind of eccleſiaſtical tyranny, the candidates for the miniſtry were obliged to ſign an act of orthodoxy peculiar to the *Pruſſian* dominions; which certain ſcruples entertained by Mr. *De-Miſſy* and Mr. *Franc*, another candidate, who had been examined and received with him, not permitting them to do without reſerve, it was eleven months † before they could obtain their letters, at the end of which time they were allowed to ſign with every reſtriction they could wiſh. To avoid the inconvenience of this act which miniſters were then obliged to ſign alſo when they were called on to ſerve a church, notwithſtanding ſome eminent miniſters at that time at *Berlin* had never ſigned, Mr. *De-Miſſy* reſolved to quit the country; and after having preached about five years in different towns of *The United Provinces*, from whence, as well as from *Berlin*, he brought the moſt flattering teſtimonies of approbation and eſteem, he was invited to *London* in 1731, and ordained to ſerve the *French* chapel in *The Savoy*; and in 1762 he was named by the Biſhop of *London* to ſucceed Mr. *Serces* as one of the *French* chaplains to his Majeſty in his chapel at *St. James's*. Several little poetical pieces, ſome of which have been ſet to muſic, eſſays both in ſacred and profane literature, epitomes of books, memoirs, diſſertations, &c. by Mr. *De-Miſſy*, with his initials *C. D. M.* or ſome aſſumed name, and frequently anonymous, appeared in different collections and periodical journals in *Holland*, *France*, and *England*, from 1721. He ſeldom publiſhed any thing except occaſionally, or in conſequence of certain unforeſeen engagements, or the importunity of friends. Such was a little piece printed in *March*, 1722, on the recovery of *Lewis* XV. compoſed by the author while at college at the ſolicitation of his muſic-maſter; ſome pieces in the " Mereure de *France*," and Mr. *Jordan's* " Recueil de Literature, de " Philoſophie, & d'Hiſtoire, 1730; the Verſes to *Voltaire* in *Jordan's* " Voyage Literaire, " fait en 1733," printed in 1735; the Addreſſes to the Queen of *England* and the Princeſs of *Wales*, printed in the *Dutch Gazette*, 1736; the four poetical pieces in the *French* tranſlation of *Pamela*, 1741, and ſome in the " Bibliotheque *Britannique*," and the " Magazin *Francois de Londres*;" a *Greek* epigram, with a tranſlation and letters relating to it, in the Public Advertiſer, *May* 31, *June* 4, 15, 21, 1763. In 1725, at the invitation of Meſſ. De *Beauſobre*, he wrote a little poem on the tragical affair at *Thorn* ‡, which, after having been printed by their order in *Holland*, with their tranſlation of *Jablonſki's* " *Thorn* affligée," was ſuppreſſed without their knowledge before the book was publiſhed. The ſame year he tranſcribed and tranſlated, for the elder *De Beauſobre*, ſome old MS. *German* letters for his Hiſtory of the Reformation in *Germany*, which ſtill remains in MS. probably becauſe no bookſeller (notwithſtanding the author's reputation) has been found willing to engage in it on liberal terms. In 1728 or 1729, being at *Amſterdam*, he aſſiſted his friend Mr. *De Chevriere* in his Hiſtory of *England*. Among other authors who are indebted to him were the late Profeſſor *Wetſtein* in his ſplendid edition of the *Greek* Teſtament ‖, the late Dr. *Jortin* in his Life of *Eraſmus* §, Mr. *Bowyer* and the Writer of theſe Anecdotes in " Two Eſſays on the Origin of Printing, 1774," and

* *Candidat* is the title given at *Berlin* to ſuch gentlemen as, after examination, are acknowledged capable of the holy miniſtry, but have not yet any living or eccleſiaſtical preferment.

† This time was paſſed in examinations and altercations; and the affair probably would not have terminated as it did, had it not been for the death of a prime miniſter, who was uncommonly ſtrenuous for the act, which was peculiarly diſtreſſing to delicate conſciences, even though orthodox. There yet exiſts (in ſome copies of letters written at the time) a full account of this petty perſecution, which is curious enough, but perhaps not an object of attention here.

‡ The perſecution there of the Proteſtants was, at the time, thought ſo remarkable, that it was ſaid to have been foretold in the Revelations.

‖ See Tom. I. p. 46. n. 12. p. 50. n. 44. p. 53. n. 69. p. 58. n. 106. Tom. II. p. 271.
§ See Vol. II. p. 20. 89. 414.

2   the

the new edition with additions, 1776. In 1728 a bookseller at *Amsterdam* proposed to him to undertake a 4to volume, to connect the History of the Councils by *Lenfant* and Father *Paul*; but from this he excused himself, and recommended Mr. De *Beausobre*, senior, whose critical Essay on the History of *Manicheism* was the fruit of this negociation. In 1735 Mr. *De-Missy* was appointed to preach in the *French* church, called the *Patente*, in *Soho*, on the Anniversary of the Revocation of the Edict of *Nantes* (for a pastor of that church, who a month before had broke his leg), and he was requested to publish a sermon, which is now out of print, but has passed through several editions, the best of which is that of 1751 *. Some critics have very bitterly reproached him for a little 4to piece, intituled, " Remarques de *Pierre le Motteux* sur " *Rabelais*, traduites librement de l'*Anglois* par *C. D. M.* & accompagnées de di- " verses Observations du Traducteur. Edition revue, &c. à *Londres*, 1740," or rather 1741; in which work he engaged from motives of pure friendship and honour, of which he had no more reason to be ashamed than of the work itself †. In the " Bibliotheque *Britannique*" are several other pieces by Mr. *De-Missy*, as critiques on new books, dissertations, and pieces in verse; and in the " Journal *Britannique*," among others, some letters on the Vatican MS. cited by Father *Amelot*, concerning the *three that bear record in heaven*; one by way of answer to a kind of anonymous criticism, which, after having appeared in the additions to the *Dutch* edition of the " Journal des Sçavans," and in a certain periodical paper printed at *The Hague* ‡, still fuller of falsehoods and the greatest abuse, appeared a little divested of these ornaments even in Dr. *Maty's* Journal, which false hoods and abuse Mr. *Prosper Marchand*, or his editor, thought proper to re-print in his note under the name of *David Martin*, in his " Dictionaire Historique," 1758. In 1749 and 1750 appeared two little *English* Poems by Mr. *De-Missy*, on the political feuds of the time, composed while a pretty severe fit of the gout forbad him any great application: one intituled, " *Dick and Tim*;" the other " Bribery, a Satire §." —Towards the close of 1765 he was consulted by his learned friend Mr. *Bowyer* about a preface, which the latter undertook to draw up for Mr. *Vaillant* the bookseller, who proposed to publish a work, or rather prolegomena of a posthumous work, of Father *Harduoin*, the MS. of which he had purchased abroad, which preface Mr. *Bowyer* solicited his friend to draw up; and Mr. *De-Missy* having made some curious remarks on this extraordinary work, found himself in a manner obliged by Mr. *Bowyer's* preface to publish them in 1766 in a pamphlet, intituled, " De *Joannis Harduini* " Jesuitæ Prolegomenis cum autographo collatis Epistola, quam ad amicissimum " virum *Wilhelmum Bowyerum*, iisdem nondum prostantibus, scripserat *Cæsar Missiacus* " [vulgo *Cæsar De-Missy*], Reg. *Brit.* à sacris *Gallicè* peragendis. Prostant *Harduini* " Prolegomena *Londini* apud *P. Vaillant*, 1766." In 1769 appeared a first, and in 1770 a second, edition of " Paraboles ou Fables & autres petites narrations d'un Citoyen de la " Republique Chretienne du dixhuitieme siécle mises en vers par *Cæsar De-Missy* ‖, &c."

* Concerning the first, see Biblioth. Brit. Tom. VII. where is also a Dissertation on the 137th Psalm, whence the text is taken; and on the latter, the Journal Brit. Tom. V. p. 226.

† On this see Biblioth. Brit. Tom. XVII. p. 420. and Journal Brit. XI. 92—95.

‡ The good people at *The Hague*, who printed these things, went so far as to send copies by the post to *London*, accompanied with a letter written in the name of a respectable lady, whose signature they were not ashamed to forge. But this proceeding met with the treatment it deserved. A late learned *English* prelate, who sometimes spent an hour in Mr. *De-Missy's* library, and had been informed of the whole affair, said to him, taking him by the hand, " Make yourself easy, sir; it is the lot of " men of merit to be attacked by those who have none: good men will esteem you the more."

§ Of these see the *Nouvelles Litteraires*, in the " Magazin *François de Londres*," I. 113—116.

‖ Of which a third edition, with considerable corrections, was ready for publication when the author died, and was published in 1776 with a head of him in a medallion. In this collection are interspersed the most sublime, serious, useful, Christian ideas, such as the author always strove to inculcate in his sermons and conversation, expressed with all the charms of poetry.

M*r.*

Mr. *De-Miſſy's* firſt wife was a lady of a conſiderable *French* family which had taken refuge in *England*; and on her death he took a ſecond wife, who ſurvived him, and to whom his memory will be for ever dear. In his youth he was 'perſonally acquainted with the moſt diſtinguiſhed ſcholars of his native country, Mr. *La Croze*, Mr. *Chauvin*, Mr. *Lenfant*, and Meſſrs. Dr. *Beauſobre*; and correſponded with the latter after he left *Berlin*, as he did alſo with the celebrated Mr. *Jordan*, his friend and relation Mr. *Benjamin Godeffroy*, paſtor of the *French* church at *Dreſden*, ſince deceaſed, his brother-in-law Mr. *Emanuel Focke*, firſt paſtor of the church of *Ballenſtat*, with ſome *French* clergymen of *The United Provinces*, with Profeſſor *Wetſtein*, with the biſhop of *Lombès*, who was a relation of his firſt wife, and died 1771, and with Mr. *Formey* at Berlin. In *England* he enjoyed the eſteem and friendſhip of ſeveral perſons of eminence both in the literary world and the church, moſt of whom he ſurvived. There are ſtill remaining ſeveral letters which paſſed between him and Mr. *De Voltaire*, from 1741 to 1743, which may perhaps ſome time or other be publiſhed. Mr. *De-Miſſy* was a determined Chriſtian, without ſuperſtition or bigotry. With much natural gaiety of temper, and the moſt ſociable and communicative diſpoſition, he poſſeſſed a ſolid though lively turn of mind, a ſtrong judgement, a very delicate taſte, and the moſt diſintereſted love for truth, and was capable of the cloſeſt application. The advancement of Chriſtianity, which he called the TRUTH by way of eminence, was the great object of his life and wiſhes. His character was ſuch as muſt command the warmeſt love and eſteem. On *Sunday, July* 30, 1775, he preached twice with his uſual zeal and vivacity; and in the evening was ſeized with the painful diſorder, which carried him off the 10th of *Auguſt* following. We cannot draw a better character of him than in the words of one of his friends, in a ſermon preached ſoon after his deceaſe *. In 1780 there came out three volumes of ſermons by Mr. *De-Miſſy* on divers texts of ſcripture. There remain among his papers ſeveral pieces of poetry, detached remarks on the original text of ſcripture, and many claſſic authors, ſome diſſertations, &c. which, though they did not receive his finiſhing hand, deſerve, in the opinion of his friends, to ſee the light in their preſent ſtate. A collation of ſome *Greek* MSS. of the New Teſtament, with notes, &c. by him is preparing for the preſs in *Germany*.

P. 456. note, l. 19. read, " *Framfield*."

P. 457. At the beginning of the fourth volume of *Somers's* Tracts, is advertiſed, " A Collection of Debates in Parliament before the Reſtoration from MSS. by Sir *Joſeph* " *Ayloffe*, bart." This, I ſuppoſe, never appeared.

Ibid. note, l. 28, *add*, daughter and heireſs of *Thomas Railton*, Eſq; of *Carliſle*, in the county of *Cumberland*.—In 1742, Sir *Joſeph* reſided at *Acton*.—Such of his MSS. as had not been claimed by his friends and acquaintance were ſold by auction, by *Leigh*, *February* 27, 1782 †.

---

* " After mentioning his talents and knowledge, it is but juſtice to his memory to ſay ſome-
" thing of his virtues. At the head of theſe might be placed his love of truth, his indefatigable
" aſſiduity in ſeeking it, and the exquiſite pleaſure he felt in communicating it to others. We muſt
" next ſpeak of his ardent zeal for the glory of God, and the intereſts of religion and revelation,
" and the moſt eſſential parts of both. This zeal made him attentively watch the progreſs and arts
" of irreligion and its partizans: his univerſal juſtice extended itſelf even to the enemies of truth,
" and his diſintereſtedneſs made him overlook every other uſe of money than that of ſatisfying his
" wants and doing good to others. In his humanity, charity, compaſſion, and beneficence, all were
" equally ſharers; the poor, ſtrangers, and even his enemies, and the undeſerving. It was a grief
" to him not to be able to do all the good he wiſhed, and to afford relief in every caſe."

† On this occaſion, a friend wiſhes me to take notice of the unjuſtifiable proceeding, at too many literary ſales, of perſons who take upon them at the moment of ſale to claim articles after they have been timely expoſed to view, to the manifeſt prejudice of ſuch purchaſers as cannot attend in perſon.

 P. 458.

P. 458. To the books of Sir *William Browne*, add, " Oratio *Harveiana* *, Principibus Medicis parentans; Medicinam, Academias utrasque laudans; Empiricos, eorum cultores perstringens; Collegium usque à natalibus illustrans : In Theatro Collegii Regalis Medicorum *Londinensium* habita Festo Divi *Lucæ*, MDCCLI, à *Gulielmo Browne*, Equite Aurato, M. D. *Cantab.* & *Oxon.* hujusce Collegii Socio, Electo, Censore, F. R. S. et à Consiliis. Solidorum duorum pretio venalis," 4to. This oration was embellished with Sir *William's* arms in the title-page ; a head-piece †, representing the theatre at *Oxford*, the senate-house at *Cambridge*, and the College of Physicians ; and an emblematic initial letter. These ornaments accompanied all his future publications.—On his *Cambridge* prize-medal is his portrait, and D. GVLIELMVS BROWNE EQVES. NAT. III. NON. A. I. MDCXCIII. Motto, ESSE ET VIDERI.—Reverse, *Apollo* presenting a wreath to a physician, SVNT SVA PRAEMIA LAVDI. ELECTVS COLL. MED. LOND. PRAESES. AS. MDCCLXXV.

P. 465. *Richard Blyke*, Esq; F. R. and A. S. S. (son of *Theophilus Blyke*, Esq; who was deputy secretary at war, paymaster of the widows pensions, and had been commissary of the stores at *Barcelona*) was Deputy-Auditor of Mr. *Aislabie's* office of the Imprest ; and had the honour of being god-son to Mr. Secretary *Craggs*. He had been long engaged in collecting materials for an history of *Hereford*, his native city, and of that county at large. Some of the valuable records, papers, &c. which he had collected for this purpose, were ready for the press in 1776, when death deprived his friends of this most excellent person, who was universally beloved. The collections were purchased at the sale of his library at Mr. *Baker's* for 30l. by the present Earl of *Surrey*, with a view of encouraging any person that shall undertake the history of that county, in which he has such considerable interest, and which had been unsuccessfully attempted by Mr. *Hill* and Mr. *Walwyn*. See British Topography, vol. I. p. 410. On the death of Mr. *Blyke's* father, his mother married a clergyman who had a living in *Gloucestershire*.

P. 468. note, l. penult. read, " 1748." Bishop *Gibson* died *Sept.* 6, 1748.

P. 469. note, l. 2. The exact date of the two shocks is *Feb.* 8, and *March* 8, 1749-50. Ibid. note *, Archbishop *Herring* was assisted in his answer to Bishop *Sherlock's* " Option," by Mr. Archdeacon *Denne*, and *Paul Jodrell*, Esq; to a brother of whom he bequeathed in return the Option of Dr. *Denne's* archdeaconry of *Rochester*, which Mr. *Jodrell* disposed of (in reversion) to the present archdeacon Dr. *Law.*

P. 470. sub-note, l. 2. read, " singly in *November*, 1753."

P. 472. l. 5. add, " under the tuition of Mr. *Charles Skottowe*;" and l. 6, read, " Mr. *Salter's* natural and acquired abilities were such as occasioned him to be taken notice of, not only in the university, but elsewhere; insomuch that his friends, who were proper judges of, and well acquainted with his merit, recommended him to Sir *Philip Yorke*," &c. About the time of his quitting *Cambridge*, he was one of the writers ‡ in the " *Athenian* Letters," printed for private use in 1741, and of which 100

* This Oration (inscribed, " Præsidi dignissimo, colendissimo; doctissimis, amicissimis Collegis;. hanc Orationem, quam edi voluerunt, officium, amorem, præstans, dat, dicat, uti par est, Orator *Harveianus*)" was accompanied with the following admonitory distich :
    " Docti & justi nomen parvi penderet,
    " Qui Sermonem hunc, invito me, verteret."

† Inscribed, " Et cantare pares, & respondere parati;" and under a figure of the sun, " Mihi magnus *Apollo.*"

‡ The other writers, I am informed, in this agreeable collection, were the Hon. *Philip Yorke* (now Earl of *Hardwicke*), the Hon. *Charles Yorke*, the late Bishop of *Lincoln* (Dr. *Green*), the Rev. *George Henry Rooke*, D. D. master of *Christ's*, the Rev. *Henry Heaton*, M. A. (afterwards prebendary of *Ely*), the Rev. *John Lawry*, M. A. (afterwards prebendary of *Rochester*), *Daniel Wray*, Esq; and Dr. *Heberden.* Of these only the first and two last survive. How desirable a present to the publick is a volume from such characters !

copies have lately been re-printed for select friends by the present Earl of *Hardwicke*. To Dr. *Whichcote's* " Aphorisms" were added some Letters that passed between him and Dr. *Tuckney*, concerning the use of Reason in Religion, &c ; and in the Preface was given a good historical account of both these Doctors, as well as of their two contemporaries and friends, Doctors *Hill* and *Arrowsmith*.

P. 472. note †, read, " good portrait by *Vivares*."

P. 475. Dr. *John Henry Hampe*, a well-known and remarkable physician, who for many years resided in obscure lodgings in *The King's-Mews* near *Charing-Cross*, had the honour of being physician to the late Princess Dowager of *Wales*. He spent great part of a long and laborious life in vainly seeking the philosopher's stone. After having by uncommon abstinence attained the age of fourscore, he determined to communicate to the world the experience he had acquired in the valuable art of MAKING GOLD (an art which had unfortunately reduced our venerable physician to poverty) ; and with this view began in 1776 to print his " Treatise on Experimental Metallurgy ;" in which but small progress was made at the press, when the learned author was released from his labours and penury in the beginning of the year 1777. The volume of " Ex-" periments" was however finished under the correction of *John Seyferth*, Esq; and published in 1777 by Mr. *Nourse*, in a small folio volume, with an excellent portrait of the author, scraped by *Burke*, from a painting by *Angelica Kauffman*, and the following remarkable inscription, written by the Doctor himself :

ΓΑΣΤΡΟΣ ΚΡΑΤΕΙΝ.

IOHANNES HENRICVS HAMPE,
Siegena-Nassovicus,
Medicinæ Doctor *Duisburgensis Clivorum*,
Medicus regius tricenarius
Practicus *Londinensis* quinquagenarius
Acad. Imper. Nat. Cur. Societat. Reg. *Lond.* socius
Perantiquus
Senex octogenarius temperatissimus sanissimus
Per quindecim annos vixit
Quoad liquida invinius υδροποτης
Quoad solida Λαχανι-μαζοφαγς
Sola ciborum Αναιμαχτων et paucitate et simplicitate
Perviridem senectutem assecutus

Rarissimè per diem ultra duodecim solidorum uncias consumens
Corporis siccitate et mira agilitate conspicuus,
Externorum et internorum sensuum integritate
Animaque perturbationibus vacua beatissimus
(Ρωμη ψυχης σωφροσυνη)
Ad longævitatem mortemque sanam omni morborum
Genere vacuam (ευθανασια) aspirans
Utpote felicitatem mundanam veram et unicam
Necnon extremam artis salutaris metam
Ad quam contingendam nulla datur via
Nisi per illud Πυθαγορι Γαςρος Κρατων
Systematis metallurgiae experimentalis *Angl.* idiom. autor."

P. 476. l. ult. read, " in this year."

Ibid. Of several of Mr. *Durand's* earlier publications notice has been already taken in PP. 45. 58. 154, 155. He was also author of " La Vie & les Sentimens de *Lucilio Vanini*," printed at *Rotterdam*, 1727, 12mo ; and editor of *Telemachus*, printed by *Watts*, 1745. A little poem of his, under the title of " Avis aux Predicateurs ; ou Idée Generale " de la vraie Prédication," is prefixed to the Life of *Ostervald*. The Preface, containing a short account of Mr. *Durand*, was written by the late Rev. Mr. *Samuel Beuzeville* * of *Bethnal Green*, a *French* Clergyman of great learning and piety, lately deceased, who represents him as " one of the most distinguished and eloquent " among the *French* Protestant preachers, as is amply proved," he says, " by the " very favourable reception given to a volume of Sermons published by him when " he was but 30 years old. No less favourable was that which his translation of " two books of *Pliny* on gold and silver, with that on ancient painting, and of the " Academics of *Cicero*, and his History of the 16th Century, met with. He was a " universal scholar, a deep divine, a devotee to truth, and, to crown all, a most bene-

* His funeral sermon was preached on the 13th of *January*, 1782, by Mr. *Moore*, one of the minor canons of *St. Paul's* ; and has since been printed in small 8vo.

" volent

" volent difinterefted man. Many of his valuable MSS. perifhed at *London* in an acci-
" dental fire." There exift among Mr. *Beuzeville's* papers in MS. by Mr. *D. Durand,*
" Des Notes fur le N. Teftament de Mr. *Le Cène,* & fur le N. Teftament de *Génève.*"
" Idée Générale de l'H.ftoire ;" and " La Vie de Mr. *Jaquelot* ;" which laft the poffeffor would be glad to fee printed.

P. 478. fub-note, l. 30. read, " noftratium."

P. 480. Dr. *Matthew Maty* was born in *Holland* in the year 1718. He was the fon
a clergyman, and was originally intended for the church ; but in confequence of fome
mortifications his father met with from the Synod on account of fome particular fentiments he entertained about the doctrine of the Trinity, turned his thoughts to phyfic.
He took his degree of M. D. at *Leyden,* and in 1740 came to fettle in *England,* his father having determined to quit *Holland* for ever. In order to make himfelf known, in
174 he began to publifh in *French,* an account of the productions of the *Englifh* prefs,
printed at *The Hague* under the name of the " Journal *Britannique.*" This journal,
which continues to hold its rank amongft the beft of thofe which have appeared fince the
time of *Bayle,* anfwered the chief end he intended by it, and introduced him to the
acquaintance of fome of the moft refpectable literary characters of the country he had
made his own. It was to their active and uninterrupted friendfhip he owed the
places he afterwards poffeffed. In 1758 * he was chofen fellow, and in 1765, on the
refignation of Dr. *Birch,* who died a few months after and made him his executor,
fecretary to the Royal Society. He had been appointed one of the under-librarians
of *The Britifh Mufeum* at its firft inftitution in 1753, and became principal librarian at
the death of Dr. *Knight* in 1772. Ufeful in all thefe pofts, he promifed to be eminently
fo in the laft, when he was feized with a languifhing diforder, which in 1776 put an end
to a life which had been uniformly devoted to the purfuit of fcience and the offices of
humanity. He was an early and active advocate for inoculation ; and when there was
a doubt entertained that one might have the fmall-pox this way a fecond time, tried it
upon himfelf unknown to his family. He was a member of the medical club (with the
Doctors *Parfons, Templeman, Fothergill, Watfon,* and others) which met every fortnight
in *St. Paul's Church Yard.* He was twice married, *viz.* the firft time to Mrs. *Elizabeth
Boifragon* ; and the fecond to Mrs. *Mary Deners.* He left a fon and three daughters.
A portrait of Dr. *Maty,* by his own order, has been engraved fince his death by *Bartolozzi,* to be given to his friends ; of which no more than 100 copies were taken off,
and the plate deftroyed.

Ibid. note ‡, for " whom" read " who."

P. 483. Mr. *Bowyer's* eftate at *Danby-Dale* had long before been fubjected to the
charitable bequeft defcribed below †, by his only furviving fon.

P. 485.

---

* Some *French* verfes by Dr. *Maty,* on the death of the Count *de Gifors,* were printed in " The
" Gentleman's Magazine," 1758, p. 435.

† " To the Curate, Church-wardens, and Overfeers of the Poor, of the Parifh of *Danby-Dale,* in
" *Cleveland,* in the County of *York.*

" Whereas *Samuel Rabanks* left by Will, dated the 15th of *May,* 1633, part of his eftates at
" *Danby-Dale* and *Great Broughton* in *Cleveland,* in the County of *York,* to his Nephew *Samuel Pru-
" dom,* and gave out of the faid eftates a charity for ever to nine poor people of *Danby-Dale* and
" *Glais-Dale* to be annually chofen as mentioned in the faid Will ; I, *Thomas Bowyer,* furviving
" heir of the faid *Samuel Prudom,* have printed a few copies of that part of the Will refpecting the
" aforefaid charity, for your better information. Being a ftranger to the neighbourhood of *Danby-
" Dale,* I defire, as the final choice now centers in me, that you will be particularly careful to at-
" tend ftrictly to that part of the Will refpecting the perfons and quality of the eighteen you nomi-
" nate ; for fhould you nominate other than fuch perfons as are fpecified in the faid Will, as nearly
" fuch as fuch can be found, the fault, which will be no fmall one, muft be entirely yours. I would
" chufe

P. 485. Mr. *Wallis* was living in 1738. See p. 557.

" chuse no one should have the benefit of the said charity more than two years together, a yearly
" election being appointed, so that every fit person may receive a benefit from the said charity,
" T. BOWYER."

" Extract of such part of the Will of *Samuel Rabanks*, as relates to a charity he gives to the Poor
" of *Danby* and *Glais-Dale* in *Cleveland*, 15 *May*, 1635.—Now I, the said *Samuel Rabanks*, for a
" direction and declaration, to what intents and purposes, and in what manner and form, the rents,
" issues, and profits of the said Messuages, Lands, Tenements, Hereditaments, and Premises,
" by me the said *Samuel Rabanks* to the said *Samuel Prudom* and *Thomas Reeve* conveyed or men-
" tioned to be conveyed as aforesaid, shall be after my decease employed according to the said trust,
" do, by this my last Will and Testament in writing, limit and appoint that the said *Samuel Prudom*
" and *Thomas Reeve*, and the heirs and assigns of the said *Samuel Prudom*, shall, from and after my
" decease, out of the rents, issues, and profits of the said messuages, lands, tenements, and
" hereditaments, to them conveyed or mentioned to be conveyed as aforesaid, upon the 9th
" day of *June*, or the 9th day of *December*, which of them shall first happen after my
" decease, and from thenceforth upon every 9th day of every month, monthly, for ever
" hereafter, pay, or cause to be paid, to nine poor people, to be from time to time nominated and
" elected in the manner herein by me appointed, and not otherwise, to every of them nine-pence a
" week, which comes to every of them three shillings by the month, and amounteth in all to £.17
" 11s. for the whole year: and also, for ever, after my decease, upon every 9th day of *December*,
" pay the sum of ten shillings of lawful *English* money to some godly and able preacher, to be from
" time to time nominated by the said *Samuel Prudom* and his heirs, who, upon every 9th day of *De-*
" *cember*, yearly, shall preach the word of God in the parish-church of *Danby* aforesaid : and the said
" *Samuel Prudom*, his heirs or assigns, shall, immediately after such sermon ended, give and deliver
" one peck of rie, not only to every such of the said nine poor people as shall be then present in the
" said church during all the time of the said sermon, but also to such other of them who shall be
" then absent, and not able to repair to the church, by reason of sickness or otherwise. And I do
" hereby further limit and appoint that the said *Samuel Prudom*, his heirs and assigns, shall and may
" from time to time, and all times hereafter, after my decease, receive and retain the residue of the
" said rents, issues, and profits of the said premises to him conveyed as aforesaid, to his and their own
" use and uses for ever. And touching the nomination and election of such poor people, to whose
" benefit I appoint and intend the said rie and monthly payments, I do hereby limit and appoint that
" on every 9th Day of *December* in every year for ever after my decease, the curate, church-wardens,
" and overseers of the poor of *Danby* for the time being, shall in the said church of *Danby*, after
" the sermon and distribution of the said rie, made according to my said appointment, publicly, in
" the presence of the said *Samuel Prudom*, his heirs and assigns, if they will be then and there pre-
" sent, and of such other of the parishioners of the said parish as will be there present, nominate
" eighteen poor persons of the said parish of *Danby*, whereof six shall be named by the curate, six by
" the church-wardens, and six by the said overseers of the poor for the time being, and shall set
" down in writing their names; and of those eighteen so to be named, there shall be nine then and
" there forthwith and immediately elected by the said *Samuel Prudom*, his heirs or assigns. And
" if the said *Samuel Prudom*, his heirs or assigns, shall be then absent, or refuse to make such elec-
" tion of such nine persons, or any of them, then such nine persons, or so many of them whereof
" no such election shall be made by the said *Samuel Prudom*, his heirs or assigns, as aforesaid, shall
" be elected and chosen on the next Sabbath-day after by the curate and overseers of the said parish
" for the time being, or any three of them, whereof the curate shall be one. And, as touching the
" persons so from time to time to be nominated and elected, I neither prefer men, nor exclude wo-
" men; but as touching their quality, whether men or women, I desire and appoint that no person
" or persons shall be nominated or elected to take any benefit of this my gift, but such only as are
" of the poorest sort for estate, and the best report for their good life and conversation; and of those
" so to be elected and qualified, I desire, limit, and appoint, that they shall be all of *Danby* only, if
" there be so many there · and if in case there shall not be so many there of the poorest and
" most needful persons, the number wanting shall be supplied out of *Glais-dale*, so that supply
" exceed not the number of three persons at any time: and to such nine persons so to be
" elected and qualified I intend the said payments and rie, and no other; but for their persons,
" estates, lives, and places of dwelling, as aforesaid. And I desire all such to whose care I have
" entrusted the disposition hereof, and the nomination and election of the said persons, that they
" would perform the same with the same respect of charity I intend it."

P. 485.

P. 485. Mrs. *Elianor James* (mother, I believe, to the three brothers * mentioned in p. 585) was a very extraordinary character, a mixture of benevolence and madness; an assertion that a perusal of the two letters † transcribed below will fully justify.

P. 486.

* *Harris James*, originally a letter-founder, and related to these brothers, was formerly of *Covent-Garden* theatre, where he represented fops and footmen.

† " To the Lords Spiritual and Temporal assembled in Parliament.

" MAY IT PLEASE YOUR LORDSHIPS,

" I have read a Case that is before your Lordships, relating to one *Dye*; and I find he has been
" greatly baffled, and it appears to me that he is the injured person : and the consideration that he
" has been twenty years, and has borrowed two thousand pounds, which if he should lose, his chil-
" dren would be ruined ; and these considerations moved me to humbly entreat your Lordships, for
" the love of justice, to consider the length of time, and the great charge, that right may take place,
" and that an end may be put to this suit : for justice is beautiful ; and the God of justice bless
" your Lordships. My heart is wounded to think, that *England* will be ruined if your Lordships
" don't stand in the gap : for what advantage can it be to *England* for *Scotland* to be united to it ?
" Is the cruel usage wherewith they used the Episcopal church-men there so soon forgot ? Surely
" there is not a miracle wrought in them, that their natures should be changed : Therefore let *Eng-
" land* be *England*; and let *Scotland* be as it is. And 'tis in your Lordships power to do good to
" the church and kingdom ; for the King leaves it wholly to you, and to the House of Commons :
" Therefore so act, as you will answer before God, who has committed the Talent of power to your
" trust ; that you may employ it to his glory, and for the good of your country : and therefore give
" not the power out of your own hand : and God Almighty give your Lordships such wisdom, that
" you may be more than conquerors for the glory of God, and the good of the kingdom ! Which
" that the Lord may grant, is the prayer of your humble servant, and soul's well-wisher,

" ELIANOR JAMES."

" Mrs. *James's* advice to all printers in general.

" I have been in the element of printing above forty years, and I have great love for it, and am
" a well-wisher to all that lawfully move therein, and especially to you that are masters ; therefore
" I would have you wise and just, and not willingly break the laws of God nor man, but that you
" would do by all men as you would desire they should do by you : and you cannot be ignorant of
" the great charge in bringing up of servants in the art of printing, neither can you be insensible
" how remiss, provoking and wasteful some servants are, especially when they are encouraged there-
" in, by the unjust hope of getting away from their masters, and having over-work from other
" masters that have not had the charge and trouble of bringing them up, which is too frequently
" practised among you, to the ruin of the trade in general, and the spoiling of youth. For when a
" boy has served half his time, and has gained some experience in his trade, he presently begins to
" set up for conditions with his master ; then he will not work unless he has so much for himself,
" and liberty to go where he pleases ; which if his master denies, he then strives to vex his master,
" and waste his time and goods ; and then when he beats him, away he runs with great complaints,
" when the master is all the while the sufferer ; and it is no wonder to hear a boy that wants an
" honest principle to do his own duty, rail against and bely his master and mistress ; for he thinks
" to excuse himself by blackening them. Now I would have this great evil prevented, and that
" you may easily do, if you will resolve to take no man's servant from him, and then a master may
" (as he ought) have the benefit of the latter part of his time to make him amends for his trouble
" and charge, which is according to the will of God and good men. For if it should happen, that
" an apprentice by any trick should get away from his master, I would not have you give any en-
" couragements, as money, but that he should serve the term of his indenture as an apprentice
" without ; for giving him money makes him a journey-man before his time : for indeed, if there
" be any consideration, it ought to be given to the master that had the trouble and charge of bring-
" ing him up ; and who will serve seven or eight years, if they can get off before ? For besides,
" boys will have a thousand tricks to provoke their masters to anger, in trifling away their time,
" and flinging their houses into pie, except their masters will be under conditions to give them en-
" couragements, and to give them that liberty to go where they will, and have money to spend, and
" this is to make the master the servant, and the boy the master ; therefore, pray, brother, do not be
" guilty in destroying of youth, for it is the destruction of the trade. I desire you to take care not
" to bind any boy except he be above the age of fourteen, and the fewer the better. So I rest your
" sister and soul's well-wisher, ELIANOR JAMES,

" Now to you, journey-men ; you are my brothers, for my husband was a journey-man before he
" was a master, and therefore I wish you well, and take care that you are not guilty of any ill thing,

4 H " as

P. 486. Of Mrs. *Markland*, the worthy sister of the excellent old friend of Mr. *Bowyer*, I cannot resist the temptation of giving a short account, in her own expressive words : " I have been struggling many years with a weak constitution, and, added to this, the " infirmities of old age have made a severe attack upon me. But these vicissitudes must " inevitably happen at 73, which is 3 years beyond the time allotted by the Royal " Psalmist for trouble and sorrow. I cannot expect any relief for my complaints but " through the gate of death. I return you my most grateful thanks, good Sir, for your " kind offer to do me any service in *London*; you have given me too strong proofs of " your integrity and diligence, to have the least doubt of your good will in the perform- " ance of any friendly office to the distressed or afflicted. My connections, to my great " sorrow, are all at an end in your part of the world by the loss of my best friends, and " at a time of life we are the least able to support ourselves under such a calamity, as " the mind is always a fellow-sufferer with the enervated body. In the hands of a wise " Providence, these chastisements may turn out for the best; and I ought to submit to " the Divine Dispensations, and think whatever is, is right, in the moral sense of the " word. I hope you enjoy your health; and may you have added to it, every blessing " this world can afford, is the sincere wish of your much obliged humble servant,

" *Liverpool, Nov.* 19, 1779. CATHARINE MARKLAND."

P. 490. The picture of " *Alfred* the Great, dividing his loaf with the Pilgrim *," was painted by *Benjamin West*, Esq; Historical-painter to his Majesty, and presented to the Company of Stationers in 1779 by Mr. *John Boydell*, who has since published an engraving from it. This painting, with the two portraits mentioned in p. 492, and one of *Tycho Wing* †, make a complete list of the Company's pictures.

" ' as shewing servants ill examples, and giving bad counsels; for if you should, you would be like " *Judas* in betraying your master that employs you; for sober men, they scorn to be guilty of this " crime; but for you of the worser sort, you are like devils, for you study how to do all manner of " mischief to a good husband; for you hate them because they are better than yourself: had not you " better imitate them, and pray to God to make you like them? For what benefit have you in " starving your wives and children, and making yourselves sots only fit for hell? Pray, brothers, " mend your faults, and pray to God to give you repentance, and to mend for the time to come, that " 'you may be reconciled to God and man, which I heartily wish. ELIANOR JAMES."

* While the *Danes* were ravaging all before them, *Alfred*, with a small company, retreated to a little inaccessible island in *Somersetshire*, called *Athelney*; where his first attention was to build a fortress : thither he afterwards moved his family, whose security gave him the most pungent concern. He had early married a lady, who, by her birth, accomplishments, and beauty, was worthy of the high station to which he had raised her. *Alfred* loved with the sincerest affection, and had the happiness to find his love returned with equal sincerity. Heaven too had blessed him with children. The principal inconvenience he laboured under, in this forlorn situation, arose from a scarcity of provisions. It happened one day as he was reading, that he found himself disturbed by the voice of a poor pilgrim, who with the greatest earnestness begged for somewhat to satisfy his hunger. The humane king (whose attendants had been all sent out in search of food) called to *Elswitha*, and requested her to relieve the miserable object with a part of what little there remained in the fort. The queen, finding only one loaf, brought it to *Alfred*; but at the same time represented to him the distresses that the family would be driven to, should the attendants prove unsuccessful. The king, however, not deterred, but rather rejoicing at the trial of his humanity, divided the loaf, and gave to the poor Christian half of it : consoling the queen with this pious reflection, ' That he who could feed five thousand with five loaves and two fishes, could make, if it so please him, the half of a loaf suffice for more than their necessities.' The pilgrim departed; the king resumed his studies; and felt a satisfaction that ever results from beneficent actions. His attendants returned with a vast quantity of fish; which greatly encouraged the king, and put him upon those glorious undertakings which restored the lustre of the *Saxon* diadem.

† Son of *Vincent*, the celebrated almanack-maker; of whom, though no painting is known to exist, there is preserved in *Stationers Hall* (by the attention of Mr. *Lockyer Davis* when Master of the Company) an engraved portrait, from his " Astronomia *Britannica*, 1669," folio, inscribed, " *Vincentius Wing, Luffenhamensis*, in com. *Rutlandiæ*; natus anno 1619, die 9 *Aprilis*." His life was written by *Gadbury*, who informs us that he died *Sept.* 20, 1668.

S

P. 497. Mr. *Nelson's* epitaph is here annexed :

" H. S. E.
ROBERTUS NELSON, Armiger,
Qui,
Patre ortus *Johanne,* cive *Londinenſi,*
Ex ſocietate Mercatorum cum *Turcis* commercium
Habentium, matre *Deliciis* ſorore
Gabrielis Roberts, equitis aurati, ex eâdem
Civitate & eodem ſodalitio, uxorem habuit
Honoratiſſimam dominam *Theophilam
Lucy, Kingſmilli Lucy* Baronetti viduam,
Prænobilis *Johannis* comitis de *Berkeley*
Filiam, quam *Aquiſgranum* uſque valetudinis
Recuperandæ cauſa proficiſcentem lubentér
Comitatus, ad extremum vitæ terminum
Summo amore fovit : morte divulſam
Per novem annos ſuperſtes plurimum deſideravit.
Literis *Græcis* et *Latinis,*
Quas partim in ſcholâ *Paulinâ,*
Partim intra domeſticos parietes didicerat,
Linguarum *Gallicæ* et *Italicæ* peritiam
Lutetiæ et *Romæ* agens facilè adjunxit.
In omni ferè literarum genere verſatus,
Ad theologiæ ſtudium animum præcipuè appulit;
Et felici pariter memoriâ atque acri judicio pollens,
Antiquitatum ecclesiaſticarum ſcientiâ
Inter clericos enituit laicus.
Peragratâ ſemel atque iterum *Europâ,*
Poſtquam diverſas civitatum
Et religionum formas exploraverat,
Nullam reipublicæ adminiſtrandæ rationem
Monarchiæ domi conſtitutæ præpoſuit,
Cæteras omnes eccleſias *Anglicanæ* longè poſthabuit:
Hanc ipſi ſemper charam
Beneficiis auxit,
Vitâ exornavit,
Scriptis defendit,
Filius ipſius obſequentiſſimus,
Et propugnator imprimis ſtrenuus.
Nulla erat bonorum virorum communitas,
Aut ad pauperum liberos ſumptu locupletiorum
Bene inſtituendos,

Aut ad augendam utilitatem publicam,
Aut ad promovendam Dei gloriam inſtituta,
Cui non ſe libenter ſocium addidit.
Hiſce ſtudiis et temporis et opum
Partem longè maximam impendit.
Quicquid facultatum ſupererat,
Id ferè omne ſupremis tabulis
In eoſdem uſus legavit.
Dum id ſibi negotii unicè dedit, Deo ut placeret,
Severam interim Chriſtianæ religionis
Ad quam ſe compoſuit diſciplinam
Suaviſſimâ morum facilitate ita temperavit,
Ut hominibus perrarò diſpliceret :
In illo enim, ſi in alio quopiam mortalium,
Forma ipſa honeſti mirè elucebat,
Et amorem omnium facilè excitabat.
Cum naturæ ſatis et gloriæ,
Bonis omnibus et eccleſiæ,
Parum diu vixiſſet,
Fatali aſthmate correptus,
Kenſingtoniæ animam Deo reddidit,
Vitæ jam actæ recordatione lætus,
Et futuræ ſpe plenus.
Dum Chriſtianum Sacrificium ritè celebrabitur,
Apud ſanctæ cœnæ participes,
Nelſoni vigebit memoria.
Dum ſolennia recurrent Feſta & Jejunia,
Nelſoni Faſtos jugiter revolvent pii ;
Illum habebunt inter hymnos et preces,
Illum inter ſacra gaudia et ſuſpiria
Comitem pariter et adjutorem.
Vivit adhuc, et in omne ævum vivet,
Vir pius, ſimplex, candidus, urbanus :
Adhuc in ſcriptis poſt mortem editis,
Et nunquam morituris,
Cum nobilibus et locupletibus miſcet colloquia
Adhuc eos ſermonibus
Multâ pietate et eruditione refertis
Delectare pergit et inſtruere.
Ob. 16 *Jan.* An. Dom. 1714.
Ætat. ſuæ 59."

Ibid. Mr. *Gabriel Hanger* was afterwards created lord *Coleraine.*
P. 501. Mr. *Ballard's* epitaph deſerves to be perpetuated :

" H. S. E.
GEORGIUS BALLARD,
Campoduni ſui haud vulgare ornamentum,
Qui diurnâ artis illiberalis exercitatione
ita victum quæritabat,
Ut animum interea diſciplinis liberalibus
excultum redderet.
In celebritatem et literatorum amicitiam
Eruditionis famâ aliquando evocatus,
Et inter academicos *Oxoniæ* adſcriptus,

Otio floruit nec ignobili,
Nec reipublicæ literariæ inutilis ;
Quippe fœminarum,
Quotquot *Britanniam* ſcriptis illuſtrarunt,
memoriam,
Scriptor ipſe poſteris commendavit.
Sed, dum ſtudiis intentus,
Vitæ umbratili nimium indulgeret,
Renûm calculo confectus obiit
Anno 1755."

P. 502. l. 7. read, " 1703, 1705."

P. 504. add,

"*Epitaphium*
JOHANNIS URRY,
Æd. Chrift. Oxon. Alumni à feipfo fcriptum,
1714.

Juftitiæ ac libertatis amans, licentiam abominatus;
 Famæ bonæ non averfatus;
Nullam, quam malam, maluit.
Divitiis et gloriolæ quietam mentem prætulit.
Patriæ patri et ecclefiæ matri fidelis ufque filius
 Extremum ad vitæ fpiritum perduravit.
Dominum fuum ferre, atque dura ipfius juffa
 Audire, non gravatus eft,
Quippe hoc numini parere ratus eft.
Confervo fervire ægrè tulit;

At alieno domino nefas piaculare duxit;
Nec crimen gravius patrare humanum genus
 potuiffe,
Quam datam fidem fallere putavit.
Decus effe quum non potuerit fodalitati huic
 regiæ et amplæ,
 Dedecus effe ftudiosè vitabat:
Et quoad potuit decorare ædes ab *Aldrichio* fundatas,
Ad quas itaque abfolvendas magnam reiculæ fuæ
 partem moriens legavit.
Et quamvis memorabile nihil perfecit unquam;
 Juffu tamen eft aggreffus opus ultra vires
  Magnum *Chaucerum*,
Nec abfolvit *, magno fed aufu excidit."

Ibid. l. 14. read, "Dr. *Charlet's*."

Ibid. fub-note, read, "His patron's wife, and mother to the Dutchefs Dowager of "*Portland*."

P. 506. There is a portrait of Dr. *Gower*, in his doctor's robes. *Jac. Fellowes pinx.* *G. Vertue fculp.*

Ibid. fub-note, l. 9. "*Bagford's* collections are locked up in a large cubical deal box, " and probably have never been opened fince they have been at *Cambridge*." T. F.

P. 507. l. 31. "Dr. *Newcome* had a print fcraped for Mrs. *Newcome* after her death, which he gave away: it was from a very bad picture, and probably never was like her. The young artift would not put his name. She was the very learned lady mentioned by Dr. *Grey* in his *Hudibras*, for her note about *Penguins* in Book I. She publifhed " An " Enquiry into the Evidence of the Chriftian Religion, *Cambridge*, 1728," 8vo, in 150 pages; and had the character of being very learned: all I know of that matter is, that as often as I have been in company with her, and when things were thrown out defignedly to tempt her to fpeak, and difcover herfelf, as the armour produced to *Achilles*, it never took effect. So that I cannot fpeak of her learning from my own knowledge: but if fhe was not that, fhe was fomething better; a very good woman." *T. F.*

Ibid. l. 37. read, "fome gentleman, a member of the fociety."

P. 508. fub-note, l. 2. "*Oxford*, in 1662."

P. 510. l. 34. read, "blue flate ftone."

Ibid. l. 36. Mr. *Madox's* large and valuable collection of tranfcripts, in 94 volumes in folio and quarto, confift chiefly of extracts from records in *The Exchequer*, the Patent and Claufe Rolls in *The Tower*, the *Cotton* Library, the Archives of *Canterbury* and *Weftminfter*, the Collections of *Chrift's College*, *Cambridge*, &c. made by him, and intended as materials for a feudal hiftory of *England* from the earlieft times. Thefe collections were the labour of 30 years; and Mr. *Madox* frequently declared, that when young he would have given 1500 guineas for them.—59 volumes of *Rymer's* Collection of Public Acts relating to the Hiftory and Government of *England* from 1115 to 1698 (not printed in his Fœdera, but of which there is a Catalogue in vol. XVII.) are depofited in *The Mufeum* by order of the Houfe of Lords.

P. 512. On the 20th of *December*, 1714, Mr. *R. Gale's* name was added to the commiffioners of ftamp-duties; and was continued in a fubfequent commiffion, dated *May* 4, 1715. "A Copy of an ancient Chirograph or Conveyance of a Sepulchre " cut in marble, lately brought from *Rome*, and now in the poffeffion of Sir *Hans Sloane*,

---

* Mr. *Urry* dying before the work was completed, the tafk of editorfhip devolved on his friend *William Brome*, Efq; of *Chrift Church*, *Oxford*. See his agreement with *Lintot*, in p. 503.

"with

" with some observations on it by *Roger Gale*, Esq;" is in Phil. Transf. N° 441, p. 211.——
The name of Mr. *S. Gale* was in *Peck's Stanford* as contributor of the plate of the
Bishop of *Elphin's* seal.

P. 513—520. The numbering of eight pages has been accidentally omitted.

P. 521. The Duchess of *Portland* has the copy of *Burnet* that was Lord *Dartmouth's* [*],
who was secretary of state at the time: and he has written at the end of vol. I. " So far
" I read, and did not perceive any design in the writer to pervert or mislead ; but this was
" not the case in the succeeding volume. Now Lord *B*—— tells me, that a man must
" be a simpleton to talk so, because all the anecdotes are in the first volume, and conse-
" quently there was the opportunity for taking liberties ; but that the subsequent ones
" are a mere compilation from news-papers." *T. F.*—Another copy of *Burnet's* History
of his own Times [†] is mentioned in this page, line the last, to be in the library of the
Earl of *Shelburne*, with MS. remarks by Dean *Swift*. In the same valuable library is
the Dean's copy of " Lord *Herbert's* Life of *Henry* VIII." with MS. notes, remarkable for being the first in the list of the books *Swift* has given us, as having been read by
him at *Moor Park* [‡].—Mr. *Astle* has the Dean's MS. remarks on " *Macky's* Characters;"
and I have myself those on " *Gibbs's* Psalms."

Ibid. l. 20. read, " p. 532."—Subnote, l. 2. read, " detracting."

P. 529. Mr. *Thomas Baker* was descended from a family ancient and well-esteemed,
distinguished by its loyalty and affection for the crown. His grandfather Sir *George
Baker*, knt. almost ruined his family by his exertions for *Charles* I. Being recorder of
Newcastle, he kept that town, 1639, against the *Scots* [||] (as they themselves wrote to the
Parliament) with " a noble opposition." He borrowed large sums upon his own credit,
and sent the money to the king, or laid it out in his service [§]. His father was *George
Baker*, Esq; of *Crook*, in the parish of *Lanchester*, in the county of *Durham*, who married
Margaret daughter of *Thomas Forster* of *Edderston*, in the county of *Northumberland*, Esq.
Mr. *Baker* was born at *Crook*, September 14, 1656 [**]. He was educated at the free-school
at *Durham*, under Mr. *Battersby*, many years master, and thence removed with his elder
brother *George* to St. *John's College, Cambridge*, and admitted, the former as pensioner,
the latter as fellow commoner, under the tuition of Mr. *Sanderson*, *July* 9, 1674 [††]. He
proceeded B. A. 1677; M. A. 1681; was elected fellow *March* 1679-80; ordained
deacon by bishop *Compton* of *London*, *December* 20, 1685; priest by Bishop *Barlow* of
Lincoln, *December* 19, 1686. Dr. *Watson*, tutor of the college, who was nominated, but
not yet consecrated, bishop of *St. David's*, offered to take him for his chaplain, which he
declined, probably on the prospect of a like offer from Lord *Crew* bishop of *Durham*,
which he soon after accepted. His Lordship collated him to the rectory of *Long-Newton*

---

[*] Sir *John Dalrymple* acknowledges his obligations to the present Earl of *Dartmouth*, for the use
of a copy of his ancestor's MS. notes on *Burnet*.

[†] Or, as *Swift* calls it, " The History of *Scotland* in my own Time." Speaking of the Εἰκὼν
Βασιλικὴ, he says, " it is a poor performance, and unworthy of the reputed author."

[‡] See " Supplement" to his Works, 4to. p. 739.

[||] *Lloyd's* Memoirs, p. 689.

[§] Mr. *Thomas Baker* erected a monument to him at his own expence in the great church at *Hull*,
with an epitaph, after he had lain there disregarded 40 years. See the epitaph in *Le Neve's* Mon-
Angl. from 1615 to 1679, p. 123.

[**] *Heath's* Chron. p. 68. *Rushworth's* Collections, p. iii. vol. II. p. 647. Register of Births in
Lanchester church, there being at that time no register of baptisms.

[††] Mr. *Thomas Baker's* admission is entered in the College Register, *June* 13, 1674, ætat. 16.
But if the parish register may be depended on, he must at that time have been near 18; and he has
been heard to say, that coming up at the same time with his elder brother *George*, who was two years
older, that it might not be known how late he was admitted, their true ages were concealed.

in

in his diocefe, and the fame county, *June* 1687 ; and, as Dr. *Grey* was informed by fome of the bifhop's family, intended to have given him that of *Sedgefield*, worth 6 or 700*l*. a year, with a golden prebend, had he not incurred his difpleafure, and left his family, for refufing to read King *James* the Second's declaration for liberty of confcience. Mr. *Baker* himfelf gives the following account of this matter : " When the king's declara-" tion was appointed to be read, the moft condefcending thing the bifhop ever did me " was coming to my chambers (remote from his) to prevail with me to read it in his " chapel at *Auckland*, which I could not do, having wrote to my curate not to read it " at my living at *Long-Newton*. But he did prevail with the curate at *Aukland* to read " it in his church when the bifhop was prefent to countenance the performance. When " all was over, the bifhop (as a penance, I prefume) ordered me to go to the dean (as " archdeacon) to require him to make a return to court of the names of all fuch as " did not read it, which I did, though I was one of the number." The bifhop, who dif-graced him for this refufal, and was excepted out of King *William's* pardon, took the oaths to that king, and kept his bifhoprick till his death. Mr. *Baker* refigned *Long Newton Aug.* 1, 1690, refufing to take the oaths* ; and retired to his fellowfhip at *St. John's*, in which he was protected † till *Jan.* 20, 1716-17, when, with 21 others ‡, he was difpoffeffed of it. This hurt him moft of all, not for the profit he received from it, but that fome whom he thought his fincereft friends came fo readily into the new meafures, particularly Dr. *Robert Jenkin* the mafter ‖, who wrote a defence of the profeffion of Dr. *Lake* bifhop of *Chichefter*, concerning the new oaths and paffive obedience, and refigned his pre-centorfhip of *Chichefter*, and vicarage of *Waterbeach*, in the county of *Cambridge*. Mr. *Baker* could not perfuade himfelf but he might have fhewn the fame indulgence to his fcruples on that occafion as he had done before while himfelf was of that way of thinking. Of all his fufferings none therefore gave him fo much uneafinefs. In a letter from Dr. *Jen-kin*, addreffed " to Mr. *Baker*, fellow of *St. John's*," he made the following remark on the fuperfcription : " I was fo then ; I little thought it fhould be by him that I am " now no fellow : but God is juft, and I am a finner." After the paffing the Regiftring Act, 1723, he was defired to regifter his annuity of 40*l*. which the laft act required before it was amended and explained. Though this annuity, left him by his father for his for-tune, with 20*l. per annum.* out of his collieries by his elder brother from the day of his death, *Aug.* 1699, for the remaining part of the leafe which determined at *Whitfuntide* 1723, was now his whole fubfiftence, he could not be prevailed on to fecure himfelf againft the act, but wrote thus in anfwer to his friend : " I thank you for your kind " concern for me ; and yet I was very well apprifed of the late act, but do not think " it worth while at this age, and under thefe infirmities, to give myfelf and friends fo " much trouble about it. I do not think that any living befides myfelf knows furely " that my annuity is charged upon any part of my coufin *Baker's* eftate ; or if they do,

* The following memorandum was extracted from the regifter-book of *Long-Newton* by the cu-rate of that parifh : " Mr. *John Oliver*, rector of *Long-Newton*, died in *February*, 1686, and was " fucceeded by Mr. *Thomas Baker*, fellow of *St. John's College* in *Cambridge*; who, refufing to take " the oaths to King *William* and Queen *Mary*, at *Candlemas* 1689, returned to his college again.— " Mr. *James Finny*, M. A. of *St. John's College* in *Oxford*, chaplain to the Right Honourable the " Earl of *Burlington* and *Cork*, afterwards D. D. and prebendary of *Durham*, was inducted into the " rectory of *Long-Newton* on the 30th of *January*, 1690."

† See his Preface to Lady *Margaret's* Funeral Sermon.

‡ Mentioned in the Appendix to *Kettlewell's* Life.

‖ " Mr. *Baker* was quite wrong in fancying that the mafter, &c. could do more for him than he did. He was fcreened, till notice came from above that it would not be overlooked there any longer. Now did Mr. *Baker*, as a fcrupulous man, reconcile to his confcience, the holding of his fellowfhip with his annuity of 40*l. per annum* ? Was not this *certi reditus*?" *T. F.*

" I can

" I can hardly believe that any one for fo poor and uncertain a reward will turn in-
" former; or if any one be found fo poorly mean and bafe, I am fo much acquainted
" with the hardfhips of the world, that I can bear it. I doubt not I fhall live under
" the fevereft treatment of my enemies; or, if I cannot live, I am fure I fhall die, and
" that's comfort enough to me. If a conveyance will fecure us againft the act, I am
" willing to make fuch a conveyance to them, not fraudulent or in truft, but in as full
" and abfolute a manner as words can make it; and if that fhall be thought good fecu-
" rity, I defire you will have fuch a conveyance drawn and fent to me by the poft, and
" I'll fign it and leave it with any friend you fhall appoint till it can be fent to you."
He retained a lively refentment of his deprivations; and wrote himfelf in all his books,
as well as in thofe which he gave to the college library, " focius ejectus," and in fome
" ejectus rector." In 1730 he contributed a fine common-prayer book to Mr. *Willis's*
new chapel*. He continued to refide in the college as commoner-mafter till his
death, which happened *July* 2, 1740, of a paralytic ftroke, being found on the floor of
his chamber. " In the afternoon, being alone in his chamber, he was ftruck with a
" flight apoplectic fit, which abating a little, he recovered his fenfes, and knew all
" about him, who were his nephew *Burton* †, Doctors *Bedford* and *Heberden*. He feemed
" perfectly fatisfied and refigned; and when Dr. *Bedford* defired him to take fome me-
" dicine then ordered, he declined it, faying, he would only take his ufual fuftenance,
" which his bed-maker knew the times and quantities of giving: he was thankful for
" the affection and care his friends fhewed him, but, hoping the time of his diffolution
" was at hand, would by no means endeavour to retard it. His diforder increafed, and
" the third day from this feizure he departed. His accuftomed regularity and abftemi-
" ous way of living had, one would have imagined, been a fecurity from a diforder of
" this nature; though perhaps, when it did come, it rendered him lefs able to ftruggle
" with it. But it happened at this very time his great nephew, the prefent Mr. *Baker*
" of *Crook*, was juft come from *Eton* fchool to be admitted at *St. John's*, upon which
" occafion, befides the great joy he expreffed in feeing him, he frequented company
" more than ufual, and had entertainments in his own chambers (which he very rarely
" practifed): fo that this unufual hurry deftroyed that æquilibrium of fpirits his wonted
" tranquillity had kept up, and, like any violent excefs, proved too much for him to
" bear. I recollect it always as one of the fortunate incidents of my life that I hap-
" pened to be thrown in the way at this time, both as I had an opportunity of feeing
" my much honoured and great friend in his laft minutes, as alfo of having an occafion
" of exerting myfelf in his fervice; who, when I was a ftudent, had left no act of
" friendfhip or relation undone towards me; and next, I am extremely glad of this
" further and public opportunity of owning the great obligation and honour I had in
" being known to, and in my youth regarded by, fo great and learned a man, fo kind
" and affectionate a relation." *Letter from Dr. John Bedford* (of whom fee an account
hereafter) *to Dr. Grey, Durham, July* 27, 1755. He was buried in *St. John's* outer chapel, near the monument of Mr. *Afhton*, who founded his fellowfhip. No memorial has

---

* See above, p. 245.—" Mr. *Baker* defires me to convey his prefent of a fine common-prayer
" book for Mr. *Willis's* new chapel by the coach that goes from hence. He bids me further add,
" that he hath now by him Mr. *Strype's* laft volume of Annals in MS.; which, had you been here,
" he thinks you was fitter to have examined than himfelf, whether he hath been guilty of making
" repetitions, a fault he is too fubject to; it is to remain in his cuftody till the laft day of this month,
" and no longer." Dr. *William Baker* ‡ to Dr. *Grey, dated Cambridge, Oct.* 15, 1730.

† Mr. *Richard Burton*, of *Elamore-Hall*, Mr. *Baker's* nephew and executor.

‡ Fellow of *St. John's College, Cambridge.* Mr. *Bowyer* printed for him a 30th of *January* Sermon, 1726. He
publifhed alfo two other fingle Sermons, in 1716 and 1728.

yet been erected over him, he having forbidden it in his will. Being appointed one of the executors of his eldest brother's will, by which a large sum was bequeathed to pious uses, he prevailed on the other two executors, who were his other brother *Francis* and the Hon. *Charles Montagu,* to lay out 1310*l.* of the money upon an estate to be settled upon *St. John's* college for six exhibitioners. He likewise gave the college 100*l.* for the consideration of 6*l.* a year (then only legal interest) for his life; and to the library several choice books, both printed and MS. medals, and coins; besides what he left to it by his will; which were " all such books, printed and MS. as he had, and were " wanting there." All that Mr. *Baker* printed was, 1. " Reflections on Learning, shew- " ing the insufficiency thereof in its several particulars, in order to evince the useful- " ness and necessity of Revelation, *London,* 1709-10," (which went through 8 editions; and Mr. *Boswell,* in his " Method of Study" ranks it among the *English* classics for purity of style); and 2. " The Preface to Bishop *Fisher's* Funeral Sermon for *Margaret* " countess of *Richmond* and *Derby,* 1708;" both without his name. Dr. *Grey* had the original MS. of both in his own hands. The latter piece is a sufficient spesimen of the editor's skill in antiquities to make us regret that he did not live to publish his " History " of *St. John's* college, from the foundation of old *St. John's* house to the present time ; " with some occasional and incidental account of the affairs of the university, and of such " private colleges as held communication or intercourse with the old house or college : " collected principally from MSS. and carried on through a succession of masters to the " end of Bishop *Gunning's* mastership, 1670." The original, fit for the press, is among the *Harleian* MSS. N° 7028. His MS. collections relative to the History and Antiquities of the University of *Cambridge,* amounting to 39 volumes in folio and 3 in quarto, are divided between *The British Museum* and the public library at *Cambridge;* the former possesses 23 volumes, which he bequeathed to the Earl of *Oxford,* his friend and patron; the latter 16 in folio and 3 in quarto, which he bequeathed to the university. A particular detail of the contents of those in *The British Museum* may be seen in the *Harleian* Catalogue, from N° 7028 to 7054. Dr. *Knight* * styles him " the greatest master of the " antiquities of this our university;" and *Hearne* † says, " Optandum est ut sua quo- " que collectanea de antiquitatibus *Cantabrigiensibus* juris faciat publici Cl. *Bakerus,* " quippe qui eruditione summâ judicioque acri & subacto polleat." Mr. *Baker* intended something like an *Athenæ Cantabrigienses* on the plan of the *Athenæ Oxonienses.* Had he lived to have completed his design, it would have far exceeded that work, notwithstanding the reflection, as unjust as severe, with which the writer of *Anthony Wood's* article in the first edition of the " Biographia *Britannica*" insults *Cambridge,* by saying, " that Mr. " *Baker's* feeble attempt of the like kind undoubtedly reflects the highest honour on Mr. " *Wood's* performance." With the application and the industry of *Wood* Mr. *Baker* united a penetrating judgement and a great correctness of style; and these improvements of the mind were crowned with those amiable qualities of the heart, candour and integrity ‡.

* Life of *Erasmus,* p. 88.
† Pref. ad *Rosf. Warw.* p. 6.
‡ Dr. *Grey* collected materials for a life of him, which were given by his widow to Mr. *Masters,* who thought them hardly sufficient to make a work by themselves, but would have prefixed them to Mr. *Baker's* History of *St. John's* college, and applied to Dr. *Powell,* the late master, for the use of the transcript taken, at his predecessor Dr. *Newcome's* expence, from the original in *The British Museum.* But this was declined, as the history, though containing several curious matters, is written under the influence of partiality and resentment. It is probable, however, that Mr. *Baker's* Collections will some time or other be laid before the public.—In an unpublished letter of Bishop *Warburton,* written towards the close of Mr. *Baker's* life, he says, " Good old Mr. *Baker* of *St. John's* " has indeed been very obliging. The people of *St. John's* almost adore the man; for, as there is " much in him to esteem, much to pity, and nothing (but his virtue and learning) to envy; he has " all the justice at present done him that few people of merit have till they are dead."

Among

Among his contemporaries who diftinguifhed themfelves in the fame walk with himfelf, and derived affiftance from him, may be reckoned Mr. *Hearne*, Dr. *Knight*, Dr. *John Smith*, *Hilkiah Bedford**, *Browne Willis*, Mr. *Strype*, Mr. *Peck*, Mr. *Ames*, Dr. *Middleton*, and Profeffor *Ward*. Two large volumes of his letters to the firft of thefe antiquaries are in the *Bodleian* library. There is an indifferent print of him by *Simon* from a memoriter picture; but a very good likenefs of him by *C. Bridges*. *Vertue* was privately engaged to draw his picture by ftealth. Dr. *Grey* had his picture, of which Mr. *Burton* had a copy by Mr. *Ritz*. The Society of Antiquaries have another portrait of him. It was his cuftom in every book he had, or read, to write obfervations † and an account of the author. Of thefe a confiderable number are at St. *John's* college, and feveral in the *Bodleian* library, among Dr. *Rawlinfon's* bequefts. I have a fair tranfcript of his felect MS. obfervations on Dr. *Drake's* edition of Archbifhop *Parker*, 1729; which fhall appear in fome future number of the " Bibliotheca Topographica." Dr. *John Bedford* of *Durham* had his copy of the " Hereditary Right" greatly enriched by Mr. *Baker*. (*MS. Letter to Dr. Grey, Durham, July* 27, 1755.)—Dr. *Grey*, who was advifed with about the difpofal of the books, had his copy of *Spelman's* Gloffary ‡. Mr. *Crow* married a fifter of Mr. *Baker's* nephew *Burton*; and, on *Burton's* death inteftate in the autumn after his uncle, became poffeffed of every thing. What few papers of Mr. *Baker's* were among them, he let Mr. *Smith* of *Burnhall* fee; and they being thought of no account were deftroyed ||, except the deed concerning the exhibitions at St. *John's*, his own copy of the Hiftory of the college, notes on the foundrefs's funeral fermon, and the deed drawn for creating him chaplain to Bifhop *Crew* in the month and year of the revolution, the day left blank, and the deed unfubfcribed by the Bifhop as if rejected by him.

---

* Of whom, fee hereafter, p. 629.

† " His obfervations that he wrote in books were often very trifling. When Dr. *Taylor* publifhed " his *Lyfias*, he told me (I think) that he gave him a large-paper copy; and when he died was very " defirous to get a fight of it to fee what he had written: but found only the copy of his own ad- " miffion and Mr. *Morton's* to whom it is dedicated. It fhould be obferved, however, that *Baker* " did not live long after the publication." T. F.

‡ " I return you a thoufand thanks for the trouble you have had with my uncle's catalogue, and " for your kind endeavours to procure me a better price for the remaining part of his books, than " what has been offered at *Cambridge*. I find they are like to raife little money at beft: and my " coufin *Baker* feeming defirous to purchafe them, and have them preferved in memory of his uncle, " and to prevent their being expofed in fhops; I think to bring them into the country, which I " hope may be done without a great expence, as we have water-carriage the whole way: fhould the " young man happen to change his mind when he comes to age, the lofs (it is likely) cannot be " great. I am told, Mr. *Thurlbourne* fays he would give any (even my own) price for fome of the " books in the catalogue. After fo much trouble as I have given you, I am really afhamed to take " any further liberties of that fort. Yet, I muft confefs, I fhould be very thankful to you, if, at " your leifure, you would be fo good as to mark a few of the moft valuable of them: the books of " low (or no) price, I beg you will give yourfelf no trouble about. So foon as I am able to write, " I will defire Dr. *Williams* to look out *Spelman's* Gloffary, which you will give me leave to beg a " place for in your ftudy, where I fhall be proud to have it preferved, as a memorial of our common " friend; and a mark of that efteem with which I am, &c. RICHARD BURTON." *Letter to Dr.* *Grey, Jan.* 16, 1740-1.

|| " Some time fince I did myfelf the pleafure of anfwering your obliging letter, and am forry to " find it has not reached your hands. In it I did acquaint you that I have made diligent fearch " after the effects and papers my uncle left, but can find none, as I believe they were all confumed " after Mr. *Burton's* death by an accident when in his brother *Crow's* cuftody, fo that I am afraid " I can give you no light whatfoever of his correfpondence or life. I am greatly obliged to you for " your kind intention of perpetuating the memory of my uncle; and am, &c. GEORGE BAKER." *Letter to Dr. Grey, dated Elemore, Sept.* 18, 1755.

P. 529. Another unnoticed publication of Mrs. *Aſtell* appeared in 1706, intituled, " Six Familiar Eſſays upon Marriage, Croſſes in Love, and Friendſhip, written by a " Lady," 12mo. Some pamphlet which ſhe had publiſhed in 1705 was ſuſpected to be the work of Biſhop *Atterbury* ∗.

P. 532. l. 13. read, " Aliquot Vetuſtorum ;" though *Newton* prints it " Vetuſtis."

P. 536. Dr. *Taylor* left an exhibition at *St. John's* for a ſcholar at *Shrewſbury* ſchool. Ibid. In the inſcription, col. 2. l. 2. read, " reliquerunt ;" and it is remarkable that " *ſex* latrones" are here mentioned, on the pyramid (p. 81) *ſeptem*.

P. 539. Dr. *Madden's* " Memoirs †" are addreſſed, in an ironical dedication, to *Frede-rick* Prince of *Wales.*—There is a later mezzotinto of him, by *Richard Purcell*, from a painting by *Robert Hunter*, with his arms, and this inſcription :

" SAMUEL MADDEN, D. D. ætatis ſuæ 68, 1755.
" Fortior qui ſe, quam qui fortiſſima vincit moenia."

Monſ. *Groſley*, a lively *French* traveller, ſpeaking of a city in the centre of *France,* " which at the beginning of the fifteenth century ſerved as a theatre to the grandeſt " ſcene that *England* ever acted in that kingdom," mentions ſeveral *Engliſh* families as lately extinct, or ſtill ſubſiſting there. " This city," he adds, " in return, has given the " *Britiſh* dominions an illuſtrious perſonage, to whom they are indebted for the firſt " prizes which have been there diſtributed for the encouragement of agriculture and " arts. His name was *Madain :* being thrown upon the coaſt of *Ireland* by events of " which I could never hear any ſatisfactory account, he ſettled in *Dublin* by the name " of *Madden*, there made a fortune, dedicated part of his eſtate, which amounted to " four or five thouſand pounds a year, to the prizes which I have ſpoken of, and left a " rich ſucceſſion : part of this ſucceſſion went over to *France* to the *Madains* his rela-" tions, who commenced a law-ſuit for the recovery of it, and cauſed eccleſiaſtical cen-" ſures to be publiſhed againſt a merchant, to whom they had ſent a letter of attorney " to act for them, and whom they accuſed of having appropriated to himſelf a ſhare of " their inheritance." *Tour to London*, 1772, vol. II. p. 100.

P. 544. Bp. *Warburton's* opinion ‡ of *Webſter* (which Mr. *Maty* has communicated to the publick among his " Literary Curioſities)" is too important to be omitted. It is extracted from various Letters to Dr. *Birch*.

Ibid. l. ult. *add*, " I heartily wiſh we had a new edition of Father *Paul*. Such a " thing, I remember, was propoſed ſome years ago ; but, I know not by what chance, " it miſcarried. I could wiſh that Mr. *Johnſon* would give us the original on one ſide, " and his tranſlation on the other. But this won't hit the public taſte." Biſhop *War-burton*, MS.

P. 544.

∗ " I am informed this day that you have put out in print a mighty ingenious pamphlet ; but that " you have been pleaſed to father it upon one Mrs. *Aſtell*, a female friend and witty companion of " your wife's." *Lord Stanhope to Dr. Atterbury*, MS.

† The extraordinary circumſtances attending the printing and ſuppreſſion of theſe Memoirs have been already mentioned in p. 83 ; but the reaſons for it are not very evident. The whole of the bu-ſineſs was tranſacted by Mr. *Bowyer*, without either of the other printers *(Roberts* ‖ and *Woodfall)* ever ſeeing the author. The book was finiſhed at the preſs *March* 24, 1732-3 ; and 100 copies were that day delivered to the author. On the 28th a number of them was delivered to the ſeveral bookſellers mentioned in the title-page ; and in four days after, all that were unſold were recalled, and 800 of them given up to Dr. *Madden* to be deſtroyed. The copy mentioned in p. 539 is now in the library of Mr. *Bindley*.

‡ " I do not know what you think in town of the Miſcellany papers ; but, I proteſt, the ſurpriſing " abſurdity made me think that people would imagine I got ſomebody to write booty, had not the

‖ Mr. *James Roberts* died *Nov.* 2, 1754, aged 85.—Mr. *John Watts*, another printer of firſt-rate eminence, died *Sept.* 26, 1763. aged 83.

" equal

P. 544. fub-note, l. ult. read, " by Sir *Nathaniel Brent* in 1616."

P. 547. l. 2. *add*, " Mr. *Holmes* was barrack-mafter of *The Tower*. He died *Feb.* 16,
" 1748-9."

Ibid. l. 4. read, " Vol. I. p. 295. The Life is written with the Bifhop's own hand,
" ending with his birth-day when he was 80 years old."

P. 549. Among Dr. *Birch's* MSS. (N° 4270) is " Some Account of the Tithes belong-
" ing to the parifh of *Debden* in *Effex*, and receipts for repairs done by Dr. *Birch* the
" rector," &c.

P. 553. Dr. *Colbatch*, in a Commemoration Sermon, 1717, fpeaks thus of Dr. *Laughton*:
" We fee what a confluence of nobility and gentry the virtue of one man daily draws
" to one of our leaft colleges."

Ibid. Dr. *Warton* having obferved, that in a little piece written by Lord *Lyttelton* in
his youth, the " Obfervations on the Life of *Tully*," there is a more difpaffionate and
impartial character of the orator than in the panegyrical volumes of *Middleton*; a new
Reviewer * (who treads in the footfteps of *Bayle* and Dr. *Maty*) has well obferved, that
" this

" equal virulency fhewn the writer to be in earneft.—I hope you read my laft; you might perceive
" I was in a paffion againft *Webfter* when I wrote; but his laft letter againft me has cured me of it,
" and I defign to take no manner of notice of him in the preface of my Sermon. You will won-
" der at this odd kind of cure. But there is a certain point, at which when any thing arrives, it
" lofes its nature; fo that what was before only fimple calumny, appears now to be madnefs; and
" I fhould have an ill-office to endeavour the cure of it."—" It is a great pleafure to me that fuch
" judges as you approve of my Sermon, and almoft as great that my enemies are fuch as *Webfter*. As
" I am refolved, for the future, not only not to anfwer, but even not to read what that wretch writes
" againft me; his putting his name to what he does will be of ufe to me. I wifh you could con-
" trive that that fhould come to his ear."—In the fame letter, which (as Mr. *Maty* obferves) is no
Warburtoniana, but the *Ana* of every man who ever lived, " I have not feen *Webfter's* circular
" letter. Pray, when you go by Mr. *Gyles's* fhop, defire him to fend it me."—" What a happy
" thing it would be if we could fend over on a miffion fome of our hot zealots to cool themfelves
" in an *Indian* Savanna! Don't you think *Venn* and *Webfter* would make a proper as well as plea-
" fant figure in a couple of bear-fkins! Methinks I fee them march in this terror of equipage,
" like the *Pagan* priefts of *Hercules* of old,

" Jamque facerdotes, primufque *Potitius*, ibant
" Pellibus in morem cincti, flammafque ferebant.

" The fanaticifm of fome of thefe miffionaries gave birth to a very ferious thought, which you will
" find in the fecond edition of the Divine Legation, now printing; therefore I fhall not repeat it
" here. You fee I have publifhed a fecond edition of my firft volume: there are feveral additions
" in fupport of my fcheme, and reafonings on it, which I hope will not difpleafe you, as likewife
" feveral omiffions of paffages which were thought vain, infolent, and ill-natured, particularly that
" againft the author of the Enquiry into the Demoniacks, which I hope will lefs difpleafe you.—
" Mr. *Gyles* has fent me word, that *Webfter* has publifhed all his letters; and thinks it proper to do the
" fame by thofe news-papers wrote in defence of me. I have returned anfwer, that it was a matter
" of the utmoft indifference, but that if he thought it worth his while, I gave my confent, fo I have
" left it to him to do what he thinks proper.—To think I will ever enter into a controverfy with
" the weakeft as well as wickedeft of all mankind, is a thing impoffible. This I fhall do indeed,
" in a fhort preface to the fecond volume. I fhall hang him and his fellows as they do vermin in
" a warren, and leave them to pofterity to ftink and blacken in the wind; and this will I do, was the
" Pope himfelf their protector. Other bufinefs with them in the way of argument I fhall never
" have any."—" I mentioned the fecond volume: it is now in the prefs, I have received two fheets,
" two more are coming, and they cry out for more copy. *Inter nos*, I only write from hand to
" mouth, as they fay here; fo that an Eaft-wind, a fit of the fpleen, want of books, and a thoufand
" other accidents, will frequently make the prefs ftand ftill. This will be an inconvenience to Mr.
" *Gyles*: but I told him what he was to expect; and his hands are fo full of great works, that I may
" well be fpared, amongft the firft-rate of the fleet, and cruize at my leifure on a lee-fhore, fafe
" from *Webfter*, and the reft of thefe *Guarda-Coftas*."

* See Mr. *Maty's* Review for *March*, 1782, p. 81.—From the fame publication, p. 128, I fhall
copy a fragment of Bifhop *Warburton*; " We fhall now foon have Dr. *Middleton's Tully*: the follow-

" ing

" this is a controvertible propofition;" and adds, " As to the affertion, that *Middleton*
" faw the book *de Tribus Luminibus*, and availed himfelf much of it ; I have been told
" by a gentleman who lived much with him at the time, that he did fee it, but did not
" find it much to his purpofe."

P. 554. Mr. *Bowyer* begins his remarks on Dr. *Middleton* by the paragraph tranfcribed below *.

P. 559. *Samuel Haynes*, M. A. (fon of *Hopton Haynes* †, Efq;) was tutor to the Earl of
Salifbury, with whom he travelled, and who rewarded him, in *June* 1737, with the valuable rectory of *Hatfield, Herts*. In *March*, 1743, on the death of Dr. *Snape*, he fucceeded to a canonry at *Windfor* ; and in *May*, 1747, he was prefented alfo by his noble
patron to the rectory of *Clothall* (the parifh in which the Earl of *Salifbury's* feat called
Quickfwood is fituated) where Mr. *Haynes* re-built the parfonage-houfe. He was an
amiable man and a chearful companion ; as may be judged from his being prefident of
a club of gentlemen at *Baldock*, to which no other clergyman was admitted. He died
June 9, 1752.

P. 563. fub-note, read, " A MS. note of Dr. *Ward*, in his copy of thofe Memoirs,
" now in the hands of *John Loveday*, Efq."

P. 565. l. 1. Dr. *Ward's* copy gave it, " for the ufe of his fucceffors," &c.

Ibid. l. 32. read, " the civility and vivacity of his converfation."

Ibid. l. 37. Mr. *Folkes's* treatife on Perfpective is now in the collection of Mr. *Gough*.

" ing paffage relating to it I tranfcribe from one of his laft ‡ letters to me, becaufe I believe it will
" pleafe you. ' I feem now determined for a fubfcription, efpecially as I have got an additional
" charge fince I faw you, two fmall girls about eight years old, who are now in the houfe with me,
" left by an unfortunate brother, who had nothing elfe to leave ; but they are fine children, and
" have gained already fo much upon our affections, that, inftead of thinking them a burthen, we
" begin to think them a bleffing : my fubfcription therefore is like to be of the charitable kind, and
" *Tully* to be their portion.' What think you of this? I think it more edifying than all *Water-*
" *land's* books of controverfy.
      " For modes of faith let gracelefs zealots fight,
      " He can't be wrong, whofe life is in the right.
" You fee, this, if known, would much advantage his fubfcription; but I have no reafon to think
" he has a mind it fhould be known : and therefore keep it fecret." *Letter to Dr. Birch*.

* " As cenfure is a tax paid by great writers to little, I defire thefe ftrictures may be looked upon,
not fo much a proof of my detraction from Dr. *Middleton's* merit, as a teftimony of my homage to it:
I fhall fometimes make his enquiries only an introduction to new ones; and if I am for placing his
in a different point of light, I would propofe to do fo from the fame principle which I fuppofe actuated him, a fincere defire after truth. But at the fame time that I allow this to have been his firft
motive in writing, I cannot allow he always kept that motive in his fight. His heart was never open
to the glory of retracting." *W. B.*

† This gentleman was affay-mafter of the Mint near 50 years, and principal tally-writer of the
Exchequer for above 40 years ; in both which places he always behaved himfelf highly worthy of
the great truft repofed in him, being indefatigable and moft faithful in the execution of his offices.
He died at his houfe in *Queen-Square, Weftminfter, Nov.* 19, 1749. He was a moft loyal fubject,
an affectionate hufband, a tender father, a kind mafter, and a fincere friend ; charitable and compaffionate to the poor, a complete gentleman, and confequently a good Chriftian. The following
tribute was paid to his memory by Mr. *Egelfham*, a worthy old printer, author of " A Short Sketch
" of *Englifh* Grammar, 1779," 8vo ; a pleafant little volume of Songs, intituled, " *Winkey's* Whims,
" 1769 ;" and many fugitive effays in the public prints.

On the Death of HOPTON HAYNES, Efq;
  Affay-mafter of his Majefty's Mint.

" Worthy the ableft Mufe ! accept the lays,
Accept my tribute, not thy due, of praife !
Mean tho' my verfe, my theme fhall be approv'd,
Praifing of thee—whom every good man lov'd.

Who can repeat the virtues of thy mind ?
Or who a virtue, thou poffefs'd not, find ?
Great univerfal friend of all mankind !
  O could my pen depict the glowing thought,
With which my warm, but heavy heart is fraught,
Pleas'd with the tafk, I'd all thy virtues paint,
But I defift, where *Pope's* ftrong Mufe might faint."

‡ This letter is fince printed in *Middleton's* Works.

P. 569.

P. 569. l. 9. read, " 1602."—Sub-note, l. 14. read, " *Villers.*"

P. 572. l. 13—15. This story is told, by *Swift*, of *Daniel Purcell*, a Nonjuror.

P. 582. Dr. *William Stukeley*, descended from an ancient family * in *Lincolnshire*, was born at *Holbech* in that county, *November* 7, 1687. After having had the first part of his education at the free-school of that place, under the care of Mr. *Edward Kelsal*, he was admitted into *Bene't College* in *Cambridge*, *Nov.* 7, 1703, under the tuition of Mr. *Thomas Fawcett*, and chosen a scholar there in *April* following. Whilst an under-graduate, he often indulged a strong propensity to drawing and designing; but made physic his principal study, and with that view took frequent perambulations through the neighbouring country, with the famous Dr. *Hales*, Dr. *John Gray* of *Canterbury*, and others, in search of plants; and made great additions to Mr. *Ray's* " Catalogus Plantarum circa *Cantabrigiam* ;" which, with a map of the county, he was solicited to print; but his father's death and various domestic avocations prevented it. He studied anatomy under Mr. *Rolfe* the surgeon; attended the chemical lectures of Signor *Vigani*; and, taking the degree of M. B. in 1709, made himself acquainted with the practical part of medicine under the great Dr. *Mead* at *St. Thomas's* hospital. He first began to practise at *Boston* in his native county, where he strongly recommended the chalybeate waters of *Stanfield* near *Folkingham*. In 1717 he removed to *London*, where, on the recommendation of his friend Dr. *Mead*, he was soon after elected a fellow of the Royal Society, and was one of the first who revived that of the Antiquaries †, in 1717-18, to which last he was secretary for many years during his residence in town. He took the degree of M. D. at *Cambridge* in 1719, and was admitted a fellow of the college of physicians in the year following, about which time (1720) he published an account of " *Arthur's* Oon" in *Scotland*, and of " *Graham's* dyke," with plates, 4to. In the year 1722, he was appointed to read the *Gulstonian* Lecture, in which he gave a description and history of the Spleen: and printed it in folio, 1723, together with some anatomical observations on the dissection of an elephant, and many plates coloured in imitation of nature. Conceiving there were some remains of the *Eleusinian* mysteries in free-masonry, he gratified his curiosity, and was constituted master of a lodge (1723), to which he presented an account of a *Roman* amphitheatre at *Dorchester*, 4to. After having been one of the censors of the College of Physicians, of the council of the Royal Society, and of the committee to examine into the condition of the astronomical instruments of the Royal Observatory at *Greenwich*, he left *London* in 1726, and retired to *Grantham* ‡ in *Lincolnshire*; where he soon came into great request. The Dukes of *Ancaster* and *Rutland*, the families of *Tyrconnel*, *Cust*, &c. &c. and most of the principal families in the country, were glad to take his advice. During his residence here, he declined an invitation from the Earl of *Hertford* ‖ to settle

as

---

* His father, *John*, was of the family of the *Stukeleys*, lords of *Great Stukeley* near *Hurtingdon*. His mother, *Frances*, daughter of *Robert Bullen*, of *Weston*, *Lincolnshire*, descended from the same ancestors with *Anne Bullen*.

† He was also one of the earliest members of the Gentlemen's Society at *Spalding*; and held a regular correspondence with *Maurice Johnson*, Esq; and the learned *Gales*. Several of his letters to those gentlemen adorn the parts already published of the " Reliquiæ *Galeanæ*;" and others (which still remain among his MSS.) will, it is hoped, be communicated in future numbers of that work.

‡ In this town Sir *Isaac Newton* (one of the early friends of Dr. *Stukeley*) received the first part of his education, and intended to have ended his days, if he could have met with a suitable house. Dr. *Stukeley*, by his residence there, had an opportunity of collecting some memoirs of the earlier part of Sir *Isaac's* life and family, which he communicated to Mr. *Conduit*, who then proposed publishing his life. These papers, through the marriage of a daughter, fell afterwards into the hands of the late Lord *Lymington*.

‖ *Algernon Seymour*, Earl of *Hertford*, eldest son to *Charles* duke of *Somerset* by *Elizabeth* lady *Percy*, was born *Nov.* 11, 1684. He was appointed custos rotulorum of *Sussex*, *Jan.* 1705-6; made a campaign in *Flanders* in 1708, and was present at the victory of *Oudenard*, and taking of *Lisle*; was at the taking of *Tournay* and *Mons* in 1709; appointed colonel of a regiment of foot, *Oct.* 23, that year, and.

as a physician at *Marlborough*, and another to succeed Dr. *Hunton* at *Newark*. In 1728 he married *Frances* daughter of *Robert Williamson*, of *Allington*, near *Grantham*, gent. a lady of good family and fortune. He was greatly afflicted with the gout, which used generally to confine him during the winter months, on account of which, for the recovery of his health, it was customary with him to take several journeys in the spring, in which he indulged his innate love of antiquities, by tracing out the footsteps of *Cæsar's* expedition in this island, his camps, stations, &c. The fruit of his more distant travels was his " Itinerarium Curiosum; or, an Account of the Antiquities " and Curiosities in Travels through *Great Britain*, Centuria I." adorned with one hundred copper-plates, and published in folio, *London*, 1724. This was reprinted after his death, 1776, with two additional plates; as was also published the second volume (consisting of his description of *The Brill*, or *Cæsar's* camp at *Pancras*, *Iter Borcale* 1725, and his edition of *Richard of Cirencester* *, with his own and Mr. *Bertram's* † notes) illustrated with 103 copper-plates engraved in the Doctor's life-time. Overpowered with the fatigue of his profession and repeated attacks of the gout, he turned his thoughts to the church; and, being encouraged in that pursuit by archbishop *Wake*, was ordained at *Croydon*, *July* 20, 1729; and in *October* following was presented by Lord Chancellor *King* to the living of *All Saints*, in *Stamford* ‡. At the time of his entering on his parochial cure (1730), Doctor *Rogers* of that place had just invented his Oleum Arthriticum; which Dr. *Stukeley* seeing others use with admirable success, he was induced to do the like, and with equal advantage: for it not only saved his joints, but, with the addition of a proper regimen, and leaving off the use of fermented liquors, he recovered his health and limbs to a surprising degree, and ever after enjoyed a firm and active state of body, beyond any example in the like circumstances, to a good old age. This occasioned him to publish an account of the success of the external application of these oils in innumerable instances, in a letter to Sir *Hans Sloane*, 1733; and the year after he published also " A Treatise on the Cause and Cure of the Gout, from a new Rationale;" which, with an abstract thereof, has passed through several editions. He col-

and served in every campaign till the peace of *Utrecht*; was appointed governor of *Tinmouth Fort* in *Feb.* 1710-11; colonel and captain of the second troop of horse-guards, and gentleman of the bed-chamber to the prince of *Wales*, on the accession of *George* I. In 1722, on the death of his mother, he became baron *Percy*, *Lucy*, *Poynings*, *Fitzpayne*, *Bryan*, and *Latimer*. His Lordship was elected president of the Society of Antiquaries in 1724; was appointed brigadier-general, *March* 19, 1726-7; major-general of the horse, *Nov.* 11, 1735; governor of *Minorca*, *Sept.* 26, 1737; lieutenant-general of horse, *July* 2, 1739; colonel of the royal regiment of horse-guards, *May* 6, 1740; governor of *Guernsey*, *March* 13, 1741-2; general of the horse, *March* 24, 1746-7; became duke of *Somerset*, on the death of his father, *Dec.* 2, 1748; and was created, *Oct.* 2, 1749, earl of *Northumberland* and baron *Warkworth*; and next day earl of *Egremont* and baron *Cockermouth*. Dying *February* 1, 1749-50, without issue male, the baronies of *Percy*, *Lucy*, *Poynings*, *Fitzpayne*, *Bryan*, and *Latimer*, devolved on the lady *Elizabeth* his only daughter; the titles of duke of *Somerset* and baron *Seymour* fell to Sir *Edward Seymour*, baronet; those of earl of *Egremont* and baron *Cockermouth* to his nephew Sir *Charles Wyndham*, bart. the earldom of *Northumberland* and barony of *Warkworth* to Sir *Hugh Smithson*, bart. who had married the duke's daughter in 1740; and who obtained an act of parliament, *April* 11, 1750, to take and use the name, and bear and quarter the arms, of the *Percys* earls of *Northumberland*; and *Oct.* 18, 1766, was created earl *Percy* and duke of *Northumberland*. The earldom of *Hertford* and barony of *Trowbridge* were revived, in the person of *Francis Seymour* lord *Conway*, *Aug.* 3, 1750.—Duke *Algernon* was uniformly through life the patron of Dr. *Stukeley*, and was attended by him during his last illness.

* Published in 1757 under this title: " An Account of *Richard of Cirencester*, monk of *West-
" minster*, and of his Works: with his ancient Map of *Roman Britain*; and the Itinerary thereof."

† See " *Britannicarum* Gentium Historiæ Antiquæ Scriptores tres: *Ricardus Corinensis*, *Gildas
" Badonicus*, *Nennius Banchorensis*. Recensuit Notisque & Indice auxit *Carolus Bertramus* Societatis
" Antiquariorum *Londinensis* Socius, &c. *Havniæ*, 1757." 8vo. See also Dr. *Stukeley's* publication,
p. 12, 13. The Doctor's letters to Mr. *Bertram* (which were in being *Dec.* 24, 1773, at *Copenhagen*)
would be a curiosity. Those of Mr. *Bertram* to the Doctor are safely preserved.

‡ He had the offer of that of *Holbech*, the place of his nativity, from Dr. *Reynolds*, bishop of
Lincoln; and of another from the Earl of *Winchelsea*; but he declined them both.

lected

lected some remarkable particulars at *Stamford* in relation to his predecessor Bp. *Cumberland*; and in 1736 printed an explanation, with an engraving, of a curious silver plate of *Roman* workmanship in basso relievo, found under ground at *Risley Park* in *Derbyshire*; wherein he traces its journey thither, from the church of *Bourges*, to which it had been given by *Exsuperius*, called *St. Swithin*, bishop of *Thoulouse*, about the year 205. He published also the same year his " Palæographia Sacra, Nᵒ I. or, Discourses on the Mo- " numents of Antiquity that relate to Sacred History," in 4to, which he dedicated to Sir *Richard Ellys*, bart. " from whom he had received many favours." In this work (which was to have been continued in succeeding numbers *) he undertakes to shew, how Heathen Mythology is derived from Sacred History ; and that the *Bacchus* in the Poets is no other than the *Jehovah* in the Scripture, the conductor of the *Israelites* through the wilderness. In his country retirement he disposed his collection of *Greek* and *Roman* coins according to the order of the Scripture History ; and cut out a machine in wood † (on the plan of an Orrery) which shews the motion of the heavenly bodies, the course of the tide, &c. In 1737 he lost his wife ; and in 1738 married *Elizabeth* the only daughter of Dr. *Gale* dean of *York*, and sister to his intimate friends *Roger* ‡ and *Samuel Gale*, Esquires ; and from this time he often spent his winters in *London*. In 1740, he published an account of *Stonehenge*, dedicated to the Duke of *Ancaster*, who had made him one of his chaplains, and given him the living of *Somerby* near *Grantham* the year before. In 1741 he preached a Thirtieth of *January* Sermon before the House of Commons ; and in that year became one of the founders of the *Egyptian* society ‖. In 1743 he printed an account of Lady *Roisia's* sepulchral cell lately discovered at *Royston*, in a tract, intituled, " Palæographia *Britannica*, Nᵒ I." to which an answer was published by Mr. *Parkin* § in 1744. The Doctor replied in " Palæographia *Britannica*, Nᵒ II." 1746, giving an account therein of the origin of the universities of *Cambridge* and *Stamford*, both from *Croyland Abbey* ; of the *Roman* city *Granta*, on the North-side of the river, of the beginning of *Cardike* near *Waterbeach*, &c. To this Mr. *Parkin* again replied in 1748 ; but it does not appear that the Doctor took any further notice of him. In 1747 the benevolent Duke of *Montagu* (with whom he had become acquainted at the *Egyptian* Society **) prevailed on him to vacate his preferments in the country,

* " In the progress of this work, one of my views is an attempt to recover the faces or resem- " blances of many great personages in antiquity, mentioned in the Scriptures. If novelty will please, " I need not fear of success : but it will not appear so strange a matter as it seems at first sight, when " we have once ascertained the real persons characterised by the Heathen Gods and Demi-gods." *Dr. Stukeley to Mr. Gale, MS. May* 9, 1737.—" I have wrote this summer a Discourse on the Myste- " ries of the Ancients, and would willingly communicate it to you, as a second number to my " Palæographia Sacra.—Poor *Maittaire* is now at *Belvoir* with the Duke. I think the Critic is in " a declining state of health.—I visited *Meadus* ; and found the man, as usual, beset with a parcel " of sycophants, puffs, and what not ?" *Ibid. July* 30, 1738.

† He also cut out a *Stonehenge* in wood, arranged on a common round trencher ; which at his sale was purchased by *Edward Haistwell*, Esq; F. S. A. for 1l. 12s.

‡ Whom he frequently accompanied in antiquarian excursions, p. 107.

‖ Of which see above, p. 107. The great and learned Earl of *Pembroke*, the first patron of this society, accompanied Dr. *Stukeley* in opening the burrows on the *Wiltshire* Downs ; and drawings of his Lordship's antique marbles at *Wilton* were taken by the Doctor.

§ *Charles Parkin*, M. A. rector of *Oxburgh*, who continued Mr. *Blomfield's* History of *Norfolk*.

** Of this Society, which has been mentioned p. 107, the following short history by Dr. *Stukeley* is preserved in the Dedication to his *Carausius*, p. vi. " Dec. 11, 1741, an *Egyptian* Society was begun, " under the presidentship of Lord *Sandwich*. The purpose of it was to enquire into *Egyptian* Anti- " quities ; Lord *Sandwich* was met by Dr. *Pococke*, Dr. *Perry*, Capt. *Norden* the *Swedish* gentleman, " all having been in *Egypt* : they nominated Mr. *Martin Folkes*, Mr. *Charles Stanhope*, Dr. *Stukeley*, " Dr. *Milles*, Mr. *Dampier* ††, Mr. *Mitchell* ‡‡ associates, and with them founders of the society. " The Dukes of *Montagu* and *Richmond*, Lord *Stanhope*, Mr. *Dayrolles* ‖‖, and some others, were no- " minated candidates. A sistrum was laid before the president as the *insigne* of office. At one of

†† Q. the late master of *Eton* school. ‡‡ Q. the late resident at *Berlin*.

‖‖ *Solomon Dayrolles*, Esq; the friend and correspondent of Lord *Chesterfield*.

" these

country, by giving him the rectory of *St. George, Queen Square*; from whence he frequently retired to *Kentish Town* *, where the following inscription † was placed over his door:

" Me dulcis faturet quies ;
" Obfcuro pofitus loco
" Leni perfruar otio
" *Chyndonax* ‡ Druida.
" O may this rural folitude receive,
" And contemplation all its pleafures give,
" The Druid prieft !"

He had the misfortune to lofe his patron in 1749; on whofe death he publifhed fome verfes, with others on his entertainment at *Boughton*, and a " Philofophic Hymn on " *Chriftmas-Day*." Two papers by the Doctor, upon the Earthquakes in 1750, read at the Royal Society, and a Sermon preached at his own parifh church on that alarming occafion, were publifhed in 8vo, 1750, under the title of " The Philofophy of Earth- " quakes, Natural and Religious ;" of which a fecond part was printed with a fecond edition of his Sermon on " the Healing of Difeafes as a Character of the *Meffiah*, " preached before the College of Phyficians *Sept.* 20, 1750." In 1751 (in " Palæo- graphia *Britannica*, N° III.") he gave an account of *Oriuna* the wife of *Caraufius*; in

" thefe meetings, *Jan.* 22, 1742, the Duke of *Montagu* was pleafed to afk me the purport of that fo " celebrated inftrument. I fpoke of it to the fatisfaction of thofe prefent, but particularly of the " Duke, and he requefted me afterwards to give it him in writing." And fee *Reliquiæ Galeanæ*, pp. 102. 316, where it appears that the meetings were held at *The Lebeck's Head* in *Chandos-Street*.

* The following verfes (written, I am informed, by Mr. *James Holcombe*, then one of Dr. *Stukeley's* parifhioners) were addreffed to him from *Queen-Square*, *Oct.* 5, 1761:

" To a BROTHER DRUID.

" Dear Sir, your patience I folicit,
While, in a fhort poetic vifit,
I thanks return for the repaft
You gave two friends, on *Thurfday* laft,
At your delicious country feat,
With truly rural charms replete ;
And, a few thoughts with rhyme adorning,
Tell you, how well I paft my morning.
  With joy, I fipp'd the fable fluid,
As calm as a contented Druid,
And, while I view'd the fairy fpot,
The hurry of the town forgot.
The winding walk, the rifing ground,
With nobly fpreading fun-flowers crown'd ;
The Tumulus, the Temples twain,
The Hermitage, the *Gothic* Fane,
Whofe ufe fo richly you explain,
And all your garden's glorious treafure,
Gave me variety of pleafure,
Which, if I could *Apollo* bribe,
I would more feelingly defcribe.
  Thrice happy you, who can employ
Your time, in fcenes which never cloy ;
Who now and then from crouds can fteal,
And raptures in retirement feel.
The curious plants you nurfe with care,
Which ftrike the eye, and fcent the air,

At once our admiration win,
And ftir up moral thoughts within.
For who can Nature's charms explore,
And not the Ruling Power adore ?
The Power Supreme, without whofe aid,
The whole creation foon would fade !
  Your motto is with meaning fraught,
Tho' not, I truft, by many fought,
And while 'tis in a *Roman* drefs.
Few paffengers the purport guefs.
However 'tis moft *apropos*,
And makes one think of mifletoe.
  Adieu, dear fir, I have not time,
To drefs my thoughts in better rhyme.
No poet by profeffion, I
Hope, you will not my numbers try
By criticifm's rigid rules,
Which nature cramps, and genius cools.
Unfkill'd in any tricks of art,
I only fcribble from the heart ;
And therefore, while my verfe you read,
Let candid favour for me plead ;
For candor I fubmiffive fue,
That fure is to a neighbour due.
  May placid peace, and buxom health,
Which wife men covet more than wealth,
Long fhed on you their bleffings down,
In *Ormond-Street*, or *Kentifh-Town* !"

† After Dr. *Stukeley's* death, this infcription was taken down by his fon-in-law *Richard Fleming*, Efq.
‡ Alluding to an urn of glafs fo infcribed found in *France*, which he was firmly perfuaded con- tained the afhes of an arch-druid of that name (whofe portrait forms the frontifpiece to *Stonehenge*), though the *French* Antiquaries in general confidered it as a forgery; but Mr. *Tutet* has a MS. vin- dication of it, by fome learned *French* antiquary, 43 pages in fmall 4to.

Phil.

Phil. Tranf. vol. XLVIII. art. 33, an account of the Eclipfe predicted by *Thales*; and in the Gentleman's Magazine, 1754, p. 407, is the fubftance of a paper read at the Royal Society in 1752, to prove that the coral-tree is a real fea-vegetable. On *Wednefday* the 27th of *February*, 1765, Dr. *Stukeley* was feized with a ftroke of the palfy, which was brought on by attending a full veftry, at which he was accompanied by Serjeant *Eyre* *, on a contefted election for a lecturer. The room being hot, on their return through Dr. *Stukeley's* garden, they both caught their deaths; for the Serjeant never was abroad again, and the Doctor's illnefs came on that night. Soon after this accident his faculties failed him; but he continued quiet and compofed until *Sunday* following, the 3d of *March*, 1765, when he departed, in his feventy-eighth year, which he attained by remarkable temperance and regularity. By his own particular directions, his corpfe was conveyed in a private manner to *Eaft-Ham* in *Effex*, and was buried in the church-yard, juft beyond the eaft-end of the church, the turf being laid fmoothly over it, without any monument. This fpot he particularly fixed on, in a vifit he paid fome time before to the vicar of that parifh †, when walking with him one day in the church-yard. Thus ended a valuable life, daily fpent in throwing light on the dark remains of antiquity. His great learning and profound fkill in thofe refearches enabled him to publifh many elaborate and curious works, and to leave many ready for the prefs. In his medical capacity, his " Differtation on the " Spleen" was well received. His " Itinerarium Curiofum," the firft fruits of his juvenile excurfions, prefaged what might be expected from his riper age, when he had acquired more experience. The curious in thefe ftudies were not difappointed, for, with a fagacity peculiar to his great genius, with unwearied pains and induftry, and fome years fpent in actual furveys, he invefigated and publifhed an account of thofe ftupendous works of the remoteft antiquity, *Stonehenge* and *Abury*, in 1743, and hath given the moft probable and rational account of their origin and ufe, afcertaining alfo their dimenfions with the greateft accuracy. So great was his proficiency in Drui-dical hiftory, that his familiar friends ufed to call him, " The Arch-Druid of this age." His works abound with particulars that fhew his knowledge of this celebrated *Britifh* priefthood, and in his Itinerary he announced a " Hiftory of the ancient *Celts*, particu-" larly the firft inhabitants of *Great Britain*," for the moft part finifhed, to have con-fifted of four volumes folio, with above 300 copper-plates, many of which were engraved. Great part of this work was incorporated into his *Stonehenge* and *Abury*. In his " Hiftory " of *Caraufius*" in two vols. 4to, 1757, 1759, he has fhewn much learning and ingenuity

* *William Eyre*, Efq; called to the degree of ferjeant at law *Jan.* 23, 1741. That gentleman was educated at *Winchefter* fchool, and formerly fellow of *New-College*; he was a good lawyer, and an eminent antiquary; and had a very noble collection of gold and filver *Greek*, *Roman*, and *Englifh* coins, which he bequeathed, by will, to *Winchefter College*, after the death of his brother the Rev. Dr. *Eyre*, F. R. & A. SS. who very foon after the Serjeant's death delivered them up to the aforefaid college, where they now remain.

† This was the Rev. *Jofeph Sims*, B. D. of *Catharine-Hall*, *Cambridge*, formerly chaplain to Bifhop *Wilcocks*, whom he had fucceeded as chaplain to the *Englifh* factory at *Lisbon* ‡. He was rector of *St. John the Evangelift*, in *Weftminfter*; and obtained the vicarage of *Eaft-Ham* *January* 9, 1756; and re-built the parfonage-houfe there at his own expence. He was alfo a prebendary of *Lincoln* and of *St. Paul's*; a learned divine; and publifhed a Sermon on the rebellion, 1745, 4to, and a volume of excellent Sermons in 8vo, 1772. He died *April* 28, 1776, at the rectorial-houfe at *St. John*, *Weftminfter*, aged 84, and was buried at *Eaft Ham*. See his Tithe-caufe in *Burn's* " Ecclefi-" aftical Law;" by which Mr. *Sims* claimed tithe of beans and peafe; but which was determined againft him both in Chancery and on appeal to the Houfe of Lords.

‡ In his five months abfence from which, Mr. *Tindal*, tranflator of *Rapin*, officiated for him. See before, p. 553.

in

in settling the principal events of that emperor's government in *Britain*. To his interest and application we are indebted for recovering from obscurity *Richard* of *Cirencester's* Itinerary of *Roman Britain*, which has been mentioned in p. 622. His discourses, or sermons, under the title of " Palæographia Sacra, 1763," on " the vegetable crea-" tion," &c. bespeak him a botanist, philosopher, and divine, replete with ancient learn-ing, and excellent observations ; but a little too much transported by a lively fancy and invention. He closed the last scenes of his life with completing a long and laborious work on ancient *British* coins, in particular of *Cunobelin*, and felicitated himself on hav-ing from them discovered many remarkable, curious, and new anecdotes, relating to the reign of that and other *British* kings. The 23 plates of this work were published after his decease ; but the MS. (left ready for publishing) remains in the hands of his daughter Mrs. *Fleming*, relict of *Richard Fleming*, Esq; an eminent solicitor, who was the Doctor's executor. By his first wife Dr. *Stukeley* had three daughters ; of whom one died young ; the other two still survive him ; the one, Mrs. *Fleming* already mentioned ; the other, wife to the Rev. *Thomas Fairchild*, rector of *Pitsey* in *Essex*. By his second wife Dr. *Stukeley* had no child. To the great names already mentioned among his friends and patrons, may be added those of Mr. *Folkes*, Dr. *Berkeley* Bishop of *Cloyne* (with whom he corresponded on the subject of Tar-water), Dr. *Pocock* Bishop of *Meath*, and many others of the first rank in literature at home ; and among the eminent foreigners with whom he corresponded were Dr. *Heigertahl*, Mr. *Keysler*, and the learned Father *Montfaucon*, who inserted some of his designs (sent him by archbishop *Wake*) in his " Antiquity explained." A good account of Dr. *Stukeley* was, with his own permission, printed in 1755, by Mr. *Masters*, in the second part of his " History of *Corpus Christi College* ;" and very soon after his death a short but just character of him was given in the Gentleman's Magazine for 1765, by his friend *Peter Collinson*. Of both these, the compiler of the present note has availed himself ; and has been favoured with several additional particulars from respectable authority. After his decease, a medal of him was cast and repaired by *Gaub* ; on one side the head adorned with oak leaves, inscribed REV. GVL. STVKELEY, M. D. S. R. & A. S. Exergue, *æt*. 54. Reverse, a view of *Stonehenge*, OB. MAR. 4, 1765, ÆT. 84 ; [but this is a mistake, for the Doctor was but 78.] There is a portrait of him after *Kneller* in mezzotinto by *J. Smith* in 1721, before he took orders, with his arms, *viz.* Argent, a Spread Eagle double-headed Sable. Mrs. *Fleming* has another portrait of him in his robes, by *Wills* ; and Mrs. *Parsons* (relict of Dr. *James Parsons**), has a fine miniature, which is esteemed a good likeness.

P. 582. The last words of eminent men are frequently thought worth recording. Dr. *Jortin*, in answer to a female attendant who offered him some nourishment, said, with great composure, " No ; I have had enough of every thing !"

P. 583. To the article of Mr. *Lyons* (in p. 294.) add, " The Scholar's Instructor, " or *Hebrew* Grammar, by *Israel Lyons*, Teacher of the *Hebrew* Tongue in the " University of *Cambridge*. The second edition, with many Additions and Emendations " which the Author has found necessary in his long Course of teaching *Hebrew*. Cam-" bridge, 1757," 8vo, was the production of his father ; as was a treatise printed at the *Cambridge* press†, under the title of " Observations and Enquiries relat-

* Who was among the very intimate friends of Dr. *Stukeley* in the latter part of his life.
† " I am now publishing a small book of five sheets, and am obliged to quote a shekel of *Simon* " with *Samaritan* characters, which is in Dr. *Morton's* Tables of Alphabets, which tables I do not " doubt but you have them. I shall take it as a great favour of you if you could send me the let-" ters of the inscription, either in *hollow* letters, if you have such, but if you have them not, then " you will be pleased to send me the letters of the inscription in the common *Samaritan* characters." *Letter to Mr. Bowyer, July 4, 1768.*

" ing

"ing to various Parts of Scripture History *, 1768," published by subscription at 2s. 6d.
—After the death of the younger *Lyons*, his name appeared in the title-page of "A
"Geographical Dictionary," of which the Astronomical parts were said to be "taken
"from the papers of the late Mr. *Israel Lyons*, of *Cambridge*, Author of several valuable
"Mathematical Productions, and Astronomer in Lord *Mulgrave's* Voyage to the Northern Hemisphere." His first work, the "Fluxions," made him talked of at a very early
early age. He was a wonderful young man for parts and memory.

P. 589. *George Costard*, whose oriental and astronomical learning is too well known
to need encomium, was born about the year 1710; and in or before 1726† was entered of
Wadham College, Oxford, where he took the degree of M. A. *June* 28, 1733, and became a
fellow of that society, and tutor there. His first ecclesiastical preferment was the curacy
of *Islip* in *Oxfordshire*. He published, 1. "Critical Observations on some Psalms, 1733,"
8vo. 2. "A Letter to *Martin Folkes*, Esq; President of the Royal Society, concerning the
"Rise and Progress of Astronomy amongst the Ancients ‡," 1746, 8vo. His name is
signed at the conclusion of this learned and ingenious letter, though not inserted in the
title-page. 3. "Some Observations tending to illustrate the Book of *Job* ‖, and in par-
"ticular the words, *I know that my Redeemer liveth*, &c. *Job* xix. 25. 1747," 8vo.

Annexed

* The subjects of the Observations were these : *Abraham* offering up his son. God not the author
of human sacrifices. 1. Of the Empire of the *Assyrians*. 2. The sins of the fathers not punishable
in their children. 3. When cloathing was first introduced. 4. Confusion of languages not at one
time. 5. A future state. 6. *Jephtha* did not sacrifice his daughter. 7. The time in which *Job*
lived. 8. The antiquity of letters. 9. The *Hebrew* letters not changed. 10. Music discovered
without design. 11. The establishment of property. 12. The rise of sacrifices. 13. The real serpent not cursed. And many others.

† In several of his books Mr. *Costard* has written his name and college, of this date; and in some
of them, "ex dono M. *Freke* nepoti suo *Geo. Costard, Wadh. Coll.* 1726."

‡ Of the articles mentioned Nᵒ 2—5, I have an epitome in MS. by Mr. *Bowyer*.

‖ "The composition under consideration," says Mr. *Costard*, "is an exalted and regular piece of
"Eastern poetry, and of the dramatick kind. The persons speaking are *Eliphaz, Bildad*, and *Zo-
"phar*; who regularly take their turns in the debate, which is upon a question no less important
"than how—' to vindicate the ways of God to men.' What methods are pursued by them, in
"order to do this, doth not at present fall under my design to observe. 'Tis apparent, however,
"that their several answers to *Job's* pleas may be looked on as three distinct acts. These replica-
"tions and rejoinders continue to the 32ᵈ chapter, where *Elihu* begins the share he takes in the
"conference. This brings us to the 38ᵗʰ chapter, which concludes the fourth act, when the Deity
"appears and closeth the scene in the fifth. I will not say, that this is the first tragedy that we
"know of as extant in the world, or that any Eastern productions of this nature laid the foundation
"of the *Greek* stage. It may not be improper to observe, however, that two rules laid down by a
"very great master of the art of poetry are exactly maintained. It is not, as was said,
"   —quinto productior actu;
"nor is God introduced, 'till it becomes
"   —dignus vindice nodus.
"The narration at the beginning and end may be looked on as the prologue and epilogue; and
"the part assigned *Job's* wife § seems intended for a short and refined satire on those that, without
"proper accomplishments or abilities, impertinently interpose their judgements in subjects of the
"highest importance, and which it is impossible they should understand. But if this is a proper re-
"presentation of the case, will it not be a farther proof of the lateness of the composition? Poetry,
"no doubt, such as it was, must have been of very ancient original. But then it seems to have been
"confined for a long time to songs, short hymns, panegyricks, and the like; rather taught and

§ "The next person in the drama is *Job's* wife. She acts a short part indeed, but a very spirited one. *Curse
God*, says she, *and die*. Tender and pious! He might see by this specimen of his wife what he was to expect
from his friends. The Devil, we are told, tempted *Job*, but he seems to have taken possession of his wife," &c.
Bishop *Warburton*.

"treasure

Annexed to these observations is " The Third Chapter of *Habakkuk*, paraphrastically translated into *English* Verse," by Mr. *Costard*, some years before, for his own amusement. 4. " A Further Account of the Rise and Progress of Astronomy amongst the Ancients [*], in " Three Letters to *Martin Folkes*, Esq; President of the Royal Society. By the Author " of the First, 1748," 8vo. The immediate subjects of these letters were, the *Chaldæan* Astronomy, the Constellations in the Book of *Job*, and the Mythological Astronomy of the Ancients. 5. " Two Differtations : I. containing an Enquiry into the Meaning of the word " *Kefitah*, mentioned in *Job*, chap. xlii. ver. 11. In which is endeavoured to be proved, " that though it most probably there stands for the Name of a Coin, yet that there is no " reason for supposing it stamped with any Figure at all, and therefore, not with that of " a Lamb in particular. II. On the Signification of the Word *Hermes*; in which is " explained the Origin of the Custom, among the *Greeks*, of erecting Stones called *Her-* " *mæ*; together with some other Particulars, relating to the Mythology of that People, " 1750 [†]," 8vo. 6. " Differtationes II. Critico-Sacræ [‡], quarum prima explicatur " *Ezek.* xiii. 18. Altera vero 2 *Reg.* x. 22. 1753," 8vo. 7. His " Letter to Dr. *Shaw*, " on the *Chinese* Chronology and Astronomy," is printed in Phil. Transf. N.° 483, p. 477. 8. " A Letter on a Fiery Meteor, seen *July* 14, 1745," Ib. N.° 477, p. 522. (observed by him near *Stanlake Broad*, in returning from his living). 9. " Letter to Dr. *Bevis*, " concerning the Year of the Eclipse foretold by *Thales*," Phil. Transf. vol. XLVIII. p. 17. 10. " Letter on an Eclipse mentioned by *Xenophon*," Ib. p. 155. 11. " A " Letter on the Ages of *Homer* and *Hesiod*," Ib. p. 441. At the end of article 6, was announced what appeared in 1765, in 4to, under the title of (12.) " The Use of " Astronomy in History and Chronology, exemplified in an Enquiry into the Fall of the " Stone into *Ægofpotamos*, said to be foretold by *Anaxagoras*. In which is attempted " to be shewn, that *Anaxagoras* did not foretell the Fall of that Stone, but the Solar " Eclipse in the first year of the *Peloponnesian* War; that what he saw was a Comet " at the Time of the Battle of *Salamis*; and that this Battle was probably fought the " year before Christ 478; or two years later than is commonly fixed by Chronologers." 13. " The History of Astronomy, with its Application to Geography, History, and Chro- " nology, occasionally exemplified by the Globes, 1767," 4to. 14. " Astronomical and " Philological Conjectures on a Passage in *Homer*, 1768," 4to. 15. " A Letter to *Na-*

" treasured up in the memory, like those of the Druids, than committed to writing. Regular " poems must have been owing to leisure, education, and the establishment of schools and acade- " mies. There men of letters, and lovers of retirement, might without interruption give scope to " their fancy, and cultivate its suggestions into an orderly well digested system. 'Twas then, and " not before, that abstruse metaphysical subjects began to employ men's thoughts, and which were " by every one treated according to his different inclination and abilities."

* On this most curious subject, see Messrs. *Gentil, Bailly,* &c.

† These differtations were inscribed to his friend Professor *Hunt*. In the conclusion of them, Mr. *Costard* observes, " The study of the Oriental languages seems to be gaining ground in *Europe* " every day; and provided the *Greek* and *Latin* are equally cultivated, we may arrive in a few years " at a greater knowledge of the ancient world, than may be expected, or can be imagined. But " without this foundation, I may venture to pronounce, from the little experience I have had, that " all will be darkness and perplexity. It is beginning at the wrong end, which can never be at- " tended with success in any thing. It may not, perhaps, be improper to add, before I have done, " that for such researches as these I have here been speaking of, few places, if any, in *Europe* are so " well adapted as the University of *Oxford*."

‡ The latter of these was republished under the title of " A Differtation on 2 *Kings* x. 22, translated " from the *Latin* of Rabbi C———d, with a Dedication, Preface, and Postscript, Critical and Ex- " planatory, by the Translator, 8vo, 1752." In the Preface and Dedication, Mr. *Costard* is at- tempted to be placed in a very ludicrous light.

" *thanie*

" thaniel Braſſey Halhed *, Eſq; containing ſome Remarks on his Preface to the Code of " Gentoo Laws lately publiſhed, 1778," 8vo; a letter evidently dictated, not by the " ſpirit of criticiſm," but by the love of truth, and for which Mr. Coſtard deſerved the thanks of every friend to revelation.—In June, 1764, he obtained the vicarage of Twickenham in Middleſex, by the favour of lord chancellor Northington; Biſhop Terrick, who held it in commendum with the ſee of Peterborough, having vacated it by his tranſlation to that of London. The fellows of Wadham-College hold their fellowſhips for a limited number of years. He died Jan. 10, 1782. His library, Oriental MSS. and philoſophical inſtruments, were ſold by auction by Mr. Paterſon March 19—21.

P. 590. l. 15. read, " Howgrave."

P. 592. " Peck's advertiſement," ſays Biſhop Warburton, " has been an inexhauſtible " fund of mirth in this place [Newark], and I don't doubt but our good friend Mr. Ray † " has had his ſhare of it. He ſeems to have had a deſign of confirming what I ſaid of " the poem, that it was his own, when he ſays that, being his own property, he will " give the reaſons that induced him to pitch upon Milton for the author; which im " plies, that, being his own property, he had a right to give it to whom he pleaſed; and " he pitched upon Milton as the moſt in his favour whilſt he was writing blank verſe. " But his joining Herod the Great ‡ to it, which is undoubtedly his own, aſcertains the " property; a poem, as well as a man, being to be known by his company. On which " I will venture to pronounce condemnation in due form of law, that it ſhall return " from whence it came. From a dunghill, he ſays, he received it, and to a dunghill it " ſhall go, let him print upon as ſtiff paper as he pleaſes. In this caſe I am as clear " and poſitive as the famous Etymologiſt ‖, who ſaid he not only knew from whence " words came, but whither they were going §."

P. 596. l. 4. read " plight."

P. 607. l. 7. read " ſon of."

P. 610. Another of Mr. Markland's ſiſters (Mary) was married to Robert Foley, Eſq; father to the late Sir Robert.

P. 613. note, l. 9. for " 1615" read " 1650."

P. 617. The name of Bedford has occurred ſo often in this volume, that it becomes neceſſary to give ſome account of the family. Hilkiah Bedford, of Sibſey, in Lincolnſhire, a Quaker, came to London, and ſettled there as a ſtationer, between the years 1600 and 1625. He married a daughter of Mr. William Plat of Highgate, by whom he had a ſon Hilkiah, a mathematical inſtrument-maker in Hoſier-Lane, near Weſt-Smithfield. In this houſe (which was afterwards burnt in the great fire of London 1666) was born the famous Hilkiah, July 23, 1663; who in 1679 was admitted of St. John's college, Cambridge, the firſt ſcholar on the foundation of his maternal grandfather William Plat. Hilkiah was afterwards elected fellow of his college, and patronized by Heneage Finch Earl of Winchelſea, but deprived of his preferment (which was in Lincolnſhire) for refuſing to take the oaths at the revolution, and afterwards kept a boarding-houſe for the

* To this gentleman the publick is indebted for " A Grammar of the Bengal Language, printed " at Hoogly in Bengal, 1778," 8vo; which is a remarkable curioſity in typography; the Bengal types uſed in it having been incomparably well cut by Mr. Wilkins, a gentleman in the Eaſt India Company's civil ſervice at that ſettlement.

† A native of Spalding, and member of the Gentlemen's Society there. He was educated at St. John's college, Cambridge, and died at Spalding.

‡ This was a tranſlation of the " Baptiſta" of Buchanan, printed by Peck, with his " Memoirs of " Milton." Prefixed to it are ſeveral very inconcluſive reaſons for aſcribing it to Milton.

‖ Dr. Bentley. See p. 636.

§ The firſt of Biographers has uſed a ſimilar expreſſion in the cloſe of his critique on Parnell.

Weſtminſter

Weſtminſter ſcholars. In 1714, being tried in the Court of King's-bench, he was fined 1000 marks, and impriſoned three years, for writing, printing, and publiſhing "The "Hereditary Right of the Crown of *England* aſſerted, 1713," folio ; the real author of which was *George Harbin*, a Nonjuring clergyman, whom his friendſhip thus ſcreened, and on account of his ſufferings he received 100*l.* * (ſee p. 507) from the late Lord *Weymouth*, who knew not the real author. His other publications were, a tranſlation of an anſwer to *Fontenelle's* Hiſtory of Oracles, and a *Latin* Life of Dr. *Barwick*, which he afterwards tranſlated into *Engliſh.* He died in 1724. By his wife *Alice*, daughter of *William Cooper*, Eſq; he had three ſons ; 1. *William* †, educated at *St. John's* college (appointed phyſician to *Chriſt's Hoſpital* 1746, and regiſter of the College of Phyſicians, *London*, of which he was fellow and cenſor, and died *July* 11, 1747, leaving by his ſecond wife an only daughter *Elizabeth*, married 1778 to *John Claxton*, Eſq; of *Lincoln's-Inn*, and of *Shirley* near *Croydon*, *Surrey*, F. A. S.) 2. *Thomas*, a divine, of whom an account has been given in p. 340. And 3. *John* ‡, phyſician at *Durham*. He had alſo three daughters, of whom *Chriſtian* the eldeſt married *George Smith* ‖, Eſq; of *Burnhall* ; *Elizabeth* married 50 years to the Rev. Mr. *Gordoun*, who died advanced in years within a week after her, *Oct.* 1779 ; *Mary* married to Mr. *John Soleby*, druggiſt, in *Holbourn.*

* Perhaps the pocketing of the 100*l.* required no ceremony ; for *Bedford* "was proſecuted, and "ſuffered impriſonment for fathering" the book (ſee p. 17) ; which notorious fact, known to Lord *Weymouth* and all the world, might ſufficiently account for the benefaction to *Bedford*, whether he were looked upon to be the author of the book, or not. But the ſtrange part of the ſtory is, that *Harbin*, the author of the book, ſhould carry the money to him as the real author.

† I have a number of this gentleman's letters to Dr. *Z. Grey* in MS.

‡ Who uſed to ſign himſelf " *John Bedford*, M. D. Univ. *Patav.*" About the year 1761 he retired from practice, and lived remarkably recluſe. He was deſcribed by a gentleman who viſited him in 1766, as " near in his expences, ſober and regular in his living, exact in his payments, and "punctual to his promiſes." He had at that time an intention of putting up a monument to his father in the church of which he was deprived. He was thrice married ; died in 1776, very rich ; and left a ſon, *Hilkiah*, who was entered in the ſummer of 1768 of *St. John's College, Cambridge*, became a fellow of that colege, and a counſellor, and died, greatly beloved, in 1779. Dr. *John Bedford* had alſo two daughters ; one of whom died ſingle in 1765 ; the other (born in 1748) was married in 1766.

‖ The following inſcription is copied from a black marble tomb-ſtone in *Elvet* church-yard, *Durham.*

" Here lies the body
Of GEORGE SMITH, of *Burnhall*, Eſq;
The venerable remains of a moſt valuable perſon,
Whoſe manners, life, and writings,
Gave a luſtre to his birth and ſtation,
And ſhewed, that with the name
He had all the qualifications
of a Gentleman, a Chriſtian, and a Scholar.

He died *Nov.* 4, 1756, in the 64th year of his age.
Near him are alſo buried
Twelve of his children, who died infants, viz.
Seven ſons and five daughters.
Alſo CHRISTIAN,
Wife of the ſaid GEORGE SMITH,
Who died the 23d of *July*, 1781,
Aged 79."

⁂ A

⁎⁎⁎ A few articles of information having come to hand too late to be inserted in their regular places; they are here submitted to the reader.

P. 1. The first book printed by the elder Mr. *Bowyer* was the " Defence" here mentioned. The author of it was *Thomas Wagstaffe*, an eminent Nonjuror, of a good family in *Warwickshire*. He was born *Feb.* 5, 1645; educated at the *Charter-House* school; and in 1660 admitted commoner of *New-Inn-Hall* at *Oxford*. He took the degrees of B. A. and M. A. and, going into orders, became rector of *Martin's-Thorp* in the county of *Rutland*. After that, he lived in the family of Sir *Richard Temple*, at *Stow* in *Buckinghamshire*; and in 1684 was presented by the King to the Chancellorship of the church of *Litchfield*, with the annexed prebend of *Alrewas*. The same year the King gave him the rectory of *St. Margaret Pattens* in *London*. Upon the Revolution in 1688, he was deprived of his preferments for not taking the new oaths; and afterwards practised physic many years, wearing his gown all the while. *Feb.* 23, 1693, he was consecrated a Nonjuring Bishop by the deprived Bishops of *Norwich*, *Ely*, and *Peterborough (Lloyd, Turner, and White)*; which solemnity was performed at the Bishop of *Peterborough's* lodgings in the house of the Reverend Mr. *Giffard* at *Southgate*, *Henry* Earl of *Clarendon* being present: Mr. *Wagstaffe* was consecrated by the title of suffragan of *Ipswich*, and Dr. *Hickes* at the same time by that of *Thetford*. In 1711 he published in 4to, from the press of Mr. *Bowyer*, " A Vindication of King *Charles* the Martyr: proving that his Majesty " was the author of ΕΙΚΩΝ ΒΑΣΙΛΙΚΗ, against a Memorandum, said to be written by " the Earl of *Anglesey*; and against the Exceptions of Dr. *Walker* and others. To " which is added a Preface, wherein the bold and insolent assertions published in a Pas- " sage of Mr. *Bayle's* Dictionary, relating to the present Controversy are examined and " confuted. The third Edition; with large Additions, together with some original " Letters of King *Charles* the First, under his own Hand, never before printed; and " faithfully copied from the said Originals." Mr. *Wagstaffe* died *October* 17, 1712, after having given many proofs of good parts and learning: for he wrote and published many pieces, in defence of the constitution of the church and state according to the Nonjuring system.—As many tracts have been written to prove that King *Charles* could not be the author of ΕΙΚΩΝ ΒΑΣΙΛΙΚΗ, and still more to confirm his title to that book, I will transcribe below ⁎ an epitome of the controversy; and add here such new testimonies as have occurred

---

⁎ On one side it is said, that in the year 1686, when the Earl of *Anglesea's* books were selling by auction, this book presented itself among others. The bidders being cold, the company had time to turn over the leaves; and there they found a declaration, under his lordship's own hand, that King *Charles* the Second and the duke of *York* both assured him that it was not of the King's own compiling, but made by Dr. *Gauden*† bishop of *Exon*. This made a noise; and Dr. *Walker* being ques-

† *John Gauden* was born at *Mayland* in *Essex*; made dean of *Bocking* and master of *The Temple* in the beginning of the reign of *Charles* I.; bishop of *Exeter* in 1660; and translated to *Worcester* two years after, which see he enjoyed but four months, dying at his palace there, *Sept.* 20, 1662, aged 57. A portrait of him is given by Dr. *Nash*, in which his character is strongly marked, though by a bad artist, and taken from a bad bust, placed over his grave in the cathedral church at *Worcester*. *Gauden* published a book, intituled, " Ἱερὰ δάκρυα, Ecclesiæ " *Anglicanæ* Suspiria: The tears, sighs, complaints, and prayers of the Church of *England*." In the frontispiece is drawn a tree, on whose branches is set forth the history and chronology of Episcopacy, Presbytery, and Independancy, as pretenders to church government: the whole book is wrote something in this style, and is more debased with the pedantry than embellished with the elegances of learning. Some other of his works are " Hieraspistes." A sermon intituled, " Funerals made Cordial." " The Case of the Ministers Maintenance " by Tythe." Some Sermons; and other books.

tioned

curred to me from the MSS. of Mr. *Bowyer :* " Mr. *Royston*, who first printed the book, informed Sir *William Dugdale*, that, about the beginning of *October* 1648, he was sent

tioned about it, as known to be very intimate with *Gauden*, he owned that the bishop had imparted to him the plan in the beginning, and several chapters actually composed; and that he, on the other hand, had disapproved the imposing in such a manner on the publick; and in his treatise, intituled, " A True Account of the Author, &c." Dr. *Walker* says, " I know and believe the book was written by Dr. *Gauden*, except the " sixteenth and twenty-fourth chapters, which were written by Dr. *Duppa*." *Gauden* delivered the MS. to *Walker*, who carried it to the press. A merchant of *London* of the name of *North*, a man of good credit, married the bishop's son's lady's sister, and after young *Gauden's* death his papers came into *North's* hands, being his brother-in-law. There he found one packet relating entirely to ΕΙΚΩΝ ΒΑΣΙΛΙΚΗ, containing among other things, original letters, and a narrative written by Dr. *Gauden's* own wife. Bishop *Burnet* says, that, as he had once an occasion to quote this book, when in conference with king *Charles* the Second, and the duke of *York*, in 1673, they both declared that their father never wrote it, but that it was written by *Gauden*, whom they rewarded with a bishoprick. See " A Letter from Major-General *Ludlow* to Sir E. S. 1691," 4to; " *Ludlow* " no Lyar, 1692," 4to; *Walker's* " True Account, &c. 1692," 4to; *Toland's* and *Richardson's* " Life of *Milton*," and *Bayle's* " General Dictionary;" and more particularly *Neale's* " History " of the Puritans," vol. II. chap. 10.—To this evidence has been opposed, the public testimony of both *Charles* II. and *James* II. to the contrary, under the great seal in their patent to Mr. *Royston*, for printing all the works of King *Charles* I. And though it is highly probable that neither of these princes were likely to know any thing of the contents of patents, this circumstance deserves at least as much credit as a private memorandum unattested, purporting it to be written with a view that it could not answer: " I assert this," says Lord *Anglesea*, " to undeceive " others:" but if his intention had been " to undeceive others," why did he leave his declaration in the privacy of his study, on a single leaf that might be obliterated or torn out; where indeed it was known to exist but by accident, the slow sale of the books affording time to the company to turn over the leaves? why did he not authenticate his declaration by proper witnesses, and publish it to the world, or leave it in some trusty hand, with a charge to publish it at some more convenient season? As to *Gauden's* pretensions to this book, they are easily to be accounted for, supposing them to be ill founded. After the death of Dr. *Bryan Duppa*, bishop of *Winchester*, *Gauden*, presuming on the favour of some persons at court, solicited, with great eagerness, for the vacant see, though he had openly abjured the whole episcopal order, and was said to have advised King *Charles* II. by letter to suppress it in *Scotland*: to strengthen his claim to this favour, he is said to have whispered among his friends, and attempted, without witness or credit, to persuade the King and his brother the Duke of *York*, that their father was obliged to him for the credit which he derived from the ΕΙΚΩΝ ΒΑΣΙΛΙΚΗ. But this was 15 years after the death of *Charles* I. nor was any person then living who could give evidence concerning the book. It is however urged, that Dr. *Walker*, at the age of 70, and 40 years after the King's death, appeared in defence of this fiction; but must *Walker's* evidence, in favour of *Gauden*, be deemed indisputable, as has been insinuated, merely because *Gauden* was his preceptor, and afterwards his intimate? This surely is rather a reason why it ought to be suspected. Besides, *Walker's* evidence is defective, and, in some instances, scarce consistent; for, though he says Dr. *Gauden* shewed him the plan, and several chapters actually composed, yet he does not say that they were in the doctor's hand; and he afterwards expresses himself doubtfully, whether he read any part of the manuscript, or only saw it with the title of the chapters, though surely, if *Gauden* shewed him some part actually composed, as his own work, he could not have mortified him with such coldness and want of curiosity as not to read it: besides, for what other purpose was it shewn? and how could *Walker* be supposed to live at this time in the house with *Gauden*, and know so much, without knowing more? As to the evidence of Mr. *North* and Mrs. *Gauden*, it can stand for little, if the following positive evidence in favour of the book be considered : M. *de la Pla*, minister of *Finchingfield*, in a letter to Dr. *Goodall*, informs him, that *William Allen*, a man of repute and veracity, who had been many years a servant to *Gauden*, declared, that *Gauden* told him he had borrowed the book, and that being obliged to return it in a certain time, he sate up in his chamber one whole night to transcribe it, *Allen* himself sitting up with him, to make up his fire and snuff his candles. It is also recorded by Sir *William Dugdale*, who was perfectly acquainted with the transactions of his own times, that these meditations had been begun by his majesty at *Oxford*, long before he went thence to the *Scots*, under the title of *Suspiria Regalia*; and that the manuscript itself, in the King's own hand-writing, being lost at *Naseby*, was restored to him at *Hampton-Court*, by Major *Huntingdon*, who had obtained it from *Fairfax*. That Mr. *Thomas Herbert*, [afterwards Sir *Thomas*, the traveller,] who waited on his majesty in his bed-chamber in the *Isle of Wight*, and

William

sent to by the King to prepare all things ready for the printing some papers, which he purposed shortly after to convey to him; and which was this very copy, brought to him the 23d of *December* next following by Mr. *Edward Symmons*; in the printing whereof Mr. *Royston* made such speed, that it was finished before the 30th of *January*, on which his Majesty's life was taken away. Mr. *Edward Symmons*, who conveyed both the copies *(viz.* that written by Mr. *Odart* and that by the King) to the press, declared upon his death-bed, that it was the King's work, and assured several of his friends at *Fowey*, when he sent them some of the books, that he had printed them from the King's own copy *.—There were seventeen editions printed of the book in 1648, without the Prayers; and twelve more in 1649, in which year there were at least six editions † with the Prayers. These were first printed by *Dugard*, who was *Milton's* intimate friend, and happened to be taken printing an edition of the King's book. *Milton* used his interest to bring him off, which he effected by the means of *Bradshaw*, but upon this condition, that *Dugard* should add *Pamela's* prayer to the aforesaid book he was printing, as an atonement for his fault, they designing thereby to bring a scandal upon the book, and blast the reputation of its authority. (Dr. *Gill's* Letter to Mr. *Wagstaffe.)* To the same purpose Dr. *Bernard*, who (as well as *Gill*) was physician to *Hills*, *Oliver's* printer, and told him this story, adding, " that he had often heard *Bradshaw* and *Milton* ‡ laugh at their inserting this prayer out of Sir *Philip Sydney's Arcadia*." These Prayers are said in their title to have been " delivered to Dr. *Juxon*," &c. If so, they must have been handed to the press by the King's enemies; for Dr. *Juxon* and all his papers were immediately seized upon the King's death; even the minutest scraps were examined, the King's cloaths, cabinets, and boxes, were rifled. They were first printed at *Dugard's* press, and afterwards

William Levet, a page of the back-stairs, frequently saw it there, read several parts of it, and saw the king divers times writing farther on in that very copy which Bishop *Duppa*, by his majesty's direction, sent to Mr. *Royston*, a bookseller, at the *Angel* in *Ivy-Lane*, on the 23d of *December*, 1648, who made such expedition, that the impression was finished before the 30th of *January*, on which his majesty died. Lastly, it is improbable, that, if this book had been the work of *Gauden*, King *Charles* II. would have expressed himself with so little esteem and affection, when he heard of his death; " I doubt not," said he, " it will be easy to find a more worthy person to fill " his place." See *Wagstaffe's* " Vindication, 1711;" *Bedford's* Appendix to his " Life of Dr. " *Barwick*;" Dr. *Hollingworth's* " Defence of *Eikoon Basilike*, 2 parts, 4to, 1692;" another " Defence," by *Thomas Long*, B. D. 4to, 1693; and *Dugdale's* " Short View."

* Archbishop *Herring*, comparing the work with *Anti-Machiavel*, says, " In my opinion, this " book of the King of *Prussia* is much more in the style and character of a great prince than the ce- " lebrated ΕΙΚΩΝ ΒΑΣΙΛΙΚΗ, unless we are to suppose every christian prince to support the two cha- " racters of king and priest; for the book last mentioned is more agreeable to the sacred function, " as, I believe, in real truth, it was the work of one of us." *Letters to Mr. Duncombe.—Swift's* opinion of it has been already given in p. 613.

† The *sixth* is said, in the title, to be " printed by *W. D.* in *R. M.* Anno Dom. 1649." There were *fifty* editions in various languages within twelve months.

‡ " *Milton*," says his greatest Biographer, " is suspected of having interpolated the book called " *Icon Basilike*, which the Council of State, to whom he was now made *Latin* secretary, employed " him to censure, by inserting a prayer taken from *Sidney's Arcadia*, and imputing it to the King; " whom he charges, in his *Iconoclastes*, with the use of this prayer as with a heavy crime, in the in- " decent language with which prosperity had emboldened the advocates for rebellion to insult all " that is venerable and great : ' Who would have imagined so little fear in him of the true all-seeing " Deity—as, immediately before his death, to pop into the hands of the grave bishop that attended " him, as a special relique of his saintly exercises, a prayer stolen word for word from the mouth of " a heathen woman praying to a heathen god ?' The papers which the King gave to Dr. *Juxon* on " the scaffold the regicides took away, so that they were at least the publishers of this prayer ; and " Dr. *Birch*, who examined the question with great care, was inclined to think them the forgers. " The use of it by adaptation was innocent ; and they who could so noisily censure it, with a little " extension of their malice could contrive what they wanted to accuse."

were

were quickly tranflated to Mr. *Rovfion's*, for every thing that was fuppofed to come from the King quickened the fale of the impreffion. Mrs. *Fotherly* of *Rickmanfworth* in *Hertfordfhire*, daughter of Sir *Ralph Whitfield*, firft ferjeant-at-law to King *Charles* I. and grand-daughter to Sir *H. Spelman*, declared to Mr. *Wagftaffe*, that within two days after the King's death, fhe faw, in a *Spanifh* leather cafe, three of thefe prayers, faid to be delivered to the bifhop of *London* at his death, from whom they were taken away by the officers of the army ; and it was from one of thofe officers, in whofe cuftody they then were, that fhe had the favour to fee them ; and that the perfon who fhewed her thofe prayers, fhewed her alfo the *George* with the Queen's picture in it, and two feals which were the King's. Three of the prayers therefore were the King's, the other added by the publifher." *W. B.*—The late worthy Dr. *John Burton*, in an Appendix to " The Ge-" nuinenefs of Lord *Clarendon's* Hiftory," &c. has given fome remarks on the grounds upon which the King's title to this book was called in queftion ; which he concludes by obferving, that, " confidering only the characters of the perfons, and abftracting from " the proofs of the facts, the account which afcribes the honour of the performance to " Dr. *Gauden* appears on the face of the thing altogether incredible, and that in favour " of King *Charles* will at leaft appear probable. But when all the evidences on both " fides of the queftion are ftated in a fair light *, the point will be at once determined, " the King's right will be for ever eftablifhed : even prejudiced men may at laft receive " conviction, and be afhamed of their own credulity, and the impudence of the aftonifh- " ing accufation."—Dr. *Nafh* alfo, in his fecond volume of *Worcefterfhire*, p. clvii. has drawn together the principal arguments on each fide of this curious queftion ; and finds reafon to conclude from fome obfervations of Bifhop *Warburton* †, and the whole of the

evidence

* Mr. *Hume*, who takes occafion to mention the book in queftion, fays, " With regard to the " genuinenefs of that production, it is not eafy for an hiftorian to fix any opinion, which will be " entirely to his own fatisfaction. The proofs brought to evince that this work is or is not the " King's, are fo convincing, that, if an impartial reader perufes any one fide apart, he will think it " impoffible that arguments could be produced fufficient to counter-balance fo ftrong an evidence : " and when he compares both fides, he will be fome time at a lofs to fix any determination. " Should an abfolute fufpence of judgement be found difficult or difagreeable in fo interefting a " queftion, I muft confefs, that I much incline to give the preference to the arguments of the Roy- " alifts. The teftimonies, which prove that performance to be the King's, are more numerous, " certain, and direct, than thofe on the other fide. This is the cafe, even if we confider the ex- " ternal evidence : but when we weigh the internal, derived from the ftyle and compofition, there " is no manner of comparifon. Thefe meditations refemble in elegance, purity, neatnefs, and fim- " plicity, the genius of thofe performances, which we know with certainty to have flowed from the " royal pen : but are fo unlike the bombaft, perplexed, rhetorical, and corrupt ftyle of Dr. *Gauden*, " to whom they are afcribed, that no human teftimony feems fufficient to convince us that he was " the author. Yet all the evidences, which would rob the King of that honour, tend to prove, that " Dr. *Gauden* had the merit of writing fo fine a performance, and the infamy of impofing it on the " world for the King's. It is not eafy to conceive the general compaffion excited towards the King, " by the publifhing, at fo critical a juncture, a work fo full of piety, meeknefs, and humanity. " Many have not fcrupled to afcribe to that book the fubfequent reftoration of the royal family. " *Milton* compares its effects to thofe which were wrought on the tumultuous *Romans* by *Anthony's* " reading to them the will of *Cæfar*. The *Icon* paffed through fifty editions in a twelvemonth ; " and, independent of the great intereft taken in it by the nation, as the fuppofed production of their " murdered Sovereign, it muft be acknowledged the beft profe compofition, which, at the time of its " publication, was to be found in the *Englifh* language." *Hiftory of England*, 8vo, vol. VII. p. 160.

† In the public library at *Durham* may be feen a MS. note written by Bifhop *Warburton* in the margin of *Neal's* Hiftory, wherein he fays, " There is full as ftrong evidence on the other fide, which " Mr. *Neale* does not produce ; evidence of the King's bed-chamber, which fwear they faw the " progrefs of the work, faw the King write it, heard him fpeak of it as his, and tranfcribed part of it " for him. It appears by the wretched falfe tafte of compofition in *Gauden's* other writings, and by

" his

evidence both external and internal, that *Gauden* was not the author of the book in question. " As he had the character of a proud, ambitious man," says Dr. *Nash*, " he
" might be tempted to encourage, if not invent this forgery, which tended so much to
" gain him interest at court. The only similitude I could find between the *Eikoon Ba-*
" *silikè* and *Gauden's* other works, consists in the quaint *Greek* title *, which, perhaps,
" might not be given to the former by the King, or whoever wrote the book, but by the
" publisher to humour the false taste of the times." And the late worthy Mr. *Granger*
says, " Whoever examines the writings of the King and the Divine, will find that *Charles*
" could no more descend to write like *Gauden*, than *Gauden* could rise † to the purity and
" dignity of *Charles*." But, after all, it may be observed, that in the volume of " King
" *Charles's* Works," there are some other pieces which have since been proved not to
have been written by him.

In a copy of *Wagstaffe's* " Vindication" and " Defence," formerly belonging to Dr.
Rawlinson, and now to Mr. *Gough*, are autographs of the following testimonies :

" The author of the following tracts was the Right Reverend Mr. *Wagstaffe*, who
" was consecrated a Bishop by the Right Reverend the deprived Bishops of *Norwich*,
" *Ely*, and *Peterborough*, and the Right Reverend *George Hickes* Suffragan Bishop of
" *Thetford*; the Honourable *Henry* Earl of *Clarendon* being a witness thereto.

" J. Creyk, Chaplain to Lord Winchelsea.

" *Winchelsea, Aug.* the 12, 1722. I do affirm that, in the year 1688, Mrs. *Mom-*
" *pesson* (wife to *Thomas Mompesson*, Esq; of *Bruham* in *Somersetshire*, a worthy and a very
" good woman) told me and my wife, that Archbishop *Juxon* assured her, that to his
" certain knowledge the ΕΙΚΩΝ ΒΑΣΙΛΙΚΗ was all composed and written by King
" *Charles* the First.—Although in the following book the King's book is thoroughly
" vindicated, and proved to be of his Majesty's composing, I was willing to add this
" circumstance, from Mrs. *Mompesson*, with whom and her husband my wife and I at
" that time sojourned. Winchelsea."

P. 12. To the list of books, l. 3. add, " An Introduction to the Classics; contain-
" ing a short Discourse on their Excellences; and Directions how to study them to
" Advantage; with an Essay on the Nature and Use of those emphatical and beautiful
" Figures which give Strength and Ornament to Writing. By *Anthony Blackwall*,
" M. A. ‡, 1719," 2d edition, 12mo.

P. 32.

" his unchaste language, that he was utterly incapable of writing this book. Again, consider what
" credit was to be given to *Gauden's* assertion of his authorship. He confesses himself a falsary and
" an impostor, who imposed a spurious book on the public in the King's name. Was not a man so
" shameless capable of telling this lye for a bishoprick, which he was soliciting on the pretended
" merit of this work ? As to *Walker*, it is agreed that *Gauden* told him, that he (*Gauden*) was the
" author of the book, and that he (*Walker*) saw it in *Gauden's* hand-writing; which is well ac-
" counted for by a servant, a tithe-gatherer of *Gauden*, who swears that *Gauden* borrowed the book
" of one of the King's friends, to whom it was communicated by the King for their judgement; that
" he (*Gauden*) sat up all night to transcribe it, and that he (the tythe-gatherer) sat up with him to
" snuff the candles, and to mend his fire. It is agreed that *Charles* II. and the Duke of *York* be-
" lieved on the word of *Gauden*, when he solicited his reward, that he (*Gauden*) wrote it; but then
" this favoured their prejudices, and what they believed Lord *Clarendon* would believe likewise.
" On the whole, it is so far from being certain, as the Historian (*Neale*) pretends, that the book is
" spurious, that it is the most uncertain matter I ever took the pains to examine. There is strong
" evidence on both sides; but I think the strongest, and most unexceptionable, is on that which
" gives the book to the King." *History of Worcestershire*, vol. II. p. clviii.

* The history of " the quaint *Greek* title" is given in *Wagstaffe*, p. 105.

† " If we could be sure of this, the matter would be determined at once, as there is no third
" claimant. It is likely that *Charles* wrote some, or much; and that *Gauden* made a book of it." *T. F.*

‡ This excellent and learned gentleman, after completing his academical education at *Emanuel-*
4 L 2
College,

P. 32. "You mention Mr. *Waſſe* * as the publiſher of "Bibliotheca Literaria," which "he was not, but Dr. *Jebb*. *Waſſe* contributed ſeveral pieces, as many others did; "and at laſt knocked it up by ſending too long pieces, which had not variety enough to "pleaſe the capricious taſte of the world; *viz.* the Life of *Juſtinian*, which took up "two whole numbers, not finiſhed then." Bowyer, *MS. Letter to a Friend.*

P. 37. note †, A friend obſerves, "I have now before me *Midleton's* "De Medi-"corum apud veteres *Romanos* degentium Conditione Diſſertatio, 1726," and "Notæ "breves —— 1726," moſt undoubtedly written by Dr. *Joſeph Letherland*, (notwith-

College, Cambridge, was appointed head-maſter of the free-ſchool at *Derby,* and lecturer of *All-Hallows* there, where he firſt diſtinguiſhed himſelf in the literary world by an edition of *Theognis,* printed at *London* in 1706, and was afterwards head-maſter of the free-ſchool at *Market-Boſworth* in *Leiceſterſhire,* The Grammar whereby he initiated the youth under his care into *Latin* was of his own compoſing, and ſo happily fitted for the purpoſe, that he was prevailed on to make it public, though his modeſty would not permit him to fix his name to it, becauſe he would not be thought to preſcribe to other inſtructors of youth. It is intituled, "A New *Latin* Grammar; being a ſhort, clear, and eaſy "Introduction of young Scholars to the Knowledge of the *Latin* Tongue; containing an exact "Account of the two firſt Parts of Grammar." In his "Introduction to the Claſſics," firſt pub-liſhed in 1718, 12mo, he diſplayed the beauties of thoſe admirable writers of antiquity, to the un-derſtanding and imitation even of common capacities; and that in ſo conciſe and clear a manner as ſeemed peculiar to himſelf. But his greateſt and moſt celebrated work was, "The Sacred Claſſics "defended and illuſtrated; or, an Eſſay humbly offered towards preſerving the Purity, Propriety, "and True Eloquence of the Writers of the New Teſtament. Vol. I. In Two Parts. In the Firſt "of which thoſe Divine Writings are vindicated againſt the Charge of barbarous Language, falſe "*Greek,* and Soleciſms. In the Second is ſhewn, that all the Excellencies of Style, and ſublime "Beauties of Language and genuine Eloquence do abound in the Sacred Writers of the New Teſ-"tament. With an Account of their Style and Character, and a Repreſentation of their Superi-"ority, in ſeveral Inſtances, to the beſt Claſſics of *Greece* and *Rome.* To which are ſubjoined pro-"per Indexes. By *A. Blackwall,* M. A." firſt printed in 4to, 1725; and of which a ſecond volume (completed but a few weeks before his death) was publiſhed in 1731, under the title of "The "Sacred Claſſics defended and illuſtrated. The Second and Laſt Volume. In Three Parts. "Containing, I. A farther Demonſtration of the Propriety, Purity, and ſound Eloquence of the "Language of the New Teſtament Writers. II. An Account of the wrong Diviſion of Chapters "and Verſes, and faulty Tranſlations of the Divine Book, which weaken its Reaſonings, and ſpoil "its Eloquence and Native Beauties. III. A Diſcourſe on the Various Readings of the New "Teſtament. With a Preface; wherein is ſhewn the Neceſſity and Uſefulneſs of a New Verſion "of the Sacred Books. By the late Reverend and Learned *A. Blackwall,* M. A. Author of the "Firſt Volume. To which is annexed, a very Copious Index." To this volume was prefixed an admirable Preface, and a portrait of the Author, by *Vertue,* from an original painting. Both vo-lumes were printed at *Leipſick,* 1736, in one volume 4to, tranſlated by *Chriſtopher Wolle,* who has added various obſervations, &c. Mr. *Blackwall* had the felicity to bring up many excellent ſcho-lars in his ſeminaries at *Derby* and *Boſworth;* among others, the celebrated *Richard Dawes* †, author of the "Miſcellanea Critica," and one gentleman (whoſe name I ſhould be happy to record), who, being patron of the church of *Clapham* in *Surrey,* preſented him to that living, as a mark of his gratitude and eſteem. This happening late in life, and *Blackwall* having occaſion to wait upon the Biſhop of the dioceſe, he was ſomewhat pertly queſtioned by a young chaplain as to the extent of his learning. "Boy," replied the indignant veteran, "I have forgot more than ever you knew!" He died at *Market Boſworth, April* 8, 1730. His ſon, *John Blackwall,* gent. died *July* 5, 1763, aged 56; and was buried at *Stoke* in *Leiceſterſhire.* See his epitaph in the Hiſtory of *Hinckley,* p. 97.

* Of *Aynhoe* in *Northamptonſhire;* an eminent critic at the end of the laſt and beginning of the preſent century.

† Born in 1708, and admitted of *Emanuel College, Cambridge,* in 1725. In 1736 he publiſhed a Specimen of a *Greek* Tranſlation of Paradiſe Loſt; of which, in his Preface to the Miſcellanea Critica, he had candour enough to point out the imperfections himſelf. The blot of his life was taking part againſt *Bentley,* from whom the preſent father of *Greek* literature in this country, Mr. *Toup,* acknowledges to have learnt more than from all the critics of all the ages before. Mr. *Dawes* died in 1766, and left ſome manuſcripts, to which Mr. *Burgeſs* (who has lately publiſhed a new and improved edition of the "Miſcellanea Critica") had acceſs. There are ſome others in Dr. *Aſkew's* collection, who bought Mr. *Dawes's* library. See *Maty's* Review for *February,* 1782.

ſtanding

ſtanding the diſguiſe of *P. W.*) as was alſo "Animadverſio brevis, 1727." But your Nº 6 was, I can warrant, Profeſſor *Ward's*; as in a ſub-note you rather ſuppoſe it to be. There is an 8vo. with this title, all I know of it, "*Dan. Vink* Amœnitates Phyſico-"medicæ, in quibus Medicina a ſervitute liberatur. *Traject.* 1730."—In the ſame note, l. 6, for "1734" read "1724."

P. 48. Dr. *Wilkins* died Sept. 6, 1745, aged 62.

P. 99. note. In Dr. *Knight's* epitaph, l. 6, read, "Concionando."

P. 103. Biſhop *Tanner*, in 1733, married a ſecond wife, Miſs *Scottow* of *Thorp*, near *Norwich*, with whom he had a fortune of 15,000*l.* His only ſon (by his firſt wife) *Thomas Tanner*, D. D. (who married a daughter of Archbiſhop *Potter*) is now preben-dary of *Canterbury*, and ſucceſſor to Dr. *Wilkins* in the rectories of *Hadleigh* and *Monks Eleigh, Suffolk.*

Ibid. note, l. 14. *alphabet of graduates*] Dr. *Caryl** did the ſame, and brought it down lower. The two catalogues, it is much to be hoped, will be incorporated at the expence of the Univerſity. The writer of this paragraph would willingly contribute his aſſiſtance in the taſk, however laborious it may be.—Since p. 103 was printed, Dr. *Robert Richardſon* (to whom I was indebted for the account of his excellent father) is alſo dead †. Dr. *Richardſon's* attachment to *Frederick* Prince of *Wales*, occaſioned that ſarcaſm in the Capitade, "He prays for *George*, to *Frederick's* cauſe adheres." His car-rying his option-cauſe by appeal into the Houſe of Lords was entirely owing to Mr. *Yorke*, who inſiſted upon it, offering to plead it *gratis.*

P. 123. note *, l. 3, read, "now (1782) Lord *Fairfax* of *Scotland*, by the death of "his elder brother."

P. 127. Dr. *Chandler*, a friend informs me, was not originally brought up to the profeſſion of a bookſeller; it was in conſequence of having loſt his wife's fortune in the *South Sea* bubble that he took it up, and continued in it but two or three years.

P. 138. Dr. *Warburton*, in a letter to Dr. *Birch*, ſays, "I am glad that the Society "for the Encouragement of Learning is in ſo hopeful a condition; though methinks it "is a little ominous to ſet their preſs a-going with the arranteſt Sophiſt ‡ that ever "wrote, prepared by ſo arrant a critic."

P. 150.

---

* *Lyndford Caryl*, D. D. prebendary of *Canterbury, Lincoln,* and *Southwell*, maſter of *Jeſus College, Cambridge,* and regiſtrar of that univerſity. He died at *Canterbury*, aged 75, and was buried in the chapel belonging to *Jeſus College.*

† He died, aged 50, at his houſe in *Dean-Street, Soho,* of a moſt uncommon and diſtreſſing com-plaint. His rectory of *Wallington, Herts,* was given to him by Sir *Joſeph Yorke*, with whom he had reſided as chaplain many years at *The Hague.*—"Whilſt in that employ, the papers on both ſides, "previous to the trial of the great cauſe, *Douglas* againſt *Hamilton*, being ſent over to his Excel-"lency, the Doctor, for his own curioſity, digeſted them and drew up the ſtate of the queſtion, "which was printed in 4to, and ſo well approved of by the gentlemen of the profeſſion, that it was "put into the hands of the counſel for the party he eſpouſed as their brief; of which perhaps there "never was a ſimilar inſtance. The Doctor had the happineſs and honour to ſee the opinion "he ſupported confirmed by the almoſt unanimous ſuffrages of the Houſe of Peers, with this "rare circumſtance, that two of the ableſt law lords that ever met in that place, whoſe political "opinions generally divide them, appeared ably and warmly on the ſame ſide of the queſtion. Nor "would any thing have been wanting to make the triumph complete, had Mr. *Andrew Stewart* "never committed his thoughts to print; however, ſo due a ſenſe was entertained of the Doctor's "ſervices, that after the trial he was offered 400*l.* in the handſomeſt manner, which he was adviſed, "I can't tell why, to refuſe." *T. F.*

‡ This probably alludes to Mr. *Markland's* edition of *Maximus Tyrius*; at leaſt the following quotation from another letter ſhews Dr. *Warburton's* opinion of that able critic: "I have a poor "opinion both of *Markland's* and *Taylor's* critical abilities, between friends: I ſpeak from what "I have ſeen. Good ſenſe is the foundation of criticiſm; this it is that has made Dr. *Bentley* and

"Biſhop

P. 150. *Nathaniel Salmon*, fon of the Rev. *Thomas Salmon*, M. A. rector of *Mepfall* (a living of confiderable value in *Bedfordfhire*, and now in the patronage of *St. John's College* in *Cambridge*) was admitted of *Bene't College*, *June* 11, 1690, under the tuition of Mr. *Beck*, and took the degree of LL. B. in 1695. Soon after which he went into orders, and was for fome time curate of *Weftmill* in *Hertfordfhire*, but, although he had taken the oaths to King *William*, he would not do it to his fucceffor Queen *Anne*; and when he could officiate no longer as a prieft, he applied himfelf to the ftudy of phyfic, which he practifed firft at *St. Ives* in *Huntingdonfhire*, and afterwards at *Bifhop's Stortford* in the county of *Hertford*. He did not, however, take this turn out of neceffity, but by choice, fince he had the offer of a living of 140*l. per annum* from a friend in *Suffolk*, if his confcience would have permitted him to qualify himfelf for it by taking the legal oaths. He was the elder brother of Mr. *Thomas Salmon* the hiftoriographer; who, dying fuddenly in *London* in *April* 1743, was buried in *St. Dunftan's Church*. *Nathaniel* (who left three daughters) was the author of, 1. " A Survey of the *Roman* " Antiquities in the Midland Counties of *England*, 1726," 8vo.—2. " A Survey of the " *Roman* Stations in *Britain*, according to the *Roman* Itinerary, 1728," 8vo.—3. " The " Hiftory of *Hertfordfhire*, defcribing the county and its ancient monuments, particu-" larly the *Roman*, with the characters of thofe that have been the chief poffeffors of " the lands, and an account of the moft memorable occurrences. *London*, 1728," folio. This was defigned as a continuation of Sir *Henry Chauncey's* Hiftory, and dedicated to the Earl of *Hertford*.—4. " The Lives of the *Englifh* Bifhops from the Reftoration to " the Revolution, fit to be oppofed to the Afperfions of fome late Writers of Secret " Hiftory. *London*, 1731—1733.—5. " A Survey of the *Roman* Stations in *England*, " 1731," (an improved edition probably of N° 1. and 2.) 2 vols. 8vo.—6. " The Anti-" quities of *Surrey*, collected from the moft Ancient Records, and dedicated to Sir *John* " *Evelyn*, Bart. with fome Account of the Prefent State and Natural Hiftory of the " County. *London*, 1736," 8vo.—7. " The Hiftory and Antiquities of *Effex*, from the " Collections of Mr. *Strangeman*," in folio, with fome Notes and Additions of his own; but death put a ftop to this work, when he had gone through about two-thirds of the county, fo that the hundreds of *Chelmsford*, *Hinkford*, *Lexdin*, *Tendring*, and *Thurftable*, are left unfinifhed.

P. 215. " A remarkable cafe of a perfon cut for the ftone in a new way, commonly " called the *lateral*, *March* 13, 1741-2, by Mr. *Chefelden*," is in Phil. Tranf. N° 478, p. 33.—" The effects of the *Lixivium Saponis*, taken inwardly by a man aged 75, who " had the ftone, and in whofe bladder, after his deceafe, were found 214 ftones." Ibid. p. 36.

P. 291. To the books of 1759 add, Mr. *Murden's* " Collection of State Papers," folio. The publication of this work, which had been long delayed through the pecuniary difficulties of the editor, was at length completed in confequence of the following agreement: " Mr. *Bowyer* undertakes to finifh Mr. *Murden's* State Papers, and to deliver " them when printed, on receiving the fubfcription-money which fhall remain unpaid " when the book is finifhed, and on being paid for printing the laft 50 fheets, exclufive " of the faid fubfcription money." *From the Original.*

" Bifhop *Hare* the two greateft critics that ever were in the world. Not that good fenfe alone will " be fufficient; for that confiderable part of it, emending a corrupt text, there muft be a certain fa-" gacity, which is fo diftinguifhing a quality in Dr. *Bentley*. Dr. *Clarke* had all the requifites of a " critic but this, and this he wanted. *Lipfius, Jof. Scaliger, Faber, If. Voffius, Salmafius*, had it in " a great degree; but thefe are few amongft the infinite tribe of critics."

P. 295.

P. 295. Mr. *Arnald* was born at *London*, and admitted a penſioner of *Bene't College*, *Cambridge*, under the tuition of Mr. *Waller*, in 1714. After taking the degree of B. A. being diſappointed of a fellowſhip, he removed to *Emanuel College*, March 10, 1718, where he proceeded M. A. and was elected fellow in 1721. He commenced B. D. ſeven years after, as the ſtatutes of that houſe required, and continued there till the ſociety preſented him to the rectory of *Thurcaſton*. Whilſt fellow of that college, he printed two copies of Sapphics on the death of King *George* ; a Sermon preached at *Biſhop Stortford* ſchool-feaſt, *Aug.* 3, 1726; and another at the Archdeacon's Viſitation at *Leiceſter*, *April* 22, 1737. His third Sermon, preached at *Thurcaſton*, *Oct.* 9, 1746, has been already particularly mentioned. His widow died *April* 11, 1782.

P. 310. note, l. 5. read, " a Day in Vacation."

P. 334. The circumſtance of Mr. *Club's* death, I am informed by a gentleman who knew him well, is erroneous. He died a natural death, of age and infirmities.

P. 341. l. 4. add, Mr. *Shepheard* has alſo lately publiſhed *(May,* 1782) " An Eſſay " on Education, in a Letter to *William Jones*, Eſq;" 8vo.

P. 357. ſub-note, l. ult. read, " 1773, p. 21."

P. 425. *George* the firſt Lord *Lyttelton* was born at ſeven months, and thrown away by the nurſe as a dead child, but upon cloſer inſpection was found to be alive. Dr. *Naſh*, Appendix to vol. II. p. 24.

P. 505. To the extracts from *Wanley's* Diary, add, " Mr. *Browne Willis* came, want-
" ing to peruſe one of *Holmes's* MSS. marked L, and did ſo; and alſo L 2, L 3, and L 4,
" without finding what he expected. He would have explained to me his deſign in his
" intended book about our Cathedrals ; but I ſaid I was about my Lord's neceſſary buſi-
" neſs, and had not leiſure to ſpend upon any matter foreign to that. He wanted the
" liberty to look over *Holmes's* MSS. and indeed over all this library, that he might
" collect materials for amending his former books, and putting forth new ones. I ſigni-
" fied to him that it would be too great a work ; and that I, having buſineſs appointed
" me by my Lord, which required much diſpatch, could not in ſuch a caſe attend upon
" him. He would have teazed me here this whole afternoon, but I would not ſuffer
" him. At length he departed in great anger, and I hope to be rid of him." *December*
13, 1725.

P. 509. l. 6. Biſhop *Keene* *, maſter of his college.

P. 543. *Iſaac Maddox*, born at *London* of obſcure parents, whom he loſt whilſt he was young, was taken care of by an aunt, who placed him in a charity-ſchool, and after-wards put him on trial to a paſtry-cook ; but, before he was bound apprentice, the maſter told her that the boy was not fit for trade ; that he was continually reading books of learning above his (the maſter's) comprehenſion, and therefore adviſed that ſhe ſhould take him away, and ſend him back to ſchool to follow the bent of his incli-nation †. He was on this ſent, by an exhibition of ſome Diſſenting friends, to one of the

---

* " The ſee of *Ely* was Biſhop *Keene's* great object, the aim and end of all his ambition ; and upon
" the vacancy in 1771, he ſucceeded," ſays Dr. *Newton*, " to his heart's deſire, and happy it was
" that he did ſo ; for few could have borne the expence, or have diſplayed the taſte and magnifi-
" cence, which he has done, having a liberal fortune as well as a liberal mind ; and really meriting
" the appellation of a builder of palaces : for he built a new palace at *Cheſter*, he built a new *Ely*-
" houſe in *London*, and in great meaſure a new palace at *Ely*, left only the outer walls ſtanding,
" formed a new inſide, and thereby converted it into one of the beſt epiſcopal houſes, if not the very
" beſt, in the kingdom. He had indeed received the money which aroſe from the ſale of old *Ely*-
" houſe, and alſo what was paid by the executors of his predeceſſor for dilapidations, which alto-
" gether amounted to about 11,000l. : but yet he expended ſome thouſands more of his own upon
" the buildings, and new houſes require new furniture." *Life of Biſhop Newton, by himſelf,* 1782.

† See Dr. *Norvell's* Anſwer to " Pietas Oxonienſis, 1768," p. 49.

7   univerſities

universities in *Scotland*; but, not caring to take orders in that church, was afterwards, through the patronage of Bishop *Gibson*, admitted of *Queen's College, Cambridge*, and was favoured with a Doctor's degree at *Lambeth*. After entering into orders, he first was curate of *St. Bride's*, then domestick chaplain to Dr. *Waddington*, bishop of *Chichester*, whose niece he married; and was afterwards promoted to the rectory of *St. Vedast* in *Foster-Lane, London*. His other preferments are pointed out in his character at large in the epitaph transcribed below *, from the Historian of *Worcestershire*. In 1733 he published the first part of the "Review of *Neal*" (as mentioned in p. 356) under the title of "A Vindication of the Government, Doctrine, and Worship of the Church of *England*, "established in the Reign of Queen *Elizabeth*." He was a great benefactor to the *London* hospitals, and the first promoter of the *Worcester* infirmary in 1745, which has proved of singular benefit to the poor, and a great advantage to medical and chirurgical knowledge in that neighbourhood. He was also a great encourager of trade,

* His monument in the South transept of the great aile in the cathedral of *Worcester* consists of a female figure of white marble, leaning with her right elbow on a sarcophagus of black marble, on which is the story of the merciful *Samaritan*, in white basso-relievo. In her left hand she holds an inverted torch, behind which rises a pyramid of grey marble, about twenty-four feet in height, as a back ground; on the top of which are the arms of the see of *Worcester*. On a tablet is the following inscription:

"May this marble record to future times
The excellent endowments and beneficent virtues
of Dr. *Isaac Maddox*, bishop of this diocese.
An exact knowledge of the constitution
of this national church,
And an active zeal for its support and prosperity,
Manifested in a variety of occasions,
And especially in writing a judicious vindication
of the plan of the Reformation adopted by
Queen *Elizabeth*,
Eminently qualified him for the prelacy:
All the extensive and important duties of which
function
He perfectly understood and conscientiously
discharged
With fervor, prudence, and integrity.
The love of his country
(The ruling passion of his truly *English* heart)
Urged him to promote, with unwearied care,
Loyalty, industry, sobriety,
And whatever might secure and increase
the public welfare.
A father to his clergy—
He directed them by his counsel,
Supported them by his authority,
And assisted them by his liberality:
A rare example!
After many other bountiful donations,
He assigned 200*l. per annum*, during his life,
For the augmentation of the smaller benefices
of his diocese.

A guardian of the poor,
He abounded in private charities,
And encouraged every public one.
Long may the sick and impotent bless the patron,
And those of this county the institutor,
Of Infirmaries!
Hospitality and generosity,
Enlivened with chearfulness, affability,
and good-nature,
Were the distinguished virtues of the man
and the friend;
And the piety and fortitude of the Christian
Were brought to the test and stood the trial
In two most afflicting circumstances—
The death of a lovely daughter,
In whom at 11 years of age
All the graces of the mind,
Dwelling in the most elegant form,
Not only began to dawn,
But seemed to be hastening to maturity;
And the death of a most accomplished son,
at the age of 17,
Whose virtuous disposition,
and uncommon attainments in learning,
Deserved and received the favour and applause
of *Eton* and *Christ Church*.
Conjugal and maternal affection,
Weeping over the mingled ashes
of her much honoured and much lamented Lord
and of her dear children,
Erected this monument to their memory.

He was born *July* 27, 1697; was appointed clerk of the closet to Queen *Caroline* 1729; was made dean of *Wells* in 1733; was consecrated bishop of *St. Asaph* 1736; and was translated to the see of *Worcester* in 1743. He married in 1731 *Elizabeth* daughter of *Richard Price*, of *Hayes*, in the county of *Middlesex*, Esq; and died *Sept.* 27, 1759, leaving to a tender mother's care one surviving beloved daughter, since given in marriage to the honourable and reverend Mr. *Yorke*, dean of *Lincoln*."

engaging

engaging in the *British* Fishery, by which he lost some money. He likewise was a strong advocate for the act against vending spirituous liquors. A gentleman once dining with him at *Hartlebury*, after a handsome entertainment came some tarts; he very much pressed the company to taste his pastry, saying pleasantly, "that he believed they were very " good, but that they were not of his own making." This was a joke he was fond of repeating. Bishop *Maddox* published 14 single Sermons, all in 4to, preached on pub-lic occasions between the years 1734 and 1752.

P. 554. " One of Dr. *Bentley*'s most formidable enemies was Dr. *Middleton*, as appears " from several parts of his works, and particularly from his remarks upon Dr. *Bentley*'s " projected edition of the New Testament, which remarks are supposed to have been one " principal obstacle to the publication of that work. But, length of time having overcome " all prejudices, it is much wished that the person who possesses the MS. would oblige the " learned world by setting forth so curious a performance. By the death of Dr. *King*, " there was a vacancy of the mastership of *The Charter House*, a place which some consi-" derable persons at different periods have desired to fill. Bishop *Benson* and Dr. *Jortin* " used to say, that there was a certain time in their lives, when of all preferments they " wished for it the most. And now the competitors to succeed Dr. *King* were Dr. *Mid-*" *dleton* and Mr. *Mann*. When Dr. *Middleton* applied to Sir *Robert Walpole* for his vote " and interest, Sir *Robert* honestly told him, that, talking with Bishop *Sherlock*, he found " the Bishops were generally against his being chosen master. Mr. *Mann* had been tutor " to the Marquis of *Blandford*; and it was through the interest of the *Marlborough* fa-" mily that he gained the ascendant over Dr. *Middleton*.....Dr. *Middleton* was much hurt " and provoked at the disappointment; and thinking Bishop *Sherlock* to be the primary " cause of it, he wreaked his malice in his ill-natured and ill-timed animadversions upon " the Bishop's Discourses on Prophecy, pretending that he had never seen them before, " though they had been published several years, and had gone through several editions. " Nor did he afterwards spare the Archbishop and his chaplains, but took every opportu-" nity of making *Lambeth-House* the subject of his wit and satire. It is also well known " that he wrote a treatise on the inutility and inefficacy of prayer, which was communi-" cated to Lord *Bolingbroke*, who much approved it, and advised the publication of it. " Mrs. *Middleton*, however, never thought proper to publish it in her life-time; and the " Bishop has heard that Dr. *Heberden*, a particular friend of Dr. *Middleton*, and to whom " his widow left all his papers, has since committed it to the flames; an act worthy of so " good a man, and the fittest end of such a work." Bishop *Newton*.

P. 558. In *Chambers*'s Epitaph l. 1. read " Multis;" and in col. 2. " putavit." And see p. 149; where it appears that Mr. *Bowyer* had conceived an extensive design for improving the Dictionary of Mr. *Chambers**.

P. 559. *Henry Fletcher*, Esq; was created a baronet *April* 24, 1782.

Ibid. sub-note, l. 1. read, μητροπολίτης—l. 2. a comma after the second word, a period after the fourth.

P. 560. sub-note, read, 1717.——P. 567. l. 5. from bottom, read p. 192.

. P. 581. The title of Mr. *Cooke*'s book is, " The Medallic History of *Imperial Rome*; " from the first Triumvirate, under *Pompey, Crassus*, and *Cæsar*, to the removal of the " Imperial Seat by *Constantine the Great*. With several Medals and Coins, accurately " copied and curiously engraven. To which is prefixed an Introduction, containing a " General History of the *Roman* Medals, in two volumes. By *William Cooke*, M. A. " Vicar of *Enford* in *Wiltshire*, and Rector of *Oldbury* and *Didmarton* in *Glouceste-*" *shire*, 1781," 2 vols. 4to †.

* The anecdote in the second sub-note, p. 558, should have been omitted, having been before introduced in p. 148.

† The merit of this work is greatly lessened by the want of new and correct engravings of the coins, which are for the most part taken from the *Pembroke* collection. Mr. *Cooke* also vindicates *Goltzius* from the charge brought against him by *Patin*, that no man had seen one-third of the coins exhibited by him.

P. 586. l. 8. read, " one of the two daughters of *Samuel De Langle*, D. D. who had " a benefice in the neighbourhood of *Oxford*, and taught the *French* language to " young gentlemen in the university. The other was married to Dr. *Smalridge*." [See the next note.]—A niece of Dr. *R. Freind* * was married to a son of Dr. *Bentley*, who, after that event, conceived a better opinion of the *Chrift Church* men, and declared, that " *Freind* had more good learning in him than ever he had imagined."

P. 587. l. 2. " The epitaph to *Smalridge* at *Chrift Church*," fays Bifhop *Newton*, " was drawn up moft probably by Dr. *Freind*, the head-mafter of *Weftminfter* school, " and alfo his brother-in-law; the Bifhop and he having married two fifters †. Dr. *Freind* " was at that time the celebrated writer of *Latin* epitaphs; which yet Mr. *Pope*, who " was as great a compofer of epitaphs in *Englifh* verse, and could not well bear a " rival in any way, thought too prolix and too flattering, if Dr. *Freind* be really in- " tended, as he was generally fuppofed to be intended, in that epigram :

" *Freind*, for your epitaphs I'm griev'd,
" Where ftill fo much is faid,
" One half will never be believ'd,
" The other never read."

P. 588. Dr. *Freind* had once a fee of 300 guineas for a journey from *London* to *In- geftree* in *Staffordfhire*, to attend Mr. *Pulteney*, who lay there dangeroufly ill, but recovered before Dr. *Freind* arrived.

Ibid. l. 14. The traditional ftory is thus confirmed by Bifhop *Newton*: " Dr. *William* " *Freind*, brother to Dr. *Robert Freind*, mafter of *Weftminfter* school, and to Dr. *John* " *Freind*, the famous phyfician, had a prize of 20,000l. in Queen *Anne's* time, and " another confiderable prize of 5 or 10,000l. in the reign of *George* I. but yet with thefe " lucky hits he would have died a prifoner in *The Fleet* ‡, if his old fchool-fellow the " Earl of *Winchelfea*, when he was at the head of the Admiralty, had not made him " chaplain to a fhip of 100 guns."

Ibid. l. 33. Mr. *Spence's* ‖ explanation of an antique marble at *Clandon-Place* in *Surrey* is printed in Gent. Mag. 1772, p. 176.

P. 598. Bifhop *Newton's* delineation of a learned Prelate will be no bad companion to that by Dr. *Johnfon* : " Bifhop *Warburton* was in a great meafure loft to the world and " to his friends fome years before his death, by the decay of his intellectual faculties, the " body preffing down the mind that mufed upon many things; which hath been the " cafe of many a great Genius as well as himfelf. For he was indeed a great Genius,

---

* This gentleman's fon (fee p. 330, note, l. 1.) married, in *April* 1739, *Grace*, youngeft fifter to the late Sir *Thomas Robinfon*, &c.—The following Impromptu is afcribed to Mr. *Hawkins Browne*, on feeing Mr. *Highmore's* picture of this lady :

" I, whom no living beauty yet could warm,
" Am now enamour'd of an empty form."

† The Bifhop left three children, a fon named *Philip*, and two daughters.

‡ Rather *The King's Bench*, a circumftance which Mrs. *Pilkington* could not miftake.

‖ " Mr. *Spence's* character," fays a friend who had feen the note in p. 332, " is properly deline- " ated; and his *Polymetis* is juftly vindicated from the petty criticifms of the faftidious *Gray*. In " Dr. *Johnfon's* mafterly Preface to *Dryden*, he obferves, that ' we do not always know our own " motives.' Shall we then prefume to attribute the frigid mention of the truly learned and inge- " nious Mr. *Spence*, in the Preface to *Pope*, to a prejudice conceived againft him on account of his " preference of blank verfe to rhyme in his Effay on Mr. *Pope's* Odyffey; a work, which for found " criticifm and candid difquifition is almoft without a parallel. The judicious Dr. *Warton's* fenti- " ments with refpect to it may be feen in his admirable Effay on *Pope*, ii. 301, juft publifhed : and " Bifhop *Lowth*, whofe learning and genius are indifputable, expreffes himfelf in the following " manner in a note on his twelfth Præelection on *Hebrew* poetry : ' Hæc autem vide accurate et " fcienter explicata à Viro Doctiffimo *Jofepho Spence* in Opere erudito juxta atque eleganti cui " Titulus *Polymetis*.'

5

" of the moſt extenſive reading, of the moſt retentive memory, of the moſt copious
" invention, of the livelieſt imagination, of the ſharpeſt diſcernment, of the quickeſt
" wit, and of the readieſt and happieſt application of his immenſe knowledge to the
" preſent ſubject and occaſion. He was ſuch an univerſal reader, that he took delight
" even in romances; and there is ſcarce one of any note, ancient or modern, that he
" had not read; he ſaid himſelf, that he had learned *Spaniſh* to have the pleaſure of
" reading *Don Quixote* in the original. He was excellent and admirable both as a
" companion and a friend. As a companion, he did not dwell upon little trivial mat-
" ters, but diſcloſed a nicer vein of converſation, was lively and entertaining, was in-
" ſtructive and improving, abounded with pleaſant ſtories and curious anecdotes; but
" ſometimes took the diſcourſe too much to himſelf, if any thing can be ſaid to be too
" much of ſuch an inexhauſtible fund of wit and learning. As a friend, he was inge-
" nuous and communicative, would anſwer any queſtion, would reſolve any doubts, de-
" liver his ſentiments upon all ſubjects freely without reſerve, laid open his very heart,
" and the character which he was pleaſed to give Mr. *Pope*, of being *the ſoul of friend-*
" *ſhip*, was more juſtly applicable to him, and more properly his own. The ſame
" warmth of temper which animated his friendſhip, ſharpened likewiſe his reſentment:
" but even to his enemies, if he was eaſily provoked, he was as eaſily reconciled, eſpe-
" cially after the leaſt acknowledgement and ſubmiſſion, ſo that his friends truly applied
" to him the ſaying,

" *Iraſci facilis, tamen ut placabilis eſſet.*

" He was rather a tall, robuſt, large-boned man, of a frame that ſeemed to require a
" good ſupply of proviſions to ſupport it; but he was ſenſib'e, if he had lived as other
" people do, he muſt have uſed a good deal of exerciſe; and if he had uſed a good deal
" of exerciſe, it muſt have interrupted the courſe of his ſtudies, to which he was ſo de-
" voted as to deny himſelf any other indulgence, and ſo became a ſingular example, not
" only of temperance, but even of abſtinence in eating and drinking; and yet his ſpirits
" were not lowered or exhauſted, but were rather raiſed and increaſed by ſuch low
" living..... The beſt and moſt valuable memorials of Biſhop *Warburton* will be his
" own works. And yet his capital work, The Divine Legation of *Moſes*, is left unfi-
" niſhed, to the loſs and regret of all who have any regard for religion or learning.
" It is indeed a loſs much to be lamented, whatſoever was the cauſe, whether he was
" diſguſted at the ill reception which was given to the work by ſeveral of the clergy,
" for whoſe uſe and ſervice it was principally intended; or whether he was diverted
" from it by the numerous controverſies wherein he was engaged in defence of it. But
" he ſhould have cared for none of theſe things, but ſhould have proceeded di-
" rectly and ſteadily to the end. The viper might have faſtened upon his hand, but,
" like St. *Paul*, he ſhould have ſhaken off the beaſt into the fire; and, like him too,
" would certainly have felt no harm. Whatever was the cauſe, the misfortune is, that
" out of nine books, ſix only are compleated. Of the three remaining, he judged the
" ninth to be the moſt material, and had therefore written the whole, or the greater
" part of it, and had cauſed it to be printed, but could not be prevailed upon to pub-
" liſh it in his life-time. It is hoped that ſome of his friends, and thoſe whom it may
" concern, will, for their own emolument, as well as for the public benefit, ſet forth a
" handſome edition of all his works * together, as a κτημα ις αει, a poſſeſſion for ever."
—" The works of Biſhop *Warburton* and Dr. *Jortin*," ſays Biſhop *Newton* in another
paſſage with wonderful acuteneſs, " will ſpeak for them better than any private
" commendation. They were really two very extraordinary men; and though their
" characters were much alike in ſome reſpects, yet they were very different in others.

* I have anticipated the worthy Biſhop's wiſh in p. 599.

" They

" They were both men of great parts and abilities, both men of uncommon learning
" and erudition, both able critics, both copious writers. But the one was the more
" univerfal, the other, perhaps, the better *Greek* and *Latin* fcholar; the one had the
" larger comprehenfion of things, the other the more exact knowledge of words; the
" one had his learning more like cafh ready at hand, the other had his more like bills
" in his common-place-book; the one was the more rapid and flowing, the other the
" more terfe and correct writer; the one was more capable of forming the plan and
" fyftem of a large work, the other excelled more in little loofe detached pieces; the
" fermons of the one are not the moft valuable, thofe of the other are the moft valuable,
" of all their writings. And in themfelves, the one was more open and communicative,
" more inviting and engaging in his manner; the other was more clofe and referved,
" more fhy and forbidding in his appearance; the one was warmer in his commenda-
" tions, a more zealous friend, and a more generous enemy; the other was more
" fparing of his praife, cooler both in friendfhip and enmity, and rather carping and
" undermining than freely judging or cenfuring. But their little failings will die with
" them, their fuperior excellences will live in the mouths and memories of men."

P. 620. Dr. *John Savage* *, the predeceffor of Mr. *Haynes* at *Clothall*, (and alfo lecturer of *St. George, Hanover-Square*), died *March* 24, 1747. He was called the
Ariftippus of the age.—It was *Savage*, and not *Haynes*, that built the rectory at *Quickfwood*; was the pleafant companion, and prefident of the club at *Royfton*.

P. 629. l. 6. read, " *commendam.*"—P. 636. note, l. 11. for " preferving" read
" proving."—l. 31. read, " tranflated into *Latin*."

P. 637. note *, read " formerly regiftrar."—P. 638. twice, read *Murdin*.

* " In his younger days," fays Bifhop *Newton*, " he had travelled with an Earl of *Salifbury*,
" to whom he was indebted for a confiderable living in *Hertfordfhire*; and in his more advanced
" years was a lively, pleafant, facetious old man. One day at the levee *George* I. afked him, ' How
" long he had ftayed at *Rome* with Lord *Salifbury*?' Upon his anfwering how long; ' Why,'
" faid the King, ' you ftayed long enough, why did not you convert the Pope?'—' Becaufe, Sir,'
" replied he, ' I had nothing better to offer him.' Having been bred at *Weftminfter*, he had always
" a great fondnefs for the fchool, attended at all their plays and elections, affifted in all their public
" exercifes, there grew young again, and among boys was a great boy himfelf. The King's
" fcholars had fo great a regard for him, that, after his deceafe, they made a collection among
" themfelves, and at their own charge erected a monument to his memory in the Cloifters." The
monument the Bifhop mentions is a fmall tablet of white marble on the right-hand fide of the door
leading into *The Chapter-houfe*, and is thus infcribed:

" JOHANNI SAVAGE, S. T. P.   Ipfe loci Genius te moeret Amicus Amicum,
Alumni Scholæ *Weftmonafterienfis*   Et luctu Pietas nos propiore ferit.
Pofuerunt,   Nobifcum affueras docto puerafcere lufu,
MDCCL.   Fudit & ingenitos cruda fenecta fales.
Tu noftræ memor ufque Scholæ, dum vita manebat; Chare Senex, Puer hoc te faltem carmine donat,
Mufa nec immemores nos finit effe Tui.   Ingratum Pueri nec tibi carmen erit."

Dr. *Savage* ufed to attend the fchool, to furnifh the lads with extempore epigrams at the elections.

MORE LAST WORDS.

P. 36. note, l. 5, 6. I have been referred by a worthy friend to the following short paragraph in the Preface to *Chishull's* Travels : " The Infcriptions here said to be re-" ported in *Prideaux* are to be found in the Doctor's edition of the *Marmora Arun-*" *deliana*. And as to thofe referred to at the end of our author's book, fuch of them " will be here fubjoined as are not in the large collection defigned by him for a fecond " part of his *Antiquitates Afiaticæ*, of which a few fheets only, containing thofe which " relate to *Ephefus*, were printed by him a little before his death, and the reft are now " in *my* poffeffion. R. MEAD." It appears by this Preface, that the world was in-debted to Dr. *Mead* for much more than the patronage of this learned work ; almoft all the citations from ancient authors having been filled up, and the whole work revifed and methodized by him.—Mr. *Chishull* had an only fon, *Edmund*, whom Dr. *Mead* calls " the induftrious fon of a learned father."

P. 155. note, l. 5. read *three* * editions of Mr. *Chefelden's* Anatomy.

P. 246. An Epitaph, by Mr. *Browne Willis*, on his grandfather, in *Fenny-Stratford* chapel, is in Gent. Mag. 1760, p. 291.

P. 248. l. 19. Mifs *Talbot's* character is thus drawn by the Dutchefs of *Somerfet* in a letter to Lady *Luxborough* : " She is all the world has faid of her, as to an uncommon " fhare of underftanding : but fhe has other charms, which I imagine you will join " with me in giving the preference even to that ; a mild and equal temper, an unaffected " pious heart, and the moft univerfal good-will to her fellow creatures that I ever " knew. She cenfures nobody, fhe defpifes nobody, and whilft her own life is a pattern " of goodnefs, fhe does not exclaim with bitternefs againft vice . . . . . We are at prefent " very highly entertained with the Hiftory of Sir *Charles Grandifon* †, which is fo vaftly " above *Pamela* or *Clariffa*, that I fhall not be eafy till you have read it, and fent me " your fentiments upon it."

P. 298. fub-note, l. 20. for *Anne*, read *Catharine*.

P. 340. Mr. *Stackhoufe's* " Hiftory of the Bible" has been thus briefly characterized : " In the new Hiftory of the Bible, lately publifhed, written by the Rev. Mr. *Thomas* " *Stackhoufe*, is given a plain and eafy narrative of the matters contained in the Holy " Scriptures, from the beginning of the World, to the full eftablifhment of Chriftianity : " In the notes is digefted the fenfe of the beft Commentators, in order to explain the " feveral difficult Texts, rectify the Mif-tranflations, and reconcile the feeming Contra-" dictions, that any where occur : In the objections, all the material exceptions which " are made to the facts recorded in each period of hiftory, are fairly ftated and anfwered : " And in the Differtations, which attend each chapter, the moft remarkable paffages " are illuftrated, and the Prophane and Sacred Hiftory all along connected. The whole " is adorned with proper Maps and Sculptures, and all matters referred to in Scriptural, " Chronological, and Alphabetical tables." Gent. Mag. 1740, p. 251.

P. 354. I am happy to correct the third line of this page, by reading " Bifhop of *Dro-*" *more*," inftead of " Dean of *Carlifle*," after the name of my worthy friend Dr. *Percy*.

P. 416. note, l. 4. add, We are indebted to Mr. *Folkes* for the firft introduction of the Polypus into *England*. Mr. *Leeuwenhoek* had firft noticed it in *Holland* in 1703; and Monf. *Trembley* made further difcoveries of its amazing properties 1739. Mr. *Folkes* no fooner received fome fpecimens from abroad than he fet about making experiments with them, the refult of which was communicated to the Royal Society, and printed in their Tranfactions. Mr. *Baker* alfo made experiments on three which Mr. *Folkes* gave

---

* When the *third* edition was printed by Mr. *Bowyer* in 1725, the following remarkable adver-tifement appeared in *The Daily Courant :* " The additions being too numerous to be printed fepa-" rate, books of this edition will be changed for either of the former editions, at 2s. in fheets, though " never fo much defaced or imperfect. There are alfo fome printed on the fineft royal paper, " which will be changed at 5s. in fheets."

† " I am, like the reft of the world, perufing Sir *Charles Grandifon*. I don't know whether that " world joins me in preferring the author's *Clariffa*. He wants the art of abridgement in every " thing he has yet wrote." *Mr. Shenftone to Mr. Jago.*

him,

him, 1743; and soon after the animal was discovered in *England*. When Mr. *Folkes's* other engagements in the pursuit of science prevented him from continuing his researches on the polype, Mr. *Baker* took them intirely on himself, and published the result in a professed treatise, 1743, 8vo, which has gone through several editions. The figures cut in wood were drawn from the microscope by Dr. *Parsons*. In *The British Museum* are the two following MSS. by Mr. *Baker*:

4435. Experiments and Observations on a Beetle that lived three years without food; printed in Phil. Transf. vol. XLI p. 241.

4436. Letter and Discovery of a perfect plant *in semine*.

P. 442. The family of *Jennens* is one among the many who have acquired ample fortunes at *Birmingham*, where they were equally famous for industry and generosity. *John Jennens* gave, in 1651, 3l. 10s. for the use of the poor; and Mrs. *Jennens* 10l. to support a lecture. The land on which the neat and elegant church of *St. Bartholomew* was built in 1749 was the gift of *John Jennens*, Esq; of *Gopsal*, then possessor of a considerable estate in and near *Birmingham*; and Mrs. *Jennens* gave 1000l. towards the building. The family seat at *Gopsal* is now the property of *Assheton Curzon*, Esq.

P. 446. A most capital article is omitted among the books of 1773; the splendid edition of " Bishop *Hoadly's* Works," in 3 volumes, folio, published by his son the late worthy Chancellor of *Winchester*. Of these Works 12 copies only (for his Majesty, and for public libraries) were printed on a beautiful writing paper.

P. 456. Proposals for a History of *Suffolk* were printed in 1751 by Sir *Joseph Ayloffe*; who drew up likewise about the same time Proposals (still in MS.) for a new " Encyclopedie."

P. 463. l. 27, read, " Miss *Susannah Kett*." The sale of Mr. *Ives's* curiosities produced more than 2000l. There is a second portrait of Mr. *Ives*, *J. S. pinx. P. S. Lamborn fec.* without his name, but with his arms, and a motto, MORIBUS ANTIQUIS.

P. 465. Add to the books of 1772, Mr. *Gough's* edition of *Perlin's* " Description des " Royaulmes d'*Angleterre* & d'*Escosse*," with *De la Serre's* " Histoire de l'Entrée de la " Reine du Mere du Roy tres Chrestien dans la *Grande Bretagne*," 4to; and to those of 1777 (p. 476), his " Dissertation on the Coins of *Canute*," 4to.

P. 533. Mr. *Spinckes* was editor of Dean *Hickes's* Sermons, 2 vols. 8vo. 1741.

P. 555. sub-note, l. 5. for " present" read " same."

P. 557. In the MS. Library of the Earl of *Shelburne* (N° 752), are " Topographical " Notes of Parishes in *Northamptonshire*, collected for the Use of *John Bridges*, Esq; of " *Barton Segrave*, in that County;" and also (N° 772, 773.) " More particular En- " quiries, containing an Account of 32 Parishes in *Northamptonshire*, collected for *John* " *Bridges*, Esq; 1719-20," 2 vols. 4to.

P. 590. sub-note, l. 11. read 22.

P. 621. The following articles by Dr. *Stukeley* are among the MSS. in *The Museum*:

4064. Account of a Silver Plate found in *Risley Park*, *Derbyshire*; read before the Society of Antiquaries, *April* 8, 1736.

4432. 14. Miscellaneous Observations on his Travels through *England* in 1721.

51. Account of a Shower of Wheat, 1732.

75. Account of his Book on the Cause and Cure of the Gout.

4437. Account of a Chaise that may be worked by a Man carried upon it, 1740-1; with a Drawing.

P. 626. Mr. *Fairchild* died, of an apoplectic stroke, *May* 31, 1782.

P. 628. An Essay by Mr. *Costard* on the *Sphæra Barbarica* is among the MSS. in *The Museum*, N° 4440.

P. 636. As there are other *Claphams*, Q. whether it was that in *Surrey* to which Mr. *Blackwall* was presented?

P. 637. The rectory of *Wallington*, I have been informed, was given to Dr. *Richardson* by his father, as master of *Emanuel College*, who is patron, and must give it to a fellow. Sed Q?———P. 643. l. 8. read, " and as a friend."

INDEX.

4

INDEX.

Barnard,

Opened

4 N

Carte,

7

Ferguson,

Hurd,

Morris,

Parkin,

Printers,

Epigram

Lately published, by the EDITOR of these ANECDOTES,

1. CONJECTURES and OBSERVATIONS on the NEW TESTAMENT. Collected from various Authors, as well in regard to Words as Pointing. By W. BOWYER. The Third Edition, much enlarged, and printed in a handsome Quarto, by J. NICHOLS.

2. Biographical Anecdotes of WILLIAM HOGARTH, and a Catalogue of his Works chronologically arranged. By J. NICHOLS. Octavo. Price 3s. sewed.

3. Biographical Memoirs of WILLIAM GED. By J. NICHOLS. Octavo. Price 1s.

4. A Select Collection of Poems, with Notes Biographical and Historical. By J. NICHOLS. In Eight Volumes, adorned with elegant Portraits. Price One Guinea in boards.

5. A SUPPLEMENT to SWIFT's WORKS. By J. NICHOLS. In one large Quarto Volume; and reprinted in every smaller Size, to suit the various Editions.

6. The Original Works in Prose and Verse of WILLIAM KING, LL.D. of Doctors-Commons, and Judge of the High Court of Admiralty in Ireland. Now first collected, with Historical Notes, by J. NICHOLS. In Three Volumes, 8vo. Price 10s. 6d. in boards.

7. A Collection of all the WILLS, now known to be extant, of the Kings and Queens of ENGLAND, Princes and Princesses of Wales, and every Branch of the Blood Royal, from the Reign of William the Conqueror to that of Henry the Seventh exclusive, with Explanatory Notes, and a Glossary. By J. NICHOLS. Quarto. Price Eighteen Shillings in boards.

8. The Origin of Printing, by W. BOWYER and J. NICHOLS, complete in one Volume, 8vo. Price 4s. 6d. in boards.

9. Five Numbers of a valuable Collection of Local Antiquities, under the Title of BIBLIOTHECA TOPOGRAPHICA BRITANNICA — TUNSTALL — RELIQUIÆ GALEANÆ — ABERDEEN — HAWKWOOD — ST. KATHARINE's. — [To be continued in subsequent Numbers.] By J. NICHOLS.

10. BRITISH TOPOGRAPHY; or, an Historical Account of what has been done for illustrating the Topographical Antiquities of Great-Britain and Ireland. By Mr. GOUGH. Two Volumes, Quarto, Price 2l. 12s. 6d. in boards.

11. The History of THETFORD. By the late Mr. THOMAS MARTIN of Palgrave. Quarto. Price One Guinea in boards.

** A Volume of Mr. BOWYER's MISCELLANEOUS TRACTS is in the Press, and will be published in the ensuing Winter; with an accurate and handsome Edition, in Quarto, of the New Testament in Greek, faithfully printed from a Copy prepared for that purpose by Mr. BOWYER.

BRIEF MEMOIRS

OF

JOHN NICHOLS;

WITH

A LIST OF HIS PUBLICATIONS.

Nichols and Son, Printers, Red Lion Passage, Fleet Street.
Sept. 24, 1804.

JOHN NICHOLS, fon of EDWARD and ANNE NICHOLS, of Iflington, was born Feb. 2, 1744-5; and received his education in that village at the academy of Mr. John Shield. His original defignation was to the Royal Navy; which in 1751 was rendered abortive by the death of his maternal uncle, Mr. Thomas Wilmot, firft lieutenant of the Seahorfe, a twenty-gun fhip, under captain Barrington, afterwards the celebrated Admiral, who himfelf died, full of years and honour, Aug. 16, 1800.

At the age of thirteen he was placed under the care of the late very learned and eminent Printer, Mr. WILLIAM BOWYER; who, in a fhort time difcovering him to be induftrious and attentive, as well as eager for improvement, received him into his confidence, and fuperintended his ftudies with the kindeft affiduity.

In the autumn of 1765 he was fent to Cambridge, to treat with the Univerfity for a leafe of their exclufive privilege of printing Bibles, &c.; but that learned body having determined to keep the property in their own hands, he in the following year entered into partnerfhip with his mafter; with whom in 1767 he removed from White Friers into Red Lion Paffage, Fleet Street. This union continued till diffolved by the death of Mr. Bowyer; in whofe will Mr. Nichols found himfelf remembered in a manner that demonftrated the regard in which he was held by the teftator. Every grateful acknowledgement has fince been returned. A monument to the memory of Mr. Bowyer was erected in the church of Low Leyton; a tombftone placed in the church-yard there; and a handfome brafs-plate, with a buft of the deceafed, in Stationers Hall, accompanied by good portraits of the
elder

elder Mr. Bowyer and the pious Mr. Nelſon; to which have ſince been added thoſe of Archbiſhop Chichley, and of Steele and Prior.

In December 1784, he was elected into the common council for the Ward of Farringdon Without; whence, in 1786, on a violent colliſion of parties, he was ouſted; but, in the ſummer of 1787, was unanimouſly re-elected; and, receiving from Mr. Alderman Wilkes the unſolicited appointment of one of the Deputies of the ward, was nominated a governor of the London Workhouſe, a corporation governor of the Royal Hoſpitals of Bridewell and Bethlehem, and treaſurer of St. Bride's Charity-ſchools.

At the end of 1797, finding his health impaired, and wiſhing in ſome degree to retire from the buſtle of public life, he declined all civic honours; but was once more prevailed on in 1798 to reſume a ſeat in the common council; in 1799 was elected by ballot one of the three repreſentatives of that court at the board of commiſſioners for the general purpoſes of the Income Act; and in 1800, by ballot alſo, a corporation governor of Chriſt's Hoſpital.

In the ſummer of 1803, he in a conſiderable degree withdrew from the trammels of buſineſs, to a houſe in his native village; where he hopes *(Deo volente)* to paſs the evening of a laborious life in the calm enjoyment of domeſtic tranquillity; and that his earthly remains may (at a period which he neither looks forward to with terror, nor wiſhes to anticipate) be depoſited with thoſe of ſeveral near relations whoſe loſs he has long deplored, in the church-yard where many of his happieſt days were paſſed in harmleſs ſports.

If it be worth while to open a literary career in a poetic character; among other youthful votaries of the Mufes, Mr. Nichols very early afpired to diftinction; and employed fome leifure hours in writing verfes, which generally found their way into the newspapers and magazines of the time, to moft of which (and in the Gentleman's and Ladies Diaries) he was an occafional contributor from 1761 to 1766, when the term of his apprenticefhip expired.

At an early part of that period he furnifhed Mr. Kelly with a few numbers of " The Babler ;" and his old friend Mr. Redmayne, then printer of the Weftminfter Journal, with a feries of Letters from " The Cobler of Alfatia."

He affifted Mr. Bowyer in the publication of " Verfes on the Coronation of King George the Second, 1761 ;" and tranflated many of the Latin epigrams.

In 1763, he publifhed two poetical pamphlets in 4to; the one, intituled, " Iflington, a Poem ;" the other, " The Buds of Parnaffus ;" re-publifhed in 1764, with fome additional Poems.

In 1765, he contributed feveral poems to a mifcellaneous collection, publifhed by Dr. Perfect of Town Malling under the title of " The Laurel Wreath," 2 vols. 12mo.

The other works of which he has been either the author or the editor are the following :

" The Origin of Printing," 1774, 8vo; re-printed in 1776; and a Supplement added in 1781. The original defign of this work was by Mr. Bowyer ; the completion of it by Mr. Nichols. The two learned friends noticed in the advertifement were the Rev. Dr. Henry Owen and the Rev. Cæfar De Miffy.

B   " The

" The Seventeenth Volume of Swift's Works, with Notes, 1775, 8vo.

" Index to the Miscellaneous Works of Lord Lyttelton, 1775," 8vo.

" Index to Lord Chesterfield's Letters to his Son, 1776," 8vo.

" The original Works, in Prose and Verse, of William King, LL. D. now first collected, with Historical Notes, 1776," 3 vols. small 8vo.

" Supplement to Swift's Works, with Notes and Index, vols. XXIV. XXV. 1776, 1779," 8vo.

In 1778, he gave, in the Public Advertiser, a few numbers of " Modern Characters," selected from the Works of Dean Swift; and in the middle of that year became associated with his friend David Henry, esq. in the management of " The Gentleman's Magazine;" a work which has the merit of having given birth to every similar publication.

" Brief Memoirs of Mr. Bowyer," 8vo. were circulated early in 1779, as a tribute of respect, amongst a few select friends.

" History of the Royal Abbey of Bec, near Rouen [from a MS. communicated by Dr. Ducarel], 1779," small 8vo.

" Some Account of the Alien Priories, and of such Lands as they are known to have possessed in England and Wales, 1779," 2 vols. small 8vo. These volumes, originally compiled from the MSS. of John Warburton, esq. were revised through the press by Dr. Ducarel and Mr. Gough; many valuable notes were added by both, and a Glossary by Mr. Gough.

" Six Old Plays," on which Shakespeare grounded a like number of his; selected by Mr. Steevens, and revised by Mr. Nichols, 1779, 2 vols. small 8vo.

The late learned Edward Rowe Mores, M. A. and F. R. S. having left at his death a small unpublished impression of " A Dissertation upon English Typographical Founders and Founderies;" all the copies

of

of this very curious pamphlet were purchafed at his fale by Mr. Nichols; and given to the publick in 1779, with the addition of a fhort explanatory " Appendix."

" A Collection of Royal and Noble Wills;" in which he was affifted by the late Dr. Ducarel; and by Mr. Gough, who contributed the Preface and the Gloffary; 1780, 4to.

" A Select Collection of Mifcellaneous Poems, with Hiftorical and Biographical Notes, 1780;" 4 vols. fmall 8vo; to which four other volumes, and a general Poetical Index, were added in 1782.

Some notes, communicated by him to the re-publication of Mr. Dodfley's Collection of Old Plays in 1780, are acknowledged by Mr. Reed in the Preface to that Work.

In the fame year, on the fuggeftion, and with the affiftance, of his firm friend Mr. Gough, and with him concurring in a wifh to fave from the chandler and the cheefemonger any valuable articles of Britifh Topography, MS or printed, he opened a new fource of literary amufement, in the " Bibliotheca Topographica Britannica;" which was completed (in LII Numbers) in 1790.

" Biographical Anecdotes of William Hogarth, 1781," 8vo; republifhed in 1782; and again in 1785; each edition being confiderably enlarged. In this work he was indebted for nearly every critique on the plates of Hogarth to the late George Steevens, efq. who wrote the Prefaces to the fecond and third editions; and by whom large additions for a fourth were made, in a copy purchafed at his fale by Mr. Baker of St. Paul's church-yard. A tranflation into German of the fecond edition was publifhed at Leipfic in 1783.

" Biographical and Literary Anecdotes of William Bowyer, Printer, F. S. A. and of many of his learned Friends, 1781," 4to.

B 2   " Biographical

" Biographical Memoirs of William Ged, including a particular Account of his Progress in the Art of Block-printing, 1781," 8vo.

A third edition [much enlarged] of Mr. Bowyer's " Conjectures and Observations on the New Testament, 1782," 4to. In this edition he was honoured with the advice and assistance of the Hon. and Right Reverend Dr. Shute Barrington, the present Bishop of Durham, the late Dr. Heberden (who furnished many new notes by Mr. Markland), the late Dr. Owen, the Rev. Dr. Gosset, Rev. Stephen Weston, &c.

" The History and Antiquities of Hinckley, in Leicestershire, 1782," 4to.

Mr. Bowyer's " Apology for some of Mr. Hooke's Observations concerning the Roman Senate, with an Index to the Observations, 1782," 4to.

In 1783, he collected " The principal Additions and Corrections in the Third Edition of Dr. Johnson's Lives of the Poets, to complete the Second Edition" (of 1781).

" Bishop Atterbury's Epistolary Correspondence, with Notes, vol. II. 1783; vol. III. 1784; vol. IV. 1787. A new edition of this work, corrected and much enlarged, was published in 1799, with Memoirs of the Bishop; and a Fifth Volume, entirely new.

In conjunction with Dr. Heathcote, he revised the second edition of the " Biographical Dictionary," 12 vols. 8vo, 1784; and added several hundred new lives.

" A Collection of Miscellaneous Tracts, by Mr. Bowyer, and some of his learned Friends, 1785," 4to.

" History and Antiquities of Lambeth Parish, 1786," compiled principally from papers communicated by Dr. Ducarel, in return for assistance which had been given him by Mr. Nichols in the Histories of the Two Archiepiscopal Palaces of Lambeth and Croydon.

" The Tatler," *cum Notis Variorum*, 1786, 6 vols. small 8vo. The principal merit of this edition is due to the Rev. Dr. John Calder, who was furnished with
the

the Notes of a learned and refpectable Prelate; but Mr. Nichols wrote the Preface, and contributed feveral Notes.

" The Works, in Verfe and Profe, of Leonard Welfted, efq. now firft collected, with Notes and Memoirs of the Author, 1787," 8vo.

" Hiftory and Antiquities of Afton Flamvile and Burbach, in Leicefterfhire, 1787," 4to.

" Sir Richard Steele's Epiftolary Correfpondence, now firft publifhed, with Biographical and Hiftorical Notes, 1788, 2 vols. fmall 8vo.

" The Progreffes and Royal Proceffions of Queen Elizabeth, 1788," 2 vols. 4to. Of this Collection a Third Volume is intended to be publifhed in 1804.

" Hiftory and Antiquities of Canonbury, with fome Account of the Parifh of Iflington, 1788," 4to.

" The Lover and Reader, by Sir Richard Steele, now firft collected, and illuftrated with Notes, 1789," 8vo.

" The Town Talk, Fifh Pool, Plebeian, Old Whig, Spinfters, &c. by Sir Richard Steele; now firft collected, and illuftrated with Notes, 1790," 8vo.

" Collections towards the Hiftory and Antiquities of the Town and County of Leicefter, 1790," 2 vols. 4to. Very few copies of this work were printed, merely with a view of foliciting communications towards a regular Hiftory of that County.

An edition of " Shakefpeare's Works, 1790," in feven volumes, 12mo; accurately printed from the Text of Mr. Malone; with a Selection of the more important Notes.

" The Theatre and Anti-theatre, &c. of Sir Richard Steele, illuftrated with Notes, 1791," 8vo.

" Mifcellaneous Antiquities, in Continuation of the *Bibliotheca Topographica Britannica*," Six Numbers, 4to, 1792—1798.

" The Hiftory and Antiquities of the Town and County of Leicefter;" Parts I. and II. 1795, Folio.
A Third

A Third Part was publifhed in 1798; a Fourth in 1800; a Fifth in 1804; and Two more Parts (one of which is now in the prefs) will complete the Work.

" Illuftrations of the Manners and Expences of antient Times in England, 1797," 4to.

" Bifhop Kennett's Funeral Sermon, with Memoirs of the Cavendifh Family, 1797." 8vo; from a corrected copy of the former edition in the poffeffion of the Rev. Mr. Freeman, &c. &c.

" Chronological Lift of the Society of Antiquaries of London;" compiled in conjunction with Mr. Gough, 1798, 4to; to which was intended to have been added biographical memoirs of the feveral members, " quique fui memores alios fecere merendo."

An edition of " Shakefpeare's Works, 1799," in eight volumes, 12mo; accurately printed from the Text of Mr. Steevens; with a Selection of the more important Notes.

Having recovered the MS. of the Reverend Kennet Gibfon's " Comment upon Part of the Fourth Journey of Antoninus through Britain" (which in 1769 Mr. Gibfon propofed to publifh by fubfcription, but which upon his death was fuppofed to have been loft); Mr. Nichols publifhed it in 1800, with the Parochial Hiftory of Caftor and its Dependencies; and an Account of Marham, and feveral other places in its neighbourhood."

In the fame year he completed " The Antiquaries Mufeum," which had been begun in 1791 by his friend Jacob Schnebbelie; who dying in 1792, before the Third Number was completed, the work was continued, for the benefit of his family, to XIII Numbers (the laft of which contains Memoirs of the Author) by Mr. Gough and Mr. Nichols.

In 1801, he publifhed " An Hiftorical Account of Beauchief Abbey, in the County of Derby;" the MS. of which had been entrufted to him for that purpofe in 1796 by his late venerable and much refpected friend

friend the Rev. Samuel Pegge, LL.D. F.S.A. not long before his death.

In the fame year, he publifhed a new and complete Edition of the " Works of Dean Swift," in XIX vols. 8vo; which in 1803 were reprinted in XXIV volumes, 18mo.

In 1802, Mr. Hutton of Birmingham, in a Dedicatory Epiftle, addreffed to him a pleafant " Hiftory of the Roman Wall," 8vo.

In 1803, in conformity to the laft will of his worthy friend Samuel Pegge, efq. (fon of the learned Antiquary already named), he ufhered into the world a very excellent octavo volume, under the title of " Anecdotes of the Englifh Language, &c."

Journal of a very young Lady's Tour from Canonbury to Aldborough, through Chelmsford, Sudbury, and Ipfwich, and back through Harwich, Colchefter, &c. Sept. 13—21, 1804; written haftily on the Road, as Occurrences arofe. [Not intended for publication; but a very few copies only printed, to fave the trouble of tranfcribing.]

[Nichols and Son, Printers, Red Lion Paffage, Fleet-Street.]

MEMOIR

OF

JOHN NICHOLS, ESQ. F.S.A.

By A. C.

EXTRACTED FROM THE GENTLEMAN'S MAGAZINE
FOR DECEMBER 1826.

MEMOIR OF JOHN NICHOLS, ESQ. F.S.A.

JOHN NICHOLS, a man who afforded au eminent exemplar of personal probity, and whose long life was spent in the promotion of useful knowledge, was the descendant of a respectable family. His grandfather was Bartholomew Nichols, of Piccadilly, in the parish of St. James's, Westminster. His father, Edward Nichols, was born in the same place, Oct. 18, 1719, but resided during the greater part of his life at Islington, in Middlesex, where he died Jan. 29, 1779, in the sixtieth year of his age. He married Anne, daughter of Thomas Wilmot of Beckingham, near Gainsborough, Lincolnshire. She was born in the same year with her husband, and died Dec. 27, 1783, aged sixty-four. Of all their children, two only survived, John, the subject of this Memoir, and Anne, still living, wife of Edward Bentley, Esq. of the Accountant's Office in the Bank of England.

Our Author was born at Islington, Feb. 2, 1744-5. To the place of his nativity he always retained a great affection. It was the scene of the happy days of his childhood, to which he adverts in the following affecting lines, part of a sketch of his life, printed, but not published, in 1803 :—" In the summer of 1803, he in a considerable degree withdrew from the trammels of business, to a house in his native village, where he hopes *(Deo volente)* to pass the evening of a laborious life in the calm enjoyment of domestic tranquillity ; and that his earthly remains may (at a period which he neither looks forward to with terror, nor wishes to anticipate,) be deposited with those of several near relations, whose loss he has long deplored, in the church-yard where many of his happiest days were passed in harmless sports." How little do we see of the future ! Mr. Nichols had then before him twenty-three years devoted to as arduous labour as any which he had ever sustained.

He was educated at an academy at Islington, kept by Mr. John Shield, a man of considerable learning, who appears to have taken great pains in cultivating the talents of such as, like the subject of this Memoir, recommended themselves by attention and docility.

The profession which Mr. Nichols followed, with so much success and reputation during the whole of his long life, was not that for which he was originally destined by some part of his family. It is frequently the case with the guardians of youth, or their advisers, to be determined by petty circumstances and indistinct prospects, in the disposal of those who are under their care. Mr. Nichols had a maternal uncle, Lieutenant Thomas Wilmot, a brave officer, who in 1747 was serving under Captain, afterwards· Admiral Barrington, when he captured the Duke of Chartres East Indiaman, and was in a fair way to higher promotion. This appears to have induced the friends of Mr. Nichols, who was of a good constitution and lively temper, to propose that, at a proper time, he should be taken under this uncle's protection, and educated for the naval service. Mr. Wilmot's death, however, which happened in 1751, put an end to the hopes derived from this scheme. Our author remarks, but with no great regret : " Had his life been spared, I should, instead of having been employed as a pioneer of literature, probably have been engaged under the banners of the gallant Admiral, in the naval defence of my country."

He was too young when his uncle died, to feel the loss, or to indulge dreams of naval glory, and soon had the happiness to be placed in a situation which proved more suitable to his inclinations, and more adapted to his talents. The kindness of Providence guided him to a Master who soon discerned his worth, and to a branch of literature in which his success and industry have never been exceeded.

This master was the celebrated Mr. WILLIAM BOWYER, who, at his death, was termed "the last of learned English printers," a title which may now be dropt, while it is still allowed that he was almost the first of that distinguished class in England, and qualified both by education and learning, to be the companion and adviser of the most eminent scholars who flourished in the early part of the eighteenth century. He came into business with the advantages of an university education, and an intercourse with many learned men who had been his contemporaries at Cambridge.

It was in 1757, before Mr. Nichols was quite thirteen years of age, that he was placed under Mr. Bowyer, who appears to have quickly discovered in his pupil that amiable and honourable disposition which distinguished him all his life. He had a tenacious memory, which was but little impaired even in his latter days. He was likewise very early a lover of books, although, like most youths, who think more of gratifying curiosity than of procuring permanent advantages, his reading was desultory, and for some years his choice depended on the works submitted to his Master's press, few of which, happily for him, were of a trifling, and none of a pernicious kind. From the moment he became Mr. Bowyer's apprentice, he was intent on the acquisition of solid knowledge, and to this he was continually prompted, not only by the instructions of his Master, but by the nature of his employment. He was gradually inspired with a certain degree of ambition, of which he probably knew neither the extent or end, in consequence of intercourse with the men of learning for whom Mr. Bowyer printed.

Mr. Nichols had not been long in this advantageous situation, when his Master gladly admitted him into his confidence, and intrusted him with cares which, in case of many young men, would have been considered as unsuitable to their age, and requiring a more lengthened trial. But, besides the indispensable qualities of industry and integrity, Mr. Bowyer found in his young apprentice another merit which was of great importance to his press. Mr. Nichols brought with him no small portion of classical knowledge and taste, acquired at school, and cultivated at his leisure hours.

Of this he speaks with his accustomed modesty: "He never affected to possess any superior share of erudition; content, if in plain and intelligible terms, either in conversation or in writing, he could contribute his quota of information or entertain-

ment." The present writer, however, has seen some early as well as later proofs, that his acquaintance with Latin was never dropt, and it is certain that his employment was a continual excitement to acquire some knowledge of the learned languages. At a very advanced period of life he speaks with exultation of his having been first employed, as a compositor, on Toup's "Emendationes in Suidam," and other works of classical criticism.

Mr. Bowyer appears to have been not only the instructive master, but the kind and indulgent friend to his apprentice, and was often anxious to amuse him by conveying a taste for poetry; of which Mr. Nichols had afforded some specimens. Of these Mr. Bowyer thought so favourably, that in 1760, when our author was only in his sixteenth year, he enjoined him, as an evening's task, to translate a Latin poem of his own, published in 1733, and entitled " *Bellus homo et Academicus.*" This Mr. Nichols executed with considerable spirit and humour, and in the following year (1761) Mr. Bowyer associated him with himself in translating the Westminster Verses which had been spoken on the previous Coronation of George the Second.

The applause bestowed on these efforts very naturally led Mr. Nichols to become a more constant votary of the Muses, and from 1761 to 1766, his productions made no inconsiderable figure in the periodical journals. In 1763 he published two poetical pamphlets in 4to., the one entitled " Islington, a Poem," and the other " The Buds of Parnassus," which was republished in 1764, with some additional poems. In 1765, he contributed several poems to a miscellaneous collection, published by Dr. Perfect of Town-Malling, under the title of " The Laurel Wreath," 2 vols. 8vo. His occasional productions of this kind, when further advanced, will be noticed hereafter.

During his minority he produced some prose essays on the manners of the age, such as they appeared to one who had been no inattentive observer. These were published in a periodical paper, written chiefly by Kelly, entitled " The Babbler," and in the Westminster Journal, a newspaper, under the signature of " The Cobbler of Alsatia."

These were merely his amusements, and indicative of an ambition which at his early age was surely pardonable. His more serious hours were devoted to the business of the press. His leading object was to please his master in the superintendance of the learned works printed by Mr. Bowyer, and in this he succeeded so well, that the relative situations of master and servant soon merged in a friendship, the compound of affection on the one side, and of reverence on the other.

So amply had he fulfilled Mr. Bowyer's expectations, as to prudence and judgment, that before his apprenticeship expired, he sent him to Cambridge to treat with that University for a lease of their exclusive privilege or printing Bibles. This was a negociation which required great delicacy and presence of mind, and these Mr. Nichols preserved on every interview. His endeavours proved unsuccessful only because the University determined, on a due consideration of the matter, to keep the property in their own hands.

This journey, however, to our young aspirant was delightful. He had never before travelled but a very few miles from his native place, and in Cambridge and its colleges he found every thing that could increase his enthusiasm for literary pursuits. He made minutes of this tour, which he used to say, afforded him the most pleasing recollections at a far distant period of life. His remarks on the passing objects on the journey, prove that he had already imbibed somewhat of the topographer's inquisitive spirit; and at Cambridge he indulged in the delights of " local emotion," by contemplating with reverence the colleges in which some eminent scholars, with whom he had already become acquainted, had studied. On one occasion he says, " Visited Peter-house, not without a respectful thought of Mr. Markland." During his return likewise he exhibited some promising appearances of the *viator curiosus*.

Soon after, Mr. Bowyer gave another proof of the value he placed on Mr. Nichols' services, when the period of them expired, by returning to his father half of his apprentice-fee. But the high estimate he had formed of him did not end here. He appears to have been long convinced that Mr. Nichols' assistance was of great im-portance in his printing establishment. Accordingly in 1766, he took him into partnership, and in the following year, they removed their office from White Friars to Red-lion-passage, Fleet-street, where it remained until a very few years since. This union, one of the most cordial that ever was formed, lasted until the death of Mr. Bowyer in 1777.

As Mr. Bowyer continued to be not only the printer, but the intimate friend and assistant in the learned labours of some of the first scholars of the age, Mr. Nichols had frequent opportunities, which he never neglected, of acquiring the notice and esteem of those gentlemen. He had not, indeed, been long associated with Mr. Bowyer, as a partner, before he began to be considered as his legitimate successor, and acquired the esteem and patronage of Mr. Bowyer's friends in no common degree. This he lived to repay by handing down to posterity many important circumstances of their lives, frequently derived from personal knowledge, which but for his industry and research, and the confidence bestowed upon him by their families, must have been lost to the world.

The first publication in which he was concerned as an author, was " The Origin of Printing, in two Essays: 1. The substance of Dr. Middleton's Dissertation on the Origin of Printing in England. 2. Mr. Meerman's account of the invention of the art at Harleim, and its progress to Mentz, with occasional remarks, and an Appendix," 8vo, 1774. Mr. Nichols informs us that the " original idea of this pamphlet was Mr. Bowyer's; the completion of it his Partner's." Mr. Nichols' share, therefore, must have been very considerable. It was published without a name, and at first was attributed to Mr. Bowyer, but the respective shares of him and his partner were soon discovered. A second edition, with many improvements, appeared in 1776, and a supplement in 1781. The foreign journals spoke with as much respect of this work as those at home.

Mr. Nichols derived considerable fame from it. He was now enabled to add to the number of his literary friends the names of Sir James Burrough and Sir John Pringle, as he had before acquired the esteem and acquaintance of Dr. Birch, Dr. Parsons, Dr. Warton, Dr. Farmer, and the Earl of Marchmont. Sir John Pringle was accustomed to submit his prize-medal speeches, which he intended for the Royal Society, to Mr. Nichols's perusal, before delivery, an honour of which so young a man may be forgiven if he was somewhat proud.

As the works which passed through Mr. Bowyer's press engaged a more than common attention on the part of Mr. Nichols, he happened very early in life to conceive a high opinion of the merits of Dean Swift, in consequence of Mr. Bowyer's having printed the 13th and 14th volumes of his works in the year 1762. Of Dean Swift Mr. Nichols appears never to have lost sight from this time, and, applying himself closely in search of materials, published, in 1775, a supplemental volume to Dr. Hawkesworth's edition. This was republished afterwards so as to correspond with Hawkesworth's 4to, 8vo, and 12mo editions, and afterwards incorporated, with many additions and valuable biographical notes, in what may be now justly considered as the standard edition, first printed in 19 vols. 8vo, in 1800, and reprinted in 1808. Mr. Nichols's accuracy and judgment as an editor, were so completely established by the appearance of the first mentioned volume, that information respecting unpublished letters and tracts was sent to him from all quarters. Sheridan's Life was the only part which he considered necessary to retain as originally published, since it was supposed by many, (but certainly not by the writer of this Memoir,) to furnish a defence of the objectionable parts of Swift's personal history. But, whatever the merits of this celebrated author, it appears incontestibly from the preface to the second volume, that the public is indebted to Mr. Nichols for the very complete state in which his works are now found.

The next publication of our author, the "Original Works, in Prose and Verse, of William King, LL.D. with Historical Notes," 3 vols. small 8vo, 1776, afforded another decided proof of that taste for literary history and illustration, to which we owe the more important obligations, which Mr. Nichols conferred by his recent and voluminous contributions to the biography of men of learning. It is evident that he must have been very early accustomed to inquiry and investigation, which enabled him to satisfy the cu-

riosity of the reader so amply as he has done in King's Works. This publication likewise exhibits an extraordinary proof of diligence both in business and study, when we consider that at this time he had scarcely reached his thirty-first year, and had the cares of a young family, just deprived of their maternal parent, to perplex and afflict his mind, with the numerous engagements in which his partnership with Mr. Bowyer, and intimacy with their common friends, necessarily involved him. But it may be noticed here, although not for the last time, that Mr. Nichols possessed not only extraordinary judgment in the allotment of his hours, but had equally extraordinary health and spirits to sustain him, amidst the intenseness of industry, and the frequent calls of complicated avocations. In both the above-mentioned works, he acknowledges having been assisted by his friend Isaac Reed of Staples Inn, a man who never was consulted on points of literary history without advantage.

In 1778, Mr. Nichols obtained a share in the Gentleman's Magazine, of which he became the editor. This was an event of the greatest importance to all his subsequent pursuits, as well as to the publick at large. Of this publication it would be superfluous to say much in this place, after the ample history of its rise and progress published by its Editor in 1821, as a Preface to the General Index from 1787 to 1818. It had not been long under his care before it obtained a consequence which it had never before reached, although the preceding volumes were formed from the contributions of some of the most able scholars and antiquaries of the time. The celebrated Burke entitled it "one of the most chaste and instructive Miscellanies of the age." This Mr. Nichols found it, and this he left it, with such improvements, however, as rendered it of paramount importance to men of literary curiosity, and of great effect in the promotion of right principles. In 1782, Dr. Warton complimented him in these words: "Your Magazine is justly in the greatest credit here (Winchester), and under your guidance is become one of the most useful and entertaining Miscellanies I know."

It might be easy, were it necessary, to add to these the suffrages of some of the most eminent writers of the last half century. As a repository of Literary history, and of public transactions for a much longer period, it is without a rival, a circumstance at which we cannot be surprized, when we consider that it contains the early, as well as the more mature lucubrations of many hundred authors in every department of Literature. In the history of the Magazine, noticed above, Mr. Nichols has given a list of above five hundred men of note, who had been correspondents in his time, and whom he had survived. Nearly an equal number might be added of those who have died since this list was made out, and of those who are still living, and lamenting the loss of one who afforded many of them the means of being first introduced to public notice.

In order to render the various information contained in this Magazine more easily accessible, Mr. Nichols had published in 1786, a complete Index to the first fifty-four volumes, compiled by the late Rev. Samuel Ayscough. This was given to the publick at a very moderate rate, but its importance was so soon acknowledged that before it was reprinted we remember the price had risen to eight and nine guineas: and both Indexes served to increase the demand for complete sets of the Magazine, which, from various causes, are not easy to be procured in a perfect state.

Gibbon, the historian, had such a value for this Miscellany, that he recommended to Mr. Nichols a Selection of the most curious and useful articles. Mr. Nichols was too much employed to have leisure for such an undertaking; but it has, however, been since accomplished, and we understand with great judgment, in 4 vols. 8vo, by a learned gentleman of New College, Oxford.

In noticing the Gentleman's Magazine, while under Mr. Nichols's care, the present writer will not attempt that which Mr. Nichols would have disdained, any comparison between it and its rivals. This indeed becomes the less necessary, as they have all dropt into oblivion, with the exception of a few of recent date, in which no rivalship seems intended. It may be added, however, that his plan was calculated for permanence. It depended on none of the frivolous fashions of the age. Its general character was usefulness combined with rational entertainment. Its supporters were men of learning, who found in its pages an easy mode of communicating their doubts and their inquiries, with a certainty that their doubts would be resolved, and their inquiries answered by men equal to the task. The Miscellany was particularly recommended by the impartiality of the Editor, who admitted controversialists to the most equal welcome, and never interfered but when, out of respect to his numerous readers, it became his duty to check the rudeness of personal reflection. In the course of such controversies, he must not be suspected of acceding to every proposition advanced either in warmth or in calmness, and much was no doubt admitted of which he could not approve. But his own principles remained unshaken, principles early adopted, and favourable to piety and political happiness; and such he preserved and supported amidst the most alarming storms to which his country had ever been exposed. Whatever anomalies may be occasionally perceived in the effusions of some of his correspondents, if the whole of his administration be examined, it will be found that the main object and tendency of the Magazine was to support our excellent Constitution in Church and State, especially when in some latter years both were in danger from violence without, and treachery within.

The sentiments of two very eminent and learned dignitaries of the Church, with the perusal of which we have been favoured since Mr. Nichols' death, may, we hope, without breach of confidence, be added to the above. Mr. Nichols "was an able, and what is much more, he was a perfectly honest man. We can ill afford to lose him. As an excellent Antiquary, as a friend to literary men, and as a liberal, but thoroughly attached son of the Church of England, his memory will long live in the esteem and recollection of his friends."—"It is my firm opinion, that in the various productions which during so long a period issued from his press, not a line escaped which could he detrimental to the influence of Christianity; but on the contrary, particularly in the conduct of that leading work, the 'Gentleman's Magazine,' the genuine principles of orthodox religion have been advocated and diffused in this nation by its channel for the longest portion of a century. And even in the amusing and instructive articles of a literary and antiquarian cast, this leading purpose seems not to have been lost sight of. While he (Mr. Nichols) sojourned with us, he was by the kindness and benevolence of his heart the delight of his friends, and must be considered as an eminent benefactor to his country."

There was no part of the Magazine on which Mr. Nichols bestowed more attention than on the record of deaths, now known by the name of OBITUARY. In order to render this an article of authority, and often indeed it has been quoted as such, he was indefatigable in his inquiries, anxiously consulted his numerous friends, and had very often the advantage of original documents from the relatives of persons of various classes, whose history might be interesting to the public. In this he not only gratified immediate curiosity, but laid the foundation of those more extended accounts which afterwards appeared in works professedly biographical. The warmth of friendship and the recency of grief might no doubt sometimes give a high colouring to these reports, which became chastened on further reflection and inquiry; but corrections or additions were impartially admitted, and the Editor at least was accessible to every communication which tended to establish the truth.

It may here be noticed that many of the additional articles in the Biographical Dictionary which he edited, in conjunction with Dr. Heathcote, in 1784, came from Mr. Nichols. How ably, and kindly, he assisted in the late edition of that work, completed in 1817, 32 vols. 8vo. can never be forgotten by its Editor, who hopes hereafter to acknowledge it more amply than merely by a reference to Mr. Nichols' printed works.

Although Mr. Bowyer's press had not issued many works interesting to English Antiquaries, Mr. Nichols appears, before the period to which we are now arrived, to have formed such connections as gradually encouraged what was early in his mind, until his inquiries became fixed on subjects relating to the antiquities of his own country. Among these preceptors we may notice Dr. Samuel Pegge, Borlase, Hutchins, Denne, and Dr. Ducarel. With the latter he was long linked in friendship, and in conjunction with him, published in 1779 the "History

of the Royal Abbey of Bec, near Rouen," and "Some account of the Alien Priories, and of such Lands as they are known to have possessed in England and Wales," 2 vols. But he had another coadjutor in these two works, of incalculable value, the celebrated RICHARD GOUGH, esq.

This very eminent antiquary, justly entitled the Camden of the Eighteenth Century, was, like Bowyer, an early discerner of Mr. Nichols's worth, and saw in him an able and useful assistant in his multifarious endeavours to illustrate the antiquities of Great Britain. Mr. Gough was his senior by ten years, and a higher proficient in his favourite studies. At what precise time they became acquainted, we have not been able to discover, but it seems, with much probability, to have been about the year 1770, when the first volume of the Archæologia was printed by Mr. Nichols, to whom Mr. Bowyer, from declining health, had almost entirely resigned the business of the press. Some years before this, Mr. Gough had been a frequent correspondent in the Gentleman's Magazine, a publication constantly read by Mr. Nichols, when there was little prospect of his becoming its chief support, or of Mr. Gough's taking so active a part in the management of it, as to become nearly a co-editor. It is probable that their intimacy was perfected whilst Mr. Gough was superintending his friend Mr. Hutchins's "History of Dorsetshire" through the press. That work was issued in two volumes, fol. 1774.

Their connexion, at whatever time begun, ended in a strict intimacy and cordial friendship, which terminated only in the death of Mr. Gough in 1809. It was a friendship uninterruptedly strengthened by congeniality of pursuits, mutual esteem, and the kindness of domestic intercourse. On their final separation Mr. Nichols says with unfeigned feeling: "The loss of Mr. Gough was the loss of more than a brother—it was losing a part of himself. For a long series of years he had experienced in Mr. Gough the kind, disinterested friend; the prudent, judicious adviser; the firm, unshaken patron. To him every material event in life was confidentially imparted. In those that were prosperous, no man more heartily rejoiced; in such as were less propitious, no man more sincerely condoled, or more readily endeavoured to alleviate." Mr. Nichols has since lost no opportunity of honouring the memory of his departed friend, both in his "Literary Anecdotes," and in his "Illustrations of Literary History." His last office of duty was to select and transfer to the Bodleian Library, Oxford, the valuable collection of Topography, printed and MS. which Mr. Gough bequeathed to that noble repository.

In 1780, Mr. Nichols published a very curious "Collection of Royal and Noble Wills," 4to. In this work he acknowledges his obligations to Mr. Gough and to Dr. Ducarel, for obtaining transcripts and elucidating by notes. It was a scheme originally suggested by Dr. Ducarel, probably in consequence of the publication of the Will of Henry VII. by Mr. Astle some years before. To this work, in 1794, Mr. Nichols added the will of Henry VIII. which is now seldom to be found with the preceding, itself a work of great rarity.

Amidst these more serious employments, Mr. Nichols diverted his leisure hours by compiling a work, which seems to have been entirely of his own projection, and the consequence of early predilection. This appeared in 1780, with the title of "A Select Collection of Miscellaneous Poems, with Historical and Biographical Notes," 4 vols. small 8vo. To these were added, in 1782, four other volumes, with a general poetical Index.

In this curious work, he has not only revived many pieces of unquestionable merit, which had long been forgotten, but produced some originals from the pens of men of acknowledged genius. In so large a collection are some which might perhaps have been allowed to remain in obscurity without much injury to the public, but even in the production of these he followed the opinion, and had the encouragement, of some of the best critics of the time, Bishops Lowth and Percy, Dr. Warton, Mr. Kynaston, &c.

The biographical notes were deemed very interesting, and were happily the occasion of a similar improvement being made to Dodsley's Collection of Poems, in the edition of 1782, if we mistake not, by Isaac Reed. In Mr. Nichols's collection are a few of his juvenile attempts at versification, of which he says, "they will at least serve as a foil to the beauties with which they are surrounded." Mr. Nichols never claimed a high rank among poets, but there is evidently too much disparagement in the above opinion.

In the same year (1780), on the suggestion, and with the assistance of Mr. Gough, he began to publish the "Bibliotheca Topographica Britannica," a work intended to collect such articles of British Topography, MS. or printed, as were in danger of being lost, or were become so scarce as to be out of the reach of most collectors. His reputation was now so fully established that he had ready assistance from most of the eminent Antiquaries of that day; and in 1790, the whole was concluded in fifty-two parts or numbers, making eight large quarto volumes, illustrated by more than three hundred plates, with great exactness and accuracy, both in these and in the letter-press. A complete copy of this work is very rarely to be found, and when found, valued at an enormous price. A continuation was begun some time after, under the title of "Miscellaneous Antiquities," of which six numbers were published.

It is to be feared Mr. Nichols was a considerable loser by this work, not only in the expenses of printing and engraving, but in the purchase of manuscripts and drawings. He could not indeed have been long connected with Mr. Gough, without imbibing a portion of his disinterested spirit, and looking for his best reward in the pleasure of the employment, and the consciousness that he was contributing much valuable information for the use of posterity, and the honour of his country. Mr. Nichols thought as little of expence as of fatigue, and to the fear of either he seems to have been an entire stranger. His success, however, was not different from that of his brethren, for we know no class of writers worse rewarded than Antiquaries.

The publication of the Bibliotheca Topographica took up ten years, and in some hands might have been quite sufficient to employ the whole of those years. But such was the unwearied industry of our author, that within the same period no less than eighteen publications issued from his press, of all which he was either editor or author.

As a complete list of his works will be appended to this article, we shall only notice here those which are more particularly connected with his researches as a Biographer. In 1781 he published in 8vo, "Biographical Anecdotes of William Hogarth." This was republished in 1782, again in 1785, and a fourth and most complete edition in 1810—1817, in 3 vols. 4to, with very elegant reduced plates. Of this work, on its first appearance, the testimony of Lord Orford may be considered as decisive:—"Since the first edition of this work (the Anecdotes of Painting), a much ampler account of Hogarth and his Works has been given by Mr. Nichols; which is not only more accurate, but much more satisfactory than mine: omitting nothing that a collector would wish to know, either with regard to the history of the painter himself, or to the circumstances, different editions, and variations of his prints. I have completed my list of Hogarth's Works from that source of information." * In 1822, Mr. Nichols superintended a superb edition of Hogarth's works, from the original plates, restored by James Heath, esq.; and furnished the Explanations of the subjects of the Plates. Let it not be forgotten that these Explanations were written by Mr. Nichols in his seventy-eighth year.

In the same year (1781) he was the author of " Biographical Memoirs of William Ged, including a particular account of his progress in the art of Block-printing." But what in the course of years and by slow gradations, almost imperceptibly became the most important of all Mr. Nichols's biographical labours, was his " Anecdotes of Bowyer, and of many of his literary Friends," 4to, 1782. He had printed in 1778, twenty copies of " Brief Memoirs of Mr. Bowyer," 8vo, for distribution, " as a tribute of respect, amongst a few select friends." Gratitude to so kind a benefactor induced Mr. Nichols to make, from time to time, additions to this little work, quite unconscious that it would at last extend to the noblest monument raised

to his own memory, as well as that of his friend.

The second and much enlarged edition of 1782 was welcomed with ardour by all classes of men of literature, and soon rose to more than double the price at which it was originally offered to the publick. The author was consequently again anxious to enlarge what was so generally acceptable, but had to encounter many interruptions from other extensive designs which he now began to meditate.

Of these the most important of all was his " History of Leicestershire," of which it has been justly said that it might have been the work of a whole life. Although generally devoted to subjects of the topographical kind, he acknowledged to the present writer that he had been induced to fix upon Leicestershire, as his *magnum opus*, from circumstances of a domestic kind, both his amiable wives having sprung from respectable families in that County.

This, however, like the other extensive work just mentioned, was not the accomplishment of a complete design, distinctly laid down in plan, and regularly executed. It grew from lesser efforts, among which we may enumerate " The History and Antiquities of Hinckley," which he published in 1782, 4to. " The History and Antiquities of Aston Flamvile and Burbach, in Leicestershire," 1787, 4to. " Collections towards the History and Antiquities of the Town and County of Leicester," 1790, 2 vols. 4to. It was in the preface to these volumes that he first intimated his intention to give the publick a much more complete work of the kind, soliciting assistance, which appears to have been tendered so liberally, that about 1792, he was enabled to begin to print his great work of " The History and Antiquities of the Town and County of Leicester," of which Parts I. and II. were published in 1795. Of this a third part was published in 1798, a fourth in 1800, a fifth in 1804, a sixth in 1807, the seventh and concluding part in 1811, and an Appendix in 1815, in which he was assisted by his son ; the whole making four large volumes, elegantly printed in folio, and illustrated by a profusion of views, portraits, maps, &c. and complete Indexes.

* Lord Orford's Works, 4to, vol. III. p. 458.

If any proofs were wanting of Mr. Nichols's *power* of literary labour, and, what is equally necessary, the frequent *revision* of that labour, the History of Leicestershire might be allowed to remain as completely decisive. But even this extensive undertaking cannot be allowed to stand alone. During the years in which he was preparing his materials, travelling into all parts of the county, and corresponding with, or visiting every person likely to afford information, he appeared as editor or author of no less than forty-seven articles. Among these were a second edition of " Bowyer's Greek Testament." " Bishop Atterbury's Correspondence," 5 vol. 8vo. illustrated, as usual, with topographical and historical notes, the result of arduous research and frequent correspondence with his learned friends. " A Collection of Miscellaneous Tracts by Mr. Bowyer." " The History and Antiquities of Lambeth Parish." " The Progresses and Royal Processions of Queen Elizabeth," 2 vol. 4to. and a third in 1804. " The History and Antiquities of Canonbury, with some account of the parish of Islington," 4to. " Illustrations of the Manners and Expences of Ancient Times in England," 4to. In 1815, the author speaks of this volume : " I have no hesitation in saying, in a case where it can neither promote my interest, nor hazard my veracity, that this is not only one of the scarcest publications of the eighteenth century, but, in its way, is also one of the most curious."

During the same period Mr. Nichols published an edition of " The Tatler," 6 vols. 8vo. with notes respecting biography, but particularly illustrative of manners. From the sources that had supplied many of these, he edited afterwards, " Sir Richard Steele's Epistolary Correspondence," 2 vol. 8vo. " The Lover and Reader." " The Town Talk, &c." " The Theatre and Anti-Theatre," by the same author, 3 vols. all illustrated with notes, furnished from many forgotten records, and family communications. Mr. Nichols appears to have first turned his attention to the British Essayists in consequence of his connexion with Bishop Percy, Dr. Calder, and others who intended to publish editions of the Tatler, Spectator, and Guardian, with the same species of annotation, explanatory of the man-

ners and spirit of the times, and including memoirs of the authors. When they entered on their work, there was a possibility of recovering much information, and much information was recovered ; a considerable part of which we have since seen added to various editions of these periodical writings, frequently without the candour of acknowledgment.

The extent of Mr. Nichols' literary productions will yet appear more extraordinary, when we add that, during the period we have hastily gone over, he became engaged in some of those duties of public life which necessarily demanded a considerable portion of time and attention ; and it may be asked, without much hazard of a ready answer, where could he find that time ? Certain it is, that he did find it, without any apparent injury to his usual pursuits, and that for many years he enjoyed a well-earned reputation as a member of the Corporation of London.

In December 1784, the respect he had acquired in the City induced his friends to propose him as a member of the Common Council for the Ward of Farringdon Without. He was accordingly elected on the 21st of that month, and with the interval of only one year, held this situation, (10 years as Deputy, under Alderman Wilkes,) until the year 1811, when he resigned all civic honours. He had previously declined the solicitation of his fellow-citizens of the Ward to become their Alderman on the death of Wilkes. A considerable time before his resignation he had felt it his duty to seek health and quiet in retirement, but it is also more than probable that the prevalence of party-spirit among those with whom he had been accustomed to act, but could act no longer, had its effect in precipitating a measure which many of his friends wished he had taken much sooner. The writer of this memoir hopes he will not be thought anxious to take from the number of Mr. Nichols' useful accomplishments, when he adds that his highly-respected friend was not qualified for political life, as it too frequently appeared among many with whom he was obliged to associate. He could not indulge asperity of thought or of language ; he had nothing of the malevolence of party-spirit, and never thought worse of any man for differing from him, ever so widely, in opinion. Unfit, however, as he was to join in the clamour of the day, he retained the respect of his colleagues, as an amiable and honest man, and an honour to the situation he had filled.

In 1804 his views were directed to an honour more in unison with his literary pursuits. He had for some time been a member of the Court of Assistants of the Stationers' Company, and in the above year attained what he called "the summit of his ambition, in being elected Master of the Company." Nor can any one think such ambition of the trivial kind who recollects how nearly connected this Company is with the literature of the age, and that among its members are to be found the liberal and munificent patrons of learned men, who are no longer dependant on the petty rewards which in former days flowed, tardily enough sometimes, from the blandishments of *dedication.*

How well Mr. Nichols discharged the duties of Master, not only on this occasion, but for many years after as *Locum Tenens,* has been repeatedly acknowledged, and still lives in the memory of the Court. Their rooms are decorated by portraits presented at various times by Mr. Nichols, among which are those of Robert Nelson, esq. the elder and younger Bowyer, Archbishop Chichele, Sir Richard Steele, and Matthew Prior; with a bust of Mr. Bowyer, and with the quarto copper-plate, finely engraved by the elder Basire, that an impression of it may be constantly given to every annuitant under Mr. Bowyer's will.

On the 8th of January 1807, by an accidental fall, at his house in Red Lion Passage, Mr. Nichols had one of his thighs fractured; and on the 8th of February, 1808, experienced a far greater calamity, respecting not only himself but the publick, in the destruction, by fire, of his printing office and warehouses, with the whole of their valuable contents. "Under these accumulated misfortunes," we use his own words, "sufficient to have overwhelmed a much stronger mind, he was supported by the consolatory balm of friendship, and offers of unlimited pecuniary assistance;—till, cheered by unequivocal marks of public and private approbation (not to mention motives of a higher and far superior na-

ture *), he had the resolution to apply with redoubled diligence to literary and typographical labours."

It would be difficult perhaps to find many instances of a " stronger mind " than Mr. Nichols displayed, at his advanced age, while suffering under both the above calamities. In the case of the fracture, the present writer had an opportunity to witness an instance of patient endurance and of placid temper, which he can never forget. Only three days after the accident, he found Mr. Nichols, supported by the surgical apparatus usual on such occasions, calmly reading the proof of a long article which he had that morning dictated to one of his daughters, respecting the life and death of his old friend Isaac Reed, which went to press as he left it, and indeed wanted no correction†. This accident left some portion of lameness, and abridged his usual exercise, but his general health was little impaired, and his vigour of mind remained unabated, when he had to endure the severer trial of the destruction of his printing-office and warehouses.

This, it might have been naturally expected, would have indisposed him for all future labours. He was now in his sixty-third year, and could not be far from the age when " the grasshopper is a burthen." For fifty years he had led a life of indefatigable application, and had produced from his own efforts, works enough to have established character, and content ambition. He was not desirous of accumulating wealth, and the reward of his industry had been tardy; but it seemed now approaching, and he had reason to expect a gradual advantage from his various productions, and a liberal encouragement in his future efforts. It was therefore a bitter disappointment, when, at the close of a cheerful day, and reposing in the society of his family, he heard that his whole property was consumed in a few short hours.

The present writer had on this occasion a striking proof of the uncertainty of sublunary enjoyments. In the afternoon of that fatal day, Mr. Nichols sent to him one of the most lively letters

---

* Here Mr. Nichols quotes a passage from Bishop Hough, "I thank God, I had the hope of a Christian, and that supported me."

† See Gent. Mag. January, 1807, p. 80.

he had ever received.—On the following morning, he hastened to visit Mr. Nichols, and found him, as was to be expected, in a state of considerable depression : but in a few days his mind appeared to have recovered its tone. He felt the power of consolation, and was excited to fresh activity.—Thus, in two remarkable instances, he displayed a temper and courage rarely to be found ; in the case of his personal accident, when his recovery was doubtful, and of his subsequent calamity, when his loss was irreparable ‡.

Hopeless as such a return to accustomed pursuits may appear, Mr. Nichols resumed his labours with an energy equal to what he had ever displayed when in the prime of life. Besides completing his " History of the County of Leicester," already mentioned, he returned to his " Life of Bowyer," of which one volume had been printed, but not published, just before his fire, under the title of " Literary Anecdotes of the Eighteenth Century, comprising Biographical Memoirs of William Bowyer, Printer, F.S.A. and many of his learned friends; an incidental view of the progress and advancement of Literature in this Kingdom during the last century ; and Biographical Anecdotes of a considerable number of eminent Writers and ingenious Artists."

This he lived to extend to nine large volumes, 8vo ; to which he afterwards, finding materials increase from all quarters, added four volumes, under the title of " Illustrations of the Literary History of the Eighteenth Century, consisting of authentic Memoirs and Original Letters of Eminent Persons ; and intended as a Sequel to the Literary Anecdotes." It was one of the last actions of his life, to show the writer of this memoir a fifth volume nearly printed, and to announce a sixth volume in preparation. Of these it is hoped the publick will not be long deprived, as Mr. Nichols had the happiness to leave a son, fully acquainted with his designs, equally respected by his friends and correspondents, and amply qualified to perpetuate the reputation which has attached to his name.

It is very difficult for the present writer to speak of this extraordinary and satisfactory work, in measured terms. Himself an ardent lover, and an humble inquirer into the biography of Great Britain, he has enjoyed in this extensive collection a fund of information which it would be in vain to seek elsewhere. It is original in its plan and in its execution, nor perhaps will there soon arise an Editor, to whom manuscripts of the most confidential kind, epistolary correspondence, and other precious records will be intrusted with equal certainty of their being given to the publick accurately and minutely, and yet free from injury to the characters of the deceased, or the feelings of the living.

By the vast accumulation of literary correspondence in these volumes, Mr. Nichols has released the biographical inquirer from much of the uncertainty of vague report, and has in a great measure brought him near to the gratification of a personal acquaintance. These records embrace the memoirs of almost all the learned men of the eighteenth century, and there are scarce any of that class with whom Mr. Nichols's volumes have not made us more intimate. Candid biographers of future times must be ready to acknowledge with gratitude that their obligations are incalculable. Already indeed the publick has done justice to the merits of this work ; for of all Mr. Nichols's publications it has been the most successful, and is soon likely to be one of the *recherchès* among book collectors. As in the present memoir we have confined ourselves to the notice of such of his various labours as involve somewhat of his personal character, we may refer to the " Anecdotes" and " Illustrations" for many traits of the most amiable kind, which will now be viewed with affectionate interest by those who knew him, and will ensure the highest respect from those who had not that happiness.

The fourth volume of the " Illustrations" was published in 1822, before which he had published, among other works, " Hardinge's Latin, Greek, and English Poems," 8vo, 1818 ; " Miscellaneous Works of George Hardinge, Esq. 1819," 3 vols. 8vo ; a new edition of his " Progresses of Queen Elizabeth," with considerable additions, 3 vols. 4to; which was followed by the " Progresses of King James the First," 3 vols. 4to, which

---

‡ Some particulars of the valuable works destroyed by this fire, most of which are now difficult to be procured even at a high price, may be seen in the Gent. Mag. 1808, p. 99.

had engaged his attention almost to the hour of his death. These are both works of great curiosity, comprehend a great many rare and valuable fragments of royal history, a large collection of rare tracts, and much illustration of the manners and customs of the sixteenth and seventeenth centuries.

In Mr. Nichols's death, which took place on Sunday, Nov. 26, there was much cause for affliction, and much to afford consolation. It was sudden beyond most instances we have ever heard of. He had passed some cheerful hours with his family, and was retiring to rest about 10 o'clock at night. He had reached a step or two of the lower staircase, accompanied by his eldest daughter, when he said, but with no particular alteration of voice, "Give me your hand," and instantly, but gently, sunk down on his knees, and expired without a sigh or groan, or any symptom of suffering.

On the Monday before, he complained as if he had caught cold; and on Thursday, when the writer of this memoir saw him for the last time, he mentioned something of the kind, but said nothing of pain, or of any internal feeling that could give alarm. Before parting he conversed in his usual lively manner, about many things past and to come, and when the interview ended, he bid his visitor farewell, as one whom he fully expected to see, with some other friends, within a few days. He had no presentiment of death, and during his last week wrote two or three articles for the Magazine with his accustomed ease and spirit.

Sudden as his death was, and there is something in sudden death to which no argument can reconcile the greater part of survivors, it could not fail even upon a slight reflection to administer consolation. When the first impression was over, it was felt as a great blessing that Mr. Nichols had outlived the common age of man with entire exemption from the pains and infirmities he had witnessed in the case of some of his dearest friends. There was here none of that imbecility so afflicting to friends and relatives; memory and judgment were strong to the last.

For several years he had been accustomed to write some lines on the return of his birth-day, for the amusement of his family. These were ge-

nerally contemplative and serious, affectionate as regarding his family, and pious as regarding himself, his advanced age, his probable dissolution, and his firm reliance on the merits of his Redeemer. All came from the heart, and delighted those whom he wished to delight, a family eminent for mutual affection. The last of these verses, printed in the Magazine for 1824, may be considered as his dying words and his dying prayer.

His old age, at whatever period the reader may date it, imposed no necessity of leaving off his accustomed employments, or discontinuing his intercourse with society. He had no chronic disorder, hereditary or acquired, and his occasional illnesses were of short duration. He was always ready to gratify his anxious family by applying to medical advice, and was never wanting in such precautions as became his advanced years. His constitution to the last exhibited the remains of great strength and activity. If, as asserted, a healthy old man is "a tower undermined," it was not easy in him to discover what had given way.

His natural faculties remained unimpaired during the whole course of his life, with the exception of his sight, which for several years past had become by degrees less and less distinct. Three days only before his death he made a very extraordinary declaration to the writer of this article: "I cannot now read any printed book, but I can read manuscript."

Although we are not desirous to report miracles in order to embellish the life of this worthy man, yet it may be allowed, and he felt it as such, to be an extraordinary instance of the kindness of Providence that a degree of sight was still left which enabled him to peruse and select from the vast mass of literary correspondence now before him, such articles as were proper for his "Illustrations." As to printed books, he had the assistance of his amiable daughters, who were his amanuenses and his librarians. Those who knew the ardour of his parental affection could easily perceive that, amidst a privation which would have sunk the spirits of most men, he had now a new source of domestic happiness and thankful reflection. He lived also to see his son advancing to reputation, in the same business and the same literary pursuits in which himself delighted, and a grandson eagerly pursuing his footsteps. We may well exclaim, *O fortunate senex!*

As much of Mr. Nichols' personal character has been introduced in the preceding pages, it only remains to be added that it was uniformly remarkable for those qualities which procured universal esteem. The sweetness of his temper, and his disposition to be kind and useful, were the delight of his friends, and strangers went from him with an impression that they had been with an amiable and benevolent man. During his being a Member of the Corporation, he employed his interest, as he did elsewhere his pen, in promoting charitable institutions, and in contributing to the support of those persons who had sunk from prosperity, and whose wants he relieved in a more private manner. For very many years he filled the office of Registrar, or Honorary Secretary of the Literary Fund, which gratified his kind feelings by enabling him to assist many a brother author in distress. Nor was his assistance less liberally afforded to those of his own profession, whom he respected and whom he encouraged, either in their outset in life, or when in difficulties. In all this he experienced what all men of similar character have experienced. He sometimes met with those who availed themselves of his unsuspicious temper and known benevolence, yet he was rarely heard to complain of ingratitude. He never introduced the subject; but, when closely pressed, he would acknowledge some instances in his own experience, yet with great reluctance, and an apparent willingness to have it thought that his bounty had not been injudicious.

His literary transactions were uniformly conducted on the best principles. His early associations were mostly with honourable men, whom he was ambitious to copy; and those who have been longest connected with him in business acknowledge with pleasure and respect that Mr. Nichols never discovered the least symptom of what is mean or selfish. He performed nothing, indeed, during his long life, of which he might not have delighted to hear. His friendships were never dissolved, for they were never unequal. By those of superior rank

he was treated with the respect due to the character of a gentleman and a man of talent; while his inferiors found him useful, kind, and benevolent, always a friend, and often a patron.

By what means he preserved the *mens sana in corpore sano* for so many years of unequalled literary labour has been incidently hinted in the preceding pages. The subject might perhaps admit of more discussion, if this article had not already extended further than the writer originally intended. As to health, medical writers have given us no rules for procuring longevity, but what experience proves to be fallacious. All that requires to be said here, and it may afford a useful lesson, is, that Mr. Nichols had originally a good constitution, which he preserved by exercise, and the vicissitudes of constant employment. His mind was always employed on what was useful; and such a mind is made to last. Both mind and body there is every reason to think were preserved in vigour by the uncommon felicity of his temper. He had none of the irascible passions, nor would it have been easy to have provoked him to depart from the language and manners which rendered his company delightful.

There was much in the division of his time which enabled him to perform the arduous tasks which he imposed on himself. He began his work early, and despatched the business of the day before it became necessary to attend to publick concerns, or join the social parties of his friends. He had another habit which may be taken into the account. From his youth, he did every thing quickly. He read with rapidity, and soon caught what was important to his purpose. He spoke quickly, and that whether in the reciprocity of conversation, or when, which was frequently the case, he had to address a company in a set speech. He had also accustomed himself to write with great rapidity; but this, he used jocularly to allow, although a saving of time, did not tend to improve his hand.

Upon the whole, if usefulness be a test of merit, no man in our days has conferred more important favours on the republic of letters.

Mr. Nichols was twice married. First, in 1766, to Anne, daughter of Mr. William Cradock. She died in

1776, leaving two daughters, one of whom married the Rev John Pridden, M.A. F.S.A., and died in 1815 ; the other is still living : and secondly, in 1778, to Martha, daughter of Mr. William Green, of Hinckley, in Leicestershire. She died in 1788, leaving one son, John Bowyer Nichols, Esq. and four daughters, three of whom are still living, and the eldest of them is married to John Morgan, Esq. of Highbury-place.

He was interred in Islington Church-yard, where his parents and all his children who died before him are deposited. Mr. Nichols, at the time of his death, was probably the oldest native of Islington, and his grave is only a very few yards from the house in which he was born.

His funeral was, (as he would have wished,) as private as possible ; attended only by *all* his male relatives who had arrived at man's estate, and by his attached friends, James and William Morgan, and Wm. Herrick, Esqrs. ; W. Tooke, Esq. F.R.S. ; A. Chalmers, Esq. F.S.A. ; H. Ellis, Esq. F.R.S. ; Charles and Robert Baldwin, George Woodfall, and J. Jeaffreson, Esqrs.

There are several good portraits of Mr. Nichols :—1. painted by Towne, 1782, æt. 37, and engraved by Cook, published in "Collections for Leicestershire ; " 2. painted by V. D. Puyl, 1787, (unpublished); 3. drawn by Edridge, published in Cadell's " Contemporary Portraits ; " 4. drawn by J. Jackson, Esq. R.A. and engraved by Heath, 1811, æt. 62, published by Mr. Britton, and inserted in the " Literary Anecdotes ;" 5. another painted by Jackson, mezzotinted by Meyer, published in " History of Leicestershire ;" 6. painted and engraved by Meyer, 1825, æt. 80, and published with this Magazine. Several small copies have been made from the above prints. There is also a faithful bust of Mr. Nichols, by Giannelli. A. C.

The very numerous Publications of which Mr. Nichols was either the Author or the Editor, we shall set down in chronological order :

1. " Islington, a Poem, 1763," 4to.

2. "The Buds of Parnassus, 1763," 4to ; republished in 1764, with additional Poems.

3. " The Origin of Printing, 1774," 8vo ; the joint production of Mr. Bowyer and himself ; reprinted in 1776 ; and a Supplement added in 1781.

4. " Three Supplemental Volumes to the Works of Dean Swift, with Notes, 1775, 1776, 1779," 8vo.

5. " Index to the Miscellaneous Works of Lord Lyttelton, 1775," 8vo.

6. " Index to Lord Chesterfield's Letters to his Son, 1776," 8vo.

7. " The Original Works, in Prose and Verse, of William King, LL D. with Historical Notes, 1776," 3 vols. small 8vo.

8. " Brief Memoirs of Mr. Bowyer, 1778," 8vo ; distributed, as a tribute of respect, amongst a few select friends.

9. " History of the Royal Abbey of Bec, near Rouen, 1779," small 8vo.

10. " Some Account of the Alien Priories, and of such Lands as they are known to have possessed in England and Wales, 1799," 2 vols. small 8vo.

11. " Six Old Plays," on which Shakspeare grounded a like number of his ; selected by Mr. Steevens, and revised by Mr. Nichols, 1779, 2 vols. small 8vo.

12. Mr. Rowe-Mores having left at his death a small unpublished impression of " A Dissertation upon English Typographical Founders and Founderies;" all the copies of this very curious pamphlet were purchased at his sale by Mr. Nichols ; and given to the publick in 1779, with the addition of a short explanatory " Appendix."

13. " A Collection of Royal and Noble Wills, 1780," 4to.

14. " A Select Collection of Miscellaneous Poems, with Historical and Biographical Notes, 1780 ;" 4 vols. small 8vo ; to which four other volumes, and a general Poetical Index by Mr. Macbean, were added in 1782.

15. " The Bibliotheca Topographica Britannica," 4to ; in conjunction with Mr. Gough (in LII Numbers), 1780—1790.

16. " Biographical Anecdotes of William Hogarth, 1781," 8vo ; republished in 1782, again in 1785 ; and a fourth edition, in three very handsome quarto volumes, with CLX genuine Plates, 1810—1817.

17. " Biographical Memoirs of William Ged, including a particular Account of his Progress in the Art of Block-printing, 1781," 8vo.

18. A Third Edition, much enlarged, of Mr. Bowyer's " Conjectures and Observations on the New Testament, 1782," 4to ; and a Fourth Edition in 1812.

19. " Biographical and Literary Anecdotes of William Bowyer, Printer, F.S.A. and of many of his learned Friends, 1782," 4to.

20. " The History and Antiquities of Hinckley, in Leicestershire, 1782," 4to ; of which a second edition, in folio, extracted from the " History of Leicestershire," was printed in 1812.

21. Mr. Bowyer's " Apology for some of Mr. Hooke's Observations concerning the Roman Senate, with an Index to the Observations, 1782," 4to.

22. " Novum Testamentum Græcum, ad fidem Græcorum solùm Codicum MSS. expressum; adstipulante Joanne Jacobo Wetstenio: juxta Sectiones Jo. Alberti Bengelii divisum; et novâ Interpunctione sæpiùs illustratum. Editio Secunda, Londini, curâ, typis, & sumptibus Johannis Nichols, 1783."

23. In 1783, he collected " The principal Additions and Corrections in the Third Edition of Dr. Johnson's Lives of the Poets, to complete the Second Edition" (of 1781).

24. " Bishop Atterbury's Epistolary Correspondence, with Notes," vols. I. and II. 1783; vol. III. 1784; vol. IV. 1787.—A new Edition of this Work, corrected and much enlarged, was published in 1799, with Memoirs of the Bishop; and a Fifth Volume, entirely new.

25. In conjunction with the Rev. Dr. Ralph Heathcote, he revised the second edition of the " Biographical Dictionary," 12 vols. 8vo, 1784; and added several hundred new lives.

26. " A Collection of Miscellaneous Tracts, by Mr. Bowyer, and some of his learned Friends, 1785." 4to.

27. " The History and Antiquities of Lambeth Parish, 1786."

28. " The Tatler, 1786," *cum Notis Variorum*, 6 vols. small 8vo.

29. " The Works, in Verse and Prose, of Leonard Welsted, Esq. with Notes and Memoirs of the Author, 1787," 8vo.

30. " The History and Antiquities of Aston Flamvile and Burbach, in Leicestershire, 1787," 4to.

31. " Sir Richard Steele's Epistolary Correspondence, with Biographical and Historical Notes, 1788," 2 vols. small 8vo; and an enlarged Edition, in 1809, 2 vols. 8vo.

32. " The Progresses and Royal Processions of Queen Elizabeth, 1788." 2 vols. 4to.—Of this Collection a Third Volume was published in 1804; and Part of a Fourth Volume in 1821.

33. " The History and Antiquities of Canonbury, with some Account of the Parish of Islington, 1788," 4to.

34. " The Lover and Reader, by Sir Richard Steele, illustrated with Notes, 1789," 8vo.

35. " The Town Talk, Fish Pool, Plebeian, Old Whig, Spinster, &c. by Sir Richard Steele; illustrated with Notes, 1790," 8vo.

36. " Collections towards the History and Antiquities of the Town and County of Leicester, 1790," 2 vols. 4to.

37. " An Edition of Shakspeare, 1790," in seven vols. 12mo; accurately printed from the Text of Mr. Malone; with a Selection of the more important Notes.

38. " The Theatre and Anti-theatre, &c. of Sir Richard Steele, illustrated with Notes, 1791," 8vo.

39. " Miscellaneous Antiquities, in continuation of the Bibliotheca Topographica Britannica," Six Numbers, 4to. 1792—1798.

40. " The History and Antiquities of the Town and County of Leicester;" Parts I. and II. 1795. Folio.—A Third Part was published in 1798; a Fourth in 1800; a Fifth in 1804; a Sixth in 1807 (reprinted in 1810); and the Seventh in 1811; and an Appendix and General Indexes in 1815.

41. " Illustrations of the Manners and Expences of Antient Times in England, 1797," 4to.

42. " Bishop Kennett's Funeral Sermon, with Memoirs of the Cavendish Family, 1797," 8vo.

43. " Chronological List of the Society of Antiquaries of London, 1798," 4to. compiled in conjunction with Mr. Gough.

44. " An Edition of Shakspeare, 1799," in eight vols. 12mo; accurately printed from the Text of Mr. Steevens: with a Selection of the Notes.

45. Having recovered the MS. of the Reverend Kennett Gibson's " Comment upon Part of the Fourth Journey of Antoninus through Britain" (which in 1769 Mr. Gibson proposed to publish by subscription, but which upon his death was supposed to have been lost), Mr. Gough and Mr. Nichols jointly published it in 1800, with the Parochial History of Castor and its Dependencies; and an Account of Marham, and several other places in its neighbourhood. A new and improved Edition of this Work was printed in 1819.

46. In 1800, he completed " The Antiquaries' Museum," which had been begun in 1791 by his friend Jacob Schnebbelie.

47. In 1801, he published Dr. Pegge's " Historical Account of Beauchief Abbey, in the County of Derby."

48. In the same year, he published a new and complete Edition of the " Works of Dean Swift," in XIX vols. 8vo; which in 1803 were reprinted in XXIV vols. 18mo; again in XIX vols. 8vo, in 1808.

49. In 1803, in conformity to the last will of Samuel Pegge, esq. (son of the learned Antiquary already named), he ushered into the world, " Anecdotes of the English Language, &c." 8vo; and a new edition, with improvements, in 1814, 8vo; and in 1818, another work by the same gentleman, intituled, " Curialia Miscellanea, or Anecdotes of Old Times," &c. 8vo.

50. " Journal of a very young Lady's Tour from Canonbury to Aldborough, through Chelmsford, Sudbury, Ipswich; and back, through Harwich, Colchester, &c. Sept. 14—21, 1804; written hastily on the

Road, as occurrences arose;" not intended for publication; but a very few copies only printed, to save the trouble of transcribing.

51. In 1806, he published, from the MSS. of his Friend Mr. Samuel Pegge, " The Fourth and Fifth Parts of Curialia: or, An Historical Account of some Branches of the Royal Household, &c." 4to.

52. In 1809 he printed from the Originals, and illustrated with Literary and Historical Anecdotes, " Letters on various subjects, to and from Archbishop Nicolson," 2 vols. 8vo.

53. In the same year he edited another posthumous Work of Dr. Pegge's, under the title of " *Anonymiana;* or, Ten Centuries of Observations on various Authors and Subjects," 8vo; and a Second Edition in 1818.

54. A new edition of " Fuller's History of the Worthies of England," with brief Notes, 1811, 2 vols. 4to.

55. " Literary Anecdotes of the Eighteenth Century," 1812—1815, 9 volumes, 8vo.

56. " Literary Illustrations of the Eighteenth Century," a Sequel to the above Work, 4 vols. 1817—1822.

57. A new Edition of his friend Sir John Cullum's " History and Antiquities of Hawsted " 1 vol. 4to. 1813.

58. A Third Edition of Rev. Thomas Warton's " History of Kiddington, in Oxfordshire;" revised through the press with the assistance of H. Ellis, esq. 1 vol. 4to, 1815.

59. " Hardinge's Latin, Greek, and English Poems," 1818, 8vo.

60. " Miscellaneous Works of George Hardinge," 3 vols. 8vo. 1819.

61. In 1818 he prefixed to the third volume of General Index to the Gentleman's Magazine, a Prefatory Introduction, descriptive of the rise and progress of the Magazine, with Anecdotes of the Projector and his early associates.

62. " Taylor and Long's Music Speeches at Cambridge," 3 vols. 1819, 8vo.

63. " Four Sermons, by Dr. Taylor, Bps. Lowth and Hayter," 1822, 8vo.

64. Explanations of the subjects of Hogarth's Plates, for the splendid and complete Edition of them, published by Messrs. Baldwin, Cradock, and Joy, in 1822.

65. " Progresses of Queen Elizabeth," new edition, with very considerable improvements, 3 vols. 4to. 1823,

66. " The Progresses of King James the First," in 3 vols. 4to, were printing at the time of Mr. Nichols's death; and he lived to see the greater part of them published.

67. A Fifth Volume of " Literary Illustrations" is left by Mr. Nichols, nearly completed at the press.

A TRIBUTE TO THE MEMORY OF THE LATE J. NICHOLS, Esq.

LATE in the vale of life, and full of years,
　Cheerful and happy was his cloudless day,
When, lo! bewept by Friendship's grateful
　　tears,
　He slept in peace—his spirit pass'd away.

While Earth admir'd the Historian of his
　　time,
　Domestic virtues were his highest praise,
These gave to life an energy sublime,
　A beauteous lustre to his lengthen'd days.

Unfeign'd affection liv'd within his heart,
　A store of blessings which he freely gave,
Blessings that he delighted to impart
　　To numerous friends now mourning o'er
　　　his grave.

Various his talents, as his heart was kind,
　The page of ancient lore he lov'd to scan;
Learning's bright gems enrich'd his liberal
　　mind,　　　　　　　　　　[man.
　And form'd his studies thro' the age of

With patient industry and wondrous toil,
　Thro' dark antiquity he sought his way;
And, persevering in the hard turmoil,
　He brought its treasures to the light of day.

In later years instruction from his pen
　Delighted thousands by his pleasing page;
A faithful painter of the lives of men,
　He gave the history of a learned age.

His labours o'er, he rests beneath the sod,
　His lamp consum'd, his various studies
　　cease,
His happy spirit soars to meet his God,
　And rest for ever in the realms of peace.
　　　　　　　　　　　W. Hersee.

EPITAPH

ON THE LATE JOHN NICHOLS, ESQ.

By JOHN TAYLOR, ESQ.

HERE Nichols rests, whose pure and
　　active mind
Thro' life still aim'd to benefit mankind.
For useful knowledge eager from his youth,
To lengthen'd age in keen pursuit of Truth.
What ruthless time had destin'd to decay,
He well explor'd and brought to open day.
Yet still he search'd not with a Bigot's zeal
To gain what Time would for Oblivion steal,
But that such works recorded should remain
As taste and virtue gladly would retain.
And though intent to merit public fame,
Warmly alive to each domestic claim:
He like the Patriarchs rever'd of yore,
To all his kindred due affection bore.
Prompt with good humour all he knew to
　　cheer,
And wit with him was playful, not severe.
Such was the Sage whose reliques rest below,
Belov'd by many a friend, without one foe.

A TRIBUTE TO THE MEMORY OF JOHN NICHOLS, Esq. F.S.A.

By the Rev. Dr. Booker.

WHEN die the Good, Affliction's tear
    will flow,
To soothe the heart that bleeds with ten-
    derest woe,
And, round whose urn may we that title
    bind?
Round theirs who reverenc'd God, and
    bless'd mankind.

    Such, honour'd Sage! whose multifarious
      lore,
Tho' unexampled, still acquiring more,
Render'd thy years, when others' work is
    done,
Like the mild radiance of a setting Sun.

    To bless and serve thy country was the
      aim
Of all thy views: and now a deathless
    name
Awaits thee.—Sculptur'd marbles shall de-
    cay,
And votive lines of Genius fade away;
Yet shall thy useful labours these supply,—
And while thy country lives, shall never
    die.

    From the profound abyss of hoary Time,
Thou many a buried truth and mouldering
    rhyme
Didst rescue,—throwing light on ages past,
Whose rays will shine while History's page
    shall last.

    Around the throne thy safeguards didst
      thou bring,
To shield from fell disloyalty thy King;
Around the forms of consecrated law,
Which shield the good, and keep the bad
    in awe,
Thou, as a faithful Watchman, plac'd on
    high,
Didst lurking danger to those forms des-
    cry;
Around the altar, where thy Christian vow,
In youth was made, and thou in age didst
    bow,—
The *first* confirming (on conviction due)
What the long patriarchal *last* found true,—
There a Palladium, from all feet profane,
Thou more than half a century didst main-
    tain;
Nor did the lengthen'd term of duty close,
When feebler minds would have desired re-
    pose;
But in the hallow'd path thou didst pro-
    ceed,   [meed.
Till Heaven approving, call'd thee to thy
Then, like a golden shock of ripen'd grain,
Fresh reap'd in autumn, from some spacious
    plain,
Death did thy venerable frame convey,
Softly to slumber in thy parent clay,
Till by thy Saviour's awful fiat given,
Angels transport it to thy home in Hea-
    ven.

J. B. NICHOLS, 25, PARLIAMENT STREET.